World Scripture

and the

Teachings

of

Sun Myung Moon

World Scripture
and the
Teachings
of
Sun Myung Moon

UNIVERSAL PEACE FEDERATION

New York

Published in the United States of America by

Universal Peace Federation
200 White Plains Road
Tarrytown, NY 10591
www.upf.org

Copyright © 2007, 2011 Universal Peace Federation

All rights reserved. No part of this publication may be reproduced, stored in a retrieval system or transmitted in any form or by any means electronic, mechanical, photocopying, recording or otherwise without the prior written permission of the publisher.

Separate sources of copyright material included in these volumes are noted in the Acknowledgements, page 1149. None of this material may be reprinted except by permission of the owners of the original copyright.

PUBLISHER: Dr. Thomas G. Walsh

EDITOR   Dr. Andrew Wilson

ASSOCIATE EDITORS
                 Dr. Sung-Bae Jin
                 Dr. Theodore Shimmyo
                 Rev. Hee Hun Oh Standard

PRODUCTION DIRECTOR
                 Dr. Gordon L. Anderson

LIBRARY OF CONGRESS CATOLOGING-IN-PUBLICATION DATA

World Scriptures and the Teachings of Sun Myung Moon; editor, Andrew Wilson, 1184 pages

ISBN 978-1-930549-57-9 (paper)

This volume is dedicated to
the Rev. Dr. Sun Myung Moon and Dr. Hak Ja Han Moon,
True Parents of Heaven, Earth and Humankind

Contents

Preface — XI
Invocation — 1

Part One: God and Creation

Chapter 1: God — 5

Knowledge of God ∗ 5
The One God ∗ 10
Formless, Invisible, Mystery ∗ 13
Transcendent Reality ∗ 17
Sovereign and Omnipotent ∗ 20
Omniscient and Omnipresent ∗ 25
Immanent and Dwelling within the Heart ∗ 27
Unchanging and Eternal ∗ 30
The Original Cause ∗ 34
God's Goodness ∗ 36
Divine Love and Compassion ∗ 41
The Creator ∗ 46
Heavenly Father and Mother ∗ 53

Chapter 2: Truth and Universal Law — 57

Eternal Truth ∗ 57
The Moral Law ∗ 62
The Golden Rule ∗ 67
The Ten Commandments ∗ 69
Beyond the Law ∗ 72
Duality ∗ 75
Interdependence ∗ 83
Cause and Effect ∗ 85

Chapter 3: The Purpose of Human Life — 91

For God's Good Pleasure ∗ 91
The Image of God ∗ 94
The Temple of God ∗ 99
Sons and Daughters of God ∗ 102
The Value of Human Life ∗ 106
Conscience and Inborn Goodness ∗ 112
Perfection ∗ 117
Joy ∗ 124

Chapter 4: God's Creation and Human Creativity — 129

The Sanctity of Nature ∗ 129
Reverence for Life ∗ 136
Nature as Teacher ∗ 141
Microcosm and Macrocosm ∗ 142
The Lord of Creation ∗ 146
Stewardship ∗ 153
Beauty ∗ 159
Creativity and Art ∗ 163
Health and Disease ∗ 169

Chapter 5: Life after Death and the Spirit World — 175

The Spirit World ∗ 175
The Immortal Soul ∗ 179
Preparation for Eternity ∗ 184
Dreams ∗ 192
The Passage Beyond ∗ 195
The Judgment ∗ 201
Heaven ∗ 207
Hell ∗ 214
Angels ∗ 222
Spirits of the Departed ∗ 227
Reincarnation ∗ 232
Spiritual Error and the Occult ∗ 234
Uniting Heaven and Earth ∗ 238

Part Two: Sin and Salvation

Chapter 6: Evil, Sin and the Human Fall — 245

The Human Fall * 245
Cain and Abel * 256
The Devil and His Activities * 259
Sin * 268
Inherited Sin and Karma * 271
Collective and Historical Sin * 277
Selfish Desires and Fallen Nature * 279
The War Within * 284
Egoism and Pride * 286
Ignorance and Atheism * 290
Idolatry and Materialism * 296
Suffering * 298
God's Grief * 304

Chapter 7: Salvation – Liberation – Enlightenment — 313

Grace * 313
Forgiveness * 319
Atonement * 322
Enlightenment * 325
Liberation * 330
Emptiness—Nirvana * 335
Spiritual Union * 339
Healing * 344
The Refining Fire * 348
Help and Deliverance * 351
Reversal and Restoration * 358
Rebirth * 363
Resurrection * 368
Eternal Life * 372
Universal Salvation * 376

Chapter 8: Religion — 381

The Purpose of Religion * 381
One Truth, Many Paths * 386
Tolerance, Religious Freedom and
    Interfaith Solidarity * 391
Shamanism, Polytheism and Animism * 397
Buddhism * 402
Confucianism * 406
Judaism * 410
Christianity * 416
Islam * 424

Chapter 9: History of God's Providence — 429

Founders, Prophets and Saints * 429
Noah * 436
Abraham * 439
Isaac * 445
Jacob * 448
Joseph * 455
Moses * 462
Women of the Bible * 468
Buddha * 481
Confucius * 484
Jesus * 487
Muhammad * 516

Chapter 10: Eschatology and Messianic Hope — 519

Tribulation * 519
The Last Judgment * 527
New Revelation * 532
Recognizing the Day of the Lord * 537
The Messiah * 543
The Kingdom of Heaven * 553

Part Three: The Path of Life

Chapter 11: Growth, Responsibility and Destiny — 563

Spiritual Growth * 563
The Seasons of Life * 566
Cultivating the Good * 569

Decision * 574
Good and Evil * 576
Individual Responsibility * 581

Predestination * 588
Synergy of Grace and Effort * 594
Preparation and Making a
    Good Beginning * 596
Perseverance and Patience * 600

Chapter 12: Morality   605

Self-Control * 605
Restraint * 609
Integrity * 611
Righteousness * 616
Sincerity and Authenticity * 621
Honesty * 625
Caution and Vigilance * 628
Prudent Speech * 631
Moderation * 634
Modesty * 637
Chastity * 640
Sobriety and Temperance * 647

Chapter 13: Love   653

True Love * 653
Living for Others * 662
Sacrificial Love * 668
Universal Love * 673
Love Your Enemy * 678
Forgiveness * 682
A Good Heart * 685
Good Deeds * 688
Giving and Receiving * 690
Charity * 695
Hospitality * 700
The Great Commandment * 702

Chapter 14: Wisdom   705

The Primary Ends of Education * 705
The Search for Knowledge * 709
Tradition * 715
Scripture and Interpretation * 717
Intellectual Knowledge and
    Spiritual Wisdom * 724
The Teacher * 731
Discipleship * 736
Learning and Practice * 740

Chapter 15: Faith   743

Faith * 743
Witness * 754
Hope * 759
Assurance * 762
Gratitude and Indebtedness * 765
The Fear of God * 770
Doubt * 773
Hypocrisy * 775
Heresy * 777
Arguing with God * 781
Testing * 785

Chapter 16: Prayer and Worship   795

Prayer * 795
Meditation * 803
Praise * 814
Devotion * 818
Purity of Intention * 824
Offerings and Tithes * 828
Ritual * 833
Beyond Ritual * 840

Chapter 17: Obedience and Sacrifice   845

Call and Mission * 845
Obedience and Submission * 849
Self-Sacrifice * 853
War against Evil * 857
Persecution * 865
Martyrdom * 870

Chapter 18: Humility and Self-Denial   875

Humility * 875
Turn the Other Cheek * 881
Repentance * 884
Judge Not * 889
Self-Denial * 892
Subduing the Desires of the Flesh * 894
Non-Attachment to Wealth and
    Possessions * 899
Separation from Family * 904
Separation from the World * 909
Asceticism, Monasticism and Celibacy * 913

Part Four: Family and Society

CHAPTER 19: FAMILY   925

The Basic Form of Life ✳ 925
Filial Piety ✳ 933
Sibling Love ✳ 938
Friendship ✳ 940
Conjugal Love ✳ 944
Ethics of Married Life ✳ 957
Parental Love ✳ 967
The Love of Grandparents ✳ 973

CHAPTER 20: SOCIETY   977

Family as the Cornerstone of Society ✳ 977
The Moral Foundations of Society ✳ 980
Patriotism and Public Service ✳ 985
Labor ✳ 990
Freedom ✳ 994
Equality ✳ 1001
Women's Rights ✳ 1009
Justice ✳ 1015
Economic Justice ✳ 1017
Unity and Community ✳ 1030
World Citizenship ✳ 1035

CHAPTER 21: LEADERSHIP AND GOVERNMENT   1039

God-Fearing Leadership ✳ 1039
Righteous Leadership ✳ 1041
Exemplary Leadership ✳ 1046
Government for the People ✳ 1051
Law and Punishments ✳ 1058
Prophets and Messengers ✳ 1065

CHAPTER 22: PEACE   1075

The Peace of God ✳ 1075
Inner Peace ✳ 1077
Reconciliation and Peacemaking ✳ 1080
Restitution ✳ 1084
The Futility of War ✳ 1087
The Rise and Fall of Nations ✳ 1091
World Peace ✳ 1097

NOTES   1105
LIST OF SOURCES   1149

Preface

World Scripture and the Teachings of Sun Myung Moon builds on the foundation of *World Scripture: A Comparative Anthology of Sacred Texts* (1991). That volume was in many ways a pioneering work of religious literature, systematically examining the scriptures of the world's religions to illuminate their universal teachings and underscore their common ground, and drawing on sacred texts to articulate a vision of interreligious compatibility and harmony.

Conventional textbooks often treat each religion separately, comparing similarities and differences. The religions come to be viewed as outgrowths of humanity's diverse cultures and historical contexts. According to this pluralistic and somewhat relativistic perspective, the religions may propose irreconcilable truth claims. Such a manner of presentation does little to disclose the common ground among religions, or the fact that the unifying force behind all religion is the one God, who in His love has been raising people of every culture to knowledge of His truth.

In the past it was fashionable to believe that religious differences were indeed irreconcilable and that, therefore, in the march of history towards globalization and a technologically advanced world civilization, religions were destined to decline and disappear. Nevertheless, Rev. Dr. Sun Myung Moon commissioned *World Scripture* based upon the firm conviction that religions have a key role to play in building world peace in the 21st century.

Knowing the fundamental power of religion to mold thought and culture, from the beginning of his ministry he advocated interreligious understanding, respect and unity as necessary pre-requisites for world peace. In the 1970s, after his ministry had expanded beyond Asia to the West, Father Moon began to sponsor annual dialogues for reconciliation among religions, including the Assembly of the World's Religions in 1985, 1990 and 1992. It was shortly after the first of these Assemblies that he outlined his concept for *World Scripture: A Comparative Anthology of Sacred Texts*. He enlisted the support of an Editorial Board of forty distinguished scholars drawn from the religions of the world, and with their guidance that book was published six years later.

Although initially Father Moon's vision and activism on behalf of interreligious unity was misunderstood and considered to be impractical and unrealistic, today people are coming to recognize that the world has no viable alternative. We experience the violence, fear and anxiety of a world in travail, as global linkages of communication and commerce are undermined by tensions that arise from persistent cultural and religious misunderstanding, prejudice and conflict.

If a new global civilization of peace is to survive its birth pangs, people must forge bonds of fraternity across civilizations and especially between religions. And to enlist the religions in peacebuilding requires an awareness of the shared values widespread in scriptures and the daily practice of the faithful. This can help defuse tribalism, intolerance and fear of difference. These values include: the Golden Rule, respect for the rights of every human being, self-mastery, moral restraint, family, charity, forgiveness and peace under the gracious sovereignty of the one God.

By highlighting these shared values, *World Scripture: A Comparative Anthology of Sacred Texts* showed that the common ground among religions is in reality vast and deep. It called on believers to focus on these points of shared understanding, rather than fixating on the differences. It was written with the hope that when believers of every tradition are informed by these common values, they can defuse religious enmity and mobilize their religions as positive forces for world peace.

Sun Myung Moon and His Teachings

The present volume, the second in the World Scripture series, brings together these sacred texts with selections from Father Moon's teachings. It is no exaggeration to say that his teachings cover the multitude of topics espoused by the world's religions. As a native of Korea, a land blessed with deep roots in Buddhism, Confucianism and traditional religions, and which has seen the explosive growth of Christianity as well as the emergence of Islam, Father Moon in his youth drank deeply from their fountains of wisdom. His deep respect for the religious traditions is evident in his teachings. Often he affirms a particular religion's doctrine and demonstrates its application in the contemporary world. Occasionally he takes issue and offers a different explanation. And not infrequently, he takes a traditional religious concept and adds further dimensions.

For the many people who have come to know and respect Father Moon for his interreligious work and his efforts for world peace, these pages offer a doorway into his thought. For those who are already well acquainted with his teachings, this book reveals the rich connections between his thought and the heritage of the world's religions.

While the truth of God is universal, every religion offers a specific path whereby one may find the truth, practice the truth, and embody it in one's life. It is a great blessing for anyone to follow such a path that leads to salvation and the fullness of spiritual realization. For this reason, *World Scripture and the Teachings of Sun Myung Moon* affirms the great wisdom of the world's religious traditions and the believers who adhere closely to their chosen path. This volume, therefore, is not designed for a spiritual dilettante who only wishes to pick and choose from among the world's religions just the teachings that are pleasing to him. At the same time, this volume counsels believers on the path of religion to chart a course that avoids the pitfalls of narrow-mindedness, exclusivism and triumphalism.

Father Moon's words are not the musings of an academic who studies about the world's religions. He is a true practitioner of religion: one who lives by what he teaches, who has tested his words in the fire of experience, and proclaims them as a path to God and God's love. At the same time, the life-giving truth taught by Father Moon is aligned with the teachings of all the world's faiths. Therefore, as we further study the world's religions in the light of his teachings, we can attain a deep faith and a life-giving connection to Ultimate Reality without falling into exclusivism.

People may wonder: What sort of religious leader is Father Moon? How can he advocate unity and harmony at a time when religions seem so diametrically at odds with one another? Why does he pursue interfaith work with the fervor that other committed religionists pour into evangelizing and making converts? The answer to this question lies in his view of God.

Father Moon knows God as the God of love and sacrifice, always willing to give first, forever living for the sake of others. He is the God who, ever since the time of the tragic Fall of humanity, has been desperately seeking to reunite with us. From this perspective, all the major religions are God-made; each is an expression of God's effort to elevate humanity. Further, being God-made, they each have, transcending cultural and historical differences, certain core elements that reflect

God's divine nature of love and sacrifice. Hence, it is to be expected that we can find common values among the religions of the world, not just one or two, but many.

Chief among God's attributes, according to Father Moon, is parental love. God's parental love is evident in His founding of religions in diverse cultural and historical circumstances, for the purpose of awakening and educating human beings everywhere to attain fellowship with Him. In this sense, the religions of the world are like brothers and sisters in God's family. When the children get along well together, their parents are pleased. Why should religions promote charity and cooperation with other religions? It is first of all to please God, who is their common Parent and who wants them to live in harmony and peace.

Here is the source of Father Moon's revolutionary view of the relationship among religions. Religions should align themselves with the ultimate wish of God, the Parent of humankind, whose love is higher and more comprehensive than any human love. Our Parent's desire is not that religions exist only for themselves, as if it were enough that their rituals and teachings connect their adherents to God above. They also need to relate to the other religions as their brothers and sisters. Instead of remaining separate from one another and even fighting with one another, religions should live for the sake of one another with the common purpose of liberating the world together: "We should not pursue our own self-interest but rather seek for the welfare of other religious groups. Religions should walk the path of self-denial, self-sacrifice, and service to others."[1]

Distinctive Features of This Volume

As regards the selection of texts from the world's traditions, there are some notable developments in this volume as compared with the first *World Scripture*. First, texts are included from the Hellenistic tradition of classical Greece and Rome. Father Moon classifies Socrates, the greatest exemplar of classical philosophy and a martyr to truth, as one of the world's great saints alongside Buddha, Confucius, Jesus and Muhammad. As the *World Scripture* series aims to establish common ground among religions, this volume extends the common ground to include classical philosophers such as Plato, Aristotle and the Stoics. There are indeed shared values between Athens and Jerusalem.

Second, this volume goes further than the first volume of *World Scripture* in seeking to address pressing contemporary issues, including democracy, women's rights, the meaning of freedom, economic justice, the environment, the arts, and more. Father Moon speaks frequently about the problems of the contemporary world, advocating new solutions grounded in timeless spiritual principles. To better explore this side of his thought and its connections with the world's religious traditions, it seemed appropriate to supplement the scriptures with selected quotations from world-level figures who applied their faith to their social context. They include: Mahatma Gandhi, Martin Luther King, Jr., the Dalai Lama, Susan B. Anthony, various Roman Catholic Popes, Islamic teachers such as Rumi and Al-Ghazzali, and others.

Third, one of the pillars of Father Moon's thought is divine providence, which he sees as carried out in an historical line extending from Adam, to Noah, Abraham, Isaac and Jacob, Moses and Jesus. God's providence includes as well the lives and teachings of Buddha, Confucius and Muhammad, whose roles were to expand the fruits of the central line of providence outward to the rest of the world. To better explore this aspect of his thought, this volume recasts the *World Scripture* chapter The Founder into a new chapter, History of God's Providence, where each of these figures is treated in turn. As regards the biblical figures, wherever possible scriptural testimony is drawn from the texts of all three Abrahamic faiths.

Translation

A special challenge in preparing this volume was to establish accurate translations of Father Moon's teachings. This was a considerable undertaking, occupying the work of the editors and their staff for two full years. Korean and English are such dissimilar languages that translation between them is extremely difficult, and furthermore Father Moon has a unique vocabulary and gives his Korean words special meanings. Few people have both the requisite skills in translation and familiarity with Father Moon's thought as to be qualified for the task. Although thousands of pages of Father Moon's words exist in English, the translations are largely unreliable. Many were simultaneous translations made in the heat of delivering a sermon, where the translator was oftentimes reduced to paraphrasing a complex thought. Sometimes the translator adjusted the content on purpose to be more understandable to a Western audience; this was especially the case for certain well-known public speeches delivered in 1973 and 1974.

Hence, it was not surprising that when English passages selected for the book were checked against the Korean text, eighty percent of them had to be completely re-translated.[2] The American and Korean editors met together on a weekly basis to review the translations, identify difficulties, and come up with renderings that satisfied both the criteria of accuracy and good English sense. Nevertheless, no translation can be perfect; there is always something lost or misunderstood in going from one language to another, one culture to another, one way of thinking to another. The editors regret where their work may fall short and cause misunderstanding.

Acknowledgements

World Scripture and the Teachings of Sun Myung Moon would not have been possible without the support and labor of many dedicated people whom we wish to acknowledge. Particularly, we would like to thank Dr. Andrew Wilson, who has been leading this task with a deep sense of commitment ever since the publication of the first *World Scripture*, for his profound knowledge and wise judgment in planning this volume and in selecting and arranging its text. We would also like to recognize Dr. Theodore Shimmyo and Hee Hun Oh Standard for guiding the overall direction of the book and for their exceptional endeavors to attain an accurate translation of Father Moon's teachings that is both faithful to the original language and intelligent in its English expression.

We are also grateful to all those who supplied new passages from diverse traditions in order to fill out the World Scripture in areas where it was lacking, especially Elio Roman, Dr. Muhammad Habash, Dr. Thomas Selover, David Eaton, Dr. Charles Selengut, Mark Callahan and Dr. Dietrich Seidel; and we wish to thank once again all the editors and contributors to the first *World Scripture*, which served as the basis upon which this new compilation was created. Furthermore, we are grateful to Dr. Sung-Bae Jin and his team of scholars in Korea, including Dr. Taek-Yong Oh and Prof. Jae-Il Lee of Sun Moon University, who provided key texts from Father Moon's voluminous speeches. Acknowledgment is also due to Hyanghwa Oh, Tim Elder, Lym-Sung Kim, YoungAe Cotter, Moonsook Choi Yoon and Michiko Kim, who made dedicated efforts to translate these passages from Korean to English; to Julian Gray, Dr. Clinton Bennett, Dr. David Carlson, David Fraser-Harris and Kyoungho Kim, who gave valuable advice on a wide range of editorial and translation matters; to the staff of the Universal Peace Federation who provided organizational support; to Dr. Tyler Hendricks and the Unification Theological

Seminary which offered its generous assistance; and finally, to Dr. Gordon Anderson and Jeff Anderson, who worked to lay out and produce the book, and pursued the difficult task of obtaining permissions, and went the extra mile to meet some very tight deadlines.

Universal Peace Federation
Publisher

Invocation

WE OPEN WITH REPRESENTATIVE PRAYERS from the world's religions. They invoke, give thanks, and affirm the efficacious influence of Absolute Reality in human life. Many of these prayers, including the Lord's Prayer, the Fatihah, the Kaddish, the Gayatri, and the Family Pledge of Father Moon, are recited daily or weekly as part of regular worship.

Our Father who art in heaven,
Hallowed be Thy name.
Thy kingdom come, Thy will be done,
On earth as it is in heaven.
Give us this day our daily bread;
And forgive us our debts,
As we also have forgiven our debtors.[1]
And lead us not into temptation,
But deliver us from evil.
Matthew 6.9-13, The Lord's Prayer

In the name of God, the Beneficent, the
   Merciful.
Praise be to God, Lord of the Worlds,
The Beneficent, the Merciful,
Owner of the Day of Judgment.
Thee alone we worship; Thee alone we ask for
   help.
Show us the straight path:
The path of those whom Thou hast favored;
Not of those who earn Thine anger
Nor of those who go astray.[2]
Qur'an 1, The Fatihah

Glorified and sanctified be God's great name throughout the world which he has created according to his will. May he establish his kingdom in your lifetime and during your days, and within the life of the entire house of Israel, speedily and soon; and say, Amen.[3]

May his great name be blessed forever and to all eternity.

Blessed and praised, glorified and exalted, extolled and honored, adored and lauded be the name of the Holy One, blessed be he, beyond all the blessings and hymns, praises and consolations that are ever spoken in the world; and say, Amen.

May the prayers and supplications of the whole house of Israel be accepted by their Father who is in heaven; and say, Amen.

May there be abundant peace from heaven, and life, for us and for all Israel; and say, Amen.

He who creates peace in his celestial heights, may he create peace for us and for all Israel; and say, Amen.
The Kaddish (Judaism)

OM.
We meditate upon the glorious splendor
Of the Vivifier divine.
May He Himself illumine our minds.
OM.[4]
Rig Veda 3.62.10, The Gayatri Mantra (Hinduism)

Homage to Him, the Exalted One, the
   Arahant, the All-enlightened One.
To the Buddha I go for refuge.
To the Norm I go for refuge.
To the Order I go for refuge.[5]
Khuddaka Patha (Buddhism)

From the unreal lead me to the Real!
From darkness lead me to light!
From death lead me to immortality!
OM.
>   Brihadaranyaka Upanishad 1.3.28 *(Hinduism)*

May the Lord bless you and keep you;
May the Lord make his face to shine upon you,
   and be gracious to you;
May the Lord lift up his countenance upon
   you, and give you peace.
>   Numbers 6.24-26, The Aaronic Benediction

Teachings of Sun Myung Moon

1. Our family, the owner of Cheon Il Guk, pledges to seek our original homeland and build the Kingdom of God on earth and in heaven, the original ideal of creation, by centering on true love.[6]

2. Our family, the owner of Cheon Il Guk, pledges to represent and become central to heaven and earth by attending God and True Parents; we pledge to perfect the dutiful family way of filial sons and daughters in our family, patriots in our nation, saints in the world, and divine sons and daughters in heaven and earth, by centering on true love.

3. Our family, the owner of Cheon Il Guk, pledges to perfect the Four Great Realms of Heart, the Three Great Kingships and the Realm of the Royal Family, by centering on true love.

4. Our family, the owner of Cheon Il Guk, pledges to build the universal family encompassing heaven and earth, which is God's ideal of creation, and perfect the world of freedom, peace, unity and happiness, by centering on true love.

5. Our family, the owner of Cheon Il Guk, pledges to strive every day to advance the unification of the spirit world and the physical world as subject and object partners, by centering on true love.

6. Our family, the owner of Cheon Il Guk, pledges to become a family that moves heavenly fortune by embodying God and True Parents, and to perfect a family that conveys Heaven's blessing to our community, by centering on true love.

7. Our family, the owner of Cheon Il Guk, pledges, through living for the sake of others, to perfect the world based on the culture of heart, which is rooted in the original lineage, by centering on true love.

8. Our family, the owner of Cheon Il Guk, pledges, having entered the Completed Testament Age, to achieve the ideal of God and human beings united in love through absolute faith, absolute love and absolute obedience, and to perfect the realm of liberation and complete freedom in the Kingdom of God on earth and in heaven, by centering on true love. *(The Family Pledge)*

Part One

God and Creation

Chapter 1

GOD

Knowledge of God

HOW CAN HUMAN BEINGS RECOGNIZE the existence of the Absolute Being? Philosophers have ever pondered this question; some offering proofs while others are skeptical that any such knowledge can be had. Although such discussion is beyond the scope of this anthology, certain arguments are put forth in scripture. God has left evidence of His existence and provided ways for people to know Him, if they only look.

The first of these is evidence of God's handiwork in the creation. Numerous scientists testify that the more they studied nature, the more certain they were of a Designer. Inventor Thomas Edison remarked, "The universe is permeated by Intelligence. I tell you, no person can be brought into close contact with the mysteries of nature or make a study of chemistry without being convinced that behind all, there is a supreme Intelligence."[1]

The second path to God is the doorway of contemplation, that innermost self which senses God's reality. The apprehension of God is mystical, not intellectual. Blaise Pascal said, "It is the heart which perceives God, and not the reason."[2] Father Moon teaches that God is most essentially our Parent; hence we should experience Him with the same immediacy that we know our own parents. The third type of evidence is supernatural. Few of us have access to this source, but we regard those who have such experiences as trustworthy guides. They are the founders of religion and people who have journeyed into the spiritual realms.

1. Traces of God in the Creation

For what can be known about God is plain to [all], because God has showed it to them. Ever since the creation of the world his invisible nature, namely, his eternal power and deity, has been clearly perceived in the things that have been made. So they are without excuse.

Romans 1.19-20

We shall show then Our signs on the horizons and within themselves until it becomes clear to them that it is the Truth.

Qur'an 41.53

And of His signs is that He created you from the dust; now behold you are human beings, ranging widely.

And of His signs is that He created for you, of yourselves, spouses that you might find repose in them, and He has planted love and kindness in your hearts. Surely there are signs in this for people who reflect.

And of His signs is the creation of the heavens and the earth and the variety of your tongues and hues, surely there are signs in this for people who have knowledge.

And of His signs is your slumber by night and day, and your seeking of His bounty. Surely there are signs in this for people who hear.

The lightning which He shows you for fear and hope is yet another of His signs; He sends down water from the sky, thereby reviving the earth after it is dead. Surely in this there are signs for people who understand.

And of His signs is that space and the earth stand firm by His command; then when He calls you, suddenly, from the earth you shall emerge.

Qur'an 30.20-25

For each and every form he is the Model;
it is his form that is to be seen everywhere;
Indra moves multiform by his creative charm;
the bay steeds yoked to his car are a thousand.

                    Rig Veda 6.47.18 *(Hinduism)*

Too many people have a microscopic idea of the Creator. If they would only study his wonderful works as shown in nature herself and the natural laws of the universe, they would have a much broader idea of the great Engineer. Indeed, I can almost prove [God's] existence by chemistry. One thing is certain: the universe is permeated by Intelligence. I tell you, no person can be brought into close contact with the mysteries of nature or make a study of chemistry without being convinced that behind all, there is a supreme Intelligence.

                    Thomas Edison

So also did We show Abraham the power and the laws of the heavens and the earth, that he might have certitude. When the night covered him over, he saw a star; he said, "This is my Lord." But when it set, he said, "I love not those that set." When he saw the moon rising in splendor, he said, "This is my Lord," but when the moon set, he said, "Unless my Lord guide me, I shall surely be among those who go astray." When he saw the sun rising in splendor, he said, "This is my Lord; this is the greatest of all," but when the sun set, he said, "O my people! I am indeed free from your [error] of ascribing partners to God. For me, I have set my face firmly and truly towards Him who created the heavens and the earth, and never shall I ascribe partners to God."

                    Qur'an 6.75-79

All things are made to bear record of Me, both things which are temporal and things which are spiritual; things which are in the heavens above, and things which are on the earth, and things which are in the earth, and things which are under the earth, both above and beneath: all things bear record of Me.

                    Pearl of Great Price, Moses 6.63
                    (Latter-day Saints)

The heavens are telling the glory of God;
and the firmament proclaims his handiwork.
Day to day pours forth speech,
and night to night declares knowledge.
There is no speech, nor are there words,
neither is their voice heard;
Yet their voice goes out through all the earth,
and their words to the end of the world.[3]

                    Psalm 19.1-4

Teachings of Sun Myung Moon

How can we know the divine nature of the incorporeal God? One way to fathom His deity is by observing the universe which He created. Thus, St. Paul said:

> Ever since the creation of the world His invisible nature, namely, His eternal power and deity, has been clearly perceived in the things that have been made. So they are without excuse. (Rom. 1.20)

Just as a work of art displays the invisible nature of its maker in a concrete form, everything in the created universe is a substantial manifestation of some quality of the Creator's invisible, divine nature. As such, each stands in a relationship to God. Just as we can come to know the character of an artist through his works, so we can understand the nature of God by observing the diverse things of creation. (*Exposition of the Divine Principle*, Creation 1.1)

The human body reflects the mystery of God. Analyze and dissect it using your intellect, and even after millions of years you would not know all there is to know about your body. Despite thousands of eye doctors, there are still innumerable mysteries about the eye. Do you think medical science knows all there is to know about the eye? No, their knowledge is still in its infancy. How, then, can these "infants" say there is no God? (95:123, November 6, 1977)

Look at the eye. Before it was formed, the eye must have been designed by someone who realized that it would be functioning in an atmosphere of dust and wind. It was designed in such a way to adjust to such conditions. Do you think the eye knew ahead of time what conditions it would face? If it did not, there must be Someone who knew, and who created the eye with the means to protect it. There must be some Intelligence, operating behind the scenes, which had cosmic knowledge. It knew that the earth's heat would cause moisture to evaporate from the surface of the eye, so it made tear ducts to lubricate it. There is Reason within the design of nature. Look at the eyelids, designed to prevent the serious problem of dust entering the eye. Look at the eyebrows; they were designed to block sweat from running down into the eye. Did the eyebrows appear knowing that they would have this function? Or did the eyes put on eyebrows because they knew this of themselves?

No. There is an Intelligence that knew in advance the environment in which the eye would be functioning and designed the eye precisely for it. (117:78, February 1, 1982)

One way to prove the existence of God is by observing the abundant evidence that God is trying to promote world citizenship and the concept of the world as one nation. Can you find a certain universal ingredient in religion that encourages loyalty beyond the level of nation or race? That evidence alone is sufficient for us to recognize the existence of God, who through the course of history has been promoting unity. (95:63, October 23, 1977)

2. Evidence for God within the Self

Eye cannot see him, nor words reveal him;
by the senses, austerity, or works he is not known.
When the mind is cleansed by the grace of wisdom,
he is seen by contemplation—the One without parts.

Mundaka Upanishad 3.1.8 (Hinduism)

The thing that is called Tao is eluding and vague.
Vague and eluding, there is in it the form.
Eluding and vague, in it are things.
Deep and obscure, in it is the essence.
The essence is very real; in it are evidences.
From the time of old until now, its manifestations ever remain,
By which we may see the beginnings of all things.
How do I know that the beginnings of all things are so?
Through this.[4]

Tao Te Ching 21 (Taoism)

As the Holy One I recognized Thee, O Wise Lord,
When He came to me as Good Mind;
The Silent Thought taught me the greatest good
so that I might proclaim it.

Avesta, Yasna 45.15 (Zoroastrianism)

Who knows truly, and who will now declare,
what paths lead together to the gods?
Only their lowest aspects of existence are seen,
who exist on supreme, mystical planes.

Rig Veda 3.54.5 (Hinduism)

Confucius said, "The power of spiritual forces in the universe—how active it is everywhere! Invisible to the eyes and impalpable to the senses, it is inherent in all things, and nothing can escape its operation." It is the fact that there are these forces which make men in all countries fast and purify themselves, and with solemnity of dress institute services of sacrifice and religious worship. Like the rush of mighty waters, the presence of unseen Powers is felt; sometimes above us, sometimes around us.

In *The Book of Songs* it is said,

> The presence of the Spirit:
> It cannot be surmised,
> How may it be ignored!

Such is the evidence of things invisible that it is impossible to doubt the spiritual nature of man.

Doctrine of the Mean 16 *(Confucianism)*

Teachings of Sun Myung Moon

Before I came into being, God exists. Before I was able to think about God, God exists. God rules over my whole being, including my senses. This is the most important key to understanding.

It is a principle that experience precedes understanding. We do not know what cold is until we feel cold. First we feel the cold weather, and consequently we form a notion of cold.

Likewise, to know that God exists, you should feel His presence in your very cells. To what degree do you experience God? To what degree does your actual experience confirm God's existence? That is the question. (58:291-92, June 25, 1972)

God is alive; so is the Devil. How do you know that God exits, or that the Devil exists? Communism and philosophy in general raises this question. It is the philosophical argument of idealism versus realism. In the latter perspective, anything invisible is not real, but merely an abstract idea. Even the conscience is thought of as a mere concept.

It is the same with love. Love is also an abstract idea from that point of view, yet in truth, love is not an idea. Love connects with everything in our actual life. (186:67, January 29, 1989)

Do you have love? Do you have life? Do you have lineage and conscience? Then, have you ever seen love? Can you see life, lineage or conscience? You know these exist, but you must acknowledge that you cannot see or touch them. You know them because you sense them with your mind. A similar logic applies to the question of whether God exists, or whether a person can see God. Anyone can recognize God and confirm that He exists. Once God comes into your heart, your heart knows Him. (May 1, 2004)

Just as you understand the true meaning of filial piety only after having your own children, you can sense the value of your faith and experience the concrete existence of God only after you have put your faith into practice. (29:198, February 28, 1970)

Had humans not fallen, no one would question whether God exists. Each of us would know the answer through our original minds. Had humans been born from good parents whose original nature was fully developed, they would know God's existence naturally from birth. Doesn't a baby emerge from the womb knowing how to suck its mother's breasts? When the newborn is presented with the breast it begins sucking instinctively. Likewise, had the Human Fall not occurred, we would instinctively know God. Firmly relating with God, we would know how to solve any problem and understand the right path to follow. However, because of the Fall, that original relationship was forgotten. Humankind created a world in which people doubt the existence of God. This is, indeed, a miserable situation. (20:306-07, July 14, 1968)

Just as an electron revolves around a proton, human beings are made to revolve around God. God can pursue the providence for restoration because the human mind, as an electron, naturally relates to God's mind as its nucleus, its proton.

Hence, when we search for the truth, even all by ourselves, we begin to feel the vibration of God's life and the harmony of God's love. (2:137, March 17, 1957)

What is the world we long for in our hearts? It is not the world that we perceive through the outward five senses. Nor is it a world created by concepts. We long for the world of heart, filled with God's love. In that world, we can feel the love of God in even the smallest subatomic particle. You must experience this world. Jesus said, "He who has ears to hear will hear." You cannot experience this multi-dimensional, transcendent world with your everyday feelings. (7:255, September 20, 1959)

God's true homeland is the spirit world… If you want to truly know God, first know the spirit world where God lives and works. (365:302, January 14, 2002)

3. Evidence of God in History

No one has ever seen God; the only Son, who is in the bosom of the Father, he has made him known.[5]

John 1.18

And you shall know that I am the LORD, when their slain lie among their idols round about their altars, upon every high hill, on all the mountain tops, under every green tree, and under every leafy oak, wherever they offered pleasing odor to all their idols. And I will stretch out my hand against them, and make the land desolate and waste, throughout all their habitations, from the wilderness to Riblah. Then they will know that I am the LORD."

Ezekiel 6.13-14

All thy works shall give thanks to thee, O LORD,
and all thy saints shall bless thee!
They shall speak of the glory of thy kingdom,
and tell of thy power,
to make known to the sons of men thy mighty deeds,
and the glorious splendor of thy kingdom.
Thy kingdom is an everlasting kingdom,
and thy dominion endures throughout all generations.

The LORD is faithful in all his words,
and gracious in all his deeds.
The LORD upholds all who are falling,
and raises up all who are bowed down.
The eyes of all look to thee,
and thou givest them their food in due season.
Thou openest thy hand,
thou satisfiest the desire of every living thing.
The LORD is just in all his ways,
and kind in all his doings.

Psalm 145.10-17

Teachings of Sun Myung Moon

The Absolute Being is not conceptual, but rather a real existence who has been revealing Himself throughout human history. The saints, sages and religious leaders who appeared at various times and places have, without exception, appealed to the human conscience and heart, urging the people to practice love of neighbor. When the people responded and followed their teachings, they and their nations enjoyed peace and prosperity; but when they refused, they fell into confusion and decline. Even in today's confusion and chaos, humankind is waiting, consciously or unconsciously, for the appearance of modern saints and sages who will reveal the path of love.

All this shows that the Absolute Being is a real existence who operates behind the scenes of history. He is the Subject of love, who has worked through saints, sages and religious leaders of every age. He works to fulfill His plan: to establish a world of moral values, a world where love is the norm. (69:238, November 21, 1973)

The One God

THE UNITY AND UNIQUENESS OF GOD COMPRISE the theme of the passages collected in this section. They come from every religion, the avowedly monotheistic Abrahamic faiths and Eastern religions also. The divine unity may be hidden under a multiplicity of appearances; nevertheless there is a single Source and a single Principle that brings order and meaning to the phenomenal world. In particular, many of these texts affirm that the various concepts of Ultimate Reality in the world's religions are manifestations of the same one God.

The readings from Father Moon affirm the one God at the root of all true religion. In addition, they point to the ethical teachings implicit in this truth.

Hear, O Israel, the LORD our God, the LORD is One.[6]

     Deuteronomy 6.4: The Shema

Say: He is God, the One!
God, the eternally Besought of all!
He neither begets nor was begotten.
And there is none comparable unto Him.

     Qur'an 112

He is the Sole Supreme Being; of eternal manifestation;
Creator, Immanent Reality; Without Fear, Without Rancor;
Timeless Form; Unincarnate; Self-existent;
Realized by the grace of the Holy Preceptor.

     Japuji p. 1, The Mul Mantra (Sikhism)

He is the one God, hidden in all beings, all-pervading, the Self within all beings, watching over all works, dwelling in all beings, the witness, the perceiver, the only one, free from qualities.

     Svetasvatara Upanishad 6.11 (Hinduism)

They have called him Indra, Mitra, Varuna, Agni,
and the divine fine-winged Garuda;
They speak of Indra, Yama, Matrarisvan:
the One Being sages call by many names.

     Rig Veda 1.164.46 (Hinduism)

To God belong all creatures in the heavens and on the earth: even those who are in His very Presence are not too proud to serve Him, nor are they ever weary. They celebrate His praises night and day, nor do they ever flag or intermit. Or have they taken gods from the earth who can raise the dead? If there were, in the heavens or in the earth, other gods besides God, there would have been confusion in both! But glory to God, the Lord of the Throne; high is He above what they attribute to Him!

     Qur'an 21.19-22

There is everywhere not disorder but order, proportion and not disproportion, not disarray but arrangement in an order perfectly harmonious.

Therefore we must infer and be led to perceive the Master that put together and compacted all things, and produced harmony in them. For though He be not seen with the eyes, yet from the order and harmony of things contrary it is possible to perceive their Ruler, Arranger and King… In the order and harmony of the Universe we perceive God the governor of it all, and that He is one and not many.

Athanasius (Christianity)

The sage clasps the Primal Unity,
Testing by it everything under heaven.

Tao Te Ching 22 (Taoism)

Paul, standing in the middle of the Areopagus, said, "Men of Athens, I perceive that in every way you are very religious. For as I passed along, and observed the objects of your worship, I found also an altar with this inscription, 'To an unknown god.' What therefore you worship as unknown, this I proclaim to you. The God who made the world and everything in it, being Lord of heaven and earth, does not live in shrines made by man, nor is he served by human hands, as though he needed anything, since he himself gives to all men life and breath and everything. And he made from one every nation of men to live on the face of the earth, having determined allotted periods and the boundaries of their habitation, that they should seek God, in the hope that they might feel after him and find him. Yet he is not far from each one of us, for 'In him we live and move and have our being'; as even some of your poets have said, 'For we are indeed his offspring.' "

Acts 17.22-28

When appearances and names are put away and all discrimination ceases, that which remains is the true and essential nature of things and, as nothing can be predicated as to the nature of essence, is called the "Suchness" of Reality. This universal, undifferentiated, inscrutable Suchness is the only Reality, but it is variously characterized as Truth, Mind-essence, Transcendental Intelligence, Perfection of Wisdom, etc. This teaching of the imagelessness of the Essence-nature of Ultimate Reality is the teaching which has been proclaimed by all the Buddhas, and when all things are understood in full agreement with it, one is in possession of Perfect Knowledge.[7]

Lankavatara Sutra (Buddhism)

God said to Israel, "Because you have seen Me in many likenesses, there are not therefore many gods. But it is ever the same God: I am the LORD your God." Rabbi Levi said, "God appeared to them like a mirror, in which many faces can be reflected; a thousand people look at it; it looks at all of them." So when God spoke to the Israelites, each one thought that God spoke individually to him.

Pesikta Kahana 109b-110a (Judaism)

The Hindus and the Muslims have but one and the same God.

Adi Granth, Bhairo, p. 1158 (Sikhism)

There can be no doubt that whatever the peoples of the world, of whatever race or religion, derive their inspiration from one heavenly Source, and are the subjects of one God. The difference between the ordinances under which they abide should be attributed to the varying requirements and exigencies of the age in which they were revealed. All of them, except for a few which are the outcomes of human perversity, were ordained of God, and are a reflection of His Will and Purpose.

Gleanings from the Writings of
Baha'u'llah 111 (Baha'i Faith)

Teachings of Sun Myung Moon

What is the source of all beings? God, the One Being, unique and absolute. (262:51, July 23, 1994)

What is the one true existence in heaven and earth? He is the Absolute Being. The Korean language refers to Him as the Only Being, the Owner and Lord, which when abbreviated is "The One Lord" (*Hananim*), God.[8] (39:302, January 16, 1971)

God is called by many different names, yet regardless of what names He is called, there cannot be many gods. Since the origin is only one, there can be only one God. Due to the many different languages of the world, there are many different names for God. Yet God, the original entity, is only One.

The purpose that God pursues is manifested through religions. Hence, no matter how many religions exist, their purpose is one—the peace of the Kingdom of Heaven. (210:199-200, December 23, 1990)

All the 'absolute beings' worshiped until now are not different gods, but actually one and the same God. Each religion's theology grasps but an aspect of God's attributes. A correct understanding of the entirety of God clarifies that all religions are brothers, all established by the one God. (122:304, November 25, 1982)

Each religion has an absolute being as a basis for its doctrine. The absolute being of Judaism is Jehovah, of Christianity, God, and of Islam, Allah. Confucianism and Buddhism do not specify an absolute being. However, because the basic Confucian virtue of benevolence (*jen*) is linked to the mandate of Heaven, Heaven may be regarded as the absolute being in Confucianism. Buddhism teaches that all phenomena are in constant change while the truth is found in the 'Suchness' that lies behind all phenomena.[9] Thus, Suchness functions as the absolute being of Buddhism. (122:301, November 25, 1982)

The basic cause of religious conflict lies in the ambiguity of their doctrines about Ultimate Reality. The Absolute Being is only one; there cannot be two absolute beings. However, when the leaders of each religion claim that only their absolute being is the true God, it leads to the contradiction that there is more than one absolute being. We would then conclude that the god of each religion is only a relative god, and that there is no basis for believing that the Absolute Being exists.

Consequently, although God has been promoting through the various religions a universal teaching about God's love and truth, their various perspectives remain only relative. We can conclude that religions have been incapable of establishing the absolute value perspective that can bring the prevailing confusion under control. This is the inevitable result of the fact that no religion has been able to present the correct explanation about the Absolute Being. (122:300-01, November 25, 1982)

Each religion has pride in its own teachings and jealously guards its traditions, regarding itself as superior to all others. However, religious teaching has universal elements, which come from God. The one God is the God of all religions. Therefore, religions should purify themselves and elevate themselves through universal principles.

The central value in religion is true love, which we can sum up by the teaching, "Live for the sake of others." The individual lives for the sake of the family; the family lives for the sake of the community; the community lives for the sake of the nation; the nation lives for the sake of the world. Likewise, my religion should live for the sake of other religions. This is the principle of principles.

The source of this universal principle is God. In creating the universe, God invested Himself totally for the sake of His creatures. Throughout history, God has been continually sacrificing Himself in order to save fallen human beings, who have been living just as they desire. The prophets, saints and sages who knew God's will have followed this divine principle in their own lives. (234:222, August 20, 1992)

In God's way of thinking, there is no concept of an enemy. If there were, it would imply Dualism (two origins). Because God does not have such a concept, He does not fight. (225:123, January 5, 1992)

Formless, Invisible, Mystery

GOD IS FORMLESS AND INVISIBLE. He is beyond any human concept, hidden and inscrutable: "My thoughts are not your thoughts, neither are your ways my ways." In the monotheistic religions, the prohibition of images is a statement about the utter transcendence of God, for to represent God by an idol is to reduce the infinite to finitude. Eastern religions likewise assert that no words or intellectual concepts can properly convey the nature of Ultimate Reality. How can finite human knowledge comprehend the supreme Knower and source of mind itself?

Father Moon affirms that God is formless, invisible and beyond human knowledge, but then adds something more: God is not content to remain that way. The invisible God's ultimate purpose is to manifest Himself in the visible form of Man. Accordingly, God does not leave us forever in ignorance, but in the Last Days He reveals all matters hidden in His heart. What is more, we will advance to the point where we can fully embody God's nature and become His representatives on earth.

No vision can grasp Him,
but His grasp is over all vision;
He is above all comprehension,
Yet is acquainted with all things.
Qur'an 6.103

The way that can be spoken of
Is not the eternal Way;
The name that can be named
Is not the eternal name.
The nameless was the beginning of heaven and
 earth;
The named was the mother of the myriad
 creatures.
Hence always rid yourself of desire in order to
 observe its secrets;
But always allow yourself to have desires in
 order to observe its manifestations.
These two are the same
But diverge in name as they issue forth.
Being the same they are called mysteries,
Mystery upon mystery—
The gateway of the manifold secrets.
Tao Te Ching 1 (Taoism)

The eye cannot see it; the mind cannot grasp
 it.
The deathless Self has neither caste nor race,
Neither eyes nor ears nor hands nor feet.
Sages say this Self is infinite in the great
And in the small, everlasting and changeless,
The source of life.
Mundaka Upanishad 1.1.6 (Hinduism)

The Supreme Soul is neither long nor short, nor a circle nor a triangle, nor a quadrilateral nor a sphere. He is neither black nor blue nor red nor yellow nor white. He is neither a pleasant smell nor an unpleasant smell. He is neither pungent nor bitter nor astringent nor sour nor sweet. He is neither hard nor soft, neither heavy nor light, neither cold nor hot, neither rough nor smooth. He is bodiless. He is not subject to birth. He is free from attachment. He is neither female nor male nor neuter. He is immaculate knowledge and intuition. There exists no simile to comprehend him. He is formless existence. He is what baffles all terminology. There is no word to comprehend him. He is neither sound nor form nor odor nor taste nor touch. Only so much I say.

Acarangasutra 5.126-40 *(Jainism)*

Here, O Shariputra, form is emptiness, and the very emptiness is form; emptiness does not differ from form, form does not differ from emptiness; whatever is form, that is emptiness, whatever is emptiness, that is form. The same is true of feelings, perceptions, impulses, consciousness.

Heart Sutra *(Buddhism)*

Truly thou art a God who hidest thyself.

Isaiah 45.15

Can you find out the deep things of God?
Can you find out the limit of the Almighty?
It is higher than heaven—what can you do?
Deeper than Sheol—what can you know?
Its measure is longer than the earth,
and broader than the sea.

Job 11.7-9

The Intelligence which reveals all—by what shall it be revealed? By whom shall the Knower be known? The Self is described as "not this, not that" *(neti, neti)*. It is incomprehensible, for it cannot be comprehended; undecaying, for it never decays; unattached, for it never attaches itself; unbound, for it is never bound. By whom, O my beloved, shall the Knower be known?[10]

Bhrihadaranyaka Upanishad 4.5.15 *(Hinduism)*

Who sees me by form,
Who seeks me in sound,
Perverted are his footsteps upon the Way;
For he cannot perceive the Tathagata.

Diamond Sutra 26 *(Buddhism)*

For my thoughts are not your thoughts,
neither are your ways my ways, says the LORD.

Isaiah 55.8

Invent not similitudes for God; for God knows, and you know not.

Qur'an 16.74

Moses said, "I pray thee, show me thy glory." And [the LORD] said, "I will make all my goodness pass before you, and will proclaim before you my name 'The LORD'; and I will be gracious to whom I will be gracious, and will show mercy on whom I will show mercy." "But," he said, "you cannot see my face; for man shall not see me and live." And the LORD said, "Behold, there is a place by me where you shall stand upon the rock; and while my glory passes by I will put you in a cleft of the rock, and I will cover you with my hand until I have passed by; then I will take away my hand, and you shall see my back; but my face shall not be seen."

Exodus 33.18-23

Since you saw no form on the day that the LORD spoke to you at Horeb out of the midst of the fire, beware lest you act corruptly by making a graven image for yourselves, in the form of any figure, the likeness of male or female, the likeness of any beast that is on the earth, the likeness of any winged bird that flies in the air, the likeness of anything that creeps on the ground, the likeness of any fish that is in the water under the earth.

Deuteronomy 4.15-18

In the beginning was God,
Today is God
Tomorrow will be God.
Who can make an image of God?
He has no body.

He is as a word which comes out of your
   mouth.
That word! It is no more,
It is past, and still it lives!
So is God.

Pygmy Hymn (African Traditional Religions)

Teachings of Sun Myung Moon

You cannot see God even in the spirit world. Can you see energy? God is the original source of energy. Therefore, even in the spirit world He cannot be seen. (105:193, October 21, 1979)

God is formless. He is infinitely greater than any concept of bigness and infinitesimally smaller than any concept of smallness. (35:157, October 13, 1970)

What is the shape of love? If love had a certain shape, like a square, then it could only accommodate a square-shaped person. But because love is like the air, without shape or form, it can fill any shape or form. Love can be sometimes round, sometimes thin. It can be stretched like an elastic thread, even thousands of miles. Yet love never complains, "I'm already too stretched. Don't pull me any more!"

    Love always has the attitude, "Pull me more. Stretch me further." That is opposite from, "Too much! Stop it!" Even if the love thread breaks, God would want to keep unwinding it from its spool. That love string will pull God and stretch Him out. Even if God felt pain at this, His "Ouch!" would be a joyful one. (167:115, July 1, 1987)

How heavy do you think God is? How many kilograms does He weigh? A hundred billion tons? Were God that heavy, He would have a serious problem trying to move around. Rather, it is ideal that God is invisible. Even if you carried Him inside your wallet, you would not feel any weight.

    Being invisible, God can pass through the eye of even the smallest needle. He can move around at will. Being infinitely large yet also infinitely small, He can freely move about anywhere in the universe. (136:106)

You should be grateful that God is invisible. If you could see Him [as He commented on your every action and every word], you would have a nervous breakdown and would be dead within an hour. This is no laughing matter. I tell you this from my own poignant experience. (38:244)

God is very smart. He thought, "The most convenient way to exercise My sovereignty is to be invisible. Then I can do as I wish without being seen or caught by anyone." Despite not having a body, "it is enough," He considered, that I can fulfill my duty as the Lord."

    Suppose God had a body. If He said to the cosmos, whose span is 21 billion light years, "Come to my bosom and rest inside of Me," could God do His duty? Imagine the vast distances! How long would it take God's mind to reach His body? God could foresee that He would be miserable.

    Having conceived all possibilities, God decided to take dominion as a formless, invisible existence. Being invisible, God can move about at His convenience. Moreover, nobody feels troubled when God travels about the physical world. Even if God were to step on your body, you would not notice. How convenient! It is simple logic that God chose to be an invisible God because that resulted in the most convenience...

Suppose you could see God with your physical eyes—see Him as He commented on your every move and every word, and intervened in everything you did. Do you think you could survive even one day without having a nervous breakdown?

Countless particles are passing through your body at this moment, yet you cannot see or feel them. How, then, could you ever see the work of the invisible God as He passes right through you? Rather foolishly saying that you would believe in God if only He showed Himself to you, you should rather be grateful that He is invisible. (138:168, January 21, 1986)

If God, the great Lord of heaven and earth, were visible to human eyes, people would fight each other to possess God. There would be no way to stop the battle...

If God were visible, America and the Soviet Union would fight over Him, each claiming that God was theirs. Who could stop the fighting? The omniscient God stays invisible lest such fights break out. To wish that God were visible is foolish. It is better that He is not. (41:260)

God alone is absolute, unchanging and eternal. Do you think it is easy for the eternal God to relate to fallen human beings? Do people have any idea how to relate to Him? (92:299, April 24, 1977)

God's thoughts, as He leads His Providence, are different from our thoughts, as we encounter the Providence. This is a problem. How can we, who are immersed in the satanic world, find our way to God's Providence? We certainly cannot find the way to fulfill God's purposes by our own concepts. Rather, we must understand the world God originally intended and then transform [ourselves and our world] into God's world. (161:109, January 11, 1987)

God is formless and invisible. His ideal of creation is to manifest Himself into beings with form. In fulfilling this purpose, God would not rest content to be a Being visible only to the spirit world. He would want to be a Being with the substance of the visible world as well. (298:106, January 1, 1999)

The invisible and formless God is the origin of energy. Yet, to have complete dominion over the physical world, God needs an instrument that possesses physical form. If Adam had reached perfection without falling, he would have entered the spirit world as fully the image of God. The spirit of Adam would have become one with the invisible God, and God would have taken on the image of Adam. Had that come to pass, when Adam laughed, God would be laughing and the entire universe would be laughing as well.

The process of creation is the projection of the invisible God into physical forms. It is like a magnet, which needs a south pole as well as a north pole in order to function. There are two aspects of God, external and internal. Thus, God's idea was for the invisible God and the visible God—Adam—to be in harmony. Their give and take would create a circuit. Through their give and take of love, the internal would become external and the external would become internal, back and forth, in circular motion. Thus the internal God and the external God would be united as one. (105:193-94, October 21, 1979)

> In the course of history
> so many saints and sages have come and gone,
> yet none knew the circumstances of Heaven;
> none knew the heart of God.

May we discover the path
to know Heaven's circumstances
and be familiar with God's heart:
knowledge revealed as the Last Days draw near. (7:286, October 11, 1959)

Transcendent Reality

TRANSCENDENCE IS AN ESSENTIAL ATTRIBUTE of the Absolute Being. God's glory fills the world, but the world cannot exhaust God. God is the Ground of Being and the Source of energy within every atom and the life of all creatures. He is the center of the universe and holds all things together. Yet God's involvement in the world in no way limits or affects His transcendence and absoluteness.

How can finite human beings connect with the transcendent God? Some passages recommend that we apply the principle of transcendence in our daily life, by overcoming the limitations of nation and race in our dealings with others. Others speak of getting in touch with the deepest part of our own mind, where the Absolute Being chooses to make His dwelling place.

Holy, holy, holy is the LORD of hosts;
the whole earth is full of his glory.

Isaiah 6.3

God! there is no God but He,
the Living, the Everlasting.
Slumber seizes Him not, neither sleep;
to Him belongs all that is in the heavens and
    the earth.
Who is there who shall intercede with Him
save by His leave?
He knows what lies before them
and what is after them,
and they comprehend not anything of His
    knowledge
save such as He wills.
His throne comprises the heavens and earth;
the preserving of them oppresses Him not;
He is the All-high, the All-glorious.

Qur'an 2.255: The Throne Verse

Who has measured the waters in the hollow of
    his hand
and marked off the heavens with a span,
enclosed the dust of the earth in a measure
and weighed the mountains in scales
and the hills in a balance?

Who has directed the Spirit of the LORD,
or as his counselor has instructed him?
Whom did he consult for his enlightenment,
and who taught him the path of justice,
and taught him knowledge,
and showed him the way of understanding?

Behold, the nations are like a drop from a
    bucket,
and are accounted as the dust on the scales…
All the nations are as nothing before him,
they are accounted by him as less than nothing
    and emptiness.

Isaiah 40.12-17

The Supreme Being is thousand-headed,
Thousand eyed, thousand footed;
Pervading the earth on all sides,
He exists beyond the ten directions.

The Supreme Being, indeed, is all this,
What has been and what will be,
The Lord of immortality
As well as of mortal creatures.

Such is his magnificence, but
The Supreme Being is even greater than this;
All beings are a fourth of him,

Three-fourths—his immortality—lie in heaven.

Three-fourths of the Supreme Being ascended;
The fourth part came here again and again,
Diversified in form, it moved
To the animate and the inanimate world.

      Rig Veda 10.90.1-4 (Hinduism)

Thou art the fire
Thou art the sun
Thou art the air
Thou art the moon
Thou art the starry firmament
Thou art Brahman Supreme;
Thou art the waters—thou, the Creator of all!

Thou art woman, thou art man,
Thou art the youth, thou art the maiden,
Thou art the old man tottering with his staff;
Thou facest everywhere.

Thou art the dark butterfly,
Thou art the green parrot with red eyes,
Thou art the thundercloud, the seasons, the seas.
Without beginning art thou,
Beyond time and space.
Thou art he from whom sprang
The three worlds.

    Svetasvatara Upanishad 4.2-4 (Hinduism)

The Self is one. Ever still, the Self is
Swifter than thought, swifter than the senses.
Though motionless, He outruns all pursuit.
Without the Self, never could life exist.

The Self seems to move, but is ever still.
He seems far away, but is ever near.
He is within all, and He transcends all.

The Self is everywhere. Bright is the Self,
Indivisible, untouched by sin, wise,
Immanent and transcendent. He it is
who holds the cosmos together.

      Isha Upanishad 4-8 (Hinduism)

There was something undifferentiated and yet complete,
which existed before heaven and earth.
Soundless and formless, it depends on nothing and does not change.
It operates everywhere and is free from danger.
It may be considered the mother of the universe.
I do not know its name; I call it Tao.
If forced to give it a name, I shall call it Great.
Being great means functioning everywhere.
Functioning everywhere means far-reaching.
Being far-reaching means returning to the original point.

      Tao Te Ching 25 (Taoism)

Divinity existed before the appearance of heaven and earth and gives form to them; it surpasses the yin and the yang, yet has the quality of them. Divinity is thus the absolute existence, governing the entire universe. Yet at the same time it dwells within all things, where it is called spirit; omnipresent within human beings, it is called mind.

  In other words, the human mind communes with Divinity, which is ruler of heaven and earth; mind and Divinity are one and the same.

  Divinity is the root origin of heaven and earth, the spiritual nature of all things, and the source of human destiny. Itself without form, Divinity nurtures things with form.

    Kanetomo Yoshida, An Outline of Shinto

Beyond the senses is the mind, beyond the mind is the intellect, higher than the intellect is the Great Atman [the original mind], higher than the Great Atman is the Umanifest. Beyond the Unmanifest is the Person, all-pervading, and imperceptible.[11]

    Katha Upanishad 2.3.7-8 (Hinduism)

Buddha abides in the infinite, the unobstructed, ultimate realm of reality, in the realm of space, in the essence of True Thusness, without birth or death, and in ultimate truth...

How should enlightening beings see the body of Buddha? (*Dharmakaya*) They should see the body of Buddha in infinite places. Why? They should not see Buddha in just one thing, one phenomenon, one body, one land, one being—they should see Buddha everywhere.

Just as space is omnipresent, in all places, material or immaterial, yet without either arriving or not arriving there, because space is incorporeal, in the same way Buddha is omnipresent, in all places, in all beings, in all things, in all lands, yet neither arriving nor not arriving there, because Buddha's body is incorporeal, manifesting a body for the sake of sentient beings.[12]

Garland Sutra 37 (Buddhism)

The Way is like an empty vessel
That yet may be drawn from
Without ever needing to be filled.
It is bottomless; the very progenitor of all
　things in the world.
In it all sharpness is blunted,
All tangles untied,
All glare tempered,
All dust smoothed.
It is like a deep pool that never dries.

Tao Te Ching 4 (Taoism)

Teachings of Sun Myung Moon

God transcends space. He encompasses the world and the entire universe. Such also is His unlimited love. (94:282-83, October 9, 1977)

God is the origin of heaven and earth. There is nothing that does not originate from Him. Because everything belongs to God, the whole cosmos senses its bond with God and lives in connection with Him.

By analogy, we humans have four hundred billion cells, and whatever each cell feels, its feeling is communicated to our brain. All creatures are in such a relationship with their Creator. (140:123, February 9, 1986)

Not my parents, my community or my nation gave me life. My life originated rather from the one Origin—God, the Absolute Being, transcending all these. Therefore, my life must be firmly connected to the transcendent Cause, to the axis of the Absolute Being. Relational factors such as time, circumstances and social conditions should not restrict it. Only when we unite our life to the transcendent Cause, the transcendent Purpose, can we transcend the bonds of time, circumstances and social conditions, and extricate ourselves in one leap. (36:64, November 15, 1970)

A human being attains perfection when he centers his life on his mind; likewise, the creation attains perfection only when God stands as its center. Thus, the universe is one organic body that moves only according to God's purpose of creation. As one organic body, the universe exists in a relationship of internal nature and external form, with God as the internal nature and the created universe as the external form. (*Exposition of the Divine Principle,* Creation 1.1)

Everything revolves. Atoms and even elementary particles rotate. Electrons revolve around protons. The solar system revolves around the sun, and the Milky Way rotates around its galactic core. They are revolving around something that remains still. This universe, with all its varied phenomena, is a huge complex of myriads of these relationships. Therefore, we can think that this universe also revolves around a single core: God, the origin of all creation. All things revolve because they resemble their Master, God, who is always revolving. (173:134-35, February 14, 1988)

God, the Creator of heaven and earth, is the Parent and Origin of all beings. He gives value to all existence. Because He is, this world of phenomena came to be. The Absolute Being does not change because the times change—what is absolute does not change. Nor is He restricted by time and space. From a position transcending all restrictions, God has dominion over all restrictions. (21:249, November 24, 1968)

A human being has both mind and body. Beyond his mind is his spirit, and beyond his spirit is God. Therefore, a person becomes perfect only after becoming completely one with God.

One human being, even though apparently only an insignificant individual, represents all of human history and all of the future. Therefore, he has a cosmic value…

As he pursues the ultimate goal, each person must attend his own deep mind. This is an ironclad rule of Heaven. Heaven will punish a person who fails to obey his original mind's command.

In the course of history, the voice of God has been saying, "Live by your deep mind. Live according to your conscience and belong to the side of goodness. Be careful not to be caught in materialistic, evil conditions."

Then, is the standard of a person's conscience able to receive the heart of Heaven 100 percent? No, it is not. In fact, many restrictions impede fallen people's conscience. At the entrance to the heaven of our hopes stand many gates, each a saga of our shortcomings. Borrowing a Christian expression, they are gates of judgment. Our course is made all the more difficult because we are currently in a historical period of fear, anxiety, and confusion. We live in an era when even though we may struggle to achieve goodness, we many times cannot.

These days we should not possess so many material things. When God created human beings, He first created the material, the body, and then breathed into it of His spirit. Therefore, although human beings are composed of both body and spirit, the spirit is the center.

As the world moved towards exalting the authority of material, a period of ideological struggle became inevitable. In fact, this phenomenon was conspicuous right after World War II. Eventually, however, a new age will come based upon spiritual teachings.

Then, what will be the nature of this teaching? It will penetrate matter, penetrate mind, and center on the Spirit. The course of restoration is heading towards an age when thought will center on the Spirit. (4:268, August 3, 1958)

Sovereign and Omnipotent

GOD IS SOVEREIGN OVER THE UNIVERSE. He rules over the affairs of men and women; He decides their destinies. At the same time, since human beings have freedom whether to submit to God's sovereignty, the proper course is to recognize God's authority over our lives and make Him our Lord.

This leads to the question of whether God's sovereignty can be absolute. In this world, the claim that God invariably establishes justice by punishing evil and rewarding goodness is difficult to maintain. Nevertheless, God's ultimate sovereignty is certain. Father Moon teaches in some depth about this matter. He asserts the principle that God can be sovereign only when people are in a state of perfection where they can freely submit to His dominion, yet due to the Human Fall this condition was not obtained. Instead, the Devil took possession of this world by usurping the human heart. Therefore, it is first necessary to expel the power of evil from the world and make it a domain over which God can reign without limitation. That day, Father Moon asserts, is now at hand.

1. Almighty God

The Creator of the heavens and the earth; and when He decrees a thing, He but says to it "Be," and it is.

Qur'an 2.117

All that is in the heavens and the earth
   magnifies God;
He is the All-mighty, the All-wise.
To Him belongs the Kingdom of the heavens
   and the earth.
He gives life, and He makes to die,
and He is powerful over everything.
He is the First and the Last, the Outward and
   the Inward;
He has knowledge of everything.
It is He that created the heavens and the earth
   in six days
then seated Himself upon the Throne.
He knows what penetrates into the earth, and
   what comes forth from it,
what comes down from heaven, and what goes
   up into it.
He is with you wherever you are;
and God sees the things you do.
To Him belongs the kingdom of the heavens
   and the earth;
and unto Him all matters are returned.
He makes the night enter into the day
and makes the day enter into the night.
He knows the thoughts within the breasts.

Qur'an 57.1-6

If He so will, He can remove you and put in your place a new creation; that is surely no great matter for God.

Qur'an 14.19-20

You are the one imperishable
paramount necessary core of knowledge,
The world's ultimate foundation;
you never cease to guard the eternal tradition.
You are the everlasting Divine Being.

There is no telling what is
beginning, middle, or end in you.
Your power is infinite;
your arms reach infinitely far.
Sun and moon are your eyes.
This is how I see you.
Your mouth is a flaming sacrificial fire.
You burn up the world with your radiance.

For you alone fill the quarters of heaven
and the space between heaven and earth.
The world above, man's world,
and the world in between
are frightened at the awesome sight of you,
O mighty being!

Bhagavad-Gita 11.18-20 *(Hinduism)*

O mankind! It is you that have need of God: but God is the One Free of all wants, worthy of all praise.

Qur'an 35.15

Teachings of Sun Myung Moon

What is God like? [You say,] He is omnipotent, omniscient, omnipresent, who can destroy or create worlds with just one word. However, we do not need this kind of God. What kind of God does our original mind desire? We long for a God about whom we can say, "I love Him more than I love my own father and mother." (147:271)

God is almighty. It was not due to His shortcoming or lack of ability that He has been imprisoned in great pain and has endured immense suffering behind the scenes of history. It was because there are provisions in the Principle of Restoration, which He was not free to disclose, that called Him to wait with forbearance until Adam and Eve's positions, lost at the human fall, were recovered with the appearance of the perfected Second Adam. Although God is all-powerful, He will not set aside the eternal laws and principles that He Himself established. (September 12, 2005)

Many people rattle off words about God's absoluteness, omnipotence and glory. Nonetheless, through my lifelong search for truth, I have found that to be way off the mark. When the first human ancestors fell, God became a bereaved Parent who lost His beloved children. Think of it: if your children were in prison, could you as a parent live in glory? So you can understand how God's heart could be in deep pain and sadness. Furthermore, God also had to hand over to Satan the beautiful creation which He had made for His children.

From the moment He lost His object partners of love, the God of true love became the God of loneliness. From that moment on, God was in no position to exercise His power as the Lord of the universe. He had no opportunity to display His authority as the Creator of all things, while fallen people go about boasting over their petty creations. Although God is the Lord of all that has breath, He could not display His dignity. Although God is the Owner of all that lives, He was never able to manifest His supreme glory. Although God is Author of the Principle, how could He operate freely in a world that had fallen and become unprincipled?

Human beings, living with all degrees of distrust and rebellion, mock God as non-existent or dead. Even those who say they believe mostly ignore God as they go about their daily life. God has endured this long history with a heart full of excruciating pain.[13] (January 29, 2001)

We need a God who transcends evil and everything, who has absolute power to subjugate all. Even though the Devil exists, he should not be able to hinder God; rather God should transcend the Devil and be completely unrestricted. Until we find such a God, we will not be able to overcome the present state of conflict.

God has been fighting with the Devil throughout history, and religions have been relegated to an internal, spiritual role. That condition has not provided a way to establish a new culture. Only when God is absolute and transcendent, when the Devil cannot interfere in any way, can there be the new beginning that can resolve the problems of today's world.

Yet consider the present position of God. He is not a transcendental Being who rules over human history or the history of providence. Why? It is because human beings fell. God stands in the position of a doctor who seeks to cure human beings of this sickness. He is the repairman, mending us of this defect. Not having yet raised up perfected individuals, He could not be the God who stands in the absolute position and guides humankind towards the one goal. (140:18-19, February 1, 1986)

> Father! Mayest Thou become the Lord of this heaven and earth which have no lord;
> the Center who can be responsible for this nation and lead it to its future destiny,
> the Center of our families' hopes,
> and our individual hopes.
> What the world needs, the nation needs, the family needs and the individual needs
> art Thou, our Father, the Lord who created all of heaven and earth.
>
> Thou art the Being of infinite might.
> Thou art the omnipotent Being,

unlimited in the world of time and space,
the Creator of everything.
Thou art the Subject Partner endowing everything with meaning.
Everything exists according to its destined relationship with Thee.
Nothing that exists is without purpose:
each is an object partner to Thee, the Subject Partner.
We know that we ourselves, our families, nations and the world,
find their position in relation to Thee.

When the sun shines,
the life of all beings springs forth from that light.
Even microorganisms seek to unite with the light, facing one center.
In the same way, we must attend Thee as the Lord of our lives,
our Father who brightens the path on which we must tread.
Unless we unite with Thee,
and become one with Thee,
our path of life will be blocked. (59:65-67, July 9, 1972)

2. The Lord Who Rules Over Human Affairs

The LORD will reign for ever and ever.
Exodus 15.18

Unto God belongs the sovereignty of the heavens and the earth and all that is therein, and it is He who has power over all things.
Qur'an 5.120

All that are rulers, kings, potentates, lords,
    chiefs, officials—
All are God's creation.
Their will is subject to God's;
On God are they all dependent.
Adi Granth, Bilaval-ki-Var 6, M.4, p. 851
(Sikhism)

Then did I recognize Thee in mind,
to be the first and the last, O Lord,
Father of good thought,
when I apprehended Thee in my eye,
True creator of Right,
the Lord over the actions of life!
Avesta, Yasna 31.8 (Zoroastrianism)

Revere the anger of Heaven,
And presume not to make sport or be idle.
Revere the changing moods of Heaven,
And presume not to drive about at your
    pleasure.
Great Heaven is intelligent,
And is with you in all your goings.
Great Heaven is clear-seeing,
And is with you in your wanderings and
    indulgences.[14]
Book of Songs, Ode 254 (Confucianism)

The Wise One is the most mindful of the plans,
which, indeed, were wrought in the past,
By demons and by men,
    and which will be wrought hereafter!
He, the Lord, is the sole decider,
so may it be unto us as He wills!
Avesta, Yasna 29.4 (Zoroastrianism)

Whoever vows to tyrannize over the humble
    and the meek,
The Supreme Lord burns him in flames.

The Creator dispenses perfect justice
And preserves His devotee.
Adi Granth, Gauri, M.5, p. 199 (Sikhism)

Never mind if the people are not intimidated by your [correct] authority. A mightier Authority will deal with them in the end.
Tao Te Ching 72 (Taoism)

The great day of the LORD is near,
near and hastening fast;
the sound of the day of the LORD is bitter,
the mighty man cries aloud there.
A day of wrath is that day,[15]
a day of distress and anguish,
a day of ruin and devastation,
a day of darkness and gloom,
a day of clouds and thick darkness,
a day of trumpet blast and battle cry
against the fortified cities
and against the lofty battlements.
I will bring distress on men,
so that they shall walk like the blind,
because they have sinned against the LORD;
their blood shall be poured out like dust,
and their flesh like dung.
Neither their silver nor their gold
shall be able to deliver them
on the day of the wrath of the LORD.
In the fire of his jealous wrath,
all the earth shall be consumed;
for a full, yea, sudden end
he will make of all the inhabitants of the earth.
Zephaniah 1.14-18

Teachings of Sun Myung Moon

Have we only regarded God as a concept? Have we only honored Him as Lord in worship? That is not right. God is the Lord of our life, the Ruler of our daily affairs and the Subject of our thought. (11:87, February 12, 1961)

In order to understand ourselves and give a full account of ourselves, we need a standard upon which to evaluate and judge ourselves. This is the Absolute Being, whom we worship in our faith. When we enter into a relationship with Him, we can assess ourselves in comparison to Him; then we can understand who we are and what we are. Therefore, we should be able to deeply experience that there is a God, who reigns over us and moves our mind. (7:207-08, September 13, 1959)

God gave His Word to the Israelites who left Egypt in order to recreate them as God's people. However, when they did not follow His Word, He appeared to them as the terrifying God who struck and punished them. During the Old Testament Age, before the appearance of the Messiah, Satan still reigned as king; it was an age of the Devil's power. Therefore, Jehovah God appeared to Moses as a terrifying, vengeful and jealous God. He appeared with the Law to strike the people who had become servants of sin, mercilessly punishing anyone who violated the Law. This was the situation in the Old Testament Age.

Look at the attributes of Jehovah, the God of the Old Testament Age. He was a jealous God who terrified those Israelites who worshipped other gods. He was a cruel God who ordered the Israelites to exterminate the seven Canaanite tribes leaving no survivors. He was a merciless God who wiped out any Israelite who violated the commandments of the Mosaic Law. Does the loving God who created the universe have the character to feel such jealousy, exact such revenge, instill such terror, and exhibit such cruelty as to exterminate the seven Canaanite tribes? No. God appeared in that way because during the Old Testament Age, he tasked His angels to serve as mediators in the role of God. The vengeful legalism summed up in the saying, "A life for a life, an eye for an eye, a tooth for a tooth, a hand for a hand, a foot for a foot, a burn for a burn, a wound for a wound, and a stripe for a stripe" cannot stem from the character of the Creator God. God is the God of love and forgiveness. (124:202, February 15, 1983)

Please pay attention to my prophetic proclamation. Humankind is now at a historical turning point. Now the God of power and authority, who in the past seemed so powerless or even not to exist, can manifest in our life. Now is an amazing time, when human beings in their everyday life can experience the absolute realm of God, the sovereign Lord whose divine principle governs all things and the universe.

People will increasingly be able to perceive God. They will perceive the spirit world and the works of spirits. As they naturally understand the public laws of the universe through their own experiences, people will undergo definite changes to their character and become true individuals. They will no longer be self-centered in relating to greater wholes in the universal order of being. They will learn to be altruistic, living for the sake of others. (February 6, 2004)

We are transcending Satan's limited realm. Once that work is completed, God can take dominion over the universe without any difficulty. Then, Satan's realm will be gone from the earth, and the new sovereignty of Heaven will arrive. With God on high, Satan will disappear and Heaven's new sovereignty will be established. God's dominion will extend from individuals to the cosmos, and God will reign for the first time in human history.

The time is at hand when all-transcendent, all-encompassing, all-sovereign and almighty God can do all that He desires. Being all encompassing, God will reign over the entire world that formerly had been in Satan's possession. Being almighty, God will do whatever He pleases, holding all authority over Satan. (295:254, September 8, 1998)

Omniscient and Omnipresent

NOTHING IS HIDDEN FROM GOD, because He sees everything. He knows our past, our present and our future. There is no place to escape from God, because He is everywhere. Therefore, we should be sincere in our thoughts and careful about our actions. Not only is God aware of what we do; He also sympathizes with our difficulties. He is our companion in every situation; we are never alone. See also Chapter 11: *Predestination*.

To God belong the East and the West;
wherever you turn, there is the Face of God;
God is All-embracing, All-knowing.
Qur'an 2.115

You know when I sit down and when I rise up;
you discern my thoughts from afar.
You search out my path and my lying down,
and you are acquainted with all my ways.
Psalm 139.2-3

Our Lord! Lo! You know that which we hide and that which we proclaim. Nothing in the earth or in heaven is hidden from God.
Qur'an 14.38

In *The Book of Songs* it is said,

> In your secret chamber even you are judged;
> See you do nothing to blush for,

Though but the ceiling looks down upon
    you.

Therefore the moral man, even when he is not doing anything, is serious; and, even when he does not speak, is truthful.
Doctrine of the Mean 33 (Confucianism)

Mark well three things and you will not fall into the clutches of sin: know what is above you—an eye that sees, an ear that hears, and all your actions recorded in the book.
Mishnah, Avot 2.1 (Judaism)

Surely God—He knows what is in the wombs.
No soul knows what it shall earn tomorrow, and
no soul knows in what land it shall die.
Surely God is All-knowing, All-aware.
Qur'an 31.34

The great Ruler of all these worlds,
beholds as if from near at hand
the man who thinks he acts by stealth:
the Gods know all this of him.

When one stands or walks or moves in secret,
or goes to his lying down or uprising,
when two sitting together take secret counsel,
King Varuna knows, being there the Third...

If one will go away beyond the heavens,
still he cannot escape King Varuna;
his envoys move about here from the heavens,
and, thousand-eyed, they look upon the earth.

King Varuna observes all that which lies
between heaven and earth and beyond them;
the twinklings of men's eyes have been counted
    by him;
as a dicer the dice, He measures everything.
Atharva Veda 4.16.1-8 (Hinduism)

See you not that God knows all that is in the heavens and on earth? There is not a secret consultation between three unless He is their fourth, nor between five unless He is their sixth, nor between fewer or more unless He is in their midst, wherever they be.
Qur'an 58.7

Whither shall I go from thy Spirit?
Or whither shall I flee from thy presence?
If I ascend to heaven, thou art there!
If I make my bed in Sheol, thou art there!
If I take the wings of the morning
and dwell in the uttermost parts of the sea,
even there thy hand shall lead me,
and thy right hand shall hold me.
Psalm 139.7-10

You who dive down as if under water to steal,
Though no earthly king may have seen you,
The King of heaven sees.
Yoruba Proverb (African Traditional Religions)

Teachings of Sun Myung Moon

When God looks at a person, He sees the person's mind. He sees his past, his present, and based on that He sees his future. (100:93, October 8, 1978)

God transcends time, and He has no regard for your 24-hour timeframe. God does not sleep. Apply this principle in your activities, and you will develop without limit. (94:282-83, October 9, 1977)

God's mind is not only in His Word, but also in everything He created. For this reason, God exists everywhere. Truly, He is omnipresent. (8:182, December 13, 1959)

You have a mind. Mind is invisible, and may not appear to exist; yet it exists. Where is your mind? Is it in your head or in your heart? In truth, your mind extends throughout every part of your body.

Likewise, this world is like God's body, and He is present everywhere in the world. Yet [like mind], you cannot see God. (89:72, July 11, 1976)

God's love is more than enough to embrace the universe. God's love is at the center of everything. God as the central being of love maintains the great foundation. When God moves, everything moves with Him, even the smallest things. Everything is contained within one great circle. Thus does God embrace the whole world, the entire universe. (205:33, July 7, 1990)

If God did not exist, the universe would feel completely empty. But because God exists, the universe feels completely full. Why? Because there is love. Hence, even when we are alone, because we know God, we feel the universe's fullness. We feel God in every place. Hence, within love we can know the deep inspiration that comes from God's omnipresence. But if we did not know God, we would feel an all-pervading emptiness, as if nothing existed. (91:323, March 1, 1977)

How do you experience God's omnipresence? Feel the air as the breath from God's mouth. Feel a typhoon as God blowing His nose. Feel the stream as God's sweat pouring out from going through the suffering course of restoration for the sake of the world. Learn the love of God from the sun, which symbolizes the elements of life throughout the cosmos. Nature is a textbook for experiencing God's heart, a textbook for the happiness of His beloved children. Speak to the plants; feel that their leaves are as your children; you are not crazy. You are close to being a saint. (59:102-03, July 9, 1972)

Consider that our Father is the living God, who watches over us from the beginning to the end of our life. He foresees our life in the eternal spirit world, as well as our present life on earth. When He looks at you spiritually, what do you think He sees? (118:38, May 2, 1982)

Immanent and Dwelling within the Heart

ABIDING WITHIN THE HEART, God is near at hand to each of us, if only we would notice. In the Bible, God's immanence is described in the revelation to Elijah, where instead of a grand manifestation in earthquake and storm, God appeared as "a still small voice." Through faith and humility we can sense God's presence within. Yet God is in fact near to all, even though most are blind and deaf to His reality.

In the Abrahamic religions, God's immanence rarely leads to identification with the soul itself, but Eastern traditions teach more thoroughgoing notions of divine immanence. Sufis interpret the qur'anic parable of the Lamp as expressing God's presence in the heart as a light illuminating the body. In Hinduism, divine immanence is ontological: Ultimate Reality is the Self, the Atman. In Buddhism, it is realization by the mind of its true nature: the Essence of Mind *(Tathata)* or Buddha-nature. Yet these conceptions in no way make a simple identification of God with the individual soul *(jiva)*, which is beclouded and deluded by an egoistic sense of self; see also Chapter 7: *Enlightenment*.

The complete realization of the God within is a potential and ideal, because that is our God-given purpose. As Father Moon teaches, God created each of us to encompass the universe and correspond with God's heart.

Behold, the kingdom of God is within you.

Luke 17.21

We indeed created man; and We know what his soul whispers within him, and We are nearer to him than the jugular vein.

Qur'an 50.16

For the word of God is living and active, sharper than any two-edged sword, piercing to the division of soul and spirit, of joints and marrow, and discerning the thoughts and intentions of the heart. And before him no creature is hidden, but all are open and laid bare to the eyes of him with whom we have to do.

Hebrews 4.12-13

That mind which gives life
to all the people in the world—
such is the very mind which nourishes me!

Moritake Arakida, One Hundred Poems about the World (Shinto)

Why do you go to the forest in search of God?
He lives in all and is yet ever distinct;
He abides with you, too,
As a fragrance dwells in a flower,
And reflection in a mirror;
So does God dwell inside everything;
Seek Him, therefore, in your heart.

Adi Granth, Dhanasri, M.9, p. 684 (Sikhism)

For thus says the high and lofty One
who inhabits eternity, whose name is Holy,
"I dwell in the high and holy place,
and also with him who is of a contrite and
  humble spirit,
to revive the spirit of the humble,
and to revive the heart of the contrite."

Isaiah 57.15

In the golden city of the heart dwells
The Lord of Love, without parts, without stain.
Know him as the radiant light of lights.

There shines not the sun, neither moon nor
  star,
Nor flash of lightning, nor fire lit on earth.
The Lord is the light reflected by all.
He shining, everything shines after him.

Mundaka Upanishad 2.2.10-11

God is the Light of the heavens and the earth.
The parable of His Light
is as if there were a Niche,
and within it a Lamp;
the Lamp enclosed in Glass:
The Glass as it were a brilliant star:
Lit from a blessed Tree,
an olive neither of the East nor of the West,
whose oil is well-nigh luminous,
though fire scarce touched it.
Light upon Light!
God guides whom He will to His Light:
God sets forth parables for men, and God
  knows all things.

Qur'an 24.35

The Lord takes his stand upon
hearing, sight, touch, taste, smell,
and upon the mind.
He enjoys what mind and senses enjoy.

Deluded men cannot trace his course.
Only the eye of wisdom sees him
clothed in the states of existence, going forth,
being in the body, or taking in experience.

Disciplined men can also make an effort
and see his presence in themselves.

Bhagavad-Gita 15.9-11 (Hinduism)

I am in my Father, and you in me, and I in you.

John 14.20

Daibai asked Baso, "What is Buddha?"
Baso answered, "This very mind is the
  Buddha."

Mumonkan 30 (Buddhism)

Within our Essence of Mind the Three Bodies of Buddha (*Trikaya*) are to be found, and they are common to everybody. Because the mind labors under delusions, he knows not his own inner nature; and the result is that he ignores the Trikaya within himself, erroneously believing that they are to be sought from without. Within yourself you will find the Trikaya which, being the manifestation of the Essence of Mind, are not to be sought from without.[17]

Sutra of Hui Neng 6 (*Buddhism*)

God said to Elijah... "Go forth, and stand upon the mount before the Lord." And behold, the Lord passed by, and a great and strong wind rent the mountains, and broke in pieces the rocks before the Lord, but the Lord was not in the wind; and after the wind an earthquake, but the Lord was not in the earthquake; and after the earthquake a fire, but the Lord was not in the fire; and after the fire a still small voice.[18]

1 Kings 19.11-12

Teachings of Sun Myung Moon

Where does God exist? He is not in heaven, but in our heart—the center of our heart. (145:310, June 1, 1986)

God is not merely a concept. God is alive in each of our lives, and we can feel His touch. I constantly hear the beating of God's pulse. I breathe as He breathes. I can feel the warmth of His body against my own. I have come to know the heart of God, and have shed rivers of tears from the knowledge that His heart is bursting with the sorrow of having lost humankind through the Fall. (234:233, August 22, 1992)

When we forget to eat and sleep, yearning for our beloved Heavenly Father and calling out, "Father!" He holds our hand, even though we do not notice Him. We call out, "Father," and Heavenly Father clasps us to His bosom. It is precious to have these experiences in our life of faith.

With a heart of love, even before you say, "Please be with me while I do this," God is already with you. Experience this, and you will know that God is Gracious and Merciful. (58:299, June 25, 1972)

How does God love? It is not hard to answer. Since God is without form, He can go anywhere—inside a lady's eyes, inside her heart, anywhere at all. Where does God live? He dwells in the midst of our heart. God's masculine aspect lives in the heart of a man, and God's feminine aspect lives in the heart of a woman. (128:325)

Many Christians today think that because God the Creator is unique and absolute, the Supreme Being, it is impossible for human beings, His creatures, to relate with God in a full partnership. They reason that creatures are profane while God is absolute and holy. Consider this matter, however, from the concept of love. To form relationships of love, even the lofty and supremely good God and lowly created beings must share common attributes of character. To love, they must share the same heart. That is, the personal God must have the same qualities as the human personality. (138:247, January 24, 1986)

The universe is vast, as great as 21 billion light-years across... Yet when we search within for the best place to receive God, our greatest treasure, the natural conclusion is, "The heart is the only appropriate place." No place can be safer or more comfortable for Him.

The heart is able to stand in the position of God's object partner and exist for eternity by engaging in spherical motion, and this is the reason that human beings can have eternal life. (May 1, 2004)

God is immeasurably huge, but a human being, though tiny in comparison, is a microcosm of the universe. Therefore, we can experience that God is within us as we go into God. We can experience that we are within God and God is within us. That is why Jesus said, "I am in the Father and the Father is in me." Although God is infinitely big, only when human beings dwell within Him, can God work. (31:210, May 31, 1970)

Thou dost relate to us at the dividing line between joy and sorrow. (24:245, August 24, 1969)

Now is the time when people must reflect on themselves and listen to the voice from Heaven. Through the benefit of the providence, the living God has now drawn near to us. From now on, people will have many spiritual experiences that they could not have earlier. That is to say, they will communicate with the transcendent world. Through these frequent spiritual experiences, people will be influenced directly and indirectly. Especially people who experience the inspiration of God and good spirits will have their spiritual senses developed centered on God, and they will experience major changes in their character. People whose character is thus transformed to fit the way of Heaven are the true people God has been hoping for. (February 6, 2003)

> Thou dost not live in some distant, relative world.
> Thou art in the middle of our hearts;
> Thou surroundest our bodies
> unnoticed, like the air all around us;
> Thou hast been embracing our entire lives.
> When we receive that power which surrounds us,
> infinite power is mobilized.
> When we absorb that power—eternal power—
> it impacts and stimulates us anew. (27:41-42, November 23, 1969)

Unchanging and Eternal

UNCHANGING AND ETERNAL—the Absolute Being in all religions is depicted as having these qualities. Conversely, all beings, things and phenomena in the world are transient, impermanent and relative; from that perspective, they cannot have a reciprocal relationship with the Absolute Being. Human beings have both types of qualities: we value what is unchanging, but at the same time we have changeable elements that make us less than trustworthy. Becoming a person of steadfastness and unchanging devotion is thus a key ingredient in making a relationship to God.

Father Moon's teaching on this point focuses on true love, which likewise has the qualities of unchangeability, absoluteness and eternity. He explains that even in God, these attributes exist mainly for the purpose of relating to His creatures in true love. Moreover, the demands of love test God's unchangeability every day as He relates to human beings who are inconstant and treacherous.

I am the Alpha and the Omega, the first and the last, the beginning and the end.

Revelation 22.13

He is the First and the Last,
the Outward and the Inward;
and He is Knower of all things.

Qur'an 57.3

Jesus Christ is the same yesterday and today and forever.

Hebrews 13.8

Nothing can ever destroy the Buddha Nature.

Mahaparinirvana Sutra 220 *(Buddhism)*

The great, unborn Self is undecaying, immortal, undying, fearless, infinite.

Brihadaranyaka Upanishad 4.4.25 *(Hinduism)*

Moses said to God, "If I come to the people of Israel and say to them, 'The God of your fathers has sent me to you,' and they ask me, 'What is his name?' what shall I say to them?" God said to Moses, "I Am Who I Am."[19]

Exodus 3.13-14

Subhuti, if anyone should say that the Tathagata comes or goes or sits or reclines, he fails to understand my teaching. Why? Because 'Thus Gone' (Tathagata) has neither whence nor whither, and therefore he is called 'Tathagata.'[20]

Diamond Sutra 29 *(Buddhism)*

With the Lord one day is as a thousand years, and a thousand years as one day.

2 Peter 3.8

Who knows the Eternal's day
and the Eternal's night,
Each lasting a thousand ages, truly
knows day and night.

At daybreak all things are disclosed;
they arise from the unmanifest.
At dusk they dissolve into
the very same unmanifest.

Again and again, the whole multitude
of creatures is born, and when night falls,
Is dissolved, without their will,
and at daybreak, is born again.[21]

Beyond that unmanifest is
another, everlasting Unmanifest
Which has no end, although
every creature perish.

This is called the Imperishable
Unmanifest and the Highest Goal.
Who reaches it does not return.
It is my supreme abode.

Bhagavad-Gita 8.17-21 *(Hinduism)*

All that is on the earth will perish:
But will abide forever the face of thy Lord—
full of Majesty, Bounty, and Honor.

Qur'an 55.26-27

In primal time, in all time, was the Creator;
Nothing is real but the Eternal.
Nothing shall last but the Eternal.

Adi Granth, Japuji 1, M.1, p. 1 *(Sikhism)*

All flesh is grass,
and all its beauty is like the flower of the field.
The grass withers, the flower fades,
when the breath of the Lord blows upon it…
The grass withers, the flower fades,
but the word of our God will stand forever.

Isaiah 40.6-8

Even ornamented royal chariots wear out. So too the body reaches old age. But the Dhamma of the Good grows not old. Thus do the Good reveal it among the Good.

Dhammapada 151 *(Buddhism)*

By detachment from appearances, abide in Real Truth. So I tell you, "Thus shall you think of all this fleeting world:

> A star at dawn, a bubble in a stream;
> A flash of lightning in a summer cloud,
> A flickering lamp, a phantom, a dream."[22]
>
> Diamond Sutra 32 *(Buddhism)*

There is, monks, a condition where there is neither the element of extension, the element of cohesion, the element of heat, nor the element of motion, nor the sphere of the infinity of space, nor the sphere of the infinity of consciousness, nor the sphere of nothingness, nor the sphere of neither-perception-nor-non-perception; neither this world, nor a world beyond, nor sun and moon.

There, monks, I say, there is neither coming nor going nor staying nor passing away nor arising. Without support or mobility or basis is it. This is indeed the end of suffering.

> That which is Selfless, hard it is to see;
> Not easy is it to perceive the Truth.
> But who has ended craving utterly
> Has naught to cling to, he alone can see.

There is, monks, an unborn, a not-become, a not-made, a not-compounded. If, monks, there were not this unborn, not-become, not-made, not-compounded, there would not here be an escape from the born, the become, the made, the compounded. But because there is an unborn, a not-become, a not-made, a not-compounded, therefore there is an escape from the born, the become, the made, the compounded.[23]

Udana 80 *(Buddhism)*

Teachings of Sun Myung Moon

God is eternal. He was eternal in the past, He is eternal in the present, and He will be eternal in the future. (22:317, May 11, 1969)

Eternity cannot be captured within time, but time exists within eternity. (41:285)

God's ideal is eternal. God is the center of absolute and eternal life. Yet the center of that ideal is true love, with "me" as its counterpart. (216:115, March 9, 1991)

To love means to take responsibility for eternity. Love is unchanging. If God changed the way people do, how could we ever trust Him? But God is unchanging and eternal. He wants to make a relationship with mankind through true love. Nevertheless, people are constantly changing, day in and day out. How can God trust us? (31:210, May 31, 1970)

Eternal life is essentially an attribute of love. Even God, when He created the universe, adhered to the standards of absolute faith, absolute love and absolute obedience. God lives this way, always desiring to invest more love for the world, even though everything in the world is transient. For this reason, every creature without exception attends Him as the absolute, unique, unchanging and eternal Lord. (330:262, August 18, 2000)

How old is God? For billions of years He has been growing old, waiting. If God had a beard, I am sure it would have grown all the way down to His feet, and if God grew taller every year, there's no telling how tall He would have grown. By what power has He been able to endure and wait for so long? It is nothing else but love. (111:77, January 25, 1981)

If your day-to-day life has only a transient value, you cannot make a connection with eternity. Your life should connect with God's eternal love. Only then will the eternal God be with you. (2:13, January 6, 1957)

When God decides something, His decision is unchanging for eternity. Can you meet God's standard if you change your mind a dozen times a day?

Truth is truth whether you live or die; it is eternal. Truth is beyond death, beyond changeability. Thus, in order for you to be a true person, you should be beyond death, and be unchangeably steadfast. This means there will be a collision at some point between your changeability and unchangeability. Unchanging elements will overcome changing elements. Changing elements will vanish. It is as if life and death collide. When you overcome death you will have life. Once you pass through this stage, then you can have a connection with God. (66:43-44, March 18, 1973)

Being absolute, God is tested continually by the world. Everyone—even Satan—tests whether God's love is unchanging. If God were ever unable to overcome a test and stopped loving, then He would be changeable. Yet God remains calm and unperturbed by anything. When I contemplated why God permits Himself to be put through intolerable difficulties, I realized that He had to endure them in order to secure His unchangeability.

Satan and God are completely opposite. God is eternal, while Satan is transient; God is unchanging, while Satan is ever changing; God is unique, while Satan is not. There is a clear contrast between the characteristics of God and Satan.

Is your mind changing or unchanging? An unchanging mind is closer to God. You prefer to be unchanging, not changing, to be absolute, not relative, because you want to take after God's character. You would resemble God because you wish to be His object partner.

God is unchanging, eternal, unique and absolute, but for what end? If God possessed these attributes purely for His own sake, they would have no meaning. These attributes are for the sake of His object partners. Likewise, we seek to be unchanging and absolute for the sake of our counterpart, not for ourselves.

Therefore, no matter how many people in the world oppose God, He must endure in silence. Evil people swear, accuse and lash out at God, but He just takes it all in and remains silent.

All people are meant to make the journey to true love. Therefore, even evil people seek to become absolute, unique, eternal and unchanging. Were we solitary beings, what difference would it make if we were changing or unchanging? When we say we want to be unchanging, we automatically have a relationship in mind. Because of the unchanging relationship between God and human beings, love can be possible. And love—true love—is eternal. (123:330-32, January 9, 1983)

> All the ideologies, doctrines and rights that people hold—
> all these will disappear.
> But Father, we yearn that Thou dost put in our minds
> power ever flowing and ever bursting forth,
> the Eye of resurrection,
> that our minds and bodies may rise
> to the place where we can live eternally. (4:65, March 9, 1958)

The Original Cause

THE FIRST CAUSE OF ALL EXISTENCE did not merely create the world long ago and let it run on its own steam ever since. God is sustaining and moving the world, continually causing reality from moment to moment. Furthermore, as the Cause, God determines the purpose and qualities of all beings. In this regard, Father Moon teaches that as the Cause of human beings, God is a personal God who created human beings with characteristics resembling Himself.

Nothing exists apart from a pre-ordained purpose and goal, towards which it moves by God's unseen hand. This means that God is also the cause of history. Father Moon points out that history moves in accordance with God's purpose—a divine providence governed by definite laws and that advances towards a clear goal. When the world reaches that goal, the Cause (God) and the effect (humanity) will be one.

1. The Cause of All Existence

I am the nucleus of every creature, Arjuna; for without me nothing can exist, neither animate nor inanimate...

Wherever you find strength, or beauty, or spiritual power, you may be sure that these have sprung from a spark of my essence.

Bhagavad-Gita 10.39, 41 (Hinduism)

There is one God, the Father, from whom are all things and for whom we exist.

1 Corinthians 8.6

The loving sage beholds that Mysterious
   Existence
wherein the universe comes to have one home;
Therein unites and therefrom issues the whole:
The Lord is the warp and woof in created
   beings.

White Yajur Veda 32.8 (Hinduism)

Surely it is He who originates, and brings again, and He is the All-forgiving, the All-loving, Lord of the Throne, the All-glorious, Performer of what He desires.

Qur'an 85.13-16

Eternally He doles out gifts;
Those receiving them at last can receive no
   more.
Infinitely the creation receives from Him
   sustenance.
He is the Ordainer;
By His Ordinance the universe He runs.
Says Nanak, Ever is He in bliss,
Ever fulfilled.

Adi Granth, Japuji 3, M.1, p. 2 (Sikhism)

If God removed His hand the world would end.

Proverb (African Traditional Religions)

Teachings of Sun Myung Moon

Before we were born, God designed our eyes, ears, mouth, etc., so that they might perceive and know all that exists in this world. Could human beings have known beforehand everything they needed to live? There must be a Being, omniscient and transcendent of human beings, who knew everything. That Being is God. (*Way of God's Will*)

God is the Causal Being of the universe. He is the Causal Being of all faculties. He is the Causal Being who adds energy. He is the Causal Being who gives direction and purpose... He presents a purpose with a direction always centered on His deep motivation, and He keeps this position without wavering. That is why, if we begin from the Cause and fix on His direction, we can move to the world that fulfills His purpose. (89:75-76, July 11, 1976)

Everything about human beings—alive with consciousness, pursuing goodness and higher value, and having a sense of sorrow and sadness—began from their Origin, not from themselves. In this resultant human life, we are going through the process of connecting with the original Cause. (140:123, February 9, 1986)

For anything on this earth to exist, there must be a cause that enables it to exist. The community in which we live, our nation and the entire visible world are each different levels of effect. The complexity of connections that form each of these environments must have developed from a cause.

Human beings create societies, nations and the world. Yet, the fundamental cause that formed human beings does not lie within us. Without a doubt, we are resultant beings. We were formed from some preexisting motivation and content. We came from a cause.

God is the First Cause. How do you think He created human beings? God made us in His image, like Himself. That means the Father resembles us just as we resemble the Father. So when someone asks you, "What kind of being is God?" you can answer, "He is someone like me." This answer will hit the mark. (127:233)

Every individual has unlimited hope, unlimited ambition, and unlimited ideals. For we resultant beings to be this way, there first had to be a causal being that possesses these qualities. The causal being is a real existence. We call it God.

God is a personal God; therefore, God can be the total motivation and cause for us human beings. Because God, the Cause, possesses such a nature, human beings, who are the effect, must necessarily possess the same nature. It stands to reason that one day, God—the cause—and we human beings—the effect—will become so inseparable that nothing can tear us apart. That day of reunion must appear in the human world. God has kept this cherished desire as He sought for humanity. (28:282-83, February 11, 1970)

2. The Cause behind History

For I am God, and there is no other;
I am God, and there is none like me,
declaring the end from the beginning
and from ancient times things not yet done,
saying, "My counsel shall stand,
and I will accomplish all my purpose,"
calling a bird of prey from the east,
the man of my counsel from a far country.
I have spoken, and I will bring it to pass;
I have purposed, and I will do it.

Isaiah 46.9-11

On the day when We shall roll up heaven as a scroll is rolled for the writings; as We originated the first creation, so We shall bring it back again—a promise binding on Us; so We shall do. For We have written in the Psalms, after the Remembrance, "The earth shall be the inheritance of My righteous servants."

Qur'an 21.104

I testify that Thou art the Lord of all creation, and the Educator of all beings, visible and invisible. I bear witness that Thy power hath encompassed the entire universe, and that the hosts of the earth can never dismay Thee, nor can the dominion of all peoples and nations deter Thee from executing Thy purpose. I confess that Thou hast no desire except the regeneration of the whole world, and the establishment of the unity of its peoples, and the salvation of all they that dwell therein.

Gleanings from the Writings
of Bahá'u'lláh 115 *(Baha'i Faith)*

Teachings of Sun Myung Moon

God is the First Cause and Creator of the universe—this is the starting-point of religion. Moreover, God is good, and He is eternal and unchanging, unique and absolute. As such a God created this world, He must have first formed a purpose for the creation. This purpose of creation would also have to be eternal, unchanging, unique, and absolute. (100:241, October 19, 1978)

A human being manifests the result. No one insists that human beings are the First Cause. Even if we do not know our cause, we know that we are the result of some existence, because we were born.

In order to know what a human being is, we should know the Being who made human beings as resultant beings. Therefore, we should have a clear answer to the question of God, the First Cause. Only by knowing God, the Causal Being, is it possible to set our direction in life. Only with God can we find the teaching for how we should live, how our family should live, how society, the nation and the world should function. It concerns not only my individual direction, but also the way the world is going in these Last Days. (100:234, February 26, 1986)

Of everything that happens in the flow of history, nothing occurs without a relationship to Thy providence. (140:62, February 1, 1986)

Although the direction of history appears to be heading toward evil, that is not true. History progresses as human beings, through the operation of the mind, restrain their bodies and determine with resolve the direction they will go. Thus does God work in the background to govern and direct history's development over certain times and periods. (4:191, April 20, 1958)

In the past, the present and the future, the eternal God directs His providence. Therefore, the sagas recorded in God's heart pattern the history of every age, and the sagas that shaped those ages foreshadow the future. (16:253, June 19, 1966)

God's Goodness

SCRIPTURES OF EVERY RELIGION PRAISE GOD'S GOODNESS. Many describe the Absolute Being's good attributes in personal terms: God is merciful, loving, beautiful, gracious, compassionate and faithful. Yet the standard of absolute goodness is beyond the ordinary. Universal, impartial and all-embracing, it touches all people whether they are good or bad. Common metaphors thus liken God's goodness to the beneficial influences of the sun and rain that comes down everywhere. The abundance and fecundity of the creation is yet another testimony to God's goodness. Wishing to dwell amidst goodness, the God of goodness promotes goodness both in nature and in the minds of human beings.

1. God's Goodness to Human Beings

The LORD is gracious and merciful,
slow to anger and abounding in steadfast love.
The LORD is good to all,
and his compassion is over all that he has made.

Psalm 145.8-9

Allah is kind and loves whoever is kind;
Allah is clean and loves whoever is clean;
Allah is generous and loves whoever is generous.

Hadith of Muslim 913.2 *(Islam)*

God is not the author of all things, but of good only.

Plato, The Republic 2 *(Hellenism)*

God the Rescuer,
God the Savior,
Almighty, whom we joyfully adore,
Powerful God,
Invoked by all men,
May he, the bounteous, grant us his blessings!

Rig Veda 7.100.4 *(Hinduism)*

The Lord and Cherisher of the Worlds—
Who created me, and it is He who guides me;
Who gives me food and drink,
And when I am ill, it is He who cures me;
Who will cause me to die, and then to live again;
And who, I hope, will forgive me my faults on the Day of Judgment.

Qur'an 26.77-82

Always created beings He cherishes;
The Creator looks to the weal of all.
Lord! invaluable are Thy blessings;
Without extent is His bounty.

Adi Granth, Kirtan Sohila, M.1, p. 12 *(Sikhism)*

Lo! We have shown man the way, whether he be grateful or disbelieving.

Qur'an 76.3

He makes his sun rise on the evil and on the good, and sends rain on the just and on the unjust.

Matthew 5.45

It is the Way of Heaven to show no favoritism.
It is forever on the side of the good man.[24]

Tao Te Ching 79 *(Taoism)*

The Tao is the refuge for the myriad creatures.
It is that by which the good man protects,
And that by which the bad is protected.

Tao Te Ching 62 *(Taoism)*

I have no corporeal existence,
but Universal Benevolence is my divine body.
I have no physical power,
but Uprightness is my strength.
I have no religious clairvoyance beyond what is bestowed by Wisdom,
I have no power of miracle other than the attainment of quiet happiness,
I have no tact except the exercise of gentleness.

Oracle of the Kami of Sumiyoshi *(Shinto)*

Teachings of Sun Myung Moon

God is the Father and Mother of all emotions—joy, anger, sorrow, and pleasure. He is our Owner, who prepares a place of comfort for us when we are sad and protects us when we face difficulty. He is our absolute Parent, whose love surpasses that of anyone who ever lived. (203:228, June 26, 1990)

If God were a being of destruction, causing heaven and earth to decrease, people would want nothing to do with God. The eternal God should always provide what is needful and appropriate to human beings and all creatures. That is why He was needed in the past, is needed in the present, and will be needed in the future. Otherwise, our worship and our desire for relationship with God would be in vain and to no purpose. (22:317, May 11, 1969)

All religions of the world begin with the recognition that God, the Lord and Creator, is the First Cause of the universe. If this God exists, He must be good; He must be eternal and unchanging; and He must be unique and absolute. The God who created the universe must have, from the first, a purpose for creating. This purpose of creation must also be eternal, unchanging, unique, and absolute.

God's purpose of creation is joy. He created human beings and the universe to experience joy. Joy cannot be experienced alone. To experience joy, it is always necessary to have an object partner, or counterpart. It is only when a subject partner and object partner establish a common base and engage in give and take action that joy can be experienced. Giving and receiving love is to experience the supreme joy. In sum, God created us to become His object partners, that He might experience joy eternally by relating with us in love. This is His purpose of creation. (100:241, October 19, 1978)

Each of us desires to be good. There is not a single person in the world that does not desire goodness. We know that the direction of history has been toward goodness, as educators and people of faith have labored and fought to set standards of goodness. We are born seeking for goodness and live seeking for goodness—that is the purpose of our life. Since our lives are the warp and woof of history, it is the goal of history as well. (24:13, June 22, 1969)

How can we fallen human beings return to the God of goodness? First, we must grow to the point where our conscience resembles God's original goodness. Next, we must behave in accordance with God's word, thus manifesting God's goodness and confirming the value of His word. When we do this, God will rejoice on seeing the ideal of the goodness for which He created all things. We humans have long pursued goodness, but finally we will experience the value of God's goodness by substantially embodying goodness ourselves. (2:131, July 21, 1957)

How are we to live in God's Kingdom? We are to live with the attitude to accept anyone who comes our way. Although occasionally a thief may enter and take something, you just close your eyes to it as he leaves through the gate, knowing that at least you have something that he could take. God thinks this way. Why? Because God feels, "Though he may be a petty thief, he is still living in My domain. Even if he takes something, he is only moving it about within the realm where I am the Owner of everything." Do you think there are fences and locks in heaven? No, there are none. (224:327-28, December 29, 1991)

2. God's Goodness Manifest in the Creation

God saw everything that he had made, and behold, it was very good.

Genesis 1.31

He has created the seven heavens in harmony. You cannot see a fault in the Beneficent One's creation; look again, can you see any flaws? Look again and yet again, and your sight will grow dim and weak [without finding any.]

Qur'an 67.3-4

This world is a garden,
The Lord its gardener,
Cherishing all, none neglected.

Adi Granth, Majh Ashtpadi, M.3, p. 118 (Sikhism)

Abundant is the year, with much millet and
    much rice;
And we have our high granaries,
With myriads, and hundreds of thousands, and
    millions of measures;
For spirits and sweet spirits,
To present our ancestors, male and female,
And to supply all our ceremonies.
The blessings sent down on us are of every
    kind.

Book of Songs, Ode 279 (Confucianism)

It is He who sends down to you out of heaven water of which you may drink, and by which grow trees, for you to pasture your herds, and thereby He brings forth for you crops, and olives, and palms, and vines, and all manner of fruit. Surely in that is a sign for a people who reflect.

And He subjected for you the night and day, and the sun and moon; and the stars are subjected by His command. Surely in that are signs for a people who understand.

And He has multiplied for you in the earth things of diverse hues. Surely in that is a sign for a people who remember.

It is He who subjected for you the sea, that you may eat of it fresh flesh, and bring forth out of it ornaments for you to wear; and you may see the ships cleaving through it; that you may seek of His bounty, and so haply you will be thankful…

If you count God's blessing, you can never number it; surely God is All-forgiving, All-compassionate.

Qur'an 16.10-18

The great Tao flows everywhere;
It can go left; it can go right.
The myriad things owe their existence to it,
And it does not reject them.
When its work is accomplished,
It does not take possession.
It clothes and feeds all,
But does not pose as their master.
Ever without ambition,
It may be called Small.
All things return to it as their home,
And yet it does not pose as their master,
Therefore it may be called Great.
Because it would never claim greatness,
Therefore its greatness is fully realized.

Tao Te Ching 34 (Taoism)

Let me tell you then why the Creator made this world of generation. He was good, and the good can never have any jealousy of anything. And being free from jealousy, he desired that all things should be as like himself as they could be. This is in the truest sense the origin of creation and of the world, as we shall do well in believing on the testimony of wise men: God desired that all things should be good and nothing bad, so far as this was attainable.

Wherefore also finding the whole visible sphere not at rest, but moving in an irregular and disorderly fashion, out of disorder he brought order, considering that this was in every way better than the other.

Now the deeds of the best could never be or have been other than the fairest; and the Creator, reflecting on the things which are by nature visible, found that no unintelligent creatures taken as a whole were fairer than the intelligent taken as a whole; and that intelligence could not be present in anything that was devoid of soul. For which reason, when he was framing the universe, he put intelligence in soul, and soul in body, that he might be the creator of a work which was by nature fairest and best. Wherefore, using the language of probability, we may say that the world became a living creature truly endowed with soul and intelligence by the providence of God.

Plato, Timaeus *(Hellenism)*

The primary cause of the pure unity of Enlightenment and Nirvana that has existed from beginningless time is the principle of integrating compassion, the indrawing, unifying principle of purity, harmony, likeness, rhythm, permanency, and peace. By the indrawing of this Principle within the brightness of your own nature, its unifying spirit can be discovered and developed and realized under all varieties of conditions.

Surangama Sutra *(Buddhism)*

Teachings of Sun Myung Moon

When looking at reality from the perspective of love, God is the root. The root communicates through the stem to the sprouting leaves, which spread out in all directions: east, west, south and north. As the plant spreads out, its leaves sprout more abundantly, the stem grows stronger and the root grows larger. Live like this, and you will discover that God is the loving vertical Father of our human world. God is our Creator and Father who bestows true love in abundance. (203:352, June 28, 1990)

Everything exists for the sake of something greater than itself, and the greater thing for something still greater. It is wrong to think that life is simply about the strong eating the weak, as Charles Darwin taught. That perspective on life is dead wrong. The Lord of the universe—the Creator of the universe—created all things for the sake of human beings. All creatures were created with that specific purpose in mind. (217:204, June 1, 1991)

God is the omnipotent and omniscient King of wisdom. In creating the universe of subject-object relationships, He had to decide whether the origin of true love, true happiness, true peace and the true ideal of the human world should be in the subject partner or in the object partner. God had to decide on this matter with the eternal ideal world in mind.

If God had set things up in such a way that all object beings must serve Him, then human beings would establish that same tradition: "Everyone must serve me." This would have created serious problems. There would be no way to achieve unity, harmony or development.

Thus we understand: rather than demanding that object partners attend the subject partner, God invariably takes the position that He exists for the sake of His object partners. This way, everything becomes one; there is progress and development. Hence, the almighty God decided to set up the standard of peace, happiness, love and the ideal as "living for the sake of others." (72:14, May 7, 1974)

Divine Love and Compassion

OF ALL GOD'S ATTRIBUTES, love is the most attractive and compelling. Most people who believe in God do so because of the mysterious moments when they felt His love, comfort and grace. It moved their hearts to faith, even amidst the mind's doubts. Because of the Creator's love, the creation is a benevolent place that upholds and protects life. Indeed, the good creation is an expression of that love.

Love is the essence of God; it is even more than that. As Father Moon teaches, love is the very motivation behind God's creation; it is the "why" of God. Love is also the reason God has pursued the history of salvation through many tortuous paths. Love teaches God to be patient and forgiving with us ignorant creatures who long ago lost our way and became inured to the gracious melodies of the Spirit. Despite our deafness and blindness, God never ceases to embrace us and lead us forward.

1. Love: The Essence of God

God is love, and he who abides in love abides in God, and God in him.

1 John 4.16

My mercy embraces all things.

Qur'an 7.156

To love is to know me,
My innermost nature,
The truth that I am.

Bhagavad-Gita 18.55 (Hinduism)

The Great Compassionate Heart is the essence of Buddhahood.

Gandavyuha Sutra (Buddhism)

Lord! You are the uninvoked savior, motiveless compassionate being, a well-wisher even when unprayed, a friend even when unrelated.

Vitaragastava 13.1 (Jainism)

Bright but hidden, the Self dwells in the heart.
Everything that moves, breathes, opens, and
    closes
lives in the Self. He is the source of love
and may be known through love but not
    through thought.
He is the goal of life. Attain this goal!

Mundaka Upanishad 2.2.1 (Hinduism)

Love is the firstborn, loftier than the gods, the
    Fathers and men.
You, O Love, are the eldest of all, altogether
    mighty.
To you we pay homage!

Greater than the breadth of earth and heaven,
    or of waters and Fire,
You, O Love, are the eldest of all, altogether
    mighty.
To you we pay homage!...

In many a form of goodness, O Love, you show
    your face.
Grant that these forms may penetrate within
    our hearts.
Send elsewhere all malice!

Atharva Veda 9.2.19-20, 25 (Hinduism)

O good man! Compassion acts as parent to all
    beings.
The parent is compassion.
Know that compassion is the Tathagata.

O good man! Compassion is the Buddha
    Nature of all beings.
Such a Buddha Nature is long overshadowed
    by illusion.
That is why beings cannot see.

The Buddha Nature is Compassion.
Compassion is the Tathagata.[25]

Mahaparinirvana Sutra 259 (Buddhism)

The Bull of Dharma is born of compassion;[26]
Content of mind holds creation together.
Whoever understands this is enlightened;
How great is the load under which this Bull
    stands!

Japuji 16, M.1, p. 3 (Sikhism)

O Son of Man! Veiled in My immemorial being and in the ancient eternity of My essence, I knew My love for thee; therefore I created thee, have engraved on thee Mine image, and revealed to thee My beauty.

*Hidden Words of Bahá'u'lláh,
Arabic 3 (Baha'i Faith)*

Teachings of Sun Myung Moon

God is the Lord of love. He exists to spread love throughout the universe and make it eternal. (298:304, January 17, 1999)

God is the Womb of love. He is the Source of love's emotion, out of which emanates parental love, children's love, sibling love, love of kin and love of country. These different kinds of love are like branches and leaves growing from the main trunk. They are like waves that eventually turn into ripples. The further away from the Source, the fainter the emotion becomes. (50:267, November 8, 1971)

How does it feel to experience the realm of God's love? It is like walking through a garden on a warm spring day. You see all different kinds of flowers and become intoxicated with all their fragrances. Lying on the grass, you feel something indescribable as you look up at the sky and see the towering cumulus clouds shaped like clumps of cotton. You feel your cells dancing, breathing.

God's love is the wellspring of power and happiness for all beings; it endows each one with the energy of life. God's love is the absolute requirement for faith. It is the necessary element for joy, pleasure, peace, and everything else human life desires. Moreover, God's love is the principle of the spirit world. (24:325, September 14, 1969)

What is God's heart? It refers to God's perfect foundation for love. All of God's creations welled up from His heart, as did all His ideals for them. Thus, God's heart is the perfect foundation for everything. God's heart also springs forth into the perfect completion of everything. There can be no perfection or completion apart from God's heart. (82:292, February 1, 1976)

God is the Subject of heart. For this reason, God can feel limitless sorrow as well as limitless joy. Just because He is God doesn't mean that He possesses only joy and positive emotions. When God is sad, His heart of sorrow is deeper and wider than any person can ever comprehend. (11:89, February 12, 1961)

God exists for love and lives for love. God does not live for Himself, but for love. Likewise, all things are born from love. Thus, in the world of love, there cannot be a concept that we should live for ourselves. (303:287, September 9, 1999)

God knows everything. Omniscient and omnipotent, He is the Supreme King of knowledge and power. Omnipresent, He exists everywhere. What does God need? Diamonds? He can make them any time. Gold or jewels? No. What God needs is love. Dwelling all by Himself, would God say, "I have love and it's great" and laugh? No, there is something that God needs.

God is a personal God; then He should have a mouth, shouldn't He? He also should have a nose, eyes, ears, hands and feet, a mind—and a heart. Surely, God must have them, because He is a personal God. (142:30)

God is the Original Being of love, and out of love He created human beings. A solitary being cannot love. Therefore, there is one thing that even God absolutely needs: a partner whom He can love. He can only love in a relationship with a counterpart. God, the Original Being of love and heart, created the universe with love as His motivation.

In doing so, He created human beings in His image as His substantial object partners, as it is recorded in Genesis 1:27, "So God created man in his own image, in the image of God he created him; male and female he created them." God is our eternal, formless and internal Parent, and [he created] Adam and Eve to be perfected as our visible and external parents. (135:10-11, August 20, 1985)

If what God needs is love, then He needs object partners with whom He can relate and share love. What sort of beings could these be? Animals? God would love beings that resemble Him. If God's partners are indeed human beings, then we are led to the conclusion that God has a human-like personality. God, who is in complete harmony within Himself, must also have attributes that can harmonize one hundred percent with the innate faculties of the human mind and body. Hence, God must have intellect, emotion and will. (162:271, April 17, 1987)

Love cannot be completed without a partner. Even God absolutely needs a counterpart in order to attain the most precious love; that is why He created. God seeks out a partner, so that He can experience absolute love through relating with another. In this sense, God exists for human beings and human beings exist for God. True love begins when we live for the sake of another.

What is the origin of human beings? God's love. We were born for love. Love is the origin.

Life is not the most precious thing. Our life derived from God's idea of love; therefore, love precedes life. Love is the root of life. We are born from love, grow up in love, and meet a partner for love—that should be our life.

If God is the first generation, then human beings are the second generation. God always loves us, His sons and daughters, but do we experience God's love? Human beings need to experience that love if we are to become God's perfect partners. (143:310, March 21, 1986)

2. Divine Mercy

God is All-gentle to His servants, providing for whomsoever He will.

Qur'an 42.19

If we are faithless, he remains faithful—for he cannot deny himself.

2 Timothy 2.13

God is the best to take care of man, and He is the Most Merciful of those who show mercy!

Qur'an 12.64

No one is more patient over injury which he hears than God.

Hadith of Bukhari and Muslim *(Islam)*

God drives away flies for a cow that has no tail.
Yoruba Proverb (African Traditional Religions)

God is faithful, and he will not let you be tempted beyond your strength, but with the temptation will also provide the way of escape, that you may be able to endure it.
1 Corinthians 10.13

God charges no soul save to its capacity; standing to its account is what it has earned, and against its account what it has deserved.
Our Lord! Take us not to task if we forget, or make mistake.
Our Lord! Charge us not with a load as that which You laid upon those before us.
Our Lord! Burden us not beyond what we have the strength to bear.
Pardon us, forgive us, and have mercy on us.
Qur'an 2.286

Teachings of Sun Myung Moon

What is God? God is the existence that absolutely lives for others. (175:158, March 16, 1988)

No matter what happens in the human world, God is patient because He is who He is. He sees tragic and heart-breaking things, yet He remains calm and composed, never losing His dignity. If God were to open His mouth and express His suffering, He could pour out tragic stories for millions of years, weeping all the while. Would God weep out of self-pity? No, God weeps only for humankind, His children. (124:60, January 23, 1983)

What kind of being is God? Does He say, "I am God Almighty! I created you to serve Me, to love Me and sacrifice everything for Me"? Such a being cannot be God.

In fact, God has set the tradition of humbly serving and loving the world. His tradition is that of changing diapers and cleaning up the baby's feces, and washing the dirt off a sick and infirm old man. That tradition should form the core of our education. (116:90-91, December 20, 1981)

God, the Creator of the universe, still remembers the wonderful process by which His creation unfolded, how each creature arose and what He did to further their development. He invested such great love for His creation; love was the motivation, and love the goal.

Even though humankind fell, God just cannot put aside His abiding love for human beings; to do so would be against His Principle and His standard of love. Therefore, when He sees fallen people living in misery, He does not condemn. Rather, He is merciful to them. (115:320-21, November 29, 1981)

3. God's Loving Heart toward Humanity

When Israel was a child, I loved him,
and out of Egypt I called my son.
The more I called them,
the more they went from me;
they kept sacrificing to the Baals,
and burning incense to idols.

Yet it was I that taught Ephraim to walk,
I took him up in my arms;
but they did not know that I healed them.
I led them with cords of compassion,
with the bands of love,
and I became to them as one
who eases the yoke on their jaws,
and I bent down to them and fed them.[27]

Hosea 11.1-4

In the perilous round of mortality,
In continuous, unending misery,
Firmly tied to the passions
As a yak is to its tail;
Smothered by greed and infatuation,
Blinded and seeing nothing;

Seeking not the Buddha, the Mighty,
And the Truth that ends suffering,
But deeply sunk in heresy,
By suffering seeking riddance of suffering;
For the sake of all these creatures,
My heart is stirred with great pity.

Lotus Sutra 2 (*Buddhism*)

Teachings of Sun Myung Moon

How hard is it to educate just one child? Children share their parents' flesh and blood. Their hearts are linked to their mother, so when mother cries they cry too. Their hearts are naturally connected to their father, so they respond to his cares and sorrows. Even so, it is still extremely hard to teach and raise them, is it not?

Then consider the magnitude of God's task. Today's human beings are not God's children. Although God cries out in bitterness, they act as if they do not hear anything. Although God weeps with grief and sorrow, they just ignore it. This is because human beings stem from Satan's flesh and blood. They may sense God's grief, yet all they do is praise Him. They may notice that other people are perishing, yet still they laugh and make merry.

Think how difficult it is for God, who has to train workers and raise leaders from among such people. Without a heart of utmost compassion, God would not have even a foothold to develop His providential work. Yet it is God's heart to consider every single detail—from one to one hundred to one thousand to even ten thousand—in arranging things for you. (42:257, March 21, 1971)

God elected Cain and Abel, Noah, and many other families as He pursued the providence of restoration. At every dispensation God led of this providential history, His heart was fretful beyond description. Nevertheless, controlling His feelings, God endured with great patience.

Who on this earth today feels the fretful heart of our patient God? Who would hug God and weep with Him? Anyone who knows God's heart like this and shed tears would understand: God rejoiced at the time of the creation of all things in heaven and earth, but due to the Human Fall God now grieves; His sorrow encompasses all in heaven and earth. (4:239, May 18, 1958)

[Until the coming of Jesus], what had been God's heart toward humanity? He did not have the attitude to live for His own sake. Although we fallen human beings deserved to suffer and die, God poured out all of His heart and strength to save us. Persevering through the four thousand years of Old Testament history, He fought every step of the way to separate humanity from Satan. You should understand the nature of God who loved us, persevered for us and fought for us with an unchanging heart…

During Jesus' life of 33 years, he did not try to distinguish himself before the people, but in silence he sought to experience the heart of God… At difficult moments Jesus might have felt the urge to seek his own welfare, but because he was ever immersed in God's heart, he could not even think of doing it. Jesus knew that God had persevered for four thousand years for the purpose of finding one man—Jesus himself. Knowing that, Jesus spent thirty years preparing himself, so that he could emerge as the man of substance who could liberate God from that history.

God never made excuses for His situation or complained about His suffering, not to anyone. Because Jesus was trying to understand everything about the heart of God, when he was lonely he too persevered and never made any excuses. You should follow the example of his life. (1:78, May 27, 1956)

Even though human beings sinned, God does not accuse us, saying, "Hey, you! Why did you sin?" He knows the situation of sinners. He cares about humanity more than for Himself. He comes in sorrow to sorrowful people, in suffering to suffering people, and in sympathy with those who feel victimized and angry.

How much have you empathized with God's situation? God comes into our sphere of life in this way. Not only that—he comes to us with His heart: "Although you betrayed Me, I am your Father. With a father's heart I have been searching for you for six thousand years." (9:231, May 29, 1960)

> Father! We have been like pitiful orphans,
> knocked about this way and that,
> ignorant of our purpose, our direction, and our historical situation,
> unable to grasp the center of life, pushed here and there—
> still Thou didst hold on to us.
> Yet we did not know that Thou wast there,
> sorrowful when we were sad,
> not averse to toiling day and night to seek us out,
> even as we were ensnared and groaning in the realm of death. (5:337, March 8, 1959)

The Creator

THIS SECTION ON GOD AS THE CREATOR includes classic accounts of the creation of the universe and the creation of human beings. Some describe creation as beginning with a word; others from a desire within the Absolute Being. In some texts the Creator forms the universe out of nothing *(ex nihilo)*, in others the world originated as an emanation from the Absolute, a portion of which emerged out of the void to take on the attributes of form and matter. Several texts describe the root of creation in the appearance of Mind, which then molds physical matter into its abode; others mention the motive of Love, which sought to divide Being from Non-Being in order to manifest itself. (For more texts on creation by the interaction of two poles which emerged from the One, see Chapter 2: *Duality*.) Finally, scriptures from Hinduism and Taoism describe creation in terms of divine self-emptying and sacrifice.

These creation stories are not mere explanations of how things came to be in the far remote past. They are to instruct us on the workings of God who even today governs this world by the same creative principle that He used in the beginning. As the biblical scholar Rudolph Bultmann said, "The real purpose of the creation story is to inculcate what God is doing all the time."[28] This in turn informs us about who we are. Father Moon, for his part, emphasizes the effort and love God invested in the creative process. If we are God's children, then just as God invested effort and sincerity in creating, we too should invest 100 percent of our effort in order to realize fully our potential as creative beings. As creation proceeds from mind to matter, so too our life can accord with the cosmic order when it is centered on the mind. As God was motivated to create out of love, searching for a counterpart in the world of being with whom to rejoice, so we should strive to become God's beloved, able to please His heart.

1. In the Beginning

In the beginning God created the heavens and the earth. The earth was without form and void, and darkness was upon the face of the deep; and the Spirit of God was moving over the face of the waters.

And God said, "Let there be light"; and there was light. And God saw that the light was good; and God separated the light from the darkness. God called the light Day, and the darkness he called Night. And there was evening and there was morning, one day.

And God said, "Let there be a firmament in the midst of the waters, and let it separate the waters from the waters." And God made the firmament and separated the waters which were under the firmament from the waters which were above the firmament. And it was so. And God called the firmament Heaven. And there was evening and there was morning, a second day.

And God said, "Let the waters under the heavens be gathered together into one place, and let the dry land appear." And it was so. God called the dry land Earth, and the waters that were gathered together he called Seas. And God saw that it was good. And God said, "Let the earth put forth vegetation, plants yielding seed, and fruit trees bearing fruit in which is their seed, each according to its kind, upon the earth." And it was so. The earth brought forth vegetation, plants yielding seed according to their own kinds, and trees bearing fruit in which is their seed, each according to its kind. And God saw that it was good. And there was evening and there was morning, a third day.

And God said, "Let there be lights in the firmament of the heavens to separate the day from the night; and let them be for signs and for seasons and for days and years, and let them be lights in the firmament of the heavens to give light upon the earth." And it was so. And God made the two great lights, the greater light to rule the day, and the lesser light to rule the night; he made the stars also. And God set them in the firmament of the heavens to give light upon the earth, to rule over the day and over the night, and to separate the light from the darkness. And God saw that it was good. And there was evening and there was morning, a fourth day.

And God said, "Let the waters bring forth swarms of living creatures, and let birds fly above the earth across the firmament of the heavens." So God created the great sea monsters and every living creature that moves, with which the waters swarm, according to their kinds, and every winged bird according to its kind. And God saw that it was good. And God blessed them, saying, "Be fruitful and multiply and fill the waters in the seas, and let birds multiply on the earth." And there was evening and there was morning, a fifth day.

And God said, "Let the earth bring forth living creatures according to their kinds, cattle and creeping things and beasts of the earth according to their kinds." And it was so. And God made the beasts of the earth according to their kinds, and the cattle according to their kinds, and everything that creeps upon the ground according to its kind. And God saw that it was good.

Then God said, "Let us make man in our image, after our likeness; and let them have dominion over the fish of the sea, and over the birds of the air, and over the cattle, and over all the earth, and over every creeping thing that creeps upon the earth." So God created man in his own image, in the image of God he created him; male and female he created them. And God blessed them, and God said to them, "Be fruitful and multiply, and fill the earth and subdue it; and have dominion over the fish of the sea and over the birds of the air and over every living thing that moves upon the earth." And God said, "Behold, I have given you every plant yielding seed which is upon the face of all earth, and every tree with seed in its fruit; you shall have them for food. And to every beast of the earth, and to every bird of the air, and to everything that creeps on the earth, everything that has the breath of life, I have given every green plant for food." And it was so. And God saw everything that he had made, and behold, it was very good. And there was evening and there was morning, a sixth day.[29]

Thus the heavens and the earth were finished, and all the host of them. And on the seventh day God finished his work which he had done, and he rested on the seventh day from all his work which he had done. So God blessed the seventh day and hallowed it, because on it God rested from all his work which he had done in creation.

Genesis 1.1-2.3

God it is who created the heavens and the earth,
and that which is between them, in six days.
Then He mounted the throne.
You have not, beside Him, a protecting friend or mediator.
Will you not then remember?
He directs the ordinance from the heaven to the earth;
then it ascends to Him in a Day, whose measure is a thousand years of your reckoning.
Such is the Knower of the invisible and the visible, the Mighty, the Merciful,
who made all things good which He created.[30]

Qur'an 32.4-7

Tao gave them birth;
The power of Tao reared them,
Shaped them according to their kinds,
Perfected them, giving to each its strength.

Therefore of the ten thousand things there is not one that does not worship Tao and do homage to its power. Yet no mandate ever went forth that accorded to Tao the right to be worshipped, nor to its power the right to receive homage. It was always and of itself so.[31]

Tao Te Ching 51 (Taoism)

As the web issues out of the spider
And is withdrawn, as plants sprout from the earth,
As hair grows from the body, even so,
The sages say, this universe springs from
The deathless Self, the source of life.

The deathless Self meditated upon
Himself and projected the universe
As evolutionary energy.
From this energy developed life, mind,
The elements, and the world of karma,
Which is enchained by cause and effect.

The deathless Self sees all, knows all. From him
Springs Brahma, who embodies the process
Of evolution into name and form
By which the One appears to be many.

Mundaka Upanishad 1.1.7-9 (Hinduism)

The Holy One went about creating worlds and destroying them until He created heaven and earth, of which He said, "These please Me."[32]

Genesis Rabbah 9.2 (Judaism)

Teachings of Sun Myung Moon

Christians today believe that the omnipotent God created by speaking words, saying "Let there be…" and the creation appeared as if it were a magic show. On the contrary, God totally invested His entire self into the work of creation. He invested, expressing His total love. Don't we give our utmost sincerity and invest our flesh and blood for sake of the people we love? Likewise, in creating human beings, God invested His entire Being in us; we are the bone of His bones, the flesh of His flesh and the ideal of His ideals. Therefore, God can relate with us as His beloved object partners and His hope. (78:111-12, May 6, 1975)

When God created heaven and earth, after each day of creation, "God saw that it was good." This means He felt joy. What is the experience of joy? It is the feeling of satisfaction we have when we accomplish a certain purpose. Because the created universe embodies God's purposeful consciousness, God rejoiced at its creation. (9:169, May 8, 1960)

Every result begins from a motive or cause. Every existence begins from a motive and unfolds through a process before it materializes as a result. This is the case with all natural phenomena. Human beings did not make it so; rather, this is a basic principle and heavenly law, God's law. For this reason, there is no such thing as the evolution of new species by random mutation. All things exist in order. The world was created by design, in which every existence, as an object-partner of God, arose through a principled process out of that motive [in the mind of God].

Consider successful people: could they succeed without a firm determination in their minds? Starting with a motive and plan in their mind, they prepare the ground and steadfastly push forward to reach their objective. Since this is necessary for an individual to succeed, would it not also be necessary for God, the Creator of this great universe, to attain His objectives? It is the same principle. (9:227, May 29, 1960)

The natural world contains such a wide diversity of creatures. What was the process by which each was created? They were created through the Creator's heart of dedication and sincerity. Even the microscopic organisms were created through God's heart of love and His cherished desire to exhibit His own splendor. (20:248, July 7, 1968)

God carried out His work of creation with the utmost sincerity, dedication and investment. He established the standard of absolute faith, absolute love and absolute obedience, and then invested absolutely. All created beings are God's beloved object partners, whom He created by investing with utmost sincerity. (400:81, December 27, 2002)

Each of you wishes for your partner of love to be better than you in every way. By the same token, God is looking to create something and someone greater than Himself. Do you suppose God would expend only 90 percent of His energy in creating the universe, or would He give His full 100 percent? How about 100 percent a thousand times over? Indeed, He would invest and forget what He gave, and give again and again a thousand times over. Know that this is how our universe was created: God invested 100 percent of His energy, giving and forgetting what He gave, and repeating the process tens of thousands of times. (254:266, February 15, 1994)

2. The Creation of Human Beings

Then the LORD God formed man of dust from the ground, and breathed into his nostrils the breath of life; and man became a living being.

Genesis 2.7

We created man of an extraction of clay,
then We set him, a drop, in a receptacle secure,
then We created of the drop a clot
then We created of the clot a tissue
then We created of the tissue bones
then We garmented the bones in flesh;
thereafter We produced him as another creature.
So blessed be God, the fairest of creators!

Qur'an 23.14

Creating the universe himself, He has remained unattached.
The compassionate Lord too has made the holy center [the human being].
Combining air, water, and fire, He created the citadel of the body.
The Creator fashioned the Nine Abodes [of sensation];
In the Tenth is lodged the Lord, unknowable, limitless.[33]

The illimitable Lord in His unattributed state of void assumed might;
He, the infinite One, remaining detached:
Displaying His power, He himself from the void created inanimate things.
From the unattributed void were created air and water.
Raising creation, He dwells as monarch in the citadel of the body.
Lord! In the fire and water [of the body] exists Thy light;
In Thy state of void was lodged the power of creation.

Adi Granth, Maru Sohale, M.1, p. 1037 *(Sikhism)*

Teachings of Sun Myung Moon

God first made the soil and then used it to create human beings. God created the universe by this principle, forming the internal on the basis of the external. From existing beings, God seeks to create greater beings. Creation is thus a process from things of lesser value to things of greater value. Likewise, in the creation of humans, God created first the body and then the spirit. (152:319-20, August 18, 1963)

Investing all His heart and mind, God formed the human body out of dust as the dwelling-place of the eternal spirit, where it is to live and grow. No work of art, however beautiful, can compare with the human body. God did not create it thoughtlessly, saying, "Hey, get up!" Rather, God invested all of His heart and mind into forming it. Then He completed the human being by breathing a living spirit into it. (8:80, November 8, 1959)

God's purpose in creating human beings was to rejoice with them… However, they cannot become the object partners who inspire God with joy unless they understand His Will and make effort to live accordingly. Hence, human beings are endowed with emotional sensitivity to the heart of God, intuition and reason to comprehend His Will, and the requisite abilities to practice it. (*Exposition of the Divine Principle*, Eschatology 1.1)

What if God had placed our eyes on our feet, or our mouth on the back of the head? God gave much thought to the human body's design. The mouth is where it is on the face so the two eyes can watch what we put into it and the hands can best function to feed it. Suppose your eyes were in the back of your head; your mouth might bite your finger and they wouldn't see it happening, and you would lose a finger! You have to admit that God is truly the master scientist!

Everyone has little valleys on either side of their mouths, so that when they perspire the sweat doesn't run into their mouths. If the mouth were set deeper into the face then you would constantly have to blow away your sweat, but you don't have to because God prepared better contours for your face. What a mess it would be on a rainy day if your nose were set upside down!

Think about it: everything about you is well made, from the hair inside your nose to your teeth. Everything has its role in the order of the body… Is God's thinking random or confused? No, the universe follows His order and logic. (104:207-08, May 6, 1979)

3. The Work of Creation Required Love and Sacrifice

The spirit of the valley never dies.
It is called the subtle and profound female.
The gate of the subtle and profound female
Is the root of heaven and earth.
It is continuous, and seems to be always existing.
Use it and you will never wear it out.

Tao Te Ching 6 (Taoism)

At first was neither Being nor Nonbeing.
There was not air nor yet sky beyond.
What was its wrapping? Where? In whose protection?
Was Water there, unfathomable and deep?

There was no death then, nor yet deathlessness;
of night or day there was not any sign.
The One breathed without breath, by its own impulse.
Other than that was nothing else at all.

Darkness was there, all wrapped around by darkness,
and all was Water indiscriminate. Then
that which was hidden by the void, that One, emerging,
stirring, through the power of ardor (*tapas*), came to be.

In the beginning Love arose,
which was the primal germ cell of the mind.[34]
The Seers, searching in their hearts with wisdom,
discovered the connection of Being in Nonbeing.

A crosswise line cut Being from Nonbeing.
What was described above it, what below?
Bearers of seed there were and mighty forces,
thrust from below and forward move above.

Rig Veda 10.129 (Hinduism)

When with the Supreme Being as the offering
the gods performed a sacrifice,
spring was the molten butter, summer
the fuel, and autumn the oblation.

On the grass they besprinkled him,
the Sacrificed Supreme Being, the first born.
With him the gods sacrificed,
and those Sadhyas and the sages.

From that sacrifice, fully offered,
was gathered mixed milk and butter.
And the birds of the air arose,
the forest animals and the domestic.

From that sacrifice, fully offered,
the Rig and the Saman Vedas were born,
the Chandas [Atharva Veda] was born of that,
and from that were born the Yajur Vedas.

From that were born horses, and the
animals with two rows of teeth;
yea, kine were born of that, and
of that were born the goat and the sheep...

From his mind was born the moon, and
from his eye the sun. From his mouth
were Indra and Agni born,
and Vayu (wind) was born from his breath.

From his navel came the mid-air,
from his head the sky was fashioned,
from his feet the earth, and from his ear
the quarters. Thus they formed the worlds.[35]

Rig Veda 10.90.6-10, 13-14 (Hinduism)

Teachings of Sun Myung Moon

God established living for the sake of others as the basic principle of creation. What does this mean? Suppose we take a volume of air where pressure is evenly distributed and create a vacuum in one place. The more the air pressure in that area approaches a vacuum, the faster the high-pressure air will rotate around the area of low pressure. Do you understand what I mean? When God has invested Himself over and over again in search of His objects of love, He can simply remain in His place and everything will naturally come back to Him. This is also the logical basis upon which God created all creatures in a pair system. (199:276, February 20, 1990)

Which comes first, life or love? Love comes first. Although our planet Earth came into being from God's life, we do not hold that life comes first; rather, we declare that love is first. Why? Although God began the creation of heaven and earth with life, the source of life and the motive for life is love. The reason life came into being is because of love.

Why did God create heaven and earth? Although He is the Absolute Being, God cannot feel joy as long as He is alone. Although He might sense it, He cannot experience its stimulation; this is why He created. God may say, "I am the Absolute Being, the Master of love and Master of life!" yet as long as He remains solitary, He cannot feel love's stimulation. He cannot feel the stimulation of life, the experience that all of heaven and earth are within Him. (38:152, January 3, 1971)

When God created each thing, He invested energy. Investing energy is to deplete oneself. Though God is omniscient and almighty, if He were to give out all His energy with nothing returning to Him, then God would be depleted.

If you engage in strenuous labor right after eating breakfast, you quickly become hungry and tired. Why? Investing energy is a negative for the subject partner. No one likes to suffer loss all the time. Enjoyment comes when there is a positive return on the investment. God created all things in the heavens and the earth for enjoyment, not so that He could weep or be sorrowful. Hence, something must return to God as a positive benefit...

Then, when does God receive a positive benefit? This is the measure of perfection in created beings. A being can be said to have reached perfection at the point when God begins to receive a return on His investment.

Isn't this the case in business? We plan to invest a certain amount, expecting that after a certain point we will begin to realize profits. Or when we study, we think that after putting in a certain number of hours we will be adequately prepared to pass the exam. This is true with everything; it is a universal law. When we have a desire, if we work hard and challenge our limit to reach a goal, then we can cross the finish line and receive something in return.

The same is true with God. What did He expect to gain by creating human beings? In creating them He invested His energy and consumed something of Himself. God spent everything possible for our sake. Yet there is no loss; once we become perfect, there is a return. We should understand this basic rule.

If 100 units were invested but the return was valued at less than 100 units, God would not have continued His work of creation. The return should be 110, 200, or 300 units, something valued more than the 100 units invested. Even better, the return should be unlimited. When this happens, God experiences joy even as He invests. Considering this, we conclude that the return should be something with a higher dimension of value. What form would it take? What, when it returns, gives joy? The answer is love. (65:22-23, November 13, 1972)

If God had thought only of Himself, would He have created heaven and earth? To create means to invest energy. The cherished desire of an artist is to create a masterpiece. To do this, the artist will invest all of his heart and soul. He will want to reach the point where he cannot do anything more. Only by thus investing himself completely can he create the perfect masterpiece. (78:111, May 6, 1975)

God created the universe, first, with absolute faith. Second, He created with absolute love, cherishing each creation as His beloved object partner. Third, God created with absolute obedience, which means that He totally emptied Himself. God gave His total investment, forgetting what He had given and repeatedly giving still more. He gave up even any concept [that something might come of what He had given]. After thus emptying Himself, God reached the zero point. Since He had invested all of His absolute faith, God reached the zero point. Since He had invested all of Himself with absolute love, in total obedience to the principle of love, God reached the zero point. (313:114-15)

Heavenly Father and Mother

THE ABSOLUTE BEING RELATES TO human beings as parent to child. The Jewish and Christian scriptures call God our Heavenly Father; in the Lotus Sutra the Buddha is called "Father of the World." In some traditions the Absolute Being is also identified as the Divine Mother. Even religions that customarily employ patriarchal imagery for God also describe a motherly aspect: God as Nurturer, Fount of compassion and Sustainer. "There is something in the nature of God that corresponds to our maleness and our femaleness," remarks Bishop Desmond Tutu.[36] God's fatherhood and motherhood may be identified with heaven and earth, cooperating to create and nurture all living things.

God's parental role is not limited to the act of creation; it is an enduring affective relationship of the heart. Love reveals God's parental aspect better than anything. Even Islam, which avoids describing God as a divine father, in light of its strong rejection of polytheism in which gods physically procreate, includes traditions that describe God's love by analogy to a father's love for his son.

Love is central to Father Moon's teaching about the parenthood of God: "The relationship of the Father and His children is the foundation of the universe." Elaborating, he teaches that we can and should establish a genuinely filial relationship to God, attending Him and sharing His heart. God, for His part, is ever searching for children who can meet Him in that intimate embrace.

Our Father who art in heaven, hallowed be thy name.
Matthew 6.9

You men are all my children,
And I am your Father.
For age upon age, you
Have been scorched by multitudinous woes,
And I have saved you all.[37]
Lotus Sutra 3 (Buddhism)

The Great Principle, the Divine, is my womb;
I cast the seed into it;
There is the origin of all creatures.
Whatever forms originate in any wombs — The real womb is the Divine, the Great Principle.
I am the Father that gives the seed.
Bhagavad-Gita 14.4 (Hinduism)

Thou art Father, Mother, Friend, Brother.
With Thee as succorer in all places, what fear have I?
Adi Granth, Majh M.5, p. 103 (Sikhism)

For God, people of the whole world are all my children. All of you equally must understand that I am your Parent.

The daily concern of the Parent is single-heartedly how best I can advance arrangements to save all of you.
Ofudesaki 4.79; 14.35 (Tenrikyo)

Our Father, it is thy universe, it is thy will,
Let us be at peace, let the souls of the people be cool.
Thou art our Father; remove all evil from our path.

        Nuer Prayer *(African Traditional Religions)*

Heaven and Earth are the father and mother of the ten thousand things.
People are the sensibility of the ten thousand things.

        Book of History 5.1.1: The Great Declaration *(Confucianism)*

What man of you, if his son asks him for bread, will give him a stone? Or if he asks for fish, will give him a serpent? If you, then, who are evil, know how to give good gifts to your children, how much more will your Father who is in heaven give good things to those who ask him!

        Matthew 7.10-11

Once a man came to the Messenger with his son. The Messenger embraced they boy and said, "Do you have mercy upon him?" The father said, "Yes." Then the Messenger replied, "Allah is more merciful upon him than you."

        Hadith of Bukhari *(Islam)*

Do you thus requite the LORD,
you foolish and senseless people?
Is not he your father, who created you,
who made you and established you?...

He found him in a desert land,
in the howling waste of the wilderness;
He encircled him, he cared for him,
he kept him as the apple of his eye.
Like an eagle that stirs up its nest,
that flutters over its young,
Spreading out its wings, catching them,
bearing them on its pinions,
The LORD alone did lead him,
and there was no foreign god with him.

        Deuteronomy 32.6-12

All ye under heaven! Regard heaven as your father, earth as your mother, and all things as your brothers and sisters.[38]

        Oracle of the Kami of Atsuta *(Shinto)*

Mother Earth, have pity on us and give us food to eat!
Father Sun, bless all our children and may our paths be straight!

        Blackfoot Prayer *(Native American Religions)*

That breast of Thine which is inexhaustible, health-giving,
by which thou nursest all that is noble,
containing treasure, bearing wealth, bestowed freely;
lay that bare, O Divine Mother, for our nurture.

        Rig Veda 1.164.49 *(Hinduism)*

As one whom his mother comforts,
so will I comfort you;
You shall be comforted in Jerusalem.

        Isaiah 66.13

O Mother of Imupa, advocate for the whole [feminine] world!
What a remarkable Mother I have!
O Mother, a pillar, a refuge!
O Mother, to whom all prostrate in greeting
Before one enters her habitation!
I am justly proud of my Mother.
O Mother who arrives,
Who arrives majestic and offers water to all!

        Yoruba Prayer *(African Traditional Religions)*

Teachings of Sun Myung Moon

God is our Friend, our greatest Friend. God is our Father, Elder Brother, King, and Creator. How proud we should be to have such a God! (293:161, May 26, 1998)

Why did God create the universe? The reason is that God wants to engage in the loving relationship of a father with his children. The relationship of father and children is, in fact, the foundation of the universe. (118:290, June 20, 1982)

What is the Creator like, the Lord who created us? He is the lord of our body and mind. He is the lord of our ideas and the world of emotions. He is the lord of our hearts. We absolutely need such a God. We do not just need Him conceptually; we do not just need to recognize He exists; we need Him absolutely. Losing the Lord is sorrow.

God is more than our Lord. Taking one more step, God is our Father. God is Lord because He created us and created the heavens and the earth, but He did not stop at being our Lord. He is our Father. Therefore, He seeks to clarify the bond between us by revealing, "I am your Father, and you are my sons and daughters." He longs to rejoice in that relationship, singing songs of happiness. This hope is the center of the Father's daily living, the center of His thought, and the purpose for which He created human beings. (7:48-49, July 12, 1959)

We should call God, "Father." God is the Father who originally created you. Due to the Human Fall we also need rebirth, but God engendered your first birth. Your physical father was only the bridge over which you came into this world. When you go to dwell in the spirit world, you will not call Him "father" but rather "older brother." You will also not call your physical mother "mother."

People of firmly rooted faith in the spirit realms all call God "Father," just as Christians do on earth. In any given family, the grandfather calls God "Father," the father calls God "Father," the grandchild calls God "Father"—every member of the family calls God "Father." Since God is the Father of all people, all people are brothers and sisters to one another. (21:249, November 24, 1968)

Heaven represents father and Earth represents mother. Your first mother is the woman who gave you birth. Your second mother is the Earth, which supplies all the resources for life. Like a woman, the earth digests everything without complaint… Your third mother is the Holy Spirit. (279:171, August 4, 1996)

When you go to the spirit world, you will not only have a Heavenly Father but also a Heavenly Mother. Can a new life be born without both a father and a mother? The dual characteristics of God are as divine Father and Mother, who were to be united as one in Adam and Eve. Therefore, we can say that through either our father or our mother there lies a gate to heaven.

Had Adam and Eve become one, who would be the leading lights of the Kingdom of God in the spirit world? They would be our father and mother. Having lived on earth in the body, they would be the King and Queen of the eternal Kingdom of Heaven in the other world.

Hence, in the Unification Church…you have spiritual experiences where I, Reverend Moon, appear in your visions or dreams, and so does True Mother. You can experience that Mother and I are truly living with you throughout your life. How does the invisible God appear to earthly people?

You should know that He can appear in the image of True Father and True Mother, to show Himself to His children throughout the world. (90:196-97, January 1, 1977)

Human beings lost God. What is this God? He is our Parent. He is the ultimate First Ancestor and King, such as whom there never was and never will be another. What, then, are we? We are God's sons and daughters. We are the sons and daughters of the King who rules the universe. This means we are princes and princesses. Then, what should we princes and princesses do? We should be educated in love and live with love under God's sovereign authority. This is the world's ideal. (105:26, July 8, 1979)

God's purpose of creation is to create an ideal family where God can dwell with human beings. Although human beings fell, in their hearts they long for the day when God can live as the Father of the human family and they can live as members of God's family. We long to attend God as our eternal Father, become members of His family and live with God eternally. That is our hope, our ideal, our life, and our joy. That will be the completion of God's long-sought purpose. (7:264-65 September 27, 1959)

Don't simply serve God. Become God's object partner, who says, "Father, here I am. How anxiously Thou hast waited for this moment for 6,000 years! How many tears Thou hast shed! How desperately Thou hast yearned for me! Now, here I am." This is what God has desired to hear from you.

After such a reunion, when God blesses you with dominion over all things in heaven and on earth, He would like to forget all the pain of the past and say, "I rejoice, for today is the day of My birth."[39] God wants to put all the pain of the past 6,000 years behind him and sing songs of heartfelt love with His children in the new heaven and new earth. Then we will clearly know that God is our Father, and we are His children. (7:171, August 30, 1959)

Chapter 2

Truth and Universal Law

Eternal Truth

THE ETERNAL WORD, TRUTH, OR DIVINE WISDOM pre-existed the creation of the universe. The Word is all-pervasive; it guided the creation of the universe and continues to function in the principles of nature. It operates through physical, moral and spiritual laws. For some, truth is to be grasped by reason. For others, its essence is the Word, which is manifested completely only in Christ, the perfect man.

The Word gives the universe its purpose. This touches the mystery of why God created the universe. As the Absolute Being, omnipotent and omnipresent, what did God gain by creating something apart from Him? The texts in the last group suggest that the primary theme was love. Love, which arises only in relationship, is imprinted in the cosmos by the pervasive duality of plus and minus, male and female. God, too, to experience the joy of love, would create objects apart from Himself with which to have a relationship. Here lies the purpose of creation, the root Idea in the mind of God that lies behind the blueprint of creation.

1. In the Beginning Was the Word

He has created the heavens and the earth with truth.

                    Qur'an 16.3

When Heaven creates a thing, it gives each thing a principle of truth.

                    Chu Hsi *(Confucianism)*

The sun and the moon are made punctual, the stars and the trees adore, and the sky He hath uplifted; and He hath set the measure.

                    Qur'an 55.5-7

The LORD by wisdom founded the earth;
by understanding he established the heavens;
by his knowledge the deeps broke forth,
and the clouds drop down the dew.

                    Proverbs 3.19-20

By Truth is the earth sustained,
and by the sun are the heavens;

By Order the gods stand
and Soma is set in the sky.

                    Rig Veda 10.85.1 *(Hinduism)*

In the beginning was the Word, and the Word was with God, and the Word was God.[1] He was in the beginning with God; all things were made through him, and without him was not anything made that was made. In him was life, and the life was the light of men. The light shines in the darkness, and the darkness has not overcome it.

                    John 1.1-5

This, [in the beginning] was the only Lord of the universe. His Word was with Him. This Word was His second. He contemplated. He said, "I will deliver this Word so that she will produce and bring into being all this world."

                    Tandya Maha Brahmana 20.14.2 *(Hinduism)*

He [Christ] is the image of the invisible God, the first-born of all creation; for in him all things were created, in heaven and on earth, visible and invisible, whether thrones or dominions or principalities or authorities—all things were created through him and for him. He is before all things, and in him all things hold together.

Colossians 1.15-17

The LORD created me at the beginning of his work,
the first of his acts of old.
Ages ago I was set up,
at the first, before the beginning of the earth...
When he marked out the foundations of the earth,
then I was beside him, like a little child;[2]
I was daily his delight,
rejoicing before him always;
rejoicing in his inhabited world,
and delighting in the sons of men.

Proverbs 8.22-31

In human practice, when a mortal king builds a palace, he builds it not with his own skill but with the skill of an architect. The architect moreover does not build it out of his head, but employs plans and diagrams to know how to arrange the chambers and the doors. Thus God consulted the Torah and created the world.

Genesis Rabbah 1.1 (Judaism)

The Tao has its reality and its signs but is without action or form. You can hand it down but you cannot receive it; you can get it but you cannot see it. It is its own source, its own root. Before heaven and earth existed it was there, firm from ancient times. It gave spirituality to the spirits and to God; it gave birth to heaven and to earth. It exists beyond the highest point, and yet you cannot call it lofty; it exists beneath the limit of the six directions, and yet you cannot call it deep. It was born before heaven and earth, and yet you cannot say it has been there for long; it is earlier than the earliest time, and yet you cannot call it old.

Chuang Tzu 6 (Taoism)

Teachings of Sun Myung Moon

With what was the world created? In the beginning, there was God's Will. There was God's idea. Along with it, there was God's plan. God's original Will was to create humans and the human world according to His plan. Therefore, human beings... no matter how fallen, should stand within the Will and plan of God. (76:92, February 1, 1975)

Even the most advanced science cannot attain or surpass what God has made. The immense universe operates in an orderly way according to its laws. Since God created and governs the immense universe, whose comprehension is beyond the reach of human thought and science, we conclude that God is the absolute Scientist. (127:10, May 1, 1983)

Even the greatest scientist or scholar in the world today possesses only miniscule knowledge. The deeper you go, the more you will find principled actions based on eternal laws. Considering this, we see that these laws could not have come about by chance. In every case, they uphold a certain content of the origin. Their direction is aligned with, and never contradictory to, the whole purpose of the universe. This lawful universe is infinitely vast, and at the same time so subtle. Hence, no one can deny that God, who created this universe, is the King of wisdom and the King of knowledge. (127:11, May 1, 1983)

Before God created the heavens and the earth and human beings, there was a time when He functioned centering on Himself. Because we humans resemble God, we also have times when we think only about ourselves.

Then God began to create all things in heaven and on earth; this means that He spread out the universe [as the environment for human beings], His object partners. In due course, He would create His object partners. All this investment by the invisible God was for the purpose of manifesting as the visible God. (69:81-82, October 20, 1973)

God created human beings as the model, expanding His creations to the four directions, East, West, South and North. (173:212, February 18, 1988)

Before creating human beings, God created the natural world by expressing partial reflections of the internal nature and external form He had conceived for human beings, who were yet to be created. Hence, a human being, as the manifest image of God, contains the sum total of the essences of all things. (*Exposition of the Divine Principle*, Creation 3.2)

Even before the creation, the first thing that God thought of was true parents, and the family where true parents, true couple, and true children are united as one. (339:212, December 26, 2000)

2. Truth Is Absolute

From the bosom of the sacred Word He
   brought forth the world.
On high, below, He abides in His own laws.
Atharva Veda 4.1.3 (Hinduism)

There is no changing the words of God; that is the mighty triumph.
Qur'an 10.64

Righteousness and justice are the foundations
   of thy throne;
steadfast love and faithfulness go before thee.
Psalm 89.14

Truth is victorious, never untruth.
Truth is the way; truth is the goal of life,
Reached by sages who are free from self-will.
Mundaka Upanishad 3.1.6 (Hinduism)

By Divine Law are all forms manifested;
Inexpressible is the Law.
By Divine Law are beings created;
By Law are some exalted.
By Divine Law are beings marked with nobility
   or ignominy;
By the Law are they visited with bliss or bale.
On some by His Law falls grace;
Others by His Law are whirled around in cycles
   of births and deaths.
All by the Law are governed,
None is exempt.
Says Nanak, Should man realize the power of
   the Law,
He would certainly disclaim his ego.
Japuji 2, M.1, p. 1 (Sikhism)

Absolute truth is indestructible. Being indestructible, it is eternal. Being eternal, it is self-existent. Being self-existent, it is infinite. Being infinite, it is vast and deep. Being vast and deep, it is transcendental and intelligent. It is because it is vast and deep that it contains all existence. It is because it is transcendental and intelligent that it embraces all existence. It is because it is infinite and eternal that it perfects all existence.
Doctrine of the Mean 26 (Confucianism)

What is meant by an eternally-abiding reality? The ancient road of reality has been here all the time, like gold, silver, or pearl preserved in the mine. The Dharmadhatu (Absolute Truth) abides forever, whether the Tathagata appears in the world or not. As the Tathagata eternally abides, so does the Reason of all things. Reality forever abides, reality keeps its order, like the roads in an ancient city.

For instance, a man who is walking in a forest and discovering an ancient city with its orderly streets may enter into the city, and having entered into it, he may have a rest, conduct himself like a citizen, and enjoy all the pleasures accruing therefrom. What do you think? Did this man make the road along which he enters into the city, and the various things in the city? [No.]

Just so, what has been realized by myself and the other Tathagatas is this Reality, this eternally-abiding reality, the self-regulating reality, the Suchness of things, the Realness of things, the truth itself.

Lankavatara Sutra 61 (*Buddhism*)

Teachings of Sun Myung Moon

Since God is an eternal, unchanging and unique Being, the love, ideals, peace and happiness that He desires must be likewise. (74:161, December 7, 1974)

God is absolute. Even after the Fall, God continues to relate to what He has made according to the laws and principles He established. (52:87, December 22, 1971)

The life of true love is living for the sake of others... [without] hopes of receiving something in return... as Jesus said, "Greater love has no man than this, that a man lay down his life for his friends," and "Whoever exalts himself will be humbled, and whoever humbles himself will be exalted." This is the very Principle of Creation, which God Himself set up. God is the almighty Creator, yet He will not destroy what He created at a whim and start over again, for to do so he would have to negate His own Principle.[3] (January 27, 2004)

The components that make up the universe were not created blindly. This vast universe exists and moves by the relative relationships between subject and object partners, whose unceasing give and take following the track of the law enables the universe to continue in perpetuity. To continue in perpetuity, we, too, must follow the track of the law. If we do not, we will not continue but will perish. For our physical life to continue, we need to eat, digest normally, and have good circulation to distribute the nutrients throughout our body. Thus, a being can continue only when there is smooth give and take. (182:117, October 16, 1988)

Ontology should clarify... the motivation, purpose, and laws of creation, and show that they govern the movement of all beings. The normative laws that govern human beings should be in unity with the laws of the universe—the way of Heaven.

Just as the laws by which the sun, moon and stars were created—the way of Heaven—set up a system of vertical order, so also in the family there is a vertical order extending from grandparents to parents and children, and likewise a horizontal order formed by the siblings. The laws of Heaven and the values or norms of [family life] correspond.

With a theoretical structure consistent with the natural sciences, and with a self-evident nature acceptable to the human conscience, ontology must attest to the historical validity of the proposition, "Those who betray Heaven will perish, and those who are faithful to Heaven will live." On the basis of this ontology we can establish absolute values in the true sense. Establishing them—absolute truth, absolute goodness and absolute beauty—then understanding them and practicing them, we will bring about humanity's spiritual revolution. Then the chaos in today's world will gradually disappear. (122:303-04, November 25, 1982)

3. The Law of Love

Love, the divine Principle, is the Father and Mother of the universe, including man.
Science and Health, p. 256 (Christian Science)

Love is the great law that rules this mighty and heavenly cycle, the unique power that binds together the diverse elements of this material world, and the supreme magnetic force that directs the movements of the spheres in the celestial realms. Love reveals with unfailing and limitless power the mysteries latent in the universe. Love is the spirit of life unto the adorned body of mankind, the establisher of true civilization in this mortal world, and the shedder of imperishable glory upon every high-aiming race and nation.
'Abdu'l Bahá (Bahá'í Faith)

That which lets now the dark (yin), now the light (yang) appear is Tao.

As continuer, it is good. As completer, it is the essence.
The kind man discovers it and calls it benevolence (jen).
The wise man discovers it and calls it wisdom.
The people use it day by day and are not aware of it, for the way of the superior man is rare.
It manifests itself as benevolence but conceals its workings.
It gives life to all things, without sharing the anxieties of the holy sage.
Its glorious power, its great field of action, are of all things the most sublime.
It possesses everything in complete abundance: this is its great field of action.
It renews everything daily: this is its glorious power.
I Ching, Great Treatise 1.5 (Confucianism)

Teachings of Sun Myung Moon

The universe is created centering on love and the principles of love. It dances to that rhythm, not to the rhythm of the individual. (131:124, April 22, 1984)

The omniscient and omnipotent God, who has no need for gold or knowledge, the God who has everything—what was it He yearned for that He would create human beings? What was the fundamental motivation for the act of creation? It was not power, it was not knowledge, and it was not wealth. What God lacked was a foundation for love. Even God cannot bring about love by Himself. Thus, the motivation for the creation of the heavens and the earth was love. (149:149, November 21, 1986)

The creation of the universe began with love. Love preexisted the creation. If the idea of love did not exist, then there would have been no purpose to the principle of male and female. The mineral kingdom consists of positive and negative ions—like male and female. The world of insects consists of male and female. The animal world consists of male and female. Human beings, likewise, are men and women. Before the principle of male and female, there was the idea of love, that things made male and female would become one through love.

If the idea of love didn't exist, this universe pervaded by the duality of male and female would not have arisen. Which came first: male and female physical beings or the emotion and idea of love? This is the old philosophical problem of Realism vs. Idealism... We should know that the idea of love came first.

Women are not born for their own sake. Men are not born for their own sake. They both exist for the sake of love. For this reason, the chief concern of both men and women is love. (218:339-40, August 22, 1991)

The created world contains subject and object partners, and for this reason there are men and women and male and female creatures. The subject-object relationship is found in flowers with stamen and pistil, in molecules with positive and negative ions, and in atoms with protons and electrons. Everything exists in a pair system.

Nothing else but love fulfills the value and carries on the history of existing beings. Through love men and women procreate. Other beings—insects, plants, and minerals—also love according to their kind.

Why is everything in a pair system? Why are there always subject and object partners? The reason is love. Which came first, love or subject and object partners? Does love exist because there are women and men, or do we exist as women and men because of love? Which is it? We exist as women and men because of love. (227:268, February 14, 1992)

Without God's investment of love, the cosmos could not have come into being. The law of the cosmos is that the subject partner lives for the sake of the object partner. However, in the fallen world, the subject does not live for the sake of the object; instead, the subject misuses the object for his own sake. That is why the world is destined to decline. Religions must teach the heavenly principle that you are happy only when your counterpart is happy. (271:70, August 21, 1995)

The Moral Law

DIVINE LAW, THE IMMUTABLE LAW OF NATURE, is inherently moral. It embraces in one principle the cosmological, ethical, social and legal spheres. Religion, therefore, cannot accept the modern distinction between fact and value; rather the moral law governing human life is as absolute as the law of gravity.

Since the order of the universe and the order of life cohere; establishing right order in our lives is the way to prosperity and longevity. Following the moral law leads to life and heaven; ignoring the law leads to decline, suffering and death.

The moral norms of human life are revealed in sacred Scriptures are variously called the Law or Torah (Judaism), Dhamma (Theravada Buddhism), Tao (Taoism), Dharma (Hinduism), and Moral Order (Confucianism). Yet these are but expressions of a natural law, inherent to our being and written on the heart, which transcends religion or social circumstance. In fact, as Father Moon teaches and Confucian texts confirm, it finds its foremost expression in the family. The fundamental principle is to establish harmonious relationships, and this is achieved by practicing unselfishness and living for the sake of others.

1. Living by the Law

The LORD commanded us to do all these statutes, to fear the LORD our God, for our good always, that he might preserve us alive, as at this day.

Deuteronomy 6:24

Easily known is the progressive one, easily known the one who declines. He who loves Dhamma progresses, he who hates it declines.

Sutta Nipata 92 (Buddhism)

God has revealed the fairest of statements, a Scripture consistent, [with reward] paired [with punishment], at which creeps the flesh of those who fear their Lord, so that their flesh and their hearts soften to God's reminder. Such is God's guidance, with which He guides whom He will.

Qur'an 39.23

The night passes; it is never to return again.
The night passes in vain
for one who acts not according to the law.

Uttaradhyayana Sutra 14.24 (Jainism)

The law of the LORD is perfect,
reviving the soul;
The testimony of the LORD is sure,
making wise the simple;
The precepts of the LORD are right,
rejoicing the heart;
The commandment of the LORD is pure,
enlightening the eyes;
The fear of the LORD is clean,
enduring for ever;
The ordinances of the LORD are true,
and righteous altogether.
More to be desired are they than gold,
even much fine gold;
Sweeter also than honey
and drippings of the honeycomb.

Psalm 19.7-10

Those who live in accordance with the divine laws without complaining, firmly established in faith, are released from karma. Those who violate these laws, criticizing and complaining, are utterly deluded, and are the cause of their own suffering.

Bhagavad-Gita 3.31-32 (Hinduism)

Every one then who hears these words of mine and does them will be like a wise man who built his house upon the rock; and the rain fell, and the floods came, and the winds blew and beat upon that house, but it did not fall, because it had been founded on the rock. And every one who hears these words of mine and does not do them will be like a foolish man who built his house upon the sand; and the rain fell, and the floods came, and the winds blew and beat against that house, and it fell; and great was the fall of it.

Matthew 7.24-27

The blessed Buddhas, of virtues endless and limitless, are born of the Law of Righteousness; they dwell in the Law, are fashioned by the Law; they have the Law as their master, the Law as their light, the Law as their field of action, the Law as their refuge...

The Law is equal, equal for all beings. For low or middle or high the Law cares nothing. So I must make my thought like the Law.

The Law has no regard for the pleasant. Impartial is the Law. So I must make my thought like the Law....

The Law does not seek refuge. The refuge of all the world is the Law. So I must make my thought like the Law.

The Law has none who can resist it. Irresistible is the Law. So I must make my thought like the Law.

The Law has no preferences. Without preference is the Law. So I must make my thought like the Law.

The Law has no fear of the terrors of birth-and-death, nor is it lured by Nirvana. Ever without misgiving is the Law. So I must make my thought like the Law.

Dharmasangiti Sutra (Buddhism)

What Tao plants cannot be plucked,
What Tao clasps cannot slip.
By its virtue alone can one generation after another carry on the ancestral sacrifice.

Apply it to yourself and by its power you will be freed from dross.
Apply it to your household and your household shall thereby have abundance.
Apply it to the village, and the village will be made secure.
Apply it to the kingdom, and the kingdom shall thereby be made to flourish.
Apply it to an empire, and the empire shall thereby be extended.

Tao Te Ching 54 (Taoism)

Teachings of Sun Myung Moon

The way of prosperity is to follow God's law. The reason is simple: God protects and helps anyone who follows God's law because He wants to see His purpose of creation fulfilled. Hence, if we observe God's law we will prosper. If we oppose God's law and follows Satan's law instead, we will perish, for God will strike us. (103:275, March 11, 1979)

How do we describe a person who lives in accordance with the law? Do we say he is arrogant? No, we say he or she is as an honest person. The Korean word for honesty (*jeongjik*) is composed of two Chinese characters, 正 meaning "right" and 直 meaning "straight." The law establishes what is straight. With the law we separate good from evil and distinguish between right and wrong. (37:112, December 23, 1970)

This is a meter ruler. You cannot arbitrarily make your own meter different from the standard length. You have to measure distance according to the standard of the original meter. In other words, you should measure your words and deeds according to the original standard. (51:80, November 11, 1971)

The law of the universe, which upholds the welfare of the whole, is a proper standard of judgment. All human beings come before its court, and at the trial each is judged according to its statutes. What sort of people will be justified before the law of the universe? They are men and women who willingly sacrifice themselves for the benefit of the whole. On the other hand, those who dislike sacrifice, who pursue their individual interests and even take advantage of others, will be found guilty. Do you understand?

So what kind of people are good people? They are people who work for the sake of others. What kind of acts are good acts? Surely, they are acts of self-sacrifice and service to benefit others. From this point of view, are today's young people who live lives of self-indulgence good people or bad people? They are bad people, without a doubt.

The law of the universe applies not only to human beings, but to the all beings in the material world. For instance, the cells of the eye cannot act as though everything in the body exists only for the eye. If the eye were to say to its owner, "Submit to me. If you as a human being, employ me for your sake, I, your eye, will rebel against you!" that kind of attitude would lead to its destruction. Rather, the cells of the eye exist for the benefit of the entire body. The eye should think, "Although my cells are precious, serving my owner is the public purpose, so I will follow the law of the universe."

That which is public has greater value. This can be affirmed in every instance. Since we know this principle, we cannot complain. (105:93, September 30, 1979)

2. Natural Law

The moral law is to be found everywhere, and yet it is a secret.

The simple intelligence of ordinary men and women of the people may understand something of the moral law; but in its utmost reaches there is something which even the wisest and holiest men cannot understand. The ignoble natures of ordinary men and women of the people may be able to carry out the moral law; but in its utmost reaches even the wisest and holiest of men cannot live up to it.

Great as the Universe is, man is yet not always satisfied with it. For there is nothing so great but the mind of the moral man can conceive of something still greater which nothing in the world can hold. There is nothing so small but the mind of the moral man can conceive of something still smaller which nothing in the world can split.

The Book of Songs says,

> The hawk soars to the heavens above
> Fishes dive to the depths below.

That is to say, there is no place in the highest heavens above nor in the deepest waters below where the moral law is not to be found. The moral man finds the moral law beginning in the relation between man and woman; but ending in the vast reaches of the universe.

Doctrine of the Mean 12 *(Confucianism)*

Law is twofold—natural and written. The natural law is in the heart, the written law on tables. Therefore all are under the law, the natural law, but it does not belong to all men that each should be a law unto himself. However, that man is a law unto himself who does the commandments of the law of his own accord and manifests the work of the law written in his own heart...

Nature herself is the teacher of good conduct. You know that one must not steal, and if your servant has stolen from you, you beat him, while if someone has lusted after your wife, you think he should be punished. Now, what you condemn in others you perpetrate yourself...

Saint Ambrose of Milan[4] *(Christianity)*

The life of the moral man is an exemplification of the universal moral order. The life of the vulgar person, on the other hand, is a contradiction of the universal moral order.

The moral man's life is an exemplification of the universal order, because he is a moral person who unceasingly cultivates his true self or moral being. The vulgar person's life is a contradiction of the universal order, because he is a vulgar person who in his heart has no regard for, or fear of, the moral law.

Doctrine of the Mean 2 *(Confucianism)*

The principle of Tao is just as close as what is right in front of our eyes, in our everyday lives, in eating and drinking, and in the maintaining of normal social relationships—between ruler and subject, and father and son, and between brothers, and spouses, and friends.

Chu Hsi *(Confucianism)*

Teachings of Sun Myung Moon

Like it or not, human beings live within a cyclical existence: people grow old and return to their original elements, and new people are born. Through this cycle, humanity develops and increases.

All things that exist move and function within their limited realm in accordance with the laws of nature that establish nature's cycles.

The nine planets of the solar system revolve about the sun. Can a planet say, "I will go where I please"? No, it cannot leave its orbit. When spring comes, can any animal or plant say, "I refuse to grow"? No. Spring is the time to grow. Summer is the time for plants to become thick with foliage and their flowers to bloom. Then in autumn, they must bear fruit. (207:61, November 1, 1990)

The solar system turns in a great, cosmic circle. What is its center? It is love—true love. Therefore, at home, we are taught to love and honor our parents, an expression of love called filial piety. We are taught to love our nation; that love is called patriotism. We are taught to love humankind; that is to love as a saint. In other words, in the various orbits of our life, love should be at the center. When true love takes the center seat, everything else falls into its proper place. The right order is created around that eternal and unchanging axis. (146:166, June 15, 1986)

Just as the laws by which the sun, moon and stars were created—the way of heaven—set up a system of vertical order, so also in the family there is a vertical order extending from grandparents to parents and children, and likewise a horizontal order formed by the siblings. The laws of heaven and the values or norms of [family life] correspond. (122:304, November 25, 1982)

In springtime the flowers bloom, in summer the plants grow, and in autumn they bear fruit. Likewise, when you live according to the laws of nature, it is a shortcut to the Kingdom of Heaven. (393:215, February 20, 2004)

What is the heavenly law? Have you ever heard of this religious term? You know what human morals are, but have you ever heard of heavenly morals? What is the origin of the human morals? Is it the Korean constitution? No, the origin of human morals is the conscience.

Human laws today are based on Roman law, and Roman law is the foundation of world culture. However, human morals are based on the conscience. Conscience precedes law.

Goodness is the foundation of conscience. When we deviate from goodness and go astray, our conscience tries to correct us. Our concept of goodness sets the standard for our conscience. Hence, a universal society needs the moral law, because its members seek a social order that is in accord with the untainted conscience. Ultimately, the root of human morals is the heavenly law. (33:44, August 2, 1970)

Human morals are rooted in the heart. Relationships in the family, norms of behavior, social systems, the social order and such should be rooted in the heart. Human morals begin from parents loving their children. Then, by children loving their parents, they establish a true human relationship. A second true human relationship is established by a husband loving his wife and a wife loving her husband. Love is like the leaven for morality in all its aspects.[5] (64:124-25, October 29, 1972)

Formulas rooted in laws have made possible the development of our technological civilization. Whether a scientific idea can be accepted as law depends on how widely it can be applied in its field. Likewise, in our religious lives, we should not go by blind faith. God always carries out His Providence through formulaic laws, so we must understand these formulas. There is a clear formula running through the history of the Providence of Restoration from the past up to the present. This is one of the most important teachings of the Unification Principle. (16:119, October 22, 1978)

The Golden Rule

THE GOLDEN RULE is found in the scriptures of nearly every religion. It is often regarded as the most concise and general principle of ethics. Though sometimes called "reciprocity," the Golden Rule is proactive, not reactive. It teaches us to initiate acts of kindness and consideration for the other, not to react to an insult by returning the same. Hence, this is a challenging ethic, requiring considerable moral integrity to practice.

There are three levels of this ethic: First, the negative expression, "do not do to others what you do not want them to do to you," teaches us to refrain from harming others, as we would not wish to be harmed. Next, the positive form, "whatever you wish that men would do to you, do so to them" or "you shall love your neighbor as yourself" requires us to consider the other person's needs and feelings and to act towards him or her in a loving manner. Finally, Father Moon's teaching elevates the Golden Rule to his statement of the fundamental principle to live for the sake of others. This ethic calls us to continual acts of service and sacrifice. It requires a selfless orientation of character, which ultimately stems from our vertical connection to God and His endless love.

Whatever you wish that men would do to you, do so to them.

Matthew 7.12

Tsekung asked, "Is there one word that can serve as a principle of conduct for life?" Confucius replied, "It is the word *shu*—reciprocity: Do not do to others what you do not want them to do to you."

Analects 15.23 (Confucianism)

You shall love your neighbor as yourself.[6]

Leviticus 19.18

Not one of you is a believer until he loves for his brother what he loves for himself.

Forty Hadith of an-Nawawi 13 (Islam)

Try your best to treat others as you would wish to be treated yourself, and you will find that this is the shortest way to benevolence.

Mencius VII.A.4 (Confucianism)

One should not behave towards others in a way which is disagreeable to oneself. This is the essence of morality. All other activities are due to selfish desire.

Mahabharata, Anusasana Parva 113.8 (Hinduism)

In happiness and suffering, in joy and grief, regard all creatures as you regard your own self, and do not injure others with that which would injure yourself.

Yogashastra 2.20 (Jainism)

Comparing oneself to others in such terms as "Just as I am so are they, just as they are so am I," he should neither kill nor cause others to kill.

Sutta Nipata 705 (Buddhism)

One going to take a pointed stick to pinch a baby bird should first try it on himself to feel how it hurts.

Yoruba Proverb (African Traditional Religions)

Act only on that maxim through which you can at the same time will that it should become a universal law.

Immanuel Kant, *Groundwork for the Metaphysics of Morals*

A certain heathen came to Shammai and said to him, "Make me a proselyte, on condition that you teach me the whole Torah while I stand on one foot." Thereupon he repulsed him with the rod which was in his hand. When he went to Hillel, he said to him, "What is hateful to you, do not do to your neighbor: that is the whole Torah; all the rest of it is commentary; go and learn."

Talmud, Shabbat 31a *(Judaism)*

Here am I, fond of my life, not wanting to die, fond of pleasure and averse from pain. Suppose someone should rob me of my life… it would not be a thing pleasing and delightful to me. If I, in my turn, should rob of his life one fond of his life, not wanting to die, one fond of pleasure and averse from pain, it would not be a thing pleasing or delightful to him. For a state that is not pleasant or delightful to me must also be to him; and a state that is not pleasing or delightful to me, how could I inflict that upon another?

Samyutta Nikaya 5.353 *(Buddhism)*

Teachings of Sun Myung Moon

Even looking at contemporary morals and social ethics, a certain principle applies. It is the standard that we live for the sake of others and not insist that others live for us. (71:125, April 29, 1974)

What is the path for us to live a true life? As we go on the path, the main thing we should keep in mind is to live for the sake of others. Confucius, Jesus, Muhammad and Buddha all affirm this truth. Living for the sake of others is the universal principle that defines the way we should live our lives—the one law of the true way of life. (133:18, July 1, 1984)

What should you do to others if you want them to serve you? [Serve them.] Should you serve them first, or let them serve you first? [I'll serve others after they serve me.] That won't do. Isn't there a saying that if you want others to serve you, you should first serve them? [Yes.] The basic rule is that you should be the first to serve. What about me? Do I, Father Moon, seek to serve you, or do I seek to have you serve me? I never have the slightest thought of wanting you to serve me. It is not good to be indebted to others. (50:339, November 8, 1971)

What is a life of true love? In a nutshell, it is living for the sake of others. It is living for the sake of another before you wish that the other would do something for you. In living for others, you give and forget that you ever gave. You do not give in hopes of receiving something in return. You give and give to the point where you have no regrets for not having given more. Even as you give, you bow your head in humility. Thus, Jesus said, "Greater love has no man than this, that a man lay down his life for his friends." (January 27, 2004)

According to the universal law, a subject partner should care for its object partner as parents care for their children or teachers for their students. However, people in the fallen world instead try to use others in self-centered ways. That is why they perish. Through their good example, religious people should educate others in Heaven's principle that we should place the happiness of others before our own happiness. (271:72, August 21, 1995)

The Ten Commandments

THE TEN COMMANDMENTS are known the world over as the basis of Jewish and Christian ethical values. Yet similar lists of ethical principles are found in most religions. The Qur'an contains more than one list of ethical precepts that has been termed the Islamic Decalogue. Jesus in the Sermon on the Mount commented that these commandments are not merely laws to be obeyed, but should be lived from the heart.

In Buddhism, Hinduism and Jainism there are lists of "ten charges" or "ten precepts" for monks and laypeople, and these are further condensed into lists of five universal dharmas called *samanya dharma*. Another comparable list is the Buddhist Eightfold Path. As befitting their Eastern perspective, most include inward elements, e.g., self-control and generating a heart of compassion. Confucianism has its own list of five—the Five Relations—with a distinctive emphasis on relationships rather than laws.

Father Moon himself has promulgated three commandments of the Kingdom of Heaven: Keep purity, do not violate the rights of others and do not steal. They can be compared to the Commandments specifically against adultery, murder and theft, but the second of these goes deeper into matters of the heart, reflecting the Confucian emphasis on proper relationships as well as Jesus' teachings on the interior aspects of the Ten Commandments.

I am the LORD your God, who brought you out of the land of Egypt, out of the house of bondage.

You shall have no other gods before me.

You shall not make for yourself a graven image, or any likeness of anything that is in heaven above, or that is in the earth beneath, or that is in the water under the earth; you shall not bow down to them or serve them; for I the LORD your God am a jealous God, visiting the iniquity of the fathers upon the children to the third and fourth generation of those who hate me, but showing steadfast love to thousands of those who love me and keep my commandments.

You shall not take the name of the LORD your God in vain: for the LORD will not hold him guiltless who takes his name in vain.

Remember the sabbath day, to keep it holy. Six days you shall labor, and do all your work; but the seventh day is a sabbath to the LORD your God; in it you shall not do any work, you, or your son, or your daughter, your manservant, or your maidservant, or your cattle, or the sojourner who is within your gates; for in six days the LORD made heaven and earth, the sea, and all that is in them, and rested on the seventh day; therefore the LORD blessed the sabbath day and hallowed it.

Honor your father and your mother, that your days may be long in the land which the LORD your God gives you.

You shall not kill.

You shall not commit adultery.

You shall not steal.

You shall not bear false witness against your neighbor.

You shall not covet your neighbor's house; you shall not covet your neighbor's wife, or his manservant, or his maidservant, or his ox, or his ass, or anything that is your neighbor's.[7]

Exodus 20.1-17

Say, Come, I will recite what God has made a sacred duty for you:

Ascribe nothing as equal with Him;

Be good to your parents;

Kill not your children on a plea of want—we provide sustenance for you and for them;

Approach not lewd behavior whether open or in secret,

Take not life, which God has made sacred, except by way of justice and law. Thus does He command you, that you may learn wisdom.

And approach not the property of the orphan, except to improve it, until he attains the age of maturity.

Give full measure and weight, in justice—No burden do we place on any soul but that which it can bear.

And if you give your word, do it justice, even if a near relative is concerned; and fulfill your obligations before God. Thus does He command you, that you may remember.

Verily, this is my straight Path: follow it, and do not follow other paths which will separate you from His Path. Thus does He command you, that you may be righteous.

Qur'an 6.151-53

Seven precepts were commanded to the children of Noah: social laws [civil justice]; to refrain from blasphemy; idolatry; adultery; bloodshed; robbery; and eating flesh cut from a living animal.[8]

Talmud, Sanhedrin 56a (Judaism)

You have heard that it was said to the men of old, "You shall not kill; and whoever kills shall be liable to judgment." But I say to you that every one who is angry with his brother shall be liable to judgment; whoever insults his brother shall be liable to the council, and whoever says, "You fool!" shall be liable to the hell of fire...

You have heard that it was said, "You shall not commit adultery." But I say to you that every one who looks at a woman lustfully has already committed adultery with her in his heart.

Matthew 5.21-22, 27-28

Forgiveness, humility, straightforwardness, purity, truthfulness, self-restraint, austerity, renunciation, non-attachment and chastity [with one's spouse] are the ten duties.

Tatthvarthasutra 9.6 (Jainism)

Not killing, no longer stealing, forsaking the wives of others, refraining completely from false, divisive, harsh and senseless speech, forsaking covetousness, harmful intent and the views of Nihilists—these are the ten white paths of action, their opposites are black.

Nagarjuna, Precious Garland 8-9 (Buddhism)

Nonviolence, truthfulness, not stealing, purity, control of the senses—this, in brief, says Manu, is the Dharma for all the four castes.[9]

Laws of Manu 10.63 (Hinduism)

The Noble Truth of the Path leading to the cessation of suffering is this Noble Eightfold Path, namely: right view, right aspiration, right speech, right action, right livelihood, right effort, right mindfulness, right concentration.

What is right view? Knowledge of suffering, knowledge of the arising of suffering, knowledge of the cessation of suffering, knowledge of the path leading to the cessation of suffering—this is called right view.

What is right aspiration? Aspiration for renunciation, aspiration for non-malevolence, aspiration for harmlessness—this is called right aspiration.

What is right speech? Refraining from lying speech, refraining from slanderous speech, refraining from harsh speech, refraining from gossip—this is called right speech.

What is right action? Refraining from violence against creatures, refraining from taking what has not been given, refraining from going wrongly among the sense-pleasures, this is called right action.

What is right livelihood? A disciple of the Noble Ones, getting rid of a wrong mode of livelihood, makes his living by a right mode of livelihood. This is called right livelihood.

What is right effort? A monk generates desire, effort, stirs up energy, exerts his mind and strives for the non-arising of evil unskilled states that have not arisen... for the getting rid of evil unskilled states that have arisen... for the arising of skilled states that have not arisen... for the maintenance and completion of skilled states that have arisen. This is called right effort.

What is right mindfulness? A monk fares along contemplating the body in the body... the feelings in the feelings... the mind in the mind... the mental states in the mental states... ardent, clearly conscious of them, mindful of them so as to control the covetousness and dejection in the world. This is called right mindfulness.

And what is right concentration? A monk, aloof from the pleasures of the senses, aloof from unskilled states of mind, enters on and abides in the first meditation which is accompanied by initial thought and discursive thought, is born of aloofness, is rapturous and joyful. By allaying initial thought and discursive thought, with the mind subjectively tranquilized and fixed on one point, he enters on and abides in the second meditation which is devoid of initial thought and discursive thought, is born of concentration, and is rapturous and joyful. By the fading out of rapture... he enters on and abides in the third meditation... the fourth meditation. This is called right concentration.

Majjhima Nikaya 3.251-52:
The Eight-Fold Path (Buddhism)

There are five universal ways in human relations... those governing the relationship between ruler and minister, between father and son, between husband and wife, between elder and younger brothers, and those in the intercourse between friends. These five are the universal ways in the world.

Doctrine of the Mean 20.79 (Confucianism)

Teachings of Sun Myung Moon

Heavenly law leads humanity to pursue goodness by setting up divine commandments and moral teachings. Without a doubt, Heaven reveals them for our education... Heaven has prompted saints and sages to propound moral teachings for pitiful humanity immersed in fallen life; thus [Confucius taught] the Three Bonds and the Five Moral Disciplines[10] in human relations, and Moses introduced the Ten Commandments. Numerous people on the spiritual path toiled to establish these ways of life. (7:16-23, July 5, 1959)

From now on, we have to recognize and abide by three immutable laws:

The first law: Do not defile the blood lineage, even at the point of death. The blessed blood lineage that has been bequeathed through God's love and life must not be contaminated by actions immersed in the habitual patterns of the fallen world. Can you abide by this rule? All couples, even if your spouse is deceased, must pledge today that you will not defile your lineage.

The second law: Do not infringe upon human rights. Whether female or male, black or white, everyone is equal. One must not discriminate or violate human rights, [for example] by dismissing a person from his post out of a wrong motivation... The person that practices true love, honoring human rights in the correct way, living for the sake of others, is in the mainstream. The creation of heaven and earth began from that point. Whoever commits an act that dilutes or squanders this main current of thought is not to be tolerated. Violation of this is the second of all sins.

The third law: Refrain from stealing money or misusing public funds for selfish purposes. [For example,] if you are entrusted with a public mission but slack off and leave your post, then your stay in an expensive hotel is a violation of this law. It is destroying the public environment. It is something as fearful as misappropriating national assets. People who live this way can never be successful no matter how hard they try. Even if they pray hard, their prayers will not reach God.

Seventy percent of the people in jail are there because they violated these commandments. If you are imprisoned, you will see it is true. Human rights infringements and lineage violations are problems that concern man and woman. Then come the money problems.

What's the first law? Keep your purity! Second? Don't abuse human rights! Third? Don't misuse public money! On this historic day, I declare that keeping these laws is absolutely necessary to maintain the sovereign power and kingship of heaven, and to stand before it as a people, and as parents, wives, children, and brothers and sisters.

Therefore, you cannot neglect your older brother. You cannot neglect your younger brother merely because he is handicapped. In the secular world people may not care, but we cannot neglect in-laws or relatives. If you who graduated from a university neglect those who only completed high school, it is a sin. These are violations of human rights.

You should live a good life. Can you live a good life by yourself? No, you should live with others. Within an environment governed by God's official laws, with whom should you live to be living a good life? The answer is simple. You should have good relationships between parents and children, between husband and wife, and among siblings...

When you are exemplary to one another, it can be called a good life. If you are not a good example, you are not living a good life. Live a good life by being exemplary in front of your parents, your spouse and your children.

Even if you are accused as a traitor and executed in public view, if you keep these commandments absolutely, your family will belong to the heavenly royal family that possesses eternal freedom, unity and liberation.

I want you to remember this clearly. Keep it as a motto, the motto of the third millennium: Pure lineage, equality of human rights, and guarding public assets—do not be a thief. What is next? Be an example! Be an exemplary parent, exemplary spouse, exemplary child and exemplary sibling. If you form such a family, people in your neighborhood will say, "We should follow that person. I want to live with him." That person is surely a citizen of Kingdom of Heaven, and Heaven will remember that family forever.

I explained to you on this historic day, the day of the Coronation Ceremony of God's Kingship, the three most important things that humankind must uphold and by which you can be truly liberated in your family and in your nation. I hope you can remember these contents and keep them as the goals of your life. (January 13, 2001)

Couples must never fall. If they do, it is a serious problem. I cannot emphasize this enough. Next, you should love human beings. Third, you should be careful not to misuse public funds. Matters of heart, relationships with human beings, and with material are very important. When the Heavenly Constitution is installed, [these will be its] first provisions. (169:217, October 31, 1987)

Beyond the Law

LAWS DEFINE THE PATH TO GOD, yet the ideal of divine life in many religions is to live beyond all boundaries. Therefore, as much as the law is a teaching that liberates, it can also be a fetter. Paul, for example, contrasts the Mosaic Law, which educates but confines, with the liberating grace available through Jesus Christ. Fulfilling the obligations of the law cannot save, because they do not touch the deepest promptings of the mind, which are still engulfed in the endless conflict between good and evil. Laws, therefore, are at best of provisional value, a concession to sin. Moreover, in situations where earthly laws are flawed or abused, the conscience guides us to follow a higher law.

Beyond the law lies a higher relationship with the Absolute, where a person is free to do what he or she likes, confident that the promptings of the conscience are always in agreement with what God requires.

However, life in the spirit should not be misconstrued as a license to sin. Even in a state of complete freedom, there are still heavenly standards and principles. All the same, a truly enlightened person is one with those principles and hence does not feel constrained by them.

I will put my law within them, and I will write it upon their hearts; and I will be their God, and they shall be my people. And no longer shall each man teach his neighbor and each his brother, saying, "Know the LORD," for they shall all know me, from the least of them to the greatest.

Jeremiah 31.33-34

One who is rich in the enlightenment will not indulge in any sinful action, since his conscience is guided by the intellect fully illumined with Truth.

Acarangasutra 1.174 (Jainism)

No one born of God commits sin; for God's nature abides in him, and he cannot sin because he is born of God.

1 John 3.9

Now we know that whatever the law says it speaks to those who are under the law, so that every mouth may be stopped, and the whole world may be held accountable to God. For no human being will be justified in his sight by works of the law, since through the law comes knowledge of sin. But now the righteousness of God has been manifested apart from law, although the law and the prophets bear witness to it, the righteousness of God through Jesus Christ for all who believe...

While we were living in the flesh, our sinful passions, aroused by the law, were at work in our members to bear fruit for death. But now we are discharged from the law, dead to that which held us captive, so that we serve not under the old written code but in the new life of the Spirit.

Romans 3.19-22, 7.5-6

The man of superior virtue is not conscious of his virtue,
and in this way he really possesses virtue.
The man of inferior virtue never loses sight of his virtue,
and in this way he loses his virtue...

Therefore, only when Tao is lost does the doctrine of virtue arise.
When virtue is lost, only then does the doctrine of humanity arise.
When humanity is lost, only then does the doctrine of righteousness arise.
When righteousness is lost, only then arise rules of propriety.
Now, propriety is a superficial expression of loyalty and faithfulness, and the beginning of disorder.

Tao Te Ching 38 (Taoism)

People under delusion accumulate tainted merits but do not tread the Path.
They are under the impression that to accumulate merits and to tread the Path are one and the same thing.
Though their merits for alms-giving and offerings are infinite,
They do not realize that the ultimate source of sin lies in the three poisons within their own mind.

Sutra of Hui Neng 6 (Buddhism)

Finite and transient are the fruits of sacrificial rites. The deluded, who regard them as the highest good, remain subject to birth and death... Considering religion to be observance of rituals and performance of acts of charity, the deluded remain ignorant of the highest good. Having enjoyed in heaven the reward of their good works, they enter again into the world of mortals. But wise, self-controlled, and tranquil souls, who are contented in spirit, and who practice austerity and meditation in solitude and silence, are freed from all impurity, and attain by the path of liberation to the immortal, the truly existing, the changeless Self.

Mundaka Upanishad 1.2.7-11 (Hinduism)

Subhuti, if you should conceive the idea that anyone in whom dawns the Consummation of Incomparable Enlightenment declares that all manifest standards are ended and extinguished, do not countenance such thoughts.

Diamond Sutra 27 *(Buddhism)*

"All things are lawful for me," but not all things are helpful. "All things are lawful for me," but I will not be enslaved by anything... The body is not meant for immorality, but for the Lord, and the Lord for the body.

1 Corinthians 6.12-14

Teachings of Sun Myung Moon

True love transcends the law. True love has such a privilege. Since we know this, we should practice it. If we do, then we will enjoy the unlimited freedom of the Kingdom of Heaven. (116:249, January 1, 1982)

When the mind and body become one, the universe is like putty in our hands. Since we become a microcosm of the universe, we can understand everything. We will not need anyone to teach us. No one will need to teach us how to live, or lay out rules of ethics and morality. Do the sparrows and the animals need lessons in morality? Animals know how to protect themselves and physiologically group themselves in their own species. Why are human beings, the lords of creation, so ignorant in this regard? It is because of the Human Fall. Because of the Fall, struggle and conflict came into existence. (162:223, April 12, 1987)

Moral laws spring from the mind. Those who live with a good mindset and do not suffer from a guilty conscience have no fear in anything. Even if they are dragged before the cruelest tyrant, they can stand tall before him. (19:288, March 10, 1968)

Goodness is something the universe protects and raises. It holds freedom and peace within it, accompanied by life and authority. There is nothing in heaven and earth that can subjugate goodness. When we are good, we are not afraid of anyone, even the president of a nation. No matter what laws are applied against us, we are not influenced. That is why secular laws cannot reach the standard of the conscience. Therefore, worldly laws cannot intrude upon the authority of goodness. (16:134, January 2, 1966)

Can you find anywhere in the world a constitution or law code that would condemn someone who sacrifices himself in service for others? Would a court of law convict him, declaring him a criminal? [No.] If such a law existed, it would be denounced as a bad law. Rather, the nation's president would recognize and honor him. (105:93, September 30, 1979)

As Unification Church members, you may say, "I do not have any boundaries; I do not have to guard myself from anything; I am really free." But this is not so. In our way of life there are certain boundaries we are not allowed to cross—for example, the line of the Fall. If we cross that line, inevitably our internal nature and status is changed and we are transferred to a different owner [from God to Satan]. (90:9, December 5, 1976)

God does everything according to a rule. In the natural sciences, people solve the mysteries of the universe using the formulas of mathematics. Since that is so, wouldn't there be formulas in the world of love? Were there no formulas, there would be no way to govern the people streaming into the Kingdom from every corner of the world. (170:256, November 22, 1987)

Duality

DUALITY IS A CONSISTENT THEME throughout the cosmos. All existing beings display duality or polarity: male and female, light and dark, heaven and earth, mind and body, subject and object, the self and the whole, being and non-being. The dynamic interactions between these poles are a source of generative and creative power. This is seen in the regular cycles of nature, the alternation of day and night, and the changing seasons. Duality is portrayed mythically by the cosmic union of god and goddess, and recognized by science in the electromagnetic interactions that construct atoms and molecules. Some religions, notably Confucianism and Taoism, regard the polarity of yang (masculine) and yin (feminine) as a governing principle of nature, one that can instruct human beings on the proper way of life.

Father Moon devotes considerable attention to duality, which he develops into a systematic relational ontology. He observes the interactions in nature and sees in them the basis for the principle of altruism; as giving precedes receiving in all successful relationships. Even the forces of repulsion in nature have the effect of reducing threesomes to twosomes, thus protecting the realm of creative and loving relationships that duality provides. On that basis, he also critiques the Marxist dialectic for teaching a flawed conception of reality, rooted in conflict.

1. The Duality of Masculine and Feminine

And all things We have created by pairs, that you may receive instruction.
Qur'an 51.49

All things are twofold, one opposite the other, and He has made nothing incomplete.
One confirms the good things of the other, and who can have enough of beholding His glory?
Ecclesiasticus 42.24-25 (Christianity)

The Originator of the heavens and the earth; He has appointed for you of yourselves spouses, and pairs also of the cattle, by means of which He multiplies you.
Qur'an 42.11

The Great Primal Beginning generates the two primary forces [yang and yin]. The two primary forces generate the four images. The four images generate the eight trigrams. The eight trigrams determine good fortune and misfortune. Good fortune and misfortune create the great field of action.
I Ching, Great Commentary 1.11.5-6 (Confucianism)

The Creator, out of desire to procreate, devoted Himself to concentrated ardor (tapas). Whilst thus devoted to concentrated ardor, He produced a couple, Matter and Life (prana), saying to Himself, "these two will produce all manner of creatures for me." Now Life is the Sun; Matter is the Moon.
Prasna Upanishad 1.4-5 (Hinduism)

By the transformation of Yang and its union with Yin, the five agents arise: water, fire, wood, metal and earth. When these five forces are distributed in harmonious order, the four seasons run their course. The five agents constitute the system of Yin and Yang, and Yin and Yang constitute one Great Ultimate.
Chou Tun-i, Explanation of the Diagram of the Great Ultimate (Confucianism)

Mujahid said, "God has created all things in pairs: He created man and woman, heaven and earth, sun and moon, night and day, light and dark, mankind and jinn, good and evil, morning and evening, also all different kinds of foods and winds and sounds. God has made all these as signs of His greatness."

Al-Qurtubi, Al-Thuriat Surat 17 *(Islam)*

So God created man in his own image, in the image of God he created him; male and female he created them.

Genesis 1.27

"Male and female He created them." From this we learn that every figure that does not comprise male and female elements is not a true and proper figure... Observe this: God does not place His abode in any place where male and female are not found together, nor are blessings found save in such a place.

Zohar 1.55b *(Judaism)*

All life, all pulsation in creation throbs with the mighty declaration of the truth of Shiva-Shakti, the eternal He and the eternal She at play in manifestation.[11]

Kularnava Tantra 3 *(Hinduism)*

When the upper world was filled and became pregnant, it brought forth two children together, a male and a female, these being heaven and earth after the supernal pattern. The earth is fed from the waters of heaven which are poured into it. These upper waters, however, are male, whereas the lower are female, and the lower are fed from the male and the lower waters call to the upper, like a female that receives the male, and pour out water to meet the water of the male to produce seed.

Zohar 1.29b *(Judaism)*

The Innate is twofold, for Wisdom is the woman and Means is the man. Thereafter these both become twofold, distinguished as relative and absolute. In man there is this twofold nature: the thought of enlightenment [relative] and the bliss arising from it [absolute]; in woman too it is the same, the thought of enlightenment and the bliss arising from it.

Hevajra Tantra 8.26-29 *(Buddhism)*

Teachings of Sun Myung Moon

The entire world of being exists in a pair system. Human beings exist as men and women, and animals as male and female. Insects also exist as male and female. So do butterflies, birds, ants, and even minerals. The 107 elements do not come together randomly; when one element finds another that can be its reciprocal partner, nothing can stop them from uniting. But not even God can bring together two positives that repel each other. If there is a reciprocal quality between two things, they will come together automatically, and nothing can stop them. (203:353, June 28, 1990)

When we study the universe, we see that all beings exist by forming reciprocal relationships between masculine (yang) and feminine (yin). This holds in all cases. On the level of minerals, the bonding of positive and negative ions forms molecules. In plants, existence and propagation occur through the cooperation of pistil and stamen.

This duality is even more pronounced in animals. Birds, mammals, and all other types of animals exist as male and female. Finally, we human beings, who are God's highest creation, are differentiated as men and women. The first man, Adam, and the first woman, Eve, were the first ancestors of humankind.

For what purpose did God create the universe with duality? The Creator separated all things into masculine and feminine so that the two could join by giving and receiving love. All species increase their numbers and carry on life through acts of love. (201:204-05, April 9, 1990)

The universe emerged out of relationships— between up and down, right and left, and front and back. Therefore, from insects to animals and humans, heaven and earth exist in a pair system.

Even the five sensory organs exist in a pair system. So do the hands, feet, mind and body (however our mind and body are not united as one, and this is a most critical problem). Our eyes blink together. Our nostrils breathe together. Our lips move together when we speak. Sound resonates in both ears when we hear. We use both hands to make things. We cannot walk with one foot alone but require two feet. Everything in the universe needs a partner in order to function and act. Nothing can function alone. Hence, a being by itself cannot resemble God. (391:174, August 21, 2002)

When God created, He worked centering on human beings. With human beings as His model, He expanded the creation in all directions. Hence, He created all creatures—minerals, plants, and animals—in pairs. The act of creation proceeded by weaving together in pairs the vertical paths and the horizontal paths. Some moved straight, some in a zigzag, others engaged in all manner of actions, but all were arranged in a pair system to create the natural world. It is teaching material for people to learn about ideal love. (173:211)

Inside the seed of a plant are two parts in a reciprocal relationship. The two are completely one inside a single shell. They engage in give and take action through the embryo in order to propagate life. In an egg, too, there is an embryo between yolk and white, and they form one body within the single shell. The same is true for the human fetus.

Whether human beings or plants, life forms through a harmonious union of subject and object partners by means of give-and-take action. These multiply in a way that resembles their causal being, thus connecting to the foundation of their existence. Ultimately we resemble the First Cause. Therefore, the First Cause must be the basic model, with subject and object partners forming a perfect harmonious union, and having the status of Subject Partner in relation to all beings. (89:226, November 27, 1976)

Even though a person may have many possessions, many children and great power, there is no joy if he or she lives alone. Likewise, although God is the Subject and the Absolute Being, without a partner He also is lonely.

Why did God create heaven and earth? God is the Absolute Subject, but He cannot experience joy as long as He remains alone. Joy cannot be experienced alone; it arises only in the context of a relationship. Peace, too, and happiness, only exist in the context of relationships. For this reason, God cannot function as God as long as He is alone. (58:210, June 11, 1972)

Throughout the universe, love is something that no being can possess by itself. Once a being meets its counterpart, however, and they relate with love, they can obtain all the things that love provides. For example, even though a couple may love children, until they have children of their own, they cannot experience parental love. They cannot become the owners of the kind of love that parents have for their children. From this perspective, we can understand why God created human beings and the universe: He created them as His object partners in order to realize true love.

All types of love—including the love of children, love of siblings, love of husband and wife, and love of parents—come about through the unity of subject and object partners. Once subject and object partners become one, nothing can separate them. If they could be divided, we could not say that true love is indestructible. Among married couples, there should not be even the thought of divorce. (*True Family and World Peace*, March 14, 1999)

God created everything in complementary pairs so that they could receive God's true love. God wanted them to receive this one love as a partnership. If a man and a woman perfect God's love, embody God's love, and share that love with each other from the same ground of complementarity as God, then they will definitely become an ideal couple. (26:155-56, October 25, 1969)

For the sake of love, God created human beings as His partners. God created all things in the universe in pairs so that God's love may be eternal, man's love may be eternal, woman's love may be eternal, and children's love may be eternal. They are all God's family; hence they should be eternal. (201:193, April 1, 1990)

2. The Duality of Spirit and Matter

Know that *prakriti* (nature, energy) and *Purusha* (spirit) are both without beginning, and that from prakriti come the *gunas* (qualities of the phenomenal world) and all that changes. Prakriti is the agent, cause, and effect of every action, but it is Purusha that seems to experience pleasure and pain. Purusha, resting in prakriti, witnesses the play of the gunas born of prakriti. But attachment to the gunas leads a person to be born for good or evil. Within the body the supreme Purusha is called the witness, approver, supporter, enjoyer, the supreme Lord, the highest Self... Whatever exists, Arjuna, animate or inanimate, is born through the union of the field and its Knower.[12]

        Bhagavad-Gita 13.19-22, 26 *(Hinduism)*

By a marvelous mating, He brings a spiritual nature into union with one that is material and makes the soul and body active and passive principles, respectively, of a single human whole. This operation of God, so marvelous and mysterious, He performs not only in the case of man, who is a rational animal and the highest and noblest of all animals on earth, but also in the case of the tiniest insects. And no one can reflect on this marvel without a sense of astonishment and some expression of admiration for the Creator.

        Saint Augustine, City of God 22.24 (Christianity)

Our body is just a shell. Inside and outside, there is nothing but the energy of heaven and earth, and yin and yang.

        Chu Hsi *(Confucianism)*

Teachings of Sun Myung Moon

The human body consists of 40 trillion cells. They are connected by the body's circulatory system that is constantly in motion, with blood circulating through arteries and veins. At the same time, electrical energy circulates up and down through the nervous system. In sum, the body contains dual systems of circulation: one visible, the other invisible. (262:126, July 23, 1994)

There is another pair of dual characteristics in reciprocal relationship, which are even more fundamental to existence than the dual characteristics of yang and yin. Every entity possesses both an outer form and an inner quality. The visible outer form resembles the invisible inner quality. The inner quality, though invisible, possesses a certain structure that manifests visibly in the particular outer form…

Let us take human beings as an example. A human being is composed of an outer form, the body, and an inner quality, the mind. The body is a visible reflection of the invisible mind. Because the mind possesses a certain structure, the body that reflects it also takes on a particular appearance. This is the idea behind a person's character and destiny being perceived through examining his outward appearance by such methods as physiognomy or palm reading. Here, mind is the internal nature (*sungsang*) and body is the external form (*hyungsang*). Mind and body are two correlative aspects of a human being; hence, the body may be understood as a second mind. Together, they constitute the dual characteristics of a human being. Similarly, all beings exist through the reciprocal relationships between their dual characteristics of internal nature and external form…

The body resembles the mind and moves according to its commands in such a way as to sustain life and pursue the mind's purposes. Mind and body thus have a mutual relationship of internal and external, cause and result, subject partner and object partner, vertical and horizontal.

Similarly, all created beings, regardless of their level of complexity, possess an intangible internal nature, which corresponds to the human mind, and a tangible external form, which corresponds to the human body. Within each being, the internal nature, which is causal and subject, commands the external form. This relationship allows the individual being to exist and function purposefully as a creation of God. (*Exposition of the Divine Principle*, Creation 1.1)

This created world in which we live has two axes: a visible axis and an invisible axis. They form a dual structure. The object partner revolves around its subject partner, but the subject partner also revolves. An example is the body and mind of a human being engaging in give-and-take action. All beings exist according to this principle.

Fallen humans in the world must correct their axis in order to be restored. The correct human structure has the mind at the center of the body and the spirit dwelling in the center of the mind. The body revolves around the mind and moves in accordance with the mind's commands. If his mind says, "Go to the east," his body heads east, and if his mind says, "Go to the west," his body heads west. His body cannot make a move by itself. (136:14, December 20, 1985)

3. Duality Operates by Giving and Receiving

Not a handful of rain descends from above without the earth sending up two handfuls of moisture to meet it.
      Genesis Rabbah 13.13 *(Judaism)*

Love works in a circle, for the beloved moves the lover by stamping a likeness, and the lover then goes out to hold the beloved in reality.

Who first was the beginning now becomes the end of motion.
      Thomas Aquinas, Summa Theologica[13] *(Christianity)*

Verily in the creation of heaven and earth and the alternation of night and the day are signs for people of understanding.
      Qur'an 3.190

Observe how all God's creations borrow from each other: day borrows from night and night from day, but they do not go to law one with another as mortals do... The moon borrows from the stars and the stars from the moon... the sky borrows from the earth and the earth from the sky... All God's creatures borrow from the other, yet make peace with one another without lawsuits; but if man borrows from his friend, he seeks to swallow him up with usury and robbery.

Exodus Rabbah 31.15 (Judaism)

When the sun goes, the moon comes; when the moon goes, the sun comes. Sun and moon alternate; thus light comes into existence. When cold goes, heat comes; when heat goes, cold comes. Cold and heat alternate, and thus the year completes itself. The past contracts. The future expands. Contraction and expansion act upon each other; hereby arises that which furthers.

The measuring worm draws itself together when it wants to stretch out. Dragons and snakes hibernate in order to preserve life. Thus the penetration of germinal thought into the mind promotes the workings of the mind. When this working furthers and brings peace to life, it elevates a man's nature.[14]

I Ching, Great Commentary 2.5.2-3 (Confucianism)

Difficult and easy complete one another.
Long and short test one another;
High and low determine one another.
Pitch and mode give harmony to one another,
Front and back give sequence to one another.

Tao Te Ching 2 (Taoism)

For everything there is a season, and a time for every matter under heaven:
a time to be born, and a time to die;
a time to plant, and a time to pluck up what is planted;
a time to kill, and a time to heal;
a time to break down, and a time to build up;
a time to weep, and a time to laugh;
a time to mourn, and a time to dance;
a time to cast away stones, and a time to gather stones together;
a time to embrace, and a time to refrain from embracing;
a time to seek, and a time to lose;
a time to keep, and a time to cast away;
a time to rend, and a time to sew;
a time to keep silence, and a time to speak;
a time to love, and a time to hate;
a time for war, and a time for peace.

Ecclesiastes 3.1-8

Heaven and earth come together, and all things take shape and find form. Male and female mix their seed, and all creatures take shape and are born." In the Changes it is said, "When three people journey together, their number decreases by one. When one man journeys alone, he finds a companion.

I Ching, Great Commentary 2.4.13 (Confucianism)

Heaven is high, the earth is low; thus the Creative and the Receptive are determined. In correspondence with this difference between low and high, inferior and superior places are established.

Movement and rest have their definite laws; according to these, firm and yielding lines [of the hexagrams] are differentiated.[15]

Events follow definite trends, each according to its nature. Things are distinguished from one another in definite classes. In this way good fortune and misfortune come about. In the heavens phenomena take form; on earth shapes take form. In this way change and transformation become manifest.

Therefore the eight trigrams succeed one another by turns, as the firm and the yielding displace each other.

Things are aroused by thunder and lightning; they are fertilized by wind and rain. Sun and moon follow their courses and it is now hot, now cold.

The way of the Creative brings about the male; the way of the Receptive brings about the female.

> The Creative knows the great beginnings;
> the Receptive completes the finished things.
>
> I Ching, Great Commentary 1.1.1-5 *(Confucianism)*

> Thirty spokes share one hub to make a wheel.
> Through its not-being (*wu*),
> There being (*yu*) the use of the carriage.
>
> Mold clay into a vessel.
> Through its not-being,
> There being the use of the vessel.
>
> Cut out doors and windows to make a house.
> Through its not-being
> There being the use of the house.
>
> Therefore in the being of a thing,
> There lies the benefit;
> In the not-being of a thing,
> There lies its use.[16]
>
> Tao Te Ching 11 *(Taoism)*

Teachings of Sun Myung Moon

What is the heavenly law of the universe? What is the law of existence? It is giving and receiving. (157:266, April 10, 1967)

For an action to be structured, there must be a subject-object relationship. For the action to continue, the subject and object partners must share a common purpose that is beneficial to both. Under conditions that are less than this, the action will not happen. This is an ironclad rule and a law of the universe's existence. (56:134-35, May 14, 1972)

Personally, would you rather receive or give? This is a serious question. In the Divine Principle's concept of give-and-take action, does "give" come first, or "take?" Giving comes first. Do parents give for the sake of their children, or children for their parents? Parents give first. Then it is logical that the act of giving began with the Origin of all existence, and through the links of the chain of existence it has been passed down to us. (239:59, November 23, 1992)[17]

Everything is in motion. How does the motion start, by giving or taking? You all want to receive, don't you? You desire to pull in some money. To see whether this is right or wrong, we have to analyze the principle of the universe. If it is the Principle, not even God can deny it. When God created, did He begin with a pulling force that sought to receive, or a force that sought to give? It was a giving force. He invested energy.

Ladies, when you knead dough, what happens? You press it down again and again, in order that it may expand. (239:223, November 25, 1992)

What happens when there is no difference between what is given and what is received? The action goes on and on… But if there are impurities, then complete give and take is impossible, and the action cannot last long. The greater the difference between give and take, the sooner the action will break apart. (157:266-67, April 10, 1967)

All things originate from one Source, divide into many entities, and then finally rejoin into one great whole. This is how things make progress. From one they divide into many, and then come together as one. From there they divide again and then become a larger being. This means that all will enter a world of oneness that is greater than before. (26:189, October 25, 1969)

There is force of attraction and force of repulsion in this universe. Things are attracted to things that relate with them and repel those things that contravene them. God's power of creation[18] acts to protect the universe from anything that tries to harm it. A reciprocal realm can only form in keeping with this basic logic. When some other being approaches that might harm the reciprocal realm, it is repelled. The force of repulsion is not a bad thing; it is a secondary protective force… to facilitate and perfect God's power of creation. If there were not a reaction to every action, it would be impossible even to walk. (227:37, February 10, 1992)

When a wife dies, or a husband dies, why does the surviving spouse feel sorrow? When a woman's husband dies, why does she make a big scene by crying "Wah!" at the top of her lungs? She doesn't just cry; she completely loses her mind. Why does this happen? She and her husband formed a reciprocal realm and, centering on love, entered into the universe's realm of eternal principle. But the death of the husband caused that reciprocal realm to break apart, and the wife feels a force pushing against her with such force that it makes her skin turn red. That force makes her feel sorrow and pain…

Unmarried girls will go around playing, and sometimes you see a group of girls hanging on to each other, embracing each other and such. The same is true with boys. Wrestling with each other, rolling around on the ground like calves, they make all sorts of noise in the village. But on the day one of those young men marries and takes a wife, will he want one of his handsome friends to come and stand next to him in front of his wife? Would any man want that? No, he will kick his friend away, saying, "Don't ever come here again! Get out of here! Now!"

It's not a bad thing for him to tell his friend to go. He is actually telling him, "You should do as I do, and stand in a position where you can welcome the universal principle." By kicking his friend away, he guides him to the path to perfection. (218:335, August 22, 1991)

Knowing this is the principle, the theory of evolution cannot be sustained. The supposed evolutionary link from amoebas to monkeys to human beings ignores the fact that each of the countless relationships between male and female had to pass through the gate of love and establish a realm of reciprocity.

Take sparrows, for example. During the winter, they know nothing about having relationships, so they play around and all become their own positives. But in the spring, when they start making nests and forming reciprocal realms, they become absolute. Both the male and the female of an established pair will repel a third sparrow that approaches. If a female approaches them, the male will repel it; if a male approaches, the female will repel it. Why is that? They repel the third sparrow because it threatens to break up their reciprocal realm and is an aggressor on the realm of the law of the universe. (218:338, August 22, 1991)

Hegel and especially Engels, philosophers who came up with the law of the dialectic, saw universal law as decreeing conflict and opposition. Unless we successfully resolve the question of the dialectic within the universe, we cannot find the true formula for the ideal world, nor can we establish peace and harmony with hierarchical order in organizations structured with up and down relationships. We must demonstrate the falsity of such principles as "survival of the fittest," "the strong eat the weak," and "power causes progress." Otherwise, people would think that mistreating others is not a sin. (132:142, May 31, 1984)

Some people say the universe is made of energy. It is true that all beings are formed of energy, but what is needed for that energy to exist?

No being is energy itself. There is always a reciprocal standard or common base. Before we acknowledge energy, we must acknowledge the common base. If we acknowledge the common base, we must acknowledge subject and object partners...

"Relative relationship" does not refer to a thesis-antithesis-synthesis relationship, where a standard called "thesis" and something called "antithesis" oppose each other and become unified as one. Instead, it refers to a relationship where the object partner responds to the subject partner. That is, it means that a subject and object partner respond to each other and engage in action centering on a common purpose. When they engage in perfect give-and-take action and achieve a reciprocal realm, energy comes into being, and only then is the center determined. Even if there is a great deal of action, if the action is going in opposite directions, it will eventually destroy the world. (15:53, February 7, 1965)

Interdependence

ALL BEINGS, GREAT AND SMALL, are linked in a web of interdependent relationships. Apart from the whole, no individual could exist. Therefore, to think of "myself" as a separate individual is a fundamental error of cognition. Einstein called it an "optical delusion of consciousness... a kind of prison for us, restricting us to our personal desires, and to affection for a few persons nearest to us." He said we should "free ourselves from this prison, by widening our circle of compassion to embrace all living creatures, and the whole of nature in all its beauty."

In reality, every being is immersed in a web of cause and effect—a chain of "concatenation" according to a Buddhist text—that stretches to the ends of the universe. This understanding is the basis of the Buddhist teaching of "no-self." Recognizing that all beings are "I" and "I" am all beings, it is the root of the Buddhist ethic of compassion. It is a remedy for the malady of individualism, which leads people to believe that the goal is "my" salvation. In fact, no human being can attain ultimate peace as long as other people are suffering.

We are members one of another.
Ephesians 4.25

This world of men, given over to the idea of "I am the agent," bound up with the idea "another is the agent," understand not truly this thing; they have not seen it as a thorn. For one who looks at this thorn with caution, the idea "I am the agent" exists not, the idea "another is the agent" exists not.
Udana 70 (Buddhism)

All things are devoid of self-nature [separate existence], have never been born, and in their original nature are [transparent] like the sky; things separated from concatenation belong to the discrimination of the ignorant. When this entire world is regarded as concatenation, as nothing else but concatenation, then the mind gains tranquility.[19]
Lankavatara Sutra 78 (Buddhism)

Why should I be unable
To regard the bodies of others as "I"?
It is not difficult to see
That my body is also that of others.

In the same way as the hands and so forth
Are regarded as limbs of the body,
Likewise why are embodied creatures
Not regarded as limbs of life?

Only through acquaintance has the thought of "I" arisen
Towards this impersonal body;
So in a similar way, why should it not arise
Towards other living beings?

When I work in this way for the sake of others,
I should not let conceit or [the feeling that I am] wonderful arise.
It is just like feeding myself—
I hope for nothing in return.

              Shantideva, Guide to the Bodhisattva's
                  Way of Life 8.112-16 *(Buddhism)*

It is because every one under heaven recognizes beauty as beauty that the idea of ugliness exists. And if every one recognized virtue as virtue, this would merely create fresh conceptions of wickedness.

For truly, Being and Not-being grow out of one another.

                        Tao Te Ching 2 *(Taoism)*

All humans are caught in an inescapable network of mutuality, tied in a single garment of destiny. Whatever affects one directly, affects all indirectly. I can never be what I ought to be until you are what you ought to be, and you can never be what you ought to be until I am what I ought to be.

                Martin Luther King, Jr. *(Christianity)*

Teachings of Sun Myung Moon

In the universe, everything is linked and related, from the minutest things to the largest. (16:119, January 2, 1966)

Every existence is linked to another through dual purposes. One purpose pertains to internal character and the other to external form. The purpose pertaining to internal character is for the whole, while the purpose pertaining to external form is for the individual. These relate to each other as cause and effect, internal and external, and subject and object. Therefore, there cannot be any purpose of the individual apart from the purpose of the whole, nor any purpose of the whole that does not include the purpose of the individual. All the creatures in the entire universe form a vast complex linked together by these dual purposes. (*Exposition of the Divine Principle,* Creation 1.3.1)

When all beings in the whole universe, with subject and object partners well adjusted to each other, are linked to one another in harmony for a common purpose, there is completion and perfection. The universe is a balanced whole composed of reciprocal relationships, large and small. Without reciprocal relationships, nothing can exist. Anything that ceases to relate becomes extinct. (391:174, August 21, 2002)

Heavenly fortune[20] rejects those who live for their own sake and embraces those who live for the sake of others. It is like a person who is nearly blind suddenly seeing with 20-20 vision; his eyes exclaim for joy: "Wow! We can see everything very clearly!" Through Heaven's power we are connected to the entire universe and can see all for eternity. This power penetrates everything infinitely; hence our scope of action expands infinitely… By living for the sake of others, we can make relationships with everything. (244:107, January 31, 1993)

In the human body, the eye looks very simple, but it is actually complex. Each cell that makes up the eye is complex as well. All the organs are complex, but in living together as a single organism, they do not conflict with each other. Instead, they function together interdependently. No part of the body can say that it likes only the hand and does not like the eye. Each organ has its lawful place, and each accommodates itself to the limitations of its position and rank, relating to the others front and back, left and right, and above and below. That is the only way it can function; there is no other way. (49:193, October 10, 1971)

Each human being is like a cell. They do not exist separately, each doing their own thing. Rather, they come together and form a whole, creating an axis. Then humankind can enter into a partnership with God, the Center of the whole. The force of love flowing in this partnership motivates them to pursue a common objective. Cause and effect correspond to each other and fulfill their purpose. When the cause and effect are thus united, God and the whole of humankind manifest their value and complete their one common purpose. (110:73, November 9, 1980)

The supreme element that we human beings pursue is love. Therefore, we should make it so the give and take of love proceeds smoothly. The universe should be linked by one axis, formed when each person centers on his or her subject partner. Then, just like an electrical circuit, everything can engage in good give and take action through the axis. It is similar to a tree whose parts engage in give and take action centering on the trunk. Through that axis, every cell, from the bottommost tip of the central root to the terminal bud at the very top, relate to each other continually. If that give and take action is good, the tree will grow; if not, the root will shrivel and the whole tree will decline. (165:177, May 20, 1987)

Cause and Effect

THE MAXIM THAT A PERSON REAPS what he has sown, belief in divine retribution, and the doctrine of karma, are diverse expressions of a common idea: that the world is governed by justice. Religions give various teachings regarding the specific manner in which justice is meted out, e.g. through one's fate in this life, by reincarnation, or in the afterlife. Yet all agree that one way or another, justice will be served. It is inherent in the nature of the universe, as designed by a benevolent Creator, that good deeds be rewarded and evil deeds punished. This is the principle of cause and effect.

The principle of cause and effect bears the same ambiguous relationship to Ultimate Reality as divine law generally. In the eastern religions the principle of justice is inherent in the fabric of the cosmos and is therefore subordinate to the ultimate goal of liberation. Karma and the wheel of samsara display the operation of cause and effect, yet these are part of the hellishness of human existence and have nothing to do with the ultimate goal of Nirvana and Enlightenment, where the cycle of rebirth is broken. On the other hand, the monotheistic religions portray God as the divine Judge who visits punishments upon the guilty to maintain justice. Nevertheless, it is not the Heavenly Father's purpose to act as a judge against His children; rather with love and truth He guides them on the path to salvation. Therefore, as Father Moon does, we can ascribe God's judgments to the operation of His creation, a cosmos that is designed to administer justice through the operation of cosmic law.

The passages in this chapter describe two aspects of cause and effect. First is the aspect of justice: people reap what they sow. Father Moon draws instances of this principle not only in the lives of individuals, but also from the history of nations and races, who collectively have committed sins that must bear requital. Even though this world seems to tolerate injustice and permit wrongs to go unpunished, scriptures assert that the ultimate individual recompense is in the afterlife, where he or she is destined either for heaven or hell. Here Father Moon's teachings give a deeper explanation for why sinners are destined for hell, not by the decree of any angelic judge but by the conditions they made for themselves during earthly life.

Second, there are passages on cause and effect as a universal principle that operates in the growth and completion of all beings. We learn that the effect is not separate from the cause; rather, they are closely tied together. The core Buddhist doctrine of Dependent Origination expresses the negative of this idea, as ignorance develops through a causal chain to the whole human condition of suffering (*dhukka*). A Taoist text puts it positively, that cause and effect form a circuit, the movement of Heaven. Father Moon teaches that God is immanent in the world, working everywhere as the cause and revealing Himself in human beings as the effect. Ultimately, God and humans, cause and effect, are to be united as the Alpha and the Omega—through love.

1. We Reap the Consequences of Our Actions

Do not be deceived; God is not mocked, for whatever a man sows, that he will also reap.
         Galatians 6.7

Whatever affliction may visit you is for what your own hands have earned.
         Qur'an 42.30

All who take the sword will perish by the sword.
         Matthew 26.52

Suffering is the offspring of violence—realize this and be ever vigilant.
         Acarangasutra 3.13 *(Jainism)*

Ashes fly back in the face of him who throws them.
     Yoruba Proverb (African Traditional Religions)

They sow the wind, and they will reap the whirlwind.
         Hosea 8.7

An ignorant man committing evil deeds does not realize the consequences.

The imprudent man is consumed by his own deeds, like one burnt by fire.
         Dhammapada 136 *(Buddhism)*

Unto God belongs the sequel of all things.
         Qur'an 31.22

God is not hornless;
He is horned:
He exacts punishment for every deed.
     Ovambo Proverb *(African Traditional Religions)*

Unrighteousness, practiced in this world, does not at once produce its fruit; but, like a cow, advancing slowly, it cuts off the roots of him who committed it.
         Laws of Manu 4.172 *(Hinduism)*

There are no special doors for calamity and happiness [in men's lot]; they come as men themselves call them. Their recompenses follow good and evil as the shadow follows the substance.
     Treatise on Response and Retribution 1 *(Taoism)*

Not in the sky, nor in mid-ocean, nor in a mountain cave, is found that place on earth where abiding one may escape from the consequences of one's evil deed.
         Dhammapada 127 *(Buddhism)*

The net of Heaven is cast wide. Though the mesh is not fine, yet nothing ever slips through.
         Tao Te Ching 73 *(Taoism)*

Beloved, never avenge yourselves, but leave it to the wrath of God; for it is written, "Vengeance is mine, I will repay, says the Lord."
         Romans 12.19

Let not their conduct grieve you, who run easily to disbelief, for lo! they injure God not at all. It is God's will to assign them no portion in the hereafter, and theirs will be an awful doom.

And let not those who disbelieve imagine that the rein We give them bodes good for their souls. We only give them rein that they may grow in sinfulness. And theirs will be a shameful doom.

Qur'an 3.176, 178

Everything is given on pledge, and a net is spread for all the living; the shop is open; and the dealer gives credit; and the ledger lies open; and the hand writes; and whosoever wishes to borrow may come and borrow; but the collectors regularly make their daily round, and exact payment from man whether he be content or not; and they have that whereon they can rely in their demand; and the judgment is a judgment of truth; and everything is prepared for the feast.

Mishnah, Avot 3.20 (Judaism)

Further, as Heaven and Earth are the greatest of things, it is natural, from the point of view of universal principles, that they have spiritual power. Having spiritual power it is proper that they reward good and punish evil. Nevertheless their expanse is great and their net is wide-meshed. There is not necessarily an immediate response as soon as this net is set in operation.

Pao-p'u Tzu[21] (Taoism)

Holy, then, did I recognize Thee, O Wise Lord.
I perceived Thee foremost at the birth of life,
When Thou didst endow acts and words with retribution:
Bad unto bad, good blessing unto holy,
Through Thy wisdom, at the final goal of life!

Avesta, Yasna 43.5 (Zoroastrianism)

According as one acts, according as one conducts himself, so does he become. The doer of good becomes good. The doer of evil becomes evil. One becomes virtuous by virtuous action, bad by bad action.

But people say, "A person is made [not of acts, but] of desires only." [I say,] as his desire, such is his resolve; as is his resolve, such the action he performs; what action he performs, that he procures for himself. On this point there is this verse,

> Where one's mind is attached—the inner self
> goes thereto with action, being attached to it alone.
> Obtaining the end of his action,
> whatever he does in this world,
> he comes again from that world
> to this world of action.[22]

So the mind that desires.

Brihadaranyaka Upanishad 4.4.5-6 (Hinduism)

Teachings of Sun Myung Moon

In order for life to be sustained centering on this body, all the different parts must engage in give and take action as subject and object partners. If everything engaged in this action does what it is supposed to do, then the physical body will function smoothly, and existence will continue. But what happens when this is blocked somewhere?

This universe protects anything that engages in give and take in accord with God's ideal. If an opposing element appears, something becomes lacking, or there is a blockage, there will be a failure within that realm of interaction. Hence, in order to protect the universe, there will be a reaction to expel it. This reaction is not a bad thing. It may be seen as something bad, but it truly functions to protect the larger realm.

For example, if your stomach hurts, it means there is a blockage in a circuit of give and take action between some subject and object partner. The blockage causes it to be pushed away to the same extent as it is blocked. A cosmic force to push it out acts on the stomach, and it hurts. All you need to do is open the place that is blocked, and you will feel fine.

Likewise, the world of our conscience and the entire human world are in pain. Why? There are elements that do not meet the standards of the cosmic force, and the universe is trying to push them out. Hence, we feel pain in our conscience. While the conscience was going in the proper direction, something stood opposing it and blocked the conscience's function. We experience a reaction, resulting in pain. If the problem is not solved, that reaction will send the person into hell. (165:176-77, May 20, 1987)

The law of cause and effect cannot be avoided in history. America is an extension of Great Britain… thus America is in a position to indemnify what Britain did wrong in history. What did Britain do when she colonized Asia, especially China? She killed countless Asians through pushing the opium trade. Britain adopted that policy to dominate the Chinese and profit off of them, while totally unconcerned that whole populations became helpless addicts. Someone today has to indemnify that sin. Americans, especially American youth, should indemnify that historical debt; otherwise young people here will be plagued by drugs as a result. (105:134, October 4, 1979)

God abhors sin, and misuse of love is the sin God abhors the most. God regards sinners who commit such transgressions and do not repent as His enemies, and He visits them with destruction. It is the Principle that whoever indulges in illicit love will perish. In Italy, the lustful and immoral city of Pompeii was destroyed by instant calamity. Sodom and Gomorrah perished under the same law. The Roman Empire once prevailed in the world with unparalleled power, but it collapsed for the same reason. From the vantage point of history, America today is on the same path. Unless it repents for its violations of the law of God's love, it too will perish. (104:141, April 29, 1979)

I was involved in the underground resistance movement against Japanese imperial rule, and from that perspective the Japanese were my enemies. They were the enemies of the Korean people in general and my enemies in particular. Yet, after Japan was defeated at the end of World War II, I loved the Japanese. Some time earlier, certain Japanese policemen had arrested me for my activities in the resistance and tortured me severely. When the war ended I could have reported them, and they all would have been executed. Yet, when I came across those same policemen running for their lives, I helped them escape to safety.

Do you know why so many young people in Japan place their eternal lives in my hands and pledge their loyalty to me? It is because there is a principle of cause and effect, which dictates that they must return what was given. (*True Family and World Peace*, February 10, 2000)

2. The Chain of Causation

The world exists because of causal actions, all things are produced by causal actions and all beings are governed and bound by causal actions. They are fixed like the rolling wheel of a cart, fixed by the pin of its axle shaft.

Sutta Nipata 654 (Buddhism)

Rousing himself from his concentration of mind, the Exalted One gave close attention to causal uprising in direct order:

This being, that becomes; by the arising of this, that arises, namely: Conditioned by ignorance, activities; conditioned by activities, consciousness; conditioned by consciousness, mind and body; conditioned by mind and body, the six sense-spheres; conditioned by the six sense-spheres, contact; conditioned by contact, feeling; conditioned by feeling, craving; conditioned by craving, grasping; conditioned by grasping, becoming; conditioned by becoming, birth; conditioned by birth, old age and death, grief, lamentation, suffering, sorrow and despair come into being. Thus is the arising of this mass of Ill. [23]

Udana 1.1 (Buddhism)

The ten thousand things all come from the same seed, and with their different forms they give place to one another. Beginning and end are part of a single ring and no one can comprehend its principle. This is called Heaven the Equalizer.

Chuang Tzu 27 (Taoism)

Behold, I am coming soon, bringing my recompense, to repay every one for what he has done. I am the Alpha and the Omega, the first and the last, the beginning and the end.

Revelation 22.12-13

Teachings of Sun Myung Moon

In everything, there is cause and effect. The effect appears as the result of a process. Passing through that process is a condition for the effect to become one with its cause. This is because the process is aligned with the cause and accepts the effect. It brings them to the point where they can unite and fulfill their purpose. Conversely, without a proper beginning, there can be no destination. (15:130, October 3, 1965)

The relationship between the world of essence and the world of phenomena can be compared to that between mind and body. It is a relationship of cause and result. (*Exposition of the Divine Principle*, Introduction)

God abides in the causal realm and in the resultant world. He is "the Alpha and the Omega," who exists as both the cause and the result.

By recognizing that human beings exist within a process that moves from cause to result, we can understand the relationship between God and humanity. History proceeds from the causal world to the resultant world. The human conscience also proceeds along this path, but [these days] the flow of history is so fast that the conscience must hurry twice as quickly to keep pace.

God, being the Cause, must establish human beings as the result. If [the first] human beings had not fallen, they would have been the cause of history. The Fall was a failure to possess the cause. (11:114, February 19, 1961)

Just as subject and object partners must become one, the cause and the result must also become one. In the Bible, God states: "I am the Alpha and the Omega, the first and the last, the beginning and the end." If God is the Alpha, we human beings are the Omega. If God is the first, we are the last, and if God is the beginning, then we are the end. Should the two remain separated? The verse promises that they are to unite. (69:76, October 20, 1973)

Anyone who denies the Origin cannot bring a result. The origin of all children is their [Heavenly] Parent, but if the children deny their Parent, it is logical that they cannot become an acceptable result. When the cause and the result become one, the ideal appears, full of joy. (328:185, August 3, 2000)

When a man connects with his wife in all aspects of her life [and vice-versa], the two become one. First they orbit around each other; then they meet. When they meet, they are elevated.

In other words, a man and a woman meet together by living for the sake of each other. Then, once they marry, they should sacrifice for God. We call this origin-division-union action. God divided people into two different sexes for love; therefore they should come together for love. Thus, their union should also be the unity of cause and result. Where the cause and the result became one, there can be a seed. Thus there arises an endless cycle of give and take between cause and result. Their oneness is the basis for a unified world. (389:303, August 7, 2002)

Chapter 3

The Purpose of Human Life

For God's Good Pleasure

AS CREATURES, HUMAN BEINGS ARE CREATED with a purpose determined by their Creator. The monotheistic religions in particular recognize that God created human beings to serve, love and glorify Him. We can thus find fulfillment through service and obedience. However, as our heavenly Father, God would also want us to be children who reflect His image and likeness in the world by spreading love and benevolence throughout the human race.

God is the Enjoyer of all phenomena in some texts; specifically, we can speak of God's joy when His purpose of creation is fulfilled. It is our privilege as human beings to return such joy to God. Father Moon explains God's purpose for creating human beings as a creative partnership, where we take after God's loving nature and God in turn rejoices to see countless images of Himself as we establish loving families and relate to one another and to all God's creatures with divine love. Nevertheless, due to the Fall of the first ancestors, people do not form loving families or treat the creation with love. Therefore, God has never experienced the fullness of joy. (See Chapter 6: *God's Grief*.)

1. Our Purpose Is to Serve God

I have created the jinn and humankind only that they may serve Me. No sustenance do I require that they should feed Me. For God is He who gives all sustenance, the Lord of Power, Steadfast.

Qur'an 51.56-58

All that God created in His world He created only for His glory, as it is said, "All that is called by my name, for my glory I created and fashioned and made it" (Isaiah 43.7).

Avot 6.11 (Judaism)

There is one God, the Father, from whom are all things and for whom we exist.

1 Corinthians 8.6

The greatest bliss is the good pleasure of God: that is the supreme felicity.

Qur'an 9.72

Why, is he better who founds his building upon the fear of God and His good pleasure, or he who founds his building upon the brink of a crumbling bank that will tumble with him into the fire of hell? And God does not guide the people of the evildoers.

Qur'an 9.109

If you obey the commandments of the LORD your God which I command you this day, by loving the LORD your God, by walking in his ways, and by keeping his commandments and his statutes and his ordinances, then you shall live and multiply, and the LORD your God will bless you in the land.

Deuteronomy 30.16

Do not try to develop what is natural to man; develop what is natural to Heaven. He who develops Heaven benefits life; he who develops man injures life.

Chuang Tzu 19 (Taoism)

If it be your wish, O people, to know God and to discover the greatness of His might, look, then, upon Me with My own eyes, and not with the eyes of anyone besides Me. You will, otherwise, be never capable of recognizing Me, though you ponder My Cause as long as My Kingdom endures.

Gleanings from the Writings of Bahá'u'lláh 127 (Bahá'í Faith)

Teachings of Sun Myung Moon

Originally, human beings were created to be happy, full of life and joy before God their Parent. Our existence should be for the glory of God. (52:36, December 12, 1971)

What should we human beings set as our purpose? Rather than setting our purpose on the individual, family, community, nation, world, or even the cosmos, we should set our purpose on God. Our purpose should be to bring God and humankind together. (41:323, February 18, 1971)

For what purpose were we born? What should be our center as we go through life, and what should be our ultimate goal? These questions absolutely cannot be answered if we exclude God. Without God, our life will have no connection to the Cause. Even if he makes some success in his life, a person who lacks a connection to the Cause cannot reap the result, and the value of his result cannot be recognized. A building is constructed according to a blueprint created by an architect. A building built without a blueprint cannot become what the Architect intends. (21:100, November 17, 1968)

My life is for the sake of God and the world. You also should think to live for God and the world. You should not think to live merely for yourself… Always check how closely you are aligned to the life that God wants you to live. (147:115, August 31, 1986)

2. God's Joy in Human Beings

God saw everything that he had made, and behold, it was very good.

Genesis 1.31

I was a secret treasure, and I created the creatures in order that I might be known.

Hadith (Islam)

O Lord of all, hail unto Thee!
The Soul of all, causing all acts,
Enjoying all, all life art Thou!
Lord of all pleasure and delight!

Maitri Upanishad 5.1 (Hinduism)

Happiness is spiritual, born of Truth and Love. It is unselfish; therefore it cannot exist alone, but requires all mankind to share it.

Science and Health, 57 (Christian Science)

As the bridegroom rejoices over the bride,
so shall your God rejoice over you.

Isaiah 62.5

When all human beings have accomplished the purification of their minds and come to lead a life full of joy, I, *Tsukihi* (God), will become cheered up. And when I become cheered up, so will all human beings. When the minds of all the world become cheered up, God and human beings will become altogether cheered up in one accord.

Ofudesaki 7.109-111 (Tenrikyo)

What is man that thou art mindful of him,
and the son of man that thou dost care for him?
Yet thou hast made him little less than God,
and dost crown him with glory and honor.

Psalm 8.4-5

The Messenger of Allah said: "God says: I have created human beings to win, not for Me be the winner."

al-Ghazzali, Revival of Religious Science (Islam)

Brahma's creative activity is not undertaken by way of any need on His part, but simply by way of sport.

Vedanta Sutra 2.1.32-33 (Hinduism)

We created not the heaven and the earth and all that is between them in play. If We had wished to find a pastime, We could have found it in Our presence—if We ever did. Nay, but We hurl the true against the false, and it prevails over it, and lo! [the false] vanishes...

To Him belongs whosoever is in the heavens and the earth. And those who dwell in His presence are not too proud to worship Him, nor do they weary.

Qur'an 21.16-19

Having created the world and all that lives and moves therein, He, through the direct operation of His unconstrained and sovereign Will, chose to confer upon man the unique distinction and capacity to know Him and to love Him—a capacity that must needs be regarded as the generating impulse and the primary purpose underlying the whole of creation.

Gleanings from the Writings of Baha'u'llah 27 (Baha'i Faith)

Teachings of Sun Myung Moon

God came to us in order to feel joy through our daily life. (*Way of God's Will* 2.2)

Though God is the Absolute Being, He cannot be happy alone. Adjectives such as "good" and "happy" cannot apply to any being that lives in isolation. They apply only where there is a robust mutual relationship. Imagine a professional singer who finds herself exiled to an uninhabited island. She may sing at the top of her voice, but with no one to listen, will it bring her happiness? In the same way, even the self-existent God absolutely needs a partner to share love with in order to experience joy and be happy. (September 12, 2005)

God's creation was a necessary act. The ideal of true love that God is creating cannot be realized by a solitary being. This ideal exists so that God can share with human beings the joy of His exalted and righteous Will. When we understand the God of true love correctly, it is self-evident that this unhappy world of sin and strife was not His original plan. (400:81, December 27, 2002)

Just as in a family, where the basis of the parents' happiness is when they have children, it is likewise unmistakable that God's purpose in searching for humanity is to attain His own happiness through His children. There is no basis for God's happiness if human beings are excluded. Therefore, God strives to connect with human beings and bring them to Himself, establishing a realm where God and human beings are in unity. Just as we do, God experiences happiness when all the varieties of heart are present in the family. (32:197, July 15, 1970)

If we were to ask God to tell us why He created this world, He would no doubt answer, "Because I liked it." Because He liked it. Because it gave Him joy. God created this world to obtain joy. This state of liking, this joy, is obtained through love.

God wanted to rejoice; therefore He created this world for the realization of love. God wanted to rejoice over a world of warm and harmonious love, where human beings and all creatures would dwell as one in God's love. God wanted to rejoice over men and women who would form true conjugal relationships in His love, and then build families, tribes, nations and a world of love; and God would taste the joy of love through the loving oneness of these human beings. This was the very ideal of God's creation.

If human beings had accomplished everything for God exactly as He had envisioned and according to His Will, then God would have become the God of joy, God of glory, and God of happiness. (113:312)

God did not create human beings as objects for His amusement or as a hobby. It is impossible to express in words how hard God worked and the efforts He devoted to create human beings and establish them as the center of all created beings.

In creating human beings, God devoted Himself, making many efforts. He gave them all His heart and soul and the essence of His life. He totally invested His love and affection. He created them to be in a relationship that no force can ever undo or sever. Because God created them in such a way, only when He beholds them [in their original unfallen state] can He finally feel at peace. (20:207, June 9, 1968)

God created all things in heaven and earth because it pleased Him to behold them.

Many Christians today say, "God is the Creator, and we are His creatures. There can be no parity or resemblance between the Creator and His creatures." This would mean that God is always absolute and alone, in a position without an object partner. Nothing would be greater unhappiness.

Consider a man of authority, even the president of a country; his wife has died and he lives alone. Would his son say to him, "Father, you must be so happy to be living alone"? Surely his father would reply, "You rascal. How can I be happy?" Rather the son should say, "Father, would you like me find you a new wife?" That would be a filial son. (57:247, June 4, 1972)

God's purpose in creating the universe was to feel joy when He saw the purpose of goodness fulfilled in the Heavenly Kingdom, which the whole creation, including human beings, could have established… The purpose of the universe's existence centered on human beings is to return joy to God, the Creator. (*Exposition of the Divine Principle*, Creation 3.1)

The Image of God

HOW CAN WE DESCRIBE A HUMAN BEING'S LIKENESS to the divine? This and the following sections explore this topic from three aspects: Human beings are created in God's image; we are vessels for God's indwelling Spirit; and we are God's beloved children.

Jewish and Christian scriptures teach that man was created in the image and likeness of God. The image of God speaks to the ideal of holiness, truthfulness, righteousness, and charity. The saint or self-realized person is like heaven, manifesting the character of God. To reach this ideal requires a transformation of the inner man, or as Father Moon puts it, a "revolution of character."

Father Moon's teaching seeks to get at some of the ways that human beings resemble God. He examines God's attributes: omnipotence, omniscience, absoluteness, eternity, etc. and explains that human beings strive for these same qualities. Moreover, possessing these qualities is our heavenly birthright.

Furthermore, the scriptures affirm that men and women are equally in the image of God. Since God created human beings to be nothing less than His counterparts with whom to share His complete love, human beings should resemble God to the fullest extent. Thus, had human beings not been marred by the Fall, we could attain the fullest manifestation of God's image as a man and woman in the union of marriage.

1. How Human Beings Resemble God

God said, "Let us make man in our image, after our likeness."[1]

       Genesis 1.26

O Son of Man! Veiled in My immemorial being and in the ancient eternity of My essence, I knew My love for thee; therefore I created thee, have engraved on thee Mine image, and revealed to thee My beauty.

   Hidden Words of Bahá'u'lláh, Arabic 3
       (Baha'i Faith)

Rabbi Akiba said: Beloved is man, for he was created in the image of God. But it was by a special love that it was made known to him that he was created in the image of God; as it is taught, "For in the image of God made He man." (Gen. 9.6)

     Mishnah, Avot 3.18 (Judaism)

So set your purpose for religion as a man by nature upright—the nature [framed] of God, in which He has created man. There is no altering the laws of God's creation. That is the right religion.

       Qur'an 30.30

Conform yourselves to the character of God.

     Hadith of Abu Nuaym (Islam)

Fire blazing from the earth.
The Superior man reflects in his person
 Heaven's virtue.

     I Ching 35 (Confucianism)

If we keep unperverted the human heart—which is like unto heaven and received from earth—that is God.

   Revelation to Mikado Seiwa (Shinto)

Looking first at absolute Justice, Beauty and Temperance, and again at the human copy, they will mingle and temper the various elements of life into the image of a man. Thus is a human being conceived according to that other Image, which, when existing among men, Homer calls the form and likeness of God.

     Plato, The Republic (Hellenism)

As God is called merciful and gracious, so you be merciful and gracious, offering gifts gratis to all; as the Lord is called righteous and loving, so you be righteous and loving.

     Sifre Deuteronomy (Judaism)

God is never in any way unrighteous—he is perfect righteousness; and he of us who is the most righteous is most like him.

     Plato, Theaetetus (Hellenism)

That which is the finest essence—this whole world has that as its soul. That is Reality. That is the Self. That art thou.

Chandogya Upanishad 6.8.7 (Hinduism)

Veiled by ignorance,
The minds of man and Buddha
appear to be different;
Yet in the realm of Mind Essence
they are both of one taste.

Milarepa (Buddhism)

And the LORD said to Moses, "Say to all the congregation of the people of Israel, 'You shall be holy; for I the LORD your God am holy.'"

Leviticus 19.1-2

Father, O mighty Force,
That Force which is in everything,
Come down between us, fill us,
Until we become like Thee,
Until we become like Thee.

Susu Prayer (African Traditional Religions)

"Now what do you think, Vasettha... is Brahma [the supreme Being] in possession of wives and wealth, or is he not?"[2]

"He is not, Gotama."

"Is his mind full of anger, or free from anger?"

"Free from anger, Gotama."

"Is his mind full of malice, or free from malice?"

"Free from malice, Gotama."

"Is his mind tarnished, or is it pure?"

"It is pure, Gotama."

"Has he self-mastery, or has he not?"

"He has, Gotama."

"Now what do you think, Vasettha, are the brahmins versed in the Vedas in possession of wives and wealth, or are they not?"

"They are, Gotama."

"Have they anger in their hearts, or have they not?"

"They have, Gotama."

"Do they bear malice, or do they not?"

"They do, Gotama."

"Are they pure in heart, or are they not?"

"They are not, Gotama."

"Have they self-mastery, or have they not?"

"They have not, Gotama."

"Can there, then, be agreement and likeness between the brahmins with their wives and property, and Brahma, who has none of these things?"

"Certainly not, Gotama!"

"Then that these brahmins versed in the Vedas, who also live married and wealthy, should after death, when the body is dissolved, become united with Brahma, who has none of these things—such a condition of things is impossible!"...

"Now what do you think, Vasettha, will the monk who lives according to the Dhamma be in possession of women and wealth, or will he not?"

"He will not, Gotama!"

"Will he be full of anger, or free from anger?"

"He will be free from anger, Gotama!"

"Will his mind be full of malice, or free from malice?"

"Free from malice, Gotama!"

"Will his mind be tarnished, or pure?"

"It will be pure, Gotama!"

"Will he have self-mastery, or will he not?"

"Surely he will, Gotama!"

"Then as you say, the monk is free from household and worldly cares, free from anger, free from malice, pure in mind, and master of himself; and Brahma also is free from household and worldly cares, free from anger, free from malice, pure in mind, and master of himself. Is there then agreement and likeness between the monk and Brahma?"

"There is, Gotama!"

"Then verily, that the monk who is free from household cares should after death, when the body is dissolved, become united with Brahma, who is the same—such a condition of things is in every way possible!"

Digha Nikaya 13.31-34, Tevigga Sutta (Buddhism)

What is man? Man is not matter; he is not made up of brain, blood, bones, and other material elements. The Scriptures inform us that man is made in the image and likeness of God. Matter is not that likeness. The likeness of Spirit cannot be so unlike Spirit. Man is spiritual and perfect; and because he is spiritual and perfect, he must be so understood in Christian Science. Man is idea, the image, of Love; he is not physique.

Science and Health, 475 *(Christian Science)*

Teachings of Sun Myung Moon

God made us in His image, like Himself. That means the Father resembles us just as we resemble the Father. So when someone asks you, "What kind of being is God?" you can answer, "He is someone like me." This answer will hit the mark. (127:233)

God created all creatures to take after His image, and among them He particularly created human beings to represent His character and be co-creators.

Human beings should have the same attributes of feeling and thinking as God does. If God rejoices, human beings should rejoice with Him, and if God grieves, human beings should grieve with Him. Unless people are able to experience the same feelings as God, no matter how much God loves them they cannot attain a state of harmony and oneness with Him.

In sum, God necessarily had to create object partners to share His love. Hence, God created human beings with the capacity to rejoice with God and experience His love. Again, God created human beings with the same value as the Absolute Being, that they might stand as His object partners. (39:9, January 9, 1971)

People are fond of things that resemble them. Whom does the world resemble? In the future, whom should the ideal world resemble? It must resemble God. It says in Genesis 1:27, "God created man in His own image, in the image of God He created him; male and female He created them." Indeed, God created men and women in His image. We like things that resemble us, and we can surmise that God likes us because we resemble Him. God created all creatures in heaven and on earth, and He is pleased when they resemble Him. (26:167, October 25, 1969)

Since we are created to resemble God, we want to make ourselves like Him. God is omniscient, omnipotent, and omnipresent, so what must we be like in order to resemble God? As God is eternal, we also must be eternal. As God is omnipresent, we also must be omnipresent. That is why we want to live anywhere in the world. We want to be omniscient and omnipotent to embrace the entire world at once...

In what respect would God most like us to resemble Him? More than omnipresence, more than omniscience and omnipotence, more than uniqueness, He most wants us to resemble Him in love. The day when we come to resemble Him in love, we can lose everything and still it will follow us wherever we go. A woman can be so ugly as to be not worth a penny, but if she has love a young man as handsome as a stallion will pursue her. (26:167, October 25, 1969)

A true person is one who resembles God. To establish a world abounding in true people, what we need is not a political revolution but a "revolution of character." A revolution of character is the revolution that transforms us into true human beings who resemble God's character. It uplifts people's character to the standard of God's character. (149:271, November 28, 1986)

God is the most public-minded being, whereas Satan is the most self-centered being, private and selfish to his bone marrow. Thus, God's formula to restore human beings aims for us to become God-like. This means that we must sacrifice what is personal and uphold what is public. Each of us must embody the spirit of altruism and service to others.

A selfless and public-minded person will prosper because he or she is the image of God. The selfish, self-centered person will decline because he is the opposite of God, in the image of the betrayer. This is a law of Heaven. (88:209, September 18, 1976)

3. God's Image More Completely Reflected in the Family

So God created man in his own image, in the image of God he created him, male and female he created them.

Genesis 1.27

I am He, you are She;
I am Song, you are Verse,
I am Heaven, you are Earth.
We two shall here together dwell,
becoming parents of children.

Atharva Veda 14.2.71 (Hinduism)

The gospel of Love... presents the unity of male and female as no longer two wedded individuals, but as two individual natures in one; and this compounded spiritual individuality reflects God as Father-Mother, not as a corporeal being. In this divinely united spiritual consciousness, there is no impediment to eternal bliss—to the perfectibility of God's creation.

Science and Health, 576 (Christian Science)

Teachings of Sun Myung Moon

It is only when a man and woman become one that they come to resemble God, who created us male and female in His image. (135:122)

In human beings, God's internal nature and external form are manifested separately as man and woman. When the time is ripe, they are to become a father and a mother, Parents of Heaven and Earth. Then, God dwells in their bones. (341:239, January 2, 2001)

God is the harmonious union of the dual characteristics of masculinity and femininity. Creation occurs by the principle that God's internal nature divides into two separate characteristics, which then re-unite in a form that resembles God's original internal nature. Man and woman are born each resembling one of God's characteristics. That is, the union of God's son and God's daughter is the union of God's masculinity and God's femininity. In their harmonious union they resemble God. For this reason, husband and wife are a unified body that represents God in His entirety. (9:83, April 16, 1960)

Even secular people wish that their loved ones would live forever. They want to go through life with one partner only, and would dislike it if he or she were to change. If even fallen human beings want their beloved partners to be eternal, unchanging, absolute, and unique, how much more so would God, who is the Center of the universe? There is no possibility that God would want His beloved partners, human beings, to be changeable. Nor would God want His object partners to be limited in any way. Instead, God wants us to be absolute. God wants us to be unchanging. (77:185, April 6, 1975)

What is God's purpose in creating human beings? He did not create them just to watch them go about their daily lives. He did not create them to just grow old and die. God created human beings to have us build a God-centered haven of love. We are created to grow to maturity in love, communicate with each other through heart, and then build God's Kingdom on earth. Adam, the male, represents heaven, and Eve, the female, represents earth. Therefore, when the two become one horizontally in God's love, they bring unity to the entire cosmos, heaven and earth. (21:44-45, September 1, 1968)

Since we human beings resemble God, by the power of God's omniscient and almighty love we can do anything. Just as God created Adam and Eve, we human beings receive the power to create when we give birth to sons and daughters. (57:111, May 29, 1972)

The Temple of God

HUMAN BEINGS ARE MEANT TO BE the living temples of God. At the creation of man God injected a special element of His Spirit that endows the human mind with divine qualities, such as love, creativity, and the desire for the eternal. God wants to make His home in human beings. With the Spirit of God resonating with the mind, the body sees, hears and acts as God would see, hear and act. By thus acting on behalf of the formless and invisible God, human beings are sanctified, and through them God is able to sanctify others.

In Hinduism and other eastern faiths, this indwelling presence of Ultimate Reality is called the Self or Atman. However, most people live in ignorance of the Self, and they live entirely from egoistic motives. To misconstrue the personal ego as the Holy Spirit would be a serious error and even a mark of insanity. For Father Moon, we are like temples that suffered desecration due to the tragedy of the human fall. God's Spirit cannot dwell in fallen people. Originally, Adam and Eve were to become temples of God and act as God's earthly body to beautify this world and transform it into a Garden of Eden. Jesus came as God's temple; therefore he could reveal God in his person. Through God's grace and human efforts at restoration, we too can attain the position of God's temples.

Do you not know that you are God's temple and that God's Spirit dwells in you?

1 Corinthians 3.16

Let a man always consider himself as if the Holy One dwells within him.

Talmud, Ta'anit 11b (Judaism)

I have been crucified with Christ; it is no longer I who live, but Christ who lives in me.[3]

Galatians 2.20

Heaven and earth contain Me not, but the heart of my faithful servant contains Me.

Hadith of Suhrawardi (Islam)

Just as God fills the whole world, so the soul fills the body. Just as God sees but is not seen, so the soul sees but is not itself seen. Just as God feeds the whole world, so the soul feeds the whole body. Just as God is pure, so the soul is pure. Just as God dwells in the innermost precincts [of the Temple], so also the soul dwells in the innermost part of the body.

Talmud, Berakot 10a *(Judaism)*

When I love him, I am his hearing by which he hears, his sight by which he sees, his hand by which he strikes, and his foot with which he walks.

40 Hadith of an-Nawawi 38 *(Islam)*

I have breathed into man of My spirit.

Qur'an 15.29

The LORD God formed man of dust from the ground, and breathed into his nostrils the breath of life; and man became a living being.

Genesis 2.7

Smaller than the smallest, greater than the greatest, this Self forever dwells within the hearts of all. When a man is free from desire, his mind and senses purified, he beholds the glory of the Self and is without sorrow.

Though seated, he travels far; though at rest, he moves all things. Who but the purest of the pure can realize this Effulgent Being, who is joy and who is beyond joy.

Formless is he, though inhabiting form. In the midst of the fleeting he abides forever. All-pervading and supreme is the Self. The wise man, knowing him in his true nature, transcends all grief.

Katha Upanishad 1.2.20-22 *(Hinduism)*

Bright but hidden, the Self dwells in the heart.
Everything that moves, breathes, opens, and
    closes
lives in the Self. He is the source of love
and may be known through love but not
    through thought.
He is the goal of life. Attain this goal!

The shining Self dwells hidden in the heart.
Everything in the cosmos, great and small,
lives in the Self. He is the source of life,
truth beyond the transience of this world.
He is the goal of life. Attain this goal!

Mundaka Upanishad 2.2.1-2 *(Hinduism)*

The rich build temples to Shiva,
What shall I, a poor man, do?
O my Lord! my legs are the pillars,
My torso, the shrine,
And my head, the golden pinnacle!
Things standing shall fall,
But the moving ever shall stay![4]

Basavanna, Vacana 820 *(Hinduism)*

Abdullah bin Omar saw the Messenger (PBUH) walking around the Ka'ba saying, "How blessed you are, O Ka'ba, and your fragrant wind. How great, how great is your sacredness! By Allah, owner of my soul, to Allah the sacredness of a believer has greater holiness than you."

Sunnan Ibn Majah[5] 2.3932 *(Islam)*

Man was also in the beginning with God. Intelligence, or the light of truth, was not created or made, neither indeed can be. All truth is independent in that sphere in which God has placed it, to act for itself, as all intelligence also; otherwise there is no existence.

Behold, here is the agency of man, and here is the condemnation of man; because that which was from the beginning is plainly manifest unto them, and they receive not the light. And every man whose spirit receives not the light is under condemnation.

For man is spirit. The elements are eternal, and spirit and element, inseparably connected, receive a fullness of joy; and when separated, man cannot receive a fullness of joy. The elements are the tabernacle of God; yea, man is the tabernacle of God, even temples; and whatsoever temple is defiled, God shall destroy that temple.[6]

Doctrine and Covenants 93.29-35
(Latter-day Saints)

Teachings of Sun Myung Moon

A human being is a temple of God, and inside that temple dwells a mind which is a microcosm of the infinite God. (107:172, April 27, 1980)

First Corinthians 3:16 says: "Do you not know that you are God's temple and that God's Spirit dwells in you?" If you enter into a deep mystical state, you will recognize this to be true. If you ask, "Heavenly Father, where are you?" God will answer you from the original root of your mind. (362:190, December 12, 2001)

As written in I Corinthians 3:16, Adam and Eve were created as the dwelling place of God, as holy temples. What of God was to dwell within them? God's love was to dwell within those holy temples.

As God's temples [had they not fallen], Adam and Eve would be God's body. When they loved each other, it would be God loving through them as His body. This is the secret of the universe. (161:44, January 1, 1987)

Had there been no Fall, God would be dwelling in our hearts and we would be His temples... Our faces would express God's pure joy. We would see things with God's eyes and for God's sake; we would listen with God's ears and for God's sake; we would feel with God's touch for God's sake; we would speak on God's behalf, and so on. Everything we did and thought would be an expression of the living God inside us. (95:247, December 4, 1977)

Ever since the fall of Adam and Eve, God has been hoping to find men and women who could empathize with God's heart, be united in God's heart, and be the temples in which God can dwell. (3:298, January 26, 1958)

Jesus' mind and body were not simply his own. His mind was the mind of God. His body was not his, but God's. Also, Jesus' words were not his own, but were the law of Heaven, representing God's Will and the hope of all humankind. Jesus came to this earth as God's substantial temple, as the divine Word, and as the representative who could sit on God's throne. (3:264, January 12, 1958)

The relationship between God and a person who has attained individual perfection can be compared to that between the mind and the body. The body is the dwelling place of the mind and moves according to the mind's direction. Likewise, God abides within the mind of a fully mature person. Such a person becomes a temple of God and leads his life in harmony with His Will. A perfect individual is fully attuned to God, just as the body resonates with the mind. For this reason it is written, "Do you not know that you are God's temple and that God's Spirit dwells in you?" (I Cor. 3.16) and "In that day you will know that I am in my Father, and you in me, and I in you." (John 14.20) A person who has perfected his individual character becomes a temple of God, and the Holy Spirit abides within him. Living in oneness with God, he acquires a divine nature. (*Exposition of the Divine Principle*, Eschatology 1.1.1)

When you go to bed and your head is snuggled into the pillow, have you ever thought, "Ah, I am sleeping with God"? Have you ever thought, "I feel so good that God is sleeping next to me"? And then in the morning as you wake up and get out of bed, do you say to yourself, "Wake up, God! Oh,

You are already awake. Good morning, Father"? You should live with the feeling that when you wake up, God is already awake, ready to greet you. (92:153, April 1, 1977)

Each human being can contain the entire universe. Therefore, prepare a space within yourself where God can come and take a nap, comfortably stretching His legs. Become a person within whom God can feel completely free. Though he kicks and stretches, he feels no walls or obstructions. If you are like that, you can be God's temple.

Knowing this, you should love yourself and respect yourself as the temple of God that you are. (125:101, March 13, 1983)

A human being has a body and a definite shape, while the invisible God has no shape or body. However, without having a body, God cannot reign over the spiritual and physical worlds. God also needs a substantial body in order to manifest as the Parent of humankind. God created Adam and Eve to manifest Himself through these substantial beings.

Thus, unfallen Adam and Eve were not only to be the progenitors of the human race; they were also to be God's substantial body through which He could reign over heaven and earth. They were responsible to exercise dominion over the world on behalf of God in the position of parents. (133:91-92, July 10, 1984)

God has no shape or form. Even in the spirit world, you cannot see God. The reason why God created Adam centering on love is because this created world around us has form. [Through Adam], God was to become a Father with a form.

As a result of God becoming a Father possessing form, that which is invisible and that which is visible are united into one. This, in turn, symbolizes the unity of the universe. Thus, God created Adam and Eve so that He could take on form. So, what is the decisive element in His taking on form? This can only be love. Adam and Eve came into the world with an appearance such that they could have a form resembling God's external aspect.

In that case, the features of Adam and Eve would have been elevated to the palace and the throne of the Kingdom of Heaven. God would have then dwelled within the hearts of this king and queen, and from there He would have ruled over the physical world and the invisible world. This would have created God's Kingdom—a kingdom of love. Only love can bring spirit and flesh together. Nothing else will suffice. (143:93-94, March 16, 1986)

Sons and Daughters of God

JEWISH AND CHRISTIAN SCRIPTURES CALL GOD our "heavenly Father"; this insight can be found in most of the world's faiths. Therefore, human beings are supposed to be God's sons and daughters. How genuine that Parent-child relationship can be is the subject of the passages in this section.

Father Moon teaches that the depth and emotive power of our relationship with God should be even greater than the filial affection and obligation we feel toward our physical parents who gave us birth. The notion that a human being can and should share God's heart, God's situation, and God's sense of responsibility for the world in the same way that a filial son carries burdens for his aging father—what profound implications this can have for our life with God!

1. Our Birthright as God's Sons and Daughters

You are the children of the LORD your God.
Deuteronomy 14.1

For all who are led by the spirit of God are sons of God. For you did not receive the spirit of slavery to fall back into fear, but you have received the spirit of sonship. When we cry, "Abba! Father!" it is the Spirit himself bearing witness that we are the children of God, and if children, then heirs, heirs of God and fellow heirs with Christ, provided that we suffer with him in order that we may also be glorified with him.
Romans 8.14-17

Anas and 'Abdullah reported God's Messenger as saying, "All [human] creatures are God's children, and those dearest to God are those who treat His children kindly."
Hadith of Baihaqi (Islam)

We are the children of our Maker
And do not fear that He will kill us.
We are the children of God
And do not fear that He will kill.
Dinka Prayer (African Traditional Religions)

See what love the Father has given us, that we should be called children of God; and so we are.
1 John 3.1

Let the children come to me, and do not hinder them, for to such belongs the kingdom of God. Truly, I say to you, whoever does not receive the kingdom of God like a child shall not enter it.
Luke 18.16-17

I say, "You are gods,
sons of the Most High, all of you.
Psalm 82.6

May the words of the prophet Asaph apply—"Ye are gods, and all of you are children of the most High,"—lest we, abusing the Father's most indulgent generosity, render that unfettered choice which He gave us harmful rather than beneficial. May some holy aspiration enter our hearts, so that we are not content with middling things, but pant for the highest and strain to achieve them, since we can if we will.
Pico della Mirandola, On the Dignity of Man (Christianity)

Teachings of Sun Myung Moon

We are told that God is the God of love. We humans seek the supreme position where the God of love can truly love us. When we can occupy that position, God, from His position, cannot but love us. It is the place where the human heart and the divine Heart are united as one. It can only be attained when we are relating with God in a parent-child relationship.

I am not referring to the relationship we have with our own father and mother who gave us birth and raised us. I am speaking about the original relationship, between the absolute God who created the cosmos and human beings had they not fallen. It is the ultimate relationship human beings can have with God: God is our Father and we are truly His sons and daughters. God intends that we attain this incredible position. (53:286, March 4, 1972)

Once I entered a mystic state and asked God in prayer, "What is the basis of the universe?" God answered, "It is the relationship between father and child." This does not mean our relationship with the parents who gave us birth, but to the relationship between God and human beings.

What is the exact content of this relationship? There is nothing closer, nothing deeper, than when the Father and His child are one: one in love, one in life, and one in ideals. In that unity, God's love is my love, God's life is my life, and God's ideal is my ideal. This is the first and original father-child relationship, where unification occurs. (69:78, October 20, 1973)

After creating Adam and Eve, God showered true love upon them. Who initiated true love? It was not Adam and Eve. It was God, loving them as His children. It is like a newborn baby who dwells in the warmth of its parents' love; however, it is ignorant of love and thinks that its parents exist for it alone. It knows nothing of its parents' other concerns. God's parental love encompasses everything, yet we first come into an awareness of God's love just as babies come into an awareness of their parents' love. They smile to see their parents and are grateful for their protection. This is how the love of the Parent and His children grows. (149:312, December 21, 1986)

God created human beings out of His absolute love, to be His partners in love. This relationship forms an axis of love, linking God the Father with human beings as His sons and daughters.

Is there anything higher or more precious than to be a son or daughter of God? If anything were higher, then surely human desire would aspire to attain it. But there is nothing higher. Do you think that when the omniscient and omnipotent God created Adam and Eve, He secretly reserved the highest position for Himself and made Adam and Eve to be only second best? We cannot imagine that God would do that to His children, to His partners who share absolute love with Him. As our eternal True Parent, God invested Himself one hundred percent into the creation of human beings and endowed us with the right to have equal status with Him, to participate in His work as equals, to live with Him, and to inherit from Him. God bestowed upon human beings all of His attributes. (September 12, 2005)

God is the Father of human beings, and we are His children. Then suppose someone said to God, "Your child is more handsome than you." Would God be happy to hear that remark, or would it make Him feel bad? If He were to feel bad, then God would be beneath the level of humans. Of course, He would be happy. That is the logic of love. (40:343, February 11, 1971)

The horizontal love between a husband and a wife blossoms with God's ideal love, and the fragrance of their love oscillates throughout the universe even as God's love is added on to their love: This is the truth of the relationship of the Father with His children at its perfection. (101:34-35, October 28, 1978)

2. Recovering the Dignity of Sons and Daughters of God

Sons have I reared and brought up,
but they have rebelled against me.

Isaiah 1.2

The Rock, his work is perfect;
for all his ways are justice.
A God of faithfulness and without iniquity,
just and right is he.

They have dealt corruptly with him,
they are no longer his children because of their blemish;
they are a perverse and crooked generation.
Do you thus requite the LORD,
you foolish and senseless people?
Is not he your Father, who created you,
who made you and established you?

Deuteronomy 32.4-6

We are all as the Buddha's sons. The Buddha has always declared that we are his sons. But because of the three sufferings, in the midst of births-and-deaths we have borne all kinds of torments, being deluded and ignorant and enjoying our attachment to trifles. Today the World-honored One has caused us to ponder over and remove the dirt of all diverting discussions of inferior things. In these we have hitherto been diligent to make progress and have got, as it were, a day's pay for our effort to reach Nirvana. Obtaining this, we greatly rejoiced and were contented… but still we did not perceive that we are really Buddha's sons.

Lotus Sutra 4 *(Buddhism)*

For since in prayer we call God our Father, it is our duty always to deport and demean ourselves as godly children, that He may not receive shame, but honor and praise from us.

Martin Luther, *The Large Catechism* *(Christianity)*

Teachings of Sun Myung Moon

The original relationship between God and human beings is that of eternal Parent and child. Restoration, therefore, means recovering that relationship. (316:236, February 13, 2000)

Since God is the King of faith, He seeks a prince of faith, and since He is the King of love, He looks for a prince of love. (*Way of God's Will* 2.2)

In relating to God, we should follow the way of children of filial piety. God is serious about the world situation. Is there someone who, with even greater seriousness, is desperate to experience God's heart, and who forgets himself and spends sleepless nights in the struggle to become God's child? This is what the question comes down to. (62:35, September 10, 1972)

God is your Father and you are your Father's daughters. How much God has longed to embrace His daughters in His bosom? For that reason, you should become God's filial daughters… If each of you becomes a filial daughter, all your family members will follow suit. By the same token, the entire nation, world and cosmos will unite with you. You will become God's number one victorious daughter, a saint to the world, a holy daughter to the cosmos. That is how you become a mistress in the realm of the royal family. (293:208, May 26, 1998)

> Mayest we become Thy simple and pure children
> who can penetrate to Thy heart of longing and love which desires to embrace us…
> Father! Although we called Thee "Father,"
> our voice did not flow out of a sincere mind and heart
> springing forth from our flesh and bones.
> There was never a time when we could rush to Thee
> and cling to Thee out of such an emotion. (20:199, June 9, 1968)

> Only after climbing over hills of sorrow,
> hills of suffering and hills of resentment…
> can we hold on to Thy heart and say:
> "Father, Thy sorrow is my sorrow,
> thy suffering is my suffering,
> and Thy troubles are my troubles.

Please entrust all Thy suffering to me,
while Thou dost dwell in joy." (4:294, September 14, 1958)

The Value of Human Life

HUMAN BEINGS HAVE PRICELESS VALUE. Although in many fallen societies life is regarded as cheap, and despite the worldly illusion that a person's value is determined by wealth, status, education or beauty, God endows every person with the absolute value of His love. He created us as His beloved children, infinitely precious—even equal to God. The texts gathered here express this exalted value of a human being.

A single person has the value of the whole world. Unique in all creation, he or she is irreplaceable. Moreover, the love of God, family, nation and all creation embrace each individual. Each individual is needed by all existence. The death of any individual brings loss to all existence. For this reason, taking life by murder, suicide and abortion has no place in God's world. Furthermore, since physical life provides the opportunity for growth (See Chapter 5: *Preparation for Eternity*), taking a life robs the individual and the universe of a way to attain perfection.

Still, in a world fixated on materialism, few people have realized their exalted potential value, which derives from the capacity to love God and humanity. Therefore, it is incumbent upon us all to cultivate the true wellsprings of value and become the children of God who are esteemed by the world and God.

1. More Precious than Gold

For what will it profit a man, if he gains the whole world and forfeits his life?

Matthew 16.26

Why should I fear in times of trouble,
when the iniquity of my persecutors surrounds me,
men who trust in their wealth
and boast of the abundance of their riches?
Truly no man can ransom himself,
or give to God the price of his life,
for the ransom of his life is costly,
and can never suffice.

Psalm 49.5-8

"I got me slaves and slave-girls." For what price, tell me? What in the world is worth as much as a human being? What price can you put on a rational intellect? How many drachmas do you reckon equals the value of one made in the likeness of God? How many gold pieces should you be able to get for selling a being shaped by God? God said, "Let us make man in our own image and likeness." (Gen. 1.26) Since man is in the likeness of God, and is ruler over the whole earth, and has been granted this authority over everything from God who is his Buyer, tell me, who is his seller? To God alone belongs this power.

Gregory of Nyssa, Homily on Ecclesiastes 4
(*Christianity*)

Teachings of Sun Myung Moon

People in this world believe that the good life is to live in comfortable surroundings, wear good clothes, drive a fancy car, and fly to any destination anytime they wish. You should know that their standard of judging what is the good life is a bad habit of worldly people. (131:171, May 1, 1984)

Americans may love material things, but I love people more. The winners are people who love people. Even if you lose all you possess, if you keep your human relations intact, the things will return. Though we lose money, through people we will be able to obtain money. But if we break our connection to people, we will lose everything. (February 17, 2001)

What is exceedingly valuable in the world? It is not treasure such as gold or silver, nor is it worldly fame or power. The most valuable thing in all heaven and earth is you.

Nevertheless, when people are asked what certification they have that they are valuable, they cannot answer. Still, despite their many deficiencies, people want to put themselves before heaven and earth as the most valuable existence. It is our original human nature to do so.

Maybe you think you are already living for the sake of the nation and the world. However, have you considered whether other people regard you as a valuable person? If they do not, then you need to make a new determination and a new beginning. Ask yourself, "What do others see as valuable about me?"

Can you become a jewel, one of a kind in the universe, a true treasure that God and Jesus would long to possess? The myriads of saints who formerly lived on earth, and all the philosophers who planted their thought in the world, no matter how important they may have been during their earthly lives, would long for your treasure. All humanity presently living, and even people of the future, would also want it. They would adore its value. Yet who has believed that they could be such a jewel? (17:13-14, November 6, 1966)

2. A Human Being Has the Value of the Universe

In heaven and on earth, I alone am the Honored One.[7]

Ch'ang A-han Ching (Buddhism)

When I look at Thy heavens, the work of Thy fingers,
the moon and the stars which Thou hast established;
What is man that Thou art mindful of him,
and the son of man that Thou dost care for him?
Yet Thou hast made him little less than God,
and dost crown him with glory and honor.

Psalm 8.3-5

Surely We have honored the children of Adam, and We carry them on land and sea, and We provide them with good things, and We make them to excel highly most of those whom We have created.

Qur'an 17.70

The whole world was created only for the sake of the righteous man. He weighs as much as the whole world. The whole world was created only to be united to him.

Talmud, Shabbat 30b (Judaism)

We prescribed for the Children of Israel that whoever kills a human being, except to retaliate for manslaughter or for corruption done in the land, it shall be as if he had killed all of humankind; and whoso saves the life of one, it shall be as if he had saved the lives of all humankind.

Qur'an 5.32

Only one single man [Adam] was created in the world, to teach that, if any man has caused a single soul to perish, Scripture imputes it to him as though he had caused the whole world to perish, and if any man saves alive a single soul, Scripture imputes it to him as though he had saved the whole world.

Also, man [was created singly] to show the greatness of the Holy One, Blessed be He, for if a man strikes many coins from one mold, they all resemble one another, but the King of Kings, the Holy One, made each man in the image of Adam, and yet not one of them resembles his fellow. Therefore every single person is obligated to say, "The world was created for my sake."

Mishnah, Sanhedrin 4.5 (Judaism)

Teachings of Sun Myung Moon

An individual human being is more precious than the universe. Each person's value is infinite, because he or she is created as God's partner of love. (262:145, July 23, 1994)

One human being, although seemingly an insignificant individual, has the potential to represent all of human history and all relationships with the future. Therefore, he or she has cosmic value. (4:268, August 3, 1958)

What value does God bestow on human beings? God created us to be His partners of love. Therefore, human beings are meant to share God's absolute, unique value. Yet people are ignorant of this amazing truth. These days, what is a human life worth? Yet, God created men and women as His partners of love, with a precious value that cannot be exchanged even for the whole universe! (142:143, March 8, 1986)

Even God cannot have true love, peace and happiness, or attain His ideal, apart from His object partners. What would be the use of peace or happiness to God if He were alone?… Please understand that each of you is indispensable for completing God's true love, God's peace, God's happiness and God's ideal. We have been unaware of our value. When you experience your precious, awesome and lofty value, which can bring love, peace, happiness and the ideal even to God, you can praise yourself and feel reverence for yourself. (77:314, April 30, 1975)

When you marry, you want your spouse to be better than you. You hope that your sons and daughters will marry spouses who are better than them. Whose trait does this resemble? It is God's! Heavenly Father wishes for His partners and objects of love to be better than Him. Can we deny this? Human value is supreme. From the viewpoint of love, it can be even greater than God!

For this reason, your mind desires what is highest. This is not inconceivable. All human beings could have attained this value, had there been no fall. Dwelling in that supreme, heavenly state, they were to manage and lead the universe. (211:272, December 30, 1990)

Every human being possesses a unique individuality. No matter how many billions of people are born on the earth, no two will ever have exactly the same personality. Each person is God's substantial object partner who manifests a distinctive aspect of God's dual characteristics. Hence, that person is the only one in the entire universe who can stimulate that distinctive aspect of God's nature to bring Him joy. Every person who has completed the purpose of creation is thus a unique existence in the cosmos. We can thus affirm the Buddha's saying, "In heaven and on earth, I alone am the honored one." (*Exposition of the Divine Principle*, Christology 1)

Above and below, front and rear, and right and left—everyone is related to me. These relationships are not temporary but life-long. They extend from the beginning of human history, and connect me to my posterity thousands of generations into the future. If I were to be broken, my relationship with God would also be broken. My family would be damaged, as would my clan and the whole world. That is why I am a microcosm, representing heaven and earth.

My heart desires to embrace Heaven, and my body to possess the earth. I want to be enraptured by the heart of the Sovereign Lord. I want to be His representative, who cannot be defeated by anyone or anything in heaven and earth. If I deeply analyze myself in the context of these relationships, I can understand that I am the greatest being, with infinite value. (8:10-11, October 25, 1959)

The question, however, is whether we are in a condition to receive the value that God intends to give. If we were beautiful both internally and externally, we would illuminate heaven and earth like a diamond or a brilliant gem. (352:25-26, September 16, 2001)

3. Murder, Suicide and Abortion: Crimes against Life

You shall not kill.
Exodus 20.13

A man who contributes to the killing of a believer—even with a single word—will meet Allah on the Judgment Day, with the judgment upon his forehead, "excluded from the mercy of his Lord."
Sunnan Ibn Majah 2.2620 (*Islam*)

Do not take life—which God has made sacred—except for just cause.
Qur'an 17.33

A man once came before Raba and said to him, "The ruler of my city has ordered me to kill a certain person, and if I refuse he will kill me." Raba told him, "Be killed and do not kill; do you think that your blood is redder than his? Perhaps his is redder than yours."
Talmud, Pesahim 25b (*Judaism*)

All tremble at the rod. All fear death. Comparing others with oneself, one should neither strike nor cause to strike.

All tremble at the rod. Life is dear to all. Comparing others with oneself, one should neither strike nor cause to strike.

Whoever, seeking his own happiness, harms with the rod other pleasure-loving beings, experiences no happiness hereafter.

Whoever, seeking his own happiness, harms not with the rod other pleasure-loving beings, experiences happiness hereafter.
Dhammapada 129-32 (*Buddhism*)

And do not kill yourselves, for verily God has been to you Most Merciful.
Qur'an 4.29

"Surely your blood of your lives will I require" [Genesis 9.5]. This includes suicide, except in a case like that of Saul.
Genesis Rabbah 34.13 (*Judaism*)

A monk who intentionally deprives a human being of his life, or provides the means for suicide, or praises death, or incites one to commit suicide, saying, "Of what use to you is this evil, difficult life? Death is better for you than life"… commits an offense entailing loss of monkhood.
Vinaya Pitaka (*Buddhism*)

Slay not your children, fearing a fall to poverty. We shall provide for them and for you. Truly, the slaying of them is a great sin.
Qur'an 17.31

A bhikkhu who intentionally kills a human being, down to procuring abortion, is no ascetic and no follower of the Fraternity of the Buddha.

Vinaya, Mahavagga 1.78.4 (Buddhism)

When the sacredness of life before birth is attacked, we still stand up and proclaim that no one ever has the authority to destroy unborn life.

Pope John Paul II[8] (Christianity)

Indeed for us murder is forbidden once and for all, so it is not permitted even to destroy what is conceived in the womb. To prohibit the birth of a child is only a faster way to murder; it makes little difference whether one destroys a life already born or prevents it from coming to birth. It is a human being, who is to be a human being, for the whole fruit is already present in the seed.

Tertullian, Apology 9.8 (Christianity)

Teachings of Sun Myung Moon

The preservation of human rights and human dignity must be the measure of all ethics and morality. (168:238, September 21, 1987)

How does the present administration[9] handle the issue of human rights? In North Korea, the regime of Kim Il-Sung has exterminated three million people. Mao Zedong is responsible for the deaths of 150 million people. In Russia during the Bolshevik Revolution seven million lost their lives. *The New York Times* reported that 600,000 people have been killed since the fall of Vietnam... How can we talk about human rights while ignoring communism that tramples on the right to life itself? Which is more important: human rights or the right to life? (91:255, February 23, 1977)

If on the street you met an enemy, a person whom your family hates and even all Americans hate, would it be alright to murder him? How could it be a sin? Yet no matter how vile or detestable that person might be, he has the same cosmic value as you, because he was made by the Creator. Killing him is a crime, a violation of the universal law. (105:92, September 30, 1979)

Why is a human being's physical life so precious? Without it, the cosmos cannot be brought to perfection, and even God cannot attain perfection. Our physical life is so precious... that it cannot be exchanged for the entire universe. This is the meaning of the Bible verse, "For what will it profit a man if he gains the world and forfeits his life?" (91:19, February 13, 1977)

Your most worthy parents need you. Your spouse needs you. Your brothers need you. Your family needs you. The nation needs you. The world needs you. Even the spirit world and the whole cosmos need you. Even God needs you. How can you think that you are unimportant?...

When you say, "No one needs me," you are doing wrong to all of them. You are doing wrong to your parents, your future spouse, your brothers, your family, the nation, the world, heaven and earth, and God. You are violating their love and the law of love.

A person who commits suicide sins in all these ways. So many people commit suicide—how can they do such a thing! You should never even dream of killing yourself. (74:30 November 10, 1974)

Once a baby is conceived, you must not abort it. You never know who that baby could grow up to be: maybe a saint, maybe someone who could save America, maybe even the President of the United States. So how can you destroy it as you wish? What if my mother had exercised her "right to choose" like people do today? I would not have been born.

Therefore, abortion [within a proper marital relationship] is a sin. Each fetus represents the parents' love, life and lineage. It is human; how can anyone consider it merely an animal? What is that cell that forms at conception? It is very much a human being! Within that single cell are human beings' love, life and lineage. Therefore, it represents the parents and has the same value as the parents. The father's love and mother's love are contained within that would-be baby.[10] (230:120, April 26, 1992)

Suppose a husband and wife give birth to a child with a deformity. Do they terminate its life and say, "Well, we can try again"? Is that true love? No, of course it is not. (117:292, April 11, 1982)

4. To Realize One's True Value

Verily the most honored among you in the sight of God is he who is the most righteous.
    Qur'an 49.13

The way to gain a good reputation is to endeavor to be what you desire to appear.
    Socrates, in Xenophon *(Hellenism)*

Not by matted hair, nor by family, nor by birth does one become a brahmin. But in whom there exist both truth and righteousness, pure is he, a brahmin is he.
    Dhammapada 393 *(Buddhism)*

Whose deeds lower him, his pedigree cannot elevate.
    Nahjul Balagha, Saying 21 *(Islam)*

Four are the castes—brahmin, khatri, sudra, and vaishya;
Four the stages of life—
Out of these, whoever on the Lord meditates, is superior.
    Adi Granth, Gaund, M.4, p. 861 *(Sikhism)*

The wise ones who are intent on meditation, who delight in the peace of renunciation, such mindful, perfect Buddhas even the gods hold most dear.
    Dhammapada 181 *(Buddhism)*

Teachings of Sun Myung Moon

We can gauge a person's value by seeing the quality of his or her love. (99:63, July 23, 1978)

Become such men and women of character that God will say He cannot live without you. (*Way of God's Will* 2.2)

When an individual is united with true love, it opens the way to elevate his or her value and dignity to the highest point. This is the state of mind-body unity, where the conscience and the body are resonating continually. Take two tuning forks of the same frequency: when one is struck the other one resonates with it; likewise, when true love strikes the conscience, the body will resonate with it. Such an individual requires no instruction about how to behave. (223:356, November 20, 1991)

Had Adam and Eve not fallen, their bodily desires would not have led them on a path contrary to their mind. Rather, their body would have acted in total obedience to their mind. Because this did not happen, people today cannot attain God's true love nor can they realize true human value. (399:153, December 22, 2002)

The ultimate goal of fallen man is to restore the autonomy, dignity and value of the self, the potential that God gave him as the purpose of creation. (*Way of God's Will* 2.2)

Conscience and Inborn Goodness

THE CONSCIENCE IS A GLEAM OF THE DIVINE WITHIN, prompting us to do good deeds and opposing our inclination to do evil. Buddhism describes this faculty as the "enlightening mind" or "Buddha nature" which can be uncovered through the eye of wisdom. Confucianism regards it as the heart of benevolence; this is illustrated by a well-known passage from Mencius about people's spontaneous reactions to a child falling into a well. Islam likewise regards the human heart as inherently upright, and St. Paul wrote that the conscience allows even those unschooled in religion to distinguish right from wrong.

The conscience operates positively, encouraging self-betterment and the idealistic search for a better society. It also operates negatively, scolding and admonishing us for acting selfishly and hurting others. In this regard, Father Moon speaks of the conscience as a "precious teacher" that knows us better than our parents, our teachers, and even God. The conscience is God-given, enabling us to improve and ultimately realize our full purpose as God intended. It must constantly struggle, however, against the self-centered desires of the body.

It is possible to speak of a corrupted conscience, because although its essence is God-given, upbringing and education can affect its judgment. To indoctrinate the conscience with false judgments of right and wrong is indeed of the worst defilements of the human spirit. Yet there are levels of conscience. The more superficial level of conscience is relative, adhering to a person's concept of truth. Yet at a deeper level is the Original Mind, which maintains a connection to the absolute God. Therefore, someone like Saul of Tarsus, who had persecuted Christians in good conscience, could be awakened to a higher vision of truth and change his direction in life to become St. Paul. This divine quality at the root of the conscience is the basis for Father Moon's optimistic view that all human beings will ultimately be saved.

1. The Original Mind and Heart—Rooted in Goodness

Gentleness and goodness are the roots of humanity.
  Book of Ritual 38.18 (*Confucianism*)

Religion is basically virtue, which is grounded ultimately in the spiritual nature of man.
  Kundakunda, Pravacanasara 7 (*Jainism*)

Behold, the kingdom of God is within you.[11]
  Luke 17.21

When Gentiles who have not the Law do by nature what the Law requires, they are a law to themselves, even though they do not have the Law. They show that what the Law requires is written on their hearts, while their conscience also bears witness and their conflicting thoughts accuse or perhaps excuse them on that day when, according to my gospel, God judges the secrets of men by Christ Jesus.[12]
  Romans 2.14-16

Wabisah ibn Ma`bad said, "I went to see the Messenger of God and he said to me, 'You want to question me on the subject of virtue?' 'Yes,' I replied, and he went on, 'Question your heart.

Virtue is that by which the soul enjoys repose and the heart tranquility. Sin is what introduces trouble into the soul and tumult into man's bosom—and this despite the religious advice which men may give you.' "

40 Hadith of an-Nawawi 27 *(Islam)*

For him who... knows his own mind and sees intuitively his own nature, he is a Hero, a Teacher of gods and men, a Buddha.

Sutra of Hui Neng 1 *(Buddhism)*

Your eye is the lamp of your body; when your eye is sound, your whole body is full of light; but when it is not sound, your body is full of darkness. Therefore be careful lest the light in you be darkness. If then your whole body is full of light, having no part dark, it will be wholly bright, as when a lamp with its rays gives you light.

Luke 11.34-36

The Purpose of the one true God, exalted be His glory, in revealing Himself unto men is to lay bare those gems that lie hidden within the mine of their true and inmost selves.

Gleanings from the Writings of Bahá'u'lláh 132
(Baha'i Faith)

Every being has the Buddha Nature. This is the self. Such a self is, since the very beginning, under cover of innumerable illusions. That is why a man cannot see it. O good man! There was a poor woman who had gold hidden somewhere in her house, but no one knew where it was. But there was a stranger who, by expediency, speaks to the poor woman, "I shall employ you to weed the lawn." The woman answered, "I cannot do it now, but if you show my son where the gold is hidden, I will work for you." The man says, "I know the way; I will show it to your son." The woman replies, "No one in my house, big or small, knows where the gold is hidden. How can you know?" The man then digs out the hidden gold and shows it to the woman. She is glad, and begins to respect him. O good man! The same is the case with a man's Buddha Nature. No one can see it. It is like the gold which the poor woman possessed and yet could not locate. I now let people see the Buddha Nature which they possess, but which was hidden by illusions. The Tathagata shows all beings the storehouse of enlightenment, which is the cask of true gold—their Buddha Nature.

Mahaparinirvana Sutra 214-15:
Parable of the Hidden Treasure *(Buddhism)*

All men have this heart that, when they see another man suffer, they suffer, too... A man looks out; a child is about to fall into a well. No matter who the man is, his heart will flip, flop, and he will feel the child's predicament; and not because he expects to get something out of it from the child's parents, or because he wants praise from his neighbors, associates, or friends, or because he is afraid of a bad name, or anything like that.

From this we can see that it is not human not to have a heart that sympathizes with pain. Likewise not to have a heart that is repelled by vice: that is not human, either. Not to have a heart that is willing to defer: that's not human. And not to have a heart that discriminates between true and false is not human, either.

What is the foundation of natural human feeling for others (*jen*)? The heart that sympathizes with pain. What is the foundation of a commitment to the common good (*i*)? The heart that is repelled by vice. What is the foundation of respect for social and religious forms (*li*)? The heart that is willing to defer. And what is the foundation for a liberal education (*chih*)? The heart that can tell true from false.

People have these four foundations like they have four limbs. A man who says he cannot practice them is calling himself a criminal. A man who says the ruler cannot practice that is calling the ruler a criminal.

Everybody has these four foundations in himself. If these four foundations can be filled in on a broad scale, it will be like a fire starting up, it will be like a spring bursting through. If they can be filled in, it will be enough to create and preserve the world order. Leave them unfilled, it will be impossible for a man to take care of his father and mother.[13]

Mencius II.A.6 *(Confucianism)*

Teachings of Sun Myung Moon

The human conscience is the faculty of mind that represents God. It does not exist for personal benefit, but for the righteousness of Heaven. It always strives for goodness. (219:118, August 28, 1991)

The Buddha said that all beings have a Buddha-mind. What is this Buddha-mind? It refers to the pure, original mind. (33:45; August 2, 1970)

Your attitude should be: "God is the source of my mind. I am God's object partner who strives to move according to God's mind." (162:40, March 22, 1987)

Human morals and ethics should develop on the right path to Heaven, and this is motivated by the conscience. Your conscience is striving to develop toward an ideal world, higher than the world of today. (90:161, December 26, 1976)

As we human beings strive to follow moral laws, there is a mind that tries to protect us from falling into ruin. This mind was with God from the very beginning, before human beings were created. It is called the conscience. The conscience is not a self-made law. When I justify what I do, will my conscience accept my arguments? Will it be convinced by my speech? Although we do not clearly know the source of the conscience, clearly it is not from human beings, but from elsewhere. Our conscience ever discerns whether our lives are public or private. (31:241, June 4, 1970)

All people, in all ages and places, including even the most evil, have an original mind which inclines them to repel evil and seek goodness. People's intellectual understanding of what goodness is and how goodness is achieved has differed according to time, place and individual viewpoint; this has been a source of the conflicts which have made history. Nevertheless, everyone cherishes the same fundamental goal of finding and establishing goodness. Why does the original mind irrepressibly induce people of every age and every place to do what is good? God, the Subject of goodness, created human beings as His good and worthy object partners in order to fulfill the purpose of the good. Despite Satan's crippling efforts, which have rendered fallen human beings incapable of leading a life of total goodness, the original mind remains intact within them and prompts them toward goodness. Hence, the ultimate desire of the ages is to attain a world of goodness. (*Exposition of the Divine Principle*, Eschatology 2.3)

All people have a conscience, something we cannot deny even though we may doubt the existence of God.

If we assume that God exists and that He created human beings, He must have provided a way that creatures and Creator can form a union, that is, to present a common purpose. This required that God place within them a faculty whose action enables His creatures to accord with His intended purpose for them. This original foundation, by which we human beings can unite with God the Absolute Being, is none other than the conscience...

The conscience always acts to push us to a higher level, saying, "Become better!" It urges us to reach for a higher level; it never urges us to sink to a lower level. It acts that we might be better tomorrow than we are today, and better the day after tomorrow than we will be tomorrow. It acts that we might be better next year than we are this year, better when we are in our twenties than we were in our teens, and better during our thirties than we were during our twenties. The conscience by its operation urges us continually to elevate ourselves and make ourselves increasingly value-oriented. (56:137-39, May 14, 1972)

What is the direction of the conscience, and what is its ultimate purpose? It has to be love—true, unchanging love. The essence of the conscience steers us towards love as our ultimate goal. (216:311-12, April 15, 1991)

God loves by investing Himself one hundred percent and more. Something of that nature still remains in the fallen world. It is not paternal love, but maternal love. It remains like a seed fire. If a seed fire is well guarded, it can be used later to kindle another fire. Likewise, salvation is possible only because the seed of God's original nature still remains in us. (199:276, February 20, 1990)

2. Struggling with One's Conscience

Keep your conscience clear.
1 Peter 3.16

You may not see yourself growing up, but you definitely know it when you are sinning.
Akan Proverb (African Traditional Religions)

The mind is said to be twofold:
The pure and also the impure;
Impure—by union with desire;
Pure—from desire completely free.
Maitri Upanishad 6.34 (Hinduism)

And I do call to witness the self-reproaching spirit.
Qur'an 75.2

A certain person has done no lovely deed, has done no profitable deed, has given no shelter to the timid; he has done evil, cruel, wrongful deeds. At the thought, "I have done no lovely deed," he is tormented. At the thought, "I have done evil," he is tormented. These two thoughts sear the conscience.
Itivuttaka 25 (Buddhism)

My conscience hath a thousand several tongues,
And every tongue brings in a several tale,
And every tale condemns me for a villain.
William Shakespeare, Richard III

Every judgment of conscience, be it right or wrong, be it about things evil in themselves or morally indifferent, is obligatory, in such wise that he who acts against his conscience always sins.
St. Thomas Aquinas (Christianity)

If a superior give any order to one who is under him which is against that man's conscience, although he does not obey it yet he shall not be dismissed.
Saint Francis of Assisi, Third Admonition of the Order (Christianity)

To the pure all things are pure, but to the corrupt and unbelieving nothing is pure; their very minds and consciences are corrupted.
Titus 1.15

The glory of a good man is the testimony of a good conscience. Therefore, keep your conscience good and you will always enjoy happiness, for a good conscience can bear a great deal and can bring joy even in the midst of adversity. But an evil conscience is ever restive and fearful.

Thomas à Kempis, *Imitation of Christ* (Christianity)

Is it not the fact that there is in the body a clot of blood which, if it is in good condition, the whole body is, too; and if it is in rotten condition, so too is the whole body? Is not this the heart?

40 Hadith of an-Nawawi 6 (Islam)

I myself had reason for confidence… as to the law a Pharisee, as to zeal a persecutor of the church, as to righteousness under the law blameless. But whatever gain I had I counted as loss for the sake of Christ. Indeed I count everything as loss because of the surpassing worth of knowing Christ Jesus my Lord.

Philippians 3.4-8

Teachings of Sun Myung Moon

As he pursues his life's course, a person must attend his own deep mind. This is an ironclad rule of Heaven. Heaven will punish a person who fails to follow his original mind's order. (4:260, August 8, 1958)

A guilty conscience is evidence that you have broken the heavenly law. (17:36, November 6, 1966)

No one can help me be reconciled with my conscience; it is up to me, to each individual. For instance, if I wronged my brother, I would be ashamed to go near him. Even if he doesn't know that I wronged him, my conscience already knows it. Because I feel pangs of conscience, I keep myself at a distance, feeling all the while that I should go to him and confess. That is how the principle of heaven and earth operates. Due to the Human Fall we were desensitized, but anyone whose sensitivity is keen and sharp already knows it. (400:382, January 11, 2003)

Every human being, throughout his life, has a most precious teacher within himself. Yet we do not treat this teacher well. We mistreat it, trample on it and abuse it. That teacher is the human conscience. Our conscience always gives us helpful words of advice, trying to connect us to true love. Like a parent, our conscience urges us to be good, unselfish people, and guides us to do the Will of God. But within each person there is also a rebel who always goes against the conscience. That rebel is the physical body.

The body tramples and abuses the conscience miserably. Knowing this, how can you continue to side with your body, the enemy of your conscience, as it weakens your character and damages your life?

Your conscience should be your constant internal teacher and parent, leading you to complete unity with the ultimate Parent of humankind, God. Your conscience is the agent of God within you. Do you think you should indulge and go along with your body, the enemy of the conscience? Or should you control and restrain your body and vindicate your conscience? Your body seeks only after carnal desire. It always seeks for comfort, and wants to take advantage of others. To conquer the realm of the body is an awesome responsibility, which every person must undertake. (201:208, April 10, 1990)

God is the great King of wisdom. He did not place the path to perfection in some far off place. Instead, He prepared it in the place that is nearest to us, the place that is most private and safe—your conscience.

Ladies and gentlemen, your conscience is your master. It is your teacher. It stands in the place of your parents. Your conscience is the first to know everything about you. Your conscience knows all your thoughts. It knows before your teacher, your parents or even God knows. Think how much advice your conscience gives you over your lifetime. Day and night, every time you have an evil thought, it scolds you, saying, "Hey you!" It never grows tired as it works constantly to pull you over rivers and mountains. The conscience always stands as the true master, protecting you and trying to help you. Yet, how often have you betrayed your own conscience? What should be done about your body, which has thoroughly mistreated this precious, irreplaceable teacher that the universe bequeathed to you? Do you intend to idle your life away, clinging to your physical body and enslaved by its desires while it continues to brutally trample your conscience? Don't you realize that your conscience was given to you as the representative of your heavenly Parent, to enable you to inherit His original love? (May 1, 2004)

You say that you are people of good character. You are self-satisfied and believe that there is nothing wrong with your conscience. However, your conscience is asleep…

Let's wake up our sleeping conscience. Let's wake up the conscience of the nation that sleeps in ignorance of God's heart. Let's wake up the conscience of humanity around the world that sleeps in ignorance of God's heart. Let's wake up the conscience of people, who cannot avoid their fated encounter with the Last Days, that they might act in obedience to the Will of God who seeks to embrace heaven and earth and build one united world.

Is the religion we follow today capable of awakening humanity's sleeping conscience? Do we have a philosophy that possesses such content? When the conscience is awakened, the shock, determination, and resolve that rush in must be so strong that in an instant it can properly rearrange everything in the world. It has no fear of the sword or of death. Who will dare to stand in the way of the power rising up from our conscience? No one can block it. (10:284, November 6, 1960)

Perfection

SCRIPTURES DESCRIBE THE VIRTUES of a person who is one with the Absolute, who is firmly established in truth, who is without sin or bondage to worldly corruption, and who exhibits the fullness of sanctifying grace. He or she may be called a saint, a sage, a Buddha, or a divine man. This state of perfection is not beyond our reach; it is a goal to be attained, if we only make the effort. Gandhi once said, "Life is an aspiration. Its mission is to strive after perfection, which is self-realization. The ideal must not be lowered because of our weaknesses or imperfections."

The passages in this section describe the excellent qualities of a person who has attained the state of perfection. Three characteristics of perfection in particular stand out: The first is mind-body unity. The saint has dominion over him or herself, having overcome selfish desires and been purified of any feelings of lust, greed or other cravings. As a result, he only wishes to do what is right—in accord with God's will and the dictates of conscience. In Saint Augustine's words, he is one who can "love God and do what you will."

Second, perfection is a state of unity with God. God is the pattern and model for the highest human aspirations. Thus, the saint participates in God's own perfection and comes to embody God's attributes—absoluteness, unchangeability, compassion, righteousness, etc.

Third, perfection means to embody God's true love. Love or compassion is the core of God's being, as expressed in His untiring efforts to save sinful people. Therefore, a man or woman of perfection delights in the well-being of others and selflessly works for their benefit. Saintly love has no partiality, regards no one as an enemy, but always repays evil with good. (See also Chapter 13: *True Love*.)

1. Perfection Begins with Unity of Mind and Body

A novice asked the Buddha, "What is goodness and what is greatness?" The Buddha replied, "To follow the Way and hold to what is true is good. When the will is in conformity with the Way, that is greatness."

Sutra of Forty-two Sections 15 (Buddhism)

None of you truly believes until his inclination is in accordance with what I have brought.

Forty Hadith of an-Nawawi 41 (Islam)

One who is rich in the enlightenment will not indulge in any sinful action, since his conscience is guided by the intellect fully illumined with Truth.

Acarangasutra 1.174 (Jainism)

Whose minds are well perfected in the Factors of Enlightenment, who, without clinging, delight in the giving up of grasping, they, the corruption-free, shining ones, have attained Nibbana even in this world.

Dhammapada 89 (Buddhism)

He whose senses are subdued, like steeds well-trained by a charioteer, he whose pride is destroyed and is free from the corruptions—such a steadfast one even the gods hold dear.

Like the earth, a balanced and well-disciplined person resents not... He is like a pool, unsullied by mud; to such a balanced one, life's wanderings do not arise.

Calm is his mind, calm is his speech, calm is his action, who, rightly knowing, is wholly freed [from defilements], perfectly peaceful and equipoised.

The man who is not credulous but truly understands the Uncreated (*Nibbana*), who has cut off the links, who has put an end to occasion [of good and evil], who has eschewed all desires, he indeed is a supreme man.

Dhammapada 94-97 (Buddhism)

Arjuna: Tell me of those who live established in wisdom, ever aware of the Self, O Krishna. How do they talk? How sit? How move about?

Lord Krishna: They live in wisdom who see themselves in all and all in them, who have renounced every selfish desire and sense craving tormenting the heart.

Neither agitated by grief nor hankering after pleasure, they live free from lust and fear and anger. Established in meditation, they are truly wise. Fettered no more by selfish attachments, they are neither elated by good fortune nor depressed by bad. Such are the seers.

Even as a tortoise draws in its limbs, the wise can draw in their senses at will. Aspirants abstain from sense pleasures, but they still crave for them. These cravings all disappear when they see the highest goal. Even of those who tread the path, the stormy senses can sweep off the mind. They live in wisdom who subdue their senses and keep their minds ever absorbed in Me.

Bhagavad-Gita 2.54-61 (Hinduism)

Abu Huraira reported God's Messenger as saying, "The believers whose faith is most perfect are those who have the best character."

Hadith of Abu Dawud and Darimi (Islam)

The monk who has destroyed the cankers, lived the life, done what was to be done, laid down the burden, won the goal, burst the bonds of becoming, and is freed by the fullness of gnosis, cannot transgress nine standards: a monk in whom the cankers are destroyed cannot deliberately take the life of any living thing; cannot, with intention to steal, take what is not given; cannot indulge in carnal intercourse; cannot intentionally tell a lie; cannot enjoy pleasures from memories as of yore when a householder; a monk in whom the cankers are destroyed cannot go astray through desire; cannot go astray through hate; cannot go astray through delusion; cannot go astray through fear.

Anguttara Nikaya 4.370 (*Buddhism*)

He who has achieved it cannot either be drawn into friendship or repelled,
Cannot be benefited, cannot be harmed,
Cannot either be raised or humbled,
And for that reason is highest of all creatures under heaven.

Tao Te Ching 56 (*Taoism*)

Teachings of Sun Myung Moon

"Before you desire to have dominion over the universe, you should first have dominion over yourself": This is the first article in the life of faith. To attain self-perfection you should have dominion over your self. In other words, you should reach the state of self-mastery, controlling your body, with no conflict or opposition between your mind and body. (37:122, December 23, 1970)

The structure of a human being consists of dual aspects: mind and body. The mind relates to the vertical standard, while the body relates to the horizontal standard. Had human beings attained God's ideal standard at the beginning, always receiving God's love, then whenever the bell of God's love would ring in their vertical mind, their bodies on the earth plane would resonate with it and feel everything. Whenever the mind-like spirit self resonated vertically with true love, the body on the horizontal plane would naturally respond.

When you strike an "A" on a tuning fork, it sends waves of a certain frequency through space, and when they match the frequency of another object, that object sends its waves back. This is called resonance. Likewise, there is resonance between the mind and the body at the frequency of love. When love strikes the mind or spirit self, the body responds. Had human beings not fallen, it would have been this way. By what standard would resonance occur? The resonant frequency has to be true love. (177:216, May 20, 1988)

When your mind and body become one, God will be with you. This is a fundamental principle. Why would God be with you at that point? Because that is where love is. Love begins when mind and body become one. For love to flow, subject and object are necessary. Therefore, God is with the person who has established mind-body unity. Then his or her body becomes God's temple.

What sort of place is God's temple? It is a place of Sabbath rest. In what can God rest? Love. God's temple is the place to rest in the love of God.

The highest human aspiration is to abide in the place of love—the world of heart. It is like a fountain: there is no end to love no matter how much pours out. Why does love have no end? Because God dwells there. (91:78, January 30, 1977)

God is like pure gold; there is nothing false about God. What should we do to be united with God? We should not be false people. That means our mind and body should be united, just as God's [internal nature and external form are united]. That is the meaning of Matthew 5:48: "You, therefore, must be perfect, as your heavenly Father is perfect." (91:321, March 1, 1977)

Each member of the family first needs to perfect his or her individual character. This requires removing the fallen nature, which has been passed down through the generations since the Human Fall. In other words, each person must be victorious in the struggle between the mind and the body. Then the world of harmony will bear fruit in that individual's perfected character—a state of one heart, one mind and one thought. Fallen nature, which causes jealousy, envy, greed, hatred and all other evils, will never again take root in a person who has achieved that state. (March 23, 2004)

The purpose of religion is to cultivate people of character who live by the laws of the world of the heart and all the principles of the cosmos, and thereby govern the emotions of life. (6:349, May 24, 1959)

Unless you can perfectly love yourself, you cannot perfectly love God. (22:97-98, January 26, 1969)

2. Perfection Is Unity with God

You, therefore, must be perfect, as your heavenly Father is perfect.

Matthew 5.48

No one born of God commits sin; for God's nature abides in him, and he cannot sin because he is born of God.

1 John 3.9

Sincerity [Absolute Truth] is the Way of Heaven; the attainment of Sincerity is the Way of man. He who possesses Sincerity achieves what is right without effort, understands without thinking, and naturally and easily is centered on the Way. He is a sage.

Doctrine of the Mean 20.18 *(Confucianism)*

Yea, come unto Christ, and be perfected in him, and deny yourselves of all ungodliness; and if you shall deny yourselves of all ungodliness; and love God with all your might, mind, and strength, then is His grace sufficient for you, that by His grace you may be perfect in Christ; and if by the grace of God you are perfect in Christ, you can in no way deny the power of God.

Book of Mormon, Moroni 10.32-33
(Latter-day Saints)

Blessed is the man who trusts in the LORD,
whose trust is the LORD.
He is like a tree planted by water,
that sends out its roots by the stream,
and does not fear when heat comes,
for its leaves remain green,
and is not anxious in the year of drought,
for it does not cease to bear fruit.

Jeremiah 17.7-8

The Master is a tree of contentment and forbearance;
Righteousness its flower, enlightenment the fruit.
This tree by joy in God keeps ever fresh and green;
By practice of meditation is it ripened.
With joy in the Lord is it consumed,
By such as dispense the supreme charity of selfless action.

Adi Granth, Var Majh, M.1, p. 147 *(Sikhism)*

By fullness of leadership,
the Wise Lord shall grant powerful communion
Of perfection and Immortality,
of Right, Dominion and Good Thought—
To him who is a sworn friend;
to him by spirit and by actions!

Clear are these to the man of insight,
as to a knowing one by mind.
He upholds good Dominion,
and Right by words and by actions.
He, O Lord of Wisdom,
shall be Thy most helping associate!

Avesta, Yasna 31.21-22 (Zoroastrianism)

Lao Tan said, "I was letting my mind wander in the beginning of things."

"What does this mean?" asked Confucius.

Lao Tan said, "It means to attain Perfect Beauty and wander in Perfect Happiness. He who attains Perfect Beauty and wanders in Perfect Happiness may be called the Perfect Man."

Chuang Tzu 21 (Taoism)

The Supreme Soul (*Paramatman*) is free from birth, old age and death; he is supreme, pure and devoid of the eight karmas; he possesses infinite knowledge, intuition, bliss and potency; he is indivisible, indestructible and inexhaustible. He transcends the senses and is supreme; he is free from obstructions, merit, demerit and rebirth; he is eternal, steady and independent.

Kundakunda, Niyamasara 176-77 (Jainism)

Teachings of Sun Myung Moon

Jesus taught his disciples, "You, therefore, must be perfect, as your heavenly Father is perfect." (Matt. 5.48) According to the Principle of Creation, a person who has realized the purpose of creation does not commit sin, because he is in full harmony with God and possesses a divine nature. With respect to the purpose of creation, such a person is perfect as Heavenly Father is perfect. Jesus gave this teaching to his disciples with the hope that they could be restored as people who had realized the purpose of creation and become citizens of the Kingdom…

What will people be like once they have been restored as those who have realized the purpose of creation and become perfect as Heavenly Father is perfect? Such people are fully attuned to God and experience God's heart within their innermost self. They possess a divine nature and live their life with God, inseparable from Him. (*Exposition of the Divine Principle*, Messiah 1.1)

For a person to realize his or her true nature, he or she must have a relationship with God, the cause of everything—life and death, fortune and misfortune. Without a relationship with God, a true pattern cannot be formed within the self. To become true,[14] we must be centered upon God. People can realize their true selves only when God has established the foundation to lead them and reign over all aspects of their lives…

God is the origin of everything true. Only in God can we become true. Should God leave us, we cannot remain true. There then comes into existence something untrue—the origin of evil.

People cannot comprehend their true nature by themselves. Fallen people are in no position to judge whether they are true; rather the truth of our being should determine us. Therefore, we should always be obedient to our true self. We should prize it and follow it. (24:315, September 14, 1969)

We can truly say that we know God only when we experience the reality of His existence in our daily life through our five senses. That is, we should know His real being through experience. Then we will naturally be able to sense what God's will is from moment to moment, and we will be able to act in accordance with His will in every matter. In that state of perfection, even though we sometimes may feel an urge to sin, we cannot do it. Then, God will be able to take on the physical form of human beings who are equipped with the character and qualities of lords of creation. Thus we will enable the incorporeal God to exercise dominion over all things on earth—the corporeal world—as well as over the spirit world. This is why the highest priority and most important element in human life is to know God with certainty…

Once we come to know God with certainty, and know not just the concept of the spirit world but also its reality, our life can move forward as smoothly as a car on an expressway. Just as the car reaches its destination safely as long as the driver follows the rules of the road, keeps his hands on the steering wheel and doesn't fall asleep, so too we only need to live in line with the direction from our conscience, which is given by Heaven. This is where our mind and body become one. This is where the flower of human perfection blooms and bears fruit. (May 1, 2004)

What is a true human being? Playing with God, resting with God, sleeping with God and living with God: whoever wishes to do all these with God is the supreme, true human being. God is looking for such true human beings. By the same token, we human beings are searching for what is true, and for a true world. A world where everyone lives with God is a world of true love and true happiness. (60:284, August 18, 1972)

3. Perfection Is to Love as God Loves

You have heard that it was said, "You shall love your neighbor and hate your enemy." But I say to you, Love your enemies and pray for those who persecute you, so that you may be sons of your Father who is in heaven; for he makes his sun rise on the evil and on the good, and sends rain on the just and on the unjust. For if you love those who love you, what reward have you? Do not even the tax collectors do the same? And if you salute only your brethren, what more are you doing than others? Do not even the Gentiles do the same? You, therefore, must be perfect, as your heavenly Father is perfect.

Matthew 5.43-48

God says, "Resemble me; just as I repay good for evil so do you also repay good for evil."

Exodus Rabbah 26.2 (Judaism)

Beloved, let us love one another; for love is of God, and he who loves is born of God and knows God. He who does not love does not know God; for God is love… God is love, and he who abides in love abides in God, and God abides in him.

1 John 4.7-8, 16

That devotee who looks upon friend and foe with equal regard, who is not buoyed up by praise nor cast down by blame, alike in heat and cold, pleasure and pain, free from selfish attachments, the same in honor and dishonor, quiet, ever full, in harmony everywhere, firm in faith—such a one is dear to me.

Bhagavad-Gita 12.18-19 (Hinduism)

The fruits of the Spirit are love, joy, peace, patience, kindness, goodness, faithfulness, gentleness, self-control; against such there is no law.

Galatians 5.23

Be universal in your love. You will see the universe to be the picture of your own being. Complete and total perfection will come about only when we feel that our perfection is not perfection as long as the rest of humanity remains imperfect. If we call ourselves children of God, then others are also children of God. If we do not share with them what little we have, then what right have we to call them our brothers? They may be traveling a few miles behind us, or they may be fast asleep. But they must reach the Goal before perfect perfection can dawn on earth.

Sri Chinmoy *(Hinduism)*

Teachings of Sun Myung Moon

Love is the standard for perfect character. Character is perfected through the infinite and absolute love of God. (33:79, August 9, 1970)

To pioneer this path, Jesus emphasized love as never before in history. He taught that we must overcome every difficult situation with patience. He stressed that we must be more faithful to God's Will than sinners are committed to doing evil. These are the fundamental points of what Christians call the nine fruits of the Spirit. From a life of love arises joy, happiness, and peace. From patience arises mercy and goodness. From a life of faithfulness arises humility and gentleness.

Jesus emphasized the love of heaven, the patience of heaven, and the faithfulness of heaven to remove the evil elements from human beings dwelling in the fallen world. Through this practical philosophy, we can be elevated to the heavenly way of life. Nevertheless, does Christ's love exist in your hearts today? (2:345, August 4, 1957)

What makes God true?[15] God likes both good and bad people on earth. Don't even condemned criminals cry out, "Oh God, have mercy on me! I love you!" just before their execution? Why would a condemned man pledge to God with a good and sincere heart, hoping for a new start? Why does he yearn to grasp God fully, trust Him, try to be with Him, and share with Him his feelings and difficulties more than he would with his parents or brothers and sisters? It is because God is true.

A true person, then, loves not only those whom he likes, but also the enemies who are trying to kill him. He should be a person whom we can trust fully, with whom we want to share all our problems and through whom we can wish for everything.

Is a person who hates someone a true person or a false person? Definitely, he is a false person. Then, are most people in this world true people or false people? They are false people.

To be a true person, you must be true in all dimensions. If you members love the people who love me and hate the people who hate me, are you good members or bad members? You are bad members.

Therefore, I am teaching you to love those who hate you. If you love them, sooner or later they will come to like you. If you return good three times for every time someone does you wrong, eventually that person will bow his head. Try it yourself and see if I am right or not. Everyone has a conscience. (39:302-04, January 16, 1971)

Is God's love so deeply rooted in your minds that you cannot pull out no matter how hard you try? Can you say, "I am completely bound by God's love; I cannot do whatever my body wants to do. Since God's love is rooted so deeply in my body, I cannot live any way I like. I cannot live without centering on God's love. When I eat, I eat with God's love. Whatever I do, both my mind and body are centered on God's love"? Is it that way for you? (140:24-25, February 1, 1986)

❖

Joy

THE SEARCH FOR HAPPINESS is basic to human life, and to the religious quest as well. Union with Ultimate Reality can bring transcendental joy. It is a state variously characterized as bliss (*ananda*) Nirvana, or even the mystic marriage with the divine Lover. In the monotheistic faiths, God created human beings for joy. The unity of God and His creatures makes that joy complete.

The section opens with passages that describe heavenly joy, when the human heart and God's heart beat in unison. Second are passages that contrast the greatness of heavenly joy with the paltry pleasures of the senses. This insight should not be overlooked in discussions of ethics; George Washington once asserted that there is "an indissoluble union between virtue and happiness." We conclude with passages describing the synergy between a joyous life and heavenly joy. A cheerful and optimistic attitude, accompanied by efforts to spread happiness to others, can attract the joy of the Holy Spirit. This can be experienced in the mystic connection between conjugal love and divine love. (See Chapter 19: *Conjugal Love*).

1. Heavenly Joy

Thou dost show me the path of life;
in Thy presence there is fullness of joy,
in Thy right hand are pleasures for evermore.

Psalm 16.11

I created you human beings because I desired to see you lead a joyous life.

Ofudesaki 14.25 (Tenrikyo)

Happiness is spiritual, born of Truth and Love. It is unselfish; therefore it cannot exist alone, but requires all mankind to share it.

Science and Health, 57 (Christian Science)

No eye has seen, nor ear heard,
nor the heart of man conceived,
what God has prepared for those who love
    Him.

1 Corinthians 2.9

No person knows what delights of the eye are kept hidden for them—as a reward for their good deeds.

Qur'an 32.17

I am the Tathagata,
The Most Honored among men;
I appear in the world

Like unto a great cloud,
To pour enrichment on all
Parched living beings,
To free them from their misery
To attain the joy of peace,
Joy of the present world,
And joy of Nirvana.

Lotus Sutra 5 (Buddhism)

The soul which is free from the defect of karma gets to the highest point of the universe, knows all and perceives all, and obtains the transcendental bliss everlasting.

Kundakunda, Pancastikaya 170 (Jainism)

Without doubt, in the remembrance of God do hearts find satisfaction.

Qur'an 13.28

Mother mine! Bliss have I attained in union
    with the Divine Master:
Spontaneously has union with the Divine
    Master come about—
In my mind resounds joyous music.
Fairies of the family of jewel harmony have
    descended to sing holy songs;
Sing all ye the Lord's song, who have lodged it
    in heart!

Says Nanak, Bliss have I attained on union with the Divine Master.
   Adi Granth, Ramkali, Anandu, M.3, p. 917 *(Sikhism)*

And may the sovereign Good be ours!
According as one desires bliss may one receive bliss

Through Thy most far-seeing Spirit, O Lord,
The wonders of the Good Mind which Thou wilt give as righteousness,
With the joy of long life all the days!
   Avesta, Yasna 43.2 *(Zoroastrianism)*

Teachings of Sun Myung Moon

Joy begins in the heart of God, and it is fulfilled in human beings. The heart of the invisible God is manifested in the hearts of visible human beings. (27:29, November 15, 1969)

Why are human beings born? It is to experience love with God and with all creation. Conversely, because human beings exist, God can love and be loved, and love can fill the universe. (81:334, December 29, 1975)

What is God's purpose of creation? Is it analogous to what we human beings aspire? God created out of the desire to rejoice and be happy. What brings God joy? Money? His creatures? Certainly it is not the material things that people like to own. God created heaven and earth so that He could experience joy through love.
   Then, what do all creatures desire more than anything else? Because God's purpose of creation is to experience joy through love, all creatures likewise seek a relationship of love with God, to experience joy. Accordingly, all creatures interact with one another in order to be linked with God's love. (114:63, May 16, 1981)

The meeting point of the human heart and God's heart is the starting point of happiness. (*Way of God's Will* 1.8)

When people feel good, they want to be with their parents, siblings, and relatives so they can share their joy. Happiness is eternal, and what is eternal is of the heart.
   The center of the universe is the parent-child relationship, that is, between God the Father and each one of us as His sons and daughters. The ultimate purpose of human life is to find our Father, form an unbreakable bond with Him, and experience joy. (12:104, December 16, 1962)

When God sees you loving His creatures, He says, "Wonderful! You are doing something that I cannot do"; and He loves you. God will want to show His love to you. Maybe He will stretch out His arms and hug you from behind, whispering, "Yes, you are great!" This happens. God will hug you out of joy.
   Suppose that while God is embracing you from behind, you turn around and hug Him. Would God say, "You shouldn't do that"? What do you think? What if you give God a long, long bear hug? God would say, "It's good! I like it! I like it!" God cannot but like it. He and everyone, everything, will like it. You would be in ecstasy.
   After that experience, what if you just lie around aimlessly, smitten with love-sickness? Would God be displeased? No, He would burst into laughter, saying, "Ah, My love must be really good! Ha, Ha, Ha!" Then He would say, "Amen."…

What might happen the next time you meet God? God is as smitten with you as you are with Him, so you can do anything together; it doesn't matter. You and God might hug each other, or ride around on each other's back, or wrestle on the floor one on top of the other. If you took God out somewhere, He might attach Himself to your hip like a tail. Wouldn't that be the ultimate state of bliss? God, humanity and all things of creation want to experience it. (111:170, February 15, 1981)

2. Divine Joy Surpassing the Pleasures of the Senses

The kingdom of God is not food and drink but righteousness and peace and joy in the Holy Spirit.

    Romans 14.17

The Infinite is the source of joy. There is no joy in the finite. Only in the Infinite is there joy. Ask to know the Infinite.

    Chandogya Upanishad 7.23 (Hinduism)

God has promised to believers… beautiful mansions in Gardens of everlasting bliss. But the greatest bliss is the good pleasure of God: that is the supreme felicity.

    Qur'an 9.72

The bliss of lusts and heaven-world equal not
One sixteenth of the bliss of craving's ending.

    Udana 11 (Buddhism)

Having tasted the flavor of seclusion and the flavor of pacifying the passions, he becomes free from anguish and stain, imbibing the taste of the joy of the Dhamma.

    Dhammapada 205 (Buddhism)

Anybody can enjoy the pleasures of the body, a slave no less than the noblest of mankind; but no one allows a slave any measure of happiness, any more than a life of his own. Therefore happiness does not consist in pastimes and amusements, but in activities in accordance with virtue.

    Aristotle, Nicomachean Ethics 10.6 (Hellenism)

When totally free from outer contacts
a man finds happiness in himself,
He is fully trained in God's discipline
and reaches unending bliss.
The experiences we owe to our sense of touch
are only sources of unpleasantness.
They have a beginning and an end.
A wise man takes no pleasure in them.

    Bhagavad-Gita 5.21-22 (Hinduism)

The Self-existent is the essence of all felicity… Who could live, who could breathe, if that blissful Self dwelt not within the lotus of the heart? He it is that gives joy.

    Of what is the nature of joy? Consider the lot of a young man, noble, well-read, intelligent, strong, healthy, with all the wealth of the world at his command. Assume that he is happy, and measure his joy as one unit.

    One hundred times that joy is one unit of the gandharvas; but no less joy than gandharvas has the seer to whom the Self has been revealed, and who is without craving.

    One hundred times the joy of the gandharvas is one unit of the joy of celestial gandharvas [angels]… One hundred times the joy of the celestial gandharvas is one unit of the joy of the pitris… joy of the devas… of Indra… of Brihaspati… of Prajapati… of Brahma, but no less joy than Brahma has the seer to whom the Self has been revealed, and who is without craving.

    It is written: He who knows the joy of Brahman, which words cannot express and the mind cannot reach, is free from fear. He is not distressed by the thought, "Why did I not do what is right? Why did I do what is wrong?" He who knows the joy of Brahman, knowing both good and evil, transcends them both.

    Taittiriya Upanishad 2.7-9 (Hinduism)

Teachings of Sun Myung Moon

What is the way to live in joy and ecstasy? Most people's eyes are too dim to see, their ears are too dull to hear, their noses are too numb to smell, their tongue too numb to taste, and their limbs too heavy to move. What is the way to live in unity—my eyes, my ears, and all my sense organs all knit together with my nervous system, all united into one? What is the shining way that will not only satisfy me in my personal life, but will also satisfy my family, clan, country, world, and even God? (95:181, November 13, 1977)

People living ordinary, self-centered lives lack stimulation. But if your life is filled with God's grace, you will feel newness in your spirit every day and experience your surroundings as ever new and fresh. Every morning there is something new; every evening there is something new. When God's grace is rolling in like waves, you can feel the mystery in three dimensions. Anyone who experiences life like this is a happy person. (30:134, March 21, 1970)

When you become a child of God and dwell in His love, your joy has no limit. You breathe in and out with the entire universe. We are meant to be intoxicated by the love of God. Can the artificial intoxication provided by drugs or alcohol even remotely compare? In the realm of God's love, every need is satisfied. All your body's forty trillion cells are dancing together. Your eyes and ears, your hands, and all the parts of your body revel in the rapture of joy. Nothing else can ever match it. God's love is real, and it is our highest aspiration to pursue this love. We must have it. (69:79-80, October 20, 1973)

> The fact that we can rejoice this day is something to be grateful for.
> But we must understand:
> If we cannot link today's joy with the joy of tomorrow,
> today's joy becomes for us as an enemy,
> a condition for sorrow, difficulty and lamentation.
> Joy, we know, is not only good,
> and sorrow is not only bad;
> the question is our investment of inner effort
> to link joy and sorrow to the accomplishment of our purpose,
> and how much our joy and sorrow connect
> with the values of God's Will. (43:10, April 18, 1971)

3. Leading a Joyous Life

The Holy Spirit rests on him only who has a joyous heart.

Jerusalem Talmud, Sukkot 5.1 (Judaism)

Let us live happily, without hate amongst those who hate. Let us dwell unhating amidst hateful men.

Let us live happily, in good health amongst those who are sick. Let us dwell in good health amidst ailing men.

Let us live happily, without yearning for sensual pleasures amongst those who yearn for them. Let us dwell without yearning amidst those who yearn.

Let us live happily, we who have no impediments.
We shall subsist on joy even as the radiant gods.

Dhammapada 197-200 (Buddhism)

Awake, O north wind,
and come, O south wind!
Blow upon my garden,
let its fragrance be wafted abroad.
Let my beloved come to his garden,
and eat its choicest fruits.

I come to my garden, my sister, my bride,
I gather my myrrh with my spice,
I eat my honeycomb with my honey,
I drink my wine with my milk.

Eat, O friends, and drink:
drink deeply, O lovers!

Song of Solomon 4:16-5:1

Teachings of Sun Myung Moon

God comes and extends His blessing to whatever thing you do with pleasure. (308:214, January 5, 1999)

If two-thirds of your life of seventy or eighty years was sorrowful, to compensate for the sorrow of those years, why don't you make the remainder of your life a joyful time centering on God? Live your life as you would in the Kingdom of God. The Kingdom of God is where one gives, and gives again. God is giving. Parents give to their children. The parental heart is such that even after giving, it wants to give and give again when there is something better to give. (34:141, August 30, 1970)

Why does a man need a woman, and a woman need a man? It is so they can resonate with God's love. It is to reach a state of ecstasy where they exclaim, "Wow, it is wonderful!" They are too happy even to eat or sleep. A man and woman need each other because only in the fullness of conjugal love can they resonate in full consonance with God's love. (102:21, November 19, 1978)

The horizontal love between a husband and wife blossoms with God's ideal love, and the fragrance of their love resonates throughout the universe even as God adds His love to their love. This is the perfection of the parent-child relationship between God and human beings.

    The heavenly Parent sings of His children's happiness, their hopes and everything about them. Together the Parent and His son and daughter sing of love.

    It does not end there. To that precious gift, the love they possess, God adds a third dimension of love. Then their universe expands like a balloon when air is blown into it. Their world used to be flat, but now it is big enough to hold all the created beings in the world with room to spare. It materializes with the power of their love, permeating the whole. (101:35, October 28, 1978)

CHAPTER 4

God's Creation and Human Creativity

The Sanctity of Nature

NATURE IS SACRED; ALL CREATURES GREAT AND SMALL are endowed with God's life and a modicum of God's spirit. This insight, shared by all religious traditions, is the basis of reverence and respect for all living things. In the Abrahamic religions, God created every creature according to His purpose and imbued with His loving heart. Therefore, every existence, down to a grain of sand or a blade of grass, contains elements of the divine. Furthermore, nature exhibits a marvelous balance. Hence, nature is a reliable source of poetic and religious inspiration. By contemplating nature in its original purity, we can touch God.

As sensitive people recognize, all creatures possess some level of conscious awareness. The diverse species of animals and plants form tribes and nations like the races and nations of man. They are our brothers and sisters, supported by the same Mother Earth that lent us the elements that constitute our bodies and sustain our life. When thinking of all the things nature provides, we have much to be thankful for. Not only that; as Father Moon teaches, each creature, a precious living masterpiece of God, exists for me—for my enjoyment, inspiration and instruction, to love and care for.

1. Divinity within the Natural World

The earth is the LORD's and the fullness
   thereof,
the world and those who dwell therein.
                              Psalm 24.1

Even in a single leaf of a tree, or a tender blade of grass, the awe-inspiring Deity manifests itself.
                    Urabe-no-Kanekuni (Shinto)

This earth is a garden,
the Lord its gardener,
cherishing all, none neglected.
     Adi Granth, Mahj Ashtpadi 1, M.3, p. 118 (Sikhism)

My energy enters the earth,
Sustaining all that lives:
I became the moon,
Giver of water and sap,
To feed the plants and trees.
               Bhagavad-Gita 15.13 (Hinduism)

The solid sky,
the cloudy sky,
the good sky,
the straight sky.

The earth produces herbs.
The herbs cause us to live.
They cause long life.
They cause us to be happy.

The good life,
may it prevail with the air.
May it increase.
May it be straight to the end.

Sweet Medicine's earth is good.
Sweet Medicine's earth is completed.
Sweet Medicine's earth follows the eternal ways.
Sweet Medicine's earth is washed and flows.

Cheyenne Song (Native American Religion)

Thou makest springs gush forth in the valleys;
they flow between the hills,
they give drink to every beast of the field;
the wild asses quench their thirst.
By them the birds of the air have their habitation;
they sing among the branches.
From thy lofty abode thou waterest the mountains;
the earth is satisfied with the fruit of thy work.

Thou dost cause the grass to grow for the cattle,
and plants for man to cultivate,
that he may bring forth food from the earth,
and wine to gladden the heart of man,
oil to make his face shine,
and bread to strengthen man's heart.
The trees of the LORD are watered abundantly,
the cedars of Lebanon which he planted.
In them the birds build their nests...
O LORD, how manifold are thy works!

Psalm 104.10-24

The stream crosses the path, the path crosses the stream:
Which of them is the elder?
Did we not cut the path to go and meet this stream?
The stream had its origin long, long ago.
It had its origin in the Creator.
He created things pure, pure, *tano*.

Ashanti Verse (African Traditional Religion)

Teachings of Sun Myung Moon

God's hand has touched every small blade of grass that grows in the field. Every growing tree received the touch of God's infinite heart. (6:338, June 28, 1959)

Everything in the universe arose from the heart of God. The universe in its entirety is the result of God's creative idea, whose motivation is divine love. A poet who senses this is a truly great poet. If on seeing a single leaf shaking in the wind, he senses the cosmic Heart and expresses it, then he would be a poet for the entire universe.

When viewed while in a mystical state, a single grain of sand contains within itself the principles of the universe. A single atom contains the boundless harmony of the universe.

All things that exist, though maybe not aware of it, are resultant beings that formed through the action of complex forces. The smallest molecules, atoms, and even subatomic particles do not exist unconsciously, but contain a certain consciousness and purpose. Thus, all things that exist have come into being through God's loving hand, and necessarily possess a bond of heart with God. (9:168, May 8, 1960)

Did the Absolute Being create all the creatures in heaven and earth with a heart of sorrow? No. He created with a heart of joy. God rejoiced as He watched the creation unfold. How joyful was He? If we knew, we could begin to recognize the supreme value of each one of God's creatures. Yet, people do not know how much God values His creation. We do not know, because we are still searching for God. (27:223, December 14, 1969)

People love nature; they may prefer nature to other people. Nature, because it still carries its original God-given nature, is much purer than human beings. Even people who live in great houses and enjoy all the conveniences of civilized living want to vacation at the beach or camp in the mountains. Why? Their original form is looking for some comparable companion, and nature comes closest. (107:311-12, June 8, 1980)

Human civilization is inconceivable apart from nature. People display their power and authority, yet without nature nothing is possible.

Nature makes our life valuable; it is absolutely necessary for our life. Therefore, if we do not feel the heart that flows in nature, we cannot enjoy true happiness. Nor can we be close to God and partake of His glory.

The next time you look at a flower or a patch of grass, see it from God's point of view, reflecting God's heart. Whenever you look at an insect, a bird or an animal, a feeling should arise within you that connects you with God. (6:340-41, May 28, 1959)

> Father! May all creatures of heaven and earth eternally offer hymns of praise
> to Thee, the Lord of the universe.
> Every created being is related to Thee.
> Owing to Thee, all things of heaven and earth,
> molded through Thy heart,
> raise up Thy glory,
> reveal Thy holiness and profundity,
> and display Thine infinite value. (20:243, July 7, 1968)

2. Alive with Consciousness, Endowed with Purpose

No creature is there crawling on the earth,
no bird flying with its wings,
but they are nations like yourselves.

Qur'an 6.38

I say: Just as the consciousness of a man born blind, deaf and dumb is not manifest, likewise the consciousness of beings of earth-body [e.g., minerals] is also not manifest. Nevertheless such a man experiences pain when struck or cut by a weapon, and so also do the beings of earth-body. Likewise for water-beings... fire-beings... plants... animals... air beings: their consciousness and experiences of pain are actual, though not manifest.

Acarangasutra 1.28-161 (Jainism)

If these [my disciples] were silent, the very stones would cry out.

Luke 19.40

Every part of this soil is sacred in the estimation of my people. Every hillside, every valley, every plain and grove, has been hallowed by some sad or happy event in days long vanished.

Even the rocks, which seem to be dumb and dead as the swelter in the sun along the silent shore, thrill with memories of stirring events connected with the lives of my people, and the very dust upon which you now stand responds more lovingly to their footsteps than yours, because it is rich with the blood of our ancestors

Chief Seattle (Native American Religion)

The explanation of the goodness of creation is the goodness of God... Nevertheless, certain heretics remain unconvinced, on the ground that many things in creation are unsuitable and even harmful to that poor and fragile mortality of the flesh, which of course is no more than the just penalty for sin. The heretics mention, for example, fire, cold, wild beasts, and things like that, without considering how wonderful such things are in themselves and in their proper place and how beautifully they fit into the total pattern of the universe, making their peculiar contributions to the commonweal of cosmic beauty. Nor have they observed how valuable they are even to us if only we use them well and wisely. Consider, for instance, poison. It is deadly when improperly used, but when properly applied it turns out to be a health-giving medicine.

Saint Augustine, City of God 11.22 *(Christianity)*

Teachings of Sun Myung Moon

Human beings themselves are a part of nature. Perfect nature is sacred. (90:24, December 10, 1976)

When a stamen of a flower kisses its pistil, it exclaims, "Ah, it feels so good!" Do you think it feels such a sensation or not? The sensation of male and female for each other is the best sensation, composed of all five senses linked together.

Insects may be invisibly small, yet they have eyes, ears, noses, mouths and hands, don't they? Look carefully at the lawn; so many insects are there! With their ears they hear; with their mouths they taste; with their reproductive organs they copulate and produce offspring—in this they are like humans, only the class is different.

When insects reproduce and produce offspring so tiny you cannot see them, will the parents kill them, or protect and love them? [They protect them.] When they make love, do they do it with great pleasure? Or do they say, "I dislike it"? Which? In this they are just like humans!

There is no denying that God gave all creatures the sensibility to love through their five senses. With respect to love, God created male and female to have equal value. Love is the common denominator, equalizing the low-level world of insects with the high-level human world. Whether men and women, or male and female creatures, all share this God-given common denominator. (217:306, June 13, 1991)

The human body, though consisting of matter, fully responds physiologically to the emotion, intellect and will of the human mind. This demonstrates that matter has within itself elements that resonate with emotion, intellect and will—elements which constitute the internal nature of matter. This is the reason all things in the universe respond to human emotion, intellect and will, albeit to different degrees. We become intoxicated with the beauty of the natural world and experience the rapture of mystical union. We experience this because we are the center of the internal natures of all things in the natural world. (*Exposition of the Divine Principle*, Creation 2.3.3)

God created every species of animal and insect to be preserved, that none becomes extinct. The food chain is balanced. While larger creatures eat smaller creatures, the larger ones do not reproduce as often. Many beasts of prey bear offspring only once every two years. For lions and tigers it is two years and eight months, almost three years. In contrast, rabbits bring forth their young every three months. By having many offspring, they provide food for the larger beasts as well as continue their own species.

Adam and Eve create on behalf of God, and all things were created for the growth and perfection of Adam and Eve. They may sacrifice their lives, but they are assisting in the perfection of Adam and Eve's bodies. For this reason, people are permitted to eat anything, whether plant or animal.

Greek philosophy looks at the world as a constant struggle, every creature an enemy to one another. On the contrary, they are not enemies. Such ideas arose only as a result of the Human Fall. The Marxist dialectic as described in *Das Kapital* states that development comes about through struggle, but that is not true.

Even the vilest germs disappear when faced with their natural enemies. Do you understand what I mean by natural enemy? A tiger is the natural enemy of a dog. When a dog sees a tiger, it freezes and trembles and crawls back into its dwelling to hide. Natural enemies balance each other; thus nature takes care of every circumstance that comes along. (May 10, 2003)

3. Mother Earth and Her Children

And God said, "Let the earth bring forth vegetation, plants yielding seed, and fruit trees bearing fruit in which is their seed, each according to its kind, upon the earth." And it was so. The earth brought forth vegetation, plants yielding seed, and fruit trees bearing fruit in which is their seed, each according to its kind. And God saw that it was good.

Genesis 1.11-12

Perhaps if we are lucky,
Our earth mother
Will wrap herself in a fourfold robe of white meal,
Full of frost flowers;
A floor of ice will spread over the world,
The forests because of the cold will lean to one side,
Their arms will break beneath the weight of snow.
When the days are thus,
The flesh of our earth mother will crack with cold.
Then in the spring when she is replete with living waters,
Our mothers,
All different kinds of corn,
In their earth mother we shall lay to rest.
With their earth mother's living waters
They will be made into new beings;
Into their sun father's daylight
They will come out standing;
Yonder to all directions
They will stretch out their hands calling for rain.
Then with their fresh waters

The rain makers will pass us on our roads.
Clasping their young ones [the ears of corn] in their arms,
They will rear their children.
Gathering them into our houses,
Following these toward whom our thoughts bend,
With our thoughts following them,
Thus we shall always live.

Zuni Song (*Native American Religions*)

Set me, O Earth, amidst thy center and thy navel,
and vitalizing forces that emanate from thy body.
Purify us from all sides.
Earth is my Mother; her son am I;
and Heaven my Father: may he fill us with plenty…

Whatever I dig from thee, Earth,
may that have quick growth again.
O purifier, may we not injure thy vitals or thy heart…

As a horse scatters dust, so did Earth, since she was born,
scatter the people who dwelt on the land,
and she joyously sped on, the world's protectress,
supporter of forest trees and plants.

What I [Earth] speak, I speak with sweetness;
what I look at endears itself to me;
and I am fiery and impetuous: others who fly at me with wrath
I smite down.

Peaceful, sweet-smelling, gracious, filled with milk,
and bearing nectar in her breast,
may Earth give with the milk her blessings to me.

Thou art the vessel, the Mother of the people,
the fulfiller of wishes, far-extending.
Whatever is wanting in thee is filled
by Prajapati, first-born of Eternal Order [the first god].

May those born of thee, O Earth,
be, for our welfare, free from sickness and waste.
Wakeful through a long life, we shall become bearers of tribute for thee.

Earth, my Mother! set me securely with bliss
in full accord with Heaven. Wise One,
uphold me in grace and splendor.

Atharva Veda 12.1 (Hinduism)

Most High, omnipotent, good Lord,
All praise, glory, honor, and blessing are yours.
To you alone, Most High, do they belong,
And no one is worthy to pronounce your name.

Be praised, my Lord, with all your creatures,
Especially Sir Brother Sun,
Who brings the day, and you give light to us through him.
How handsome he is, how radiant, with great splendor!
Of you, Most High, he bears the likeness.

Be praised, my Lord, for Sister Moon and the Stars.
In heaven you have formed them, bright, and precious, and beautiful.

Be praised, my Lord, for Brother Wind,
And for Air, for Cloud, and Clear, and all weather.
By which you give your creatures nourishment.

Be praised, my Lord, for Sister Water,
She is very useful, and humble, and precious, and pure.

Be praised, my Lord, for Brother Fire,
By whom you light up the night.
How handsome he is, how happy, how powerful and strong!

Be praised, my Lord, for our Sister, Mother Earth.
Who nourishes and governs us,
And produces various fruits with many-colored flowers and herbs.

St. Francis of Assisi, Canticle of the Sun (Christianity)

Teachings of Sun Myung Moon

When we were created, the universe lent us its elements to constitute our bodies. This means the universe gave birth to us. It is our first parent. Our fathers and mothers are our second parents, the parents who brought us into the world. God, who gave each of us a spirit, is our third parent. Thus, human beings have three sets of parents. (106:84, December 9, 1979)

People in ancient times had a close relationship with nature. Then the natural world and the spirit world were close to human beings—not distant and foreign as they are to people living in modern times. When people entered a grove of giant trees, they looked at them reverently and thought, "For thousands of years these trees have been here; through countless cycles of quickening in spring and dying in autumn they remain unchanged; their shade makes a pleasant environment for all creatures." Observing them, they recognized that they were deficient in many aspects, and so they worshipped tall trees, great rocks and high mountains.

They saw tall persimmon trees, thick with foliage in the summer and bare in the winter. With the arrival of spring their branches sprouted with new life: first buds, then blossoms, and finally delicious and fragrant fruit. They marveled at this, and sensed that those trees were better than they.

Where is the fragrance in human existence? Do humans give off a fragrance that beautifies their surroundings, attracting birds and insects to nest in their branches? No, compared to nature, man is humbled and recognizes his inadequacy. (November 4, 1990)

When we look at the creation, we feel a religious emotion welling up from deep in our hearts and naturally bow down before it. Gazing up at the constellations of the night sky or exploring nature around us, we experience awesome and mysterious feelings surging up from deep in our hearts. This state is the starting point of religion. While gazing at living things and the phenomena of nature, we can sing songs that arise from the precious world of the heart within.

Playing nature's music, displaying nature's art and reciting nature's poetry, all living things resonate in our hearts. Then we can relate with God, who rules the heavenly bodies. Experience the feeling that you are intimately connected to everything; then you can enter a state of the heart to rightly appreciate them. You enter a mystical state in which you can feel everything in its reality.

God created human beings to connect with all His creation, which He had made inseparably interrelated with Himself. Externally we appear to be extremely small and insignificant, but when we behold nature from this understanding, we can feel a human being's true dignity and value. (5:344-45, March 8, 1959)

I once asked God, "For whom didst Thou create this universe?" God replied, "Sun Myung Moon, I created it for you." As God is my God, so the universe is my universe. These are not only words; I feel it to my bones.

In springtime, I behold the beauty of the universe in the beautiful flowers and fragrances, and in the butterflies and bees flying about. These creatures show us God's love and God's precious value; they display the harmony of His angels. I feel connected to everything. A bird chirps; it is asking me to feed it. It wants me to help it find a mate.

I am very sensitive to the world of nature. When butterflies are fluttering together in pairs, or when a male and female bird sing together for joy, I see it as a lesson that men and women should live together with even greater beauty… and happiness than these.

When the birds and flowers stimulate me with their joy and love, I would in turn stimulate God in heaven with my songs of joy and love. I may be penniless and my clothes may be rags, yet I never feel poor. I think, "The sky is my blanket, the flowing brook is my water faucet, and the plants growing nearby are my food." When you feel that the house of God is your house, how can you feel poor?

When I see a small stream, I feel behind it the dignity of the great ocean. When I see a blade of grass, I think its beauty is greater than the greatest masterpieces in the world's museums. A painting may cost millions of dollars, but it is merely man-made. It cannot compare with this small creation of God. Once I caught a bird and kissed it, saying, "You are more precious than anything in the world." (106:137, December 23, 1979)

Reverence for Life

PASSAGES IN THIS SECTION PRESCRIBE the ethic proper to reverence for life. Taoist and Buddhist texts remark on the artificiality of the human world and call us to return to the innocence and purity of nature. Living in nature is purifying and conducive to the spiritual life, in contrast to the dark and dirty environment of the city. For anyone who spends time in nature, reverence for the natural world and respect for all its creatures is not something forced, but flows naturally from a loving heart. Then there is the doctrine of *ahimsa*, non-violence towards all living beings, which arose on the Indian subcontinent. Vegetarianism is often motivated by this ethic. Moreover, among nature's creatures, none gives more completely and without complaint than the cow, which is rightly revered by Hindus and many native peoples.

Father Moon's teachings touch on many of these points, but especially emphasize love of nature, which he regards as the starting point for environmental ethics. However, he offers an interesting dissent from vegetarianism, based upon the concept that creatures of lower order seek to come closer to God's love through being eaten and absorbed by creatures of higher order. Ideally they would strive to be nourishment for humans, who stand at the summit of creation because they embody God's love. Nevertheless, people who do not practice true love are unworthy to consume their food.

1. Care and Reverence for All Living Things

As a mother with her own life guards the life of her own child, let all-embracing thoughts for all that lives be thine.

            Khuddaka Patha, Metta Sutta *(Buddhism)*

The mode of living that is founded upon total harmlessness towards all creatures, or upon a minimum of such harm, is the highest morality.

            Mahabharata, Shantiparva 262.5-6 *(Hinduism)*

The Prophet said, "There is neither harm nor cause for harm in Islam."

            Majma' al-Zawa'd 4.6536 *(Islam)*

One should not injure, subjugate, enslave, torture, or kill any animal, living being, organism, or sentient being. This doctrine of nonviolence is immaculate, immutable, and eternal. Just as suffering is painful to you, in the same way it is painful, disquieting, and terrifying to all animals, living beings, organisms, and sentient beings.

            Acarangasutra 4.25-26 *(Jainism)*

A certain priest had been killed by the bite of a snake, and when they announced the matter to the Blessed One, he said, "Surely now, O priests, that priest never suffused the four royal families of snakes with his friendliness. For if that priest had suffused the four royal families of the snakes with his friendliness, that priest would not have been killed by the bite of a snake…

> Creatures without feet have my love,
> And likewise those that have two feet,
> And those that have four feet I love,
> And those, too, that have many feet.

            Vinaya Pitaka, Cullavagga 5.6 *(Buddhism)*

The moral person accepts as being good: to preserve life, to promote life, to raise to its highest value life which is capable of development; and as being evil: to destroy life, to injure life, to repress life which is capable of development. This is the absolute fundamental principle of the moral.

A man is ethical only when life, as such, is sacred… that of plants and animals as well as that of his fellow man, and when he devotes himself helpfully to all life that is in need of help.

            Albert Schweitzer

Rear them, but do not lay claim to them;
Control them, but never lean upon them,
Be their steward, but do not manage them.
This is called the Mysterious Power.

Tao Te Ching 51 (Taoism)

A horse or a cow has four feet: that is Nature. Put a halter around the horse's head or put a rope through the cow's nose: that is man. Therefore it is said, "Do not let man destroy Nature. Do not let cleverness destroy destiny [the natural order]."

Chuang Tzu 17 (Taoism)

In the land of Yamato there are many
    mountains;
ascending to the heaven of Mount Kagu,
I gaze down on the country, and see
smoke rising here and there over the land,
sea gulls floating here and there over the sea.

A fine country is this,
the island of dragonflies, this
province of Yamato.[1]

Man'yoshu I (Shinto)

On the eastern side of this Himalaya, the king of mountains, are green-flowing streams, having their source in slight and gentle mountain slopes; blue, white, and the hundred-leafed, the white lily and the tree of paradise, in a region overrun and beautified with all manner of trees and flowing shrubs and creepers, resounding with the cries of swans, ducks, and geese, inhabited by troops of monks and ascetics.[2]

Jataka (Buddhism)

Come back, O Tigers, to the woods again,
and let it not be leveled with the plain.
For without you, the axe will lay it low.
You, without it, forever homeless go.

Khuddaka Patha (Buddhism)

Teachings of Sun Myung Moon

Unless you love nature and human beings, you cannot love God. (70:182, February 9, 1974)

Those who cannot love nature cannot love human beings, the owners of nature. We should love nature and other people more than ourselves. (375:20, April 13, 2002)

You love your wife, but do you love the air, sun, light, water and vegetation from which your wife is benefiting?...Unless you love nature, you cannot love yourself. If you eat the things of nature while mistreating nature, you may get sick. (385:200-01, July 11, 2002)

Nature is the closest thing to our body. We should fulfill the desire of nature, which languishes in lamentation...
    If you love the natural environment of your hometown, you can know how to love your body. If you love your body, you can know how to love your own heart and mind. If you love your own heart and mind, you can know how to love God. Do so and you will not perish. (14:102, June 20, 1964)

We should love the ocean. Yet how can we, when dangers abound and so much about the ocean is unknown? By searching it out and learning its secrets, our love for the ocean will grow and grow. Likewise, there are many dangers lurking in the mountains. Yet we want to explore the mountains and brave their challenges. Then our hearts will grow deeper and wider. (391:218, August 26, 2002)

Only those who love the mountains can worship what is high. Confucius, Buddha, Jesus, and all the prophets loved the mountains... Indeed, many people treading the path of God's providence received comfort from nature. (14:102, June 20, 1964)

New York City and the Washington D.C. metropolitan areas are truly dark, living hells. It is better to live on an island where you have to travel three miles[3] before meeting another soul, and if you walk all day, you might see ten people at most. If you live in such a place, perhaps the eye of your original mind will open. Even in a rural area where you are with nature for 80 percent of your day and with people only 20 percent of the time, it is not easy to keep a balance.

    I recommend that city dwellers spend time in the wilderness. We must resolve the problems of air and water pollution; otherwise, how can humanity survive even 300 more years?

    Today we can enjoy a civilized life even in a rural area. With the Internet and the telephone, even if you were to live on top of a 7000-meter-high peak in the Rocky Mountains, you could still reach everywhere in the world. I am going to the jungles of South America. Although there are many mosquitoes, there is clear air, clean water and bright sunshine. Sometimes I go to an island in the Pacific Ocean, where the air is good and the water is clear. I go where the environment is good and there is no pollution, so I can converse with nature. When I am with nature, I am close to God. (339:164, December 10, 2000)

2. The Sacred Cow

The cows have come and brought us good
    fortune,
may they stay in the stall and be pleased with us;
may they live here, mothers of calves,
    many-colored,
and yield milk for Indra on many dawns...

They are not lost, nor do robbers injure them, nor
the unfriendly frighten, nor wish to assail them;
the master of cattle lives together long
with these, and worships the gods and offers
    gifts.

The charger, whirling up dust, does not reach
    them,
they never take their way to the slaughtering
    stool,
the cows of the worshipping man roam about
over the widespread pastures, free from all
    danger.

To me the cows are Bhaga, they are Indra,
they [their milk] are a portion of the first-
    poured Soma.
These that are cows are Indra, O people!
the Indra I long for with heart and spirit.

Ye cows, you fatten the emaciated,
and you make the unlovely look beautiful,
make our house happy, you with pleasant
    lowings,
your power is glorified in our assemblies.[4]

    Rig Veda 6.28 *(Hinduism)*

Behold this buffalo, O Grandfather, which You
    have given us.
He is the chief of all four-leggeds upon our
    Sacred Mother.
From him the people live and with him they
    walk the sacred path.

    Sioux Prayer *(Native American Religion)*

Teachings of Sun Myung Moon

When I was a boy living in the country, I used to hate to feed the cows. The cows know when it is lunchtime. But I didn't want to stop playing, so I said to myself, "Cows, wait 30 minutes," and then continued playing for another hour or two. The cows waited for me, wondering, "Where is our master, the one who was supposed to bring us in?" If I had been a cow whose master came very late, I would have gotten angry and become violent. Yet when I arrived, the cows just looked at me without saying a word. Then I thought, "Oh cows, you are great! I'm sorry." That happened many times.

I then realized, "Cows are better than me," and I said to them, "Now that I know that you have an aspect greater than me, I will feed you a great deal and atone for my shortcomings." I kept feeding them until after sunset. The cows continued to eat because their master was feeding them.

Like this, I learned many things from cows. Cows sometimes appear great and kingly as they lie in the burning sunlight on a midsummer's day, shedding sweat and looking over the remote mountains, meditating calmly.

This is why people all over the world like to eat cow meat, not the meat of dogs or tigers. In those days toothbrushes were made of cow bone. Every part of the cow was utilized. Nothing was discarded; even their manure was used as fertilizer. Therefore everything about a cow is good. (109:40-41, October 26, 1980)

3. Vegetarianism

This is the quintessence of wisdom: not to kill anything. Know this to be the legitimate conclusion from the principle of reciprocity with regard to non-killing. He should cease to injure living beings whether they move or not, on high, below, and on earth. For this has been called the Nirvana, which consists in peace…

A true monk should not accept such food and drink as has been especially prepared for him involving the slaughter of living beings. He should not partake of a meal which contains but a particle of forbidden food: this is the Law of him who is rich in control. Whatever he suspects, he may not eat. A man who guards his soul and subdues his senses, should never assent to anybody killing living beings.

Sutrakritanga 1.11.10-16 *(Jainism)*

Without doing injury to living beings, meat cannot be had anywhere; and the killing of living beings is not conducive to heaven; hence eating of meat should be avoided.

Laws of Manu 5.48 *(Hinduism)*

If one is trying to practice meditation and is still eating meat, he would be like a man closing his ears and shouting loudly and then asserting that he heard nothing… Pure and earnest monks, when walking a narrow path, never so much as tread on the growing grass beside the path. How can a monk, who hopes to become a deliverer of others, himself be living on the flesh of other sentient beings? Pure and earnest monks never wear clothing made of silk, nor boots made of leather, for it involves the taking of life. Neither do they indulge in eating milk or cheese, because thereby they are depriving the young animals of what rightfully belongs to them.

Surangama Sutra *(Buddhism)*

Teachings of Sun Myung Moon

Animals and vegetables are like an orchestra of love, feeding the universe. When human beings eat them, they are eating the fruits of love. If at mealtime you eat them with tearful eyes and a loving heart, they will say, "Thank you. Because you eat me and assimilate me into your flesh and blood, I am being transformed into elements with which to love God. Please eat me. It is my honor."

When you are eating beef, you should think, "This piece of meat has come to me as the fruit of love, from a cow that was raised from a calf by a loving, caring mother." Eat it with gratitude, making sure that you are aligned with God's essential love. Then, you will not get sick. (217:307-08, June 12, 1991)

Where do the animals and plants come from that comprise your meals? Someone had to ruthlessly cut down various plants. Then you chew them up with your teeth and swallow them. The vegetables in your salad bowl will not protest, however, because they know the universal law and think that they are there to serve a greater purpose. With that attitude, they can thank you for eating them so that you can serve the public purpose.

There is a harmony of purpose here. The food on your plate has a certain appreciation of what you live for and is willing to serve your body. That is the only way there can be harmony between you and your food. Otherwise, your food would hate you for eating it and resent it when you laugh in enjoyment. The key point is that your food accepts you only because it knows you are living for the public purpose. Food will resent the laughter of a greedy person who wants to eat it.

If you are not living for a public purpose, then sometimes your food will stage a demonstration against you inside your stomach. Then you get sick, and in some cases even die. (105:94-95, September 30, 1979)

The theory that lower beings sacrifice themselves in striving to unite with a higher existence seems to correspond to the law of the jungle that the strong devour the weak. Then, is it a sin for people to slaughter cows and pigs and eat them? It can be, unless they eat those animals in order to live for the sake of God and His love. In that case, it is certainly in accordance with the law of existence. Everything will condone their actions, even the animals they slaughtered. (124:320, March 1, 1983)

Plants absorb minerals and animals eat plants. When a lower creature is eaten by a higher creature, it is elevated to a higher realm of existence. Then, by providing nourishment to human beings, plants and animals can reach the very nerve cells that can love God. That is the highest ideal for a plant or animal. All things are seeking God's love.

By the same token, human beings should be willing and able to sacrifice themselves for the sake of God. The power of love strives to sacrifice. If the love continues to grow, it eventually reaches God's love.

A couple loving each other with such a concept is the universe's treasure. The entire universe protects them, heaven and earth protect them, and all things protect them. Therefore, we human beings should also learn how to protect the universe. (201:123, March 27, 1990)

Nature as Teacher

NATURE HAS MUCH TO TEACH US. From ants industriously storing food to birds sweetly calling for their mates, observing the ways of nature's creatures provides lessons about the basic morality of life. Cultivating the earth and caring for animals teaches about patience, sacrifice, and God's dependable grace when the harvest yields its abundance. Father Moon teaches that through plants and animals God provided even the earliest humans with sufficient instruction to live a life of love and value.

But ask the beasts, and they will teach you;
the birds of the air, and they will tell you;
or the plants of the earth, and they will teach
    you;
and the fish of the sea will declare to you.
Who among all these does not know
that the hand of the LORD has done this?
Job 12.7-9

After the sacred volumes of God and the Scriptures, study, in the second place, that great volume of the works and the creatures of God.
Francis Bacon[5]

Have you considered the soil you till?
Do you yourselves sow it, or are We the
    Sowers?
Did We will, We would make it broken orts,
    and you will remain bitterly jesting—
"We are debt-loaded; nay, we have been
    robbed."

Have you considered the water you drink?
Did you send it down from the clouds, or did
    We send it?
Did We will, We would make it bitter; so why
    are you not thankful?

Have you considered the fire you kindle?
Did you make its timber to grow, or did We
    make it?
We ourselves made it for a reminder,
and a boon to the desert-dwellers.
Qur'an 56.63-73

Truly, truly, I say to you, unless a grain of wheat falls into the earth and dies, it remains alone; but if it dies, it bears much fruit.
John 12.24

Let us know, let us press on to know the LORD;
his going forth is sure as the dawn;
he will come to us as the showers,
as the spring rains that water the earth.
Hosea 6.3

Teachings of Sun Myung Moon

Human beings experience interest and curiosity when observing nature. From its creatures we learn about the nature of love. Observing the insects and animals, we see that they all live in pairs. In this respect, nature is a museum where God prepared exhibits to teach human beings, God's object partners of love, about the ideal of relationships. (137:212, January 3, 1986)

All creatures love one another. Animals, insects, plants and minerals all love one another. They sing, dance, fly and crawl for their mates. Watch them and learn what they do. Adam and Eve were educated in the museum of nature, a living textbook…

    Adam and Eve watched male and female animals kissing each other; they saw and learned. Nature is a natural source of our education. (134:194, July 20, 1985)

We can learn by watching the birds loving each other, building their nests to lay their eggs, and feeding their young. We have to do more than birds for the sake of our own children, even hundreds of times more. Male and female insects mate with each other and bear their young. Some even risk their lives to raise them. This is how they teach us. (229:287, April 13, 1992)

The salmon has a truly amazing lesson for human beings. It loves once and dies. It becomes food to nourish its offspring. What a wonderful example of a creature that gives up its life for the sake of love! (132:81, May 20, 1984)

I discovered 80 percent of the Divine Principle from nature. (374:235, April 10, 2002)

Trees and grass are the best of all nature's teaching materials. The seeds that are sown in spring grow, blossom and bear fruit, thus paying back the farmer for his labor. Then, they die away, yet the next year, they propagate more branches and bear more fruits for the harvest. Thus, they teach us the way to grow and prosper. (386:298, July 18, 2002)

In my village, I used to watch flocks of migratory birds come and go with the seasons. People who live in a big city like Seoul may not be familiar with them. Not experiencing the ebb and flow of nature, they lack in the area of emotion. Without the opportunity to experience the mystery and beauty of nature, their heart does not fully develop.

When the season turned and beautiful birds flew around, I would spy on them, observing how they laid their eggs and hatched their chicks. It was not unusual for me to spend a week observing a nest. (137:223-24, January 3, 1986)

Do birds recognize national borders? Do they need a visa when they migrate? Would a hurricane stop in the Gulf of Mexico because it didn't have a visa to enter the United States? Is the weather constrained by American law? It is amazing when you think of it—ants and lizards can cross the Mexican border as often as they please, but human beings cannot cross the border without a visa! Must American ants and Mexican ants get government authorization to mate? Animals do not care about national sovereignties, but people's lives are complicated with such things. (106:138, December 23, 1979)

Microcosm and Macrocosm

A HUMAN BEING IS A MICROCOSM of the universe, encapsulating in him or herself the essences of all things. Conversely, the entire universe resembles a human being in macrocosm. The world's scriptures express this insight in both mythological and philosophical language.

As a microcosm, linked to all space and time, a human being has the foundation to know, use, and enjoy all things. Of all creatures, humans have the widest scope of thought and action, encompassing all things, knowing and appreciating all things, guiding and prospering all things, and transcending all things. Nevertheless, as Father Moon teaches, being a microcosm also brings with it the responsibility to love the universe and uphold the universe.

What is the source of the correspondence between macrocosm and microcosm? The Upanishads and other mystical texts describe a primordial Person—Purusha, Metatron—a cosmic Man which pre-existed the creation and gave it shape. Father Moon speaks of a pre-existing human "prototype" in the mind of God. From that starting point, it was inevitable that all the elements of nature would recombine in human beings, when they arose. He goes on to describe the spirit world as shaped like a gigantic Person.

All that the Holy One created in the world He created in man.

Talmud, Abot de Rabbi Nathan 31 (*Judaism*)

The whole of existence arises in me,
In me arises the threefold world,
By me pervaded is this all,
Of naught else does this world consist.

Hevajra Tantra 8.41 (*Buddhism*)

The human form is built into the world structure; indeed, even the cosmos.

Hildegard of Bingen, Scivias (*Christianity*)

One who knows the inner self knows the external world as well. One who knows the external world knows the inner self as well.

Acarangasutra 1.147 (*Jainism*)

Man is the product of the attributes of Heaven and Earth, by the interaction of the dual forces of nature, the union of the animal and intelligent souls, and the finest subtle matter of the five elements...[6]

The five elements in their movements alternately displace and exhaust one another. Each one of them, in the revolving course of the twelve months of the four seasons, comes to be in its turn the fundamental one for the time.

The five notes of harmony, with their six upper musical accords and twelve pitch-tubes, come each, in their revolutions among themselves, to be the first note of the scale.

The five flavors, with the six condiments and twelve articles of diet, come each one, in their revolutions in the course of the year, to give its character to the food.

The five colors, with the six elegant figures which they form on the two robes, come each one, in their revolutions among themselves, to give the character of the dress that is worn.

Therefore Man is the heart and mind of Heaven and Earth, and the visible embodiment of the five elements. He lives in the enjoyment of all flavors, the discriminating of all notes of harmony, and the enrobing of all colors.

Book of Ritual 7.3.1-7 (*Confucianism*)

Consider a man's body: his head rises up and is round and resembles the shape of heaven. His hair resembles the stars and constellations. His ears and eyes, quick in their senses, resemble the sun and the moon. The breathing of his nostrils and mouth resembles the wind. The penetrating knowledge of his mind resembles the spiritual intelligence [of Heaven].

Tung Chung-Shu, Luxuriant Gems of the Spring and Autumn Annals 56 (*Confucianism*)

In the beginning the Self alone was here—no other thing that blinks the eye at all. He thought, "What if I were to emanate worlds?"

He emanated these worlds, water, rays of light, death, the waters. Water is up there beyond the sky; the sky supports it. The rays of light are the atmosphere; death the earth; what is underneath, the waters.

He thought again, "Here now are these worlds. What if I were to emanate guardians?" He raised a Man (*Purusha*) up from the water and gave him a form. [7]

He brooded over him; when He had finished brooding over him, a mouth broke open on him the likeness of an egg. From the mouth came speech and from speech Fire.

Nostrils broke open, from the nostrils came breath, from breath the Wind.

Eyes broke open, from the eyes came sight, from sight the Sun.

Ears broke open, from the ears came hearing, from hearing the Points of the Compass.

Skin broke out, from skin grew hairs, from the hairs plants and trees.

A heart broke out, from the heart came mind, from the mind the Moon.

A navel broke open, from the navel came the out-breath, from the out-breath Death.

A phallus broke forth, from the phallus came semen, from semen Water...

Those deities [the macrocosmic beings], Fire and the rest, after they had been sent forth, fell into the great ocean. Besieged with hunger and thirst, they begged, "Allow us a place in which we may rest and take food."

He led a cow towards them. They said, "This is not enough." He led a horse towards them. They said, "This is not enough." He led man towards them. Then they said, "Well done, indeed." Therefore man is well done. He said to them, "Enter the man, each according to his place."

Then Fire, having become speech, entered the mouth; the Wind, having become breath, entered the nostrils; the Sun, having become sight, entered the eyes; the regions, having become hearing, entered the ears; the plants and trees, having become hairs, entered the skin; the Moon, having become mind, entered the heart; Death, having become out-breathing, entered the navel; Water, having become semen, entered the phallus...

The Self considered, "How could these guardians exist without Me?... If, without Me, speech is uttered, breath is drawn, eye sees, ear hears, skin feels, mind thinks, sex organs procreate, then what am I?" Whereupon, opening the center of the skull, He entered. The door by which He entered is called the door of bliss.[8]

Aitareya Upanishad 1.1-3.12 (*Hinduism*)

Teachings of Sun Myung Moon

A human being is a small universe, the microcosm of the great universe of God's creation. God, the Source of the great universe, is also the source of our energy. As small individual universes, each of us stands in the presence of the great universe and receives its energy into our heart. Thus, we are connected to a source of unending power, and as its counterpart we are endowed with cosmic value. (121:193, October 27, 1982)

As human beings are a microcosm of the universe, the body represents the earth while the mind and spirit represent heaven. (8:78, November 8, 1959)

Up and down, front and rear, right and left: everything is related to me. Furthermore, these relationships are not temporary, but are linked to the entire course of my life. I stem from a line of ancestors stretching back to the beginning of time, and I am linked to descendants a thousand generations into the future. We have to think that we stand on the altar of all these connections.

If one day I am shattered into pieces, all those heavenly relationships will also be shattered into pieces. All relationships in the family, the tribe and the world will likewise be shattered. Such is the significance of being a microcosm, representing heaven and earth.[9] (8:10-11, October 25, 1959)

Look at our hands. Each finger has three knuckles [symbolizing the three stages of growth]. Each arm has three sections: upper arm, forearm and hand. The whole body is composed of three parts: head, torso and legs. Make a fist like an infant does, with the thumb inside. The thumb symbolizes

God, the center of the universe. The four fingers symbolize the four compass directions and four seasons. The twelve knuckles, three on each of the four fingers, symbolize the twelve months.

To strongly make a point, you make a fist and shake it in the air. It is like shaking the whole universe. To strike something with your fist means that you are striking it as a representative of the universe. From this, we can see that human beings are the counterparts of the Lord who created the universe.

These are just a few of the reasons each human being is a microcosm. Although a human body is very small, it contains everything in the universe. The circulatory system is like the trunk of a tree; the heart is like its root and lungs are like leaves. Our body is indeed a microcosm, representing all things of the universe. (54:96, March 20, 1972)

We are born to resonate with the beat of the universe in all its rotations and revolutions. Ocean waves strike the shore, and my heart beats in time. The wind sighs serenely, and my heart feels serene. A flower releases a pleasing fragrance; it stirs a fragrance in my heart and I feel enraptured. (104:123, April 22, 1979)

You are the planet Earth in miniature, a universe in miniature. Your body is composed of all the Earth's elements. Who, then, created you? The universe loaned you all the elements that make up your body. The universe gave you birth and made you; hence you should regard the universe as your first parent.

It is amazing! You contain all the elements of the universe. Furthermore, you are mobile, a universe that can move about, whereas the cosmic universe is stationary. Because you move and act, you can govern the universe. (105:106-07, September 30, 1979)

If you could see the entire spirit world, it would look like a gigantic Person. As this huge person unites with God, its Subject Partner, then the spirit world and physical world will intermingle with each other. Then, when God runs, the earth will also run. When God laughs, the earth will also laugh.

Each of us can become a center of the universe. What does this mean? Consider the tiny cells in your finger. Each one of those cells communicates with your entire body. Although your body is huge in comparison to those cells, their functioning is vital for the body; in that sense they are equal to the whole body. Do you understand? I am talking about what it means to the center of the universe. Each of us relates to the universal body as one cell, yet we can be qualified to be its center.

Blood circulates throughout your whole body, from the head down to the soles of your feet. When that blood that went to the feet comes to the head, can the head say, "Don't come near me"? In the same way, as we circulate through the entire universe, there cannot be any discrimination between black, white and yellow people. The parts of the body are variously colored. Are brown eyes prejudiced against black hair? Do white nails say to yellow skin, "You are of a different kind"?[10] Just so, if you could go to the spirit world, you would see that all people constitute the body of one Person. Saints and holy men may perform the role of the eyes or the ears, but even though they have important roles, they are still only components of that one macrocosmic Person.

Hell in the spirit world is like an infected wound in the body. Do you think God wants hell to exist for eternity? If you had a wound, what would you do? You would draw out the pus and clean it up. In the same way God wants to clean up and eliminate hell. (91:280, February 27, 1977)

When heaven and earth are in harmony, there is mutual affection among all subject and object partners throughout the cosmos. All are linked to the human family, which is the nucleus of cosmos.

Men are larger and stronger, but women have love. The sun is large, but it cannot neglect the earth. There is mutual give and take everywhere, from which arises joy and all the perfections of heaven and earth. Thus we can see the larger significance of love between a man and a woman: it is a microcosm of the solar system and an encapsulation of the animal and plant kingdoms. It is the epitome of the pair system by which all things exist. The animal, plant and mineral kingdoms are all based on the pair system. God set up all male-female pairs to be represented by this one nucleus—human conjugal love. What, then, would happen if this center were in conflict?

You would like to be the center of the cosmos, right? Do animals have this desire? Does the solar system? No; it is evident that humans are the only beings who have this aspiration. (216:157, March 10, 1991)

The Lord of Creation

ALTHOUGH HUMAN BEINGS ARE BUT A PART OF THE NATURAL WORLD, we occupy a unique position as lords of creation. In the Bible, Adam and Eve were granted the blessing of dominion over all things, and the Qur'an accords to each human being the status of God's "vicegerent." This means also that God created the natural world for our benefit, as nature provides us with everything we need to live and thrive. Nevertheless, the blessing of dominion is not divine permission to pollute the earth and create artificial environments at nature's expense. In the agricultural societies where this mandate was first given, human creativity was seen as essentially in harmony with nature's ebb and flow. We are truly lords of creation when we practice love for all things and use our creativity to enhance nature's abundance even as we adapt it to our use.

The basis of humankind's sovereignty over nature is not a matter of size or strength. On that scale of things we are but infinitesimal specks on a planet that is itself but a speck in the infinite reaches of the universe. Rather, it is due to our unique spiritual endowment. Humans seek after God; they seek to better themselves and aspire to a better world. This makes us different in kind from animals. In our awareness of and intimacy with the Creator of the universe, we humans are potentially more valuable than the entire world of creation.

Do we deserve this honor? As Father Moon teaches, since we receive the Creator's abundant love, we should, in turn, love the creation on God's behalf. Then we become the bridge between God and the natural world. God loves His creatures through us, and through us the entire natural world is perfected.

1. Human Beings Are Given Dominion over All Things

I will create a vicegerent on earth.

Qur'an 2.30

And God blessed them, and God said to them, "Be fruitful and multiply, and fill the earth and subdue it; and have dominion over the fish of the sea and over the birds of the air and over every living thing that moves upon the earth."

Genesis 1.28

Do you not see that God has subjected to your use all things in the heavens and on earth, and has made His bounties flow to you in exceeding measure, both seen and unseen?

Qur'an 31.20

When I look at thy heavens, the work of thy fingers,
the moon and the stars which thou hast established;

What is man that Thou art mindful of him,
and the son of man that thou dost care for
him?
Yet thou hast made him little less than God,
and dost crown him with glory and honor.

Psalm 8.3-5

God is He who created the heavens and the earth, and sends down rain from the skies, and with it brings forth fruits to feed you; it is He who made the ships subject to you, that they may sail through the sea by His command; and the rivers He has made subject to you. And He made subject to you the sun and the moon, both diligently pursuing their courses; and the night and the day He has made subject to you. And He gives you of all that you ask for. But if you count the favors of God, never will you be able to number them. Verily, man is given up to injustice and ingratitude.

Qur'an 14.32-34

Out of the ground the LORD God formed every beast of the field and every bird of the air, and brought them to the man to see what he would call them; and whatever the man called every living creature, that was its name.

Genesis 2.19

Teachings of Sun Myung Moon

God, the Creator, created human beings as the lords of all things. (323:165, June 1, 2000)

The ideal world is a world that reflects God and fulfills God's purpose of creation. Hence, human beings ever seek a harmonious and peaceful life filled with God's love, and to improve their environment by continually creating new things. Creativity does not mean merely production, but rather all manner of creative actions such as originating new ideas, planning, improving, and producing.

Humans have come to reflect God's creativity through outstanding scientific progress, but so far have not learned His love. Therefore, this world is still filled with sorrow, pain, and distress. (65:259, November 26, 1972)

Who is enlightened? He can embrace a tree and, marveling at its value, exclaims "Oh, God! I bow before Thy greatness that is disclosed in this tree."… On seeing nature's incredible variety, he recognizes the exquisite beauty of God's variegated love and heart. His heart draws him to be a friend to all beings, and every cell in his body rejoices to be their company. If you attain this state, you represent the entire universe. You are the lord of creation…

St. Francis preached to the animals and birds. This is no idle tale; it is fact. (9:168, May 8, 1960)

All beings desire true love. This is why human beings, as the lords of creation, should embrace and love all creatures, God's masterpieces, and teach them how to love. All creation is longing to receive and experience God's love through men and women who have become one with God at the pinnacle of true love. We should feel ashamed that we have not yet realized this degree of love.

All beings exist at a certain level in mutual attraction. At the same time, all beings want to be absorbed into higher levels of love. Thus, minerals want to be absorbed into plants, plants want to be absorbed into animals, and finally all of creation wants to be absorbed into human beings. Through this process they ultimately reach the position where they can experience the essence of true love, which is the love that is nearest to God – the origin of love. God created everything with an intrinsic nature to provide value to a higher level. For example, eels and worms that fish like to eat also provide ingredients for natural medicines for humans. Creatures on a higher level are meant to consume beings on a lower level. Without this process, the universe could not exist.

Darwin's theory regarding the survival of the fittest needs to be reexamined in the context of this logic of love. Even ants and microorganisms want true love so much that they will die to become part of an entity of greater love. Because of this principle, human beings, created as the highest partners of God's love, can consume all creatures. We can enjoy everything we desire, on one condition: that we do so with a heart that represents the love of God, the Creator. (March 14, 1999)

God created all things with forms, but God does not have any form… In order to have dominion over all beings—creatures on earth and angels in heaven—God needed a counterpart who could be their master. That is why He created human beings. Adam [and Eve] were to be the center of God's dominion over both the spirit world and the physical world. This was God's purpose for creating human beings. As they relate with the substantial personal Being, the perfection of Adam [and Eve] is the perfection of God's form. Accordingly, God created Adam and Eve in His image, resembling His character and form. Without humans as His form, God could not have dominion over the world of forms. (35:157, October 13, 1970)

2. Human Beings Are Superior to All Other Creatures

Verily We have honored the children of Adam. We carry them on the land and the sea, and have made provision of good things for them, and have preferred them above many of those We created with a marked preferment.
Qur'an 17.20

What a piece of work is a man! How noble in reason! How infinite in faculties! In form and moving how express and admirable! In action how like an angel! In apprehension how like a god! The beauty of the world, the paragon of animals.
William Shakespeare, Hamlet, Act II. Scene ii

Having created the world and all that lives and moves therein, He, through the direct operation of His unconstrained and sovereign Will, chose to confer upon man the unique distinction and capacity to know Him and to love Him… Upon the inmost reality of each and every created thing He has shed the light of one of His names, and made it a recipient of the glory of one of His attributes. Upon the reality of man, however, He has focused the radiance of all of His names and attributes, and made it a mirror of His own Self. Alone of all created things man has been singled out for so great a favor, so enduring a bounty.
Gleanings from the Writings of Baha'u'llah 27 (Baha'i Faith)

Man, as the manifestation of God, is the leader of all things, and no creature is more honorable than man. All things upon the earth, following their own individual names, fashioning their true way, will know that Thou hast brought them to sight for man's sake. All things whatsoever, forgetting not their source, deviating not from their determined pattern, are made to work as well as to understand their part; humbling themselves and honoring man, without anger, without haste, without anxiety, without grief, neither linked nor parted, they are made to work out their true personality.
The Ritual Prayer (Perfect Liberty Kyodan)

The human body is a revelation of the goodness of God and the providence of the body's Creator.

It is a body obviously meant to minister to a rational soul, as you can see from the arrangement of the human organs of sense and of man's other members. This is obvious, too, in man's specific appearance, form, and stature. The bodies of irrational animals are bent toward the ground, whereas man was made to walk erect with his eyes on heaven, as though to remind him to keep his thoughts on things above.

Saint Augustine, City of God 22.24 *(Christianity)*

Man was equipped with [three] souls... By virtue of the animal soul he shares with the animals; his physical soul links him with the plants; his human soul is a bond between him and the angels...

The function of the human, rational soul is the noblest function of all, for it is itself the noblest of spirits. Its function consists of reflecting upon things of art and meditating upon the things of beauty: its gaze being turned towards the higher world, its loves not this lower abode and meaner station. Belonging as it does to the higher side of life and to primal substances, it is not its business to eat and drink, neither does it require luxury and coition; rather its function is to wait for the revelation of truths.

Avicenna (Ibn Sina), Katib al-Najat *(Islam)*

We did indeed offer the Trust to the heavens and the earth and the mountains; but they refused to undertake it, being afraid of it. But man undertook it; he was indeed unjust and foolish.[11]

Qur'an 33.72

Teachings of Sun Myung Moon

What is the difference between humans and animals? Human beings are special because they possess a spirit, not because of any feature of their physical bodies. As spiritual beings, humans are distinct from all creatures that are merely physical beings. It is the spirit that endows humans with great value; the physical body is of little value in comparison.

Compare a man with an ape. An ape eats, sleeps, and brings forth its young; when it grunts it is mainly for food. Does an ape cry out yearning for its parents? Does an ape sacrifice its life for its siblings or parents? How about a man? Does a man sacrifice his life for others, or not? He does! Men and apes are different in kind.

Do apes gather to recount stories about their ancestors' brave deeds? Do they gather to worship God? Do they ponder about the spirit world? Do they dream about a peaceful world, an ideal world flourishing with love? Apes and human beings are qualitatively different.

From of old, human beings have aspired for something greater. From the very beginning, human beings have worshipped God. There is not a tribe of man that has not done so. Thinking on God, humans have pursued a better life and a better world. No ape can think such things. It is utterly impossible even after passing through a million evolutionary stages. (39:333, January 16, 1971)

Is it not true that God created human beings as the lords of creation? Didn't He give us the central position representing all things in heaven and earth? As the central beings in the universe, we humans have the right to exercise sovereignty over all its creatures. Know that such a right does not pertain in the anthropoid apes' world, or in the world of lions, tigers and such.

Then I ask the question: Do people in today's world live like human beings or more like animals? (117:35, January 31, 1982)

Who is a person of character? Someone who only lives to eat? Or someone with artistic or poetic talents who appreciates fully the beauty of the world, who whispers to the mountains and fields and sings to the flowing water? (85:143, March 3, 1976)

What does it mean that human beings are the lords of creation? Surely, God is the Lord of creation. You understand that God endowed each human being with a spirit. As the human spirit is the chief among all spirits, humans can have a direct connection to God. That is why a human being can be the lord of creation.

Nevertheless, a human being cannot be the lord of creation by himself. He is merely a created being. How can a created being be the lord of creation? Created beings are resultant beings. Apart from a relationship with the Causal Being, they cannot correspond with the Cause, nor can they possess the Cause. Rather, the Cause should possess the result. Surely humans are resultant beings. Nevertheless, we are called lords of creation and the center of all spirits. This indicates that human beings are supposed to be in relationship with God and become one with Him. (32:137, July 5, 1977)

To fulfill the ideal of love, God made all creatures and placed human beings at the center of the universe. We are called the lords of creation because we have the privilege of receiving God's love first. Then, as representatives of the God of love, we are in the central position, acting for the sake of the entire created world. We cannot be the lords of creation without first becoming God's counterparts and participating in the realm of God's love. Our special value derives from having the privilege of love... Without love, everything will pass away. (132:246, June 20, 1984)

Among animals and plants, sex is only for the purpose of reproduction. Human beings are the exception; within the conjugal relationship they can enjoy sexual love freely. This is a privilege of human beings as the lords of creation. God blessed His children to enjoy love infinitely. Yet, this God-given freedom is accompanied by responsibility. What if every person insisted on freely making love with whomever they wanted? The world would descend into chaos. It is possible for human beings to attain perfection and realize supreme love only when they take responsibility for their love. (282:213, March 13, 1997)

3. Human Beings Are Worthy to Receive Honor from All Creatures, for They Lead All Creatures to Completion

The whole world was created only for the sake of the righteous man. He weighs as much as the whole world. The whole world was created only to be united to him.

Talmud, Shabbat 30b (Judaism)

His movement is of Heaven, his stillness of Earth. With his single mind in repose, he is king of the world; the spirits do not afflict him; his soul knows no weariness. His single mind reposed, the ten thousand things submit—which is to say that his emptiness and stillness reach throughout Heaven and Earth and penetrate the ten thousand things. This is what is called Heavenly joy. Heavenly joy is the mind of the sage by which he shepherds the world.

Chuang Tzu 13 (Taoism)

Elijah... went and dwelt by the brook Cherith that is east of the Jordan. And the ravens brought him bread and meat in the morning, and bread and meat in the evening; and he drank from the brook.

1 Kings 17.5-6

Thus I have heard, on a certain occasion the Exalted One was staying near Uruvela, on the bank of the river Neranjara, at the root of the mucalinda tree, having just won the highest wisdom. Now on that occasion the Exalted One was seated for seven days in one posture and experienced the bliss of release. Then arose a great storm of rain out of due season, and for seven days there was rainy weather, cold winds, and overcast skies. So Mucalinda, King of the snakes, coming forth from his haunt, encircled the body of the Exalted One seven times with his coils and stood rearing his great hood above the Exalted One's head, thinking, "Let not heat or cold or the touch of flies, mosquitoes, wind, or creeping things annoy the Exalted One."

Now after the lapse of those seven days the Exalted One roused himself from that concentration of mind. Then Mucalinda, King of the snakes, seeing that the sky was clear and free of clouds, unwrapped his folds from the Exalted One's body, and, withdrawing his own form and creating the form of a youth, stood before the Exalted One, holding up his clasped hands and doing reverence to him.

Udana 10 (Buddhism)

The earth's condition is receptive devotion.
Thus the superior man who has breadth of
    character
Carries the outer world.

I Ching 2 (Confucianism)

Only those who are absolutely sincere can fully develop their nature. If they can fully develop their nature, they can then fully develop the nature of others. If they can fully develop the nature of others, they can then fully develop the nature of things. If they can fully develop the nature of things, they can then assist in the transforming and nourishing process of Heaven and Earth. If they can assist in the transforming and nourishing process of Heaven and Earth, they can thus form with Heaven and Earth a trinity.

Doctrine of the Mean 22 (Confucianism)

"The flowers appear on the earth, the time of song has come, and the voice of the turtledove is heard in our land" (Song of Songs 2.12):

When God created the world, He endowed the earth with all the energy requisite for it, but it did not bring forth produce until man appeared. When, however, man was created, all the products that were latent in the earth appeared above ground. Similarly, the heavens did not impart strength to the earth until man came. So it is written, "All the plants of the earth were not yet on the earth, and the herbs of the field had not yet sprung up, for the LORD God had not caused it to rain upon the earth, and there was not a man to till the ground." (Gen. 2.5)... When, however, man appeared, forthwith "all the flowers appeared on the earth," all its latent powers being revealed; "the time of song has come," the earth being now ripe to offer praises to the Almighty, which it could not do before man was created. "And the voice of the turtledove is heard in our land": this is the word of God, which was not in the world until man was created.

Zohar, Genesis 97a (Judaism)

Teachings of Sun Myung Moon

If you are completely united with God's Will, you may have a mysterious experience: the feeling that God recognizes you as His own. At that moment, you will see the things of creation bowing their heads to you. On the day when all creatures recognize that you are a son or daughter of God and God's treasured possession, the countless spirits of the spirit world, as well as all creatures on the earth, will bow their heads in praise. When God and all things recognize you, then everyone with a true conscience will also be in harmony with you. (4:102, March 16, 1958)

God said to the Earth, "O Earth, I made you the first mother. Now bear sons and daughters for me, and they will convey my eternal love to you."

The Earth agreed, and they entered into a covenant. Then the Earth said, "God, I long for Thy love. Thou didst ask me to make mediators who can build the bridge for Thy love. Having agreed to this covenant, I shall willingly comply with it by investing all of myself." With that, the Earth provided the material for the human body.

Now, if my body establishes a living connection with God's love, experiences God's love and loves God, then the Earth will say, "I am pleased to have created such glorious human beings." (97:143, March 12, 1978)

The things of creation manifest their beauty to support the original love of human beings. The flowers with their red, yellow and multi-colored hues stimulate our love; they are nature's way of praising love. They are God's gifts to us…

A husband and wife may dance round and round… but which ever way they turn, they do not forget the center. Likewise, all kinds of flowers have one thing in common: amidst the profusion of their petals, there is a center—the stamen and pistil. All things exist in pairs, and long to exclaim, "Ah!" as they come together.

All things in nature symbolize the ideal of love between man and woman, and all things praise that love. That is the original purpose of their existence. Flowers and foliage deck themselves out as best they can to celebrate and welcome the love of human beings. It is the same with animals: birds sing their love songs to praise human beings in love. The sight of a man and woman loving each other inspires them to sing with more ardor. And as both male and female harmonize their birdsong to the couple's love, it encourages the couple to love with even more passion.

In love's embrace, all creatures and human beings are united into one, and God, too, sings for joy… This universe is so beautiful! The clouds are love; the breezes blow love; the brooks babble love; the birds sing of love…! If you were to ask a flower, "Where do you want to go? Would you like to go to a place where you can manifest your utmost beauty and make others happy?" It will answer, "Yes, put me in the foremost place in the world!" Where is that place? Surely it is the master bedroom of a home where God's love dwells, where it can praise such love. What a marvelous place for a flower to be! Nothing is more delightful to a flower than to bloom in the bedroom of a couple that loves each other with true love. Since God dwells in that place, the flower is not only providing decoration for that couple, but also for God. What an honor! (146:107, June 7, 1986)

The human body is a microcosm of the universe. There are minerals, plant and animal substances within your small universe. When true love knocks at the door of the human body, all the billions of cells are immediately activated and become ecstatic. The five senses come alive—every cell of your lips wants to kiss your beloved; every cell in your eyes want to gaze into your lover's eyes…

Keep your eyes wide open and observe the life of males and females in the animal world. Consider also the coupling between pairs in the world of microbes, the world of cells and the world of minerals. Then, when you become the embodiment of true love, when every cell of your body and all your senses are alive with true love, what happens? You become like a gigantic magnet, pulling all the paired elements of nature to you. Everything will line up centering upon you because you are the center of true love.

Everything in the universe responds to true love. Therefore, all the animals, plants, and minerals will follow you wherever you go. Nature will protect you and your loving family. In the original world of true love, there are no barriers. You enjoy total freedom. Wherever you go, you find only harmony and complete cooperation. (163:44, April 1, 1987)

In the universe are galaxies, vast beyond imagining. The universe is vast beyond counting; yet, God's purpose of creation cannot be found by gazing at the universe. God's purpose of creation—to build a world where all people live with one accord—can be found on the Earth, which is only a small planet inside the solar system, and within human beings, who when compared to the vast universe are smaller than dust particles. Have you ever thought about this amazing fact? Once we know it, we should feel delighted, grateful and glorious! (5:343, March 8, 1959)

Stewardship

THE BIBLICAL IMAGE OF MAN'S PRIMORDIAL HOME is not a wild place, but a Garden. God gave the natural world to humans as a trust—to be tended, maintained and shaped into a garden of abundance. The ethic of stewardship is described by the passages in this section. They exhort kindness to animals in distress, the proper management of natural resources, preservation of endangered species, responsible fishing practices and sustainable development. They teach us to respect nature's balance, not to over-fish the seas, cut down the forests, or pollute the water and air. We should avoid over-consumption and generating excessive waste, but live in harmony with nature's capacity to provide.

However, there is a precondition for good stewardship of nature: we must learn to live in harmony with other human beings. The biblical promise that "the wolf shall dwell with the lamb" is predicated on people living peaceably with one another according to Heaven's principles.

1. Care for All Creatures

"He that is wise, wins souls" [Proverbs 11.30]. The rabbis said, "This refers to Noah, for in the Ark he fed and sustained the animals with much care. He gave to each animal its special food, and fed each at its proper period, some in the daytime and some at night. Thus he gave chopped straw to the camel, barley to the ass, vine tendrils to the elephant, and grass to the ostrich. So for twelve months he did not sleep by night or day, because all the time he was busy feeding the animals."

Tanhuma, Noah 15a (Judaism)

According to Abu Hurairah, the Messenger of God said, "A man traveling along a road felt extremely thirsty and went down a well and drank. When he came up he saw a dog panting with thirst and licking the moist earth. 'This animal,' the man said, 'is suffering from thirst just as much as I was.' So he went down the well again, filled his shoe with water, and taking it in his teeth climbed out of the well and gave the water to the dog. God was pleased with his act and granted him pardon for his sins."

Someone said, "O Messenger of God, will we then have a reward for the good done to our animals?" "There will be a reward," he replied, "for anyone who gives water to a being that has a tender heart."

Hadith of Bukhari (Islam)

May no living creatures, not even insects,
Be bound unto samsaric life; nay, not one of
   them;
But may I be empowered to save them all.

Milarepa (Buddhism)

At the openings of ant hills
Please have trustworthy men
Always put food and water,
Sugar and piles of grain.

Before and after taking food
Offer appropriate fare
To hungry ghosts, dogs,
Ants, birds, and so forth.
Nagarjuna, Precious Garland 249-50 (Buddhism)

Confucius fished with a line but not with a net. While fowling he would not aim at a roosting bird.
Analects 7.26 (Confucianism)

To you did the soul of the ox complain,
"For whom did you create me? Who made me?
Fury and violence oppress me, and cruelty and tyranny.
I have no shepherd other than you: then obtain good pastures for me."

Then the Creator of the ox asked Right, "Have you a judge for the ox,
That you may give him, with the pasture, the care for the raising of the cattle?
Whom did you appoint his master who shall put to flight Fury together with the wicked?"

As Righteousness, reply was made, "No companion is there for the ox
That is free from hatred. Men do not understand
How the great deal with the lowly.
Of all beings he is the strongest
To whose aid I come at his call...

"With hands outstretched we pray to the Lord,
We two, my soul and the soul of the mother-cow,
Urging the Wise One to command that no harm shall come to the honest man,
To the herdsman, in the midst of the wicked who surround him."

Then spoke the Wise Lord himself, he who understands the prayers in his soul:
"No master has been found, no judge according to Righteousness,
For the breeder and the herdsman has the Creator fashioned you...

"Whom hast thou, as Good Mind, who may take care of us two for men?"
"I know but this one, Zarathustra Spitama, the only one who has heard our teaching;
He will make known our purpose, O Wise One, and that of Righteousness.
Sweetness of speech shall be given to him."

And then moaned the ox-soul: "That I should have to be content
With the powerless word of a man without strength for a guardian,
I who wish for a strong master!
Will he ever be, he who shall help him with his hands?"[12]
Avesta, Yasna 29.1-9 (Zoroastrianism)

Teachings of Sun Myung Moon

Loving God starts from below your own feet. It means to love the things you possess and the natural environment. You absorb the things that you love as your life elements. Love all things equally. The entire universe exists in love, and you are part of it. Therefore, if you live for the universe, it will return to your bosom. (290:129, February 15, 1998)

There are languages in the animal world. If you sing to your plants, they will grow better and their flowers will generate more fragrance. Even flowers appreciate music and art. (262:127, July 23, 1994)

In the old days when people drove oxen to till the soil, they might whip the animal's butt, hollering, "You rotten beast! Why are you so lazy? I raised you for this time of the year, you good-for-nothing!" Instead, you would do well to speak gently to the ox, "I am very sorry that I have to use you like this after a long winter of inactivity and poor feeding." Have a heart more tolerant and patient than the animal, and God will draw near to you. (127:89, May 5, 1983)

Human beings, the center of the creation, want love. Animals also want love; so do plants. Animals want human love. Plants want love from animals. Humans, as the masters of creation, should love animals; those animals should love plants and other creatures. True love thus links everything in a hierarchical order, with God on the top, then human beings, then animals, then plants and finally minerals. (166:51-52, May 28, 1987)

When I go fishing, I release the first fish I catch. When I release it, however, I ask it a question based on the Principle: "You were born through love, so you should die for love; that is the way. Wouldn't you like to live and die for the sake of human beings who love you?" (93:189, May 29, 1977)

Animals, male and female, should be liberated. Even fish should be liberated. We should build a world where people prepare food for the animals as their owners rather than kill them and eat them. (388:270, August 2, 2002)

2. Conservation and Sustainable Development

Never does a Muslim plant trees or cultivate land, and birds or men or beasts eat out of them, but that is a charity on his behalf.
Hadith of Muslim (Islam)

The earth feels happy in the place where one of the faithful cultivates wheat, grass and fruit, where he waters ground that is dry, or dries out ground that is too wet.
Avesta, Vendidad 3.1.4 (Zoroastrianism)

If you do not allow nets with too fine a mesh to be used in large ponds, then there will be more fish and turtles than they can eat; if hatchets and axes are permitted in the forests on the hills only in the proper seasons, then there will be more timber than they can use… This is the first step along the kingly way.
Mencius I.A.3 (Confucianism)

One day Honi the Circle-Drawer was journeying on the road when he saw a man planting a carob tree. He asked him, "How long does it take for this tree to bear fruit?" The man replied, "Seventy years." He then further asked him, "Are you certain that you will live another seventy years?" The man replied, "I found ready grown carob trees in the world; as my ancestors planted these for me, so I too plant these for my children."
Talmud, Taanit 23a (Judaism)

The sacred hoop of any nation is but one of many that together make the great circle of creation. In the center grows a mighty flowering tree of life sheltering all the children of one mother and one father. All life is holy.

People native to this land have long lived by the wisdom of the circle, aware that we are part of the Earth and it is part of us. To harm this Earth, precious to God—to upset the balance of the circle—is to heap contempt on its Creator. Therefore, with all our heart and mind, we must restore the balance of the Earth for our grandchildren to the seventh generation.
Black Elk (Native American Religion)

The LORD said to Moses on Mount Sinai, "Speak to the Israelites and say to them: 'When you enter the land I am going to give you, the land itself must observe a sabbath to the LORD. For six years sow your fields, and for six years prune your vineyards and gather their crops. But in the seventh year the land is to have a sabbath of rest, a sabbath to the Lord. Do not sow your fields or prune your vineyards.'"

Leviticus 15.1-4

There is a type of man whose... aim everywhere is to spread mischief through the earth and destroy crops and cattle. But God loves not mischief.

Qur'an 2.205

When you besiege a city for a long time, making war against it in order to take it, you shall not destroy its trees by wielding an axe against them; for you may eat of them, but you shall not cut them down. Are the trees in the field men that they should be besieged by you?

Deuteronomy 20.19

The destruction of vegetable growth is an offense requiring expiation.[13]

Pacittiya 11 (Buddhism)

Rajah Koravya had a king banyan tree called Steadfast, and the shade of its widespread branches was cool and lovely. Its shelter broadened to twelve leagues... None guarded its fruit, and none hurt another for its fruit. Now there came a man who ate his fill of fruit, broke down a branch, and went his way. Thought the spirit dwelling in that tree, "How amazing, how astonishing it is, that a man should be so evil as to break off a branch of the tree, after eating his fill. Suppose the tree were to bear no more fruit." And the tree bore no more fruit.

Anguttara Nikaya 3.368 (Buddhism)

Teachings of Sun Myung Moon

Nature always seeks balance, and has been doing so unceasingly for billions of years. What about you Americans: are you in balance or not? You waste excessively. Once when I went to a public restroom, I saw someone tear off a long strip of toilet paper and use only the end of it, leaving two-thirds unused on the floor. (339:165, December 20, 2000)

Wasting anything is a sin, from the principled viewpoint. When we were born, we are allotted only a certain amount of material for our use. If we use more than the allotted amount, we are committing sin. We should conserve resources for our posterity. (June 13, 2000)

How to solve environmental pollution is one of the biggest problems facing humanity. According to scientists, once the ozone layer is depleted, humankind will not be able to survive the sun's ultraviolet rays. Pollution is even changing the climate. We should, therefore, change our lifestyle. We should live a simple life in nature, as people did in the ancient times. We should even go to the bathroom in nature, which recycles human waste as fertilizer, rather than causing pollution to the environment. (203:56, June 14, 1990)

We should not allow animal species to become extinct. We should nurture them and then set them free. Zoos should not just exhibit animals; they should breed them to set free in the wild.

We should likewise protect insect species. We should protect and nurture all the species of plants, which are food for animals. We should protect the seeds of the world, that no plant species becomes extinct. (324:118, June 17, 2000)

Already, some species of insects, fish and animals have become extinct. If this phenomenon continues unabated, then in 600 years, or even 300 years, human beings will also become extinct. (326:152, July 7, 2000)

We should raise fish in farms and then let them loose. We can hatch them from eggs like we raise chickens. After letting them loose, we love them, then catch and eat them. The things of creation serve as living offerings to compensate their owner for the love they have received: thus does the creation provide food for people. Now, instead of just catching fish, we should first farm them…

Krill is high in protein; it is a good resource that can be food for animals. This foodstuff exists for the sake of humanity. By supplying the world with krill, we can solve the world's food problems.

We can lay water pipelines to the desert and create fish farms. Just as petroleum is brought to the American mainland from Alaska, it should be possible to pipe seawater or freshwater to any place in the world. Amazon River water can be piped to the desert. Then it can be developed for fish farming. We should breed and grow fish with a loving heart, before we eat them.

By creating fish farms in the desert, we can also use the water to irrigate the land to grow vegetables and grass. Every year, more land is turning into desert. Through human ingenuity, by establishing fish farms, the desert will become a place of marshes and trees. I am not just thinking small-scale; I envision transforming a huge desert into fish farms that will produce an infinite supply of food. (324:114-15, June 17, 2000)

Solutions to the world's environmental problems cannot be arrived at through the efforts of scientists alone, or by the efforts of any one individual, organization, or nation… They call for sacrifice and cooperation among all peoples of the world, transcending the interests of any one community or nation. Such a spirit of cooperation will be attained only when all people view themselves as members of the same human family. This revolutionary change in human consciousness has long been needed, and is vital to humanity's survival today. (74:108-09, November 21, 1974)

3. To Restore the Garden of Eden

The LORD God took the man and put him in the Garden of Eden to till it and keep it.

Genesis 2.15

When God created the first man, He took him and led him round all the trees of the Garden of Eden, and said to him, "Behold My works, how beautiful and commendable they are! All that I have created, for your sake I created it. Pay heed that you do not corrupt or destroy My universe; for if you corrupt it there is no one to repair it after you."

Ecclesiastes Rabbah 7.13 *(Judaism)*

In the days when natural instincts prevailed, men moved quietly and gazed steadily. At that time, there were no roads over mountains, nor boats, nor bridges over water. All things were produced, each for its own proper sphere. Birds and beasts multiplied; trees and shrubs grew up. The former might be led by the hand; you could climb up and peep into a raven's nest. For then man dwelt with the birds and beasts, and all creation was one. There were no distinctions of good and bad men; being all equally without knowledge, their virtue could not go astray. Being all equally without evil desires, they were in a state of natural integrity, the perfection of human existence.

Chuang Tzu 9 *(Taoism)*

The wolf shall dwell with the lamb,
and the leopard shall lie down with the kid,
and the calf and the lion and the fatling together,
and a little child shall lead them.
The cow and the bear shall feed;
their young shall lie down together;
and the lion shall eat straw like the ox.
The sucking child shall play over the hole of the asp,
and the weaned child shall put his hand on the adder's den.
They shall not hurt or destroy
in all My holy mountain;
for the earth shall be full of the knowledge of the LORD
as the waters cover the sea.[14]

Isaiah 11.6-9

Teachings of Sun Myung Moon

Our planet Earth faces serious environmental problems. Environmental pollution and injury to nature show contempt for the beautiful and holy world that God created. People without true love abuse the natural world; they take it as merely something to be used.

One serious consequence of the Fall is that Adam and Eve could not inherit God's true love. As a result, people are unable to love their fellow human beings, and they are unable to love the creation.

All creatures still yearn to receive true love from human beings. I would like to build an ideal community in South America, one that demonstrates the appropriate relationship of love between human beings and nature. (271:75-76, August 22, 1985)

Live in the countryside rather than in the city. Embrace, nurture and protect the natural world with the same love that God had when He first created it. You and I have the responsibility to protect endangered species from becoming extinct. Only when we love all creation and all people in God's stead can we return to our rightful positions as owners.

Love nature. Love the sea, the mountains and the fields—all three. Love all living things, so that they may grow. As the descendants of Adam and Eve, you have the responsibility to love the water, the air and the earth in God's stead, restoring them to their original condition before the Fall. They will supply nutrients for all things to grow, and all creation will return to the blessed world of Eden. (May 10, 2003)

This planet earth is becoming barren. Year by year the deserts are growing, and plants are disappearing. Therefore, we should collect all the varieties of seeds that God created and sow them. With the loving heart that God had when He created all things on earth, we should increase the trees and plants, transplanting them and propagating their cuttings. We should protect the land. The land should contain a balance of plants, animals and human beings. If the plants die away, then human life and civilization will inevitably perish.

We are now faced with a situation in which the purpose of creation is being trampled. Therefore, as we love God, His nation and His sovereignty, we should also love and protect His people and His land. By restoring the entire creation, we should create a lush and prosperous natural world where animals roam free, as God originally intended us to build. (304:254-55, November 8, 1999)

Beauty

BEAUTY ABOUNDS IN NATURE: the majestic mountains, the delicate hues of a flower, the brilliant colors of a sunset, the sparkle of dew on the morning grass. There is harmony of shape and color, light and shadow, sound and silence.

Harmony is an aspect of beauty. Harmony is inherent in the very structure of the universe. The ancients found mathematics to be the basis of music, and today scientists are learning more about the "music of the spheres" in the motions of the stars and the properties of the atom. Singing birds and chirping insects sound nature's music as they seek for love. They are expressing its inherent harmony; human music cannot compare with it. The dissonance of our fallen condition condemns us to strike discordant notes. Were that human beings as harmonious as nature!

Human beings, God's supreme creations, should manifest supreme beauty. People sing, dance, and create beautiful art, but more than that, we find beauty in one another, in expressions of love. There is inner beauty in a loving couple, a filial child caring for aged parents, and a loyal citizen making sacrificial efforts for the welfare of his or her nation. The beauty that people manifest in these ways also glorifies God, who delights to see beauty abounding in His works. This inner beauty becomes apparent in the spirit world—where beauty abounds for those who are worthy.

1. The Beauty of Nature

Nature is the art of God.
  Dante Alighieri

Consider the lilies of the field, how they grow; they neither toil nor spin; yet I tell you, even Solomon in all his glory was not arrayed like one of these.
  Matthew 6.28-29

God is beautiful and loves beauty
  Hadith of Muslim *(Islam)*

It is God who has made for you the earth as a resting place, and the sky as a canopy, and has given you shape—and made your shapes beautiful—and has provided for you sustenance of things pure and good; such is God, your Lord. So glory to God, the Lord of the Worlds!
  Qur'an 40.64

Known by the name of Protectress
is the Goddess girt by Eternal Law;
by her beauty are these trees green
and have put on their green garlands.
  Atharva Veda 10.8.31 *(Hinduism)*

The One who, Himself without color,
by the manifold application of His power
Distributes many colors in His hidden purpose,
And into whom, its end and its beginning, the
  whole world dissolves—
He is God!
  Svestasvatara Upanishad 4.1 *(Hinduism)*

Beauty is before me.
Beauty is behind me.
Beauty is below me.
Beauty is above me.
I walk in beauty.
  Navajo Song *(Native American Religions)*

God created the seven heavens in harmony.
  Qur'an 71.15

In the cosmic Void is He absorbed,
Where plays the unstruck mystic music—
Beyond expression is this miraculous wonder.
  Adi Granth, Gauri Sukhmani 23.1,
  M.5, p. 293 *(Sikhism)*

The origin of music lies far back in time. It arises out of two poles: the two poles give rise to the powers of darkness and light. The powers of darkness and light undergo change; the one ascends into the heights, the other sinks into the depths; heaving and surging they combine to form bodies. If they are divided they unite themselves again; if they are united they divide themselves again. That is the eternal way of heaven. Heaven and earth are engaged in a circle. Every ending is followed by a new beginning; every extreme is followed by a return. Everything is coordinated with everything else. Sun, moon, stars move in part quickly, in part slowly. Sun and moon do not agree in the time which they need to complete their path. The four seasons succeed each other, bringing heat and cold, shortness and length, softness and hardness. That from which all beings arise and in which they have their origin is the Great One; that whereby they form and perfect themselves is the duality of darkness and light... Sound arises out of harmony. Harmony arises out of relatedness. Harmony and relatedness are the roots from which music, established by the ancient kings, arose.

Book of Ritual 19 *(Confucianism)*

Teachings of Sun Myung Moon

No matter how precious a work of art in a museum may be, can it be equal to a living work of art? This world is God's work of art; it is like a museum containing all God's beloved creations. (175:187, April 16, 1988)

Listen to the sound of the cicada. When it sings, all other creatures sing along with it. No orchestra on earth can compare to the orchestra of nature. (285:243, June 5, 1997)

Beholding all things of the natural world, nature's beauty and harmony through the changing seasons, we should appreciate their profundity. A bird in flight, a butterfly or bee, the flowing streams and the towering mountains—know that each is God's creation and a manifestation of God's inner heart. (5:343, March 3, 1959)

If you ever feel as if you are dying of loneliness, go out into a garden and find a flower. Smell its fragrance and talk with it, "What a beautiful fragrance! Where are you from?" It might respond, "I come from my grandma and grandpa." This means its ultimate origin was from God.

God created this world as a beautiful garden for us; it is a museum of living things, given for our enjoyment. Picasso's paintings may be beautiful, but he could not create even a patch of grass. Have you ever considered that you are looking at God's museum?

Have you ever been astonished at the beauty of a pussy willow? It blooms on a cold spring day by the ice-melting stream. How marvelous! Have you wondered for whom is it blooming? Imagine: when your beloved child is thirsty, he breaks the ice with his fist and drinks the water. Afterwards he sees that pussy willow in bloom, a symbol of spring, and sings its praises. It is wonderful! Seeing it enriches our life.

Our living environment is a museum of love. Talk with its exhibits and make them your friends. Once you understand that you were born on earth to build relationships with this world of love, how can you be lonely? (112:220, April 12, 1981)

> God of creation! Thy beauty is manifested in all the created beings:
> Everywhere Thy hands have touched teems with mysterious and radiant beauty.
> Let us fathom the distressed heart of the Father

who, even today, ceaselessly tries to find beauty in us, who were created for this purpose. Allow us, we pray, to return beauty to Thee, for Thy love. (1:102, June 10, 1956)

2. The Beauty of Human Beings

Confucius said, "It is goodness that gives to a neighborhood its beauty."

Analects 4.1 (Confucianism)

The perfume of flowers blows not against the wind, nor does the fragrance of sandalwood, tagara and jasmine, but the fragrance of the virtuous blows against the wind; the virtuous man pervades every direction.

Dhammapada 54 (Buddhism)

Whether in village or in forest, in vale or on hill, wherever monks dwell—delightful, indeed, is that spot.

Dhammapada 98 (Buddhism)

Purified, for spiritual might, by God's impulse, we think of all beautiful things.

Rig Veda 5.82.6 (Hinduism)

I will greatly rejoice in the LORD,
my soul shall exult in my God;
for he has clothed me with the garments of
    salvation,
he has covered me with the robe of
    righteousness,
as a bridegroom decks himself with a garland,
and as a bride adorns herself with her jewels.

Isaiah 61.10

Let not yours be the outward adorning with braiding of hair, decoration of gold, and wearing of fine clothing, but let it be the hidden person of the heart with the imperishable jewel of a gentle and quiet spirit, which in God's sight is very precious.

1 Peter 3.3-4

When anyone, having the right kind of love, mounts up and begins to see the beauty present in the beautiful person, he is not far from the final goal. For the right way of love, whether one goes alone or is led by another, is to begin with the beautiful things that are seen here, and ascend ever upwards, aiming at the beauty that is above, climbing as it were, on a ladder from one beautiful body to two, and from two to all bodies, and from beautiful bodies to beautiful actions and from beautiful actions to beautiful forms of knowledge, till the last from these one reaches that knowledge which is the knowledge of nothing else but Beauty itself, and so knows at last what Beauty really is.

Plato, Symposium (Hellenism)

Indeed there are three types of music. The first type is the music of the universe (*musica mundana*), the second type that of the human being (*musica humana*), and the third type is that created by certain instruments (*musica instrumentis constituta*)... producing melodies.

Now the first type, the music of the universe, is best observed in those things which one perceives in heaven itself, or in the structure of the elements, or in the diversity of the seasons... Thus there must be some fixed order of musical modulation in this celestial motion.

Now one comes to understand the music of the human being by examining his own being. For what unites the incorporeal existence of reason with the body except a certain harmony and, as it were, a careful tuning of low and high pitches in such a way that they produce one consonance?

Boethius

Teachings of Sun Myung Moon

People appear beautiful when they receive God's grace, when God loves them. They are beautiful because they radiate light. In a world where all things radiate love's light, no one would discriminate between beauty and ugliness. (33:88, August 9, 1970)

What is original beauty? It is to become embodiments of beauty, to express our beauty through laughter, dance and song, and with it to glorify God. This was the beauty God intended for the original Garden of Eden. (2:245, June 9, 1957)

If you look at people with the glasses of love, there is no one who displeases you. Even an ugly woman looks beautiful; even a misshapen man looks handsome. (162:47, March 22, 1987)

There is nothing attractive about a lake filled with muddy water. Yet if a lotus blooms in the midst of the mud, it makes the lake truly amazing. One flower can make a lake come alive. One flower can transform an ugly lake into a beautiful lake. From this point of view, evil human beings, if they have even an ounce of love in their hearts, can be beautiful. (354:21, September 16, 2001)

A woman may have great beauty, but if there is no purpose to her beauty, does it have meaning? Would any of the women here like to be a beautiful doll that stayed all day in a glass box? None of you could tolerate it. Beauty is not a passive thing just to be admired; it is active, pursuing a goal.

Some think that the purpose for a woman's beauty is to attract a husband. If that were all, would she be happy? No. In her beauty a woman dreams of something more than merely securing a man; she dreams of finding something within that man—love. The goal of beauty is love. Beauty's dream comes true in the happiness of love. (116:10-11, December 1, 1981)

Looking with a genuine heart of love, who is more beautiful, the smiling face of a woman who has artfully adorned herself with makeup or the smile of a woman who suffers and works hard to care for her family? The hard-working woman has the more beautiful smile. Although she is busy day and night with laundry, cleaning the house and looking after her children, she has a most noble appearance. (129:176, October 30, 1983)

How serious we are to live for others in this world determines the beauty of our character in the next world. It does not matter if a person is plump or slender; his or her heart to live for others is the supreme beauty of all beauty, because it is the way to perfect love. (307:166, November 8, 1998)

The major topic in the spirit world is harmony. It is balance and unity. What is the center of harmony? Could you say, "Since my face is beautiful, the harmony of the universe should revolve around me?" In the spirit world, though you may boast of your beauty, you will meet many who are more beautiful than you. The environment there is exceptionally beautiful. You should learn to appreciate it; nevertheless, because you tend to see only one dimension you are likely to miss its multidimensionality. (217:143, May 19, 1991)

Creativity and Art

ARTISTS, SCIENTISTS AND INVENTORS take after the creativity of God. The universe was created beginning with an idea in the divine Mind, followed by the expenditure of energy to make that idea a reality. Likewise, artists and scientists give all their heart and effort to create a new existence that manifests the images and thoughts in their mind.

This section focuses on the arts, and so includes alongside scripture some selected passages from famous artists reflecting on the meaning of their art. Yet, creativity is not the sole possession of these elite personages; we find creativity in the athlete who plays exuberantly for the love of sport, in the merchant who finds better ways to market his wares, and in children as they dance and sing. Father Moon, who has established ballet companies and art schools and who himself loves to sing duets with his wife, is cognizant of the role the arts can play in creating a God-centered culture.

Topics include: art as harmony of opposites, art's emotional core and emotional power; the muse, or spirituality of art; and the problem of art and values.

1. The Spirituality of Art

All art is concerned with coming into being.
Aristotle, Nicomachean Ethics 6.4 (Hellenism)

Life is art.
The whole life of man is Self-Expression.
The individual is an expression of God.
We suffer if we do not express ourselves.
Precepts 1-4 (Perfect Liberty Kyodan)

We composers are projectors of the infinite into the finite.
Edvard Grieg

The sole and end aim of figured bass should be nothing else than God's glory and the recreation of the mind.
Johann Sebastian Bach

True art is made noble and religious by the mind producing it... the endeavor to create something perfect; for God is perfection, and whoever strives after perfection is striving for something divine.
Michelangelo

Be filled with the Spirit, addressing one another in psalms and hymns and spiritual songs, singing and making melody to the Lord with all your heart.
Ephesians 5.18-19

And whenever the evil spirit from God was upon Saul, David took the lyre and played it with his hand; so Saul was refreshed, and was well, and the evil spirit departed from him.
1 Samuel 16.23

Men can be evil—more evil than their animal brothers can ever be—but they can also rise in the ecstasy of creation. The cathedrals of England stand as monuments to man's worship of what is above himself.

One does feel proud to belong to the human race when one sees the wonderful things human beings have fashioned with their hands. They have been creators—they must share a little the holiness of the Creator, who made the world and all that was in it, and saw that it was good. But He left more to be made.
Agatha Cristie

In eloquence there is magic, in knowledge ignorance;
in poetry wisdom, and in speech weariness.

                Hadith of Abu Dawud *(Islam)*

If I create from the heart, nearly everything works; if from the head, almost nothing.

                Marc Chagall

Let our artists be those who are gifted to discern the true nature of the beautiful and graceful; then will our youth dwell in a land of health, amid fair sights and sounds, and receive the good in everything; and beauty, the effluence of fair works, shall flow into the eye and ear, like a health-giving breeze from a purer region, and insensibly draw the soul from earliest years into likeness and sympathy with the beauty of reason.

    Musical training is a more potent instrument than any other, because rhythm and harmony find their way into the inward places of the soul, on which they mightily fasten, imparting grace, and making the soul of him who is rightly educated graceful.

                Plato, The Republic *(Hellenism)*

Teachings of Sun Myung Moon

Human beings are meant to inherit the creative nature of God and participate with God in His great work of creation. (*Exposition of the Divine Principle,* Creation 5.2.2)

A culture develops from words. It begins with speech; then the words are written down to become literature. Then they are expressed in paintings and other works of art. Art and culture are thus expressions of the invisible word. This is the principle of creation through the Word, emerging as visible form and substantial existence. (107:317, June 8, 1980)

Songs, dancing and art are ways that human beings respond to God's joy and laughter. On the other hand, without love, singing, dancing and art are to no purpose. The core of art is love. For the love of the world God comes down and resonates with us through singing, dancing and art. (225:128-29, January 5, 1992)

When professionals in the art world seek for something profound and need inspiration, they fall back on their religious background. That is why the culture of art developed centered on religion. Take Christian culture, for example. If you have a chance to travel in Europe, visit the Vatican. You will see the essence of European culture in each work of art. (198:281; February 5, 1990)

Art is worthless unless there is profound emotion in the background. A great work of art should be capable of arousing deep emotion, whether one views it today or a thousand years from now. A painting that can stimulate such a feeling deep in our hearts is called a masterpiece. (142:274-75, March 13, 1986)

To be an artist is to make one's life a work of art. Children's education should be imbued with art. A wife should be an artist of the emotions in the way she honors and shows appreciation to her husband. I believe that it is a greater art than the paintings that hang in museums. The greatest value of art is to beautify and elevate love in the family. (100:139, October 9, 1978)

Human beings value love more than anything. Have you ever heard of animals creating art or literature? The theme of great literature is simple: the joys and sorrows of love relationships. Great literature is good at describing love—in history, in society, in ordinary life and in the future.

Next, great literature is good at using metaphors, for instance, a majestic river evokes love flowing into eternity... What better way of describing the beauty of love than using nature's metaphors? God created all things in nature to stimulate our sense of love. All creatures are woven together with love.

A masterpiece of literature has as its central theme a love which connects all of the beauty and wonder of nature—the heavenly bodies, the beauty of rivers, mountains, trees and flowers—all of which come together to stimulate the expression of human love. A novel may be well written, but unless it expresses the beauty of love, the reader easily loses interest. The central theme of literature is always how to manifest the human passion of love. Poetry is no exception; poems just use fewer words. Young people in particular are sensitive to poetic feelings and are readily intoxicated by the emotions evoked in poetry and literature. They are responding to the universal human desire to relate to love. (94:60, July 3, 1977)

How can peoples from diverse nations and languages share their feelings in a short time? It cannot be done with literature or fine arts. It can be done only through song. A song, though short, can express all kinds of feelings and capture anyone's heart.

What songs make us the happiest? Songs that praise the most precious Central Being of the universe. They attract the greatest attention of all beings, including all things in nature. When we sing God's praises in the evening under the setting sun, we can move God's heart to empathize with our emotions. Therefore, when you sing, do not sing casually, but place yourself in the positions of the composer and lyricist and feel their emotions. Then sing with a heart to praise God.

Some songs are joyful and some songs are sad. When you sing joyful songs with a joyful heart, you harmonize with Heaven and rejoice alongside nature in the garden of joy. When you sing sad songs, you should open your chest as wide as possible and sing loudly in order to melt the world's griefs and clean up the world's sorrows. (270:11, May 3, 1995)

2. Harmony

Music expresses the harmony of the universe, while rituals express the order of the universe. Through harmony all things are influenced, and through order all things have a proper place. Music rises to heaven, while rituals are patterned on the earth... Therefore the Sage creates music to correlate with Heaven and creates rituals to correlate with the Earth. When rituals and music are well established, we have the Heaven and Earth functioning in perfect order.

Book of Ritual 19 (*Confucianism*)

Music creates order out of chaos; for rhythm imposes unanimity upon the divergent, melody imposes continuity upon the disjointed, and harmony imposes compatibility upon the incongruous. Thus, a confusion surrenders to order and noise to music, and as we through music attain that greater universal order which rests upon fundamental relationships of geometrical and mathematical proportion, direction is supplied to mere repetitious, power to the multiplication of elements, and purpose to random association.

Yehudi Menuhin

True poetry, complete poetry, consists in the harmony of contraries. Hence, it is time to say aloud—and it is here above all that exceptions prove the rule—that everything that exists in nature exists in art.

Victor Hugo

Teachings of Sun Myung Moon

Always bear in mind that you stand in relation to others. A dancer expresses the beauty of her art while always standing in the position of an object to her partner. Like a dancer, you should live with the feeling of being embraced in God's bosom. With such a mind, you can become a handsome man or a beautiful woman. Bring love's activity and beauty's receptivity into harmony. (15:171, 1965.10.07)

We need a realm of partners. When man and woman love each other, all kinds of harmony emerge in heaven and on earth. Literature and art emerged centering on the love between man and woman. Literature deals with their yearning to find the original Being (through their love). What is art? It is that which beautifies love. (354:21, September 16, 2001)

A good singer knows the art of harmony, balancing her highs and lows. When she sings her highest note beyond which she can go no higher, she must then come down to a lower note. No one wants to listen to a soprano who keeps ascending; when she skillfully lowers her voice you feel relieved. A soprano who knows how to lower her voice at the right time is a good singer. Likewise, the art of happiness in human life is the ability to go up and down smoothly. (98:50, April 9, 1978)

3. Inspiration

Not by wisdom do poets write poetry, but by a sort of genius and inspiration; they are like diviners or soothsayers who also say many fine things, but do not understand the meaning of them.

Socrates, in Plato, Apology (Hellenism)

When in my most inspired moods, I have definite inspiring visions, involving a higher selfhood. I feel at such moments that I am tapping the source of infinite and eternal energy from which you and I and all things proceed. Religion calls it God.

Richard Strauss

I have very definite impressions while in that trance-like condition, which is the prerequisite of all true creative effort. I feel that I am one with this vibrating Force, that is omniscient, and that I can draw upon it to an extent that is limited only by my own capacity to do so.

Richard Wagner

The most beautiful experience one can have is the mysterious. It is the fundamental emotion that stands at the cradle of art and science.

Albert Einstein

The LORD has called by name Bezalel the son of Uri, son of Hur, of the tribe of Judah; and he has filled him with the Spirit of God, with ability, with intelligence, with knowledge, and with all craftsmanship, to devise artistic designs, to work in gold and silver and bronze, in cutting stones for setting, and in carving wood, for work in every skilled craft.

Exodus 35.30-33

Woodworker Ch'ing carved a piece of wood and made a bell stand, and when it was finished, everyone who saw it marveled, for it seemed to be the work of gods or spirits. When the Marquis of Lu saw it, he asked, "What art is it you have?" Ch'ing replied, "I am only a craftsman—how would I have any art? There is one thing, however. When I am going to make a bell stand, I never let it wear out my energy. I always fast in order to still my mind. When I have fasted for three days, I no longer have any thought of congratulations or rewards, of titles or stipends. When I have fasted for five days, I no longer have any thought of praise or blame, of skill or clumsiness. And when I have fasted seven days, I am so still that I forget I have four limbs and a form and body. By that time, the ruler and his court no longer exist for me. My skill is concentrated and all outside distractions fade away. After that, I go into the mountain forest and examine the Heavenly nature of the trees. If I find one of superlative form, and I can see a bell stand there, I put my hand to the job of carving; if not, I let it go. This way I am simply matching up 'Heaven' with 'Heaven.' That's probably the reason that people wonder if the results were not made by spirits."

Chuang Tzu 19 *(Taoism)*

Teachings of Sun Myung Moon

When your mind and body become united and you reach the point where you open the gate of love, your mind will resonate with the universe. Then you can become a writer or a poet. In that state, you open to relate to everything in all its dimensions. Then, even watching a fallen leaf tossed by the wind will bring you to laughter. (137:232, January 3, 1986)

World-famous scientists usually have deeply sensitive minds, by which they harmonize with the heart of nature. With that sensitivity they unexpectedly receive intuitions, inspirations and dreams. These phenomena occur especially when they are completely absorbed in their research. (6:341-42, June 28, 1959)

Before you write anything, first make a spiritual condition to enter a mystical state; then you can produce beautiful writing. When painting, do not just work alone in your room. Instead, make a spiritual condition and ask a great painter's spirit to come and help you; then your work will generate great admiration from people. Great scientists and artists inevitably have a spiritual connection; it exists because they made spiritual efforts. (100:123, October 9, 1978)

An artist should have a clear mind and spirit. Then with clear conscience he should invest everything. (77:319, April 30, 1975)

4. Art and Morality

As for the poets, those who follow them stray into evil. Have you not seen how they stray in every valley, and how they say what they do not? Except for those who believe and do good works, and remember God much.

Qur'an 26.224-227

Singing produces hypocrisy in the heart as water produces crops.

Hadith of Baihaqi *(Islam)*

'A'isha told that when the subject of poetry was mentioned to God's messenger, he said, "It is speech, and what is good in it is good and what is bad is bad."

Hadith of Daraquni (Islam)

Emotions of any kind are produced by melody and rhythm; therefore by music a man becomes accustomed to feeling the right emotions; music has thus power to form character, and the various kinds of music based on various modes, may be distinguished by their effects on character—one, for example, working in the direction of melancholy, another of effeminacy; one encouraging abandonment, another self-control, another enthusiasm, and so on.

Aristotle (Hellenism)

If one should desire to know whether a kingdom is well governed, if its morals are good or bad, the quality of its music will furnish the answer.

The noble-minded man's music is mild and delicate, keeps a uniform mood, enlivens and moves. Such a man does not harbor pain or mourn in his heart; violent and daring movements are foreign to him.

Yo Ki, Memorial of Music (Confucianism)

The final purpose of art is to intensify, even, if necessary, to exacerbate, the moral consciousness of people.

Norman Mailer

Under the effect of music, the five social duties are without admixture, the eyes and the ears are clear, the blood and the vital energies are balanced, habits are reformed, customs are improved, the empire is at complete peace.

Spring and Autumn Annals (Confucianism)

Teachings of Sun Myung Moon

Humankind struggles in frustration, longing in the world of the heart, because they have defiled the heart's law. People strive to fill that longing through hobbies, art, knowledge, and love objects, but they are never fully satisfied. This is the sorrow and tragedy of the human condition since the Human Fall. (6:348, May 24, 1959)

After World War II, the trend developed, especially among American women, to worship Lucifer-like men. Who are they? Movie stars, singers and actors… These people are actually last in line to enter heaven, yet women came to worship them.

I have a vision for the arts far beyond secular art. The secular world's art is rotten; especially the recording artists and Hollywood set who are immersed in free sex. Many have contracted HIV/AIDS. I am promoting absolute sex, and members of my ballet company should not be involved in immoral love affairs. It is a wedge to protect American people from rotting away because of these artists. (339:152-53, December 10, 2000)

In America, you can watch movies on television 24 hours a day. You can watch any kind of movie: war movies, movies about love, even pornographic movies. Young people are readily attracted to them and influenced. Since they do not have a clear viewpoint of life or thought, they copy what they see in these movies.

Youth today live in a permissive environment and have abandoned traditional values that might restrain them from seeking out the stimulating things that they see in the movies. Since their parents do not pay them much attention, family ties are not strong enough to sway them. Teachers and public officials avoid giving them proper education on these matters. Therefore, there is nothing to stop young people from trying free sex, drugs, violence—copying everything they see in the movies. If this continues, the family will disappear and the world will soon be doomed...

Therefore, we should quickly establish the standard of a new tradition for the building of a new culture. It is a most urgent matter for unifying the world. (241:197-98, December 26, 1992)

God's heart of true love—to give and give more, and forget and forget again, to give unconditionally and live for the sake of others—is the foundation of the world of heart. God's ideal out of which He created the world began from His heart. The arts, which spring from this Origin, should resemble this heart. Hence, in the world of art, there can be no barriers. Art cannot be used as propaganda or the instrument of a particular ideology. Harmony and unity are its basic principles. Divisions and conflicts are the fruits of fallen nature. Accordingly, in the world of art, East and West should understand and accept each other, through art whose character is universal and inclusive. (316:70-71, February 9, 2000)

Health and Disease

THE HUMAN BODY IS CERTAINLY AMONG the Creator's crowning achievements. The body is like a small universe, whose parts are in constant interaction to maintain balance and the motion of life. It operates by natural principles to preserve health and fight disease. Yet much about its marvelous functioning remains a mystery. When an imbalance or blockage disturbs the interactions among the body's cells and organs, disease and pain result. The entire body is then mobilized to aid the infected part. In this, the body illustrates universal moral laws: living for the sake of the greater good, and attending to a deficiency in a part before it compromises the whole. Furthermore, the importance of the mind, or the psychological component in healing, can never be understated.

Medical science has done much to improve health, and the role of the physician is affirmed in the scriptures. In this section, we have added to sacred writings passages from some of the foundational authorities in medicine: Hippocrates, Galen, Paracelsus and the Classic of the Yellow Emperor. Father Moon calls for a holistic approach to medicine that utilizes the best of both East and West, scientific medicine and spiritual healing. If you wish to live a long life, you should eat healthy food, drink pure water, breathe clean air, and exercise regularly. And, Father Moon adds, love all people.

1. The Healing Power of the Body

Great thanks are due to Nature for putting into the life of each being so much healing power.

Johann Wolfgang von Goethe

The human body contains blood, phlegm, yellow bile and black bile. These... make up its constitution and cause its pains and health. Health is... that state in which these... substances are in the correct proportion to each other... When one of these is separated from the rest and stands by itself, not only the part from which it has come, but also that where it collects and is present in excess, should become diseased, and because it contains too much of the particular substance, cause pain and disease.

Hippocrates

There are many parts, yet one body. The eye cannot say to the hand, "I have no need of you," nor again the head to the feet, "I have no need of you." On the contrary, the parts of the body which seem to be weaker are indispensable, and those parts of the body which we think less honorable we invest with the greater honor, and our unpresentable parts are treated with greater modesty, which our more presentable parts do not require. But God has so composed the body, giving the greater honor to the inferior part, that there may be no discord in the body, but that the members may have the same care for one another. If one member suffers, all suffer together; if one member is honored, all rejoice together.

1 Corinthians 12.20-26

In the whole world it is said that some part of the body is afflicted and painful. It is truly a signpost or guidance from God, though you are ignorant of it.

Ofudesaki 2.22 (Tenrikyo)

Teachings of Sun Myung Moon

Truly, the human body is a treasure house of truth, a microcosm of the vast universe, and a palace of mysteries. (203:327, June 28, 1990)

The human body is like a comprehensive kingdom of heaven, where all the parts interact with one another in harmonious subject-object relationships. Therefore the universe protects the body, and you do not get sick. People do not realize that air pressure of one kilogram per square centimeter is squeezing every cell. Yet everything is in balance.

When we get sick, it means that something is lacking in a particular part of the body. Some subject and object partners have lost their ideal relationship, and the universe tries to pull these failed ones down. An expelling force pushes them out; this is expressed as sickness. (204:112, July 1, 1990)

Why do you get sick?... In order for the body to sustain its life, all its parts engage in good interactions, with each part performing its function well. Then the body functions smoothly, and its life continues. However, what happens if there is a blockage somewhere?

This universe protects anything whose elements engage in give and take in accord with God's ideal pattern. However, should an opposing element appear, something becomes lacking, or there is a blockage someplace, those elements no longer move within the realm that the universe is protecting. Hence, there is a reaction to expel the offending elements. This reaction is not a bad thing; it happens for the universe to protect itself. People mainly view sickness as something bad, but it is a natural function to protect the greater organism. So we should change the way we view sickness.

Therefore, if you have a stomach-ache, this means that there is a blockage in a circuit of give-and-take action between some subject and object partner. Your body tries to expel it to the same degree as it is blocked. An expelling force is acting on that place, and so it hurts. Once you release the blockage, you will recover. (165:176, May 20, 1987)

When you get sick, why do you feel pain? It is because the balance in your body has broken down. Once the balance is out of kilter, a universal force acts to expel. Even if you did not feel pain, since you have a conflict within your system, the universal force would still act to repel, and you could die. The pain warns you of your condition.

Likewise, the reason you feel a pang of conscience is because of the action of this same universal force. Therefore, you should not do or even think of anything that can cause such a result. (400:113, December 28, 2002)

2. The Mind's Power to Heal

A cheerful heart is a good medicine,
but a downcast spirit dries up the bones.
Proverbs 17.22

Passion makes the bones rot.
Proverbs 14.30

Nowadays people... use wine as beverage and they adopt reckless behavior... Their passions exhaust their vital forces; their cravings dissipate their true (essence); they do not know how to find contentment within themselves; they are not skilled in the control of their spirits. They devote all their attention to the amusement of their minds, thus cutting themselves off from the joys of long (life). Their rising and retiring is without regularity. For these reasons they reach only one half of the hundred years and then they degenerate.
The Yellow Emperor's Classic of Internal Medicine

Neither ought you to attempt to cure the body without the soul; and this is the reason why the cure of many diseases is unknown to the physicians of Hellas, because they are ignorant of the whole which ought to be studied also; for the part can never be well unless the whole is well... For this is the great error of our day in the treatment of the human body, that physicians separate the soul from the body.
Plato (Hellenism)

Teachings of Sun Myung Moon

Your mental attitude toward your situation is all-important. Diseases and bodily sicknesses can be controlled by your mind. When you get sick, if you think, "I will die soon," you very well might! Rather, you should think, "This illness came not to kill me but to make me stronger by fighting it off. Maybe it will even give me a blessing." Then you will soon be healthy. Conquer your sickness in your mind, and you will regain your health. (118:327, June 20, 1982)

If you think you are too old, you are finished. Then you will age very rapidly. Although I am aging, I am always thinking of things to do so that I will not lose my spirit and energy. Because I don't loose my spirit, I can overcome any obstacles and maintain my health. Your mental outlook is a powerful thing. (205:91, July 7, 1990)

No matter how healthy your mind may be, if you do not have a healthy body, you cannot fulfill your responsibility as a human being. Therefore, I bid you to constantly make efforts to bring unity in your mind and body. (271:151, August 27, 1995)

In order to become a revolutionary, you should be healthy. If you are weak physically, you cannot carry out your revolutionary mission. (203:177, June 24, 1990)

3. Medicine

The physician is Nature's assistant.
Galen

The book of Nature is that which the physician must read; and to do so he must walk over the leaves.[15]
Paracelsus

Servants of God, make use of medical treatment, for God has not made a disease without appointing a remedy for it, with the exception of one disease: old age.
Hadith of Ahmad, Tirmidhi and Abu Dawud (Islam)

Give the physician his place, for the Lord created him;
let him not leave you, for there is need of him.
There is a time when success lies in the hands of physicians,
for they too will pray to the Lord
that he should grant them success in diagnosis and in healing, for the sake of preserving life.
Ecclesiasticus 38.11-14

The medicine men learn their medicines from the spirits in a vision. The spirits tell them what to use and how to use it. Their medicines are nearly always herbs (*wato*) or roots (*hutkan*)... They drive the disease out in the sweat, in the vomit, in the defecation, in the urine, and in the breath.
Oglala Sioux Tradition (Native American Religions)

The *hekura* [guardian spirits]... help you bring back stolen souls; thanks to them you don't lose your way. You can repel the demons of disease; they enable you to recognize them by their smell. Each one has its particular odor, and their hammocks are impregnated with it; it comes from the *watota*, which they all possess. A high-quality hallucinogen enables you to see and name the demon who has just stolen a soul. You think, "It is so-and-so who is guilty!" And it is your turn to hurl your familiar hekura after him.
Yanomami Shaman's Instruction (Native American Religions)

Teachings of Sun Myung Moon

Even the vilest germs disappear when faced with their natural enemies. All we need to do is introduce several of the germs' natural enemies to mop them up and restore the body's balance. Yet today's doctors, in their ignorance, cut and slice in order to cure diseases like SARS. I am establishing a unified medical science, a combination of Eastern and Western medicines. It is a preventative medical science. I believe that by employing the principle of natural enemies, people can protect themselves from disease proactively. We should not have to undergo surgery in order to be healed of disease. In God's love, our bodies are not meant to be cut and sliced. (May 10, 2003)

What is medicine? It is the disease's natural enemy. If you have a disease in your head, the medicine would be the tail of its natural enemy. It is interesting to examine the materials and methods of Oriental medicine. If you get sick in the right side of your body, the treatment for it may involve the left side.[16] (325:148, June 30, 2000)

We need to develop a unified medical science as a field of Unification Thought. It will cure the diseases of the body, even those that originated from the Human Fall. Furthermore, it should help to heal the conflict between Eastern and Western medicine by harmonizing Eastern and Western cultures. When we can combine Eastern and Western medicine, we will be able to cure incurable diseases like HIV/AIDS.

In Korea, among people of the countryside with no formal medical education, there are many gifted healers. The spirit world instructs them about special treatments for curing diseases such as AIDS that are incurable with modern medicine. Conventional medicine ignores such things. (287:38, August 10, 1997)

4. Good Hygiene

Nothing is to be found that can substitute for exercise in any way… Exercise will expel the harm done by most of the bad regimens that most men follow. Not all motion is exercise. Exercise is powerful or rapid motion or a combination of both, vigorous motion which alters breathing and increases its rate.

Maimonides, Mishneh Torah (Judaism)

Diseases caused by over-eating are cured by fasting; those caused by starvation are cured by feeding up. Diseases caused by exertion are cured by rest; those caused by indolence are cured by exertion. To put it briefly: the physician should treat disease by the principle of opposition to the cause of the disease according to its form.

Hippocrates

Those children who are nourished by their mother's milk enjoy the most appropriate and natural food.

Galen

Teachings of Sun Myung Moon

Are you doing exercises in the morning? Some might say, "Why should I? I am still tired, and I need my rest." However, those who do not make efforts to keep their health will gradually grow infirm. It is the law of nature. (380:164, June 7, 2002)

Whenever my physical condition is poor, I know how to improve it with exercise and massage. For instance, if I feel an ache in my lower back, I massage it like this—a sort of acupuncture. If I examine myself, I can tell what is wrong with my body. I've trained myself to manage my health. (203:176, June 23, 1990)

Before you love God directly, you should love the food you eat, love material, all things, and your body from head to toe. Through loving all things, you come to love your body, because your body absorbs the elements of all things. (138:99, January 19, 1986)

Appreciate the grass growing in the earth, made by Heavenly Father's hands. Fresh air is far more fragrant than any man-made perfume. Anyone who knows the taste of fresh air, sunshine and clean water, will not get sick. If we live with a heart to appreciate nature, we shall remain always healthy. (9:177, May 8, 1960)

If you want to be healthy, you should love people, giving and forgetting what you have given continually. People who live this way will be happy and enjoy their life during their sojourn on earth. (331:23, August 23, 2000)

Chapter 5

Life after Death and the Spirit World

The Spirit World

WHAT IS THE SPIRIT WORLD? INVISIBLE TO EARTHLY EYES, it is not easily fathomed, yet it is a vital part of our existence and a place to which we will all journey one day. Father Moon teaches that knowing about the spirit world is second in importance only to knowing God. Three definite notions about the spirit world are represented here: First, knowing the spirit world is essential to finding and keeping the proper direction in our earthly life. Second, the spirit world corresponds by analogy to the earthly world. It maintains the quality of life and love cultivated on earth. Its harmony or lack of harmony is the result of the love, or lack of love, of its citizens, who cultivated various tendencies and prejudices while on earth. Third, the spirit world is composed of a multiplicity of societies and realms—though today these are in the process of being unified into one universal heaven.

1. The Spirit World Corresponds to the Physical World

I [Paul] know a man in Christ who fourteen years ago was caught up to the third heaven—whether in the body or out of the body I do not know, God knows. And I know that this man was caught up into Paradise—whether in the body or out of the body I do not know, God knows—and he heard things that cannot be told, which man may not utter.

2 Corinthians 12.2-4

No one in heaven or on the earth knows the Unseen save God; and they know not when they will be raised. Does [human] knowledge extend to the Hereafter? No, for they are in doubt concerning it. No, for they cannot see it.

Qur'an 27.65-66

To fear death, gentlemen, is no other than to think oneself wise when one is not, to think one knows what one does not know. No one knows whether death may not be the greatest of all blessings for a man, yet men fear it as if they knew that it is the greatest of evils. And surely it is the most blameworthy ignorance to believe that one knows what one does not know.

Socrates, in Plato, Apology 29 *(Hellenism)*

God created the seven heavens in harmony.

Qur'an 71.15

What is here [the phenomenal world], the same is there [in Brahman]; and what is there, the same is here.

Katha Upanishad 2.1.10 *(Hinduism)*

Thou who exists beyond the wide firmament, mighty in Thine own splendor and strong of mind,

175

hast made, for our help, the earth a replica of Thy glory.

Rig Veda 1.52.12 *(Hinduism)*

We have such a high priest, one who is seated at the right hand of the throne of the Majesty in heaven, a minister in the sanctuary and the true tabernacle which is set up not by man but by the Lord... There are priests who offer gifts according to the law. They serve a copy and shadow of the heavenly sanctuary; for when Moses was about to erect the tabernacle, he was instructed by God, saying, "See that you make everything according to the pattern which was shown to you on the mountain."¹

Hebrews 8.1-5

The system of Change is tantamount to Heaven and Earth, and therefore can always handle and adjust the way of Heaven and Earth. Looking up, we observe the pattern of the heavens; looking down, we examine the order of the earth. Thus we know the causes of what is hidden and what is manifest. If we investigate the cycle of things, we shall understand the concepts of life and death.

Essence and material force are combined to become things. The wandering away of Spirit becomes change. From this we know that the characteristics and conditions of spiritual beings are similar to those of Heaven and Earth and therefore there is no disagreement between them. The knowledge [of Spirit] embraces all things and its way helps all under heaven, and therefore there is no mistake. It operates freely and does not go off course. It rejoices in Nature and understands destiny. Therefore there is no worry. As [things] are contented in their stations and earnest in practicing kindness, there can be love. It molds and encompasses all transformations of Heaven and Earth without mistake, and it stoops to bring things into completion without missing any.

I Ching, Great Commentary 1.4.1-4 *(Confucianism)*

Teachings of Sun Myung Moon

Human life does not end with the death of the physical body. It continues in the spirit world, where saints and sages and also all of our ancestors live as spirit selves. It is a form of human existence of a higher order than in life in the physical body. This earthly world where our physical bodies dwell is only a minuscule part of the infinite and eternal world—the fundamental world that God created. (July 10, 2003)

You should clearly know God and the spirit world. Even if fallen people forget about everything else, they should know these two well. The [heavenly] spirit world is the eternal fatherland, our eternal original home. However, we cannot establish this original home once we arrive at the spirit world; we must do it while on earth. (398:145, December 9, 2002)

Do you know that the Bible mentions the third heaven? Saint Paul saw it fourteen years before [he wrote the epistle]. During those fourteen years, Paul built himself up, holding onto his experience of seeing the third heaven. Paul not only talked about the third heaven; he could keep going because he had glimpsed a realm higher than the world around him. (62:47, September 10, 1972)

The spirit world is connected with the physical world. The focal point and common factor linking them is true love. (137:54, December 18, 1985)

The quality of your internal life on earth will be visible in the spirit world. Love is central, because the love within God and human beings joins them like the cells of the body. In the spirit world we each become one of the cells. Once you enter that dimension, God will surely come inside your heart. When you call, "God!" He will answer in your heart, "Who is calling me? What do you want?" (218:129, July 14, 1991)

Where is the spirit world? Is it outside your body, or does it come inside your body? It penetrates even inside your body. You are walking around with the spirit world on your shoulders; you are carrying it and holding it wherever you go. Can you get away from it? Impossible. That is why my heart is always confident wherever I go, and why opposition cannot affect me. (162:116, March 30, 1987)

2. The Many Levels and Realms in the Spirit World

In my Father's house are many rooms.
John 14.2

Of the nether worlds and heavens has He created millions;
Men exhaust themselves trying to explore them.
Adi Granth, Japuji 22, M.1, p. 5 (Sikhism)

There are celestial bodies and there are terrestrial bodies; but the glory of the celestial is one, and the glory of the terrestrial is another. There is one glory of the sun, and another glory of the moon, and another glory of the stars; for star differs from star in glory.[2]
1 Corinthians 15.40-41

The church of the Firstborn... are they into whose hands the Father has given all things— they are they who are priests and kings, who have received of His fullness, and of His glory; and are priests of the Most High, after the order of Melchizedek, which was after the order of the Only Begotten Son. Wherefore, as it is written, they are gods, even the sons of God... These are they whose bodies are celestial, whose glory is that of the sun, even the glory of God, the highest of all, whose glory the sun of the firmament is written of as being typical.

And again, we saw the terrestrial world, and behold and lo, these are they who are of the terrestrial, whose glory differs from that of the church of the Firstborn who have received the fullness of the Father, even as that of the moon differs from the sun in the firmament. Behold, these are they who died without law... who received not the testimony of Jesus in the flesh, but afterwards received it. These are they who are honorable men of the earth, who were blinded by the craftiness of men.

These are they who receive of His glory, but not of His fullness. These are they who receive of the presence of the Son, but not of the fullness of the Father. Wherefore, they are bodies terrestrial, and not bodies celestial, and differ in glory as the moon differs from the sun...

And again, we saw the glory of the telestial, which glory is that of the lesser, even as the glory of the stars differs from that of the glory of the moon in the firmament. These are they who received not the gospel of Christ, neither the testimony of Jesus. These are they who deny not the Holy Spirit. These are they who are thrust down to hell. These are they who shall not be redeemed from the devil until the last resurrection, until the Lord, even Christ the Lamb, shall have finished his work.

These are they who receive not of His fullness in the eternal world, but of the Holy Spirit through the ministration of the terrestrial; and the terrestrial through the ministration of the celestial. And also the telestial receive it of the administering of angels who are appointed to minister for them, or who are appointed to be ministering spirits for them; for they shall be heirs of salvation.[3]
Doctrine and Covenants 76.54-88 (Latter-day Saints)

When King Solomon "penetrated into the depths of the nut garden" (Song of Solomon 6.11), he took up a nut shell and studying it, he saw an analogy in its layers with the spirits that motivate the sensual desires of humans...

God saw that it was necessary to put into the world so as to make sure of permanence all things having, so to speak, a brain surrounded by numerous membranes. The whole world, upper and lower, is organized on this principle, from the primary mystic center to the very outermost of all the layers. All are coverings, the one to the other, brain within brain, spirit inside of spirit, shell within shell.

The primal center is the innermost light, of a translucence, subtlety, and purity beyond comprehension. That inner point extends to become a "palace" which acts as an enclosure for the center, and is also of a radiance translucent beyond the power to know it. The "palace" vestment for the incognizable inner point, while it is an unknowable radiance in itself, is nevertheless of a lesser subtility and translucency than the primal point. The palace extends into a vestment for itself, the primal light. From then outward, there is extension upon extension, each constituting a vesture to the one before, as a membrane to the brain. Though membrane first, each extension becomes brain to the next extension.

Likewise does the process go on below; and after this design, man in the world combines brain and membrane, spirit and body, all to the more perfect ordering of the world.

Zohar (Judaism)

All kingdoms have a law given;

And there are many kingdoms; for there is no space in which there is no kingdom; and there is no kingdom in which there is no space, either a greater or a lesser kingdom.

And unto every kingdom is given a law; and unto every law there are certain bounds also and conditions.

All beings who abide not in those conditions are not justified.

For intelligence cleaves unto intelligence; wisdom receives wisdom; truth embraces truth; virtue loves virtue; light cleaves unto light; mercy has compassion on mercy and claims her own; justice continues its course and claims its own; judgment goes before the face of Him who sits upon the throne and governs and executes all things.[4]

Doctrine and Covenants 88.36-40 (Latter-day Saints)

Teachings of Sun Myung Moon

The entire spirit world appears as one person. When this gigantic Person becomes one with God as its Subject partner, then the entire spirit world and physical world will melt together. When God jumps, the earth will jump. When God laughs, the earth will laugh...

The spirit world is structured and functions as one person. Saints take the role of eyes and ears. (91:280, February 27, 1977) [5]

In the spirit world, everything is linked centering on God. Although people have different ranks and inhabit different regions, they all know that they should follow God and make Him their center. Even spirits in the lower realms have an alignment toward God, reflected in their life goals like a concept of faith. (161:220, February 15, 1987)

Just as people in earthly society have different ranks, there are also different ranks in the spirit world. You do not know much about spirit world now, but when you understand its geography, you will recognize that it contains thousands of different levels. (91:269-70, February 27, 1977)

In the spirit world, there is an abundance of flowers wherever you go. Amazingly, the flowers are laughing and dancing. Yet they receive human beings depending upon the level of their perfection: laughing and dancing, or dancing but not making any sound, or standing still, etc. On seeing them, you will finally realize: "Ah, I wish I would have understood the Father's love and practiced it!" Yet by then it would be too late. That is why I am training you and educating you to pass the tests on earth, to help you be tuned to the right frequency of love. (227:100, February 10, 1992)

The spirit world is still incomplete. Its hierarchical system was originally supposed to be centered on God, the True Parents and true children. Everyone was supposed to have a position in this hierarchy, but it is not realized yet; neither is it the case on earth. The hierarchy must be established on earth first. If the conditions on earth are met, then the spirit world will automatically follow…

So far, the spirit world has been organized hierarchically into the Buddhists Club, the Confucians Club, the Muslims Club, the Christians Club, etc… Now, as the work of the True Parents on earth proceeds at the worldwide level, the boundaries between all the religions are disappearing. The movement for unification will progress on earth, along with similar activities in the spirit world. (161:223, February 15, 1987)

Barriers divide the spirit world. There are no nations like Korea, Japan and America; however, there are different realms based on the different religions. Those who practiced Buddhism [on earth] dwell in the Buddhist realm. Those who practiced Confucianism dwell in the Confucian realm. Those who believed in Jesus live in the Christian realm. Those who followed Islam enter the Muslim realm, and so forth. With the passage of time, the people of each group built up their respective realms and surrounded themselves with walls. These walls, products of the Fall, stand firm until the day of Christ's return, when he comes to break them down. (89:101, October 4, 1976)

The Immortal Soul

SPIRIT OR SOUL IS THE IMMORTAL HUMAN ESSENCE. Originating in the eternal God, it returns to God in the end. The body, on the other hand, is made from clay and is but a vestment that clothes the spirit. This is a rather universal conception, widespread in all religions although they differ on the details. The soul may ascend to heaven, descend into hell, merge with the Godhead, sleep until the general resurrection, or transmigrate into another earthly body; regardless, survival of the spirit is a common thread in all faiths.

These texts include descriptions of a "spiritual body" that clothes the soul in the next life. Others conceive of the spirit as having its own form and structure. Coterminous with the flesh during life, it then separates and ascends to the spirit world after death. Father Moon offers additional insight into how people on earth already live in both worlds, by virtue of the resonance between their spirit and flesh. This speaks to how people with spiritual gifts can perceive the spirit world during earthly life.

The spirit truly finds its wings after death, when it is no longer tied down to the body and can travel freely at will. Nevertheless, earthly life is important as the training-ground where the qualities of spirit needed for fulfillment in heaven are developed; that is the subject of the next section.

1. Soul and Body

The body is the sheath of the soul.
Talmud, Sanhedrin 108a (Judaism)

Then the LORD God formed man out of the dust of the ground, and breathed into his nostrils the breath of life; and man became a living being.
Genesis 2.7

And He originated the creation of man out of clay,
then He fashioned his progeny of an extraction of mean water,
then He shaped him, and breathed His spirit in him.
Qur'an 32.8-9

The soul is characterized by knowledge and vision, is formless, an agent, has the same extent as its own body, is the enjoyer of the fruits of karmas, and exists in samsara. It is also enlightened and has a characteristic upward motion.
Nemichandra, Dravyasangraha 2 (Jainism)

Ts'ai-wu said, "I have heard the names *kuei* and *shen*, but I do not know what they mean." The Master said, "The [intelligent] spirit is of the *shen* nature, and shows that in fullest measure; the animal soul is of the *kuei* nature, and shows that in fullest measure. It is the union of *kuei* and *shen* that forms the highest exhibition of doctrine.

"All the living must die, and dying, return to the ground; this is what is called *kuei*. The bones and flesh molder below, and, hidden away, become the earth of the fields. But the spirit issues forth, and is displayed on high in a condition of glorious brightness. The vapors and odors which produce a feeling of sadness, and arise from the decay of their substance, are the subtle essences of all things, and also a manifestation of the *shen* nature."
Book of Ritual 21.2.1 (Confucianism)

Someone will ask, "How are the dead raised? With what kind of body do they come?" You foolish man! What you sow does not come to life unless it dies. And what you sow is not the body which is to be, but a bare kernel, perhaps of wheat or some other grain. But God gives it a body as He has chosen, and to each kind of seed its own body. For not all flesh is alike, but there is one kind for men, another for animals, another for birds, and another for fish. There are celestial bodies and there are terrestrial bodies; but the glory of the celestial is one, and the glory of the terrestrial is another.
1 Corinthians 15.35-40

Teachings of Sun Myung Moon

Investing all His heart and mind, God formed the human body out of dust as a place where the spirit self, a life manifesting the principle of eternity, can live and grow. No work of art could be greater. God did not make it by saying to the dust, "Arise!" No, God invested all of His heart, mind and energy into forming this body. Then, He completed the human being by blowing a life spirit into it. God created the first man with a special blessing, as a being that could live forever in the corporeal and incorporeal worlds within God's dominion. But he fell. (8:80, November 8, 1959)

Our spirit self, or spirit, is a substantial yet incorporeal reality, which can be apprehended only through the spiritual senses. It is the subject partner to our physical self. Our spirit can communicate directly with God and is meant to govern the incorporeal world, including the angels. In appearance our spirit self matches our physical self. After we shed the physical self, we enter the spirit world and live there for eternity. The reason we desire an eternal life is because our innermost self is the spirit self which has an eternal nature.

Our spirit self consists of the dual characteristics of spirit mind (subject partner) and spirit body (object partner). The spirit mind is the center of the spirit self, and it is where God dwells.

The spirit grows through give and take action between two types of nourishment: *life elements* (생소) of a yang type that come from God, and *vitality elements* (생력) of a yin type that come from the physical self...

The spirit can grow only while it abides in the flesh. Thus, the relationship between the physical self and the spirit self is similar to that between a tree and its fruit. (*Exposition of the Divine Principle*, Creation 6.3.2)

Human beings consist of a dual structure: a mind-like self and a body-like self. The mind grasps the vertical standard. The body holds a horizontal standard. Consider an ideal person, living by God's ideal standard and receiving God's love. When God's love sounds vertically in the mind or spirit self, it resounds horizontally through the body. The spirit self, with its vertical standard, picks up the vibration of God's true love and transmits it to the physical self, where it resonates through the person's relations with his or her surroundings. (177:216, May 20, 1988)

Our spirit self and physical self should resonate like a tuning fork. When a tuning fork is struck, it makes a nearby tuning fork resonate at the same frequency. By the same principle, once God's love moves in our spirit, our body automatically responds.

What causes our mind and body to resonate 100 percent and brings them into the realm of oneness? It is not God's wisdom or power. It is only love. (138:255, January 24, 1986)

Both the body and the mind are composed of cells. Do you know that you have a spirit self, and that it has five spiritual senses? The cells of the inner self and the cells of the outer self resonate with each other.

The spirit self, our inner self that lives for eternity, and the physical self, our outer self that can live on earth only, should resonate with each other in love. When they resonate with God's love, their spiritual cells and physical cells are linked together in the same vibration. Therefore, as the cells of the eyes vibrate, they can see everything in the spirit world as clearly as the physical world. They can see by virtue of their perfect resonance. (171:103, December 13, 1987)

2. Death: Transition to a New Life

The hour of departure has arrived, and we go our ways—I to die, and you to live. Which is better God only knows.

    Socrates, in Plato, Apology 42 (*Hellenism*)

The dust returns to the earth as it was, and the spirit returns to God who gave it.

    Ecclesiastes 12.7

It is We who give life, and make to die, and to Us is the homecoming.

    Qur'an 50.43

Now my breath and spirit goes to the Immortal, and this body ends in ashes;
OM. O Mind! Remember. Remember the deeds.
Remember the actions.

    Isha Upanishad 17 (*Hinduism*)

Man's real nature is primarily spiritual life,
which weaves its threads of mind to build a cocoon of flesh,
encloses its own soul in the cocoon,
and, for the first time, the spirit becomes flesh.
Understand this clearly: The cocoon is not the silkworm;
in the same way, the physical body is not man but merely man's cocoon.
Just as the silkworm will break out of its cocoon and fly free,
so, too, will man break out of his body-cocoon and ascend to the spirit world when his time is come.
Never think that the death of the physical body is the death of man.
Since man is life, he will never know death.[6]

    Nectarean Shower of Holy Doctrines (Seicho-no-Ie)

One man believes he is the slayer, another believes he is the slain. Both are ignorant; there is neither slayer nor slain. You were never born; you will never die. You have never changed; you can never change. Unborn, eternal, immutable, immemorial, you do not die when the body dies. Realizing that which is indestructible, eternal, unborn, and unchanging, how can you slay or cause another to be slain?

As a man abandons his worn-out clothes and acquires new ones, so when the body is worn out a new one is acquired by the Self, who lives within.

The Self cannot be pierced with weapons or burned with fire; water cannot wet it, nor can the wind dry it. The Self cannot be pierced or burned, made wet or dry. It is everlasting and infinite, standing on the motionless foundation of eternity. The Self is unmanifest, beyond all thought, beyond all change. Knowing this, you should not grieve.[7]

    Bhagavad-Gita 2.19-25 (Hinduism)

You prefer this life, although the life to come is better and more enduring. All this is written in earlier scriptures; the scriptures of Abraham and Moses.

    Qur'an 87.16-19

I inquired of Africanus whether he himself, my father Paulus, and others whom we look upon as dead, were really living. "Yes, truly," replied he, "they all enjoy life who have escaped from the chains of the body as from a prison. But as to what you call life on earth, that is no more than a form of death. But see, here comes your father Paulus towards you!"[8]

    Cicero, On the Republic 6.14 (Hellenism)

Onyame[9] does not die; I will therefore not die.

    Akan Proverb (African Traditional Religions)

Meet the Fathers, meet Yama, and meet with the
fulfillment of wishes in the highest heaven;
casting off imperfections, find anew thy dwelling,
and be united with a lustrous body.

    Rig Veda 10.14.8 (Hinduism)

Though our outer nature is wasting away, our inner nature is being renewed every day. For this slight momentary affliction is preparing us for an eternal weight of glory beyond all comparison, because we look not to the things that are seen but to the things that are unseen; for the things that are seen are transient, but the things that are unseen are eternal.

For we know that if the earthly tent we live in is destroyed, we have a building from God, a house not made with hands, eternal in the heavens. Here indeed we groan, and long to put on our heavenly dwelling, so that by putting it on we may not be found naked. For while we are still in this tent, we sigh with anxiety; not that we would be unclothed, but that we would be further clothed, so that what is mortal may be swallowed up by life. He who has prepared us for this very thing is God, who has given us the Spirit as a guarantee.

So we are always of good courage; we know that while we are at home in the body we are away from the Lord, for we walk by faith, not by sight. We are of good courage, and we would rather be away from the body and at home with the Lord. For we must all appear before the judgment seat of Christ, so that each one may receive good or evil, according to what he has done in the body.

2 Corinthians 4.16-5.10

Teachings of Sun Myung Moon

In the Korean language, the word *toraganda* means, "to die," but its literal meaning is, "to return." To where do we return? Not to the soil of the cemetery. It means to return to the original place of departure, the place of origin. It is a place beyond the origin of history… even the dwelling-place of the Creator. Since we originated from God, we should return to Him.

The universe has natural cycles. The snow covering the mountains melts, flows down through many small valleys into streams and rivers and on into the ocean. Then it evaporates and becomes vapor. Through this circulation, water thus returns to a higher state. Likewise, we want to return to a higher and better place. (299:61, February 4, 1999)

Humans originate from God's mind, grow up and mature in God's bosom of love, and make a family on earth which can embrace the whole world with love. Through this process, they will return to God's bosom of love as mature persons. This is the path of our life. (135:267-68, December 15, 1985)

A human being's essence is spiritual. When you go to the spirit world you will recognize more deeply that the essence of being human is to live for the sake of others.

Then, why do people deal with everything so selfishly? It is because humans have a blood relationship with Satan, the angel who violated the law of heaven. (2:138, March 17, 1957)

People are meant to live on earth in good families and, after perfecting their internal spirit self, go to the Kingdom of Heaven in the spirit world. The Kingdom of Heaven in the spirit world is our original homeland, where we live eternally as spirit beings in God's love. Due to the Human Fall, human beings no longer have a properly functioning spirituality. They live in ignorance of their spirit self and the spirit world. Nevertheless, human beings, unlike any other animal, possess a spirit self and go to the spirit world. If only people understood this! (343:196, January 29, 2001)

We were born as an eternal life, and therefore go to the spirit world after death. Life there will be on a totally different dimension. In this limited world we cannot move freely, but the other world is a higher dimensional place where we can do anything. You can jump beyond time. With true love, whatever you desire you will receive, anytime and anywhere. The spirit world is boundless.

We are created as eternal beings. Each of us is that way because we are the object partners of the eternal God, participating in His true love. If we become such object partners of true love, then when we go to the spirit world we will be completely free.

However, to realize this you must be trained in true love here on earth. You are not yet ready. Without fulfilling your responsibility to prepare yourselves well, you cannot go to the realm of freedom in the spirit world. But once you perfect true love on the earth, you can go there anytime. (216:116, March 9, 1991)

Preparation for Eternity

RELIGIONS DO NOT EXPOUND ON THE REALITY OF A FUTURE LIFE merely as a comfort to the bereaved or as an opiate to the oppressed in this life. Rather, the fact of a future life enhances the purpose and sharpens the meaning of earthly existence. How a person lives on earth mainly determines his or her ultimate destiny. A wise person lives in this world with an eye toward eternity.

Indeed, it is generally taught that life in this world is the only chance we have to prepare for life in the next world. The link between deed and retribution is not severed by death; rather we reap in the eternal world the fruits of our actions in this life. Just as importantly, a person's qualities of character survive death: As a person in this life was hard-working or lazy, generous or miserly, courageous or timid, forgiving or begrudging, so will he or she continue to be in the afterlife.

Therefore, the wise person lives with an eye to eternity by following religious precepts, repenting for misdeeds, and seeking to clear up all accounts before the day of his death. For one who is prepared, death is not to be feared. But for those who are heedless and do not prepare, death comes suddenly, fearfully and leaving them with regret. As Father Moon teaches, souls in the spirit world breathe the air of love; therefore, unless they have cultivated on earth the capacity for love, they will find the spirit world suffocating. Hence, the measure of our future happiness in the eternal world is the ability to love that we cultivate during earthly life.

1. Live this Short Earthly Life in the Light of Eternity

This world is like a vestibule before the World to Come; prepare yourself in the vestibule that you may enter the hall.

Mishnah, Avot 4.21 (Judaism)

The Marrying Maiden:
The superior man understands the transitory
In the light of the eternity of the end.[10]

I Ching 54 (Confucianism)

Better is one hour of repentance and good works in this world than all the life in the world to come, and better is one hour of calmness of spirit in the world to come than all the life of this world.

Mishnah, Avot 4.22 (Judaism)

A rare chance, in the long course of time, is human birth for a living being; hard are the consequences of actions; Gautama, be careful all the while!

Uttaradhyayana Sutra 10.4 (Jainism)

And we see that death comes upon mankind... nevertheless there was a space granted unto man in which he might repent; therefore this life became a probationary state; a time to prepare to meet God; a time to prepare for that endless state which has been spoken of by us, which is after the resurrection of the dead.

Book of Mormon, Alma 12.24 (Latter-day Saints)

If any do wish for the transitory things of life, We readily grant them such things as We will, to such persons as We will. But in the end We have provided hell for them; they will burn therein, disgraced and rejected. But those who wish for the things of the hereafter, and strive for them with all due striving, and have faith—they are the ones whose striving is acceptable to God.

Qur'an 17.18-19

We are on a market trip to earth:
Whether we fill our baskets or not,
Once the time is up, we go home.

Igbo Song (*African Traditional Religions*)

As the fallow leaf of the tree falls to the ground, when its days are gone, even so is the life of men; Gautama, be careful all the while!

As the dewdrop dangling on the top of a blade of grass lasts but a short time, even so the life of men; Gautama, be careful all the while!

A life so fleet, and existence so precarious, wipe off the sins you ever committed; Gautama, be careful all the while!

Uttaradhyayana Sutra 10.1-3 (*Jainism*)

In the evening do not expect [to live till] morning, and in the morning do not expect evening.

Prepare as long as you are in good health for sickness, and so long as you are alive for death.

Forty Hadith of an-Nawawi 40 (*Islam*)

O people! Fear God, and whatever you do, do it anticipating death. Try to attain everlasting blessing in return for transitory and perishable wealth, power and pleasures of this world.

Be prepared for a fast passage because here you are destined for a short stay. Always be ready for death, for you are living under its shadow. Be wise like people who have heard the message of God and have taken a warning from it.

Beware that this world is not made for you to live forever, you will have to change it for hereafter. God, glory be to Him, has not created you without a purpose and has not left you without duties, obligations, and responsibilities…

You must remember to gather from this life such harvest as will be of use and help to you hereafter.

Nahjul Balagha, Khutba 67 (*Shiite Islam*)

Teachings of Sun Myung Moon

As we live out our earthly life, we are at the same time moving toward the eternal world. Most people pass through life like this: they are born, grow from youth to teen age to their 20s and 30s, reach middle age, and then gradually fade into old age. They live their lives like a setting sun.

We, on the other hand, know the existence of the spirit world. We know that this earthly life is short, while the world after death is eternal. Therefore, we live our earthly lives as the time to prepare ourselves for the eternal world.

Our life in the physical body is a preparation period. It is like taking a course at school where the tuition is the price of our entire life. Knowing this, we cannot but strive to fulfill our responsibility in order to achieve a result that would properly represent our life. (140:121, February 9, 1986)

Which is more important, the flesh or the spirit? It is the spirit. The flesh can live within a limited timeframe of seventy or eighty years, but the spirit transcends time and space.

No matter how good a life you may enjoy in the flesh, you will die in the end. The flesh is meant to die. Hence, we should not live according to measures of physical life. The flesh exists for the spirit, not the spirit for the flesh. You should not cling to physical things as people in the secular world commonly do. (20:326, July 14, 1968)

In spirit world we breathe love. Those who fail to love on earth will suffocate in the other world. Earthly life is a training ground where we train ourselves to breathe in the other world. That is why we should love others more than our own spouse. (121:294, October 29, 1982)

It takes good nurture in the mother's womb to be born as a good-natured and healthy baby. Likewise, to be born well into the spirit world from the "womb" of earthly life, you should grow by taking after God's divine heart and character. In the process you should work hard to overcome obstacles, even if it means risking your life. (14:17, April 19, 1964)

Religion is a means for us to learn the laws of heaven while we are alive on earth. It exists to train us while on earth to possess the character whereby we can adapt to the laws of the original homeland when we arrive there one day. (77:189, April 6, 1975)

How precious it is to be alive on the earth! It is only one moment, our only one chance. Compared to eternity, our earthly life is nothing but a dot, so short. Therefore we should rise above any thought for our physical life and prepare for the spirit world. (207:99, November 1, 1990)

You all think, "I am young. Surely I will live another 40 or 50 years." Do you have a guarantee from God? Rather, it would be better if you thought you might die soon—maybe within a year—and you had only a short time left to prepare everything. Live with this kind of concept. The sooner you expect to die, the better. Then you would be busy preparing the true substance that will enable you to build your "house" of eternal life.

How serious would you be if you really believed that you had only two more years to live? Visit a cemetery; go to a funeral and see death. It is necessary to do this in a life of faith. Jesus said, "Whoever would save his life will lose it, and whoever loses his life for my sake will find it." Expecting to die soon, you would determine to die for God's Will and for Heaven. Then you will live eternally. (102:122, November 27, 1978)

2. Store Up Treasures in Heaven

Do not lay up for yourselves treasures on earth, where moth and rust consume and where thieves break in and steal, but lay up for yourselves treasure in heaven, where neither moth nor rust consumes and where thieves do not break in and steal. For where your treasure is, there will your heart be also.

Matthew 6.19-21

Men who have not led a religious life and have not laid up treasure in their youth perish like old herons in a lake without fish.

Men who have not lived a religious life and have not laid up treasure in their youth lie like worn-out bows, sighing after the past.

Dhammapada 155-56 (Buddhism)

O shrewd businessman, do only profitable business:

Deal only in that commodity which shall accompany you after death.

Adi Granth, Sri Raga, M.1, p. 22 (Sikhism)

Beautified for mankind is love of the joys [that come] from women and offspring, and stored-up heaps of gold and silver, and horses branded, and cattle and land. That is comfort of the life of the world. God! With Him is a more excellent abode. Say, Shall I inform you of something better than that? For those who keep from evil, with their Lord are Gardens underneath which rivers flow, and pure companions, and contentment from God.

Qur'an 3.14-15

Relatives and friends and well-wishers rejoice at the arrival of a man who had been long absent and has returned home safely from afar.

Likewise, meritorious deeds will receive the good person upon his arrival in the next world, as relatives welcome a dear one on his return.

Dhammapada 219-20 (Buddhism)

Leaving the dead body on the ground like a log of wood or a clod of earth, the relatives depart with averted faces; but spiritual merit follows the soul.

Let him therefore always slowly accumulate spiritual merit, in order that it may be his companion after death; for without merit as his companion he will traverse a gloom difficult to traverse.

That companion speedily conducts the man who is devoted to duty and effaces his sins by austerities, to the next world, radiant and clothed with an ethereal body.

Laws of Manu 4.241-243 (Hinduism)

And [Jesus] told them a parable, saying, "The land of a rich man brought forth plentifully; and he thought to himself, 'What shall I do, for I have nowhere to store my crops?' And he said, 'I will do this: I will pull down my barns, and build larger ones; and there I will store all my grain and my goods. And I will say to my soul, Soul, you have ample goods laid up for many years; take your ease, eat, drink, be merry.' But God will say to him, 'Fool! This night your soul is required of you; and the things you have prepared, whose will they be?' So is he who lays up treasure for himself, and is not rich toward God."

Luke 12.16-21

I see men of wealth in the world—
acquiring property, from delusion they give not
    away;
out of greed a hoard of wealth they make,
and hanker sorely after more sense pleasures...

Heirs carry off his wealth;
but the being goes on according to kamma.
Wealth does not follow him who is dying,
nor child or wife, nor wealth or kingdom.

Long life is not gained by wealth,
nor is old age banished by property.
"For brief is this life," the wise say,
non-eternal, subject to change.

Rich and poor feel the touch [of death],
fool and wise are touched alike.
But the fool, as though struck down by folly,
    prostrate lies,
While the wise, touched by the touch, trembles
    not.
Wherefore better than wealth is wisdom
by which one here secures the
    Accomplishment.

Majjhima Nikaya 2.72-73 (Buddhism)

Teachings of Sun Myung Moon

The way to riches in the other world is not complicated. Those who invested much love on earth are rich. (205:347, October 2, 1990)

When you die, you leave everything behind, except your love for God and your love for yourself, that is, your effort to cultivate good character, to develop love for your spouse, and to extend the love for your family to the world. Your record of loving God and loving people remains to the end and becomes the measure to decide your property rights in the next world. (127:38, May 1, 1983)

What gifts will you bring to heaven with you? When you arrive at the spirit world, you will stand before many martyrs and saints of great merit. Can you open your bag of gifts before such great figures? Please reflect deeply. Could you present gifts that resemble a beggar's things?... When you arrive at the spirit world, you should be able to open your gift box and say, "This is what I have prepared all my life, so please receive it." Even a woman brings a full dowry when she gets married, so how can you go to the spirit world empty-handed? (32:71, June 21, 1970)

In the next world, the result of true love that you accumulated throughout your life on earth appears like a label. You will, therefore, dwell in the appropriate level, depending on the merit that you accomplished during your lifetime. (211:288, December 30, 1990)

To enter heaven, we should live for the sake of others. We can never enter if we live self-centered lives. (91:173, February 6, 1977)

What is the final goal of life? It is not merely a matter of meeting the Lord in heaven. The real issue is whether you are able to dwell together with the Lord. What will be your condition when you meet Him? Will you be in a state where you can live comfortably with Him?

You will find the Lord in the centermost position. If you want to live with Him, you must be able to live in the central position.

That central position is the place of God's love. For this reason, the ultimate goal sought by the human conscience is to connect with heavenly fortune[11] and follow it to the point where we become one with God and make God's love our own. (24:17, June 22, 1969)

What you bring to the spirit world is not money... Rather, it is the sons and daughters you restore from Satan's world and raise to be loved by God. Through them your merit will be connected to your ancestors, making a condition to liberate them. This is the greatest gift you can obtain in the process of restoration.

You should go to the other world after educating many spiritual children on earth. Then the scope of your activity in the spirit world will be great. You will be the center of an expansive network of relationships extending throughout the entire spirit world. The spiritual standard you made on earth will be the basis for your activities there.

If your spiritual standard is lacking, you will be pushed into a corner, barely able to do anything. Therefore, do you have time to just sleep and idle away your life? Just providing for your family and raising your children does not count for much in the spirit world. Rather, you should be seeking out people whom you can raise to heaven. They will become your assets in the Kingdom of Heaven. (230:24, April 15, 1992)

3. As We Live on Earth, So Shall We Live in Heaven

Tzu-lu asked how one should serve ghosts and spirits. The Master said, "Till you have learnt to serve men, how can you serve ghosts?" Tzu-lu then ventured upon a question about the dead. The Master said, "Till you know about the living, how are you to know about the dead?"

Analects 11.11 (Confucianism)

Jesus said, "Truly, truly, I say to you, whatever you bind on earth shall be bound in heaven, and whatever you loose on earth shall be loosed in heaven."[12]

Matthew 18.18

Now man is made of determination (*kratu*); according to what his determination is in this world so will he be when he has departed this life.

Shankara, Vedanta Sutra 1.2.1 (Hinduism)

Both life and death of such as are firm in their penance and rules are good. When alive they earn merit and when dead they attain beatitude.

Both life and death of such as indulge in sins are bad. When alive they add to malice and when dead they are hurled into darkness.

Dharmadasaganin, Upadesamala 443-44 (Jainism)

Here he grieves, hereafter he grieves. In both states the evil-doer grieves. He grieves, he is afflicted, perceiving the impurity of his own deeds.

Here he rejoices, hereafter he rejoices. In both states the well-doer rejoices. He rejoices, exceedingly rejoices, perceiving the purity of his own deeds.

Here he suffers, hereafter he suffers. In both states the evil-doer suffers. "Evil have I done"—thinking thus, he suffers. Having gone to a woeful state, he suffers even more.

Here he is happy, hereafter he is happy. In both states the well-doer is happy. "Good have I done"—thinking thus, he is happy. Upon going to a blissful state, he rejoices even more.

Dhammapada 15-18 (Buddhism)

As for that abode of the Hereafter, We assign it to those who seek not oppression in the earth, nor corruption. The sequel is for those who ward off evil. Whoever brings a good deed, he will have better than the same; while as for him who brings an ill deed, those who do ill deeds will be requited only what they did.

Qur'an 28.83-84

Teachings of Sun Myung Moon

The value of your life is not determined after living it to the end. It is determined by the life that you live each day. (197:186, January 14, 1990)

A person cannot suddenly change his way of life in the other world. There is a saying that the habit of a three-year old continues until he turns eighty. Inborn personality is hard to change. Hence, spirit people cannot live very differently from the way they lived on earth. After all, the inhabitants of the spirit world are the souls of people who formerly lived on earth. From this perspective, the spirit world is not so different from the physical world. (141:268, March 2, 1986)

All the sensibilities of a spirit are cultivated through the reciprocal relationship with the physical self during earthly life. Therefore, only when a person reaches perfection and is totally immersed in the love of God while on earth can he fully delight in the love of God as a spirit after his death. All the qualities of the spirit self are developed while it abides in the physical self: Sinful conduct during earthly life aggravates evil and ugliness in the spirit of a fallen person, while the redemption of sins granted during earthly life opens the way for his spirit to become good. This was the reason Jesus had to come to the earth in the flesh to save sinful humanity.

We must lead a good life while we are on the earth. Jesus gave the keys to the Kingdom of Heaven to Peter, who remained on the earth, and said, "Whatever you bind on earth shall be bound in heaven, and whatever you loose on earth shall be loosed in heaven," because the primary objective of the providence of restoration must be carried out on the earth. (*Exposition of the Divine Principle*, Creation 6.3.2)

Is it easy or difficult to change your habits? Yet you have lived with selfish habits, according to the satanic world's idea of right and wrong. These habits have congealed in you. They are stronger than the craving we Koreans have for *kimchee*.

Ever since the day Satan began his reign over humanity, people have been establishing self-centered habits and traditions. They are like a rotten root. How can we pull it out? You say you understand the Principle and know what to do. Yet try as you may to dig a hole and pull out that root, you cannot. It is taller than you are. It is so long that even if you were to stand at the top of a tree you cannot pull it out. Can you, nevertheless, loudly proclaim that you have pulled it out? This is a serious matter.

Do you have confidence to go to heaven? To go to heaven, you must have God-centered habits and tradition. (213:20, January 13, 1991)

How much you have lived for the Will of God throughout your life will determine your position in the spirit world. Therefore, you yourself know very well whether or not you can enter the heavenly realms. For what purpose did you eat and sleep, like and dislike, come and go? This will determine whether you can enter heaven. (*Way of God's Will* 1.8)

The Kingdom of God, the hope of humanity, is composed according to the principle of living for the sake of others. Like it or not, you are destined to go to the spirit world. Everyone takes that journey according to his or her way of life. What is the fundamental issue in your life? It is whether you are living more for the sake of others or for yourself. If you lived more for the sake of others, you will go to the Kingdom of God. If the opposite is true, you will go to hell. You may be unable to believe this fundamental formula now, but once you die, you will understand. (74:51, November 27, 1974)

4. The Finality of Death

You can climb up the mountain and down again;
you can stroll around the valley and return; but
you cannot go to God and return.
        Nupe Proverb (*African Traditional Religions*)

The untrustworthy lord of death
Waits not for things to be done or undone;

Whether I am sick or healthy,
This fleeting life span is unstable.

Leaving all I must depart alone.
But through not having understood this
I committed various kinds of evil
For the sake of my friends and foes.

Yet my foes will become nothing.
My friends will become nothing.
I too will become nothing.
Likewise all will become nothing.

Just like a dream experience,
Whatever things I enjoy
Will become a memory.
Whatever has passed will not be seen again.

Even within this brief life
Many friends and foes have passed,
But whatever unbearable evil I committed for
    them
Remains ahead of me…

While I am lying in bed,
Although surrounded by my friends and
    relatives,
The feeling of life being severed
Will be experienced by me alone.

When seized by the messengers of death,
What benefit will friends and relatives afford?
My merit alone shall protect me then,
But upon that I have never relied.

Shantideva, Guide to the Bodhisattva's Way of Life
2.33-41 (Buddhism)

Teachings of Sun Myung Moon

No friends accompany you on the path of death. You journey without your beloved parents, beloved brothers, beloved spouse or beloved children. You journey all alone. Once you go down that path, you can never return. With what kind of heart will you make the journey?

If you do not have hope that you can overcome death, when you meet your death it will be the end. The numerous people who believed and followed God's Will did not retreat before death. Rather, they mocked death and overcame it with dignity. Throughout history, such people exalted the way of Heaven.

Each one of you likewise has to maintain hope to overcome the death that awaits you. You should aspire to stand before God with dignity at the end of your journey. You should be able to run with joy to the heavenly world, the original homeland your heart desperately longs for. Then you will conquer death. (6:53, March 22, 1959)

It is not enough to live with a vague belief in the existence of the spirit world. On earth we must know how to prepare for life in the spirit world, where whether we like it or not, we shall live for eternity. Once we know, we should thoroughly prepare ourselves for that day. A child who develops a problem while in the womb will suffer after his birth from a handicap that lasts his entire life. So too, if we fail to recognize Heaven's Will during our short life on earth and commit sin or carry out evil deeds, we will eventually pay the price in the spirit world according to the universal principle of cause and effect. In the spirit world our souls will have to suffer indescribable pain and make many efforts at atonement.[13] Yet once we shed our physical body, it will be too late.

When the physical body dies, it returns to the earth as a handful of dirt, but do you think that our life, our mind, our heart, and our hopes are also buried? It is absolutely not so. Our 100-year-long life is recorded, photographed and automatically evaluated without fail in our personal supercomputer, built by God, called the spirit self. This is why all of us, during life on earth, should stop and check ourselves again and again, and ask our unsteady mind and heart: "Where are you going?" (May 1, 2004)

Dreams

BETWEEN THIS WORLD AND THE NEXT IS THE WORLD OF DREAMS. Not all dreams are spiritual, but some definitely are, and they are often the most vivid and memorable. During such a dream, the spirit leaves the body for a time and mounts up into the spirit world, where it experiences various phenomena. Some of these are of God and convey meaningful messages. Other dreams are encounters with low or evil spirits; these include nightmares, sexual dreams and the like. These passages describe the spiritual process of dreaming and give instructions on how to discern whether a dream is from God. Through a dream God can reveal life-changing information and guidance, as He did to Jacob and Joseph in the Bible. Thus, paying attention to significant dreams is an important discipline of the religious life.

Jacob... came to a certain place, and stayed there that night, because the sun had set. Taking one of the stones of the place, he put it under his head and lay down in that place to sleep. And he dreamed that there was a ladder set up on the earth, and the top of it reached to heaven; and behold, the angels of God were ascending and descending on it! And behold, the LORD stood above it and said, "I am the LORD, the God of Abraham your father and the God of Isaac; the land on which you lie I will give to you and to your descendants... Behold, I am with you and will keep you wherever you go, and will bring you back to this land; for I will not leave you until I have done that of which I have spoken to you." Then Jacob awoke from his sleep and said, "Surely the LORD is in this place; and I did not know it."

Genesis 28.10-16

When a man lies down in bed, his soul leaves him and begins to mount on high, leaving with the body only the impression of a receptacle which contains the heartbeat. The rest of it tries to soar from grade to grade, and in doing so it encounters certain bright but unclean essences. If the soul is pure and has not defiled itself by day, it rises above them, but if not, it becomes defiled among them and cleaves to them and does not rise any further. There they show it certain things which are going to happen in the near future, and sometimes they delude her and show it false things. Thus it goes about the whole night until the man wakes up, when it returns to its place.

Happy are the righteous to whom God reveals His secrets in dreams, so that they may be on their guard against sin! Woe to the sinners who defile their bodies and their souls! As for those who have not defiled themselves during the day, when they fall asleep at night their souls begin to ascend, and first enter those grades which we have mentioned, but they do not cleave to them and continue to mount further. The soul thus privileged to rise finally appears before the gate of the celestial palace, and yearns with all its might to behold the beauty of the King and to visit His sanctuary... Thus it is written, "With my soul have I desired Thee in the night (Isaiah 26:9)," to pursue after Thee and not to be enticed away after false powers.

Zohar 1.83a (Judaism)

God takes the souls of men at death; and those that die not He takes during their sleep. Those on whom He has passed the decree of death He keeps back, but the rest He returns to their bodies for a term appointed. Verily in this are signs for those who reflect.

Qur'an 39.42

While one is in the dream state, the golden, self-luminous being, the Self within, makes the body to sleep, though He Himself remains forever awake and watches by his own light the impressions of deeds that have been left upon the mind. Thereafter, associating Himself again with the consciousness of the sense organs, the Self causes the body to awake.

While one is in the dream state, the golden, self-luminous being, the Self within, the Immortal One, keeps alive the house of flesh with the help of the vital force, but at the same time walks out of this house. The Eternal goes wherever He desires.

The self-luminous being assumes manifold forms, high and low, in the world of dreams. He may seem to be enjoying the pleasure of love, or laughing with friends, or looking at terrifying sights. Everyone is aware of the experiences; no one sees the Experiencer.

Some say that dreaming is but another form of waking, for what a man experiences while awake he experiences again in his dreams. Be that as it may, the Self, in dreams, shines by Its own light...

The Self, having in dreams enjoyed the pleasures of sense, gone hither and thither, experienced good and evil, hastens back to the state of waking from which he started.

Brihadaranyaka Upanishad 4.3.11-16 *(Hinduism)*

Once upon a time, Chuang Tzu dreamed that he was a butterfly, a butterfly fluttering about, enjoying itself. It did not know that it was Chuang Tzu. Suddenly he awoke with a start and he was Chuang Tzu again. But he did not know whether he was Chuang Tzu who had dreamed that he was a butterfly, or whether he was a butterfly dreaming that he was Chuang Tzu. Between Chuang Tzu and the butterfly there must be some distinction. This is what is called the transformation of things.

Chuang Tzu 2 *(Taoism)*

If there is a prophet among you, I the LORD make myself known to him in a vision, I speak with him in a dream.

Numbers 12.6-7

God's messenger said, "A believer's vision is a forty-sixth part of prophecy, and what pertains to prophecy cannot be false." He held that visions were of three types: ideas which come from within, terrifying dreams caused by the devil, and good news from God; so when one sees anything he dislikes he should not tell it to anyone, but should get up and pray.

Hadith of Bukhari and Muslim *(Islam)*

The vision flutters over a man as long as it is not interpreted, but when it is interpreted it settles. Tell it only to one who loves him or one who has judgment.

Hadith of Abu Dawud *(Islam)*

Pharaoh said to Joseph, "I have had a dream, and there is no one who can interpret it; and I have heard it said of you that when you hear a dream you can interpret it." Joseph answered Pharaoh, "It is not in me; God will give Pharaoh a favorable answer." Then Pharaoh said to Joseph, "Behold, in my dream I was standing on the banks of the Nile; and seven cows, fat and sleek, came up out of the Nile and fed in the reed grass; and seven other cows came up after them, poor and very gaunt and thin, such as I had never seen in all the land of Egypt. And the thin and gaunt cows ate up the first seven fat cows, but when they had eaten them no one would have known that they had eaten them, for they were still as gaunt as at the beginning. Then I awoke. I also saw in my dream seven ears growing on one stalk, full and good; and seven ears, withered, thin, and blighted by the east wind, sprouted after them, and the thin ears swallowed up the seven good ears. And I told it to the magicians, but there was no one who could explain it to me."

Then Joseph said to Pharaoh, "The dream of Pharaoh is one; God has revealed to Pharaoh what he is about to do. The seven good cows are seven years, and the seven good ears are seven years; the dream is one. The seven lean and gaunt cows that came up after them are seven years, and the seven empty ears blighted by the east wind are also seven years of famine. It is as I told Pharaoh, God has shown to Pharaoh what he is about to do. There will come seven years of great plenty throughout all the land of Egypt, but after them there will arise seven years of famine, and all the plenty will be forgotten in the land of Egypt; the famine will consume the land, and the plenty will be unknown in the land by reason of that famine which will follow, for it will be very grievous. And the doubling of Pharaoh's dream means that the thing is fixed by God, and God will shortly bring it to pass.

Genesis 41.15-32

Teachings of Sun Myung Moon

Dreams are one means that God uses to reveal Himself. Hence, dreams may give important revelations... some dreams are correct and come true.

Because of the Human Fall, we belong to the satanic lineage or bloodline. As we move about, that satanic blood circulates through our bodies. It stirs up like muddy water in a glass tube. However, when we sleep the body is at rest, and the blood circulation slows. It can be compared to the sediment settling to the bottom of the tube and clear water rising to the top. Then our original, clear mind can be touched by Heaven. This is why revelations usually come through dreams. At that time, God may teach us using images and symbols.

How do you distinguish whether a particular dream is just a random dream, a revelation from God or an image from Satan? Satanic dreams do not have a clear picture, direction, or central theme. They are jumbled, and when you get up you easily forget them. In contrast, a heavenly dream is coherent and contains a clear theme. It often continues a message from one dream to the next. If you have consistent dreams three nights in a row, then you should recognize it as a revelation from God. A heavenly dream will be so clear in your mind that you will recall it vividly when you wake up. You do not forget it, because God and human beings are meant to be united for eternity.

On the other hand, satanic dreams are quickly forgotten because any relationship with Satan is temporary. They do not sway those of you who remain in constant contact with the good spirit world, because you have experienced heavenly dreams and know how to recognize them. Still, you are beset by nightmares and temptations from Satan's world. Psychologists call them manifestations of the subconscious. Still, they are easily forgotten. They are not like dreams from God, which are vivid, unexpected and unforgettable. (91:272-75, February 27, 1977)

Don't ignore revelations or dreams. Pray and make sincere devoted efforts to receive such experiences. How to adapt them to our real lives, and how to apply them to the practical reality: this is most important in a life of faith. (76:153, February 2, 1975)

First you may have a premonition (*amshi*). For instance, while casually walking down the street, you see a sitting bird on the wall of a house suddenly fly away in front of you. You sense something unusual; it is an indirect hint that something special is about to happen.

The next stage is to have unusual dreams (*mongshi*). They are not like the dreams you normally have in a deep sleep. Saint Paul experienced the third heaven in a dream-like state. Never let such an experience slip by. You should, instead, put it all together and analyze it from a scientific perspective, seeking to understand its meaning for you. When it can speak to you about what direction you should take, you will definitely see a result. These unforgettable dreams are 100 percent accurate. Have such experiences in your life.

If you reach that level, what will happen next? You will receive a revelation (*gyeshi*) or a direction (*jishi*). Revelations require interpretation but directions do not; that is the difference between the two. God can teach you through a voice or a vision. You may have a vision of a pair of deer drinking water at a brook and looking at the distant mountains on a beautiful spring day; this is a very good sign that something good might happen. Soon after you have the vision, a corresponding event will occur; it is never a coincidence. Through this, God is cultivating the field of your heart.

Beyond the stage of revelations, you will reach the stage of trance (*mookshi*).[14] A trance is like traveling to the spirit world and experiencing its wonders. When you can connect to that world, you can even arrive at the realm of God's feelings. Treasure all these experiences, and apply their lessons to your life. Your life of faith is precious, and you should cultivate it.

Finally, you reach the point where you can experience the great resultant world of God in your daily life. At this stage, God's instructions will be in your mind. You try to talk pleasantries to someone, but you cannot speak. You want to say a few words of encouragement, but instead you utter a reproach. When such incomprehensible phenomena take place, you must learn to control the situation. Otherwise, people might think you are insane. (76:130-35, February 2, 1975)

The Passage Beyond

AT THE MOMENT OF DEATH, THE PASSAGE INTO THE NEXT LIFE is a nearly impenetrable mystery. Published accounts of near-death experiences by people who have been resuscitated from clinical death may give a clue. They report passing through a tunnel into another world, meeting a being of light, and feeling great warmth and accepting love. While these people did not, by definition, die, they may have experienced the first stage of the passage. Who can know how it ends?

What can be known with some certainty is that there is survival after death. In fact, many people who die do not at first realize that they are dead, as they continue to experience themselves as conscious, sentient beings.

Physical death is but a transition to a higher stage of existence. It is the putting on of a new body, like the metamorphosis of a caterpillar into a butterfly. Father Moon calls it a second birth, by analogy to the birth of an infant who must leave the comfortable world of the womb. As the womb nourished the fetus until birth, when it is destroyed and the baby leaves it for life on the earth, the physical body nourishes the soul until death, when it expires and the soul departs for life in the spirit world. Hence there are three stages of life: in the water-world of the womb, in the air-world of earthly existence, and in the spirit world where we breathe an atmosphere of love.

Therefore, death is not something to be feared. On the other side it is celebrated as the soul's birthday. The chief issue is whether we have adequately prepared our soul with the spiritual faculties to exist comfortably in that world. There, nothing matters but one's ability to love.

1. The Second Birth

For this perishable nature must put on the imperishable, and this mortal nature must put on immortality. When the perishable puts on the imperishable, and the mortal puts on immortality, then shall come to pass the saying that is written:

"Death is swallowed up in victory."
"O death, where is thy victory?
O death, where is thy sting?"

1 Corinthians 15.53-55

One who identifies himself with his soul regards bodily transmigration of his soul at death fearlessly, like changing one cloth for another.

    Pujyapada, Samadhishataka 77 *(Jainism)*

Look upon life as a swelling tumor, a protruding goiter, and upon death as the draining of a sore or the bursting of a boil.

    Chuang Tzu 6 *(Taoism)*

Have you seen the seed which you emit?
Is it you who create it, or are We the Creator?
We have decreed death to be your common lot,
and We are not to be frustrated from changing your forms
and creating you again in forms that you know not.
And you certainly know already the first form of creation:
Why then do you not celebrate His praises?

    Qur'an 56.58-62

There is birth, there is death, there is issuing forth, there is entering in. That through which one passes in and out without seeing its form—that is the Portal of God.

    Chuang Tzu 23 *(Taoism)*

The world beyond is as different from this world as this world is different from that of the child while still in the womb of its mother. When the soul attains the Presence of God, it will assume the form that best befits its immortality and is worthy of its celestial habitation.

    Gleanings from the Writings of Bahá'u'lláh 81 *(Baha'i Faith)*

The silver cord is snapped, or the golden bowl is broken, or the pitcher is broken at the fountain, or the wheel broken at the cistern, and the dust returns to the earth as it was, and the spirit returns to God who gave it.

    Ecclesiastes 12.6-7

As a man passes from dream to wakefulness, so does he pass from this life to the next.

When a man is about to die, the subtle body, mounted by the intelligent self, groans—as a heavily laden cart groans under its burden.

When his body becomes thin through old age or disease, the dying man separates himself from his limbs, even as a mango or a fig or a banyan fruit separates itself from its stalk, and by the same way that he came he hastens to his new abode, and there assumes another body, in which to begin a new life.

When his body grows weak and he becomes apparently unconscious, the dying man gathers his senses about him and, completely withdrawing their powers, descends into his heart. No more does he see form or color without.

He neither sees, nor smells, nor tastes. He does not speak, he does not hear. He does not think, he does not know. For all the organs, detaching themselves from his physical body, unite with his subtle body. Then the point of his heart, where the nerves join, is lighted by the light of the Self, and by that light he departs either through the eye, or through the gate of the skull, or through some other aperture of the body. When he thus departs, life departs; and when life departs, all the functions of the vital principle depart. The Self remains conscious, and, conscious, the dying man goes to his abode. The deeds of this life, and the impressions they leave behind, follow him.

As a caterpillar, having reached the end of a blade of grass, takes hold of another blade and draws itself to it, so the Self, having left behind it [a body] unconscious, takes hold of another body and draws himself to it.

As a goldsmith, taking an old gold ornament, molds it into another, newer and more beautiful, so the Self, having given up the body and left it unconscious, takes on a new and better form, either that of the Fathers, or that of the Celestial Singers, or that of the gods, or that of other beings, heavenly or earthly.

    Brihadaranyaka Upanishad 4.3.34-4.4.4 *(Hinduism)*

Teachings of Sun Myung Moon

It is natural to want to resemble God, and for God to want His children to resemble Him. Therefore, there should be a way for God to bring us to where He is. It is inevitable that humans should be reborn as beings that resemble God. Both God and human beings look forward to that day of our rebirth. How does that happen? Through death.

Then, shouldn't human beings welcome death? We die to experience God's true love. Discarding the physical body enables us to participate in the infinite realm of God's activity, and contribute to the world of God's love.

Death is to be born in the midst of God's love! Yet earthly people grieve over death. Does this make God laugh or cry? You should understand that death is the moment of your second birth. It is a joyful moment when you leave the finite realm of love and enter the infinite realm of love.

On which day is God happier, the day of your physical birth or the day when you are born as God's son or daughter to live and love in the infinite world? Why am I saying this? Unless you are liberated from the fear of death, you cannot establish a relationship with God. (116:172, January 1, 1982)

Humans grow through three stages: formation, growth and completion. Likewise, they pass through three different worlds: the water world where they float in the mother's womb, the earth world where they walk, and the air world where they can fly. Hence, we live three lives: 10 months in the womb, 100 years of life on earth, and eternal life in the spirit world. (297:257, December 19, 1998)

While in the womb you breathed through the umbilical cord. Meanwhile, your nostrils, a pipeline to the air, were being prepared so that you could breathe after you were born into the physical world. Likewise, while you live in the earthly world, what should you do to prepare for the next? You should experience love. You should breathe the 'air' of love from your father and mother. As you grow, you should pass through all the stages of love as a sibling, husband and wife, parent and grandparent.

The moment you were born, your life was destined to end. When it does, the body will be dissolved. Then, just as you were born as an infant, on the day you die you will experience a new birth as an infant.

What happens in that birth? You are pushed out of the world of the second womb and connected to the breathing organ for your third life, to breathe love. You are pushed out of the womb, a world where you experienced the love of your parents and siblings, to enter a new world of love where you will harmonize with the original Being, the God of the great universe.

The spirit world is filled with the air of love. The air of love! That is why, while you live on earth, you should be installing that pipeline you will depend upon to breathe love. Know that if you have spiritual experiences and feel spiritual love—if you are able to breathe the air of love—you shall not die. (139:213-14, January 31, 1986)

We cannot remember how difficult it was for our mother to give birth to us. Why did God make birthing so difficult? Why isn't it as easy as speaking or eating? The reason why God made giving birth a life-risking experience for the mother is because He wants her to see His radiant love.

In electricity, there is something called a current spike. The instant a switch is turned on, a twenty or thirty-fold burst of electricity flows through the circuit. By the same token, the moment when human beings are desperate, they generate an explosive amount of energy. A mother gives birth a death-like state with her eyes popping out, as if heaven and earth were being destroyed. Then the baby utters its first loud cry, and her eyes open wide; she totally forgets her pain. Having given birth in such pain, the mother naturally loves her child more than anything.

How difficult is it to be born? The amniotic sack that was our home breaks. The placenta that had nourished us is cast off. Yet these events are not disastrous; they are rather fortunate, for the sake of our happiness. Yet we do not realize that it was a new beginning of life until after the birth was over...

Again the time comes, after living our earthly life, to kick away from this physical plane and depart for a new world. Nevertheless, as a fetus does not want to leave the safety of its mother's womb, we would rather continue to live on earth. We do not want to die. Death comes, and once again we go through a big tumult.

Yet we will be born into the spirit world, an infinite world. We will escape from the bounds of time and space, able to travel instantly from one end of the spirit world to the other, faster than the speed of light. (107:42, January 20, 1980)

On the day of your birth the umbilical cord, the lifeline that was linked to your bellybutton, had to be severed. Likewise, in the world of air, the spirit self is attached to the body and sucks nutrition from it like a fetus on its placenta. There comes a day when the physical body becomes too old to feed it, and it leaves it behind...

The fetus that experiences momentary pain as it emerges from its mother's womb grows to become the object of its parents' love. In the same way, our spirit self must leave behind our crying physical body in order to be born anew as the object partner of God, who is the eternal Spirit.

On earth, the baby can grow up to become the friend of its father and mother because it was born into the physical world where it can share love with them. Before that, it was merely a fetus swimming around the mother's womb. In the same way, life on earth is breathing and living in the swaddling clothes of air... After our second birth into the spirit world, we will share love with God our Parent, who provides our spiritual link with the infinite world. (297:258-59, December 19, 1998)

Once you enter the spirit world, you breathe through the cells of the fontanel located on the top of the head.[15] The atmosphere in the spirit world is not earthly air; it is love. We breathe the elements of love.

Even while living on earth, it is not enough for us to eat food and drink water. Our earthly existence is only a shadow of our true self. Therefore, we should use this short time to cultivate a loving character. More than anything else, what we need during earthly life is love. We pity orphans, who have no parents to love them, because they do not receive the love that can connect them to the eternal spirit world. People without love are lonely, and we pity the single person who lives without a life companion.

At death, we lose the organs of the body through which we breathed during our second life. Yet it is necessary that one day we should be released from the body, that we might inherit the elements of love, which are invisible. Therefore, during earthly life we should prepare for the day of death by cultivating our inner self; this is done through experiencing children's love, sibling's love, conjugal love and parental love.

As a fetus in the womb grows healthy and strong in accordance with natural principles, people should grow well on earth by living in accordance with God's law. Therefore, we should never live a casual lifestyle. (297:260, December 19, 1998)

Consider a dragonfly. First it swims in the water as a larva, next it crawls on the land for a short time, and then it flies, catching prey on the wing. It is an existence it could never imagine when it was a larva. Yet as it flies around, the entire world is its stage…

Why don't human beings, who are the lords of all creation, have wings? Is it enough that people live limited to the earth? Actually, we have higher-dimensional wings. Once you die and shed your physical body, you will fly. Death is a happy, joyful gate to the second birth. (297:261-62, December 19, 1998)

2. First Moments in the Afterlife

The body which you have now is called the thought-body of propensities. Since you do not have a material body of flesh and blood, whatever may come—sounds, lights, or rays—are, all three, unable to harm you; you are incapable of dying. It is quite sufficient for you to know that these apparitions are your own thought-forms. Recognize this to be the *Bardo* (the intermediate state after death).

Tibetan Book of the Dead (Buddhism)

When the soul departs from this world she knows not by what path she will be made to travel; for it is not granted to all souls to ascend by the way that leads to the realm of radiance where the choicest souls shine forth. For it is the path taken by man in this world that determines the path of the soul on her departure. Thus, if a man is drawn towards the Holy One, and is filled with longing for Him in this world, the soul in departing from him is carried upward towards the higher realms by the impetus given her each day in this world.

Zohar 1.99a-b (Judaism)

If we do not improve our time while in this life, then comes the night of darkness wherein there can be no labor performed. You cannot say, when you are brought to that awful crisis, that I will repent, that I will return to my God. Nay, you cannot say this; for that same spirit which possesses your bodies at the time that you go out of this life, that same spirit will have power to possess your body in that eternal world.

Book of Mormon, Alma 34.33-35 (Latter-day Saints)

Those who remember me at the time of death will come to me. Do not doubt this. Whatever occupies the mind at the time of death determines the destiny of the dying; always they will tend toward that state of being. Therefore, remember me at all times…

Remembering me at the time of death, close down the doors of the senses and place the mind in the heart. Then, while absorbed in meditation, focus all energy upwards towards the head. Repeating in this state the divine Name, the syllable OM that represents the changeless Brahman, you will go forth from the body and attain the supreme goal.[16]

Bhagavad-Gita 8.5-7, 12-13 (Hinduism)

Teachings of Sun Myung Moon

If while walking down the street you are killed instantly in a traffic accident, you will not know that you have died. You think to yourself, "I have come to a strange place. It is a little better than my own neighborhood. It has things I have never seen before." A vast space opens before your eyes. Since you see it, you don't think that you are dead.

But what an odd place it is! Instead of seeing people around you as you normally would, they appear only when you want to see them. Unless you call them, they do not appear. You feel very much alone.

Then you meet guides, who explain to you, "You have died. You have come to the spirit world." Still, you don't believe them. You have a feeling that you collided with a car far away somewhere as in a dream, but you do not feel that you have died. You are still connected with the earth.

Dazed, and not believing you are dead and in the spirit world, you think, "I must go home." You try to go to your house in the physical world, but you cannot.

Then your ancestors from some generations back come and explain, "You are no longer on the earth. You have entered the spirit world." You finally say, "Ah, so this is the spirit world." (194:41-42, October 15, 1989)

What will be your thoughts when you pass into the spirit world? At first you will be welcomed into a vast world. Yet right away you will recognize that its way of life is not what you were used to in your small hometown. On earth there was racial discrimination and conflicts among people of different backgrounds and cultures. Some people's ways were incompatible with yours, and you handled things by insisting on your own viewpoint and affirming that your own values were best. Now that you have arrived in the spirit world, you will want to leave those outmoded values behind. But your past life does not go away. It revives in the spirit world with all vividness.

The more you feel the immensity of the spirit world, the more you long for your home and for life on earth, because you cannot easily absorb the environment of the spirit based on your limited sensibility. Yet there is where you will spend eternity. Still, can you ever forget about your earthly life?

When you first arrive, you will meet only strangers. In the midst of such an unfamiliar environment, how you will long to meet someone you knew in the past! You cannot escape your emotional connection to your past life. You think about the people you loved. You wonder how your mother and father are doing, and how your grandparents are living. Yet it is not easy to meet them. (187:285-85, February 12, 1989)

Suppose through some misfortune a man died while still searching for the ultimate goal. However, death does not mean the end of the quest. Once in the spirit world, he would say, "I died while searching for love, and now in the spirit world I will find that love." If a man dies in the bosom of God's love, then it is not a miserable death. Did death shatter his love? No. God, the subject of love, will recognize the value of his death, saying: "You died for the sake of the love that I have been searching for."...

Suppose a wife sacrificed her life for her husband. What will happen when he joins her in the spirit world? Or suppose an elder brother arrives in the spirit world after his younger brother had died for him. Would they be happier or less happy than they were when they were together on earth? Can the depth of love they formerly shared on earth even compare with that precious love for which one offered his life? It would certainly transcend that earthly level of love...

So, in searching for the path of love, death is not a problem. Though you die, it would not be the end, but new life. By this kind of sacrificial death, you would pass through the tollgate to reach a world of love that is eternal and of a higher dimension. From this perspective, there is no reason to fear death. (67:173-74, June 3, 1973)

The Judgment

AFTER THE INITIAL PASSAGE INTO THE AFTERLIFE, there is another, less comfortable event. Each individual undergoes a judgment where he must review his life with unsparing honesty. There is a ledger recording every deed, and its consequences on the people it affected. Now that book is opened and read. The movie that recorded the person's life is projected onto the screen of his mind. Everything comes to light.

The main criterion of judgment seems to be the deeds. Did the person live more to benefit others, or did he use others to benefit himself? Scriptures describe a trial scene, with God as judge, Jesus or Muhammad as defense attorney, and sometimes the devil as prosecutor. God is bound to pass sentence based upon the evidence. On this point, Father Moon offers a unique insight: to overcome Satan's accusation at the judgment, we should win over the person or persons who most hate and accuse us on earth. He calls it loving 'Cain.'

Scriptures describe a gate that only the righteous may enter, a "bridge of the separator" that only the righteous may cross, and a fire that burns up all falsehood and leaves only what is genuine. The spirit world has various abodes, heavens and hells, welcoming the soul according to its condition. Spirits are sorted out, and each goes to its appropriate place. No guards are required to keep out the unworthy; no policemen to direct traffic, for each person naturally goes to the place most fitting to his or her character and past life.

1. The Life Review

For God will bring every deed into judgment, with every secret thing, whether good or evil.
                                Ecclesiastes 12.14

For nothing is covered that will not be revealed, or hidden that will not be known.
                                Matthew 10.26

Then I saw a great white throne and Him who sat upon it; from His presence earth and sky fled away, and no place was found for them. And I saw the dead, great and small, standing before the throne, and books were opened. Also another book was opened, which is the book of life. And the dead were judged by what was written in the books, by what they had done.
                                Revelation 20.11-12

When the earth is shaken with her earthquake
And the earth yields up her burdens,
And man says, "What ails her?"
That day she will relate her chronicles
Because your Lord inspires her.
That day mankind will issue forth in scattered groups to be shown their deeds.
And whoever has done good, an atom's weight will see it then,
And whoever has done ill, an atom's weight will see it then.
                                Qur'an 99

And every man's augury have We fastened to his own neck, and We shall bring forth for him on the Day of Resurrection a book which he will find wide open. "Read your book! Your soul suffices as a reckoner against you this day."
                                Qur'an 17.13-14

After you depart this life, God shall demand a reckoning of your deeds
That in His ledger are recorded.
Those that are rebellious, shall be summoned.
Azrael, the angel of death, will hover over them,
And trapped in a blind alley they will know not any escape.
Saith Nanak, Falsehood must be destroyed;
Truth in the end shall prevail.
    Adi Granth, Ramkali-ki-Var 13, M.1, p. 953 *(Sikhism)*

On the day when man's time arrives to depart from the world, when the body is broken and the soul seeks to leave it, on that day man is privileged to see things that he was not permitted to see before, when the body was in full vigor. Three messengers stand over him and take an account of his life and of all that he has done in this world, and he admits all with his mouth and signs the account with his hand... as it is written, "that every man should acknowledge his works." (Job 37:7)

Zohar 1.79a (Judaism)

Teachings of Sun Myung Moon

At the fateful moment of death, all the facts of a person's past life will pass through his mind as images. No one needs to explain to him what kind of person he is; he will know it by himself. The life he inherited from his ancestors, the circumstances he faced, the situation he leaves behind, and all his past will appear as images in his mind at the last moment of his life.

A person who left behind a valuable moment during his earthly life will recognize it: "There was truth. I left behind something more precious than my life." However, another person will admit, "I spent my whole life course from birth to death as merely a passerby." Reflecting on all his past actions and feeling no desire to remember them, he feels miserable. For the person whose face is filled with joy as he reflects on his past, death is not to be feared; it is a moment of comfort. His past will not die and his reality will not die...

If a person gave his life while struggling to save his brother, a kinsman or a stranger, at the moment of death that fact will appear as an unforgettable image. But times of self-centered happiness, even moments of basking in the glory and acclaim of many people, will not bring any effect.

What does it mean to be good, to be persons of truth who can stand on their own before God? Truth and goodness do not begin from us or end in us. Truth and goodness are established when something begins in us and brings results for others, or begins in others and brings results in us. It is the same with all existences in heaven and earth; they have to establish reciprocal relationships of give and take according to the Principle.

If one's past life was entirely a life of giving, there will be no fear on the path of death. A shining past is a life of giving everything to others, sacrificing for others, shedding tears for others, investing life for others, desiring for others, concentrating all one's vitality and investing it for others...

For ordinary people facing the vicissitudes of the fallen world, their path of life is sometimes up and sometimes down. They make plans from one year to the next, or maybe plan their future for ten or twenty years, but always centered on themselves. However, when they meet their final destiny, all their records of sacrificing others for their own benefit will bind them. (31:308-10, June 7, 1970)

2. The Sorting, for Heaven or Hell

The hour is coming when all who are in the tombs will hear his voice and come forth, those who have done good, to the resurrection of life, and those who have done evil, to the resurrection of judgment.

John 5.28-29

Towards the wicked man and the righteous one
And him in whom right and wrong meet
Shall the Judge act in upright manner,
According to the laws of the present existence.

Avesta, Yasna 33.1 (Zoroastrianism)

He, having effected an activity of body that is harmful, effected an activity of speech that is harmful, effected an activity of mind that is harmful, arises in a world that is harmful. Because he has uprisen in a world that is harmful, harmful sensory impingements assail him. He, being assailed by harmful sensory impingements, experiences a harmful feeling, without exception painful, even as do creatures in Niraya Hell. In this way, there is the uprising of a being from what he has come to be; he uprises according to what he does; when he has uprisen sensory impingements assail him. So I speak thus: Creatures are heir to deeds.

Majjhima Nikaya 1.389-90, Kukkuravatikasutta (Buddhism)

For the Son of man is to come with his angels in the glory of his Father, and then he will repay every man for what he has done.

Matthew 16.27

Naturally every Hopi wants to join the spirits of his loved ones who have passed beyond. To that end he keeps his heart pure and is kind and generous to other people.

When a bad person, one who is known as "not-Hopi," dies, his fate is very different. Witches called the "Two Hearts" take him by the hand as soon as the breath is out of his body, and they lead him away to their own country. The country of the Two Hearts is as bad as they are themselves.

Hopi Tradition (Native American Religions)

The Trumpet will be sounded, and whoever is in heaven and whoever is on earth will be stunned, except for someone God may wish. Then another [blast] will be blown and behold, they will stand there watching! The earth will shine through its Lord's light and the Book will be laid open. Prophets and witnesses will be brought in, and judgment will be pronounced among them formally, and they will not be harmed. Every soul will be repaid for whatever it has done; He is quite aware of what they are doing.

The ones who disbelieve will be driven along to hell in throngs until, just as they come up to it, its gates will swing open and its keepers will say to them, "Did not messengers come to you from among yourselves reciting your Lord's verses to you and warning you about meeting [Him] on this day of yours?" They will say, "Of course!" But the Sentence about torment has still come due for disbelievers. Someone else will say, "Enter hell's gates to remain there. What an awful lodging will it be for the overbearing!"

The ones who have heeded their Lord will be driven along to the Garden in throngs until just as they come up to it, its gates will swing open and its keepers will tell them, "Peace be upon you! You have been good, so enter it to remain there." They will say, "Praise be to God who has held true to His promise for us and let us inherit the earth! We shall settle down anywhere we wish to in the Garden. How favored are such workers' wages!"

Qur'an 39.68-74

At the gates of the land of the dead
You will pass before a searching Judge.
His justice is true and He will examine your feet,
He will know how to find every stain,
Whether visible or hidden under the skin;
If you have fallen on the way He will know.
If the Judge finds no stains on your feet
Open your belly to joy, for you have overcome
And your belly is clean.

Fon Song (African Traditional Religions)

Teachings of Sun Myung Moon

How is it determined whether we shall go to heaven or hell? It doesn't matter how religious we are. The answer is simple: if we lived mainly for ourselves, we shall go to hell. On the other hand, if on the balance, even by just one percent, our life was mainly dedicated for a public purpose, we shall overcome hell and arrive in heaven. (75:330, January 16, 1975)

Is the standard of a person's conscience able to receive the heart of Heaven one hundred percent? No, it is not that way at all. In fact, the conscience of a fallen person is oppressed by so many restrictions. Nevertheless, at the entrance to heaven, our hoped-for destination, stands a gate of judgment. (4:269, August 8, 1958)

It is a gate that only those who lived for the sake of others can pass through. There are guards at the gate. Please understand well that whatever I ask of you is to enable you to pass through that gate. (203:193, June 24, 1990)

Heaven is a vast world, and it consists of three levels. Who will go to the highest level? It is those who most lived for others. It is the law there. If you lived for others, then wherever you go, people will welcome you.

However, for those who lived for themselves, the opposite scene will unfold. No matter where a self-centered person goes, the people will drive him out, saying "Huh! We don't like your kind of people." Everyone will reject a person who lived for himself, and everyone will welcome someone who lived for others. That is for sure.

You should know clearly whether you are on the path to heaven or to hell. This is not my casual viewpoint. I know the spirit world. People lead all manner of lives on earth, but no one can avoid death. Those who lived for themselves will go to hell, and those who lived for others will go to heaven. At death people are sorted into these two worlds. (203:100-01, June 17, 1990)

3. The Court of Judgment

Who shall bring any charge against God's elect? It is God who justifies; who is to condemn? Is it Christ Jesus, who died, yes, who was raised from the dead, who is at the right hand of God, who indeed intercedes for us? Who shall separate us from the love of Christ?

Romans 8.33-35

When I die my death will be a mercy and a blessing for you: After death, your deeds will be sent to me and I will look at them: If you worked righteousness, I will praise God for this. If you worked evil, I will ask God that you be forgiven.

Hadith of Ibn Sa'd (Islam)

They that are born are destined to die; and the dead to be brought to life again; and the living to be judged, to know, to make known, and to be made conscious that He is God, He the Maker, He the Creator, He the Discerner, He the Judge, He the Witness, He the Complainant; He it is that will in future judge, blessed be He, with whom there is no unrighteousness, nor forgetfulness, nor respect of persons, nor taking of bribes. Know also that everything is according to reckoning; and let not your imagination give you hope that the grave will be a place of refuge for you. For perforce you were formed, and perforce you were born, and perforce you live, and perforce you will die, and perforce you will in the future have to give account and reckoning before the King of kings, the Holy One, blessed be He.

Mishnah, Avot 4.29 (Judaism)

Teachings of Sun Myung Moon

Jesus is working as an attorney in the spirit world. He would say to God, "This person did such and such good deeds with faith in my name. Isn't it true, based upon the agreement fixed between you and the Devil, that the Devil cannot take a person who strived to be good and who observed public righteousness?" Then, God has to agree with him. (149:98, November 17, 1986)

God brings each individual into judgment based on the degree to which he or she lived centered on the mind or centered on the body. An individual is completely restored when he or she becomes the very incarnation of the scriptures, established in truth and guiltless of every law in the book of judgment.

Now, on the foundation of individual perfection, it is time to establish a family that can pass through the judgment. All the family's records will be presented as evidence… God takes position of the judge, Satan will be the prosecutor, and Jesus will be our defense attorney. Therefore, we should establish a pure family that Satan cannot accuse of any wrong. (13:211, March 15, 1964)

Do you love Cain? Cain is in the position of Satan's son. Satan, who is spiritual, challenges us through people who take the role of Cain. They are grinding their teeth, hating us even though we never did them any wrong. If Satan is not to hook you, you should subjugate Cain; that is, win him over. This will require you to love Cain all the way to the end; otherwise, you cannot save him.

For this reason, in order to enter the Kingdom of Heaven, you need to obtain a certificate from Satan. What is Satan's certificate? For a convicted criminal to be released he should first go through an attorney, then a prosecutor, and finally he can be released by the judge. Satan is in the position of the prosecutor, God is the judge, and Jesus is the attorney.

If Satan accuses a defendant with convincing evidence, God cannot do anything about it. Then Jesus, the attorney, says, "Heavenly Father, since this person is accused of such and such counts, let him be given an indemnity condition proportionate to his offenses, and then liberate him." For this reason [proving he has fulfilled the indemnity condition], he needs to procure a certificate from Satan. (48:316-17, September 26, 1971)

4. You Are Your Own Judge

The self is the maker and non-maker, and itself makes happiness and misery, is its own friend and its own foe, decides its own condition good or evil, and is its own river Veyarana [the river in which hell-beings are tormented].

Madaghishloka (Jainism)

The sacrificers and the sorcerer princes
Have subdued mankind to the yoke of their
    dominion,
To destroy existence through evil deeds:
They shall be tortured by their own soul and
    their own conscience,

When they come to the Bridge of the
    Separator,
Forever to be inmates of the House of Evil.

Avesta, Yasna 46.11 (Zoroastrianism)

The Good Spirit, who was born simultaneously with you, will come now and count out your good deeds with white pebbles, and the Evil Spirit, who was born simultaneously with you, will come and count out your evil deeds with black pebbles. Thereupon you will be greatly frightened, awed, and terrified, and will tremble; and you will attempt to tell lies, saying, "I have not committed any evil deed."

Then the Lord of Death will say, "I will consult the Mirror of karma." He will look in the Mirror, wherein every good and evil act is vividly reflected. Lying will be of no avail.

Then one of the executive furies of the Lord of Death will place a rope around your neck and drag you along; he will cut off your head, extract your heart, pull out your intestines, lick up your brain, drink your blood, eat your flesh, and gnaw your bones; but you will be incapable of dying. Although your body be hacked to pieces, it will revive again. The repeated hacking [symbolizing the pangs of the deceased's conscience] will cause intense pain and torture.

Even at the time that the pebbles are being counted out, be not frightened; tell no lies; and fear not the Lord of Death.

Your body being a mental body is incapable of dying even though beheaded and quartered. In reality, your body is of the nature of voidness; you need not be afraid. The Lords of Death are your own hallucinations. Your desire-body is a body of propensities, and void. Voidness cannot injure voidness; the qualityless cannot injure the qualityless. Apart from one's own hallucinations, in reality there are no such things existing outside oneself as Lord of Death, or god, or demon. Act so as to recognize this.

Tibetan Book of the Dead *(Buddhism)*

Teachings of Sun Myung Moon

God does not decide whether a person's spirit enters heaven or hell upon his death; the spirit himself decides it. Humans are created so that once they reach perfection they will fully breathe the love of God. Those who committed sinful deeds while on earth become crippled spirits who are incapable of fully breathing in the love of God. They find it agonizing to stand before God, the center of true love. Of their own will, they choose to dwell in hell, far removed from the love of God. (*Exposition of the Divine Principle*, Creation 6.3.2)

Running through each of you is the boundary line dividing heaven and hell. One step to the right and you go to heaven, one step to the left is hell. Heaven is not so far away, and neither is hell. You are the deciding factor.

In spirit world there is no policeman directing traffic. We each find our own place. Since you go there of your own free will, you cannot complain. In hell, you cannot protest, "God, why did you send me here?" because you decided your own dwelling place. Even at this moment, each of you knows whether you should go to heaven or hell. (201:225-26, April 22, 1990)

How is it decided whether my journey will end at heaven or hell? I decide it. If I feel guilt-stricken in my conscience for having lived only to enjoy the pleasures of the senses, I will be in hell. However, if I lived according to my conscience, preferring a life of integrity of heart, I will dwell in the heavenly spheres. For this reason, people should abandon the aspiration for material things and deny their evil desires. The correct way is to live by one's conscience and strive to uphold the ethics of heaven. (7:238, September 20, 1959)

People bound for heaven do not need to be taught the way. Having lived according to their conscience, they will arrive there automatically. When the sun rises, don't all the buds of the trees turn to face the sun? Even plants know instinctively what direction to take. Then, as the lord of all creation, how could you not know where to go? You will experience this after you enter the spirit world. (75:42, January 1, 1975)

Heaven

CONCEPTIONS OF HEAVEN AND HELL ARE FOUND UNIVERSALLY among the religions of the world. Descriptions of these abodes are often full of graphic and fanciful imagery, conveying in metaphor a reality that can hardly be part of the ordinary experience of mortals. Are these realms objectively real? The scriptures are unanimous in affirming they are. Yet they do not have any physical location: "up" or "down" is a matter of spiritual geography, not of astronomy or geology. The view found in some texts, that heaven or hell is derived from one's state of mind, does not make it any less real. For the attitudes and desires of people's hearts, which may be hidden by the external features of mortal life, constitute the spirit world's "matter."

The world's scriptures describe Heaven as a place of rest, or as an exalted spiritual state, full of divine grace, whose inhabitants live in communion with God and in harmony with one another. A number of texts describe it as a place of fellowship with the spirits of the departed or a fellowship of saints. There are also descriptions using more graphic and materialistic imagery: gardens of delights, with riches and pleasures abounding. Father Moon's colorful descriptions of heaven are in agreement with these themes of scripture. What's more, he adds a distinctive note, affirming that heaven is also a place where families dwell together, enjoying perfect love.

We conclude with visions or tours of Heaven: a Buddhist description of the Pure Land, Muhammad's Night Journey through the seven heavens, an Iroquois Native American journey in the Code of Handsome Lake, as well as Father Moon's own descriptions. They describe a paradisiacal existence, a word of eternal youth and health where every wish is granted, where the senses are flooded with vibrant colors and melodious music.

1. Realms of Grace

No one who does good deeds will ever come to a bad end, either here or in the world to come. When such people die, they go to other realms where the righteous live.

Bhagavad-Gita 6.40-41 (Hinduism)

Those who have faith and do righteous deeds, they are the best of creatures. Their reward is with God: Gardens of Eternity, beneath which rivers flow; they will dwell therein for ever; God well pleased with them, and they with Him; all this for such as fear their Lord and Cherisher.

Qur'an 98.7-8

Rabbi Joseph... was ill and fell into a coma. When he recovered, his father asked him, "What did you see?" He replied, "I beheld a world the reverse of this one; those who are on top here were below there, and vice versa." He said to him, "My son, you have seen a corrected world."

Talmud, Pesahim 50a (Judaism)

Not like this world is the World to Come. In the World to Come there is neither eating nor drinking, nor procreation of children or business transactions, no envy or hatred or rivalry; but the righteous sit enthroned, their crowns on their heads, and feast on the radiance of the Divine Splendor (Shekhinah).

Talmud, Berakot 17a (Judaism)

To the highest regions, in due order, to those regions where there is no delusion, and to those regions which are full of light where the glorious gods dwell—who have long life, great power, great luster, can change their shape at will, are beautiful as on their first day, and have the brilliance of many suns—to such places go those who are trained in self-control and penance, both monks and householders who have obtained liberation by absence of passion.

Uttaradhyayana Sutra 5.26-28 (Jainism)

Higher than all stands the Realm of Grace—
None can have access there except heroes of supreme might,
Inspired by God-consciousness.
In that sphere abide numberless heroines like Sita of surpassing praise
And beauty indescribable.
Those to God united suffer neither mortality nor delusion.
In that sphere abide devotees assembled from the various universes,
Cherishing the holy Eternal ever in their hearts.
In everlasting bliss.

The formless Supreme Being abides in the Realm of Eternity.
Over His creation He casts His glance of grace.
In that realm are contained all the continents and universes,
Exceeding in number all count.
Of creation, worlds upon worlds abide therein—
All obedient to His Will;
He watches over them in bliss,
And has each constantly in mind.
Saith Nanak, Such is that realm's [glory] that to try to describe it is to attempt the impossible.

Adi Granth, Japuji 37 M.1, p. 8 *(Sikhism)*

Teachings of Sun Myung Moon

How is heaven—the spirit world where God resides—organized? Its ordering principle is simple. No one who lived a self-centered life can be admitted to Paradise or the heavenly spheres. Heaven is the dwelling-place of people who lived for the sake of the whole.

You may not have experienced the spirit world, but by the grace of God, I experienced the richness of that world. If you enter heaven, you will not find a single person who lived for him or herself. Its citizens are all people who lived for God and humanity. (77:189, April 6, 1975)

Heaven is an ideal realm centered on God; it is a place where everything moves to the rhythm of God's love, tuned to its frequency. Therefore, unless we prepare on earth the appropriate elements that can tune to God's frequency, we will not be able to harmonize with the beings in that world. For this purpose, while on earth we should perfect three different kinds of love: children's love, conjugal love and parental love.[17] (19:335, March 29, 1968)

Heaven begins from a heart that overcomes the world. Although heaven may exist all around us, if our own mind is evil we cannot perceive it, we cannot be harmonized with it, and it would be meaningless to us. Therefore, the basis for receiving the Kingdom of Heaven is not the environment, but I, myself. The pillar for maintaining the Kingdom of Heaven is not my circumstances, but my own heart. (46:24, July 18, 1971)

In the Kingdom of Heaven you will see green grass everywhere. There are mountains, lakes and prairies. Birds sing, flowers bloom in profusion, and animals play happily together. The air is fresh and filled with fragrances like lilac. Bright light shines throughout, more beautiful than diamond and clear as crystal. Just standing there makes you feel comfortable and refreshed. You are naturally filled with feelings of love and happiness. Unlike in earthy life where happiness comes and goes, in heaven you feel happy continually.

In the Kingdom of Heaven there is no anxiety or suffering. All the spirits have bright and peaceful expressions; they naturally care for each other without needing to say a word. There is no fighting, no fallen nature of jealousy, hate or arrogance. Everyone is filled only with true love and lives for the sake of others. (Heung Jin Moon, *Message from the Spirit World*, January 1, 2002)

2. Fellowship with the Saints and Our Ancestors

Where men of goodwill and good deeds rejoice,
Their bodies now made free from all disease,
Their limbs made whole from lameness or defect—
In that heaven may we behold our parents and our sons!

Atharva Veda 6.120.3 (Hinduism)

All who obey God and the Apostle are in the company of those on whom is the grace of God—of the Prophets who teach, the sincere lovers of Truth, the witnesses [martyrs] who testify, and the righteous who do good: Ah! what a beautiful fellowship!

Qur'an 4.69

You have come to Mount Zion and to the city of the living God, the heavenly Jerusalem, and to innumerable angels in festal gathering, and to the assembly of the first-born who are enrolled in heaven, and to a judge who is God of all, and to the spirits of just men made perfect, and to Jesus, the mediator of a new covenant.

Hebrews 12.22-24

When you die, you will be again with those you love who have gone before you. Again you will be young and strong, though you might have been old and feeble on the day you died. In the spirit land the corn will grow and all will be happy, whether they were good or bad when they were alive. So death is not something to be afraid of.

Yuma Tradition (Native American Religions)

And those Foremost [in faith] will be Foremost [in the hereafter].
These will be those nearest to God;
In Gardens of Bliss;
A number of people from those of old,
and a few from those of later times.
They will be on thrones encrusted, reclining on them, facing each other.
Round about them will serve youths of perpetual freshness,
with goblets, shining beakers, and cups filled out of clear-flowing fountains;
No after-ache will they receive therefrom, nor will they suffer intoxication;
And with fruits, any that they may select,
And the flesh of fowls, any that they may desire.
And there will be companions with beautiful, big and lustrous eyes,
Like unto pearls well-guarded:
A reward for the deeds of their past life.

Qur'an 56.10-25

For [the ancestors] Soma is purified,
some accept the molten butter;
to the company of those, for
whom the honey flows, let him go!

To the company of those who
are invincible by spiritual discipline *(tapas)*,
and through spiritual discipline have gone to heaven,
to men of great spiritual fire, let him go!

To the company of those who
fight contested battles, heroes
who cast away their lives, to those who
made a thousand gifts, let him go!

To those ancient followers
of the Law, steadfast in the Law,
who furthered the Law, to the Fathers, Yama,
great in their spiritual fire, let him go![18]

To the sage-poets, the leaders
of thousands, those who protect the sun,
to the Rishis of great spiritual discipline,
born of spiritual discipline, Yama! let him go!

Rig Veda 10.154.1-5 (Hinduism)

Teachings of Sun Myung Moon

The Kingdom of Heaven is an extension of family life. (*Way of God's Will* 1.8)

The Chinese character "heaven" (天) is written by combining two characters: the character 二 means "two," and 人 means "person." In other words, heaven consists of two people. All beings in heaven live in mutual relationships with corresponding entities. (92:309, April 24, 1977)

In heaven you do not age, since you are in the supreme state, your mind intoxicated with love. My mother should be old by now, but when I glimpse her [in the spirit world] she looks beautiful, as she did in the prime of her life. (201:103, March 11, 1990)

What is heaven like? It is a realm centered on love. There you enjoy being loved. You enjoy receiving love endlessly and never tire of it...

Captivated by love, the sleepers awaken, the deaf hear and the dumb speak. There are no barriers to communicating with anyone, and you can continue speaking endlessly for tens of millions of years. All your cells and all your senses are activated one hundred percent. (102:160-61, December 17, 1978)

In the afterlife it is no problem to travel hundreds of millions of miles in an instant. The power of love is the speediest. If you call someone whom you are yearning to see with true love, that person will immediately appear before your eyes. It doesn't matter that your beloved is a hundred million light-years away. As long as you have love, you can see that person any time. A mother at one end of the universe and a son is at the other end can meet each other in an instant. If you long to meet a person who lived tens of millions of years ago, he or she will appear immediately. Past and future do not exist in heaven. Only the present exists. A thousand years ago is as the present. Such is the spirit world, transcending time and space. (194:133-34, October 17, 1989)

What is the best way to greet God, returning joy and glory to Him? In the Garden of Eden, Adam and Eve would have greeted God best by loving each other in God's presence. Likewise, in the spirit world, a couple stands before God wearing their wedding garments; then they embrace and make love, and in that moment they become one with God. That is the best way to greet God. (314:25, December 30, 1999)

The Kingdom of Heaven is a world of relations. Therefore, our entire family should be included. So should all members of our clan and all the people of our nation. (18:331, August 13, 1967)

If only parents were to enter heaven without their children accompanying them, it would not be heaven. In the Kingdom of Heaven, parents enjoy the love and support of their entire family. They live together and relate with each other with God as the center.

Thus, we cannot enter the Kingdom of Heaven by ourselves. Parents and children enter heaven together. Suppose you were in heaven while your mother was in hell and screaming for help, "My child, please save me!" Would you say, "Heaven is wonderful, but Mother, you deserve to be in hell and suffer in pain"? Heaven is not such a place.

According to God's purpose of creation, all family members, parents and children, should dwell together in heaven. Not only your immediate family, but also your clan and your entire nation should enter there. Everyone in the world should dwell together there. (15:265, October 17, 1965)

In the spirit world you do not need formal introductions. On meeting someone, you immediately know who he or she is. That person may have lived a thousand years ago or even many millions of years ago, yet still you will recognize him or her. People believe that biblical history is 6000 years, but that number is only symbolic. When you know the spirit world, you will understand the actual length of human history. It could stretch back millions or tens of millions of years.

You can call for an ancestor from a certain era, and he or she will appear in front of you. You recognize that person at a glance, without speaking a word. You instantly grasp all the essentials, including the manner of respect you should use when addressing him.[19] Hence, you do not need formal introductions like on earth. Everyone automatically observes the hierarchical order.

What can keep the order? By living with love. Love determines position. Therefore, unless you become a child of God, you cannot enter the Kingdom of Heaven. (208:142-43, November 17, 1990)

3. Heaven's Delights

He who enters paradise will be in affluent circumstances and will not be destitute, his clothing will not wear out and his youth will not pass away.

Hadith of Muslim (Islam)

The Pure Land (Sukhavati) is fragrant with many sweet-smelling odors, rich in manifold flowers and fruits, adorned with jewel trees, and frequented by flocks of various birds with sweet voices, which have been produced by the miraculous power of the Tathagata. The jewel trees have various colors, many colors, many hundreds of thousands of colors. They are composed of varying combinations of the seven precious things: gold, silver, beryl, crystal, coral, red pearls, and emerald... Their roots, trunks, branches, leaves, flowers, and fruits are pleasant to touch, and fragrant. And when these trees are moved by the wind, a sweet and delightful sound proceeds from them, which one never tires of hearing...

Many kinds of rivers flow along in this Pure Land... whose banks are lined with variously scented jewel trees, and from them hang bunches of flowers, leaves, and branches of all kinds. When beings wish to indulge in sports full of heavenly delights on those riverbanks, then as they step into the water, the water rises as high as they wish it to—up to the ankles, or to the knees, or to the hips, or to their sides, or to their ears. If beings wish the water to be cold, for them it becomes cold; if they wish it to be hot, for them it becomes hot; if they wish it to be hot and cold, for them it becomes hot and cold, to suit their pleasure.

Those rivers flow along, full of water scented with the best perfumes, covered with lilies, lotus, and all manner of beautiful flowers, resounding with the sounds of peacocks, sparrows, parrots, ducks, geese, herons, cranes, swans, and others, with small islands inhabited by flocks of birds, easy to ford, free from mud, and with golden sand on the bottom. And all the wishes those beings may think of, they will be fulfilled, as long as they are rightful.

Larger Sukhavativyuha Sutra 15-18 (Buddhism)

The Messenger of God said, "While I was at Mecca, the roof of my house opened and Gabriel entered. He opened my chest, washed me with the water of Zamzam, brought a golden basin full of faith and wisdom and emptied all of it into my chest. After that he closed it, took me by the hand and raised me towards the lowest heaven.

"When I arrived at the lowest heaven, Gabriel said to the doorkeeper, 'Open.' 'Who is there?' he asked. 'Gabriel,' the angel replied. 'Is there anyone with you?' responded the doorkeeper. 'Yes,' replied Gabriel, 'Muhammad is with me.' 'Has he been commanded?' added the doorkeeper. 'Yes,' said the angel.

"When the doorkeeper had opened to us, we rose up within the lowest heaven, and suddenly we saw a man sitting, having some spirits on his right and others on his left. Every time he looked to the right he smiled, but as soon as he looked to the left he wept. He said, 'Welcome virtuous prophet and virtuous son.' 'Who is this?' I asked Gabriel. 'This man,' he replied, 'is Adam, and those spirits on the right are destined to Paradise, while the spirits on his left are destined to hell. That is why, when he looks to the right, he smiles, and when he looks to the left, he weeps.'

"Then Gabriel raised me up to the second heaven and said to the doorkeeper, 'Open.' He asked the same questions as the first, and then opened to us." The Prophet found in the various heavens Adam, Idris, Moses, Jesus, and Abraham...

"Then the angel raised me until he brought me to a height where I heard the beating of wings... Then Gabriel led me away and brought me to the Lote-Tree of the Boundary, which is covered with unspeakably beautiful colors. Next I entered Paradise. There are domes of pearls, and the sun there is made of musk."[20]

Hadith of Bukhari *(Islam)*

For all there is heaven; earth is heaven, and sea heaven; and animal and plant and man; all is the heavenly content of that heaven: And the gods in it, despising neither men nor anything else that is there where all is of the heavenly order, traverse all that country and all space in peace.

To "live at ease" is there; and, to these divine beings, verity is mother and nurse, existence and sustenance; all that is not of process but of authentic being they see, and themselves in all: For all is transparent, nothing dark, nothing resistant; every being is lucid to every other, in breadth and depth; light runs through light. And each of them contains all within itself, and at the same time sees all in every other, so that everywhere there is all, and all is all and each all, and infinite the glory. Each of them is great; the small is great; the sun, there, is all the stars; and every star, again, is all the stars and sun. While some one manner of being is dominant in each, all are mirrored in every other.

Plotinus, Enneads 5.8.3 *(Hellenism)*

Then they went out upon the narrow road and had not gone far when a brilliant light appeared. It was then that they smelled the fragrant odors of the flowers along the road. Delicious looking fruits were growing on the wayside, and every kind of bird flew in the air above them. The most marvelous and beautiful things were on every hand. All these things were on the heaven road. *Eniaiehuk.*

They continued on their journey, and after a short time they came to a halt. Then spoke the messengers, "This place is called The Spring, and it is a place for rest." Then behold, he saw the spring and he thought that he had never seen so beautiful and clear a fount of water. Then said the four, "This is a place of refreshment." One of the four drew a bottle from his bosom, so it seemed and it was, and dipped it in the spring. Then he said, "You must partake first," and so he took it, but when he looked at it he thought it was not enough. So he said, "I think that this is not sufficient." When he had said this, the messengers looked at one another and smiled, and one said, "Truly it is enough. If it lacks, there is still the spring and the vessel may be refilled." So all took and drank, and all the drink that all wished was in the bottle... *Eniaiehuk.*

They proceeded on their journey, and had gone but a short way when they saw someone coming toward them, and it was not long before they met. He saw it was a dog, and when they met, the dog began to wag its tail and sprang upon him. Then he recognized the animal as his own dog, appearing just as it had when he had decorated it for the sacrifice in the New

Year's ceremony. Then said the four, "This thing attests to the value of our thank-offering to the Creator." So they said. *Eniaiehuk.*

They took up their journey again, and in a short time came to a halt. In the distance before them a man appeared to be coming, and soon he came nearer. Then he saw that the man was guiding two others, one on either side. As he looked, he saw that one was the daughter of Gaiant'waka, and it appeared that she was a large child. With her was Ganio'dai'io', his own son, an infant. The son and the daughter greeted one another. One could see that they were not strangers, for they were friendly. Moreover a fourth person was leading them all. *Eniaiehuk.*

Now that person spoke and said, "I brought them with me to testify to the truth that those of the lower world when they pass away come hither."

The Code of Handsome Lake 112-116
(*Native American Religion*)

The inhabitants of paradise will eat and drink in it, but they will not spit or pass water or void excrement, or suffer from catarrh.

Hadith of Muslim (*Islam*)

Teachings of Sun Myung Moon

What is it like to live in the other world? There is no need to worry about what to eat, where to live or what to wear. Anything is possible just by thinking about it or wishing it. People eat in the spirit world. They can feel the pulse in the veins. Although theirs is a spiritual body, they can feel it just the same as the pulse in a physical body.

Whatever you want to eat, it immediately appears. Make a list of the foods you would like to enjoy, and they will be set out on the table before your eyes. Where does it come from? The spirit world is active and self-organizing; it assembles the elements that are needed. What is the governing and active force that can mobilize the whole? It is not power, nor is it knowledge or money. It is love, only love.

God is supreme, yet if you call for Him with deep and heart-felt sincerity, He immediately replies, "Yes, my child. What do you want?" If you ask, "Where are you?" God answers, "Where else could I be, other than in your heart?" God is the origin of all creation. God is in the root of heart.

In heaven, if you wish, you can hold celebrations millions of times a day. In the ecstasy of love, whatever you desire is done at your command. (194:42, October 15, 1989)

Dogs can follow their masters to the heavenly realms. Pets and beloved articles can accompany their owners wherever they go. (78:337, June 10, 1975)

Are there automobile factories in the other world? Here on earth, people are proud of their Mercedes Benzes. Will you brag about your car in the spirit world? Cars are not necessary over there…

By the power of your imagination alone, you can have anything you want. If you wish for a car encrusted with diamonds, it will appear. Yet why would you need a car? Even without a car, you can travel billions of light years in an instant. As long as you have the heart of true love, that is enough. (207:94-95, November 1, 1990)

When God created this vast universe, there were neither cars nor food. Yet, just as the Creator God made all kinds of things to realize the ideal of true love, we too, centering on love, can create by exercising our original innate powers and abilities.

Centering on love, when you think of something in your mind, whatever you name will appear before your eyes. You can gather millions of people for a banquet and request particular dishes, and they will appear on the table. If you want to wear a golden formal gown, you can have it, too. How fantastic! After such a delicious meal, your tongue might hang out!

What would your tongue do at that point? It wants to taste true love. It wants to reach a higher plane, jumping up and up, exclaiming, "I like it! I like it! That is enough for me. Now I want to enjoy these things with my loving spouse." As long as you are standing within love's sovereignty, standing as one of God's companions, whatever you desire can be realized in a moment.

Everything looks beautiful, everything sounds wonderful, and you feel content with everything around you. Sleeping is sound and sweet, and waking up is wonderful.

Yet in the spirit world you do not need sleep. Even in the middle of the night, every cell of your body can dance. Each cell is like your partner; it dances accompanied by melodies whose beauty far surpasses any earthly music...

In heaven, love connects you with everything. You breathe the air of love, eat the food of love, and wear the clothes of love. God your Parent provides you with all these, out of His true love. (217:293, June 2, 1991)

Do you think that people urinate in the spirit world? I am telling you that we do; when you get there you will see for yourself. What about defecating? Yes, we do, but afterwards the waste immediately returns to its elements. [There are 107 known elements in the universe.] Hence, it is not necessary to clean it up. With a mind of love, all you do is make a motion with your hand and all the waste returns to its origin. (212:30, January 1, 1991)

Hell

NO ONE LIKES TO THINK THAT THEY OR THEIR LOVED ONES are destined for hell. Yet it is a painful truth that most people live out their lives far away from the original standard of God's love. The human condition is too often this: we allow our thoughts and desires to be captive to the will of the flesh; our mentality is continually self-seeking; we habitually ignore the promptings of conscience. We betray those we love and then run away from facing the consequences, as well as the truth about ourselves. Having lived this way for seventy-plus years, is there any hope of fitting in to the crystal-clear society of heaven?

What is hell? Some traditions describe it as a place deep underground, with rivers of fire and sulfur. Some say that hell is but a state of mind, yet as anyone knows who has experienced the pangs of intense loneliness, remorse, shame, guilt, or loss, such states of mind can be excruciatingly vivid. Furthermore, it is said that in the spirit world it will not be possible to avoid such feelings, as is usually done while in the body, through such devices as forgetting, rationalization, or losing oneself in sense-pleasures or drink. There is no respite from unpleasant feelings, which remain to torture the unfortunate soul continually. To describe such pain beyond comprehension, scriptures use concrete images: burning fire, boiling water, bitter cold, being crushed, hacked and dismembered, trampled, burned, and eaten alive.

We conclude with several passages that hold out the possibility of rescue from hell. The Eastern religions regard all states of hell as purgatories, designed to mete out punishments for a period of time, that evil karma might be burned up and the soul have a future opportunity to find the Path. Father Moon teaches that God did not create hell; indeed its very existence is an affront to God's goodness and a nail driven into His loving heart. If we have sufficient love, we will do whatever it takes to turn others away from hell. We will even, like Jesus who "harrowed hell" during his three days in the tomb or the Hindu hero Vipascit, rescue the people imprisoned in its dungeons.

1. Torments of Hell

Hell, where their worm does not die, and the fire is not quenched.

Mark 9.47-48

As for the cowardly, the faithless, the polluted, as for murderers, fornicators, sorcerers, idolaters, and all liars, their lot shall be in the lake that burns with fire and sulfur, which is the second death.

Revelation 21.8

There is a stream of fire from which emerge
   poisonous flames.
There is none else there except the self.
The waves of the ocean of fire are aflame
And the sinners are burning in them.

Adi Granth, Maru Solahe, M.1, p. 1026 (Sikhism)

Hell is before him, and he is made to drink festering water, which he sips but can hardly swallow. Death comes to him from every side, yet he cannot die—before him is a harsh doom.

Qur'an 14.15-16

Hell will lurk in ambush
to receive home the arrogant,
who will linger there for ages.
They will taste nothing cool in it nor any drink
except hot bathwater and slops,
a fitting compensation
since they have never expected any reckoning
and have wittingly rejected Our signs.
Everything We have calculated in writing.
"So taste! Yet We shall only increase torment
   for you!"

Qur'an 78.21-30

Some of the sinful are cut with saws, like firewood, and others, thrown flat on the ground, are chopped into pieces with axes. Some, their bodies half buried in a pit, are pierced in the head with arrows. Others, fixed in the middle of a press, are squeezed like sugarcane. Some are surrounded close with blazing charcoal, enwrapped with torches, and smelted like a lump of ore. Some are plunged into heated butter, and others into heated oil, and like a cake thrown into the frying pan they are turned about. Some are thrown in the path of huge maddened elephants, and some with hands and feet bound are placed head downwards. Some are thrown into wells; some are hurled from heights; others, plunged into pits full of worms, are eaten away by them...

Having experienced in due order the torments below, he comes here again, purified.[21]

Garuda Purana 3.49-71 (Hinduism)

Then the man of unwholesome deeds boils in water infested with worms. He cannot stay still—the boiling pots, round and smooth like bowls, have no surfaces which he can get hold of. Then he is in the jungle of sword blades, limbs mangled and hacked, the tongue hauled by hooks, the body beaten and slashed. Then he is in Vetarani, a watery state difficult to get through, with its two streams that cut like razors. The poor beings fall into it, living out their unwholesome deeds of the past. Gnawed by hungry jackals, ravens and black dogs, and speckled vultures and crows, the sufferers groan. Such a state is experienced by the man of unwholesome deeds. It is a state of absolute suffering. So a sensible person in this world is as energetic and mindful as he can be.

Sutta Nipata 672-76 (Buddhism)

There men were dismembering one another, cutting off each of their limbs, saying, "This to you, this to me!" When asked about it, they replied, "In this way they have treated us in the other world, and in the same way we now treat them in return."

Satapatha Brahmana 11.6.3 (Hinduism)

There are divers regions in the hollows on the face of the globe everywhere, some of them deeper and also wider than that which we inhabit, others deeper and with a narrower opening than ours, and some are shallower and wider; all have numerous perforations, and passages broad and narrow in the interior of the earth, connecting them with one another; and there flows into and out of them, as into basins, a vast tide of water, and huge subterranean streams of perennial rivers, and springs hot and cold, and a great fire, and great rivers of fire, and streams of liquid mud, thin or thick... pour into a vast region of fire, and form a lake larger than the Mediterranean Sea, boiling with water and mud; and proceeding muddy and turbid, and... after making many coils about the earth plunge into Tartarus...

And when the dead arrive at the place to which the genius of each severally conveys them, first of all they have sentence passed upon them, as they have lived well and piously or not... Those who appear to be incurable by reason of the greatness of their crimes—who have committed many and terrible deeds of sacrilege, murders foul and violent, or the like—they are hurled into Tartarus, which is their suitable destiny, and they never come out. Those again who have committed crimes, which, although great, are not unpardonable—who in a moment of anger, for example, have done violence to a father or mother, and have repented for the remainder of their lives, or who have taken the life of another under like extenuating circumstances—these are plunged into Tartarus, the pains of which they are compelled to undergo for a year, but at the end of the year the wave casts them forth... and they are borne to the Acherusian Lake, and there they lift up their voices and call upon the victims whom they have slain or wronged, to have pity on them, and to receive them, and to let them come out of the river into the lake. And if they prevail, then they come forth and cease from their troubles; but if not, they are carried back again into Tartarus and from thence into the rivers unceasingly, until they obtain mercy from those whom they have wronged: for that is the sentence inflicted upon them by their judges.

Plato, Phaedo (*Hellenism*)

Teachings of Sun Myung Moon

Hell is a place where everyone is totally self-centered, each insisting that he or she is the best and highest. With that attitude, they argue and fight continually. (360:185, November 16, 2001)

Hell is the realm of Satan's love. Satan adores only hatred, jealousy, division and destruction. That is why only these things fill Satan's realm. These characteristics of Satan manifest as wars. (214:282, February 3, 1991)

Hell is full of people who are proud of their power, their money and themselves. A person's original mind desires to love and be loved, and to pursue goodness. The people living in hell do just the opposite, and face continual conflict. Yet being in hell does not remove the human desire to be loved. Actually, the yearning for love is felt even more strongly. (102:160, December 17, 1978)

What, then, will you do in the afterlife? Will you eat? Yes, you will eat. But it should be centered on love. Those who do not have love cannot open their mouths, no matter how much they try. That is the law. If you love only yourself and not the whole, you may try to eat, but your mouth will not open. If you try to eat with chopsticks, the chopsticks will swerve sharply to the right or the left. It is a miserable existence. In the spirit world, anything is possible with love, but only with love. Otherwise, nothing is possible. (207:94-95, November 1, 1990)

In the spirit world, most people dwell in various levels of hell. How did they end up living there? Some failed to practice filial piety as befits good sons and daughters. Some had the mission of patriots yet did not fulfill their mission and live for the sake of their country. Some were chosen to become saints and live for the sake of the world, but they did not attune themselves to that rhythm and hence failed to reach that level. (147:183-84, September 21, 1986)

The accusations we could face in the spirit world are far more fearful than the severest persecution on earth. Because I know that earthly persecution, no matter how heavy, is easier to endure than the accusations in the spirit world, I am clear about the path I should go. (189:247, April 9, 1989)

Heaven is a world of light, and hell is a world of darkness. You may have enjoyed your earthly life, but once you arrive in hell the darkness will quickly overcome you. It is like drinking: for awhile you are in high spirits, but later you feel regret as your conscience tells you it was the wrong thing to do. It will also ask, "Where are you going?" People who suffer continually from pangs of conscience belong to the world of darkness. If only their conscience were pleased with them; then they would display the original nature within themselves to relate to the world of light. (400:104, December 28, 2002)

This world is in chaos. How about the spirit world? The same confused people live there; therefore, the spirit world must likewise be in chaos. It is logical. A thief with a criminal record cannot just drop his bad habits when he crosses over to the spirit world. There too he would be a thief, wanting to own things without making effort to earn them. People like him are unable to fit in with heaven, so they went off and formed the realms of hell.
    God did not create hell. Human beings formed hell. Do people design their new house to be a garbage dump? No! They build a nice house, but after living in it for a while it becomes like a garbage dump. Hell is like that. (148:28, October 4, 1986)

Many people on earth think that there are only two different places: heaven and hell. But in reality there are many different levels, from very evil places to very good places. Heaven is a place of comfort, but life in any of the levels below heaven is difficult and uncomfortable because the people fight each other continually, everyone insisting on their own opinion. Each region is filled with people who are of the same type, so after awhile living there becomes tedious.
    For example, people who on earth were accustomed to stealing things dwell in a region of the spirit world where people are always suspicious, thinking that everyone around them is looking to steal from them. Their lives are forever filled with distrust and anxiety. Likewise, people who on earth were accustomed to fighting live in a region where fighting goes on continually...
    If you descend further into the lower regions, you come to regions of hell that are suffocating, dark and scary. They smell horribly, worse than the smell of rotten meat or fish. Deformed figures appear in front of you, biting each other, yelling at each other with hate-filled voices. There is a region filled with burning holes, and in each one a wrathful person is held fast. The worst regions are reserved for those who were sexually corrupt or who committed suicide. They seem to be filled with snakes, but on close examination each snake is an ugly deformed human being slithering about. People living on the earth do not realize how frightening the regions of hell really are. They would not be able to stand it even for a minute...
    From the Kingdom of Heaven to hell, the various regions of the spirit world have colors of differing hues. The Kingdom of Heaven is a bright realm, transparent and white. It is without any

stain, clean like flawless white jade. But as we descend the colors become darker and darker and dirtier—first beige, then darker shades of purple. Descending to still lower regions the color becomes brown, then gray, dark gray, black, and pitch black. The more sins committed, the darker the color. Also, spirits who committed many sins with a certain part of their body show dirtier and darker colors on that part. (Heung Jin Moon, *Message from the Spirit World*, January 1, 2002)

People who denied God on earth are more pitiful than people who starve to death. Those who died of hunger may, depending on their merit, be granted a certain standing in the other world. But atheists have no standing because they deny the spirit world exists. They become wandering spirits, wandering about the spirit world like clouds. Just as clouds gather and produce rain, they gather and create evil influence. They dwell in hell and inflict pains there. (205:355, October 2, 1990)

2. Warnings about Hell

Rivalry in worldly increase distracts you
Until you visit the graves.
Nay, but you will come to know!
Again, you will come to know!
Would that you knew now with certainty of mind!
For you will behold hell-fire;
Indeed, you will behold it with sure vision.
Then, on that day, you will be asked concerning pleasure.

                                    Qur'an 102

There was a rich man, who was clothed in purple and fine linen and who feasted sumptuously every day. And at his gate lay a poor man named Lazarus, full of sores, who desired to be fed with what fell from the rich man's table; moreover the dogs came and licked his sores. The poor man died and was carried by the angels to Abraham's bosom. The rich man also died and was buried; and in Hades, being in torment, he lifted up his eyes, and saw Abraham far off and Lazarus in his bosom. And he called out, "Father Abraham, have mercy upon me, and send Lazarus to dip the end of his finger in water and cool my tongue; for I am in anguish in this flame." But Abraham said, "Son, remember that you in your lifetime received your good things, and Lazarus in like manner evil things; but now he is comforted here, and you are in anguish. And besides all this, between us and you a great chasm has been fixed, in order that those who would pass from here to you may not be able, and none may cross from there to us."

And he said, "Then I beg you, father, to send him to my father's house, for I have five brothers, so that he may warn them, lest they also come into this place of torment." But Abraham said, "They have Moses and the prophets; let them hear them." And he said, "No, father Abraham; but if some one goes to them from the dead, they will repent." He said to him, "If they do not hear Moses and the prophets, neither will they be convinced if someone should rise from the dead."

                                    Luke 16.19-31

In the garden of the city of Sieu-Shui-Siuen, there once lived a man by the name of Fan Ki, who led a wicked life. He induced men to stir up quarrels and lawsuits with each other, to seize by violence what did not belong to them, and to dishonor other men's wives and daughters. When he could not succeed easily in carrying out his evil purposes, he made use of the most odious stratagems.

One day he died suddenly, but came back to life twenty-four hours afterward and bade his wife gather together their relatives and neighbors. When all were assembled he told them that he had seen the king of the dark realm who said to him, "Here the dead receive punishment for their deeds of evil. The living know not the lot that is reserved for them. They must be thrown into a bed of coals whose heat is in proportion to the extent of their crimes and to the harm they have done their fellows."

The assembled company listened to this report as to the words of a feverish patient; they were incredulous and refused to believe the story. But Fan Ki had filled the measure of crime, and Yama, the king of hell, had decided to make an example of him so as to frighten men from their evil ways. At Yama's command Fan Ki took a knife and mutilated himself, saying, "This is my punishment for inciting men to dissolute lives." He put out both his eyes, saying, "This is my punishment for having looked with anger at my parents, and at the wives and daughters of other men with lust in my heart." He cut off his right hand, saying, "This is my punishment for having killed a great number of animals." He cut open his body and plucked out his heart, saying, "This is my punishment for causing others to die under tortures." And last of all he cut out his tongue to punish himself for lying and slandering.

The rumor of these occurrences spread afar, and people came from every direction to see the mangled body of the unhappy man. His wife and children were overcome with grief and shame, and closed the door to keep out the curious crowd. But Fan Ki, still living by the ordeal of Yama, said in inarticulate sounds, "I have but executed the commands of the king of hell, who wants my punishment to serve as a warning to others. What right have you to prevent them from seeing me?"

For six days the wicked man rolled upon the ground in the most horrible agonies, and at the end of that time he died.

Treatise on Response and Retribution *(Taoism)*

Teachings of Sun Myung Moon

People can never escape from hell; [without help] they are trapped there forever. Yet, do you realize that your own mother, father and relatives will likely end up going to hell? You vaguely think that things will somehow work out. However, the reality is that your beloved parents and relatives are headed for hell. In this life, if they should go to prison, wouldn't you cry out desperately and do whatever it takes to free them? Yet truly, your own children, parents, siblings and kinfolk are bound for an eternal prison from which there is no escape. If you really knew that, wouldn't you feel desperate to save them?

This means you are not certain whether or not hell truly exists. You might think that it probably exists, but you really do not know what it is like. Now you may be uncertain, but once you die you will know for sure. Then it will be too late. (34:267, September 13, 1970)

What would happen if God were to bring all believers to heaven, even though they were ignorant of heaven's laws and [had not prepared themselves to fit with] the structure of the ideal realm? They would face difficulties living there. (390:260, August 13, 2002)

God's mind has room to accommodate everyone; He wants to welcome every human being to live within His mind. But should He open the door to wicked people and permit them to enter His domain? Or should He close the door and keep them out? This is God's problem.

God abides at the highest place, where everyone wants to enter. However, the mind of God has many levels, with walls or mountains separating them. This is the reality of the spirit world: there are many different levels, each walled off from the next. On one side of the wall is hell; on the other side is heaven. Should the spirit world have walls? Or shouldn't they exist? What do you think?

In the spirit world, groups of people with the same mindset live together; this creates a wall. It is very difficult to go up to the next higher level, and nearly as hard to go down. Most people cannot even dream of leaving their limited domain. Only the most highly developed spirits can freely travel down to the hells and back. They have the mind of God, who wants to embrace all people.

Yet God's situation is difficult. The people on His right are good, while the people on His left are bad. Although He wants to embrace good and bad alike, He has no other choice but to separate them. God declares, "Anyone who is greedy and selfish will be placed upside-down." Don't you think this will happen to you if you are self-centered and insist on your own way? Self-centered people think nothing of trampling and beating up others as they scramble to reach the top. They would push away the good people and leave them in misery. Therefore, God sets up walls between the different regions of the spirit world, to keep the evil spirits from breaking through. These walls are absolutely necessary. Were evil spirits given freedom and equality with good spirits, they would cause such havoc in heaven that even God would have to escape.

The only way to avoid being blocked by walls in the spirit world is to train yourself during your earthly life. Once you get to the spirit world, it will take tens of thousands of years to climb up each step. (November 4, 1990)

The perfection of man and woman is for the two to abide in love with God as the third—the unity of a man, a woman and God. Yet ever since the Human Fall, not one human being could reach that exalted state of love. Having fallen into a world of darkness, don't people nevertheless aspire to regain the heights? The goal of true love is extremely high, but in reality the standard of human life is extremely low. Knowing the ideal but recognizing that they live very far from it, people feel heartbreak, emptiness and misery. That is truly hell. (92:197, April 10, 1977)

3. Rescuing Souls from Hell

For Christ also died for sins once for all, the righteous for the unrighteous, that he might bring us to God, being put to death but made alive in the spirit; in which went and preached to the spirits in prison.[22]

1 Peter 3.18-19

As for those who will be wretched, they will be in the Fire, sighing and wailing will be their portion; they will abide there as long as the heavens and the earth endure, save for that which your Lord wills. Lo! Your Lord is the Doer of what He will.

And as for those who will be glad, they will be in the Garden; they will abide there as long as the heavens and the earth endure, save for that which your Lord wills—a gift unfailing.[23]

Qur'an 11.106-08

When Allah has finished His Judgments among the people, He will take whomever He will out of Hell through His Mercy... They will come out of the Fire, completely burnt and then the water of life will be poured over them and they will grow under it as does a seed that comes in the mud of the torrent...

Those people will come out like pearls, and they will have (golden) necklaces, and then they will enter Paradise whereupon the people of Paradise will say, "These are the people emancipated by the Beneficent. He has admitted them into Paradise without them having done any good deeds and without sending forth any good (for themselves)."

Hadith of Bukhari 9.93.532 *(Islam)*

"Ho! servant of Yama! Say, what sin have I committed, for which I have incurred this deepest hell, frightful for its torments? Known as King Vipascit, I protected the earth with uprightness; I let no fighting rage; no guest departed with averted countenance; nor did I offend the spirits of the ancestors, the gods, ascetics, or my servants; nor did I covet other men's wives, or wealth, or aught else belonging to them. How, then, have I incurred this very terrible hell?"

Yama's officer: "Come then, we go elsewhere. You have now seen everything, for you have seen hell. Come then, let us go elsewhere."

Thereupon the king prepared to follow him; but a cry went up from all the men that abode in torment: "Be gracious, O king! Stay but a moment, for the air that clings to thy body gladdens our mind and entirely dispels the burning and the sufferings and pains from our bodies, O tiger-like man! Be gracious, O king!"

Vipascit: "Neither in heaven nor in Brahma's world do men experience such joy as arises from conferring bliss on suffering creatures. If, while I am present, torment does not hurt these men, here then will I remain, firm as a mountain."

Yama's officer: "Come, O king; we proceed. Enjoy the delights won by your own merit; leave here the evildoers to their torments."

Vipascit, "As long as these beings are in sore suffering, I will not go. From my presence the denizens of hell grow happy. Fie on the sickly protection-begging life of that man who shows no favor to one distressed, even though he be a resolute foe! Sacrifices, gifts, austerities do not work for the welfare of him who has no thought for the succor of the distressed... To grant deliverance to these men excels, I consider, the joy of heaven. If many sufferers shall obtain happiness while only I undergo pain, shall I not in truth embrace it?"

Dharma [the Law]: "These evil-doers have come to hell in consequence of their own deeds; you also, O king, must go to heaven in consequence of your meritorious deeds. I lead you to heaven; mount this heavenly chariot and linger not; let us go."

Vipascit: "Men in thousands, O Dharma, suffer pain here in hell; and being in affliction they cry to me to save them; hence I will not depart."

Dharma: "O king! Your merit is truly beyond reckoning. In evincing now this compassion here in the hells, your merit has amounted even higher. Come, enjoy the abode of the immortals; let these unfortunates consume away in hell the sin arising from their own actions!"

Vipascit: "Whatever good deeds I possess, O Lord of the Thirty Gods, by means thereof let the sinners who are undergoing torment be delivered from hell!"

Indra: "So be it, O king! You have gained an even more exalted station: see too these sinners delivered from hell!"

Markandeya Purana 13-15 (Hinduism)

Teachings of Sun Myung Moon

God is a God of love. When God looks down from His throne and sees spirits in hell crying out to Him in their misery, "Please, God, save me!" what would He say? Would He say, "You deserve a lot worse"? Or does He have mercy on them? Surely, God will do everything possible to liberate hell. (98:116, May 7, 1978)

Only through love can we transform hell into heaven. We can renovate hell only if we possess love. (90:314, January 15, 1977)

Since people do not live longer than 100 years, out of the five billion people on earth, fifty million go to the spirit world each year—even to hell. What shall we do about this? God wants to harvest to His side what Satan has sown, but how many of them have gone to hell during the past forty years?

Perhaps two billion? This is serious. When I go to the spirit world, they may say, "Reverend Moon, when you were alive on earth, why didn't you fulfill your responsibility for us?" How am I supposed to reply to them? At least I should determine in my heart to take responsibility to save them, if not now, then through my followers who come after me. (205:356, October 2, 1990)

> From Judas Iscariot and Emperor Nero down to today's communist party,
> countless people have betrayed Heaven.
> Although we are destined for victory in relating with the entire cosmos,
> at this time for the complete dissolution of grief,
> we recognize that when the divine judgment befalls them
> we cannot just sweep them up and throw them away.
> Mayest Thou, through Thy name, and with the solemn authority of Thy universal victory,
> enable us to form relationships even with them, as is also our destiny...
> Although they were hated enemies who pierced Thy heart with nails,
> who killed Thy son Jesus, and killed many of Thy beloved people,
> let this be a place where we can love them.
> Open the gates of heaven and earth and reach out to them with Thy heart,
> Thy mind of magnanimous love.
> We know that by liberating them, the doors of hell will be opened,
> and the way will gradually be paved to abolish hell. (78:18-19, May 1, 1975)

Angels

ANGELS AND SPIRITUAL BENEFACTORS ARE A FEATURE OF ALL RELIGIONS. They may be recognized as gods, devas, kami, the spirits of animals and mountains (Shamanism), or dignitaries like the Jade Emperor (China) and the Buddhist bodhisattvas. In the latter group are the spirits of human beings who lived exemplary lives on earth and were then elevated to the status of deity and assigned the mission of angels. Nevertheless, in the monotheistic faiths these benefactors, no matter how exalted, are regarded as subordinate to and servants of the one Ultimate Reality.

In many traditions, these benevolent spirits dispense blessings to the human world and protect people from harm. Angelic visitors communicate God's instructions, as the angel Gabriel spoke to Muhammad and to the Virgin Mary. Thus angels take the role of "ministering spirits," serving God and assisting human beings—God's children.

Angels have power, and hence they are often the objects of worship. Yet within Judaism, Islam and Christianity are teachings that human beings are superior to angels. Along this line, Father Moon teaches that the angels assisted God in every step of creation, up to His ultimate goal of creating human beings. God placed angels in the Garden of Eden to educate and assist Adam and Eve as they grew from childhood to mature adulthood, when they were to become perfect and fulfill the ideal of creation. Chief among them was the archangel Lucifer, who however became corrupt and caused his charges to fall. (See Chapter 6: *The Devil and His Activities*) It still remains for human beings to judge the angels and regain their lost dignity.

1. The Identity and Mission of Angels

Who makes His angels spirits; His ministers a flaming fire.

Psalm 104.4

He created man of clay like the potters, and the Jinn did He create of smokeless fire.[24]

Qur'an 55.14-15

Are they [the angels] not all ministering spirits sent forth to serve, for the sake of those who are to obtain salvation?

Hebrews 1.14

The angels celebrate the praises of their Lord, and pray for forgiveness for all beings on earth.

Qur'an 42.5

Those who have said, "Our Lord is God," then have gone straight, upon them the angels descend, saying, "Fear not, neither sorrow; rejoice in Paradise that you were promised. We are your friends in the present life and in the world to come; therein you shall have all that your souls desire."

Qur'an 41.30-31

For He will give His angels charge over you, to guard you in all your ways.
On their hands they will bear you up, lest you dash your foot against a stone.

Psalm 91.10-11

I [the Bodhisattva Samantabhadra] relieve the distress of the beings of all evil realms, and equally bestow happiness on them. I continue to do so through the lapse of boundless kalpas, and in the extent of the ten quarters of the universe. The benefits of all are eternal, and omnipresent.[25]

Gandavyuha Sutra 39 (Buddhism)

Anything evil refrain from doing; all good deeds do! So you will be released forever from the influence of evil stars, and always be encompassed by good guardian angels.

Tract of the Quiet Way (Taoism)

When a man walks on the highway, a company of angels goes before him, proclaiming, "Make way for the image of the Holy One!"

Midrash on Psalm 17.8 (Judaism)

It [the Qur'an] is naught but an inspiration that is inspired,
which one of mighty powers [Gabriel] has taught him,
one vigorous; and he grew clear to view when he was on the uppermost horizon.
Then he drew near and came down till he was two bows' length away or even nearer, and he revealed unto His slave that which He revealed.[26]

Qur'an 53.4-10

The angel Gabriel was sent from God to a city of Galilee named Nazareth, to a virgin betrothed of a man whose name was Joseph, of the house of David; and the virgin's name was Mary. And he came to her and said, "Hail, O favored one, the Lord is with you!" But she was greatly troubled at the saying, and considered in her mind what sort of greeting this might be. And the angel said to her, "Do not be afraid, Mary, for you have found favor with God. And behold, you will conceive in your womb and bear a son, and you shall call his name Jesus.

Luke 1.26-31

Lord Scripture Glory says, "For seventeen generations I have been incarnated as a high mandarin, and I have never oppressed my people nor maltreated my subordinates. I have helped them in misfortune; I have rescued them from poverty; I have taken compassion on their orphans; I have forgiven their transgressions; I have extensively practiced secret virtue which is attuned to Heaven above. If you are able to keep your hearts as I have kept mine, Heaven will surely bestow upon you blessings."[27]

Tract of the Quiet Way (Taoism)

Teachings of Sun Myung Moon

God created the angelic world prior to creating the physical universe. Then, with the help of the angels, God utilized the elements of creation to form human beings. (83:155, February 8, 1976)

Angels, like all beings, were created by God. God created them prior to any other creation. In the biblical account of the creation of heaven and earth, we find that God spoke in the plural: "Let us make man in our image, after our likeness." (Gen. 1.26) This is not because God was referring to Himself as the Holy Trinity, as many theologians have interpreted the passage. Rather, He was speaking to the angels, whom He had created before human beings.

God created angels to be His retainers, who would assist Him in creating and sustaining the universe. In the Bible we find many instances of angels working for the Will of God. Angels conveyed to Abraham important words of God's blessing (Gen. 18.10); an angel heralded the conception of Christ (Matt. 1.20); an angel unchained Peter and led him out of prison and into the city. (Acts 12.7-10) The angel who escorts John in the Book of Revelation calls himself "a servant" (Rev. 22.9), and in Hebrews angels are referred to as "ministering spirits." (Heb. 1.14) The Bible often portrays angels honoring and praising God. (Rev. 5.11-12, 7.11-12)

Let us investigate the relationship between human beings and angels from the perspective of the Principle of Creation. Because God created us as His children and gave us dominion over all creation (Gen. 1.28), we are meant to rule over the angels as well. It is written in the Bible that we have the authority to judge the angels. (1 Cor. 6.3) Many who communicate with the spirit world have witnessed hosts of angels escorting the saints in Paradise. These observations illustrate the fact that angels have the mission to minister to human beings. (*Exposition of the Divine Principle*, Fall 2.2.1)

In front of God, the angels were supposed to fulfill the duties of servants and serve as a protective fence for Adam and Eve. They were supposed to create a glorious environment for them to live eternally in God's Kingdom. Then they would have lived happily with Adam and Eve in God's love. In short, God created the angels and archangels for the sake of Adam and Eve. God, in His parental love for Adam and Eve, created the angels for their sake. (15:238, October 17, 1965)

Good spirits who passed away after living on Earth belong to the realm of angels in terms of their mission. Why? God created angels before creating Adam. Therefore, before the perfection of [the new] Adam on earth, good people are assigned the role of angels by a certain procedure. (76:324, March 15, 1975)

Men are in the position of an archangel—not the archangel who caused the Fall but a restored archangel.[28] The angels in the Garden of Eden were given the mission to protect and nurture Adam and Eve to fulfill the ideal of God's family, and assist them to enter the Kingdom of Heaven. However, they failed to fulfill their mission, and instead they became gangsters, following the king of hell. (281:313, March 9, 1997)

For this reason, the angels should come down to the earth and work hard, sacrificing themselves for the citizens of the Kingdom to be established by the coming Messiah. Through shedding sweat in this way, they can be restored. The spirit world is the world of angels, and the physical world is Adam's world. Since both worlds have fallen under the power of the Devil, angels in the spirit world and "substantial" angels in the physical world should work for their liberation. Liberation is not possible only through the activities of angels in the spirit world. We need to create a substantial world of [people fulfilling the mission of] angels. (62:247, September 25, 1972)

2. War among the Angels

Now war arose in heaven, Michael and his angels fighting against the dragon; and the dragon and his angels fought, but they were defeated and there was no longer any place for them in heaven.

Revelation 12.7-8

Say: It has been revealed to me that a company of the jinn gave ear. Then they said, "We have indeed heard a Qur'an wonderful, guiding to rectitude. We believe in it, and we will not associate with our Lord anyone. He—exalted by our Lord's majesty! —has not taken to Himself either consort or a son.

"The fools among us spoke against God outrage, and we had thought that men and jinn would never speak against God a lie. But there were certain men of mankind who would take refuge with certain men of the jinn, and they increased them in vileness, and they thought, even as you also thought, that God would never raise up anyone.

"And we stretched towards heaven, but we found it filled with terrible guards and meteors. We would sit there on seats to hear; but any listening now finds a meteor in wait for him. And so we know not whether evil is intended for those in the earth, or whether their Lord intends for them rectitude.

"Some of us are righteous, and some of us are otherwise; we are sects differing... Some of us have surrendered, and some of us have deviated." Those who have surrendered sought rectitude; but as for those who have deviated, they have become firewood for hell.

Qur'an 72.1-15

Teachings of Sun Myung Moon

Because the archangel's Fall led Adam and Eve to their ruin and the ruin of the human world, [others of] the angelic world have been working on God's behalf, fighting against Satan. The good angels fight against the evil Satan [and his minions]. Whenever the side of the good angels wins a battle, there is a step forward. (109:18, October 26, 1980)

Good spirits are fighting their way to advance progress towards God's original world... while evil spirits are struggling to block the way. The evil spirit world and evil physical world are in a constant communication. Good spirits are the spirits of people who were opposed and persecuted in the sinful world. They are religious believers. (134:10, January 1, 1985)

God and Satan fight over human beings, vying to claim them for their side. The spirits of people who have passed away add their forces to the struggle. Good spirits help good people, while evil spirits help evil people. In this way, evil people are pulled to the side of Satan, while the good people go to the side of God. The physical and the spiritual team up in this manner and cause all manner of conflict, although people are ignorant of it. (161:14, January 1, 1987)

3. Man's Superiority to Angels

Do you not know that we are to judge angels?

    1 Corinthians 6.3

Behold, your Lord said to the angels, "I will create a vicegerent on earth." They said, "Wilt Thou place therein one who will make mischief therein and shed blood? —while we do celebrate Thy praises and glorify Thy holy name?" He said, "I know what you know not."

And He taught Adam the names of all things; then He placed them before the angels, and said, "Tell me the nature of these, if you are right."

They said, "Glory to Thee! Of knowledge we have none, save what Thou hast taught us: in truth it is Thou who art perfect in knowledge and wisdom."

He said, "O Adam, tell them their natures." When he had told them, God said, "Did I not tell you that I know the secrets of heaven and earth, and I know what you reveal, and what you conceal."

    Qur'an 2.30-33

When Moses ascended on high, the ministering angels spoke before the Holy One, blessed be He, "Sovereign of the Universe! What business has one born of woman among us?" "He has come to receive the Torah," He answered them. They replied, "That secret treasure, which You have hidden for nine hundred and seventy-four generations before the world was created, You desire to give to flesh and blood! 'What is man, that Thou art mindful of him, And the son of man, that Thou visitest him?' 'O LORD our God, How excellent is Thy name in all the earth! Who hast set Thy glory [the Torah] upon the heavens!'" (Psalm 8.5, 2).

"Reply to them," said the Holy One to Moses...

Moses then spoke before Him, "Sovereign of the Universe! The Torah which You give me, what is written in it?" "I am the LORD your God, which brought you out of the Land of Egypt" (Exodus 20.2). He said to the angels, "Did you go down to Egypt; were you enslaved to Pharaoh; why then should the Torah be yours? Again, what is written in it? 'You shall have no other gods' (Exodus 20.3); do you dwell among peoples that engage in idol worship? Again, what is written in it? 'Remember the Sabbath day, to keep it holy' (Exodus 20.8); do you perform work, that you need to rest?... Again, what is written in it? 'You shall not murder. You shall not commit adultery. You shall not steal' (Exodus 20.13-15); is there any jealousy among you; is the evil Tempter among you?" Straightaway the angels conceded to the Holy One, blessed be He, for it is said, "O LORD our God, How excellent is Thy name in all the *earth*," (Psalm 8.10) whereas "Who hast set Thy glory upon the *heavens*" is not written.[29]

    Talmud, Shabbat 88b-89a (Judaism)

Teachings of Sun Myung Moon

Angels are beings that serve God. Hence, should the sons and daughters of God appear, they should rule the angels. It is the dignity of human beings to rule the angels. (84:98, February 22, 1976)

It was not only to prevent their fall that God gave immature human beings the commandment.[30] God also wanted them to enjoy dominion over the natural world—including the angels—by inheriting His creative nature. In order to inherit this creatorship, human beings should perfect themselves through their faith in the Word as their own portion of responsibility.

God gave the commandment not to the Archangel but only to the human beings. God wished to exalt the dignity of human beings as bestowed by the Principle of Creation, which entitled them to stand as God's children and govern even the angels. (*Exposition of the Divine Principle*, Fall 3.2)

Spirits of the Departed

SOULS WHO HAVE PASSED ON DO NOT REALLY LEAVE US. They remain with us as more than mere memories. The souls of people whom we loved on earth continue to seek our welfare us much as they are able. The souls of people we wronged on earth harbor resentment against us and would avenge themselves if given the chance. Thus, the dead are not really dead. They may be living with us. Sometimes sensitive people can call them down to earth, as in the Bible when Saul employed a medium to call up the ghost of the prophet Samuel.

Most people are ignorant of spiritual influences on the living, yet they are real. The philosopher Immanuel Kant once said, "The human soul stands even in this life in indissoluble connection with all immaterial natures in the spirit world, that it reciprocally acts upon these and receives impressions and help from them." They include not only spirits of the dead, but also nature spirits—sprites, fairies and their ilk. The first peoples know them well, and their shamans are trained to sense their presence and employ them for human benefit. Their influence can be benign, or it can be beneficial, as the muse that inspires great art or the sudden insight that begets scientific discovery and invention. Spiritual influence can also be terribly destructive; for example, the passions that inflame age-old conflicts into modern-day ethnic violence.

Intercourse between heaven and earth works both ways. Spirits can be mobilized to assist earthly people for a righteous cause; conversely spirits need help from earthly people to resolve their own difficulties. Many religions promote the idea that the living should make offerings to benefit the dead; the Latter-Day Saints even promote baptism for the dead as a way to bring them closer to the perfection of the end-times. In this regard, Father Moon teaches a doctrine of "returning resurrection," by which spirits descend to assist the living, and the living in turn assist the dead by shouldering the burden of their unfinished business and resolving it.

1. Spirits among Us

Do not say, "They are dead!" about anyone who is killed for God's sake. Rather they are living, even though you do not notice it.[31]

Qur'an 2.154

The scent of the *sakaki* leaves is fragrant;[32]
Drawing near, I see countless kinsmen
Assembled all around,
Assembled all around.

Kagura-Uta (*Shinto*)

The light which these souls [of departed saints] radiate is responsible for the progress of the world and the advancement of its peoples. They are like leaven which leavens the world of being, and constitute the animating force through which the arts and wonders of the world are made manifest... These souls and symbols of detachment have provided, and will continue to provide, the supreme moving impulse in the world of being.

Gleanings from the Writings of Bahá'u'lláh 81
(*Baha'i Faith*)

Then the woman said, "Whom shall I bring up for you?" He said, "Bring up Samuel for me." When the woman saw Samuel, she cried out with a loud voice; and the woman said to Saul, "Why have you deceived me? You are Saul." The king said to her, "Have no fear; what do you see?" And the woman said to Saul, "I see a god coming up out of the earth." He said to her, "What is his appearance?" And she said, "An old man is coming up; and he is wrapped in a robe." And Saul knew that it was Samuel, and he bowed with his face to the ground, and did obeisance. Then Samuel said to Saul, "Why have you disturbed me by bringing me up?"

1 Samuel 28.11-15

Those who are dead are never gone:
they are there in the thickening shadow.
The dead are not under the earth:
they are there in the tree that rustles,
they are in the wood that groans,
they are in the water that runs,
they are in the water that sleeps,
they are in the hut, they are in the crowd,
the dead are not dead.

Those who are dead are never gone:
they are in the breast of the woman,
they are in the child who is wailing,
and in the firebrand that flames.
The dead are not under the earth:
they are in the fire that is dying,
they are in the grasses that weep,
they are in the whimpering rocks,
they are in the forest, they are in the house,
the dead are not dead.

Birago Diop (African Traditional Religions)

"The path of the *hekura* is visible, luminous; there arises from it something like a fiery breath that makes the air heavy and almost unbreathable. One does not see the hekura, one feels the wind they raise when they move. During the hunt from which I just returned, I scattered the hekura who were in me."

"Ordinary men are unable to recognize them. Yet the wind tells us that they are there."

"I see them only at night, when I close my eyes."

"One can see them only then."

"Their paths become luminous for me. I am sleeping; they approach and summon me to answer them. They suddenly wake me by shaking my arm or pulling on my ankle."

"Those who are not truly shamans do not hear them. He who is really a shaman hears a kind of buzzing, 'bouu...' during his sleep, and this song echoes, rebounding off the celestial vault. He opens his eyes and says to himself, 'I am going to see them now!' The parrotlets sing, 'bre, bre, bre,' he knows that it is they. A cool breeze then glides along his legs..."

"I saw the hekura walk on a rotten branch; I was passing right underneath."

"Indeed, it was they; but they were not friendly toward you. The strong odors of the smoking grill, the smell of singed hair, of scorched meat near the fire, all this drives them off. Yet they did seem inclined to approach you."

"They give off a heady perfume; it comes from the dyes and the magic plants they carry with them. Suddenly, I stopped smelling these aromas, my nostrils no longer perceived them."

"Therefore when one is at the end of the initiation, it is advisable not to hunt. If a flock of toucans takes flight and one of them lands near you, then all the others immediately follow suit. Be sure not to frighten them: stare at them fixedly and continue on your way; you be sure that they are hekura. Of course, there are those you drove away during the hunt; but don't be overly concerned, I foresee that those were not the good ones. The others remain, who came into your breast while you were lying in your hammock. Those are truly yours, they are in you." 33

Yanomami Shaman's Instruction
(Native American Religion)

And when the last Red Man shall have perished, and the memory of my tribe shall have become a myth among the white men, these shores will swarm with the invisible dead of my tribe, and when your children's children think themselves alone in the field, the store, the shop, upon the highway, or in the silence of the pathless woods, they will not be alone. In all the earth there is no place dedicated to solitude. At night when the streets of your cities and villages are silent and you think them deserted, they will throng with the returning hosts that once filled them and still love this beautiful land. The White Man will never be alone.

Chief Seattle[34] (Native American Religion)

Teachings of Sun Myung Moon

You are ignorant of the original life of God's creation. You are unable to speak with confidence in the presence of the Creator, the spirits in heaven and all things on earth. Yet even at this hour, God and some spirits in heaven and on earth are helping you. (8:43, November 1, 1959)

At the peak of your spirituality, if you resolve and act upon your resolution for God, good spirits will descend from the spirit world and assist you. However, if your spiritual level drops, those spirits that had been assisting you will begin to leave, one by one. As they depart they are sorrowful, mournfully thinking that they might never again descend to the earth and assist earthly people. Indeed, once they leave you, it is hard for them to return. Act, therefore, to increase the number of spirits who can assist you. Then your work will make smooth and rapid progress, and heavenly fortune will be with you. (161:273-74, February 26, 1987)

Spirit people cannot come here and work just as they wish; their way is blocked. Only a few particular spirits can return to earth, unless earthly people through their religious life build a bridge enabling more to cross. (102:29, November 19, 1978)

When our ancestors entered the spirit world, they were judged guilty. Unable to make progress in the spirit world, they should again descend to earth and make restitution. It would be better for you not to follow the same path. (146:224, July 1, 1986)

In the past, a person who prayed and made numerous conditions of devotion could meet the deceased founder of his religion for a short time, but then they had to separate, because the religious leader had to return to the spirit world. However, now is the time when all spirits can descend to earth, to people of their respective religions. (161:199-200, February 3, 1987)

2. Helping the Spirits and Gaining Spiritual Merit

Choosing an auspicious day and making purifications
you prepare the sacrifices.
You present them filially,
in spring, summer, autumn and winter,
to your ancestors, the former kings...
The spirits come,
and confer on you many blessings.

Book of Songs 2.1.6 (Confucianism)

Outside the walls they stand, at the crossways and outside doors, to their own home returning. But when a plenteous meal is spread, of food and drink, no man remembers them [the dead]. Such is the way of things.

Wherefore do those who have pity on their kin make offerings due, of choice food and drink at seasonable times, saying, "Be this a gift to kinsmen, may our kinsmen be well pleased with it!" Then do those earth-bound [ghosts], kinsmen, gather there where a plenteous meal is spread of food and drink, and fail not to render thanks, saying, "Long live our kinsmen, thanks to whom we have this gift! To us this offering is made; not without fruit are they who give!"

For [in ghostland] no cattle-keeping, no ploughing of fields is seen. There is no trading there, as on earth, no trafficking with gold. We ghosts that have departed there exist on what is given here. Even as water gathered on high ground flows down into the marsh, so are offerings given here on earth of service to the ghosts...

Of a truth, wailing and grief and all manner of lamentation avail not anything. It helps not the ghosts that kinsmen stand lamenting thus.

Moreover, [if] this gift of charity is bestowed on the Order, it is bound to be of service [to the ghosts] for a long, long time.

Thus this duty done to kinsmen has been declared: unto the ghosts it is no mean offering of worship; unto the Brethren of the Order it is strength conferred; unto yourselves no small merit has been won.

Khuddaka Patha, Tirokudda-sutta *(Buddhism)*

The rice and water no longer are offered,
the ancestors also must fall dishonored
from home in heaven.

Bhagavad-Gita 1.42 *(Hinduism)*

All these [saints of the Old Testament Age], though well attested by their faith, did not receive what was promised, since God had foreseen something better for us, that apart from us they should not be made perfect.

Therefore, since we are surrounded by so great a cloud of witnesses, let us also lay aside every weight, and sin which clings so closely, and let us run with perseverance the race that is set before us.

Hebrews 11.39-12.1

It is sufficient to know, in this case, that the earth will be smitten with a curse unless there is a welding link of some kind or other between the fathers and the children, upon some subject or other—and behold what is that subject? It is the baptism for the dead. For we without them cannot be made perfect; neither can they without us be made perfect. Neither can they nor we be made perfect without those who have died in the gospel also; for it is necessary in the ushering in of the dispensation of the fullness of times, which dispensation is now beginning to usher in, that a whole and complete and perfect union, and welding together of dispensations, and keys, and powers, and glories should take place.[35]

Doctrine and Covenants 128.18 *(Latter-day Saints)*

Teachings of Sun Myung Moon

According to the Principle of Creation, the growth of the human spirit requires two kinds of nourishment: life elements received from God and vitality elements received through give and take action with the physical self. Spirits can neither grow nor be resurrected apart from a physical self. Consequently, the spirits of people who died before they could reach perfection during their earthly life, can be resurrected, only by returning to earth and completing their unaccomplished responsibility through cooperation with earthly people. By assisting people of faith living on the earth to fulfill their missions, the spirits may complete their mission at the same time. Herein lies the meaning behind the verse, which foretold that in the Last Days the Lord would come "with His holy myriads." (Jude 1.14)

How do spirits help people on earth fulfill the Will of God? When people become receptive to spirits through prayer or other spiritual activities, the spirits descend to them to form a common base with their spirit selves and work with them. Spirits perform various works. For example, they pour spiritual fire on earthly people and give them the power to heal diseases. They help people enter states of trance and perceive the realities of the spirit world. They give people revelations and the gift of prophecy. They can also give deep inspiration to the soul. In these various works, spirits act on behalf of the Holy Spirit, guiding people on the earth to accomplish the Will of God. (*Exposition of the Divine Principle,* Resurrection 2.3.1)

If you went to the other side, to the spirit world, do you think you would see people living happily or people fighting each other? Murderers and their victims are there together. Don't you think they would be ready to fight, brandishing swords or knives and seeking revenge? However, there are many walls that block them. For this reason, evil spirits go to the descendants of their enemies and cause sudden deaths by accidents in order to fetch them to the spirit world.

The quarrels between spirits should all be resolved. Yet for this to happen, the resolution must first take place on earth. It requires that we offer something precious—something more precious than the memory of their murder or their grudge against their enemy. Only in this way can quarrels among the spirits be resolved.

With what offering can the spirit world be liberated? With what can God be liberated? Our ancestors bound themselves, thus making a mess of the spirit world. Therefore, we, their descendants, should now resolve our ancestors' wrongdoing.

We have learned the proper tradition of filial sons and daughters: we should pay back our parents' debts. In that light, who should knock down all the walls that our ancestors erected in the spirit world? We should do it. In doing this work, we have to make our ancestors come down to meet us directly, and teach us. It sounds like a dream, but it is real.

We are not alone. If I look at you, I can see what kind of people your ancestors are, and what they did. The faces of your ancestors appear and quickly disappear. I can distinguish which of them are good spirits and which are evil. (191:205-06, June 24, 1989)

During Jesus' advent on earth, there was a special opportunity for good spirits who had lived previously to resurrect. They could rise from the form-spirit level of the spirit world to the life-spirit level of the spirit world. Likewise, your ancestors in the spirit world also have a special opportunity[36] to resurrect by returning to earth, based on the condition afforded by your earthly life.

Your ancestors are eager to return to earth and do the work of returning resurrection. Isn't it wonderful that you give them that opportunity? Among the ancestors of your family and clan were loyal patriots, filial sons and faithful wives. Call them in prayer, and they will come. They can come because the time is right, when your ancestors should cooperate with you. (14:22-23, April 19, 1964)

The question is whether we have set the standard to mobilize the spirits of the spirit world, and have them bear witness. The spirit world is also demanding to be mobilized. The spirit world is aware of the heart of God. Therefore, if people on earth appeal on behalf of God's sorrowful heart, then the spirit world will mobilize many spirits. They will help in the work of realizing the teachings of the Kingdom of Heaven.

Why can't spirits in the spirit world come to this earth plane? It is because the earth is beset by barriers of lamentation. If the earthly environment were free of the conditions of lamentation, if we were free from the miserable conditions that beset our flesh, and if we would enter a state of peace, unafraid of Satan's threats, then God would help us. (4:60, March 2, 1958)

Reincarnation

BELIEF IN REINCARNATION IS COMMON to the religions born in India: Buddhism, Hinduism and Jainism. This is the belief that the individual soul passes from one earthly life to another, each life conditioned on the deeds of the previous lives. Differences in fortune, wealth, social position, and endowments are the consequences of actions done in previous lives. As the cosmos revolves in its cycles, the wheel of *samsara* turns for each human being as he or she rises and falls through countless births and deaths—sometimes as humans, sometimes as animals or even insects.

On the other hand, Christianity largely rejects reincarnation, holding that God provides everyone the opportunity for salvation within a single lifetime. Even the Buddha spoke against easy reliance on reincarnation as a comfort to misbehaving sinners, thinking that they could easily obtain a second chance.

According to the doctrine of reincarnation, souls have the opportunity to progress to the ultimate goal of perfection only when they are incarnated as human beings. Thus, spirits seek out human bodies in which to be reincarnated, in hopes of a chance to right wrongs and make progress on the path. Father Moon also teaches that spirits can only progress while linked to a human body. However, instead of souls transmigrating from one body to another, he describes a process of spirits descending to cooperate with earthly people, which he calls "returning resurrection." Through assisting people on earth who face similar difficulties, spirits can resolve their unfinished business and be liberated to rise to a higher level. Sometimes this is a painful and even punishing encounter for earthly people, who have to deal with ancestors whose agonizing experiences they never imagined. Believers in reincarnation simply misconstrue the spirits' thoughts and experiences as if they were their own deeds in an earlier lifetime. Regardless of where the truth lies, to see oneself as inextricably bound up with the lives of others—extending from the distant past into the future endless future—leads to an attitude of humility and patient endurance.

According to his deeds (*karma*) the embodied one successively
Assumes forms in various conditions.
Coarse and fine, many in number,
The embodied one chooses forms according to his own qualities.
Each subsequent cause of his union with them is seen to be
Because of the quality of his acts and of himself.
    Svetasvatara Upanishad 5.11-12 (*Hinduism*)

The universe is peopled by manifold creatures who are, in this round of rebirth, born in different families and castes for having done various actions.

Sometimes they go to the world of the gods, sometimes to the hells, sometimes they become demons in accordance with their actions.

Sometimes they become soldiers, or outcastes and untouchables, or worms or moths....

Thus, living beings of sinful actions, who are born again and again in ever-recurring births, are not disgusted with the round of rebirth, but they are like warriors, never tired of the battle of life.

Bewildered through the influence of their actions, distressed and suffering pains, they undergo misery in non-human births.

But by the cessation of karma, perchance, living beings will reach in due time a pure state and be born as men.
    Uttaradhyayana Sutra 3.1-7 (*Jainism*)

"Frequently I have been born in a high family, frequently in a low one; I am not mean, nor noble, nor do I desire social preferment." Thus reflecting, who would brag about his family or about his glory, or for what should he long? Therefore a wise man should neither be glad nor angry about his lot: he should know and consider about the happiness of all living creatures. Carefully conducting himself, he should mind this: "I will always experience blindness, deafness, dumbness, be one-eyed, hunchbacked, black, white, and every color; because of my carelessness I am born in many births, experience many feelings."

Acarangasutra 2.50-55 (Jainism)

There is no such thing as a return to this life for the punishment of souls... How can the return to bodies which are gifts of God be punishment?

Saint Augustine, City of God 12.27 (Christianity)

Sooner, do I declare, would a one-eyed turtle, if he were to pop up to the surface of the sea only once at the end of every hundred years, chance to push his neck though a yoke with one hole than would a fool, who has once gone to the Downfall, be reborn as a man.

Samyutta Nikaya 5.455 (Buddhism)

Teachings of Sun Myung Moon

Nature has its causes, its directives, and it moves in cycles seeking for results. In the course of its cycles, complex directives are gathered together and mature as completed things. The universe rotates. History likewise moves in cycles, even as it progresses. The four seasons revolve—spring, summer, fall and winter. From this perspective, how can the theory of evolution be correct when it calls only for linear progress? Why shouldn't the process be cyclical?

Recognition that the world is continually revolving may have led to the belief of reincarnation. It provides some reason for the belief that human beings are transformed into animals, insects or plants [and then rise again as humans] as the universe makes its revolutions. (94:11-12, June 19, 1977)

Regardless of time and place, religious people as well as all the other people live in circumstances where they are intertwined with the spirit world according to its karma. This is an indubitable fact of human life. People in every age, whether or not they believe in a religion, witness the fact through dreams and other mysterious experiences. (131:167, May 1, 1984)

Why should we return to earth? Because our relationships were bound on earth; therefore, they should be loosed on earth. Religions such as Buddhism call such phenomena reincarnation. However, an ascended saint like Buddha or Confucius can appear in spirit at any moment. Therefore, it cannot be that the actual Buddha returns as another person. Phenomena that can be mistaken for reincarnation take place when a person who has not completed his responsibility in a certain field descends through returning resurrection to fulfill it by utilizing another individual. (91:276-77, February 27, 1977)

The Buddhist theory of reincarnation does not see the whole picture; it recognizes only one aspect of returning resurrection. Spirits in the spirit world want to benefit through returning to earthly people.

But for the Human Fall, humans would be creatures of great value, having dominion over the angelic world and the universe. Instead, because of the Fall they plummeted down, even several levels below zero. It remains for them to return to the original position, but it cannot be done all at once. They should go through many stages, step by step...

In order to go over even one stage, a price, called an indemnity condition, must be paid. Suppose a person cooperated in God's providence to reach a certain point. Yet he or she cannot automatically rise to a next stage. There may be an indemnity period, requiring a principled number such as 7 years, 40 years, 70 years, or even several centuries. Since that person cannot be elevated any further until the indemnity period has matured, he or she passes on to the spirit world. That person, now a spirit, would then want an earthly person, let's call him A, to complete laying the foundation. Then if that person also dies before fulfilling it, he would work through another person, B, whom he had chosen. Thus the same spirit cooperates with both person A and person B.

For example, suppose the spirit is Saint Paul. For Saint Paul to be elevated to a higher level, he has to return to someone of his choosing on earth, person A. However, if person A dies without fulfilling his mission, he will have to return again to a person B and cooperate with him. If this person B finally completes his mission on earth, then the spirit, Saint Paul, can resurrect to a higher level.

There must be an indemnity period based on principled numbers. This period cannot be completed in a short time. Thus, if even person B, the second person chosen for the mission, does not complete it, the spirit will have to return through returning resurrection to assist yet a third person, person C. Some people might regard person C as the reincarnation of Saint Paul. At the same time, if person B had left some writings or special works, people might claim that he was the reincarnation of Saint Paul…

In such a way, the spirit of Saint Paul might come down and work with a number of different people throughout the world. Some people, seeing the phenomenon superficially, call it reincarnation. But if they could grasp the whole picture they would not regard it so. (54:277-79, March 26, 1972)

Spiritual Error and the Occult

THERE IS A CURRENT OF DEEP DISTRUST FOR SPIRITS and their communications within the major religions. Since they are not comparable to Ultimate Reality, spirits are not privy to the highest truth. Christianity, Judaism, and Islam teach that ranks of angels fell into error and sin. Buddhism even regards the creator god (the Hindu god Brahma) as one of these subordinate deities, subordinate to the *Dhamma* revealed by the Buddha.

Spirits are often fallible, motivated by selfish ends, and liable to mislead people who rely on them for guidance. Furthermore, the spirit world is also populated by evil spirits, demons and fallen angels, as well as intermediate spiritual beings including the jinn, spirits of the dead, and various classes of ghosts. Occult practices, such as seeking information from mediums, witches and shamans, can lead people astray through communication with spirits from the lower realms. Father Moon has experience of this from Korea, a society where shamanism is still widespread. He also recognizes an insidious connection between occultism and the Human Fall, where Eve placed herself under the power of a spirit.

Therefore, we are advised to "test the spirits to see whether they are of God," based on the higher authority of revealed truth. Faith, purity, adherence to revealed truth, and performance of good deeds are superior ways to insure fellowship with spiritual beings of the highest levels.

1. Spirits, Being Fallen Themselves, are False Guides

O Lord, how can a god or a demon know all the extent of Your glory? You alone know what You are, by the light of Your innermost nature.

Bhagavad-Gita 10.14 (Hinduism)

Even in His servants He puts no trust,
and His angels He charges with error.

Job 4.18

Alas for the blindness of the sons of men, all unaware as they are how full the earth is of strange and invisible beings and hidden dangers, which could they but see, they would marvel how they themselves could survive on the earth.

Zohar 1.55a (Judaism)

God has taken his place in the divine council;
in the midst of the gods he holds judgment:
"How long will you judge unjustly
and show partiality to the wicked?
Give justice to the weak and the fatherless;
maintain the right of the afflicted and the
    destitute.
Rescue the weak and the needy;
deliver them from the hand of the wicked."
They have neither knowledge nor
    understanding,
they walk about in darkness,
all the foundations of the earth are shaken.
I say, "You are gods,
sons of the Most High, all of you;
nevertheless you shall die like men,
and fall like any prince."

Psalm 82

Teachings of Sun Myung Moon

Spiritual phenomena include the activities of ghosts or evil spirits. However, these do not lead to resolving our relationship with God. Unless we are taught the correct relationship with God, and unless we understand the influences of evil spirits on us, we cannot find our proper place in the universe. (191:11, June 24, 1989)

The spirit world is in the Cain position and the earth is in the Abel position.[37] Up to now, the spirit world, in the Cain position, has been dominating humankind. When people allow themselves to be guided by spiritual mediums, they are only allowing spirits to command earthly people for their own benefit. (83:15, February 5, 1976)

Today many people are suffering from psychological disorders, and some mutter to themselves. Do you know why this happens? It is caused by the spirit world. Spirits from the lower realms cannot ascend to the higher realms on their own, so they manipulate earthly people. But low spirits do not have a good viewpoint or direction; [therefore their influences always have an adverse affect on people]. Good spirits, on the other hand, have a clear direction. (91:273, February 27, 1977)

2. Dangers of Occultism

Men of ignorance worship spirits and ghosts.
Bhagavad-Gita 17.4 (Hinduism)

Do not turn to mediums or wizards; do not seek them out, to be defiled by them: I am the LORD your God.
Leviticus 19.31

Confucius never discussed abnormal phenomena, physical exploits, disorderly conduct, or spiritual beings.
Analects 7.20 (Confucianism)

My follower does not study the practice of magic and spells. He does not analyze dreams and signs in sleep and movements in the Zodiac.
Sutta Nipata 927 (Buddhism)

As we were going to the place of prayer, we were met by a slave girl who had a spirit of divination and brought her owners much gain by soothsaying. She followed Paul and us, crying, "These men are servants of the Most High God, who proclaim to you the way of salvation." And this she did for many days. But Paul was annoyed, and turned and said to the spirit, "I charge you in the name of Jesus Christ to come out of her." And it came out that very hour.
Acts 16.16-18

Aisha told that when God's messenger was asked by some people about fortune-tellers he replied, "They are of no account." They said, "Messenger of God, they sometimes tell a thing which is true." He replied, "That is a word pertaining to truth which a jinn snatches and cackles into the ear of his friend as a hen does; then they mix more than a hundred lies with it."
Hadith of Bukhari and Muslim (Islam)

When the unclean spirit has gone out of a man, he passes through waterless places seeking rest, but he finds none. Then he says, "I will return to my house from which I came." And when he comes he finds it empty, swept, and put in order. Then he goes and brings with him seven other spirits more evil than himself, and they enter and dwell there; and the last state of that man becomes worse than the first.
Matthew 12.43-45

Teachings of Sun Myung Moon

People want to believe in a higher power, without knowing what it is. Unable to relate to it by themselves, they may seek out a shaman, who leads them in shamanistic rituals. Or, they may latch on to superstitions. Thus they grope in the darkness, seeking for something. People have this tendency, though they don't know why. (101:90, October 22, 1978)

Mediums and fortunetellers will tell your fortune and predict your future. They can do this because they are in contact with certain spirits standing behind them, who can see and reveal to them some aspects of your reality. (176:286, May 13, 1988)

Spiritual mediums are often confused and fall into conflict among themselves, because the levels of the spirit world with which they are in communication and the content of the revelations they receive differ. Although spiritually perceptive people are in contact with the same spirit world, because their circumstances and positions vary and their character, intellect and spirituality are at different levels, they will perceive the spirit world in different ways. These differences give rise to conflicts among them. (*Exposition of the Divine Principle*, Resurrection 2.2.6)

Why do the "gods" in the spirit world—the angelic world—try to relate with the world of human beings? You have heard of mediums, fortune telling and superstitions. They are religious forms that do not make clear distinctions between good and evil. As God prepared religious forms, Satan too prepared religious forms as a countermeasure.

More than 80 percent of mediums and fortune-tellers are women. With whom are they working? When Eve fell, she was overcome by the power of an angel to do wickedness. The same path is repeated during the time of restoration: definitely, there are angels in the spirit world who descend to the earth to relate with women and instruct them. The work of fortune-tellers and mediums is to teach what angels instruct them to say. Just like fallen Eve, they live with spirits. (76:95, February 1, 1975)

If a spiritualist with low spirituality treats your ailment, the spirits in the spirit world will be temporarily comforted, but the problem will not be fundamentally resolved. Your soul will be comforted and peaceful for a while, but after some time passes it will be disturbed with the same problem. (293:249-50, June 1, 1998)

3. Wisdom in Dealing with Spirits

Beloved, do not believe every spirit, but test the spirits to see whether they are of God; for many false prophets have gone out into the world.

1 John 4.1

Now concerning spiritual gifts, brethren, I do not want you to be uninformed. You know that when you were heathen, you were led astray to dumb idols, however you may have been moved. Therefore I want you to understand that no one speaking by the Spirit of God ever says "Jesus be cursed!" and no one can say "Jesus is Lord!" except by the Holy Spirit.

1 Corinthians 12.1-3

Evil spirits have power over fearful men but cannot disturb the fearless.

Holy Teaching of Vimalakirti 7 *(Buddhism)*

A Muslim is not turned back from anything because of an omen. When he sees something indicating misfortune he should say, "O God, You alone bring good things, You alone avert evil things, and there is no might or power but in God."

Hadith of Abu Dawud *(Islam)*

To maintain the existence of a ghost,
Only brings about mischief;
To understand the non-existence of a ghost
Is the way of Buddha;
To know that ghost and Reality are one
Is the way to Liberation.
Knowing that the ghosts are all one's parents
Is the right understanding;
Realizing that the ghost itself is Self-mind
Is glory supreme.

Milarepa *(Buddhism)*

Teachings of Sun Myung Moon

Since a fallen person stands in the midway position between God and Satan and relates with both of them, the works of a good spirit may be accompanied by the subtle influences of an evil spirit. In other cases, phenomena which begin as the works of evil spirits may, as time passes, merge with the works of good spirits. Discerning the spirits is thus very difficult for those who do not understand the

Principle. It is a pity that many religious authorities, in their ignorance, condemn the works of good spirits by lumping them together with evil spirits. This may place them in inadvertent opposition to God's Will. In the present era, spiritual phenomena are becoming ever more prevalent. Unless religious leaders can correctly distinguish the works of good spirits from the works of evil spirits, they cannot properly instruct and guide those who experience spiritual phenomena. (*Exposition of the Divine Principle*, Fall 4.4)

Do you think that when I meet spiritualist ladies, I simply follow their advice? No way. They do not know the whole picture. They can testify to the present situation, but they do not know how things operate. (68:276, August 5, 1973)

Spiritualists differ among themselves because they each insist on their own viewpoint. This is a common problem among spiritual people. One hundred spiritualists will have one hundred different viewpoints. Being self-centered, each believes that his or her view is the best one. However, they should be the best by centering on the Center, not on themselves. (325:289, July 2, 2000)

Through spiritualists, shamans, fortune-tellers and the like who are in touch with the spirit world, the spirit world has been taking advantage of earthly people. In the future this will no longer be permitted. The time is coming when earthly people will have dominion over the spirit world. (219:78, August 25, 1991)

Uniting Heaven and Earth

HUMAN BEINGS ARE COMPOSED OF BOTH SPIRIT AND BODY; hence we stand astride both the earthly world and the spirit world. With this unique endowment, we can be the mediators between the two worlds. Instead of regarding the spirit world with fear, we have the power to exercise dominion over both worlds. Saints and sages have been known to command the heavenly hosts to assist them in a righteous cause. Even ordinary believers have this ability, by virtue of a human being's status as lord of creation and God's "vicegerent."

Native peoples have long understood this. Through ceremony and dance they realize a living relationship with both worlds. Through intense spiritual disciplines, Hindu yogis and ascetics of all traditions obtain the power to fly with the spirits and do miraculous feats. Christianity acknowledges dominion over heaven and earth in Jesus Christ, whose victory over death is the ground of salvation. Father Moon teaches that the Kingdom of God will be established through a grand unification of the spiritual and the physical dimensions of existence.

For he has made known to us in all wisdom and insight the mystery of his will, according to his purpose which he set forth in Christ as a plan for the fullness of time, to unite all things in him, things in heaven and things on earth.

Ephesians 1.9-10

His movement is of Heaven, his stillness of Earth. With his single mind in repose, he is king of the world; the spirits do not afflict him; his soul knows no weariness. His single mind reposed, the ten thousand things submit—which is to say that his emptiness and stillness reach throughout Heaven and Earth and penetrate the ten thousand things. This is what is called Heavenly joy. Heavenly joy is the mind of the sage by which he shepherds the world.

Chuang Tzu 13 (Taoism)

The Sky blesses me, the Earth blesses me;
Up in the Skies I cause to dance the Spirits;
On the Earth, the people I cause to dance.

Cree Round Dance (Native American Religions)

Thy kingdom come,
Thy will be done,
On earth as it is in heaven.

Matthew 6.10

The ascetic bears fire, he bears water,
the ascetic upholds earth and heaven,
the ascetic sees all visions of luster,
the ascetic is called the Light.

Munis [yogis] with the wind for their girdle
wear the soiled yellow robe;
they go along the course of the wind
where the gods have gone before.

"In the ecstasy of Munihood
we have ascended on the wind,
and only these bodies of ours
are what you mortals ever see."

The Muni flies through mid-air
while he looks at varied forms,
and he is of every deva
a comrade in doing good.

Rig Veda 10.136.1-4 (Hinduism)

Heaven possesses yin and yang and man also possesses yin and yang. When the universe's material force of yin arises, man's material force of yin arises in response. Conversely, when man's material force of yin arises, that in the universe should also arise in response. The principle is the same. He who understands this, when he wishes to bring forth rain, will activate the yin in man in order to arouse the yin in the universe. When he wishes to stop rain, he will activate the yang in man in order to arouse the yang of the universe. Therefore the bringing forth of rain is nothing supernatural. People suspect that it is supernatural because its principle is subtle and wonderful.

It is not only the material forces of yin and yang that can advance or withdraw according to their kind. Even the way misfortunes, calamities and blessings are produced follows the same principle. In all cases one starts something himself and other things become active in response according to their kind. Therefore men of intelligence, sageliness and spirit introspect and listen to themselves, and their words become intelligent and sagely. The reason why introspection and listening to oneself alone can lead to intelligence and sageliness is because one knows that one's original mind lies there.

Therefore when the note of F is struck on a seven-stringed or twenty-one stringed lute, the F note on other lutes sound of themselves in response. This is a case of things being activated because they are similar in kind. Their activity takes place in sound and is invisible. Not seeing the form of their activity, people say that they sound of themselves. Furthermore, since they activate each other invisibly, it is thought that they do so themselves. In reality, it is not that they do so themselves, but that there is something that causes them. In reality things are caused, but the cause is invisible.

Tung Chung-shu, Luxuriant Gems of the
Spring and Autumn Annals (Confucianism)

Only those who are absolutely sincere can fully develop their nature. If they can fully develop their nature, they can then fully develop the nature of others. If they can fully develop the nature of others, they can then fully develop the nature of things. If they can fully develop the nature of things, they can then assist in the transforming and nourishing process of Heaven and Earth. If they can assist in the transforming and nourishing process of Heaven and Earth, they can thus form with Heaven and Earth a trinity.

Doctrine of the Mean 22 (Confucianism)

Stick to the One and the ten thousand tasks will be accomplished; achieve mindlessness and the gods and spirits will all bow down.

Chuang Tzu 12 (Taoism)

Since therefore the children share in flesh and blood, he himself likewise partook of the same nature, that through death he might destroy him who has the power of death, that is, the devil, and deliver all those who through fear of death were subject to lifelong bondage.

Hebrews 2.14-15

Teachings of Sun Myung Moon

God created human beings to live both in the spirit world and on earth through the harmony of spirit and flesh. God, who is spirit, communicates with the human spirit; the human spirit communicates with the flesh; and through this harmony of spirit and flesh a person attains dominion over the creation. This is the Principle of Creation. (2:80, March 3, 1957)

The spirit world transcends time and space. Hence, if we are united in our mind and body, if our mind and body are in resonance, we can experience telepathy. It is like tuning our radio to a certain frequency; then we can hear the sound.

In that state of resonance, when you desire to go somewhere, you will be taken there in spirit. If you want to see someone, that individual will appear instantaneously before your eyes. If you are close to that person, he or she will appear with a friendly appearance, but if you have a hostile relationship, he or she will appear as an enemy. Regardless, the vision will be something unforgettable. (187:311, February 12, 1989)

God began His creation from His own essence, investing for the sake of love, investing repeatedly and forgetting what He had invested. Therefore, if God's partner is to receive it, he must likewise invest and forget. Thus there is investing from above and also from below. In this way, heaven and earth join together harmoniously and become one. They become one centering on the love that can embrace and move heaven and earth. This generates great power. (237:130, November 13, 1992)

The universe does not of itself have internal sensibility toward God. Hence, God does not govern the universe directly. Rather, God endowed human beings with sensibilities to all things in the universe and gave them the mandate to rule over the universe directly. God created the human body with elements from the physical world—such as water, clay and air—to allow us to perceive and govern it. To make it possible for us to perceive and govern the spirit world, God created our spirits with the same spiritual elements that compose the spirit world... Human beings, composed of flesh which can dominate the physical world and spirit which can dominate the spirit world, likewise have the potential to rule both worlds.

God created human beings to be the mediator and the center of harmony of the cosmos. When a person's flesh and spirit unite through give and take action and become God's substantial object partner, the physical world and spirit world can also begin give and take action with that person as their center. They thus achieve harmonious integration to construct a cosmos that is responsive to God. Like the air that enables two tuning forks to resonate with each other, a true person acts as the mediator and center of harmony between the two worlds.

However, due to the human Fall, the universe has lost its master. St. Paul wrote, "the creation waits with eager longing for the revealing of the sons of God" (Rom. 8.19) —that is, people who have been restored to the original state. Tragically, with the Fall of human beings, who should have served as the center of universal harmony, the give and take between the physical and spiritual worlds was severed. The two worlds have been rendered utterly unable to achieve integration and harmony. Since they remain divided, Paul continued, "the whole creation has been groaning in travail." (Rom. 8:22) (*Exposition of the Divine Principle,* Creation 6.2)

The spirit world and the physical world should be united by true love. Yet because true love did not appear, the spirit world and physical world were not united; because true love did not appear, the mind and the body of each individual were divided; and because true love was not erected, religions and politics were separated.
    Through true love, all can be united. Through true love, individuals, families, societies, nations, the world and cosmos can be connected. We must make it happen. Otherwise, we cannot inherit the original Kingdom of Heaven in the spirit world and on earth. (216:105-06, March 9, 1991)

If there is a man who can gain dominion over Satan, he can liberate both the spirit world and the physical world. (161:243; February 22, 1987)

You should be able to mobilize the spirit world. However, when you reach such spirituality, you will face things that are difficult for you to handle. In that situation, your attitude should be, "I am acting on behalf of God." It is not enough for you to do things by your own power; the question is how you can mobilize the spirit world, and carry out your mission in multi-dimensional ways. (102:117, November 27, 1978)

There are people in this world who can perform wondrous feats. Some can fly through the air. Some can walk on water. Some can travel thousands of miles in an instant. Soon the day will come when I will summon them from the Himalayas and other places where they are pursuing the path to enlightenment. (60:195, August 17, 1972)

To restore the physical world and spirit world means to bring them back to their original state. It may cost me 70 to 80 years of my life to restore both the earthly world and the spirit world. I could have become a successful businessman, yet there is no greater business than this. I have spent my entire youth trying to accomplish it. (15:146, October 3, 1965)

Without unifying the spirit world, it is impossible to bring unity on the earth. If unity is not attained on earth, oneness will also not be found in the spirit world. They share a common destiny.
    It is a very good thing that Western people are marrying Asians and Asians marrying Westerners. When their ancestors look down from the spirit world, how pleased they are! Why? In the spirit world, white people have clustered only among white people, black people dwelt among other blacks, [and yellow people lived only with others of the yellow race]. The spirit world has been all divided, therefore on earth the races have been in conflict continually. But because earthly people are now marrying interracially, those in the spirit world are being softened up to the idea of becoming one, and unification is proceeding there. All are being unified, making one world. Like the prayer, "Thy will be done on earth, as it is in heaven," because this is happening in the spirit world, even more of the same will occur on the earth. (99:188, September 18, 1978)

PART TWO

SIN AND SALVATION

Chapter 6

Evil, Sin and the Human Fall

The Human Fall

THE ABRAHAMIC FAITHS TEACH THAT HUMANITY FELL from a primordial state of unity with God, and similar beliefs are found the world over. Christianity links the Fall with the doctrine of Original Sin, as the sin of Adam and Eve is imputed to all humanity, causing an enduring separation between humans and God which can only be remedied by Christ. In Islam, on the other hand, Adam's sin was his alone, and he, like all human beings, could return to a position of acceptance by submission *(islam)* to God. Still, the Fall brought into existence Satan, setting up for all humanity a trial which only some are able to endure. Finally, in Judaism we find a mixture of beliefs: passages gathered in this section affirming that the fall of Adam and Eve brought a curse into the world are counterbalanced by other passages emphasizing individual responsibility and denying that we are culpable for the sins of our first ancestor.

The human fall explains the discrepancy between the cosmos' pure origin and its present state of suffering. It is logically necessary for religions in which (1) God is the only Creator, (2) the Creation was purposed to be good, and (3) evil is regarded as real and contrary to the purpose of creation. These postulates hold in Christianity, Judaism and Islam. They do not obtain in Buddhism, which lacks a doctrine of Creation, nor in Hinduism, which regards matter as base and a limitation to be overcome on the path to self-realization. Nevertheless, we find even in these religions speculation on a primordial fall from grace to explain the origin of evil karma.

The biblical and Qur'anic accounts of the Human Fall are full of symbolism and open to varying interpretations. The serpent—variously called Satan, Lucifer or Iblis—instigates Adam and Eve to disobey God's commandment, often with the hint of sexual misconduct. Father Moon directly attributes the Human Fall to sexual immorality, teaching that it poisoned the potential of humans for true, godly love. Other accounts of the origin of evil that ascribe or hint at a sexual transgression are presented from Greek myth, Buddhism, Shinto and African tradition.

1. Adam and Eve's Transgression

The LORD God took the man [Adam] and put him in the Garden of Eden to till it and keep it. And the LORD God commanded the man, saying, "You may freely eat of every tree of the garden; but of the tree of the knowledge of good and evil you shall not eat, for in the day that you eat of it you shall die."

Then the LORD God said, "It is not good that the man should be alone; I will make him a helper fit for him." So out of the ground the LORD God formed every beast of the field and every bird of the air, and brought them to the man to see what he would call them; and whatever the man called every living creature, that was its name. The man gave names to all cattle, and to the birds of the air, and to every beast of the field; but for the man there was not found a helper fit for him. So the LORD God caused a deep sleep to fall upon the man, and while he slept took one of his ribs and closed up its place with flesh; and the rib which the LORD God had taken from the man he made into a woman and brought her to the man. Then the man said, "This at last is bone of my bones and flesh of my flesh; she shall be called Woman, because she was taken out of Man." Therefore a man leaves his father and his mother and cleaves to his wife, and they become one flesh. And the man and his wife were both naked, and were not ashamed.

Now the serpent was more subtle than any other wild creature that the LORD God had made. He said to the woman, "Did God say, 'You shall not eat of any tree of the garden'?" And the woman said to the serpent, "We may eat of the fruit of the trees of the garden; but God said, 'You shall not eat of the fruit of the tree which is in the midst of the garden, neither shall you touch it, lest you die.'" But the serpent said to the woman, "You will not die. For God knows that when you eat of it your eyes will be opened, and you will be like God, knowing good and evil." So when the woman saw that the tree was good for food, and that it was a delight to the eyes, and that the tree was to be desired to make one wise, she took of its fruit and ate; and she also gave some to her husband, and he ate. Then the eyes of both were opened, and they knew that they were naked; and they sewed fig leaves together and made themselves aprons.

And they heard the sound of the LORD God walking in the garden in the cool of the day, and the man and his wife hid themselves from the presence of the LORD God among the trees of the garden. But the LORD God called to the man, and said to him, "Where are you?" And he said, "I heard the sound of Thee in the garden, and I was afraid, because I was naked; and I hid myself." He said, "Who told you that you were naked? Have you eaten of the tree of which I commanded you not to eat?" The man said, "The woman whom Thou gavest to be with me, she gave me fruit of the tree, and I ate." Then the LORD God said to the woman, "What is this that you have done?" The woman said, "The serpent beguiled me, and I ate." The LORD God said to the serpent, "Because you have done this,

> Cursed are you above all cattle,
> and above all wild animals;
> Upon your belly you shall go,
> and dust you shall eat all the days of your life.
> I will put enmity between you and the woman,
> and between your seed and her seed;
> He shall bruise your head,
> and you shall bruise his heel."

To the woman He said,

> "I will greatly multiply your pain in childbearing,
> in pain you shall bring forth children,
> Yet your desire shall be for your husband,
> and he shall rule over you."

And to Adam he said, "Because you have listened to the voice of your wife, and have eaten of the tree of which I commanded you, 'You shall not eat of it,'

> cursed is the ground because of you;
> in toil you shall eat of it all the days of your life;
> Thorns and thistles it shall bring forth to you;
> and you shall eat the plants of the field.
> In the sweat of your face you shall eat bread
> till you return to the ground,
> for out of it you were taken;
> you are dust,
> and to dust you shall return."

The man called his wife's name Eve, because she was the mother of all living. And the LORD God made for Adam and for his wife garments of skins, and clothed them.

Then the LORD God said, "Behold, the man has become like one of us, knowing good and evil; and now, lest he put forth his hand and take also of the tree of life, and eat, and live forever"—therefore the LORD God sent him forth from the Garden of Eden, to till the ground from which he was taken. He drove out the man; and at the east of the Garden of Eden he placed the cherubim, and a flaming sword which turned every way, to guard the way to the tree of life.

Genesis 2.15-3.24

It is We who created you and gave you shape; then We bade the angels, "Bow down to Adam," and they bowed down; not so Iblis, he refused to be of those who bow down. [God] said, "What prevented you from bowing down when I commanded you?" He said, "I am better than he; You created me from fire, and him from clay." God said, "Get down from this place; it is not for you to be arrogant here; get out, for you are of the meanest of creatures." He said, "Give me respite till the day when they are raised up." God said, "Be among those who are to have respite."

He said, "Because you have thrown me out of the Way, lo! I will lie in wait for them on Your Straight Way: Then will I assault them from before them and behind, from their right and their left: nor will You find, in most of them, gratitude." God said, "Get out from this, disgraced and expelled. If any of them follow you, I will fill hell with all of you.

"And Adam, dwell, you and your wife, in the Garden, and enjoy its good things as you wish, but approach not this tree, or you will run into harm and transgression."

Then Satan began to whisper suggestions to them, bringing openly before their minds all their shame that was previously unnoticed by them. He said, "Your Lord only forbade you this tree, lest you should become angels or such beings as live forever." And he swore to them both, that he was their sincere advisor. So by deceit he brought about their fall: when they tasted of the tree, their shame [private parts] became apparent to them, and they began to sew together the leaves of the Garden over their bodies.

And their Lord called unto them: "Did I not forbid you that tree, and tell you that Satan was an avowed enemy unto you both?" They said: "Our Lord! We have wronged our own souls. If You do not forgive us and do not grant us Your mercy, we shall certainly be lost." God said, "Get you down, with enmity between yourselves. On earth will be your dwelling place and your means of livelihood—for a time. Therein shall you live, and therein you shall die; but from it shall you be brought forth at last."

O Children of Adam! We have bestowed raiment upon you to cover your shame, as well as to be an adornment to you. But the raiment of righteousness—that is the best. Such are among the signs of God, that they may receive admonition.

O Children of Adam! Let not Satan seduce you in the same manner as he got your parents out of the Garden, stripping them of their clothing in order to expose their private parts. He and his tribe watch you from where you cannot see them! We have made the devils friends only to those without faith.

Qur'an 7.11-27

If I have covered my transgressions as Adam,
By hiding my iniquity in my bosom,

Job 31.33 (NKJV)

Why does the scripture not place the verse "And the LORD God made for Adam and his wife garments of skin" (Genesis 3.21) immediately after "And they were both naked, and were not ashamed" (Genesis 2.25)? It teaches you through what sin that wicked creature inveighed them: Because the serpent saw them engaged in their natural relations, he conceived a lust for her.

Midrash Rabbah, Genesis 18.6 (Judaism)

The serpent followed Eve, saying, "Her soul comes from the north, and I will therefore quickly seduce her." And how did he seduce her? He had intercourse with her.

Bahir 199 (Judaism)

What was the wicked serpent contemplating at that time? He thought, "I shall go and kill Adam and wed his wife, and I shall be king over the whole world."

Talmud, Avot de Rabbi Nathan 1 (Judaism)

The first man of our race did not bide his time, desired the favor of marriage before the proper hour, and fell into sin by not waiting for the time of God's Will.

Clement of Alexandria, Stromata 3.14.94 (Christianity)

Dreams of falling are most frequently characterized by anxiety. Their interpretation when they occur in women offers no difficulty, because they nearly always accept the symbolic meaning of falling, which is a circumlocution for giving way to an erotic temptation.

Nothing can be brought to an end in the unconscious; nothing is past or forgotten.

Sigmund Freud, *The Interpretation of Dreams*

Teachings of Sun Myung Moon

Could the Human Fall have been the result of eating a fruit of a tree? Adam and Eve fell by the sin of illicit love, a transgression that violated God's ideal of true love. Prior to the fall, when they were constrained by the commandment [not to eat the fruit], Adam and Eve were in an imperfect state, that is, in their growing period. The archangel Lucifer, symbolized by the serpent, tempted Eve, and she spiritually fell with him. She then tempted Adam to eat the fruit before the time was ripe, and they fell physically.

Adam and Eve had been living in joy in the Garden of Eden and conversing with God. The only possible sin that they would be tempted to commit at the risk of their lives was a sin involving wrongful love.

The consummation of human ancestors' first love was also to be God's own completion. Therefore, it naturally should have been the moment of joy and jubilation for God, Adam and Eve, and all creation. They were to have rejoiced together in continuous festivities of love and blessing. On that joyous occasion, God's love, life and lineage was to be firmly settled in the first human ancestors.

Instead, Adam and Eve covered their lower parts and hid in the bushes, trembling with fear. By their illicit act, they had violated the Way of Heaven, forming a relationship that was the origin of false love, false life and false lineage. Consequently all humankind ever since, as descendants of fallen Adam and Eve, came to be born with original sin, from generation to generation.

The reason why every person experiences inner conflict between the mind and the body is due to the Fall. The reason why human beings act against their original mind, and form societies where the order of love is corrupted, is also due to the Fall. (277:200, April 16, 1996)

What was the forbidden fruit? What sort of fruit could cause countless generations of humanity to groan in misery? Why would God create a fruit that could cause misery, destruction and war? My teaching is logical: the fruit is a symbol for love. So many evils spring from love. From love can spring either good or evil fruit, therefore it is called "the fruit of the knowledge of good and evil." (128:86, June 5, 1983)

We read that before the Fall, Adam and Eve were both naked, and were not ashamed. (Gen. 2.25) After the fall, however, they felt ashamed of their nakedness and sewed fig leaves together into aprons to cover their lower parts. If they had committed a crime by eating some actual fruit from a tree called the tree of the knowledge of good and evil, then they certainly would have covered their hands or mouths instead. It is human nature to conceal one's faults. Thus, the act of covering their lower parts shows that these parts, and not their mouths, were the source of their shame.

In Job 31.33-34, it is written, "If I have concealed my transgressions like Adam, by hiding my iniquity in my bosom." Adam concealed his lower parts after the Fall; this indicates that his blemish was in his lower parts. Adam and Eve's sexual parts were the source of their shame because those were the instruments of their sinful deed.

In the world before the Human Fall, what act would one be willing to carry out even clearly at the risk of one's life? It could be nothing else but the act of love. God's purpose of creation, described in the blessing "be fruitful and multiply," (Gen. 1.28) can be achieved only through love. Accordingly, from the viewpoint of God's purpose of creation, love should be the most precious and sacred act. But because the sexual act was the very cause of the Fall, people often regard it with shame and even contempt. In conclusion, human beings fell through an act of illicit sexual intercourse. (*Exposition of the Divine Principle,* Fall 1.3.2)

Everything in the universe is created to be governed by God through love. Thus, love is the source of life, the key to happiness, and the essence of the ideal to which all beings aspire. The more one receives love, the more beautiful one appears to others. When the angel, created as God's servant, beheld Eve, the daughter of God, it was only natural that she looked beautiful in his eyes. Moreover, when Lucifer saw that Eve was responding to his temptation, the angel felt the stimulation of her love to be deliciously enticing. At this point, Lucifer was seducing Eve with the mind to have her, regardless of the consequences. Lucifer, who left his proper position due to his excessive desire, and Eve, who wanted to open her eyes and become like God before the time was ripe, formed a common base and began give and take action. The power of the unprincipled love generated by their give and take led them to consummate an illicit sexual relationship on the spiritual plane.

All beings are created based on the principle that when they become one in love, they exchange elements with each other. Accordingly, when Eve became one with Lucifer through love, she received certain elements from him. First, she received feelings of dread arising from the pangs of a guilty conscience, stemming from her violation of the purpose of creation. Second, she received from Lucifer the wisdom which enabled her to discern that her originally intended spouse was to be Adam, not the angel. (*Exposition of the Divine Principle,* Fall 2.2.1)

How did Eve feel while the archangel Lucifer was raping her? She felt pangs of conscience. She disliked what was happening, but let herself be pulled along as he seduced her.

When we make love, we are supposed to feel joy with every cell in our body. Our passion should be like a flower at the height of spring. Eve, however, grimaced as she made love, her heart shriveling and her every cell withering. (33:330, August 23, 1970)

Eve was to become the future wife of God. This is because Adam was to be one body with God—that is, God Himself… From this perspective, the Fall was Satan violating God's wife. (22:208, February 4, 1969)

Once Eve had united with the Archangel through their illicit sexual relationship, she stood in the position of the Archangel with respect to Adam. Thus, Adam, who was still receiving God's love, appeared very attractive to her. Seeing Adam as her only hope of returning to God, Eve turned to Adam and tempted him, playing the same role as the Archangel had played when he had tempted her. Adam responded and formed a common base with Eve, and they began give and take action with each other. The power of the unprincipled love generated in their relationship induced Adam to abandon his original position and brought them together in an illicit physical relationship of sexual love.

When Adam united in oneness with Eve, he inherited all the elements Eve had received from the Archangel. These elements in turn have been passed down to all subsequent generations without interruption... and humanity has multiplied in sin to the present day, perpetuating the lineage of Satan. (*Exposition of the Divine Principle*, Fall 2.2.2)

2. Catastrophic Consequences of the Human Fall

When Zeus was angry with mankind, he devised the worst punishment he could think of, and invented Woman. Hephaestus, the smith of the gods, was instructed to form her from the earth and make her irresistibly beautiful. Each of the gods gave her his own special gift of skill, and from this she was called Pandora, "all gifted."

When she was perfected with every gift and arrayed in all her loveliness, this treacherous treasure was taken down to earth by Hermes, the messenger god, and given to Prometheus' foolish brother Epimetheus. Now Prometheus had warned his brother not to accept anything from Zeus, even if it looked like a gift sent in friendship; but Epimetheus as usual acted first and thought afterwards. He accepted the maiden from Hermes and led her into his house, and with her a great jar—some say a box or chest—which the gods had sent with her, telling her to keep it safely but never open.[1]

This was too much for Pandora, who among her gifts was endowed with feminine curiosity. After restraining it for a little while, she at last gave in and lifted the lid from the jar, and from that moment began the sorrows of mankind. For each of the gods had stored in it the worst thing he was able to give, and wonderful as had been the gifts with which they endowed her, just as dreadful were the evils that rushed eagerly from the jar in a black stinking cloud like pestilent insects—sickness and suffering, hatred and jealousy and greed, and all the other cruel things that freeze the heart and bring on old age.

Pandora tried to clap the lid on the jar again, but it was too late. The happy childhood of mankind had gone forever, and with it the Golden Age when life was easy. From then on man had to wrest a hard living by his own labor from the unfriendly ground.

Only one good thing came to man in the jar and remains to comfort him in his distress, and that is the spirit of Hope.

Myth of Pandora's Box (Hellenism)

In the olden days, when God still lived among men, Death did not live among men. Whenever he happened to stray onto the earth, God (*Imana*) would chase it away with his hunting dogs. One day during such a chase, Death was forced into a narrow space and would have been caught and destroyed. But in his straits he found a woman, and promised her that if she hid him he would spare her and her family. The woman opened her mouth and Death jumped inside.[2] When God came to her and asked her if she had seen Death, she denied ever seeing him. But God, the All-Seeing One, knew what happened, and told the woman that since she had hidden Death, in the future Death would destroy her and all her children. From that moment death spread all over the world.

Hutu tradition (African Traditional Religions)

If Adam had not sinned, he would not have begotten children from the side of the evil inclination, but he would have borne offspring from the side of the Holy Spirit. But now, since all the children of men are born from the side of the evil inclination, they have no permanence and are but short-lived, because there is in them an element of the 'other side.' But if Adam had not sinned and had not been driven from the Garden of Eden, he would have begotten progeny from the side of the Holy Spirit—a progeny holy as the celestial angels, who would have endured for eternity, after the supernal pattern. Since, however, he sinned and begat children outside the Garden of Eden, these did not take root.

Zohar, Genesis 61a (Judaism)

After [they fell] God clothed Adam and Eve in garments soothing to the skin, as it is written, "He made them coats of skin (עוֹר, 'or) [Gen. 3.21]. At first they had coats of light (אוֹר, or), which procured them the service of the highest of the high, for the celestial angels used to come to enjoy that light; so it is written, "For you made him but little lower than the angels, and crowned him with glory and honor" [Psalm 8.5]. But after their sins they had only coats of skin, good for the body but not for the soul.

Zohar 1.36b (Judaism)

The deities Izanagi and Izanami descended from Heaven to the island Ono-goro and erected a heavenly pillar and a spacious palace.

At this time Izanagi asked his wife Izanami, "How is your body formed?" She replied, "My body, though it be formed, has one place which is formed insufficiently." Then Izanagi said, "My body, though it be formed, has one place which is formed to excess. Therefore, I would like to take that place in my body which is formed to excess and insert it into that place in your body which is formed insufficiently, and thus give birth to the land. How would this be?" "That will be good," said Izanami. "Then let us, you and me, walk in a circle around this heavenly pillar and meet and have conjugal intercourse," said Izanagi. "You walk around from the right, and I will walk around from the left and meet you."

After having agreed to this, they circled around; then Izanami said first, "How delightful! I have met a lovely lad!" Afterwards, Izanagi said, "How delightful! I have met a lovely maiden!" After each had spoken, Izanagi said to his wife, "It was not proper that the woman should speak first." Nevertheless, they commenced procreation and gave birth to a leech-child. They placed this child into a boat made of reeds and floated it away.

Then the two deities consulted together, "The child which we have just borne is not good. It is best to report this before the heavenly gods." So they ascended together and sought the will of the heavenly gods. The gods thereupon performed a grand divination, and said, "Because the woman spoke first, the child was not good. Descend once more and say it again."[3]

Kojiki 4.1-6.1 (Shinto)

Teachings of Sun Myung Moon

How could the original sin arise from eating a literal fruit? If the first ancestor committed sin by eating a fruit, what could bequeath that sin to thousands of generations of his descendants? The generations are related through lineage. If the root of sin is planted in the lineage, the sin continues forever by the law of heredity. Only a problem of love could make this happen. Wrongful love was the cause of the Human Fall. (23:167, May 18, 1969)

Love is supposed to bring human beings to perfection. However, when something goes wrong with love, even God steps back. Then it becomes a serious problem. In this respect, we discover that something went wrong with love. Nothing else could become such a serious problem for God, for humankind and for history. The failure of love was the greatest catastrophe in the whole universe. (128:87, June 5, 1983)

Were you to truly know love, you would be well acquainted with everything. You would not only know the facts of the earth plane, but also your spiritual eyes would be open and you would understand the cosmos in all its dimensions. You would reach the level where you could experience God directly. God endowed human beings with the potential to develop their senses of love to that degree.

However, Adam and Eve fell before they could reach that level. (137:129, January 1, 1986)

When Adam and Eve were in adolescence, at the age of 16, 17 or 18, their eyes were not supposed to wander about. They were supposed to look into each other's eyes and say, "You are the one I have been looking for! It was you all along!" Gazing into each other's eyes filled with mystery and touching each other's noses, they would have felt a spark of electricity. Would their minds and body have been completely united at that moment? Yes they would have been.

When a man and a woman become one in the mind and the body and establish goodness in the universe, they are like flowers in full bloom. The fragrance of their love fills the entire universe, enthralling all its creatures. Every creature stretches its body and perks up its nose to smell the alluring scent. What about God? He would exclaim, "Wow! This is awesome!" Even God is captivated. He is naturally drawn to them. He gives them all His attention. He urges them on.

Up to the moment when God joined Adam and Eve, they were not prepared to experience the electricity of love. They would have felt clumsy around each other; their physical touch would have come as a shock. But once their minds and bodies would be totally united in God's love, once the three—God, Adam and Eve—would be united as one, they would have experienced love like a flash of lightening. At that moment, they would have become the nucleus of the universe. They would have orbited about each other in love, forming the nucleus for governing all things by love. Yet Adam and Eve were derailed from this orbit…

Had Adam and Eve become the nucleus, God would have nestled them in His bosom. He would have been with them always. Even if His body tried to leave, His feet would have stayed with them. The couple would have been inseparable, ever embracing each other. Their sons and daughters would have been connected to them by cords of love, and wherever they went they would come together again… The families, tribes, peoples, nations, and world descended from them were supposed to be established from that nucleus. As descendants of a man and woman in complete oneness, they too would have embraced one another in true love as they built their own families, tribes, peoples, nations and world. What a wonderful world it would be! Everything would be marvelous. It would be the Kingdom of Heaven on earth. Don't you think so?

Am I a dreamer, or do I speak truth? My elucidation of the Human Fall as the reason for the [corruption] of love is logical and correct, based upon a proper assessment of history. Knowing it, we can resolve all human problems. Even so, it is not an easy task.

Because the nucleus of love was not established, and instead the Fall occurred, the whole world became contrary to God's ideal, its unity shattered into pieces. Stemming from that initial disorder, all human beings became separated from one another. We cannot deny that the world today is beset by divisions. That is to say, we are all fallen. It is only appropriate to conclude that we are living in the world that resulted from the Fall.

Since people live in a condition of separation, they deny that God exists. Moreover, they deny their parents, their brothers and sisters, their husband and wives. The world is in chaos. In such a state, human beings can never achieve oneness by their own efforts. Although there are always people who seek for the ideal, they cannot possibly attain it… Meanwhile, others despair, saying that humanity is facing destruction, that there is no hope, and that utopian ideals are merely vain figments of the human imagination. (128:88, June 5, 1983)

If the first human beings did not fall, they would have received God's vertical love, and they would have become, as it were, the bodies of God. It would be as if God were the bones, and Adam and Eve the flesh.

God would be the internal Parent in the internal position, and Adam and Eve the external parents in the external position. The internal and the external would become one through love... Without the union of vertical and horizontal love, no one can be perfected.

Our first ancestors should have become the human beings whom God intended to create according to His original Will. We should have descended from such persons. We should have been born from persons with a divine nature. Then we would possess both God's divine nature and our parents' human nature.

Adam and Eve could become perfect and bear perfect fruit only when connected to the love of God. Without that connection, it is not possible. The connecting point of God's vertical love and Adam and Eve's horizontal physical love was to be the very root of our ancestors' lineage. All of humanity was supposed to have arisen from that beginning point.

The Fall, however, severed man's love, woman's love and God's love. Because of the Fall, man's love, woman's love and God's love were not connected. If there had been no Fall, man and woman would be tied together by God's love—without doubt.

Why do a man and a woman try to become one? They do it for love. What do they want after uniting in love? They want to receive God's blessing. That is the purpose. (184:71, November 13, 1988)

3. Corruption of Sexual Love

Lust requires for its consummation darkness and secrecy; and this not only when unlawful intercourse is desired, but even such fornication as the earthly city has legalized. Where there is no fear of punishment, these permitted pleasures still shrink from the public eye...

Even the parental duty, done as it is in accordance with Roman law for the procreation of children, and, therefore, is both legally right and morally good, looks for a room from which all witnesses have been carefully removed. It is only after the best man and bridesmaids, the friends and the servants, have gone from the room that the bridegroom even begins to show any signs of intimate affection... Not even the children who have been born because it was done are allowed to be witnesses while it is being done. Yes, it is a good deed; but it is one that seeks to be known only after it is done, and is ashamed to be seen while it is being done. The reason can only be that what, by nature, has a purpose that everyone praises involves, by penalty, a passion that makes everyone ashamed...

Now, in the Garden, before the Fall... the passions of anger and lust were never so roused counter to the commands of the rational will that reason was forced, so to speak, to put them in harness. It is different now, when even people who live a life of moral and religious self-control have to bridle these passions. This may be easy or difficult, but the bit and bridle are always needed. Now, the present condition is not that of healthy human nature; it is a sickness induced by sin...

No one, then, should dream of believing that the kind of lust which made the married couple in the Garden ashamed of their nakedness was meant to be the only means of fulfilling the command which God gave when He "blessed them, saying: Increase and multiply, and fill the earth." (Gen. 1.28) The fact is that this passion had no place before they sinned; it was only after the Fall, when their nature had lost its power to exact obedience from the sexual organs, that they fell and noticed the loss and, being ashamed of their lust, covered these unruly members. But God's blessing on their marriage, with the command to increase and multiply and fill the earth, was given before the Fall. The blessing remained even when they had sinned, because it was a token that the begetting of children is a part of the glory of marriage and has nothing to do with the penalty for sin...

We conclude, therefore, that, even had there been no sin in the Garden, there would still have been marriages worthy of that blessed place and that lovely babies would have flowered from a love uncankered by lust. Unfortunately, to show just how that could be we have no present experience to help us. Nevertheless, when we consider how many other human organs still obey the will even after the Fall, we have no reason for doubting that the one unruly member could have done the same, as long as there was no defiance from lust. After all, we move our hands and feet to their appropriate functions whenever we choose and with no rebellion on their part... But the peculiarity of the passion of lust which we are here discussing is that the soul can neither sufficiently control itself so as to be free of lust, nor in any way control the body when lust takes over the control of sexual excitement in defiance of the will. This defiance is precisely what makes both lust itself and the organs it controls such sources of shame.

Saint Augustine, City of God 14.18-23 (*Christianity*)

You must know, monks, that after the floods [that put out the conflagration that ended the last cosmic cycle] receded and the earth came back into being, there was upon the face of the earth a film more sweet-smelling than ambrosia. Do you want to know what was the taste of that film? It was like the taste of grape wine in the mouth. And at this time the gods of the Abhasvara Heaven said to one another, "Let us go and see what it looks like in Jambudvipa now that there is earth again." So the young gods of that heaven came down into the world and saw that over the earth was spread this film. They put their fingers into the earth and sucked them. Some put their fingers into the earth many times and ate a great deal of this film, and these at once lost all their majesty and brightness. Their bodies grew heavy and their substance became flesh and bone. They lost their magic and could no longer fly. But there were others who ate only a little, and these could still fly about in the air. And those that had lost their magic cried out to one another in dismay, "Now we are in a very sad case. We have lost our magic. There is nothing for it but to stay here on earth; for we cannot possibly get back to heaven." They stayed and fed upon the film that covered the earth, and gazed at one another's beauty. Those among them that were most passionate became women, and these gods and goddesses fulfilled their desires and pleasure in one another. And this was how it was, monks, that when the world began love-making first spread throughout the world; it is an old and constant thing...

And the gods who had returned to heaven looked down and saw the young gods that had fallen, and they came down and reproached them, saying, "Why are you behaving in this unclean way?" Then the gods on earth thought to themselves, "We must find some way to be together without being seen by others." So they made houses that would cover and hide them. Monks, that was how houses first began.

[Now the people] seeing this thing of husbands and wives had begun, hated and despised such couples and seized them with the left hand, pushed them with the right hand and drove them away. But always after two months or maybe three they would come back again. Then the people hit them or pelted them with sticks, clods of earth, tiles or stones. "Go and hide yourselves! Go and hide yourselves properly!"

That is why today when a girl is married she is pelted with flowers or gold or silver or pieces of clothing or rice, and the people as they pelt her say, "May peace and happiness, new bride, be yours!" Monks, in former times ill was meant by these things that were done, but nowadays good is meant.

Ekottara Agama 34 and Ch'i-shih Ching[4] (Buddhism)

Teachings of Sun Myung Moon

Sexual love caused human beings to fall. Therefore, our sexual organs are most fearful things. Religion holds adultery to be the cardinal sin. Is free sex in America and throughout the world the expression of God's philosophy of the Kingdom or the devil's philosophy of hell? It is the philosophy of hell run rampant, creating hell both on earth and in heaven. Everyone who follows this trend is doomed. (261:304, July 24, 1994)

How can God's love be linked to this world? True love coming down from above brings unity by the most direct and shortest path, making a 90-degree angle. Once that direct connection is made with the vertical God, the love of human beings can correspond to it—true love traveling by the most direct and shortest path. Induced by that vertical love, a man and a woman move on the horizontal plane toward the vertical line, creating a right angle: this is love's final destination. What was the Human Fall? It bent this right angle. (218:219, July 29, 1991)

God's purpose of creation, described in the blessings "be fruitful and multiply," (Gen. 1.28) can be achieved only through love. Accordingly, from the viewpoint of God's purpose of creation, love should be the most precious and sacred act. But because the sexual act was the very cause of the Fall, people often regard it with shame and even contempt. (*Exposition of the Divine Principle*, Fall 1.3.2)

There is ample evidence which helps us recognize that the root of human sin stems from sexual immorality. We know that the original sin has been perpetuated through lineal descent from one generation to the next. This is because the root of sin was solidified by a sexual relationship that binds one in ties of blood. Furthermore, those religions which emphasize the need to purge sin regard fornication as a cardinal sin, and they have taught the virtues of chastity and restraint in order to curb it. This is an indication that the root of sin is found in lustful desires. The Israelites performed the rite of circumcision as a condition for sanctification. They qualified themselves as God's chosen people by draining blood, because the root of sin lies in having taken in through an unchaste act the evil blood which permeates our being.

Sexual promiscuity is a principal cause of the downfall of numerous heroes, patriots and nations. Even in the most outstanding people, the root of sin—illicit sexual desire—is constantly active in their souls, sometimes without their conscious awareness. We may be able to eradicate all other evils by establishing moral codes through religion, by thoroughly implementing various educational programs, and by reforming the socio-economic systems that foster crime. But no one can prevent the plague of sexual promiscuity, which has become increasingly prevalent as the progress of civilization makes lifestyles more comfortable and indolent. Therefore, the hope of an ideal world is an empty dream as long as this root of all evils has not been eradicated at its source. Christ at his Second Advent must be able to solve this problem once and for all. (*Exposition of the Divine Principle*, Fall 1.5)

Cain and Abel

THE FIRST MURDER IN HUMAN HISTORY followed close on the heels of the human fall; indeed, the tension between the brothers can be attributed to the situation they inherited from their parents. The story of Cain and Abel raises the inescapable human problem of inequality. It asks: how should people cope with differences in wealth, talent, love, fortune, and in this case, blessing.

The Bible regards Abel as one of the righteous; the Qur'an portrays him as a man of peace who refuses to take up a weapon to fight his brother Cain. Hence comes the tradition that there are two kinds of people: Abel-type people are good and faithful, while Cain-type people are evil, atheistic and violent. In Father Moon's teaching, however, Cain and Abel are most essentially brothers. Moreover, both had flaws: Abel's arrogance over being the favored one contributed to Cain's hatred, and Cain's hatred had a history, too.

Father Moon teaches that God's purpose in accepting only Abel's offering was not to express His disdain for Cain, but rather to promote a process of *restoration:* by Cain yielding to Abel, Cain and Abel were to reverse the mistake of their parents when Adam was wrongly dominated by the Archangel. Had this restoration been successful, there would have been no murder; instead even Cain's offering would have been accepted by God.

Inequality is inevitable; how we deal with it is where choice comes into play. Cain had a choice: to react with violence or to humbly seek his brother's help. Abel also had a choice: to glory in his favored status or to have compassion on his less favored brother, comfort him and raise him up. The choices we make in these Cain-Abel situations can make the difference between peace and war.

Now Abel was a keeper of sheep, and Cain a tiller of the ground. In the course of time Cain brought to the LORD an offering of the fruit of the ground, and Abel brought of the firstlings of the flock and of their fat portions. And the LORD had regard for Abel and his offering, but for Cain and his offering He had no regard. So Cain was very angry, and his countenance fell. The LORD said to Cain, "Why are you angry, and why has your countenance fallen? If you do well, will you not be accepted? And if you do not do well, sin is couching at the door; its desire is for you, but you must master it."

Cain said to Abel his brother, "Let us go out into the field." And when they were in the field, Cain rose up against his brother Abel, and killed him. Then the LORD said to Cain, "Where is Abel your brother?" He replied, "I do not know; am I my brother's keeper?" And the LORD said, "What have you done? The voice of your brother's blood is crying to me from the ground. And now you are cursed from the ground, which has opened its mouth to receive your brother's blood from your hand. When you till the ground, it shall no longer yield to you its strength; you shall be a fugitive and a wanderer on the earth." Cain said to the LORD, "My punishment is greater than I can bear. Behold, you have driven me this day away from the ground; and from your face I shall be hidden; and I shall be a fugitive and a wanderer on the earth, and whoever finds me will slay me." Then the LORD said to him, "Not so! If any one slays Cain, vengeance shall be taken on him sevenfold." And the LORD put a mark on Cain, lest any who came upon him should kill him. Then Cain went away from the presence of the LORD, and dwelt in the land of Nod, east of Eden.

Genesis 4.3-16

And recite for them the story of the two sons of Adam truthfully, when they offered a sacrifice, and it was accepted of one of them, and not accepted of the other. "I will surely slay you," said one. "God accepts only of the god-fearing," said the other.

"Yet if you stretch out your hand against me, to slay me, I will not stretch out my hand against you, to slay you; I fear God, the Lord of all Beings. I desire that you should be laden with my sin and your sin, and so become an inhabitant of the Fire; that is the recompense of the evildoers."

Then his soul prompted him to slay his brother, and he slew him, and became one of the losers.

Then God sent forth a raven, scratching into the earth, to show him how he might conceal the vile body of his brother. He said, "Woe is me! Am I unable to be as this raven, and so conceal my brother's vile body?" And he became one of the remorseful.

Qur'an 5.27-31

By faith Abel offered to God a more acceptable sacrifice than Cain, through which he received approval as righteous, God bearing witness by accepting his gifts; he died, but through his faith he is still speaking.

Hebrews 11.4

When Adam and Eve begot children, the firstborn was the son of the serpent's slime. For two beings had intercourse with Eve, and she conceived from both and bore two children. Each followed one of the male parents, and their spirits parted, one to this side and one to the other, and similarly their characters. On the side of Cain are all the haunts of the evil species, from which come evil spirits and demons and necromancers. From the side of Abel come a more merciful class, yet not wholly beneficial—good wine mixed with bad. The right kind was not produced until Seth came, who is the first ancestor of all the generations of the righteous...

Cain rose up against Abel and killed him because he inherited his nature from the side of Samael, who brought death into the world. He was jealous of Abel on account of his female, as indicated by the words, "and it came to pass when they were in the field (Gen. 4.8)," the word "field" signifying woman. According to the text, Cain was angry because his offering was not accepted, but this is a further reason.[5]

Zohar 1.36b (Judaism)

Teachings of Sun Myung Moon

The biblical account of Cain and Abel reveals the beginnings of human conflict right in Adam's family. It provides the archetype for humankind's unending history of struggle, war and conflict. We are conflicted on many levels, beginning with the war between the body and mind within each individual and extending to wars between nations and even to the global conflict between materialism and theism. (September 12, 2005)

Originally, God alone was to govern human beings. God was to be our only Lord. Nevertheless, Satan became our lord through his immoral relationship with the first ancestors.

The Principle teaches that love carries governing, sovereign power. That is why Satan has a right to claim ownership over human beings even though his love is immoral. However, God is the original owner through the Principle of Creation. Thus, God and Satan could both claim ownership over human beings. Yet it is physically impossible to divide Adam into two—one piece for God and the other for Satan. Therefore, God had to set up a certain rule to divide a human being. God set up the rule for separation in terms of the polarities of internal and external and subject and object, with God in the position of the internal being and the creation the external being.

By this principle, God divided fallen Adam and Eve into two through their two children. Cain represented Satan, and Abel represented sinless Adam. Hence God placed Abel, the second son, in the internal position. Abel represented the second love between Adam and Eve, which contained fewer evil elements, while Cain was the fruit of the first love. God took Abel because Adam and Eve's relationship was more principled than the first relationship between Eve and the archangel.

The original order of love was to flow from God to Adam and then to the archangel. Hence the positions in restoration must also be ordered: first God, then Abel and last Cain. By restoring these positions, relationships, to the original order, God intends to restore the lost principle...

God led the providence to restore the birthright of the elder son through these two brothers. Cain must go down to Abel's position, and Abel must go up to Cain's position—the first son's position.

However, Cain killed Abel. His action was a repetition of Adam and Eve's fall. It repeated the condition by which Satan came to control Adam. It was the opposite of restoration. (55:109-10, April 1, 1972)

The Bible attests to the discrimination between first- and second-born sons. For example... it is written that God loved the second son Jacob and hated the first son Esau even while they were still inside their mother's womb. (Rom. 9.11-13) They were placed in the positions of Cain or Abel based solely upon the distinction of who was to be the firstborn son. When Jacob was blessing his two grandchildren, Ephraim and Manasseh, he crossed his hands and laid his right hand on the head of Ephraim, the second son in the position of Abel, to give him the first and greater blessing. (Gen. 48.14) According to this principle, God placed Cain and Abel in a position where each could deal with only one master, and had them offer sacrifices.

When Cain and Abel offered their sacrifices, "The Lord had regard for Abel and his offering, but for Cain and his offering he had no regard." (Gen. 4.4) Why did God accept Abel's offering but reject Cain's? God received Abel's sacrifice because he stood in a proper relationship with God. Also, he made the offering in an acceptable manner—through faith (Heb. 11.4) and in line with God's Will. In this way, Abel successfully laid the foundation of faith in Adam's family. He serves as an example that any fallen person can make an offering acceptable to God provided he satisfies the necessary conditions.

God did not reject Cain's sacrifice because He hated him. Rather, because Cain stood in a position to relate with Satan, which gave Satan rights over the sacrifice, God could not accept Cain's sacrifice unless he first made some condition justifying its acceptance. (*Exposition of the Divine Principle,* Foundation 1)

When Cain found out that God accepted only Abel's offering, he struck and killed Abel out of hatred. You have to understand, however, that already while they were preparing their offerings, Cain nursed feelings of resentment against Abel. Cain did not strike Abel in a sudden flash of anger over God accepting only Abel's offering. Rather, even before that incident, Cain hated Abel and wanted to kill him. (3:205, November 1, 1957)

It seems that God was discriminating between Cain and Abel, but that was not the case. If Cain had even the slightest desire to go through Abel, who represented Heaven's position, then God would have accepted Cain's offering. Although his acceptance would have come later, God desired to relate to them in fairness.

You must not repeat the mistake of Abel, who prolonged the providence of God by not being able to cope with the mission Heaven gave to him. (3:205, November 1, 1957)

Cain should have appealed to Abel, asking him to show him the way to approach God that his offering might also be accepted. He should have kept a mind of absolute faith, absolute love and absolute obedience to God; then he would have totally united with his brother. Only then could he have entered the realm of God. (378:206-07, May 12, 2002)

God placed Abel in the position to save Cain. God expected that Abel would love Cain, and share with him all the love that he received from God, as well as his own love. (18:277, June 12, 1967)

When God accepted only Abel's offering, Abel became arrogant. Through that condition, Satan could make accusation against him. Satan influenced Cain to lose his temper and his reason, driving him to kill his own brother. (374:12-13, April 4, 2002)

All the conflicts and wars that the world has witnessed since the beginning of history have been, in essence, battles between the Cain side, which is relatively evil, and the Abel side, which is more on the side of goodness. (299:105, February 6, 1999)

Yet Cain and Abel must never be divided. They are like the right hand and the left hand. Everyone should live with the attitude, "My God is also your God"; "The God who loves me also loves you." (3:207, November 1, 1957)

Think about the moment when Cain killed Abel. The pain of it seared God's heart, and His tears continue to this day. God intended that the elder son love his younger brother, but instead he murdered him. That one murder broke God's heart. Yet look at the world today: every day tens of thousands of people are being killed or dying of starvation. Do you think God's heart is at peace? (March 2, 2003)

The Devil and His Activities

SCRIPTURES OF ALL RELIGIONS TESTIFY TO DEMONIC BEINGS and powers. Their chief is known by various names: Satan, Lucifer, Iblis, Mara, Samael, Beelzebub and Angra Mainyu, among others. Some of them we met in the accounts of the Human Fall and the origin of evil. Yet the Devil is continually active, drawing people's hearts to do wickedness. While rationalists have difficulty accepting the reality of the Devil, a glance at the history of the twentieth century and its horrors makes plain that the capability of human beings to inflict evil on one another transcends reason. Pope Paul VI said of the Devil,

> We know that this dark and disturbing spirit really exists, and that he still acts with treacherous cunning; he is the secret enemy that sows errors and misfortunes in human history… who finds his way into us by way of the senses, the imagination, lust, utopian logic, or disorderly social contacts in the give and take of life. [6]

The Devil's hooks are many and various. Scriptures teach that when a person desires to do a small evil, the Devil has a claim and can influence him to do something far worse. Conversely, people on a religious path experience the Devil's temptations precisely at the point where they are about to make great progress.

Belief in the power of the Devil does not imply dualism, although in some religions—Zoroastrianism most notably—God and the Devil are in eternal rivalry. For the monotheistic faiths that teach the goodness of God's creation, the demons themselves are resultant beings, angels who fell from their original status as God's servants to become the enemies of God. Father Moon explains that the fall of the angel Lucifer occurred at the Human Fall, at which time he becomes Satan, the powerful demon who asserts dominion over human beings.

Following these are passages describing the Devil's nature and the various temptations and stratagems he uses to capture human beings. We should be aware that the key to overcoming Satan is to purify ourselves of every characteristic that resembles him—selfishness, arrogance, greed, craving for sensual pleasures—and instead live a life fixed on God and eternity.

1. The Fall of the Angels

And the great dragon was thrown down, that ancient serpent, who is called the Devil and Satan, the deceiver of the whole world—he was thrown down to the earth, and his angels were thrown down with him.

Revelation 12.9

How you are fallen from heaven,
O Lucifer, son of the morning!
How you are cut down to the ground,
you who weakened the nations!
For you said in your heart,
"I will ascend into heaven,
I will exalt my throne above the stars of God;
I will sit also upon the mount of the
   congregation,
in the sides of the north;
I will ascend above the heights of the clouds;
I will be like the Most High."
Yet you shall be brought down to hell,
to the depths of the pit.

Isaiah 14.12-15 (KJV)

And when We said to the angels, "Bow yourselves to Adam," they bowed themselves, save Iblis; he said, "Shall I bow myself to one whom You have created of clay?" He said, "What do you think? This [creature] You have honored above me, if You defer me until the Day of Resurrection I shall assuredly master his seed, save a few."

Said We, "Depart! Those of them that follow you—surely hell shall be your recompense, an ample recompense! And startle any of them whom you can with your voice; and rally against them your horsemen and your foot [soldiers], and share with them in their wealth and their children, and promise them!" But Satan promises them naught, except delusion.

Qur'an 17.61-64

The Lord God spoke to Moses, saying, "That Satan... is the same who was from the beginning, and he came before me, saying, 'Behold, here am I; send me, I will be thy son, and I will redeem all mankind, that not one soul shall be lost. Surely I will do it; therefore give me my honor.'

"But my Beloved Son, who was my Beloved and Chosen from the beginning, said to me, 'Father, Thy will be done, and the glory be Thine forever.'

"Therefore, because that Satan rebelled against me, and sought to destroy the agency of man, which I, the Lord God, had given him, and also, that I should give to him my own power; by the power of my Only Begotten [Christ], I caused that he should be cast down; and he became Satan, yea, even the devil, the father of all lies, to deceive and to blind men, and to lead them captive at his will, even as many as would not hearken unto my voice."[7]

Pearl of Great Price, Moses 4.1-4 (Latter-day Saints)

And the angels that did not keep their own position but left their proper dwelling have been kept by Him in eternal chains in the nether gloom until the judgment of the great day; just as Sodom and Gomorrah and the surrounding cities, which likewise acted immorally and indulged in unnatural lust, serve as an example by undergoing a punishment of eternal fire.

Jude 6-7

Teachings of Sun Myung Moon

God is the owner, and we human beings are His sons and daughters. Angels, on the other hand, were created as God's servants; hence they are also the servants of His children. Among all the angels, the archangel Lucifer was the closest to God as well as to Adam and Eve. He knew all the stories behind the scenes. During the process of creating the universe, prior to the creation of Adam and Eve, God would discuss things with the archangel and send him to do his errands. In other words, the archangel was like a servant of a wealthy lord. He was also in the position of a servant to his master's children, no matter how young or immature they were. (53:331, March 6, 1972)

God created the angelic world and assigned Lucifer (Isa. 14.12) to the position of archangel. Lucifer was the channel of God's love to the angelic world, just as Abraham was the channel of God's blessing to the Israelites. In this position he virtually monopolized the love of God. However, after God created human beings as His children, He loved them many times more than He had ever loved Lucifer, whom He had created as His servant. In truth, God's love toward Lucifer did not change; it was the same before and after the creation of human beings. Yet when Lucifer saw that God loved Adam and Eve more than him, he felt as if there had been a decrease in the love he received from God. This situation is similar to that in the biblical parable of the laborers in the vineyard. (Matt. 20.1-15) Although the laborers who had worked since morning received a fair wage, when they saw that those who came later and worked less received just as much, they felt underpaid. Lucifer, feeling as though he were receiving less love than he deserved, wanted to grasp the same central position in human society as he enjoyed in the angelic world, as the channel of God's love. This was why he seduced Eve, and this was the motivation of the spiritual fall. (*Exposition of the Divine Principle*, Fall 2.2.1)

God cursed the fallen angel, saying, "Upon your belly you shall go, and dust you shall eat all the days of your life." (Gen. 3.14) "Upon your belly you shall go" means that the angel would become a miserable being, unable to function properly or to perform its original service. To "eat dust" means that ever since the angel was thrown down from heaven (Isa. 14.12, Rev. 12.9), he has been deprived of life elements from God. Instead, he has had to subsist on evil elements gleaned from the sinful world. (*Exposition of the Divine Principle*, Fall 1.4)

2. Works of the Devil

When a man grasps at things, Mara stands beside him.[8]

Sutta Nipata 1103 *(Buddhism)*

Shall I inform you on whom it is that the devils descend?

They descend on every lying, wicked person, into whose ears they pour hearsay vanities, and most of them are liars.

Qur'an 26.221-223

The foremost of your armies is that of Desire, the second is called Dislike. The third is Hunger-Thirst and the fourth is Craving. The fifth is the army of Lethargy-Laziness and the sixth is Fear. The seventh is Doubt and the eighth is Obstinacy-Restlessness. Then there are Material Gain, Praise, Honor, and Fame... These, O Mara, are your forces, the attackers of the Evil One. One less than a hero will not be victorious over them and attain happiness.

Sutta Nipata 436-39 (Buddhism)

For we are not contending against flesh and blood, but against the principalities, against the powers, against the world rulers of this present darkness, against the spiritual hosts of wickedness in the heavenly places.

Ephesians 6.12

The Evil Ruler spoils the Word,
the plan of life, by his teachings.
He, indeed, deprives me
of the exalted goal of Good Thought.

Avesta, Yasna 32.9 (Zoroastrianism)

Never did We send an apostle or a prophet before you, but, when he framed a desire, Satan threw some vanity into his desire. But God will cancel anything vain that Satan throws in, and God will confirm His signs—for God is full of knowledge and wisdom: that He may make the suggestions thrown in by Satan but a trial for those in whose hearts is a disease and who are hardened of heart.

Qur'an 22.52-53

The Messenger of God said, "There is none among you with whom is not an attaché from among the *jinn* (evil spirits)." The Companions said, "With you, too?" He said, "Yes, but God helps me against him and so I am safe from his hand."

Hadith of Muslim (Islam)

He who commits sin is of the devil; for the devil has sinned from the beginning. The reason the Son of God appeared was to destroy the works of the devil. No one born of God commits sin; for God's nature abides in him, and he cannot sin because he is born of God. By this it may be seen who are the children of God, and who are the children of the devil: whoever does not do right is not of God, nor he who does not love his brother.

1 John 3.8-10

You are of your father the devil, and your will is to do your father's desires. He was a murderer from the beginning, and has nothing to do with the truth, because there is no truth in him. When he lies, it is according to his own nature, for he is a liar and the father of lies. But, because I [Jesus] tell the truth, you do not believe me.

John 8.43-45

Through me you pass into the city of woe:
Through me you pass into eternal pain:
Through me among the people lost for aye.
Justice the founder of my fabric moved:
To rear me was the task of power divine,
Supremest wisdom, and primeval love.
Before me things create were none, save things
Eternal, and eternal I shall endure.
All hope abandon, ye who enter here.

Dante Alighieri, The Divine Comedy

Teachings of Sun Myung Moon

What is the meaning of the Fall? Humankind fell under Satan's control. Imprisoned within the realm of Satan's dominion, the descendants of Adam and Eve have lived out their miserable history. (168:300, October 1, 1987)

The Devil demands that others live for his sake. That is the reason why all dictators throughout history have demanded that others serve them. (222:138, October 28, 1991)

A human being's essence is spirit. When you go to the spirit world, you will vividly realize that the essence of being human is to live for the sake of others. Why, then, do people treat every matter so selfishly? It is because humankind has a blood relationship with Satan, the angel that violated the law of Heaven. (2:138, March 17, 1957)

Evil started from Satan, who infused into Eve the attitude, "I am the subject; I am the center." It started with the mentality to boast of oneself, which is evil. God's original Principle of Creation is, "Live for the sake of others." Satanic fallen nature is, "Live for myself."

You must know the origin of good and evil clearly. Evil people expect others to live for them; God wants to tear down this nature. Jesus also wants to it tear down; that is why he taught: Do not be arrogant, live for others and serve others. (69:84-85, October 20, 1973)

The Fall means that human beings fail to connect with God's vertical true love and cannot fulfill horizontal true love in their relationships with others. This is because the archangel Lucifer invaded human horizontal love.

As the result of the Fall, God lost His children, and we were born into a dysfunctional life, suffering from conflict between mind and body. On this condition, the Devil can inappropriately subjugate human beings. (198:158, February 1, 1990)

In John 8.44, Jesus says: "You are of your father the Devil... He is a liar and the father of lies." Our lineage from Satan is a result of the Fall. Lucifer (who became Satan) seduced Eve, who then seduced Adam. As a result, human history began with a tragedy brought about by deception. (73:202-03, September 18, 1974)

When Eve united with the archangel Lucifer and they fell, the archangel became Satan, the Devil, and Eve was bonded to his blood lineage. Originally, Adam and Eve's children should have been the elder and younger sons of God. However, once Eve had fallen with Satan, he claimed her body as his. According to the Principle of Creation, love determines ownership. By this principle, once two people enter into a love relationship, each partner has ownership rights over the other. Therefore, once Eve fell, the archangel could rightfully claim ownership over her and over all her descendants, fallen human beings. (110:216, November 18, 1980)

Due to the Fall, human beings could not become temples of God; instead, they united with Satan and became his dwelling places. By being united with Satan, they failed to cultivate the divine nature; instead, they acquired an evil nature. People with evil nature have propagated evil through their children, constituting evil families, evil societies and an evil world. This is the hell on earth in which we have been living. In this hell, we cannot properly form cooperative horizontal relationships with one another because our vertical relationships with God have been severed. We perform deeds harmful to others because we cannot feel the pain and suffering of our neighbors as our own.

Since humans are living in hell on earth, after shedding their physical body, they naturally enter hell in the spirit world. We have not built the Kingdom of God, but instead established the sovereignty of Satan. For this reason, Satan is called the "ruler of this world" (John 12.31) and the "god of this world." (2 Cor. 4.4) (*Exposition of the Divine Principle*, Eschatology 1.1)

Father! We cannot feel in our daily life how much the foundation of Satan's power and authority remains.
We go about our walk of faith, hour after hour, day after day,
yet we do not recognize the extent that Satan's power and authority
has invaded our daily life and the circumstances in which we live. (19:185, January 17, 1968)

3. Satan the Accuser

When a man sins, he draws to himself numbers of evil spirits and emissaries of punishment, before whom he shrinks back in fear. Solomon was conversant with the mysteries of wisdom, and God set upon his head the crown of royalty, and the whole world feared him. When, however, he sinned, he drew to himself multitudes of evil and punitive spirits, of whom he was much frightened, so that they could maltreat him and take away his precious possessions. In truth, a man by his actions is always drawing to himself some emissary from the other world, good or evil according to the path which he treads.

Zohar 1.53b (Judaism)

Now there was a day when the sons of God came to present themselves before the LORD, and Satan also came among them. The LORD said to Satan, "Whence have you come?" Satan answered the LORD, "From going to and fro on the earth, and from walking up and down on it."

And the LORD said to Satan, "Have you considered my servant Job, that there is none like him on the earth, a blameless and upright man, who fears God and turns away from evil?" Then Satan answered the LORD, "Does Job fear God for naught? Hast Thou not put a hedge about him and his house and all that he has, on every side? Thou hast blessed the work of his hands, and his possessions have increased in the land. But put forth Thy hand now, and touch all that he has, and he will curse Thee to thy face." And the LORD said to Satan, "Behold, all that he has is in your power."⁹

Job 1.6-12

And Satan says, when the issue is decided, "God surely promised you a true promise; I also promised you, then I failed you, for I had no authority over you, but that I called you, and you answered me. So do not blame me, blame yourselves."

Qur'an 14.22

Teachings of Sun Myung Moon

Satan is constantly accusing all people before God, as he did Job, in order to drag them into hell. However, even Satan cannot perpetrate his evil activity unless he first finds an object partner with whom he can form a common base and engage in give and take action. Satan's object partners are evil spirits in the spirit world. The object partners to these evil spirits are the spirit selves of evil people on the earth, and the vehicles through which these evil spirit selves act are their physical selves. Accordingly, the power of Satan is conveyed through evil spirits and is manifested in the activities of earthly people. For example, Satan entered into Judas Iscariot (Luke 22.3), and Jesus once called Peter "Satan." (Matt. 16.33) In the Bible, the spirits of evil earthly men are called "angels" of the devil. (Matt. 25.41)

The Kingdom of Heaven on earth is a restored world in which Satan can no longer instigate any activity. To realize this world, it is necessary for all humanity to eliminate their common base with Satan and not engage in give and take action with him. The prophecy that in the Last Days God will confine Satan in a bottomless pit signifies that Satan will be utterly incapable of any activity, since there will no longer be any counterparts with whom Satan can relate. (*Exposition of the Divine Principle*, Fall 4.2)

Why doesn't Satan release his claim on human beings? He asserts to God, "Didn't You set up the principle of creation that dominion is based on love? Whether my love was lawful or unlawful doesn't matter; I definitely loved Adam and Eve. Isn't love the original basis for dominion? Since I loved Adam and Eve, I have a right to claim them [and their descendants] under my dominion. I will not relinquish my claim over human beings to You unless You love me more than I loved them." (128:90, June 5, 1983)

God says to Satan, "Satan, when human beings were originally created you could not accuse them; you could not even put one finger on them." Satan counters, "I already know that. However, according to the Principle, once we come to love someone, we should belong to that person for eternity. Isn't that the law of love? I won humans by love, even though it was illicit love, so their relationship to me has to be eternal." God retorts, "According to the Principle, since I created human beings, they should be My sons and daughters. The relationship you made with them was unlawful." God is speaking out of truth, but Satan is also basing his argument on the Principle. (111:147, February 10, 1981)

God has been fighting against Satan internally and against evil people externally, but in fighting He does not act capriciously in violation of His own laws. God never fights in a way that would violate the laws of the universe. Jesus also never fought outside the laws of Heaven.

Accordingly, when we wage the universal fight in the Last Days, we must understand the laws of Heaven and learn how to fight in accordance with those laws. Although you might not be aware of it, Satan also cannot be so insolent as to fight in a way that transgresses the laws of Heaven.

For this reason, when you set conditions of restoration and fight Satan, if you deviate from the Will of God, then Satan will accuse you. Even Jesus was not exempt. Whoever violates the principle, Satan will attack without mercy. (2:176-77, April 14, 1957)

4. Human Beings Must Choose between God and the Devil

The LORD said to Cain, "Why are you angry, and why has your countenance fallen? If you do well, will you not be accepted? And if you do not do well, sin is couching at the door; its desire is for you, but you must master it."

Genesis 4.6-7

Be sober, be watchful. Your adversary the devil prowls around like a roaring lion, seeking someone to devour.

1 Peter 5.8

Whoever lives contemplating pleasant things, with senses unrestrained, in food immoderate, indolent, inactive, him verily Mara overthrows, as the wind blows down a weak tree.

Whoever lives contemplating the impurities of the body, with senses restrained, in food moderate, full of faith, full of sustained energy, him Mara overthrows not, as the wind cannot shake a rocky mountain.

Dhammapada 7-8 (Buddhism)

O men, God's promise is true; so let not the present life delude you, and let not the Deluder delude you concerning God. Surely Satan is an enemy to you; so take him for an enemy. He calls his party only that they may be among the inhabitants of the Fire.

Qur'an 35.5-6

O believers, follow not the steps of Satan; for whoever follows the steps of Satan will assuredly be bid to indecency and dishonor. But for God's bounty to you and His mercy not one of you would have been pure ever; but God purifies whom He will; and God is All-hearing, All-knowing.

Qur'an 24.21

Yes, there are two fundamental spirits, twins which are renowned to be in conflict. In thought and in word, in action, they are two: the good and the bad. And between these two, the beneficent have correctly chosen, not the maleficent.[10]

Furthermore, when these two spirits first came together, they created life and death, and now, in the end the worst existence shall be for the deceitful but the best thinking [Heaven] for the truthful person.

Of these two spirits, the deceitful one chose to bring to realization the worst things. But the very virtuous spirit, who is clothed in the hardest stones, chose the truth, and so shall mortals who shall satisfy the Wise Lord continuously with true actions.

Avesta, Yasna 30.3-5 (Zoroastrianism)

When Israel stood before Mount Sinai, the impurity of the serpent was removed from them, so that carnal passion was suppressed among them, and in consequence they were able to attach themselves to the Tree of Life, and their thoughts were turned to higher things and not to lower. Hence they were given heavenly illuminations and knowledge which filled them with joy and gladness. Further, God girded them with cinctures of the letters of the Holy Name, which prevented the serpent from gaining power over them and defiling them as before.

But when they sinned and worshipped the golden calf, they were degraded from their high estate and lost their illumination, they were deprived of the protective girdle of the Holy Name and became exposed to the attacks of the evil serpent as before.

Zohar 1.52b (Judaism)

The Essence of Mind or Suchness is the real Buddha,
While heretical views and the three poisonous elements [greed, anger, delusion] are Mara.
Enlightened by right views, we call forth the Buddha within us.
When our nature is dominated by the three poisonous elements
We are said to be possessed by the devil;
But when right views eliminate from our mind these poisonous elements
The devil will be transformed into a real Buddha.

Sutra of Hui Neng 10 (Buddhism)

Teachings of Sun Myung Moon

God is supremely selfless and supremely public minded; whereas Satan is absolutely self-centered and only out for himself. (88:209, September 18, 1976)

God has no capacity to be corrupted—He is eternal, unchanging, and unique. Therefore, regardless of his power, Satan can never bring God under his control, because God is true, and Satan cannot digest a true being.

Then, why does God, who aspires to be lord of all creation, not bring Satan under His control? It is because Satan does not have God's unchanging nature—quite the opposite. God is unchanging while Satan is always changing to suit himself. God is unique and Satan is not; God is eternal while Satan is temporal. This, in essence, is their dividing line.

Why, then, are human beings the objects of both God's desire and Satan's desire? People stand between God and Satan. They have qualities that can relate to both God's world and Satan's world.

Is someone who changes from moment to moment more on God's side or Satan's side? Is someone who is constantly creating divisions and fights in the home more susceptible to God or to Satan? What about the person who is immersed in his daily affairs and does not think about the whole, or the world, or history, or eternity, or any kind of long-term vision? What about a father who neglects his wife and children, who only goes off to the local bar and drinks every night, seeking his own pleasure? Certainly, Satan will claim such people. (124:243-44, February 20, 1983)

We are living in a fallen realm. That is why we need to live a life of faith. Remember this, and always be aware that Satan governs this fallen world. This is not merely a concept; it is reality. (161:218, February 15, 1987)

The Bible exhorts us to pray ceaselessly. The Devil can attack us and even work through us twenty-four hours a day. Although God is with us, He stays in a vertical relationship with only the mind as His base; how effectively, then, can He work with us? Satan can come at us from any direction, from 360 degrees; hence we are bound to be overwhelmed. (200:227, February 25, 1990)

Evil activity in the spirit world had been increasing gradually ever since the Human Fall. But the situation changed drastically in the 1980s, when hosts of evil spirits descended to the earth and greatly increased their activities there.

Why did this happen? In former times, when the central figures of the Providence did not know the identity of Satan, the root of sin, or the nature of the Original Sin, Satan felt at ease and could take his time creating his self-centered world. However, when the True Parents came into the world the situation began to change. The True Parents revealed the identity of Satan, the root of sin, and that the Original Sin was fornication. They figured out all Satan's traits and all his tricks, facts that not even God had revealed to humanity. Then the True Parents began making conditions so that Satan could no longer stand on his feet on the earth. As they achieved victory after victory in the Providence of Restoration, Satan was taken aback; then he began to get nervous. In response, Satan mobilized evil spirits in the spirit world to work with evil spirits in the bodies of people on the earth, by stimulating their resentment and their desire to take revenge on the descendants of the people who had caused them pain.[11]

In particular, Satan watched closely for opportunities to invade Blessed families. Whenever he found any bad conditions, he put evil spirits into them. He wanted to block them from advancing and turn them from a God-centered life. God expected that Blessed families would make unity of heart with God and True Parents by living with absolute faith, absolute love and absolute obedience. Satan cannot invade such families. But when Blessed families acted in unprincipled ways, they made conditions for Satan to invade them. Most of them expected that the victory of True Parents would protect them; they didn't look deeply at themselves to check whether they had anything for which Satan could accuse them. They didn't reflect on whether they still had any fallen nature. Therefore, at least from now on, we must work hard to purify ourselves from evil and sin and be reborn as original, true children. (Heung Jin Moon, *Message from the Spirit World*, January 1, 2001)

Sin

THE BIBLICAL MEANING OF SIN IS TO "MISS THE MARK." Thus, sin denotes how human beings deviate from the true standard of life. There are many ways to conceive of sin; here we present four. The first is evil deeds, which typically comprise murder, stealing, sexual immorality, lying and drunkenness. The world's religions are unanimous in condemning these sins. The second meaning of sin is a self-centered mindset, by which we do harm to others whether intentionally or unintentionally. This is a more subtle understanding; it invites introspection about the motives behind our behavior and the way our daily life impinges on others. Sin has power: it binds us and blocks our approach to God. A third way to understand sin is to see it as all-pervasive imperfection and fallenness, a universal condition of humankind. In this light, Father Moon explains that all sin is the result of Human Fall, which severed our original relationship with God and left us in a state of alienation and strife.

1. The Meaning of Sin

Whoso in this world destroys life, tells lies, takes what is not given, goes to others' wives, and is addicted to intoxicating drinks, such a one digs up his own root in this world.

Dhammapada 246-47

Do you not know that the unrighteous will not inherit the kingdom of God? Do not be deceived; neither the immoral, nor idolaters, nor adulterers, nor sexual perverts, nor thieves, nor the greedy, nor drunkards, nor revilers, nor robbers will inherit the kingdom of God.

1 Corinthians 6.9-10

The plunderer of gold, the liquor-drinker,
the invader of a teacher's bed, the
   brahmin-killer:
These four sink downward in the scale—
And, fifth, he who consorts with them.

Chandogya Upanishad 5.10.9

The Prophet said, "When a man commits fornication he is not a believer, when a man steals he is not a believer; when a man drinks wine he is not a believer; when he takes plunder on account of which others raise their eyes at him he is not a believer; and when a man defrauds his neighbor he is not a believer; so beware, beware!"

Hadith of Bukhari and Muslim (Islam)

If you, Rahula, are desirous of doing a deed with the body, you should reflect on that deed of your body, thus: "That deed that I am desirous of doing with the body is a deed of my body that might conduce to the harm of self and that might conduce to the harm of others and that might conduce to the harm of both; this deed of body is unskilled, its yield is anguish, its result is anguish." If you, Rahula, reflecting thus, should find it so, a deed of body like this, Rahula, is certainly not to be done by you.

Majjhima Nikaya 1.415 (Buddhism)

Behold, the LORD's hand is not shortened, that
   it cannot save,
or his ear dull, that it cannot hear;
but your iniquities have made a separation
   between you and your God,

and your sins have hid his face from you so that he does not hear.

Isaiah 59.1-2

Bound by the fetters of the fruits of good and evil, like a cripple;
without freedom, like a man in prison.

Maitri Upanishad 4.2 (Hinduism)

When we choose to sin, what we want is to get some good or get rid of something bad. The lie is in this, that what is done for our good ends in something bad, or what is done to make things better ends by making them worse. Why this paradox, except that the happiness of man can come not from himself but only from God, and that to live according to oneself is to sin, and to sin is to lose God?

Saint Augustine, City of God 14.4 (Christianity)

Teachings of Sun Myung Moon

What is sin? It is what emerges from self-centered living and not living for the sake of others. Why is stealing wrong? A thief steals out of his personal desire—the wrong of the act begins there. What is wrong with stealing a dress from a big department store, where no one will miss it? That dress has value imparted by the people who invested their sacrifice and service in making it. Thus the dress has public value. Stealing it is a sin, because taking something without paying for it nullifies its value. (105:92, September 30, 1979)

We have to recognize and abide by three immutable laws:

The first law: Do not defile the blood lineage, even at the point of death. The blessed blood lineage, bequeathed through God's love and life, must not be contaminated by actions immersed in the habitual patterns of the fallen world...

The second law: Do not infringe upon human rights... Whether female or male, black or white, everyone is equal... Violation of this is the second of all sins.

The third law: Refrain from stealing money or misusing public funds for selfish purposes. (January 13, 2001)[12]

What is sin? People think sin is to disobey God's word, but in truth, sin is to make any condition by which Satan can accuse us. While it is wrong not to believe the word of God, it becomes a sin when there is a condition upon which the enemy can grab hold of us. Hence, once we transgress the law, not even God can do anything about it. (22:257, May 4, 1969)

The human tradition of love as it has been passed down through history is evil. It is sinful, unacceptable to God. It is the enemy of God. Of all sins, fallen love is the by far the worst; it is the sin God abhors the most. Those who indulge in fallen love are God's worst enemies, whom God abhors the most. Unless we correct the ways of love, God will always treat it as a sin and those who engage in love as enemies, and they are bound to perish. It is only natural that they perish. Have you seen Pompeii in Italy? Because of its decadent and immoral social life, the city was destroyed by instant calamity. Sodom and Gomorrah, too, were destroyed for the same reason. The Roman Empire, too, perished for the same reason.

Looking at this historical evidence, America will also surely perish unless she repents and repudiates its immoral way of love. (104:140, April 29, 1979)

❖

2. The Pervasiveness of Sin

If we say we have no sin, we deceive ourselves, and the truth is not in us.

    1 John 1.8

Nor do I absolve my own self of blame; the human soul is certainly prone to evil, unless my Lord do bestow His mercy.[13]

    Qur'an 12.53

All men, both Jews and Greeks, are under the power of sin, as it is written,

> None is righteous, no, not one;
> no one understands, no one seeks for God.
> All have turned aside, together they have gone wrong;
> no one does good, not even one.

    Romans 3.9-12

No creature, whether born on earth or among the gods in heaven, is free from the conditioning of the three states of matter (*gunas*).[14]

    Bhagavad-Gita 18.40 *(Hinduism)*

Confucius said, "I for my part have never yet seen one who really cared for Goodness, nor one who really abhorred wickedness. One who really cared for Goodness would never let any other consideration come first. One who abhorred wickedness would be so constantly doing Good that wickedness would never have a chance to get at him. Has anyone ever managed to do Good with his whole might even as long as the space of a single day? I think not. Yet I for my part have never seen anyone give up such an attempt because he had not the strength to go on." [15]

    Analects 4.6 *(Confucianism)*

As sin came into the world through one man, and death through sin, and so death spread to all men because all men sinned.

    Romans 5.12

Behold, I was brought forth in iniquity,
and in sin did my mother conceive me.[16]

    Psalm 51.5

When the first couple were punished by the judgment of God, the whole human race, which was to become Adam's posterity through the first woman, was present in the first man. And what was born was not human nature as it was originally created but as it became after the first parents' sin and punishment... so changed and vitiated that it suffers from the recalcitrance of a rebellious concupiscence and is bound by the law of death.

    Saint Augustine, City of God 13.3 *(Christianity)*

Teachings of Sun Myung Moon

Is there anyone in the world whose righteousness is complete and perfect for all eternity? Who can be proud of his or her justice before heaven and earth? No such person exists. Is there anyone who, after finding a religion, has attained a self that will never deviate from the eternal way? You cannot confidently answer Yes. No one has such integrity that he or she can be eternally and inseparably united with Heaven's principles. (4:135, March 30, 1958)

God is good; therefore human beings should naturally be good. However, we are people with many complications and impurities; we are unable to be good. Thus, there is a large gap between the God of goodness and us humans. When mud or grease sticks to your clean clothes, you want to immediately wash it out or even cut it off, because you hate to see it. God feels the same way when He sees these dirty humans clinging to the hem of His garment. You do not need to know the Bible to realize that we humans are stained. (92:58, March 13, 1977)

Due to the fall, the relationship between God and humankind was completely severed. No matter how people try to return to God, they cannot. Likewise, God cannot relate with us—the gap is so wide.

We are penned in behind a wall, confined behind a boundary line. What is that wall? It prevents us from approaching God, our Parent, to attend Him. It blocks even God from doing what He would want to do. That wall is a serious problem for religious people.

That wall also separates each individual's mind and body. That wall, with various historical contents, comes between husband and wife. That wall divides families, tribes, peoples, nations, and the whole world. It divides the spirit world from physical world. It stands between heaven and hell. Even if God dwells in heaven on His glorious throne, unless that wall is removed, people on earth can never surmount the walls that surround them on every side. This is the tragedy of human life on earth. (135:268, December 15, 1985)

The Fall meant that Adam and Eve, who should have become one with each other centering on God, instead became one with the archangel Lucifer, who was a mere servant of God. Instead of inheriting God's lineage, human beings inherited the servant's bloodline. Therefore, no matter how much fallen people call God "my Father," they do not feel it as true to life. (91:242, February 23, 1977)

The family created by the relationship between fallen Adam and Eve had no relationship to God. That family became the root of God's deep sorrow, and the base through which the enemy Satan could claim his rights and exercise his authority over humanity. One man and one woman caused the Fall, but its effect was not limited to that couple only. It extends throughout the cosmos and holds sway throughout all of human history. (46:196, August 15, 1971)

We human beings are still slaves to the fallen nature that we inherited from our first ancestors, Adam and Eve. We have not escaped that yoke. This is evidenced by the confessions of saints and sages. Although they spent their entire lives in fasting and abstinence and unceasingly pursued paths of incredible suffering, they invariably confess that they could not root out the desires of the flesh before they had to leave this world. Their confessions remain as pitiful cries to their disciples who still insist on following in their footsteps. (May 1, 2004)

Inherited Sin and Karma

RELIGIONS OFTEN EXPLAIN DIFFERENCES in people's fortunes and native endowments as the consequence of an inheritance from the past. It is conceived in two ways, either as karma from past lives or as the sins of the fathers visited on their descendants. These doctrines encourage people to accept their lot in life and suffer it patiently, in order to expiate past deeds and earn merit for the benefit of future generations.

Karma means action, specifically one's own actions committed either in this life or in past lives. In Hinduism and Buddhism, religions that hold to a belief in reincarnation, it is taught that people are bound to reap the fruit of their actions in another lifetime. However, these religions part company over whether a person's situation is fated by karma. For Hinduism indeed it is. Karma determines one's present circumstances. Hence inequalities of wealth, race, gender or caste are only apparent; in fact the universe is absolutely just and fair.

Buddhism, on the other hand, denies that karma is a deterministic principle. As but one of the twenty-four factors *(paccaya)* that condition a person's life, karma need not be actualized when other conditions are fulfilled. Through spiritual discipline and meditative practice, a Buddhist aspirant seeks to attain liberation and be released from the bonds of karma.

Most other religions, in both the East and the West, recognize sin to be inherited through the lineage. An individual is burdened by the sins of his or her ancestors, who also bequeath their traditions, attitudes and personality traits, not to mention physical traits. Their lives leave an impression that can endure through the centuries, coloring the experiences of many generations to come. A wise person, therefore, seeks to resolve these inherited problems, so they will not plague his offspring. He would rather leave merit for his children's benefit. Father Moon teaches many insights about inherited sin, how it comes to pass and how it can be resolved.

1. *The Legacy of Past Deeds*

For I the LORD your God am a jealous God, visiting the iniquity of the fathers upon the children to the third and the fourth generation of those who hate me, but showing steadfast love to the thousandth generation of those who love me and keep my commandments.

Exodus 20.5-6

Loose us from the yoke of the sins of our fathers
and also of those which we ourselves have committed.

Rig Veda 7.86.5 *(Hinduism)*

If at death there remains guilt unpunished, judgment extends to the posterity... When parties by wrong and violence take the money of others, an account is taken, and set against its amount, of their wives and children and all the members of their families, when these gradually die. If they do not die, there are disasters from water, fire, thieves, and robbers, from losses of property, illnesses, and evil tongues to balance the value of their wicked appropriations.

Treatise on Response and Retribution 4-5 *(Taoism)*

You who are so powerful as to enter inside the small medicine gourd to shelter yourself from danger,
Have you forgotten your children?
Have you forgotten your wife?
The evil seeds a man sows
Shall be reaped by his offspring.

Cruelty is never without repayment.
However late it is,
The repayment will come when it will.

Yoruba Song *(African Traditional Religions)*

In this world the fate of every posterity is similar to that of its ancestors. Neither death leaves of the work of destruction, nor the survivors give up their sinful activities. Human beings follow in each others' footsteps; groups after groups and nations after nations end their days without mending their ways.

Nahjul Balagha, Sermon 86 *(Shiite Islam)*

Happy are the righteous! Not only do they acquire merit, but they bestow merit upon their children and children's children to the end of all generations, for Aaron had several sons who deserved to be burned like Nadab and Abihu, but the merit of their father helped them.

Woe unto the wicked! Not alone that they render themselves guilty, but they bestow guilt upon their children and children's children unto the end of all generations. Many sons did Canaan have, who were worthy to be ordained like Tabi the slave of Rabbi Gamaliel, but the guilt of their ancestor caused them [to lose their chance].

Talmud, Yoma 87a *(Judaism)*

Subha, the son of Toddeya, asked the Exalted One, "What is the cause and what is the reason, O Gotama, for which among men and the beings who have been born as men there is found to be lowness and excellence? For some people are of short life span and some of long life span; some suffer from many illnesses and some are free from illness; some are ugly and some beautiful; some are of little account and some have great power; some are poor and some are wealthy; some are born into lowly families and others into high families; some are devoid of intelligence and some possess great wisdom. What is the cause, what is the reason for which among men and the beings who have been born as men there is to be found lowness and excellence?"

"Men have, O young man, deeds as their very own, they are inheritors of deeds, deeds are their matrix, deeds are their kith and kin, and deeds are their support. It is deeds that classify men into high or low status.

"Here, O young man, some woman or man is a taker of life, fierce, with hands stained by blood, engaged in killing and beating, without mercy for living creatures. As a result of deeds thus accomplished, thus undertaken, he is reborn on the breakup of the body, after death, into a state of woe, of ill plight, of purgatory or hell, or if he comes to be born as a man, wherever he may be reborn he is of a short life span. This course—that he is a taker of life, fierce, with hands stained by blood, engaged in killing and beating, without mercy for living creatures, leads to shortness of life.

"Here, on the other hand, O young man, some woman or man gives up killing, totally refraining from taking life… This course… leads to longevity.

"Here some woman or man is by nature a tormentor of living creatures… As a result of the deeds thus accomplished… wherever he is reborn he suffers much from sickness… But here some woman or man is not by nature a tormentor of living beings… wherever he may be reborn he is free from sickness.

"Here some woman or man is wrathful… wherever he is reborn he is ugly… But here some woman or man is not wrathful… wherever he may be reborn he is handsome.

"Here some woman or man is jealous-minded… wherever he is born he is of little account… But here some woman or man is not jealous-minded… wherever he may be reborn he has great power.

"Here some woman or man is not a giver to ascetic or brahmin… wherever he is born he is poor… Here some woman or man is a giver… wherever he may be reborn he is wealthy.

"Thus men have, O young man, deeds as their very own, they are inheritors of their deeds, their deeds are their kith and kin, and their deeds their support. It is their deeds that classify men into this low or high status."

Majjhima Nikaya 3.202-206 *(Buddhism)*

The Reactive Mind is a portion of a person's mind which works on a totally stimulus-response basis, which is not under his volitional control, and which exerts force and the power of command over his awareness, purposes, thoughts, body, and actions. Stored in the Reactive Mind are engrams, and here we find the single source of aberrations and psychosomatic ills.[17]

L. Ron Hubbard, *Scientology 0-8* (Scientology)

Teachings of Sun Myung Moon

Our ancestors, through the ages of history, all died after living a hundred years or less. If they thought and worked for the sake of the whole, for the benefit of the whole, what they did remains even after a thousand years. Yet most of them did not. They lived centered on themselves, and everything they did perished with them. Having fallen and committed sins continually, they created problems destructive to the whole. (200:91, February 24, 1990)

Human beings throughout history have committed innumerable sins. First there was the Original Sin committed by Adam and Eve… it is like the root. Even that root is of various kinds: a central taproot and peripheral roots. From that root has grown a trunk; it started small with but a few branches but now it has grown and sprouted tens of thousands of branches, all tangled with each other. The overall amount of accumulated human sin is so huge. How can it be forgiven? Yet this huge mass of sin is connected to each one of you. (258:84-85, March 17, 1994)

Who do we resemble, that we should look and act the way we do? Each person takes after his or her parents. Then, who do our parents resemble, that they should look and act as they do? They take after the grandparents. If we keep going back through the generations, we will eventually come to humanity's first ancestors. We are the way we are, because of what humanity's first ancestors were like. Who, then, did the first ancestors resemble that they became the way they were? This is the question.

You naturally resemble your mother and father. If a person doesn't resemble his parents, then there must be a trait somewhere a few generations back that was hidden until it made its appearance, according to the laws of genetics. Traits do not just appear without any connection or source.

You may think that you are in control of the way you develop, but the fact is that thousands of generations of ancestors already came before you… So you can be compared to exhibits in a museum, where all the physical traits, qualities and values of your ancestors over thousands of generations are gathered in one place. They are the source of your appearance, personality and values. You are like exhibits put out by your ancestors, who are saying, "Look! This is our descendant." Have you ever thought of it this way? Each of you is unique in the world. No matter how many men and women there may be under heaven, each of you was born a unique overall representation and fruit of your ancestors. (41:139, February 14, 1971)

You all have different ancestries. They took various paths and lived in various circumstances. Some were evil; others were good; they are all intermingled in your family tree. You are their fruits. Because of your varied backgrounds, you stand in different positions, with different merits. God is just and fair. But since each individual has a different background, can God really say, "All people are absolutely equal"? Is that a correct concept?

It would have been different had there been no Fall. It would have been different if our lineages had all proceeded within the realm of God's love. Certainly, we are all destined to find God's love. However, since every fallen human being has to travel along a uniquely different life course in his or her quest to reach the ideal, we cannot expect to find equality among us.

For the same reason, we can understand that people are bound for various destinations in the spirit world: heaven, hell, or the thousands of different levels in between. They are situated according to the accumulated good or evil of their own lives added to that of their particular ancestral line. (91:269-70, February 27, 1977)

2. Breaking the Chain of Demerit

The wise priest knows he now must reap
The fruits of deeds of former births.
For be they many or but few,
Deeds done in covetousness or hate,
Or through infatuation's power,
Must bear their needful consequence.
Hence not to covetousness, nor hate,
Nor to infatuation's power
The wise priest yields, but knowledge seeks
And leaves the way to punishment.

Anguttara Nikaya 3.33 (Buddhism)

If it be that good men and good women are downtrodden, their evil destiny is the inevitable retributive result of sins committed in their past mortal lives. By virtue of their present misfortunes the reacting effects of their past will be thereby worked out, and they will be in a position to attain the Consummation of Incomparable Enlightenment.

Diamond Sutra 16 (Buddhism)

My father was a merchant in Ujjeni, and I was his only daughter, dear, charming and beloved. Then a wealthy merchant from Saketa sent men to woo me; to him my father gave me as a daughter-in-law...

I myself adorned my lord like a servant-girl. I myself prepared the rice gruel; I myself washed the bowl; as a mother to her only son, so I looked after my husband. Yet my husband was offended by me, who in this way had shown him devotion, an affectionate servant, with humbled pride, an early riser, not lazy, virtuous. He said to his parents, "I shall not be able to live together with Isidasi in one house... She does me no harm, but to me she is odious. I have had enough; I am leaving her." Hearing this utterance my father-in-law and mother-in-law asked me, "What offense has been committed by you? Speak confidently how it really was." "I have not offended at all; I have not harmed; I have not said any evil utterance; what can be done when my husband hates me?" I said. Downcast, overcome by pain, they led me back to my father's house, saying, "While keeping our son safe, we have lost the goddess of beauty incarnate."

Then my father gave me to the household of a second rich man for half the bride price for which the merchant had taken me. In his house too I lived a month, then he too rejected me, although I served him like a slave girl, virtuously. Then my father spoke to one wandering for alms, a tamer of others and self-tamed, "Be my son-in-law; throw down your cloth and pot." He too, having lived with me for a fortnight, returned me to my father...

I begged my father, "Evil indeed was the action done by me [the karma leading to my misfortune]; I shall destroy it." Then my father said, "Attain enlightenment and the foremost doctrine and obtain quenching, which the best of men have realized." Saluting my parents and relatives, I went forth [as a nun]. In seven days I attained the Three Knowledges.

I know now my own last seven births; I shall relate to you the actions of which this misfortune is the fruit and result; listen to it attentively. In the city of Erakaccha I was a wealthy goldsmith. Intoxicated by pride in my youth, I had sexual intercourse with another's wife. Having fallen from there, I was cooked in hell; I cooked for a long time; and rising up from there I entered the womb of a female monkey. A great monkey, leader of the herd, castrated me when I was seven days old; this was the fruit of the action of having seduced another's wife. I died in the Sindhava forest and entered the womb of a one-eyed, lame she-goat. As a goat I was castrated, worm-eaten, tail-less, unfit, because of having seduced another's wife. Next I was born of a cow belonging to a cattle-dealer; a lac-red calf. I was castrated after twelve months and drew the plough, pulled the cart, and became blind, tail-less, unfit, because of having seduced another's wife. Then I was born of a household slave in the street, neither as a woman or a man, because of having seduced another's wife. In my thirtieth year I died; I was born as a girl in a carter's family which was poor and much in debt. To satisfy the creditors, I was sold to a caravan leader and dragged off, wailing, from my home. Then in my sixteenth year when I had arrived at marriageable age, his son, Giridasa by name, took me as a wife. But he had another wife, virtuous and possessed of good qualities, who was affectionate towards her husband; with her I stirred up enmity. These [my misfortunes] were fruit of that last action, that men rejected me though I served like a slave girl. Even of that I have now made an end.

Therigatha 400-447, Isidasi Sutta *(Buddhism)*

If you have fulfilled a command, do not seek its reward from God straightaway, lest you not be acquitted of sin, but be regarded as wicked because you have not sought to cause your children to inherit anything. For if Abraham, Isaac, and Jacob had sought the reward of the good deeds which they performed, how could the seed of these righteous men [e.g., Israel] have been delivered?

Exodus Rabbah 44.3 *(Judaism)*

Teachings of Sun Myung Moon

For thousands of years our ancestors have been building up walls of sorrows, and as the days go by these walls are not getting lower; rather, through his many deceptions Satan has been raising the walls higher.

Today all the people of the world have the responsibility to take down the walls of grudges and resentments their ancestors built up; we take this on as our responsibility. (1:305, December 23, 1956)

Original sin, personal sin, collective sin, and hereditary sin inherited from our ancestral line—we should cleanse all sin before we pass on to the spirit world. It doesn't matter that you have become a follower of the Lord; an indemnity course remains for each individual. None of you has the same course. Some suffer a great deal; some even die on the way; while others have an easier time. Why? Everyone's indemnity course differs. Although we may practice the same standard of faith, our paths are not the same because the amount of indemnity to be paid varies. (251:131, October 17, 1993)

We are burdened with sins inherited from our ancestors even though we personally did not commit them, and we are also responsible for collective sins that were committed by the nation or people we belong to. In a word, being a fallen person means being the result of six thousand years of fallen human history—a mixture of good and evil. We inherit good and evil characteristics from our ancestors, but since they lived in the world where there was more evil than good, we mostly inherit evil. It is no surprise that we end up adding to that evil, trapped in a vicious cycle.

There is a story behind every sin, and someone was its cause. Maybe an ancestor of yours, while living on earth, gave much difficulty and pain to someone, and that person died carrying resentment. Now this resentful spirit comes down to you, a descendant of that ancestor, to get revenge. He could have gone to any of a number of descendants, but he alights on you. He influences you, driving you to the edge, until you commit the sin.

Resentful spirits can also afflict you with sickness and pain. All modern diseases have spiritual causes connected to the sins of ancestors. By looking at the sicknesses and difficulties of descendants, we can infer about the life of their ancestors. If the ancestors stole from others or misused public things or money, their descendants may suffer from stomach problems. If they committed sins of lust and fornication, their descendants may suffer from genital diseases, or be unable to bear children, or have difficulty being faithful, or get divorced. Ancestors who did not see things about others correctly and hurt them, or who misjudged others based on bad rumors and violated their hearts, will have descendants born blind, mute or deaf. In other words, according to the way the pain was given—to a certain part of the body—the descendants suffer with the same kind of troubles. The heavier the ancestors' sins, the more difficult it is to heal the resulting sickness; it may even be incurable.

If people on the earth do not clear up these sins through paying the required indemnity, the suffering is passed down to their children. Later, when those people come to the spirit world and watch their children suffer they regret that they did not clear things up for them. They lament, "If only I had borne my suffering on earth, my children would not need to suffer now." Therefore, unless you clear up all the sins passed down from your ancestors, as well as your personal sins, your children cannot escape from sickness and pain. (Heung Jin Moon, *Message from the Spirit World*, January 1, 2002)

Your ancestors committed a great many sins. On top of it, how much more sin did you commit? If you truly knew the weight of it all, you would despair. Surely you should do your best to indemnify those sins [and leave a clean slate] for your descendants. If you cannot cleanse them completely, you should be willing to devote your life as a sacrificial offering. For example, you might marry an ugly woman and determine to make your life together with her better than the most handsome couple in the world. (116:150, December 27, 1981)

> The altars of sorrow continuing for six thousand years or more are due to the mistakes of our ancestors,
> but we fear we might leave that sorrow to our descendants by once again not fulfilling our responsibility today.
> Today we learned that we are responsible to stop the history of misfortune in this generation and to dissolve the grief in Heaven's heart unto joy. (8:262-63, February 7, 1960)

Collective and Historical Sin

INDIVIDUALS ARE ALSO INEXTRICABLY BOUND TO THE COLLECTIVES to which they belong: nation, race, tribe and religion. Whether guilty or blameless in their personal lives, individuals prosper or suffer with the fortunes of these collectives. The evils descend on the community—war, famine, epidemic diseases and rampant drug use—bring hardships to everyone in the community. Father Moon terms this collective sin. People are responsible to recognize collective sin and atone for it. They can atone by first making efforts to understand the grievances of those populations that have been oppressed and mistreated by their nation. They can then work to resolve them through sacrifice and love.

Even those who are pious and innocent suffer for the misdeeds of others through their contact, as fish in a snake-infested lake.
    Ramayana, Aranya Kanda 38 *(Hinduism)*

When God causes punishment to descend on a people, those righteous ones among them will be smitten by the punishment, but afterwards they will be resurrected according to their deeds.
    Hadith of Bukhari and Muslim *(Islam)*

All of you are pledges for the other: all of you, aye the world, exist through the merit of a single righteous man among you, and if but one man sins, the whole generation suffers.

Tanhuma (Judaism)

Justice is turned back,
and righteousness stands afar off;
for truth has fallen in the public squares,
and uprightness cannot enter.
Truth is lacking,
and he who departs from evil makes himself a prey.

Isaiah 59.14-15

I am full of the wrath of the LORD;
I am weary of holding it in.
"Pour it out upon the children in the street,
and upon the gatherings of young men, also;
both husband and wife shall be taken,
the old folk and the very aged.
Their houses shall be turned over to others,
their fields and wives together;
for I will stretch out my hand
against the inhabitants of the land," says the LORD.

"For from the least to the greatest of them,
every one is greedy for unjust gain;
and from prophet to priest,
every one deals falsely.
They have healed the wound of my people lightly,
saying, 'Peace, peace,'
when there is no peace.
Were they ashamed when they committed abomination?
No, they were not at all ashamed;
they did not know how to blush.
Therefore they shall fall among those who fall;
at the time that I punish them, they shall be overthrown," says the LORD.

Jeremiah 6.11-15

Fondly do we hope—fervently do we pray—that this mighty scourge of war may speedily pass away. Yet, if God wills that it continue until all the wealth piled by the bondsman's two hundred and fifty years of unrequited toil shall be sunk, and until every drop of blood drawn with the lash shall be paid with another drawn by the sword, as was said three thousand years ago, so still it must be said, "The judgments of the Lord are true and righteous altogether."

Abraham Lincoln, Second Inaugural Address

Teachings of Sun Myung Moon

Sin—it is intertwined like a gigantic steel net, woven through this person and that person, this organization and that organization, this society and that society, this nation and that nation. (1:167, July 11, 1956)

What should America do to indemnify all her historical sin? Americans massacred the Indians and enslaved Black people. Since the Indians are of the Oriental race, one way for America to indemnify her sin is to live for the sake of Oriental people. (101:336, November 12, 1978)

In sports these days, more and more blacks are the prominent world champions. Every year more blacks are emerging at the top, replacing whites. If blacks are equipped with God's teaching, then, coupled with their sense of physical power, I think they have a glorious future surpassing that of white people.

Hence, the more that the whites oppose black people, the more they will lose God's blessings and the more blacks shall receive them. God does not lose in the end.

When Jesus stumbled while carrying his cross to Calvary, a black person, Simon of Cyrene, took up Jesus' burden. That act was very significant; when the Last Days come, God will raise up black people for a great mission. Yet, they should be equipped with Heaven's teaching. (91:219, February 20, 1977)

Selfish Desires and Fallen Nature

PASSION, GREED, COVETOUSNESS, HATRED, LUST: these emotions dominate the soul, causing blindness and leading to destruction. Every major religion recognizes that suffering and evil are caused by excessive desires or desires directed toward a selfish purpose. Buddhism has summed up this principle in the second of the Four Noble Truths and denotes these desires by the term "craving." Craving is a fetter: poisoning the heart, deluding the mind, and binding us to evil courses of action.

While all religions view selfish desire as baneful and the cause of much suffering, they differ in explaining these selfish desires in relation to human psychology. Buddhism and Jainism reject desire of all kinds, even the grasping for existence itself, as harmful and a source of bondage. In the monotheistic religions: Christianity, Judaism, Islam, and in some texts from Sikhism and Hinduism, the passions of the flesh—which are evil—are distinguished from the healthy ambition for goodness and the passion for God. Chinese religion condemns only excessive desire and selfish desire: Desires themselves may be good if they are in harmony with the Tao. This is also Father Moon's teaching: God created desire that people might aspire for goodness, but it was perverted into self-centered grasping as a result of the Human Fall.

Father Moon teaches that selfish desires are manifestations of 'fallen nature,' satanic qualities and attitudes that were implanted into Adam and Eve at their fall. Various scriptures testify to the fact that humans have corrupted their original nature and deviated from their true calling. Instead, we have sunk to the level of beasts, or even lower. Beset with inner contradiction, we allow arrogance, violence, greed, and lust to dominate our lives.

1. Selfish Desires and Passions

The Noble Truth of the Origin of suffering is this: It is craving that leads back to birth, bound up with passionate greed. It finds fresh delight now here and now there, namely, craving for sense pleasures, craving for existence and becoming, and craving for non-existence.[18]

Samyutta Nikaya 56.11 (Buddhism)

Lust, hatred, and delusion
ruin the man of wicked heart.
They are begotten in himself
like the lush growth of pith in the stem.

Itivuttaka 45 (Buddhism)

Let no one say when he is tempted, "I am tempted by God"; for God cannot be tempted with evil and he himself tempts no one; but each person is tempted when he is lured and enticed by his own desire. Then desire when it has conceived gives birth to sin; and sin when it is full-grown brings forth death.

James 1.13-15

What causes wars, and what causes fighting among you? Is it not your passions that are at war in your members? You desire and do not have; so you kill. And you covet and cannot obtain; so you fight and wage war. You do not have, because you do not ask. You ask and do not receive, because you ask wrongly, to spend it on your passions.

James 4.1-3

No more deadly curse than sensual pleasure has been inflicted on mankind by nature, to gratify which our wanton appetites are roused beyond all prudence or restraint. It is a fruitful source of treasons, revolutions, secret communications with the enemy. In fact, there is no crime, no evil deed, to which the appetite for sensual pleasures does not impel us.

Cicero, De Senectute 12 (Hellenism)

Arjuna: What is the force that binds us to selfish deeds, O Krishna? What power moves us, even against our will, as if forcing us?

Krishna: It is selfish desire and anger, arising from the state of being known as passion; these are the appetites and evils which threaten a person in this life.

Just as a fire is covered by smoke and a mirror is obscured by dust, just as an embryo is enveloped deep within the womb, knowledge is hidden by selfish desire—hidden, Arjuna, by this unquenchable fire for self-satisfaction, the inveterate enemy of the wise.

Selfish desire is found in the senses, mind, and intellect, misleading them and burying wisdom in delusion.

Bhagavad-Gita 3.36-40 (Hinduism)

Confucius said, "I have never seen anyone whose desire to build up his moral power was as strong as sexual desire."

Analects 9.17

They say that woman is an enticement.
No, No, she is not so.
They say that money is an enticement.
No, No, it is not so.
They say that landed property is an enticement.
No, No, it is not so.
The real enticement is the insatiable appetite
   of the mind,
O Lord Guheswara![19]

Allama Prabhu, Vacana 91 (Hinduism)

Five are the robbers lodged in this body—
Lust, wrath, avarice, attachment, and egoism.[20]

Adi Granth, Sorath, M.3, p. 600 (Sikhism)

Blinded are beings by their sense desires
spread over them like a net;
covered are they by cloak of craving;
by their heedless ways caught
as a fish in the mouth of a funnel-net.
Decrepitude and death they journey to,
just as a sucking calf goes to its mother.

Udana 75-76 (Buddhism)

Teachings of Sun Myung Moon

What is the greatest danger in our life? It is getting pulled off the right track. Think: what can pull you off the track? There are two aspects of vulnerability, external and internal. Externally, the number one temptation is probably money, followed by knowledge, and then power. Any of these can pull you off the track.

    Will you succumb to the temptation of money? Under what conditions does money tempt you? This has to do with the internal aspect—your greed and ambition. I am speaking of self-centered greed and ambition. Ambition is not necessarily bad, but when it is self-centered, it is bad. (90:9, December 5, 1976)

People feel joy when their desires are fulfilled. The word "desire," however, is often not understood in its original sense, because in the present circumstances our desires tend to pursue evil rather than good. Desires which result in injustice do not emanate from a person's original mind...

Has anyone realized the joy in which the original mind delights by pursuing evil desires? Whenever such desires are sated, we feel unrest in our conscience and agony in our heart. Would a parent ever instruct his child to be evil? Would a teacher deliberately instill unrighteousness in his students? The impulse of the original mind, which everyone possesses, is to abhor evil and exalt goodness. (*Exposition of the Divine Principle*, Introduction)

Human beings are God's substantial object partners. Therefore, God wants to rejoice through us. However, if we are defective partners, always expressing our fallen nature as jealousy, envy and arrogance, how can God feel happiness through us? (Way of God's Will 2.2)

The human condition has been such that love of the flesh—which is external—betrays God's love, and betrays the ideal and eternal origin of life based in the mind—which is internal. Therefore, to establish unity between mind and body, we have to eradicate this external love—satanic love—and in its place inherit internal love—God's original love. (20:179, June 9, 1968)

2. Degraded and Fallen Nature

Human nature is analogous to water: originally, it is pure. If we fill a clear vessel then the water will be clear, but if we fill a dirty vessel then the water will be sullied. Its original purity is always there, but once it becomes dirty or turbid it is very difficult to regain its purity.

Chu Hsi (Confucianism)

God made man upright, but they have sought out many devices.

Ecclesiastes 7.29

Delusion is a sort of demonic force. People's original mind is pure but it becomes perverted due to delusion and other karmas.

Kundakunda, Pancastikaya 38 (Jainism)

I enquired what iniquity was, and found it to be not a substance, but the perversion of the will, turned aside from Thee, O God, the Supreme, toward these lower things, and casting out its bowels and puffed up outwardly.

Saint Augustine, Confessions 7.16 (Christianity)

Satan said, "I will take of Thy servants a portion marked off; I will mislead them, and I will create in them false desires; I will order them... to deface the fair nature created by God." Whoever, forsaking God, takes Satan for a friend, has of a surety suffered a loss that is manifest. Satan makes them promises, and creates in them false desires; but Satan's promises are nothing but deception.

Qur'an 4.118-20

Your mind, having become diseased and bewildered because of the false sense-conceptions accumulated since beginningless time, has developed many desires, attachments and habits. From these there have arisen, incident to the ever-changing processes of life, arbitrary conceptions concerning self and no-self and as to what is true and what is not true. These arbitrary conceptions have not developed in a normal way from your pure Mind Essence, but in an abnormal way because of the prior false conceptions that had their origin in the sense organs, like the sight of blossoms in the air that come to diseased minds. They falsely appear to have had their origin in the enlightening and Essential Mind but, in truth, they have arisen because of diseased conditions.

Surangama Sutra (Buddhism)

Slight is the difference between man and the brutes. The common man loses this distinguishing feature, while the gentleman retains it.

Mencius IV.B.19 (Confucianism)

The heart is deceitful above all things, and desperately corrupt; who can understand it?

Jeremiah 17.9

And recite to them the tiding of him to whom We gave Our signs, but he cast them off, and Satan followed after him, and he became one of the perverts. And had we willed, We would have raised him up, but he inclined towards the earth and followed his lust. So the likeness of him is as the likeness of a dog; if you attack it it lolls its tongue out, or if you leave it it lolls its tongue out. That is that people's likeness who cried lies to Our signs...

They have hearts, but understand not with them; they have eyes, but perceive not with them; they have ears, but they hear not with them. They are like cattle; nay, rather they are further astray. Those—they are the heedless.

Qur'an 7.175-179

That man in whom there never kindles
One spark of the love of God,
Know, Nanak, that his earthly vesture
Is no better than that of a swine or dog!

Adi Granth, Slok, M.9, p. 1428 (Sikhism)

Most men, and men of the most vulgar type, seem (not without some ground) to identify the good, or happiness, with pleasure; which is the reason why they love the life of enjoyment. For there are, we may say, three prominent types of life—that just mentioned, the political, and thirdly the contemplative life. Now the mass of mankind are evidently quite slavish in their tastes, preferring a life suitable to beasts.

Aristotle, Nicomachean Ethics 1.5 (Hellenism)

Hear, O heavens, and give ear, O earth,
for the LORD has spoken:
"Sons I have reared and brought up,
but they have rebelled against me.
The ox knows its owner,
and the ass its master's crib;
but Israel does not know,
my people does not understand."

Isaiah 1.2-3

Teachings of Sun Myung Moon

When God's one son and daughter, who should have been the true ancestors of humankind, committed sin, they were expelled from His Kingdom. From that moment, all men and women lost their potential to become God's temples. Instead, they became dens of Satan, headquarters of selfishness. (219:117, August 28, 1991)

Human beings were degraded by the Fall to a status lower than the things of creation, as it is written, "the heart is deceitful above all things." (Jer. 17.9) (*Exposition of the Divine Principle,* Restoration 1.2.1)

Have you heard that when an ocean-going ship is about to be wrecked, the rats on board the ship try to escape along the mooring ropes to the land, seeking safety? Even lowly creatures are aware of their destiny in terms of life and death, but what about human beings, who are the masters of all creation? Having fallen, they became as dull as a baby squid. (215:53, February 6, 1991)

Our mind and body can become completely one through the power of God's love, but we have never really experienced that oneness because of the division between them that resulted from the Fall of the human ancestors. If not for the Fall, our mind and body would have completely united based on God's intrinsic love. In the world of love centered around that intrinsic love, there would be no need for moral education. God would suffice as a teacher. People would know love without being taught.

When the mind and body become one, we understand everything. There would be no need for education about how human beings should live. There would be no need for instruction in ethics and the rules of morality. Do the animals need to be taught moral lessons? They know how to protect themselves and group themselves among members of their own species. Why are human beings, the lords of creation, so ignorant in this regard? It is because of the Fall that we fight and struggle. (162:223, April 12, 1987)

We have fallen nature. What are the four aspects of fallen nature? They are arrogance, jealousy, anger and lying. We should remove all of them. (150:126, September 4, 1960)

Eve inherited from the Archangel all the proclivities incidental to his transgression against God when he bound her in blood ties through their sexual relationship. Adam in turn acquired the same inclinations when Eve, assuming the role of the Archangel, bound him in blood ties through their sexual relationship. These proclivities have become the root cause of the fallen inclinations in all people. They are the primary characteristics of our fallen nature.

The fundamental motivation which engendered these primary characteristics of the fallen nature lay in the envy the Archangel felt toward Adam, the beloved of God. How can there be anything such as envy and jealousy in an archangel, whom God created for a good purpose? The Archangel was endowed with desire and intellect as a part of his original nature. Because the Archangel possessed an intellect, he could compare and discern that God's love for human beings was greater than the love God gave to him. Because he also possessed desires, he had a natural yearning for God to love him more. This desire of the heart was naturally conducive to envy and jealousy. Envy is an inevitable byproduct of the original nature, like the shadow cast by an object in the light.

After human beings reach perfection, however, they will never be induced to fall because of incidental envy. They will know deep inside that the temporary gratification they might feel by attaining the object of their desire is not worth the agony of self-destruction that would ensue. Hence, they would never commit such crimes...

The primary characteristics of the fallen nature can be divided broadly into four types: The first is failing to take God's standpoint. A principal cause of the Archangel's fall was his failure to love Adam with the same heart and perspective as God; instead, he felt jealous of Adam. This led him to tempt Eve. An example of this characteristic of the fallen nature is when a courtier feels jealous of the king's favorite instead of sincerely respecting him as one whom the king loves.

The second is leaving one's proper position. Seeking more of God's love, Lucifer desired to enjoy the same position of love in the human world. This unrighteous desire caused him to leave his position and fall. People are induced by unrighteous desires to step beyond the bounds of what is right and overreach themselves because of this primary characteristic of the fallen nature.

The third is reversing dominion. The angel, who was supposed to come under the dominion of human beings, instead dominated Eve. Then Eve, who was supposed to come under the dominion of Adam, dominated him instead...

The fourth is multiplying the criminal act. After her fall, had Eve not repeated her sin by seducing Adam, Adam would have remained whole. The restoration of Eve alone would have been relatively easy. However, Eve spread her sin to others by inducing Adam to fall. The proclivity of evil people to entangle others in an expanding web of crime stems from this primary characteristic of the fallen nature. (*Exposition of the Divine Principle*, Fall 4.6)

We now know the characteristics of fallen nature: The Fall began, first with self-centered ownership; next, speaking lies; next, an immoral relationship; next, taking all things from God; and finally, in the second generation, murder. All dictators throughout history lied, violated love, stole others' possessions, and murdered good people. Considering this, we should not follow the same pattern of historical error. We wish to inherit a heavenly tradition of love by overcoming these transgressions within ourselves. (121:257-58, October 27, 1982)

The War Within

THE HUMAN CONDITION IS BESET BY INNER CONFLICT between two opposing inclinations, one good and the other evil. As long as people are plagued by this inner contradiction, they can neither realize their divine self nor achieve a state of wholeness. Paradoxically, people immersed in worldly life may not always recognize the war within themselves—except in the glimmerings of a guilty conscience. On the other hand, those who strive to lead a conscientious or religious life are directly confronted by this problem.

Father Moon teaches that this inner contradiction is a direct result of the Human Fall. It cannot be that God created human beings with such a contradiction, he maintains, or God would not be a God of goodness and humans would have no hope to reach perfection. No, this inner contradiction is evidence of a distortion in human nature, caused by the Human Fall. The war between mind and body will never end until the problem of the Fall is solved.

I do not understand my own actions. For I do not do what I want, but I do the very thing I hate. Now if I do what I do not want, I agree that the law is good. So then it is no longer I that do it, but sin which dwells within me. For I know that nothing good dwells within me, that is, in my flesh. I can will what is right, but I cannot do it. For I do not do the good I want, but the evil I do not want is what I do. Now if I do what I do not want, it is no longer I that do it, but sin which dwells within me.

So I find it to be a law that when I want to do right, evil lies close at hand. For I delight in the law of God, in my inmost self, but I see in my members another law at war with the law of my mind and making me captive to the law of sin which dwells in my members. Wretched man that I am! Who will deliver me from this body of death?

Romans 7.15-24

I know what is good
but I am not inclined to do it;
I know also what is bad,
but I do not refrain from doing it;
I just do as I am prompted to do
by some divine spirit
standing in my heart.[21]

Mahabharata (*Hinduism*)

Rabbi Isaac said, "Man's evil inclination renews itself daily against him, as it is said, 'Every imagination of the thoughts of his heart was only evil every day.' [Genesis 6.5]." And Rabbi Simeon ben Levi said, "Man's evil inclination gathers strength against him daily and seeks to slay him… and were not the Holy One, blessed be He, to help him, he could not prevail against it."

Talmud, Kiddushin 30b (Judaism)

By the fetters of envy and selfishness are all bound—gods, men, demons… so that although they wish, "Would that we might live in friendship, without hatred, injury, enmity or malignity," they still live in enmity, hating, injuring, hostile, malign.

Digha Nikaya 2.276 (Buddhism)

All vices are like chains thrown around the neck.

Adi Granth, Sorath, M.1 p. 595 (Sikhism)

Whatever harm a foe may do to a foe, or a hater to a hater, an ill-directed mind can do one far greater harm.

Dhammapada 42 (Buddhism)

Surely God wrongs not men anything, but men wrong themselves.

Qur'an 10.44

The spirit is indeed willing, but the flesh is weak.

Matthew 26.41

Man should discover his own reality
and not thwart himself.
For he has the self as his only friend,
or as his only enemy.
A person has the self as a friend
when he has conquered himself,
But if he rejects his own reality,
the self will war against him.

Bhagavad-Gita 6.5-6 (Hinduism)

The Prophet declared, "We have returned from the lesser holy war (al jihad al-asghar) to the greater holy war (al jihad al-akbar)." They asked, "O Prophet of God, which is the greater war?" He replied, "Struggle against the lower self."[22]

Hadith (Islam)

What is the life of virtue save one unending war with evil inclinations, and not with solicitations of other people alone, but with evil inclinations that arise within ourselves and are our very own… And when we seek final rest in the supreme good, what do we seek save an end to this conflict between flesh and spirit, freedom from this propensity to evil against which the spirit is at war? Yet, will as we may, such liberty cannot be had in mortal life.

Saint Augustine, City of God 19.4 (Christianity)

Teachings of Sun Myung Moon

Human beings inherently tend to avoid evil and seek goodness. Our minds are ever eager to establish a world of goodness and eradicate the world of evil. On the other hand, we also experience an evil mind within us, which struggles powerfully against our good mind. To the degree that we hold fast to our good mind, our evil mind opposes with proportionate strength. (36:51, November 15, 1970)

Since the beginning of time, not even one person has abided strictly by his original mind. As St. Paul noted, "None is righteous, no, not one; no one understands, no one seeks for God." (Rom. 3.10-11) Confronted with the human condition, he lamented, "For I delight in the law of God, in my inmost self, but I see in my members another law at war with the law of my mind and making me captive to the law of sin which dwells in my members. Wretched man that I am!" (Rom. 7.22-24)

We find a great contradiction in every person. Within the self-same individual are two opposing inclinations: the original mind that desires goodness and the evil mind that desires wickedness. They are engaged in a fierce battle, striving to accomplish two conflicting purposes. Any being possessing such a contradiction within itself is doomed to perish. Human beings, having acquired this contradiction, live on the brink of destruction.

Can it be that human life originated with such a contradiction? How could beings with a self-contradictory nature come into existence? If burdened by such a contradiction from its inception, human life would not have been able to arise. The contradiction, therefore, must have developed after the birth of the human race. Christianity sees this state of destruction as the result of the Human Fall. (*Exposition of the Divine Principle*, Introduction)

The conscience is that faculty of the mind that presents God's thought. It does not exist for you, but for the righteousness of Heaven. Your conscience always pursues goodness. The body rebels against the conscience. Your body is self-centered; it seeks its own comfort; it follows instinctive desires. Your conscience strives to have your body obey the mind and reproaches it when it does not. From this point, conflicts and struggles arise within the self. (219:118, August 28, 1991)

Our body has become the stage of Satan's activities. It has become Satan's dance hall. Had there not been the Human Fall, our mind and body would be one. They would become one automatically centering on God's love, life and lineage. (235:203, September 20, 1992)

Why do human beings need religion? We need religion to conquer our body. Otherwise, due to the body, human history would be doomed; due to the body, society would be doomed; and due to the body, humankind would be doomed. Accordingly, you should deeply realize that your body is the womb of the enemy and the seedbed of sins and evils. (18:322, August 13, 1967)

Regard yourself as the problem. You can be your own worst enemy. If you cannot unite your mind and body, you become your own enemy. (128:108, June 5, 1983)

Even though [at the Fall] we received Satan's evil seed, each person, deep in his original mind, covets God's original, ideal seed of life. This is the basis of our internal struggles. Within each individual, two opposing elements are struggling: the original mind on God's side, and the body on Satan's side. For this reason, as long as we do not bring oneness in our mind and body, we cannot enter the Kingdom of Heaven. (235:203, September 20, 1992)

Egoism and Pride

EGOISM, THE INORDINATE PREOCCUPATION WITH ONE'S OWN SELF, makes people blind to the reality of God. The problem is compounded by pride—pride in oneself, pride in one's wealth, knowledge or power. Egoism and pride close us off from God. Thinking ourselves to be independent, we cannot recognize that our very existence is dependent upon Ultimate Reality. Pride makes us blind to the needs of others and too stubborn to accept help from others. Pride makes us unable even to take an accurate measure of ourselves.

In Christianity, pride is regarded as the first step to the fall and rebellion against God. In Buddhism, grasping after the self and the sense of ego is the chief of all cravings and the deepest root of ignorance. In the Indic religions egoism is a fetter that binds people to the wheel of rebirth.

Father Moon reiterates these universal teachings, but with particular emphasis on the social manifestations of pride and egoism among the affluent people of today's wealthy and powerful nations. He warns America in particular that it had better repent for its arrogance, which is seeping into every cranny of the social fabric, or inevitably it will decline. He also links egoism and pride to the Human Fall, which implanted that wicked propensity deep in the human mind.

Verily man is rebellious
For he thinks himself independent.
Lo! unto thy Lord is the return.

Qur'an 96.6-8

Pride goes before destruction,
and a haughty spirit before a fall.

Proverbs 16.18

Woe to those who are wise in their own eyes,
and shrewd in their own sight!

Isaiah 5.21

Selfishness may be sweet for oneself, but no harmony of the whole can come from it.

Osashizu (Tenrikyo)

We maintain that all pain and suffering are results of want of Harmony, and that the one terrible and only cause of the disturbance of Harmony is selfishness in some form or another.

Helena Blavatsky, The Key to Theosophy

In thinking, "This is I" and "That is mine," he binds himself with his self, as does a bird with a snare.

Maitri Upanishad 3.2 (Hinduism)

"Sons have I; wealth have I": Thus is the fool worried. Verily, he himself is not his own. Whence sons? Whence wealth?

Dhammapada 62 (Buddhism)

Where egoism exists, Thou are not experienced,
Where Thou art, is not egoism.

Adi Granth, Maru-ki-Var, M.1, p. 1092 (Sikhism)

But Jeshurun waxed fat, and kicked;
you waxed fat, you grew thick, you became sleek;
then he forsook God who made him,
and scoffed at the Rock of his salvation.

Deuteronomy 32.15

Nzame [God] is on high, man is on the earth.
Yeye O, Yalele, God is God, man is man.
Everyone in his house, everyone for himself.[23]

Fang Tradition (African Traditional Religions)

For the LORD of hosts has a day
against all that is proud and lofty,
against all that is lifted up and high;
against all the cedars of Lebanon
lofty and lifted up;
and against all the oaks of Bashan;
against all the high mountains
and against all the lofty hills;
against every high tower,
and against every fortified wall;
against all the ships of Tarshish,
and against all the beautiful craft.
And the haughtiness of man shall be humbled,
and the pride of men shall be brought low;
and the LORD alone will be exalted in that day.

Isaiah 2.12-17

The fool who thinks he is wise is called a fool indeed.

Dhammapada 63 (Buddhism)

Whoever proclaims himself good,
know, goodness approaches him not.

Adi Granth, Gauri Sukhmani 12, M.5, p. 278 (Sikhism)

Confucius said, A faultless man I cannot hope ever to meet; the most I can hope for is to meet a man of fixed principles. Yet where all around I see Nothing pretending to be Something, Emptiness pretending to be Fullness, Penury pretending to be Affluence, even a man of fixed principles will be none too easy to find.

Analects 7.25 (Confucianism)

He who tiptoes cannot stand;
He who strides cannot walk.
He who shows himself is not conspicuous;
He who considers himself right is not
    illustrious;
He who brags will have no merit;
He who boasts will not endure.
From the point of view of the Way, these are
    like "excessive food and useless excres-
    cences" which all creatures detest.
He who has the Way does not abide in them.

Tao Te Ching 24 (Taoism)

Pride has seven forms:
Boasting that one is lower than the lowly,
Or equal with the equal, or greater than
Or equal to the lowly
Is called the pride of selfhood.

Boasting that one is equal to those
Who by some quality are better than oneself
Is the pride of being superior. Thinking
That one is higher than the extremely high,

Who fancy themselves to be superior,
Is pride greater than pride;
Like an abscess in a tumor
It is very vicious.

Conceiving an "I" through ignorance
In the five empty [aggregates]
Which are called the appropriation
Is said to be the pride of thinking "I."

Thinking one has won fruits not yet
Attained is pride of conceit.
Praising oneself for faulty deeds
Is known by the wise as wrongful pride.

Deriding oneself, thinking
"I am senseless," is called
The pride of lowliness.
Such briefly are the seven prides.

Nagarjuna, Precious Garland 406-12 (Buddhism)

Teachings of Sun Myung Moon

In your walk of faith, regard arrogance as the enemy, regard stubbornness as the enemy, and regard insisting on your own way as the enemy. (67:139, June 1, 1973)

Because people are self-centered in their thinking, they speak ill of others. When others have something good, they want to take it from them. Such people are doomed. What about you? Is your mind self-centered or other-centered? No one can solve this problem but you. (36:183, November 29, 1970)

People whose philosophy of life is "me first" are doomed to perish. In pursuing their own desires they harm others and damage their nation—such people will perish. Individuals should not take advantage of their nation; rather, individuals should offer themselves for their nation. That is a duty of citizens.

    People are not meant to live for themselves. Yet today many live only for their own sake. They say, "I live for me." They are people to be pitied, like orphans who have no parents or siblings. (24:20-21, June 22, 1969)

The first step towards the Fall was the appearance of individualism. It was thinking that nothing in the world matters but me. The next step was to think people have unlimited freedom: "What's this with God telling us we cannot eat that fruit? Why should there be any rules to restrict us? We can do as we please." Is it freedom when people do just as they please? It should not be that way. (49:190, October 10, 1971)

From the day the first human ancestors fell and received the blood of Satan, people unconsciously became arrogant and have used others to satisfy their needs. They have pursued that direction throughout human history. (46:142, August 13, 1971)

What is the Fall? It is to unlawfully take what belongs to someone else. Self-centeredness ruined the world. Knowing this universal principle, human beings should return to the world of oneness, but instead they continue to play the game of pulling the world for themselves. That is evil. (170:174, November 15, 1987)

Human beings have inherited Satan's nature: the inclination to regard everything, even God, from a self-centered viewpoint. (91:242, February 23, 1977)

Are Americans proud of their money? Do not be proud of it before God. God can create money as much as He wants. Nor should Americans be proud of their power and military might: God is all-powerful. God is all-knowing: who can challenge Him with knowledge? It doesn't matter that you earned a Ph.D. from Harvard; you are all the same when you stand naked before Him. Your knowledge will not gain you admission into the Kingdom of Heaven. All who are proud of these things will fall into hell. (358:162, October 14, 2001)

I know that American culture upholds individualism. However, there must not be individualism that disregards the relationship between God, the Subject, and human beings, His objects. Selfish individualism is destructive, and its prevalence is driving America into a corner.

Now America should recover the essence of Christianity by seeking for God's original way of life: The individual lives for the sake of the family; families contribute to the community; communities give their strength to the nation; nations exist to benefit the world; and the world exists for the sake of God. These are God's heavenly ethics. If we practice it, then what is God's is also mine, and whatever I do for God also benefits me. Living for the sake of God is ultimately living for my own benefit. (69:88-89, October 20, 1973)

Selfish individualism is Satan's creation, a result of the Fall. As Satan centers on himself, he divides people by having them center on themselves. Thus one [an individual] becomes two [mind and body in conflict.] Two [a couple] become four [the man's mind, the man's body, the woman's mind and the woman's body.]

Why did America become such an individualistic nation? It is because Satan is exerting his dominion there. The so-called right of privacy is at the heart of American individualism. Yet this individualism is causing the family to break down, the society to break down, and the nation to weaken. Individualism is a most fearful thing; it leads people to hell. (361:234, November 25, 2001)

What is the origin of the dirt that has stained human history? It begins from ourselves. Dirt did not just fall on our first ancestors; they made themselves dirty. How did they become dirty? They thought of themselves as being the center of everything; egoism and selfishness are what stained them.

If our ancestors had lived in service to what is more precious than themselves, then they would not have taken the path to defilement. What is more precious than oneself? We are resultant beings; therefore, we should live for the Causal Being. God is that most precious existence, and we should live for Him. Had people truly lived for God and thought of God before thinking of themselves, we could never have become evil. (92:58-59, March 13, 1977)

Many of you soon become arrogant and think, "I am a member of the Unification Church. I have worked for the church for three years, so it's about time that Reverend Moon gives me the Blessing. Then he should recognize me, and so should the church." What a pity if you think that way! In our church there are two ways of life: arrogance and humility. The way of arrogance leads to hell, while the way of humility leads to heaven. What about you: do you belong to heaven or to hell? (92:71, March 13, 1977)

Ignorance and Atheism

MANY RELIGIONS REGARD IGNORANCE AS THE CAUSE OF EVIL in human life. Being ignorant of God and the purpose of life, people's values become confused, and consequently they act wrongly. The apostle Paul taught that ignorance of God lay at the root of all forms of license and immorality. In Islam it is called "forgetting God," causing people to deviate from the path and lose their souls. In Buddhism, this ignorance leads to grasping after self and begets delusion (*moha*). Many scriptures warn against the illusory goals and vanities that infect worldly life.

In their search for knowledge, people have embraced various philosophies, yet it is clear that none of them have illuminated the truth one hundred percent. Oftentimes, valid insights are mixed with false views, leading to confusion and conflict over values, to skepticism and even atheism. This too is the result of humanity's fundamental ignorance, whose source stems from the Human Fall, according to Father Moon. As a prophet of the twentieth century who lived through the struggle with communism, he is particularly concerned about this contemporary form of ignorance.

The concluding passages describe humanity's spiritual blindness. They describe ignorance as a veil that obscures the faculty of insight. The Buddha used metaphors such as moths drawn to perish in a lamp to represent people's attraction to the illusory vanities of this world. In Hinduism and Jainism, this blindness (*avidya*) is what binds people to the wheel of birth-and-death (*samsara*), binding them sense pleasures instead of seeking Reality itself. Plato's famous Myth of the Cave speaks to this topic. Father Moon likewise describes a pervasive delusion, born of the Human Fall, that leaves human beings blind to spiritual truth and totally unable to know God's inner heart.

1. Ignorance of God

Be not like those who forget God, and therefore He made them forget their own souls!

Qur'an 59.19

Although they knew God they did not honor him as God or give thanks to him, but they became futile in their thinking, and their senseless minds were darkened. Claiming to be wise, they became fools, and exchanged the glory of the immortal God for images resembling mortal man or birds or animals or reptiles. Therefore God gave them up in the lusts of their hearts to impurity, to the dishonoring of their bodies among themselves, because they exchanged the truth about God for a lie and worshipped and served the creature rather than the Creator, who is blessed forever! Amen.

Romans 1.21-25

The fool says in his heart,
"There is no God."
They are all corrupt, they do abominable deeds,
there is none that does good.
The LORD looks down from heaven
upon the children of men,
to see if there are any that act wisely,
that seek after God.
They have all gone astray,
they are all alike corrupt;
there is none that does good,
no, not one.
Have they no knowledge,
all the evildoers
who eat up my people as they eat bread,
and do not call upon the LORD?

Psalm 14.1-4

Whoever wants to do some evil against another does not remember God.

Proverb (African Traditional Religions)

He who does not clearly understand Heaven will not be pure in virtue. He who has not mastered the Way will find himself without any acceptable path of approach. He who does not understand the Way is pitiable indeed!

Chuang Tzu 11 (Taoism)

No man lies to his neighbor until he has denied the Root. It happened once that Rabbi Reuben was in Tiberias on the Sabbath, and a philosopher asked him, "Who is the most hateful man in the world?" He replied, "The man who denies his Creator." "How so?" asked the philosopher.

Rabbi Reuben answered, "'Honor thy father and thy mother, thou shalt not murder, thou shalt not commit adultery, thou shalt not steal, thou shalt not bear false witness against thy neighbor, thou shalt not covet.' No man denies the derivative [the Ten Commandments] until he has previously denied the Root [God], and no man sins unless he has denied Him who commanded him not to commit that sin."

Tosefta Shevuot 3.6 (Judaism)

The demonic do things they should avoid and avoid the things they should do. They have no sense of uprightness, purity, or truth.

"There is no God," they say, "no truth, no spiritual law, no moral order. The basis of life is sex; what else can it be?" Holding such distorted views, possessing scant discrimination, they become enemies of the world, causing suffering and destruction.

Hypocritical, proud, and arrogant, living in delusion and clinging to deluded ideas, insatiable in their desires, they pursue their unclean ends. Although burdened with fears that end only with death, they still maintain with complete assurance, "Gratification of lust is the highest that life can offer."

Bound on all sides by scheming and anxiety, driven by anger and greed, they amass by any means they can a hoard of money for the satisfaction of their cravings.

"I got this today," they say; "tomorrow I shall get that. This wealth is mine, and that will be mine too. I have destroyed my enemies. I shall destroy others too! Am I not like God? I enjoy what I want. I am successful. I am powerful. I am happy. I am rich and well-born. Who is equal to me? I will perform sacrifices and give gifts, and rejoice in my own generosity."

This is how they go on, deluded by ignorance. Bound by their greed and entangled in a web of delusion, whirled about by a fragmented mind, they fall into a dark hell.

Bhagavad-Gita 16.7-16 (Hinduism)

Teachings of Sun Myung Moon

Humanity fell into ignorance of God at its beginning, and we are still ignorant of God today. We do not know God, God's ideal of creation, or the family that was to be the basis of our fulfillment. For this reason, everything goes wrong. Human life, from the family level to the world level, is a mess. (325:220, July 1, 2000)

Many people think that food, clothing and survival are the chief ends of life. Of course, they do develop some good elements through moral human relationships with each other. However, the standards of their morality and social arrangements differ according to culture and background. Hence, while everyone has an innate desire to establish the original standard of morality, we face the reality that existing moralities and ways of life are scattered in many directions. There is no consensus about it—this is a problem.

People are unsure about their ultimate destination after earthly life is finished. They are uncertain about the existence of the spirit world. They are even ignorant of the existence of God. (140:122-23, February 9, 1986)

When people believe there is nothing after death, they want to experience everything they possibly can of earthly life. They want to excel everyone else in building an ideal environment for themselves before they die. They want to do something significant on the world stage and to experience all manner of relationships. Inevitably, their life becomes nothing but the pursuit of physical pleasure. That is why in affluent countries like the United States today, ethics and morality have all become decadent.

The loss of values is serious, even to the extent that people reject their historical traditions and destroy the family structure of parents, siblings, husband and wife. In their pursuit of physical pleasures, people throw away what is needed for lasting relationships. Children pursue these pleasures and their parents oppose; husbands seek them out and their wives object. People lose the desire to marry, as life becomes more casual every day. (172:15-16, January 3, 1988)

Adam and Eve fell into a state of ignorance: ignorant of the ideal world of oneness and ignorant of God's purpose to realize that world. Born as descendants of ancestors who fell into ignorance, we also do not know where we are supposed to go. (140:14, February 1, 1986)

If we are created in such a way that we cannot live apart from God, then surely our ignorance of God consigns us to walk miserable paths. Although we may diligently study the Bible, can we claim that we really know the reality of God? Can we ever grasp the heart of God? (*Exposition of the Divine Principle*, Introduction)

Religions have helped fallen people gradually overcome their spiritual ignorance by stimulating their latent original mind to activity. They have been teaching people to focus their lives on the invisible, causal world of God. Since not everyone feels an immediate need for religion, only a few exceptional people attain spiritual knowledge rapidly. For the vast majority, spiritual growth remains a slow process. We see this from the fact that even today, with religions widespread throughout the world, people's spiritual level is often no better than that of people in ancient times. (*Exposition of the Divine Principle*, Parallels 7.2.2)

Ask young people whether they really love God. If they are honest their answer must be "No." Why? Because their views are different from God's. Young people like to enjoy their life, indulging in free sex and drugs, but God does not allow it. As long as they are doing those things, they cannot say they love God. (91:22, January 16, 1977)

2. False Views

Woe to those who call evil good and good evil,
who put darkness for light and light for darkness,
who put bitter for sweet and sweet for bitter!

Isaiah 5.20

Beings who are ashamed of what is not shameful, and are not ashamed of what is shameful, embrace wrong views and go to a woeful state.

Beings who see fear in what is not to be feared, and see no fear in the fearsome, embrace false views and go to a woeful state.

Beings who imagine faults in the faultless and perceive no wrong in what is wrong, embrace false views and go to a woeful state.

Dhammapada 316-18 *(Buddhism)*

Whenever people are deceived and their notions are at variance with reality, it is clear that the error slips in through resemblances [to reality].

Plato, Phaedrus *(Hellenism)*

When the Tao was lost, there was virtue;[24]
When virtue was lost, there was benevolence;
When benevolence was lost, there was rectitude;
When rectitude was lost, there were rules of propriety.
Propriety is a wearing thin of loyalty and good faith,
And the beginning of disorder.

Tao Te Ching 38 *(Taoism)*

Teachings of Sun Myung Moon

Philosophers, saints and sages set out to pave the way of goodness for the people of their times. Yet so many of their accomplishments have become added spiritual burdens for the people of today. Consider this objectively. Has any philosopher ever arrived at the knowledge that could solve humanity's deepest anguish? Has any sage ever clearly illuminated the path by resolving all the fundamental questions of human life and the universe? Have not their teachings and philosophies raised more unsettled questions, thus giving rise to skepticism? (*Exposition of the Divine Principle*, Introduction)

Despite the fact that human beings are meant to live attending God as their Parent and to follow His guidance day by day, many people are ignorant of God's existence. Taking one more step, they proclaim, "God is dead." More and more, God is being removed from human society. Who made such a world, God or human beings? (135:268, December 15, 1985)

Serious problems are rampant in society, including the confusion of value systems, moral corruption, drug addiction, terrorism, racial discrimination, unequal distribution of wealth, atheistic communism, violations of human rights, war and genocide. These evils, which threaten humanity's destruction, are the inevitable consequences of atheistic materialism, secular humanism and hedonism, which have at their core the rejection of God. All these are the effects of the declining faith and spiritual exhaustion of this generation. (135:221, November 16, 1985)

I am not one to condemn humanism altogether, but the problem with the humanism we see today is that it is based on a thoroughly atheistic outlook. Once we deny the existence of God and the significance of the Creator's creative acts, human beings are reduced to just a handful of dust. It is a perspective that considers human beings no better than mere machines. This was precisely the fallacy in Marxist-Leninism. If we say there is no God, and that human beings are no better than machines or animals, then there is no basis for morality. Without a belief in the spirit and eternal life, people cease to feel responsible for each other and commit atrocities against other human beings. (234:232, August 22, 1992)

3. Spiritual Blindness and Delusion

The unbelievers... are like the depths of
   darkness
In a vast deep ocean,
Overwhelmed with billow,
Topped by billow,
Topped by dark clouds:
Depths of darkness,
One above another:
If a man stretches out his hand, he can hardly
   see it!
For any to whom God gives not light,
There is no light!

Qur'an 24.40

Blind is this world. Few are those who clearly
   see.
As birds escape from a net, few go to a blissful
   state.

Dhammapada 174 (Buddhism)

This vast universe is a wheel, the wheel of Brahman. Upon it are all creatures that are subject to birth, death, and rebirth. Round and round it turns, and never stops. As long as the individual self thinks it is separate from the Lord, it revolves upon the wheel in bondage to the laws of birth, death, and rebirth...

   The Lord supports this universe, which is made up of the perishable and the imperishable, the manifest and the unmanifest. The individual soul, forgetful of the Lord, attaches itself to pleasure and thus is bound.

Svetasvatara Upanishad 1.6-8 (Hinduism)

On a certain occasion the Exalted One was seated in the open air, on a night of inky darkness, and oil lamps were burning. Swarms of winged insects kept falling into these oil lamps and thereby met their end, came to destruction and utter ruin. Seeing this, the Exalted One saw the meaning in it and uttered this verse of uplift,

> They hasten up and past, but miss the real;
>   a bondage ever new they cause to grow.
> Just as the flutterers fall into the lamp,
>   so some are bent on what they see and hear.

Udana 72 (Buddhism)

To the pure all things are pure, but to the corrupt and unbelieving nothing is pure; their very minds and consciences are corrupted.

Titus 1.15

The god of this world has blinded the minds of the unbelievers, to keep them from seeing the light of the gospel of the glory of Christ, who is the likeness of God.

2 Corinthians 4.4

Fools dwelling in darkness, but thinking themselves wise and erudite, go round and round, by various tortuous paths, like the blind led by the blind.

Katha Upanishad 1.2.5 (Hinduism)

The soul is only able to view existence through the bars of a prison, and not in her own nature; she is wallowing in the mire of all ignorance. Philosophy sees the terrible nature of her confinement, and that the captive through desire is led to conspire in her own captivity.

Plato, Phaedo (Hellenism)

Teachings of Sun Myung Moon

Are any among you caught in the abyss of despair? You have no connection whatsoever to the ideal world. Are you in such darkness that you cannot distinguish front from back, left from right, up from down? Amidst your confused, turbulent and disorderly lives, you have forgotten the center and continue to violate Heaven's laws and principles. As long as this is the case, you cannot make any connection with God's ideal Garden. (2:246, June 9, 1957)

The world has become a wretched place, far from God's presence. Yet humanity to this day lives in ignorance of this. People are deluded into believing that the lineage of the enemy is the lifeline upon which the world depends. This is the wretched truth about humanity descended from the Fall. That is why we refer to this world as hell on earth. God views humanity's tragic situation with a heart full of pain. (September 12, 2005)

Most of the six billion people in the world are blind. Though they appear normal, they cannot see even an inch in front of themselves. But this does not keep people from acting as though they are philosophers and theologians who understand the truth of Heaven. It has been this way throughout history, and it has caused God much grief. (May 1, 2004)

With the Fall of the first human ancestors, human beings were cast into a hopeless hell from which they cannot escape by their efforts alone. They should have become true owners, true parents and true kings and queens, who communicate directly with God through their five spiritual senses and freely exercise dominion over all things through their five physical senses; thus they were to be God's representatives to both the spirit world and the physical world. But due to the Fall their five spiritual senses became largely paralyzed. They fell into a state similar to that of a blind man whose sightless eyes appear normal to an observer. Forced to live mainly by their five physical senses, they became only half human. They could not see God, or see Him only dimly. They could barely hear His voice or feel His touch. So how could they experience His love as their own Parent or know His suffering heart? (January 27, 2004)

> The greatest sorrows of humankind are:
> our inability to form a relationship with Thy love,
> the loss of our original conscience,
> which could communicate with Thy heart,
> and our inability to harmonize our minds and bodies,
> which would enable us to live in accordance with our conscience and Thy heart.

Because of the Fall, the sensibility by which we could communicate with Thy heart left us, and the mind which could love all things through experiencing Thy heart is no longer with us. (6:298-99, June 14, 1959)

Idolatry and Materialism

LITERALLY THE WORSHIP OF IMAGES, IDOLATRY in the broader sense means allegiance to false values that substitute for God. In the Qur'an idols are regarded as evil spirits and Satan; those who worship them are therefore enemies to God. The Bible views idols as human artifacts, not as representations of deity. Hence idol worship is regarded as a form of materialism, and, conversely, any false reliance on human power or wealth is a form of idolatry. A more spiritual conception of idolatry is to identify it with egoism and human craving, since attachment to these false realities separates us from our true nature. The biblical story of the golden calf describes the worship of the idol as accompanied by orgiastic rites.

In the twentieth century, the idols of nationalism, racism, and especially materialism have captivated millions, with horrible results. Father Moon explicitly calls materialism modern-day idolatry and regards it as one of Gods' biggest "headaches." His passages on this topic are a contemporary counterpoint to the classic texts.

Lo, Abraham said to his father Azar, "Do you take idols for gods? For I see you and your people are in manifest error."

Qur'an 6.74

Shun the abomination of idols, and shun the word that is false—being true in faith to Allah, and never assigning partners to Him: if anyone assigns partners to God, he is as if he had fallen from heaven and been snatched up by birds, or the wind had swooped down and thrown him to a distant land.

Qur'an 22.30-31

Our God is in the heavens;
he does whatever he pleases.
Their idols are silver and gold,
the work of men's hands.
They have mouths, but do not speak;
eyes, but do not see.
They have ears, but do not hear;
noses, but do not smell.
They have hands, but do not feel;
feet, but do not walk;
and they do not make a sound in their throat.²⁵

Those who make them are like them;
so are all who trust in them.

Psalm 115.3-8

For many... live as enemies of the cross of Christ. Their end is destruction, their god is the belly, and they glory in their shame, with minds set on earthly things.

Philippians 3.18-19

"There shall be *in* you no strange god and you shall not worship a foreign god" [Psalm 81.10]. What is the "foreign god" within a man's body? It is the evil impulse.

Talmud, Shabbat 105b (Judaism)

Have you seen him who makes his desire his god, and God sends him astray purposely, and seals up his hearing and his heart, and sets on his sight a covering? Who, then, will lead him after God [has condemned him]? Will you not then heed?

Qur'an 45.23

When the people saw that Moses delayed to come down from the mountain, the people gathered themselves together to Aaron, and said to him, "Up, make us gods, who shall go before us; as for this Moses, the man who brought us up out of the land of Egypt, we do not know what has become of him." And Aaron said to them, "Take off the rings of gold which are in the ears of your wives, your sons, and your daughters, and bring them to me." So all the people took off the rings of gold which were in their ears, and brought them to Aaron. And he received the gold at their hand, and fashioned it with a graving tool, and made a molten calf; and they said, "These are your gods, O Israel, who brought you up out of the land of Egypt!" When Aaron saw this, he built an altar before it; and Aaron made proclamation and said, "Tomorrow shall be a feast to the LORD." And they rose up early on the morrow, and offered burnt offerings and brought peace offerings; and the people sat down to eat and drink, and rose up to play.

Exodus 32.1-6

Teachings of Sun Myung Moon

What is idolatry? It is to abandon God and worship something else, to revere it more than God. Today numerous people are worshipping the idol called "civilization" without being aware of it... They take as their idols material things; they become slaves of civilization. Hence, they do not know where to find the center of their life. Without seeking Heaven they make frantic efforts, yet they do not know what direction to go or what goal to aim for. They are no different than the benighted Israelites in the days of Ahab and Jezebel. (6:31, March 15, 1959)

The world should center on the mind, but instead it is devoted to matter... Look at the reality of education, focused as it is on the needs and values of material civilization. The precious and invisible mind is being neglected for the sake of money that is visible to the eyes. (19:287, March 10, 1968)

First theism appeared; it emerged as a spin-off of history. Next, humanism emerged as a spin-off of history, and then materialism. They each appeared as separate and incompatible ways of thinking. Thus separated, each in turn perished.

Human beings consist of body, mind and spirit. Our body consists of matter, our mind consists of character, and with our spirit we are to unite with God. When we try to become one with God without considering the material world and human beings we do not succeed, because that way does not fit our nature. We need God, but we also need human beings and the material world. For this reason, theism, humanism and materialism should not be separate. We need them all. Therefore, religion in the future should be equipped in all three areas, guiding us to fulfill the whole of human life in all its aspects.

Human beings, having a complex culture, are higher than matter. God is higher than human beings. Therefore, God should govern human beings and all things; that is in keeping with the Principle.

In earlier times, when people placed religion at the center of their life, they tended to deny the value of human beings. As a result, humanism emerged, putting human beings at the center and denying the importance of God. More recently, humanism has declined as people value material above all else. For materialists, money is everything. Nothing is as valuable as money, not even human beings. They see everything in terms of money.

Yet after living materialistic lives, people find that material things are not everything. They begin to re-examine the human being to discover their original nature. They are faced with the limitations of materialism and realize that they need to recover human beings... They begin asking questions,

"What is a human being? Is there something about human beings that needs to be restored? Do we need to once again consider the question of God?" We are living in a transitional period when these trends are evident. American young people, hippies and yippies, do all sorts of things, and many are in search of religion. (103:226, March 1, 1979)

Suffering

THE FIRST OF THE BUDDHA'S FOUR NOBLE TRUTHS is that human existence is suffering (Pali *dukkha*). Suffering is the pervasive human condition, a sort of illness generated by the self through its false attachments. Buddhist texts—echoed in other scriptures—describe it by the metaphor of a universal fire engulfing the world. In Hinduism, the human lot is to go through an endless cycle of death and rebirth, conditioned by the results of past actions.

Ecclesiastes is in many ways the most Buddhist of books in the Bible in its theme of the vanity of human works. Few are those who ever fulfill all their desires, yet even those who do are not satisfied, ever wanting more. Akin to this is the observation in Chinese texts that even when people begin with the best of intentions, their behavior usually degenerates and ends in acrimony, betrayal, or violence.

In Christianity, the doctrine of Original Sin conveys a similar idea: by their fallen condition people are unable to fulfill their life's purpose. Father Moon often laments about the interminable misery of the human condition and explains how the Human Fall brought this about.

1. Sorrow Is Everywhere

The Noble Truth of Suffering (*Dukkha*) is this: Birth is suffering; aging is suffering; sickness is suffering; death is suffering; sorrow and lamentation, pain, grief, and despair are suffering; association with the unpleasant is suffering; dissociation from the pleasant is suffering; not to get what one wants is suffering—in brief, the five aggregates of attachment are suffering.[26]

Samyutta Nikaya 56.11 (Buddhism)

Affliction does not come from the dust,
nor does trouble sprout from the ground;
but man is born to trouble
as the sparks fly upward.

Job 5.6-7

This world, become ablaze, by touch of sense afflicted,
utters its own lament. Whatever conceit one has, therein is instability. Becoming other, bound to becoming, yet in becoming it rejoices. Delight therein is fear, and what it fears is Ill.

Udana 32 (Buddhism)

Brothers, all is burning. And what is the all that is burning? Brothers, the eye is burning, visible forms are burning, visual consciousness is burning, visual impression is burning, also whatever sensation, pleasant or painful or neither-painful-nor-pleasant, arises on account of the visual impression, that too is burning. Burning with what? Burning with the fire of lust, with the fire of hate, with the fire of delusion; I say it is burning with birth, aging, and death, with sorrows, with lamentations, with pains, with griefs, with despairs.

The ear is burning, sounds are burning, auditory consciousness is burning... Burning with what? Burning with the fire of lust, with the fire of hate, with the fire of delusion; I say it is burning with birth, aging, and death, with sorrows, with lamentations, with pains, with griefs, with despairs.

    The nose is burning, odors are burning…

    The tongue is burning, flavors are burning…

    The body is burning, tangible things are burning, tactile consciousness is burning…

    The mind is burning, thoughts are burning… Burning with what? Burning with the fire of lust, with the fire of hate, with the fire of delusion;

I say it is burning with birth, aging, and death, with sorrows, with lamentations, with pains, with griefs, with despairs.

    Samyutta Nikaya 35.28: The Fire Sermon (*Buddhism*)

Farid, I thought I alone had sorrow;
Sorrow is spread all over the whole world.
From my roof-top I saw
Every home engulfed in sorrow's flames.

    Adi Granth, Shalok, Farid, p. 1382 (*Sikhism*)

Teachings of Sun Myung Moon

Humanity lost the original garden and fell into the world of death. There, we struggle against the darkness. We live in the midst of lamentation and hopelessness, entrapped in the power of the enemy. Still, in our conscience, the remnant of the original mind, we long for the original homeland. (6:291, June 14, 1959)

The world we live in is not a joyful world but a miserable world; it is not a world of delight but a world of sorrow; it is not a world where people live with gratitude but a world where people live with grudges. If you cannot overcome this unfortunate world, then you will never find the path to happiness.

    How can you know that you are unhappy? You can understand it through your mind. In your mind, is there a grieving heart that you cannot get rid of? This is proof that Satan is our ancestor. Do you have hatred and resentment toward other people? This is like Satan entangling our minds in steel nets to prevent us from going toward the original Garden of Eden.

    Human beings are living in the world of death where there is no life, the world of despair and pitch darkness. Although human beings should be singing of the preciousness of life and living in harmony with God's eternal ideal, people today are living in despair. They are cut off from the hope of standing before the ideal of God. (2:246, June 9, 1957)

We are surrounded by evil elements. The way to evil does not need to be taught. Everyone can go that way without education, because history started from an evil foundation. Does anyone need to be taught how to be bad? Because humans fell by their own decision, society educates people to act according to their conscience based on the prevailing morality. Even so, how many people are able to live in accordance with that education? Evil things can be done without education; anyone can score 100 points.

    The conscience always tells us to be good people, but have we actually become good? Unable to solve this problem, our life is one of continual lamentation. Today is lamentation, tomorrow is lamentation, and the whole year is lamentation. Youth is lamentation, middle age is lamentation, old age is lamentation, and we die with lamentation. Evil marks our whole life. (36:57, November 15, 1970)

Due to the Human Fall, history started from a point of sadness. The saddest thing about the starting point was that we had to leave God. God was to be the source of our happiness and the center of our life, His grace pervading everything. Due to the Fall, however, humankind lost happiness, life and all things. People fell into deep despair, darkness, and unhappiness. Having lost any vision or hope, tears filled their eyes. With those tears came despair, and utter darkness. (52:36, December 12, 1971)

2. The Futility of Human Life

Vanity of vanities! All is vanity. What does man gain by all the toil at which he toils under the sun?

Ecclesiastes 1.2-3

Parable of those who reject their Lord: their works are as ashes on which the wind blows furiously on a stormy day. No power have they over aught that they have earned. That is straying far, far from the goal.

Qur'an 14.18

Men think much of their own advancement and of many other worldly things; but there is no improvement in this decaying world, which is as a tempting dish, sweet-coated, yet full of deadly gall within... It is as intangible as a mist; try to lay hold of it, and it proves to be nothing!

Yoga Vasishtha (Hinduism)

Not by a shower of gold coins does contentment arise in sensual pleasures.

Dhammapada 186 (Buddhism)

Desire never rests by enjoyment of lusts, as fire surely increases the more butter is offered to it.

Laws of Manu 2.94 (Hinduism)

The benighted one is incompetent to assuage sufferings, because he is attached to desires and is lecherous. Oppressed by physical and mental pain, he keeps rotating in a whirlpool of agony. I say so.

Acarangasutra 2.74 (Jainism)

Intoxicated by the wine of illusion, like one intoxicated by wine; rushing about, like one possessed of an evil spirit; bitten by the world, like one bitten by a great serpent; darkened by passion, like the night; illusory, like magic; false, like a dream; pithless, like the inside of a banana-tree; changing its dress in a moment, like an actor; fair in appearance, like a painted wall—thus they call him.

Maitri Upanishad 4.2 (Hinduism)

I the Preacher have been king over Israel in Jerusalem. And I applied my mind to seek and to search out by wisdom all that is done under heaven; it is an unhappy business that God has given to the sons of men to be busy with. I have seen everything that is done under the sun; and behold, all is vanity and a striving after wind.

> What is crooked cannot be made straight,
> and what is lacking cannot be numbered.

I said to myself, "I have acquired great wisdom, surpassing all who were over Jerusalem before me; and my mind has had great experience of wisdom and knowledge." And I applied my mind to know wisdom and to know madness and folly. I perceived that this also is but a striving after wind.

> For in much wisdom is much vexation,
> and he who increases knowledge increases sorrow.

I said to myself, "Come now, I will make a test of pleasure; enjoy yourself."... Whatever my eyes desired I did not keep from them; I kept my heart from no pleasure, for my heart found pleasure in all my toil, and this was my reward for all my toil. Then I considered all that my hands had done and the toil I had spent in doing it, and behold, all was vanity and a striving after wind...

So I turned about and gave my heart up to despair over all the toil of my labors under the sun, because sometimes a man who has toiled with wisdom and knowledge and skill must leave all to be enjoyed by a man who did not toil for it. This also is vanity and a great evil. What has a man from all the toil and strain with which he toils beneath the sun? For all his days are full of pain, and his work is a vexation; even in the night his mind does not rest. This also is vanity.

Ecclesiastes 1.12-2.23

How vast is God,
The ruler of men below!
How arrayed in terrors is God,
With many things irregular in his ordinations.
Heaven gave birth to the multitudes of the people,
But the nature it confers is not to be depended upon.

All are good at first,
But few prove themselves to be so at the last.

Book of Songs, Ode 255 (Confucianism)

When men get together to pit their strength in games of skill, they start off in a light and friendly mood, but usually end up in a dark and angry one, and if they go on too long they start resorting to various underhanded tricks. When men meet at some ceremony to drink, they start off in an orderly manner, but usually end up in disorder, and if they go on too long they start indulging in various irregular amusements. It is the same with all things. What starts out being sincere usually ends up being deceitful. What was simple in the beginning acquires monstrous proportions in the end.

Chuang Tzu 4 (Taoism)

Teachings of Sun Myung Moon

People think, "Let us seek our pleasure during this life of less than 100 years. We have only one chance at adolescence. So, let's eat as we wish, play as we wish, and do as we wish while we are young." Most people who live on this earth think this way. However, even if they do everything their physical bodies desire, eventually all will come to naught. In a matter of a few years they will be bored with it all. Their life will have been in vain. (41:143, February 14, 1971)

Religions have made strenuous efforts to deny life in this world in their quest for the life eternal. They have despised the pleasures of the body for the sake of spiritual bliss. Yet, however hard they may try, people cannot cut themselves off from the reality of this world or annihilate the desire for physical pleasures, which follows them like a shadow and cannot be shaken off. This world and its desires tenaciously grab hold of religious people, driving them into the depths of agony. Such is the contradiction which plagues their devotional lives. Even many enlightened spiritual leaders, still torn by this contradiction, have met a sad end. (*Exposition of the Divine Principle,* Introduction)

Suppose a man devotes his life to earning money and becomes a millionaire. It requires strenuous effort; he must labor through his 20s, 30s, 40s and 50s to become a millionaire in his 60s. However, at age 60, the day of his death is not distant. Having worked hard to earn money all his life, the age of retirement draws near. When he looks at all the money he has accumulated, does he feel hope or despair? As he thinks about the past, he might feel a heaviness in his spirit. As he reviews all the efforts he made at earning money, he might feel an emptiness in his heart. When it dawns on him that he lived his whole life for money, wouldn't he feel extremely miserable?...

Suppose a man goes to a university and earns a Ph.D. He might think it a great accomplishment. To obtain that degree he studied day and night without eating, playing or taking rest. Maybe he even becomes a world-famous Nobel laureate. However, if we look closely at his life, we find many miserable things.

Although he has the knowledge of a Nobel laureate, it is all within a small field of specialization. His research in his field is like digging a small cave in the wide world. Staying within the limits of his specialization, he realizes that compared with the whole world he is extremely small. Even though he boasts that he knows something, it is an extremely small thing.

Does knowledge give human beings happiness and peace? No. Knowledge is such that we realize that the more we study, the more we do not know.

Suppose he becomes a famous professor at the university. Every day he holds a chalk and writes on the blackboard. He writes books and takes on various academic responsibilities. Yet while he inhales chalk powder and becomes a leading voice in his field, he has no idea what kind of influence he has in the world. He does not know what will happen to the world in the future. Lacking the mind to comprehend God's Will, he does not think about what perspective he should take in viewing the world. In fact, he is more ignorant than ordinary ignorant people, because he is so caught up in his own studies.

Even with all his knowledge, he spends his entire life as a mere bookworm. He lacks the self-confidence to assert his own ideas; mostly he just represents and compares the ideas of others in his field. His life commitment consists of little more. Hence, even if he becomes a famous professor, what is the point? Life is too precious to invest it all for something like that.

Another man covets power; he dreams of becoming a big shot, like the President of the United States. Yet even if he attains that power, does it last forever? The President of the United States holds power for only four years. Compared with the expanse of history, it is like the blink of an eye. Though he enjoys his power—eating the finest food, drinking the finest wine, dancing—once the power is gone, he is nothing. He no longer matters to anyone. People with ordinary aspirations are better off than he. (98:82-85, April 30, 1978)

3. The Path of Tears

Kisa Gotami had an only son, and he died. In her grief she carried the dead child to all her neighbors, asking them for medicine, and the people said, "She has lost her senses. The boy is dead."

At length Kisa Gotami met a man who replied to her request, "I cannot give you medicine for your child, but I know a physician who can. Go to Sakyamuni, the Buddha."

Kisa Gotami repaired to the Buddha and cried, "Lord and Master, give me the medicine that will cure my boy."

The Buddha answered, "I want a handful of mustard seed." And when the girl in her joy promised to procure it, the Buddha added, "The mustard seed must be taken from a house where no one has lost a child, husband, parent, or friend."

Poor Kisa Gotami now went from house to house, and the people pitied her and said, "Here is the mustard seed, take it!" But when she asked, "Did a son or daughter, a father or mother, die in your family?" they answered her, "Alas! the living are few, but the dead are many. Do not remind us of our deepest grief." And there was no house but some beloved one had died in it.

Kisa Gotami became weary and hopeless, and sat down at the way-side, watching the lights of the city as they flickered up and were extinguished again. At last the darkness of night reigned everywhere. And she considered the fate of men, that their lives flicker up and are extinguished. And she thought to herself, "How selfish am I in my grief! Death is common to all; yet in this valley of desolation there is a path that leads him to immortality who has surrendered all selfishness."

Putting away the selfishness of her affection for her child, Kisa Gotami had the dead body buried in the forest. Returning to the Buddha, she took refuge in him and found comfort in the Dharma.

Buddhaghosa, Parable of the Mustard Seed
(Buddhism)

Teachings of Sun Myung Moon

Adam and Eve and certainly God shed tears over their fall. Adam and Eve wept for themselves. God also shed tears, but for whom? The Father of mankind shed tears for His children, who faced expulsion from the Garden of Eden due to their violation of the heavenly law. God wept not for Himself, but for His children.

Those tears themselves were tragic. Human history began in tears, and for God also, history began with tears. Human beings live in misery, but so does God. Humans truly deserved to shed tears for their sin, but God does not deserve to shed tears.

The history of tears that began with the first human ancestors has expanded down through the generations to all mankind throughout the world. Human history is stained with repeated tears, of suffering and struggle and broken-heartedness. People hurt each other and suffer oppression by those above them. No one has been able to put a stop to the tears of history.

People ordinarily grieve for their own misfortunes. Nevertheless, more than for ourselves, or for our family's misfortunes, or our nation's misfortunes, we should grieve for the world's pain… Everyone has been grieving over his or her own misery, or at best over their family's sorrows or their nation's suffering, but what they should focus on is the sorrow of the world. For this, we have to change and reverse the purpose of tears. We still grieve but for a different purpose. We need a reorientation to the other kind of tears—the tears that God sheds when He weeps in sorrow over the situation of humankind. God's eyes are always filled with tears, but His tears are for others, never for Himself.

Where can we truly find happiness? First, we should find a way to overcome our own tears; then we should overcome the conditions over which God sheds tears. Then we can find happiness. Why? The history of tears for both God and humans began as a result of the Human Fall; therefore we should return to the time before the Fall when there were no tears…

It is our destiny to go over these two hills of sorrowful tears—human tears and God's tears. Those who are traveling the road of truth should climb these two hills of tears. We should shed tears over the misery of humanity and taste many situations of human suffering. While others may live in blissful ignorance, we should grieve over the problems of human life, from fundamental questions down to the prevailing conditions of society. Some young people in particular agonize about such things; those who do not have such experiences cannot live a true life.

While we overcome our own sorrows, we should also seek ways to alleviate the suffering of the world. Nevertheless, grappling with the suffering and misery of human live is not sufficient to bring a lasting solution. We must go deeper and uproot the fundamental cause of tears. This means reversing the initial tragedy that caused God and human beings to shed tears. Yet no one could comprehend a method for doing this.

The tears we shed for ourselves or for our nation, on the human level alone, cannot be helpful for reaching the ideal world. They are still within the realm of selfishness, being merely the continuation of the tears that fallen Adam and Eve shed for themselves.

What, then, should we do? We should discover another realm of tears, the tears of God's sorrow. We should deeply experience their taste then surmount them. Otherwise we cannot establish the basis for human happiness. This means learning how to shed tears that transcend our own suffering. First we should discover God and experience His tears; then we should willingly walk the path to alleviate God's suffering. (94:306-10, October 16, 1977)

God's Grief

IF GOD IS OUR DIVINE PARENT and we human beings are His children, then surely God must feel great sadness of heart over His children's bondage, degradation and rebellion. Thus, religious traditions that revere a personal, compassionate God recognize God to have an aspect of sorrow. In Christianity, Jesus' Passion has regularly represented the suffering of God, as the Father is one with His Son. Although the biblical witness to God's grief is sometimes eclipsed by the Aristotelian conception that perfection requires that God be impassible, contemporary theologians are affirming that the Creator also suffers. In Mahayana Buddhism, the compassion of Shakyamuni and the commiseration of the bodhisattvas for human suffering stems from the heart of the cosmic Buddha who is the Father of all humanity.

For Father Moon, to know God means to experience God's painful and grieving heart: broken at the Fall, sorrowful that His children continue to live in darkness, tortured by the power and arrogance of evil that holds His children in thrall, and agonized at the thorny path that His saints must walk as they strive to fulfill the providence and attain liberation. By attaining such knowledge, we can become compassionate ourselves, and persevering in the struggle to liberate humanity.

1. God's Grief over the Human Fall and Humankind's Sinful Condition

The LORD saw that the wickedness of man was great in the earth, and that every imagination of the thoughts of his heart was only evil continually. And the LORD was sorry that He had made man on the earth, and it grieved Him to His heart.[27]

Genesis 6.5-6

And it came to pass that the God of heaven looked upon the residue of His people, and He wept; and Enoch bore record of it, saying, "How is it that the heavens weep, and shed forth their tears as the rain upon the mountains?" And Enoch said unto the Lord, How is it that you can weep, seeing you are holy, and from all eternity to all eternity?"...

The Lord said unto Enoch, "Behold these your brethren; they are the workmanship of My own hands, and I gave to them their knowledge... and commandment, that they should love one another, and that they should choose Me, their Father; but behold, they are without affection, and they hate their own blood; and the fire of My indignation is kindled against them; and in My hot displeasure will I send in the floods upon them... misery shall be their doom; and the whole heavens shall weep over them, even all the workmanship of My hands; therefore should not the heavens weep, seeing these shall suffer?"[28]

Pearl of Great Price, Moses 7.28-37
(Latter-Day Saints)

Abu Dharr reported God's Messenger as saying, "I see what you do not see and I hear what you do not hear; heaven has groaned, and it has a right to groan."

Hadith of Ahmad, Tirmidhi and Ibn Majah (Islam)

Whatever kind of regret I, Tsukihi [God], may have borne, until now I have overlooked it and kept still patiently...

Never think of this regret as slight! It is the result of the regret that has been accumulated and piled up.

All people of the whole world are My children. Although I single-heartedly love them, unaware of this, each and every one of them equally is thinking only of dust.

Think of the regret of God over these dusty minds! It is far beyond expression of My words.[29]

Ofudesaki 17.64-70 (Tenrikyo)

Abuk, mother of Deng,
Leave your home in the sky and come to work in our homes,
Make our country to become clean like the original home of Deng,
Come make our country as one: the country of Akwol
Is not as one, either by night or by day,
The child called Deng, his face has become sad,
The children of Akwol have bewildered their Chief's mind.[30]

Dinka Song (African Traditional Religions)

Teachings of Sun Myung Moon

God's heart was torn asunder and broken with indescribable grief and tears the moment Adam and Eve fell. (7:292, October 11, 1959)

Love is endless. Had God not established the principle of love, He would be alone. Dwelling by Himself, He would be unable to experience joy, anger, sorrow or happiness.

Although God's love is absolute, once God lost His partners of love, He unexpectedly found Himself in an absolutely miserable and grim situation, such as no one in history has ever experienced. No one can comfort Him over this, ever. (204:101, July 1, 1990)

If Adam and Eve had not fallen, God their Creator would have been their eternal Lord. But due to the Fall, Satan became their lord. The Fall made this outcome unavoidable. Suppose a girl of noble birth, raised within the walls of her house, is raped by a gangster; to whom does she belong? She belongs to him. The same principle applies.

Adam was to have been the king of heaven and Eve his queen. To restore these original positions requires following the principle of creation. From the beginning of creation God laid down the law of eternal love to be fulfilled by Adam and Eve, so it has to be observed. Were God to disregard this law, it would be tantamount to destroying the law of Heaven.

God set up this heavenly law. If He were to negate it, that would be tantamount to negating humankind and to negating Himself as the absolute Creator. That is why God had no alternative but to bring order through a course of re-creation. Who has known its long and painful history? (207:272, November 11, 1990)

How grieved was God that His enemy deprived Him of His throne! Unable to become the glorious God, He became the long-suffering and sorrowful God. Although He is rightfully the King of His kingdom and the King of the universe, God has been mistreated as if He were dead. His enemy robbed Him of His ideal and violated His beloved children. The planet Earth has fully become His enemy's plaything. (105:199, October 21, 1979)

Why is God's heart full of grief? It is because of Satan. It is because human beings planted Satan's blood and flesh through partaking of his false love. It is because they sowed the Devil's seeds, which propagated as the Devil's families. God wished to rejoice, singing, "May my families live with true love for ten thousand years under Heaven's dominion!" However, with the appearance of the Devil's families multiplying throughout the world, God's dreams were shattered. (214:282, February 3, 1991)

Can you imagine how much it breaks God's heart to observe human misery every hour of every day? What happened to God's dignity when His sons and daughters, whom He intended to glorify as princes and princesses, became cripples, fell into a pit filled with dung and were stuck upside-down in hell? What became of the dignity of the omniscient and omnipotent God, of the absolute God? Can He show His face? (218:240, August 19, 1991)

As long as human beings live in despair, God also lives in despair. As long as Satan shackles human beings on earth, the world of darkness under his dominion will remain also in the spirit world. (2:246, June 9, 1957)

2. God's Painful Struggle to Save Humankind

When man is sore troubled, the Shekhinah says, "How heavy is My head, how heavy is My arm." If God suffers so for the blood of the wicked, how much more for the blood of the righteous.

Mishnah, Sanhedrin 6.5 (Judaism)

O Jerusalem, Jerusalem, killing the prophets and stoning those who are sent to you! How often would I have gathered your children together as a hen gathers her brood under her wings, and you would not!

Matthew 23.37

"In all their afflictions He was afflicted" (Isaiah 63.9). So God said to Moses, "Do you not notice that I dwell in distress when the Israelites dwell in distress? Know from the place whence I speak with you, from the midst of thorns [the Burning Bush], it is as if I stand in their distresses."

Exodus Rabbah (Judaism)

When Israel was a child, I loved him,
and out of Egypt I called My son.
The more I called them,
the more they went from Me;
they kept sacrificing to the Baals,
and burning incense to idols.

Yet it was I that taught Ephraim to walk,
I took him up in My arms;
but they did not know that I healed them.
I led them with cords of compassion,
with the bands of love,
and I became to them as one
who eases the yoke on their jaws,
and I bent down to them and fed them.

Hosea 11.1-4

The Enlightened One, because He saw mankind drowning in the great sea of birth, death and sorrow, and longed to save them, for this was moved to pity.

Because He saw the men of the world straying in false paths, and none to guide them, for this He was moved to pity.

Because He saw that they lay wallowing in the mire of the Five Lusts, in dissolute abandonment, for this He was moved to pity.

Because He saw them still fettered to their wealth, their wives and their children, knowing not how to cast them aside, for this He was moved to pity.

Because He saw them doing evil with hand, heart, and tongue, and many times receiving the bitter fruits of sin, yet ever yielding to their desires, for this He was moved to pity.

Because He saw that they slaked the thirst of the Five Lusts as it were with brackish water, for this He was moved to pity.

Because He saw that though they longed for happiness, they made for themselves no karma of happiness; and though they hated pain, yet willingly made for themselves a karma of pain; and though they coveted the joys of heaven, would not follow His commandments on earth, for this He was moved to pity.

Because He saw them afraid of birth, old age, and death, yet still pursuing the works that lead to birth, old age, and death, for this He was moved to pity.

Because He saw them consumed by the fires of pain and sorrow, yet knowing not where to seek the still waters of samadhi, for this He was moved to pity.

Because He saw them living in an evil time, subjected to tyrannous kings and suffering many ills, yet heedlessly following after pleasure, for this He was moved to pity.

Because He saw them living in a time of wars, killing and wounding one another; and knew that for the riotous hatred that had flourished in their hearts they were doomed to pay an endless retribution, for this He was moved to pity.

Because many born at the time of His incarnation had heard Him preach the Holy Law, yet could not receive it, for this He was moved to pity.

Because some had great riches that they could not bear to give away, for this He was moved to pity.

Because He saw the men of the world plowing their fields, sowing the seed, trafficking, huckstering, buying, and selling; and at the end winning nothing but bitterness, for this He was moved to pity.[31]

Upasaka Sila Sutra (*Buddhism*)

Teachings of Sun Myung Moon

It is natural that we want to protect our loved ones, even with our very life. Such is the original ideal of creation. The same is true for God, who loves His children. He became a sorrowful God who has had to invest His very life. (206:24, October 3, 1990)

I cannot count the days I spent in tears and lamentation after I came to know this world of God's inner heart. Who could even dare to imagine that God was stricken with grief? He created the first human ancestors as His children and tried to raise them to be His eternal object partners in true love, yet they took the path of the Human Fall. Who could imagine God's misery and humiliation, even as He walked His providence of salvation for tens of thousands of years? Anger exploded within Him over the injustice of it all. His heart sighed in lamentation. God should be the Father and King of glory, but the enemy Satan stole His throne and His position as Parent. Although God is clearly alive and carrying out His providence, people say, "God is dead," and they mock and mistreat Him. Still, He perseveres on the path with patient endurance, waiting for the day when human beings will come to understand this truth.

Because God conducts His providence on a foundation of true love—which calls us to live for the sake of others—and on the basis of eternity, He does not just annihilate the universe and begin again after seeing His children descend into the bottomless pit of the Human Fall. With the power of His omniscience and omnipotence, He could have judged the world and Satan at once, smashing them to pieces. Though He has this power, He chose to absorb all the contempt and accusation into Himself. He voluntarily placed Himself in a prison-like environment, because He is our Father.

Ladies and gentlemen, have you spent even one day before our God, our Father, shedding tears of repentance because you empathize with Him? How can you stand before God and still close your eyes as if to block out how He bites His tongue and endures us human beings, who inherited the lineage of the Devil and became the tools of Satan? How can you be so insensitive to how God anxiously looks forward to the day of His liberation and release? (May 1, 2004)

When Jesus was on the cross, God had to turn away and allow His beloved Son to be killed. Who knew the wretchedness in God's mind and heart at that moment? The Bible does not explain it, but wasn't there some reason why God could not intervene to prevent His Son's death?...

Likewise, we think that God should have stood on the side of His chosen ones. Seeing them suffer persecution wherever they went—beaten, decapitated, and burned in pitch—we might ask, "Why was God not able to prevent this?"[32] Instead, you should think how grievous and distressed God was that He could not exercise His almighty power to save them. How can we still say that He is the Most High God? (64:222, November 12, 1972)

What kind of God is our Father? He has walked the most tragic path through the course of history. He has suffered tragedies more horrible than any human tragedy.

When God saw His children languishing in sorrow and suffering and despair, He did not say, "You deserve it." Our Father worked to save His children pierced with sorrow by placing Himself in greater sorrow; He worked to save His children moaning in pain by going to a place of even greater pain. He did not hesitate even to go to His death to save His children who were on the verge of death.

Once we understand this, how should we live? If we see a pitiful old person on the street, bent over with age, we should think, "That is what my Father must look like as He seeks after me."

When we see a laborer's swollen hands, we should think, "My Father's hands are even more torn up and swollen than his." When we see a pitiful beggar, we should think, "This beggar is not a beggar; instead he is my Father," and humbly bow our heads. God's heart is embedded even in lives that appear insignificant and wretched. We should shed tears with the understanding that each of these people is our Father, and then we should cast aside our dignity and help them. This is the only way we will come to know God. (8:345-46, February 28, 1960)

3. Sharing God's Tears

My grief is beyond healing,
my heart is sick within me.
Hark, the cry of the daughter of my people
from the length and breadth of the land:
"Is the LORD not in Zion?
Is her King not in her?"
Why have they provoked me to anger with
their graven images, and with their foreign
idols?
"The harvest is past,
the summer is ended,
and we are not saved."

For the wound of the daughter of my people is
    my heart wounded,
I mourn, and dismay has taken hold on me.
Is there no balm in Gilead?
Is there no physician there?
Why then has the health of the daughter of my
    people not been restored?
O that my head were waters,
and my eyes a fountain of tears,
that I might weep day and night
for the slain of the daughter of my people![33]

                              Jeremiah 8.18-9.1

Let not those who hope in thee be put to
    shame through me,
O Lord GOD of hosts;
let not those who seek thee be brought to dis-
    honor through me,
O God of Israel.
For it is for thy sake that I have borne
    reproach,
that shame has covered my face.

I have become a stranger to my brethren,
an alien to my mother's sons.
For zeal for thy house has consumed me,
and the insults of those who insult thee have
    fallen on me.

                              Psalm 69.6-9

Do not pray for a thing that you lack, for your prayer will not be accepted. Rather when you wish to pray, pray for the heaviness that is in the Head of the world. For the want of the thing that you lack is [a want] in the indwelling Glory. For man is a part of God, and the want that is in the part is in the whole, and the whole suffers the same want as the part. Therefore let your prayer be directed to the want of the whole.

    Pray continually for God's glory that it may be redeemed from its exile.

                       Israel Baal Shem Tov[34] (Judaism)

Teachings of Sun Myung Moon

People who experience the heart of God in their lives cannot come before God without shedding tears, no matter where they are. They know the original Will of God and struggle to become His sons and daughters. If you are among them, sharing God's Will and desire, He will visit you and weep with you.

    Where are the roots of God's grief? They are inside us. They are inside our nation, this world and all things of creation. We must carry on a movement to eradicate them and restore God's joy. For us, the center of our life of faith should be to experience God's grief. (4:60, March 2, 1958)

Is God deserving of pity? Many people would question why the all-knowing and almighty God needs to be pitied. Still, regardless of how all-knowing and almighty He may be, nothing can relieve Him from the shock of losing His beloved children. If there had been a way for God to find relief from that shock by Himself, He would not have had to suffer through a six-thousand-year course of history. (35:88, October 4, 1970)

God seeks people thirsting for faith and hope and burning with love, who say, "God is in shackles on account of humankind, including me; God was accused by Satan because of me; Jesus died on the cross for me; the Holy Spirit went through a bloody history of struggle on my behalf. God, please give me the strength. I will bring rest and liberation to the Father, to the Son, and to the Holy Spirit." (7:162, August 30, 1959)

God our Parent cannot free Himself from lamentation until all people are free from lamentation. How can any parents be comfortable while their beloved children are in misery? This explains why we should liberate God, who exists in such a state.

How shall we liberate God? Since we live in a realm beset by restrictions, which also restrict God from loving all people, we are responsible to restore the realm of liberation where God can freely love all people. Since we were corrupted through the Fall, we must liberate God by becoming children who are victorious over the Fall. (65:100, November 13, 1972)

As long as God, the Center of the universe, is in anguish, human beings have no way to salvation. Who can lift away the suffering of God? Only someone who experiences the depth of God's suffering in his own life and suffers even beyond that. If God were joyful and happy, then all beings immersed in suffering could hope to find a way to happiness. But how can salvation be possible while God, the center of the universe, is suffering? Therefore, at all cost, we must not let God remain in suffering.

There is no question that the fall of God's children, Adam and Eve, was the pinnacle of God's suffering. God is the Father of humankind and Adam and Eve were His first children. Their fall had a direct impact on God. The resulting separation caused God incredible pain—physically, mentally and emotionally. When they departed [from the Garden of Eden], God must have wept bitter tears. That pain in God's body, mind and heart was the beginning of human suffering; it has continued through history...

However, Adam and Eve did not understand the seriousness of their sin. They might have felt some anguish in their minds and hearts because the left the bosom of God their Father, but they were unable to grasp the gravity of the pain and suffering they caused God. Ever since, God has had to relate to human beings who lack any perception of His suffering heart. For God, this is the ultimate agony.

How can you possibly experience God's heart? By listening to a sermon like this you may feel it conceptually, but you still do not feel His sorrow down to your bones. Consider a woman who loses her parents, husband, and children, as well as all her possessions, in a tragic accident. How would she feel? Although during her lifetime in the fallen world she could see and experience many types of evil and sin, her pain and grief at losing her entire family would be unbearable. How much more shock and grief God must have felt, being completely pure and never having experienced any sin, suffering, or crime.

Today many people commit suicide. Do you think the despair that drives people to commit suicide can be compared to God's despair at the moment Adam and Eve fell? No one but God is truly entitled to use the word 'suffering'... We may experience tragedies in our life, yet as time passes the pain and grief will ease. However, God is a spiritual being. He has no concept of time. During one thousand years or even ten thousand years, the pain of the Human Fall has never left God's mind and heart. Nevertheless, could God not simply cast His suffering out of His heart? More than omniscient and omnipotent, God is absolute in love. (94:34-36, June 26, 1977)

How many tears have you shed for God? Have you ever sought out a way to take on suffering and toil on behalf of God's pain and toil, even though your own limbs might be torn off? You have not tried. In seeking to become God's sons and daughters, you have to shed tears for the purpose of the whole. When you meet God, you should comfort Him with unending tears. Representing the original ancestors, you should say, "Father, I am Thy son (daughter). How great was Thy sorrow upon losing me! How many times throughout history until the present day hast Thou suffered humiliation, pain and extreme hardship from my descendants!"

The almighty, all-knowing God certainly has the authority to judge the entire world and even Satan. Yet God cries out in pain, knowing that even though He is capable of bringing judgment, He cannot destroy the world He toiled to create. Our hearts break when we think of God in this situation. God is not dwelling in a heavenly place. He stands lonely and desolate, accused by Satan, robbed of His foothold by the satanic world… How much have you wept in sympathy with God's situation? The issue comes down to this. (51:111, November 18, 1971)

Father! Humankind knows not Thy sorrowful heart permeating the earth.
Humankind does not know Heaven's sad tears soaking the footprints of human history;
hence we are ignorant of Heaven's endless lamentations encircling our minds and bodies.
We confess that we are descendants of rebellion
who cannot establish our dignity before Heaven or be trusted by Heaven.
Father, no one on earth can stop Thy tears;
no one can hold and comfort Thee in Thy sorrow;
no one can protect Thee on Thy path.
Therefore, the grief on this earth is Heaven's grief permeating the earth;
the sorrow on this earth is Heaven's sorrow permeating the earth;
the frustration on this earth is Heaven's frustration permeating the earth…

When in these last days we despair,
we turn towards Heaven and cry out, "O God, please help us!
"Father, please have compassion on humankind!"
Yet who in this age clings to Thy heart, sharing Thine anguish?
Who clings to Thy mind, weeping with Thee?
If there were such a person,
Thou wouldst call him Thy true son or Thy true daughter,
grasping him or her as Thine object partner on earth. (6:235-36, May 24, 1959)

CHAPTER 7

SALVATION – LIBERATION – ENLIGHTENMENT

Grace

DUE TO HUMANITY'S FALLEN AND DEGRADED CONDITION, IT IS DIFFICULT if not impossible for people to attain the goal and purpose of life unaided. In fact, help is available; God's grace is sufficient support on the journey of faith. The scriptures often emphasize the priority of divine grace; it is present prior to even a glimmer of faith, prompting faith in people who would otherwise be lost and unable to escape their miserable existence.

We have selected passages that describe God as the savior of sinful people. Grace is entirely God's initiative, given regardless of a person's attitude or merit. Furthermore, God's grace far overshadows the merit gained by good works; indeed, nothing can come of a person's good works or austerities endured for the purpose of salvation, in the absence of divine grace.

The section ends with the two parables of the Prodigal Son, one from the New Testament and one from the Lotus Sutra. The teachings of these two stories differ in some respects, yet the theme of divine compassion for errant humanity shines through both. The Buddhist parable's depiction of the father as searching desperately for his son and then patiently working to recover him whole over many years is a fitting description of God's toil through human history to save fallen humanity, according to the teachings of Father Moon.

1. Grace Needful for Salvation

For by grace you have been saved through faith; and this is not your own doing, it is the gift of God—not because of works, lest any man should boast.

Ephesians 2.8

Abu Huraira reported God's Messenger as saying, "There is none whose deeds alone would entitle him to get into Paradise." Someone said, "God's Messenger, not even you?" He replied, "Not even I, but that my Lord wraps me in mercy."

Hadith of Muslim (Islam)

By assuming numerous garbs [of ascetics],
    learning, induced meditation, or stubborn practices,
Has none attained Him.
Says Nanak, By His grace alone does one attain
    to sainthood and enlightenment.

Adi Granth, Gauri Bavan Akkhari, M.5, p. 251 (Sikhism)

The Self is not to be obtained by instruction,
Nor by intellect, nor by much learning.
He is to be obtained only by the one whom He
    chooses.
To such a one the Self reveals His own person.

Mundaka Upanishad 3.2.3; Katha Upanishad 1.2.23 (Hinduism)

Even if you cry your heart out, hurt your eyes by constant weeping and even if you lead the life of an ascetic till the end of the world, all these untiring efforts of yours will not be able to make compensation for a tithe of His good will and kindness, for His bounties and munificence and for His mercy and charity in directing you towards the path of truth and religion.

Nahjul Balagha, Khutba 57 (Shiite Islam)

Now, if it had not been for the plan of redemption, which was laid from the foundation of the world, there could have been no resurrection of the dead. [1]

Book of Mormon, Alma 12.25 (Latter-day Saints)

Since all have sinned and fall short of the glory of God, they are justified by his grace as a gift, through the redemption which is in Christ Jesus, whom God put forward as an expiation by his blood, to be received by faith.

Romans 3.23-25

If, because of one man's trespass, death reigned through that one man, much more will those who receive the abundance of grace and the free gift of righteousness reign in life through the one man Jesus Christ.

Romans 5.17

My grace is sufficient for you, for my power is made perfect in weakness.

2 Corinthians 12.9

We who live in the world, still attached to karmas, can overcome the world by Thy grace alone.

Srimad Bhagavatam 11.2 (Hinduism)

All need grace, for even Abraham, for whose sake grace came plenteously into the world, himself needed grace.

Genesis Rabbah 60.2 (Judaism)

Through Thy power, O Lord,
Make life renovated, real at Thy will.

Avesta, Yasna 34.15 (Zoroastrianism)

Teachings of Sun Myung Moon

Almighty God is the God of love and the God of mercy. He is deeply concerned and grieved over the living death of His children. He knows that people are incapable of breaking their chains and getting rid of their sin by their own efforts. He knows that only one power can bring people to salvation—God Himself. And God, in His mercy, is determined to save this world. (September 18, 1974)

Because God must, in the end, accomplish His Will[2] on earth, He has preserved us although we were perishing. (*Way of God's Will* 1.3)

God is not the kind of God to just stand by while human beings live a fallen existence. He has worked until today to lay the foundation for re-creation through religion, in order to recreate the ideal world that He has purposed from the very beginning. This is God's providence for salvation. (May 10, 1981)

Our ancestors who were expelled from the Garden of Eden were the worst criminals in human history; they have no basis to be proud of themselves. However, because God still has a relationship of heart with them, He endures all ordeals while leading the providence of restoration from Adam, Noah, Moses and Jesus to the present day. Thinking of this grace of God, we should appeal to Him with gratitude for His mercy upon humanity throughout history, not merely for His mercy in the current moment. (16:236, June 19, 1966)

We have nothing that would enable us to relate with the all-knowing and almighty Being. Born as fallen people, our eyes are defiled. Our five senses and all our emotions belong to the secular. We have nothing that would enable us to relate with God. By the principle of heavenly righteousness we have nothing. And yet, one path remains through which we can relate to God: by the principle of love. (149:37, November 11, 1986)

Salvation fundamentally begins when we connect with God's love. However, we became fallen human beings having nothing to do with God's lineage. Atonement is required; this means nothing less than the removal of the original sin. However, since the original sin is carried in the lineage, we fallen human beings cannot resolve this problem on our own, no matter what we do. That is why we need the Messiah. (35:159, October 13, 1970)

> Not due to our own will do we exist,
> not due to our own selves do we enjoy the glory of life,
> and not due to our own efforts can we rejoice today in the presence of our Father,
> but due to the grace mercifully bestowed by our Father,
> who hast toiled through thousands of years of history. (2:280, June 23, 1957)

2. Grace for the Prodigal Son

There was a man who had two sons; and the younger of them said to his father, "Father, give me the share of property that falls to me." And he divided his living between them. Not many days later, the younger son gathered all he had and took his journey into a far country, and there he squandered his property in loose living. And when he had spent everything, a great famine arose in that country, and he began to be in want. So he went and joined himself to one of the citizens of that country, who sent him into his fields to feed swine. And he would gladly have fed on the pods that the swine ate; and no one gave him anything. But when he came to himself he said, "How many of my father's hired servants have bread enough and to spare, but I perish here with hunger! I will arise and go to my father, and I will say to him, 'Father, I have sinned against heaven and before you; I am no longer worthy to be called your son; treat me as one of your hired servants.'" And he arose and came to his father. But while he was yet at a distance, his father saw him and had compassion, and ran and embraced him and kissed him. And the son said to him, "Father, I have sinned against heaven and before you; I am no longer worthy to be called your son." But the father said to his servants, "Bring quickly the best robe, and put it on him; and put a ring on his hand, and shoes on his feet; and bring the fatted calf and kill it, and let us eat and make merry; for this my son was dead, and is alive again; he was lost, and is found." And they began to make merry.

Now his elder son was in the field; and as he came and drew near to the house, he heard music and dancing. And he called one of his servants and asked what this meant. And he said to him, "Your brother has come, and your father has killed the fatted calf, because he has received him safe and sound." But he was angry and refused to go in. His father came out and entreated him, but he answered his father, "Lo, these many years I have served you, and I never disobeyed your command; yet you never gave me a kid, that I might make merry with my friends. But when this son of yours came, who has devoured your living with harlots, you killed for him the fatted calf!" And he said to him, "Son, you are always with me, and all that is mine is yours. It was fitting to make merry and be glad, for this your brother was dead, and is alive; he was lost, and is found."³

Luke 15.11-32: Parable of the Prodigal Son

It is like a youth who, on attaining manhood, leaves his father and runs away. For long he dwells in some other country, ten, or twenty, or fifty years. The older he grows, the more needy he becomes... From the first the father searched for his son but in vain, and meanwhile has settled in a certain city. His home becomes very rich...

At this time, the poor son, wandering through village after village, and passing through countries and cities, at last reaches the city where his father has settled. Always has the father been thinking of his son, yet, though he has been parted from him over fifty years, he has never spoken of the matter to any one, only pondering over it within himself and cherishing regret in his heart, as he reflects, "Old and worn, I own much wealth—gold, silver, and jewels, granaries and treasuries overflowing; but I have no son. Some day my end will come and my wealth will be scattered and lost, for there is no one to whom I can leave it... If I could only get back my son and commit my wealth to him, how contented and happy should I be, with never a further anxiety!"

Meanwhile the poor son, hired for wages here and there, unexpectedly arrives at his father's house... Seeing his father possessed of such great power, he was seized with fear, regretting that he had come to this place, and secretly reflects, "This must be a king, or someone of royal rank; it is no place for me to obtain anything for hire of my labor. I had better go to some poor hamlet, where there is a place for letting out my labor, and food and clothing are easier to get. If I tarry here long, I may suffer oppression and forced service." Reflecting thus, he hastens away.

Meanwhile the rich elder on his lion-seat has recognized his son at first sight, and with great joy in his heart has also reflected, "Now I have some one to whom I may bequeath my treasuries of wealth. Always I have been thinking of this my son, with no means of seeing him; but suddenly he himself has come and my longing is satisfied. Though worn with years, I yearn for him as of old."

Instantly he dispatches his attendants to pursue him quickly and fetch him back. Thereupon the messengers hasten forth to seize him. The poor son, surprised and scared, loudly cries his complaint, "I have committed no offense against you; why should I be arrested?" The messengers all the more hasten to lay hold of him and compel him to go back. Thereupon the poor son, thinking within himself that though he is innocent yet he will be imprisoned, and that now he will surely die, is all the more terrified, faints away and falls prostrate on the ground. The father, seeing this from afar, sends word to the messengers, "I have no need for this man. Do not bring him by force. Sprinkle cold water on his face to restore him to consciousness and do not speak to him any further." Wherefore? The father, knowing that his son's disposition is inferior, knowing that his own lordly position has caused distress to his son, yet convinced that he is his son, tactfully does not say to others, "This is my son."

A messenger says to the son, "I now set you free; go wherever you will." The poor son is delighted, thus obtaining the unexpected. He rises from the ground and goes to a poor hamlet in search of food and clothing. Then the elder, desiring to attract his son, sets up a device. Secretly he sends two men, doleful and shabby in appearance, saying, 'You go and gently say to the poor man, "There is a place for you to work here...we will hire you for scavenging, and we both also will work along with you."' Then the two messengers go in search of the poor son and, having found him, place before him the above proposal. Thereupon the poor son, having received his wages beforehand, joins with them in removing a refuse heap.

His father, beholding the son, is struck with compassion for, and wonder at, him. Another day he sees at a distance, through a window, his son's figure, gaunt, lean, and doleful, filthy and unclean with dirt and dust; thereupon he takes off his strings of jewels, his soft attire, and puts on a coarse, torn and dirty garment, smears his body with dust, takes a basket in his right hand, and with an appearance fear-inspiring says to the laborers, "Get on with your work, don't be lazy." By such a device he gets near to his son, to whom he afterwards says, "Ay, my man, you stay and work here, do not go again elsewhere; I will increase your wages; give whatever you need, bowls, utensils, rice, wheat-flour, salt, vinegar, and so on; have no hesitation; besides there is an old and worn-out servant whom you shall be given if you need him. Be at ease in your mind; I am, as it were, your father; do not be worried again. Wherefore? I am old and advanced in years, but you are young and vigorous; all the time you have been working, you have never been deceitful, lazy, angry or grumbling; I have never seen you, like the other laborers, with such vices as these. From this time forth you shall be as my own begotten son."

Thereupon the elder gives him a new name and calls him a son. Then the poor son, though he rejoices at this happening, still thinks of himself as a humble hireling. For this reason, during twenty years he continues to be employed in scavenging. After this period, there grows mutual confidence between them, and he goes in and out and at his ease, though his abode is still in a small hut.

Then the elder becomes ill and, knowing that he will die before long, says to the poor son, "Now I possess abundance of gold, silver, and precious things, and my granaries and treasuries are full to overflowing. The quantities of these things, and the amounts which should be received and given, I want you to understand in detail. Such is my mind, and you must agree to this my wish. Wherefore? Because now I and you are of the same mind. Be increasingly careful so that there be no waste."

The poor man accepts his instruction and commands, and becomes acquainted with all the goods... but has no idea of expecting to inherit as much as a meal, while his abode is still the original place and he is yet unable to abandon his sense of inferiority.

After a short time has again passed, the father notices that his son's ideas have gradually been enlarged, his aspirations developed, and that he despises his previous state of mind. On seeing that his own end is approaching, he commands his son to come, and gathers together his relatives, and the kings, ministers, warriors, and citizens. When they are all assembled, he addresses them saying, "Now, gentlemen, this is my son, begotten by me. It is over fifty years since, from a certain city, he left me and ran away to endure loneliness and misery. His former name was so-and-so and my name was so-and-so. At that time in that city I sought him sorrowfully. Suddenly in this place I met and regained him. This is really my son and I am really his father. Now all the wealth which I possess belongs entirely to my son, and all my previous disbursements and receipts are known by this son."

When the poor son heard these words of his father, great was his joy at such unexpected news, and thus he thought, "Without any mind for, or effort on my part, these treasures now come of themselves to me."

World-honored One! The very rich elder is the Tathagata, and we are all as the Buddha's sons. The Buddha has always declared that we are his sons. But because of the three sufferings, in the midst of births-and-deaths we have borne all kinds of torments, being deluded and ignorant and enjoying our attachment to trifles. Today the World-honored One has caused us to ponder over and remove the dirt of all diverting discussions of inferior things. In these we have hitherto been diligent to make progress and have got, as it were, a day's pay for our effort to reach Nirvana. Obtaining this, we greatly rejoiced and were contented, saying to ourselves, "For our diligence and progress in the Buddha-law what we have received is ample"... The Buddha, knowing that our minds delighted in inferior things, by his tactfulness taught according to our capacity, but still we did not perceive that we are really Buddha's sons... Therefore we say that though we had no mind to hope or expect it, yet now the Great Treasure of the King of the Law has of itself come to us, and such things that Buddha-sons should obtain, we have all obtained.[4]

Lotus Sutra 4: Parable of the Prodigal Son
(Buddhism)

Teachings of Sun Myung Moon

Parents suffer deeply if their child commits a crime. If he is sent to jail, the parents would not say, "You deserve it!" Instead, they would forgive their child, sympathize with him and shed tears of compassion. Such is parental love. If their child were sentenced to death, the parents—especially the mothers—would wail. They would desperately search for some way to save their child's life, even up until the last minute at the execution site. They would gladly trade their own life for his. That is the precious unchanging love of a parent.

If the heart of human parents moves in this way towards their children, then do you think that God, the Parent of humankind, would do any less? Never! God's love is far greater than human love. Surely the love of God surpasses the love of any earthly parent. (91:148, February 6, 1977)

God has been toiling to recover humankind, even though we deserve to die thousands of times in the realm of death. Never forget that when God comes to us in the realm of death, He bring us something more precious than anything in the world. Understand that when He saves us from the realm of death, He does so with anguish and a worried heart. To claim us from the realm of death, God is willing to sacrifice everything. (6:115-16, April 12, 1959)

No matter what happens in the human world, God is patient because He is who He is. He sees many tragic and heart-breaking things, yet He remains calm and composed, never losing His dignity. If God were to open His mouth and express His suffering, He could pour out tragic stories for millions of years, weeping all the while. Would God weep out of self-pity? No, God weeps only for humankind, His children. (124:60, 830123)

God is our Parent; that is why He loves us although He is high above us. We can draw an analogy to the parents of a disabled child, whose disability is so severe that he cannot recognize their love. The parents feel miserable, yet they cannot help but love their child. Even though their child is unable to appreciate even one one-hundredth of their love, and it grieves the parents to face that, they nevertheless love their child, giving all the time. They yearn to give love one hundred times more, and when they see that their child is unable to appreciate any of it, they experience grief and frustration one hundred times more. Parents yearn to love a child who can fully unite with their love, but parents of a child who cannot relate to their love experience only pain and sorrow. Truly there is no greater heartbreak... Now, can you imagine if it were not a matter of only one child's lifetime, but forever? That is God's miserable and heartbreaking situation, trying to love human beings...

Where is the supreme relationship between Heaven and human beings, linking their deepest hearts? No matter how high we climb and search, since God is the Parent, we humans must seek the position of God's children. Hence in Christianity, God is called Father and we are called God's children.

What is the standard of that parent-child relationship? Is it below or above the line of the Human Fall? It cannot be below it. The standard should be above the level of the Fall.

Even among fallen people today, whose love is below the line of the Fall, the parent-child relationship suffers when children are not dutiful. Imagine, then, how miserable it would be for parents who had never fallen. When we think about the difficult relationships between parents and children around us, we can fathom something of God's situation.

God surely intended to love His children with a love above the line of the Fall. How strong would that love be? Yet since no one has ever stood above the line of the Fall, nobody knows. (62:20, September 10, 1972)

Heavenly Father has been searching for His lost children for six thousand biblical years, while enduring suffering upon suffering. However, if the children whom He finally found were weak and pathetic, how would He feel? It is conceivable that God might lament, "It would have been better had I not found them." Are you confident that you are not children like that? (*Blessing and Ideal Family* 7.4.1)

> Allow us to feel Thy merciful touch,
> the touch of our Father who seeks us,
> carrying the burden of providence for 6,000 years.
> Still, Thou hast not cast us aside,
> although we are foolish and inadequate. (3:258-59, January 12, 1958)

Forgiveness

SOILED BY SIN AND UNWORTHY to enter the presence of God, or corrupted by evil deeds and hence unable to realize our true inner nature, we cry out to God for forgiveness of sins. The experience of divine forgiveness and pardon is universal, reaching to supplicants in all the world's religions. God is always desirous to forgive sins; it is His loving will to do so as our loving Parent.

The opening passages express God's forgiving nature; the concluding texts describe removing sins as a process of cleansing.

1. *God's Forgiveness*

O My servants who have transgressed against their souls! Despair not of the mercy of God: for God forgives all sins: for He is Oft-forgiving, Most Merciful.

Qur'an 39.53

I, I am he who blots out your transgressions for my own sake, and I will not remember your sins.

Isaiah 43.25

In him we have redemption through his blood, the forgiveness of our trespasses, according to the riches of his grace which he lavished upon us.[5]

Ephesians 1.7-8

Though a man be soiled with the sins of a lifetime, let him but love me, rightly resolved, in utter devotion. I see no sinner, that man is holy. Holiness soon shall refashion his nature to peace eternal. O son of Kunti, of this be certain: the man who loves me shall not perish.

Bhagavad-Gita 9.30-31 *(Hinduism)*

God the Almighty has said, "O son of Adam, so long as you call upon Me and ask of Me, I shall forgive you for what you have done, and I shall not mind. O son of Adam, were your sins to reach the clouds of the sky and were you to ask forgiveness of Me, I would forgive you. O son of Adam, were you to come to Me with sins nearly as great as the earth and were you to face Me, ascribing no partner to Me, I would bring you forgiveness nearly as great as it."

Forty Hadith of an-Nawawi 42 (Islam)

Let him utter the name, Buddha Amitayus. Let him do so serenely with his voice uninterrupted; let him be continually thinking of Buddha until he has completed ten times the thought, repeating, "Adoration to Buddha Amitayus." On the strength of [the merit of] uttering the Buddha's name he will, during every repetition, expiate the sins which involve him in births and deaths during eighty million kalpas.[6]

Meditation on Buddha Amitayus 3.30 (Buddhism)

Shining brightly, Agni, drive away
our sin, and shine wealth on us.
Shining bright, drive away our sin.

For good fields, for good homes, for wealth,
we made our offerings to Thee.
Shining bright, drive away our sin...

So that Agni's conquering beams
may spread out on every side,
Shining bright, drive away our sin.

Thy face is turned on every side,
Thou pervadest everywhere.
Shining bright, drive away our sin.[7]

Rig Veda 1.97.1-6 (Hinduism)

Teachings of Sun Myung Moon

God has already forgiven us our sins. Do you think it would be possible for God to forgive us if He still thought that we were sinners? He forgives us because He looks at us with endless compassion. You should know that through forgiveness, all can be united as one. (41:333, February 18, 1972)

Great forgiveness is possible only when one understands the other person's situation one hundred percent. Because God knows our situation, He forgives us. (2:220, May 26, 1957)

No one can criticize a parent who forgives a child who repents for his or her sin. No one can accuse that parent for not punishing the child. That is why Satan cannot accuse God for loving humankind and trying to save them. Satan cannot make accusations against a person of perfect love. On the contrary, Satan voluntarily surrenders before him. The law requiring punishment yields to Heavenly Father's love, by which He forgives repentant sinners. (62:52, September 10, 1972)

We know the shame of our first human ancestors before Heaven; we know that throughout history people have lived shameful lives; we know that the world we are living in is shameful. What can we be proud of before God? Can we be proud of ourselves as individuals? No… we are not qualified to approach God. Therefore, we should be willing to do anything that God wants us to do, anything that will make Him happy, anything that will allow Him to overlook our shame, in order that we might be forgiven of our sins. (66:18, March 11, 1973)

2. Cleansing and Purification

On this day shall atonement be made for you, to cleanse you; from all your sins you shall be clean before the LORD.

Leviticus 16.30

Have mercy on me, O God,
according to thy steadfast love;
according to thy abundant mercy blot out my transgressions.
Wash me thoroughly from my iniquity,
and cleanse me from my sin!
For I know my transgressions,
and my sin is ever before me.

Against thee, thee only, have I sinned,
and done that which is evil in thy sight,
so that thou art justified in thy sentence
and blameless in thy judgment.
Behold, I was brought forth in iniquity,
and in sin did my mother conceive me.

Behold, thou desirest truth in the inward being;
therefore teach me wisdom in my secret heart.
Purge me with hyssop, and I shall be clean;
wash me, and I shall be whiter than snow.
Fill me with joy and gladness;
let the bones which thou hast broken rejoice.
Hide thy face from my sins,
and blot out all my iniquities.
Create in me a clean heart, O God,
and put a new and right spirit within me.

Psalm 51.1-10

Thus hearing the litany, and that there be no blot of sin in the court or the country,
May the deities bestow their purification that no offense remain, and
As the wind blows from its origin to carry away the clouds of heaven,
Even as the wind of morning and the wind of evening clears away the morning and evening mists,
As the ship in harbor casts off its moorings stem and stern to be borne out onto the great plain of the sea, and
As the rank grasses beyond the river are swept away with the clean stroke of the scythe—
Even so, may the deity Seoritsuhime-no-kami,
Dwelling in the swift-flowing stream that falls from the high mountains and low hills,
Carry away these sins and pollutions without remain, to the wide sea plain.

Our sins thus swept away, may the goddess Hayaakitsuhime-no-kami,
Who lives in the stream of the sea plain,
Open wide her great mouth to engulf those sins and impurities, and
When they are thus imbibed,
May the god Ibukidonushi-no-kami,
Dwelling in the place where breath is breathed,
Blow them out with a great rushing breath.
And when he has thus banished them to the underworld,
May the goddess Hayasasurahime-no-kami disperse them once and all.

Even in this way, may the sins of all in the realm,
from officials of the court on down,
every transgression within the land be washed away.[8]

Engishiki 8 (Shinto)

Teachings of Sun Myung Moon

Just as the ocean takes in all manner of sewage and muddy water and then cleanses it, God, the original entity of absolute true love, resolutely works to cleanse the human world that deviated from the principles of His creation. (December 27, 2002)

Father! Please purify the minds and hearts of all Thy children who kneel before Thee.
Work with Thy purifying touch in the soul of each one here.
Please reveal all that is in each of our minds and bodies, Father, and sanctify everything.
Since it will not do unless all improper elements are separated out and cast away,
O Father, please personally be the Lord who purifies us
and the Lord of our hearts. (1:162, July 11, 1956)

Atonement

SIN CANNOT BE REMOVED UNLESS SOMEONE TAKES RESPONSIBILITY to make expiation for the transgression. This is the concept of atonement. Atonement is required because of God's lawful nature, which requires that the object of His love be worthy to receive it. The predicament of the sinner is made worse by Satan's accusation, which serve to remind God of sins he might rather overlook. Therefore, some act of sacrifice is needed to pay the debt, clear away the sin, and remove the obstacle to full forgiveness and fellowship between God and human beings.

In Christianity, Jesus Christ offers himself on the cross as atonement for sin. This is the ultimate atonement: a sinless man dying to save sinners. And yet, Jesus' atoning death on the cross is an example of a larger principle, as vicarious atonement can occur in many situations: a priest offers a sacrifice for sins of the worshippers, a good man pays with his life for the sins of the community, or a patriot sheds his blood on the altar of his nation. In each case, a righteous person's sacrifice provides atonement for many.

1. The Principle of Atonement

When God desires to give healing to the world He smites one righteous man among them with disease and suffering, and through him gives healing to all... A righteous man is never afflicted save to bring healing to his generation and to make atonement for it. The 'other side' prefers that punishment should light upon the virtuous man rather than on any other; it would disregard the world on account of the joy it finds in having power over him.

Zohar 5.218a (Judaism)

Aaron shall offer the bull as a sin offering for himself, and shall make atonement for himself and for his house. Then he shall take the two goats, and set them before the LORD at the door of the tent of meeting; and Aaron shall cast lots upon the two goats, one lot for the LORD and the other lot for Azazel. And Aaron shall present the goat on which the lot fell for the LORD, and offer it as a sin offering; but the goat on which the lot fell for Azazel shall be presented alive before the LORD to make atonement over it... He shall kill the goat of the sin offering which is for the people, and bring its blood within the veil, and sprinkle it upon the mercy seat and before the mercy seat; thus he shall make atonement for the holy place, because of the uncleanness of the people of Israel... And Aaron shall lay both his hands upon the head of the live goat, and confess over him all the iniquities of the people of Israel, and all their transgressions, all their sins; and he shall put them upon the head of the goat, and send him away into the wilderness by the hand of a man who is in readiness. The goat shall bear all their iniquities upon him to a solitary land... And it shall be a statute to you forever that in the seventh month, on the tenth day of the month... on this day shall atonement be made for you, to cleanse you; from all your sins you shall be clean before the LORD.⁹

Leviticus 16.6-30

Surely he has borne our griefs and carried our sorrows;
yet we esteemed him stricken,
smitten by God, and afflicted.
But he was wounded for our transgressions,
he was bruised for our iniquities;
upon him was the chastisement that made us whole,
and with his stripes we are healed.
All we like sheep have gone astray;
we have turned every one to his own way;
and the LORD has laid on him the iniquity of us all.[10]

Isaiah 53.4-6

Teachings of Sun Myung Moon

In the Old Testament Age, the chosen people of Israel made atonement through offering ceremonies involving the shedding of blood. But they did not know the principle behind it. God is the owner of all creation. However, the sacrificial offering represented the people. It was divided into two: one part was taken by God and the other, by Satan. (309:203, May 30, 1999)

What is meant by indemnity? No human being could possibly pay all his debt of sin. Even if he tried for his entire lifetime, he would die with the debt still unpaid. Therefore, salvation requires that there be a way to lighten the debt and shorten the period to pay it off. God would shorten the period to, say, one year. However, at that point Satan makes accusations and insists that God cannot be so lenient; he demands a greater payment, one that might require ten years. Then what happens? God and Satan agree to a compromise.

In other words, there is a struggle between God and Satan. Satan demands that human beings pay a great deal of the debt as is their due, while God only asks people to pay a small amount as a condition to forgive the whole debt. Actually, Satan is correct from the viewpoint of principle: debts should be paid in full. Yet, God is correct from the viewpoint of love, in seeking a way to reconnect human beings with His love. And love is the very core of the principle. (111:147, February 10, 1981)

We received the amazing grace of forgiveness of our sins thanks to the altars of blood erected by the many saints and sages.[11] (9:161, May 8, 1960)

Why has God patiently made sacrifice after sacrifice, developing His providence to the worldwide level? For whom has God made these sacrifices? Not for America, nor for Christianity; God did it to save me. God sent the Jesus Christ and allowed him to die on the cross for me, for my salvation. God then raised up the Christian church, established it throughout the world, and prepared it for the Second Coming in these Last Days—all for me. (77:46, March 30, 1975)

There are several categories of people who go to the spirit world. One group lives out their full span of life; another group does not. Among those who go to the spirit world earlier than their given life span, there are two categories: those who are being punished for their sins, and those who are taken as indemnity conditions for the sins of the world.

There is a saying that if in a village three exemplary young men die in their prime, great blessings will come to that village. The same is true for a clan: if three great young men die in a clan, that clan will receive many blessings. That is, to deserve blessings a price must be paid. This is by the law of cause and effect: it applies everywhere.

When God lets one central person, worthy of one thousand people, go the path of death, if those one thousand people are moved by his love and are determined to live like him, taking after his example, they will enter that person's realm of benefit. People want to follow the path of a patriot or a saint because they want to enter the same realm of benefit.

Last year, many of our church members went to the spirit world, and it will be the same this year as well. Although I do not speak of it, I am already aware it will happen. Why is it so? Every time we take another step forward, we must pay indemnity for it. (33:11, July 28, 1970)

You should become like a chief priest, repenting of the past on behalf of your people and making an offering of atonement before God. In order to make such an offering, you should share your people's path of tribulation. This is a principle in approaching God. (13:265, April 12, 1964)

2. Atonement by the Sacrifice of Jesus Christ

Since all have sinned and fall short of the glory of God, they are justified by his grace as a gift, through the redemption which is in Christ Jesus, whom God put forward as an expiation by his blood, to be received by faith. This was to show God's righteousness, because in his divine forbearance he had passed over former sins; it was to prove at the present time that he himself is righteous and that he justifies him who has faith in Jesus.

Romans 3.23-26

But when Christ appeared as the high priest of the good things that have come, then through the greater and more perfect tent (not made with hands, that is, not of this creation) he entered once and for all into the Holy Place, taking not the blood of goats and calves but his own blood, thus securing an eternal redemption. For if the sprinkling of defiled persons with the blood of goats and bulls and with the ashes of a heifer sanctifies for the purification of the flesh, how much more shall the blood of Christ, who through the eternal Spirit offered himself without blemish to God, purify your conscience from dead works to serve the living God.[12]

Hebrews 9.11-14

In this is love, not that we loved God but that he loved us and sent his Son to be the expiation for our sins. Beloved, if God so loved us, we also ought to love one another.

1 John 4.10-11

For it is impossible to restore again to repentance those who have once been enlightened, who have tasted the heavenly gift, and have become partakers of the Holy Spirit, and have tasted the goodness of the word of God and the powers of the age to come, if they then commit apostasy, since they crucify the Son of God on their own account and hold him up to contempt.

Hebrews 6.4-6

Teachings of Sun Myung Moon

Jesus Christ came to the earth to save humanity, bringing with him the glory, love and eternal life of God. Yet there was one condition that obstructed his way. This was none other than sin—sin intertwined like a gigantic steel net, woven through this person and that person, this organization and that organization, this society and that society, this nation and that nation. Jesus willingly offered himself to eradicate sin; otherwise we could not see the glory of God on this earth; nor could we know the love of God or the life of God. (1:167, July 11, 1956)

When someone owes a huge debt, if the creditor displays good will in forgiving a portion of the debt, then the debtor can pay back less than the total amount and still satisfy the entire debt. The outstanding example of this is redemption through the cross. Merely by fulfilling a small indemnity condition of faith in Jesus, we receive the much greater grace of salvation, which entitles us to participate with Jesus in the same resurrection. (*Exposition of the Divine Principle*, Restoration 1.1)

Many Christians believe that the omniscient, omnipotent, benevolent and loving God forgives us even though we commit sins tens of thousands of times. Then as soon as they go outside the church door they start fighting again. A church is not a house of forgiveness, dispensing forgiveness to people who commit sins unceasingly.

If God could forgive sins so lightly, why would He not forgive the one sin that was committed in the Garden of Eden? Furthermore, if God could find a way to forgive Satan, would He not have done it? Surely He would. Nevertheless, God cannot forgive Satan's sin, which transgressed the core principle of the universe. For God to forgive that sin would be to fundamentally undermine the universal law of love, causing the world, which was created for love, to fall into chaos. Satan violated God Himself. This cannot be forgiven.

This is why God had to set up the Providence of Restoration to enable humans to reach the standard prior to the Human Fall. By this means, when people reach that standard, Satan can be expelled and a new perfect Adam can appear. It has taken God six thousand years to prepare that foundation. (19:161, January 1, 1968)

Enlightenment

ENLIGHTENMENT MEANS DISPELLING THE DARKNESS OF IGNORANCE. According to the manner in which Reality is perceived in the different traditions, enlightenment may be either the intuitive grasping of inner wisdom, illumination by the truth of the Word, or direct apprehension of transcendent Reality. The true self, formerly obscured by false habits of thinking and vain desires, is suddenly revealed. The inner eye, which was blinded by defilements of worldly living, opens to a vision of the true Reality. From that moment life can never be the same, as the enlightened person begins to live by the knowledge he has acquired.

There is rational enlightenment, the cognition of truth. Knowledge of God's Word enlightens the mind, lighting a marked-out path to a person formerly lost in the darkness of ignorance. Father Moon is one with the Christian tradition in teaching that the Word of God can transform lives.

A second group of passages describe enlightenment as self-realization, the inward experience of finding one's original mind, the God within. This describes the experience of salvation in Hinduism and Buddhism, yet is common to most religions. This can be a soul-shaking experience, as the mind opens to receive massive amounts of energy. Having stripped away everything false, the enlightened mind corresponds to the standard of the Divine Mind, setting up a powerful connection. Father Moon encourages every person to gain such an experience on the path to wholeness and completion. He teaches that no amount of conceptual knowledge or faith can substitute for realization of the God within.

Finally, there is shamanistic enlightenment, which opens the five spiritual senses and enables one to see, hear and sense the invisible spirit world. With proper training, anyone can access this knowledge and source of spiritual power.

1. The Light of True Knowledge

Your word is a lamp to my feet and a light to my path.

Psalm 119.105

The truth has come, and falsehood has vanished away. Surely falsehood is ever certain to vanish.

Qur'an 17.85

Jesus spoke to them, saying "I am the light of the world; he who follows me will not walk in darkness, but will have the light of life."

John 8.12

You will know the truth, and the truth will make you free.

John 8.32

As sight is in the body, so is reason in the soul.

Aristotle, Nicomachean Ethics 1.6 (Hellenism)

The holy Preceptor by the Word lighted a lamp;
Thereby was shattered darkness of the temple
    of the self,
And the unique chamber of jewels thrown open.
Wonderstruck were we in extreme on
    beholding it—
Its greatness beyond expression.

Adi Granth, Bilaval, M.5, p. 821 (Sikhism)

To know the eternal is called enlightenment
Not to know the eternal is to act blindly, to
    result in disaster.
He who knows the eternal is all-embracing.
Being all-embracing, he is impartial.
Being impartial, he is kingly [universal].
Being kingly, he is one with Nature.
Being one with nature, he is in accord with Tao.
Being in accord with Tao, he is everlasting,
And is free from danger throughout his lifetime.

Tao Te Ching 16 (Taoism)

It is wonderful, Lord! It is wonderful, Lord! It is as if, Lord, one might set upright that which had been upturned, or might reveal what was hidden, or might point out the path to one who had gone astray, or might bring an oil lamp into the darkness so that those with eyes might see material shapes.

Udana 49 (Buddhism)

When they listen to that which has been revealed unto the Messenger, you see their eyes overflow with tears because of their recognition of the Truth. They say, "Our Lord, we believe. Inscribe us as among the witnesses."

Qur'an 5.83

Teachings of Sun Myung Moon

For fallen people, knowledge is the light of life holding the power of revival, while ignorance is the shadow of death and the cause of ruin. Ignorance cannot beget true sentiments, and in the absence of knowledge and emotion the will to act cannot arise. Without the proper functioning of emotion, intellect and will, one cannot live the life of a true human being.

If we are created in such a way that we cannot live apart from God, then surely our ignorance of God consigns us to walk miserable paths. Though we may diligently study the Bible, can we really say that we know clearly the reality of God? Can we ever grasp the heart of God?...

The heart of God: His heart of joy at the time of creation; the broken heart He felt when humankind, His children whom He could not abandon, rebelled against Him; and His heart of striving to save them throughout the long course of history. (*Exposition of the Divine Principle*, Introduction)

Today the world is in need of a great spiritual enlightenment. Individuals, nations and the world as a whole must achieve a new understanding of the existence of God. We should have an encounter with God, through which we can restore and secure our original inseparable relationship with Him. (234:241, August 22, 1992)

The day of the Second Coming is the time when we wake up to the reality that God is our Parent, and we shed tears with Him. We open our eyes to discover that God is our True Parent, and for six thousand years He has grieved over the sorrow of humankind and wandered in search of us. God grieved for us long before we knew of our plight. When everything that has inflicted deep pain in the historical heart of God is thus revealed, I can truly call God "My Father" and He can call me "My son." This is the day of the final awakening.

On that day, our hearts are filled with tremendous hope and determination to right the wrongs of history and stand up for God's providence. On that day, we experience joy as if God's entire purpose were fulfilled. It is like the feeling we would have experienced had we reached perfection, never having fallen. (6:155, April 19, 1959)

2. Inner Enlightenment

Brahman is all in all.
He is action, knowledge, goodness supreme.
To know Him, hidden in the lotus of the heart,
is to untie the knot of ignorance.
Mundaka Upanishad 2.1.10 (Hinduism)

In the golden city of the heart dwells
The Lord of Love, without parts, without stain.
Know Him as the radiant light of lights.

There shines not the sun, neither moon nor star,
Nor flash of lightning, nor fire lit on earth.
The Lord is the light reflected by all.
He shining, everything shines after Him.
Mundaka Upanishad 2.2.10-11 (Hinduism)

God is the Light of the heavens and the earth.
The parable of His Light
is as if there were a Niche,
and within it a Lamp;
the Lamp enclosed in Glass:
The Glass as it were a brilliant star:
Lit from a blessed Tree,
an olive neither of the East nor of the West,
Whose oil is well-nigh luminous,
though fire scarce touched it.
Light upon Light!
God guides whom He will to His Light:
God sets forth parables for men, and God knows all things.[13]
Qur'an 24.35

Even as a mirror stained by dust
Shines brilliantly when it has been cleansed,
So the embodied one, on seeing the nature of the Self,
Becomes unitary, his end attained, from sorrow freed.
Svetasvatara Upanishad 2.14 (Hinduism)

The Self within the heart is like a boundary which divides the world from That. Day and night cross not that boundary, nor old age, nor death; neither grief nor pleasure, neither good nor evil deeds. All evil shuns That. For That is free from impurity: by impurity can it never be touched.

Wherefore he who has crossed that boundary and has realized the Self, if he is blind, ceases to be blind; if he is wounded, ceases to be wounded; if he is afflicted, ceases to be afflicted. When that boundary is crossed, night becomes day; for the world of Brahman is light itself.

Chandogya Upanishad 4.1-2 *(Hinduism)*

The Sixth Patriarch was pursued by the monk Myo as far as Taiyu Mountain. The patriarch, seeing Myo coming, laid the Robe and bowl [of office] on a rock and said, "This robe represents the faith; it should not be fought over. If you want to take it away, take it now." Myo tried to move it, but it was as heavy as a mountain and would not budge. Faltering and trembling, he cried out, "I came for the Dharma, not for the robe. I beg you, please give me your instruction."

The patriarch said, "Think neither good nor evil. At this very moment, what is the original self of the monk Myo?" At these words, Myo was directly illuminated. His whole body was covered with sweat. He wept and bowed, saying, "Besides the secret words and secret meaning you have just now revealed to me, is there anything else, deeper still?" The patriarch said, "What I have told you is no secret at all. When you look into your own true self, whatever is deeper is found right there."[14]

Mumonkan 23 *(Buddhism)*

Teachings of Sun Myung Moon

Whatever difficulties you face, do not ask others, but ask your own conscience. When you pray, do not pray vaguely. God gave you an original mind, so you should be united with that precious gift. Once you are united with it, you will know everything about yourself. Once you have cultivated your heart and mind, you can be tuned to God's heart and mind. (307:216, November 21, 1998)

Even though I am your teacher, my teachings cannot connect you eternally to God. It is your task to find your original heart. You have to hear the calling of Heaven through your mind's ears. You have to see the divine nature through your mind's eyes. You have to feel the heart of Heaven through your mind's senses…

We have thought that God was the only precious existence, but now we should understand that our minds are just as precious. By finding the nucleus of your mind, you can attain the high standard of value by which God can make a relationship with you. Otherwise, how can you be in alignment with Heaven's principles?…

Today's believers frequently take comfort from their conceptual beliefs and their world of faith. Yet although we are fallen, our minds contain elements of the ideal of creation by which we can commune with the eternal God. What, after all, is the purpose of prayer? Why do Buddhists seek a state of emptiness through Zen meditation? It is to awaken the elements that lie at the nucleus of the mind. (2:192-93, May 19, 1957)

Shakyamuni Buddha said, "In heaven and earth, I alone am the Honored One." In what state did he teach this? If you were to enter that state of resonance, you would become one with God. In that state, you would be able to see thousands of years of human history unfold before your eyes. You would experience yourself as having that incredible value.

How can we humans escape from the painful cycle of suffering, life after life? How can we escape from our miserable life's destiny that ends in the cemetery? This is the homework given to each of us. In order to solve this, we have to receive training to enter the realm of resonance.

When mind and body have the same power, they fight. We must establish the mind over the body. There are two ways: The first way is by weakening the body through conditions such as fasting, prayer vigils, etc., and then to drag about the weakened body for several months. After a while, even when the body is comfortable, it will obey the mind out of its newly acquired habit. If you reach that state, you will experience Heaven's help bringing you success in what you do…

The second way to establish the mind's dominion over the body… is to give more energy to the mind. Make continual efforts to give energy to the mind. When these efforts accumulate to a certain point, the door of your mind will open. Once that door opens, you will gain immense power. If you strengthen the mind's power at least three times over, then you will have no problem with the body. People make many conditions in the religious life to focus the mind's power to lead the body.

Once you attain spiritual enlightenment, you gain great power in your mind. Then, if you yield to your body's desires, you will feel nauseous and want to vomit. A person who has attained spiritual enlightenment has strong mental power; hence his body follows the mind's desires automatically…

All religions teach this as the way to reach an advanced stage in the life of a human being. Following this way, and centered on God's love, you will enter a realm of high dimension—when you realize on your own that you are sons and daughters of God. That is why Buddha said, "In heaven and earth, I alone am the Honored One." A person who has attained enlightenment is the source of his own authority; that is why he has the right to boast of how precious he is.

By becoming a son or daughter who receives the unique love of God, you are in a position to inherit everything that is God's. You realize that you are of yourself an elevated being. The path of every human being ends here, in the realm of God's love. (38:270-73, January 8, 1971)

3. Opening the Third Eye

I am blind and do not see the things of this world; but when the light comes from above, it enlightens my heart and I can see, for the Eye of my heart sees everything; and through this vision I can help my people. The heart is a sanctuary at the center of which there is a little space, wherein the Great Spirit dwells, and this is the Eye. This is the Eye of the Great Spirit by which He sees all things, and through which we see Him. If the heart is not pure, the Great Spirit cannot be seen.

Black Elk (Native American Religions)

The enlightenment consists of a mysterious light which the shaman suddenly feels in his body, inside his head, within the brain, an inexplicable searchlight, a luminous fire…for he can now, even with closed eyes, see through darkness and perceive things and coming events which are hidden from others: thus they look into the future and into the secrets of others.

The candidate obtains this mystical light after long hours of waiting, sitting on a bench in his hut and invoking the spirits. When he experiences it for the first time, it is as if the house in which he is suddenly rises, he sees far ahead of him, through mountains, exactly as if the earth were one great plain, and his eyes could reach to the end of the earth. Nothing is hidden from him any longer; not only can he see things far, far away, but he can also discover souls, stolen souls, which are either kept concealed in far, strange lands or have been taken up or down to the Land of the Dead.

Iglulik Eskimo Shaman Initiation
(Native American Religions)

Teachings of Sun Myung Moon

Most people do not know the spirit world. They know only the world they perceive through their five senses. However, when we directly relate to God in true love, we can cultivate our ten senses— the five physical senses and beyond them, the five spiritual senses. This will enable us to resonate with the spirit world.

People who only seek self-centered love cannot achieve it. Fallen love is dark; it is destruction itself. The more you immerse yourself in fallen love, the more darkness will envelop you. It is as if an insulator covered your electrical terminal; no electricity can flow. (399:220, December 24, 2002)

Cognition of spiritual reality begins when it is perceived through the five senses of the spirit self. These perceptions resonate through the five physical senses and are felt physiologically. Cognition of truth, on the other hand, arises from the knowledge gleaned from the physical world as it is perceived directly through our physiological sense organs. Cognition thus takes place through both spiritual and physical processes.

Human beings become complete only when their spirit self and physical self are unified. Hence, the experience of divine inspiration gained through spiritual cognition and the knowledge of truth obtained through physical cognition should become fully harmonized and awaken the spirituality and intellect together. It is only when the spiritual and physical dimensions of cognition resonate together that we can thoroughly comprehend God and the universe. (*Exposition of the Divine Principle*, Eschatology 5.1)

Liberation

THE SPIRITUAL FREEDOM EXPERIENCED BY PEOPLE WHO ARE RELEASED from the fetters of desires and attachments to worldly things is called Liberation (*moksha*). It is an inner experience of freedom that can arise regardless of the person's external circumstances: The saint is free even in prison, while people living in comfort and affluence may be caught in dire bondage to runaway desires, addictions, and bad relationships. The Christian scriptures speak of a comparable experience of Christian liberty.

Yet liberation goes beyond the individual. Jesus spoke about liberating the prisoners and a Kingdom of freedom. When people live in the spirit of love and self-giving, they can be very free with one another. If everyone in a family or society enjoyed the inner freedom of a God-centered life, they then could live and act in freedom. Therefore, Father Moon teaches, liberating others also expands our own realm of liberation. That liberation should expand to encompass societies, nations, the entire world, and beyond to the realm of God. Jewish Kabbalistic doctrine describes the task of liberating of the "divine sparks" residing in each thing, that they may rise up and rejoin the divine unity. God's liberation is contingent upon human liberation, teaches Father Moon, because human suffering and oppression binds God in fetters of grief and pain. Liberating humanity also liberates God, and when God is liberated, humanity can be truly free.

1. The State of Inner Freedom

That disciplined man with joy and light within,
Becomes one with God and reaches the freedom that is God's.

Bhagavad-Gita 5.24 (Hinduism)

Desire is a chain, shackled to the world, and it is a difficult one to break. But once that is done, there is no more grief and no more longing; the stream has been cut off and there are no more chains.

Sutta Nipata 948 (Buddhism)

The fetters of the heart are broken, all doubts are resolved, and all works cease to bear fruit [of karma], when He is beheld who is both high and low.

Mundaka Upanishad 2.2.8 (Hinduism)

Yea, happily he lives, the brahmin set free,
Whom lusts defile not, who is cooled and loosed from bonds,
Who has all barriers burst, restraining his heart's pain.
Happy the calm one lives who wins peace of mind.

Anguttara Nikaya 1.137 (Buddhism)

Open yourself, create free space;
release the bound one from his bonds!
Like a newborn child, freed from the womb,
be free to move on every path!

Atharva Veda 6.121.4 (Hinduism)

Now the Lord is the Spirit, and where the Spirit of the Lord is, there is freedom.

2 Corinthians 3.17

Immediately after attaining release from all karmas, the soul goes up to the end of the universe. Previously driven [by karmas], the soul is free from the bonds of attachment, the chains have been snapped, and it is its nature to dart upwards. The liberated self, in the absence of the karmas which had led it to wander in different directions in different states of existence, darts upwards as its nature is to go up.

Ratnakarandasravakacara 10 (Jainism)

The wind blows where it wills, and you hear the sound of it, but you do not know whence it comes or whither it goes; so it is with every one who is born of the Spirit.

John 3.8

He whose corruptions are destroyed, he who is not attached to food, he who has Deliverance, which is void and signless, as his object—his path, like that of birds in the air, cannot be traced.[15]

Dhammapada 93 (Buddhism)

One that the Lord's command in mind cherishes,
Is truly to be called *Jivan-mukta* (liberated while living).
To such a one are joy and sorrow alike;
Ever in joy, never feels he sorrow.
Gold and a clod of earth to him are alike,
As also nectar and foul-tasting poison.
To him are honor and dishonor alike;
Alike also pauper and prince.
One that such a way practices,
Says Nanak, a Jivan-mukta may be called.

Adi Granth, Gauri Sukhmani 9, M.5, p. 275 (Sikhism)

Teachings of Sun Myung Moon

According to the perspective of religion, humanity does not dwell in a liberated state. People today do not live in the realm of God's freedom; rather they are constrained within the fallen world under Satan's control. In other words, the world is in bondage. Christians in the established churches and we Unification Church members have the same understanding: we are in bondage.

This bondage is manifest as the persistent struggle between our mind and body. If human beings were made from the beginning with their minds and bodies in conflict, it would be absolutely impossible for them to perfect their character or attain liberation. In fact however, humans were created with harmonious internal elements, by which they could have attained the ideal state of liberation. They only fell into bondage during the course of their growth, when as a result of the Fall they were driven into a state of disorder, where we remain to this day. Therefore, it is entirely possible to be liberated from bondage and attain the ideal state. (85:227, March 3, 1976)

What does it feel like to experience the being of God? The interminable struggle between your mind and the body, which formerly plagued your self-centered life when you put yourself as number one in everything you did, will completely disappear. Instead, you will live the life that God wants you to live: living for the sake of others and giving yourself for the whole. Then, true love will continue forever, and God's joy will be displayed in the spirit world. You will experience such satisfaction and happiness as you have never felt before, because it will be connected to the whole. Thus, you will discover yourself in the state of liberation. (329:301-02, August 11, 2000)

The body has a limit, but the mind is infinite. The world of the mind is beyond form, beyond any philosophy or viewpoint. Still greater than the mind is the world of the heart. It has no restrictions. The world of the mind has certain restraints, conditioned by its relationships. Yet nothing can restrain the world of the heart. What could ever restrain a parent's love for his or her children? Even a barrier as daunting as a huge mountain cannot block the way. (7:246, September 20, 1959)

It is written in the Bible, "Where the Spirit of the Lord is, there is freedom." (2 Cor. 3.17) The Father is a Spirit of freedom, liberation and unification. How, then, can the spirit of freedom, which transcends any trials, be instilled in your hearts? How can you find the point of liberation where you overcome all the walls of suffering? When will you experience that peaceful moment of total unification, which is your ultimate hope?

In thinking about these important questions, consider that God is not free. Since God is not free, liberated and unified, the freedom people pursue today is not true freedom. The liberation people are proclaiming is not complete liberation, and the unification people are promoting is not complete unification...

God created us. Therefore, the complete freedom, liberation and unification that we desire can be realized only when God is free and becomes the master of liberation and unification. God's freedom, liberation and unification are the standards for humanity's freedom, liberation and unification; that is only logical. (4:314-15, October 12, 1958)

2. Universal Liberation

And [Jesus] came to Nazareth, where he had been brought up; and he went to the synagogue, as his custom was, on the sabbath day. And he stood up to read; and there was given to him the book of the prophet Isaiah. He opened the book and found the place where it was written,

> The Spirit of the Lord is upon me,
> because he has anointed me to preach good news to the poor.
> He has sent me to proclaim release to the captives
> and recovering of sight to the blind.
> to set at liberty those who are oppressed,
> to proclaim the acceptable year of the Lord.

And he closed the book, and gave it back to the attendant, and sat down; and the eyes of all in the synagogue were fixed on him. And he began to say to them, "Today this scripture has been fulfilled in your hearing."[16]

Luke 4.16-21

For the creation waits with eager longing for the revealing of the sons of God; for the creation was subjected to futility, not of its own will but by the will of Him who subjected it in hope; because the creation itself will be set free from its bondage to decay and obtain the glorious liberty of the children of God. We know that the whole creation has been groaning in travail together until now; and not only the creation, but we ourselves, who have the first fruits of the Spirit, groan inwardly as we wait for adoption as sons, the redemption of our bodies.

Romans 8.19-23

The holy sparks that fell when God built and destroyed worlds, man shall raise and purify upward from stone to plant, from plant to animal, from animal to speaking being, purify the holy sparks that are imprisoned in the world of shells (*kelippot*)[17] That is the basic meaning of the service of each one in Israel.

It is known that each spark that dwells in a stone or plant or another creature has a complete figure with the full number of limbs and sinews and, when it dwells in the stone or plant, it is in prison, cannot stretch out its hands and feet and cannot speak, but its head lies on its knees. And who with the good strength of his spirit is able to raise the holy spark from stone to plant, from plant to animal, from animal to speaking being, he leads it into freedom, and no setting free of captives is greater than this. It is as when a king's son is rescued from captivity and brought to his father.

All that a man owns, his servant, his animals, his tools, all conceal sparks that belong to the roots of his soul and wish to be raised by him to their origin.

All things of this world that belong to him desire with all their might to draw near him in order that the sparks of holiness that are in them should be raised by him.

Man eats them, man drinks them, man uses them; these are the sparks that dwell in the things. Therefore, one should have mercy on his tools and all his possessions for the sake of the sparks that are in them; one should have mercy on the holy sparks.

Take care that all you do for God's sake be itself service of God. Thus eating: do not say that the intention of eating shall be that you gain strength for the service of God. That is also a good intention, for course; but the true perfection only exists where the deed itself happens to heaven, that is where the holy sparks are raised.

In all that is in this world dwell holy sparks, no thing is empty of them. In the actions of men also, indeed even in the sins that a man does, dwell holy sparks of the glory of God. And what is it that the sparks await that dwell in the sins? It is the turning [repentance]. In the hour where you turn on account of sins, you raise to the higher world the sparks that were in it.

Israel Baal Shem Tov *(Judaism)*

Teachings of Sun Myung Moon

Liberation means that all hazardous conditions in our world are transformed into harmonious relationships. Our world becomes unified, without any sharp edges, where up and down, right and left, and front and rear have equal value.

Once liberation comes, grandfathers and grandmothers will like it, quarreling husbands and nagging wives will be satisfied, children and grandchildren will be glad. The multitudes will rejoice, and people of all nations will cheer. (341:161-62, January 1, 2001)

Before trying to liberate North Korea, you should ask yourself whether you are liberated. The liberation of the self is based on the unity of your body and mind. The liberation of the nation is the fifth level after the liberation of the individual, family, tribe and people.[18] (187:126, February 5, 1989)

All things that were supposed to be united into one were shattered into pieces. They were turned upside down throughout humanity's fragmented history, because countless indemnity courses blocked heaven and earth and passed each other in all directions. Therefore God has been leading a course of re-creation. To walk that course, True Parents came to the earth.

Heavenly Father, we know how hard Thou hast striven throughout history, in Thy providence of recreation which Thou hast conducted through our forbearers, to reconnect all the divisions in the mineral world, the world of microscopic organisms, the plant kingdom, the animal kingdom, the human world, and even in the heavenly world…

Therefore, centering on the love that is proper to God's ideal of creation, we should restore back what was lost in the world of minerals, the world of microscopic organisms, the plant kingdom, the animal kingdom, the human world, and the heavenly world. Thou, Heavenly Father, and we, True Parents, should create the realm of oneness… I sincerely hope and ask Thee to guide us to create one unified world, joining the heavenly world and earthly world. (May 4, 2003)

Throughout history, human beings have been searching for their own liberation and salvation, but who has been concerned about God's situation? Does God dwell in blissful joy for eternity, not in need of liberation? God is the Parent who has been mourning over human beings as they suffered in sin and evil throughout history. How, then, can God rejoice with a liberated heart? It is impossible. Depending on the degree of earthly liberation, God's heart can also be liberated. Only when God is liberated can human beings be liberated, be free to enjoy a family life of true love, and bring liberation to the creation. Furthermore, only when God is liberated can the beings in the spirit world be liberated and released. (April 30, 2004)

The ultimate goal of God's providence of salvation goes beyond the individual; it is to liberate and save the family, tribe, nation, physical world and the spirit world including hell. Until this is done, God Himself is not liberated. When the purpose of God's providence of salvation is fully attained, in other words, when even hell and all the spirit world are liberated, on that day, God will declare the completion of His ideal, proclaiming, "My will is done! Hallelujah! March forward into one world, under the dominion of my love." (114:78, May 17, 1981)

Emptiness—Nirvana

EMPTINESS, NIRVANA—THE ULTIMATE STATE OF INNER PEACE in Buddhism—is a state without self, without passions, without desires. It is a state beyond thought, beyond words, beyond any intellectual attempt to grasp what it is. Yet paradoxically, in this emptiness there is fullness, fearlessness and enlightenment. It is a marvelous, mystical state, almost impossible to describe.

Father Moon calls the state of Emptiness the 'zero point.' He explains its mystical feeling as a resonant connection with God, who also dwells in Emptiness when He creates the world. Father Moon also teaches an active way of self-emptying in the service of others. Self-giving, living for others, giving even when it is difficult to give: these practices can lead to the zero point just as surely as meditation.

"All states are without self." When one sees this in wisdom, then he becomes dispassionate towards the painful. This is the path to purity.

Dhammapada 279

The Man of the Way wins no fame,
The highest virtue wins no gain,
The Great Man has no self.

Chuang Tzu 17 (Taoism)

Where egoism exists, Thou art not experienced,
Where Thou art, is not egoism.

Adi Granth, Maru-ki-Var, M.1, p. 1092 (Sikhism)

Torah abides only with him who regards himself as nothing.

Talmud, Sota 21b (Judaism)

The Plain of High Heaven is not a specific place localized here or there, but refers rather to a pure state without any anomaly or excess. In terms of the human body, it is a state within the human breast without thought, contemplation, or passions.

Masamichi Imbe, *Secret Oral Tradition of the Book of the Divine Age* (Shinto)

This is Peace, this is the excellent, namely the calm of all the impulses, the casting out of all 'basis,' the extinction of craving, dispassion, stopping, Nirvana.[19]

Anguttara Nikaya 5.322 (Buddhism)

When a man is free from all sense pleasures and depends on nothingness he is free in the supreme freedom from perception. He will stay there and not return again.

It is like a flame struck by a sudden gust of wind. In a flash it has gone out and nothing more can be known about it. It is the same with a wise man freed from mental existence: in a flash he has gone out and nothing more can be known about him.

When a person has gone out, then there is nothing by which you can measure him. That by which he can be talked about is no longer there for him; you cannot say that he does not exist. When all ways of being, all phenomena are removed, then all ways of description have also been removed.[20]

Sutta Nipata 1072-76 (Buddhism)

For him who has completed the journey, for him who is sorrowless, for him who from everything is wholly free, for him who has destroyed all ties, the fever of passion exists not.

He whose senses are subdued, like steeds well-trained by a charioteer, he whose pride is destroyed and is free from the corruptions—such a steadfast one even the gods hold dear.

Like the earth, a balanced and well-disciplined person resents not... He is like a pool, unsullied by mud; to such a balanced one, life's wanderings do not arise.

Calm is his mind, calm is his speech, calm is his action, who, rightly knowing, is wholly freed [from defilements], perfectly peaceful and equipoised.

The man who is not credulous but truly understands the Uncreated (*Nibbana*), who has cut off the links, who has put an end to occasion [of good and evil], who has eschewed all desires, he indeed is a supreme man.

Dhammapada 90, 94-97 (Buddhism)

Here, O Shariputra, form is emptiness, and the very emptiness is form; emptiness does not differ from form, form does not differ from emptiness; whatever is form, that is emptiness, whatever is emptiness, that is form. The same is true of feelings, perceptions, impulses, consciousness.

Here, O Shariputra, all dharmas are marked with emptiness; they are not produced or stopped, not defiled or immaculate, not deficient or complete.

Therefore, O Shariputra, in emptiness there is no form, nor feeling, nor perception, nor impulse, nor consciousness... There is no suffering, no origination, no stopping, no path. There is no cognition, no attainment, and no non-attainment.

Therefore, O Shariputra, it is because of his indifference to any kind of personal attainment that a bodhisattva, through having relied on the perfection of wisdom, dwells without thought-coverings. In the absence of thought coverings he has not been made to tremble, he has overcome what can upset, and in the end he attains to Nirvana.

Heart Sutra (Buddhism)

Nan-po Tzu-k'uei said to the woman Nü Yü, "You are old, and yet your complexion is like that of a child. How is this?"[21]

Nü Yü replied, "I have learned Tao."

"Could I get Tao by studying it?" asked the other.

"I fear not," said Nü Yü. "You are not the sort of person. There was Pu-liang Yi. He had the qualifications of a sage... so I began teaching him. In three days, all distinctions of high and low, good and bad, had ceased to exist. Seven days more, and the external world had ceased to be. In nine more days, he became unconscious of his own existence. He first became ethereal, next possessed of perfect wisdom, then without past and present, and finally was able to enter where life and death are no more—where killing does not take away life, nor does giving birth add to it. In that state, there is nothing he does not welcome, nothing he does not send off, nothing he does not destroy, nothing he does not construct. This is to be at Peace in Strife. He who can be at peace in strife is on the way to perfection."

Chuang Tzu 6 (Taoism)

The Perfect Way is only difficult for those who pick and choose;
Do not like, do not dislike; all will then be clear.
Make a hairbreadth difference, and Heaven and Earth are set apart;
If you want the truth to stand clear before you, never be for or against.
The struggle between 'for' and 'against' is the mind's worst disease;
While the deep meaning is misunderstood, it is useless to meditate on Rest.
It [the Original Mind] is blank and featureless as space...

At the ultimate point, beyond which you can go no further,
You get to where there are no rules, no standards,
To where thought can accept Impartiality,
To where effect of action ceases,
Doubt is washed away, belief has no obstacle.
Nothing is left over, nothing remembered;
Space is bright, but self-illumined; no power of mind is exerted.
Nor indeed could mere thought bring us to such a place.
Nor could sense or feeling comprehend it.
It is the Truly-so, the Transcendent Sphere, where there is neither He nor I.

For swift converse with this sphere use the concept 'Not Two';
In the 'Not Two' are no separate things, yet all things are included.
The wise throughout the Ten Quarters have had access to this Primal Truth;
For it is not a thing with extension in Time or Space;
A moment and an aeon for it are one.
Whether we see it or fail to see it, it is manifest always and everywhere.
The very small is as the very large when boundaries are forgotten;
The very large is as the very small when its outlines are not seen.
Being is an aspect of Non-being; Non-being is an aspect of Being.
In climes of thought where it is not so the mind does ill to dwell.
The One is none other than the All, the All none other than the One.
Take your stand on this, and the rest will follow of its own accord;
To trust in the Heart is the Not Two, the Not Two is to trust in the Heart.
I have spoken, but in vain; for what can words tell
Of things that have no yesterday, tomorrow, or today?[22]

Seng Ts'an, On Trust in the Heart (*Buddhism*)

Teachings of Sun Myung Moon

While seeking for absolute love, you should not have consciousness of self. (279:146, August 4, 1996)

If we could totally subjugate our body, if our actions were always in conformity with our will, then we would not need religion. Jesus came in order to correct the disunity between the mind and the body. This is also the purpose of the Buddha's teaching that we should return to the state of nothingness—the zero point. If the mind and body are united, you do not feel [any distinction]. Why should we return to a state of emptiness? It is so we may experience Being. In a state of emptiness, the zero point, there emerges a counterpart with whom you can be in total harmony. Hence, at the zero point you can experience Being one hundred percent. (256:212, March 13, 1994)

God dwells in the 'king zero point.' Since God has such a nature, to meet Him you must become even lower than zero. Then you must guard that king zero point. The king zero point is like the mind, and as the flesh surrounds the mind, you should surround and protect the zero point.

Have you reached the state where you can guard the zero point? Can you go even lower than the zero point? This is what Buddhist meditation is about—to search the God-like mind for the deepest point. (230:134, May 1, 1992)

The [self-centered] ego has nothing to do with the ideal of creation. Therefore, we should completely deny ourselves. In order to find the true self, we should place ourselves at the zero point. That is the only place where we can be totally united in mind and body.

When God created us, He was in a state of total mind-body unity. He was in a state of total self-giving, with absolute love and absolute faith. God had no space to think of His own benefit or situation. Herein lies the origin of love: it is a state of one hundred percent giving and living for the sake of others.

Where do you think you can find your true self? You find it by practicing a life of true love, always living for the sake of others. If you dwell at the zero point—denying yourself while living for the sake of your family, all humankind throughout the world, and God—you will find your true self without doubt. It is our inevitable destiny to do so as we walk the path of restoration, which leads to salvation. (356:301-02, October 21, 2001)

Although we yearn for God and seek to love Him as the Subject of our faith, our experiences of Him are vague and indistinct. We still wonder, "Where can we find God?" Although He is definitely present, we cannot perceive Him with the certainty that we perceive things with our five physical senses. How, then, can we see God? We do not begin by looking at God, but rather by looking into ourselves.

When we look into ourselves, we find that we exist as mind and body. We should not focus on the body, but look into our mind.

Among a thousand fallen people, their fundamental nature may be the same, but each one has a different mind, a different personality each with different qualities.

When drawing a circle, you first draw a horizontal line and then a vertical line. From the point where they intersect, you draw the circle around it, starting from one degree, two degrees, and finally covering all 360 degrees. The horizontal line and the vertical line determine a 90-degree angle. How, then, do we make our mind a perfect circle? Depending on their personalities, each person draws their horizontal line in a different place. Just as our faces are different from one another, our inborn natures are different.

When drawing our circle through 360 degrees, we begin from zero degrees and trace it based on that standard. However, if the baseline of our minds is not properly fixed, we will not have the proper standard for measuring the degrees of the circle. Indeed, the baselines of people's minds are not the same. Why? As people's faces, interests and feelings differ, they each draw their horizontal and vertical lines in a different way.

How, then, can you form a circle covering all 360 degrees? You should find the zero point. Where is your zero point? Everyone has one. It is within yourself, within the core of your heart—there you will find it. When you draw a horizontal line from the zero point, you can properly fix the vertical line perpendicular to it.

We are to stand as object partners before God, our Subject Partner. Surely He has endowed human beings with a base to respond to Him as object partners. Therefore, upon the base of the horizontal mind, we should find the vertical direction, the true perpendicular. Surely there must be one.

You see the horizon in two dimensions, but if you try and estimate the perpendicular your measure could easily be off the mark. How can you find the accurate measure? If your horizontal is too high you must lower it; if it is too low you must raise it, to fix it at the zero point.

In an electrical power plant there are many meters, and each one is calibrated to a zero point. That neutral point must be set properly in order to adjust the positive and negative voltages and to measure the power levels. We, too, must accurately calibrate our zero point.

Where is our zero point located? It is a position that exists but seemingly does not exist. People who practice Zen meditation say that they attain the state of 'no-self.' That is what I am talking about. We should reach that spiritual standard, the zero point state. Once we attain it, our horizontal standard will become responsive to all things. (76:125)

Spiritual Union

SPIRITUAL UNION IS THE FINAL GOAL of the religious mystic. The experience of this unity is profound; it can hardly be described in words. A person in this state is united with God and united with all existence. All distinctions dissolve between subject and object, knower and known.

Mystical union is less common in conventional religion, particularly in the Abrahamic faiths whose uncompromising monotheism requires an absolute distinction between the infinite God and even the most saintly of His creatures. Yet the scriptures of Judaism and Christianity speak of a Beatific Vision, an encounter with God's presence that transforms the viewer. In Islam, traditions attributed to Muhammad himself undergird the unitive experiences of Sufi mystics.

Father Moon affirms all these varieties of unitive experiences. By learning to live in love, he teaches, we can draw close to God's mind and heart, share God's experiences, and move as appendages of God's body. We dwell in God, God dwells in us, and we experience mystic oneness with all His creations.

1. Becoming One with God

Do you not believe that I am in the Father and the Father in me?

John 14.10

Heaven and earth contain me not, but the heart of my faithful servant contains me.

Hadith of Suhrawardi *(Islam)*

Abide in me, and I in you. As the branch cannot bear fruit by itself, unless it abides in the vine, neither can you, unless you abide in me. I am the vine, you are the branches. He who abides in me, and I in him, he it is that bears much fruit, for apart from me you can do nothing.

John 15.4-5

As rivers flow into the sea and in so doing lose name and form, so even the wise man, freed from name and form, attains the Supreme Being, the Self-luminous, the Infinite. He who knows Brahman becomes Brahman.

Mundaka Upanishad 3.2.8-9 *(Hinduism)*

Meditate upon Him and transcend physical consciousness. Thus will you reach union with the Lord of the universe. Thus will you become identified with Him who is One without a second. In Him all your desires will find fulfillment.

The truth is that you are always united with the Lord. But you must know this.

Svetasvatara Upanishad 1.11-12 *(Hinduism)*

And we all, with unveiled face, beholding the glory of the Lord, are being changed into His likeness from one degree of glory to another; for this comes from the Lord who is the Spirit.

2 Corinthians 3.18

Bright but hidden, the Self dwells in the heart.[23]
Everything that moves, breathes, opens, and closes
Lives in the Self. He is the source of love
And may be known through love but not
 through thought.
He is the goal of life. Attain this goal!

Mundaka Upanishad 2.2.1 *(Hinduism)*

Every Buddha Tathagata is one whose body is the Principle of Nature (*Dharmadhatu-kaya*), so that he may enter into the mind of any being. Consequently, when you have perceived Buddha, it is indeed that mind of yours that possesses those thirty-two signs of perfection and eighty minor marks of excellence [which you see in Buddha]. In fine, it is your mind that becomes Buddha, nay, it is your mind that is indeed Buddha.

Meditation on Buddha Amitayus 17 *(Buddhism)*

In spontaneous joy is rising the mystic melody;
In the holy Word my heart feels joy and perpetually disports.
In the cave of spontaneous realization is it in trance,
Stationed on a splendid high cushion.

After wandering to my home [true self] have I returned,
And all of my desires have obtained.
Devotees of God! completely fulfilled is my self,
As the Master has granted a vision of the Supreme Being,
Realized by mystic illumination.

Himself is He King, Himself the multitude;
Himself the supremely liberated, Himself of joys the Relisher;
With Him seated on the throne of eternal justice,
Ended is all wailing and crying.

As I have seen, such vision of Him have I conveyed—
Only those who are initiated into this mystery have its joy.
As light is merged into Divine Light, has joy come:
Nanak, servant of God, has beheld the sole, all-pervading Supreme Being.

Adi Granth, Majh, M.5, p. 97 (Sikhism)

Teachings of Sun Myung Moon

God is huge, but a human being is a microcosm of the cosmos. By penetrating into God, we can experience God within us. When we experience this, we can say, with Jesus, "I am in the Father, and the Father in me." (John 14.10) Although God is infinitely large, He can do His work only when human beings fully dwell within Him. (31:210, May 31, 1970)

When your mind and body are united as one, you will be in your eternal dwelling place, the center where God abides. Then you can possess even God. This state arises when true love is restored; it is the supreme goal of human beings who had lost everything as the result of the Fall. (294:98-99, June 14, 1998)

The path of religion is to stop living as animalistic human beings and become humane human beings. Eventually we are to become divine human beings. We are to participate in the divine realm. We are to become people with a divine nature who practice divine love and rejoice ever more in eternal happiness. (117:37, January 31, 1982)

Love is the central point, the rope that binds God and human beings together eternally. When embodied human beings attain oneness with God, their heart is immersed in a state of profound awareness and their emotions thrill with boundless happiness. Through love, God and human beings become one. Through love, human beings and the world become one. Here is the starting point for the realization of the ideal world that fulfills God's purpose of creation. (35:356, October 13, 1970)

When you are united with God in true love, you can have dominion over all God's creation, both physical and spiritual. When you live completely for others, you are reaching the very essence of God. Then, God's will becomes your will, and God's feelings naturally come into your heart. Living this way, you become a resonant vessel of God's heart and love. You and God will always resonate together, like two tuning forks. (201:206, April 9, 1990)

As existent beings in front of Thee,
we entrust to Thee our whole selves:
We shall be Thy branches and leaves.
When Thou art sorrowful, we shall also be sorrowful;
when Thou art happy, we shall also be happy;
when Thou dost hurry to work, we shall also hurry to work.
Permit us to become Thy sons and daughters who stand beside Thee,
as Thou dost deal with every aspect of our world. (42:59, February 21, 1971)

2. God and Human Beings United in Love

God the Almighty has said… "My servant will not approach Me with anything dearer than that which I put on him as an obligation; and he continues presenting Me with works of supererogation, that I may love him. And when I love him, I am his hearing by which he hears, his sight by which he sees, his hand by which he strikes, and his foot with which he walks."

40 Hadith of an-Nawawi 38 *(Islam)*

Who shall separate us from the love of Christ?… For I am sure that neither death, nor life, nor angels, nor principalities, nor things present, nor things to come, nor powers, nor height, nor depth, nor anything else in all creation, will be able to separate us from the love of God in Christ Jesus our Lord.

Romans 8.35, 38-39

"Look at those who are clothed in the wedding garment of charity, adorned with many true virtues; they are united with Me through love. So I say, if you should ask Me who they are, I would answer," said the gentle loving Word, "that they are another Me; for they have lost and drowned their own will and have clothed themselves and united themselves and conformed themselves with Mine."

Catherine of Siena *(Christianity)*

Teachings of Sun Myung Moon

Perfect unity is possible only in the perfect love of God. (94:263, October 1, 1977)

Once God's love dwells within your heart, even when you are alone, you will be totally filled. You will be happy. Because His love fills you, you can find joy in everything. (95:39, September 11, 1977)

What is God like? He is a God of love. When Saint Paul said, "Who shall separate us from the love of Christ?" he meant the love of God in Christ. Even Christ is nothing without God's love. Hence, we cherish God's love more than anything. God's love is the source of life, happiness and peace. You will understand this if you have spiritual experiences. (24:325, September 14, 1969)

Once a person has tasted and joined himself to God's original love, would he or she ever want to separate from it? When a bee is sucking nectar and you pull on its abdomen, it will not release its mouth from the nectar even if its abdomen is pulled off. So, what will you do once you have experienced the taste of God's love? You might leave, but you would turn around, come back, and cling to it. (137:57, December 18, 1985)

Love alone can solve everything. Love alone holds the privilege to possess the ideal vertical axis. Love brings the right of possession, the right to equality, and the right of participation. When I have true love, God dwells within me, and I in God. God belongs to me, God's love belongs to me, and God's universe belongs to me. We can have such a concept of possession. Since each of us has such a value, we have an original desire to display ourselves proudly to the entire creation. (179:169, August 1, 1988)

People who experience the heart of God in their lives cannot come before God without shedding tears, no matter where they are. They know the original Will of God and struggle to become His sons and daughters. If you are among them, sharing God's will and desire, He will visit you and weep with you.

Where are the roots of God's grief? They are inside us. They are inside our nation, this world and all things of creation. We must carry on a movement to eradicate them and restore God's joy. For us, the center of our life of faith should be to experience God's grief.

When we live shedding tears for God, we can perceive God's eternal love and fulfill the mission as God's representatives. Immersed in God's sorrowful heart, we do not need to pray. We do not need to rely on doctrines. Before we pray, we already feel the heart of God…

Do not hold a grudge against anyone. Rather, weep for them. Then you shall receive the benefit of paying indemnity. Today you enjoy the privilege of being the first people to experience God's grief and shed tears for Him. Know, however, that God shed tears for you first. (4:60, March 2, 1958)

> Father! Please reach out to each of us
> and hold us with both arms in Thy loving embrace.
> How anxiously hast Thou looked forward to this,
> hoping for this moment?
> Now I can fully envision Thy heart!
> Now I can fully envision Thy heartbreak. (9:160-61, May 8, 1960)

3. Oneness with All Things

Those who see all creatures within themselves
And themselves in all creatures know no fear.
Those who see all creatures in themselves
And themselves in all creatures know no grief.
How can the multiplicity of life
Delude the one who sees its unity?

Isa Upanishad 6-7 (Hinduism)

Buddha said, "Through the Consummation of Incomparable Enlightenment I acquired not even the least thing. *This* is altogether everywhere, without differentiation or degree."

Diamond Sutra 22-23 (Buddhism)

The infinite joy of touching the Godhead is easily attained by those who are free from the burden of evil and established within themselves. They see the Self in every creature and all creation in the Self. With consciousness unified through meditation, they see everything with an equal eye.

I am ever present into those who have realized Me in every creature. Seeing all life as My manifestation, they are never separated from Me. They worship Me in the hearts of all, and all their actions proceed from Me. Wherever they may live, they abide in Me.

When a person responds to the joys and sorrows of others as if they were his own, he has attained the highest state of spiritual union.

Bhagavad-Gita 6.28-32 (Hinduism)

In the Great Beginning, there was non-being. It had neither being nor name. The One originates from it; it has oneness but not yet physical form. When things obtain it and come into existence, that is called virtue [power which gives them their individual character]. That which is formless is divided [into yang and yin], and from the very beginning going on without interruption…

By cultivating one's nature one will return to virtue. When virtue is perfect, one will be one with the Beginning. Being one with the Beginning, one becomes vacuous, and being vacuous, one becomes great. One will then be united with the sound and breath of things. When one is united with the sound and breath of things, one is then united with the universe. This unity is intimate and seems to be stupid and foolish. This is called profound and secret virtue, this is complete harmony.

Chuang Tzu 12 (Taoism)

Teachings of Sun Myung Moon

Heavenly Father is breathing. His breath is the breath of love. God continuously breathes love into the cosmos, bringing it into alignment with love. You should align yourself with love, since in loving you will find eternal life. Only then will you transcend this reality and enter the realm of Heavenly Father's breath. (201:191, April 1, 1990)

Allow yourself time to experience through your own direct senses—through your eyes, nose, mouth and ears—and believe through your own experience. It is important to give yourself enough time to have such experiences.

Self-centered people are not able to sense it well, but when people who lead a life filled with God's grace look at nature, they experience everything as brand new. In the morning it seems new, and in the evening it seems new. As God's grace slowly rolls in like waves, they feel fascination and mystery in three dimensions. A person who can experience this is a happy person. (30:134-35, March 21, 1970)

If you want to dwell in God's heart, you should have the heart to protect all creatures in heaven and on earth as if they were your own. Since God's heart dwells in all His creatures, caring for them links you with God's heart. The highest spirituality is to be possessed by God and dwell in His heart. If even looking at a flying bird or smelling a flower's fragrance prompts you to sing eternally, then you are not dwelling in the world, but in God's heart. In that state, time means nothing. (8:182, January 23, 1959)

I long for the ideal world, a world that completes the purpose of creation, a world transcendent of the world of consciousness, a world where I can feel endless peace.

What would it be like to live in that world? On seeing even a blade of grass, you would extol the value of its existence. As a human being, you are a small thing compared with the vast universe, yet all its creatures would praise you, saying, "You are truly amazing! Whenever you move, heaven and earth move, God's heart moves, and eternal life moves." All people should attain this level. (9:320, June 19, 1960)

Healing

THE CONDITION OF FALLEN HUMANITY HAS BEEN LIKENED to an infirmity and a disease of the soul. Our hearts are heavy with pain and suffering. Hence, salvation may be regarded as healing the soul of its infirmity and restoring it to health where it can realize its true potential. Religious teaching may be regarded as a sovereign remedy, and the founder who bears the truth likened to a master physician.

Yet there is also a causal, psychosomatic relationship between the health of the soul and health of the body. Physical health is thus a welcome by-product of spiritual health. Moreover, the power of God can cause miracles to happen: old women bear children, the blind see and the dead are brought back to life. Jesus performed miraculous healings and exorcisms; as did Buddha and the saints of all religions from ancient times to the present day.

Father Moon speaks realistically about the spiritual causes of disease and the way people may align themselves to mobilize God's healing power. He also warns against the careless use of healing power, for miracles come with a price.

1. Healing the Body and Soul

And when I am sick, He heals me.

    Qur'an 26.80

If you will diligently hearken to the voice of the LORD your God, and do that which is right in his eyes, and give heed to his commandments and keep all his statutes, I will put none of the diseases upon you which I put upon the Egyptians; for I am the LORD, your Healer.

    Exodus 15.26

Whatever defect I have of eye, of heart, of mind,
or whatever excess there is,
may Brishaspati remedy it.
Gracious to us be the Lord of the world.

    Yajur Veda 36.2 (Hinduism)

Is any among you sick? Let him call for the elders of the church, and let them pray over him, anointing him with oil in the name of the Lord; and the prayer of faith will save the sick man, and the Lord will raise him up; and if he has committed sins, he will be forgiven. Therefore confess your sins to one another, and pray for one another, that you may be healed.

    James 5.14-16

O God, you are great,
You are the one who created me,
I have no other.
God, You are in the heavens,
You are the only one:
Now my child is sick,
And you will grant me my desire.

    Anuak Prayer (African Traditional Religions)

Come, let us return to the LORD;
for he has torn, that he may heal us;
he has stricken, and he will bind us up.
After two days he will revive us;
on the third day he will raise us up,
that we may live before him.

    Hosea 6.1-2

The Buddha, the Truly Enlightened One, the unexcelled master physician... having developed and perfected the medicines of the Teaching over countless eons, having cultivated and learned all skills in application of means, and fully consummated the power of illuminating spells, is able to quell all sentient beings' afflictions.

    Garland Sutra 37 (Buddhism)

This man [Zarathustra], the holy one through righteousness,
Holds in his spirit the force which heals existence,
Beneficent unto all, as a sworn friend, O Wise One.

Avesta, Yasna 44.2 (Zoroastrianism)

Sickness arises from total involvement in the process of misunderstanding from beginningless time. It arises from the passions that result from unreal mental constructions, and hence ultimately nothing is perceived which can be said to be sick. What is the elimination of this sickness? It is the elimination of egoism and possessiveness.

Holy Teaching of Vimalakirti 5 (Buddhism)

Should anyone be victim of great anxiety, his body racked with maladies,
Beset with problems of home and family,
With pleasure and pain alternating,
Wandering in all four directions without peace or rest—
Should he then contemplate the Supreme Being,
Peaceful shall his mind and body become.

Adi Granth, Sri Raga, M.5, p. 70 (Sikhism)

The words of the Torah are like a perfect remedy. This may be compared to a man who inflicted a big wound upon his son, and then put a plaster on his wound, saying, "My son! As long as this plaster is on your wound you can eat and drink what you like, and bathe in cold or warm water, and you will suffer no harm. But if you remove it, it will break out into sores." Even so did God say to the Israelites, "My children! I created within you the Evil Inclination, but I created the Law as its antidote. As long as you occupy yourselves with the Torah, the Evil Inclination will not rule over you. But if you do not occupy yourselves with the Torah, then you will be delivered into its power, and all its activity will be against you."

Talmud, Kiddushin 30b (Judaism)

Those who become obedient to God, come to a realization, come closer to God, and repent, shall receive the Baptism for deep spiritual cleansing by the holy spiritual essence of fire. They shall spiritually receive directly, the True Positive Light through your triple body, which is the way to lessen their compensation. This world shall be saved from the immense number of disturbances working against people's souls.

Goseigen (Mahikari[24])

Teachings of Sun Myung Moon

What is the prescription for healing this fractured world? It is true love. (190:57, October 9, 1988)

When you get sick, you should visit a doctor and get treated. He may give you a shot and prescribe medicine. What does the divine Physician prescribe for you? It is religion. If we believe in religion and practice it, our struggles will cease. (337:57, October 22, 2000)

We live in a time when prosperity comes to those who live according to the Principle and who uphold the standard of absolute goodness. God declares that He will personally work on behalf of His children, to free us from sickness and misery, pain and misfortune, sin and evil. (Heung Jin Moon, *Message from the Spirit World*, January 1, 2002)

Human beings are supposed to live in joy by receiving elements of love (living spirit elements) from God. Instead, they are born as imperfect individuals, plagued with anxiety and sickness. Human beings from birth are connected to sinful blood relations, and hence possess inner elements that allow Lucifer to invade. They took on a diseased form, completely different from what they were supposed to be.

As a result of Lucifer's invasion, human beings were first of all diseased spiritually and secondly diseased physically. Approximately seventy to eighty percent of all illnesses have a spiritual cause. (Sang Hun Lee, *Lucifer: A Criminal against Humanity* 2.2)

When someone gets sick, the doctor first finds out the cause of the illness; then he can prescribe a treatment that will result in a cure. However, no person in history has known why we human beings are fallen. Hence, no one could come up with an effective treatment for the problem. Satan knew it, because he caused it. God also knew, but [by Himself] He could not correct it. Therefore, until the Savior comes as God's messenger to humanity and reveals the truth, humanity has no way to be saved. (367:293, January 24, 2002)

What is the most fearful among all diseases, even for God? It is the disease resulting from the Human Fall. Do you have this disease or not? Yes you have it, but most people do not even realize that they are afflicted.

These days, everyone fears cancer. In its early stages a person may not realize that he is ill. He only recognizes that he has the disease when it becomes painful, but by then the cancer has progressed to a lethal stage. Still, at least a cancer victim knows he has the disease before he dies. With the disease of the Fall, however, people do not recognize that they are ill until after they die. That is the problem. (92:185, April 10, 1977)

2. Miracles

When Elisha came into the house, he saw the child lying dead on his bed. So he went in and shut the door upon the two of them, and prayed to the LORD. Then he went up and lay upon the child, putting his mouth upon his mouth, his eyes upon his eyes, and his hands upon his hands; and as he stretched himself upon him, the flesh of the child became warm. Then he got up again, and walked once to and fro in the house, and went up, and stretched himself upon him; the child sneezed seven times, and the child opened his eyes.

2 Kings 4.32-35

I [Jesus] heal the blind and the leprous, and bring the dead to life with Allah's permission.

Qur'an 3.49

A great crowd followed [Jesus] and thronged about him. And there was a woman who had had a flow of blood for twelve years, and who had suffered much under many physicians, and had spent all that she had, and was no better but rather grew worse. She had heard the reports about Jesus, and came up behind him in the crowd and touched his garment. For she said, "If I touch even his garments, I shall be made well." And immediately the hemorrhage ceased; and she felt in her body that she was healed of her disease. And Jesus, perceiving in himself that power had gone forth from him, immediately turned about in the crowd, and said, "Who touched my garments?" And his disciples said to him, "You see the crowd pressing around you, and yet you say, 'Who touched me?'" And he looked around to see who had done it. But the woman, knowing what had been done to her, came in fear and trembling and fell down before him, and told him the whole truth. And he said to her, "Daughter, your faith has made you well; go in peace, and be healed of your disease."

Mark 5.24-34

Now Peter and John were going up to the temple at the hour of prayer, the ninth hour. And a man lame from birth was being carried, whom they laid daily at the gate of the temple which is called Beautiful to ask alms of those who entered the temple. Seeing Peter and John about to go into the temple, he asked for alms. And Peter directed his gaze at him, with John, and said, "Look at us." And he fixed his attention upon them, expecting to receive something from them. But Peter said, "I have no silver and gold, but I give you what I have; in the name of Jesus Christ of Nazareth, walk." And he took him by the right hand and raised him up; and immediately his feet and ankles were made strong. And leaping up he stood and walked and entered the temple with them, walking, and leaping, and praising God.

Acts 3.1-8

The World-honored One, the All-compassion and Guide, for the sake of King Ajatasatru, entered into the moonlight-samadhi. Having entered the samadhi, a great light issued. The light was pure and cool, and it went to the king and shone in the king's body. The boils on his body got cured and the choking pains died out. Relieved of the pains of the boils and feeling cool in body, the king said to the Buddha, "Where does this light come from? It shines on me and touches me; it cures all boils, and the body feels peace." The Buddha answered, "O great king! This is the light of the heaven of heavens. This light has no root; it is boundless… It is seen only where there is a desire to save… O King, you said before that there was no good doctor in the world who could cure the body and mind. Because of this, this light is first sent out. It first cures your body, and then, your mind." [25]

Mahaparinirvana Sutra 575-76 (Buddhism)

The physical healing of Christian Science results now, as in Jesus' time, from the operation of divine Principle, before which sin and disease lose their reality in human consciousness and disappear as naturally and as necessarily as darkness gives place to light and sin to reformation. Now, as then, these mighty works are not supernatural, but supremely natural. They are the sign of Immanuel, or "God with us,"—a divine influence ever present in human consciousness.

Science and Health (Christian Science)

Then a blind and dumb demoniac was brought to [Jesus], and he healed him, so that the dumb man spoke and saw. And all the people were amazed, and said, "Can this be the Son of David?" But when the Pharisees heard it they said, "It is only by Beelzebul, the prince of demons, that this man casts out demons."[26]

Matthew 12.22-24

Because I see danger in the practice of miracles, I loathe and abhor and repudiate them.

Digha Nikaya 9.66 (Buddhism)

A man should not rely on miracles, and even if the Holy One, blessed be He, has once performed a miracle for him he should count on it another time, for miracles do not happen every day. And whoever runs into obvious danger may thereby exhaust all his merit previously accumulated.

Zohar 1.111b (Judaism)

Teachings of Sun Myung Moon

The Bible says that Sarah, Abraham's wife, bore Isaac when she was nearly ninety years old. Do not think that it is impossible. If you women are confident, you could also conceive by spiritual power. Spiritual power is miraculous. (283:126, April 8, 1997)

The unity of mind and body generates a mysterious, invisible power. When you enter that state, miracles occur... When you are united with God's love, you can perform miracles. Healing fire comes out of your open palms. You can move your audience simply by willing it so... You can revive those who are [spiritually] dead...

What power is this? It is the power of love. All this is possible only through the power of love. Love is such that the more you practice it, the greater it becomes. But there is a condition. To obtain that power, you must subjugate your physical body. (282:229-30, March 26, 1997)

With absolute faith, anything is possible. Suppose while walking on the street you met a sick man. Feeling deep compassion for him, without a second thought you stretch out your hands over him, place your hands on him and pray for him sincerely with tears. Then, a miracle will happen.

Yet I do not want to be involved in miracles. Jesus performed many miracles, yet people did not appreciate their value. Despite all the miracles, he was driven to death. It is no use to heal those who are not worthy. More than miracles, what they need is truth. Truth is unchanging and eternal, but signs and miracles are fleeting. What is temporary cannot govern what is eternal. (252:258, January 1, 1994)

It is possible to revive a dead person by breathing his or her spirit self back into the physical body. Yet certain conditions are required. First, the person should not be dead for too long—not more than three days—so that the flesh has not decayed. Within that period, if the spirit is called back into the body the person can come back to life; it is not very difficult.

However, bringing someone back to life on earth after God has called that person to the spirit world requires paying a suitable price. It should either be compensation of greater value [than the person's life], or something to benefit the whole purpose. Maybe to revive that one person, three or four others might have to die. Therefore, you should carefully consider the benefit of bringing someone back to life. If you do not take responsibility for doing it, you will violate the heavenly law. All in all, performing miracles is not necessarily good. (15:176, October 7, 1965)

The Refining Fire

GOD'S GRACIOUS LOVE CAN BE FOUND IN THE MIDST OF HARDSHIPS and suffering. The person whose mind is fixed on God takes life's trials and challenges as a means to purify his or her faith, correct flaws and refine character. Could it be that such trials are not accidental, but actually expressions of God's love to discipline and educate His children? (See also Chapter 15: *Testing*.)

Moreover, God's word presents us with the challenge to live by it. Scripture therefore likens the word of God to a fire, which burns away everything that is false. Father Moon explains that the judgment that many Christians fear is actually an opportunity to purify ourselves in the truth and reach the point where we are one hundred percent united with the word of Christ. Thus, the purpose of judgment is to save, not to condemn.

1. Judgment by Fire

I will put this third into the fire,
and refine them as one refines silver,
and test them as gold is tested.

Zechariah 13.9

Just as a great conflagration
Can burn up all things,
So does Buddha's field of blessings
Burn up all fabrication.

Garland Sutra 10 (Buddhism)

As the heat of a fire reduces wood to ashes,
the fire of knowledge burns to ashes all karma.
Nothing in this world purifies like spiritual wisdom.

Bhagavad-Gita 4.37 (Hinduism)

Just as a fire quickly reduces decayed wood to ashes, so does an aspirant who is totally absorbed in the inner self and completely unattached to all external objects shake to the roots, attenuate, and wither away his karma-body.

Samantabadhra, Aptamimamsa 24-27 (Jainism)

Make chastity your furnace, patience your smithy,
The Master's word your anvil, and true knowledge your hammer.
Make awe of God your bellows, and with it kindle the fire of austerity.
And in the crucible of love, melt the nectar Divine.
Only in such a mint, can man be cast into the Word.

Adi Granth, Japuji 38, M.1, p. 8 (Sikhism)

"From His right hand went forth a fiery law for them" (Deuteronomy 33.2). The words of Torah are compared to fire, for both were given from heaven, both are eternal. If a man draws near the fire, he derives benefit; if he keeps afar, he is frozen, so with the words of the Torah: if a man toils in them, they are life to him; if he separates from him, they kill him.

Sifre Deuteronomy (Judaism)

For no other foundation can any one lay than that which is laid, which is Jesus Christ. Now if any one builds on the foundation with gold, silver, precious stones, wood, hay, straw—each man's work will become manifest; for the Day will disclose it, because it will be revealed with fire, and the fire will test what sort of work each one has done. If the work which any man has built on the foundation survives, he will receive a reward. If any man's work is burned up, he will suffer loss, though he himself will be saved, but only as through fire.

1 Corinthians 3.11-15

Is not my word like fire, says the LORD, and like a hammer which breaks the rock in pieces?

Jeremiah 23.29

With fire we test the gold, and with gold We test Our servants.

Hidden Words of Bahá'u'lláh, Arabic 54 (Baha'i Faith)

Teachings of Sun Myung Moon

Each of us has many different kinds of thoughts, all varieties. Do you think we can easily negate them all to uphold the standard of absolute faith, love and obedience? Is it easy or difficult? How difficult! Even if we were to die and be reborn one hundred times, it would still be difficult.

It doesn't matter how many times we say the words "absolute faith, love and obedience"; we should enter the furnace and have our impurities burned away until there is only pure gold left. (320:235, April 5, 2000)

Jesus came into the world to cast this judgment, as he said, "For judgment I came into this world." (John 9.39) Jesus also said, "I came to cast fire upon the earth." (Luke 12.49) "Fire" here represents the means of the judgment for which Jesus came into the world. Nevertheless, there is no record that in his time Jesus judged the world with literal fire. The verses referring to fire must be symbolic. It is written, "Is not my word like fire, says the Lord?" (Jer. 23.29) Therefore, judgment by fire represents judgment by the Word of God. (*Exposition of the Divine Principle*, Eschatology 3.2.2)

The words you are familiar with are connected to Satan. Your beliefs and thought processes have not escaped a relationship with Satan. All elements in the satanic world were created from a humanistic perspective, not from God's perspective. They cannot go beyond Satan's realm. That is why we need to renovate everything through the new Word of God.

Once we know God's Word, can we also live in harmony with the old words and move on with our lives? Absolutely not. We must completely rid ourselves of the old words. We must clean out all our satanic ideas, beliefs and habits. Then, by living according to the Word of God and its absolute standards, we must establish a new tradition. (21:327, January 1, 1969)

To acquire true love, you should invest yourself totally. You should be willing to burn your own name, your pictures, even your own clothes.[27] (398:328, December 17, 2002)

> Oh Father! Look upon us with Thy fiery eyes,
> and allow not the bitter roots of sin and death to remain deep in our hearts.
> Look upon us with Thy fiery eyes,
> that today we may pull out all the roots of sin and be unified before Thee. (20:10, March 31, 1968)

> Father! We pray Thou wilt remove all that is humanistic and private.
> Born as descendants of the Fall, we used to wear masks as we saw fit and relied upon our own views.
> Purge us of all these elements as we come before Thee. (21:132, November 17, 1968)

2. Heaven's Discipline

My son, do not despise the LORD's discipline
or be weary of His reproof,
for the LORD reproves him whom He loves,
as a father the son in whom he delights.

Proverbs 3.11-12

I know, O LORD, that the way of man is not in
  himself,
that it is not in man who walks to direct his
  steps.
Correct me, O LORD, but in just measure;
not in thy anger, lest thou bring me to nothing.

Jeremiah 10.23-24

Do men imagine that they will be left [at ease] because they say, "We believe," and will not be tested with affliction? Lo! We tested those who were before you. Thus God knows those who are sincere, and knows those who feign.

Qur'an 29.2-3

We rejoice in our sufferings, knowing that suffering produces endurance, and endurance produces character, and character produces hope, and hope does not disappoint us, because God's love has been poured into our hearts.

Romans 5.3-5

Yet the suffering
Involved in my awakening will have a limit;
It is like the suffering of having an incision made
In order to remove and destroy greater pain.

Even doctors eliminate illness
With unpleasant medical treatments,
So in order to overcome manifold sufferings
I should be able to put up with some discomfort.

Shantideva, Guide to the Bodhisattva's Way of Life 7.22-24 (Buddhism)

Teachings of Sun Myung Moon

All difficulties and trials confront you so that you may correctly experience and understand God's past days. Therefore, when any difficulty comes upon you, you should rejoice and be thankful. It is the proof of God's love for you. (*Way of God's Will* 3.4)

The reason why the Unification Church requires its members to live three years of public life after receiving the Blessing is to enable them to taste true love. The reason why I tour the world and give speeches, braving persecution and opposition, is to train you to make beautiful families of true love surpassing all other families.

We go the way of God's Will despite the world's harsh persecution and oppression because we love our children and want to enable them to live in the beautiful nation of God. In this way, we live for our children and love our children more than the people of the world love their children.

You must carry on this fight throughout your lives. If you see your husband or wife being persecuted and opposed, you must pledge that you will love your children more than your feeling of distress over your spouse's plight. You must be trained in this way in the midst of persecution and opposition.

A wife who has received this 'love training' will not fight with her husband. If he crosses her with a cutting remark, she will not respond with machine-gun volleys of scolding words. A husband will not beat his wife or dominate her with his authority. Why not? Having been through love training, each spouse has come to know the other's precious value. (*Blessing and Ideal Family* 4.4.8)

Make us into people to whom Thou canst entrust Thy Will
by molding us according to Thine internal nature. (2:241, June 9, 1957)

Help and Deliverance

IN TIMES OF DISTRESS, DANGER, AND OPPRESSION, the faithful look to God for support and help. In times of crisis, in combat, and when confronting death, even non-believers will pray desperately to God. And time and again, they find deliverance in ample measure. Conversely, the scriptures warn against relying on one's own power, allies, or wealth to prevail in the battle, when true strength lies in God's saving power.

The passages include expressions of confidence in divine deliverance, supplications for help, and texts which describe God's grace as an unassailable refuge. There are several accounts of God's saving deeds in history: from the Bible, Moses at the Red Sea and Paul's escape from prison; from the Qur'an, the battle of the Trench. We include the Buddhist hymn to Kuan Yin, the bodhisattva of divine compassion who is said to be ready and able to save anyone in distress.

Father Moon experienced divine deliverance on numerous occasions, notably when he was a prisoner in a North Korean labor camp. He explains why people normally receive divine help only if they have the mind of devotion and faith. God's heart of love extends to everyone. However, due to the activities of Satan, whose accusations can cause God to withdraw His protection, people oftentimes must overcome a trial before they can receive divine assistance.

1. Help in Times of Trouble

The LORD is my shepherd, I shall not want;
he makes me lie down in green pastures.
He leads me beside still waters;
he restores my soul.
He leads me in paths of righteousness
for his name's sake.

Even though I walk through the valley of the
    shadow of death,
I fear no evil;
for thou art with me;
thy rod and thy staff,
they comfort me.

Thou preparest a table before me
in the presence of my enemies;
thou anointest my head with oil,
my cup overflows.
Surely goodness and mercy shall follow me
all the days of my life;
and I shall dwell in the house of the LORD for
    ever.

                                Psalm 23

Whosoever keeps his duty to God, God will appoint a way out for him, and will provide for him in a way that he cannot foresee. And whosoever puts his trust in God, He will suffice him. Lo! God brings His command to pass. God has set a measure for all things.

                                Qur'an 65.2-3

Because you have made the LORD your refuge,
the Most High your habitation,
no evil shall befall you,
no scourge come near your tent.
For he will give his angels charge of you
to guard you in all your ways.

On their hands they will bear you up,
lest you dash your foot against a stone.

                                Psalm 91.9-12

Not by might, nor by power, but by my Spirit,
says the LORD of hosts.

                                Zechariah 4.6

United with me, you shall overcome all difficulties by my grace.

                          Bhagavad-Gita 18.58 (*Hinduism*)

Men of little ability, too,
By depending upon the great, may prosper;
A drop of water is a little thing,
But when will it dry away if united to a lake?

          Treasury of Elegant Sayings[28] 173 (*Buddhism*)

The LORD is the everlasting God,
the Creator of the ends of the earth.
He does not grow weary, he does not tire,
his understanding is unsearchable.
He gives strength to the weary,
and to him who has no might he increases
    strength.
Youths may faint and be weary,
and young men may fall, exhausted;
but they who hope in the LORD shall renew
    their strength.
They shall mount up with wings like eagles,
they shall run and not be weary,
they shall walk and not grow faint.

                                Isaiah 40.28-31

A king is not saved by his great army,
a warrior is not delivered by his great strength.

The war horse is a vain hope for victory,
and by its great might it cannot save.
Behold, the eye of the Lord is on those who fear him,
on those who hope in his steadfast love,
That he may deliver their soul from death,
and keep them alive in famine.
Our soul waits for the Lord;
he is our help and our shield.

Psalm 33.16-20

Teachings of Sun Myung Moon

How can you receive God's protection? God does not protect a person unless he has something that endears him to God. What do you have that would draw God to relate to you? Does God need your money? Does He need your power? Knowledge? God desires but one thing: love. Therefore, love gives us the privilege to move God. When He relates to us out of love, He can alter our destiny. Love can move God.

Do you think that God will forsake people who are truly striving to love Him? What if, out of love for Him, they place themselves in miserable circumstances? Will their lives end in misfortune? On the contrary, their troubles will become a condition to turn their miserable situation into a fortunate outcome. Therefore, those who endure misfortune on the path of loving God are fortunate people. It is even more fortunate for them if they are happy to follow this path. When God sees them braving waves of misfortune throughout the world as they search for God's love, He thinks it most wonderful.

When I was in prison in North Korea, I endured severe torture. Yet the more severe the torture was, the stronger I became. I thought, "Go ahead, you… The more you torture me, the more God will love me." With that attitude, although I was destined to die, I lived. Have this attitude, and, you can make your crooked way straight.

To overcome, we need but one thing. Our path of life may be troubled, insecure, full of the misery and with only fleeting pleasures, yet on this path we can bind the power of death and go beyond death's misery. What is the path to overcome all these trials and go safely straight to the goal? It is the path of loving God. Is there any other way? When we are ready to live and die for the love of God, God will be with us and protect us. (67:175-76, June 3, 1973)

Our mind seeks the world of the heart. Even radio waves do not operate just anywhere; they require a receiver that is tuned to resonate with the signal. It is the same with people. As long as a person has a true conscience, a true loving standard, and a foundation of Heaven's heart, then wherever or whenever he goes, even in conditions of oppression and misery, he will unexpectedly find a way to survive and even prosper. Even when misunderstood and mistreated, he will find a way.

The path to life cannot be found in comfortable circumstances. No one ever achieved an historical revolution, an historical discovery, or an historical success in a comfortable place. They began in circumstances where they stood face to face with death. In such situations, God reached out to them.

Therefore, when someone is about to encounter God, he will meet with a crisis. It may be material—an accident or a financial disaster. It may be a problem with other people, or it may be a problem of the heart. At that time, if he shouts out, "I will go this path no matter what," and goes forward resolutely, he will be able to lead others who struggle with similar kinds of problems. (7:333-34, October 18, 1959)

When we cannot go one step further, yet are willing to endure still more, God appears and blesses us, saying, "My son, my daughter, you don't have to endure any longer. You can rest now." This is the path of our restoration course. As we endure on our journey with hymns of thanksgiving, God comes to us and tearfully says, "Where else can I find a son or daughter like you? I will now appoint someone else to carry on for you." Then He gives us a place of rest and heavenly rewards from His fatherly heart. (44:29, May 4, 1971)

We should know at what point God works with us and at what point Satan is likely to attack us. There are always these two kinds of works. In fulfilling the will of God, people should climb up by their own efforts to the point where God can help them. That is the human portion responsibility. God gets directly involved only after human beings have reached a certain level; he does not help them below that level. As we approach that level we may receive a little help, but only when we reach it does God provide us with maximum support.

When you spin a hoop vertically on a stick, the hardest thing is to get the hoop to go over the top. As it spins upward, it almost comes to rest on top before it accelerates on the way back down. Likewise, you assemble your efforts on the way up and strain to go over the top... Yet you could not have made it to the top based on your own efforts alone. You could succeed because God added His power to yours.

However, at the top, Satan waits in ambush. At the moment you reach the goal, God no longer supports you. If He did, it would be in violation of heavenly law. At that moment, when God lets you alone, you are liable to face Satan's attack. God and Satan each keep to their own territory and do not interfere with each other.

In other words, when you are making effort to fulfill your mission, you can gain God's help. But at the moment of success, you will face Satan. But because God and Satan do not appear at the same time, when it is time to face Satan, God withdraws. This is unavoidable. In order to give you the opportunity to fulfill your portion of responsibility, you must go over this test because of the law of human responsibility and because human beings are responsible to subjugate Satan. Knowing this, you should be alert at this critical point. It is when problems most commonly arise.

Then, you will meet another problem when you are coasting downhill. Having reached the summit, it is easy to relax and descend without making effort. If so, you will just continue to descend. But like spinning a hoop, to reach the next top you have to add more force on the downward cycle. The more force you exert as the hoop goes down, the faster it rises as it loops back up. From this perspective, know that you need God's support while you are descending just as much as you need His help when you were climbing. Yet since you are still in that dark area where Satan holds sway, you have to make a special prayer condition for a certain period of time; otherwise God's help will not be forthcoming. By this method, you can gain an added spurt of Heaven's power to rise up even faster towards the next goal.

Such is a formula. For instance, after the Israelites enjoyed a time of blessing, it was followed by a time of oppression. Without fail, after each blessing they faced attacks from Satan. (73:268-70, September 29, 1974)

> As we followed the path Thou hast walked,
> we found it was the path of the cross.
> Yet as we continued on this untraced way and struggled with the heart of pioneers,
> we discovered it was not the way of destruction.

People ridiculed us, but Thou didst encourage us.
Many people opposed us, but Thou didst comfort us.
So many times Thou didst counsel us, saying, "I am with you,
and the billions of saints in the spirit world are protecting your way." (16:50, December 26, 1965)

2. Deliverance from Danger and Death

O you who believe! Remember the grace of God on you, when there came down on you hosts; but We sent against them a hurricane and forces you could not see: but God sees clearly all that you do. Behold! They came on you from above you and from below you, and behold, the eyes became dim and the hearts gaped up to the throats, and you imagined various vain thoughts about God! In that situation were the believers tried; they were shaken as by a tremendous shaking…

And God turned back the unbelievers, for all their fury; no advantage did they gain; and enough is God for the believers in their fight. And God is full of Strength, Able to enforce His will.[29]

Qur'an 33.9-11, 25

Then Moses and the people of Israel sang this song to the LORD:
I will sing to the LORD, for he has triumphed gloriously;
the horse and his rider he has thrown into the sea.
The LORD is my strength and my song,
and he has become my salvation;
this is my God, and I will praise him,
my father's God, and I will exalt him.
The LORD is a man of war;
The LORD is his name.

Pharaoh's chariots and his host he cast into the sea;
and his picked officers are sunk in the Red Sea.
The floods cover them;
they went down into the depths like a stone.

Your right hand, O LORD, glorious in power,
your right hand, O LORD, shatters the enemy.
In the greatness of your majesty you overthrow your adversaries;
you send forth your fury, it consumes them like stubble.
At the blast of your nostrils the waters piled up,
the floods stood up in a heap;
the deeps congealed in the heart of the sea.

The enemy said, "I will pursue,
I will overtake,
I will divide the spoil,
my desire shall have its fill of them.
I will draw my sword,
my hand shall destroy them."
You blew them away with your wind,
the sea covered them;
they sank as lead
in the mighty waters.

Who is like thee, O LORD, among the gods?
Who is like thee, majestic in holiness,
terrible in glorious deeds, doing wonders?[30]

Exodus 15.1-11

They threw them [Paul and Silas] into prison, charging the jailer to keep them safely. Having received this charge, he put them into the inner prison and fastened their feet in the stocks. But about midnight Paul and Silas were praying and singing hymns to God, and the prisoners were listening to them, and suddenly there was a great earthquake, so that the foundations of the prison were shaken; and immediately all the doors were opened and everyone's fetters were unfastened. When the jailer woke and saw that the prison doors were open, he drew his sword and was about to kill himself, supposing that the prisoners had escaped. But Paul cried with a loud voice, "Do not harm yourself, for we are all here." And he called for lights and rushed in, and trembling with fear he fell down before Paul and Silas, and brought them out and said, "Men, what must I do to be saved?"

Acts 16.23-30

Arms pinioned, was I thrown down in a heap.
The elephant violently was goaded in the head.
The elephant ran away trumpeting,
Declaring, "To this prostrate figure am I a
    sacrifice;
Lord, in you alone lies my strength."
The Kazi urged the mahout to goad on the
    elephant,
Threatening, "Mahout! I shall cut you to
    pieces!
Goad and drive the elephant!"
But the elephant, meditating on God, would
    not move:
In his heart was lodged the Lord.
The people queried, "What offense has this
    holy man committed,
That in bonds he is thrown to be trampled by
    an elephant?"
The elephant bowed again and again to the
    heap before it.
The benighted Kazi did not realize this;
Three times he ordered this trial
But his hard heart still was not softened.
Says Kabir, The Lord is my guardian.
In absorption in Him lies His servant's life.

Adi Granth, Gaund, Kabir, p. 870 (Sikhism)

World-honored Lord and Perfect One,
I pray thee now declare
Wherefore this holy Bodhisat
Is known as Kuan Shih Yin [Hearer of the Cries
    of the World]? [31]
To this the Perfect One replied
By uttering this song:

The echoes of her holy deeds
Resound throughout the world.
So vast and deep the vows she made
When, after countless eons
Of serving hosts of Perfect Ones,
She voiced her pure desire
[To liberate afflicted beings].

Now hearken to what came of it—
To hear her name or see her form,
Or fervently recite her name
Delivers beings from every woe.

Were you with murderous intent
Thrust within a fiery furnace,
One thought of Kuan Yin's saving power
Would turn those flames to water!

Were you adrift upon the sea
With dragon-fish and fiends around you,
One thought of Kuan Yin's saving power
Would spare you from the hungry waves...

Were you amidst a band of thieves,
Their cruel knives now raised to slay,
One thought of Kuan Yin's saving power
And pity must restrain their blows.

Suppose the king now wroth with you,
The headsman's sword upraised to strike,
One thought of Kuan Yin's saving power
Would dash the sword to pieces.

Were you close pent by prison walls,
Your wrists and ankles bound by chains,
One thought of Kuan Yin's saving power
Would instantly procure release...

True Kuan Yin! Pure Kuan Yin!
Immeasurably wise Kuan Yin!
Merciful and filled with pity,
Ever longed-for and revered!

O Radiance spotless and effulgent!
O night-dispelling Sun of Wisdom!
O Vanquisher of storm and flame!
Your glory fills the world!

Lotus Sutra 25 (Buddhism)

Teachings of Sun Myung Moon

God appears as a rescue boat at the dire moment of death. (6:152, April 19, 1959)

We humans are completely foolish. But we have a friend in God, who is infinitely wise. His heavenly host—countless spirits—accompany us and provide reinforcements. When we think about this, we can be grateful.

I really understand the feeling of David as he stood before Goliath, on the verge of the showdown. He was bold and strong. He knew God's protection would bring him victory in the battle. Things turned out well because he faced his enemy with this thought in his heart: "When you strike, you will be the one who breaks, not me." (203:192, June 24, 1990)

President Reagan was shot, yet he did not die. During the attempt on his life three people were shot, one critically, and it was thought that he might die. But he also survived. Do you know why? Pope [John Paul II] was also shot, yet he too survived. Reverend Moon has similar divine protection. Sufficient [spiritual] foundation has been laid. (116:155, December 27, 1981)

Who guides the course of war? People start wars, but God guides their outcome, bringing recompense [for aggression]. However, it is not God's will to build a peaceful world through arms. (103:184, February 25, 1979)

When we pursue a public purpose, if Satan attacks us, God will come to our aid. If we are united with God at that point, Satan will have to retreat... and those who oppose us will disappear. This is what Satan fears more than anything. As more and more individuals, families and even nations welcome the Messiah and do the will of God, Satan grows weaker; and when the world welcomes him, Satan will disappear. Therefore, to prevent his own destruction, Satan places us in life-threatening situations and makes us shed blood on the battlefield. We should survive it. (329:287, August 11, 2000)

When Satan imprisons a citizen of Heaven within his barbed wire fence, at the proper time God will destroy that fence and reclaim him. Since he is a citizen of heaven, Satan has no right to contest his release. On the contrary, God will demand that he pay compensation for imprisoning an innocent person.

God can rescue His people at any time, but He waits until the time is ripe; then He will liberate everyone and demolish Satan's prison.

Even in the worst case, should you die, you can be confident of your destiny as you carry with you the thought, "I was born a citizen of Heaven, I lived as a citizen of Heaven, and I died for God's Kingdom." You will surely go to God's Kingdom in the spirit world, where all the heavenly spirits will welcome you with cheers. (98:162, July 16, 1978)

If you are doing God's will, even prison is an opportunity to receive blessings. The day you enter prison can be a day of hope. The day you are handcuffed can be a day of hope.

When I went to prison, I had joyful heart; I was even whistling. I found everything was prepared to welcome me. People there were waiting to receive my teachings. When I felt hungry, someone brought me food. The Bible records Elijah's miracle of being fed by ravens. In my case, communists brought me food; God moved them by mobilizing the spirit world. (103:207, February 25, 1979)

On August 1, 1950, more than 100 B-29 bombers bombed Heungnam Prison Camp [where I was incarcerated], damaging it severely. Because God had alerted me that this was about to happen, I protected the other prisoners. God told me that He would protect anyone who stayed within 12 meters of me, so I instructed my followers to stay close by. While the bombs were exploding, I was in silent meditation. I did not think about the bombing; rather I was contemplating the ideal world that would come in the future. It would be a cosmic loss to God if someone like me, who was fulfilling a mission for restoration, were taken to the spirit world. For this reason, God wanted to protect me at all costs; indeed, He was obliged to do so. (35:189, October 13, 1970)

Heungnam was the first place where U.N. troops landed in North Korea. It was because the Son of God was there, and God was urgent to rescue him. The communists were gathering groups of prisoners and taking them out of the camp, promising them food but in fact intending to execute them. The prisoners did not know it and even fought with each other to go, tempted by the promise of a good meal. But I knew of the deception and thought, "You are going on your final path, but I shall not die. Even if all of you die, I shall not. No matter what tragedy and misfortune I face, even if I am led to the execution ground, I shall survive somehow!"

On October 12, 1950, about 70 prisoners who were serving sentences of at least 7 years were taken to a mountain some 7 miles[32] away from the prison camp and executed. Since I had been sentenced to 5 years, I knew that two days later it would be my turn to be taken. Given that circumstance, God must have hurried to rescue me. On the evening of the 13th, I looked outside and saw that the situation had already changed. Rumors spread that UN troops had landed in Heungnam, and the communist guards were busy packing their belongings. The next day, October 14th, they were gone and we remaining prisoners were free. We then set off on the road to the South. (22:129-30, February 2, 1969)

Reversal and Restoration

SALVATION IS SOMETIMES PICTURED AS A GREAT REVERSAL. It looks to the day when God will act to turn the existing social and political order upside down, when the wealthy and powerful will no longer tower above the honest and god-fearing. Internally, it brings the insight that the way to God is the reverse of the way of the world. An enlightened person recognizes that he should reverse his or her orientation one-hundred-and-eighty degrees. Scripture speaks of this inner reversal as dying to self in order to live, seeking darkness in order to find the light, and abasing the self in order to become prominent.

This leads to the concept of salvation as restoration. Restoration refers to the undoing of bad habits, modes of thinking, ways of behaving, and social relations that have grown corrupt and deviated from the proper way. It is a return to the origin, aimed at restoring the original way of life according to the true principles and purposes of God. An important expression of this theme of reversion to the origin is the Buddhist doctrine of Dependent Origination (*Paticcasamuppada*), which is not just a law of causality but more properly the insight that all causes leading to downfall must be reversed.

Father Moon discusses this topic at length under the teaching of Restoration through Indemnity. Indemnity, broadly speaking, means to restore mistakes by taking the opposite course. It begins with a reversal of character—from self-centeredness to other-centeredness. It extends to relationships—paying restitution for a crime to making amends for a breach of trust, from the standpoint that it is my responsibility to restore harmony with my brother, even when the original problem was not my fault. It concludes with complete restoration, the reversal of the Original Sin that happened at the Human Fall.

1. The Great Reversal

The last will be first, and the first last.
>   Matthew 20.16

Whoever exalts himself will be humbled, and whoever humbles himself will be exalted.
>   Matthew 23.12

Him who humbles himself, God exalts; him who exalts himself, God humbles; from him who searches for greatness, greatness flies; him who flies from greatness, greatness searches out: with him who is importunate with circumstances, circumstance is importunate; by him who gives way to circumstance, circumstance stands.
>   Talmud, Erubin 13b (Judaism)

The way of Heaven,
Is it not like stretching a bow?
What is high up is pressed down,
What is low down is lifted up;
What has surplus is reduced,
What is deficient is supplemented.

The way of Heaven,
It reduces those who have surpluses,
To supplement those who are deficient.
The way of man is just not so:
It reduces those who are deficient,
To offer to those who have surpluses.
Who can offer his surpluses to the world?
Only a person of Tao.
>   Tao Te Ching 77 (Taoism)

The bows of the mighty are broken,
but the feeble gird on strength.
Those who were full have hired themselves out
    for bread,
but those who were hungry have ceased to
    hunger.
The barren has borne seven,
but she who has many children is forlorn.
The LORD kills and brings to life;
he brings down to Sheol and raises up.
The LORD makes poor and makes rich;
he brings low, he also exalts.
He raises up the poor from the dust;
he lifts the needy from the ash heap,
to make them sit with princes
and inherit a seat of honor.
For the pillars of the earth are the LORD's,
and on them he has set the world.
He will guard the feet of his faithful ones;
but the wicked shall be cut off in darkness;
for not by might shall a man prevail.[33]
>   1 Samuel 2.4-9

Teachings of Sun Myung Moon

The path of the providence of salvation is the path of restoration. The path of restoration is the path of recreation…

When God created the world, He had only one concept—the concept of the zero-point. Hence, we have to return to the zero-point when walking the path of restoration and recreating God's world. We should return to the state prior to God's creation; otherwise, nothing is possible. That is why the Bible teaches, "Whoever seeks to gain his life will lose it, but whoever loses his life will preserve it." To lose your life means to cut off Satan's life [by returning to the zero-point]. Otherwise, we have no way to connect with God at the origin.

Historically, evil people have lived better than good people. Originally, good people should prosper while evil people should decline. These positions should be switched. The zero-point is the time of transition when good people go up while evil people decline. Now is the time when this transition is taking place. (218:187-88, July 28, 1991)

In America, quite a few people live perverted lives. Grandfathers have sex with their granddaughters and fathers with their daughters—even while they live with their wives. This is the fruit of Satan, who in the beginning reversed the direction of human life 180 degrees from the plan of God. In a world that abides by Heaven's principles, could homosexuality exist? Lesbianism, alcoholism, drug addiction and such came to exist because human beings suffer from emotional misalignment. They suffer in this world, which is hell on earth. We, on the other hand, are living 180 degrees different from them, as we strive to live in God's Kingdom. (243:192, January 10, 1993)

2. Restoration by Going in the Opposite Direction

Whoever seeks to gain his life will lose it, but whoever loses his life will preserve it.

Luke 17.33

To yield is to be preserved whole.
To be bent is to become straight
To be empty is to be full.
To be worn out is to be renewed.
To have little is to possess.
To have plenty is to be perplexed.
Therefore the sage embraces the One
And becomes the model of the world.

Tao Te Ching 22 (Taoism)

I will teach you Dhamma: If this is, that comes to be; from the arising of this, that arises; if this is not, that does not come to be; from the stopping of this, that is stopped.[34]

Majjhima Nikaya 2.32 (Buddhism)

The world, O Kaccana, is for the most part bound up in a seeking, attachment, and proclivity, but a monk does not sympathize with this seeking and attachment, nor with the mental affirmation, proclivity, and prejudice which affirms an Ego. He does not doubt or question that it is only evil that springs into existence, and only evil that ceases from existence, and his conviction of this fact is dependent on no one besides himself. This, O Kaccana, is what constitutes Right Belief.

That things have being, O Kaccana, constitutes one extreme of doctrine; that things have no being is the other extreme. These extremes have been avoided by the Tathagata, and it is a Middle doctrine he teaches:

On ignorance depends karma;
On karma depends consciousness;
On consciousness depends name and form;
On name and form depend the six organs of sense;
On the six organs of sense depends contact;
On contact depends sensation;
On sensation depends desire;
On desire depends attachment;
On attachment depends existence;
On existence depends birth;
On birth depend old age and death, sorrow, lamentation, misery, grief, and despair. Thus does this entire aggregation of misery arise.

But on the complete fading out and cessation of ignorance ceases karma;
On the cessation of karma ceases consciousness;
On the cessation of consciousness ceases name and form;
On the cessation of name and form cease the six organs of sense;

On the cessation of the six organs of sense
ceases contact;
On the cessation of contact ceases sensation;
On the cessation of sensation ceases desire;
On the cessation of desire ceases attachment;
On the cessation of attachment ceases existence;
On the cessation of existence ceases birth;
On the cessation of birth cease old age and death, sorrow, lamentation, misery, grief, and despair. Thus does this entire aggregation of misery cease.[35]

Samyutta Nikaya 22.90 (Buddhism)

The sage awakes to light in the night of all creatures. That which the world calls day is the night of ignorance to the wise.

Bhagavad-Gita 2.69 (Hinduism)

The Way out into the light often looks dark,
The way that goes ahead often looks as if it went back.
The way that is least hilly often looks as if it went up and down,
The virtue that is really loftiest looks like an abyss,
What is sheerest white looks sullied. [36]

Tao Te Ching 41 (Taoism)

Sights, sounds, tastes, odors, things touched and objects of mind are, without exception, pleasing, delightful, and charming—so long as one can say, "They are."

These are considered a source of happiness by the world with its gods, and when they cease, this is by them considered suffering.

The cessation of phenomenal existence is seen as a source of happiness by us Aryans—this insight of those who can see is the reverse of that of the whole world:

What others say is a source of happiness—that, we say, is suffering; what others say is suffering—that, we know, as a source of happiness. Behold this doctrine, hard to understand, wherein the ignorant are bewildered.

Samyutta Nikaya 4.127-28 (Buddhism)

Teachings of Sun Myung Moon

The path of indemnity is to deny oneself and go opposite the way of the world. In the beginning in the Garden of Eden, Adam fell because he rejected God and followed Satan. Now in reverse we must reject Satan and return to God. (73:93, August 4, 1974)

When someone has lost his original position or state, he must make some condition to be restored to it. The making of such conditions of restitution is called indemnity. For example, to recover lost reputation, position or health, one must make the necessary effort or pay the due price. Suppose two people who once loved each other come to be on bad terms; they must make some condition of reconciliation before the love they previously enjoyed can be revived. In like manner, it is necessary for human beings who have fallen from God's grace into corruption to fulfill some condition before they can be restored to their true standing. (*Exposition of the Divine Principle*, Restoration 1.1)

A snake cannot grow without shedding its skin. To shed it, the snake crawls between narrow rocks. It needs an opposing force to push off the old skin. Likewise, the force of darkness has soaked through our body and blood. We cannot just go along with it; how do we get rid of it? We need the wisdom to go the opposite way entirely. (46:83, July 25, 1971)

Humanity went astray from the very beginning when Adam and Eve went in the wrong direction. Now we have to turn it completely around. Our conventional attitudes, our ways of thinking, and our desires in all areas of life must be changed into their opposites. What, then, should be our way of thinking? Thus far we have been thinking about our family for how it can benefit ourselves, and we have been dealing with our nation in ways that advance our self-interest. However, from now on we should think, "I exist for the greater whole—for my family, not for me; for my nation, not for me; for the world, not for me." Do you understand what I am saying? We must change fundamentally. White people should live for black people and yellow people, and yellow people should live for white people and black people. Likewise, Christianity should live for Islam, and Islam for Christianity. (May 1, 1978)

The Human Fall took place because the first human ancestors were caught up with consciousness of self. Conversely, restoration requires that our awareness be reoriented away from the self and toward the cosmos and its ideal purpose. Therefore, the path to liberation requires that we willingly bear other people's burdens and take responsibility for the common good. (396:178, November 7, 2002)

3. Restoration by Returning to the Original State

If you wish to untie a knot, you must first understand how it was tied.
Surangama Sutra (Buddhism)

Sentient beings wish to return to their origin where their nature will be in perfect unity.
Surangama Sutra (Buddhism)

Confucius said, "To subdue one's self and return to propriety, is perfect virtue. If a man can for one day subdue himself and return to propriety, all under heaven will ascribe perfect virtue to him."
Analects 12.1.1 (Confucianism)

Always to know the standard is called profound and secret virtue.
Virtue becomes deep and far reaching,
And with it all things return to their original natural state.
Then complete harmony will be reached.
Tao Te Ching 65 (Taoism)

It is as if a man traveled through the forest, through the great wood, should see an ancient road traversed by men of former days... And that man brings word to the prince, "My lord, as I traveled through the forest, I saw an ancient path, an ancient road traversed by men of former days. Going along it I saw the ruins of an ancient city, an ancient prince's domain, wherein dwelt men of former days, having gardens, groves, pools, foundations of walls, a goodly spot. Lord, restore that city." The prince or his minister then restores the city, so that it becomes prosperous and flourishing, populous and teeming with people who thrive and reach old age. Even so have I seen an ancient Path, an ancient road traversed by the rightly enlightened ones of former times.
Samyutta Nikaya 2.106 (Buddhism)

For as by a man came death, by a man has come also the resurrection of the dead. For as in Adam all die, so also in Christ shall all be made alive.[37]
1 Corinthians 15.21-22

Why are idolators lustful? Because they did not stand at Mount Sinai. For when the serpent came upon Eve he injected lust into her; as for the Israelites who stood at Mount Sinai, their lustfulness departed; but as for the idolators who did not stand at Mount Sinai, their lustfulness did not depart.[38]
Talmud, Shabbat 145b-146a (Judaism)

In the messianic future the Holy One will heal the injury [of Adam's sin]. He will heal the wound of the world.
Genesis Rabbah 10.4 (Judaism)

Teachings of Sun Myung Moon

The way of restoration is to return to the origin. Therefore, unless you make the required indemnity condition, you cannot return to the origin. It is human beings, not God, who make the indemnity condition. In order for a sick person to be healed, he must take the medicine even if it is bitter. Real medicine is bitter medicine. Making the indemnity condition is like taking bitter medicine; it is difficult work. However, without making the indemnity condition, you cannot go the path of restoration. (92:254-55, April 18, 1977)

How can we be re-created as God's children? There is only one way: by going all the way back, before the many generations of your ancestors, before fallen Adam and Eve, and come to God through the gate of the True Ancestors. (96:40, January 1, 1978)

Adam and Eve took a path that resulted in their drowning. Hence, all fallen human beings are like drowned men. They cannot save themselves; someone must come and resolve the problem for them. We who are called to this task must go all the way to the root of the problem and fix it there. (248:149, August 1, 1993)

At the Fall, human beings disobeyed God's word and rebelled against Him. Hence they were subjugated by Satan's lies. Once united with Satan, human beings received Satan's nature and Satan's love instead of God's nature and God's love.

To be restored as an original human being, we must reverse the process of the Fall. This time we must separate ourselves from Satan, reach out to God whom we had lost, and obey His Word. In this way, we can receive God's nature and His love. (88:208, September 18, 1976)

> Father! All the situations of history are entangled in us today.
> Therefore we wish and pray that Thou wilt cut all those tangles
> by connecting us with the Center of liberation. (1:345-46, December 30, 1956)

Rebirth

JESUS SAID, "YOU MUST BE BORN ANEW." Rebirth in Christ transforms a worldly person into a child of God. He or she now experiences an intimacy with God and has the indwelling spirit of Christ. The reason why people must be born a second time, according to Father Moon, lies in the Human Fall. The Fall's negative effects, experienced in every generation, derives from its corruption of the lineage of the human race at its root. Through the fall, Satan was able to usurp God and occupy the position of humanity's false father. To break the devil's persistent hold over human life, we must be born again as children of God. For this purpose, God sent the Messiah, a man without sin, representing the Father, and the Holy Spirit, representing the Mother. Out of their love we can be born anew.

In eastern religions, to enter the path of the spiritual aspirant is often understood as a second, spiritual birth. In Hinduism and Buddhism, people become "twice-born" by receiving religious instruction. Their biological parents brought them forth into a world of the senses, but after their second, spiritual, birth their life is now grounded in the Dharma. Father Moon, however, treats rebirth as a specifically Christian doctrine, one that applies strictly to the work of the Messiah to sever us from the lineage of sin. He would regard the broader concept of spiritual conversion through instruction in religious truth under the concept of resurrection.

Father Moon also speaks of the conditions to be made in order to receive rebirth: repentance and renouncing worldly ways. Thus, he also likens the process of rebirth to engrafting: Before attaching the new shoot, first the arborist cuts off the old branches; likewise we must deny ourselves and cut off everything false. Then we receive the new shoot containing the life and love of God. If the tree is properly pruned, that new shoot will produce new fruit and propagate God's lineage. Thus, although rebirth is a gift from above, it requires responsibility and dedication on the part of its recipients.

1. Born Anew as God's Sons and Daughters

Now there was a man of the Pharisees, named Nicodemus, a ruler of the Jews. This man came to Jesus by night and said to him, "Rabbi, we know that you are a teacher come from God; for no one can do these signs that you do, unless God is with him." Jesus answered him, "Truly, truly, I say to you, unless one is born anew, he cannot see the kingdom of God." Nicodemus said to him, "How can a man be born when he is old? Can he enter a second time into his mother's womb and be born?" Jesus answered, "Truly, truly, I say to you, unless one is born of water and the Spirit, he cannot enter the kingdom of God.[39] That which is born of the flesh is flesh, and that which is born of the Spirit is spirit. Do not marvel that I say to you, 'You must be born anew.'"

John 3.1-7

To all who received him [Jesus], who believed in his name, he gave power to become children of God; who were born, not of blood nor of the will of the flesh nor the will of man, but of God.

John 1.12-13

He from whom the pupil gathers the knowledge of his religious duties is called the teacher. Him he should never offend. For he causes the pupil to be born a second time by imparting to him sacred learning. The second birth is the best; the father and the mother produce the body only.

Apastamba Dharma Sutra 1.1 *(Hinduism)*

Monks, I [Buddha] am a brahmin, one to ask a favor of, ever clean-handed, wearing my last body, incomparable physician and surgeon. You are my own true sons, born of my mouth, born into the doctrine, created in the doctrine, heirs to the doctrine, not carnal heirs.[40]

Itivuttaka 101 *(Buddhism)*

Teachings of Sun Myung Moon

Why do we need to be born anew? It is because of the Human Fall. What is the Fall? The Fall means that every human being is born in a fallen state, the offspring of fallen parents. You must clearly understand that you were born in fallen love from fallen parents. (95:82, November 11, 1977)

Here in the Western world, many deny that the Human Fall has anything to do with them. Yet because of the Fall, our lineage began wrongly and our love began wrongly. Without recognizing this, we cannot comprehend salvation and the purpose of the religious life. (193:54, August 20, 1989)

Before the Fall, Adam and Eve could relate to God freely and directly, but after the Fall this was no longer possible. Also, due to the Fall, Cain and Abel, the children of Adam and Eve, could not inherit

God's lineage. They inherited Satan's lineage instead. Therefore, all people should understand that they have false life flowing though their lineage, which began as the result of false love. This is why Jesus said in John 3:3, "Unless one is born anew, he cannot see the Kingdom of God." (313:220, February 10, 2000)

Jesus told Nicodemus, "Truly, truly, I say to you, unless one is born anew, he cannot see the kingdom of God." (John 3.3) Rebirth means to be born a second time. Why must fallen people be born anew?

Had Adam and Eve realized the ideal of creation and become the True Parents of humanity, they would have borne good children without original sin and formed the Kingdom of Heaven on earth. However, Adam and Eve fell and became evil parents, multiplying evil children who created this hell on earth. Hence, as Jesus told Nicodemus, fallen people cannot see the Kingdom of God unless they are first born anew—as children without original sin.

We cannot be born without parents. Who, then, are the good parents through whom we can be born again, cleansed of original sin and able to enter the Kingdom of God? Parents who have original sin cannot give birth to good children who do not have original sin. Certainly, it is impossible to find sinless parents among fallen humankind. These parents must descend from Heaven. Jesus was the Parent who came from Heaven. He came as the True Father in order to give rebirth to fallen people, transforming them into good children, thoroughly cleansed of original sin and fit to build the Kingdom of Heaven on earth... For this reason, the Bible speaks of him as "the last Adam" (1 Cor. 15.45) and the "Everlasting Father." (Isa. 9.6)

However, a father alone cannot give birth to children. There must be a True Mother, as well as a True Father, for fallen children to be reborn as good children. The Holy Spirit came as the True Mother. This is why Jesus told Nicodemus that no one can enter the Kingdom of God unless he is born anew through the Holy Spirit. (John 3.5)

There are many who have received the revelation that the Holy Spirit is feminine. This is because the Holy Spirit comes as the True Mother or second Eve. Since the Holy Spirit is the feminine aspect of divinity, without first receiving her we cannot go before Jesus as his brides. Being feminine, the Holy Spirit consoles and moves the hearts of people. (Rom. 5.5, John 14.26-27; Acts 9.31) She cleanses people's sin, thereby atoning for the sin which Eve committed. Jesus, the masculine Lord, works in heaven (yang), while the Holy Spirit, his feminine counterpart, works on the earth (yin). (*Exposition of the Divine Principle*, Christology 4.1.1)

2. Rebirth Requires Cutting Off the Old Self

All who are led by the Spirit of God are sons of God. For you did not receive the spirit of slavery to fall back into fear, but you have received the spirit of sonship. When we cry, "Abba! Father!" it is the Spirit himself bearing witness with our spirit that we are children of God, and if children, then heirs, heirs of God and fellow heirs with Christ, provided we suffer with him in order that we may also be glorified with him.

Romans 8.14-17

For the natural man is an enemy to God, and has been from the fall of Adam, and will be, forever and ever, unless he yields to the enticings of the Holy Spirit, and puts off the natural man and becomes a saint through the atonement of Christ the Lord, and becomes as a child, submissive, meek, humble, patient, full of love, willing to submit to all things which the Lord sees fit to inflict upon him, even as a child submits to his father.

Book of Mormon, Mosiah 3.19 (Latter-day Saints)

These same people, though wrapped in all these veils of limitation, and despite the restraint of such observances, as soon as they drank the immortal draught of faith, from the cup of certitude, at the hand of the Manifestation of the All-glorious, were so transformed that they would renounce for his sake their kindred, their substance, their lives, their beliefs, yea, all else save God! So overpowering was their yearning for God, so uplifting their transports of ecstatic delight, that the world and all that is therein faded before their eyes into nothingness. Have not this people exemplified the mysteries of rebirth?

Book of Certitude 155 (Baha'i Faith)

Teachings of Sun Myung Moon

We cannot be born again unless we deny our fallen selves. (244:100, January 31, 1993)

Christianity teaches that we cannot be saved unless we receive the Holy Spirit. We come before God when the Holy Spirit visits us and connects us with the Savior. The Holy Spirit comes to bring us to Heaven, to the God of goodness. But before we can receive it, first we must repent. (99:75, September 1, 1978)

Resurrection may be defined as the process of being restored from the death caused by the Fall to life, from the realm of Satan's dominion to the realm of God's direct dominion, through the providence of restoration. Accordingly, whenever we repent of our sins and rise to a higher state of goodness, we are resurrected to that degree. (*Exposition of the Divine Principle*, Resurrection 1.3)[41]

> Father! Because we were born from evil,
> we must be born again to goodness.
> The destiny of having to be born twice is a very miserable one.
> Isn't living as a stepchild very regrettable even in the world?
> Yet we are not even at the level of stepchildren;
> having been born as children of the enemy we must find our Original Parents,
> but the path is never a smooth one.
> Therefore, we receive countless attacks from Satan's spears, swords and arrows.
> We must cut the ties that bind our bodies and go forth.
> We must confront the people that bind us and cut their ties,
> whether with our teeth or with our strength. (27:161, December 7, 1969)

3. Rebirth through Jesus and the Holy Spirit

When the day of Pentecost had come, they were all together in one place. And suddenly a sound came from heaven like the rush of a mighty wind, and it filled all the house where they were sitting. And there appeared to them tongues as of fire, distributed and resting on each one of them. And they were all filled with the Holy Spirit and began to speak in other tongues, as the Spirit gave them utterance...

And Peter said to them, "Repent, and be baptized every one of you in the name of Jesus Christ for the forgiveness of your sins; and you shall receive the gift of the Holy Spirit. For the promise is to you and to your children and to all that are far off, every one whom the Lord our God calls to him."

Acts 2.1-4, 38-39

We ourselves were once foolish, disobedient, led astray, slaves to various passions and pleasures, passing our days in malice and envy, hated by men and hating one another; but when the goodness and loving kindness of God our Savior appeared, he saved us, not because of deeds done by us in righteousness, but in virtue of his own mercy, by the washing of regeneration and renewal in the Holy Spirit, which he poured out upon us richly through Jesus Christ our Savior, so that we might be justified by his grace and become heirs in hope of eternal life.

Titus 3.3-7

The Spirit and the Bride say, "Come." And let him who hears say, "Come." And let him who is thirsty come, let him who desires take the water of life without price.

Revelation 22.17

Truly, truly, I say to you, unless you eat the flesh of the Son of man and drink his blood, you have no life in you; he who eats my flesh and drinks my blood has eternal life, and I will raise him up at the last day. For my flesh is food indeed, and my blood is drink indeed. He who eats my flesh and drinks my blood abides in me, and I in him. As the living Father sent me, and I live because of the Father, so he who eats me will live because of me. This is the bread which came down from heaven, not such as the fathers ate and died; he who eats this bread will live for ever.

John 6.53-58

Teachings of Sun Myung Moon

We are reborn through the path of love. It begins when we yearn for Jesus and the Holy Spirit. The Holy Spirit is the Bride, and the resurrected Jesus is the Bridegroom. They are our spiritual parents, and their love is the basis of our rebirth. As conception and birth originate in the love between a woman and a man, we are reborn through the love of Jesus and the Holy Spirit as they become one.

Once we receive the grace of the Holy Spirit, we naturally feel great affection and yearning for Jesus. This is the work of the Holy Spirit, moving our hearts to welcome Jesus the Bridegroom. When we are spiritually united with them, rejoicing in that state of oneness, we can regain the lost standard of original love. That is the experience of rebirth in Christianity. According to the Principle, in that moment we are resurrected to new life. (October 13, 1970)

Jesus gives the bridegroom's love and the Holy Spirit gives the bride's love: that love must become my bone and flesh. That is, as Jesus said, "I am in you and you are in me." Unless this foundation of heart-felt love is established, there is no rebirth. People easily say, "You must be born again," but in fact, to be reborn you need to love Jesus more than anyone else. Satan's dominion over humankind is based on his false love, so unless your love centered on God surpasses any human love in the fallen world, there is no way for you to connect to God. (114:28, May 14, 1981)

Christianity began from Jesus' blood on the cross. Why is Jesus' blood so meaningful? Jesus came as the True Father. Jesus' blood signifies the blood of the perfected father, with no trace of the Fall. However, can a father alone bequeath a lineage? Not without a mother! That is why the goal of the Old Testament was to have the Marriage of the Lamb. (193:57, August 20, 1989)

In Christianity, the Holy Spirit has been taking the role of mother. We are born again on the spiritual level through the mother, the Holy Spirit, and the father's spirit, Jesus' spirit.

Of course, we were born from our mother's womb. However, even beyond the womb, our life originated from our father's seed. Hence, while going back to the mother's womb exchanges the false lineage for the true lineage, it does not yet give us the father's seed.

Therefore, Christians have been longing for the True Father, who appears as the Second Coming of the Lord. He is the origin of new life. As Adam before the Fall already held in his body the seed of his children, the True Father holds within His body the seed that will bear fruit as the sons and daughters of God. (55:117-18, April 1, 1972)

Resurrection

THE RESURRECTION OF THE DEAD PROPHESIED IN THE BIBLE and the Qur'an holds out the promise of a blessed future life with God. Resurrection is not simply a matter of the soul's natural transition at death from this world into the afterlife. It is God's saving act to raise the soul from the realm of death to life eternal. In resurrection, we gain not simply a new opportunity to live; we gain a new quality of life. Father Moon teaches that we are raised spiritually from a hellish existence within the realm of death to a blessed existence in the bosom of God.

Resurrection requires some condition on our part to claim the new life that God offers: dying to self, confirmed faith, even martyrdom. This is the "death" to self that severs our ties with Satan, in order that we may more completely relate with God. Just as Jesus died on the cross as a precondition to his resurrection, so we too may face a trial. Jesus' triumph over seeming defeat at the hands of the Romans demonstrates that God can turn defeat and even death into victory and life.

Scripture speaks of a Day of Resurrection in the end times, when all the souls of the righteous will be raised up to heaven. The Bible speaks of the 144,000 saints of the "first resurrection." This means that even in the afterlife, spirits are languishing in darkness, oppressed by evil conditions until the future day of their liberation. When the Messiah comes and defeats and binds Satan in prison, on that day all souls in heaven and earth will taste the freedom of resurrection and new life. But as Father Moon makes clear, the purpose of the first resurrection is not to reward certain believers with eternal glory at everyone else's expense. Rather, the saints at the first resurrection will join in the struggle to defeat all the powers of evil, until, in the words of Paul, "the last enemy to be destroyed is death," that is, until not one soul remains in the realm of death.

1. The Dead Return to Life

And listen on the day when the crier cries from a near place, the day when they will hear the Cry in truth. That is the Day of the Coming Forth (from the graves). Verily We give life and give death, and to Us is the journeying. On the day when the earth splits asunder from them, and hastening forth they come. That is a gathering easy for Us.

Qur'an 50.41-44

The hand of the LORD was upon me, and he brought me out by the Spirit of the LORD, and set me down in the midst of the valley; it was full of bones… and lo, they were very dry. And he said to me, "Son of man, can these bones live?" And I answered, "O Lord GOD, thou knowest."

Again he said to me, "Prophesy to these bones, and say to them, O dry bones, hear the word of the LORD. Thus says the Lord GOD to these bones, Behold, I will cause breath to enter you, and you shall live. And I will lay sinews upon you, and will cause flesh to come upon you, and cover you with skin, and put breath in you, and you shall live. And you shall know that I am the LORD."

So I prophesied as I was commanded; and as I prophesied, there was a noise, and behold, a rattling; and the bones came together, bone to its bone. And as I looked, there were sinews on them, and flesh came upon them, and skin covered them… and breath came into them, and they lived, and stood upon their feet, an exceedingly great host.

Then he said to me, "Son of man, these bones are the whole house of Israel. Behold, they say, 'Our bones are dried up, and our hope is lost; we are clean cut off.' Therefore prophesy, and say to them, Thus says the Lord GOD, Behold, I will open your graves, and raise you from your graves, O my people, and I will bring you home into the land of Israel… And I will put my Spirit within you, and you shall live, and I will place you in your own land. Then you shall know that I, the LORD, have spoken, and I have done it, says the LORD." [42]

Ezekiel 37.1-14

"Shall we really be restored to our first state
even after we are crumbled bones?
That would be a vain proceeding," they say.
Surely it will need but one shout,
and lo! they will be awakened.

Qur'an 79.10-14

For as in Adam all die, so also in Christ shall all be made alive.

1 Corinthians 15.22

Jesus said to her, "I am the resurrection and the life; he who believes in me, though he die, yet shall he live, and whoever lives and believes in me shall never die."

John 11.25

I know that my Redeemer lives,
and at last he will stand upon the earth;
and after my skin has been thus destroyed,
then from my flesh I shall see God.

Job 9.25-26

Truly, truly, I say to you, unless a grain of wheat falls into the earth and dies, it remains alone; but if it dies, it bears much fruit. He who loves his life loses it, and he who hates his life in this world will keep it for eternal life.

John 12.24-25

And among His signs is this: you see the earth barren and desolate, but when We send down rain to it, it is stirred to life and yields increase. Truly, He who gives life to the dead earth can surely give life to men who are dead. For He has power over all things.

Qur'an 41.39

So it is with the resurrection from the dead. What is sown is perishable, what is raised is imperishable. It is sown in dishonor, it is raised in glory. It is sown in weakness, it is raised in power. It is sown in a physical body, it is raised in a spiritual body. If there is a physical body, there is also a spiritual body. Thus it is written, "The first man Adam became a living being"; the last Adam became a life-giving spirit.

1 Corinthians 15.42-45

Teachings of Sun Myung Moon

Many have hitherto believed that the death caused by the Fall was physical death. Consequently, they have interpreted the biblical concept of resurrection as revival from physical death, and believed that resurrection of the dead involves the biological regeneration of their decomposed bodies. However, the Fall of the first human ancestors did not cause this kind of death. According to the Principle of Creation, the human body was created to return to dust after it grows old. A decomposed body cannot be restored to its original state. Furthermore, it is not necessary for a spirit to take on another physical body when he is meant to enjoy eternal life in the vast spirit world.

Resurrection may be defined as the process of being restored from the death caused by the Fall to life, from the realm of Satan's dominion to the realm of God's direct dominion, through the providence of restoration. Accordingly, whenever we repent of our sins and rise to a higher state of goodness, we are resurrected to that degree.

The Bible illustrates the process of resurrection: "He who hears my word and believes him who sent me, has eternal life; he does not come into judgment, but has passed from death to life." (John 5.24) Based on this verse, we can affirm that resurrection means to leave the bosom of Satan and return to the bosom of God. It is also written, "For as in Adam all die, so also in Christ shall all be made alive." (1 Cor. 15.22) This verse means that because we inherited Satan's lineage as a result of Adam's fall, we are dead; when we return to the lineage of God through Christ, we shall be resurrected to life...

The changes a person experiences when he is resurrected and enters the governance of God take place in his heart and spirit. These internal changes also purify his body, transforming it from a haunt of Satan into a temple of God. In this sense, we may say that our physical body is also resurrected. We may compare it to a building that was previously used for evil purposes and is now used as a place of worship. Although there may be no change in its outward appearance, it is now sanctified as a sacred building. (*Exposition of the Divine Principle*, Resurrection 1.3-4)

What happens to us after we die? Up to the moment we die, we belong to ourselves. But after we die, we belong to God. Because we were born of a fallen lineage, until death we cannot sever our ties with Satan. After death, however, we can establish ties with God. Therefore, unless we die we cannot be resurrected...

Therefore, when the Bible teaches, "Those who are willing to die shall live, while those who want to live shall die," it means by death not the end of our God-given eternal life, but rather the end of our fallen life into which we were born from a fallen lineage in a fallen world. (December 19, 1998)

The Bible teaches that those who are willing to die shall live, and those who want to live shall die. This means that in order to escape from the fallen realm we must be willing to give up our lives. There is no true life in the fallen realm. Hence, when we deny this fallen life, we can be resurrected.

Jesus was resurrected because he denied his own life. Jesus could not resurrect himself; it was God who raised him. (307:167, November 8, 1998)

2. The Resurrection of the Saints—The First Resurrection

For the Lord himself will descend from heaven with a cry of command, with the archangel's call, and with the sound of the trumpet of God. And the dead in Christ will rise first; then we who are alive, who are left, shall be caught up together with them in the clouds to meet the Lord in the air; and so we shall always be with the Lord.
1 Thessalonians 4.16-17

For as in Adam all die, so also in Christ shall all be made alive. But each in his own order: Christ the first fruits, then at his coming those who belong to Christ. Then comes the end, when he delivers the kingdom to God the Father after destroying every rule and every authority and every power. For he must reign until he has put all his enemies under his feet. The last enemy to be destroyed is death.
1 Corinthians 15.22-26

Then I looked, and lo, on Mount Zion stood the Lamb, and with him a hundred and forty-four thousand who had his name and his Father's name written on their foreheads. And I heard a voice from heaven like the sound of many waters and like the sound of loud thunder; the voice I heard was like the sound of harpers playing on their harps, and they sing a new song before the throne and before the four living creatures and before the elders. No one could learn that song except the hundred and forty-four thousand who had been redeemed from the earth. It is these who have not defiled themselves with women, for they are chaste; it is these who follow the Lamb wherever he goes; these have been redeemed from mankind as first fruits for God and the Lamb, and in their mouth no lie was found, for they are spotless…
Revelation 14.1-5

Then I saw an angel coming down from heaven, holding in his hand the key of the bottomless pit and a great chain. And he seized the dragon, that ancient serpent, who is the Devil and Satan, and bound him for a thousand years, and threw him into the pit, and shut it and sealed it over him, that he should deceive the nations no more, till the thousand years were ended. After that he must be loosed for a little while.

Then I saw thrones, and seated on them were those to whom judgment was committed. Also I saw the souls of those who had been beheaded for their testimony to Jesus and for the word of God, and who had not worshiped the beast or its image and had not received its mark on their foreheads or their hands. They came to life, and reigned with Christ a thousand years. The rest of the dead did not come to life until the thousand years were ended. This is the first resurrection. Blessed and holy is he who shares in the first resurrection!
Revelation 20.1-6

Teachings of Sun Myung Moon

The "first resurrection" spoken of in the Bible describes the fulfillment of restoration for the first time in providential history. This will be accomplished through Christ at the Second Advent. He will cleanse people of the original sin and restore them to their true, original selves, enabling each to fulfill the purpose of creation.

The hope of all Christians is to participate in the first resurrection. But who in fact shall participate? It will be those who are the first to believe in, serve and follow Christ at the Second Advent. They will assist him in fulfilling all the indemnity conditions worldwide and in accomplishing the providence of restoration. In the process, they will be the first to have their original sin removed, become divine spirits, and fulfill the purpose of creation...

In order for Christ at the Second Advent to complete the providence of restoration, he must find a certain number of people who can restore through indemnity the missions of all the past saints who, despite their best efforts to do God's Will, fell prey to Satan when they failed in their responsibilities. He must find these people during his lifetime and lay the foundation of victory over Satan's world. The total number of saints whom Christ at the Second Advent must find to accomplish this task is 144,000. (*Exposition of the Divine Principle*, Resurrection 2.2.7)

What is the secret that will enable us to chase out Satan from everywhere? It is to live for the sake of others, die for the sake of others, and practice altruistic love. When we do that, Satan will certainly flee, breaking down all the barriers and national borders that he had erected.

What will happen next? Once Satan is gone, souls who had been headed for hell will be given the opportunity to resurrect and enter heaven. Eternal life will finally become a reality.

As people who know God and the Kingdom of Heaven, we will call on God, the Source of love, as our Father. We will earnestly desire to practice God's tradition of living for others, and will continue to do so for tens of thousands of years. This is the tradition of eternal life, established in people of the eternal lineage. It is for us to share. (August 18, 2000)

Eternal Life

FOR MANY, THE GOAL OF RELIGION is immortality or eternal life. People have always chafed under the limitations of mortality, and have found in religion the means to transcend the death which seems to proscribe the possibilities of human existence. As with resurrection, eternal life is not simply about the survival of the soul at death and its journey into the afterlife. Eternal life is not about eternal existence *per se*, but rather about the quality of that existence.

We find that the scriptures of many religions give two meanings to the terms "life" and "death." There is physical life—existence on this earthly plane, and there is spiritual life—the state of blessedness which endures from life to life and transcends death. There is physical death—the dropping of the body which is an event in the voyage of every soul, and spiritual death—the condition of distance from God, ignorance, and a hellish existence in the hereafter.

"Eternal life" and "immortality" are thus ciphers to describe the condition of blessedness. This condition is present already in the physical life of the person who realizes Truth or lives in God's grace, and it will continue, unabated, in the hereafter. The person who gains eternal life has accomplished the goal of life, and hence death is not to be feared as a limitation, as it is for a worldly person who has tied all hopes to his possessions and pleasures in the world. We note, however, that Buddhist scriptures generally avoid speaking of this state of blessedness as eternal life, for Buddhism views the desire for life as a kind of grasping, and hence a fetter to liberation. Instead, they speak of Nirvana.

Father Moon's teaches that eternal life is rooted in our relationship with the eternal God, based upon God's love for us and our love for God. "Eternity does not exist apart from true love," he states. Then he expands upon this concept to describe the relationship between human lovers as aspiring for the eternal. This is so because we human beings are designed for eternal life, eternal love with God, and eternal community with the ones we love under God.

1. Eternal Life in God

For God so loved the world that He gave His only begotten Son, that whoever believes in him shall not perish but have everlasting life.

John 3.16

He who believes in me, though he die, yet shall he live, and whoever lives and believes in me shall never die.

John 11.25-26

Those who have faith and do righteous deeds, they are the best of creatures. Their reward is with God: Gardens of Eternity, beneath which rivers flow; they will dwell therein for ever; God well pleased with them, and they with Him; all this for such as fear their Lord and Cherisher.

Qur'an 98.7-8

The Supreme Being does not die; I will therefore not die.

Akan Proverb (African Traditional Religions)

Being in accord with Tao, he is everlasting.

Tao Te Ching 16 (Taoism)

Where one sees nothing but the One, hears nothing but the One, knows nothing but the One—there is the Infinite. Where one sees another, hears another, knows another—there is the finite. The Infinite is immortal; the finite is mortal.

It is written, He who has realized eternal Truth does not see death, nor illness, nor pain; he sees everything as the Self, and obtains all.

Chandogya Upanishad 7.23, 27 (Hindusm)

Those who are free from desire are free because all their desires have found fulfillment in the Self. They do not die like the others; but realizing Brahman, they merge in Brahman. So it is said:

> When all the desires that surge in the heart
> Are renounced, the mortal becomes immortal.
> When all the knots that strangle the heart
> Are loosened, the mortal becomes immortal,
> Here in this very life.

Brihadaranyaka Upanishad 4.4.6-7 (Hinduism)

For the wages of sin is death, but the free gift of God is eternal life in Christ Jesus our Lord.

Romans 6.23

From the unreal lead me to the Real!
From darkness lead me to light!
From death lead me to immortality!

Brihadaranyaka Upanishad 1.3.28 (Hinduism)

Higher than this is Brahman, the Supreme, the Great.
Hidden in all things, body by body,
The One embracer of the universe—
By knowing Him as Lord men become immortal.

I know this mighty Person
Of the color of the sun, beyond darkness.
Only by knowing Him does one pass over death.
There is no other path for going there.

Than whom there is nothing else higher,
Than whom there is nothing smaller, nothing greater,
The One stands like a tree established in heaven.
By Him, the Person, this whole world is filled.

That which is beyond this world
Is without form and without ill.
They who know That, become immortal;
But others go only to sorrow.

          Svetasvatara Upanishad 3.7-10 (Hinduism)

The supreme stage of the Soul is free from birth, old age and death; he is supreme, pure, and devoid of eight karmas; he possesses infinite knowledge, intuition, bliss, and potency; he is indivisible, indestructible, and inexhaustible. Besides, he is supersensuous and unparalleled, is free from obstructions, merit, demerit, and rebirth, and is eternal, steady, and independent.[43]

          Kundakunda, Niyamasara 176-77 (Jainism)

"For the living know that they shall die" (Ecc. 9.5): these are the righteous who in their death are called living... "but the dead know nothing": these are the wicked who in their lifetime are called dead.

          Talmud, Berakot 18ab (Judaism)

Leave the dead to bury their own dead; but as for you, go and proclaim the kingdom of God.[44]

          Luke 9.60

Teachings of Sun Myung Moon

When a follower asked Jesus if he could go home to bury his deceased father, Jesus said, "Leave the dead to bury their own dead." (Luke 9.60) From these words of Jesus, it is clear that the Bible contains two different concepts of life and death. The first concept of life and death concerns physical life. Here, "death" means the end of physical life, as was the case of the disciple's deceased father who was to be buried. "Life" in that sense means the state in which the physical self maintains its physiological functions.

The second concept of life and death concerns those living people who had gathered to bury the deceased man, those whom Jesus called "the dead." Why did Jesus refer to people whose bodies were alive and active as the dead? He meant that since they had not accepted Jesus, they were far removed from the love of God and were dwelling in the realm of Satan's dominion. This second concept of death does not refer to the expiration of physical life. It means leaving the bosom of God's love and falling under the dominion of Satan. The corresponding concept of life refers to the state of living in accordance with God's Will, within the dominion of God's infinite love. Therefore, even if a person's physical self is alive, if he dwells apart from God's dominion and is in servitude to Satan, he is dead as judged by the original standard of value. A similar conclusion can be drawn from the Lord's words of judgment upon the faithless people of the church in Sardis: "You have the name of being alive, and you are dead." (Rev. 3.1)

On the other hand, even though a person's physical life may have expired, he remains alive in the true sense if his spirit abides in the Kingdom of Heaven in heaven, a realm in the spirit world where God governs through love. When Jesus said, "He who believes in me, though he die, yet shall he live" (John 11.25), he meant that those who believe in him and live within the realm of God's dominion have life. Even after their physical bodies have returned to the soil, their spirits enjoy life in God's dominion. Jesus also said, "Whoever lives and believes in me shall never die" (John 11.26) In saying that believers will never die, he meant that those who believe in Jesus during their earthly life will obtain eternal life not in this world, but in spirit, within the bosom of God's love. They will be alive, both in this life and the next. Jesus' words assure us that death, in the sense of the end of physical life, has no effect on our eternal life. (*Exposition of the Divine Principle*, Resurrection 1.1)

Eternal life does not mean that we merely exist forever in the spirit world. It means we eternally "live." How do we cultivate such a life?

As human beings, each of us was created to be an object of God's love—God's beloved partner. God cherishes true love more than Himself. Hence, although God is the center of absolute and eternal life, His ideal of true love is even more absolute and eternal. It is the very core of God. We are the object partners of that true love.

How do we come to be in such a precious, eternal position? Love is the attribute that brings subject and object into oneness. Love unites a family. It unites the nation. In the unity of love, we can participate in anything our beloved does, follow him wherever he goes, and inherit everything he or she possesses. In the same way, we can inherit God's eternal life. We can inherit God's heart—his heart of love by which He longs to dwell within each of us and also in the creation. How precious it is to find such great value within ourselves!…

What joy! What amazing grace! What an unparalleled blessing! Now we can dwell in the same position as God. Now we can participate in God's eternal love. (216:115, March 9, 1991)

[Originally,] human beings are born from true love, grow in true love, live in true love and die in true love. We are not meant to just disappear into a void. Since God, the Subject of all created beings, is eternal, unchanging and unique, we who are His partners of love should live eternally. This is the starting-point of the logic of eternal life. Life does not begin from life. Life originates from true love, not the other way around.

If God creates something He regards as most precious, would He discard it ten years or one hundred years later, or would He want to keep it for eternity? Obviously, He would create it to last forever. Thus it is with human beings. Would God create human beings to be born and die, and their death is the end? No, He created human beings to live forever. Why? They are the object partners of the absolute God, with whom He can share joy in absolute true love…

Suppose you were fleeing to a refugee camp; if you had a precious possession, would you take it with you or leave it behind? You would want to take it with you. Once in the camp, you would treasure it. You would not enjoy it for a few days and then throw it away. You would keep it until you die, and then bequeath it to your descendants for eternity. That is human desire.

It is the same with God, the Absolute Being. God is eternal, and He desires that His object partners, whom He loves, should live eternally. That is why human beings want to live forever. For this reason also, the absolute God never ceases to seek for His children. Each human being has the value of eternity. (290:143-44, February 18, 1998)

If God only liked humans for one or two days, or even for one hundred years, and then discarded them, it would not be true love. The more you love, the more you want to be with your beloved one. For this reason you sometimes find a man whose wife died young who never remarries, preferring to live alone until his death while treasuring some article of his wife's clothing…

That is why God created human beings, His precious children, to live forever. However, for love to last forever, people should stand on the foundation of actions that can generate greater output force. In other words, as time goes by love's power gets stronger, generating more give and take action instead of consuming energy. Hence, the lovers' joy never ends, but only grows and develops more and more, to infinity. Such is the ideal world, the Kingdom of Heaven in which God dwells. (39:42)

2. Love: The Basis of Eternal Life

We know that we have passed out of death into life, because we love the brethren. He who does not love abides in death. Any one who hates his brother is a murderer, and you know that no murderer has eternal life abiding in him. By this we know love, that he [Jesus] laid down his life for us; and we ought to lay down our lives for the brethren.

1 John 3.14-16

Teachings of Sun Myung Moon

Eternity does not exist apart from true love. (August 18, 1988)

When you are united with your beloved, you do not care if the world is perishing. Even if your parents demanded that you separate, threatening you with a knife, you would not be afraid of that knife. You would be determined to stay together, even if you died and went to the next world. You are not concerned about your earthly life, because you believe that you will be together in the spirit world. You actually prefer life in eternity to finite earthly life. (380:88, June 5, 2002)

> May we discover by ourselves and prove by ourselves,
> not only by faith or conviction but also from experience,
> that Thou and I have a relationship extending front and back, right and left.
> Thou and I were living, are living and shall ever live
> in a relationship eternal and unchanging. (40:350, February 11, 1971)

Universal Salvation

THE COMPASSION AND GRACE OF GOD KNOW NO BOUNDS. The heavenly Father's heart yearns to save all His children. These passages from scripture praise the extent of God's saving work and predict it eventually to embrace all humankind. In Buddhist terms, the essential purpose of absolute Truth is to liberate all sentient beings, and Mahayana Buddhist scriptures express the universality of grace in the bodhisattva vow of the Buddha Amitabha to save all beings.

Salvation may come to all people through one central point: thus in Abraham "shall all the families of the earth be blessed" (Gen. 12.3). For those who believe in one religion as the only way, the divine mandate to save all humankind is a powerful impetus to missionary activity. On the other hand, God may express His saving will by sending multiple prophets and sages to all nations, warning each to return to God using the means suitable to their different cultures.

If salvation is to be available universally, to every soul who has ever lived regardless of his or her earthly life, the doctrine may appear at odds with beliefs about hell and the Last Judgment. If God is most essentially just, how can the wicked ever receive salvation? On the other hand, if God is most essentially gracious and compassionate, how can He permit any creature to suffer in hell eternally? To understand the heart of God our heavenly Father, Father Moon asks us to imagine how we would feel if one of our children were a condemned criminal. We would want to save our child, even take his place at the gallows.

Father Moon also discusses the difficulty of the path of salvation in terms of the methods which God is constrained to use, because He created human beings with the sovereign freedom to live and mold our lives as each sees fit. Nevertheless, ultimately God's purpose shall be done: all people will be saved and even hell will be emptied of its occupants.

The daily concern of the Parent is single-heartedly how best I can advance arrangements to save all of you.

Ofudesaki 14.35 (Tenrikyo)

The Dharma of the Buddhas
by the constant use of a single flavor
causes the several worlds
universally to attain perfection.
By gradual practice
all obtain the Fruit of the Way.

Lotus Sutra 5 (Buddhism)

The Lord is not slow about his promise as some count slowness, but is forbearing toward you, not wishing that any should perish, but that all should reach repentance.

2 Peter 3.9

God is on the watch for the nations of the world to repent, so that He may bring them under His wings.

Numbers Rabbah 10.1 (Judaism)

I testify that Thou art the Lord of all creation, and the Educator of all beings, visible and invisible. I bear witness that Thy power hath encompassed the entire universe, and that the hosts of the earth can never dismay Thee, nor can the dominion of all peoples and nations deter Thee from executing Thy purpose. I confess that Thou hast no desire except the regeneration of the whole world, and the establishment of the unity of its peoples, and the salvation of all them that dwell therein.

Gleanings from the Writings of Bahá'u'lláh 115 (Baha'i Faith)

We will make offering unto You with worship,
    O Lord, and to the Right,
That you may achieve through Good Mind the
    destiny of all creatures in the Dominion.
For the salvation of the man of insight among
    such as you,
O Wise One, will hold good for everyone.[45]

Avesta, Yasna 34.3 (Zoroastrianism)

"As I live," says the LORD God, "I have no pleasure in the death of the wicked."

Ezekiel 33.11

Turn to me and be saved,
all the ends of the earth!
for I am God, and there is no other.
By myself I have sworn,
from my mouth has gone forth in righteousness
an irrevocable decree:
"To me every knee shall bow,
every tongue shall swear."

Isaiah 45.22-23

God it is who has sent His Messenger with the guidance and the Religion of Truth, that He may cause it to prevail over all [false] religion, however much the idolaters may be averse.

Qur'an 9.33

The LORD said to Abram... "In you all the families of the earth shall be blessed."

Genesis 12.3

And there never was a people, without a warner having lived among them.

Qur'an 35.24

"Are you not like the Ethiopians to me,
O people of Israel?" says the LORD.
"Did I not bring up Israel from the land of Egypt,
and the Philistines from Caphtor and the
    Syrians from Kir?"[46]

Amos 9.7

The Tathagatas do not enter ultimate liberation until all living beings have entered ultimate liberation.

Holy Teaching of Vimalakirti 4 *(Buddhism)*

Behold my servant, whom I uphold,
my chosen, in whom my soul delights;
I have put my Spirit upon him,
he will bring forth justice to the nations.
He will not cry or lift up his voice,
or make it heard in the street;
a bruised reed he will not break,
and a dimly burning wick he will not quench;
he will faithfully bring forth justice.
He will not fail or be discouraged
till he has established justice in the earth;
and the coastlands wait for his law.[47]

Isaiah 42.1-4

I establish the Vows unexcelled,
And reach the highest path, Bodhi.
Were these Vows unfulfilled,
I would never attain Enlightenment.

I will be the great provider
Throughout innumerable ages.
Should I fail to save all in need,
I would never attain Enlightenment.

Upon my attaining Enlightenment,
If my Name were not heard anywhere
In the ten quarters of the universe,
I would never attain Enlightenment.

Practicing the Holy Way—selflessness,
Depth in right reflection and pure wisdom,
Aspiring toward the highest path,
I will be the teacher of devas and men.

My wondrous power by its great light
Brightens countless lands throughout,
Removes the darkness of the three defilements
And delivers all from suffering and pain.[48]

Larger Sukhavativyuha Sutra 9.1-5:
Juseige *(Buddhism)*

Teachings of Sun Myung Moon

The sinful world brings humankind sorrow and causes God to grieve. (Gen. 6.6) Would God abandon this world in its present misery? God intended to create a world of goodness and experience from it the utmost joy; yet due to the Human Fall, the world came to be filled with sin and sorrow. If this sinful world were to continue forever in its present state, then God would be an impotent and ineffectual God who failed in His creation. Therefore, God will save this sinful world, by all means...

    The Human Fall was undoubtedly the result of human mistakes. Nevertheless, God also assumes some responsibility for the outcome because it was He who created human beings. Therefore, God has felt compelled to conduct the providence to correct this tragic outcome and to restore human beings to their true, original state. Furthermore, God created us to live eternally. This is because God, the eternal subject partner, wanted to share eternal joy with human beings as His object partners. Having endowed human beings with an eternal nature, God could not, by the laws of the Principle, simply annihilate them just because they fell. If He were to do that, He would be violating His own Principle of Creation. The only choice left to God is to save fallen people and restore them to the original, pure state in which He initially created them. (*Exposition of the Divine Principle*, Eschatology 2.1)

The purpose of the providence of salvation, and of religion, is to save the entire world. Since God created humankind as His beloved children, He cannot just beat and kill them and leave them in hell. Therefore the goal of the providence of salvation is to save everyone, not leaving even a single person in the satanic world. God wants to take back every kind of human being. (80:283, November 2, 1975)

God is a God of love. When God looks down from His throne and sees spirits in hell crying out to Him in their misery, "Please, God, save me!" what would He say? Would He say, "You deserve a lot worse"? Or does He have mercy on them? Surely, God will do everything possible to liberate hell. (98:116, May 7, 1978)

Imagine you have a son who committed murder and was sentenced to death. As he is going to his execution, would you say, "You deserve to die. Good-bye. At last we are rid of you!" Would any parent think like that? On the contrary, you would rather want to die in his place.

Imagine now you have many children, and they are dying tragically one after another. Do you think any parent could just watch them die without doing everything possible to rescue them? Loving parents would be desperate to save their children. They would keep on trying, even though it may take an eternity.

This gives you some sense of God's misery. As He watches His children entering hell and eternal death, God is infinitely sorrowful and anxiously tries to liberate them to eternal life. Only by so doing can He fulfill His responsibility as our Heavenly Father. Therefore, it is logical to conclude that in the end God will liberate every soul in hell. (62:51, September 10, 1972)

To believe, as some do, that all humanity will receive judgment and only 144,000 Christians will be saved at the Rapture is an unusually self-centered way of thinking. (245:97, February 28, 1993)

The Unification Church's viewpoint of salvation is not for a husband to go to heaven while his wife goes to hell. Both have to go to the Kingdom of Heaven together. It is not for us to enjoy heaven while our father and mother languish in hell. We should dwell in the Kingdom of Heaven with our sons and daughters and parents together. (34:359, September 20, 1970)

God's providence of salvation is to bring [evil] to voluntary surrender. If God could have used force as He pleased, why has the providence taken thousands of years? He could have finished everything in short time—a few weeks. However, since God does not use force, instead He endures a heartbreaking situation. (394:16, October 6, 2002)

Even fallen parents cannot feel joyful when one of their children is unhappy. How much more so for God, our Heavenly Parent? It is written, "The Lord… is forbearing toward you, not wishing that any should perish, but that all should reach repentance." (2 Pet. 3.9) Accordingly, hell cannot remain forever. No trace of hell will remain in the ideal world, which is the fulfillment of God's deepest desire. In the Last Days, when the time is ripe, evil spirits will descend to evil people on earth of the same spiritual level and assist them to accomplish God's Will. Indeed, even the demons testified that Jesus was the Son of God. (Matt. 8.29). (*Exposition of the Divine Principle,* Resurrection 3.3.3)

Chapter 8

RELIGION

The Purpose of Religion

ALL RELIGIONS SHARE CERTAIN PURPOSES IN COMMON, though with different emphases. For Western religions, the primary purpose of religion is salvation. The etymology of the word "religion" derives from a Latin word meaning "to re-bind" with God. Human beings are fallen and broken, and therefore God has established religion as a means of repairing our brokenness, restoring us to our original goodness, and re-connecting us with God. In contrast, the Eastern understanding of religion is contained in its Chinese characters, which mean "foundational teaching." This describes the purpose of religion as the basic teaching for cultivating a good and virtuous character.

Father Moon recognizes both meanings, inasmuch as fallen human beings cannot finally cultivate virtuous character without resolving sin and rebinding with God. He distinguishes two valid aspects of religion: first, providential religions (Judaism and Christianity) whose purpose is to welcome the Messiah who comes to solve original sin and restore full communion with God, and second, religions the world over whose purpose is mainly to train people in virtue. The Kingdom of God is built on both of these foundations.

Religion also has a social purpose: to cultivate community. Religion teaches the ways of love and reconciliation that enable people to live in peace and harmony. By extension, the ultimate purpose of religion is to establish world peace. That is, because God is the Creator and Father of all humankind, religions that take us close to God enable us to feel part of the universal brotherhood and sisterhood that flows from His parental love.

1. Religions Provide the Way of Salvation

"Men, what must I do to be saved?" And they said, "Believe in the Lord Jesus, and you will be saved, you and your household."

Acts 16.30-31

Seek refuge with the Lord alone,
with your whole being, Bharata.
By His grace, you will reach
supreme peace, an everlasting estate.

Bhagavad-Gita 18.62 (Hinduism)

Surely the [true] religion with God is Islam [the Surrender]. Those who formerly received the Scriptures... if they argue with you, [O Muhammad], say, "I have surrendered my purpose to God, and so have those who follow me." And say to those who have received the Scriptures and those who have not read [them], "Have you also surrendered?" If they surrender, then truly they are rightly guided.

Qur'an 3.19-20

To many a refuge fear-stricken men betake themselves—to hills, woods, groves, trees, and shrines. Nay, no such refuge is safe, no such refuge is supreme. Not by resorting to such a refuge is one freed from ill.

He who has gone for refuge to the Buddha [the teacher], the Dhamma [the teaching], and the Sangha [the taught], sees with right knowledge the Four Noble Truths: Sorrow, the

Cause of Sorrow, the Transcending of Sorrow and the Noble Eightfold Path which leads to the Cessation of Sorrow. This, indeed, is refuge secure. By seeking such refuge one is released from all sorrow.

Dhammapada 188-192 (Buddhism)

Surely, the path that leads to worldly gain is one, and the path that leads to Nibbana is another; understanding this, the bhikkhu, the disciple of the Buddha, should not rejoice in wordly favors, but cultivate detachment.

Dhammapada 75 (Buddhism)

Teachings of Sun Myung Moon

Why throughout history have people needed to improve themselves through morals, ethics, and religion? Why should we observe them? It is because we sense something is wrong with us, and we desire to return to our original standing before God. (205:8, July 15, 1990)

However hard the original mind may struggle to attain goodness, we can hardly find any examples of true goodness in this world under the sovereignty of evil. Human beings have thus been compelled to seek the source of goodness in the world transcendent of time and space. This necessity has given birth to religion. Through religion, fallen people mired in ignorance have sought to meet God by ceaselessly striving toward the good. Even though the individuals, peoples and nations that championed a certain religion may have perished, religion itself survives. (*Exposition of the Divine Principle*, Eschatology 2.3)

God, the Parent of humankind, cannot remain aloof when He sees His sons and daughters in their fallen state. They are like broken radios, so God created repair shops to fix them. These repair shops are religions. Seeing the many traces of these repair shops down through history, we cannot deny the existence of God. (54:102, March 20, 1972)

If God used His almighty power, He could easily save all humanity. Then He wouldn't need religion. But why does God need religion? God wants the enemy to surrender willingly. When that happens, God can become the center and heal all beings. That is God's strategy. (207:21, October 21, 1990)

Religion does not have humankind as its primary object. Rather, religious teachings establish God, the Parent, as foremost. A life of following God's will is a course to establish and mature in a relationship with God. Therefore, holy men and women invariably support the will of Heaven and declare the heart of Heaven.

    A true religion should teach people about God. A true religion should not have some vague ideas about God; a true religion should be able to give a clear picture of God so that people can understand Him. A religion that compromises with the world cannot be called a higher order religion. That kind of religion will ultimately decline.

    A true religion should teach people the path to know God clearly, to become one with God, and finally, to reestablish the world that God originally intended at the creation. After all, the purpose of religion is to seek for the ideal world: a world without sin, a world where all people enjoy the original relationship with God. (February 6, 2003)

> We know that the main problem here is not which denomination,
> which religion or which group we belong to.

The viewpoint of truth—the entirety of truth—
is to have an inward heart that Thou canst recognize,
and to go forth with an earnest heart that can experience Thy heart.
O Father, grant us to know Thy heart! (4:236, May 18, 1958)

2. Religions Cultivate Good Character

Religion that is pure and undefiled before God and the Father is this: to visit orphans and widows in their affliction, and to keep oneself unstained from the world.

James 1.27

Whoever surrenders his purpose to God while doing good, his reward is with his Lord; and there shall be no fear come upon them, neither shall they grieve.

Qur'an 2.112

For the grace of God has appeared for the salvation of all men, training us to renounce irreligion and worldly passions, and to live sober, upright, and godly lives in this world, awaiting our blessed hope, the appearing of the glory of our great God and Savior Jesus Christ, who gave himself for us to redeem us from all iniquity and to purify for himself a people of his own who are zealous for good deeds.

Titus 2.11-14

Make your mosque of compassion, your prayer mat of sincerity;
your Qur'an of honest and legitimate earning.
Be modesty your circumcision, noble conduct your Ramadan fast—
thus shall you be a true Muslim.

Make good deeds your Kaaba; truth your preceptor;
good action your Kalima and namaz.
Make your rosary of what pleases God:
Thus will you be honored at the last reckoning.

Adi Granth, Var Majh, M.1, p. 140 (Sikhism)

What is to be avoided most in our life is vacillation and frivolity; what is most excellent is a reverential heart. Therefore, we Confucians endeavor to preserve sincerity of heart and consider reverence as most essential. It is needless to say that sincerity and reverence make us companions of heaven and earth, gods and spirits. There is, however, another class of people who adopt Buddhism as their guidance. They bow before the Buddha and recite his sutras, always bent on preserving reverence and awe. They will never relax the vigilant guard over the heart, which will by degrees become pure and bright, free from evil thoughts and ready to do good. This enlightenment is called their most happy land. What is necessary, then, for Buddhists as well as Confucians is to avoid vacillation and frivolity, which will render you unreliable. Keep the heart always restrained by reverence and awe. Otherwise what can be the use of the recitation of sutras or the discourses of Confucius?[1]

Tract of the Quiet Way (Taoism)

Teachings of Sun Myung Moon

The word "religion" in Chinese characters is 宗教 (*chongkyo* in Korean). It means a floor-like teaching, in other words, the foundational teaching for human beings. (92:309, April 24, 1977)

The church is the place where you cultivate your character and become a person of integrity. Due to the Fall we came to be in need of the church. The family and society are not sufficient to nurture a mature character; it doesn't happen automatically. Nor does school: even if you attend a good college and then go on to earn a doctor's degree, it will not restore your character. That is where the church has a role. (25:126, September 30, 1969)

Through religions, God has been teaching people how to strengthen a God-centered spirit and reverse the body's control over the mind; these further our character development. This is the reason why religions recommend that we fast, sacrifice and serve, be meek and humble, and so on. It is to weaken the power of the body and to have the body submit to the spirit. It normally takes three to five years for a person leading a life of faith to free him or herself from a body-centered, habitual lifestyle and establish a spirit-centered lifestyle. (201:208-09, April 9, 1990)

Each religion that has appeared on this earth emerged from the deep will of God's providence to teach the nature of love. (Way of Unification 1.1.4.1)

Heaven is our original homeland, where we are meant to go. We fallen human beings are exiles from our original homeland, and hence our destiny is to return there. We cannot, however, enter heaven by ourselves, so through the course of history God has to set up paths to enable us to return. This is why God created the various religions: to be training grounds for heaven, illuminating paths for every people, culture and tradition. Religions are meant to train and polish people to be qualified to enter the region of the original homeland. To cope with humankind's many different cultures, God set up paths in many directions, yet with each path related to the one standard. In this way, God is leading these various paths toward one unified religious world.

What do all religions teach to guide people to the original homeland? They promote the path of living for the sake of others. The higher the religion, the more strongly it emphasizes the importance of living for others. For example, religions teach us to be humble. Why? Because to live for others, we should be able to lift other people above ourselves. Religions also teach us to sacrifice and serve. Why? Through these ways, religions train people to fit the rules of the Kingdom of Heaven. (78:117, May 6, 1975)

3. Religions Promote Universal Community

There is neither Jew nor Greek, there is neither slave nor free, there is neither male nor female; for you are all one in Christ Jesus.
Galatians 3.28

The believers indeed are brothers; so set things right between your two brothers, and fear God; haply so you will find mercy.
Qur'an 49.10

Israel's reconciliation with God can be achieved only when they are all one brotherhood.
Talmud, Menahot 27a (Judaism)

Behold, how good and pleasant it is
when brothers dwell in unity!
It is like the precious oil upon the head,
running down upon the beard,
upon the beard of Aaron,
running down on the collar of his robes!
It is like the dew of Hermon,
which falls on the mountains of Zion!
For there the LORD has commanded the blessing,
life for evermore.
Psalm 133

Happy is the unity of the Sangha.
Happy is the discipline of the united ones.
Dhammapada 194 *(Buddhism)*

The ultimate purpose of Buddhism, and for that matter all religions, is to serve and benefit man.
Tenzin Gyatso, The Fourteenth Dalai Lama *(Buddhism)*

Teachings of Sun Myung Moon

Throughout history, the basic pillar of every civilization has been the spirit. Religion is that spiritual pillar, enduring from age to age always keeping the spirit as its center. As religion expands its influence, it guides the human conscience, leavens the social environment, and guides humankind towards the world of God's desire. (9:277, June 12, 1960)

God established religion to convey God's love and truth to humankind and to save humankind. God established various religions, each in its own time and place. For example, He founded Buddhism in India and Confucianism in China approximately 2,400 years ago, and in Judea, He founded Christianity 2,000 years ago.

It can be said assuredly that the absolute value perspective is established only through religions which revere Ultimate Reality. Conversely, no fundamental solution to today's confusion is possible through those thoughts and philosophies that are not founded on religion... In history, we have the examples of Confucianism, Buddhism, Christianity and Islam, each of which, in its own time and place, dispelled anxiety and brought peace to societies in chaos. On the foundation of peace and security, each brought forth a flourishing of culture. (122:300, November 26, 1982)

What is the true religion? It is the religion that brings the truth by which all people can enter into a genuine parent-child relationship with God. It unites all humankind in brotherly love. Further, it strives to bring about one human family centered on the love of God. These are the qualities of a true religion. People who are searching for the highest religion, the religion established by God, should seek a religion with these qualities. (91:225, February 20, 1977)

In the next world, people are divided by nationality; except religious people, who can dwell together with fellow-believers from every nation. In the religious sphere people believe in one God and long for one world; hence they can live together transcending nationality. (297:271, December 19, 1998)

Although their skin colors are different and their living circumstances are different, in relating to Thy Will they are brothers and sisters in a destined relationship of one blood. (10:150, September 25, 1960)

The ultimate purpose of all religions is to realize the ideal world of peace, which is God's desire. Religions should be concerned about the Will of God for the salvation of the world before thinking of the salvation of their own denomination or the salvation of individuals. (135:221, November 16, 1985)

One Truth, Many Paths

PASSAGES FROM DIVERSE SCRIPTURES AFFIRM that religions that do not share the faith of that scripture nevertheless contain elements of Truth. They affirm that all genuine religions worship the same God. Thus, the Qur'an affirms that Jews and Christians are People of the Book who worship the same God as the God of Muhammad. The Sikh scriptures affirm that there is one God for Muslims and Hindus. A Shinto text affirms that the chief Shinto deity is essentially the same as the Buddha.

Further, scriptures affirm that each religion is a path to the same Supreme Goal. Here we have the famous images of many rivers flowing into the same ocean or a mountain with many paths leading up to the same summit. The religions of the world begin by addressing the needs, customs and circumstances of diverse cultures, but as they elevate humanity they draw closer together as their paths converge to the One. In this regard, Father Moon affirms that God inspired each of the great religious founders with a message appropriate to the culture and times in which he lived. He honors them as humanity's true guides, who sent to the earth within the providence of God to help humanity progress towards the ultimate goal.

Certainly, every religion considers its way the best and highest path. The Bible says that Jesus is "the way, the truth and the life," and that "nobody comes to the Father but by me." The Qur'an states that it is the only accurate witness to the previous revelations—the Torah and the Gospel having suffered corruptions and interpolations. Nevertheless, we are cautioned to be humble before the higher wisdom of God. As the Parable of the Blind Man and the Elephant teaches, each way may touch the truth without seeing its entirety. Father Moon likewise sees religions at different levels, due to their appearance at different ages in the course of humanity's spiritual development. Yet the differences among religions should not obscure the core truth they hold in common. Hence, religious people can overlook their differences and find common ground.

1. All Religions Worship the Same God and Serve His Great Will

The Hindus and the Muslims have but one and the same God;
What can a mullah or a sheikh do?

Adi Granth, Bhairo, p. 1158 (Sikhism)

For from the rising of the sun to its setting my name is great among the nations, and in every place incense is offered to my name, and a pure offering; for my name is great among the nations, says the LORD of hosts.

Malachi 1.11

Those who worship other gods with faith and devotion also worship Me, Arjuna, even if they do not observe the usual forms. I am the object of all worship, its enjoyer and Lord.

Bhagavad-Gita 9.23-24 (Hinduism)

Lo! We did reveal the Torah, wherein is guidance and a light, by which the prophets who submitted to God judged the Jews, as did the rabbis and the doctors of the law, because they were required to guard God's Book, and to which they were witnesses. So fear not mankind, but fear Me. And barter not My revelations for a little gain. Whoso judges not by that which God has sent down—such are disbelievers...

And We caused Jesus, son of Mary, to follow in their footsteps, confirming the Torah before him, and We bestowed on him the Gospel, wherein is guidance and a light, confirming that which was revealed before it in the Torah—a guidance and an admonition for those who ward off evil. Let the People of the Gospel judge by that which God has revealed therein. Whosoever judges not by that which God has revealed—such are those who live in evil.

And unto thee We revealed the Scripture with the truth, confirming whatever Scripture was before it, and a watcher over it. So judge between them by that which God has revealed, and follow not their desires apart from the truth which has come unto thee.[2]

For each We have appointed a divine law and a traced-out way. Had God so willed, He could have made you all one community. But He willed it otherwise in order to test you by that which He has given you. So vie one with another in doing good works! Unto God you will all return, and He will then inform you of that wherein you differ.

Qur'an 5.44-48

This is the land of the gods. The people should revere them. In my essence I [Amaterasu] am the Buddha Vairocana. Let my people understand this and take refuge in the Law of the Buddhas.[3]

Revelation of Amaterasu to Emperor Shomu (Shinto)

There can be no doubt that whatever the peoples of the world, of whatever race or religion, derive their inspiration from one heavenly Source, and are the subjects of one God. The difference between the ordinances under which they abide should be attributed to the varying requirements and exigencies of the age in which they were revealed. All of them, except for a few which are the outcomes of human perversity, were ordained of God, and are a reflection of His Will and Purpose.

Gleanings from the Writings of Bahá'u'lláh 111 (Baha'i Faith)

As the different streams
having their sources in different places
all mingle their waters in the sea,
so, O Lord, the different paths that men take,
through various tendencies,
various though they appear,
crooked or straight, all lead to Thee.

Sanskrit hymn (Hinduism)

In whatever way and path humans worship Me, in that same path do I meet and fulfill their aspirations and grace them. It is always My Path that humans follow in all their different paths and journeys, on all sides.

Bhagavad-Gita 4.11 (Hinduism)

Those who believe in the Qur'an, those who follow the Jewish scriptures, and the Sabeans and the Christians—any who believe in God and the Last Day, and work righteousness—on them shall be no fear, nor shall they grieve.

Qur'an 5.69

There are righteous men among the Gentiles who have a share in the world to come.

Tosefta Sanhedrin 13.2 (Judaism)

And Peter opened his mouth and said, "Truly I perceive that God shows no partiality, but in every nation any one who fears him and does what is right is acceptable to him."

Acts 10.34-35

And nearest to them in love to the believers you will find those who say, "We are Christians," because among them are men devoted to learning and men who have renounced the world, and they are not arrogant. And when they listen to the revelation received by the Apostle, you will see their eyes overflowing with tears, for they recognize the truth. They pray, "Our Lord! We believe; write us down among the witnesses."[4]

Qur'an 5.82-83

Other religions found everywhere try to counter the restlessness of the human heart, each in its own manner, by proposing "ways," comprising teachings, rules of life and sacred rites. The Catholic Church rejects nothing that is true and holy in these religions. She looks with sincere reverence those ways of conduct and of life, those precepts and teachings which, though differing in many aspects from the ones she holds and sets forth, nonetheless often reflect a ray of that Truth which enlightens all men.

Vatican II, Nostra Aetate (Christianity)

Teachings of Sun Myung Moon

Although different religions have different names for God and different ways of worshipping Him, the central Being worshipped by each religion is the one and only God. (140:11, February 1, 1986)

All people know Jesus, Buddha, Confucius and Muhammad as the founders of the world's great religions. We revere them as the guides of humankind. There can be no objection to believing their teachings.

Why should people follow them? They came to this world as our guides. Each takes responsibility for one religion and guides his people to advance toward the summit. When they reach the summit and find that they are only on a low peak among a great range of mountains, these founders will lead them to another trail, and then another, as they advance upward towards the highest summit.

God does not choose only the path to the summit from the East. If God did, people from the West who cannot come around to the East would have no path. Therefore, God established religions in every direction—East, West, South and North—and revealed the major routes to reach to the peak from each direction. On the way, they each absorbed numerous peoples, as God furthered their progress towards one unified world. (81:181-82, December 28, 1975)

All four great founders of religion were centered on God. They were not their own lords, for above each was God, their Lord. God is above Jesus; likewise God is above Buddha, Confucius and Muhammad. These men knew God; that is why they could become the founders of religion. That is why they taught a common message—that message was one of righteousness, peace and justice. They worked to spread that message and to establish a world of goodness. They all lived many centuries ago, yet their teachings guide people to the present day. (130:146-47, January 8, 1984)

There are numerous religions on the earth today. God needed to set up different religions in order to gather the peoples scattered all over the world. Each people has a religion suited to its distinct history, circumstance, cultural background and customs, yet these religions are all headed towards one goal. They are like the streams of a single river. As you go downstream, the number of streams decreases as they merge into larger and larger tributaries, until finally they merge into a single great river. Likewise, all the religions are to unite as they flow towards the place where they can capture God's love; there they will stay. (23:125, May 18, 1969)

Religion provides training as we seek for God's love and ideal. The world's religions were given different responsibilities to raise people level by level back to the original state. (87:177, June 2, 1976)

The world in which we live is not the world of goodness; it is a fallen world where evil holds sway. Hence, many barriers block our relationship with the God of goodness. To remove these barriers, God needs human beings to play a mediating role. Therefore, throughout history and all over the world, God has been developing movements based on religion to transform this evil world to the world of goodness.

Among every people of the world, God developed a religion suitable to its unique culture and customs. God expanded the scope of these religions according to their suitability, from local beliefs to worldwide faiths. Today these religious roots have spawned four great civilizations: Christian civilization, Islamic civilization, Indian [Hindu] civilization, and the Far Eastern civilization rooted in Confucianism, Buddhism and Taoism.

Looking at the world today, what would be God's wish? His desire is that these four religions not remain separate; He would unite them and present one religion on the world stage. That religion should represent God's true Will to the world. (113:313, May 10, 1981)

> There is not a single person whom Thou hast not touched,
> or country that Thou hast not guided in hope.
> Thou hast been leading all peoples,
> transcending national borders,
> to the present point on the path to the original world,
> Thine eternal ideal. (76:86-87, February 1, 1975)

2. Beneath the Differences Are Universal Elements

A number of disciples went to the Buddha and said, "Sir, there are living here in Savatthi many wandering hermits and scholars who indulge in constant dispute, some saying that the world is infinite and eternal and others that it is finite and not eternal, some saying that the soul dies with the body and others that it lives on forever, and so forth. What, Sir, would you say concerning them?"

The Buddha answered, "Once upon a time there was a certain raja who called to his servant and said, 'Come, good fellow, go and gather together in one place all the men of Savatthi who were born blind… and show them an elephant.' 'Very good, sire,' replied the servant, and he did as he was told. He said to the blind men assembled there, 'Here is an elephant,' and to one man he presented the head of the elephant, to another its ears, to another a tusk, to another the trunk, the foot, back, tail, and tuft of the tail, saying to each one that that was the elephant.

"When the blind men had felt the elephant, the raja went to each of them and said to each, 'Well, blind man, have you seen the elephant? Tell me, what sort of thing is an elephant?'

"Thereupon the men who were presented with the head answered, 'Sire, an elephant is like a pot.' And the men who had observed the ear replied, 'An elephant is like a winnowing basket.' Those who had been presented with a tusk said it was a ploughshare. Those who knew only the trunk said it was a plough; others said the body was a granary; the foot, a pillar; the back, a mortar; the tail, a pestle, the tuft of the tail, a brush.

"Then they began to quarrel, shouting, 'Yes it is!' 'No, it is not!' 'An elephant is not that!' 'Yes, it's like that!' and so on, till they came to blows over the matter. The raja was delighted with the scene.

"Just so are these preachers and scholars holding various views blind and unseeing… In their ignorance they are by nature quarrelsome, wrangling, and disputatious, each maintaining reality is thus and thus."

Then the Exalted One rendered this meaning by uttering this verse of uplift:

> O how they cling and wrangle, some who claim
> For preacher and monk the honored name!
> For, quarreling, each to his view they cling.
> Such folk see only one side of a thing.[5]

Udana 68-69: Parable of the Blind Men and the Elephant (*Buddhism*)

Some Hindus had brought an elephant for exhibition and placed it in a dark house. Crowds of people were going into that dark place to see the beast. Finding that ocular inspection was impossible, each visitor felt it with his palm in the darkness.

The palm of one fell on the trunk. "This creature is like a water-spout," he said. The hand of another lighted on the elephant's ear. To him the beast was evidently like a fan. Another rubbed against its leg. "I found the elephant's shape is like a pillar," he said. Another laid his hand on its back. "Certainly this elephant is like a throne," he said.

The sensual eye is just like the palm of the hand. The palm has not the means of covering the whole of the beast.

The eye of the Sea is one thing and the foam another. Let the foam go, and gaze with the eye of the Sea. Day and night foam-flecks are flung from the sea: How amazing! You behold the foam but not the Sea. We are like boats dashing together; our eyes are darkened, yet we are in clear water.

Jalalu'l-Din Rumi, Masnavi 3.1259-1272 (Islam)

A man among the Muslims and a man among the Jews reviled one another. The Muslim said, "By Him who chose Muhammad above the universe," and the Jew said, "By Him who chose Moses above the universe." Thereupon the Muslim raised his hand and struck the Jew on his face, and the Jew went to the Prophet and told him what had happened between him and the Muslim. The Prophet summoned the Muslim and asked him about that, and when he informed him the Prophet said, "Do not make me superior to Moses, for mankind will swoon on the day of resurrection and I shall swoon along with them. I shall be the first to recover and see Moses seizing the side of the Throne; and I shall not know whether he was among those who had swooned and had recovered before me, or whether he was among those of whom God had made an exception... Do not make distinctions between the Prophets."

Hadith of Bukhari and Muslim (Islam)

Some call on the Lord, "Rama," some cry, "Khuda,"
Some bow to Him as Gosain, some as Allah;
He is called the Ground of Grounds and also the Bountiful,
The Compassionate One and Gracious.
Hindus bathe in holy waters for His sake;
    Muslims make the pilgrimage to Mecca.
The Hindus perform *puja*; others bow their heads in *namaz*.
There are those who read the Vedas and others—Christians, Jews, Muslims—who read the Semitic scriptures.
Some wear blue, some white robes,
Some call themselves Muslims, others Hindus.
Some aspire to *bahishat* [Muslim heaven], some to *swarga* [Hindu heaven].
Says Nanak, Whoever realizes the will of the Lord, He will find out the Lord's secrets!

Adi Granth, Ramkali, M.5, p. 885 (Sikhism)

Of whatsoever teachings, Gotamid, you can assure yourself thus, "These doctrines conduce to passions, not to dispassion; to bondage, not to detachment; to increase of worldly gains, not to decrease of them; to covetousness, not to frugality; to discontent, not contentment; to company, not solitude; to sluggishness, not energy; to delight in evil, not delight in good"—of such teachings you may with certainty affirm, Gotamid, "This is not the Norm. This is not the Discipline. This is not the Master's Message."

But of whatsoever teachings you can assure yourself thus, "These doctrines conduce to dispassion, not to passions... to delight in good, not delight in evil"—of such teachings you may with certainty affirm, "This is the Norm. This is the Discipline. This is the Master's Message."

Vinaya Pitaka 2.10 (Buddhism)

Teachings of Sun Myung Moon

In every culture, religion should be the core and standard of public righteousness. Hence each religion holds pride in keeping its own traditions and thinks itself superior to any other. However, the universal elements in each of their teachings come from the one God. (234:222, August 20, 1992)

Lamentable it is that the very religions that were supposed to serve as the leading elements of the human spirit and as the leading mediators of conflict have themselves become sources of conflict, thereby diminishing religious dignity and authority even further. Judaism fights Islam; Catholicism conflicts with Protestantism; Christianity contradicts Buddhism. Even within one religion, different denominations fight among themselves.

The basic cause of religious conflict lies in the ambiguity of their doctrines about Ultimate Reality. The Absolute Being is only one; there cannot be two absolute beings. However, when the leaders of each religion claim that only their absolute being is the true God, it leads to the contradiction that there is more than one absolute being. We would then conclude that the god of each religion is only a relative god, and that there is no basis for believing that the Absolute Being exists.

Consequently, although God has been promoting through the various religions a universal teaching about God's love and truth, their various perspectives remain only relative. We can conclude that religions have been incapable of establishing the absolute value perspective that can bring the prevailing confusion under control. This is the inevitable result of the fact that no religion has been able to present the correct explanation about the Absolute Being. (122:300-01, November 25, 1982)

As most people live in two dimensions, all religions appear to them to be the same. However, if looking at their backgrounds, especially from the standpoint of God's providence for the restoration of humankind, we recognize that religions are at different levels: the servant of servant-level religion, the servant-level religion, the adopted son-level religion, the half son-level religion, the son-level religion, the mother-level religion, the father-level religion, and finally the True Parent-level religion. Throughout history, religions have developed from stage to stage.

Yet all religions, regardless of their level, have something in common: Love God and serve Him as the absolute Lord. Most of their basic teachings are the same. For this reason, it is hard to distinguish the difference of their levels. If so, are all religions really the same? No, they are not. (143:75-76, December 9, 1990)

Good and evil are not determined by your beliefs and thoughts. They are determined by your daily life. Whether you are destined for heaven and hell is not determined by your doctrines and perspectives on the world, but by your daily life. (40:294-95, February 7, 1971)

Tolerance, Religious Freedom and Interfaith Solidarity

TOLERANCE BEGINS WITH HOW WE treat people of other faiths. We have gathered passages from the scriptures which urge treating non-believers and believers with equal respect. Religious disputes and doctrinal conflicts are condemnable; they are often motivated by egoism disguised as piety, and by displaying enmity they do not give fitting witness to one's faith.

By extension, governments are to respect religious freedom and avoid any manner of compulsion in matters of faith. Most people think of religious freedom as a feature of modern democracy, emerging as it did after a long period of religious intolerance marked by wars and cruelty—the Crusades, the Inquisition and the 30-Years' War. Still, each of the great civilizations has enjoyed periods of religions tolerance: in India under the tolerant Buddhist King Ashoka (3rd century B.C.) and the enlightened Mughal emperor Akbar (16th century), in 10th century *al-Andalus* (Spain under Muslim rule), and in Song dynasty China (10th-13th century). Nevertheless, it was with democracy that the ideal of religious freedom became firmly established as a global value. Father Moon regards the establishment of religious freedom one of the hard-won victories of divine providence.

Beyond tolerance and beyond religious freedom is the higher vision of cooperation and solidarity among religions. This largely modern ideal was born out of people's growing familiarity with the world's religions and the efforts of religious leaders to dialogue with each other in order to resolve disputes and eliminate ancient prejudices. Religious unity has long been advocated by the Baha'i Faith. Relations between Christians and Jews were transformed after the horrors of the Holocaust led to a widespread re-evaluation of Christian doctrines that had overtones of anti-Semitism. Still, until the late 1990s the predominant opinion was that the trend towards secularism would one day make religion—and hence religious intolerance—a relic of the past. Today that view is obsolete. Flare-ups of religious extremism and terrorism have made people realize that interfaith cooperation is a necessary condition for world peace. Yet for more than fifty years, without fanfare, Father Moon has worked for the goal of the unity of religions, regarding it as one of the chief goals of God's contemporary providence.

1. Tolerance towards Believers of Other Religions

Those who praise their own doctrines and disparage the doctrines of others do not solve any problem.

Sutrakritanga 1.1.50 (*Jainism*)

Do not dispute with the People of the Book but in the fairest manner.[6]

Qur'an 29.46

Maintain good conduct among the Gentiles, so that in case they speak against you as wrongdoers, they may see your good deeds and glorify God on the day of visitation.

1 Peter 2.12

Our rabbis have taught, "We support the poor of the heathen along with the poor of Israel, visit the sick of the heathen along with the sick of Israel, and bury the dead poor of the heathen along with the dead of Israel, in the interests of peace."

Talmud, Gittin 61a (*Judaism*)

Kapathika: "How should a wise man maintain truth?"

Buddha: "A man has a faith. If he says 'This is my faith,' so far he maintains truth.

But by that he cannot proceed to the absolute conclusion: 'This alone is Truth, and everything else is false.' "

Majjhima Nikaya 2.176 (*Buddhism*)

Like the bee, gathering honey from different flowers, the wise man accepts the essence of different scriptures and sees only the good in all religions.

Srimad Bhagavatam 11.3 (*Hinduism*)

The Jews should not be presented as rejected or accursed by God, as if this followed from the Holy Scriptures. All should see to it, then, that in catechetical work or in the preaching of the word of God they do not teach anything that does not conform to the truth of the Gospel and the spirit of Christ. Furthermore, in her rejection of every persecution against any man, the Church, mindful of the patrimony she shares with the Jews and moved not by political reasons but by the Gospel's spiritual love, decries hatred, persecutions, displays of anti-Semitism, directed against Jews at any time and by anyone.

Vatican II, Nostra Aetate (*Christianity*)

Teachings of Sun Myung Moon

The ideal of True Parents and the ideal of world peace are directly connected. We guide all nations, peoples, cultures, and religions to harmonize with one another by becoming 100 percent tolerant to one another for the sake of the ideal; this is the way to establish world peace. (205:159, August 16, 1990)

By demonstrating the goodness of their teachings, religions should set the example for all humankind. Instead, religions are fighting one another. Even different denominations within the same religion fight amongst themselves over differences in doctrine. On seeing this, God feels great anguish in His heart. (167:99, June 30, 1987)

We who are in a movement for unity must make efforts to unite with all religions. If possible, we can resolve doctrinal differences through persuasion. Otherwise, with much patience and much tolerance we have to compromise in order to cooperate with them. There are no other ways than these two. (103:125, February 18, 1979).

A religion that can bring peace to the world should not regard itself as important. It should not have self-centered views about its authority or its possessions. If it does, it will not go beyond the level of its own nation and the people who accept its doctrines.

There will be no escape from the history of conflicts and wars as long as our religion follows the conventional path of pursuing self-interest. God knows this; therefore He instructs us to deny and sacrifice ourselves. Even though we believe we have the central role, we should not pursue our own self-interest but rather seek for the welfare of other religious groups. Religions should walk the path of self-denial, self-sacrifice, and service to others. (172:143, January 10, 1988)

God wants to save the world, not just the Presbyterian Church or the Methodist Church or the Holiness Church. God does not live for the sake of any particular church or denomination; He lives for the world. A true church sacrifices itself for the sake of the world. If need be, for the sake of saving the world, a church should be willing even to let itself go out of existence. This is the way of the Principle; we must travel this road to accomplish God's Will.

On the other hand, churches that place themselves above every other church, that regard themselves as absolute while denying the validity of all other churches, will perish. (69:87, October 20, 1973)

In this age, God wants to lead the world through 'parent-level religions'—religions with a parental heart… Religions that put down or are hostile to other religions or denominations are not useful for the realization of world peace or the fulfillment of God's providence. (260:128, May 1, 1994)

2. Freedom of Religion

Congress shall make no law respecting the establishment of religion, or prohibiting the free exercise thereof.
    United States Constitution, Bill of Rights, Article 1

There is no compulsion in religion.
    Qur'an 2.256

Will you then compel mankind, against their will, to believe? No soul can believe, except by the Will of God.
    Qur'an 10.99-100

Everyone has the right to freedom of thought, conscience, and religion; this right includes freedom to change his religion or belief, and freedom, either alone or in community with others and in public or private, to manifest his religion or belief in teaching, practice, worship, and observance.
    Universal Declaration of Human Rights, Article 18

Whoever honors his own sect and disparages another man's, whether from blind loyalty or with the intention of showing his own sect in a favorable light, does his own sect the greatest possible harm. Concord is best, with each hearing and respecting the other's teachings. It is the wish of the Emperor that members of all sects should be learned and should teach virtue.
    Ashoka, Twelfth Rock Edict *(Buddhism)*

A Pharisee in the council named Gamaliel, a teacher of the law, held in honor by all the people, stood up and ordered that [Peter and the apostles] be put outside for a while. And he said to the council, "Men of Israel, take care what you do with these men. For before these days Theudas arose, giving himself out to be somebody, and a number of men, about four hundred, joined him; but he was slain and all who followed him were dispersed and came to nothing. After him Judas the Galilean arose in the days of the census and drew away some of the people after him; he also perished, and all who followed him were scattered. So in the present case I tell you, keep away from these men and let them alone; for if this plan or this undertaking is of men, it will fail; but if it is of God, you will not be able to overthrow them. You might even be found opposing God!"[7]
    Acts 5.34-39

When the Messenger of Allah arrived in Medina he made a treaty with the Jews there: "The Jews of the Bani Awf tribe are one community with the Muslim faithful. The Jews practice their religion and the Muslims practice theirs. For them shall be their own wealth, property and persons. Except for he who has committed oppression or transgression."
    Hadith *(Islam)*

The spirit can only acquiesce to that which seem to it to be true; the heart can only love that which seems to it to be good. Constraint will make a hypocrite of man if he is weak, a martyr if he is courageous. Weak or courageous, he will feel the injustice of persecution, and he will become indignant. Instruction, persuasion, and prayer: these are the only methods for the expansion of religion. Any method that excites hatred, indignation, or contempt is impious.
    Denis Diderot *(Humanism)*

Teachings of Sun Myung Moon

Democracy is the system that God laboriously prepared over the last two thousand years. Democracy is the system that respects human rights. Democracy is the system in which a minority group can survive in the midst of a [hostile] majority. Democracy is the system that guarantees freedom—freedom of speech, freedom of religion, freedom of association, freedom of press, and freedom of assembly. America is the representative democratic nation, and in the American Constitution the most absolute among all freedoms is freedom of religion. It states that the Congress and government shall not make any laws that restrict religions. (100:246, October 19, 1978)

God's spiritual providence of restoration during the two thousand years since Jesus' day has prepared a democratic social and legal environment that will protect Christ at the Second Advent. Jesus was killed after being branded a heretic by the Jews and a rebel by the Roman Empire. In contrast, even if Christ at the Second Advent is persecuted as a heretic, in the democratic society to which he will come, such accusations will not be sufficient grounds for him to be condemned to death. (*Exposition of the Divine Principle*, Moses and Jesus 3.3.2)

I am grateful to God that He is using me as His instrument to ignite a movement to spiritually awaken America, to call her to protect religious freedom in this most difficult time in human history.[8] (133:213, July 19, 1984)

3. Community and Solidarity among Religions

I came to the conclusion long ago… that all religions were true and also that all had some error in them, and whilst I hold by my own, I should hold others as dear as Hinduism. So we can only pray, if we are Hindus, not that a Christian should become a Hindu… But our innermost prayer should be a Hindu should be a better Hindu, a Muslim a better Muslim, a Christian a better Christian.

Mohandas Gandhi (*Hinduism*)

Basically all major religions of the world carry the same message; therefore harmony between different religions is both important and necessary.

Each system has its own value suited to persons of different disposition and mental outlook. At this time of easy communication, we must increase our efforts to learn each other's system. This does not mean that we should make all religions into one but that we should recognize the common purpose of the many religions and value the different techniques that they have developed for internal improvement.

Tenzin Gyatso, The Fourteenth Dalai Lama (*Buddhism*)

The Church therefore has this exhortation for her sons: prudently and lovingly, through dialogue and collaboration with the followers of other religions, and in witness of Christian faith and life, acknowledge, preserve, and promote the spiritual and moral goods found among these men, as well as the values in their society and culture.

Vatican II, Nostra Aetate (*Christianity*)

My house shall be called a house of prayer for all peoples.

Isaiah 56.7

And I [Jesus] have other sheep, that are not of this fold; I must bring them also, and they will heed my voice. So there shall be one flock, one shepherd.

John 10.16

The essential purpose of the religion of God is to establish unity among mankind. The divine Manifestations were Founders of the means of fellowship and love. They did not come to create discord, strife and hatred in the world. The religion of God is the cause of love, but if it is made to be a source of enmity and bloodshed, surely its absence is preferable to its existence; for then it becomes satanic, detrimental and an obstacle to the human world...

It is our duty in this radiant century to investigate the essentials of divine religion, seek the realities underlying the oneness of the world of humanity, and discover the source of fellowship and agreement which will unite mankind in the heavenly bond of love. This unity is the radiance of eternity, the divine spirituality, the effulgence of God and the bounty of the Kingdom.

'Abdu'l-Bahá, Promulgation of Universal Peace
(Baha'i Faith)

Teachings of Sun Myung Moon

As far as I know, God is not sectarian. He is not restricted by minor details of doctrine. We should quickly liberate ourselves from theological conflict which results from blind attachment to doctrines and rituals, and instead focus on living relationships with God. In my view, we urgently need to purify the religious atmosphere into one in which believers can have living faith and every soul can communicate with God.

In God's parental heart and His great love, there is no discrimination based on color or nationality. There are no barriers between cultural traditions, between East and West, North and South. Today God is trying to embrace the whole of humankind as His children. Through interreligious dialogue and harmony we should realize one ideal world of peace, which is God's purpose of creation and the common hope of humankind. (135:221, November 16, 1985)

Despite all efforts to the contrary, divisions and animosities among various religious groups continue. Religious wars are still being waged, as they have been for centuries. In spite of various ecumenical movements, religious arrogance, intolerance, and bigotry are still prevalent among devout believers. Thus, although most religions have professed the same God and often even the same views for centuries, their adherents have continually persecuted and warred with one another.

God is beyond denomination, doctrine or sect. God's purpose is and always has been to save the entire world, and not merely a certain race, nation, or religious group. As religious people, we cannot help God in the task of salvation as long as we fight among ourselves. Many religious leaders have realized this, but for numerous complex reasons their attempts to solve this problem have been repeatedly frustrated.

One of my essential teachings is that interreligious harmony is a necessary condition for world peace. Since no single religion has manifested God completely, religious differences have been inevitable. Yet because we are all sons and daughters of the same Heavenly Parent, we are all brothers and sisters in one great family. Therefore, conflict and divisive hatred among religions is unnecessary. (133:274-75, August 13, 1984)

Is God alienated from the world? No, God strives to save the world. Nevertheless, each religion cherishes its own believers but does not care so much about other people. Look at Islam: it tries to save the world, but it puts itself first. It is likewise with Buddhism: so far its adherents have not been active in going out to society. (99:17, August 27, 1978)

It was not God's original purpose to establish Hinduism, or Buddhism, or Christianity. God wanted to see from the beginning one family under God. (March 2, 2003)

In the Orient, people go in search of the state of Emptiness or No-self. Therefore, they look for quiet places where they can release their attachments to worldly things. In the West, on the other hand, people make efforts seeking for money and material things. Therefore they want quick results, and their eyes become large... Oriental people are small, with small eyes [that look into the distance], noses and everything. Their legs are short, too. From this, we see that the West is external and the East is internal.

One of Satan's goals is to permanently separate the internal from the external. God, on the other hand, tries to link the internal and external in a harmonious relationship. Thus we can foresee that when the West tries to unite with the East, God's day of fulfillment is near. This is gradually coming to pass. (118:46, May 2, 1982)

The purpose of religion is to lead us to a united world. Although different religions have different names for God and different ways of worshipping Him, the central Being each religion worships is the one and only God. Therefore, the purposes and directions for human life taught by each religion inevitably converge towards one standard. Ultimately, each religion has to manage its own path in order that all religions may enter the era of reformation at the same time. (140:10, February 1, 1986)

With the progress of God's providence, we witness that already in the spirit world there are no barriers between the four major religions at the level of their founders. Jesus, Buddha, Mohammed and Confucius communicate freely with each other and often visit each other's realms. Because I know these things well, I strongly encouraged all clergy... to transcend their denominations and sects and to unite as one. (May 8, 2001)

When all religions are as one family—living in one accord, cooperating as one body and treasuring the same idea—then all will be liberated. In that day, self-cultivation will no longer be necessary. (393:183, October 3, 2002)

Shamanism, Polytheism and Animism

WORLD SCRIPTURE TAKES A UNIVERSAL OUTLOOK in emphasizing the common features of all religions; nevertheless religions also have their unique characteristics and emphases. The following six topics treat specific religious traditions, pointing out their unique features and Father Moon's teachings about them. It cannot be overemphasized that any treatment of a religion's unique features in no way exhausts its spiritual riches or detracts from its universal qualities that join in common witness to the one God and one Reality.

Not all the religions are treated here; just those on which Father Moon has commented upon out of his own experience. Korea is a religiously pluralistic country, with roots in Shamanism, Buddhism and Confucianism; it has a large and vibrant Christian community and also a growing Muslim minority.

Father Moon's views on Shamanism are largely the result of his experience with the homegrown Korean variety. Shamanism remains strong in rural Korea, where its practitioners, called *mudangs*, are largely women. Their ability to communicate with spirits can be impressive. During his years in America, he befriended Eskimo shamans in Alaska and Native Americans in Brazil and Paraguay. Father Moon is very aware of the reality of the spirit world and the spiritual discipline required to be an effective channel to that world. For this reason, he does not cast dogmatic condemnations on Shamanism and Animism in the manner of Bible-centered Christians. Rather, he regards Shamanism as an authentic stage, albeit a low one, on the path of humankind's spiritual development.

Notable also is Father Moon's teaching that Shamanism and polytheism are "servant of servant" religions, whose original objects of worship were fallen angels. This can be seen rather clearly in Greek and Hindu mythology, where the gods' amorous activities with earthly women are of a piece with Satan's seduction of Eve at the Human Fall. Nevertheless, God still taught through these forms by empowering devoted practitioners to rise above their gods and attain a higher moral plane. In this way, human beings transcended the position of servants' servants to become their masters, thus opening a higher stage of religious development. Passages from Hinduism and Shinto illustrate how these traditions were thus elevated over time to form higher religions.

1. Worship of Nature Deities

O gods! All your names are to be revered, saluted and adored; all of you who have sprung from heaven and earth, listen here to my invocation.
Rig Veda 10.63.2 (Hinduism)

Our ancestors the emperors of old governed the realm by first paying worship to the *kami* with reverence and awe. Widely worshipping the *kami* of mountain and river, they thereby had natural concourse with heaven and earth. For this reason, summer and winter also turned in their season, and the works of creation were in harmony.[9]
Nihon Shoki 22 (Shinto)

Sansang suira!
There are eight peaks within the inner mountain,
and thirteen famous places in the outer mountain.
Within these famous mountains and the great heavens of all Buddhas,
the great altar of the nation is protected by the great generals.
Was not General Chae Yong one of them?
The famous general of Korea,
who was favored by his people...

Oh, I am the great mountain god.
If I sit down, I cover three thousand li [the entire land of Korea].
If I stand up, I stretch over ninety thousand li [the whole world].
If I look down with my clear mirror, I can observe ten thousand li.
Oh, I am the great mountain god.

What can you offer to satisfy me?
Is the whole pig covered with a red cloth enough?
Is the bundle of three different colored silks enough?
Offer many rich silks to me.
Oh, you, the husband and wife of this home.
Do you remember who gives you the food that sustains you?
Who gave you a home?
Who gave you wealth?
Who gave you long life?
I, the Sansang, gave you blessings and aid in times of need.[10]
Invocation of the Mountain Spirit
(Korean Shamanism)

War-bundle owners, I greet you. Ye elders, I am about to pour tobacco for the spirits.

Hearken Earthmaker, our father, I am about to offer you a handful of tobacco. My ancestor so-and-so concentrated his mind upon you. The fireplaces with which you blessed him, the small amount of life you granted to him, all, four times the blessings that you bestowed upon my ancestor, I ask of you directly. May I have no troubles in life.

Chief of the Thunderbirds, who lives in the west, you strengthened my grandfather. I am about to offer you a handful of tobacco. The food, the pair of deer you gave him for his fireplaces, that I ask of you directly. May you accept this tobacco from me and may I not meet with troubles.

Great Black Hawk, you also blessed my grandfather. I am about to offer you tobacco. Whatever food you blessed him with that I ask you directly. May I not meet with troubles...

You [night spirits] on the other side, who live in the east, who walk in darkness, I am about to offer you tobacco to smoke. Whatever you blessed my ancestor with, I ask of you. If you smoke this tobacco I will never be a weakling.

Disease-giver, you who live in the south; you who look like a man; who art invulnerable; who on one side of your body present death and on the other life, you blessed my ancestor in the daytime, in broad daylight. You blessed him with food and told him that he would never fail in anything. You promised to avoid his home. You placed animals before him that he might easily obtain food. I offer you tobacco that you may smoke it, and that I may not be troubled by anything.

To you, Sun, Light-wanderer... To you, Grandmother Moon... Hearken, all ye spirits to whom my ancestor prayed; to all of you I offer tobacco. My ancestor gave a feast to all those who had blessed him. Bestow upon us once again all the blessings you gave our ancestor, that we may not become weaklings. I greet you all.

Winnebago Invocation at the Sweat Lodge
(Native American Religion)

Ala, come and drink and eat the kola nut.
    Chukwu, come and drink and eat the kola nut.
    Ancestors, come and drink and eat the kola nut.

I was told by a man of Ngbwidi, one named Ehirim, that a man of Agunese had stolen his yams; and so I summoned the priests of Ala and Aro holders and elders in order that we might inquire into the matter. I called them, even as my father, who was priest of Njoku before me, used to do.

If any of these men, who have come to try the case, deal falsely in the matter, or if the accuser or accused or any person called to give evidence tells falsehood, then do you, Ala, Chukwu, Njoku, Ancestors, and Ofo, deal with that man.[11]

Igbo Invocation at a Trial
(African Traditional Religions)

Parvati, on seeing her son Ganesha resuscitated, embraced him joyously and clothed him with new garments and ornaments. After kissing his face, she said, "O Ganesha, you have had great distress since your very birth. You are blessed and contented now. You will receive worship before all the gods...

"All achievements certainly accrue to him who performs your worship with flowers, sandal paste, scents, auspicious food offerings, waving of lights, betel leaves, charitable gifts, circumambulations, and obeisance. All kinds of obstacles will certainly perish."

Shiva, Brahma, and Vishnu declared in unison, "O great gods, just as we three are worshipped in all the three worlds, so also Ganesha shall be worshipped by all of you. He is the remover of all obstacles and the bestower of the fruits of all rites."[12]

Shiva Purana, Rudrasamhita 18 (Hinduism)

Teachings of Sun Myung Moon

God instructs all people, from the most primitive to the most advanced, by means appropriate to their level. Thus, in the primitive religions of the past, God taught people to worship the things of creation, such as rocks and trees, as substitutes for God. This was the origin of shamanism. In this way God could teach the people and guide the direction of their lives. (91:271, February 27, 1977)

Shamans are possessed by servant-level spirits, confined within the realm of the fall. Yet through their revelations they can sometimes give accurate information from the spirit world to earthly people. There are groups of people on this earth who connect with the spirit world in this way. (76:95, February 1, 1975)

The spirit world is the world of angels. Why do the angels of the spirit world want to relate to the human world as gods? You have heard about shamanism, fortunetelling, superstition and such. They are religious forms in which there is not clear discernment of good and evil. As God leads the providence through religions, Satan also prepared religious forms to guard his world.

In general, more than eighty percent of fortunetellers are women. Who do they contact? At the time of the Fall, the archangel led Eve and caused her to bring evil into the world. Likewise, during the course of restoration the same path is repeated: angels in the spirit world come down to the earth to lead and teach women, uniting with them. Hence, a shaman's or fortuneteller's work is to follow the direction and teachings of angels—but this time for good. (76:95, February 1, 1975)

In the development of history, we see that there was always some sort of faith. The birth of faith lay in ancient beliefs that modern people would call superstition. For example, when people saw a big tree, they revered it. When they saw a magnificent mountain, they revered it. Although most people do not recognize them, guardian deities actually exist in those places. (176:287, May 13, 1988)

People in ancient times had a close relationship with nature. Then the natural world and the spirit world were close to human beings—not distant and foreign as they are to people living in modern times. When people entered a grove of giant trees, they looked at them reverently and thought, "For thousands of years these trees have been here; through countless cycles of quickening in spring and dying in autumn they remain unchanged; their shade makes a pleasant environment for all creatures." Observing them, they recognized that they were deficient in many aspects, and so they worshipped tall trees, great rocks and high mountains.

They saw tall persimmon trees, thick with foliage in the summer and bare in the winter. With the arrival of spring their branches sprouted with new life: first buds, then blossoms, and finally delicious and fragrant fruit. They marveled at this, and sensed that those trees were better than they.

Where is the fragrance in human existence? Do humans give off a fragrance that beautifies their surroundings, attracting birds and insects to nest in their branches? No. Compared to nature, man is humbled and recognizes his inadequacy. (November 4, 1990)

History knows that this is the age when the sun rises in the East. All people are turning in the direction of the light and lighting their own lamps. Some are doing it centering on God, but others are centering on low-level spirits. Even shamans are receiving the light based on their spiritual senses and experiences. Between shamans and non-believers, who is better? Believing in even low-level spirits is better than having no faith at all. (194:315, October 30, 1989)

2. Human Beings Who Achieve Mastery Rise above the Gods

It is people who make the gods important.

If a spirit [idol] becomes too troublesome, it will be shown the tree from which it was carved.

We shall continue to offer sacrifices so that the blame will lie with the deities.

African Proverbs (African Traditional Religions)

Fools misjudge me when I take a human form,
Because they do not know my supreme state as
   Lord of Beings.
Unconscious, they fall prey to a beguiling
   nature
such as belongs to ogres and demons,
For their hopes [ascribing to God human
   motives] are vain, and so
are their rituals and their search for wisdom.

Bhagavad-Gita 9.11-12 (Hinduism)

Whoever knows the self as "I am Brahman," becomes all this [universe]. Even the gods cannot prevent his becoming this, for he has become their Self.

Now, if a man worships another deity, thinking, "He is one and I am another," he does not know. He is like an animal to the gods. As many animals serve a man, so does each man serve the gods [with offerings]. Even if one animal is taken away, it causes anguish to the owner; how much more so when many are taken away! Therefore it is not pleasing to the gods that men should know the truth.

Brihadaranyaka Upanishad 1.4.10 (Hinduism)

Even the devas are jealous of a yogi, striving as he does to surpass them by attaining Brahman. They therefore try to lead him astray, in various ways, if they find him off guard.[13]

Srimad Bhagavatam 11.20 (Hinduism)

What is Shinto? Not in the shrines
the worldly minded frequent for gifts in vain,
but in good deeds, pure of heart,
lies real religion.

Genchi Kato (Shinto)

Look, you brothers, who bathe in the holy
   waters,
Look, you monks, who bathe in the stream.
Give up, give up, your unholy thoughts;
Give up lustful thoughts for another man's
   wife,
Give up coveting after another man's wealth.
If you bathe in the waters without giving up
   these,
It is as if bathing in a stream that has run dry.

Basavanna, Vacana 642 (Hinduism)

Truth is victorious, never untruth.
Truth is the way; truth is the goal of life,
Reached by the sages who are free from
   self-will.

Mundaka Upanishad 3.1.6 (Hinduism)

Teachings of Sun Myung Moon

We should clearly distinguish monotheism from polytheism. Only God is the true deity; the other divine beings that founded the polytheistic religions are angels. Among those religions, some developed through good angels' efforts to elevate human spirituality and heart—they are the higher religions. You should know that God has been cultivating people's hearts through these good religions. (237:186, November 17, 1992)

Human history can be considered to span at least 850,000 years. Even during the most primitive times, the religious movements that sprang up received persecution. Who initiated such work? It is God. He developed religions to separate human beings from the servant. God separated us from Satan step by step, starting from the very bottom—the level of a servant of servants.

Humans are created to be masters, but at the servant of servants' level, the servant dominates the master. In order to take our rightful position in the Kingdom of Heaven as the masters of that servant, humanity must inevitably receive persecution from the entire servant world and triumph over it. (124:69, January 23, 1983)

Among shamans, especially the men, some had formerly led a promiscuous love life. Then as shamans they leave their former life and strive on the path of morality. This led to the development of a [higher] realm of religion. From that starting-point, they could recognize that people should live a straight way of life and form faithful families. At least they recognized that it was not good to live a loose lifestyle, and sought after a proper way of love. Such efforts at laying the right path developed into the world's higher religions. (295:172, August 28, 1998)

Buddhism

FATHER MOON HAS THE HIGHEST RESPECT FOR BUDDHISM, a religion that has deeply influenced the culture of his native Korea. He regards the Buddhist teaching and practice of self-denial is at the summit of world religious teachings for recovering our true original self from the mire of our fallen condition. To reach that state of emptiness, what Father Moon calls the "zero point," is true enlightenment.

In Father Moon's view Buddhism is lacking two essential points: knowledge of a personal God and full comprehension of the ideal of true love. Nevertheless, it was God who taught the Buddha and set up Buddhism to give light to the Orient. People of all faiths can learn much from Buddhism, particularly about the way of self-denial to overcome false ego and uncover the true self.

1. The Values of Buddhism

The best of paths is the Eightfold Path. The best of truths are the Four Noble Truths. Non-attachment is the best of mental states. The best of human beings is the Seeing One.

This is the only Way. There is no other that leads to the purity of insight. You should follow this path, for this is what bewilders Mara.

Embarking upon that path, you will make an end of pain. I have declared this path after having learned the way for the removal of thorns.

Dhammapada 273-75

Not by matted hair, nor by family, nor by birth does one become a Brahmin. But in whom there exist both truth and righteousness, pure is he, a Brahmin is he.

I do not call him a Brahmin merely because he is born of a Brahmin womb or sprung from a Brahmin mother. Being with impediments, he should address others as "sir." But he who is free from impediments, free from clinging—him I call a Brahmin.

He who realizes here in this world the destruction of his sorrow, who has laid the burden aside and is emancipated—him I call a Brahmin.

He who has laid aside the cudgel in his dealings with beings, whether feeble or strong, who neither harms nor kills—him I call a Brahmin.

He who is friendly among the hostile, who is peaceful among the violent, who is unattached among the attached—him I call a Brahmin.

In whom lust, hatred, pride, and detraction are fallen off like a mustard seed from the point of a needle—him I call a Brahmin.[14]

Dhammapada 393, 396, 402, 405-07

Even ornamented royal chariots wear out. So too the body reaches old age. But the Dhamma of the Good grows not old. Thus do the Good reveal it among the Good.

Dhammapada 151

What, brethren, is causal happening?
"Conditioned by rebirth is decay and death."
Whether, brethren, there be an arising of Tathagatas or whether there be no such arising, this nature of things just stands, this causal status, this causal orderliness, the relatedness of this to that.

Samyutta Nikaya 2.25

I pay homage to the Perfection of Wisdom! She is worthy of homage. She is unstained; the entire world cannot stain her. She is a source of light, and from everyone in the triple world she removes darkness, and she leads away from the blinding darkness caused by the defilements and by wrong views. In her we can find shelter. Most excellent are her works. She makes us seek the safety of the wings of Enlightenment. She brings light to the blind; she brings light so that all fear and distress may be forsaken… She is the mother of the Bodhisattvas, on account of the emptiness of her own marks. As the donor of the jewel of all the Buddha-dharmas she brings about the ten powers [of a Buddha]. She cannot be crushed. She protects the unprotected, with the help of the four grounds of self-confidence. She is the antidote to birth-and-death. She has a clear knowledge of the own-being of all dharmas, for she does not stray away from it. The Perfection of Wisdom of the Buddhas, the Lords, sets in motion the Wheel of the Law.

Perfection of Wisdom in Eight Thousand Lines 7.1

Teachings of Sun Myung Moon

In ancient times, Buddhism and Buddhist culture emerged out of God's will, in order to reform the society of India. Buddhism presented a new ideal through a new understanding of subject and object relationships.[15] (144:182, April 24, 1986)

Buddhism, which emerged from India, is a world-level teaching. Only religions like Buddhism, which transcends the practical domain of life and contains a world-level point of view and a transcendental philosophy, will remain in the Last Days. (9:279, June 12, 1960)

Among the Oriental religions, Buddhism is the closest to God's providence… However, as Buddhism teaches the logic of *Sarvadharma* [the oneness of all things],[16] it is ignorant of a personal God—a major weakness. Nevertheless, God set things up this way to prepare the people of Asia to one day be united [with God's Kingdom] through the Oriental religions when Buddhism would connect with Judaism [had the latter received Christ]. (208:311, November 21, 1990)

Buddhism teaches the existence of God, but it focuses on God's lawful aspect. It does not explain that God is actively working in the world. (53:297, March 4, 1972)

The Buddha's entire philosophy is based on law (*dharma*). However, the object of dharma is the circumstances of human beings as objects, not the human being himself. Actually, the measure of a human being is love, not law. But the Buddha taught a standard based on law; hence his teachings are called Law Sutras.[17]

Buddhism teaches self-realization, but what should happen after attaining self-realization? Is that the end of it? That is why, even though Buddhists live solitary lives deep in the mountains and work hard for self-discipline and self-realization, they still are ambiguous about the ideal world of love. (50:116, November 6, 1971)

2. Buddhist Enlightenment

Strive and cleave the stream. Discard, O Brahmin, sense-desires. Knowing the destruction of conditioned things, be a knower of the Unmade.

Dhammapada 383

Since all Dharmas are immanent in our mind there is no reason why we should not realize intuitively the real nature of Suchness. The *Bodhisattva Sila Sutra* says, "Our Essence of Mind is intrinsically pure, and if we knew our mind and realized what our nature is, all of us would attain Buddhahood."

Sutra of Hui Neng 2

Every Buddha Tathagata is one whose body is the Principle of Nature (*Dharmadhatu-kaya*), so that he may enter into the mind of any being. Consequently, when you have perceived Buddha, it is indeed that mind of yours that possesses those thirty-two signs of perfection and eighty minor marks of excellence [which you see in Buddha]. In fine, it is your mind that becomes Buddha; nay, your mind is indeed Buddha. The ocean of true and universal knowledge of all the Buddhas derives its source from one's own mind and thought.

Meditation on Buddha Amitayus 17

In heaven and on earth, I alone am the Honored One.[18]

Digha Nikaya 2.15

Teachings of Sun Myung Moon

When we pray or meditate, as when Buddhists practice Zen, we are seeking a state that is void of self.[19] What is our goal in seeking this state? It is to awaken the elements that can become the nucleus of the mind. If you set that one standard and establish the center of your mind, you will see, hear and cognize everything in accord with the principles of Heaven. Then you can offer a full bow before God and return Him glory. (2:193, May 19, 1957)

Buddhism teaches that one should attain enlightenment and realize one's self-nature.[20] Buddha said, "In heaven and on earth I alone am the honored one." This means that you reach the state where you know that God exists within you and there is nothing you cannot do. This is the enlightened mind. Your mind is better than a teacher; your mind is your eternal lord. Therefore, you should not have a selfish mind, but a mind to serve the greater good. (133:179, July 10, 1984)

Shakyamuni in his mystical state, when he could declare, "In heaven and on earth, I alone am the honored one," is far from the normal thinking of ordinary people. When your committed efforts to reach the state of resonance of mind and body awaken your own self, you will attain the state in which you could say: "I am the best under the sun." (141:235, February 26, 1986)

Where does God dwell? God is the lord of the "zero point." That is where God wants to dwell—in the "king zero point." Since God has such a nature, to meet Him you must become even lower than zero. Then you must guard that king zero point. The king zero point is like the mind, and as the flesh surrounds the mind, you should surround and protect the zero point.

Have you reached the state where you can guard the zero point? It is easy to answer "yes," but in reality it is not easy. Mind you, all religions have been seeking to reach God or a position where we can correspond to God. This is what Buddhist meditation is about—to search the God-like mind for the deepest point. (230:134, May 1, 1992)

3. An Example of Buddhist Wisdom

Subhuti, do not say that the Tathagata conceives the idea: I must set forth a Teaching. For if anyone says that the Tathagata sets forth a Teaching he really slanders Buddha and is unable to explain what I teach. As to any Truth-declaring system, Truth is undeclarable; so "an enunciation of Truth" is just a name given to it.[21]

Diamond Sutra 21

What has been realized by the Tathagatas—that is my own realization, in which there is neither decreasing nor increasing; for the realm of self-realization is free from words and discriminations, having nothing to do with dualistic ways of speaking... For this reason it is stated by me that from the night of the Tathagata's Enlightenment till the night of his entrance into Nirvana, he has not in the meantime uttered, nor ever will utter, one word.

Lankavatara Sutra 61

Teachings of Sun Myung Moon

In the Orient there are many statues of Buddha. Does Buddha's statue ever say a word? It never speaks a word. It neither praises you nor chastises you; it only thinks. That is what makes it worthy of worship. Also, its gaze is always focused at one point, never looking around. When we are focused in the Ultimate, what is the point of looking around at trivial matters? It teaches us that the best way to solve complications of the world is silence. (228:77, March 15, 1992)

Confucianism

CONFUCIAN ETHICS ARE AT THE CORE OF EAST ASIAN culture. Today with the rapid Westernization of Asia many are discarding Confucian values and codes; nevertheless for thousands of years its moral philosophy has guided family life and molded the conduct of kings with the values of benevolence, righteousness and propriety. Father Moon has high regard for Confucian moral teachings; he calls them "close to the laws of Heaven." The Confucian Five Relations of parents and children, ruler and subject, husband and wife, elder and younger siblings, and among friends define what he believes is a superior ethic for all humanity.

Father Moon holds that God inspired Confucianism. He affirms that in its concept of Heaven, Confucianism presents a notion of God, however vague. Confucianism's weakness, he explains, is its vague understanding of God (Heaven) and as a consequence its inability to properly link Heaven and earth in daily life. Then, with profound insight, he proceeds to offer a solution that utilizes the best of Confucianism: The relationship between God and human beings is a parent-child relationship, and its ethic is one of Confucian filial piety. In other words, we should attend God as we would our own parents, and the Confucian ethic supplies the best description as to what that attendance requires.

1. *Confucian Ethics*

Oh, how great is the divine moral law of the sage Confucius. Overflowing and illimitable, it gives birth and life to all created things and towers high up to the very heavens. How magnificent it is! How imposing the three hundred principles and three thousand rules of conduct! They await the man who can put the system into practice.

Doctrine of the Mean 27

When one follows unswervingly on the path of virtue it is not to win advancement. When one invariably keeps one's word it is not to establish the rectitude of one's actions. A gentleman merely follows the norm and awaits his destiny.

Mencius VII.B.33

From the Son of Heaven [the emperor] down to the common people, all must regard cultivation of the personal life as the root or foundation. There is never a case where the root is in disorder and yet the branches are in order.

Great Learning

Benevolence (*jen*), rectitude (*i*), propriety (*li*), and wisdom (*chih*)... There are only these four principles. There is nothing else.

Chu Hsi

What is the foundation of natural benevolence (*jen*)? The heart that sympathizes with pain. What is the foundation of a commitment to the common good (*i*)? The heart that is repelled by vice. What is the foundation of respect for social and religious forms (*li*)? The heart that is willing to defer. And what is the foundation for wisdom (*chih*)? The heart that can tell true from false.

People have these four foundations like they have four limbs. A man who says he cannot practice them is calling himself a criminal. A man who says the ruler cannot practice them is calling the ruler a criminal.

Everybody has these four foundations in himself. If these four foundations can be filled in on a broad scale, it will be like a fire starting up, it will be like a spring bursting through. If they can be filled in, it will be enough to create and preserve the world order. Leave them unfilled, it will be impossible for a man to take care of his father and mother.

Mencius II.A.6

The gentleman works upon the trunk. When that is firmly set up, the Way grows. And surely proper behavior towards parents and elder brothers is the trunk of Goodness?

Analects 1.2

Now filial piety is the root of all virtue, and the stem out of which grows all moral teaching... Our bodies—to every hair and bit of skin—are received by us from our parents, and we must not presume to injure or wound them: this is the beginning of filial piety. When we have established our character by the practice of the filial course, so as to make our name famous in future ages, and thereby glorify our parents: this is the end of filial piety. It commences with the service of parents; it proceeds to the service of the ruler; it is completed by the establishment of [good] character.[22]

Classic on Filial Piety 1

What are "the things which men consider right"? Kindness on the part of the father, and filial duty on that of the son; gentleness on the part of the elder brother, and obedience on that of the younger; righteousness on the part of the husband, and submission on that of the wife; kindness on the part of elders, and deference on that of juniors; with benevolence on the part of the ruler, and loyalty on that of the minister—these ten are the things which men consider to be right.

Book of Ritual 7.2.19

Teachings of Sun Myung Moon

Many of Confucius' teachings are close to the laws of Heaven. (31:292, June 4, 1970)

Confucianism teaches the principled way of human life. What is its central theme? "As all things proceed according to the way of Heaven through the stages of sprout, growth, harvest and [winter] storage, a person's character develops by the principles of benevolence (*jen*), righteousness (*i*), propriety (*li*), and wisdom (*chih*)."[23] People should cultivate their character by these principles and so accord with the Way of Heaven. Confucianism thus places character as the standard for the human being, but not necessarily love.

People practice and cultivate benevolence, righteousness, propriety and wisdom in the context of the Three Bonds—[loyalty] between a king and his subjects, [filial piety] between parents and children, and [fidelity] between husband and wife—and the Five Moral Disciplines—closeness between parents and children, righteousness between a king and his subjects, distinction between husband and wife, order between elder an younger brothers, and trust between friends. (296:272, November 10, 1998)

According to Eastern thought, when two people are walking along a road, the older person should go first. Why? Because he came into the world first. There is an attempt to arrange human relationships according to the orderliness of nature. He who comes later walks behind; that which is higher is placed higher; and that which is lower is placed lower... By clearly establishing all relative positions, there is a sense of unchanging order. (168:252, September 27, 1987)

Confucianism teaches the Three Bonds and Five Moral Disciplines.[24] The Five Moral Disciplines consist of: closeness between parent and child; righteousness between the king and his subjects; distinction between [husband and wife, order] between elder and younger; trust among friends. The Three Bonds refer to loyalty, filial piety and fidelity. All people should fulfill these essential values.

Providentially, Confucius' teaching was like the proclamation of the heavenly archangel. Through the elements of Confucian morality, Heaven sought to establish social conditions that would protect against Satan and set up a society resembling the external form of Heaven. (205:179, August 28, 1998)

Who is a son of filial piety? According to Confucianism, he attends his parents with his life out of his deep love for them. What is a loyal subject? He offers himself for the king's service and even sacrifices his life for his king, who represents Heaven. (143:153, March 17, 1986)

Throughout Korean history, Confucianism taught the duty of filial piety. When the parents passed away, according to custom their children would mourn for three years while living in seclusion on a mountain. They truly had a heart to do so.

What can the Korean people be proud of before the world? Regardless of their position and worldly success, when their parents passed away they abandoned everything to fulfill the duty of filial piety. Confucianism established this good tradition. It was in fact God's preliminary education for the Korean people to go his way. There can be no objection to it. (181:217, October 3, 1988)

Our relationship with God should be a parent-child relationship. What is the nature of this relationship? It is a vertical relationship. The teachings of Confucianism provide a correct understanding.

Our relationship with God our Father is as undeniable and indisputable as the relationship with our parents. We are our parents' children: could either physical force or theoretical arguments persuade us otherwise? Likewise, the knowledge that we are born as sons and daughters of God our Heavenly Father cannot be contested by anyone. (198:298, February 5, 1990)

In our individual lives, shouldn't we relate to Heavenly Father as filial children? As regards the national-level providence, shouldn't we relate to Him as loyal subjects? The traditional Confucian values—the Three Bonds and the Five Moral Disciplines—make sense. Filial piety and loyalty towards Heavenly Father are based on these traditional values. We cannot be filial children to Heavenly Father if we are not first filial to our parents. We cannot be loyal subjects of Heavenly Father if we do not first demonstrate loyalty to our nation. (7:66, July 12, 1959)

2. The Confucian Concept of Heaven

Heaven helps the man who is devoted; men help the man who is true. He who walks in truth and is devoted in his thinking, and furthermore reveres the worthy, is blessed by Heaven.
     I Ching, Great Commentary 1.12.1

Yüeh-cheng Tzu saw Mencius. "I mentioned you to the prince," said he, "and he was to have come to see you. Amongst his favorites is one Tsang who dissuaded him. That is why he failed to come."

"When a man goes forward," said Mencius, "there is something which urges him on; when he halts, there is something which holds him back. It is not in his power either to go forward or to halt. It is due to Heaven that I failed to meet the Marquis of Lu. How can this fellow Tsang be responsible for my failure?"
     Mencius I.B.16

All a gentleman can do in starting an enterprise is to leave behind a tradition which can be carried on. Heaven alone can grant success.

Mencius I.B.14

When under siege in K'uang, Confucius said, "With King Wen dead, is not culture (*wen*) invested here in me? If Heaven intends culture to be destroyed, those who come after me will not be able to have any part of it. If Heaven does not intend this culture to be destroyed, then what can the men of K'uang do to me?"

Analects 9.5

Revere the anger of Heaven,
And presume not to make sport or be idle.
Revere the changing moods of Heaven,
And presume not to drive about at your pleasure.
Great Heaven is intelligent,
And is with you in all your goings.
Great Heaven is clear-seeing,
And is with you in your wanderings and indulgences.[25]

Book of Songs, Ode 254

Teachings of Sun Myung Moon

Confucius, through his teachings, taught about many aspects of human morals and ethics... Confucius knew about God's aspect of principled laws, but not about a personal God, a God having intellect, emotion and will. This makes Confucianism an archangel-type religion. It has influenced the world in morals and ethics, especially in East Asia. (295:174-75, August 28, 1998)

Confucianism's teaching about God is symbolic. It does not contain any concrete contents about God's character or attributes. Its teachings are focused on morals and ethics. For example, one of its main teachings is: "If you do good deeds, you will be blessed; if you do not, you will be punished." (53:231, February 28, 1972)

Confucius said, "Those who live for the sake of goodness will be blessed by Heaven, but to those who do not live for the sake of goodness, Heaven will bring misfortune." What does he mean by "Heaven"? It is ambiguous.[26] That is why his teaching sometimes appears to be a religion and other times not. (38:260, January 8, 1971)

In Korean custom, a person receiving a gift from someone his senior must take it with both hands. This symbolizes that a person can only receive when he becomes a 'level' base for the older person's love. He receives by setting himself at a ninety-degree angle to the giver. We have a saying in Korea, "the heart of the people is the heart of Heaven." Our rules and customs were formed by the logic of the [vertical] conscience, to be employed in fulfillment of the horizontal. (171:237, January 1, 1988)

This means that there must be a meeting of Heaven and earth. Heaven must connect with the [horizontal virtues of] benevolence, righteousness, propriety and wisdom. Yet, in Confucianism, they were not successfully connected. Hence, its concept of Heaven is vague, the Four Virtues are vague, and people have not known how to link them. Due to this ignorance, the substantial standards of these two forms could not be manifested in history; therefore they were washed away.

    How, according to the Unification Principle, do we manifest the dual characteristics [vertical and horizontal]? How can we then establish a realm of substance, and what form will it take in society? I am talking about the substantial realm of re-creation. What human beings desire most is not knowledge, not power and not money. We desire accomplishments of love: Love between teacher and disciple, love between parent and child, love between king and subject—does not love enter into all these relationships? By the same token, Heaven also needs loving sons and daughters. Hence the Principle speaks of love between Heaven and the sons and daughters of Heaven. (185:272, January 17, 1989)

Judaism

AS THE FIRST GREAT RELIGION IN GOD'S PROVIDENCE, Judaism holds a unique place among the world's religions. In ancient times, in an age darkened by idolatry, God called the Israelites and made with them an eternal covenant. Many Jews today are zealous to keep the laws of the covenant out of an intense faith and awe at God's favor and their special destiny as the chosen people. Yet this uniqueness has always been balanced by a conviction that Judaism has a universal mission. The prophets declared that the Jews were not chosen for their own sake, but to bear the light of God's truth to all nations. Amidst this tension between universalism and ethnocentrism that runs throughout Jewish history, Father Moon consistently calls on Judaism to take a global perspective.

The Jews have also suffered more than any other people. For two thousand years they wandered without a nation, oppressed and persecuted, culminating in the Holocaust of six million. How could they continue to cling to God in the midst of their suffering? What meaning could it have in the context of God's saving history? Father Moon addresses this question in several ways: it is God's course of training to make them strong; it is to unify the Jewish people and draw them closer to God; it is to make them fit to lead the world to God.

Christians have always had difficulty coming to terms with Judaism, on account of its rejection of Jesus as the Messiah. Nevertheless, there is no excuse for Christian anti-Semitism, particularly since Jesus and the disciples were themselves Jews. Still, the genuine anguish of Saint Paul, who never ceased to care for his Jewish brethren even though in his view they lost their way by not receiving Christ, is echoed in Father Moon's teaching. However, unlike Paul, Father Moon does *not* emphasize the conversion of the Jews. He teaches that Jews can fulfill God's contemporary Will through interfaith solidarity, whereby Judaism, Christianity and Islam each retain their identity even as they forgive each other, love each other, and unite for world peace.

Father Moon is supportive of the modern State of Israel as a particular homeland for the Jewish people, but not at other people's expense. He teaches that Israel's survival and prosperity is possible only in the context of genuine peace and reconciliation with its Arab neighbors—thereby resolving a conflict with deep historical roots extending back to Israel's biblical origin. Consistent with his restorationist approach, he calls for Jews and Arabs to extend themselves to each other in love, going beyond self-interest.

1. The Chosen People

All Israel shall have a part in the world to come, as it is said, "And they people shall all be righteous; they shall inherit the land forever, the branch of my planting, the work of my hands, that I may be glorified." (Isa. 60:21)

Mishnah, Sanhedrin 10.1

If you will obey my voice and keep my covenant, you shall be my own possession among all peoples; for all the earth is mine, and you shall be to me a kingdom of priests and a holy nation.

Exodus 19.5-6

O Children of Israel! Remember My favor with which I favored you, and fulfill your covenant, and I shall fulfill My covenant; and fear Me.

Qur'an 2.40

The Holy One desired to make Israel worthy, so He gave them many laws and commandments.

Mishnah, Makkot 3.16

For you are a people holy to the LORD your God; the LORD your God has chosen you to be a people for his own possession, out of all the peoples that are on the face of the earth. It was not because you were more in number than any other people that the LORD set his love upon you and chose you, for you were the fewest of all peoples; but it is because the LORD loves you, and is keeping the oath which he swore to your fathers, that the LORD has brought you out with a mighty hand, and redeemed you from the house of bondage, from the hand of Pharaoh king of Egypt. Know, therefore, that the LORD your God is God, the faithful God who keeps covenant and steadfast love with those who love him and keep his commandments...

And you shall remember all the way which the LORD your God has led you these forty years in the wilderness, that he might humble you, testing you to know what was in your heart, whether you would keep his commandments, or not. And he humbled you and let you hunger and fed you with manna, which you did not know, nor did your fathers know; that he might make you know that man does not live by bread alone, but that man lives by everything that proceeds out of the mouth of the LORD. Your clothing did not wear out upon you, and your foot did not swell, these forty years. Know then in your heart that, as a man disciplines his son, the LORD your God disciplines you. So you shall keep the commandments of the LORD your God, by walking in his ways and by fearing him.

Deuteronomy 7.6-9, 8.2-6

The LORD called me from the womb,
from the body of my mother he named my name,
He made my mouth like a sharp sword,
in the shadow of his hand he hid me;
He made me a polished arrow,
in his quiver he hid me away.
And he said to me, "You are my servant,
Israel, in whom I will be glorified.
"It is too light a thing that you should be my servant
only to reestablish the tribes of Jacob
and to restore the survivors of Israel;
I will make you a light to the nations,
that my salvation may reach to the end of the earth."

Isaiah 49.1-3, 6

Teachings of Sun Myung Moon

Among all religions in human history, Judaism alone was established by a people who claimed that they brought victory for God. It originated from Jacob's victory in the fight against the angel. Jacob did not win against a human being but an angel, a being from the invisible spirit world. The people of Israel stand on this tradition of spiritual victory over the fallen angelic realm... Hence, they could become the chosen people of God.

Thoroughly equipped with the belief that they are the chosen people, the Jews have never forgotten their history and tradition despite the suffering of wandering throughout the world for 2,000 years. Wherever they went, no matter what circumstances they faced, they maintained their belief that they were chosen by God. Such a history never existed among any other people on earth.[27] (149:85, November 17, 1986)

God appointed the Israelites to a central role and wanted all people to honor them. He wanted all people on earth to follow Israel's example; then they would praise Israel just as God would. However, the Israelites could not set up such an exemplary historical tradition. Israel began from Jacob, who was God's champion of love. However, subsequent generations of Israelites could not maintain his tradition.

The Israelites should have been superior to any other people in the world in loving God and fulfilling God's Will and providence. However, while they raised their awareness of being the chosen people, they forgot their mission and their calling for the Will of God.

What is the purpose of the chosen people? The chosen people should love the world on God's behalf and, as God's representatives, set the example for all in loving the world. However, the people of Israel did not fulfill their exalted calling. Though they were supposed to give God's love to all the world, they wanted to receive love instead. That was the problem. (169:265-66, November 1, 1987)

What is the path that God has decreed for Israel and Judaism? It is a path with universal significance. It is a universal mission. God chose the one specific people, Israel, to fulfill a mission not only for themselves but for humankind. (168:304, October 1, 1987)

Besides Judaism, there are numerous religions in the world, such as Buddhism, Confucianism and Hinduism. The religions differ, but they must not fight one another; instead, they must travel the road to one unified world. Likewise, the peoples of the world must not fight one another, but become one. There must be one teaching that can lead all the religions not to fight, but to unite.

The Jewish people in particular, who have the responsibility to lead the world's peoples and unite them into one, should have such a teaching. Because the realization of God's ideal of creation is universal, Judaism and the Jewish people should uphold a teaching that corresponds to God's ideal of creation. (168:304, October 1, 1987)

2. The Suffering of the Jews

Thou hast made us like sheep for the slaughter,
and hast scattered us among the nations.
Thou hast sold thy people for a trifle,
Demanding no high price for them.
Thou hast made us the taunt of our neighbors,
the derision and scorn of those about us.
Thou hast made us a byword among the nations,
a laughingstock among the peoples…

All this has come upon us,
though we have not forgotten thee,
or been false to thy covenant.
Our heart has not turned back,
nor have our steps departed from thy way,
that thou shouldst have broken us in the place
    of jackals,
and covered us with deep darkness.

If we had forgotten the name of our God,
or spread forth our hands to a strange god,
would not God discover this?
For he knows the secrets of the heart.
Nay, for thy sake we are slain all the day long,
and accounted as sheep for the slaughter.

                                  Psalm 44.11-22

The Israelites are compared to an olive tree, because as the olive yields its oil only by hard pressure, so the Israelites do not return to righteousness except through suffering.

                              Talmud, Menahot 53b

"For I am love-sick." [Song of Solomon 2.5] Said the community of Israel before the Holy One, "Sovereign of the Universe, all the maladies which Thou bringest upon me are to make me more beloved of Thee."

Another explanation: The community of Israel said before the Holy One, "Sovereign of the Universe, the reason for all the sufferings which the nations inflict upon me is because I love Thee."

Canticles Rabbah 2.5

All we [the nations] like sheep have gone astray;
we have turned every one to his own way;
and the LORD has laid on him [Israel] the iniquity of us all.[28]

Isaiah 53.6

Teachings of Sun Myung Moon

Despite suffering many difficulties throughout their history, the Jewish people have survived to this day as a homogeneous people. No other people have survived for so long. For two thousand years they wandered without a nation of their own. They have been trampled under the feet of many countries, despised and slaughtered. Yet in spite of all manner of difficulties, the Jews have survived with gusto as a homogeneous people, maintaining their unique traditions and teachings.[29]

How did the Jewish people handle their tribulations? They held to the thought that the more they were oppressed, the more they needed knowledge and money. So they made their children study, even if it meant living like beggars. They strived to earn as much money as possible. They believed that money and knowledge were the keys to power and worked together for their common purpose. This is how they could dissolve their grievances over all the miseries they suffered.

Did God make the Jews suffer to punish them, or was God training them to be a people that can endure difficulties? If God made the Jews suffer out of His love, then surely their long suffering will lead to blessings and worldwide influence.

This is God's will for the one chosen to guide others up the mountain: to fulfill his responsibility as a guide, he should first have the authority of one who has conquered the mountain.

In this respect, God gave the chosen people special dignity only because they are to fulfill the mission of humanity's guides. Their special privilege lasts only as long as their mission. Once their mission is accomplished, God would give the whole world the same privilege and honor. God's plan for the salvation of the world goes like this.

What is the characteristic of the chosen people? They must have the independent ability to embrace all of humankind. Otherwise they cannot digest the whole world. (81:190-91, December 28, 1975)

We should understand that God's will is to unite all religions. God's intention has been to make the world one, even if it required sacrificing the Jewish people. Six million lives are not the issue; the issue is to bring unity among all religions and to make all humankind as one.

Judaism has been persecuted more than any other religion. Because God allowed such suffering to come to the Jews, God expected them to be the strongest and most united religious people. What religion shall play the central role in uniting all religions? God chose the Jews and trained them for that role. This is my explanation of the suffering of the Jews from the perspective of God's providence. (105:126-27, October 4, 1979)

3. The Jewish-Christian Relationship

I am speaking the truth in Christ, I am not lying; my conscience bears me witness in the Holy Spirit, that I have great sorrow and unceasing anguish in my heart. For I could wish that I myself were accursed and cut off from Christ for the sake of my brethren, my kinsmen by race. They are Israelites, and to them belong the sonship, the glory, the covenants, the giving of the law, the worship, and the promises; to them belong the patriarchs, and of their race, according to the flesh, is the Christ...

I ask, then, has God rejected his people? By no means!... As regards the gospel they are enemies of God, for your sake; but as regards election they are beloved for the sake of their forefathers. For the gifts and the call of God are irrevocable. Just as you were once disobedient to God but now have received mercy because of their disobedience, so they have now been disobedient in order that by the mercy shown to you they also may receive mercy. For God has consigned all men to disobedience, that he may have mercy upon all.

Romans 9.1-5; 11.1, 28-32 (*Christianity*)

Teachings of Sun Myung Moon

Many Jews are alive on the earth today. Since a long time ago some of their ancestors betrayed the Will of God, has God therefore abandoned them? Surely not. While they may have traveled down a side path, they kept an unchanging heart toward God as God's chosen people... As long as the Jews hold fast to their role as God's chosen people despite any adversity, they will not disappear from the earth. Hence, there is an element of rightness that today they retain substantial economic power in the world and can exercise control in many fields. (4:243-44, May 18, 1958)

Judaism, centered upon the Old Testament, was the first work of God and is in an elder brother's position. Christianity, centered upon the New Testament, is in the position of the second brother. The Unification Church, through which God has given a new revelation, the Completed Testament, is in the position of the youngest brother.

These three religions are indeed three brothers in the providence of God. Then Israel, the United States and Korea, the nations where these three religions are based, must also be brothers. Because these three nations have a common destiny representing God's side, the Communist bloc as Satan's representative is trying to isolate and destroy them at the U.N.

Therefore these three brother nations must join hands in a unified effort to restore the United Nations to its original purpose and function. They must contribute internally to the unification of world religions and externally to the unification of the world itself. (88:211, September 18, 1976)

4. The Land of Israel

For Zion's sake I will not keep silent,
and for Jerusalem's sake I will not rest,
until her vindication goes forth as brightness,
and her salvation as a burning torch.
The nations shall see your vindication,
and all the kings your glory;
and you shall be called by a new name
which the mouth of the LORD will give.
You shall be a crown of beauty in the hand of the LORD,
and a royal diadem in the hand of your God.
You shall no more be termed Forsaken,

and your land shall no more be termed
  Desolate;
but you shall be called My delight is in her,
and your land Married;
for the LORD delights in you,
and your land shall be married.

Isaiah 62.1-4

The LORD your God will restore your fortunes, and have compassion upon you, and he will gather you again from all the peoples where the LORD your God has scattered you. If your outcasts are in the uttermost parts of heaven, from there the LORD your God will gather you, and from there he will fetch you; and the LORD your God will bring you into the land which your fathers possessed, that you may possess it; and he will make you more prosperous and numerous than your fathers.

Deuteronomy 30.3-5

And We said unto the Children of Israel after him [Moses]: Dwell in the land; but when the promise of the Hereafter comes to pass We shall bring you as a crowd gathered out of various nations.[30]

Qur'an 17.104 (Islam)

All civilizations of the world will be renewed by the renascence of our spirit. All quarrels will be resolved, and our revival will cause all life to be luminous with the joy of fresh birth. All religions will don new and precious raiment, casting off whatever is soiled, abominable and unclean; they will unite in imbibing the dew of the holy lights, that were made ready for all mankind at the beginning of time in the well of Israel. The active power of Abraham's blessing to all the peoples of the world will become manifest and it will serve as the basis of our renewed creativity in the land of Israel.

Abraham Isaac Kook, *The Zionist Idea*

Teachings of Sun Myung Moon

What has been the hope of the Jewish people? They hoped to experience the fulfillment of God's promise to unify the people and re-establish their nation. They longed for that day and kept it in their minds until the moment of death. They left behind the sorrow of not accomplishing it, and it remained their dying wish. When we see this, we recognize that the more a people has passed through a sorrowful course of history, the better they can receive the victorious foundation of world history.

Enduring centuries of misfortune without having a nation, they developed the vision for their nation and love of their people. Because they digested the sorrow, they could realize their vision of a new nation—a new society where they could break down the walls of their confined environment and pursue life in a new, liberated environment. (30:247-48, March 29, 1970)

The Jews thought that they would unify the world centered on their people once they met the Messiah. However… after the death of Jesus, they wandered for 2,000 years. They were trampled under the hoofs of the Gentiles' horses, killed by guns and swords, and suffered all manner of humiliations. Finally, with the Second Advent of Christ and the liberation of Korea, in 1948 Israel could emerge as an independent state.[31] (208:286-87, November 20, 1990)

The purpose of Jesus' coming was to build God's nation. Therefore, we who assume Jesus' role as 'tribal messiahs' should restore the nation of Israel and atone for its past failures…

Israel was divided by conflict on the national level between the ten tribes of the northern kingdom of Israel and the two tribes of Judah; this had its roots in the failure of Leah and Rachel to unite in the days of Jacob. Even in Moses' day, the tribes fought each other. Jesus passed away in the midst of such division, symbolized by the two thieves on the right and on the left of Jesus at the crucifixion. Now that conflict expanded to the world level, at which time the Christ at the Second Advent comes to resolve the situation and unify the world...

Currently, are not Judaism and Christianity enemies? In the Middle East, Israel and the Islamic nations are enemies. We should bring peace to the region. (250:331, October 15, 1993)

Christianity

CHRISTIANITY IS FATHER MOON'S OWN RELIGIOUS HERITAGE; hence he has more to say about it than any other religion. His main teachings concern the essence of the Christianity—its core tradition, the unity of the Church, and Christianity's mission to the world.

Following Christ's example, the core tradition of Christianity is love and sacrifice. The Christian is not reluctant or afraid to take up his cross and suffer for the sake of God's will, as Jesus did. Therefore, Christianity is not an easy or comfortable religion, but one that demands commitment, courage and conviction. Christian love is the second essential core tradition. Jesus taught his followers to love their enemies and forgive those who hurt them. The fellowship of Christians who practice the love of Christ is a beautiful thing.

However, because this love is practiced only imperfectly, and often does not extend to believers of other churches, the problem of disunity has plagued Christianity since its early days. Placing doctrinal purity and denominational self-interest ahead of Christian love, churches have quarreled and persecuted one another, causing great damage to Christianity as a whole. Father Moon has dedicated himself to restoring church unity through the practice of reconciling love and a clarification of essential Christian truth.

Christianity has a worldwide mission, to save all humankind. For Father Moon, this is not only a matter of preaching the Gospel and converting the heathen. In today's world of many religions, democratic values and the ethics of love and charity are Christianity's contributions to elevating the level of all civilizations around the globe. Ultimately, the mission of the church is to prepare the way for God's universal Kingdom on earth, based upon these values, which will be established when Christ returns.

The section concludes with a glimpse at Christian history, which can be viewed as a record of the church's successes and failures in fulfilling its mission. It is a history that is mostly found wanting. The church has consistently failed when it has lived by the secular values of power, wealth and worldly authority. It has made progress when it returns to Christ's tradition of sacrifice and the search for true freedom of faith. In the course of this history, God has attempted to establish a sovereign Christian civilization—first in the Middle Ages through Roman Catholicism, and today through Protestantism centered on the United States of America. Medieval civilization perished when the Vatican's leaders were more intent to pursue power and worldly glory than to live by Jesus' core tradition of love and sacrifice. America, as the current representative Christian nation with a calling to lead the world into the Kingdom, faces the same test.

1. The Core Traditions of Christianity: Love and Sacrifice

Whoever does not bear his own cross and come after me, cannot be my disciple.

Luke 14.27

Blessed are you when men revile you and persecute you and utter all kinds of evil against you falsely on my account. Rejoice and be glad, for your reward is great in heaven, for so men persecuted the prophets who were before you.

Matthew 5.11-12

More than that, we rejoice in our sufferings, knowing that suffering produces endurance, and endurance produces character, and character produces hope, and hope does not disappoint us, because God's love has been poured into our hearts through the Holy Spirit which has been given to us.

Romans 5.3-5

The blood of the martyrs is the seed of the Church.

Tertullian, Apology

And they devoted themselves to the apostles' teaching and fellowship, to the breaking of bread and the prayers. And fear came upon every soul; and many wonders and signs were done through the apostles. And all who believed were together and had all things in common; and they sold their possessions and goods and distributed them to all, as any had need. And day by day, attending the temple together and breaking bread in their homes, they partook of food with glad and generous hearts, praising God and having favor with all the people. And the Lord added to their number day by day those who were being saved.[32]

Acts 2.42-47

Beloved, let us love one another; for love is of God, and he who loves is born of God and knows God. He who does not love does not know God; for God is love. In this the love of God was made manifest among us, that God sent his only Son into the world, so that we might live through him. In this is love, not that we loved God but that he loved us and sent his Son to be the expiation for our sins. Beloved, if God so loved us, we also ought to love one another. No man has ever seen God; if we love one another, God abides in us and his love is perfected in us.

1 John 4.7-12

Love most of all brands us with a mark of blame in the eyes of some. "Look," [the pagans] say, "how [these Christians] love one another"—for they themselves hate one another—"and how they are ready to die for one another"—for they themselves are readier to kill one another.

Tertullian, Apology

Teachings of Sun Myung Moon

Christianity started from the cross, and wherever Christians went they were struck and shed blood. Christianity today can lead the world only when it takes the position of being persecuted. Behold! The palace of Christianity stands on the top of Vatican Hill where the most martyrs died. (*Way of God's Will* 3.4)

You may not know how much sacrifice Christianity endured in order to establish its worldwide foundation. The history of Christianity is so stained with blood that there may be no place on earth where the miserable cries of its sacrificial offerings did not ring out. Even to the present, the blood of Christians continues to flow on numerous altars. All humankind is entangled in the Christians' historical grievances. Therefore, we have the solemn historical responsibility to liberate God and Christianity, by inheriting this historical heart of suffering. (210:361, December 27, 1990)

It is not enough to go to church carrying your Bible and hymnal. You should know Jesus, who bled on God's behalf, wept on God's behalf, and shed sweat on God's behalf. Therefore, the tradition of

Christianity has been to win the world through self-sacrifice and martyrdom. It is the time-honored way that God has been seeking for lost humanity. (10:281, November 6, 1960)

Today Christianity should learn to digest the sufferings that lie ahead. We should be able to say, "Jesus courageously overcame the pain of the cross with the heart of God and blessed sinful humankind. Should we ever face that situation, may we have the same attitude as Jesus!" That is the crucial matter. (7:96, July 19, 1959)

Why could Christianity become a worldwide religion? More than any other religion, Christianity is compatible with God's will and has inherited God's internal heart. Christianity has correctly identified the core point of God's providence and has cherished that content through the ages. God is a worldwide God, so it is reasonable that Christianity, by virtue of its love for God, would develop throughout the world.

Do you know what is the core of God's will? God professes love. Jesus proclaimed before heaven, earth and humanity that God is not the Lord of judgment but the Father of love. Christianity is the only religion that recognizes God as the loving Father. (*God's Will and the World*, May 10, 1974)

2. Christian Unity

There is one body and one Spirit, just as you were called to the one hope that belongs to your call, one Lord, one faith, one baptism, one God and Father of us all, who is above all and through all and in all.

Ephesians 4.4-6

You are fellow citizens with the saints and members of the household of God, built upon the foundation of the apostles and prophets, Christ Jesus himself being the cornerstone, in whom the whole structure is joined together and grows into a holy temple in the Lord; in whom you also are built into it for a dwelling place of God in the Spirit.

Ephesians 2.19-22

I do not pray for these only, but also for those who believe in me through their word, that they may all be one; even as thou, Father, art in me, and I in thee, that they also may be in us, so that the world may believe that thou hast sent me. The glory which thou hast given me I have given to them, that they may be one even as we are one, I in them and thou in me, that they may become perfectly one, so that the world may know that thou hast sent me and hast loved them even as thou hast loved me.

John 17.20-23

Put on then, as God's chosen ones, holy and beloved, compassion, kindness, lowliness, meekness, and patience, forbearing one another and, if one has a complaint against another, forgiving each other; as the Lord has forgiven you, so you also must forgive. And above all these put on love, which binds everything together in perfect harmony. And let the peace of Christ rule in your hearts, to which indeed you were called in the one body. And be thankful.

Colossians 3.12-15

Teachings of Sun Myung Moon

We frequently hear that the church is the body of Christ. What is the body of Christ? Does it consist of church buildings made of wood or stone? No, the body of Christ is the congregation, the people. We who believe in Jesus are Jesus' body and Christ's representatives on earth.

If the believers are the body of Christ, then can there be more than one church? Today's church, divided as it is into numerous denominations, is a church in error. It is heartbreaking for Jesus to see the existence of so many denominations, each bearing his name. It is as though his body has been torn apart into many pieces…

Christianity should have become a single worldwide religion, based on the victorious foundation of Jesus' sacrifice. Like Jesus' own body, the church should have become a whole offering before God; then by that victorious foundation of offering, it could have become one worldwide religion, one Christian church. Instead, the heart of Jesus Christ is grieved to see his body so shamefully divided. Jesus is the mind and today's Christianity is the body. How can there be one mind and 1,000 bodies? How can the mind and body differ to such an extent? Therefore, our task is to unite them as one mind and one body.

What is the core conviction that Jesus has sought to convey to Christianity until this day? It is this: "God is our Father, all people are our brothers and sisters; the earth belongs to all of us; therefore we should be as members of one household." Today's Christians should adopt this outlook. Since it is God's teaching and Jesus' teaching, it should be Christianity's teaching. Therefore, we should not get caught up in sectarian squabbles. We should restore the people, even if to do so we have to abandon our denomination. We should restore the earth, even if our denomination must perish in the process. (93:12-25, May 8, 1977)

Why is today's Christianity divided into numerous denominations? The proliferation of denominations contradicts the Christian doctrine that we ought to love our enemies. Christian doctrine instructs us to love the brethren, but people have forgotten it. Christians may love one another within the same church, yet their churches are fighting one another. Jesus taught us to love our brethren. From Jesus' perspective, the Presbyterian Church, the Methodist Church, the Holiness Church and all other denominations are each other's brethren. (107:20, February 21, 1980)

God's heaviest burden is to create oneness among the declining remnants of Christianity and among the many religions. While God is trying hard to create oneness among the religions, some Methodists are praying, "O Father, I don't care what happens to other churches, but please bless the Methodist Church." Do you think such a prayer will reach God's ears? Methodism is only one of more than four hundred denominations. God will say, "You rascals! You denominationalists! Before praying for yourselves, you should make the Christian church one! If you do that, I will listen to your prayer."

What would God say if Christians were to unite as one and pray, "O Lord! Give us strength to resolve your biggest headache by uniting Christianity and creating oneness among all the religions. Gives us the ability! Help us to create this oneness!" Surely He would say, "Yes, I will grant your prayer." God is waiting for the appearance of people who can break down the walls surrounding the denominations and make them one. (98:114-15, May 7, 1978)

By what means can we unite Christianity throughout the world? It is by the Holy Spirit. Hence, I named our church, "The Holy Spirit Association." Not by fists or bayonets, but by the Holy Spirit.

We cannot unite the churches by human power. It is possible only by the power of the Holy Spirit, through mobilizing the hosts of heaven. (113:97, May 1, 1981)

3. The Church's Mission to the World

I am the LORD, I have called you in
    righteousness,
I have taken you by the hand and kept you;
I have given you as a covenant to the people,
a light to the nations.

Isaiah 42.6

For God so loved the world that He gave His only begotten Son, that whosoever believes in him shall not perish but shall have eternal life. For God sent the Son into the world, not to condemn the world, but that the world might be saved through him.

John 3.16-17

In Christ God was reconciling the world to himself, not counting their trespasses against them, and entrusting to us the message of reconciliation.

2 Corinthians 5.19-20

All authority in heaven and on earth has been given to me. Go therefore and make disciples of all nations, baptizing them in the name of the Father and of the Son and of the Holy Spirit, teaching them to observe all that I have commanded you; and lo, I am with you always, even to the close of the age.

Matthew 28.18-20: The Great Commission

When they had come together, they asked him, "Lord, will you at this time restore the kingdom to Israel?" He said to them, "It is not for you to know times or seasons which the Father has fixed by his own authority. But you shall receive power when the Holy Spirit has come upon you; and you shall be my witnesses in Jerusalem and in all Judea and Samaria and to the end of the earth."

Acts 1.6-9

Teachings of Sun Myung Moon

Christians enjoy reciting John 3:16, "For God so loved the world that He gave His only begotten Son, that whosoever believes in Him shall not perish but shall have eternal life." Christians emphasize the second part of the verse and forget the most important thing—that God so loved the *world*. God did not so love the church, or the Jews, that He sent His only begotten Son. It was because God so loved the world—the universe.

    Who is Jesus? He is the central person of the world. He came to save the world. Those whose faith is to believe in Jesus should have the world—including God, this planet, everything—very much on their minds. Yet most Christians are ignorant of this.

    Have you heard complaints that many Christians are worse than ordinary people? They believe in God, yet they are more selfish and wicked than nonbelievers. Was Jesus a self-centered, individualistic person? Nevertheless, why have so many American Christians, followers of Jesus in the nation that most represents the Christian faith, become individualistic? If they truly believed in Jesus well, they would not. It means that they only use faith in God and Jesus to advance their self-interest. (124:294, March 1, 1983)

God desires that all of you should become sacrificial offerings. As an offering, it is not proper for you to raise your head until the day when God and all humankind rejoice. If a Christian church raises its head before God is happy and before all humankind rejoices, it will perish. Christianity has the mission to serve all people. It exists as an offering for humanity. If not, it has not been fulfilling its mission and needs to be reformed without delay.

Jesus Christ, the King of Kings and Crown Prince of Heaven, came as such a universal offering. Therefore, although he looks from heaven and sees believers on earth rejoicing in his grace, he cannot be happy. The day will finally come when Jesus can rejoice; it will come only after God and all humankind rejoice. That is the day of the Second Coming. But first, he will have to lead the church on the sacrificial path of an offering. (5:79-80, December 21, 1958)

Jesus was chased out on the road of death, yet his road followed the way of Heaven. His path was not that of a worthless life, but rather a path of lofty and infinite value. It lifted the standard for all humankind. It contains the core teachings sought by the whole world. Jesus' teachings are definitely the standard that humankind must seek, and his path is the path humankind must follow. Indeed, his teachings are the basis of today's democracies and world community. (41:70, February 13, 1971)

Christianity will form the world's dominant cultural sphere in the Last Days. Centered on Christian civilization, the nations of the world will join in a world community. (39:44, January 9, 1971)

We should enlist the cooperation of all Christians throughout the world to build God's nation on earth, just as Jesus in his day was to fulfill his mission to build God's Kingdom by enlisting the cooperation of Judaism. Christians today should understand that they have a mission to accomplish: to build God's Kingdom on this earth. Christian thought is the basis of democracy worldwide. Christians should uphold Christian thought to build God's Kingdom based upon democracy. (3:123-24, October 13, 1957)

4. History of Christianity: Triumphalism, Corruption and Renewal

About noon, when the day was already beginning to decline, Constantine saw with his own eyes the trophy of a cross of light in the heavens, above the sun, and bearing the inscription, CONQUER BY THIS. At this sight he himself was struck with amazement, and his whole army also, which followed him on this expedition, and witnessed the miracle.

Eusebius, Life of Constantine

I tell you, you are Peter, and on this rock[33] I will build my church, and the powers of death shall not prevail against it. I will give you the keys of the kingdom of heaven, and whatever you bind on earth shall be bound in heaven, and whatever you loose on earth shall be loosed in heaven.

Matthew 16.18-19

The true faith compels us to believe there is one holy Catholic Apostolic Church, and this we firmly believe and plainly confess. Outside of her there is no salvation or remission from sins.

Now, therefore, we declare, say, determine and pronounce that for every human creature it is necessary for salvation to be subject to the authority of the Roman pontiff.

Pope Boniface VIII, Unam Sanctam

For the defense of the faith secular authorities ought publicly to take an oath that they will strive in good faith and to the best of their ability to exterminate in the territories subject to their jurisdiction all heretics pointed out by the Church.

Fourth Lateran Council, Canon 3

The Romanists have very cleverly built three walls around themselves... In the first place... temporal power had no jurisdiction over them... In the second place... only the pope may interpret the Scriptures. In the third place... no one may summon a council but the pope...

Therefore, when necessity demands it, and the pope is an offense to Christendom, the first man who is able should, as a true member of the whole body, do what he can to bring about a truly free council. No one can do this so well as the temporal authorities.

Martin Luther, On Papal Power

Religion is the sob of the oppressed creature, the heart of a heartless world, and the soul of soulless conditions. It is the opium of the people.

Karl Marx, *Critique of Hegel's Philosophy of Right*

The God of Israel is among us... when He shall make us a praise and glory, that men shall say of succeeding plantations: The Lord make it like that of New England: for we must consider that we shall be as a City upon a Hill, the eyes of all people are upon us.

John Winthrop, *A Model of Christian Charity*

No people can be bound to acknowledge and adore the invisible hand which conducts the affairs of men more than the people of the United States. Every step by which they have advanced to the character of an independent nation seems to have been distinguished by some token of providential urgency.

George Washington, First Inaugural Address

Teachings of Sun Myung Moon

In the Middle Ages great corruption appeared in the Roman Catholic Church. It allowed itself to be shackled by its own power and self-serving dogmas while forgetting about God's Will to bring salvation to the world... To save the world, Christianity should take the path of self-sacrifice, but instead the church glorified itself and its elite clung tenaciously to their positions.

Yet, God is alive, and because His desire is to save the world, He could not leave the church as it was. He had to reform it. Hence, God inspired Martin Luther to launch the Protestant Reformation. He approved when Luther came forth to confront the church and its corruption. (69:102, October 21, 1973)

Christianity, the Second Israel, had to deal with the confused situation of the Renaissance and the humanistic philosophies of the Enlightenment. Enlightenment figures like Voltaire, Rousseau and Montesquieu believed that Christianity would collapse. However, pious people from Germany advanced Christianity by raising the Pietist movement, which focused on internal, mystical experiences with God. The Pietist movement influenced the English clergyman John Wesley, who raised the Methodist movement. The Quakers contributed to the development of Christianity by elevating the value of mystical experience even further.

At the same time, due to the widespread influence of materialism, modern people forgot about loving God, lost their reason to love other human beings, and came to value material things above all else. Nevertheless, the time is coming when God will strike down all materialistic ideologies. He will surely do so, because human beings must ultimately return to their original position before the Fall. (4:18, February 16, 1958)

When ecclesiastic love waned, when waves of capitalistic greed surged across Christian Europe, when starving masses cried out bitterly in the slums, the promise of their salvation came not from heaven but from the earth. Its name was communism. Christianity, though it professed the love of God, had degenerated into a dead body of clergy trailing empty slogans. It was then only natural that a banner of rebellion would be raised, arguing that a merciless God who would allow such suffering could not exist. Hence, modern materialism was born. Western society became a hotbed of materialism; it was the fertile soil in which communism flourished. (*Exposition of the Divine Principle*, Introduction)

The first thing the Pilgrim Fathers built was a church. They invested all their effort to build it, giving everything they had. Next they built the road to the church. For the sake of God they worked day and night. They prayed, "God, we pledge ourselves to build a place where You can dwell, surpassing anyplace in the Old World. We pledge ourselves to establish Your ideal nation, surpassing any nation in the Old World."[34] The Pilgrims suffered a great deal, but the more they suffered, the more determined they were to build God's Kingdom, a godly society transcending what existed in Europe.

After their church, they built a school. For they resolved to educate their children well, surpassing what they could learn at schools in Europe. Last of all, they built their homes. Yet even these they built not for themselves, but dedicated them to God. Thus they created a society where God dwelt in the church, in the school, in the family, and even in the workplace. They surely lived a God-centered way of life, entrusting everything to God…

George Washington, Commander-in-Chief of the Continental Army in the Revolutionary War, was defeated in many battles. When he faced the heartbreaking winter at Valley Forge, I am sure George Washington prayed like this: "God, You led this people from Europe and brought us to America, where there is freedom of faith. You would not wish to deliver this people back into the hands of England, to suffer under its monarchy and the yoke of state-enforced religion. Please bless this nation to become the land that You desire to build, upholding freedom of faith and laying the foundation for Your ideal world." In his prayer, George Washington must have pledged that he would lead his nation to become the land desired by God.

Isn't it true that very day your Congress is convened in prayer? America is not merely the land where Americans live; it is the nation blessed by God. In this respect, America is unique. Your money is imprinted with the inscription, "In God We Trust." Does any other nation in the world do that? Americans promote the motto, "One nation under God." Does this motto refer only to America? Ladies and gentlemen, the Kingdom of Heaven should occupy the whole world. It was for this reason that America was born: as a nation composed of all the peoples of the world, it should be the model for one worldwide nation. Why did America establish freedom of religion where the new Protestant faiths could thrive? For what purpose did America throw off the state religions of Europe? It was not just for America's sake, but to save the world. To save the world!

Americans, do not think that you are prospering because you yourselves are great. God did not bless this nation so that you can enjoy an affluent life. You should remember God's original purpose in blessing America, to use this nation as His instrument for saving the world. (69:102, October 21, 1973)

Christianity in the Middle Age should have embraced all people regardless of class, and integrated them based on its religious ideals. However, it failed in doing so, and instead corrupted itself by becoming politicized. As a result, God had to strike it.

Had the Roman Papacy not become corrupt, and had it instantiated the teaching of living for the sake of others before seeking for its own benefit, with a sense of mission that it existed for the world and humankind, it would not have fallen down. However, due to its failure, God struck Catholicism externally through the Renaissance and internally through the Protestant Reformation.

Then the Puritans sailed across the Atlantic Ocean to the new continent of America and built a new nation based on Christian ideals. America's liberal democratic ideology that prevails throughout the democratic world is based on an integration of Roman political ideology, Christian religious ideas and Greek philosophy.

However, for America to fulfill its responsibility… she should give up her idea of being Number One in the world. For the people of the United States this is the most essential thing. (5:22-23, November 9, 1958)

Islam

TODAY ISLAM IS PLAYING A MAJOR ROLE IN GOD'S UNFOLDING PROVIDENCE. Father Moon finds in Muslims a firm faith and moral clarity that is sorely needed in this relativistic age, when Christianity has grown feeble. He totally rejects the "clash of civilizations" scenario that would see the Muslim world as an enemy of the West. Because Islam is a higher religion, it has the spiritual blessing to be one of the pillars of the Kingdom of God.

Islam is a righteous religion, and holds itself above Judaism and Christianity, which it regards as filled with errors and hypocrisy. Nevertheless, what is required in this age is reconciliation between these three religions as the spiritual mainstays of humanity. Father Moon identifies the source of their conflict neither in doctrine nor in the events surrounding Muhammad's ministry, but rather in the crucifixion of Jesus, which sowed the seeds that have borne their inevitable fruit in the contemporary world. Resolving the mistakes of that time will require the concerted efforts of all—Christians, Jews and Muslims—the descendants of the actors in that drama.

1. A Religion of Faith and Righteousness

You are the best community that has been raised up for mankind. You enjoin right conduct and forbid indecency; and you believe in God.

Qur'an 3.110

God has endeared the Faith to you, and has made it beautiful in your hearts, and He has made hateful to you unbelief, wickedness, and rebellion: such indeed are those who walk in righteousness—a grace and favor from God.

Qur'an 49.7

We believe in God, and in that which has been sent down on us and sent down on Abraham, Ishmael, Isaac and Jacob, and the Tribes, and that which was given to Moses and Jesus and the Prophets; of their Lord; we make no division between any of them, and to Him we surrender.[35]

Qur'an 2.136

This [Qur'an] is the Book which We have revealed as a blessing; so follow it and be righteous, that you may receive mercy; lest you should say, "The Book was send down to two peoples before us, and for our part, we remained unacquainted with what they learned by studying it"; or lest you should say, "If only the Book had been sent down to us, we should have followed its guidance better than they." Now then has come to you a clear proof from your Lord, and a guide and a mercy; then who could do more wrong than one who rejects Allah's revelations and turns away from them?

Qur'an 6.155-157

The true believers are those whose hearts are filled with awe at the mention of God, and whose faith grows stronger as they listen to His revelations. They put their trust in their Lord, pray steadfastly, and give in alms of that which We have given them. Such are the true believers. They shall be exalted and forgiven by their Lord, and a generous provision shall be made for them.

Qur'an 8.2-4

O you who believe, be upright for Allah, bearers of witness with justice; and let not hatred of a people incite you not to act equitably. Be just; that is nearer to observance of duty. And keep your duty to Allah. Surely Allah is aware of what you do.

Qur'an 5.8

Teachings of Sun Myung Moon

Islam is a comprehensive religion. It adopted the teachings of the Old and New Testaments of the Christian Bible, but with God alone as its center. It was founded with contents appropriate to Arab culture. (39:316, January 16, 1971)

Today Islam will become a prophetic religion to ignite this deviating world. (39:42, January 9, 1971)

The Grand Mufti of Syria is a leader of accomplished self-discipline who has highly cultivated his spirit. After World War II he received a revelation from Heaven that dreadful punishment would come unless Islam united with Judaism and Christianity. Because he kept this revelation for forty years, he was persecuted and imprisoned several times. Still, he could not fulfill Heaven's commission.

After learning of my interreligious activities, he was moved to think, "I should go and visit Father Moon." (212:324, January 11, 1991)

2. A Rival Religion, Correcting the Religions that Preceded It

Surely the true religion with God is Islam. And those who were (formerly) given the Book differed only after knowledge had come to them, out of envy among themselves. Whoever disbelieves the messages of God, God is Quick at the reckoning.

Qur'an 3.19

And the Jews say the Christians follow nothing true, and the Christians say the Jews follow nothing true; yet both are readers of the same Scripture. Even thus speak those who know not. God will judge between them on the Day of Resurrection concerning that wherein they differ.

Qur'an 2.113

[The children of Israel] alter the words from their contexts and neglect a portion of that whereof they were reminded. And you will always discover treachery in them excepting a few of them—so pardon them and forgive.[36] Surely Allah loves those who do good to others.

And with those who say, "We are Christians," We made a covenant, but they neglected a portion of that whereof they were reminded, so We stirred up enmity and hatred among them to the Day of Resurrection.[37] And Allah will soon inform them of what they did.

O People of the Book, indeed Our Messenger has come to you, making clear to you much of what you concealed of the Book and passing over much. Indeed, there has come to you from Allah a Light and a clear Book.

Qur'an 5.13-15

And when Allah says, "O Jesus, son of Mary, did you say to mankind, 'Take me and my mother for two gods beside Allah?'"[38] He says, "Be glorified! It was not mine to utter that to which I had no right. If I used to say it, then Thou wouldst know it. Thou knowest what is in my mind, and I know not what is in Thy mind. Surely Thou art the Knower of Things Hidden.

Qur'an 5.116

Fight those who believe not in God nor in the Last Day, nor hold that forbidden which has been forbidden by God and His Apostle, nor acknowledge the Religion of Truth, even if they are of the People of the Book, until they pay the tribute[39] with willing submission and acknowledge their subjection.

The Jews say, "Ezra is the son of God," and the Christians say, "Christ is the Son of God." That is a saying from their mouth; they but imitate what the unbelievers of old used to say. God's curse be upon them: how they are deluded away from the truth!

They have taken as lords besides God their rabbis and their monks and Christ the son of Mary, when they were bid to worship only one God. There is no God save Him...

It is He who hath sent His Messenger with the guidance and the religion of truth, that He may cause it to prevail over all religion, however much the idolaters may be averse.

Qur'an 9.29-33

Teachings of Sun Myung Moon

Had John the Baptist and the people of Israel accepted Jesus, they were destined to struggle against the Roman Empire, just as Jacob wrestled against the angel at the Ford of Jabbok.

At that time, Roman sovereignty was weak, and there was an opportunity for the smaller surrounding countries to win their independence. Therefore, with Jesus Christ as the commander-in-chief, the movement could have unified the Arab world in revolt against Rome.

By fighting a common enemy, God's intention was to unite the Arab people and the Jewish people. It was an opportunity for these peoples under the Roman yoke to unite as one. But first, Jesus, Judaism and John the Baptist's movement had to become one. That was the precondition to defeat Rome. However, instead John the Baptist went his own way, Jesus acted alone, and the Jews eventually revolted on their own [and were crushed]. As a result, there came to be lasting division between the Arabs and Jews. (111:151, February 10, 1981)

In the seventh century, the religion of Islam emerged in the Middle East. It was because Jesus was unable to establish his own nation that Islam appeared and took the position of a rival to Christianity. It is for Islam and Christianity to resolve this Cain-Abel relationship, and when they do they both will be perfected. Thus, you should understand that it was out of providential necessity that God raised up Islam as a rival religion. What do conventional theologians say is the reason and purpose of Islam?

The Jews had received much blessing from God after the Exodus from Egypt. Nevertheless, [after the crucifixion] Islam emerged from the central people—the descendants of Abraham—and became the Jews' adversaries. Nevertheless, the Jews should learn to live with their Muslim adversaries.

These days, Islam is expanding more rapidly than Christianity. They are strong! Their values are strong and their faith is firm! They do not sway back and forth, compromising like Christians do.

Ishmael and Isaac are brothers, both sons of Abraham. Yet their descendants became adversaries and fought throughout history. After the Jews lost Jerusalem, Christians and Muslims fought over the city at the time of the Crusades. The land of Israel should be restored for all these brother religions. However, this must not be accomplished by fighting and bloodshed.

That is why Reverend Moon, representing Christianity and as founder of the Unification Church, gave his hand to Minister Farrakhan; and also to President Wahid of Indonesia. I wanted to join President Wahid and Minister Farrakhan as brothers. I also helped Minister Farrakhan at the Million Family March. White people opened their eyes in alarm, saying that I should by no means ever help him. But I said to those people, "You oppose me now, but wait and see who is right. Just follow me as I guide you, and something good will definitely happen, something that pleases God. Close your eyes and pray. Don't open your mouth."[40] (June 21, 2001)

Jesus taught us to love our enemies. Minister Farrakhan may be an enemy to Christianity… but since we are taught to love our enemies, I am loving him. Does China love America? Does the Soviet Union love China? Between these enemies there is no love, but taking God's standpoint I love them all. That is why I have no enemies—neither Christians nor Muslims, neither blacks nor whites. (339:156, December 10, 2000)

Chapter 9

History of God's Providence

Founders, Prophets and Saints

GOD OPERATES HIS PROVIDENCE TO SAVE HUMANKIND through establishing religions; the religions in turn elevate human morality and ethics, leading to the creation of civilizations. Each of the major religions begins with its founder. Father Moon terms these founders "saints," and gives pride of place to Jesus, Buddha, Confucius and Muhammad as the four representative saints of humankind.

Each founder is unique, proclaiming the core truth for the religion he spawned. For the Christian, it is the saving work of Christ alone that saves, notwithstanding the accomplishments of other founders, great as they may be. Likewise, the Muslim's faith is defined uniquely by the message of Muhammad, the "seal" of the prophets—that is, the last and final prophet. The committed believer is confronted with one individual as the standard of truth, the exemplar and revealer who defines the true way. The declaration, "I am the way, the truth and the life; no one comes to the Father but by me" (John 14.6) is comparable to, "Outside the Buddha's dispensation there is no saint" (Dhammapada 254); "Muhammad is the Seal of the Prophets" (Qur'an 33.40) and so on. For Father Moon, however, all the founders were sent by the one God. All bear witness to the one truth of God. All stand within a single providence of God that seeks to elevate people of every culture and every nation and prepare them to enter His universal Kingdom.

Thus, Father Moon adds Buddha, Confucius and Muhammad to that more familiar roster of God's chosen ones in providential history, which in the Western tradition begins with Abel and Noah and continues with Abraham, Isaac and Jacob, Moses, David, Solomon and the prophets, up to Jesus. Judaism, Christianity and Islam all regard themselves as heirs to this illustrious lineage. Judaism omits Jesus of course, but adds a succession of great rabbis; Islam includes Jesus and adds a few Arabian prophets to its list such as Ishmael and Idris. Meanwhile, in the East, Hinduism recognizes a succession of Avatars who arise from age to age to defeat the powers of evil and return the world to righteousness. Confucianism has its own lineage of saints: King Yü, Wen and Wu and the Duke of Chou. Confucius saw himself as recovering their ancient wisdom and tradition.

This section treats the common characteristics of a saint: pursuit of the truth regardless of the cost; desire to elevate society and all humankind to a higher ideal; a universal outlook that does not discriminate by nationality, wealth or social status; faith in God or Heaven or some higher power; and willingness to bear with persecution and ostracism from ignorant society. Subsequent sections will treat these saints and prophets individually, with special attention on the Western biblical tradition.

1. God's Champions and Messengers

Whenever the Law declines and the purpose of life is forgotten, I manifest myself on earth. I am born in every age to protect the good, to destroy evil, and to re-establish the Law.[1]

Bhagavad-Gita 4.7-8 (Hinduism)

Lo! We inspired you [O Muhammad] as We inspired Noah and the prophets after him, as We inspired Abraham and Ishmael and Isaac and Jacob, and the tribes, and Jesus and Job and Jonah and Aaron and Solomon, and as

We imparted unto David the Psalms; and messengers We have mentioned to you before and messengers We have not mentioned to you... messengers of good cheer and of warning, in order that mankind might have no argument against God after the messengers. God was ever Mighty, Wise.

Qur'an 4.163-65

Inasmuch as these Birds of the Celestial Throne are all sent down from the heaven of the Will of God, and as they all arise to proclaim His irresistible Faith, they therefore are regarded as one soul and the same person. For they all drink from the one Cup of the love of God, and all partake of the fruit of the same Tree of Oneness. These Manifestations of God have each a twofold station. One is the station of pure abstraction and essential unity. In this respect, if you call them all by one name, and ascribe to them the same attribute, you have not erred from the truth. Even as He has revealed, "No distinction do We make between any of His Messengers!" For they one and all summon the people of the earth to acknowledge the Unity of God...

The other is the station of distinction, and pertains to the world of creation and to its limitations. In this respect, each Manifestation of God has a distinct individuality, a definitely prescribed mission, a predestined Revelation, and specially designated limitations. Each one of them is known by a different name, is characterized by a special attribute, fulfills a definite Mission, and is entrusted with a particular Revelation.

Book of Certitude, 152, 176 (Baha'i Faith)

To be unsnared by vulgar ways, to make no vain show of material things, to bring no hardship on others, to avoid offending the mob, to seek peace and security for the world, preservation of the people's lives, full provender for others as well as oneself, and to rest content when these aims are fulfilled, in this way bringing purity to the heart—there were those in ancient times who believed that the "art of the Way" lay in these things... They preached liberality of mind, hoping thereby to bring men together in the joy of harmony, to insure concord within the four seas. Their chief task lay, they felt, in the effort to establish these ideals. They regarded it as no shame to suffer insult, but sought to put an end to strife among the people, to outlaw aggression, to abolish the use of arms, and to rescue the world from warfare. With these aims they walked the whole world over, trying to persuade those above them and to teach those below, and though the world refused to listen, they clamored all the louder and would not give up, until men said, "High and low are sick at the sight of them, and still they demand to be seen!"[2]

Chuang Tzu 33 (Taoism)

Time would fail me to tell of Gideon, Barak, Samson, Jephthah, of David and Samuel and the prophets—who through faith conquered kingdoms, enforced justice, received promises, stopped the mouths of lions, quenched raging fire, escaped the edge of the sword, won strength out of weakness, became mighty in war, put foreign armies to flight. Women received their dead by resurrection. Some were tortured, refusing to accept release, that they might rise again to a better life. Others suffered mocking and scourging, and even chains and imprisonment. They were stoned, they were sawn in two, they were killed with the sword, they went about in skins of sheep and goats, destitute, afflicted, ill-treated—of whom the world was not worthy—wandering over deserts and mountains, and in dens and caves of the earth.

Hebrews 11.32-38

Let us now praise famous men,
and our fathers in their generations.
The Lord apportioned to them great glory,
his majesty from the beginning.

There were those who ruled in their kingdoms,
and were men renowned for their power,
giving counsel by their understanding
and proclaiming prophecies...

And there are some who have no memorial,
who have perished as though they had not lived...
but these were men of mercy,
whose righteous deeds have not been forgotten.

Ecclesiasticus 44.1-10 *(Christianity)*

Teachings of Sun Myung Moon

When God assigns a responsibility within His providential Will to human beings, He raises up for them a central figure. He raises each central figure to be the leading light of the people of his age and link them to the thought of Heaven. In other words, at key moments in history God seeks out a single individual who can represent his age, his culture, and the whole world. God calls on His chosen one to declare His teaching to Heaven and earth. (4:192, April 20, 1958)

Jesus, Mohammed, Buddha and Confucius are called the great saints of history. They left their traditions to posterity, which became organized as the time-honored religions and gave birth to the great civilizations of humankind.

Did these saints live as they wished, enjoying themselves every day? No, from an earthly point of view they lived miserable lives, far more difficult than the lives of ordinary people.

Why did they live that kind of life? The saints did not live according to their own desires, but instead lived obedient to the divine Will and for the sake of the world God desired to build through them.

Although they had individual desires, the saints lived always thinking about God and how they could inherit His tradition. They were concerned to train their character and to conform their life to God's Will. When they looked at their families, they thought about what would be the authentic family in the sight of God. They thought about how their society could be acceptable to God. They sought to understand what traditions their nation should have in the sight of God. (95:271, December 11, 1977)

What did these founders of religion teach? They taught centered on God. They taught according to God's teachings and guided their people to do God's Will. They did not teach their own will. They did not boast of their greatness. They passed away while proclaiming a God-centered worldview, a God-centered way of life, and a God-centered understanding of the universe. (41:329-30, February 18, 1971)

God is the Source of the principle that governs the universe. While creating the universe, God invested Himself totally for the sake of His creation. Throughout history, God has continually sacrificed Himself to save fallen human beings, who have been living just as they desire.

The prophets, saints, and sages who knew God's Will followed God's principle in their own lives. Furthermore, they were not content to keep the truth to themselves, but walked the way of sacrifice to teach others. Moses, Confucius, Buddha, Mohammed, Socrates and Jesus suffered hardships and persecution for their efforts to teach the people. They dedicated their lives to enlighten and liberate humanity. (234:222, August 20, 1992)

The Chinese character for "saint" (聖) has three parts, representing ears (耳), mouth (口), and king (王). The combination of these three elements signifies a saint. If you link the meanings, a saint is the "king of the mouth" and "king of the ears." What does this mean? As the king of the ears, he comprehends and interprets what he hears like a king. He does not simply repeat what he hears, for if he did it could cause many troubles. As a king of the mouth, he is careful about the words he speaks. He knows that whatever he says could become the law; it could sway the destiny of his nation. (118:44, May 2, 1982)

What is the definition of a saint? A saint is someone who transcends national boundaries. The saints of history did not live merely for their own people or for their own tribe. They transcended national boundaries to live for the sake of all humanity. They could say, "I will die for the sake of all humanity. I transcend all the boundaries that separate the thousands of ethnic groups and nations. I am beyond nations, beyond religions, and beyond races." Before they went to their deaths, these saints forged a connection to all humanity on a worldwide level. (38:350, January 8, 1971)

2. Every Prophet and Saint Endured Hardships and Rejection

A prophet is not without honor, except in his own country, and among his own kin, and in his own house.

Mark 6.4

As an elephant in the battlefield withstands the arrows shot from a bow, even so will I endure abuse.

Dhammapada 320 (Buddhism)

A scribe came up and said to him, "Teacher, I will follow you wherever you go." And Jesus said to him, "Foxes have holes, and birds of the air have nests, but the Son of man has nowhere to lay his head."

Matthew 8.19-20

The Messenger says, "O my Lord, behold, my people have taken this Qur'an as a thing to be shunned." Even so We have appointed to every Prophet an enemy from among the sinners; but your Lord suffices as a guide and as a helper.

Qur'an 25.30-31

To what land shall I flee? Where bend my steps?
I am thrust out from family and tribe;
I have no favor from the village to which I
    would belong,
Nor from the wicked rulers of the country:
How then, O Lord, shall I obtain Thy favor?

Avesta, Yasna 46.1 (Zoroastrianism)

While Confucius stood alone at the east gate of the outer city the natives reported to Tsekung, "There is a man at the east gate... He looks crestfallen like a homeless, wandering dog." Tsekung told Confucius this story, and Confucius smiled and said, "I don't know about the descriptions of my figure, but as for resembling a homeless, wandering dog, he is quite right, he is quite right!"

Ssu-ma Ch'ien, Shih Chi 47 (Confucianism)

The LORD, the God of their fathers, sent persistently to them by his messengers, because he had compassion on his people and on his dwelling place; but they kept mocking the messengers of God, despising his words, and scoffing at his prophets, till the wrath of the LORD rose against his people, till there was no remedy.

2 Chronicles 36.15-16

They say only, "Lo! We found our fathers following a religion, and we are guided by their footprints." And even so We sent not a warner before you [Muhammad] into any township, but its luxurious ones said, "Lo! We found our fathers following a religion, and we are following their footprints." And the warner said, "What! Even though I bring you better guidance than that you found your fathers following?" They answered, "Lo! In what you bring we are disbelievers." We have requited them; see what was the consequence for the deniers.

Qur'an 43.22-25

You stiff-necked people, uncircumcised in heart and ears, you always resist the Holy Spirit. As your fathers did, so do you. Which of the prophets did not your fathers persecute? And they killed those who announced beforehand the coming of the Righteous One, whom you have now betrayed and murdered.

Acts 7.51-52

Teachings of Sun Myung Moon

Of all the people throughout history, there are four great saints worthy of reverence; they are Jesus, Mohammed, Confucius, and Buddha. Did they have big, fancy houses? Did they even live a settled life in a village? No, wherever they went they were persecuted, despised and driven out. Jesus said, "Foxes have holes, and birds of the air have their nests, but the Son of Man has nowhere to lay his head." Is that a characteristic of a great man?

During his time Confucius was called a "homeless, wandering dog," as he put it, because he had to beg for food while traveling from place to place. The Buddha was born into a palace as a great prince, but he gave it all up for his spiritual quest, living as a hermit in the mountains, praying and searching for spiritual truth. None of these saints had a house to live in; they died without a nation. Yet today everyone considers them great. (115:14-16, October 25, 1981)

When a prophet spoke out strongly, warning the people not to follow the ways of the world, the people would say angrily, "That man is not one of us!" They would beat him and persecute him and cast him out from their midst. After much bitter rejection, the prophet would reach out to the failures of the world, to the crippled, the wounded, and those discarded by society. He would tell them of his mission as a prophet and describe how the people persecuted him and drove him out. Thus he would build relationships with those who were similarly rejected by society.[3]

He would give hope to people in despair, telling them of a new world, one far better than the existing society of their day. They would naturally listen closely to the message, while the stylish and well-to-do people were nowhere to be seen. Only society's rejects became his followers. None of the people with talent and good family backgrounds joined him because Satan took them all away. All that remained were those whose hearts were hurt and scarred. They were the ones with no ties to the world and who wished for a new world. They were the ones who responded to the prophet's words of hope. (106:176-77, December 30, 1979)

The founders of religion taught the true way to live. They taught the people of their age about the world to come, but the people were ignorant and could not understand. Why? The difference between the future world and the present reality was too great. Hence, the rulers of their time persecuted, expelled and even murdered them.

These saints did not harm their countries. They only wanted to rescue their countries from chaos and lead them to hope. However, the people did not understand, and drove them out. Yet, over the course of time, people began to accept their teachings because they showed the way for all people. In due course, their teachings would become the nucleus of the world's civilizations. (39:256, January 15, 1971)

3. Keeping the Tradition of the Fathers of Faith

Think not that I have come to abolish the law and the prophets; I have not come to abolish them but to fulfill them. For truly, I say to you, until heaven and earth pass away, not an iota, not a dot, will pass from the law until all is accomplished.[4]

Matthew 5.17-18

I [Krishna] told this eternal secret to Vivasat. Vivasat taught Manu, and Manu taught Ikshvaku. Thus, Arjuna, eminent sages received knowledge of yoga in a continuous tradition. But through time the practice of yoga was lost in the world. The secret of these teachings is profound. I have explained them to you today because you are my friend and devotee.

Bhagavad-Gita 4.1-3 (Hinduism)

Moses received the Torah on Sinai and delivered it to Joshua, and Joshua [delivered it] to the elders, and the elders to the prophets, and the prophets delivered it to the men of the Great Synagogue.[5]

Mishnah, Avot 1.1 (Judaism)

Confucius said, "I have transmitted what was taught to me without making up anything of my own. I have been faithful to and loved the Ancients."

Analects 7.1 (Confucianism)

Mention Abraham in the Book. He was a truthful prophet when he told his father, "My father, why do you worship something that neither hears nor perceives, and does not benefit you in any way?...

When he moved away from them and what they worshipped instead of God, We bestowed Isaac and Jacob on him. Each We made a prophet. We bestowed some of Our mercy on them and granted them a sublime tongue for telling truth.

Mention Moses in the Book. He was sincere, and was a messenger, a prophet. We called out to him from the right side of the mountain, and brought him close to confide in. We bestowed his brother Aaron on him as a prophet through Our mercy.

Mention Ishmael in the Book. He kept true to the Promise, and was a messenger, a prophet. He used to order his people to pray and pay the welfare tax; he was approved by his Lord.

Mention Idris in the Book. He was a truthful prophet; We raised him to a lofty place.

Those are some of the prophets from Adam's offspring whom God has favored, and some of those We transported along with Noah, and some of Abraham's and Ishmael's offspring, as well as some others We have guided and chosen. Whenever the Mercy-giving's signs are recited to them, they drop down on their knees and weep!

Qur'an 19.41-58

It was in this way that Emperor Yü, Kings T'ang, Wen, Wu, Ch'eng, and the Duke of Chou achieved eminence: all these six noble men paid attention to propriety, made manifest their justice, and acted in good faith. They exposed their errors, made humaneness their law and prudence their practice, thus showing the people wherein they should constantly abide. If there were any who did not follow these principles, he would lose power and position and be regarded by the multitude as dangerous.[6]

Book of Ritual 7.1.2 (Confucianism)

Of yore I followed countless Buddhas,
And perfectly trod the Ways
Of the profound and mystic Law,
Hard to perceive and perform.
During infinite kotis of kalpas,
Having followed all these Ways,
Attaining fruition on the Wisdom-throne,
I could perfectly understand.[7]

Lotus Sutra 2 (Buddhism)

Teachings of Sun Myung Moon

We should respect the tradition established by the forefathers of faith… Where is the spirit of Noah who was loyal to Heaven for 120 years? Where is the spirit of Abraham, who left the land of Ur of the Chaldeans to wander in a foreign land? Where is the spirit of Jacob, who left the land of Canaan and entered Egypt, and the spirit of the Israelites, who fled Egypt, the land of their enemy, and marched across the wilderness to the land of Canaan? Where is the spirit of Jesus, who after coming to the earth, wanted to bring all Israel into a new blessed Canaan, the new Eden? You should inherit their spirit through keeping their tradition. (8:25, October 25, 1959)

When Confucius appeared, did he ignore the traditions passed down from generation to generation and create something totally new that never before existed in history? No, he did not. Rather, he studied the traditions, systematized their ideas, and expanded upon them. (25:93, September 30, 1969)

Why should posterity revere the saints and the great men and women of the past? It is because in their hearts are concentrated all the stories of the struggle for goodness. In order to achieve the purpose of goodness, we should devote ourselves[8] through their foundations. Otherwise, we cannot connect with the path leading to the fulfillment of the divine purpose. People cherish the saints and seek to follow in their footsteps, because through them the fallen human heart is connected to the heart of Heaven. Thus, it is natural to follow these people as we pursue our original value. (17:268, February 15, 1967)

In the history of the providence of resurrection, many of those who were entrusted with a mission exerted themselves with utmost sincerity and faith to realize the will of Heaven. Even though they may not have fully carried out their responsibilities, based on their devotion, they broadened the foundation upon which subsequent generations can form a relationship of heart with God. We call this foundation the merit of the age in the providence of restoration. The merit of the age has increased in proportion to the foundation of heart laid by the prophets, sages and righteous people who came before us. (*Exposition of the Divine Principle*, Resurrection 2.1)

As an individual, each one of us is a product of the history of the providence of restoration. Hence, the person who is to accomplish the purpose of history is none other than I, myself. I must take up the cross of history and accept responsibility to fulfill its calling…

In other words, I must restore through indemnity, during my own generation, all the unaccomplished missions of past prophets and saints who were called in their time to carry the cross of restoration. Otherwise, I cannot become the individual who completes the purpose of the providence of restoration. To become such an historical victor, I must understand clearly the heart of God when He worked with past prophets and saints, the original purpose for which God called them, and the details of the providential missions which He entrusted to them. (*Exposition of the Divine Principle*, Restoration 3)

> We must become sons and daughters adequate
> to inherit the spirit of our forbearers
> who shouldered the mission of indemnity through the ages of history. (30:39, March 15, 1970)

Noah

NOAH IS THE FIRST BIBLICAL FATHER OF FAITH. His remarkable work to build an ark, believing God's command that a flood was about to destroy humanity, showed faith far beyond the ordinary. Father Moon emphasizes the incredible faith of Noah, which was difficult to comprehend even for his wife and family. Another quality of Noah was his compassion for the people whom he knew to be doomed, enabling him to follow God's command that he announce to the very people who were mocking and persecuting him that the judgment was imminent and invite them into his boat.

The story of Noah goes far back in the historical record. Diverse versions of the story go back 5,000 years, to ancient Sumer and Babylon. There is reason to believe that the account is based on historical fact, from evidence of a massive flood that wiped out a whole civilization in the region of the Black Sea some 7,500 years ago.

The biblical story of Noah ends with the sin of his son Ham. Father Moon regards this as a serious setback for God's providence. Always viewing history from a family perspective, he sees Ham's mistake as fracturing the unity of Noah's family such that it could no longer serve in God's providence.

1. Noah and the Flood

The LORD saw that the wickedness of man was great in the earth, and that every imagination of the thoughts of his heart was only evil continually. And the LORD was sorry that he had made man on the earth, and it grieved him to his heart. So the LORD said, "I will blot out man whom I have created from the face of the ground, man and beast and creeping things and birds of the air, for I am sorry that I have made them." But Noah found favor in the eyes of the LORD...

And God said to Noah, "I have determined to make an end of all flesh; for the earth is filled with violence through them; behold, I will destroy them with the earth. Make yourself an ark of gopher wood; make rooms in the ark, and cover it inside and out with pitch. This is how you are to make it: the length of the ark three hundred cubits, its breadth fifty cubits, and its height thirty cubits.

Genesis 6.5-8, 13-16

My counsel... was inspired in Noah: "None of your people will believe except those who already believe, so grieve not at what they do. Make an ark under Our eyes and by Our inspiration, and speak not to Me on behalf of those who are unjust. Surely they will be drowned."

And he began to build the ark. And whenever the chiefs of his people passed by him, they laughed at him. He said, "Though you mock us, yet we too mock you even as you mock; and you shall know to whom will come a punishment that will confound, and upon whom will fall a lasting doom."

At length when Our command came to pass and the oven gushed forth water, We said, "Load in two of every kind in pairs, and your household—but not those against whom the word has already gone forth—and those who believe. Yet but a few were they who believed with him.

He said, "Embark in it, and in the name of God may be its sailing and its anchoring. Surely my Lord is Forgiving, Merciful."

And it sailed with them amid waves like mountains. And Noah called out to his son, who was standing aloof, "O my son, embark with us, and be not with the disbelievers." He said, I will betake myself for refuge to a mountain that will save me from the water. Noah said, "This day there is no one safe from God's command, but he on whom He has mercy. And a wave came between them, so he was among the drowned.

Qur'an 11.36-43

God… did not spare the ancient world, but preserved Noah, a herald of righteousness, with seven other persons, when he brought a flood upon the ungodly.

2 Peter 2.5

Lo! We sent Noah to his people, saying, "Warn your people before there comes to them a painful doom." He said, "O my people! Verily I am a plain warner to you. Serve God and keep your duty to Him, and obey me, that He may forgive you some of your sins and grant your respite to an appointed term. Surely the term of God, when it comes, cannot be delayed. Did you but know!"

He said, "My Lord! I have called unto my people night and day, but all my calling has added to their repugnance. Whenever I call them that You may pardon them, they thrust their fingers in their ears and cover themselves with their garments and persist, magnifying themselves in pride."

Qur'an 71.1-7

Teachings of Sun Myung Moon

When God gives a command, it is not something that is easy to believe; rather it is something unbelievable. For example, God ordered Noah to build an ark for 120 years for the preparation for the flood judgment.[9] Further, God ordered him to build the ark not by a river but on a mountaintop. Was it easy for Noah to believe this direction? The human ancestors fell due to the faithlessness; therefore, God needed Noah to stand on absolute faith. That is the reason He did not give him a command that was easy to believe. (53:93, February 10, 1972)

What do you think Noah's family thought of him? Noah built the ark on the top of a mountain. If it had been on flat land it would be one thing, but building a ship on the top of a mountain is not only beyond common sense, it also certainly exceeded the limits of tolerance. In any ordinary sense, Noah was acting like a crazy man. If he wanted to build a ship, he should have built it on a riverbank, but since he built it on a mountain, his action was totally beyond common sense.

When God gave that command, do you think He did it in a joking manner? No. God knew better than anyone that Noah's course would require lifelong dedication on a path of unbearable suffering. God's anxiety at giving that command was greater than Noah's suffering. Nevertheless, God commanded Noah to go the path of suffering for 120 years, hoping thereby to gain a way to resolve His inner situation. How miserable was God's heart? His misery was indescribable.

At the decisive, tense moment, when whether or not to accept that command hung in the balance, Noah chose to obey God. At that moment, who do you think was happier, God or Noah? Had it gone the other way, God is the one who would have been saddened more than Noah. God's position is that of a Lord who takes responsibility for joy and sorrow. (48:69, September 5, 1971)

Imagine, you women here, that you were Noah's wife. Do you think you would have approved of him? Perhaps not. Every day he must have climbed up and down the mountain to build an ark, claiming that he had received a command from God. Every day his wife must have packed his lunch. Since Noah was too busy building the ark to provide for his family, she must have had to take the burden of providing for the family. In the beginning she might have been able to manage it, but within a few months family squabbles must have begun. Yet this difficult situation had to continue not for just twelve months or twelve years, but for 120 years. When she realized that she had to do it for 120 years, she must have fiercely accused her husband, saying that he had gone insane.

Why couldn't God instruct Noah to carry out His Will in ordinary circumstances? The reason is this: God cannot dwell together with evil. God's direction is 180 degrees contrary to the direction of

Satan. God abhors evil! If even a few people who are comfortable living in the satanic world have a small amount of faith in Him, God would not be pleased. In God's sight, the things that are precious to people who compromise with evil would only defile His world.

Even ordinary people have such a feeling. We do not like anything about our enemy; we do not even want to see him. If so, would the absolute God be pleased to receive praise from the evil world? Hence, God worked in a way that made it impossible for the people of the fallen world to have faith in Him. (69:94-95, October 21, 1973)

For one hundred and twenty years, Noah tolerated the faithless people who opposed and ridiculed him. Even when God told him to warn them that the earth was about to be judged, he accomplished his duty to God in faith. Because he was a righteous man, he was deeply concerned and saddened for the corrupt society in which he lived. While most people were living for their personal comfort, Noah alone struggled to uphold the commandment of public righteousness; Noah alone was concerned about the will of God; and Noah alone grieved in circumstances no one would want to endure. (3:169-70, October 25, 1957)

2. The Sin of Ham

Noah was the first tiller of the soil. He planted a vineyard; and he drank of the wine, and became drunk, and lay uncovered in his tent. And Ham, the father of Canaan, saw the nakedness of his father, and told his two brothers outside. Then Shem and Japheth took a garment, laid it upon both their shoulders, and walked backward and covered the nakedness of their father; their faces were turned away, and they did not see their father's nakedness. When Noah awoke from his wine and knew what his youngest son had done to him, he said, "Cursed be Canaan; a slave of slaves shall he be to his brothers."

Genesis 9.20-25

Teachings of Sun Myung Moon

Noah's position right after the flood was much like that of Adam after the creation of heaven and earth. Adam and Eve before the Fall were close in heart and innocently open with each other and with God; as it is written, they were not ashamed of their nakedness. Yet after they fell, they felt ashamed of their nakedness. They covered their lower parts with fig leaves and hid among the trees of the garden, fearing that God would see them. This shame was an indication of their inner reality, for they had formed a bond of blood ties with Satan by committing sin with their sexual parts. By covering their lower parts and hiding, they expressed their guilty consciences, which made them feel ashamed to come before God.

Noah, who had severed his ties to Satan through the forty-day flood judgment, was supposed to secure the position of Adam right after the creation of the universe. God expected that the members of Noah's family would react to Noah's nakedness without any feelings of shame and without any thought to conceal his body... Had Ham been one in heart with Noah, regarding him with the same heart and from the same standpoint as God, he would have looked upon his father's nakedness without any sense of shame. He thus would have fulfilled the indemnity condition to restore in Noah's family the state of Adam and Eve's innocence before the Fall.

We can thus understand that when Noah's sons felt ashamed of their father's nakedness and covered his body, it was tantamount to acknowledging that they, like Adam's family after the Fall, had formed a shameful bond of kinship with Satan and were thus unworthy to come before God. Satan, like the raven hovering over the water, was looking for a condition to invade Noah's family. He attacked the family by taking Noah's sons as his object partners when they in effect acknowledged that they were of his lineage. (*Exposition of the Divine Principle*, Foundation 2.2)

Our forefather Noah worked alone. He built the ark with absolute faith, but his family did not unite with him. Because of this, everything fell apart. If Ham had become one with his father in love, why should he have felt shame? If Ham had been one in heart with Noah, he would have had no reason to feel ashamed at seeing his father's nakedness. Wouldn't it have been wonderful if Ham had lay down to sleep naked beside his father? If so, when Noah awoke to see him naked, don't you think he would have blessed him, saying, "My son is just like me"? (268:293, April 3, 1995)

If only Noah had been more prudent after the Flood and had not lain naked! Had he been more prudent, would he have done it? Had he been more persevering, would he have allowed himself to get drunk? Certainly not! (99:38, August 27, 1978)

Abraham

ABRAHAM IS THE SOURCE OF THE THREE monotheistic religions, Judaism, Christianity and Islam. He is the ancestor of the Jewish people; for Christians he is the father of faith (Romans 4.1-3); in Islam he set up the Kaaba in Mecca and is the father of the Arab people through Ishmael. Abraham is renowned as the first monotheist, who came to the truth of the one God despite growing up in an idol-maker's household. Then he left home at God's command and obediently followed to an unknown land. He put his life and his future in God's hands, trusting that He would provide. Though sojourning as a stranger among the peoples of Canaan, he showed remarkable compassion for them, particularly when he interceded for the cities of Sodom and Gomorrah.

Father Moon teaches that God entrusted His entire providence to Abraham, and looked to him as a partner to make the conditions on earth needed to advance the work of salvation. Therefore, every act, every offering, every prayer of Abraham was fraught with significance. When Abraham did well, as when he left home at God's command without hesitation, God's providence advanced. When Abraham made a mistake, as when he failed to cut the birds in two at the important sacrifice described in Genesis chapter 15, God's providence was set back and prolonged. When there was a quarrel in Abraham's family, as between Sarah and Hagar, it created a negative condition for enmity between Jews and Arabs that has persisted to this day.

Abraham passed through many trials in his walk of faith. The culmination of these, when God asked him to sacrifice his son, is treated in the next section.

1. Abraham: A Man of Absolute Faith

Now the LORD said to Abram, "Go from your country and your kindred and your father's house to the land that I will show you. And I will make of you a great nation, and I will bless you, and make your name great, so that you will be a blessing. I will bless those who bless you, and him who curses you I will curse; and by you all the families of the earth shall bless themselves."

So Abram went, as the Lord had told him; and Lot went with him. Abram was seventy-five years old when he departed from Haran. And Abram took Sarai his wife, and Lot his brother's son, and all their possessions which they had gathered, and the persons that they had gotten in Haran; and they set forth to go to the land of Canaan.

Genesis 12.1-5

We gave Abraham of old his proper course, for We were aware of him, when he said to his father and his people, "What are these images to which you pay devotion?" They said, "We found our fathers worshippers of them." He said, "Truly you and your fathers were in plain error." They said, "Do you bring us the truth, or are you some jester?" He said, "No, but your Lord is the Lord of the heavens and the earth, who created them; and I am of those who testify to that. And, by God, I shall circumvent your idols after you have gone away and turned your backs." Then he reduced them to fragments, all save the chief of them, that perhaps they might have recourse to it.

They said, "Who has done this to our gods? Surely it must be some evildoer." [Others] said, "We heard a youth make mention of them, one called Abraham." They said, "Bring him here before the people's eyes that they may testify." They said, "Are you the one who has done this to our gods, Abraham?" He said, "No, their chief has done it. So question them, if they can speak." Then they gathered apart and said, "You yourselves are the wrongdoers," and they were utterly confounded. Then they said [to Abraham], "You know well that they do not speak." He said, "Do you worship instead of God that which cannot profit you at all, nor harm you? Fie on you and all that you worship instead of God! Have you then no sense?"

They said, "Burn him and stand by your gods, if you will!" We said, "O fire, be coolness and peace for Abraham!" They wished to set a snare for him, but We made them the greater losers. And We rescued him and Lot, and brought them to the land that We have blessed for all peoples.[10]

Qur'an 21.51-71

The word of the Lord came to Abram in a vision, "Fear not, Abram, I am your shield; your reward shall be very great." But Abram said, "O Lord God, what wilt thou give me, for I continue childless, and the heir of my house is Eliezer of Damascus?" And Abram said, "Behold, thou hast given me no offspring; and a slave born in my house will be my heir." And behold, the word of the Lord came to him, "This man shall not be your heir; your own son shall be your heir." And he brought him outside and said, "Look toward heaven, and number the stars, if you are able to number them." Then he said to him, "So shall your descendants be." And he believed the Lord; and he reckoned it to him as righteousness.

Genesis 15.1-6

By faith Abraham obeyed when he was called to go out to a place which he was to receive as an inheritance; and he went out, not knowing where he was to go. By faith he sojourned in the land of promise, as in a foreign land, living in tents with Isaac and Jacob, heirs with him of the same promise. For he looked forward to the city which has foundations, whose builder and maker is God.

Hebrews 11.8-10

Teachings of Sun Myung Moon

Abraham brought a revolution at the home of his father Terah. As a boy, he would kick the idols and say to his father, "Father, what are these idols?" He must have resolved many tens of times, "Someday, with my own hands, I am going to…" (151:62, October 7, 1962)

Abraham was the most-loved son of an idol merchant, and he lived well under his parents' care. However, one day God called him saying, "Abraham, Abraham! You must leave from the house of your father Terah and go to the land I will show you." God did not give him any advance preparation; the order came to him suddenly, like a bolt out of the blue. Yet in that circumstance, Abraham was not supposed to hesitate. He had to leave at once, as if he had been waiting for God's order. He could not say, "Lord, please give me some time to get ready." He had to depart immediately. Had he not done so, it would have been a grave mistake affecting many generations and even the course of human history. In other words, had Abraham delayed, it would have been a condition that Satan could accuse, nullifying all God's historical efforts heretofore. Knowing this, those who are to attend God's command must act right away. (43:270, May 1, 1971)

Suppose Abraham had gone to his parents and said, "Father, Mother, God has commanded me to leave Ur and travel to an unknown land. I intend to obey Him." They undoubtedly would have said, "Are you crazy?" Therefore, he could not say a word about it. Moreover, his instructions were not just to visit a nearby village. God instructed him to journey to a strange land, as far away as Egypt.

Abraham could overcome these obstacles and leave home because he had absolute faith in God's words. His love for God was absolute, greater than his love for his parents, his relatives or his homeland. To Abraham, nothing was more important that God's command; he cherished it more than his own life. I am sure he stole away in the middle of the night. Suddenly he found himself wandering like a gypsy. He lived in self-denial; he had given up everything. (69:95, October 21, 1973)

In the land of Canaan, God trained Abraham. As God advanced the dispensation, He put Abraham in circumstances where he would weep, not only for his own people but also for other peoples and even his enemies…

God conducted His work by having Abraham wander about like a gypsy in a foreign land. Though a stranger, he prayed sincerely, in tears, for the people's salvation. That is why God could establish Abraham as the ancestor of faith and to bless his descendants to prosper greatly like the stars in the sky and the sand on the seashore. (52:53, December 14, 1971)

In the wilderness, Abraham our ancestor, awaited the coming of the day when God's reign could be established. He left the fertile rivers of his homeland in hope, looking towards the day when the sons and daughters whom God had blessed would multiply and fill the earth like the stars in the sky and the sand on the seashore, and smite the evil world.

Why should we care about Abraham? We, too, are enslaved in the country of the enemy, behind its prison bars. We, too, should feel thoroughly disgusted with our lives in this fallen environment. We should also feel goose bumps at the prospect of freedom. If you cannot feel this, then you are not worthy to be called true believers before Heaven.

For what purpose did God raise Abraham? It was not for just himself and his descendants. It was to create a bridge for God to reach out to distant peoples living in the enemy camp, in Satan's world.[11] Abraham was to make a foundation for God's providence to expand outward. However, because the connection between Heaven and earth was still fragile, God had to begin by working through Abraham's direct lineage. Thus, He referred to Himself as the God of Abraham, Isaac and Jacob…

God blessed Abraham on the condition, "You must not compromise with Satan's world. You must not assimilate into Satan's world. You are My chosen people. Your life should be different; your feelings, desires and ideals should all be different. Your descendants shall live only if they overcome life's challenges by relying on Me." This was the nature of the blessing Abraham passed on to Isaac. Isaac kept it and conveyed it to Jacob, and Jacob likewise conveyed it to his descendants. (7:215-16, September 13, 1959)

2. Abraham's Mistake in Offering the Animals

And he said to him, "I am the LORD who brought you from Ur of the Chaldeans, to give you this land to possess." But he said, "O Lord GOD, how am I to know that I shall possess it?" He said to him, "Bring me a heifer three years old, a she-goat three years old, a ram three years old, a turtledove, and a young pigeon." And he brought him all these, cut them in two, and laid each half over against the other; but he did not cut the birds in two. And when birds of prey came down upon the carcasses, Abram drove them away.

As the sun was going down, a deep sleep fell on Abram; and lo, a dread and great darkness fell upon him. Then the LORD said to Abram, "Know of a surety that your descendants will be sojourners in a land that is not theirs, and will be slaves there, and they will be oppressed for four hundred years…"

Genesis 15.7-13

Teachings of Sun Myung Moon

Abraham offered three sacrifices—two birds, a ram and a she-goat, and a heifer—but he was careless and failed to cut the birds in two. If he had been more serious and mindful that this offering was for the sake of humanity and for the sake of God, not for himself, then he would not have committed that historical blunder. (93:313, June 12, 1977)

Because Abraham did not cut the dove and pigeon in two as he should have, birds of prey came down and defiled the sacrifices. As a result of his mistake, the Israelites were destined to enter Egypt and suffer hardships for four hundred years. Why was it a sin not to cut the birds in half?…

God's work of salvation aims to restore the sovereignty of goodness by first dividing good from evil and then destroying evil and uplifting the good. This is the reason Adam had to be divided into Cain and Abel before the sacrifice could be made. This is the reason why in Noah's day, God struck down evil through the flood judgment and winnowed out Noah's family as the good. God had Abraham cut the sacrifices in two before offering them, with the intention of doing the symbolic work of dividing good from evil, which was left unaccomplished by Adam and Noah… In other words, when Abraham offered the birds without first dividing them, it meant that he offered what had not been wrested from Satan's possession. (*Exposition of the Divine Principle*, Foundation 3.1.2)

God sought to change the course of human history through Abraham, by his condition of making the symbolic offering. Yet because the condition was not made, the course of Abraham's family had to pass through three stages, from Abraham to Isaac and Jacob, and the turning of history required an arduous process of symbolic, image-like and substantial conditions. (81:96, December 1, 1975)

3. Abraham, Ishmael and the Roots of Islam

Now Sarai, Abram's wife, bore him no children. She had an Egyptian maid whose name was Hagar; and Sarai said to Abram, "Behold now, the LORD has prevented me from bearing children; go in to my maid; it may be that I shall obtain children by her." And Abram hearkened to the voice of Sarai. So, after Abram had dwelt ten years in the land of Canaan, Sarai, Abram's wife, took Hagar the Egyptian, her maid, and gave her to Abram her husband as a wife. And he went in to Hagar, and she conceived; and when she saw that she had conceived, she looked with contempt on her mistress. And Sarai said to Abram, "May the wrong done to me be on you! I gave my maid to your embrace, and when she saw that she had conceived, she looked on me with contempt. May the LORD judge between you and me!" But Abram said to Sarai, "Behold, your maid is in your power; do to her as you please." Then Sarai dealt harshly with her, and she fled from her.

The angel of the LORD found her by a spring of water in the wilderness, the spring on the way to Shur. And he said, "Hagar, maid of Sarai, where have you come from and where are you going?" She said, "I am fleeing from my mistress Sarai." The angel of the LORD said to her, "Return to your mistress, and submit to her." The angel of the LORD also said to her, "I will so greatly multiply your descendants that they cannot be numbered for multitude." And the angel of the LORD said to her, "Behold, you are with child, and shall bear a son; you shall call his name Ishmael; because the LORD has given heed to your affliction.

Genesis 16.1-12

Abraham said, "My Lord! Make safe this territory [of Mecca], and preserve my sons and me from serving idols. My Lord! Truly they have led many of mankind astray. But whoever follows me, he truly is of me. And whoever disobeys me—still, You are Forgiving, Merciful.

Our Lord, I have settled some of my posterity in an uncultivable valley near your Sacred House, Lord, that they may establish proper worship; so incline some hearts of men that they may yearn toward them, and provide them with fruits in order that they may be thankful."[12]

Qur'an 14.35-37

Teachings of Sun Myung Moon

If Abraham had not failed in the symbolic offering, Isaac and his half-brother Ishmael would have stood in the positions of Abel and Cain. They would have been responsible to fulfill the indemnity condition to remove the fallen nature that Cain and Abel did not accomplish.[13] However, because Abraham failed in the offering, God set up Isaac in the position of Abraham, and Esau and Jacob in the positions originally intended for Ishmael and Isaac. (*Exposition of the Divine Principle,* Foundation 3.2)

Ishmael was the Cain-type offspring of Abraham, born from his concubine Hagar. Abraham's concubine and Abraham's wife fought and became enemies. The two women were supposed to be united as one family; then God's historical burden would have been lighter. Instead they fought, and Sarah expelled Hagar.

This division could have been restored at the time of Jesus, but it was not. As the result of Jesus' crucifixion, there arose divisions—up and down, right and left, and front and rear—which have persisted through the last 2,000 years. Among nations there would be conflict between the left wing and the right wing, and among religions Islam would emerge as the opponent of Christianity. Islam was victorious in the lands of the Middle East. (215:253, February 20, 1991)

4. Abraham's Plea for the People of Sodom and Gomorrah

The LORD said, "Shall I hide from Abraham what I am about to do, seeing that Abraham shall become a great and mighty nation, and all the nations of the earth shall bless themselves by him? No, for I have chosen him, that he may charge his children and his household after him to keep the way of the LORD by doing righteousness and justice; so that the LORD may bring to Abraham what he has promised him."

Genesis 18.17-19

The LORD said, "Because the outcry against Sodom and Gomorrah is great and their sin is very grave, I will go down to see whether they have done altogether according to the outcry which has come to me; and if not, I will know."

So the men turned from there, and went toward Sodom; but Abraham still stood before the LORD. Then Abraham drew near, and said, "Will you indeed destroy the righteous with the wicked? Suppose there are fifty righteous within the city; will you still destroy the place and not spare it for the fifty righteous who are in it? Far be it from you to do such a thing, to slay the righteous with the wicked, so that the righteous fare as the wicked! Far be that from you! Shall not the Judge of all the earth do right?"

And the LORD said, "If I find at Sodom fifty righteous in the city, I will spare the whole place for their sake."

Abraham answered, "Behold, I have taken upon myself to speak to the LORD, I who am but dust and ashes. Suppose five of the fifty righteous are lacking? Will you destroy the whole city for lack of five?"

And he said, "I will not destroy it if I find forty-five there."

"Suppose forty... thirty... twenty..."

"For the sake of twenty I will not destroy it."

"Oh let not the LORD be angry, and I will speak again but this once. Suppose ten are found there."

"For the sake of ten I will not destroy it." And the LORD went his way when he had finished speaking to Abraham; and Abraham returned to his place.

Genesis 18.20-33

Teachings of Sun Myung Moon

Sodom and Gomorrah deserved God's punishment. It was not Abraham's direct concern whether the cities of Sodom and Gomorrah understood the will of God or whether their people were doomed. Yet because he had a sense of mission for the divine dispensation, he felt that he should take responsibility for them. Day and night, Abraham felt anxious over the fate of the two cities; what is written in the Bible reveals some of his inner feelings.

Today, as we witness the concluding period of the 6,000-year history of God's providence, we can sleep in peace, wear nice clothes and eat good food, but not because of any merit on our part. The reason the world can at least sustain us is because in the background there was Abraham, and countless unknown people like him, as a hidden root. They appealed to God on behalf of their peoples, shedding tears and blood on countless altars...

If there were even a few righteous people in Sodom and Gomorrah who knew of Abraham's fervent prayer that penetrated into heaven, of his discussion with God face-to-face, Abraham could have used them as a condition when he appealed to God, "O Father, who determines and judges with justice, far be it that you should slay the righteous with the wicked!" Nonetheless, when he realized that he was the only one praying for Sodom and Gomorrah, Abraham's heart was deeply saddened. (1:138-39, July 1, 1956)

America—this Sodom and Gomorrah-like hell! Unless I can deal with it and restore it, the Kingdom of Heaven cannot be built. It has every element that can ruin the youth of the world. It is the breeding place of drugs, promiscuity, and all manner of corruption. I am trying to clean it up with my own hands. (105:324, October 28, 1979)

Since I came to America I have been working as hard as I can, and also I am pushing Americans to go through many hardships. Nevertheless, if we can prosper, it can be a blessing to America, and an indemnity condition that can cover the failure of America to fulfill its God-given mission. Then, I can pray to God, "Heavenly Father, please have regard for these Thy children and forgive America for their sakes. Although America deserves to perish, because these children are devoted to Thee, please save this nation." It is similar to Abraham's prayer when he pleaded with God to spare Sodom and Gomorrah if ten righteous people could be found. (103:200, February 25, 1979)

Isaac

OF ALL THE TESTS OF FAITH that Abraham faced, surely none was more difficult than the command that he sacrifice his son as a burnt offering. Yet, Abraham was obedient to God's order. He journeyed with his son to Mount Moriah, bound him and placed him on the altar, and was about to kill him only to be stopped at the last minute by an angel. The Bible identifies this son as Isaac, although in the Islamic tradition he is thought to have been Ishmael.

On the way to Mount Moriah, Isaac's faith was tested as much as Abraham's. He was old enough to understand what was about to happen; yet he was determined to unite with his father's wishes even at the cost of his life. He was an exemplary son in this regard.

Father Moon challenges us: Do we have the faith of Isaac, ready to die on God's altar? Do we have the faith of Abraham, ready if need be to send a beloved child into the face of death for the sake of God's will? Have we raised our children to have the faith of Isaac, ready to support their parents in faith?

After these things God tested Abraham, and said to him, "Abraham!" And he said, "Here am I." He said, "Take your son, your only son Isaac, whom you love, and go to the land of Moriah, and offer him there as a burnt offering upon one of the mountains of which I shall tell you." So Abraham rose early in the morning, saddled his ass, and took two of his young men with him, and his son Isaac; and he cut the wood for the burnt offering, and arose and went to the place of which God had told him. On the third day Abraham lifted up his eyes and saw the place afar off. Then Abraham said to his young men, "Stay here with the ass; I and the lad will go yonder and worship, and come again to you." And Abraham took the wood of the burnt offering, and laid it on Isaac his son; and he took in his hand the fire and the knife. So they went both of them together. And Isaac said to his father Abraham, "My father!" And he said, "Here am I, my son." He said, "Behold, the fire and the wood; but where is the lamb for a burnt offering?" Abraham said, "God will provide himself the lamb for a burnt offering, my son." So they went both of them together.

When they came to the place of which God had told him, Abraham built an altar there, and laid the wood in order, and bound Isaac his son, and laid him on the altar, upon the wood. Then Abraham put forth his hand, and took the knife to slay his son. But the angel of the LORD called to him from heaven, and said, "Abraham,

Abraham!" And he said, "Here am I." He said, "Do not lay your hand on the lad or do anything to him; for now I know that you fear God, seeing you have not withheld your son, your only son, from me." And Abraham lifted up his eyes and looked, and behold, behind him was a ram, caught in a thicket by his horns; and Abraham went and took the ram, and offered it up as a burnt offering instead of his son. So Abraham called the name of that place The LORD will provide; as it is said to this day, "On the mount of the LORD it shall be provided."

And the angel of the LORD called to Abraham a second time from heaven, and said, "By myself I have sworn, says the LORD, because you have done this, and have not withheld your son, your only son, I will indeed bless you, and I will multiply your descendants as the stars of heaven and as the sand which is on the seashore. And your descendants shall possess the gate of their enemies, and by your descendants shall all the nations of the earth bless themselves, because you have obeyed my voice."[14]

Genesis 22.1-18

On their way to Mount Moriah, Abraham and Isaac met Satan disguised as an old man. "Where are you going, Abraham?" asked Satan.

"I'm on my way to pray," answered Abraham.

"Why then the wood and the fire and the sacrificial knife?"

"We shall be on top of Mount Moriah several days and will use them to prepare our food."

"You are an old man and you have only one son with your wife Sarah, yet you are willing to sacrifice him," mocked Satan.

"As God told me to do, so shall it be," answered Abraham.

Satan then addressed Isaac, "Where are you going, Isaac?"

"To study God's wisdom," said Isaac.

"Do you intend to study after you are dead? For your father intends to sacrifice you."

"If God wishes to accept me as a sacrifice, I am glad to do His will."...

As they were wending their way to perform the will of God, Isaac said to his father, "O father, I am yet young, and I am fearful lest my body tremble at the sight of the knife, causing you grief; I am fearful lest the offering shall not be a perfect one, perfect as I should like it to be."[15]

Genesis Rabbah 56 (Judaism)

We gave [Abraham] tidings of a gentle son. And when he was old enough to walk with him, Abraham said: O my dear son, I have seen in a dream that I must sacrifice you. So look, what do you think? He said: O my father! Do what you are commanded. God willing, you will find me of the steadfast. Then, when they had both surrendered to God, and he had flung him down on his face, We called to him: O Abraham! You have already fulfilled the vision. Lo! Thus do We reward the good. Verily this was a clear test. Then We ransomed him with a tremendous victim.

And We left for him among the later folk the salutation, "Peace be to Abraham!" Thus do We reward the good. Surely he was one of Our believing servants. And We gave him tidings of the birth of Isaac, a Prophet of the righteous. And We blessed him and Isaac.[16]

Qur'an 37.101-107

By faith Abraham, when he was tested, offered up Isaac, and he who had received the promises was ready to offer up his only son, of whom it was said, "Through Isaac shall your descendants be named." He considered that God was able to raise men even from the dead; hence, figuratively speaking, he did receive him back.

Hebrews 11.17-19

Abraham breathed his last and died in a good old age, an old man and full of years, and was gathered to his people. Isaac and Ishmael his sons buried him in the cave of Machpelah, in the field of Ephron the son of Zohar the Hittite, east of Mamre.[17]

Genesis 25.8-9

Teachings of Sun Myung Moon

Abraham obeyed God's command to sacrifice as a burnt offering his precious son Isaac, who was born to Abraham in his old age. In giving that command, God took a great risk unprecedented in history. Whether or not Abraham would comply would be the condition that represented heaven and earth; it would decide the fate of events in heaven, events on earth, and millions of lives yet to be born. Although Abraham was ignorant of its great import, once he received the command, he made a sincere attempt to place his son Isaac on the altar and sacrifice him.

Think about the heart of Abraham as he picked up the knife to kill his beloved son. His mind truly transcended reality. In his time, who could have recognized that kind of faith? By meeting God's expectation in that moment of great risk, Abraham's daring act proved that he belonged to Heaven and his family belonged to Heaven. He demonstrated that he and his family, and all their cattle, follow God's orders. He established this reality when he made the burnt offering of his only son.

Abraham offered Isaac with the prayer in his heart, "Although Isaac is my son, he is Thine; therefore I shall offer him to Thee." The realistic consequences of what he was doing did not matter to him. You should learn the center of faith from the example of these historical forefathers. (1:265-66, December 2, 1956)

After Abraham failed in the symbolic offering,[18] God commanded him to sacrifice his only son Isaac as a burnt offering. In this way God began a new dispensation, for the purpose of restoring Abraham's earlier failure through indemnity…

Abraham's zeal to do God's will and his resolute actions, carried out with absolute faith, obedience and loyalty, lifted him up to the position of already having killed Isaac. Therefore, he completely separated Satan from Isaac. God commanded Abraham not to kill Isaac because Isaac, now severed of all ties to Satan, stood on God's side. We must also understand that when God said, "Now I know that you fear God…" He revealed both His reproach to Abraham for his earlier failure in the symbolic offering and His joy over the successful offering of Isaac. Because Abraham succeeded in his offering of Isaac, Isaac could carry on the providence of restoration in Abraham's family. (*Exposition of the Divine Principle*, Foundation 3.1.2.2)

It is not clear how old Isaac was when Abraham offered the boy as a sacrifice. He was old enough to carry the wood for the sacrifice, and when he saw there was no lamb to be offered, he inquired of his father about it. Isaac was apparently old enough to understand his father's intentions. We can infer that he helped his father, even though he knew that his father was preparing to offer him as the sacrifice.

If Isaac had resisted his father's attempt to sacrifice him, God definitely would not have accepted the offering. In fact, Isaac demonstrated a faith as great as that of Abraham. Together, their faith made the offering successful, and there was no way for Satan to retain his hold on them. In making the offering, Abraham and Isaac went through a process of death and resurrection. As a result, Abraham succeeded in the separation of Satan, who had invaded him because of his mistake in the symbolic offering… Second, by faithfully obeying God's will, Isaac inherited the divine mission.[19] (*Exposition of the Divine Principle*, Foundation 3.1.2.3)

> We should give ourselves as offerings to Thee, Father,
> yet we are unable to.

Therefore, even if Thou hast to drive us,
even if Thou hast to drag us—
please lead us to Thine altar.
Abraham brought his innocent son, Isaac, on the way to Mount Moriah.
When Isaac asked his father, "Where is the lamb for the burnt offering?"
his father answered that he need not worry about it.
Every time I try to fathom Abraham's heart,
every time I try to fathom that parent's heart,
I feel how sorrowful Thine heart must be
as Thou leadest us. (48:57, September 5, 1971)

Jacob

JACOB IS ONE OF THE MOST VICTORIOUS FIGURES in the Bible, and one of the most problematical. Clever and ambitious, he tricked his brother into selling him his birthright and deceived his father Isaac into giving him his brother's blessing. Yet, as he went through hardships in Haran and was himself deceived and mistreated by his uncle Laban, we sense a growing maturity that comes to fruition when he is able to win over his hostile brother with gifts and genuine humility. Through all the vicissitudes in his life, we can see his genuine faith in God and his desire to guard and perpetuate the godly tradition of his forefathers Abraham and Isaac.

Father Moon has the highest regard for Jacob, whom he regards as the most successful providential figure in the Old Testament. In reconciling with his brother Esau, Jacob is the first person in biblical history to win over his enemy with love and sacrifice. In Father Moon's view of God's providence as a course of restoration, to turn right-side up all the things turned upside-down by the human fall, Jacob restored much: By defeating the angel he restored for the first time Adam's defeat by the angel Lucifer, and by winning over his brother Esau he restored for the first time the failure of Cain and Abel. Jacob is a role model to Father Moon, and to anyone who understands that God entrusts to us a certain portion of responsibility—to exert ourselves to overcome adversity and restore the mistakes of the past. Therefore, his appellation "Israel," meaning "he who strives with God" is well deserved.

1. Jacob's Rivalry with Esau

Isaac prayed to the LORD for his wife, because she was barren; and the LORD granted his prayer, and Rebecca his wife conceived. The children struggled together within her; and she said, "If it is thus, why do I live?" So she went to inquire of the LORD. And the LORD said to her,

"Two nations are in your womb,
and two peoples, born of you, shall be divided;
the one shall be stronger than the other,
the elder shall serve the younger."

When her days to be delivered were fulfilled, behold, there were twins in her womb. The first came forth red, all his body like a hairy mantle; so they called his name Esau. Afterward his brother came forth, and his hand had taken hold of Esau's heel; so his name was called Jacob.

Genesis 25.21-26

When the boys grew up, Esau was a skilful hunter, a man of the field, while Jacob was a quiet man, dwelling in tents. Isaac loved Esau, because he ate of his game; but Rebecca loved Jacob.

Once when Jacob was boiling pottage, Esau came in from the field, and he was famished. And Esau said to Jacob, "Let me eat some of that red pottage, for I am famished!" (Therefore his name was called Edom.) Jacob said, "First sell me your birthright." Esau said, "I am about to die; of what use is a birthright to me?" Jacob said, "Swear to me first." So he swore to him, and sold his birthright to Jacob. Then Jacob gave Esau bread and pottage of lentils, and he ate and drank, and rose and went his way. Thus Esau despised his birthright.

Genesis 25.27-34

When Isaac was old and his eyes were dim so that he could not see, he called Esau his older son, and said to him, "My son"; and he answered, "Here I am." He said, "Behold, I am old; I do not know the day of my death. Now then, take your weapons, your quiver and your bow, and go out to the field, and hunt game for me, and prepare for me savory food, such as I love, and bring it to me that I may eat; that I may bless you before I die."

Now Rebecca was listening when Isaac spoke to his son Esau... She prepared savory food, such as his father loved. Then she took the best garments of Esau her older son, which were with her in the house, and put them on Jacob her younger son; and the skins of the kids she put upon his hands and upon the smooth part of his neck; and she gave the savory food and the bread, which she had prepared, into the hand of her son Jacob.

So he went in to his father, and said, "My father"; and he said, "Here I am; who are you, my son?" Jacob said to his father, "I am Esau your first-born. I have done as you told me; now sit up and eat of my game, that you may bless me." But Isaac said to his son, "How is it that you have found it so quickly, my son?" He answered, "Because the LORD your God granted me success." Then Isaac said to Jacob, "Come near, that I may feel you, my son, to know whether you are really my son Esau or not." So Jacob went near to Isaac his father, who felt him and said, "The voice is Jacob's voice, but the hands are the hands of Esau." And he did not recognize him, because his hands were hairy like his brother Esau's hands; so he blessed him. He said, "Are you really my son Esau?" He answered, "I am." Then he said, "Bring it to me, that I may eat of my son's game and bless you." So he brought it to him, and he ate; and he brought him wine, and he drank. Then his father Isaac said to him, "Come near and kiss me, my son." So he came near and kissed him; and he smelled the smell of his garments, and blessed him, and said,

> "See, the smell of my son
> is as the smell of a field which the LORD
>   has blessed!
> May God give you of the dew of heaven,
> and of the fatness of the earth,
> and plenty of grain and wine.
> Let peoples serve you,
> and nations bow down to you.
> Be lord over your brothers,
> and may your mother's sons bow down to you.
> Cursed be every one who curses you,
> and blessed be every one who blesses you!"...

Now Esau hated Jacob because of the blessing with which his father had blessed him, and Esau said to himself, "The days of mourning for my father are approaching; then I will kill my brother Jacob." But the words of Esau her older son were told to Rebecca; so she sent and called Jacob her younger son, and said to him, "Behold, your brother Esau comforts himself by planning to kill you. Now therefore, my son, obey my voice; arise, flee to Laban my brother in Haran, and stay with him a while, until your brother's fury turns away."

Genesis 27.1-29, 41-44

Teachings of Sun Myung Moon

What happened as a result of the fall is that Satan's son [Cain] was born as the elder son. Therefore, God had to replace the elder son with the younger one. Otherwise, there would be no way for God's Will to be bequeathed to future generations. Hence, God had to set up a dispensation of conflict between brothers, which happened in the lives of Jacob and Esau. (102:177, December 24, 1978)

In God's world it is the elder son, not the younger, who is to receive the blessing and inheritance. Thus, unless Jacob as the second son first gains the birthright and takes the position of the elder son, he is not qualified according to the standard of the Principle to receive God's blessing. What was Jacob's wisdom? Knowing that his elder brother Esau was hungry, he bought the birthright from him in exchange for some pottage of lentils. By this purchase, he was entitled to receive the inheritance of the elder son from his father, even if his father opposed or he had to deceive him to acquire it.

It was inevitable that God set up this situation, to restore through indemnity what was lost at the fall. (131:180-81, May 1, 1984)

Jacob thought, "If I am several times more persistent than my elder brother, and if I am better than my siblings in serving God, my father and my mother, then I can win the position of the elder son." It was logical for Jacob to believe that if he were better than Esau in attending God, his parents, siblings and kinsfolk, they would want to place him in the position of elder son and support him.

Jacob was wise. He envisioned this goal from the beginning and fought with this objective in mind, all the way to the end. Esau, on the other hand, was only looking at his immediate situation. (108:96, June 29, 1980)

Jacob deceived his father by wearing a goatskin to imitate his brother Esau, who was a very hairy man. Jacob approached his father, who was practically blind, and let him touch the hide on his arms to convince him that he was Esau. Then his father blessed Jacob with the blessing intended for his brother.[20]

Why did God's dispensation require this? According to the Principle of Creation, only the eldest son can receive the inheritance. Therefore, in order to receive God's inheritance, Jacob had to take the birthright from his elder brother. However, he could not just take it without a condition. Since Esau had already sold the birthright to Jacob, Jacob was simply taking possession of what was already his. That is why Jacob was not wrong; rather, Esau was wrong for having sold his birthright.

Jacob truly cherished the birthright; he was anxious to inherit it and bring together all the generations of his family. That is why the Bible speaks of "the God of Abraham, Isaac and Jacob." Jacob knew the will of God and God's dispensation, and he wanted to become the heir who could receive the inheritance…

What does this mean for us? The fallen world is in the position of the elder son. But through this course, Jacob restored the birthright of the elder son on the side of Heaven. Similarly among nations, from a worldly standpoint the leading powers have the right of the elder son, but from the standpoint of God's Will Israel is the elder son. These two elder sons would confront each other on the national level as Israel confronted the Roman Empire.[21] Even to this day, the mission of the chosen people is to restore the birthright from Esau, beginning on the individual and family level all the way to the world level. (102:177, December 24, 1978)

When their father gave his blessing to Jacob the birthright was restored. However, because of this Esau was extremely angry and wanted to kill Jacob—just as Cain had killed Abel. (55:112, April 1, 1972)

2. Jacob's Labors under His Uncle Laban

Then Laban said to Jacob, "Because you are my kinsman, should you therefore serve me for nothing? Tell me, what shall your wages be?" Now Laban had two daughters; the name of the older was Leah, and the name of the younger was Rachel. Leah's eyes were weak, but Rachel was beautiful and lovely. Jacob loved Rachel; and he said, "I will serve you seven years for your younger daughter Rachel." Laban said, "It is better that I give her to you than that I should give her to any other man; stay with me." So Jacob served seven years for Rachel, and they seemed to him but a few days because of the love he had for her.

Then Jacob said to Laban, "Give me my wife that I may go in to her, for my time is completed." So Laban gathered together all the men of the place, and made a feast. But in the evening he took his daughter Leah and brought her to Jacob; and he went in to her… And in the morning, behold, it was Leah; and Jacob said to Laban, "What is this you have done to me? Did I not serve with you for Rachel? Why then have you deceived me?" Laban said, "It is not so done in our country, to give the younger before the first-born. Complete the week of this one, and we will give you the other also in return for serving me another seven years." Jacob did so, and completed her week; then Laban gave him his daughter Rachel to wife… So Jacob went in to Rachel also, and he loved Rachel more than Leah, and served Laban for another seven years…

Then the LORD said to Jacob, "Return to the land of your fathers and to your kindred, and I will be with you." So Jacob sent and called Rachel and Leah into the field where his flock was, and said to them, "I see that your father does not regard me with favor as he did before. But the God of my father has been with me. You know that I have served your father with all my strength; yet your father has cheated me and changed my wages ten times, but God did not permit him to harm me. If he said, 'The spotted shall be your wages,' then all the flock bore spotted; and if he said, 'The striped shall be your wages,' then all the flock bore striped. Thus God has taken away the cattle of your father, and given them to me. In the mating season of the flock I lifted up my eyes, and saw in a dream that the he-goats which leaped upon the flock were striped, spotted, and mottled. Then the angel of God said to me in the dream, 'Jacob,' and I said, 'Here I am!' And he said, 'Lift up your eyes and see, all the goats that leap upon the flock are striped, spotted, and mottled; for I have seen all that Laban is doing to you. I am the God of Bethel, where you anointed a pillar and made a vow to me. Now arise, go forth from this land, and return to the land of your birth.'"

Then Rachel and Leah answered him, "Is there any portion or inheritance left to us in our father's house? Does he not regard us as foreigners? For he has sold us, and he has been using up the money given for us. All the property which God has taken away from our father belongs to us and to our children; now then, whatever God has said to you, do."

Genesis 29.15-30; 31.3-16

Teachings of Sun Myung Moon

Jacob went to the land of Haran and worked as a servant for his maternal uncle Laban for twenty-one years. His uncle had promised to give him his daughter Rachel as his wife. But after seven years, Laban deceived Jacob and gave him her sister Leah instead. If it had been you, you would have immediately protested. But Jacob kept silent, worked for another seven years, and got Rachel. Even after that, his uncle Laban deceived him again and again, trying to cheat him of the possessions that God had given him. Still, Jacob did not complain.

Here we must know that even though Jacob was in the loneliest of situations, still he thought of nothing else but God's Will. Because of that, other things in his life did not matter; the important thing was to accomplish God's Will. He grew farther from the world but came to receive more love from God. (52:64-65, December 22, 1971)

After being chased out and spurned by his relatives, how did Jacob overcome his difficulties? He never forgot the blessing he received from God, and he kept unwavering faith in God. He vowed he would not change no matter how his circumstances changed. Jacob had such faith that, even if Heaven did not believe in him, he was determined to make his family believe in him. He was determined to complete the unfinished task of the blessing given to him, and thus laid the foundation upon which God could advance His providence. With a burning desire to inherit the will of Heaven's principle that God had tried to establish through Abraham's family, Jacob could form a family of faith and return after twenty-one years. (4:139-40, March 30, 1958)

You are in the position of Jacob. You knew that God's blessing was yours, and with faith in this movement you left your homes. Those of you who faced opposition and persecution from your parents and siblings, raise your hands.... After leaving his home, could Jacob go directly to God? No, he had to go to Haran. You, too, must go to your own "Haran," the world where you must experience drudgery and there restore people and possessions. (67:123, May 27, 1973)

3. Jacob Wrestles with an Angel

And Jacob was left alone; and a man wrestled with him until the breaking of the day. When the man saw that he did not prevail against Jacob, he touched the hollow of his thigh; and Jacob's thigh was put out of joint as he wrestled with him. Then he said, "Let me go, for the day is breaking." But Jacob said, "I will not let you go, unless you bless me." And he said to him, "What is your name?" "Jacob." "Your name shall no more be called Jacob, but Israel, for you have striven with God and with men, and have prevailed." Then Jacob asked him, "Tell me, I pray, your name." But he said, "Why is it that you ask my name?" And there he blessed him. So Jacob called the name of the place Peniel, saying, "For I have seen God face to face, and yet my life is preserved." The sun rose upon him as he passed Penuel, limping because of his thigh.[22]

Genesis 32.24-31

Teachings of Sun Myung Moon

When the angel appeared, Jacob knew he was a messenger from God. He asked the angel, "Do you come to hinder me or to bless me?" The angel answered, "I have come to bless you." Jacob then asked, "If you came to bless me, then why don't you simply give me the blessing?" The angel answered, "I cannot give it to you freely, because your portion of responsibility still remains."

In other words, the angel would not bless Jacob unless he fought with desperate effort. When the angel presented that condition, Jacob wrestled with determination, "Alright, it is fine with me. Even if you break my arm I will not let you defeat me. Even if you strike me with a sword or cut my head off, I will not let go of you." How long do you think Jacob wrestled? It was all through the night.

Both God and Satan were watching that scene. Jacob was desperate, knowing that this was the final showdown. Hence, even when the angel struck him in his hip and his thigh, he did not release the angel from his grasp. He thought, "If I die, I die. Even if we both die, I will not let go of you." It was nerve-wracking for God to watch Jacob in that battle. Since the angel was fighting on behalf of Satan, God did not want Jacob to give up, but He could not say anything to Jacob. Imagine how anxious God must have been to watch each moment ticking during the battle between the two?

Jacob did not give up even to the last moment. He would not let go of the angel no matter how desperately the angel tried to shake him off. At that point, God publicly acknowledged Jacob's victory, and the angel, as Satan's representative, had to acknowledge it as well. Hence, he blessed Jacob with the name "Israel." At that moment, all the hosts of heaven shouted for joy. They deeply exhaled, now that anxiety over the outcome was relieved.

Jacob's love for God, that enabled him to hold onto God's neck, shedding tears for Him for twenty years, far surpassed God's relationship with Adam and Eve before the Fall. Therefore, he could receive the name "Israel." (20:229-30, June 9, 1968)

If Jacob had not been so well trained in Haran under the servitude of Laban, he would not have been able to defeat the angel at the ford of Jabbok. Jacob knew that those 21 years of bitter struggle were all for this moment. He knew that what happened this night would determine victory or defeat. That is what enabled him to persevere until the end and win. The strength cultivated during his 21-year course also enabled him to subjugate Esau. Then, he could be reunited with his parents. (67:126, May 27, 1973)

The Human Fall occurred when an angel, Lucifer, subjugated human beings; therefore, in restoration humans must subjugate an angel. For this reason God sent the angel and let him attack Jacob. Once Jacob defeated the angel, it would open the door to defeating Esau, the substantial being of the archangel who was under the control of the spiritual Satan...

What was the meaning of Jacob's victory over the angel? It was a spiritual victory over the entire angelic world. From that time on Jacob was assisted not only by God but also by the angelic world wherever he went. Most importantly, Satan could no longer spiritually control Esau, so when Esau confronted Jacob the next day, he was bound to submit to his younger brother. (92:285, April 18, 1977)

Why did the angel strike the hollow of Jacob's thigh? The human fall was caused by the misuse of the lower parts; therefore, the blow to the sinful part of the body was an act of restitution by the principle of "an eye for an eye, a tooth for a tooth." Once that restitution was complete, the angel was free to bless Jacob. (55:113, April 1, 1972)

4. Jacob's Reconciliation with Esau

Jacob sent messengers before him to Esau his brother in the land of Seir, the country of Edom, instructing them, "Thus you shall say to my lord Esau, 'Thus says your servant Jacob, "I have sojourned with Laban, and stayed until now; and I have oxen, asses, flocks, menservants, and maidservants; and I have sent to tell my lord, in order that I may find favor in your sight."'"

And the messengers returned to Jacob, saying, "We came to your brother Esau, and he is coming to meet you, and four hundred men with him." Then Jacob was greatly afraid and distressed; and he divided the people that were with him, and the flocks and herds and camels, into two companies, thinking, "If Esau comes to the one company and destroys it, then the company which is left will escape."

And Jacob said, "O God of my father Abraham and God of my father Isaac, O LORD who said to me, 'Return to your own country and to your kindred, and I will do you good,' I am not worthy of the least of all the steadfast love and all the faithfulness which you have shown to your servant, for with only my staff I crossed this Jordan; and now I have become two companies. Deliver me, I pray, from the hand of my brother, from the hand of Esau, for I fear him, lest he come and slay us all, the mothers with the children. But you said, 'I will do you good, and make your descendants as the sand of the sea, which cannot be numbered for multitude.'"

So he lodged there that night, and took from what he had with him a present for his brother Esau, two hundred she-goats and twenty he-goats, two hundred ewes and twenty rams, thirty milch camels and their colts, forty cows and ten bulls, twenty she-asses and ten he-asses. These he delivered into the hand of his servants, every drove by itself, and said to his servants, "Pass on before me, and put a space between drove and drove." He instructed the foremost, "When Esau my brother meets you, and asks you, 'To whom do you belong? Where are you going? And whose are these before you?' then you shall say, 'They belong to your servant Jacob; they are a present sent to my lord Esau; and moreover he is behind us.'" He likewise instructed the second and the third and all who followed the droves, "You shall say the same thing to Esau when you meet him, and you shall say, 'Moreover your servant Jacob is behind us.'" For he thought, "I may appease him with the present that goes before me, and afterwards I shall see his face; perhaps he will accept me." So the present passed on before him; and he himself lodged that night in the camp...

And Jacob lifted up his eyes and looked, and behold, Esau was coming, and four hundred men with him. So he divided his children among Leah and Rachel and the two maids. He put the maids with their children in front, then Leah with her children, and Rachel and Joseph last of all. He himself went on before them, bowing himself to the ground seven times, until he came near to his brother.

But Esau ran to meet him, and embraced him, and fell on his neck and kissed him, and they wept. And when Esau raised his eyes and saw the women and children, he said, "Who are these with you?" Jacob said, "The children whom God has graciously given your servant." Then the maids drew near, they and their children, and bowed down; Leah likewise and her children drew near and bowed down; and last Joseph and Rachel drew near, and they bowed down. Esau said, "What do you mean by all this company which I met?" Jacob answered, "To find favor in the sight of my lord." But Esau said, "I have enough, my brother, keep what you have for yourself." Jacob said, "No, I pray you, if I have found favor in your sight, then accept my present from my hand; for truly to see your face is like seeing the face of God, with such favor have you received me."

Genesis 32.3-33.10

Teachings of Sun Myung Moon

The struggle over the birthright continued even after Jacob received the blessing from his father. When he returned after twenty-one years of hardships in the land of Haran he encountered Esau, who still nursed the desire to kill him. However, in the end Esau welcomed him and embraced him.

Through this victory, the people of Israel could be established, graced with the birthright as the elder son nation of God. (102:177, December 24, 1978)

Jacob knew his brother Esau was ready to kill him. So he resolved to offer his wealth and servants to his elder brother. He wanted to give them all to Esau, all the things that he had earned during his entire life. Jacob prayed to God not to punish Esau, but asked God to bless Esau as He had blessed him. Because of that heart, Esau was moved to relinquish his desire to kill Jacob; and he too received God's blessing. (52:64-65, December 22, 1971)

When Jacob returned home and wanted to claim the position of the elder son that he had been blessed with years before, who should publicly acknowledge him? Who should sign the certificate? It is Esau, in the position of Cain, who should signify his approval. Without Esau's approval, Jacob could not receive the blessing from God.

During his twenty-one years in a foreign land, Jacob had prospered and gathered his own clan. He knew he had to make a superior foundation in every aspect in order to overcome Esau… That is why Jacob worked hard to gain cattle, servants and property; he needed to have more wealth than his brother. Then he could send gifts of servants and possessions to his brother, and to his elderly parents as well.

Through these gifts, Jacob wanted to make his elder brother think: "My brother is a fearful man. Indeed, God blessed him. It was my mistake that I sold my birthright so cheaply; hence I deserve to be less successful than my younger brother. So, when my brother comes, I should not reject him. I should rather welcome him." In this way, Jacob could move Esau to recognize that God was with him, and to acknowledge that he was in the position of Abel.[23]

This is the path we should walk; this is the tradition we should follow. It is a formula, applicable in any situation and in every age. (106:183-84, December 30, 1979)

The Bible records that God hated Esau from the womb (Romans 9:11-13), but this was only because he had been given the role of Cain, who was on Satan's side, for the purpose of setting up an indemnity condition in the providence of restoration. When he fulfilled his portion of responsibility by submitting to Jacob, he restored Cain's position and thus at last was able to receive God's love. (*Exposition of the Divine Principle*, Foundation 3.2)

Only after the reunion with his brother Esau could Jacob meet his parents whom he had missed for so many years and enjoy the peace he had longed for. We, too, can enter God's kingdom and meet God and True Parents only after we have gone through the course of Jacob and made oneness with the Esaus in our life, for such is the restoration of Cain and Abel. (67:135, May 27, 1973)

Joseph

JOSEPH, THE DREAMER, was hated by his brothers and sold into slavery in Egypt; yet years later when he rose to a high position and his brothers came to Egypt to buy food, he had the opportunity to help them in their distress. Joseph's troubles with his older brothers, and their eventual reconciliation, mirrored Jacob's life-long struggle with his older brother Esau. But Joseph is also a story of a godly man rising to a position of great power. Unlike Jacob, Joseph had the power to get revenge on his brothers, and indeed he used it to discomfit them and make them admit their former crime. Yet in the end he forgave them and helped them, because he saw some goodness in them—that they truly cared for their father Jacob.

Father Moon identifies with Joseph's life of misfortunes and supposedly chance encounters that turned out to be part of a larger divine plan. He is particularly interested in Joseph's motives for forgiveness, and he applies it to his own situation, as a leader who has endured persecution from his Christian "brothers."

1. Joseph the Dreamer

When Joseph said to his father, "O my father, I saw eleven stars and the sun and the moon—I saw them making obeisance to me." He said, "O my son, do not tell this dream to your brothers, lest they devise a plan against you. The devil is indeed an open enemy to man. And thus will your Lord choose you, and teach you the interpretation of sayings, and make His favor complete to you and to the children of Jacob, as He made it complete before to your fathers, Abraham and Isaac. Surely your Lord is Knowing, Wise."

Verily in Joseph and his brothers there are signs for the inquiring.

When they said, "Certainly Joseph and his brother (Benjamin) are dearer to our father than we, though we are a company. Surely our father is in plain error." (One said), "Slay Joseph or banish him to some other land, so that your father's regard may be exclusively for you, and that after that you may be accounted a righteous people." Another said, "Slay not Joseph, but if you must do something, cast him into the bottom of the well. Some travelers may pick him up."

They said, "O our father, why won't you trust us with Joseph, when we are good friends to him? Send him with us tomorrow that he may enjoy himself and play, and we will take good care of him." He said, "In truth it saddens me that you should take him with you, and I fear lest the wolf devour him while you are heedless of him." They said, "If the would should devour him while we are so strong a band, then surely we should have already perished."

Then when they led him off, and were of one mind that they should place him at the bottom of the well, We inspired in him (Joseph): You will tell them of this deed of theirs when they do not know you.

And they came to their father at nightfall, weeping and saying, "O father! We went off racing with one another and left Joseph by our goods, and a wolf devoured him. You won't believe us, though we are truthful." And they came with false blood on his shirt. He said, "No. Your minds have beguiled you into some matter. My course is comely patience. And God it is whose help is to be sought about that which you describe."

And there came travelers, and they sent their water-drawer. He let down his bucket into the well. He said, "Good news! Here is a youth." And they concealed him as an article of merchandise, and God was Cognizant of what they did. Then they sold him for a low price, a few pieces of silver, for they attached little value to him.

Qur'an 12.4-20

Teachings of Sun Myung Moon

Joseph once told his parents about a dream in which the sun, the moon and eleven stars bowed down to him. Years later, this dream came true.

You also have dreams, don't you? If you have a vivid, unusual dream that you cannot forget even after three years, I want you to know that it is a revelation from Heaven. Any of you who ever had that kind of dream, raise your hands.

Long before you met the Unification Church, some of you had dreams of meeting an Oriental man and following him. Later, after you joined the church, you recognized him as Reverend Moon.

These phenomena occur when the spirit world descends and tries to teach you. It may employ one of several distinct types of messages: God or Jesus may appear, an angel may convey a message, or one of your ancestors may appear and speak to you. It is not always easy to understand the meaning and significance of such dreams. (91:274, February 27, 1977)

2. Joseph's Path from Prison to a Great Destiny

When Joseph attained his full manhood, We gave him power and knowledge; thus do We reward those who do right. But the woman in whose house he lived sought to seduce him from his true self: she bolted the doors and said, "Now come, dear!" He said, "God forbid! Truly your husband is my lord! He made my sojourn agreeable! Truly to no good come those who do wrong!" And with passion did she desire him, and he would have desired her, but that he saw the evidence of his Lord: thus did We order that We might turn away from him all evil and shameful deeds, for he was one of Our servants, sincere and purified. So they both raced each other to the door, and she tore his shirt from the back; and they met her husband near the door.

She said, "What is the penalty for one who formed an evil design against your wife but prison or a grievous chastisement?" He said, "It was she that sought to seduce me—from my true self." And one of her household saw and bore witness, "If it be that his shirt is rent from the front, then is her tale true, and he is a liar! But if it be that his shirt is torn from the back, then is she the liar, and he is telling the truth!" So when he saw his shirt, that it was torn at the back, her husband said, "Behold, it is a snare of you women! Truly, mighty is your snare! O Joseph, pass this over! O wife, ask forgiveness for your sin, for truly you have been at fault."

Ladies said in the city, "The wife of the 'Aziz is seeking to seduce her slave from his true self; truly he has inspired her with violent love; we see she is evidently going astray." When she heard of their malicious talk, she sent for them and prepared a banquet for them; she gave each of them a knife and said [to Joseph], "Come out before them." When they saw him, they did extol him and cut their hands; they said, "God preserve us! No mortal is this! This is none other than a noble angel!" She said, "There before you is the man about whom you blamed me! I did seek to seduce him from his true self, but he did firmly save himself guiltless… And now, if he does not do my bidding, he shall certainly be cast into prison and be of the company of the vilest!"[24]

Qur'an 12.22-32

The chief butler said to Pharaoh, "I remember my faults today. When Pharaoh was angry with his servants, and put me and the chief baker in custody in the house of the captain of the guard, we dreamed on the same night, he and I, each having a dream with its own meaning. A young Hebrew was there with us, a servant of the captain of the guard; and when we told him, he interpreted our dreams to us, giving an interpretation to each man according to his dream. And as he interpreted to us, so it came to pass; I was restored to my office, and the baker was hanged."

Then Pharaoh sent and called Joseph, and they brought him hastily out of the dungeon; and when he had shaved himself and changed his clothes, he came in before Pharaoh. And Pharaoh said to Joseph, "I have had a dream, and there is no one who can interpret it; and I have heard it said of you that when you hear a dream you can interpret it."… Then Joseph said to Pharaoh, "The dream of Pharaoh is one; God has revealed to Pharaoh what he is about to do. The seven good cows are seven years, and the seven good ears are seven years; the dream is one. The seven lean and gaunt cows that came up after them are seven years, and the seven empty ears blighted by the east wind are also seven years of famine. It is as I told Pharaoh, God has shown to Pharaoh what he is about to do. There will come seven years of great plenty throughout all the land of Egypt, but after them there will arise seven years of famine, and all the plenty will be forgotten in the land of Egypt; the famine will consume the land, and the plenty will be unknown in the land by reason of that famine which will follow, for it will be very grievous. And the doubling of Pharaoh's dream means that the thing is fixed by God, and God will shortly bring it to pass. Now therefore let Pharaoh select a man discreet and wise, and set him over the land of Egypt. Let Pharaoh proceed to appoint overseers over the land, and take the fifth part of the produce of the land of Egypt during the seven plenteous years. And let them gather all the food of these good years that are coming, and lay up grain under the authority of Pharaoh for food in the cities, and let them keep it. That food shall be a reserve for the land against the seven years of famine which are to befall the land of Egypt, so that the land may not perish through the famine."

This proposal seemed good to Pharaoh and to all his servants... Pharaoh said to Joseph, "Since God has shown you all this, there is none so discreet and wise as you are; you shall be over my house, and all my people shall order themselves as you command... Behold, I have set you over all the land of Egypt."

Genesis 41.9-41

Teachings of Sun Myung Moon

A seemingly chance encounter may be fraught with destiny, so we should not take anything casually.

You know the story of Joseph. His brothers put him in a well thinking to kill him, but they sold him instead and he was brought to Egypt as a slave. There the wife of his master Potiphar tried to seduce him, and when he would not be tempted she had him imprisoned. While in prison and awaiting the day of his execution, he interpreted Pharaoh's dream and was raised to the rank of Prime Minister of Egypt. How, in the midst of his misery, could Joseph have even imagined that such good fortune would befall him? Yet these things opened the way for him to save the Israelites. Who could have known that it would turn out that way?

Likewise, if I had not been sent to Heung Nam prison for three years, I never would have committed myself to eradicate communism from this earth with my own hands. I would not have known the reality of communism, but would have simply dismissed it as just another philosophy. It was in prison that I experienced communism first-hand. You cannot imagine the cruelty and misery of life in that prison. Yet out of my experience there I resolved to liberate all people who suffered under the communist yoke. The inmates of that prison faced all kinds of evils, and many of them perished. Yet in that awful place a miracle occurred: something unexpected happened in my life that would one day change history [cause communism to fall].

When you consider this, how observant you should be in everything you do and at every moment! You should be able to digest any situation you encounter. This is absolutely necessary for your life as a human being. If you live your life with this attitude, success will walk by your side. If you do not, success will always be two steps ahead of you.

For example, suppose while walking down the street you trip over a crack and knock down a young lady who happens to be walking beside you, sending her to the hospital with a broken ankle. You visit her in the hospital, befriend her, and in time she becomes a church member and gains eternal life. Looking back on that accident, do you think she will curse you or be grateful that it happened? She would say, "It's amazing! I am so glad that my ankle was broken. Thank you, ankle! Amen!" and add proudly, "In all of history, there is no one who was witnessed to the way I was!"

Therefore, do not pray, "Please God, guard me from getting into a car accident." Instead, think that a car accident could be the opportunity that opens the door to many unexpected blessings. Who knows the future? You cannot see it. So how do you know whether to complain about your situation or be grateful? Since you do not know, be grateful. That is the attitude of a wise person. (November 4, 1990)

People in prison fit into two categories. One category is criminals who violated the legitimate interests of society for selfish reasons and broke the law. Even Satan's world[25] does not like such people. The second category is godly people who are disliked by people in Satan's world. Since people in Satan's world are God's enemies, they target the people on God's side for imprisonment. Everyone in prison, everyone who is executed under Satan's sovereignty, belongs to one of these two categories. This has been so throughout history.

God uses the imprisonment of godly people to cut the satanic net that covers this world and, by casting Heaven's net, to connect all people to the rope of God's love. Even though the powers of the satanic world put a godly person in prison, they cannot handle him or digest him. Eventually, they will have to pay a penalty.

When a person whom Satan's world imprisons loves God more intensely than Satan's people love in their self-centered way, he creates a problem for Satan's world. It will have to pay compensation a million-fold. Why? Satan knows that he should belong to God and be under the authority of God's realm of true love. Therefore, as long as God is alive, when someone is exhibiting true love, Satan cannot show his face. If he nevertheless causes any harm to come to that person, he will have to pay a heavy price for eternity.

This is the very strategy of God. Often in the past, God sent His beloved children into a situation where they would stand up for righteousness and purposefully make problems for the evil world. They would be imprisoned and sometimes even executed. Yet by killing God's children, the satanic world has had to pay compensation for thousands of years. By this strategy God could expand the foundation of religion throughout the world. (167:305-06, August 20, 1987)

3. Joseph Meets His Brothers and Reconciles with Them

When Jacob learned that there was grain in Egypt, he said to his sons, "Why do you look at one another? Behold, I have heard that there is grain in Egypt; go down and buy grain for us there, that we may live, and not die." So ten of Joseph's brothers went down to buy grain in Egypt. But Jacob did not send Benjamin, Joseph's brother, with his brothers, for he feared that harm might befall him. Thus the sons of Israel came to buy among the others who came, for the famine was in the land of Canaan.

Now Joseph was governor over the land; he it was who sold to all the people of the land. And Joseph's brothers came, and bowed themselves before him with their faces to the ground. Joseph saw his brothers, and knew them, but he treated them like strangers and spoke roughly to them. "Where do you come from?" he said. They said, "From the land of Canaan, to buy food." Thus Joseph knew his brothers, but they did not know him. And Joseph remembered the dreams which he had dreamed of them, and he said to them, "You are spies, you have come to see the weakness of the land." They said to him, "No, my lord, but to buy food have your servants come. We are all sons of one man, we are honest men, your servants are not spies." He said to them, "No, it is the weakness of the land that you have come to see." And they said, "We, your servants, are twelve brothers, the sons of one man in the land of Canaan; and behold, the youngest is this day with our father, and one is no more." But Joseph said to them, "It is as I said to you, you are spies. By this you shall be tested: by the life of Pharaoh, you shall not go from this place unless your youngest brother comes here."...

Now the famine was severe in the land. And when they had eaten the grain which they had brought from Egypt, their father said to them, "Go again, buy us a little food... Take also your brother, and arise, go again to the man; may God Almighty grant you mercy before the man, that he may send back your other brother and Benjamin. If I am bereaved of my children, I am bereaved." So the men took the present, and they took double the money with them, and Benjamin; and they arose and went down to Egypt, and stood before Joseph.

When Joseph saw Benjamin with them, he said to the steward of his house, "Bring the men into the house, and slaughter an animal and make ready, for the men are to dine with me at noon."... Then Joseph made haste, for his heart yearned for his brother, and he sought a place to weep. And he entered his chamber and wept there...

Then he commanded the steward of his house, "Fill the men's sacks with food, as much as they can carry, and put each man's money in the mouth of his sack, and put my cup, the silver cup, in the mouth of the sack of the youngest, with his money for the grain." And he did as Joseph told him. As soon as the morning was light, the men were sent away with their asses. When they had gone but a short distance from the city, Joseph said to his steward, "Up, follow after the men; and when you overtake them, say to them, 'Why have you returned evil for good? Why have you stolen my silver cup?' "

When Judah and his brothers came to Joseph's house, he was still there; and they fell before him to the ground. Joseph said to them, "What deed is this that you have done? Do you not know that such a man as I can indeed divine?" And Judah said, "What shall we say to my lord? What shall we speak? Or how can we clear ourselves? God has found out the guilt of your servants; behold, we are my lord's slaves, both we and he also in whose hand the cup has been found." But he said, "Far be it from me that I should do so! Only the man in whose hand the cup was found shall be my slave; but as for you, go up in peace to your father."

Then Judah went up to him and said, "O my lord, let your servant, I pray you, speak a word in my lord's ears, and let not your anger burn against your servant; for you are like Pharaoh himself. My lord asked his servants, saying, 'Have you a father, or a brother?' And we said to my lord, 'We have a father, an old man, and a young brother, the child of his old age; and his brother is dead, and he alone is left of his mother's children; and his father loves him.' Then you said to your servants, 'Bring him down to me, that I may set my eyes upon him.' We said to my lord, 'The lad cannot leave his father, for if he should leave his father, his father would die.' Then you said to your servants, 'Unless your youngest brother comes down with you, you shall see my face no more.' When we went back to your servant my father we told him the words of my lord. And when our father said, 'Go again, buy us a little food,' we said, 'We cannot go down. If our youngest brother goes with us, then we will go down; for we cannot see the man's face unless our youngest brother is with us.' Then your servant my father said to us, 'You know that my wife bore me two sons; one left me, and I said, Surely he has been torn to pieces; and I have never seen him since. If you take this one also from me, and harm befalls him, you will bring down my gray hairs in sorrow to Sheol.' Now therefore, when I come to your servant my father, and the lad is not with us, then, as his life is bound up in the lad's life, when he sees that the lad is not with us, he will die; and your servants will bring down the gray hairs of your servant our father with sorrow to Sheol. For your servant became surety for the lad to my father, saying, 'If I do not bring him back to you, then I shall bear the blame in the sight of my father all my life.' Now therefore, let your servant, I pray you, remain instead of the lad as a slave to my lord; and let the lad go back with his brothers. For how can I go back to my father if the lad is not with me? I fear to see the evil that would come upon my father."

Then Joseph could not control himself before all those who stood by him; and he cried, "Make every one go out from me." So no one stayed with him when Joseph made himself known to his brothers. And he wept aloud, so that the Egyptians heard it, and the household of Pharaoh heard it. And Joseph said to his brothers, "I am Joseph; is my father still alive?" But his brothers could not answer him, for they were dismayed at his presence. So Joseph said to his brothers, "Come near to me, I pray you." And they came near. And he said, "I am your brother, Joseph, whom you sold into Egypt. And now do not be distressed, or angry with yourselves, because you sold me here; for God sent me before you to preserve life. For the famine has been in the land these two years; and there are yet five years in which there will be neither plowing nor harvest. And God sent me before you to preserve for you a remnant on earth, and to keep alive for you many survivors. So it was not you who sent me here, but God; and he has made me a father to Pharaoh, and lord of all his house and ruler over all the land of Egypt. Make haste and go up to my father and say to him, 'Thus says your son Joseph, God has made me lord of all Egypt; come down to me, do not tarry.'"

Genesis 42.1-45.9

Teachings of Sun Myung Moon

Joseph, the eleventh son of Jacob, was sold into slavery in Egypt. However, it was God's will that he suffer in Egypt, because through Joseph he planned to preserve a future for Israel. We, too, are like Joseph. Our fate is to be mistreated, even though we are striving to save the nation and the world. Therefore, we should all be determined to suffer for the sake of God's will to restore humanity at the sacrifice of our lives and everything we own. Then our church will be aligned with God's concept.

Because I know this, despite all persecutions, I never complain or carry a grudge. Rather, I work tirelessly to overcome every obstacle all the way to the end. (146:124-25, June 8, 1986)

It must have been so painful for Joseph to see his brothers when they came to Egypt to purchase grain. They were his enemies who had tried to kill him years before. However, they were still his brothers, of the same blood; further, they loved and cared for his parents during all those years while he lived in a foreign land. Besides, his parents loved them. Thinking of all this, Joseph forgave them. (48:312, September 26, 1971)

Joseph's eleven brothers persecuted him and even attempted to kill him, yet he knew that unless he won them over, he would be unable to bring his parents to Egypt and preserve their lives. God has placed me in precisely the same situation as Joseph. Joseph suffered in Egypt to lay the foundation to save his brothers. Likewise, I am working to save the declining remnants of Christianity. Joseph represented the future of the Israelites; likewise I am taking the responsibility of Joseph to provide a future for Christianity. (137:27, January 1, 1986)

Joseph forgave his eleven brothers when they visited him in Egypt because, despite their evil, he knew that they cared for his parents during his absence. Likewise, we cannot help but bless the Christian churches that oppose us because they served God before the Unification Church came into being. (*Way of God's Will* 1.3)

Moses

MOSES LED AN ADVENTUROUS LIFE, from the comforts of the palace to the hardships of exile in Midian, from the heady days when he led the Israelites in their exodus from Egypt to his painful struggle to keep them united during their long years of wandering in the wilderness. Yet two constants guided Moses every step of the way: his zealous love for his people and his firm faith in the transcendent God who is mighty to save.

The Bible says that Moses alone knew God "face to face." Father Moon focuses on this aspect of Moses' inner life, explaining that Moses was keenly aware of God's anguished heart over the plight of His people and knew God's burning desire to free them and establish them as a nation in Canaan. Hence he was willing to sacrifice everything to relieve God's anguish and establish the Israelites in a way that would be acceptable to God.

1. Moses' Zeal to Liberate His People

One day, when Moses had grown up, he went out to his people and looked on their burdens; and he saw an Egyptian beating a Hebrew, one of his people. He looked this way and that, and seeing no one he killed the Egyptian and hid him in the sand. When he went out the next day, behold, two Hebrews were struggling together; and he said to the man that did the wrong, "Why do you strike your fellow?" He answered, "Who made you a prince and a judge over us? Do you mean to kill me as you killed the Egyptian?" Then Moses was afraid, and thought, "Surely the thing is known." When Pharaoh heard of it, he sought to kill Moses. But Moses fled from Pharaoh, and stayed in the land of Midian.

Exodus 2.11-15

Now Moses was keeping the flock of his father-in-law Jethro, the priest of Midian; and he led his flock to the west side of the wilderness, and came to Horeb, the mountain of God. And the angel of the LORD appeared to him in a flame of fire out of the midst of a bush; and he looked, and lo, the bush was burning, yet it was not consumed. And Moses said, "I will turn aside and see this great sight, why the bush is not burnt." When the LORD saw that he turned aside to see, God called to him out of the bush, "Moses, Moses!" And he said, "Here am I." Then he said, "Do not come near; put off your shoes from your feet, for the place on which you are standing is holy ground." And he said, "I am the God of your father, the God of Abraham, the God of Isaac, and the God of Jacob." And Moses hid his face, for he was afraid to look at God.

Then the LORD said, "I have seen the affliction of my people who are in Egypt, and have heard their cry because of their taskmasters; I know their sufferings, and I have come down to deliver them out of the hand of the Egyptians, and to bring them up out of that land to a good and broad land, a land flowing with milk and honey, to the place of the Canaanites, the Hittites, the Amorites, the Perizzites, the Hivites, and the Jebusites. And now, behold, the cry of the people of Israel has come to me, and I have seen the oppression with which the Egyptians oppress them. Come, I will send you to Pharaoh, that you may bring forth my people, the sons of Israel, out of Egypt." But Moses said to God, "Who am I that I should go to Pharaoh, and bring the sons of Israel out of Egypt?" He said, "But I will be with you; and this shall be the sign for you, that I have sent you: when you have brought forth the people out of Egypt, you shall serve God upon this mountain."

Then Moses said to God, "If I come to the people of Israel and say to them, 'The God of your fathers has sent me to you,' and they ask me, 'What is his name,' what shall I say to them?" God said to Moses, "I AM WHO I AM." He said, "Say this to the people of Israel, 'I AM has sent me to you.'" God also said to Moses, "Say this to the people of Israel, 'The LORD, the God of your fathers, the God of Abraham, the God of Isaac, and the God of Jacob, has sent me to you': this is my name for ever, and thus I am to be remembered throughout all generations. Go and gather the elders of Israel together, and say to them, 'The LORD, the God of your fathers, the God of Abraham, of Isaac, and of Jacob, has appeared to me, saying, "I have observed you and what has been done to you in Egypt; and I promise that I will bring you up out of the affliction of Egypt."' "

Exodus 3.1-17

And the Lord said to Moses in Midian, "Go back to Egypt; for all the men who were seeking your life are dead." So Moses took his wife and his sons and set them on an ass, and went back to the land of Egypt; and in his hand Moses took the rod of God.

And the LORD said to Moses, "When you go back to Egypt, see that you do before Pharaoh all the miracles which I have put in your power; but I will harden his heart, so that he will not let the people go. And you shall say to Pharaoh, 'Thus says the LORD, Israel is my first-born son, and I say to you, "Let my son go that he may serve me"; if you refuse to let him go, behold, I will slay your first-born son.'"

At a lodging place on the way the LORD met him and sought to kill him. Then Zipporah took a flint and cut off her son's foreskin, and touched Moses' feet with it, and said, "Surely you are a bridegroom of blood to me!" So he let him alone. Then it was that she said, "You are a bridegroom of blood," because of the circumcision...

Then Moses and Aaron went and gathered together all the elders of the people of Israel. And Aaron spoke all the words which the LORD had spoken to Moses, and did the signs in the sight of the people. And the people believed; and when they heard that the LORD had visited the people of Israel and that he had seen their affliction, they bowed their heads and worshiped.

Exodus 4.19-31

We sent forth Moses and Aaron to Pharaoh and his council with Our signs, but they waxed proud, and were a sinful people. So when the truth came to them from Us, they said, "Surely this is a manifest sorcery."... None believed in Moses, save a seed of people, for fear of Pharaoh and their council, that they would persecute them; and Pharaoh was high in the land, and he was one of the prodigals. Moses said, "O my people, if you believe in God, in Him put your trust, if you have surrendered." They said, "In God we have put our trust. Our Lord, make us not a temptation to the people of the evildoers, and deliver us by Thy mercy from the people of the unbelievers."...

Moses said, "Our Lord, You have given to Pharaoh and his council adornment and possessions in this present life. Our Lord, let them go astray from Thy way; our Lord, obliterate their possessions, and harden their hearts so that they do not believe, till they see the painful chastisement." He said, "Your prayer is answered; so go you straight, and follow not the way of those that know not."

And We brought the children of Israel over the sea; and Pharaoh and his hosts followed them insolently and impetuously till, when the drowning overtook them, he said, "I believe that there is no god but He in whom the children of Israel believe; I am of those that surrender." "Now? And before you were a rebel, one of those who did corruption. So today We shall deliver you with your body, that you might be a sign to those after you. Surely many men are heedless of Our signs."

Qur'an 10.75-92

Teachings of Sun Myung Moon

When Moses lived in the palace amidst opulence and splendor, he did not live a carefree life. He did not enjoy eating sumptuous meals or wearing luxurious clothes. Whether eating, dressing or sleeping, he was always thinking about the Israelites. Among all the Israelites, only Moses maintained an unchanging heart of loyalty toward God, even though his people did not recognize it.

You might think that Moses is a person with a bad temper, but the fury that Moses felt when he saw the Egyptian beating the Israelite was not some sudden impulse of the moment. When he saw that sight, his inner heart of sorrow with which he had appealed to Heaven on behalf of the people for forty years finally exploded. In other words, when he saw that injustice being done to the chosen people, he felt irrepressible indignation and beat the Egyptian to death. His love toward the Israelites and his righteous indignation toward the Egyptian motivated him to action. Hence the deed contained the providential Will of God.

Moreover, in killing the Egyptian, Moses was taking responsibility for the Israelites and their destiny. Compared to the Egyptians' sin of oppressing the Israelites, Moses' action was minuscule. Moses was more concerned about his people than anyone else. Hence God chose him to lead them.

However, the Israelites misunderstood Moses and divulged the fact that he had killed the Egyptian. As a result, knowing that his act would be exposed, Moses had no choice but to escape to the wilderness of Midian. (1:141-42, July 1, 1956)

Once he settled in the wilderness of Midian, Moses felt ashamed of the luxurious life he had led in the palace. He forgot those glorious days when his life was full of leisure and Pharaoh's daughter gave him whatever he wanted. He had become a nameless shepherd, who wore clothes made out of lamb's wool and drove flocks of sheep from one place to another. Yet, as he was watching the flock, he longed for the land of Canaan that had been promised to his distant ancestor, Abraham.

Moses appealed to Heaven with a penetrating heart. He prayed that although he was doing no more than driving sheep, one day he was going to guide his people, like a flock of sheep, into the land of Canaan. Abraham had prayed for the people in Sodom and Gomorrah without them being aware of it. In the same way, Moses prayed day and night, in times of feast or famine, giving every ounce of sincerity for the sake of the Israelites.

Seeing the Israelites suffering under the oppression and cruelty of the Egyptians, Moses felt such great anguish as if his bones were melting. He appealed to Heaven, "Jehovah! Please, on my behalf, have mercy on this people." Because Moses had such a heart, God chose him as the leader, to lead the multitude out of Egypt. To this seemingly insignificant shepherd in the wilderness of Midian, God bequeathed the hidden root that came down from the ancestors and made him the representative of the people. (1:142-43, July 1, 1956)

Because Moses endured a hard life in Midian while keeping unshakable resolution to do God's Will, it was possible for the Israelites, who themselves were suffering in difficult circumstances, to unite with him. Hence God could conduct His providence with Moses as their leader. (4:39, February 23, 1958)

All the footsteps Moses took were adventurous. Because he kept the transcendent center of God's providence close to his heart, his whole life transcended reality. All that he saw, and all the battles he fought, transcended reality.

As Moses was journeying to Pharaoh's palace at God's command, one would think that God would have blessed and protected him. Instead, He blocked Moses' path and tried to kill him. Why did God try to impede and kill Moses, who was, after all, carrying out His orders? This is something incomprehensible.

According to common sense, if God blocks your way there should be no way to pass. However, Moses was determined; his heart yearned to fulfill God's will even at the risk of his life. Therefore he overcame this test, one that had been set up by God and Satan. Moses, who believed firmly in the transcendent God, was an adventurous revolutionary on the universal scale, unprecedented in history. With the same conviction, Moses, went on to perform more than ten miracles in Pharaoh's palace.

With his transcendent faith, Moses did not succumb to anyone's opposition. That is why he could lead the six hundred thousand Israelites out of Egypt. Looking at it, the whole of Moses' life was a path of transcendent adventure. (1:267, December 2, 1956)

2. The Difficulties Moses Faced in Giving the Law and Guiding the Hebrews through the Wilderness

The LORD said to Moses, "Come up to me on the mountain, and wait there, and I will give you the tables of stone, with the law and the commandment, which I have written for their instruction." So Moses rose with his servant Joshua, and Moses went up into the mountain of God… Now the appearance of the glory of the LORD was like a devouring fire on the top of the mountain in the sight of the people of Israel. And Moses entered the cloud, and went up on the mountain. And Moses was on the mountain forty days and forty nights.

Exodus 14.12-18

Moses said to Israel, "Know you not with what travail I gained the Torah! What toil, what labor, I endured for its sake. Forty days and forty nights I was with God. I entered among the angels, the Living Creatures, the Seraphim, of whom any one could blast the whole universe in flame. My soul, my blood, I gave for the Torah. As I learnt it in travail, so do you learn it in travail, and as you learn it in travail, so do you teach it in travail."

Sifre Deuteronomy *(Judaism)*

The whole congregation of the people of Israel murmured against Moses and Aaron in the wilderness, and said to them, "Would that we had died by the hand of the LORD in the land of Egypt, when we sat by the fleshpots and ate bread to the full; for you have brought us out into this wilderness to kill this whole assembly with hunger."

Exodus 16.2-3

At the end of forty days and forty nights the LORD gave me [Moses] the two tables of stone, the tables of the covenant. Then the LORD said to me, "Arise, go down quickly from here; for your people whom you have brought from Egypt have acted corruptly; they have turned aside quickly out of the way which I commanded them; they have made themselves a molten image… Let me alone, that I may destroy them and blot out their name from under heaven; and I will make of you a nation mightier and greater than they."

So I turned and came down from the mountain, and the mountain was burning with fire; and the two tables of the covenant were in my two hands. And I looked, and behold, you had sinned against the LORD your God; you had made yourselves a molten calf; you had turned aside quickly from the way which the LORD had commanded you. So I took hold of the two tables, and cast them out of my two hands, and broke them before your eyes. Then I lay prostrate before the LORD as before, forty days and forty nights; I neither ate bread nor drank water, because of all the sin which you have committed... because the LORD had said that he would destroy you. And I prayed to the LORD, "O LORD God, destroy not your people and your heritage, whom you have redeemed through your greatness, whom you have brought out of Egypt with a mighty hand. Remember your servants, Abraham, Isaac, and Jacob; do not regard the stubbornness of this people, or their wickedness, or their sin, lest the land from which you brought us say, 'Because the LORD was not able to bring them into the land which he promised them, and because he hated them, he has brought them out to slay them in the wilderness.' For they are your people and your heritage, whom you brought out by your great power and by your outstretched arm."

Deuteronomy 9.11-29

Moses said, "I am a hundred and twenty years old this day; I am no longer able to go out and come in. The LORD has said to me, 'You shall not go over this Jordan.' The LORD your God himself will go over before you; he will destroy these nations before you, so that you shall dispossess them; and Joshua will go over at your head, as the LORD has spoken. And the LORD will do to them as he did to Sihon and Og, the kings of the Amorites, and to their land, when he destroyed them. And the LORD will give them over to you, and you shall do to them according to all the commandment which I have commanded you. Be strong and of good courage, do not fear or be in dread of them: for it is the LORD your God who goes with you; he will not fail you or forsake you."

Then Moses summoned Joshua, and said to him in the sight of all Israel, "Be strong and of good courage; for you shall go with this people into the land which the LORD has sworn to their fathers to give them; and you shall put them in possession of it. It is the LORD who goes before you; he will be with you, he will not fail you or forsake you; do not fear or be dismayed."

Deuteronomy 31.2-8

Teachings of Sun Myung Moon

In the conduct of his life Moses made himself a living sacrifice to save the lives of the whole people, but his people did not know it. Only God understood. God was his only friend, and his Father.

Moses knew God and related to Him as his Father. Therefore, Moses felt a sense of responsibility to erase the sorrows and sadness in the Father's heart. For that reason, he was willing even to fast for forty days. For forty days Moses appealed with all of his heart; consequently he could receive the word of God that could resurrect the Israelites.

The giving of the Ten Commandments was a happy event. However, the Israelites did not know that someone had suffered and sacrificed in the background for the sake of introducing this joy. Had they known, the 600,000 Israelites might have not fallen in the wilderness. If they had only imitated the faith of Moses, to uphold the Ten Commandments and become sacrifices for the sake of alleviating the sorrowful heart of God, then in the months that followed they would not have fallen in the wilderness. (3:287, January 19, 1958)

When Moses gave the law to the Israelites, he introduced the God of authority, power and judgment instead of the God of love. The reason he did so was to protect and raise them with the law as Heaven's people. It was to lead them to the land of Canaan, a land flowing with milk and honey, and thereby accomplish God's Will of restoration. (35:260, October 25, 1970)

Moses did not act centering on himself. From important strategic decisions to trivial details, he did nothing without seeking God's direction first. In this way, Moses could enter the palace of the Pharaoh, perform miracles and bring on ten plagues, and lead the Israelites out of Egypt and into the wilderness.

In that danger-filled wilderness, the Israelites should have united with Moses. The wilderness and its privations should not have deterred them. They should have been of one accord with Moses, who had freed them from slavery and was leading them to the land of Canaan. There should have been no disputing with him. Nevertheless, they did not unite with Moses, but deviated from God's path and perished.

Why did the Israelites perish in the wilderness? They did not know Moses' hidden devotion, who as their leader continually appealed to God on their behalf. What is more, they did not recognize the hardships and ordeals Moses suffered on their behalf, from the day he rescued them from Egypt through the years of shepherding them through the wilderness. Consequently, they felt estranged from Moses, and eventually they perished in the wilderness...

Whenever he faced the Israelites mistrust and lack of faith in him, Moses first repented in front of God for his own lack of ability. For example, [after the Israelites fell to worshipping the golden calf,] Moses again went up to Mount Sinai and offered a forty-day fast and prayer. He cried out, "Father, why is this people not able to enter the land that Thou hast promised, even when it lays before their eyes? Who does the blame fall upon? The responsibility lies with me. I could not fulfill my responsibility to lead them well. Therefore, please accept me as the sacrifice and keep the people from going down the path to destruction." If the Israelites had known that Moses was fasting with such an anguished heart, not for his own sake but for theirs, they would not have made the golden calf and worshipped it. (1:143-144, July 1, 1956)

When they were in the wilderness, they had no way to survive unless they followed Moses. But once they reached the Jordan River, Moses told them to cross ahead of him. It was beautiful to see them excitedly crossing the river and dashing into Canaan. However, Moses remained behind. Did Moses complain, "How could you do this to me, crossing the river and leaving me behind!"? No, Moses only felt, "It is alright for me to die here. You, my children, should go and occupy the land with God's blessing forevermore." He lifted up his hands and prayed, "God, look at these Israelites, more courageous than I. Please protect them and give them a hopeful future!" God was astonished to hear Moses' prayer and exclaimed, "Moses, you are a great leader. Please take a rest now. I will see that your prayer is fulfilled." What a wonderful death Moses had! (189:249-50, April 9, 1989)

Women of the Bible

WOMEN OF GREAT FAITH AND DEVOTION have played central roles in the advancement of God's providence. From the Mothers of Israel to the significant women in Jesus' life, the Bible records the lives of women who made great efforts for God's will, often at considerable personal cost. A woman's life in olden times was not easy, and these women all struggled through particularly trying circumstances while maintaining strong faith in God.

To support her husband Abraham, Sarah endured great hardships and even risked being taken into Pharaoh's harem. Bathsheba was actually taken by King David, who also killed her husband, yet she swallowed her pain with the attitude that she should honor her dead husband by being loyal to her king. Rebecca, on the other hand, went against her husband to support her son Jacob, because she knew he was chosen to carry on the divine will. Rachel and Leah struggled with a female sibling rivalry that paralleled that between Jacob and Esau. Tamar and Mary each risked their lives to bear out of wedlock the children God desired. Mary Magdalene showed exemplary devotion to Jesus, superior even to that of the twelve apostles. Father Moon hints of her intimacy with Jesus and her destiny—were it not for the crucifixion—to become Jesus' bride.

Father Moon sees a thread running through the lives of all these outstanding women: they were chosen in God's providence to prepare God's true lineage. Therefore, He had them develop great faith, and then placed them in circumstances which challenged them to restore the mistakes of the first woman, Eve.

1. Sarah

Now there was a famine in the land. So Abram went down to Egypt to sojourn there, for the famine was severe in the land. When he was about to enter Egypt, he said to Sarai his wife, "I know that you are a woman beautiful to behold; and when the Egyptians see you, they will say, 'This is his wife'; then they will kill me, but they will let you live. Say you are my sister, that it may go well with me because of you, and that my life may be spared on your account." When Abram entered Egypt the Egyptians saw that the woman was very beautiful. And when the princes of Pharaoh saw her, they praised her to Pharaoh. And the woman was taken into Pharaoh's house. And for her sake he dealt well with Abram; and he had sheep, oxen, he-asses, menservants, maidservants, she-asses, and camels.

But the LORD afflicted Pharaoh and his house with great plagues because of Sarai, Abram's wife. So Pharaoh called Abram, and said, "What is this you have done to me? Why did you not tell me that she was your wife? Why did you say, 'She is my sister,' so that I took her for my wife? Now then, here is your wife, take her, and be gone." And Pharaoh gave men orders concerning him; and they set him on the way, with his wife and all that he had.

Genesis 12.10-20

Teachings of Sun Myung Moon

What did Sarah think when Abraham suggested that when they went before Pharaoh they should be introduced as brother and sister? Not long before, she had hurriedly fled their homeland at her husband's urging. She could have thought, "What a husband! He dragged me away from a comfortable home to this foreign land, and he now does not even want me to call him my husband, but my brother!"

They had been journeying for months, and she rarely had the occasion to bathe. Living like gypsies, she could not always count on a meal. They had been wandering here today and there tomorrow. Thinking of her difficult life, Sarah could have felt, "What a lousy husband! He has only brought me misfortune morning, day and night. And now he asks me to call him my elder brother, not my husband…"

Despite such ordeals, Sarah maintained a hopeful heart and united with her husband. They did not fight during their long journeying. Beside every great man there must be a great woman. Since she was such a great wife to Abraham, if he were ever to take her for granted and try to strike her, God would have been angry with him. (49:144, October 9, 1971)

What about Abraham was better than Noah? Abraham's wife Sarah obeyed Abraham when he asked her to pose as his sister. Noah's wife, on the other hand, opposed Noah when he asked her to support him in doing something beyond common sense. From this perspective, Abraham's wife was better than Noah's wife. Noah's family members opposed Noah. His son Ham treated his father with contempt because his mother who raised him was filled with complaints against her husband. Isaac, on the other hand, was raised in the bosom of his mother Sarah who was united with her husband Abraham; hence he willingly obeyed his father even in a situation where he was to be killed. Sarah is the reason why Abraham's family was better than Noah's family. (46:322, August 17, 1971)

Without knowing it, Abraham walked this providential course to restore the positions in Adam's family. When the Archangel took Eve—capturing under his dominion all of Eve's descendants and the natural world—Adam and Eve were still brother and sister. For Abraham to make the indemnity condition to restore this, he was deprived of Sarah, who was playing the role of his sister, by Pharaoh, who represented Satan. He then had to take her back from Pharaoh as his wife, together with Lot as the representative of all humanity, and wealth symbolizing the natural world. This course which Abraham walked was a model course for Jesus to walk in his day.[26] (*Exposition of the Divine Principle*, Foundation 3.1.2.1)

2. Rebecca

Now Rebecca was listening when Isaac spoke to his son Esau. So when Esau went to the field to hunt for game and bring it, Rebecca said to her son Jacob, "I heard your father speak to your brother Esau, 'Bring me game, and prepare for me savory food, that I may eat it, and bless you before the LORD before I die.' Now therefore, my son, obey my word as I command you. Go to the flock, and fetch me two good kids, that I may prepare from them savory food for your father, such as he loves; and you shall bring it to your father to eat, so that he may bless you before he dies." But Jacob said to Rebecca his mother, "Behold, my brother Esau is a hairy man, and I am a smooth man. Perhaps my father will feel me, and I shall seem to be mocking him, and bring a curse upon myself and not a blessing." His mother said to him, "Upon me be your curse, my son; only obey my word, and go, fetch them to me."

Genesis 27.5-13

Now Esau hated Jacob because of the blessing with which his father had blessed him, and Esau said to himself, "The days of mourning for my father are approaching; then I will kill my brother Jacob." But the words of Esau her older son were told to Rebecca; so she sent and called Jacob her younger son, and said to him, "Behold, your brother Esau comforts himself by planning to kill you. Now therefore, my son, obey my voice; arise, flee to Laban my brother in Haran, and stay with him a while, until your brother's fury turns away; until your brother's anger turns away, and he forgets what you have done to him; then I will send, and fetch you from there. Why should I be bereft of you both in one day?"

Then Rebecca said to Isaac, "I am weary of my life because of the Hittite women. If Jacob marries one of the Hittite women such as these, one of the women of the land, what good will my life be to me?"

Then Isaac called Jacob and blessed him, and charged him, "You shall not marry one of the Canaanite women. Arise, go to Paddan-aram to the house of Bethuel your mother's father; and take as wife from there one of the daughters of Laban your mother's brother.

Genesis 27.41-28.2

Teachings of Sun Myung Moon

From time to time in human history, a woman appears who initiates a great revolution to find the path of God's love. She leads her people to offer their lives, possessions, attachments to cultural traditions and such, for God's sake.

Rebecca, Jacob's mother, was one such woman. Due to her efforts, Jacob could be victorious and receive the name "Israel." It was Rebecca who inspired him to claim the birthright of the elder son, and then guided him to receive the blessing from his father Isaac.

What Rebecca did was to unite with her younger son Jacob. On his behalf, she deceived her husband and her eldest son, thus enabling him to fulfill the will of God. In doing this, she was an exceptional woman.

Have you ever heard of someone trying to steal the birthright from his elder brother? From a conventional viewpoint, Jacob's mother was a liar and Jacob was a swindler. The Bible records these things clearly, as well as the fact that God approved of them. This has been a puzzle for Bible students.

This world belongs to Satan, therefore for God to bless His sons and daughters with the birthright of the elder son requires that they make a condition to restore the world from Satan's realm. Do you think anyone can persuade Satan to surrender his rights by reasoned arguments? No. Satan originally stole this world through deceit... In restoration, God's central figures can do to Satan exactly what he did to them; that is how God can take back all that Satan had stolen.

A woman who unites with God should be the one to take the initiative. The Fall happened when a woman (Eve) united with Satan. Then together they took the man (Adam). Therefore, a woman should unite with God and bring the man back. Rebecca took on that role. First she should pull Jacob to God's side; then together they should pull her husband and [eldest] son. From this perspective we can recognize the rightness of their actions. (105:118-20, October 4, 1979)

In Jacob's family, as long as Esau continued to hold resentment against Jacob [for taking his father's blessing], the family could not be united and stand before God. Therefore, Esau and his father had to be brought to a voluntary surrender. They should reach the point where they would genuinely praise Rebecca; until that day the family could not return to a position acceptable to God.

Rebecca served them devotedly and apologized with tears, "I am sorry; it is my fault." Yet even if Isaac and Esau forgave her, would even thousands of apologies be enough to calm their hearts towards Jacob when he appeared before them? They had to submit to Jacob freely, by their own will. There would be no restoration unless Esau (in the position of Cain) and Isaac (in the position of Satan) yield to Jacob (in the position of Abel), saying, "Jacob, you were right to claim the birthright. I will accept you."

Jacob worked hard for that, of course, but his mother worked even harder—hundreds of times harder. She worked hard to change their attitudes, making sure they pledged repeatedly not to kill Jacob. How much rested upon Rebecca! She fulfilled a vital mission to make the restoration possible. (244:240-41, February 14, 1993)

A woman, Eve, fell by uniting with the archangel. She denied her father God and Adam her intended husband. Therefore women, be on your guard! You should expect to take the lead in the course of restoration; you will go first on this path ahead of the men. Woman must rise up who can face down opposition from their fathers and their husbands in the satanic world. Unless you can be steadfast, the men in your life cannot return to the original world.

Religions have been developing through this formula; they are in the role of the bride. Hence, in general, women are more fervent in religious persuasion while men are more worldly. Whenever faithful women seek for God, they are bound to face opposition from both Satan and the men in their life. (89:208, November 22, 1976)

3. Rachel and Leah

Now Laban had two daughters; the name of the older was Leah, and the name of the younger was Rachel. Leah's eyes were weak, but Rachel was beautiful and lovely. Jacob loved Rachel… more than Leah…

When the LORD saw that Leah was hated, he opened her womb; but Rachel was barren. And Leah conceived and bore a son, and she called his name Reuben; for she said, "Because the LORD has looked upon my affliction; surely now my husband will love me." She conceived again and bore a son, and said, "Because the LORD has heard that I am hated, he has given me this son also"; and she called his name Simeon. Again she conceived and bore a son, and said, "Now this time my husband will be joined to me, because I have borne him three sons"; therefore his name was called Levi. And she conceived again and bore a son, and said, "This time I will praise the LORD "; therefore she called his name Judah; then she ceased bearing.

When Rachel saw that she bore Jacob no children, she envied her sister; and she said to Jacob, "Give me children, or I shall die!" Jacob's anger was kindled against Rachel, and he said, "Am I in the place of God, who has withheld from you the fruit of the womb?" Then she said,

"Here is my maid Bilhah; go in to her, that she may bear upon my knees, and even I may have children through her." So she gave him her maid Bilhah as a wife; and Jacob went in to her. And Bilhah conceived and bore Jacob a son. Then Rachel said, "God has judged me, and has also heard my voice and given me a son"; therefore she called his name Dan. Rachel's maid Bilhah conceived again and bore Jacob a second son. Then Rachel said, "With mighty wrestlings I have wrestled with my sister, and have prevailed."…

In the days of wheat harvest Reuben went and found mandrakes in the field, and brought them to his mother Leah. Then Rachel said to Leah, "Give me, I pray, some of your son's mandrakes." But she said to her, "Is it a small matter that you have taken away my husband? Would you take away my son's mandrakes also?" Rachel said, "Then he may lie with you tonight for your son's mandrakes." When Jacob came from the field in the evening, Leah went out to meet him, and said, "You must come in to me; for I have hired you with my son's mandrakes." So he lay with her that night. And God hearkened to Leah, and she conceived and bore Jacob a fifth son. Leah said, "God has given me my hire because I gave my maid to my husband"; so she called his name Issachar. And Leah conceived again, and she bore Jacob a sixth son. Then Leah said, "God has endowed me with a good dowry; now my husband will honor me, because I have borne him six sons"; so she called his name Zebulun. Afterwards she bore a daughter, and called her name Dinah. Then God remembered Rachel, and God hearkened to her and opened her womb. She conceived and bore a son, and said, "God has taken away my reproach"; and she called his name Joseph, saying, "May the LORD add to me another son!"

Genesis 29.30-35; 30.1-24

Teachings of Sun Myung Moon

For the first seven years, Jacob worked hard to gain the hand of Rachel, but Laban gave him Leah instead. We see that the intent of God was to have Jacob fulfill Adam's mission for restoration. To reverse the process of the Fall, he should first go through Leah (on Satan's side), and then he could embrace Rachel.[27]

In the world there are two types of women. One type is fallen woman, and the other is a woman in the restored position. Leah plundered, as it were, her younger sister's position. Laban, who represented Satan in this, blocked Rachel's way in the providence of salvation by favoring Leah. Jacob tried to work it out, but the problem was that these two women were fighting each other over Jacob's love.

It was a replica of the situation in Adam's family, where Cain and Abel fought each other over God's love. Rachel, like Abel, was trying to follow the purpose of God. At the same time, Satan interfered through Leah to promote his Cain-like self-centered love. Satan tried to seize the leading role in love, and in so doing tried to destroy God's ideal...

She did not know at that time, but Rebecca, as the mother, was supposed to work with Jacob's wives.[28] She was to persuade Leah to submit to Rachel, so the wives could unite with Jacob's heart. We can now see how difficult it was for her at that time; this was in addition to her mission to lift up Jacob in the position of Abel and enable him to appease Esau in the position of Cain, as well as to win over Isaac.

It was Rachel's position, not Leah's, which had to be upheld, and in that way Jacob, Rachel and Leah could be united as one. The elder sister should naturally submit to the younger. It is completely analogous to the relationship between the brothers Esau and Jacob, where the elder should surrender to the younger one hundred percent and honor the younger as though he were the elder. Likewise, for restoration to occur, the positions of Leah and Rachel as elder and younger sisters should be reversed. (244:239-40, February 14, 1993)

Among American women, are there any who are truly happy? Many are entangled in a relationship of Leah (the legal wife) and Rachel (the mistress). Some even go beyond that, to the point of practicing a life of free sex under the pretext of equality. Yet their actions are often rooted in jealousy...

During their struggle over love, Leah and her maids gave birth to ten sons, while Rachel had two.[29] This became the division between the northern kingdom of Israel and the southern kingdom of Judah—between ten tribes and two tribes—in the position of Cain and Abel. Thus, the struggle for love within Jacob's family ultimately led to a divided nation and the wars between them. (244:248-49, February 14, 1993)

4. Tamar

Judah took a wife for Er his first-born, and her name was Tamar. But Er, Judah's first-born, was wicked in the sight of the LORD; and the LORD slew him. Then Judah said to Onan, "Go in to your brother's wife, and perform the duty of a brother-in-law to her, and raise up offspring for your brother." But Onan knew that the offspring would not be his; so when he went in to his brother's wife he spilled the semen on the ground, lest he should give offspring to his brother.[30] And what he did was displeasing in the sight of the LORD, and he slew him also. Then Judah said to Tamar his daughter-in-law, "Remain a widow in your father's house, till Shelah my son grows up"—for he feared that he would die, like his brothers. So Tamar went and dwelt in her father's house.

In course of time the wife of Judah, Shua's daughter, died; and when Judah was comforted, he went up to Timnah to his sheepshearers, he and his friend Hirah the Adullamite. And when Tamar was told, "Your father-in-law is going up to Timnah to shear his sheep," she put off her widow's garments, and put on a veil, wrapping herself up, and sat at the entrance to Enaim, which is on the road to Timnah; for she saw that Shelah was grown up, and she had not been given to him in marriage. When Judah saw her, he thought her to be a harlot, for she had covered her face. He went over to her at the roadside, and said, "Come, let me come in to you," for he did not know that she was his daughter-in-law. She said, "What will you give me, that you may come in to me?" He answered, "I will send you a kid from the flock." And she said, "Will you give me a pledge, till you send it?" He said, "What pledge shall I give you?" She replied, "Your signet and your cord, and your staff that is in your hand." So he gave them to her, and went in to her, and she conceived by him. Then she arose and went away, and taking off her veil she put on the garments of her widowhood...

About three months later Judah was told, "Tamar your daughter-in-law has played the harlot; and moreover she is with child by harlotry." And Judah said, "Bring her out, and let her be burned." As she was being brought out, she sent word to her father-in-law, "By the man to whom these belong, I am with child." And she said, "Mark, I pray you, whose these are, the signet and the cord and the staff." Then Judah acknowledged them and said, "She is more righteous than I, inasmuch as I did not give her to my son Shelah." And he did not lie with her again.

When the time of her delivery came, there were twins in her womb. And when she was in labor, one put out a hand; and the midwife took and bound on his hand a scarlet thread, saying, "This came out first." But as he drew back his hand, behold, his brother came out; and she said, "What a breach you have made for yourself!" Therefore his name was called Perez. Afterward his brother came out with the scarlet thread upon his hand; and his name was called Zerah.

Genesis 38.6-30

Tamar was the daughter of a priest, and it can hardly be imagined that she set out with the intention of committing incest with her father-in-law, since she was by nature chaste and modest. She was indeed virtuous and did not prostitute herself, and it was out of her deeper knowledge and wisdom that she approached Judah, and a desire to act kindly and faithfully (towards the dead). And it was because her act was based on a deeper knowledge that God aided her and she straightaway conceived...

There were two women from whom the seed of Judah was to be built up, from were to descend King David, King Solomon and the Messiah, viz. Tamar and Ruth. These two women had much in common. Both lost their first husbands, and both took similar steps to replace them. Tamar enticed Judah because he was next-of-kin to her sons who had died... Ruth similarly enticed Boaz, as it says, "she uncovered his feet and laid her down," (Ruth 3:7)... From these two women, then the seed of Judah was built up and brought to completion, and both of them acted piously, and had for their aim to do kindness toward the dead, for the proper establishment of the world subsequently.

Zohar 1.188a-b (Judaism)

Teachings of Sun Myung Moon

Tamar was one example of how God's lineage developed through women with an unusual path of life. Why would God use women of questionable morals in the dispensation? Ordinary women who offer their bodies in love, as Eve did, belong to Satan and are 100 percent on Satan's side. Women on God's side must go the opposite way. Hence, God needed women who could deny love on Satan's side and [offer their bodies] to return to God.

Since Tamar met this criterion, God selected her and worked through her to fulfill the providence. What exactly did Tamar do? She was a righteous woman who was willing to take on the role of a sinner as she strived to fulfill God's will. As Eve lied to God and her husband-to-be at the time of the Fall, Tamar deceived her father-in-law and her husband to-be, the third son of Judah. Tamar did precisely what Eve did, risking her life, but she did it for God's will. (92:286-88, April 18, 1977)

I am sure Tamar prayed like this, "O Lord God, I miss the realm of Thy blessing. I am doing this to continue Thy blessed lineage, so God, please forgive me. Even though I may die tens of thousands of times, if only I can continue the blessed lineage of Judah through this immoral act, I have no regret."

With that desperate heart, Tamar did not mind facing even death in order to fulfill God's Will and resolve His grief. Tamar's filial piety and obedience to God's will was truly amazing. Yet it was painful for God to have to work His providence of restoration through this kind of complicated situation. (110:222-23, November 18, 1980)

Satan sowed the seed of false love within the womb of Eve, which gave birth to evil life. Therefore, God needed to purify a mother's womb from which the heavenly Son could be born. Despite Jacob's victory in winning over Esau, the forty-year period from their birth to their reconciliation still remained to be separated from Satan. The great mother who assumed the responsibility to meet this condition was Tamar.

Tamar had the single-minded conviction that she would carry on the lineage of the chosen people. To that end, she disguised herself as a prostitute and slept with her father-in-law, Judah, and became pregnant with twins. At the time of birth, one of the twin sons, Zerah, stretched out his hand from the womb to be born first. But he was pulled back into the womb; and the second son, Perez, was born first, taking the position of the elder brother. Thus, within the womb of Tamar, the first and second sons fought, and their reversal of position separated them from Satan.

This became the condition for restoration in the womb. Upon this condition, the Messiah could be conceived within the blood lineage of the chosen people, on the base of the nation of Israel that could stand up to the Roman Empire two thousand years later. The victorious foundation on the national level could then be formed in the womb of a mother free of satanic accusation, prepared for the seed of the Son of God. On this foundation, the holy mother Mary emerged in the mainstream of God's providence. (277:205-06, April 16, 1966)

5. Rahab

The book of the genealogy of Jesus Christ, the son of David, the son of Abraham. Abraham was the father of Isaac, and Isaac the father of Jacob, and Jacob the father of Judah and his brothers, and Judah the father of Perez and Zerah by Tamar, and Perez the father of Hezron, and Hezron the father of Ram, and Ram the father of Amminadab, and Amminadab the father of Nahshon, and Nahshon the father of Salmon, and Salmon the father of Boaz by Rahab, and Boaz the father of Obed by Ruth, and Obed the father of Jesse, and Jesse the father of David the king. And David was the father of Solomon by the wife of Uriah...

Matthew 1.1-6

And Joshua the son of Nun sent two men secretly from Shittim as spies, saying, "Go, view the land, especially Jericho." And they went, and came into the house of a harlot whose name was Rahab, and lodged there. And it was told the king of Jericho, "Behold, certain men of Israel have come here tonight to search out the land." Then the king of Jericho sent to Rahab, saying, "Bring forth the men that have come to you, who entered your house; for they have come to search out all the land." But the woman had taken the two men and hidden them; and she said, "True, men came to me, but I did not know where they came from; and when the gate was to be closed, at dark, the men went out; where the men went I do not know; pursue them quickly, for you will overtake them." But she had brought them up to the roof, and hid them with the stalks of flax which she had laid in order on the roof...

Before they lay down, she came up to them on the roof, and said to the men, "I know that the LORD has given you the land, and that the fear of you has fallen upon us... Now then, swear to me by the LORD that as I have dealt kindly with you, you also will deal kindly with my father's house..." Then she let them down by a rope through the window, for her house was built into the city wall.

Joshua 2.1-15

Teachings of Sun Myung Moon

The genealogy of Jesus recorded in chapter one of the Gospel of Matthew lists the names Tamar and Ruth, both of whom were in the position of concubines. It lists Solomon's mother Bathsheba, another concubine. It lists Rahab, who was a prostitute. These women, concubines and prostitutes, appear in the Bible as playing significant roles in the background of human history. (92:292, April 18, 1977)

Rahab appears in the Gospel of Matthew. What kind of person was she? She was a prostitute, but more than that, she helped a spy of her country's enemy. It is realistic for a prostitute to sympathize with her country's enemy, but she risked her life to do it. She demonstrates that for the sake of Heaven's will, we should risk our lives. Like Rahab, we should deny our life, our circumstances, and all the privileges our life affords. History progresses from that point of self-denial. (30:196, March 22, 1970)

6. Bathsheba

It happened, late one afternoon, when David arose from his couch and was walking upon the roof of the king's house, that he saw from the roof a woman bathing; and the woman was very beautiful. And David sent and inquired about the woman. And one said, "Is not this Bathsheba, the daughter of Eliam, the wife of Uriah the Hittite?" So David sent messengers, and took her; and she came to him, and he lay with her. (Now she was purifying herself from her uncleanness.) Then she returned to her house. And the woman conceived; and she sent and told David, "I am with child."

So David sent word to Joab, "Send me Uriah the Hittite." And Joab sent Uriah to David... David said to Uriah, "Go down to your house, and wash your feet." And Uriah went out of the king's house, and there followed him a present from the king. But Uriah slept at the door of the king's house with all the servants of his lord, and did not go down to his house. When they told David, "Uriah did not go down to his house," David said to Uriah, "Have you not come from a journey? Why did you not go down to your house?" Uriah said to David, "The ark and Israel and Judah dwell in booths; and my lord Joab and the servants are my lord are camping in the open field; shall I then go to my house, to eat and to drink, and to lie with my wife? As you live, and as your soul lives, I will not do this thing."...

In the morning David wrote a letter to Joab, and sent it by the hand of Uriah. In the letter he wrote, "Set Uriah in the forefront of the hardest fighting, and then draw back from him, that he may be struck down, and die." And as Joab was besieging the city, he assigned Uriah to the place where he knew there were valiant men. And the men of the city came out and fought with Joab; and some of the servants of David among the people fell. Uriah the Hittite was slain also...

When the wife of Uriah heard that Uriah her husband was dead, she made lamentation for her husband. And when the mourning was over, David sent and brought her to his house, and she became his wife, and bore him a son... And the LORD struck the child that Uriah's wife bore to David, and it became sick. David therefore besought God for the child; and David fasted, and went in and lay all night upon the ground. And the elders of his house stood beside him, to raise him from the ground; but he would not, nor did he eat food with them. On the seventh day the child died...

Then David comforted his wife, Bathsheba, and went into her, and lay with her; and she bore a son, and he called his name Solomon. And the LORD loved him.

2 Samuel 11.2-27, 12.15-18, 24

King David, of blessed memory, was a great sage and recognized transmigrations. When he saw Uriah the Hittite, he knew that he was the Serpent who had seduced Eve, and when he saw Bathsheba he knew that she was Eve, and he knew that he himself was Adam. Thus, he wished to take Bathsheba from Uriah, because she was destined to be David's mate... And the reason Nathan the prophet chastised him was because he hastened, and did not wait... for his haste caused him to go to her without performing *tikkun* (restoration), for he first needed to remove from her the contamination of the Serpent, and thereafter to go to her, and he did not do so. Therefore, his first son Bathsheba died, for he was from the impurity of the Serpent, but from there on there was no Satan and no bad effect.[31]

Sefer Peli'ah (Judaism)

Teachings of Sun Myung Moon

Bathsheba had cause to hate King David. But if she had, she could not have become the mother of King Solomon. She could have hated King David for intentionally sending her husband Uriah to the battlefield to be killed and taking her as his wife, but she accepted it as her fate, or rather as

Heaven's will. In other words, she believed that King David's act was not done out of ill intent, but rather to fulfill a greater purpose of God. Further, Bathsheba was a patriot who prayed for her nation to be victorious even if her husband Uriah might have to make the ultimate sacrifice.

Bathsheba thought that although her husband was killed, it was honorable for him to die as a loyal subject. Moreover, it was to his honor that she accepted being offered to the king with joy. She had such a high-standard viewpoint. She thought, "It is my duty to my husband that I offer myself to the king with loyalty and devotion." With this attitude, she married King David. On this foundation, she could give birth to King Solomon. (40:97, January 24, 1971)

King Solomon's mother was Bathsheba. She had been the wife of Uriah, but King David stole her from him. How, then, could the child from that union become King Solomon? Bathsheba was in the position of a second wife.[32] In terms of the providence to restore the positions in the Garden of Eden before the Fall, David was in the position of Adam and Uriah was in the position of the archangel. But the position of Eve had to be restored through a woman in the position of the wife of the Archangel. The archangel caused Eve to fall by stealing her from Adam, her original partner, and possessing her with false love. In order to indemnify this, David, Uriah and Bathsheba should repeat this triangular relationship and reverse it. The child born on the foundation of having fulfilled this condition according to the standard of the Principle would be a child of glory, blessed with Heaven's love. That child of glory was King Solomon. (35:168, October 13, 1970)

7. Mary

In the sixth month the angel Gabriel was sent from God to a city of Galilee named Nazareth, to a virgin betrothed to a man whose name was Joseph, of the house of David; and the virgin's name was Mary. And he came to her and said, "Hail, O favored one, the Lord is with you!" But she was greatly troubled at the saying, and considered in her mind what sort of greeting this might be. And the angel said to her, "Do not be afraid, Mary, for you have found favor with God. And behold, you will conceive in your womb and bear a son, and you shall call his name Jesus.

> He will be great, and will be called the Son of the Most High;
> and the Lord God will give to him the throne of his father David,
> and he will reign over the house of Jacob for ever;
> and of his kingdom there will be no end."

And Mary said to the angel, "How shall this be, since I have no husband?" And the angel said to her,

> "The Holy Spirit will come upon you,
> and the power of the Most High will overshadow you;
> therefore the child to be born will be called holy,
> the Son of God.

And behold, your kinswoman Elizabeth in her old age has also conceived a son; and this is the sixth month with her who was called barren. For with God nothing will be impossible." And Mary said, "Behold, I am the handmaid of the Lord; let it be to me according to your word." And the angel departed from her.

In those days Mary arose and went with haste into the hill country, to a city of Judah, and she entered the house of Zechariah and greeted Elizabeth. And when Elizabeth heard the greeting of Mary, the babe leaped in her womb; and Elizabeth was filled with the Holy Spirit and she exclaimed with a loud cry, "Blessed are you among women, and blessed is the fruit of your womb!"...

And Mary remained with her about three months, and returned to her home.

Luke 1.26-42, 56

The angels said, "Mary, God gives you good tidings of a Word from him, whose name is the Messiah, Jesus, son of Mary, illustrious in the world and in the Hereafter, and one of those brought near unto God. He will speak unto mankind in his cradle and in his manhood, and he is of the righteous." She said, "My Lord! How can I have a child when no mortal has touched me?" He said, "So. God creates what He will. If He decrees a thing, He says unto it only, 'Be!' And it is..."

Qur'an 3.45-47

Mary, the daughter of Imran, who preserved her chastity; We breathed some of Our spirit into it, and she acknowledged her Lord's words and books. She was so prayerful!

Qur'an 66.12

Teachings of Sun Myung Moon

Mary was a revolutionary woman in faith who could follow God's Will. Because the Human Fall came through the archangel Lucifer, another archangel [Gabriel] should assist Mary by bringing her God's revelation. Eve believed the words of the archangel and fell. This time Mary should absolutely believe the archangel's message from God and follow it. This is for restoration through indemnity. Therefore, Mary risked her life, completely believing what the angel told her: "Behold, you will conceive in your womb and bear a son, and you shall call his name Jesus... the child to be born will be called holy, the Son of God." (Luke 1.31, 35)

Mary's situation paralleled that of Eve in the Garden of Eden before the Fall. Mary and Joseph were engaged but not yet married; Adam and Eve were also in an engagement period as they were growing up—they were brother and sister, but someday to marry. An angel induced Eve to commit the Fall; now another angel brought Mary to God for the fulfillment of His Will. In these respects their situations were precisely parallel.

Since human beings have inherited the fallen act like a normal tradition, the same act should be repeated for God in the course of restoration. Therefore, Mary deceived her husband-to-be and her father. Do you think Mary could discuss with her father or Joseph about how she had conceived her baby? She was risking her life, because in those days an adulterous woman would be stoned to death.

Mary conceived Jesus after inheriting the victorious foundation of Rebecca and Tamar. Through these three women, all the indemnity conditions were fulfilled for the birth of the Son of God. Therefore, Satan could not make any accusation against the birth of the child. That is why, even in Mary's womb, Jesus was already the only begotten Son of God. (92:289-90, April 18, 1977)

Mary, who was engaged to Joseph, received from the archangel Gabriel the surprising message that the Messiah would be born through her. (Luke 1.31) In those days, if an unmarried woman became pregnant, she would be killed. But Mary accepted the will of God with absolute faith, saying, "Behold, I am the handmaid of the Lord; let it be to me according to your word." (Luke 1.38)

Mary consulted with the priest Zechariah, who was her relative and was highly respected. Zechariah's wife Elizabeth, with the help of God, was pregnant with John the Baptist. She said to Mary, "Blessed are you among women and blessed is the fruit of your womb. Why is this granted to me that the mother of my Lord should come to me?" (Luke 1.42-43) With these words she testified to the coming birth of Jesus.

In this way, God let Mary, Zechariah, and Elizabeth know about the birth of the Messiah before anyone else. All of them had the absolutely crucial mission of following the will of God and serving Jesus. Zechariah's family let Mary stay in their house. Jesus was conceived in the house of Zechariah.

Elizabeth and Mary were cousins on their mothers' side. But according to God's providence they were considered sisters, with Elizabeth as the elder (Cain) and Mary as the younger (Abel). Mary received Elizabeth's help in the presence of Zechariah. Through this cooperation, Zechariah's family, on the national level, indemnified the lack of unity between Leah and Rachel in Jacob's family. This allowed Jesus to be conceived. For the first time in history, there could be born on earth, free of satanic accusation and through a prepared womb, the seed of the Son of God—the seed of the True Father. In this way, the only begotten Son of God, the owner of the first love of God, was born.

Mary had to achieve something that could not be understood by common sense, nor easily tolerated under the law of those times. Mary, Elizabeth, and Zechariah had been spiritually moved. They were to follow the revelation that came from God, and unconditionally believe that it was the will and desire of God. (277:206-07, April 16, 1996)

8. Mary Magdalene

Six days before the Passover, Jesus came to Bethany, where Lazarus was, whom Jesus had raised from the dead. There they made him a supper; Martha served, and Lazarus was one of those at table with him. Mary took a pound of costly ointment of pure nard and anointed the feet of Jesus and wiped his feet with her hair; and the house was filled with the fragrance of the ointment. But Judas Iscariot, one of his disciples (he who was to betray him), said, "Why was this ointment not sold for three hundred denarii and given to the poor?"

John 12.1-4

But Jesus said, "Let her alone; why do you trouble her? She has done a beautiful thing to me. For you always have the poor with you, and whenever you will, you can do good to them; but you will not always have me. She has done what she could; she has anointed my body beforehand for burying. And truly, I say to you, wherever the gospel is preached in the whole world, what she has done will be told in memory of her."

Mark 14.6-9

Now on the first day of the week Mary Magdalene came to the tomb early, while it was still dark, and saw that the stone had been taken away from the tomb. So she ran, and went to Simon Peter and the other disciple, the one whom Jesus loved, and said to them, "They have taken the Lord out of the tomb, and we do not know where they have laid him."...

Then the disciples went back to their homes. But Mary stood weeping outside the tomb, and as she wept she stooped to look into the tomb; and she saw two angels in white, sitting where the body of Jesus had lain, one at the head and one at the feet. They said to her, "Woman, why are you weeping?" She said to them, "Because they have taken away my Lord, and I do not know where they have laid him." Saying this, she turned round and saw Jesus standing, but she did not know that it was Jesus. Jesus said to her, "Woman, why are you weeping? Whom do you seek?" Supposing him to be the gardener, she said to him, "Sir, if you have carried him away, tell me where you have laid him, and I will take him away." Jesus said to her, "Mary." She turned and said to him in Hebrew, Rabboni!" (which means Teacher). Jesus said to her, "Do not hold me, for I have not yet ascended to the Father; but go to my brethren and say to them, I am ascending to my Father and your Father, to my God and your God." Mary Magdalene went and said to the disciples, "I have seen the Lord"; and she told them that he had said these things to her.

John 20.1-18

Teachings of Sun Myung Moon

Why does the name of Mary Magdalene endure in Christianity? Why is her name praised throughout the generations? It is because Jesus wanted her name to be known.

During Jesus' lifetime, who could understand her behavior? She was ridiculed as a woman of a low background. When she poured perfumed oil worth 300 denarii on his feet, all the disciples mocked her and Judas Iscariot protested her actions. Yet Jesus declared that her name would be remembered wherever the Gospel is preached. He said so because her offering to Jesus at that hour was greater than the devotion of his disciples or anyone else. In fact, her act of devotion to Jesus matched Jesus' own devotion to God. (4:107, March 16, 1958)

When Jesus was petitioning to Heaven in the Garden of Gethsemane, his three disciples fell asleep; they did not listen to the voice of his prayer. However, Mary Magdalene recognized the divine value of Jesus. She washed his feet with her own hair after pouring perfumed oil on his feet. In this manner, she assured the glory of the Lord Jesus at his resurrection. At the time, his disciples ridiculed her behavior and attempted to stop her. Christians do not know that Jesus was deeply grieved at their attitude, a grievance that remains to this day.

Jesus Christ lived in sorrow, walking a lonely path that no one recognized. Only Mary Magdalene comforted him, empathizing with Jesus' divine heart for the past, the present and the future. For this reason, he blessed her with joyful grace and elevated her to stand in the forefront of God's will. (2:212, May 26, 1957)

Mary Magdalene appeared insignificant compared to the disciples, yet when Jesus passed away, she was the one who visited his tomb. Mary loved Jesus—who was still a bachelor—more than anyone else. She followed him everywhere, sharing the ridicule, the cursing and the ostracism he suffered. Because she longed for him so earnestly, when Jesus was resurrected he appeared to her first. Mary Magdalene is a role model for Christians throughout the world, showing the path that they should walk in the latter days.

What was the life of Mary Magdalene? She so loved Jesus that she forgot about what to eat or what to wear. She lived only for him, with an unchanging heart. She was not attached to her life; she did not think about saving face. Her faith was exemplary among all Jesus' disciples. Christians in the Last Days should have the faith of Mary Magdalene. If you can have the same heart as Mary Magdalene, you would have the tears God shed over the 6000 years of the providence welling up in your eyes, and you would recognize how much you are indebted to Heaven. (4:258-59, June 29, 1958)

When Jesus was resurrected after the cross, he turned Mary Magdalene away when she tried to embrace him. He was not in a position to say, "Mary, my Bride, let us go to the Father together." Jesus had worked hard to restore the Bride that [Heaven] had sought for 2,000 years, looking forward to the day when he could embrace his Bride. It was the Father's will that Jesus come before

Him rejoicing with his Bride, receive God's marriage Blessing and become the True Parents... but Jesus departed this world without receiving the Blessing by which he could restore the position of humanity's true ancestor. This is the sorrow of both God and Jesus. (5:187, January 18, 1959)

Among the disciples, Jesus loved Judas Iscariot in particular. He made Judas his object partner, through whom to restore God's primary Will. Jesus intended to use him in order to erect a woman in the position of Eve, but to do this they should fulfill the roles of the personages involved in the Fall. Specifically, God's Will required that Jesus set up Judas's wife as the new Eve. This woman was Mary Magdalene. She had been Judas' lover, but now as a disciple she was absolutely obedient to Jesus. So, just as Satan had taken Eve from Adam, Jesus [as Adam] planned to take Judas's woman to be the new Eve. That way the three of them would fulfill God's will according to the Principle.

Accordingly, Jesus first acknowledged that Mary Magdalene belonged to Judas Iscariot. Then Jesus commenced the providence by choosing her to be his Eve. While this fundamental providence was going on, in the meantime Satan was fully on the attack, mobilizing the Pharisees and scribes against Jesus. Regardless, had Judas Iscariot trusted, obeyed and attended Jesus in this matter, they would have established the foundation for the fulfillment of God's Will. But Judas was full of discontent and confronted Jesus. That was the beginning of his rebellion against his Teacher, which culminated when he sold out the One Man unique in all human history for a mere 30 pieces of silver. (*Wolli Wonbon* 242-43)[33]

Buddha

FATHER MOON HONORS SHAKYAMUNI AS THE GREATEST SAINT OF ASIA. His life is a model for anyone who leaves family and friends behind in the search for truth. He was also persecuted during his ministry for attracting young people who abandoned their families, wives, children and wealth to become monks and nuns and follow the path to enlightenment. That blissful state, experienced by the Buddha and many Buddhists since, brought him to the summit of the universe. Everyone would do well to emulate his spiritual practice and find that state.

1. The Buddha Rejects the World in Search of the Path to Truth

Although his parents were unwilling and tears poured down their cheeks, the recluse Gotama, having cut off hair and beard and donned saffron robes, went forth from home into homelessness.

Digha Nikaya 1.115

The king of the Shakya, having heard from the sage Asita that the goal of the prince was to attain supreme bliss, sought to engage the prince in sensual pleasures, lest he should wish to go off to the forest...

He ordered that all commoners suffering any affliction should be kept off the royal road lest the tender-hearted prince be distressed at the sight of them... Yet on one excursion, the prince saw the man overcome with old age, different in form from other people, and his curiosity was aroused. "Oh, charioteer! Who is this man with gray hair, supported by a staff in his hand, his eyes sunken under his eyebrows, his limbs feeble and bent? Is this transformation a natural state or an accident?" The charioteer, when he was thus asked, his intelligence being confused by the gods, saw no harm in telling the prince its significance, which should have been discreetly withheld from him, "Old age, it is called, the destroyer of beauty and vigor, the source of sorrow, the depriver of pleasures, the slayer of memories, the enemy of sense organs. That man has been ruined by old age. He, too, in his infancy had taken milk and, in due time, had crawled on the ground; he then became a handsome youth, and now he has reached old age..." For a long while, the prince kept his gaze on the decrepit man, sighing and shaking his head. "Turn back the horses, charioteer; go home quickly. How can I enjoy myself in the garden when the fear of death is revolving in my mind?"

[On a second excursion, the prince is similarly distressed at the sight of a man afflicted by disease. On a third excursion, he sees a corpse carried by mourners.]

The charioteer then said to him, "This is the last state of all men. Death is certain for all, whether they be of low, middle, or high degree." Though he was a steadfast man, the prince felt faint as soon as he heard about death. Leaning his shoulders against the railing, he said in a sad tone, "This is the inescapable end for all men; yet, people in the world harbor no fear and seem unconcerned. Men must be hardened indeed to be so at ease as they walk down the road leading to the next life. Charioteer, turn back, for this is not the time for the pleasure-ground. How can a man of intelligence, aware of death, enjoy himself in this fateful hour?"...

Longing for solitude, the prince kept his followers back and approached a lonely spot at the foot of a Jambu tree, covered all over with beautiful leaves. There he sat on the clean ground where the soft grass glittered like beryl. Contemplating the birth and death of beings, he undertook to steady his mind in meditation. In no time his mind became firm; he was released from mental distractions such as the desire for objects of sense, and attained the first trance of calmness. Having acquired the concentration of mind which springs from solitude, the prince was filled with extreme joy and bliss; then meditating on the course of the world, he thought, "Alas, wretched is he who, out of ignorance and the blindness of pride, ignores others who are distressed by old age, sickness, or death, though he himself, being likewise subject to disease, old age, and death, is helpless!"...

The prince now knew what he should do, and began thinking of a way to leave his home.

Ashvaghosha, Buddhacarita 3-5

Now at that time very distinguished young men belonging to the respectable families in Magadha were living the holy life under the Lord. People looked down upon, criticized, spread it about, saying, "The recluse Gotama gets along by making [us] childless, the recluse Gotama gets along by making [us] widows, the recluse Gotama gets along by breaking up families... Who now will be led away by him?"

Vinaya Pitaka 1.43

At one time Shakyamuni Buddha was staying in the town of Kausambi. In this town there was one who resented him and who bribed wicked men to circulate false stories about him. Under these circumstances it was difficult for his disciples to get sufficient food from their begging, and there was much abuse.

Ananda said to Shakyamuni, "We had better not stay in a town like this. There are other and better towns to go to. We had better leave this town."

The Blessed One replied, "Suppose the next town is like this, what shall we do then?"

"Then we move to another."

The Blessed One said, "No, Ananda, there will be no end in that way. We had better remain here and bear the abuse patiently until it ceases, and then we move to another place. There are profit and loss, slander and honor, praise and abuse, suffering and pleasure in this world; the Enlightened One is not controlled by these external things; they will cease as quickly as they come."

Dhammapada Commentary

Teachings of Sun Myung Moon

Shakyamuni entered the religious life in search of the true path. Leaving the palace behind, he journeyed as a solitary monk, overcoming many obstacles. He searched for the way for human beings to live according to the Way of Heaven, the Universal Law, which God sought to establish in the world. Yet when he set out on his journey a sea of tears blocked his way—tears from individuals, tears from his family, and tears from his countrymen. Surely the saintly Shakyamuni, who had to overcome all this, walked a most miserable path.[34] (101:151, October 29, 1978)

The passing joys of those who delight in the pleasures of the flesh are nothing compared to the bliss experienced by those on the path of enlightenment, who find joy in the midst of simple poverty. Gautama Buddha, who abandoned the luxuries of the royal palace and became enraptured in the pursuit of the Way, was not the only one who wandered about homeless while searching for his heart's resting place, though he knew not where it was. (*Exposition of the Divine Principle*, Introduction)

Buddha was persecuted by members of the royal family because he gave up his position as the crown prince. People persecuted him in a country where royalty was worshipped. (258:87, March 17, 1994)

Shakyamuni of India was born as a prince of his country, but when he came to understand that life was a "sea of bitterness," he gave up his position as a prince to search for the path of truth. Buddhism originated in India, but today there are not many Buddhists in India. There has never been a religious founder who was received well in his own country. No nation has treated its saints well during their lifetime. (39:255-56, January 15, 1971)

2. The Buddha's Enlightenment

Having mastered perfectly all the methods of trance, the prince recalled, in the first watch of the night, the sequence of his former births.

Next the Rightly-illumined One perceived, and thus was decisively awakened: When birth is destroyed, old age, and death ceases; when becoming is destroyed, then birth ceases; when attachment is destroyed, becoming ceases; when craving is destroyed, attachment ceases...[35]

Reflecting his right understanding, the great hermit arose before the world as Buddha, the Enlightened One. He found self nowhere, as the fire whose fuel has been exhausted. Then he conceived the Eightfold Path, the straightest and safest path for the attainment of this end.

For seven days, the Buddha with serene mind contemplated the Truth that he had attained and gazed at the Bodhi tree without blinking: "Here on this spot I have fulfilled my cherished goal; I now rest at ease in the Dharma of selflessness."

Ashvaghosha, Buddhacarita 14

Through many a birth I wandered in samsara, seeking but not finding the builder of this house. Sorrowful is it to be born again and again.

O house-builder! You are seen. You shall build no house again. All your rafters are broken. Your ridgepole is shattered. My mind has attained the unconditioned. Achieved is the end of craving.

Dhammapada 153-54

In heaven and on earth, I alone am the honored one.[36]

Digha Nikaya 2.15

Know then, that from time to time a Tathagata is born into the world, a fully Enlightened One, blessed and worthy, abounding in wisdom and goodness, happy with the knowledge of the worlds, unsurpassed as a guide to erring mortals, a teacher of gods and men, a blessed Buddha. He thoroughly understands this universe, as though he saw it face to face... The Truth does he proclaim both in its letter and in its spirit, lovely in its origin, lovely in its progress, lovely in its consummation. A higher life does he make known in all its purity and in all its perfection.

Digha Nikaya 13, Tevigga Sutta

Teachings of Sun Myung Moon

If you establish yourself at a true perpendicular angle [to Heaven] and resonate with the true love of the universe, you will become one with God's love both internally and externally. Then the universe will belong to you, you will become a great person, and everything will be under your dominion. Shakyamuni experienced this state, and said, "In heaven and on earth, I alone am the honored one." (178:299, June 12, 1988)

Shakyamuni Buddha said, "In heaven and earth, I alone am the Honored One." In what state did he teach this? If you were to enter that state of resonance, you would become one with God. In that state, you would be able to see thousands of years of human history unfold before your eyes. You would experience yourself as having that incredible value.

How can we humans escape from the painful cycle of suffering, life after life? How can we escape from our miserable life's destiny that ends in the cemetery? This is the homework given to each of us. In order to solve this, we have to receive training to enter the realm of resonance. (38:270-73, January 8, 1971)

Confucius

BORN INTO A ERA OF INCESSANT WARFARE, THE SAGE CONFUCIUS saw beyond the troubles of his own day and sought for the universal principles of morality that could be the basis of a peaceful world. He gathered a circle of disciples and traveled from kingdom to kingdom, seeking to interest the rulers in his ideas. Though he was rejected again and again, Confucius maintained an optimistic attitude, based on the faith that Heaven was using him for a higher purpose. Though not accepted in his day, Confucius' teachings became the foundation of East Asian civilization.

Father Moon respects Confucius for his faith in God, which he called "Heaven," and his single-minded focus to seek a higher truth transcending his meager circumstances. He regards Confucius as a counterpart to Jesus: he taught the outward form of social relations in the Kingdom of heaven, while Jesus taught and embodied its inward spirit.

1. Confucius Faced Hardships and Disappointments While Maintaining Conviction about His Mission

The border warden requested to be introduced to Confucius, saying, "When men of superior virtue have come to this [exile], I have never been denied the privilege of seeing them." The followers introduced him, and when he came out from the interview, he said, "My friends, why are you distressed by your master's loss of office? The kingdom has long been without the principles of truth and right; Heaven is going to use your master as a bell with its wooden tongue."

Analects 3.24

While Confucius stood alone at the east gate of the outer city the natives reported to Tsekung, "There is a man at the east gate… He looks crestfallen like a homeless, wandering dog." Tsekung told Confucius this story, and Confucius smiled and said, "I don't know about the descriptions of my figure, but as for resembling a homeless, wandering dog, he is quite right, he is quite right!"

Ssu-ma Ch'ien, Shih Chi 47

[Being surrounded and short of food], Confucius knew that his disciples were angry and disappointed at heart, so he asked Tselu to come in and questioned him. "It is said in the Book of Songs, 'Neither buffalos, nor tigers, they wander in the desert.' [A comparison to themselves] Do you think that my teachings are wrong? How is it that I find myself now in this situation?" Tselu replied, "Perhaps we are not great enough and have not been able to win people's confidence in us. Perhaps we are not wise enough and people are not willing to follow our teachings." "Is that so?" said Confucius. "Yu, if the great could always gain the confidence of the people, why did Poyi and Chuch'i have to go and die of starvation in the mountains? If the wise men could always have their teachings followed by others, why did Prince Pikan have to commit suicide?"

Tselu came out and Tsekung went in, and Confucius said, "Sze, it is said in the Book of Songs, 'Neither buffalos, nor tigers, they wander in the desert.' Are my teachings wrong? How is it that I find myself now in this situation?" Tsekung replied, "The Master's teachings are too great for the people, and that is why the world cannot accept them. Why don't you come down a little from your heights?" Confucius replied, "Sze, a good farmer plants the field but cannot guarantee the harvest, and a good artisan can do a skillful job, but he cannot guarantee to please his customers. Now you are not interested in cultivating yourselves, but are only interested in being accepted by the people. I am afraid you are not setting the highest standard for yourself."

Tsekung came out and Yen Hui went in, and Confucius said, "Hui, it is said in the Book of Songs, 'Neither buffalos, nor tigers, they wander in the desert.' Are my teachings wrong? How is it that I find myself now in this situation?" Yen Hui replied, "The Master's teachings are so great. That is why the world cannot accept them. However, you should just do your best to spread the ideas. What do you care if they are not accepted? The very fact that your teachings are not accepted shows that you are a true gentleman. If the truth is not cultivated, the shame is ours; but if we have already strenuously cultivated the teachings of a moral order and they are not accepted by the people, it is the shame of those in power. What do you care if you are not accepted? The very fact that you are not accepted shows that you are a true gentleman." And Confucius was pleased and said smilingly, "Is that so? Oh, son of Yen, if you were a rich man, I would be your butler!"

Ssu-ma Ch'ien, Shih Chi 47

This is the character of the man: so intent upon enlightening the eager that he forgets his hunger, and so happy in doing so, that he forgets the bitterness of his lot and does not realize that old age is at hand. That is what he is.

Analects 7.18

Teachings of Sun Myung Moon

Confucius was born in the House of Lu during the Warring States period several thousand years ago, a chaotic time of many battles and wars. Yet he was not concerned only for his own country or the surrounding states. Nor did he complain about the trouble-filled society and the difficult circumstances into which he was born. Although he had no siblings to help him serve his parents, he tried to support them with gratitude.

Confucius had the heart to be concerned about the future and the world. Despite frequent rejection, he persevered with gratitude. Therefore, eventually his teachings would unify the continent of China. More than that, he pioneered a way that has remained for all humankind, even beyond Asia. His aspiration and desire was to offer something truthful, and he searched for the truth that he could offer to humankind. This formed his character. This was where his teachings originated. (33:290, August 21, 1970)

Confucius intended that the House of Lu should adopt his way to govern his nation during those chaotic times. However, seeing chaos and confusion abounding throughout the world as well as in his own nation, he came up with a teaching for a way of life to be followed by all future generations of humankind. (32:260, July 19, 1970)

Confucius was persecuted; he was cursed as a "homeless, wandering dog." The reason why he and other persecuted people of Heaven could be recognized as saints is because they followed the principle. Therefore with the passage of time their day would come, when they were destined to be victors. (189:205-06, April 6, 1989)

2. Confucius' Religious Faith

When under siege in K'uang, Confucius said, "With King Wen dead, is not culture (*wen*) invested here in me? If Heaven intends culture to be destroyed, those who come after me will not be able to have any part of it. If Heaven does not intend this culture to be destroyed, then what can the men of K'uang do to me?"

Analects 9.5

Confucius said, "He who sins against Heaven has none to whom he can pray."

Analects 3.13

Though his food might be coarse rice and vegetable broth, Confucius inevitably offered a little in sacrifice, and always with solemnity.

Analects 10.8

Po-niu was ill and Confucius went to inquire of him. Having grasped his hand through a window, Confucius said, "It is killing him. It is the will of Heaven, alas! That such a man should have such a malady! That such a man should have such a malady!"

Analects 6.8

Confucius said, "Devote yourselves to the proper demands of the people, respect the ghosts and spirits but keep them at a distance—this may be called wisdom."

Analects 6.20

Confucius said, "I wish I did not have to speak at all." Tzu Kung said, "But if you did not speak, sir, what should we disciples pass on to others?" Confucius said, "Look at Heaven there. Does it speak? The four seasons run their course and all things are produced. Does Heaven speak?"

Analects 17.19

Teachings of Sun Myung Moon

No religious founder puts forth a teaching or propounds principles of living centered only on human beings. Among the teachings of Confucius, there is one: "Those who live for goodness will be blessed by Heaven, but those who live contrary to goodness will face misfortune from Heaven." That is, Heaven rewards with blessings those who do good deeds, and Heaven will recompense evildoers with disasters. Confucius could say this because he knew Heaven. He knew Heaven; therefore he could erect principles of living that are based on Heaven. Although he only vaguely knew Heaven (God), he included it in his teachings. Therefore, he is qualified to stand among the great founders of religion. (32:261, July 19, 1970)

Providentially, Confucius' teaching was like the proclamation of the heavenly archangel. Through the elements of Confucian morality, Heaven sought to establish social conditions that would protect against Satan and set up a society resembling the external form of Heaven.[37] (205:179, August 28, 1998)

Jesus

SUN MYUNG MOON REGARDS JESUS OF NAZARETH AS THE GREATEST of all the religious founders. He has made an exhaustive study of his life and work; his speeches about Jesus take up many volumes. He does not view Jesus from the conventional Christian perspective as the Savior who fulfilled everything through his atoning death on the cross. No, Father Moon's Jesus knew he had a much greater mission—to live and establish God's Kingdom on earth during his lifetime. The crucifixion cut short his mission, frustrated his aspirations, and prolonged the centuries of suffering and wars while the Kingdom tarried until the days of the Second Coming. It is through this lens that he views scripture passages about Jesus' person, preparations for his coming, his relations with his family, his ministry, the cross, and the resurrection.

Father Moon knows Jesus as the "man of sorrows." He asserts that even in his youth, during the 30 years prior to beginning his public life, Jesus was misunderstood and ridiculed by his family and his village. The fact that Jesus never married, when it was customary for all Jewish men in their twenties to do so, is taken not as a mark of special holiness but rather as the painful lot of a man of questionable birth and strange behavior who was not regarded as marriageable.

When it came time for Jesus to begin his ministry, all Heaven's attempts to prepare the Jewish people to welcome him ended in failure—notably the ministry of John the Baptist. Consequently, Jesus was never able to preach what he set out to preach: the gospel of the Kingdom of God in plain language. Instead he had to speak in obscure parables. He was never able to do what he set out to do: lead a spiritual and political movement to win Israel's independence from Rome and establish God's Kingdom throughout the world.

Jesus' sorrow only increased as the forces opposing his ministry grew stronger and he was compelled to take an alternative course, the way of the cross. His grief was exacerbated by the weakness of his disciples, who fled and scattered leaving him alone at the end. In the Garden of Gethsemane he prayed desperately, knowing the sorrow of God and the sufferings of generations to come that would ensue if he took that path and died without completing his original mission. But by that time the people's rejection was unalterable; the die was cast and he obediently accepted the cross as God's will.

Yet Jesus never changed his heart-felt love for the people, even for those who were killing him. When he forgave his enemies on the cross, it was an earth-shaking moment that changed history forever.

1. Jesus Came to Save Sinful Humankind

Christ Jesus came into the world to save sinners.

1 Timothy 1.15

From that time Jesus began to preach, saying, "Repent, for the kingdom of heaven is at hand."... And he went about all Galilee, teaching in their synagogues and preaching the gospel of the kingdom and healing every disease and every infirmity among the people.

Matthew 4.17, 23

Jesus said to him, "I am the way, the truth, and the life; no one comes to the Father, but by me."

John 14.6

Come to me, all who labor and are heavy laden, and I will give you rest. Take my yoke upon you, and learn from me; for I am gentle and lowly in heart, and you will find rest for your souls. For my yoke is easy, and my burden is light.

Matthew 11.28-30

And as he sat at table in the house, behold, many tax collectors and sinners came and sat down with Jesus and his disciples. And when the Pharisees saw this, they said to his disciples, "Why does your teacher eat with tax collectors and sinners?" But when he heard it, he said, "Those who are well have no need of a physician, but those who are sick. Go and learn what this means, 'I desire mercy, and not sacrifice.' For I came not to call the righteous, but sinners."

Matthew 9.10-13

I am the good shepherd. The good shepherd lays down his life for his sheep. He who is a hireling and not a shepherd, whose own the sheep are not, sees the wolf coming and leaves the sheep and flees; and the wolf snatches them and scatters them. He flees because he is a hireling and cares nothing for the sheep. I am the good shepherd; I know my own and my own know me, as the Father knows me and I know the Father; and I lay down my life for the sheep. And I have other sheep, that are not of this fold; I must bring them also, and they will heed my voice. So there shall be one flock, one shepherd.

John 10.11-16

Teachings of Sun Myung Moon

Jesus spent his whole life fulfilling his responsibility and mission. What he completed on earth during his 33 years of life secured an eternal and inviolable accomplishment. His Gospel of faith, and the example of his life, will remain for eternity.

Jesus took responsibility, not only for his own generation but also for all of history. Jesus single-handedly took responsibility to complete the providential will that God had been striving to fulfill for 4,000 years. (1:37, May 16, 1956)

Jesus came to answer the universal questions, resolve humanity's sins, and solve the problem of death. Jesus was the only person who could provide solutions to these problems.

Moreover, more than anyone else, Jesus lived a truthful life for the sake of God. Disregarding his personal life, he sought to elucidate the fundamental questions of the universe. Disregarding his own glory, he labored and sacrificed endlessly to fulfill the will of God. By virtue of his consistent heart and life, he was elevated before Heaven as the foremost torchbearer, representing all of history. That is why he could confidently cry out, "Believe in me." (3:14, September 8, 1957)

Jesus said, "I am the way, the truth and the life." What a bold statement! Was his way a treacherous mountain trail? No, it was a firm and solid road. Was his truth dim and obscure? No, he clearly knew everything that he spoke. He intended that his truth should be welcomed by all peoples, and it should become the measure of all truth. Was his life one of dying or thriving? He lowered himself to serve others, yet as he said, those who humble themselves will be lifted up. (106:13, November 4, 1979)

People in a state of imperfection cannot establish the ideal world. People ignorant of the truth cannot lay its foundations. Therefore, God promised to send to Israel the Messiah—the one perfected person with complete knowledge. Jesus would be the beginning of the God-centered sovereignty and nation; this would be possible once the Israelites united absolutely with him.

That is, by attending[38] the Messiah, immature people were to proceed on the path to individual perfection and establish families, communities and a nation united with Jesus. They had to obey Jesus' will in its entirety. However, the Israelites who met the Messiah did not understand that God had sent him. Neither did they know that God's work for Jesus was to save not only his own people but also the world. (54:41, March 10, 1972)

2. Jesus—the Son of God and Incarnation of the Word

For God so loved the world that he gave his only Son, that whoever believes in him should not perish but have eternal life.

John 3.16

Philip said to him, "Lord, show us the Father, and we shall be satisfied." Jesus said to him, "Have I been with you so long, and yet you do not know me, Philip? He who has seen me has seen the Father; how can you say, "Show us the Father?" Do you not believe that I am in the Father and the Father in me?...

Yet a little while, and the world will see me no more, but you will see me; because I live, you will live also. In that day you will know that I am in my Father, and you in me, and I in you.

John 14.8-11, 19-20

In this the love of God was made manifest among us, that God sent his only Son into the world, so that we might live through him...

And we have seen and testify that the Father has sent his Son as the Savior of the world. Whoever confesses that Jesus is the Son of God, God abides in him, and he in God. So we know and believe the love God has for us.

1 John 4.9, 14-16

In the beginning was the Word, and the Word was with God, and the Word was God. He was in the beginning with God; all things were made through him, and without him was not anything made that was made. In him was life, and the life was the light of men. The light shines in the darkness, and the darkness has not overcome it...

He was in the world, and the world was made through him, yet the world knew him not. He came to his own home, and his own people received him not. But to all who received him, who believed in his name, he gave power to become children of God; who were born, not of blood nor of the will of the flesh nor of the will of man, but of God.

And the Word became flesh and dwelt among us, full of grace and truth; we have beheld his glory, glory as of the only Son from the Father.

John 1.1-15

Teachings of Sun Myung Moon

After being born on this earth, Jesus claimed, "I am the only-begotten Son of God!" He made the decisive proclamation, "No one comes to the Father but by me," meaning that in history up until his coming, no one could fully receive God's love. Thus, Jesus expounded the ultimate standard, the level that God longs to see us attain. Jesus was the only person who claimed this relationship with God. We read his words in John 14, "Believe that I am in the Father and the Father in me." Thus, he declared that he is one with God. (53:231-32, February 28, 1972)

The Bible calls Jesus the "only-begotten Son." What does this mean? God's love is absolute love. Jesus was the first person in history who could receive the total love of God and represent that love to humankind.

Because God gave Jesus the title, "only-begotten Son," he could become our Savior. Jesus taught that he is the true Son of God from the standpoint of love. Therefore, only by going through Jesus can we make a relationship of love [with God]. (146:168, June 15, 1986)

Among Jesus' words, he said, "God is my Father." This is the correct teaching. It is the word that can bring complete success to human life. It is a word without precedent, which can elevate human affections to the level of heavenly heart and heavenly law.

Next, Jesus said, "I am the bridegroom, and you are the brides." He was speaking about this in a religious sense, was he not? In the human world, what can be more intimate than the relationship between husband and wife? What can be closer than the relationship between parent and child? Jesus also said that he was our brother. What relationship could be closer? With these teachings Jesus was describing God's family. He encapsulated the truth by describing relationships containing the divine heart. (39:42-43, January 9, 1971)

Jesus came as the incarnation of the Word. Jesus was the man whom God had been hoping to see over the long course of restoration history, the desire of God from the time of creation. (3:318-19, February 2, 1958)

God's original thought in creating the universe centered on human beings was to rejoice with all His creatures. This was God's desire, but it was not realized on this earth due to the Fall of Adam and Eve, our progenitors. God created all existence in six days through the Word [*logos*]. He bestowed upon all created beings a purpose: to become God's object partners by manifesting God's Word.

What then, would all created beings hope for, having been created as substantial object partners through the Word? This was for a mediator, one central being that would enable them to move in step with God. If human beings had become that center, the chaotic history that has unfolded on this earth would not have happened.

God also hoped to see the appearance of the one being who could represent Him and act on His behalf. This has been the center of God's hope—not only during the course of the providence of restoration since the Human Fall, but even since the beginning of creation.

The being God and creation hoped for would come as the incarnation of the Word... Due to the Fall of Adam and Eve, God's Word returned to Him without being manifested on the earth; meanwhile, separated from the Word, human beings still live on this earth. Therefore, God would once again bestow His Word upon humanity. (*Exposition of the Divine Principle*, Christology 4.1.1)

Because Jesus was born on the foundation of a purified lineage, having nothing to do with Satan, he is indeed the Son of God. He could finally claim: "I am the only begotten Son of God." No one like Jesus had ever appeared before in human history...

There have been other religious founders and saviors in history, but none of them was born relating to God as a son to his Parent, because they did not have a purified lineage, unstained by Satan's polluted blood. Neither Buddha nor Confucius nor Mohammed came from such a background. Therefore, Jesus' birth on earth was truly the hope of all humankind. It is through the glory of his person that we can receive new life and resurrection. (53:205-206, February 21, 1972)³⁹

3. Jesus—the True Man and the Sinless 'Second Adam'

The first man, Adam, became a living being; the last Adam [Jesus] became a life-giving spirit.

1 Corinthians 15.45

Lo! The likeness of Jesus with God is as the likeness of Adam.

Qur'an 3.59

For there is one God, and there is one mediator between God and men, the man Christ Jesus.

1 Timothy 2.5

In the days of his flesh, Jesus offered up prayers and supplications, with loud cries and tears, to him who was able to save him from death, and he was heard for his godly fear. Although he was a Son, he learned obedience through what he suffered; and being made perfect he became the source of eternal salvation to all who obey him.

Hebrews 5.7-9

And when God said, "O Jesus son of Mary, did you say to mankind, 'Take me and my mother for two gods besides Allah?' " He replied, "Be glorified! It was not mine to utter that to which I had no right. Thou wouldst have known it if I said it. Thou knowest what is in my mind, and I know not what is in Thy mind. Truly Thou alone art the Knower of Things Hidden. I spoke to them only that which Thou didst command me, saying, 'Worship Allah, my Lord and your Lord.' I was a witness to them while I dwelt among them, and when Thou didst take me Thou wert the Watcher over them. Thou art Witness over all things."

Qur'an 5.116-17

Teachings of Sun Myung Moon

Had Adam and Eve realized the ideal of creation and become the True Parents of humanity, they would have borne good children without original sin and formed the Kingdom of Heaven on earth. However, Adam and Eve fell and became evil parents, multiplying evil children who created this hell on earth. Hence, as Jesus told Nicodemus, fallen people cannot see the Kingdom of God unless they are first born anew—as children without original sin.

We cannot be born without parents. Who, then, are the good parents through whom we can be born again, cleansed of original sin and able to enter the Kingdom of God? Parents who have original sin cannot give birth to good children who do not have original sin. Certainly, it is impossible to find sinless parents among fallen humankind. These parents must descend from Heaven. Jesus was the Parent who came from Heaven. He came as the True Father in order to give rebirth to fallen people, transforming them into good children, thoroughly cleansed of original sin and fit to build the Kingdom of Heaven on earth… Jesus came as the True Father whom Adam had failed to become. For this reason, the Bible speaks of him as the "last Adam" and the "Everlasting Father." (1 Cor. 15.45, Isa. 9.6) (*Exposition of the Divine Principle*, Christology 4.1.1)

Jesus said that the value of a human life cannot be exchanged for the entire universe… Yet many Christians say that God is very high while we human beings are sinners. They say that Jesus is God while humans are creatures with no value. If that were true, how could we possibly be connected to God? How could we realize our full potential to become God-like people? That teaching creates an unbridgeable gap between God and human beings.

To connect us to God, Jesus should stand on the side of human beings. If he stood on the side of God, we would have no hope. We read from the Bible, "For there is one God, and there is one mediator between God and men, the man Christ Jesus." (1 Tim. 2.5) The passage is correct. Because Jesus is a man, he provides the way for us sinners to approach God. If Jesus were God and not man, we would have no way to approach Him. This is a fundamental issue; it requires the correct and logical understanding.

Jesus is a sinless person while we are sinful people—that is the difference between him and us. Because Jesus is sinless, he can relate with God's love, life and ideal; and as the mediator, he can connect us to God's love, life and ideal. (69:80-81, October 20, 1973)

Let me ask you a question: Was Jesus a man or a woman? Of course he was a man. When Jesus looked at a woman, do you think he saw her as a woman, or as a man? Of course, he saw her as a woman. Then, do you think he sometimes felt an attraction? There is always the force of electricity pulling plus and minus toward each other—it is the law of nature. While Jesus was standing there, an attractive woman would approach him. His body must have shaken like this [demonstrating]. His hand must have shaken, but his feet were firmly planted. He felt frustrated, but he did not move his feet. He knew that if he moved he might fall, so he remained still and unwavering. Ordinary people respond to temptation, but Jesus never budged, even if his hand might have touched her.

No matter how great we may be, we cannot consider ourselves to be greater than Jesus. Jesus experienced the vulnerability of his human nature, but each time he drew the line and said, "No, I cannot do it." "No, it is not permitted." "I had better cut it off." By continually overcoming temptation, he reached the point where he could say, "Now I am in oneness." (128:78-79, June 5, 1983)

4. Preparation for Christ's Advent and the Responsibility of John the Baptist

But you, O Bethlehem Ephrathah,
Who are little to be among the clans of Judah,
from you shall come forth for me
one who is to be ruler in Israel,
whose origin is from of old,
from ancient days.

Micah 5.2

As it is written in Isaiah the prophet,

> "Behold, I send my messenger before thy face,
> who shall prepare thy way;
> the voice of one crying in the wilderness:
> Prepare the way of the Lord,
> make his paths straight"—

John the Baptizer appeared in the wilderness, preaching a baptism of repentance for the forgiveness of sins. And there went out to him all the country of Judea, and all the people of Jerusalem; and they were baptized by him in the river Jordan, confessing their sins. Now John was clothed with camel's hair, and had a leather girdle around his waist, and ate locusts and wild honey.[40]

Mark 1.2-6

John said, "I baptize with water; but among you stands one whom you do not know, even he who comes after me, the thong of whose sandal I am not worthy to untie." This took place in Bethany beyond the Jordan, where John was baptizing.

The next day he saw Jesus coming toward him, and said, "Behold, the Lamb of God, who takes away the sin of the world! This is he of whom I said, 'After me comes a man who ranks before me, for he was before me.' I myself did not know him; but for this I came baptizing with water, that he might be revealed to Israel." And John bore witness, "I saw the Spirit descend as a dove from heaven, and it remained on him. I myself did not know him; but he who sent me to baptize with water said to me, 'He on whom you see the Spirit descend and remain, this is he who baptizes with the Holy Spirit.' And I have seen and have borne witness that this is the Son of God."

John 1.26-34

Now when John heard in prison about the deeds of the Christ, he sent word by his disciples and said to him, "Are you he who is to come, or shall we look for another?" And Jesus answered them, "Go and tell John what you hear and see: the blind receive their sight and the lame walk, lepers are cleansed and the deaf hear, and the dead are raised up, and the poor have good news preached to them. And blessed is he who takes no offense at me."

As they went away, Jesus began to speak to the crowds concerning John: "What did you go out into the wilderness to behold? A reed shaken by the wind? Why then did you go out?... To see a prophet? Yes, I tell you, and more than a prophet. This is he of whom it is written,

> 'Behold, I send my messenger before thy face,
> who shall prepare thy way before thee.'

Truly, I say to you, among those born of women there has risen no one greater than John the Baptist; yet he who is least in the kingdom of heaven is greater than he. From the days of John the Baptist until now the kingdom of heaven has suffered violence, and men of violence take it by force.

For all the prophets and the law prophesied until John; and if you are willing to accept it, he is Elijah who is to come. He who has ears to hear, let him hear."

Matthew 11.2-15

And this is the testimony of John, when the Jews sent priests and Levites from Jerusalem to ask him, "Who are you?" He confessed, he did not deny, but confessed, "I am not the Christ." And they asked him, "What then? Are you Elijah?" He said, "I am not." "Are you the prophet?" And he answered, "No."

John 1.19-21

Teachings of Sun Myung Moon

If the Messiah were sent to this fallen world without any preparations or foundation, the enemy Satan would definitely capture him and kill him. Therefore, to prepare for his coming, God worked throughout history to establish religions. God erected the major religions and separated good from evil to find the people on His side. God's plan was to raise an individual, family, tribe, people and nation that could be victorious over Satan. It would be the prepared foundation, ready to unite totally with the Messiah when he came. That foundation was the nation called Israel, which means victory. (74:59-60, November 12, 1974)

Through many prophets, God sent messages promising that He would send the Messiah to Israel. Thus God built a foundation of messianic expectation in the Jewish people. At the proper time, God fulfilled His promise by sending His Son, the Messiah. He was Jesus. (73:218, September 18, 1974)

When Jesus was born, God proclaimed his advent. He sent the three wise men from the East as well as Simon, Anna, John the Baptist and others to testify widely.

Concerning John the Baptist in particular, many people knew that an angel had appeared and testified to his conception. (Luke 1.13) The miracles surrounding his birth stirred all of Judea in expectation. (Luke 1.63-66) Furthermore, John's ascetic life in the wilderness was so impressive that many people questioned in their hearts whether perhaps he was the Christ. (Luke 3.15) God's purpose behind sending such a great personality as John the Baptist to bear witness to Jesus as the Messiah was to encourage the Jewish people to believe in Jesus. (*Exposition of the Divine Principle*, Messiah 1.3)

If the Jewish believers who respected John the Baptist as a prophet had united with Jesus, what would have happened? Jesus' disciples would have been the leading citizens of Israel, not poor fishermen. With that level of support, who would have dared arrested and killed Jesus? Was it originally God's will that Jesus' chief followers should be tax collectors and prostitutes? (74:153, November 28, 1974)

When the mind of John the Baptist was focused on God, he recognized Jesus as the Messiah and testified to him. Later, when the inspiration left him and he returned to a mundane state, his ignorance returned and exacerbated his faithlessness. Unable to acknowledge that he was the return of Elijah, John began to regard Jesus in the same disbelieving way as other Jews viewed him, particularly after he was imprisoned. Jesus' every word and deed seemed to him only strange and perplexing. At one point, John tried to resolve his doubts by sending his disciples to Jesus and asking, "Are you he who is to come, or shall we look for another?" (Matt. 11.3)...

John the Baptist had been chosen while still inside the womb for the mission of attending Jesus. He led an arduous, ascetic life in the wilderness, building his ministry in order to prepare the way for the coming Messiah. When Jesus began his public ministry, God revealed the identity of Jesus to John before anyone else and inspired John to bear witness to him as the Son of God. Yet John did not properly receive the grace that Heaven had bestowed on him. Therefore, when confronted with John's doubting question, Jesus did not answer explicitly that he was the Messiah; he instead answered in this circuitous way. (*Exposition of the Divine Principle*, Messiah 2.3)

Jesus said, "Among those born of women there has risen no one greater than John the Baptist; yet he who is least in the Kingdom of Heaven is greater than he." (Matt. 11.11) What did he mean by this? The mission of prophets through the ages was mainly to testify to the Messiah. Prophets in the past testified from a distance of time, but John the Baptist was the prophet contemporary with the Messiah, the prophet who could bear witness, in person, to the living Christ. Therefore he was the greatest among prophets. However, John failed to love and serve the Messiah. Even the least of the prophets then living in the spirit world knew that Jesus was the Son of God and served him. That is why John, who was given the greatest mission and failed, became less than the least.

From his birth, John should have lived and died in the service of Christ, but instead he died over involvement in a trivial matter, the affair of Herodias. Was that the path God intended for John the Baptist?

Jesus said, "From the days of John the Baptist until now the Kingdom of Heaven has advanced forcefully, and forceful men lay hold of it." (Matt. 11:12) In other words, Jesus said that during days of John the Baptist just prior to the appearance of Jesus, there was the possibility that the Kingdom of Heaven could be taken and claimed by forceful men.

If John the Baptist had believed in Jesus, he certainly would have become Jesus' chief disciple. Jesus' 12 disciples and 70 disciples would have been the leaders of John the Baptist's group. As Jews of good reputation, they could have won over the scribes and priests to Jesus' side.

One day John's followers came to him and asked, "Rabbi, he who was with you beyond the Jordan, to whom you bore witness, here he is baptizing, and all are going to him." (John 3.26) They carried concern in their question: Look at all the people going to Jesus. What about you? John replied, "He must increase, and I must decrease." (John 3.30) Usually this passage is interpreted as evidence of John's humility. But what it really means is that John and Jesus were not united in heart and action. If Jesus and John had been united, their destiny would be to rise or fall together. Know, then, that the reason Jesus died on the cross was due to the failure of John the Baptist. (69:139, October 23, 1973)

5. Worldwide Preparation for Christ's Advent

Now when Jesus was born in Bethlehem of Judea in the days of Herod the king, behold, wise men from the East came to Jerusalem, saying, "Where is he who has been born king of the Jews? For we have seen his star in the East, and have come to worship him." When Herod the king heard this, he was troubled, and all Jerusalem with him; and assembling all the chief priests and scribes of the people, he inquired of them where the Christ was to be born. They told him, "In Bethlehem of Judea..." They went their way; and lo, the star which they had seen in the East went before them, till it came to rest over the place where the child was. When they saw the star, they rejoiced exceedingly with great joy; and going into the house they saw the child with Mary his mother, and they fell down and worshiped him. Then, opening their treasures, they offered him gifts, gold and frankincense and myrrh.

Matthew 2.1-11

The ancient children of the East were possessed of a wisdom which they inherited from Abraham, who transmitted it to the sons of his concubines, as it is written, "Unto the sons of the concubines that Abraham had, Abraham gave gifts, and he sent them away... eastward, unto the country of the children of the East." (Gen. 25.6). In the course of time they followed the track of that wisdom into many directions.

Zohar 1.100b (Judaism)

I tell you, many will come from east and west and sit at table with Abraham, Isaac, and Jacob in the Kingdom of heaven.

Matthew 8.11

Teachings of Sun Myung Moon

Buddhism in India, Confucianism in China and Zoroastrianism in Persia were religions with leading influence in the Orient. Spiritualists of these religions could naturally recognize who Jesus was. (227:81, February 10, 1992)

In preparation for the First Coming of Christ, God sent the prophet Malachi to the chosen people 430 years beforehand to arouse in them a strong messianic expectation. At the same time... among the world's peoples, God founded religions suited to their regions and cultures by which they could make the necessary internal preparations to receive the Messiah. In India, God established Buddhism through Gautama Buddha (565-485 B.C.) as a new development out of Hinduism. In Greece, God inspired Socrates (470-399 B.C.) and opened the brilliant age of classical Greek civilization. In the Far East, God raised up Confucius (552-479 B.C.), whose teachings of Confucianism established the standard of human ethics. Jesus was to come upon this worldwide foundation of preparation, and through his teachings he was to bring together Judaism, Hellenism, Buddhism and Confucianism. He was to unify all religions and civilizations into one worldwide civilization founded upon the Christian Gospel. (*Exposition of the Divine Principle*, Parallels 6)

Jesus was born of Asian blood, but since he lost his body in Asia, his legacy moved in the opposite direction—to Western civilization centered on Rome—in a course of restoration through indemnity. Originally, had Jesus not died on the cross, He would have led Israel to create a unified religious sphere with Buddhism in India and Confucianism in the Far East, centered on his teachings. The religious realm was to be unified first. The highest leaders in the religious sphere communicate with the spirit world and know the direction of Heaven. For this reason, had Jesus won for Israel a degree of independence from Rome and unified the divided peoples in lands of the Middle East (representing the twelve tribes of Israel), he would certainly have been able to embrace Asia. (229:174-75, April 12, 1992)

6. Misunderstood by His Family

He went away from there and came to his own country; and his disciples followed him. And on the Sabbath he began to teach in the synagogue; and many who heard him were astonished, saying, "Where did this man get all this? What is the wisdom given to him? What mighty works are wrought by his hands! Is not this the carpenter, the son of Mary and brother of James and Joses and Judas and Simon, and are not his sisters here with us?" And they took offense at him. And Jesus said to them, "A prophet is not without honor, except in his own country, and among his own kin, and in his own house."

Mark 6.1-4

Now his parents went to Jerusalem every year at the feast of the Passover. And when he was twelve years old, they went up according to custom; and when the feast was ended, as they were returning, the boy Jesus stayed behind in Jerusalem. His parents did not know it, but supposing him to be in the company they went a day's journey, and they sought him among their kinsfolk and acquaintances; and when they did not find him, they returned to Jerusalem, seeking him. After three days they found him in the temple, sitting among the teachers, listening to them and asking them questions; and all who heard him were amazed at his understanding and his answers. And when they saw him they were astonished; and his mother said to him, "Son, why have you treated us so? Behold, your father and I have been looking for you anxiously." And he said to them, "How is it that you sought me? Did you not know that I must be in my Father's house?"... And he went down with them and came to Nazareth, and was obedient to them.

Luke 2.41-51

On the third day there was a marriage at Cana in Galilee, and the mother of Jesus was there; Jesus also was invited to the marriage, with his disciples. When the wine failed, the mother of Jesus said to him, "They have no wine." And Jesus said to her, "O woman, what have you to do with me? My hour has not yet come."

John 2.1-4

Then Jesus' mother and brothers arrived. Standing outside, they sent someone in to call him. A crowd was sitting around him, and they told him, "Your mother and brothers are outside looking for you." "Who are my mother and my brothers?" he asked. Then he looked at those seated in a circle around him and said, "Here are my mother and my brothers! Whoever does God's will is my brother and sister and mother."

Mark 3.31-35

Teachings of Sun Myung Moon

Today Christians easily believe that the Virgin Mary conceived a child by the Holy Spirit, but in those days who believed it? Apparently an illegitimate child, Jesus was the target of derision. His brothers cursed him, the villagers pointed fingers at him, and even children mocked him and harassed him.

Jesus lived to be 33, yet he was not married. Why? Everyone gets married, but what family would willingly give their daughter to be the bride of such a pariah, to face the miserable circumstances of life with him? (243:242-43, January 17, 1993)

Do you think that the people in the village did not suppose that Jesus was an illegitimate child? They did, and this caused great tension between Joseph and Mary. Joseph asked Mary many times, "Who is the boy's father?" Whenever he asked her, Mary could not answer. When she told him that she conceived Jesus by the Holy Spirit, Joseph must have disbelieved her, saying, "I am the one who saved your life. What kind of game are you trying to play with me?" Thus they would fight and quarrel all the time because of Joseph's suspicions. Their fighting must have continued even after Mary gave birth to other children.

At the age of 12, Jesus had a chance to go to the Temple in Jerusalem. His parents did not know that they had left him behind until three days into their journey home. When they returned and found him in the Temple with the priests, Mary asked, "Why are you here?" Jesus replied, "Where else would I be but in my Father's house?" He was complaining about his parents, who had left him behind for three days, returning home without him. (235:237-38, September 20, 1992)

Even when Jesus was helping Joseph with his carpentry work, he did not lead a comfortable life. His life was full of hardships, and his heart endured infinite sorrow. (7:334, October 18, 1959)

Mary did not help Jesus with the wedding he desired. She even opposed it. Jesus' words to Mary during the wedding at Cana, "O woman, what have you to do with me?" reveal his reproachful heart toward his mother, who helped in the weddings of others but neglected to help her own son receive a bride. Yet for Jesus to marry was the most important requirement of the providence. With this perspective, we can understand why Jesus asked, "Who is my mother and who are my brothers?" (Matt. 12:48) (277:210, April 16, 1996)

In those days it was customary for males to marry at around 18 to 20 years of age. Why did Jesus not marry? Why was he still single even at the age of 33? In fact, when Jesus was 17 years old he honestly told Mary the providential reason why he must marry: Adam fell around age 16, to restore the Human Fall he had to marry, and a certain procedure would be required. Three times he spoke of this to his mother: at age 17, then again at age 27 and again at age 30. But his mother would not listen to him. (266:193, December 25, 1994)

The reason why Jesus had to go the way of the cross was only secondarily because the leaders of Israel betrayed him and the Jews went against him. The primary reason was that Joseph's family could not prepare the day for Jesus to be blessed in a holy marriage. Had that one day come, Jesus would not have died on the cross. (30:173-74, March 22, 1970)

7. The Three Temptations in the Wilderness

Jesus was led up by the Spirit into the wilderness to be tempted by the devil. And he fasted forty days and forty nights, and afterward he was hungry. And the tempter came and said to him, "If you are the Son of God, command these stones to become loaves of bread." But he answered, "It is written,

> 'Man shall not live by bread alone,
> but by every word that proceeds from the mouth of God.'"

Then the devil took him to the holy city, and set him on the pinnacle of the temple, and said to him, "If you are the Son of God, throw yourself down; for it is written,

> 'He will give his angels charge of you,' and
>
> 'On their hands they will bear you up,
> lest you strike your foot against a stone.'"

Jesus said to him, "Again it is written, 'You shall not tempt the Lord your God.'" Again, the devil took him to a very high mountain, and showed him all the kingdoms of the world and the glory of them; and he said to him, "All these I will give you, if you will fall down and worship me." Then Jesus said to him, "Begone, Satan! for it is written,

> 'You shall worship the Lord your God
> and him only shall you serve.'"

Then the devil left him, and behold, angels came and ministered to him.

Matthew 4.1-11

Teachings of Sun Myung Moon

Jesus defeated Satan by overcoming the three temptations in the wilderness, the last of them on a mountaintop. Yet we should realize that when Jesus journeyed to the wilderness after being rejected by John the Baptist and his followers—a situation that made likely his rejection by the

Jewish people as well—he carried a heart of sorrow the like of which no one on the earth had ever experienced.

Jesus appeared as the only Son of God, who came to resolve the 4,000-year history of God's providence. He came as the seal of victory that God could boast about before that generation and countless generations to come. Yet it was with a sad heart Jesus that walked into the wilderness—alone, without a friend, leaving his family, the chosen John the Baptist, the religious authorities, and his people behind.

Jesus set out, filled with determination and sense of mission to pay the debts of history. What did he think about during his 40 days of fasting? He felt an acute sense of responsibility to restore through indemnity, by himself, the rueful course of his forbearers...

No one ever had more determination and resolution to fulfill God's will than Jesus Christ. He went to the wilderness with a burning heart to capture and subjugate Satan. He stood alone on that mountain with a firmer determination than any ancestor in history. (5:194-96, January 25, 1959)

Satan tempted Jesus three times. First, while he was fasting for forty days, Satan tempted him with food. He appeared before Jesus and asked him to change a stone into bread. This would be good news to a starving person, but Jesus refused. He clearly stated, "Man does not live on bread alone, but on every word that comes from the mouth of God." This means that Jesus refused to yield any conditions to Satan pertaining to the necessities of life.

Throughout history up until that time, people had been fighting over material wealth. However, Jesus' victory over Satan's first test made it possible to bring and end to this interminable struggle for material goods.

What trial did Jesus have to face next? Satan led him to the top of the Holy Temple. There he tested him, saying, "If you are the Son of God, throw yourself down." Jesus came with the religious teaching that could educate Judaism and the people of Israel. When Satan said, "throw yourself down," he meant for Jesus to bow down before the conventional Jewish doctrines and traditions and abandon his role to educate and lead them. But Jesus did not fall for Satan's test. Instead he won the victory.

What was the third test? "The devil took him to a very high mountain and showed him all the kingdoms of the world and their splendor. 'All this I will give you,' he said, 'if you will bow down and worship me.'" Here Jesus rejected Satan's demand in order to fulfill the Will of God. Far from needing Satan's help, Jesus came bearing the universal teaching by which he would build God's nation, the Kingdom of God. (3:121, October 13, 1957)

8. Jesus Taught in Parables

Another parable he put before them, saying, "The kingdom of heaven is like a grain of mustard seed which a man took and sowed in his field; it is the smallest of all seeds, but when it has grown it is the greatest of shrubs and becomes a tree, so that the birds of the air come and make nests in its branches."

He told them another parable. "The kingdom of heaven is like leaven which a woman took and hid in three measures of flour, till it was all leavened."

All this Jesus said to the crowds in parables; indeed he said nothing to them without a parable...

Matthew 13.31-34

The disciples came and said to him, "Why do you speak to them in parables?" And he answered them, "To you it has been given to know the secrets of the kingdom of heaven, but to them it has not been given. For to him who has will more be given, and he will have abundance; but from him who has not, even what he has will be taken away. This is why I speak to them in parables, because seeing they do not see, and hearing they do not hear, nor do they understand.

Matthew 13.10-13

Teachings of Sun Myung Moon

For what purpose did Jesus come to this earth and proclaim the Gospel? Why did he shed tears for 30 years and walk a path of tribulations? First, he wanted human beings to restore their relationship with God; and next, he wanted to lead them to the Kingdom of Heaven.

Jesus introduced the Kingdom of Heaven with the Word—the truth. Through Jesus, God bestowed the Word upon human beings, that they might establish an eternal, unchanging relationship with Him and to build the Kingdom of Heaven on earth. Through Jesus, God desired to manifest His truth. Hence, Jesus began to spread the word of truth to bring human beings back to God...

However, instead of receiving the truth, the people of Israel did not believe in Jesus... For this reason, he could not fully communicate the truth to humanity. He was left to convey the truth only in symbols and parables, while its fullness remained hidden.

Since then, numerous people throughout history have utilized all their knowledge and wisdom trying to open the gate to the hidden truth. They have been searching inwardly by the Spirit and externally by the truth. When the Last Days arrive, finally spirit and truth will meet. The truth that has been dwelling in Jesus' heart will be completely revealed, and the numerous people who had been searching for it will become Jesus' true followers. In that day, as people learn the truth both inwardly and outwardly, they will come to know Jesus truly. (2:126-27, March 17, 1957)

9. Jesus Gathered Disciples and Trained Them for the Kingdom

As Jesus was walking beside the Sea of Galilee, he saw two brothers, Simon called Peter and his brother Andrew. They were casting a net into the lake, for they were fishermen. "Come, follow me," Jesus said, "and I will make you fishers of men." At once they left their nets and followed him.

Matthew 4.18-22

He who loves father or mother more than me is not worthy of me; and he who loves son or daughter more than me is not worthy of me; and he who does not take his cross and follow me is not worthy of me. He who finds his life will lose it, and he who loses his life for my sake will find it.

Matthew 10.37-39

A man once gave a great banquet, and invited many; and at the time for the banquet he sent his servant to say to those who had been invited, "Come; for all is now ready." But they all alike began to make excuses. The first said to him, "I have bought a field, and I must go out and see it; I pray you, have me excused." And another said, "I have bought five yoke of oxen, and I go to examine them; I pray you, have me excused." And another said, "I have married a wife, and therefore I cannot come." So the servant came and reported this to his master. Then the householder in anger said to his servant, "Go out quickly to the streets and lanes of the city, and bring in the poor and maimed and blind and lame." And the servant said, "Sir, what you commanded has been done, and still there is room." And the master said to the servant, "Go out to the highways and hedges, and compel people to come in, that my house may be filled. For I tell you, none of those men who were invited shall taste my banquet."

Luke 14.16-24

Abide in me, and I in you. As the branch cannot bear fruit by itself, unless it abides in the vine, neither can you, unless you abide in me. I am the vine, you are the branches. He who abides in me, and I in him, he it is that bears much fruit, for apart from me you can do nothing. If a man does not abide in me, he is cast forth as a branch and withers; and the branches are gathered, thrown into the fire and burned. If you abide in me, and my words abide in you, ask whatever you will, and it shall be done for you. By this my Father is glorified, that you bear much fruit, and so prove to be my disciples. As the Father has loved me, so have I loved you; abide in my love. If you keep my commandments, you will abide in my love, just as I have kept my Father's commandments and abide in his love. These things I have spoken to you, that my joy may be in you, and that your joy may be full.

John 15.4-11

Behold, I send you out as sheep in the midst of wolves; so be wise as serpents and innocent as doves. Beware of men; for they will deliver you up to councils, and flog you in their synagogues, and you will be dragged before governors and kings for my sake, to bear testimony before them and the Gentiles. When they deliver you up, do not be anxious how you are to speak or what you are to say; for what you are to say will be given to you in that hour; for it is not you who speak, but the Spirit of your Father speaking through you.

Matthew 10.16-20

Teachings of Sun Myung Moon

Rejected by the prepared people, Jesus appeared as a laborer and became a friend of fishermen. He shared with them his life, heart and desires. He fought for them, determined to satisfy their hearts' desires. As a result, Peter and the other fishermen could follow him.

After selecting these uneducated disciples, what did Jesus do for three years? He served them, just as God had toiled for 4,000 years as a servant to raise the Israelites.

Jesus had great hopes for his twelve chosen disciples. He never forgot that God had sent him to influence Judaism by guiding its priests and officials. His teaching was grand, his hopes were high, and his passion was great.

After enduring the agony of rejection by the chief priests and scribes… Jesus sacrificed and served to raise up his disciples to take their place. Through the three years of his ministry he searched for them, forgetting food and drink. If he acquired new clothes, he gave them to his disciples and was content with his rags. If he found a comfortable place to sleep, he let his disciples sleep there and sat in an uncomfortable place. (5:225, February 1, 1959)

People believe in religion to find salvation, and the purpose of salvation is to reach perfection. To this end, religious people know that they should love God and the founder of their religion more than anyone in the fallen world. We should clearly know that the path of religion requires such a pledge. All religious believers should walk this path—to go beyond the love of the world—and thereby win over Satan's world.

We can connect with God's love only when we have transcended the love of the fallen world. This is the very reason Jesus said, "He who loves father or mother—or wife or husband—more than me is not worthy of me, and he who loves son or daughter more than me is not worthy of me." Why should we love Jesus more than our own family members? By so loving Christ we become people with greater love than people in the fallen world, and through our bond of love with Christ we are entitled to enter heaven. Meeting this condition is a requirement of God's Principle; therefore Jesus had to say these words. (93:326, June 17, 1977)

Hunger and suffering creates a bond of heart between us. Just socializing together while we wear good clothes and lead a comfortable life does not link us together. Rather, you and I should experience the misery of persecution and oppression, working day and night in difficult circumstances as we shoulder the enormous burden of fulfilling our responsibility. There is no way to build a bond of heart except through tears... You talk about a relationship of heart with Jesus or with True Parents, but where can you find it except through suffering? There is no other way. (94:233, October 1, 1977)

When people receive revelations about Christ at the Second Advent or hear his words, they will respond in ways similar to the way the Jews in Jesus' day responded. God did not reveal the news of the birth of Jesus to the priests and scribes, but to gentile astrologers and pure-hearted shepherds. This is like the case of a father who, due to the ignorance of his own children, has to confide in his step-child. Likewise, God may well reveal the news of the return of Christ first to lay people, to marginal spiritual groups and churches which the mainstream treats with disdain, or to conscientious non-believers. Only later may the news reach the mainstream Christian clergy who are unthinkingly keeping to their conventional ways of faith. In Jesus' day, those who sincerely received the Gospel were not the Jewish leaders, but simple common folk and Gentiles. Likewise, at Christ's return, simple Christians and non-Christians will accept the Lord's words before the Christian leadership, which regards itself as God's elect. This is the meaning of Jesus' parable of the marriage feast. (*Exposition of the Divine Principle*, Second Advent 4)

10. Jesus Performed Miracles, but They Were Not Conducive to Faith

The apostles returned to Jesus... and he said to them, "Come away by yourselves to a lonely place, and rest a while." For many were coming and going, and they had no leisure even to eat. And they went away in the boat to a lonely place by themselves. Now many saw them going, and knew them, and they ran there on foot from all the towns, and got there ahead of them. As he landed he saw a great throng, and he had compassion on them, because they were like sheep without a shepherd; and he began to teach them many things. And when it grew late, his disciples came to him and said, "This is a lonely place, and the hour is now late; send them away, to go into the country and villages round about and buy themselves something to eat." But he answered them, "You give them something to eat." And the disciples said to him, "Shall we go and buy two hundred denarii worth of bread, and give it to them to eat?" And he said to them, "How many loaves have you? Go and see." And when they had found out, they said, "Five, and two fish." Then he commanded them all to sit down by companies upon the green grass. So they sat down in groups, by hundreds and by fifties. And taking the five loaves and two fish he looked up to heaven, and blessed, and broke the loaves, and gave them to the disciples to set before the people; and he divided the two fish among them all. And they all ate and were satisfied. And they took up twelve baskets full of broken pieces and of the fish. And those who ate the loaves were five thousand men.[41]

Mark 6.30-44

When the disciples said, "O Jesus son of Mary! Is your Lord able to send down for us a table spread with food from heaven?"[42] He said, "Observe your duty to God, if you are true believers." They said, "We wish to eat of it, that we may satisfy our hearts and know that you have spoken truth to us, and that we may be witnesses thereof." Jesus son of Mary said, "O God, our Lord! Send down for us a table spread with food from heaven, that it may be a feast for us, for the first of and for the last of us, and a sign from Thee. Give us sustenance, for Thou art the Best of sustainers."

Qur'an 5.112-114

When they found him on the other side of the sea, they said to him, "Rabbi, when did you come here?" Jesus answered them, "Truly, truly, I say to you, you seek me, not because you saw signs, but because you ate your fill of the loaves. Do not labor for the food which perishes, but for the food which endures to eternal life, which the Son of man will give to you; for on him has God the Father set his seal." Then they said to him, "What must we do, to be doing the works of God?" Jesus answered them, "This is the work of God, that you believe in him whom he has sent."...

Jesus said to them, "I am the bread of life; he who comes to me shall not hunger, and he who believes in me shall never thirst... Truly, truly, I say to you, unless you eat the flesh of the Son of man and drink his blood, you have no life in you; he who eats my flesh and drinks my blood has eternal life, and I will raise him up at the last day..."

Many of his disciples, when they heard it, said, "This is a hard saying; who can listen to it?" But Jesus, knowing in himself that his disciples murmured at it, said to them, "Do you take offense at this?... The words that I have spoken to you are spirit and life. But there are some of you that do not believe." For Jesus knew from the first who those were that did not believe, and who it was that would betray him. And he said, "This is why I told you that no one can come to me unless it is granted him by the Father." After this many of his disciples drew back and no longer went about with him.[43]

John 6.25-67

Teachings of Sun Myung Moon

Jesus was willing to do anything for the sake of the Father's Will... Touring with his disciples, when he saw that the people were hungry, he performed the miracle of feeding the 5,000 with five loaves and two fishes. He gave everything he could. (4:83, March 9, 1958)

Jesus did not delight in performing miracles. If you think he performed miracles in comfort and joy, you are greatly mistaken. When he felt compelled by a painful situation to show mercy upon the people, he raised his hands and cried out, "Father!" This is when the miracles took place. They took place when Jesus cried out in excruciating sadness, as if his bones and flesh were melting. Do not think that Jesus performed miracles because he liked them or was reckless.

On the hill of Bethsaida, 5,000 people waved their arms and shouted out, "Jesus, you are our Savior! You are the chosen leader of Israel!" They sought him out because they expected to obtain some benefit from him. However, after some time passed they began to see that Jesus' standard of heart was different from theirs. They could not relate to his internal situation and ideals, which came from a different, higher realm. That was when they turned their backs on Jesus and abandoned him. Yet all the while, Jesus was giving them his utmost love. (3:291, February 1, 1959)

The multitudes that followed Jesus believed he was the Messiah and their Savior when he showed them the miracle of the loaves and fishes. Yet when Jesus was about to be killed, everyone abandoned him and scattered.

If the people who followed Jesus had understood his internal heart toward Heaven, if they had understood that he possessed a deeply penetrating heart toward God, and that he came to take responsibility for the whole of the God's historical providence, they would have understood his predicament and followed him to the end. (3:291, January 19, 1958)

11. Jesus' Wept Out of Love for the People and Agonized Over Their Unbelief, Even as His Closest Disciples Proved Faithless

Then Mary, when she came where Jesus was and saw him, fell at his feet, saying to him, "Lord, if you had been here, my brother would not have died." When Jesus saw her weeping, and the Jews who came with her also weeping, he was deeply moved in spirit and troubled; and he said, "Where have you laid him?" They said to him, "Lord, come and see." Jesus wept. So the Jews said, "See how he loved him!"

John 11.32-36

Woe to you, scribes and Pharisees, hypocrites! for you tithe mint and dill and cummin, and have neglected the weightier matters of the law, justice and mercy and faith; these you ought to have done, without neglecting the others. You blind guides, straining out a gnat and swallowing a camel!

Woe to you, scribes and Pharisees, hypocrites! for you cleanse the outside of the cup and of the plate, but inside they are full of extortion and rapacity. You blind Pharisee! first cleanse the inside of the cup and of the plate, that the outside also may be clean.

Woe to you, scribes and Pharisees, hypocrites! for you are like whitewashed tombs, which outwardly appear beautiful, but within they are full of dead men's bones and all uncleanness. So you also outwardly appear righteous to men, but within you are full of hypocrisy and iniquity.

Matthew 23.23-28

And they went to a place which was called Gethsemane; and he said to his disciples, "Sit here, while I pray." And he took with him Peter and James and John, and began to be greatly distressed and troubled. And he said to them, "My soul is very sorrowful, even to death; remain here, and watch." And going a little farther, he fell on the ground and prayed that, if it were possible, the hour might pass from him. And he said, "Abba, Father, all things are possible to thee; remove this cup from me; yet not what I will, but what thou wilt." And he came and found them sleeping, and he said to Peter, "Simon, are you asleep? Could you not watch one hour? Watch and pray that you may not enter into temptation; the spirit indeed is willing, but the flesh is weak." And again he went away and prayed, saying the same words. And again he came and found them sleeping, for their eyes were very heavy; and they did not know what to answer him. And he came the third time, and said to them, "Are you still sleeping and taking your rest? It is enough; the hour has come; the Son of man is betrayed into the hands of sinners."

Mark 14.32-41

And as Peter was below in the courtyard, one of the maids of the high priest came; and seeing Peter warming himself, she looked at him, and said, "You also were with the Nazarene, Jesus." But he denied it, saying, "I neither know nor understand what you mean." And he went out into the gateway. And the maid saw him, and began again to say to the bystanders, "This man is one of them." But again he denied it. And after a little while again the bystanders said to Peter, "Certainly you are one of them; for you are a Galilean." But he began to invoke a curse on himself and to swear, "I do not know this man of whom you speak." And immediately the cock crowed a second time. And Peter remembered how Jesus had said to him, "Before the cock crows twice, you will deny me three times." And he broke down and wept.

Mark 14.66-72

Teachings of Sun Myung Moon

Does God live only for Himself and His glory, or is God totally selfless, living for the well being of the entire creation? Which is true love? In fact, the true God comes to us fallen people, shedding tears. People weep either when they are sad or happy. What about God? Does He shed tears of grief looking at human misery, or tears of laughter as He saves people? Think about it. If you ever lost a loved one and then found him again years later, what would you do? You would weep, first with grief and then with joy.

Therefore, God wants to meet His beloved ones on the path of tears. Would you like to experience God's tears? Have you ever cried, so shaking with sobs that water runs from your nose and mouth, your entire body drenched in sweat? Until you experience what grief is, you cannot taste true love. (102:163-64, December 17, 1978)

In the world dominated by Satan, God's providence requires battles. God has to set up fights. Jesus certainly made some people angry when he criticized the Jews living in peace and comfort, calling them "hypocrites" and a "brood of vipers" and casting curses upon them. If Jesus had praised the rabbis, scribes and priests, telling them that they were doing a wonderful job for God, would he have been killed? Confucius and Mohammed—all the saints without exception—declared to the world something it did not want to hear. By doing that, they created the momentum for change. (95:276-77, December 11, 1977)

The people who were the closest to Jesus caused him the most sorrow. His sorrow was not so much from rejection by the people of Israel whom God had prepared, or from rejection by the Jewish authorities. His greatest sorrow came when his beloved disciples—some who had followed him for as long as three years—lost faith when he needed them to believe, did not testify when he needed them to testify, did not fight when he needed them to fight, and ran from death when he needed them to face death. (3:142, October 18, 1957)

Who followed Jesus to the end without forsaking him? The twelve disciples? No, even the three chief disciples among the Twelve did not keep faith and follow Jesus to the end.

Although Jesus tried to introduce the love of God to humankind and tried to put that love into practice, he died without building a substantial relationship of love with a single human being. Although Jesus conveyed words of heavenly love, and although his heart burned with love, he died without having found one person whom he could tightly embrace and exchange the affectionate words, "My son!" "My father!" sharing the love that runs between a parent and child.

Can you understand the heart and situation of Jesus as he cried in anguish through the sleepless night in the Garden of Gethsemane, even as the disciples were dozing off? Many people today appreciate Jesus' words of love, but 2,000 years ago, Jesus did not have anyone to whom he could give his love. (3:58, September 22, 1957)

Jesus lived barely thirty years, a life filled with sorrow. Jesus spent three years of public life, offering everything he had; yet who knew his heart, and who knew his situation? Not even one person.

Even the disciples, who attended him as their teacher, who shared his joys and sorrows, who were sad when he was sad and lonely when he was lonely—they did not know, either.

The disciples, who should have clung to Heaven and appealed with earnest hearts, concerned that their teacher might go the path of death, instead were confused, asking, "Who is Jesus?" (7:45, July 12, 1959)

On this earth, who knew the heart of Jesus? Not a single person recognized Jesus, a man filled with apprehension, who experienced and felt keenly Heaven's sorrow, who felt Heaven's lament over humanity. Jesus did not have even one disciple who exclaimed, "My Lord!" intimately feeling God's heart...

Enable us to sympathize with the heart of Jesus, who had to leave behind disciples ignorant of his great sorrow, with the heart of Jesus, who died without seeing his life bear fruit, even though he lived his entire life for humankind. (5:137-38, January 11, 1959)

12. The Agony of Christ's Passion and Crucifixion

From that time Jesus began to show his disciples that he must go to Jerusalem and suffer many things from the elders and chief priests and scribes, and be killed, and on the third day be raised. And Peter took him and began to rebuke him, saying, "God forbid, Lord! This shall never happen to you." But he turned and said to Peter, "Get behind me, Satan! You are a hindrance to me; for you are not on the side of God, but of men."

Matthew 16.21-23

And he came out, and went, as was his custom, to the Mount of Olives; and the disciples followed him. And when he came to the place he said to them, "Pray that you may not enter into temptation." And he withdrew from them about a stone's throw, and knelt down and prayed, "Father, if thou art willing, remove this cup from me; nevertheless not my will, but thine, be done."...

There came a crowd, and the man called Judas, one of the twelve, was leading them. He drew near to Jesus to kiss him; but Jesus said to him, "Judas, would you betray the Son of man with a kiss?" And when those who were about him saw what would follow, they said, "Lord, shall we strike with the sword?" And one of them struck the slave of the high priest and cut off his right ear. But Jesus said, "No more of this!" And he touched his ear and healed him. Then Jesus said to the chief priests and officers of the temple and elders, who had come out against him, "Have you come out as against a robber, with swords and clubs? When I was with you day after day in the temple, you did not lay hands on me. But this is your hour, and the power of darkness."

Then they seized him and led him away, bringing him into the high priest's house...

Now the men who were holding Jesus mocked him and beat him; they also blindfolded him and asked him, "Prophesy! Who is it that struck you?" And they spoke many other words against him, reviling him.

When day came, the assembly of the elders of the people gathered together, both chief priests and scribes; and they led him away to their council, and they said, "If you are the Christ, tell us." But he said to them, "If I tell you, you will not believe; and if I ask you, you will not answer. But from now on the Son of man shall be seated at the right hand of the power of God." And they all said, "Are you the Son of God, then?" And he said to them, "You say that I am." And they said, "What further testimony do we need? We have heard it ourselves from his own lips."

Then the whole company of them arose, and brought him before Pilate. And they began to accuse him, saying, "We found this man perverting our nation, and forbidding us to give tribute to Caesar, saying that he himself is Christ a king. And Pilate asked him, "Are you the King of the Jews?" And he answered him, "You have said so."…

And as they led him away, they seized one Simon of Cyrene, who was coming in from the country, and laid on him the cross, to carry it behind Jesus. And there followed him a great multitude of the people, and of women who bewailed and lamented him. But Jesus turning to them said, "Daughters of Jerusalem, do not weep for me, but weep for yourselves and for your children. For behold, the days are coming when they will say, 'Blessed are the barren, and the wombs that never bore, and the breasts that never gave suck!' Then they will begin to say to the mountains, 'Fall on us'; and to the hills, 'Cover us.' For if they do this when the wood is green, what will happen when it is dry?" Two others also, who were criminals, were led away to be put to death with him.

And when they came to the place which is called The Skull [Calvary], there they crucified him, and the criminals, one on the right and one on the left. And Jesus said, "Father, forgive them; for they know not what they do." And they cast lots to divide his garments. And the people stood by, watching; but the rulers scoffed at him, saying, "He has saved others; let him save himself, if he is the Christ of God, his Chosen One!" The soldiers also mocked him, coming up and offering him vinegar, and saying, "If you are the King of the Jews, save yourself!" There was also an inscription over him, "This is the King of the Jews."

One of the criminals who were hanged railed at him, saying, "Are you not the Christ? Save yourself and us!" But the other rebuked him, saying, "Do you not fear God, since you are under the same sentence of condemnation? And we indeed justly; for we are receiving the due reward of our deeds; but this man has done nothing wrong." And he said, "Jesus, remember me when you come into your kingdom." And he said to him, "Truly I say to you, today you will be with me in Paradise."

It was now about the sixth hour, and there was darkness over the whole land until the ninth hour, while the sun's light failed; and the curtain of the temple was torn in two. Then Jesus, crying with a loud voice, said, "Father, into Thy hands I commit my spirit!" And having said this he breathed his last.

Luke 22.39-23.46

And about the ninth hour Jesus cried with a loud voice, "Eli, Eli, lama sabachthani?" that is, "My God, my God, why hast thou forsaken me?"

Matthew 27.46

Teachings of Sun Myung Moon

People say that Jesus came to die. Was his death indeed predestined by God, or was it an event brought on by circumstances? You should know that it was something that came to pass suddenly and unexpectedly. We can discern this from the New Testament's account of the Transfiguration:

"And behold, two men talked with him, Moses and Elijah, who appeared in glory and spoke of his departure [his crucifixion] which he was to accomplish in Jerusalem." (Luke 9:30-31)

When Jesus later informed Peter that he would suffer in Jerusalem and be crucified, Peter violently protested, "God forbid, Lord! This shall never happen to you!" (Matt. 16:22) Then Jesus lashed out at him, saying, "Get behind me, Satan! You are a hindrance to me; for you are not on the side of God but of men." (Matt. 16:23)

Conventional Christians understand this passage to mean that Jesus was supposed to die on the cross, and because Peter tried to stop him, Jesus called him "Satan." What Jesus actually meant was this: Peter had witnessed the trance-like scene on the Mount of Transfiguration alongside Jesus; hence he should have heard sometime during that event, the instruction to Jesus that he should go to his death. However, Peter had dozed off and never heard it. Yet now that Jesus' death was decided, Peter had no business telling Jesus what to do or not to do.

The decision [to alter Jesus' course] been made on the Mount of Transfiguration. Jesus had originally come to fulfill God's Will both spiritually and physically, but he was driven into a situation where unless he sacrificed himself, he would have to turn the nation and the people over to Satan. In that situation, by going the way of crucifixion God strove to lay at least a spiritual foundation. In other words, God had determined to lead him on a secondary dispensation, one that would give birth to Christianity. (73:218, September 18, 1974)

Jesus walked a wretched path, the path of the cross. Evil men whipped and beat him. They ripped his clothing, drove him along the street, and forced him to the ground. In that situation, if Jesus had been like Elijah, he might have said to the people, "I am the only one of the Lord's prophets left." (1 Kings 18:22) But when Jesus left his disciples in the Garden of Gethsemane and went to pray, he said, "My Father, if it be possible, let this cup pass from me; nevertheless, not as I will, but as Thou wilt." (Luke 22:42) This was his greatness. He understood that his body was a sacrificial offering for the nation, a sacrificial offering for humanity and a sacrificial offering for God's providence.

Therefore, although Jesus felt his own bitter sorrow, he was more concerned for God's sorrow. God had sent Jesus for the sake of the nation; instead he felt God's sorrow to see him betrayed by his own people. Jesus was the Messiah. He was the Crown Prince of Heaven and the central personage of the entire universe. If he chose, he could have given way to self-pity and lamented his miserable fate. He could have set the entire universe in lamentation with him. Yet, he understood that his position was not to sigh in despair. Instead, he even went so far as to feel apologetic toward Heaven for having been rejected.

Jesus bore the responsibility to rally the religious establishment, rally the nation, build the Kingdom of Heaven and return the world to the Father's bosom. Yet when he was forced to abandon that mission and walk the way of the cross, he did not feel enmity toward anyone. He did not pray, "Let this cup pass from me," for fear of death. Rather, he prayed this way because he knew his death would add to the grief of the nation and to God's grief.

Jesus knew that if he died on the cross, there would be an even heavier cross remaining for the future generations. It would mean that humanity's sorrowful history would not end. He knew that the path of Golgotha would not end with him; those who followed him would also have to go the same way. Jesus knew that an even more difficult course lay beyond the cross.

As he was made to wear a crown of thorns, and the nails were hammered into his hands and feet, and his side was stabbed with a spear, Jesus knew that these events would have impact far beyond his own death. When he turned to God and said, "It is finished," he did not mean that the world's path of the cross was finished. He meant that his heart's tearful plea of concern over the cross had reached Heaven. We need to know that Jesus comforted God by offering himself as a living sacrifice and taking upon himself all the mistakes committed by past prophets and patriots.

More than that, as he neared death Jesus prayed, "Father, forgive them, for they do not know what they do." (Luke 23:34) God had a mind to pass judgment immediately, a judgment even more terrible than in Noah's time. But Jesus died clinging to the nation, clinging to the religious establishment and clinging to the cross. For this reason, God could not abandon humanity, but held on to us. Because this bond of heart existed between Jesus, the future generations of humanity and the remaining people of Israel, God could not abandon the religious organizations that turned against him, nor the people of subsequent generations. Instead, God has clung to them. (378:314, May 21, 2002)

When Jesus fell exhausted while carrying the cross to Golgotha, none among his disciples offered to shoulder the cross in his place. Neither did anyone from among the chosen people of Israel. Rather it was Simon of Cyrene, a Gentile, who shouldered the cross and participated in Jesus' tribulation. For this reason, Christianity flourished among the Gentiles, not the Jews…

How must Jesus have felt when he looked at Simon of Cyrene? His disciples, with whom he had shared all his joys and sorrows, had all disappeared, leaving this Gentile to suffer on his behalf. Jesus must have felt deeply embarrassed and sorrowful.

If any man among the twelve disciples had stood up to shoulder the cross in his place, then by looking at him, Jesus could have forgotten the hardships of death. He would have overcome his own agony by feeling compassion for his disciple. When this did not happen, Jesus felt even greater sorrow. (2:275, June 16, 1957)

Although the Roman soldiers nailed him to a cross and pierced him with a spear, Jesus asked God's forgiveness for them. He endured his pain with the attitude, "I am dying on their behalf. I am willing to be sacrificed on their behalf." From that moment a new realm opened; a new world was born that had never before existed in history.

Before Jesus' time the rule was to take revenge on your enemy, based on the law, "an eye for an eye, a tooth for a tooth." No one before Jesus had ever taught that we should love our enemies. Jesus demonstrated something totally new to the world when he loved his enemies on the cross. This was something amazingly great. From that single event sprouted a new era, a new world of God's desire. (130:232-33, January 29, 1984)

Can you fathom the agony in God's heart when Jesus was dying on the cross? Here, the children of the enemy were killing His only begotten Son, and yet God could not treat them as enemies. Can you imagine how difficult it was for God to swallow His pain and maintain a loving heart towards them? Jesus understood God's painful situation; he knew that God had to maintain unconditional love even for the enemy Satan; therefore he loved the enemy soldiers who were killing him and prayed that God would forgive their sin.

Because Jesus passed this test, Satan could be separated. Because Jesus kept God's tradition of unconditional love even for Satan, Satan had no grounds to accuse either Jesus or God. This was the condition to make a division between good and evil, to lift up Christianity beyond Satan's grasp.

God's providence can progress only on the condition of loving Satan and the individuals and families under Satan's dominion. Even in the place of death, we should love and pray for them, as God does. Otherwise there can be no restoration. For this reason, Christian martyrs throughout the world have followed Jesus' example and prayed for their persecutors, "Heavenly Father, please save them."

This goes back to the principle that Satan was originally an archangel, who was to receive love from God, Adam and Eve. Although he fell to become Satan, we should not change our love for him. By following this principle, we can be fully restored and be qualified to enter the Kingdom of Heaven. (244:154-55, February 1, 1993)

Why did Jesus appeal to Heaven, "My God, my God, why hast Thou forsaken me?" (Matt. 27.46) The first human beings abandoned God, and Jesus had the mission to restore their betrayal through indemnity. That is why God forsook him.

Nevertheless, although abandoned, Jesus kept a grateful heart. He prayed, "Nevertheless, not as I will, but as Thou wilt." (Matt. 26.39) Because Jesus wanted to become one with God and digest death and whatever hardships confronted him, no enemy could dominate him. Because Jesus did not change even in death, even when God and humankind turned their backs on him, he opened the door to resurrection.

Likewise, even if God were to turn away from you, you must be determined to cling to the Father and attend Him to the end. That is the only way you enter the blessed realm of resurrection that Jesus Christ opened for us. (4:144-45, March 30, 1958)

13. Jesus Bore Our Sins on the Cross

He was despised and rejected by men;
a man of sorrows, and acquainted with grief;
and as one from whom men hide their faces
he was despised, and we esteemed him not.

Surely he has borne our griefs and carried our sorrows;
yet we esteemed him stricken,
smitten by God, and afflicted.
But he was wounded for our transgressions,
he was bruised for our iniquities;
upon him was the chastisement that made us whole,
and with his stripes we are healed.
All we like sheep have gone astray;
we have turned every one to his own way;
and the LORD has laid on him the iniquity of us all.

                      Isaiah 53.3-6

Under the law almost everything is purified with blood, and without the shedding of blood there is no forgiveness of sins.

    Thus it was necessary for the copies of the heavenly things to be purified with these rites, but the heavenly things themselves with better sacrifices than these. For Christ has entered, not into a sanctuary made with hands, a copy of the true one, but into heaven itself, now to appear in the presence of God on our behalf. Nor was it to offer himself repeatedly, as the high priest enters the Holy Place yearly with blood not his own; for then he would have had to suffer repeatedly since the foundation of the world. But as it is, he has appeared once for all at the end of the age to put away sin by the sacrifice of himself.

                      Hebrews 9.22-26

Christ Jesus, who,
though he was in the form of God,
did not count equality with God a thing to be grasped,
but emptied himself,
taking the form of a servant,
being born in the likeness of men.
And being found in human form he humbled himself
and became obedient unto death,
even death on a cross.

Therefore God has highly exalted him
and bestowed on him the name which is above every name,
that at the name of Jesus every knee should bow,
in heaven and on earth and under the earth,
and every tongue confess that Jesus Christ is Lord,
to the glory of God the Father.[44]

Philippians 2.6-11

Teachings of Sun Myung Moon

Jesus accepted his destiny, taking on his shoulders the whole responsibility for the future of Israel, giving all his strength. His disciples scattered in all directions; they abandoned Jesus, concerned only to protect their own lives. Meanwhile, Jesus did not think about his own life at all. With utmost sincerity, taking more responsibility than any other person who lived for God in history, and eager to accomplish God's purpose, he went the way of the cross. He walked that path with God. (35:23, September 27, 1970)

Suppose Adam and Eve had a brother, and he had not fallen. If that brother went to Satan and tried to bring Adam and Eve back, Satan would by no means let them go without a price. Satan would want something more valuable than what he would lose by giving up those fallen siblings. Therefore, the unfallen brother would have to sacrifice himself in place of his fallen siblings; only on that condition could he liberate them. That sacrificial brother is Christ, the second Adam. (52:50, December 14, 1971)

An offering must shed blood. God does not like bloodshed, but He cannot save a person unless he sets a condition of dying and being reborn. Offering sacrificial animals and having them shed blood has served as a condition for this throughout the ages.

Thus, in the Old Testament Age, God raised the people of Israel by having them set this indemnity condition, forgiving their sins based on their offerings of animals. On that foundation, God planned to send the Messiah to open the New Testament Age and lead Israel to build the nation of God's victory.[45] However, when the people failed to believe in the Messiah, the Messiah died by offering his own self.

Animal sacrifices represent the people who offer them. Based on their accumulated offerings of animals, all Israel at the time of Jesus stood as the fruit of the Old Testament Age; this fruit was supposed to unite with Jesus. However, when it did not happen, Jesus had to offer his own self as the sacrifice. That is how Jesus came to die on the cross. (54:252-53, March 25, 1972)

The basic nature of Satan is arrogance and fury. In contrast, Jesus came before the people of the world in meekness and humility.

Jesus did not show meekness and humility because he was incapable and unworthy. He deserved to be higher and enjoy more glory than anyone else, but Jesus forsook all that and lowered himself. Satan confronted Jesus and tried to draw him into a fight, but Jesus knew that if he remained meek and humble to the end, Satan would be bound by a condition in the Principle to submit to God. Therefore Jesus maintained his humility, doing what Satan with his arrogant and wrathful nature cannot do. Then Satan, who also knew Heaven's law, realized that he would have no choice but to recognize Jesus.

In other words, if you move forward in meekness and humility, then even the satanic world will naturally submit. Jesus understood this principle, and he took a position of meekness and humility of which Satan was utterly incapable. Similarly, you can pioneer the new path to God only when you place yourself in a position of meekness and humility. (3:187-88, October 27, 1957)

Do you know Jesus' heart when he subjugated Satan? It was a heart full of compassion for God, compassion for all humanity, and compassion for all creation: "How pitiful is God, who lost His sons and daughters! How pitiful is creation, which lost its owners! How pitiful are human beings, who lost their value, purpose, and position!" Because Jesus' heart exploded with such pity, Satan retreated. (9:181, May 8, 1960)

14. The Tragedy of Jesus' Rejection

O Jerusalem, Jerusalem, killing the prophets and stoning those who are sent to you! How often would I have gathered your children together as a hen gathers her brood under her wings, and you would not!

                      Matthew 23.37

And when he drew near and saw the city he wept over it, saying, "Would that even today you knew the things that make for peace! But now they are hid from your eyes. For the days shall come upon you, when your enemies will cast up a bank about you and surround you, and hem you in on every side, and dash you to the ground, you and your children within you, and they will not leave one stone upon another in you; because you did not know the time of your visitation."

                      Luke 19.41-44

None of the rulers of this age understood this; for if they had, they would not have crucified the Lord of glory.

                      1 Corinthians 2.8

"Hear another parable. There was a householder who planted a vineyard, and set a hedge around it, and dug a wine press in it, and built a tower, and let it out to tenants, and went into another country. When the season of fruit drew near, he sent his servants to the tenants, to get his fruit; and the tenants took his servants and beat one, killed another, and stoned another. Again he sent other servants, more than the first; and they did the same to them. Afterward he sent his son to them, saying, 'They will respect my son.' But when the tenants saw the son, they said to themselves, 'This is the heir; come, let us kill him and have his inheritance.' And they took him and cast him out of the vineyard, and killed him. When therefore the owner of the vineyard comes, what will he do to those tenants?" They said to him, "He will put those wretches to a miserable death, and let out the vineyard to other tenants who will give him the fruits in their seasons."

                      Matthew 21.33-41

Teachings of Sun Myung Moon

Today it is easy to accept Jesus Christ as the Son of God, because for nearly 2,000 years Christianity has been glorifying him. But if you had lived in the days when Jesus was being pushed around and ridiculed, would you have believed? The scribes and priests of those days longed to see the Messiah, yet they did not recognize him. Do you really think that the Jewish people of that era were inferior to Christians today? In fact, we would probably have compounded their mistakes if we had lived in the days of Jesus of Nazareth. (69:100, October 21, 1973)

Jesus came with the lonely heart of Heaven to a people who were collapsing and dying, and taking compassion upon them, he came to them without holding back even his own life. But the people of

Israel, who called themselves the chosen people, did as they pleased to the Messiah whom Heaven had sent and to John the Baptist whom Heaven had prepared…

Today let us know: It was not because the people of Israel at that time were inferior to us, that they betrayed Heaven, nor was it because their desire to live for the sake of Heaven was not as great as ours, that they forgot Heaven.

Let us understand: They had a concept about the Messiah, thinking that the Lord to come would appear as a great man, but because in reality the Messiah who appeared was haggard, pitiful and unimpressively small, they rejected him.

Let us consider our position now: Today we commonly speak ill of the historical people of Israel, and like to criticize how they handled the situation at that time, but please let us understand: between the situation now and the situation then there is no difference. May we have the mind to admit: if we had been alive at that time, we would have done the same as they. (5:284-85, February 22, 1959)

After preparing humanity for four thousand years to receive the Messiah, his death was not in God's original plan. Satan was the one who dragged Jesus to the cross and killed him. The crucifixion was a total loss. Everything was lost: Israel, Judaism, John the Baptist, the twelve disciples who betrayed Jesus… No one remained on the side of Jesus or Heaven.

There is no Christianity at the place of Jesus' cross. Christianity began on the Day of Pentecost. You must know that the cross was the victory of Satan, not of God. God's victory came with the resurrection by the power of the Spirit.[46] (73:220-21, September 18, 1974)

15. Jesus' Resurrection

I am the resurrection and the life; he who believes in me, though he die, yet shall he live, and whoever lives and believes in me shall never die.
John 11.25-26

If Christ has not been raised, then our preaching is in vain and your faith is in vain… If for this life only we have hoped in Christ, we are of all men most to be pitied.
  But in fact Christ has been raised from the dead, the first fruits of those who have fallen asleep. For as by a man came death, by a man has come also the resurrection of the dead. For as in Adam all die, so also in Christ shall all be made alive.
1 Corinthians 15.14-22

On the first day of the week, at early dawn, they went to the tomb, taking the spices which they had prepared. And they found the stone rolled away from the tomb, but when they went in they did not find the body. While they were perplexed about this, behold, two men stood by them in dazzling apparel; and as they were frightened and bowed their faces to the ground, the men said to them, "Why do you seek the living among the dead? Remember how he told you, while he was still in Galilee, that the Son of man must be delivered into the hands of sinful men, and be crucified, and on the third day rise." And they remembered his words, and returning from the tomb they told all this to the eleven and to all the rest. Now it was Mary Magdalene and Joanna and Mary the mother of James and the other women with them who told this to the apostles; but these words seemed to them an idle tale, and they did not believe them.

That very day two of them were going to a village called Emmaus, about seven miles from Jerusalem, and talking with each other about all these things that had happened. While they were talking and discussing together, Jesus himself drew near and went with them. But their eyes were kept from recognizing him. And he said to them, "What is this conversation which you are holding with each other as you walk?" And they stood still, looking sad. Then one of them, named Cleopas, answered him, "Are you the only visitor to Jerusalem who does not know the things that have happened there in these days?" And he said to them, "What things?" And they said to him, "Concerning Jesus of Nazareth, who was a prophet mighty in deed and word before God and all the people, and how our chief priests and rulers delivered him up to be condemned to death, and crucified him. But we had hoped that he was the one to redeem Israel. Yes, and besides all this, it is now the third day since this happened. Moreover, some women of our company amazed us. They were at the tomb early in the morning and did not find his body; and they came back saying that they had even seen a vision of angels, who said that he was alive. Some of those who were with us went to the tomb, and found it just as the women had said; but him they did not see." And he said to them, "O foolish men, and slow of heart to believe all that the prophets have spoken! Was it not necessary that the Christ should suffer these things and enter into his glory?" And beginning at Moses and all the prophets, he interpreted to them in all the scriptures the things concerning himself.

So they drew near to the village to which they were going. He appeared to be going further, but they constrained him, saying, "Stay with us, for it is toward evening, and the day is now far spent." So he went in to stay with them. When he was at table with them, he took the bread and blessed, and broke it, and gave to them. And their eyes were opened and they recognized him; and he vanished out of their sight. They said to each other, "Did not our hearts burn within us while he talked to us on the road, while he opened to us the scriptures?" And they rose that same hour and returned to Jerusalem; and they found the eleven gathered together and those who were with them, who said, "The Lord has risen indeed, and has appeared to Simon!" Then they told what had happened on the road, and how he was known to them in the breaking of bread.

As they were saying this, Jesus himself stood among them and said to them, "Peace to you!" But they were startled and frightened, and supposed that they had seen a spirit. And he said to them, "Why are you troubled, and why do questionings rise in your hearts? See my hands and my feet, that it is I myself; handle me, and see; for a spirit has not flesh and bones, as you see that I have." And while they still disbelieved for joy, and wondered, he said to them, "Have you anything here to eat?" They gave him a piece of broiled fish, and he took it and ate before them.

Then he said to them, "These are my words which I spoke to you, while I was still with you, that everything written about me in the law of Moses and the prophets and the psalms must be fulfilled." Then he opened their minds to understand the scriptures, and said to them, "Thus it is written, that the Christ should suffer and on the third day rise from the dead, and that repentance and forgiveness of sins should be preached in his name to all nations, beginning from Jerusalem. You are witnesses of these things. And behold, I send the promise of my Father upon you; but stay in the city, until you are clothed with power from on high."

Then he led them out as far as to Bethany, and lifting up his hands he blessed them. While he blessed them, he parted from them, and was carried up into heaven. And they returned to Jerusalem with great joy, and were continually in the temple blessing God.

Luke 24.1-53

Teachings of Sun Myung Moon

On the cross, Jesus prayed for the people and determined to fulfill his responsibility for them even after his death; indeed, his concern for God's Will transcended even death. Therefore, God could resurrect Jesus, and Satan did not dare accuse the resurrected Jesus. When you attain a level of perfection that you have the same value as Jesus, Satan cannot accuse you, either. (2:141, March 17, 1957)

Satan exercised his maximum power to crucify Jesus, thereby attaining the goal he had sought throughout the four-thousand-year course of history. On the other hand, by delivering Jesus to Satan, God set up as compensation the condition to save sinful humanity. How did God achieve this? Because Satan had already exercised his maximum power in killing Jesus, according to the principle of restoration through indemnity, God was entitled to exercise His maximum power. While Satan uses his power to kill, God uses His power to bring the dead to life. As compensation for Satan's exercise of his maximum power in killing Jesus, God exercised His maximum power and resurrected Jesus. God thus opened the way for all humanity to be engrafted with the resurrected Jesus and thereby receive salvation and rebirth. (*Exposition of the Divine Principle*, Moses and Jesus 3.3.1.1)

After his death, Jesus was concerned about his scattered disciples. Even during the three days in the tomb, he was determined to protect them for eternity. Hence, he went to the shores of Galilee after his resurrection and searched for them.

Today from a humanistic perspective we might wonder how Jesus could care for his disciples, when they showed no sense of responsibility and betrayed him the moment they faced difficulty. Yet this did not stop Jesus from fulfilling his responsibility toward them by visiting them in Galilee.

This is the character of Jesus, who did not let even death stop his unwavering efforts at raising his disciples to also be unwavering. We should take a lesson from Jesus' admirable character in this regard. (1:38, May 16, 1956)

Due to the sin and blindness of the people, God permitted His Son to be a sacrifice. That was the significance of the crucifixion: God allowed Jesus to die on the cross as the ransom paid to Satan. In exchange, upon Jesus' resurrection, God could claim the souls of humankind—though redemption of the body was not possible. Therefore God's victory, and our salvation, was not in the cross but in the resurrection…

Our salvation comes from Jesus' victorious resurrection. This is Christ's victory, and Satan's power can never affect it. But the body of Jesus Christ was given up as a sacrifice and a ransom. In giving up his body, Jesus also gave up the body of humankind. Our salvation is limited to spiritual redemption, because the redemption of the body remained unfulfilled 2,000 years ago. And our world still suffers under Satan's power. Sin still rages within our bodies and dominates this world.

Therefore Paul cried out in anguish, "Wretched man that I am! Who will deliver me from this body of death? Thanks be to God through Jesus Christ our Lord! So then, I of my self serve the law of God with my mind, but with my flesh I serve the law of sin." (Rom. 7.24-25) Paul was living in the grace of the Lord. Still he confessed that he could serve God only with his mind, and his flesh served the law of sin. His body yearned to be redeemed; he still anguished over sin.

And so it is for us. By accepting Christ, we receive spiritual salvation. But our body still serves the law of sin under Satan's domain, until Christ returns and liberates us from the bondage of sin. The Lord of the Second Advent alone can give total salvation, in spirit and in body. (September 18, 1974)

Muhammad

LIVING IN POLYTHEISTIC ARABIA, Muhammad saw the truth of the one God and accepted his calling to be God's apostle. Though he knew the stories of the Bible from childhood, the Jews and Christians living in his area did not impress him, for they lacked the conviction or zeal to confront the ruling polytheistic tribes. Muhammad went through the streets of Mecca proclaiming the message of Islam to anyone who would listen. Though he suffered persecution and exile, he also found supporters. Muhammad and his companions were welcomed in Medina, where they defended the young faith against overwhelming odds. Muhammad was devoted to God and uncompromising with evil. Father Moon honors him as one of the foremost founders of religion.

1. God's Revelation to Muhammad

Muhammad is... the Messenger of God and the Seal of the Prophets.[47]

Qur'an 33.40

O Prophet, We have sent you as a witness, and good tidings to bear and warning, calling unto God by His leave, and as a light-giving lamp.

Qur'an 33.45-46

It belongs not to any mortal that God should speak to him, except by revelation, or from behind a veil, or that He should send a messenger and He reveal whatsoever He will, by His leave; surely He is All-high, All-wise. Even so We have revealed to thee [O Muhammad] a Spirit of Our bidding. You knew not what the Book was, nor belief; but We made it a light, whereby We guide whom We will of Our servants. And you, surely you shall guide unto a straight path—the path of God.

Qur'an 42.51-53

In the month of Ramadan... in the night on which God honored Muhammad with his mission and showed mercy on His servants thereby, Gabriel brought him the command of God. "He came to me," said the Apostle of God, "while I was asleep, with a coverlet of brocade whereupon was some writing, and said, 'Read!' I said, 'I cannot read.' He pressed me with it so tightly that I thought it was death; then he let me go and said, 'Read!' I said, 'I cannot read.' He pressed me with it again so that I thought it was death; then he let me go and said, 'Read!' I said, 'I cannot read.' He pressed me with it the third time so that I thought it was death and said, 'Read!' I said, 'What then shall I read?' —and this I said only to deliver myself from him, lest he should do the same to me again. He said,

> Read! In the name of thy Lord who created,
> Who created man of blood coagulated.
> Read! Thy Lord is the most beneficent,
> Who taught by the pen,
> Taught that which they knew not unto men. [Qur'an 96.1-5]

"So I read it, and he departed from me. And I awoke from my sleep, and it was as though these words were written on my heart. Now none of God's creatures was more hateful to me than an ecstatic poet or a man possessed: I could not even look at them. I thought, Woe is me, a poet or possessed—never shall the Quraysh say this of me! I will go to the top of the mountain and throw myself down that I may kill myself and gain rest. So I went forth to do so, and then, when I was midway on the mountain, I heard a voice from heaven saying, 'O Muhammad! Thou art the Apostle of God and I am Gabriel.' I raised my head toward heaven to see who was speaking, and lo, Gabriel in the form of a man with feet astride the horizon, saying, 'O Muhammad! Thou art the Apostle of God and I am Gabriel.' I stood gazing at him, moving neither forward nor backward; then I began to turn my face away from him, but toward whatever region of the sky I looked, I saw him as before...

"I said to Khadija, 'Woe is me, a poet or one possessed.' She said, 'I take refuge in God from that, O Abu'l-Qasim. God would not treat you thus, since He knows your truthfulness, your great trustworthiness, your fine character, and your kindness. This cannot be, my dear. Perhaps you did see something.' 'Yes, I did,' I said. Then I told her of what I had seen; and she said, 'Rejoice, O son of my uncle, and be of good heart.[48] Verily, by Him in whose hand is Khadija's soul, I have hope that you will be the Prophet of this people.'"

Ibn Ishaq, Sirat Rasul Allah

Teachings of Sun Myung Moon

Why did God reveal Himself to the prophets and create the great religions of the world? It was to enable the human race to return to Him, and then, in perfect oneness with His blessed Will, establish one peaceful world. Humanity must know God's original vision for the world, and know the reason why God revealed Himself to the prophets. Surely no one expressed more deeply this original ideal of God than the blessed Prophet Mohammed, not only in word but also in deed. (October 21, 1990)

Muhammad was centered on God, and based on God's revelation he founded the religion of Islam. It adopted the teachings of the Old and New Testaments of the Christian Bible with contents appropriate to Arab culture. Through Islam, Muhammad sought to give human beings the absolute truth of God. (39:316, January 16, 1971)

God always supports those serving the larger purpose... Between one who lived for his family, and one who sacrificed his beloved family for the benefit of his community, God would support the one living for the community. This is an unchanging principle of God. Once again, we can use the Prophet as a supreme example of knowing and living according to this Divine Principle. Did the Prophet live only for his own clan or tribe or even only for the Arab people? No, he always lived for the higher purpose, not limiting his message for only one group or race. The message of the Prophet was for every precious one into whom God breathes His spirit. (October 21, 1990)

2. Muhammad Overcame Persecution and Hardships to Establish Islam

By the Pen and by the record which men write, you are not, by the grace of your Lord, mad or possessed. Nay, verily for you is a reward unfailing, and you stand on an exalted standard of character. Soon you will see, and they will see, which of you is afflicted with madness. Verily it is your Lord who knows best, who among men has strayed from His path: and He knows best those who receive guidance.

Qur'an 68.1-7

When the Apostle openly displayed Islam as God ordered him, his people did not withdraw or turn against him until he spoke disparagingly of their gods. When he did that they took great offense and resolved unanimously to treat him as an enemy, except those whom God had protected by their allegiance to Islam from such evil, but they were a despised minority.

Ibn Ishaq, Sirat Rasul Allah

O you who believe! Remember the grace of God on you, when there came down on you hosts; but We sent against them a hurricane and forces you could not see: but God sees clearly all that you do. Behold! They came on you from above you and from below you, and behold, the eyes became dim and the hearts gaped up to the throats, and you imagined various vain thoughts about God! In that situation were the believers tried; they were shaken as by a tremendous shaking...

And God turned back the unbelievers, for all their fury; no advantage did they gain; and enough is God for the believers in their fight. And God is full of Strength, Able to enforce His will.

Qur'an 33.9-25

Teachings of Sun Myung Moon

Satan always establishes his evil regime first, ahead of God. Then with this mighty power Satan attacks God's side, attempting to destroy the tender shoot of God's Word and crush the lives of His gentle champions. Satan is always first: first with the established power and first to attack. In fact, aggression is the trademark of Satan. Being attacked first is the trademark of God's side. Yet God's side prospers according to this principle. By being attacked first God's side builds up great wealth through suffering and sacrifice. Through paying this price and bearing injustice, God's side ultimately gains the victory.

Perhaps you are familiar with the mighty yet corrupt powers that ruled out of Mecca during the life of the Prophet. When Muhammad brought his message of peace and brotherhood among all tribes and peoples, these mighty governments of evil power mobilized themselves to take the lives of God's Messenger and his followers. The followers of Islam endured this aggression and injustice, and by thus conforming to God's principle of indemnity, they were able to bring even these mighty powers into complete surrender. In the end Muhammad walked unmolested, as the glorious victor, to the Kaaba and dedicated it to the one true God. (October 21, 1990)

Chapter 10

Eschatology and Messianic Hope

Tribulation

MOST RELIGIONS ANTICIPATE A TIME beyond the present, when human history will be consummated by a decisive act of God. Evil will be destroyed and goodness will triumph. Millenarian teachings are most characteristic of Jewish, Christian and Islamic scriptures. Christianity began as a millenarian movement in Israel. Yet Hinduism, Buddhism and Zoroastrianism also contain teachings that the world is going through a cosmic cycle in which the decay of morals and religion presages a new Golden Age when life will be renewed and purified.

Millenarian beliefs can be a leavening influence on society, encouraging oppressed people with the hope that the evil system has finally reached its last hour and calling them to renewed faith or even to revolutionary action. From the Bar Kochba Rebellion of Jews against Roman tyranny, to the T'ai P'ing Rebellion in China and the African Independent Churches' agitation for independence against European colonial rule, these movements have fostered political and economic self-determination. Today, Father Moon's teachings express that same sense of urgency and possibility, proclaiming that humanity is now living in the Last Days and that the Kingdom of Heaven is at hand.

However, these beliefs can also have a negative aspect if they lead people to become self-righteous and judgmental. Father Moon warns that all the judgments and tribulations of the Last Days will strike the people on God's side earlier and more severely than non-believers, based on the principle that in the course of restoration it is for God's people to be struck first.

Typically, teachings about the Last Days or the end of the world anticipate a course of events in three phases: First, a time of tribulation when evil and confusion will prevail; second, a Last Judgment when God intervenes decisively to destroy all evil; and third, a new age of unparalleled bliss, often called the Kingdom of Heaven.

During the tribulation phase, wars, famines, plagues, natural disasters and widespread confusion will afflict humanity. Morals will decline as people become engrossed in hedonism and materialism. Religions will decline, as the teachings of their founders will be forgotten or misused for mean ends. Father Moon affirms that humanity faces such tribulations, and traces its root to the Human Fall. The Last Days is a time when the fruits of the Fall are to be harvested, he teaches.

In some scriptures, the last tribulation will be the appearance of the Beast, the Antichrist or the Dajjal, who will deny the reality of God and deceive millions with a counterfeit truth. Identifying the Antichrist has been the subject of much speculation, most of it fruitless, often fixing on the church's favorite opponent. Father Moon sees the activity of Satan behind the dark forces in history and identifies several of the Devil's stratagems to attack the people of God, including the rise of materialism and atheistic communism. Nevertheless, he reminds us that the first people to oppose Jesus were his own disciples; hence we should examine ourselves to see if we are not the antichrist, rather than blame others.

1. Degeneration of Faith and Morals in the Last Days

In the evil age to come, living beings will decrease in good qualities and increase in utter arrogance, coveting gain and honors, developing their evil qualities, and being far removed from deliverance.[1]

Lotus Sutra 13 *(Buddhism)*

But understand this, that in the last days there will come times of stress. For men will be lovers of self, lovers of money, proud, arrogant, abusive, disobedient to their parents, ungrateful, unholy, inhuman, implacable, slanderers, profligates, fierce, haters of good, treacherous, reckless, swollen with conceit, lovers of pleasure rather than lovers of God, holding the form of religion but denying the power of it.

2 Timothy 3.1-5

The Hour will not be established until (religious) knowledge will be taken away, earthquakes will be very frequent, time will pass quickly, afflictions will appear, murders will increase and money will overflow amongst you.

Hadith of Bukhari 2.17.146 *(Islam)*

The time is near in which nothing will remain of Islam but its name, and of the Qur'an but its mere appearance, and the mosques of Muslims will be destitute of knowledge and worship; and the learned men will be the worst people under the heavens; and contention and strife will issue from them, and it will return upon themselves.

Hadith *(Islam)*

Rabbi Mikhal of Zlotchov told, "Once when we were on a journey with our teacher, Rabbi Israel Baal Shem Tov, the Light of the Seven Days, he went into the woods to say the Afternoon Prayer. Suddenly we saw him strike his head against a tree and cry aloud. Later we asked him about it. He said, 'While I plunged into the holy spirit I saw that in the generations which precede the coming of the Messiah, the rabbis of the Hasidim will multiply like locusts, and it will be they who delay redemption, for they will bring about the separation of hearts and groundless hatred.'"

Hassidic Tale *(Judaism)*

Nevertheless, when the Son of man comes, will he find faith on earth?

Luke 18.8

With the footprints [heralding] the Messiah, presumption shall increase and dearth reach its height; the vine shall yield its fruit but the wine shall be costly; and the empire shall fall into heresy and there shall be none to utter reproof. The academies shall be given to fornication, and... the wisdom of the scribes shall become insipid, and they that shun sin shall be deemed contemptible, and truth shall nowhere be found. Children shall shame the elders, and the elders shall rise up before the children. The face of this generation shall be [brazen] as the face of a dog, and a son will not be put to shame by his father. On whom can we stay ourselves? On our Father in heaven.

Mishnah, Sota 9.15 *(Judaism)*

Then property alone will confer rank; wealth will be the only source of devotion; passion will be the sole bond of union between the sexes; falsehood will be the only means of success in litigation; and women will be objects merely of sensual gratification. Earth will be venerated but for its mineral treasures; the Brahmanical thread will constitute a brahmin; external types will be the only distinction of the several orders of life; dishonesty will be the universal means of subsistence; weakness will be the cause of dependence; menace and presumption will be substitutes for learning... Thus in the Kali age shall decay constantly proceed, until the human race approaches its annihilation.

Vishnu Purana 4.24 *(Hinduism)*

There will come a time [the Age of the Degeneration of the Law] when... immoral courses of action will flourish excessively; there will be no word for moral among humans—far less any moral agent. Among such humans, homage and praise will be given to them who lack filial and religious piety, and show no respect to the head of the clan; just as today homage and praise are given to the filial-minded, to the pious and to them who respect the heads of their clans.

Among such humans, there will be no such thoughts of reverence as are a bar to intermarriage with mother, or mother's sister, or teacher's wife, or father's sister-in-law. The world will fall into promiscuity, like goats and sheep, fowls and swine, dogs and jackals.

Among such humans, keen mutual enmity will become the rule, keen ill will, keen animosity, passionate thoughts even of killing, in a mother towards her child, in a child towards its mother, in a father towards his child and a child towards its father, in brother to brother, in brother to sister, in sister to brother. Just as a sportsman feels towards game that he sees, so will they feel.

Digha Nikaya 3.71-72 *(Buddhism)*

Teachings of Sun Myung Moon

Today we face a serious youth problem. In the Garden of Eden, when Adam and Eve fell, they were teenagers. They planted the seed of free sex when they fell by engaging in an illicit sexual relationship in the shade. That is why now, during the harvest time of the Last Days, it was inevitable that free sex would become rampant throughout the world.

Satan knows that God is trying to bring all human beings to Heaven by promoting the standard of true love—absolute love without any trace of the Fall. Because Satan knows that the returning Messiah will carry out this plan, his strategy is to utterly dismantle this standard. Therefore, as there is no longer any basis for love, people today engage in all sorts of behavior, including free sex, homosexuality and lesbianism. Homosexuals and lesbians are seeds of the archangel; therefore, like angels they have no object partner of love.[2]

These are the Last Days, when everywhere people are stripping off their clothes and perishing. It is the end of Satan's progeny. Now the earth has become hell, where life is in step with Satan's world of hell. Therefore, if you seek and follow a way 180 degrees opposite the prevailing lifestyle, it will be a path connected to Heaven. (279:121, August 1, 1996)

Adam and Eve distrusted God and betrayed God; this sowed the seeds of grief throughout the cosmos. Therefore in the Last Days, parents and the children will be in conflict. Just as the first human ancestors betrayed and distrusted God their Father, their descendants in the Last Days will likewise experience children rebelling against their parents...

That is why in today's society there is a pervasive tone of distrust, between parents and children, between husbands and wives, and between relatives. People no longer have confidence about their purpose for living, so much have those who deny its basis obfuscated the matter. As you see this happening, you should know that the Last Days are here. (2:330, July 28, 1957)

At the Fall, the archangel Lucifer acted to make Eve his enemy and Eve acted to make Adam her enemy. As a result, Adam, Eve and the archangel became enemies to one another. Therefore, in the Last Days everyone will become enemies to one another. Your children will become your enemies; mothers and fathers become enemies; brothers and sisters will become enemies. Nations will become enemies. All relationships will be torn apart, and you will not be able to trust anyone. What will become of ethics and morality? Such a hurricane of chaos will sweep the world that people will lose any sense of direction. People will not be able to tell right from wrong and good from evil. When that time comes, it is the Last Days. The Last Days are here right now!

You will see incidents where children kill their parents and parents kill their children. You will see ministers killing members of their congregation, and acrimonious battles between church members and their ministers. Everyone will be divided. Why is that? The seed of enmity sown by Adam, Eve and the archangel has resulted in the world becoming a battlefield. (50:213, November 7, 1971)

All religions have lost their footing. Because Christianity did not completely fulfill God's will, Buddhism, Confucianism and Islam are also going through a tough course. As a result, families, societies, nations and the world have become like hell. God's ideal realm of love is nowhere to be found on earth. Even in a vast country like America, God cannot find a true son or daughter whose mind and body are truly united. God cannot find a husband and wife who are united according to the original standard that God has desired since before the Fall. In every family, parents and children are fighting. The decline of religion has led to a world of selfish individualism in which everyone is divided. (January 13, 2001)

Without a clear vertical standard, the concepts of male and female are hazy. That is why, along with free sex, we see so much sexual confusion in the Last Days. It is neither this or that, neither man nor woman... the Devil and evil spirits cause this devastation, leading people into chaos. (189:127, April 1, 1989)

Since the Human Fall took place at the completion level of the growth stage, the completion stage remains unfulfilled.[3] The period of that stage is seven years... We are indemnifying this with a seven-year course. The seven-year course is what Christians call the seven years of the great tribulation. The great tribulation is when a family, which is in the domain of the Fall, receives persecution in order to be restored and rise up to become a family that has nothing to do with the dominion of the Fall. It is the great tribulation because the families receiving persecution and hardships are the families with whom God longs to dwell...

When Adam and Eve fell in the period of indirect dominion, Satan invaded the domain that had been reserved for human beings and came to dominate the entire realm of indirect dominion. To restore this, the seven-year great tribulation is not a time of suffering for those who deserve to suffer. Rather, it is a time when suffering comes to people who do not deserve it. (*Blessing and Ideal Family* 5.1.2)

In the free world today, many people are unwilling to marry. They live together without a legal marriage, jumping from one relationship to another... It seems like everyone is perishing, but through it God has a strategy to save them all. This trend somehow makes sense if you look at it from God's perspective. In God's view, our spirit and body is supposed to become one centered on true love, not on false love. Therefore, as people live together who have not found the origin of true love they will continue to be restless, with spirit and body divided. Once they pass through that stage, after awhile they will yearn for the marriage Blessing, the Blessing that only Heaven can give. (91:184, February 6, 1977)

2. Wars, Natural Disasters, and Widespread Devastation

And you will hear of wars and rumors of wars; see that you are not alarmed; for this must take place, but the end is not yet. For nation will rise against nation, and kingdom against kingdom, and there will be famines and earthquakes in various places: all this is but the beginning of the birth pangs.

Then they will deliver you up to tribulation, and put you to death; and you will be hated by all nations for my name's sake. And then many will fall away, and betray one another, and hate one another. And many false prophets will arise and lead many astray. And because wickedness is multiplied, most men's love will grow cold. But he who endures to the end will be saved.

Matthew 24.6-13

And after the sixty-two weeks, an anointed one shall be cut off, and shall have nothing; and the people of the prince who is to come shall destroy the city and the sanctuary. Its end shall come with a flood, and to the end there shall be war; desolations are decreed. And he shall make a strong covenant with many for one week; and for half of the week he shall cause sacrifice and offering to cease; and upon the wing of abominations shall come one who makes desolate, until the decreed end is poured out on the desolator.

Daniel 9.26-27

Society will be engulfed by ravaging wars, overflowing with havoc and devastation. In the beginning the conquerors will feel very happy over their successes and booties gathered therein, but it will all have a very sad end. I warn you of the wars of the future, you have no idea of the enormity of evil which they will carry.

Nahjul Balagha, Khutba 141 *(Shiite Islam)*

Therefore, son of man, prophesy, and say to Gog, Thus says the Lord GOD: On that day when my people Israel are dwelling securely, you will bestir yourself and come from your place out of the uttermost parts of the north, you and many peoples with you, all of them riding on horses, a great host, a mighty army; you will come up against my people Israel, like a cloud covering the land. In the latter days I will bring you against my land, that the nations may know me, when through you, O Gog, I vindicate my holiness before their eyes.

Ezekiel 38.14-16

Teachings of Sun Myung Moon

God always strikes His beloved children first, and then He strikes Satan. (*Way of God's Will* 3.4)

God cannot strike human beings even when they take Satan's side. God has to use the strategy of being struck first and then taking the victory. Satan always strikes first, but loses in the end. Throughout history Satan takes the side of self-centered people and incites them to hatred and conflict to try to destroy Heaven's side. Heaven, on the contrary, aims for the good of all, working to recreate the world with love and peace.

In the Last Days, when Satan is about to lose his dominion to Heaven's side, he will suggest atheism to the world, advocating that there is no God. This will result in movements to establish humanism, materialism and communism. All over the world, these ideologies of the left are in battle with Heaven's side on the right.

Ultimately, however, history will enter an era of a Great Revolution when Heaven's side will win and peace will prevail throughout the world. This could have occurred already, with the victory of Christian culture at the end of the Second World War... (270:232, June 7, 1995)

The satanic world is one step ahead of God. If God has a family, Satan already has a nation. Hence despite the dispensations from Adam to Abraham, in the history of the Israelites and in the centuries after Jesus, the wrongs committed in those ages did not disappear but instead accumulated...

Even after two thousand years, the responsibility of Christianity remained unfinished. How could it be indemnified? This was the purpose of World War I and World War II; they were dispensations to make restitution according to the law of indemnity.

That is why at the end of World War II, the two sides could unite centered on Christian civilization. Germany, Japan, and Italy joined with the United States, England and France to form one global sovereignty, unified based on Christian values. (292:180, April 12, 1998)

After World War II, humankind was struggling to overcome the pain of war and find the way for all nations to live in peace. At that time, God commanded me to start a world-level movement to establish God's Kingdom on the foundation of two thousand years of Christianity. The main point God revealed to me was the formula course to establish the True Parents and [unite humankind] as one true family.

However, to God's great disappointment, the Korean Christian leaders did not accept this truth. As a result, I had no choice but to walk the path of hardship. Although I had committed no crime, I was persecuted, opposed and imprisoned. This mistake of Christianity became the condition and spiritual foundation for evil to gain power in Korea. Herein lay the internal and providential reason for the Korean War and the division of Korea that has persisted for over half a century. (288:166, November 27, 1997)

3. Onslaught of Demons and Evil Spirits

And the fifth angel blew his trumpet, and I saw a star fallen from heaven to earth, and he was given the key of the shaft of the bottomless pit; he opened the shaft of the bottomless pit, and from the shaft rose smoke like the smoke of a great furnace, and the sun and the air were darkened with the smoke from the shaft. Then from the smoke came locusts on the earth, and they were given power like the power of scorpions of the earth; they were told not to harm the grass of the earth or any green growth or any tree, but only those of mankind who have not the seal of God upon their foreheads; they were allowed to torture them for five months, but not to kill them, and their torture was like the torture of a scorpion, when it stings a man. And in those days men will seek death and will not find it; they will long to die, and death will fly from them.

In appearance the locusts were like horses arrayed for battle; on their heads were what looked like crowns of gold; their faces were like human faces, their hair like women's hair, and their teeth like lions' teeth; they had scales like iron breastplates, and the noise of their wings was like the noise of many chariots with horses rushing into battle. They have tails like scorpions, and stings, and their power of hurting men for five months lies in their tails. They have as king over them the angel of the bottomless pit; his name in Hebrew is Abaddon, and in Greek he is called Apollyon.[4]

Revelation 9.1-11

Teachings of Sun Myung Moon

The age is at hand when the spirit world is attacking the earth. For this reason, many kinds of mental illnesses are appearing: neuroses, psychoses and new disorders unknown to science. Modern medicine has no cure for them. We need a new treatment, a tonic containing elements of Heaven and earth. (3:353, February 9, 1958)

Billions and trillions of spirits are on the offensive, trying to take over the physical world. They can cause mental illness. After the 1980s, and even more so in the new millennium, great numbers of people will develop some spiritual sensitivity. When they communicate with the spirit world, it could be either with good spirits or with evil spirits. Groups of people possessed by evil spirits may make war on others, causing bloodshed among people who otherwise do not want war.[5] As an antenna placed high up picks up a cacophony of noises, spiritually sensitive people will suffer from mental illness.

It would be a most fearful thing if only evil spirits mobilized to attack the physical world. There are more than enough evil spirits to strike every person living on earth. Can you imagine then what would happen? To counter it, God is making preparations. By mustering His hosts of good spirits, God is expanding the foundation of the good spirit world. (55:30, April 3, 1972)

4. The Beast or the Antichrist

Let no one deceive you in any way; for that day will not come, unless the rebellion comes first, and the man of lawlessness is revealed, the son of perdition, who opposes and exalts himself against every so-called god or object of worship… The coming of the lawless one by the activity of Satan will be with all power and with pretended signs and wonders, and with all wicked deception for those who are to perish, because they refused to love the truth and so be saved. Therefore God sends upon them a strong delusion, to make them believe what is false, so that all may be condemned who did not believe the truth but had pleasure in unrighteousness.

2 Thessalonians 2.3-12

And when the Word is fulfilled against the unjust, We shall produce from the earth a Beast to face them: he will speak to them, because that mankind did not believe with assurance in Our signs.

Qur'an 27.82

The Dajjal will come forth having with him water and fire, and what mankind see as water will be fire which burns and what they see as fire will be cold, sweet water. Any of you who live till that time must fall into what they see as fire, for it is sweet, fresh water.

Hadith of Bukhari and Muslim *(Islam)*

And I saw a beast rising out of the sea, with ten horns and seven heads, with ten diadems upon its horns and a blasphemous name upon its heads. And the beast that I saw was like a leopard, its feet were like a bear's, and its mouth was like a lion's mouth. And to it the dragon gave his power and great authority. One of its heads seemed to have a mortal wound, but its mortal wound was healed, and the whole earth followed the beast with wonder. Men worshipped the dragon, for he had given his authority to the beast, and they worshipped the beast, saying, "Who is like the beast, and who can fight against it?"

And the beast was given a mouth uttering haughty and blasphemous words, and it was allowed to exercise authority for forty-two months; it opened its mouth to utter blasphemies against God, blaspheming his name and his dwelling, that is, those who dwell in heaven. Also it was allowed to make war on the saints and to conquer them. And authority was given it over every tribe and people and tongue and nation, and all who dwell on earth will worship it, every one whose name has not been written before the foundation of the world in the book of life of the Lamb that was slain…

Also it caused all, both small and great, both rich and poor, both free and slave, to be marked on the right hand or the forehead, so that no one can buy or sell unless he has the mark, that is, the name of the beast or the number of its name. This calls for wisdom: let him who has understanding reckon the number of the beast, for it is a human number, its number is six hundred and sixty-six.[6]

Revelation 13.1-18

Children, it is the last hour; and as you have heard that antichrist is coming, so now many antichrists have come; therefore we know that it is the last hour. They went out from us, but they were not of us; for if they had been of us, they would have continued with us; but they went out, that it might be plain that they all are not of us. But you have been anointed by the Holy One, and you all know. I write to you, not because you do not know the truth, but because you know it, and know that no lie is of the truth. Who is the liar but he who denies that Jesus is the Christ? This is the antichrist, he who denies the Father and the Son.

1 John 2.18-22

Teachings of Sun Myung Moon

The world wars have resulted from Satan's last desperate struggle to preserve his sovereignty. Since the fall of the first human ancestors, Satan has been building defective, unprincipled imitations of God's ideal world. Aiming to restore the ideal world of His Principle, God has been in pursuit, gradually expanding His dominion by reclaiming it from the unprincipled world under Satan's bondage. Accordingly, in the course of the providence of restoration, a false representation of the ideal appears before the emergence of its true manifestation. The biblical prophecy that the antichrist will appear before the return of Christ is an illustration of this truth. (*Exposition of the Divine Principle,* Preparation 4.1)

Satan knew God's plan to unify the world through the one truth and presented a false imitation of the truth in order to unify humanity centering on him. This false truth is dialectical materialism. Dialectical materialism denies the existence of any spiritual reality, setting up an explanation of the universe based on a wholly materialistic logic. In denying the existence of God, it also denies the existence of Satan. Thus, in promoting dialectical materialism, Satan was effectively denying his own reality, even risking his own demise. Satan understood what would unfold at the close of human history and knew well that he would surely perish. Accepting that this was not the time to be worshipped, he rose in a monstrous denial of God, even at the sacrifice of himself. This is the spiritual root of dialectical materialism. As long as the democratic world lacks the truth which can overturn this evil doctrine, it will always be vulnerable and on the defensive. For this reason, someone on God's side must proclaim the perfect truth. (*Exposition of Divine Principle,* Preparation 4.4.1)

Who would have known that the disciples would stand in the position of the antichrist before Jesus? Who would have known that the chosen Israelite people and Judaism would become the antichrist?

We must be concerned about this in the Last Days, too. You must reflect on yourself whether you stand in the position of the antichrist. Now is not the time to reproach others or interfere with the affairs of others. The problem lies with you, yourselves. Other denominations that oppose us are not the problem. You must worry about the fact that you might become a satan in the Last Days.[7] Throughout the course of history, those people who blamed others for their problems have all lost themselves. (2:277, June 16, 1957)

> Father! The Day of Judgment now approaches for this city of death.
> Faced with such a period,
> struggling in this world of fear,
> wandering about without knowing which way to go,
> humankind has lost its center.
> People do not know what troubles they will face;
> they cannot find a place to rest.
> Please have compassion for all humankind,
> and guide them to return to Thine embrace. (5:60, December 21, 1958)

The Last Judgment

PEOPLE HAVE VIEWED THE PROSPECT OF JUDGMENT DAY with a mixture of hope and fear. It is a day of hope to the downtrodden, who will finally see vindication as the dominion of evil is overthrown and the guilty are punished. It is a day of fear to those who are painfully aware of their sins and in doubt about their salvation.

A last judgment of sorts comes upon every person individually at the time of death; this judgment was discussed in Chapter 5. Yet there is also a collective judgment that falls upon the entire world at the End of Days. The divine promise of the Kingdom of God requires that evil be vanquished on earth once and for all.

While many believers interpret the Last Judgment as a supernatural event at the literal end of the world, Father Moon teaches that the Last Judgment is a real process that occurs at the change of the age, when the evil traditions of the past are put away and people everywhere take up the task of building the Kingdom of God on earth. As in Jesus' parable of the wheat and the tares, although growth of goodness occurs unnoticed for a time amidst the fallen world, there will come the moment when the distinction between good and evil is clear as day. Then, as people recognize their sins and accept the judgment of God's Word, they will be able to root out their sins and fallen nature and begin to embody the Word in daily life, gradually transforming their character to become people of heaven.

1. *Everything Evil Is Exposed and Judgment is Passed*

The kingdom of heaven may be compared to a man who sowed good seed in his field; but while men were sleeping, his enemy came and sowed weeds among the wheat, and went away. So when the plants came up and bore grain, then the weeds appeared also. And the servants of the householder came and said to him, "Sir, did you not sow good seed in your field? How then has it weeds?" He said to them, "An enemy has done this." The servants said to him, "Then do you want us to go and gather them?" But he said, "No; lest in gathering the weeds you root up the wheat along with them. Let both grow together until the harvest; and at harvest time I will tell the reapers, Gather the weeds first and bind them in bundles to be burned, but gather the wheat into my barn."

Matthew 13.24-30

If anyone hears my sayings and does not keep them, I do not judge him; for I did not come to judge the world but to save the world. He who rejects me and does not receive my sayings has a judge; the word that I have spoken will be his judge on the last day.

John 12.47-48

The ones who disbelieve will be driven along to hell in throngs until, just as they come up to it, its gates will swing open and its keepers will say to them, "Did not messengers come to you from among yourselves reciting your Lord's verses to you and warning you about meeting [Him] on this day of yours?" They will say, "Of course!" But the Sentence about torment has still come due for disbelievers. Someone else will say, "Enter hell's gates to remain there. What an awful lodging will it be for the overbearing!"

The ones who have heeded their Lord will be driven along to the Garden in throngs until just as they come up to it, its gates will swing open and its keepers will tell them, "Peace be upon you! You have been good, so enter it to remain there." They will say, "Praise be to God who has held true to His promise for us and let us inherit the earth! We shall settle down anywhere we wish to in the Garden. How favored are such workers' wages!"

Qur'an 39.71-74

Those who feared the LORD spoke with one another; the LORD heeded and heard them, and a book of remembrance was written before him of those who feared the LORD and thought on his name. "They shall be mine, says the LORD of hosts, my special possession on the day when I act, and I will spare them as a man spares his son who serves him. Then once more you shall distinguish between the righteous and the wicked, between one who serves God and one who does not serve him.

For behold, the day comes, burning like an oven, when all the arrogant and all evildoers will be stubble; the day that comes shall burn them up, says the LORD of hosts, so that it will leave them neither root nor branch. But for you who fear my name the sun of righteousness shall rise, with healing in its wings. You shall go forth leaping like calves from the stall. And you shall tread down the wicked, for they will be ashes under the soles of your feet, on the day when I act, says the LORD of hosts.

Malachi 3.16-4.3

When the Trumpet shall sound one blast
And the earth with its mountains shall be lifted
   up and crushed with one crash,
Then, on that day, will the Event befall.
Heaven will split asunder, for that day it will be
   frail,
The angels will be on its sides, and eight will
   uphold the Throne of their Lord that day,
   above them.
On that day you will be exposed; not a secret of
   yours will be hidden.
Then, as for him who is given his record in his
   right hand, he will say, "Take, read my book!
Surely I knew that I should have to meet my
   reckoning."
Then he will be in blissful state
In a high Garden whose clusters are in easy
   reach.
[They will say to him,] "Eat and drink at ease
   for that you sent on before you in past days."
But as for him who is given his record in his left
   hand, he will say, "Oh, would that I had not
   been given my book
And knew not what my reckoning!
Oh, would that it had been death!
My wealth has not availed me,
My power has gone from me."
"Take him and fetter him And then expose him
   to hellfire…"

Qur'an 69.13-31

For no other foundation can any one lay than that which is laid, which is Jesus Christ. Now if any one builds on the foundation with gold, silver, precious stones, wood, hay, straw—each man's work will become manifest; for the Day will disclose it, because it will be revealed with fire, and the fire will test what sort of work each one has done. If the work which any man has built on the foundation survives, he will receive a reward. If any man's work is burned up, he will suffer loss, though he himself will be saved, but only as through fire.

1 Corinthians 3.11-15

Teachings of Sun Myung Moon

In the Last Days, evil will be judged everywhere in the world. What is evil? It is living only for oneself, self-centered individualism. The Lord will teach you how to pass the judgment: Live for something bigger than yourself. Living only for yourself will lead to your own destruction. You must live for the public good. In loving your children, you should raise them to be citizens of the Kingdom of Heaven.

In your personal life, when you take for yourself, that is evil; and when you give to benefit others, that is good. Judgment will be passed according to which side you were leaning each 24-hour day. (17:329, April 16, 1967)

We know Jesus to be full of love, but he only appears that way to those living in misery. To those who habitually commit evil and unrighteous acts, he is an unforgiving judge. Jesus was a man of love to fishermen, tax collectors and prostitutes, to the outcast and trampled upon, to those who in humility bared the sorrows of their souls. However, Jesus was the lord of judgment to the officials and Roman soldiers who used their swords against believers who were making sincere efforts to walk the path of righteousness... If Jesus were only love, how could he do the work of judgment that Christians expect him to perform in the Last Days? (14:309, January 10, 1965)

What is the meaning of the prophecy that "the heavens will be kindled and dissolved and the elements will melt with fire" (2 Pet. 3.12) in the Last Days? Malachi, prophesying of Jesus to come, spoke of a day burning with the fire of judgment. (Mal. 4.1) Jesus came into the world to cast this judgment, as he said, "For judgment I came into this world." (John 9.39) Jesus also said, "I came to cast fire upon the earth." (Luke 12.49) "Fire" here represents the means of the judgment for which Jesus came into the world. Nevertheless, there is no record that in his time Jesus judged the world with literal fire. The verses referring to fire must be symbolic. It is written, "Is not my word like fire, says the Lord?" (Jer. 23.29) Therefore, judgment by fire represents judgment by the Word of God...

What is the reason that Jesus judges by the Word? Human beings are created through the Word. (John 1.3) God's ideal of creation was that the first human ancestors fulfill the purpose of the Word by incarnating the Word. Yet they did not keep the Word of God and fell; thus, they failed to fulfill the purpose of the Word. Since then, God has tried to fulfill the purpose of the Word by recreating fallen human beings through the Word. This is the providence of restoration based on truth, the Word as revealed in the Scriptures. It is written, "The Word became flesh and dwelt among us, full of grace and truth; we have beheld his glory, glory as of the only Son from the Father." (John 1.14) Jesus completely realized the Word. He will come again as the standard of the judgment by the Word and judge the extent to which humanity has fulfilled the purpose of the Word. Judgment in this context contributes to the attainment of the goal of restoration, which is the realization of the purpose of the Word. Hence, in the course of the providence, the Word must be set up as the standard through which judgment can be carried out. Jesus lamented, "I came to cast fire upon the earth; and would that it were already kindled!" (Luke 12.49) As the incarnation of the Word (John 1.14), he was grieved that the people of Israel did not receive the life-giving words which he proclaimed. (*Exposition of the Divine Principle*, Eschatology 3.2.2)

What is the great judgment? It is to purify our entire body, beginning with our eyes, which has inherited Satan's blood lineage. The great judgment is not to kill Satan. It means to dissolve everything inside us that arose from immoral and unlawful norms, norms contrary to the conscience, norms that Satan has been promoting and that have defiled human history. (378:149-50, May 9, 2002)

In the future, there will surely be a new world, founded on the truth. To enter, we must pass through the judgment of truth. Next, we must pass the judgment of character. Unless our character is in alignment with this new world, we could be cast out from the trend of the age. Then, after bringing our character into oneness with the truth, we will pass through a judgment of heart. In the last days, we shall have to pass through the judgments of truth, of character and of heart. (14:179-80, October 3, 1964)

2. The Binding of Satan

Then I saw an angel coming down from heaven, holding in his hand the key of the bottomless pit and a great chain. And he seized the dragon, that ancient serpent, who is the Devil and Satan, and bound him for a thousand years, and threw him into the pit, and shut it and sealed it over him, that he should deceive the nations no more...

Then I saw a great white throne and him who sat upon it; from his presence earth and sky fled away, and no place was found for them. And I saw the dead, great and small, standing before the throne, and books were opened. Also another book was opened, which is the book of life. And the dead were judged by what was written in the books, by what they had done. And the sea gave up the dead in it, Death and Hades gave up the dead in them, and all were judged by what they had done. Then Death and Hades were thrown into the lake of fire. This is the second death, the lake of fire; and if any one's name was not found written in the book of life, he was thrown into the lake of fire.

Revelation 20.1-15

Teachings of Sun Myung Moon

The Kingdom of Heaven on earth is a restored world in which Satan can no longer instigate any activity. To realize this world, it is necessary for all humanity to eliminate their common base with Satan, restore their common base with God, and engage in give and take action with Him. The prophecy that in the Last Days God will confine Satan in a bottomless pit (Rev. 20.1-3) signifies that Satan will be utterly incapable of any activity, since there will no longer be any counterpart with whom Satan can relate. In order to eliminate our common base with Satan and be capable of judging him, we must understand the identity and crime of Satan and accuse him before God.

However, God endowed human beings and angels with freedom; therefore, He cannot restore them by force. Of their own free will, human beings are to bring Satan to voluntary submission by upholding the Word of God through fulfilling their responsibility. Only in this way can we be restored to the original ideal purposed by God at the creation. (*Exposition of the Divine Principle*, Fall 4.2)

3. The Transformation of This World and the Renewal of Life in God

On the day when the earth will be changed to other than the earth, and the heavens likewise, and they will come forth unto God, the One, the Almighty...

Qur'an 14.48

And then when retribution shall come for their offenses,
Then, O Wise One, Thy Kingdom shall be established by Good Thought,
For those who, in fulfillment, deliver evil into the hands of Truth!

And then may we be those who make life renovated,
O Lord, Immortals of the Wise One, and O Truth, bring your alliance,
That to us your minds may gather where wisdom would be in dispute!

Then, indeed, shall occur the collapse of the growth of evil,
Then they shall join the promised reward: blessed abode of Good Thought,
Of the Wise One, and of Right, they who earn in good reputation!

Avesta, Yasna 30.8-10 (Zoroastrianism)

But the day of the Lord will come like a thief, and then the heavens will pass away with a loud noise, and the elements will be dissolved with fire, and the earth and the works that are upon it will be burned up. Since all these things are thus to be dissolved, what sort of persons ought you to be in lives of holiness and godliness, waiting for and hastening the coming of the day of God, because of which the heavens will be kindled and dissolved, and the elements will melt with fire! But according to his promise we wait for new heavens and a new earth in which righteousness dwells.

2 Peter 3.10-13

Civilization as we know it is only transitory; it will finally pass away as the new age dawns and the true civilization is born. That will mark the end of the "provisional" world we live in today. God wills a reckoning for the old civilization and the establishment of a new one, and the time of His reckoning is at last drawing near.

Until now evil forces have had wide latitude in civilization, but in the transition from the old to the new, they will be weeded out. All people will go through an inexorable process of cleansing. The world will be terribly afflicted in payment for untold sins gathered over millennia. The great affliction is the sign that all societies and nations are being purified, and it will lift humankind to a new level of existence where good prevails.

The transition, which is actually upon us now, is the last stage before the beginning of an earthly paradise. In the upheaval, every sphere of life and every corner of civilization will be transformed. Those who believe in God and repent will witness the coming of the new world, and they will be able to start on the road to salvation. But those still heavily burdened with sin and unable to overcome their malicious ways will end this life in absolute misery and may find no salvation in the next.

Johrei (Sekai-Kyusei Kyo)

Teachings of Sun Myung Moon

The Bible states that in the Last Days the Lord will come to judge us. Catastrophic upheavals will occur, the sun and moon will fall from the heavens, and the earth will be destroyed. The concept of the Last Days is widespread among religions. In Buddhism it is called the Age of the Extinction of the Dharma. In Christianity we call it the Last Days.

Why should there be a Last Days? The world planned by the absolute God must be an absolute world. Once it begins it should last forever. We surmise that it was not God's original plan to bring the Last Days upon this world. Rather, because evil entered the world as a consequence of the Fall, the Last Days became necessary... God cannot abandon this fallen world. He must restore the world to its original state.

Therefore, the Last Days means one era passes and a new era arrives. If in the Last Days, because of Satan, God were to destroy the sun, the moon and the earth which He Himself created, He would be a God of failure. The sun and the moon are already resentful enough that they must shine upon evil humankind. Theirs would be a miserable fate if God destroyed them in the Last Days...

Actually, the end-times is when humanity will soar upward, after cleansing and renewing the entire course of history and setting up one victorious point as the consummation of human history. The words that promise the coming of the Last Days are words of blessing. The word "judgment" is not a bad word; it brings good news. The Last Days are the time to dissolve the thousands of years of resentment and sorrow buried so long in the hearts of God's children. Therefore, the coming of the Day of Judgment is good news. (Way of Unification 1.4.1)

Despite its evil beginning, the world under the sovereignty of Satan must one day be transformed into the world where goodness reigns, where the three great blessings are fulfilled centered on God. The Messiah comes at this time of transformation.

The Last Days is this time, when the evil world under satanic sovereignty is transformed into the ideal world under God's sovereignty. Hell on earth will be transformed into the Kingdom of Heaven on earth. Therefore, it will not be a day of fear when the world will be destroyed by global catastrophes, as many Christians have believed. In fact, it will be a day of joy, when the cherished hope of humankind, the desire of the ages, will be realized. (*Exposition of the Divine Principle*, Eschatology 3.1)

New Revelation

THE REVELATORY PHENOMENA OF THE LAST DAYS begin with a spiritual awakening. The twentieth century saw the birth of Pentecostalism, exhibiting speaking in tongues and other phenomena of the first Christian church. Throughout the world, many new sects have arisen based on special revelations to their founders. This spiritual awakening takes many forms, East and West.

Moreover, in the Jewish and Christian scriptures there are hints that God will reveal deeper aspects of His truth in the Last Days. They indicate that humankind's current state of knowledge of God's truth is imperfect and clouded by error. What of Islam, Buddhism and other religions? Truth is inexhaustible. Yet disputes over doctrines and teachings among the various denominations and sects have plagued each of the world's great faith traditions. It stands to reason that in the Last Days a new expression of truth will come to clearly distinguish truth from error, put an end to religious disputes, and guide all humankind on the path to God.

It may be inevitable that many believers attached to conventional doctrines will reject the new truth when it first appears, as has happened at the birth of every religion. Nevertheless, if the truth is broad enough to embrace the essential teachings of all the world's religions with respect and appreciation, it should attract support from all quarters and not become the basis for yet another new sect.

1. The Perfect and Complete Truth Will Be Revealed

I have said this to you in figures; the hour is coming when I shall no longer speak to you in figures but tell you plainly of the Father.

John 16.25

For our knowledge is imperfect and our prophecy is imperfect; but when the perfect comes, the imperfect will pass away. When I was a child, I spoke like a child, I thought like a child, I reasoned like a child; when I became a man, I gave up childish ways. For now we see in a mirror dimly, but then face to face. Now I know in part; then I shall understand fully.

1 Corinthians 13.9-12

For each [faith community] We have appointed a divine law and a traced-out way... Unto God you will all return, and He will then inform you of that wherein you differ.[8]

Qur'an 5.48

What is the difference between our times and the messianic times? Purity and attainment of knowledge.

Zohar, Genesis 139a (Judaism)

I have yet many things to say to you, but you cannot bear them now. When the Spirit of truth comes, he will guide you into all the truth; for he will not speak on his own authority, but whatever he hears he will speak, and he will declare to you the things that are to come. He will glorify me, for he will take what is mine and declare it to you. All that the Father has is mine; therefore I said that he will take what is mine and declare it to you.

John 16.12-15

And in the last days it shall be, God declares, that I will pour out my Spirit upon all flesh, and your sons and your daughters shall
    prophesy,
and your young men shall see visions, and your old men shall dream dreams;
yea, and on my menservants and my maidservants in those days
I will pour out my Spirit; and they shall
    prophesy.

Acts 2.17-18

"And God said, 'Let there be light!' and there was light." (Gen. 1.3) Although God spoke these words to the dwellers on the earth, that 'light' refers to the light made for the World to Come. The original light that God created was the higher light, the light of the eye. The Holy One gave Adam a glimpse of it, and at a glance he saw the entire world. When David beheld it, he was transported to spiritual ecstasy and exclaimed, "O how abundant is thy goodness." (Psalm 31.19) It was by this light that God showed Moses the Promised Land from Gilead to Dan. Yet from the beginning this divine light was hidden and concealed, as God perceived that the generations of men who lived in the times of Enoch, of Noah, and of the tower of Babel would use it for selfish purposes...

Rabbi Isaac said, "The light created by God in the work of creation filled the world with its splendor, but was eventually withdrawn and concealed. Why? So that transgressors of the good law might not participate in it. Therefore the Holy One conceals and preserves it for the days of the Righteous One [the Messiah], as it is written, 'Light dawns for the Righteous One...' (Psalm 97.11) When it shall prevail again throughout the world, humanity will become renewed and live the higher life and become one with angelic life. Until then, however, this divine light is concealed in darkness, which is its covering."

Zohar, Genesis 31b-32a (Judaism)

Teachings of Sun Myung Moon

The Bible... renders important parts of the truth in symbols and in parables. Since these are open to various interpretations, there have arisen numerous disagreements among believers, causing them to divide into many denominations. The primary cause of denominational divisions lies in the character of the Bible, not in the people. The strife between denominations will only grow more intractable unless a new truth emerges which can elucidate the symbols and parables obscuring the essential truths of the Bible. Without this new truth, God's providence, which comes through the unification of Christianity, can never reach its goal. This is why Jesus promised that in the Last Days he will give us the new Word of truth, "I have said this to you in figures; the hour is coming when I shall no longer speak to you in figures but tell you plainly of the Father." (John 16.25)

Due to the disbelief of the people of his time, Jesus died on the cross without being able to teach all that was in his heart. As he said, "If I have told you earthly things and you do not believe, how can you believe if I tell you heavenly things?" (John 3.12) What is more, Jesus added, "I have yet many things to say to you, but you cannot bear them now," (John 16.12) disclosing how sorrowful he was about the inability of even his closest disciples to receive all that he wanted to share.

Nevertheless, the words that Jesus left unspoken will not remain forever a secret, but one day will be divulged through the Holy Spirit as a new expression of truth. As Jesus said, "When the Spirit of truth comes, he will guide you into all truth; for he will not speak on his own authority, but whatever he hears he will speak, and he will declare to you the things that are to come." (John 16.13) (*Exposition of the Divine Principle,* Eschatology 5.1)

Because human beings fell, God's word of promise could not appear as the word of fulfillment. That was the case in the Old Testament and the New Testament, which contain promises of a word yet to appear—the word of fulfillment. The lack of this word is a most serious matter for all humanity. Faithful believers seeking Heaven should consider this problem. It is a problem for Christianity, and it is a problem for anyone who would attempt to unify all the world's religions.

Why is the world today full of division and strife? When Jesus appeared in the world, it also was beset with division. Jesus' word was meant to end the division and strife. However, because the people of that time did not believe in Jesus' word, the problems that he came to resolve were not entirely resolved. That is why today there should appear the Completed [Testament] Word: to bring order to this world filled with division and strife and to unite all doctrines and teachings. (3:326, February 2, 1958)

Amazing things occurred in the first church: speaking in tongues, spiritual works, prophesying, and more... These same spiritual phenomena will emerge in Christian history in the Last Days. Many who experience these things will be called crazy and heretics.

Yet the one upon whom the Spirit has been poured out cannot contest it. He may not know why it is happening, but Heaven will tell him. He opens his eyes and sees the spirit world. His actions are the actions of a spiritual being. He sees, thinks and behaves totally different from you. To you he may appear insane, but consider: did Jesus look like an intelligent man? In the eyes of his contemporaries he was a benighted fool.

In the future, such spiritual phenomena will sweep across the world, the peoples and the churches. (6:184, April 26, 1959)

Among the disciples of Jesus, there was not one who was overly attached to the Old Testament Scriptures. Rather, they all responded to the spiritual experiences which they sensed through their inner minds. In the Last Days, people who lead an ardent life of prayer or who live by their conscience will feel intense anxiety in their hearts. This is because in their hearts they vaguely sense a spiritual calling and want to follow the providence of the new age, yet they have not come in contact with the new truth which can guide them to act accordingly. These are the chosen ones who, once they hear the new truth, will be awakened simultaneously in their spirits and intellects by spirit and truth. They will then fully understand God's providential needs concerning the new age and will volunteer with great enthusiasm and delight.

We who are alive today are living in the Last Days. We should cultivate a humble heart and make the utmost effort to receive divine inspiration through prayer. We should not be strongly attached to conventional concepts, but rather should direct ourselves to be receptive to the Spirit, in order that we may find the new truth which can guide us to the providence of the new age. (*Exposition of the Divine Principle*, Eschatology 5.2)

2. The Truth of the New Revelation Eclipses the Truths of Former Dispensations

The glowworm shines so long as the lightbringer has not arisen. But when the shining one has come up, its light is quenched, it glows no longer. Such is the shining of the sectarians. So long as the rightly awakened ones arise not in the world, the sophists get no light, nor do their followers, and those of wrong views cannot be released from Ill.

Udana 73 (*Buddhism*)

And when We put a revelation in place of another revelation—and Allah knows best what He reveals—they say, "You are only inventing." Most of them know not.

Say, "The Holy Spirit has revealed it from your Lord with truth, that it may confirm the faith of those who believe, and as a guidance and good tidings for those who have surrendered."⁹

Qur'an 16.101-102

Now if the dispensation of death, carved in letters on stone, came with such splendor that the Israelites could not look on Moses' face because of its brightness, fading as this was, will not the dispensation of the Spirit be attended with greater splendor? For if there was splendor in the dispensation of condemnation, the dispensation of righteousness must far exceed it in splendor. Indeed, in this case, what once had splendor has come to have no splendor at all, because of the splendor that surpasses it... Yes, to this day, whenever Moses is read, a veil lies over their minds; but when a man turns to the Lord, the veil is removed.

2 Corinthians 3.7-16

Concerning His words—"The sun shall be darkened, and the moon shall not give light, and the stars shall fall from heaven" [Matthew 24.29]... is intended the divines of the former Dispensation, who live in the days of the subsequent Revelations, and who hold the reins of religion in their grasp. If these divines be illuminated by the light of the latter Revelation they will be acceptable to God, and will shine with a light everlasting. Otherwise, they will be declared as darkened, even though to outward seeming they be leaders of men, inasmuch as belief and unbelief, guidance and error, felicity and misery, light and darkness, are all dependent upon the sanction of Him who is the Daystar of Truth...

In another sense, by the terms "sun," "moon," and "stars" are meant such laws and teachings as have been established and proclaimed in every Dispensation, such as the laws of prayer and fasting. These have, according to the law of the Qur'an, been regarded, when the beauty of the Prophet Muhammad had passed beyond the veil, as the most fundamental and binding laws of His dispensation...

Hence, it is clear and manifest that by the words "the sun shall be darkened, and the moon shall not give her light, and the stars shall fall from heaven" is intended the waywardness of the divines, and the annulment of laws firmly established by [prior] divine Revelation, all of which, in symbolic language, have been foreshadowed by the Manifestation of God...

It is unquestionable that in every succeeding Revelation the "sun" and "moon" of the teachings, laws, commandments, and prohibitions which have been established in the preceding Dispensation, and which have overshadowed the people of that age, become darkened, that is, are exhausted, and cease to exert their influence.[10]

Book of Certitude 33-41 *(Baha'i Faith)*

Teachings of Sun Myung Moon

People need religion in order to seek the Ultimate Reality and realize goodness in accordance with the inclination of the original mind. Thus, the purpose of every religion is identical. However, religions have appeared in different forms according to their various missions, the cultures in which they took root, and their particular historical periods. Their scriptures have taken different forms for similar reasons. All scriptures have the same purpose: to illuminate their surroundings with the light of truth. Yet when a brighter lamp is lit, the old lamp is outshone and its mission fades. Because religions lack the power to guide modern people out of the dark valley of death into the full radiance of life, there must emerge a new expression of truth that can radiate a new and brighter light. (*Exposition of the Divine Principle*, Introduction)

In the Last Days, Jesus said, "the sun will be darkened, and the moon will not give its light, and the stars will fall from heaven." (Matt. 24.29) How are we to understand this verse? It is written that Joseph, the eleventh of the twelve sons of Jacob, had a dream:

> Then he dreamed another dream, and told it to his brothers, and said, "Behold, I have dreamed another dream; and behold, the sun, the moon, and eleven stars were bowing down to me." But when he told it to his father and to his brothers, his father rebuked him, and said to him, "What is this dream that you have dreamed? Shall I and your mother and your brothers indeed come to bow ourselves to the ground before you?" (Gen. 37.9-10)

When Joseph later became the prime minister of Egypt, his parents and brothers bowed down before him, as the dream had foretold. In his dream, the sun and moon symbolized the parents, while the stars symbolized their children. As will be explained, Jesus and the Holy Spirit are the True Parents who came to give rebirth to humanity in place of Adam and Eve. Therefore, in this prophecy from Matthew, the sun and moon represent Jesus and the Holy Spirit, while the stars represent the faithful believers who are their children. Elsewhere, Jesus is likened to the true light because he came as the incarnation of the Word and shone forth the light of truth. (John 1.9, 14) Here, the sunlight means the light of the words of Jesus, and the moonlight means the light of the Holy Spirit, who came as the Spirit of truth. (John 16.13)

For the sun to be darkened and the moon to lose its light means that the New Testament Word given by Jesus and the Holy Spirit will lose its luster. How can the Word as revealed in the New Testament possibly lose its light? The Old Testament Word was eclipsed when Jesus and the Holy Spirit came and gave us the New Testament Word, which fulfilled the Old Testament Word. (2 Cor. 3.7-11) Likewise, when Christ returns and gives the new truth in order to fulfill the New Testament Word and build a new heaven and new earth, (Rev. 21.1) the Word which he gave at his first coming will lose its light. It is said that the Word will lose its light because, with the coming of a new era, the period of the mission of the old truth will have lapsed.

The prophecy that the stars will fall from heaven signifies that in the Last Days many faithful Christian believers will make a misstep and fall from God's grace. At the time of Jesus, the leaders of the Jewish people were all yearning for the coming of the Messiah, but they met their downfall when they did not recognize Jesus as the Messiah and opposed him. Likewise, Christians who have been anxiously awaiting the return of Jesus are likely to make the same misjudgment and fall when he actually returns.

Jesus asked, "Nevertheless, when the Son of man comes, will he find faith on earth?" (Luke 18.8) On another occasion he said he would declare to devout believers, "I never knew you; depart from me, you evildoers." (Matt. 7.23) Jesus gave these warnings to the Christians of the Last Days because he foresaw that they would be likely to disbelieve and trespass against him at his Second Advent. (*Exposition of the Divine Principle*, Eschatology 3.2.5)

Recognizing the Day of the Lord

HOW CAN WE RECOGNIZE WHETHER THE LAST DAYS are at hand? Numerous millenarian movements have appeared in history proclaiming the Lord's coming, often leaving their followers disappointed when the appointed hour came and went without seeing the expected event. Part of the problem turns on the nature of what is expected: will it be a supernatural cataclysm with the Lord riding in on the clouds, or a natural process occurring over months and years like a change of seasons?

Some scripture passages discourage such speculation, saying that it is not for humans to know the details of God's plan. They caution us not to believe easily in rash claims, otherwise 'false Christs' might lead many credulous people astray. Other passages call for faith and patience, warning that only those who have prepared well will remain standing to greet the returning Lord.

Another group of passages have been widely interpreted as a basis for calculating the date of the Messiah's coming. Among them, we have selected passages from Christian and Jewish sources that speak of a Seventh Millennium, a millennium of Sabbath rest, as these are in agreement with Father Moon's teaching about the millennial age, the 'Completed Testament Age,' that is to begin at the end of 6,000 years of biblical history since Adam.

Finally, we look at Father Moon's teaching about the world-historical changes of the twentieth century that presage the Second Coming, rooted in the Bible's teaching that the end will not come until the Gospel has been preached to all nations.

1. No One Knows When the Last Days Will Arrive, Making Speculation Fruitless

As Jesus sat on the Mount of Olives, the disciples came to him privately, saying, "Tell us, when will this be, and what will be the sign of your coming and of the close of the age?" And Jesus answered them, "Take heed that no one leads you astray. For many will come in my name, saying, 'I am the Christ,' and they will lead many astray. And you will hear of wars and rumors of wars; see that you are not alarmed; for this must take place, but the end is not yet...

"But of that day and hour no one knows, not even the angels of heaven, nor the Son, but the Father only."

Matthew 24.3-5, 36

They ask you about the Hour—when will be its appointed time? Say, "The knowledge of it is with my Lord alone; none but He can reveal as to when it will occur. Heavy were its burden through the heavens and the earth. Only, all of a sudden it will come upon you." They ask you as if you were eager in search of it: say, "The knowledge of it is with God alone, but most men do not know."

Qur'an 7.187

You yourself know well that the day of the Lord will come like a thief in the night. When people say, "There is peace and security," then sudden destruction will come upon them as travail comes upon a woman with child, and there will be no escape. But you are not in darkness, brethren, for that day to surprise you like a thief. For you are all sons of light and sons of the day; we are not of the night or of darkness. So then let us not sleep, as others do, but let us keep awake and be sober.

1 Thessalonians 5.2-6

Teachings of Sun Myung Moon

Some Bible verses teach that you should not believe anyone who comes with news of the Last Days. Although a preacher may sweat and pour his heart out, do not believe him. Do not even believe me, the person who stands here speaking to you. You do not know if what I say is the truth or a lie. In the Last Days you will not be able to trust even your parents, brothers or sisters, so how can you trust a stranger?

At this time you need confidence to discern these matters with your heart. Discern each message with your heart, and reject it if your heart tells you that it is wrong. Your heart knows. But what if your heart is too clouded to discern properly? Anoint your head with oil, go into an isolated room and pray seriously to find the truth.

There are countless denominations and preachers who say, "Follow me." Who is the one whom God has prepared? Which church has created the best environment to welcome the Lord and a foundation where he can come and work? Are these people equipped to build a world filled with the Lord's teachings? Have you prayed about these things? Most people are not even aware that they are in a rut that will kill them, and yet they go on blabbing with their mouths open. (9:265, June 5, 1960)

Although Jesus said that the Lord would come like a thief, (Rev. 3.3) it is also written that for those in the light, the Lord will not come covertly, like a thief. (1 Thess. 5.4) When we reflect upon the events at Jesus' First Coming, we realize that he came like a thief to the priests and scribes who were in darkness, but to the family of John the Baptist, which was in the light, God plainly revealed Jesus' birth beforehand. When Jesus was born, God divulged this secret to the three wise men, Simon, Anna and the shepherds...

The secret of the time, place and manner of his return will be revealed to the faithful people who are vigilant, that they may prepare for the day of the Second Advent. In the providence of restoration, God always revealed to His prophets what He would do before He carried it out. (*Exposition of the Divine Principle*, Second Advent)

2. Unless People Prepare Well, They Will Not Recognize the Day When It Arrives

When the Son of man comes, will he find faith on earth?

Luke 18.8

What will be your state when the Son of Mary descends amongst you, and there will be an Imam amongst you? What would you do when the son of Mary would descend and lead you? [11]

Hadith of Muslim (Islam)

The kingdom of Heaven shall be compared to ten maidens who took their lamps and went to meet the bridegroom. Five of them were foolish, and five were wise. For when the foolish took their lamps, they took no oil with them; but the wise took flasks of oil with their lamps. As the bridegroom was delayed, they all slumbered and slept. But at midnight there was a cry, "Behold, the bridegroom! Come out to meet him." Then all those maidens rose and trimmed their lamps. And the foolish said to the wise, "Give us some of your oil, for our lamps are going out." But the wise replied, "Perhaps there will not be enough for us and for you; go rather to the dealers and buy for yourselves." And while they went to buy, the bridegroom came, and those who were ready went in with him to the marriage feast; and the door was shut. Afterward the other maidens came also, saying, "Lord, lord, open to us." But he replied, "Truly, I say to you, I do not know you." Watch therefore, for you know neither the day nor the hour.

Matthew 25.1-13

Rabbi Joshua ben Levi met Elijah at the mouth of the cave of Rabbi Simeon ben Yohai. He asked Elijah, "When will the Messiah come?" Elijah replied, "Go and ask him." "But where is he?" "At the gates of Rome." "And how shall I recognize him?" "He sits among the wretched who are suffering from sores; all the others uncover all their wounds, and then bind them all up again, but he uncovers and binds up each one separately, for he thinks, 'Lest I should be summoned and be detained.'"

Then Rabbi Joshua found him and said to him, "Peace be with you, my Master and Rabbi." The Messiah replied, "Peace be with you, son of Levi." He said, "When is the Master coming?" He replied, "Today."

Then Rabbi Joshua returned to Elijah, who said, "What did he say to you?" He replied, "Peace be with you, son of Levi." Elijah said, "Then he assured to you and your father a place in the world to come." The rabbi said, "He spoke falsely to me, for he said he would come today, and he has not come." Then Elijah said, "He meant 'today, if you hearken to His voice!' [Psalm 95.7]"[12]

Talmud, Sanhedrin 98a (Judaism)

But take heed to yourselves lest your hearts be weighed down with dissipation and drunkenness and cares of this life, and that day come upon you suddenly like a snare; for it will come upon all who dwell upon the face of the whole earth. But watch at all times, praying that you may have strength to escape all these things that will take place, and to stand before the Son of man.

Luke 21.34-36

Teachings of Sun Myung Moon

In the Last Days, where can you find the Will of God? Where can you find the truth, love and life of God? Would that all people find the one at the center that Will; he is the hope of all humanity.

But how can you find him? You must rectify your mind and purify it. If you make such preparations, then even if you are not seeking him, one day he will find you.

It is your responsibility to distinguish truth from falsehood. Do not expect that God will teach you. If God were to teach the truth, He would have to turn around and say it was false.[13] Accordingly, human beings must discern the truth on their own. They must be determined to seek it on their own and find it on their own. Learn from the Parable of the Wise and Foolish Virgins: of the ten who prepared their lamps only five could receive the Lord. (2:136, March 17, 1957)

How does the Lord come? In history, Jesus came through Judaism, the First Israel. But because it failed him, this time the Lord comes through Christianity, the Second Israel.

How, then, will he come? Many Christians believe the Bible's teaching that the Lord will come on the clouds. They have not heard that the Lord might come as a human being. However, as the Day approaches, people moved by the Spirit will testify to his coming in the flesh. Who will testify? They will be women more than men.

This current revival began with older ladies, women over sixty and seventy years old… who testified that the Lord would come as a human being, as Heaven directed them to prepare for the Last Days. (208:306, November 21, 1990)

3. The Seventh Millennium of Sabbath Rest

Blessed and holy is he who shares in the first resurrection! Over such the second death has no power, but they shall be priests of God and of Christ, and they shall reign with him a thousand years.

Revelation 20.6

As the land of Canaan had one year of release in seven, so has the world one millennium of release in seven thousand years; for it is said (Isa. 2.17), "And the LORD alone will be exalted in that day;" and again (Ps. 92.1), "A psalm or song for the Sabbath day," which means a long Sabbatic period, and again (Ps. 90.4), "For a thousand years in Thy sight are but as the day of yesterday."

The Tanna debe Eliyyahu teaches: The world is to last six thousand years. Two thousand of these are termed the period of disorder, two thousand belong to the dispensation of the Law, and two thousand are the days of the Messiah; but because of our iniquities a large fraction of the latter term is already passed and gone without the Messiah giving any sign of His appearing.

Talmud, Sanhedrin 97a (Judaism)

After six hundred years of the sixth millennium there will be open the gates of wisdom above and the fountains of wisdom below, and the world will make preparations to enter on the seventh millennium, as man makes preparations [for the Sabbath] on the sixth day of the week, when the sun is about to set…

The Holy One does not desire that so much [about the coming of the Messiah] should be revealed to the world, but when the days of the Messiah will be near at hand, even children will discover the secrets of wisdom and thereby be able to calculate the millennium; at that time it will be revealed to all…

"Let the LORD rejoice in His works" (Ps 104.31): He will cause souls to descend into the world and make them into new beings, so as to join the world into one. Happy are they who will be left alive at the end of the sixth millennium to enter the Sabbath. For it is the day set apart by the Holy One on which to effect the union of souls and to cull new souls to join those still on earth, as it is written, "He that is left in Zion... shall be called holy."

Zohar 1.117a-19a *(Judaism)*

There is a clear indication of this final Sabbath if we take the seven ages of world history as being 'days' and calculate in accordance with the data furnished by the Scriptures. The first age or day is that from Adam to the flood; the second from the flood to Abraham. (These two 'days' were not identical in length of time, but in each there were ten generations.) Then follow the three ages, each consisting of fourteen generations, as recorded in the Gospel of St. Matthew: the first, from Abraham to David; the second, from David to the migration to Babylon; the third, from then to Christ's nativity in the flesh. Thus, we have five ages. The sixth is the one in which we now are. It is an age not to be measured by any precise number of generations, since we are told: 'It is not for you to know the times or dates which the Father has fixed by His own authority.' (Acts 1.7) After this 'day,' God will rest on the 'seventh day,' in the sense that God will make us, who are to be this seventh day, rest in Him."

Saint Augustine, City of God 22.30 *(Christianity)*

Seventy weeks of years are decreed concerning your people and your holy city, to finish the transgression, to put an end to sin, and to atone for iniquity, to bring in everlasting righteousness, to seal both vision and prophet, and to anoint a most holy place. Know therefore and understand that from the going forth of the word to restore and build Jerusalem to the coming of an anointed one, a prince, there shall be seven weeks. Then for sixty-two weeks it shall be built again with squares and moat, but in a troubled time. And after the sixty-two weeks, an anointed one shall be cut off, and shall have nothing; and the people of the prince who is to come shall destroy the city and the sanctuary. Its end shall come with a flood, and to the end there shall be war; desolations are decreed. And he shall make a strong covenant with many for one week; and for half of the week he shall cause sacrifice and offering to cease; and upon the wing of abominations shall come one who makes desolate, until the decreed end is poured out on the desolator.

Daniel 9.24-27

Teachings of Sun Myung Moon

In the Old Testament Age, God taught the people through His servants and angels. In the New Testament Age, He worked through His Son. From then on, He works through the Holy Spirit. (10:197, October 2, 1960)

During the two-thousand-year period from Adam to Abraham, people had not yet fulfilled sufficient indemnity conditions to receive God's Word directly. At most, fallen people made indemnity conditions through offering sacrifices; but in doing so, they laid the foundation for the next period when God could begin to work His providence of restoration based on the Word. Hence, this period is called the age of the providence to lay the foundation for the Word.

During the two-thousand-year period from Abraham to Jesus, humanity's spirituality and intellect developed to the formation stage based on the Word revealed in the Old Testament. Hence, this period is called the formation stage of the providence, or the Old Testament Age.

During the two-thousand-year period from Jesus until the Second Coming, humanity's spirituality and intellect developed to the growth stage based on the Word revealed in the New Testament. Hence, this period is called the growth stage of the providence, or the New Testament Age.

During the period when the providence of restoration is to be completed after the Second Coming of Christ, humanity's spirituality and intellect are to develop through the completion stage based on the Completed Testament Word, which will be given for the fulfillment of the providence of restoration. Hence, this period is called the completion stage of the providence, or the Completed Testament Age. (*Exposition of the Divine Principle*, Restoration 2.2.1)

Paul said in I Corinthians 13, "And now faith, hope, and love abide, these three; and the greatest of these is love." We human beings, however, lost hope and faith through the Fall. By losing hope and faith, we also lost God-centered love. The six-thousand-year history of the providence of restoration was for the sake of restoring this love...

Examining these six thousand years, in the Old Testament Age people exerted effort in hope. In the New Testament Age people made effort in search of faith. The coming Completed Testament Age is the age for making effort in search of love.

In the Old Testament Age, circumcision was the condition made by the chosen people as they lived in hope. In the New Testament Age, baptism of water and the fire of the Holy Spirit established faith before God. In the coming Completed Testament Age, you will be able to enter into a loving relationship with God by receiving His seal of love. (5:108, January 4, 1959)

4. Signs of the Times

This gospel of the Kingdom will be preached throughout the whole world, as a testimony to all nations; and then the end will come.

Matthew 24.14

From the fig tree learn its lesson: as soon as its branch becomes tender and puts forth its leaves, you know that summer is near. So also, when you see all these things, you know that he is near, at the very gates.

Matthew 24.32-33

For behold, days are coming, says the LORD, when I will restore the fortunes of my people, Israel and Judah, says the LORD, and I will bring them back to the land which I gave to their fathers, and they shall take possession of it.

Jeremiah 30.3

And Jesus shall be a Sign of the Hour; therefore have no doubt about it, but follow Me: this is a straight way. [14]

Qur'an 43.61

Teachings of Sun Myung Moon

Through the benefit of the providence, the living God has now drawn near to us. From now on, people will have many spiritual experiences that they could not have earlier. They will communicate with the transcendent world. Through these frequent spiritual experiences, directly and indirectly, the transcendent world will influence people on earth. Especially people who are moved and inspired by God and the works of good spirits will develop their spiritual senses to center on God. Their character will go through a major transformation. People whose character is thus transformed to fit the heavenly way are the true people whom God has longed to see. (February 6, 2003)

As the time of the True Parents' advent draws near, all the nations in the world are inspired to join in brotherhood. Hence, after the Second World War the victorious countries liberated the defeated nations. They felt towards them like elder brothers. In a family, when the elder brother beats up his younger brother, afterwards he feels sorry for him and wants to deal kindly with him lest his father punish him. That is why the end of the Second World War saw events unprecedented in history. History unfolded in this way with the hope and goal of meeting the True Parents... and to prepare their way. (51:354, December 5, 1971)

The world's cultural spheres are converging toward one global cultural sphere based on one religion. Concurrently, nations are moving toward forming an apparatus for international governance, having progressed from the League of Nations to the United Nations. Today, people are envisioning plans for a world government. In the sphere of economics, the world is moving in the direction of establishing one international market. Highly developed transportation and communication technology have overcome the separation of time and space. People today can travel and communicate with each other almost as if they were all living in the same village. People of all races, from East and West, can meet with one another as easily as if they were members of a large family. People on all six continents are crossing the oceans seeking friendship and brotherly love. However, a family can be formed only when there is a father and a mother; only then can true brotherly love arise. Only when Christ comes again as the Parent of humanity will all people join together in one great family and live harmoniously in the global village.

As these events unfold, we may know that today is surely the Last Days. There is yet one final gift that history must present to humanity: it is the universal teaching which can bind together all the strangers of the global village into one family through the love and guidance of the same parents. (*Exposition of the Divine Principle*, Eschatology 4.3)

The Messiah

SCRIPTURES OF MANY RELIGIONS SPEAK OF A COMING LEADER who will consummate the fulfillment of the divine will on earth. He will manifest in his person the righteousness and compassion of God, bring about the final defeat of evil, and establish the Kingdom of Heaven on earth. The Hebrew title Messiah—Christ in Greek—means "anointed one," that person specially chosen by God for this mission and empowered to accomplish it.

While the term Messiah is specific to only Judaism and Christianity, prophecies that a leader will come and accomplish such a mission are nearly universal. Buddhists anticipate the coming of the Maitreya Buddha, and Hindu prophecies speak of a future avatar named Kalki. Muslims expect that the second advent of Jesus will be as a Muslim Imam, and Shiite Muslims look to a future Imam Mahdi. Zoroastrian scriptures prophesy the coming of the Saoshyant, and Confucian texts speak of a True Man who will bring peace to the world by perfectly instituting the Way of Confucius. Nevertheless, as this world is growing smaller and cultures increasingly interrelated, the task of world salvation should encompass all religions. Hence it is likely that God will send one person to fulfill all these religious hopes.

The next group of passages offer some specific prophecies about the Messiah's coming, along with samples of Father Moon's extensive teaching on these matters. Will the Messiah come supernaturally, as it were on the clouds, or naturally, born and raised as a human being on earth? Does the Messiah come in glory, or does he take the road of suffering and humiliation as did Jesus before him? Is the Messiah uniquely divine, or does he appear as the "first fruits" of a new, God-like humanity? How is the Messiah likened to Adam, and in what sense is he a new Adam? What is the meaning of the Marriage of the Lamb? Does the Messiah have a special mission to Israel?

The final group of passages consists of prophecies by Nostradamus and Asian mystics that speak of the Messiah appearing in the East, and even specifically in Korea. Especially the Korean prophecies relate directly to Father Moon's self-understanding of his messianic mission.

1. The Messiah and Savior Promised by All Religions

"Surely I am coming soon." Amen. Come, Lord Jesus!

Revelation 22.20

Behold, the days are coming, says the LORD, when I will raise up for David a righteous Branch, and he shall reign as king and deal wisely, and shall execute justice and righteousness in the land. In his days Judah will be saved, and Israel will dwell securely. And this is the name by which he will be called: "The LORD is our righteousness."

Jeremiah 23.5-6

In those days, brethren, there will arise in the world an Exalted One named Metteya [Maitreya]. He will be an Arahant, Fully Awakened, abounding in wisdom and goodness, happy, with knowledge of the worlds, unsurpassed as a guide to mortals willing to be led, a teacher for gods and men, an Exalted One, a Buddha, even as I am now. He, by himself, will thoroughly know and see, as it were face to face, this universe, with its worlds of the spirits, its Brahmas and its Maras, and its world of recluses and brahmins, of princes and peoples, even as I now, by myself, thoroughly know and see them. The Law, lovely in its origin, lovely in its progress, lovely in its consummation, will he proclaim, both in the spirit and in the letter; the higher life will he make known, in all its fullness and in all its purity, even as I do now. He will be accompanied by a congregation of some thousands of brethren, even as I am now accompanied by a congregation of some hundreds of brethren.[15]

Digha Nikaya 3.76 (Buddhism)

What will be your state when the Son of Mary descends amongst you, and there will be an Imam amongst you? What would you do when the son of Mary would descend and lead you? [16]

Hadith of Muslim (Islam)

The Imam [Mahdi] who will create a world state will make the ruling nations pay for their crimes against society. He will bring succor to humanity. He will take out the hidden wealth from the breast of the earth and will distribute it equitably amongst the needy deserving. He will teach you simple living and high thinking. He will make you understand that virtue is a state of character which is always a mean between the two extremes, and which is based upon equity and justice. He will revive the teaching of the Holy Qur'an and the traditions of the Holy Prophet after the world has ignored them as dead letters...

He will protect and defend himself with resources of science and supreme knowledge. His control over these resources will be complete. He will know how supreme they are and how carefully they will have to be used. His mind will be free from desires of bringing harm and injury to humanity. Such knowledge to him will be like the property which was wrongly possessed by others and for which he was waiting for the permission to repossess and use.

He, in the beginning, will be like a poor stranger unknown and uncared for, and Islam then will be in the hopeless and helpless plight of an exhausted camel who has laid down its head and is wagging its tail. With such a start he will establish an empire of God in this world.

He will be the final demonstration and proof of God's merciful wish to acquaint man with the right ways of life.

    Nahjul Balagha, Khutba 141, 187 *(Shiite Islam)*

When the practices taught by the Vedas and the institutes of law shall nearly have ceased, and the close of the Kali age shall be nigh, a portion of that divine being who exists of His own spiritual nature in the character of Brahma, and who is the beginning and the end, and who comprehends all things, shall descend upon the earth. He will be born as Kalki in the family of an eminent brahmin of Sambhala village, endowed with the eight superhuman faculties. By his irresistible might he will destroy all the barbarians and thieves, and all whose minds are devoted to iniquity. He will then reestablish righteousness upon earth; and the minds of those who live at the end of the Kali age shall be awakened, and shall be as pellucid as crystal. The men who are thus changed by virtue of that peculiar time shall be as the seeds of human beings, and shall give birth to a race that shall follow the laws of the Krita Age, the Age of Purity.

    Vishnu Purana 4.24 *(Hinduism)*

He shall be called the victorious Benefactor (Saoshyant) and World-renovator (Astavatereta). He is the Benefactor because he will benefit the entire physical world; he is the World-renovator because he will establish the physical living existence indestructible. He will oppose the evil of the progeny of the biped and withstand the enmity produced by the faithful.

    Avesta, Farvardin Yast 13.129 *(Zoroastrianism)*

It is only the man with the most perfect divine moral nature who is able to combine in himself quickness of apprehension, intelligence and understanding—qualities necessary for the exercise of command, magnanimity, generosity, benignity, and gentleness—qualities necessary for the exercise of patience, originality, energy, strength of character, and determination—qualities necessary for the exercise of endurance, piety, noble seriousness, order, and regularity—qualities necessary for the exercise of dignity, grace, method, subtlety, and penetration—qualities necessary for the exercise of critical judgment.

    Thus all-embracing and vast is the nature of such a man. Profound it is and inexhaustible, like a living spring of water, ever running out with life and vitality. All-embracing and vast, it is like Heaven. Profound and inexhaustible, it is like the abyss.

    As soon as such a man shall make his appearance in the world, all people will reverence him. Whatever he says, all people will believe it. Whatever he does, all people will be pleased with it. Thus his fame and name will spread and fill all the civilized world, extending even to savage countries, wherever ships and carriages reach, wherever the labor and enterprise of man penetrate, wherever the heavens overshadow and the earth sustain, wherever the sun and moon shine, wherever frost and dew fall. All who have life and breath will honor and love him. Therefore we may say, "He is the equal of God."

    It is only he in this world, who has realized his absolute self, that can order and adjust the great relations of human society, fix the fundamental principles of morality, and understand the laws of growth and reproduction of the universe.[17]

    Doctrine of the Mean 31-32 *(Confucianism)*

Teachings of Sun Myung Moon

Today the Jewish people long to see the Messiah and Christians also long to see the Messiah. They both wish for the Messiah. Will the Messiah of the Jews and the Messiah of the Christians be two different people? Will there be two different messiahs? No, there will be only one Messiah. Why? Because God's Will is one. Defeating Satan and fulfilling God's Will have to be done by one person. Hence, there can be only one Messiah. (73:206, September 18, 1974)

Christianity looks forward to the return of Christ; Buddhism hopes for the return of Buddha as the Maitreya, while Confucianism predicts the appearance of the True Man. Each religion describes in its way the return of the Lord.

When he comes, he will not simply restate the words of the Bible or repeat the words of an already established faith. The returning Lord awaited by these religions will come with a new truth of higher content. (7:198, September 6, 1959)

In God's sight, the world is one, only one. Therefore, the time will come when God will establish one prophet for the entire world. He could be an Asian; he could be a Westerner; he could be an African; he could be anyone. Whoever he is, this prophet will have a worldwide responsibility.

Through his leadership, the diverse religions of humankind will converge... eventually forming one world religion. The four major religions existing today will unite in one line, once they have ceased emphasizing the discordant elements that have kept them apart.

This will require the efforts of a central figure to pave the path for their unification, from bottom to top, and save all people on the planet Earth. God recognizes that person as the Messiah; therefore, we on earth proclaim that he is the Messiah. He comes as a universal religious leader, bringing a teaching that connects with the teachings of all religions.

The Messiah comes with a clear mission: to complete God's Will by fulfilling the purpose for which God created humankind. The failure of Adam and Eve broke this purpose, preventing God from establishing His Kingdom in the beginning. Therefore, the Messiah comes with the mission to attain the perfection that Adam did not attain and to complete the Will of God that Adam did not complete. Thus, the Messiah comes to consummate the Will of God on earth. (97:276, February 27, 1977)

2. The Mission of the Messiah— to Vanquish Evil and Establish God's Kingdom

Then I saw heaven opened, and behold, a white horse! He who sat upon it is called Faithful and True, and in righteousness he judges and makes war. His eyes are like a flame of fire, and on his head are many diadems, and he has a name inscribed which no one knows but himself. He is clad in a robe dipped in blood, and the name by which he is called is The Word of God. And the armies of heaven, arrayed in fine linen, white and pure, followed him on white horses. From his mouth issues a sharp sword with which to smite the nations, and he will rule them with a rod of iron; he will tread the wine press of the fury of the wrath of God the Almighty. On his robe and on his thigh he has a name inscribed, King of kings and Lord of lords.

Revelation 19.11-16

For to us a child is born,
to us a son is given,
and the government shall be upon his shoulder,
and his name shall be called
"Wonderful Counselor, Mighty God,
Everlasting Father, Prince of Peace."
Of the increase of his government and of peace
there will be no end,
upon the throne of David, and over his kingdom,
to establish it, and to uphold it
with justice and with righteousness,
from this time forth and for ever more.
The zeal of the LORD of hosts will do this.

Isaiah 9.6-7

The Imam [Mahdi] who will create a world state will make the ruling nations pay for their crimes against society. He will bring succor to humanity. He will take out the hidden wealth from the breast of the earth and will distribute it equitably amongst the needy deserving. He will teach you simple living and high thinking.

Nahjul Balagha, Khutba 141, 187 (Shiite Islam)

Then will appear the sign of the Son of man in heaven, and then all the tribes of the earth will mourn, and they will see the Son of man coming on the clouds of heaven with power and great glory; and he will send out his angels with a loud trumpet call, and they will gather his elect from the four winds, from one end of heaven to the other.

Matthew 24.30-31

Teachings of Sun Myung Moon

The Lord and Savior is coming! What will the Lord do when he comes? He is to rule the nation and the world. Will he rule arbitrarily, governing any way he pleases? No, he will rule with truth. Wherever in the world the Lord travels, he will govern with truth.

The Savior wants to make a world that is pleasing to God. More than that, he wants to make a world that rejoices the conscience. After all, since the human conscience originates from God, it knows what is pleasing to God and desires what God desires. In that world, there will be no racism or wars between nations. There will be no discrimination based on religion, ethnic background or cultural tradition. Instead, there will be universal agreement about what goodness is, and it will be in accord with God's view.

The day when we can march forward to such a world is coming; it is the time of the Savior's advent on earth. Christians call it the day of Christ's Second Coming. (160:345, June 15, 1969)

The mission of the Messiah is to complete the will of God. He comes to destroy Satan's evil sovereignty over this world. He comes to repair broken humanity and restore them to their original state of goodness and perfection. God sends him as the sovereign who will rule over the entire universe. (73:204, September 18, 1974)

Because the work of God is realistic and physical, the Messiah's coming on the clouds does not make sense. Yet interpreting the Bible literally, many Christians think, "Jesus will descend on the clouds! It will be done by God's power!" If that were true, if God could use supernatural power to do anything, then why did He need to send Jesus? Why would He call people to faith? In that case, God could simply create the Kingdom by Himself, without waiting for human beings to respond in faith… Yet, we know that even the omniscient and omnipotent God has been laboring for six thousand years and even longer to advance His providence of salvation without being able to send the [returning] Messiah until today…

Many Christians think that the Messiah will solve all the world's problems in an instant. They do not understand that when the Christ returns he will have to plough the ground and sow the seeds again. (90:141, December 25, 1976)

3. The Mission of the Messiah—To Restore True Human Beings and True Families

In the messianic future the Holy One will heal the injury [of Adam's sin]. He will heal the wound of the world.

Genesis Rabbah 10.4 (Judaism)

A man whose spirit shines brightly, a man whose mind is completely unified, a man whose virtue excels everyone—such a man will truly appear in this world. When he preaches the precious law, all the people will totally be satisfied—as if the thirsty drink sweet drops of rain from heaven. Each and every one will attain the path of liberation from struggles.

Sutra of the Great Accomplishment of the Maitreya (Buddhism)

"Hallelujah! For the Lord our God the Almighty reigns.
Let us rejoice and exult and give him the glory,
for the marriage of the Lamb has come,
and his Bride has made herself ready;
it was granted her to be clothed with fine linen, bright and pure"...

"Blessed are those who are invited to the marriage supper of the Lamb."

Revelation 19.6-9

Beloved, we are God's children now; it does not yet appear what we shall be, but we know that when he appears we shall be like him.[18]

1 John 3.2

Teachings of Sun Myung Moon

The man who comes as the Second Advent of the Lord is the primary example of a true individual. He is the first true man since the beginning of creation. (15:278, October 30, 1965)

The Lord will come as the True Parent. Because the human ancestors fell, they became false parents, and all humanity from birth has inherited the blood and flesh of these false parents.

Coming as the True Parent, the Messiah will unite humanity with God's love. Adam and Eve were supposed to marry in the love of God, but because of the Fall they could not. Now, six thousand years later, the Messiah resolves this problem by coming as the True Parent. He comes as the Bridegroom and receives his Bride. Christians refer to this as the Marriage of the Lamb. (32:266, July 19, 1970)

What is the mission of the coming Lord? He opens the path for humanity to receive God's love. Due to the fall, we lost our True Parents. Our ancestors were not supposed to fall; rather, they should have attained perfection and been installed as humanity's parents of goodness. Christ at the Second Advent reestablishes that position and hence enables humanity to receive the divine love they can have as members of the True Parents' beloved family.

Which is the greater happiness: When God's beloved sons and daughters live on earth as a family and go to heaven as a family? Or when a believing mother goes to heaven while the unbelieving father goes to hell—each family member to his or her own separate place? Truly, every human being should enter heaven, beginning with the parents and extending to all the children. That way, the whole family enters, the whole tribe enters, the whole nation enters, and the whole world enters.

Hence, these new Parents will give birth to a worldwide family. Their family relationship will be the basis for a new culture and tradition, rooted in a new teaching of love, which never before existed in human history. Once it makes its appearance on this planet Earth, this complicated sinful world will be transformed into the Kingdom of Heaven on earth. (52:324, February 3, 1972)

My teaching is that you should stand in the same position as Jesus and become a messiah to your tribe. (79:104, June 22, 1975)

The Messiah establishes the model for the ideal family of true love, which should expand to all families. All individuals are to be kings and messiahs. All individuals are to become true parents.

God is the True Parent, the True Teacher and the True Owner. Inherit the teaching of True Parents by practicing true love. Fulfill your role as a true teacher. Become like God, become the true owner. Truly, all my teachings are to enable you to fulfill the Ideal of the Three Great Subject Partners. (222:140, October 28, 1991)

4. The Messiah's Suffering Course

But first he must suffer many things and be rejected by this generation.

Luke 17.25

In the time to come... the Patriarchs will say, "Ephraim, our righteous Messiah, though we are your ancestors, you are greater than we. For you have borne the sins of our children, and you have borne heavy punishments, such as neither the former nor the latter generations have endured, and you became the laughter and the mocking of all the nations for Israel's sake, and you sat in darkness, and your eyes saw no light. And your skin shrank upon your bones, and your body withered like a tree, and your eyes grew dark from fasting, and your strength dried up like a potsherd, and all this befell you because of the sins of our children. Is it your will that your children should enjoy the felicity which God has destined to give them in abundance? Perhaps because of the pains which you have endured in overflowing measure for their sakes, and because thou hast lain fettered in prison, your mind is not at rest because of them?" The Messiah will reply, "Patriarchs, all that I have done, I have done only for your sakes and for your children, and for your honor and theirs, so that they may enjoy the felicity which God has destined for them in abundance." Then they reply, "May your mind be appeased, for you have appeased the mind of your Creator and our mind."[19]

Pesikta Rabbati 162b-63a (Judaism)

Teachings of Sun Myung Moon

Since Christ at the Second Advent must restore through indemnity the course of the providence of restoration left unfinished at Jesus' coming, he may have to follow a similar course. Jesus encountered disbelief among the Jewish people and had to walk a course of bitter suffering. Likewise, if Christians, the Second Israel, reject Christ at the Second Advent, he will have to go through tribulations comparable to those Jesus suffered. He will have to repeat Jesus' painful course and restore it through indemnity, but this time during his earthly life. For this reason, Jesus said, "But first he must suffer many things and be rejected by this generation." (Luke 17.25) (*Exposition of the Divine Principle*, Moses and Jesus 3.3.2)

Christian leaders today, like the Jewish leaders of Jesus' day, will probably be the first to persecute Christ at the Second Advent. Jesus came to found a new era which would fulfill the words of the Old Testament proclaimed by the prophets. He did not limit himself to repeating the words of the Old Testament, but gave new words of truth fit for the new era. The Jewish priests and scribes criticized

Jesus' words and deeds based on their narrow understanding of the Old Testament Scriptures. Their mistaken judgment led them to deliver Jesus to the cross.

Similarly, the purpose of Christ at the Second Advent is to build a new heaven and a new earth (Rev. 21.1-4) upon the foundation of the spiritual salvation which had been laid by Christianity in the New Testament Age. When he returns, he will not merely repeat the words of the New Testament given two thousand years ago, but will surely add new words of truth necessary for the founding of a new heaven and a new earth. However, those Christians of today whose minds are narrowly attached to the letter of the New Testament will criticize the words and deeds of Christ at his return based on their narrow understanding of the Scriptures. Therefore, it can be expected that they will brand the Lord a heretic and persecute him. This is why Jesus foretold that at the Second Advent, Christ would first suffer many things and be rejected by his generation. (Luke 17.25) (*Exposition of the Divine Principle*, Second Advent 4)

I, Reverend Moon, stood between God and Satan, always fighting to eliminate Satan. How could I proceed in this work without confronting Satan's accusation? I took the burden of restitution on myself, taking the required indemnity as my portion of responsibility. This is the human portion of responsibility [to defeat Satan], which people were not able to fulfill until now.

Satan knows that is the responsibility of the Messiah; therefore he mobilized all of his forces to attack me. By enduring and overcoming these attacks, I could destroy Satan's wall in the individual, the family, the tribe, the people, the nation, the world and the spirit world. It is the Messiah's responsibility to go through the entire course of indemnity. (131:70-71, April 16, 1984)

5. The Messiah Establishes Peace in the Middle East for Jews, Christians and Muslims

Behold, the days are coming, says the LORD, when I will raise up for David a righteous Branch,[20] and he shall reign as king and deal wisely, and shall execute justice and righteousness in the land. In his days Judah will be saved, and Israel will dwell securely... People shall no longer say, "As the LORD lives who brought up the people of Israel out of the land of Egypt," but "As the LORD lives who brought up and led the descendants of the house of Israel out of the north country and out of all the countries where he had driven them." Then they shall dwell in their own land.

Jeremiah 23.5-8

This world differs from the days of the Messiah only in respect of servitude to foreign powers.[21]

Talmud, Sanhedrin 99a (Judaism)

I will restore the fortunes of Jacob, and have mercy upon the whole house of Israel; and I will be jealous for my holy name. They shall forget their shame, and all the treachery they have practiced against me, when they dwell securely in their land with none to make them afraid, when I have brought them back from the peoples and gathered them from their enemies' lands... into their own land. I will leave none of them remaining among the nations any more; and I will not hide my face any more from them, when I pour out my Spirit upon the house of Israel, says the Lord GOD.

Ezekiel 39.25-29

Allah's Apostle said, "The Hour will not be established until the son of Mary [Jesus] descends amongst you as a just ruler, he will break the cross, kill the pigs, and abolish the *jizya* tax.[22] Money will be in abundance so that nobody will accept it (as charitable gifts)."

Hadith of Bukhari 3.656 (Islam)

Teachings of Sun Myung Moon

Had Jesus completed the providence of restoration through indemnity, then married and formed a family, he could have established at once a foundation of marriage Blessings that would have brought the people of Israel into Heaven's realm. Had he been able to go on to give the Blessing in Rome, he could have established the Kingdom of God on earth when he was in his forties.

Instead, Jesus was murdered. As a consequence, today the Israelis and Palestinians are fighting, although they are brothers. Originally, the world was supposed to have just one religion, one culture, one nation, and one realm of heart. Jesus came to make it so, but when he could not, then Islam came into being, Judaism came into being, and Christianity came into being. You need to know that these developments caused God much sorrow…

We have arrived at a time when Judaism, Islam, and Christianity should overcome their historical divisions and unite as one based on the Unification Principles. (August 15, 2003)

Jesus asks me, "Please, True Parents, save the people of Israel." That is why I am telling you Christian leaders to take down the cross. Take down your crosses, and perishing Christianity will revive. The cross was the rack of punishment and death. It has no place in the religion of the resurrection. Ask Jesus what he thinks about it. (January 1, 2003)

6. Prophecies of the Messiah's Advent in the East

No matter how long we wait there is no chance that he will come from Europe. It is Asia from whence he is to come. A great union will be born out of Hermes. He will surpass all the kings of the Orient. The country of the sun will maintain a great messianic law. A new leader of the spirit will come in the East.

Nostradamus, *Quatrains* 10.75

After three years of war,[23] when the land of Korea is devastated, there will begin to dawn the heavenly nation in the East. In the West, voices will cry out, "Cheong Do Ryeong, Cheong Do Ryeong!" and "Messiah, Messiah!" However, when that time comes, one must find the double bow and the double *ul* [the white cross], before one can partake of the great benefit.

This is the time when humankind meets the central fortune of Heaven. The eldest son of the East [Korea] meets and marries the eldest daughter of the Southeast [Japan].[24] Everyone covets and waits for the True Man, but who is he? He is the one who judges all good and evil.

The one who comes with the full power to administer Heaven and earth does not come from the mountains, nor from the fields, but from the place of the white cross. Verily, he comes with the heavenly law.

The number of the heavenly law is 21,600—the number denoting Heaven, and 14,400—the number denoting the earth. Their sum is 36,000 [the sum of yin and yang, Heaven and earth]. When good men and women in matrimony reach this number, the holy man will come.[25]

Yin and yang in harmony bring the fortune of the heavenly way. The united fortune of the East and the West is the Fortune of the Ten Victories.

This number changes the predisposition of nature. The religions of the East and the West come into good accord, and all the people of the world become as close as brothers and sisters. This is the manifest white cross, according to the principles of yin and yang, Heaven and earth.

The Great Way of the Ten Victories appears from the East. A thunderous voice calls out, offering the blessing. If you scorn this and go against it, your act will be as that of a praying mantis or cricket trying to stop a rolling wheel, and the holy man will only laugh.

Matching good men and women, the holy man will live comfortably. Receiving his matching and returning gratitude to God in prayer, they will receive precious children. Then the whole world will be united, such as has never happened from the dawn of creation.

In the East where the sun rises there will appear a white cross, and it will shine upon all corners of the world. The Cheong Do Ryeong is the Great King of the Ten Victories. Remember! He is the king of all kings!

Cheong Gam Nok

For as the lightning comes from the east and shines as far as the west, so will be the coming of the Son of man.

Matthew 24.27

Do not doubt that the heavenly Holy One will descend from Heaven in the East. If the East fails to recognize him, he will come to be known through newly educated Western people. If both East and West are unable to discern the One who is to come, both East and West will be discarded and new humankind will emerge. What can we do?

He returns from the West after receiving such regretful treatment, and looks down from the high mountain upon the world far away. In the latter half of the twentieth century, come to the East and undo all regrets...

Two holy men appear. The first one is not the real one, but the one who comes the second time is the Savior. When Heaven sends him to the earth secretively, his family name is Moon. When the message gets to the unwanted ones, they will cause problems for the Messiah because no human being wants to be defeated. Thus the Messiah appears amidst difficulties.

Kyeok Am Yu Rok

Teachings of Sun Myung Moon

The Korean people have long cherished a messianic hope, nurtured by the clear testimonies of their prophets. The First Israel believed in the testimonies of its prophets that the Messiah would come as their king, establish the Kingdom and bring them salvation. The Second Israel was able to endure an arduous path of faith due in part to their hope in the return of Christ. Similarly, the Korean people, the Third Israel, have believed in the prophecy that the Righteous King will appear and found a glorious and everlasting kingdom in their land. Clinging to this hope, they found the strength to endure their afflictions. This messianic idea among the Korean people was revealed through the *Cheong Gam Nok*, a book of prophecy written in the fourteenth century at the beginning of the Yi dynasty.

Because this prophecy foretold that a new king would emerge, the ruling class tried to suppress it. The Japanese colonial regime tried to stamp out this notion by burning the book and oppressing its believers. After Christianity became widely accepted, the idea was ridiculed as superstition. Nevertheless, this messianic hope still lives on, deeply ingrained in the soul of the Korean people. The hoped-for Righteous King foretold in the *Cheong Gam Nok* has the appellation *Cheong Do Ryeong* [The One Who Comes with the True Word of God]. In fact, this is a Korean prophecy of the Christ who is to return to Korea. Even before the introduction of Christianity to Korea, God had revealed through the *Cheong Gam Nok* that the Messiah would come to that land. (*Exposition of the Divine Principle,* Second Advent 3.3.4)

Just as the French prophet Nostradamus prophesied, and as is clearly recorded in one of the Orient's greatest books of prophesies, *Kyeok Am Yu Rok,* Reverend Moon has come as the one who has received Heaven's appointment. He is fulfilling the responsibilities of humanity's True Parent and the King of Peace. (May 1, 2004)

The surprising fact is that in the spirit world, the Founders of the five major religions gathered and declared that God is the Parent of humankind. They declared that Reverend Moon is the Savior and Messiah, the Second Coming of the Lord, and the True Parent. They also affirmed that the Unification Principle is a message of peace for the salvation of humanity. They declared that its core teaching, that we live for the sake of others with love, transcends religion, nationality, and race, and that practicing its teaching of true love will complete the peaceful unification of the cosmos. They further resolved that they would attend the True Parents and unite with one accord, devoting themselves for the sake of God's Kingdom and world peace. (July 11, 2003)

The Kingdom of Heaven

THE MILLENNIAL KINGDOM IS AN IDEAL WORLD without evil or sin, a world in which God's sovereignty is fully manifest. Hope for its advent can be found to some degree in every world religion, but it is most strongly expressed in the scriptures of Judaism and Christianity, as a firm promise of God. Sometimes the term Kingdom of Heaven denotes a spiritual ideal, a state of bliss in the afterlife (See Chapter 5: *Heaven*), but that sense of the term does not do justice to the most thoroughgoing eschatological visions. In this respect, Father Moon gives numerous clear teachings about the Kingdom to be established on earth. He has dedicated his life to fulfill God's calling to build that kingdom—not as a future vision but as a realistic program of human renewal.

These passages survey the Kingdom of Heaven from several perspectives. First, it is a world of God's absolute sovereignty. We note that this need not imply anything about the political system of such a world. No regime in history, even if it claimed to be instituting God's theocratic rule, has come anywhere close to the Kingdom in the true sense. God's dominion is by love, not political power. It is where goodness is vested with authority for its own sake, and God can rule through the hearts of good people.

Second, the Kingdom is a transfigured world—a new heaven and new earth—where all people live as one great human family. Giving and sharing is the norm; selfishness is unheard of. People know intimately the heart and will of God, rejoice in living by heaven's norms, and have no inward impediments to doing good. It is a world of peace, where nations no longer make war and people enjoy a life free from crime or oppression.

Third, the Kingdom requires a transformation of the self. Even if the world were at peace, if we still felt conflicted and disturbed, we would not feel comfortable and might continue to dwell in a private hell. Likewise, even though we might live in the most delightful environment, we could not enjoy it if our family were full of conflict and strife. Father Moon teaches that the family is a fundamental unit of the Kingdom.

Fourth, the Kingdom is a very natural place, free of artificiality or the constraint of external laws, because the spontaneous promptings of the heart would all be good. It is a place of dazzling beauty, where people's minds are like crystal, emanating divine light. Creation rejoices, as citizens of the Kingdom care for the environment with love and sensitivity to nature's ways.

Finally, the Kingdom transcends death. When the earthly world and the spirit world are united, the barrier of death will come down, allowing people to freely communicate with their loved ones on the other side.

1. The World of God's Sovereignty

The Lord will become king over all the earth; on that day the Lord will be one and His name one.

Zechariah 14.9

The sovereignty on that day will be God's. He will judge between them.

Qur'an 22.56

We therefore hope in Thee, O Lord our God, that we shall soon behold the triumph of Thy might, idolatry will be uprooted from the earth, and falsehood be utterly destroyed.

We hope for the day when the world will be perfected under the dominion of the Almighty and all mankind learn to revere Thy name; when all the wicked of the earth will be drawn in penitence unto Thee.

O may all the inhabitants of the world recognize that unto Thee every knee must bend, every tongue pledge loyalty. Before Thee, O Lord our God, may they bow in worship, and give honor to Thy glorious name.

May they all acknowledge Thy kingdom, and may Thy dominion be established over them speedily and forevermore. For sovereignty is Thine, and to all eternity Thou wilt reign in glory.

Daily Prayer Book, Alenu (Judaism)

Then the seventh angel blew his trumpet, and there were loud voices in heaven, saying, "The kingdom of the world has become the kingdom of our Lord and of his Christ, and he shall reign for ever and ever."

Revelation 11.15

Teachings of Sun Myung Moon

Once the sovereignty of Satan is expelled from the earth, then God, the eternal and absolute Being transcendent of time and space, will establish His sovereignty and His truth. In that day, God's truth will be absolute, and hence the purpose which it serves and the standard of goodness which it sets will both be absolute. This cosmic, all-encompassing truth will be firmly established by Christ at his Second Advent. (*Exposition of the Divine Principle,* Fall 4.3)

Did you find your original homeland? You did not. Actually, you never had it. Your original homeland is the Kingdom of God on earth. Is there any nation on earth that can qualify as the nation of the original homeland? No, there is no such nation. Then, where can we expect to establish the original home nation? It should encompass the whole planet Earth. It shall be the Kingdom of God on earth and the Kingdom of God in heaven as well.

    Three major elements are required to establish a country: sovereignty, land, and people. Does God have sovereignty anywhere in the world today? No! Does God have a land to govern? No! Are there any people in the world that allows itself to be governed by God? No! Therefore, we do not have our homeland. Eventually, God should have sovereignty over a nation called Earth and a people called Humanity. Until that day, this world is actually not a fit place for human beings to live. (155:26, October 6, 1964)

Father! Please bestow blessings upon this people and blessings upon all the people of the world.

Please resolve the grief of the many spirit people waiting in heaven for the day of the Second Advent.

May it quickly be realized—the world which Thou art able to govern, the Kingdom of peace on the earth, resolving Thy grief and Jesus' grief.

Earnestly, earnestly we ask Thee: may the day quickly come when we can return glory to Thee and rejoice together with Thee, when the earth is filled with glory and victory for eternity. (16:52, December 26, 1965)

2. A New World of Peace and Joy

Then I saw a new heaven and a new earth; for the first heaven and the first earth had passed away, and the sea was no more. And I saw the holy city, new Jerusalem, coming down out of heaven from God, prepared as a bride adorned for her husband; and I heard a loud voice from the throne saying, "Behold, the dwelling of God is with men. He will dwell with them, and they shall be his people, and God himself will be with them. He will wipe away every tear from their eyes, and death shall be no more, neither shall there be mourning nor crying nor pain any more, for the former things have passed away."

And he who sat upon the throne said, "Behold, I make all things new." Also he said, "Write this, for these words are trustworthy and true." And he said to me, "It is done! I am the Alpha and the Omega, the beginning and the end. To the thirsty I will give from the fountain of the water of life without payment. He who conquers shall have this heritage, and I will be his God and he shall be my son."...

And I saw no temple in the city, for its temple is the Lord God the Almighty and the Lamb. And the city has no need of sun or moon to shine upon it, for the glory of God is its light, and its lamp is the Lamb. By its light shall all the nations walk; and the kings of the earth shall bring their glory into it, and its gates shall never be shut by day—and there shall be no night there; they shall bring into it the glory and the honor of the nations. But nothing unclean shall enter it, nor any one who practices abomination or falsehood, but only those who are written in the Lamb's book of life.

Revelation 21.1-27

It shall come to pass in the latter days
that the mountain of the house of the LORD
shall be established as the highest of the
   mountains,
and shall be raised above the hills;
And all the nations shall flow to it;
and many peoples shall come, saying,
"Come, let us go up to the mountain of the LORD,
to the house of the God of Jacob;
That he may teach us his ways
and that we may walk in his paths."
For out of Zion shall go forth the law,
and the word of the LORD from Jerusalem.
He shall judge between the nations,
and shall decide for many peoples;
They shall beat their swords into ploughshares,
and their spears into pruning hooks;
Nation shall not lift up sword against nation,
neither shall they learn war any more.

Isaiah 2.2-4

In the City Joyful dwell the saints of God;
Neither suffering nor sorrow is found therein;
Neither anxiety to pay tribute nor any imposts;
Neither fear of retribution nor of fall from
   eminence.
In this happy land where my dwelling is,
Abides unending well-being.
All who therein dwell are blessed with eternal
   kingship;
None is there reckoned inferior to any.
That city knows no decline;
Its citizens are rich and fulfilled.
Unlimited their freedom—
None are alien there;
All in true liberty abide.
Says Ravidas, the emancipated cobbler,
Only a citizen of that City reckon I my friend.

Adi Granth, Gauri, Ravidas, p. 345 (Sikhism)

On the day when We shall roll up heaven as a scroll is rolled for the writings; as We originated the first creation, so We shall bring it back again—a promise binding on Us; so We shall do. For We have written in the Psalms, after the Remembrance, "The earth shall be the inheritance of My righteous servants."

Qur'an 21.104

Teachings of Sun Myung Moon

God had a purpose when He created human beings, and if that purpose had been fulfilled, this world would be one great human family, unified in love, where all humanity would live in peace as brothers and sisters attending God as their Parent...

In the ideal world, each individual's mind and body would be one, families would be one with each other, all ethnic groups would be one with each other, all nations would be one, the Orient and the Occident would be one, and God and humanity would be one. That is to say, the unified world is a world that fulfills God's purpose of creation. (81:158)

"I exist for my family, my family exists for my community, my community exists for my nation, my nation exists for the world, and the world exists for God": This is the principle of Heaven's sovereignty. The whole world is God's, but since you are living for God, the world is yours as well. What is God's—the whole world—becomes yours. Isn't it wonderful? When you offer what is yours for your family, your family offers itself for your nation, your nation for the world, and the world for God, then God gives everything to you. The whole world is yours; the entire universe is yours.

God's ultimate desire is for humanity to establish the Kingdom of Heaven on earth. There God and human beings will be totally united, from the True Parents at the center expanding to true children, true tribes and true peoples. God will be our Father and we will be His children in a consecrated relationship that is free from sin, according to the holy Will of God that does not allow for sin. The Kingdom of Heaven on earth will be established only when we make a world where everyone lives for the sake of others. (69:89, October 20, 1973)

In the future there will be no more wars. Wars until now were useless fights for selfish ends. People fought simply to take from others. However, in the unified world established under God's Kingship, everyone will live for the sake of others; therefore war will no longer be necessary. People will no longer want to take from their neighbors; instead your neighbors will try to give you so much that you will have to run away from them...

Laws will disappear. In a world where people govern themselves with love, they will automatically fulfill the law. When people live for the sake of each other, there will be no problems requiring recourse to the law. Higher and lower will become one, front and back will become one, left and right will become one—all will become one. (224:173, November 24, 1991)

The age is coming when God and humankind will live as one in the ideal world of creation, the world of heart. The age is coming when everyone will realize that living for the sake of others holds greater eternal value than living for the self. The blind age of selfish life will pass away as we build an altruistic world of interdependence, mutual prosperity and universally shared values. For this purpose, all should have correct knowledge about God and the spirit world and testify to the world about the heavenly path; then we can lead humanity appropriately to establish the universal family. Therefore, let us work to establish God's fatherland and hometown, the Kingdom of God on earth and in heaven, by investing ourselves for the sake of others with absolute love, unchanging love and eternal true love, looking to the day when we can offer all heavenly sovereignty to God. (December 27, 2002)

In the ideal society or nation, all people, transcending nationality and skin color, will cooperate with one another to live in harmony and happiness. With the awareness that they are all children of the one God, stemming from the one True Parents, they will relate as brothers and sisters in one global family. Blessed central families, who have restored their lineage, the realms of ownership and heart, and who are united with the True Parents' language and culture, will take the lead in establishing a world of freedom, peace and unity. There, all people will live in interdependence, promote mutual prosperity and share universal values, immersed in the culture of God's heart.[26]

Therefore, this world will have nothing to do with corruption, injustice, war or crime. Humankind will eliminate the sources of pollution in the global environment, and love and protect nature as its true owner. People will labor and perform their daily tasks joyfully and with a loving heart, always aiming to serve and benefit others. This will gradually equalize people's standards of living. Education will include highly developed technological and scientific material; but before knowledge, sports or technology, priority will be given to education of the heart and norms of blessed family life, in order to raise the chosen people who can follow the way of Heaven. (269:156-57, April 3, 1995, New Hope Farm Declaration)

3. A World of Godly People Who Possess the Kingdom within Themselves

For the creation waits with eager longing for the revealing of the sons of God; for the creation was subjected to futility, not of its own will but by the will of Him who subjected it in hope; because the creation itself will be set free from its bondage to decay and obtain the glorious liberty of the children of God. We know that the whole creation has been groaning in travail together until now; and not only the creation, but we ourselves, who have the first fruits of the Spirit, groan inwardly as we wait for adoption as sons, the redemption of our bodies.

Romans 8.19-23

Behold, the Kingdom of God is within you.

Luke 17.21

The kingdom of heaven may be compared to a king who gave a marriage feast for his son... But when the king came in to look at the guests, he saw there a man who had no wedding garment; and he said to him, "Friend, how did you get in here without a wedding garment?"[27] And he was speechless. Then the king said to the attendants, "Bind him hand and foot, and cast him into the outer darkness; there men will weep and gnash their teeth."

Matthew 22.1-13

Behold, the days are coming, says the LORD, when I will make a new covenant with the house of Israel and the house of Judah, not like the covenant which I made with their fathers when I took them by the hand to bring them out of the land of Egypt, my covenant which they broke, though I was their husband, says the LORD. But this is the covenant which I will make with the house of Israel after those days, says the LORD: I will put my law within them, and I will write it upon their hearts; and I will be their God, and they shall be my people. And no longer shall each man teach his neighbor and each his brother, saying, "Know the LORD," for they shall all know me, from the least of them to the greatest, says the LORD; for I will forgive their iniquity, and I will remember their sin no more.

Jeremiah 31.31-34

Confucius said, "The practice of the Great Tao and the eminent men of the Three Dynasties—this I have never seen in person, and yet I have a mind to follow them. When the Great Tao prevailed, the world was a commonwealth; men of talent and virtue were selected, mutual confidence was emphasized, and brotherhood was cultivated. Therefore, men did not regard as parents only their own parents, nor did they treat as sons only their own sons. Old people were able to enjoy their old age; young men were able to employ their talents; juniors respected their elders; helpless widows, orphans, and cripples were well cared for. Men had their respective occupations, and women their homes. They hated to see wealth lying about in waste, and they did not hoard it for their own use. They hated not to use their energies, and they used their energies not for their own benefit. Thus evil schemings were repressed, and robbers, thieves, and traitors no longer appeared, so that the front door remained open. This was called the Grand Unity (Ta-tung).

Book of Ritual 7.1.2 (Confucianism)

As earthly paradise moves into its advanced stages, people's inner attitudes towards God will directly affect more and more aspects of daily life. Those whose souls are closer to God will be so much of the same heart that they can communicate without verbalizing their thoughts and feelings. By this stage, contemplation will have become the mode of existence for everyone. God will have given them such highly refined powers of spiritual perception that they can at last see His will directly and perfectly understand what is in the hearts and minds of others.

In its ultimate phase, paradise on earth will be so perfect, so unblemished, that it may be called the Crystal World. All evil and hatred will have been cleansed away. The world will have become the final realization of absolute goodness and love. Completely free from even a hint of sin or impurity, humankind at last will dwell in the heavenly abode longed for through the ages. This is the Crystal World of unity with God.

Johrei (Sekai Kyusei Kyo)

Teachings of Sun Myung Moon

The ideal society is a place where the ideal of love is perfectly realized. It is a beautiful world, where people who have substantiated God's love in themselves live in complete satisfaction of heart. Their faces are beautiful, radiating eternal light. All perfected human beings shine with such internal beauty. (Way of God's Will 1.8)

If you have not ended the fighting within yourself, then even if you lived in a world where people ceased to fight and all the nations were at peace, you would still feel out of place, without any peace or happiness. The problem is in you. You must first solve the fundamental problem within yourself. Only then, when you encounter an ideal environment in the world outside of you, will you feel its peace seeping into your heart and its happiness encompassing your soul. Only when you create the foundation for the Kingdom of Heaven within yourself will you experience freedom and happiness in the world around you. Your outward circumstances may be perfect, but if you have not resolved your personal problems, you will not be able to fit in with those circumstances. You will not be fully happy. (20:167, June 9, 1968)

First, you have to establish the Kingdom of Heaven as an individual. Next, you have to establish the Kingdom of Heaven as a couple. What is the Kingdom of Heaven as a couple? It is the state of matrimony where a man and woman are totally united as one. It is not like a typical marriage where in the beginning you tell your spouse, "I love you," but after a few years you say good-bye and divorce... A heavenly couple is inseparable; they could lose their legs by exploding dynamite but still keep embracing with their upper bodies! That is possible only with true love. To achieve that kind of love, your mind and body must be completely united. Then you can attain the Kingdom of Heaven as a couple.

After you realize the Kingdom of Heaven as a couple, would you be satisfied? No, you would want to realize the Kingdom of Heaven as a family. When father and mother become totally one and love each other, their son will think that he wants to marry a bride just like his mother, and the daughter will think that she wants to marry a man just like her father. The father and mother acting as a plus guide their sons and daughters as a minus: that family unity is the Kingdom of Heaven as a family.

Once we realize the Kingdom of Heaven in our families, finally we will be able to establish the Kingdom of Heaven on earth, which is God's ideal. (96:29, January 1, 1978)

The original Garden was to be an ideal place. There the spirit world and physical world would be open to each other, and the feelings of siblings could be communicated freely all the way to the ends of the universe. It would not be like the present-day world, divided among ethnic sentiments, where national sovereignties clash, and where ideologies and religions are at odds with each other. In that world, people would discuss all matters from the heart. The heart does not discriminate by race, nationality, or other such things. Hence, people would easily be able to reconcile their differences, such as economic disparities and cultural misunderstandings. (7:37, July 5, 1959)

From perfected individuals and families up to the perfection of the cosmos, a beautiful world will emerge—the Kingdom of Heaven on earth and in spirit world. It will be a world of freedom. God also will be free, and He will be able to visit your family anytime He desires. Until now, there were barriers everywhere, blocking everyone from going where they wished. Now all the walls and barriers that Satan created will be torn down and everywhere will be level. Then God will form the same perpendicular connection with everyone. Around that ninety-degree axis, everything—front and back, left and right, high and low—will relate freely. All will enter the realm of liberation and unification. That is the Kingdom of Heaven. (313:243, December 19, 1999)

4. A Kingdom Encompassing Both the Earthly World and the Spirit World, Where There Is No Death

Then comes the end, when he [Christ] delivers the kingdom to God the Father after destroying every rule and every authority and power. For he must reign until he has put all his enemies under his feet. The last enemy to be destroyed is death.

1 Corinthians 15.24-26

The victorious World-Renovator and his helpers... shall make existence renovated—ageless, deathless, never decaying, incorruptible, ever living, ever benefiting, ruling at will. The dead shall rise up, life shall prevail indestructible, and existence shall be renovated at the will of God!

Avesta, Zamyad Yast 19.11 (*Zoroastrianism*)

The holy man told them, "I'll give you something to eat that will kill you, but don't be afraid; I'll bring you back to life again." They believed him. They ate something and died, then found themselves walking in a new, beautiful land. They spoke with their parents and grandparents, and with friends that the white soldiers had killed. Their friends were well, and this new world was like the old one, the one the white man had destroyed. It was full of game, full of antelope and buffalo. The grass was green and high, and though long-dead people from other tribes also lived in this land, there was peace. All the Indian nations formed one tribe and could understand each other. Kicking Bear and

Short Bull walked around and saw everything, and they were happy. Then the holy man of the Paiutes brought them back to life again.

"You have seen it," he said, "the new land I'm bringing. The earth will roll up like a blanket with all that bad white man's stuff, the fences and railroads and mines and telegraph poles, and underneath will be our old-young Indian earth with all our relatives come to life again." Then the holy man taught them a new dance, a new song, a new prayer. He gave them sacred red paint... Now everywhere we are dancing this new dance to roll up the earth, to bring back the dead. A new world is coming.

Ghost Dance *(Native American Religion)*

Teachings of Sun Myung Moon

The Kingdom of Heaven that God desires is not established only in the spirit world. The Kingdom is established first on the earth and then in the spirit world. Since the spirit world is formed by spirits of people who formerly lived on the earth, the spirit world and the physical world are inextricably linked.

If you want to have a substantial foundation to realize the teaching of the Kingdom of Heaven, you must live in accordance with the principles of heaven as well as the laws of human beings. By demonstrating the principles of heaven in your daily life, you connect heaven's laws with human laws. Furthermore, the principles of heaven do not only concern individual life; they contain the principles for families, societies, nations, the world and cosmos. You must realize these principles of heaven in yourselves. (2:226, June 2, 1957)

When as individuals we make God's love our love, and when we extend that to families, tribes, peoples and nations, we can establish the Kingdom of God on earth and the Kingdom of God in heaven. Upon that earthly foundation of true love, a corresponding foundation will form in the spirit world. When that foundation on earth reaches the national level, then the spirit world will also have a national foundation. Then it will automatically open and become one with the earth. (134:217, July 20, 1985)

The Kingdom of Heaven on earth will not be established unless we prepare a foundation on the earth through which we can move between physical and spirit worlds, beyond the limitation of death. Without the Kingdom of Heaven on earth, there will be no Kingdom of Heaven in the spirit world. You should arrange things in such a way that after you go to spirit world, you can come back to earth at will. That is the way to live in the Kingdom of Heaven on earth and create the Kingdom of Heaven in heaven simultaneously. (146:223, July 1, 1986)

Part Three

The Path of Life

Chapter 11

Growth, Responsibility and Destiny

Spiritual Growth

GROWTH IS A FACT OF NATURE; nothing springs forth fully formed but passes through a process of growth from inception to completion. The same principle that applies to the growth of the body also applies to the growth of the spirit—"from stage to stage." The stages of growth are described in many ways: by the metaphor of sprouting grain, or the four seasons, or grades at school.

Only upon reaching maturity, which is a state of spiritual perfection, can a human being fully participate in the love of God and take his or her place in God's Kingdom. What is spiritual perfection? It is unity of mind and body, when you are free from the constant struggle with the flesh to do what is right; it is, attaining the fullness of Christ; it is oneness with God's constant and loving mind.

O man! Verily you are ever toiling on towards your Lord—painfully toiling—but you shall meet Him... You shall surely travel from stage to stage.

Qur'an 84.6, 19

To the pupil training, in the straight way walking,
By ending [his sins] first comes knowledge;
Straight follows insight; by that insight freed
He knows in very truth: Sure is my freedom
By wearing out the fetter of becoming.

Itivuttaka 53 (Buddhism)

By the... soul, and Him who perfected it
and inspired it with conscience of what is
    wrong for it and right for it:
He is indeed successful who causes it to grow,
and he is indeed a failure who stunts it.

Qur'an 91.7-10

Practicing step by step,
One gradually fulfills all Buddha teachings.
It is like first setting up a foundation

Then building the room:
Generosity and self-control, like this,
Are bases of enlightening beings' practices.

Garland Sutra 10 (Buddhism)

The kingdom of God is as if a man should scatter seed upon the ground, and should sleep and rise night and day, and the seed should sprout and grow, he knows not how. The earth produces of itself, first the blade, then the ear, then the full grain in the ear. But when the grain is ripe, at once he puts in the sickle, because the harvest has come.[1]

Mark 4.26-29

Muhammad is the Apostle of God; and those who are with him are strong against unbelievers, but compassionate amongst each other... And their similitude in the Gospel is: Like a seed which sends forth its blade, then makes it strong; it then becomes thick, and it stands on its own stem, filling the sowers with wonder and delight.

Qur'an 48.29

Heaven has only spring, summer, autumn, and winter. Humans have only humanity, rectitude, propriety, and wisdom... There are only these four principles. There is nothing else. Humanity, rectitude, propriety and wisdom are origin, growth, perfection, and fulfillment. If in spring nothing has sprouted or been born, then in summer there will be no way for growth to take place, and in autumn and winter it will be impossible to harvest and store.

Chu Hsi (Confucianism)

Grace was given to each of us according to the measure of Christ's gift... to equip the saints for the work of ministry, until we all attain to the unity of the faith and of the knowledge of the Son of God, to mature manhood, to the measure of the stature of the fullness of Christ; so that we may no longer be called children, tossed to and fro on every wind of doctrine, by the cunning of men, by their craftiness in deceitful wiles. Rather, speaking truth in love, we are to grow up in every way into him who is the head, into Christ—from whom the whole body, joined and knit together by every joint with which it is supplied, when each part is working properly, makes bodily growth and upbuilds itself in love.

Ephesians 4.7-16

Becoming a Christian can be the act of a moment; being a Christian is the act of a lifetime. I have grown to understand more fully what Jesus meant when He spoke of spiritual commitment and conversion as being "born again" (John 3.3). Physical birth is a process, moving from conception through the period of gestation to the miracle of the moment of birth. But birth is not only the end of one process—it is the beginning of another, the process of growth. The same should be true spiritually. My commitment to Christ was a "spiritual rebirth," but this was to be followed by spiritual growth.

Billy Graham, *The Courage of Conviction*
(Christianity)

In regard to the principle of human life, God infused into it a capacity for reasoning and intellection. In infancy, this mental capacity seems, as it were, asleep and practically non-existent, but in the course of years it awakens into a life that involves learning and education, skill in grasping the truth and loving the good.

This capacity flowers into that wisdom and virtue which enable the soul to battle with the arms of prudence, fortitude, temperance, and justice against error, waywardness, and other inborn weaknesses, and to conquer them with a purpose that is no other than that of reaching the supreme and immutable Good.

Saint Augustine, City of God 22.24 *(Christianity)*

The desirable is called "good." To have it in oneself is called "true." To possess it fully in oneself is called "beautiful," but to shine forth with this full possession is called "great." To be great and be transformed by this greatness is called a "sage"; to be a sage and to transcend the understanding is called "divine."

Mencius VII.B.25 *(Confucianism)*

Teachings of Sun Myung Moon

All phenomena occurring in the universe bear fruit only after the lapse of a certain interval of time. All things are designed to reach completion only after passing through a set growing period...

It is written in Genesis that God warned Adam and Eve, "Of the tree of the knowledge of good and evil you shall not eat, for in the day that you eat of it you shall die." (Gen. 2.17) They had a choice either to ignore God's warning and lose their lives, or to heed the warning and live. The fact that they had the potential either to fall or to become perfect demonstrates that they were still in a state of immaturity. The universe was designed to reach perfection after a certain growing period, described in the Bible as six days. As one of God's creations, human beings are also bound to this principle. (*Exposition of the Divine Principle*, Creation 5.2)

We should not think that when God created Adam and Eve from clay, He created them as adults. Rather, God created them as infants. God went through the same process as a mother who gives birth to her baby, cradles it and raises it.

Everything in the universe develops through three stages, and humans are no exception. Beginning from infancy, Adam and Eve grew through childhood and their teenage years. The next step was to be their maturation…

An individual proceeds from an infant to an adult, marries and becomes a parent. In a human being's stage-wise growth, God wants to see the embodiment of His own lengthy growth process—his youth, His adulthood and His advanced age. Thus, every child is the substantial manifestation of God's invisible history. This shared experience binds the child and his or her vertical Parent into one. (225:198-99, January 20, 1992)

God Himself must have gone through stages of growth—infancy, childhood, etc. You should know that your wife is the invisible God grown into a substantial physical being…

As parents watching your children grow, you will relive the days when you were growing up. It is the same with God. God watched with amazement as Adam and Eve grew and created their horizontal sphere of life.[2] Likewise, when you have your children, you will experience a force of love that will expand your (horizontal) world. (297:151-53, November 19, 1998)

For a tree to bear fruit, it must go through a summer season when the growing fruits absorb vitality elements from its root, trunk and branches. Through this process it gains the perfect life force to produce fruit that will bring forth new life. In this regard, we sons and daughters… should search deeply within ourselves as to whether the fruit in our hearts is full of the power of life, by which we can be born again happily into a new world.

No matter how many years go by, how much it rains or how fiercely the wind blows, our inner life force must not be invaded by the evil of our environment but must go the path of continuous development. That is the only way we can welcome the spring and become a seed—a matrix to produce a second life wherever it is planted. (32:37, June 14, 1970)

To yield good seed, you have to go the path of love. This means that you must be born in love, grow with love as the purpose of your life, and walk the path of love your whole life long. Even at the moment when you depart this world, you should leave with the intention to return to love. (138:99, January 19, 1986)

Spiritual growth can be compared to education… When someone is studying for a Ph.D., does he deny what he learned in kindergarten? Not at all. All his prior learning, well digested, formed the foundation for his efforts to earn the Ph.D. (111:129, February 8, 1981)

You must receive an education in God's love. For how long? Until you can understand all the Father's values and standards. In other words, you grow by receiving your parents' love until you are fully mature. (51:172, November 21, 1971)

God's central concern is with human beings' internal nature and character. He intends that, as we experience true love, we will come to reflect His true love and grow to perfection. God created the power of love to be the strongest among all internal forces. Through experiencing the power of such love within the realm of Heaven's love and law, people are to increasingly resemble God, their Parent. (279:206, August 20, 1996)

We need to embody true love. The way to embody true love begins by living as a filial child, then a patriot, a saint, and finally a divine son and daughter of God. At that stage we can experience the innermost emotions of God's heart. (September 12, 2005)

The Seasons of Life

LIFE HAS ITS SEASONS: YOUTH, ADOLESCENCE, ADULTHOOD and old age. Youth is a time to learn, when one is malleable and most open to instruction; adolescence is a time of exploration that requires self-discipline; the twenties is the time to set up the foundations of family and career; and middle age is the time to accomplish one's goals. Old age finally arrives, displaying the fruits of one's life. It is a time to manifest either the wisdom gained through a lifetime of living a moral life and practicing spiritual discipline, or the decrepitude of a wasted life. Once it has drawn nigh, it is too late to change. More passages on the stages of the human life cycle are found throughout Chapter 19.

1. Childhood and Adolescence

Every child is born of the nature of purity and submission to God.

Hadith of Bukhari *(Islam)*

Let the children come to me, and do not hinder them, for to such belongs the kingdom of God. Truly, I say to you, whoever does not receive the kingdom of God like a child shall not enter it.

Luke 18.16-17

The great man is he who does not lose his child's heart.

Mencius IV.B.12 *(Confucianism)*

You can only coil a fish when it is fresh.

Nupe Proverb *(African Traditional Religions)*

Elisha ben Abuyah said: If one learns when a youth, to what is it like? It is as ink written on new paper. If one learns when an old man, it is as ink written on erased paper.

Mishnah, Avot 4.25 *(Judaism)*

For though by this time you ought to be teachers, you need some one to teach you again the first principles of God's word. You need milk, not solid food; for every one who lives on milk is unskilled in the word of righteousness, for he is a child. But solid food is for the mature, for those who have their faculties trained by practice to distinguish good from evil.

Hebrews 5.12-14

I write to you, young men, because you are strong, and the word of God abides in you, and you have overcome the evil one.

1 John 2.14

You will be running to the four corners of the universe:
To where the land meets the big water;
To where the sky meets the land;
To where the home of winter is;
To the home of rain.
Run this! Run!
Be strong!
For you are the mother of a people.

Apache Initiation Song (Native American Religions)

Teachings of Sun Myung Moon

Father! We must become children, children who implore Thee, "We are hungry" when we are hungry. Children are thirsty for their mother's love. Children are simple and innocent. The more they are raised, brought up and gently embraced, the more they grow to follow their parents' standard...

Please allow us to have hearts that long for Thee, like hungry babes longing for their mother's milk. (20:11, March 31, 1968)

Wouldn't it be wonderful if God had created Adam and Eve complete and perfect? But that is not how the universe works. All things begin from the bottom-most stage and grow to reach their proper level. Thus, Adam and Eve should begin their lives as babies and grow up. They are not meant to have a complete relationship with the universe in an instant.

When a young man reaches the age of fifteen, sixteen and seventeen, he comes to enjoy the world of male-female relationships. He feels romantic, poetic yearnings. Don't teenagers feel that way? They would like to leave home, travel all over the world and find adventure on land and sea. That is when their eyes are wide open to find a partner for love. (January 8, 1984)

Adolescence is the time to give off fragrance. It spreads far and wide, attracting the bees and butterflies. That is why young men and women want to become the top champion, the top student, the top everything. (56:262, January 2, 1972)

Today's teenagers are wild; they hook up with anyone willy-nilly. By doing so, they bring about their own ruin and society's ruin. Yet, because adolescence is a time of change, teens cannot settle with one partner; they go from one relationship to another.

Therefore, teenagers need to follow a definite discipline and be aware of the dangerous circumstances in which they live. You [parents] need to straighten them out. You need to clear up the complications in their lives. (118:197, June 1, 1982)

2. Maturity and Old Age

The Master said, "At fifteen I set my heart upon learning. At thirty, I had planted my feet upon firm ground. At forty, I no longer suffered from perplexities. At fifty, I knew what were the biddings of Heaven. At sixty, I heard them with a docile ear. At seventy, I could follow the dictates of my own heart; for what I desired no longer overstepped the boundaries of right."

Analects 2.4 (Confucianism)

Respect the young. How do you know that they will not one day be all that you are now? But if a man has reached forty or fifty and nothing has been heard of him, then I grant there is no need to respect him.

Analects 9.22 (Confucianism)

If the hair has become white, a man does not on that account become old; though a man may be young, if he is learned the gods look upon him as old.

Laws of Manu 2.136 (Hinduism)

You cannot prolong your life, therefore be not careless; you are past help when old age approaches.

Uttaradhyayana Sutra 4.1 (Jainism)

The man of little learning grows old like the ox. His muscles grow but his wisdom grows not.

Dhammapada 152 (Buddhism)

Remember also your Creator in the days of your youth, before the evil days come, and the years draw nigh, when you will say, "I have no pleasure in them"; before the sun and the light and the moon and the stars are darkened and the clouds return after the rain; in the day when the keepers of the house tremble, and the strong men are bent, and the grinders cease because they are few, and those that look through the windows are dimmed, and the doors on the street are shut; when the sound of the grinding is low, and one rises up at the voice of a bird, and all the daughters of song are brought low; they are afraid also of what is high, and terrors are in the way; the almond tree blossoms, the grasshopper drags itself along and desire fails; because man goes to his eternal home, and the mourners go about the streets; before the silver cord is snapped, or the golden bowl is broken, or the pitcher is broken at the fountain, or the wheel broken at the cistern, and the dust returns to the earth as it was, and the spirit returns to God who gave it.

Ecclesiastes 12.1-7

Before the gray descends on your cheek,
the wrinkles plow your chin,
and the body becomes a cage of bones;
Before the teeth fall off from your mouth,
the back bends to the earth,
and you become a burden to others;
Before you hold a stick in one hand
and lean heavily with the other on your knee;
Before age corrodes your bodily beauty
and you feel the pangs of death;
Adore our Lord Kudala Sangama!

Basavanna, Vacana 161 (Hinduism)

Teachings of Sun Myung Moon

What period of human life is most important? It is not childhood. It is the years when you are passing through young adulthood and into middle age, that is, between your twentieth and fortieth year. Especially during a person's twenties, before age thirty, he should lay the groundwork for his life's activities and secure a solid foundation for his life. He should also create the conditions upon which he can move forward and pursue his goals. Anyone who fails to do these things is bound to live as a mediocre, unremarkable person during his thirties and into his forties. (22:314, May 12, 1969)

The period in a person's life when he is capable of the greatest amount of activity is from his twenties to his forties, perhaps his fifties. These twenty to thirty years are a person's peak years. But once a person crosses forty, he usually starts to decline. From this perspective, you should think about how little time you have left to work for God's Will. (33:186, August 12, 1970)

Of all the precious seasons of life, the bloom of youth is beyond compare. When we enter the prime of life we have burdens to carry, and if we cannot keep up the fight, we know that our descendants, who are the fruit of that, will be miserable. Therefore, only if we live vigorously during the prime of life, and continue into old age, will our family have in its bosom descendants who will be able to greet new springs, see new summers, and prevail through the following winters without difficulties. (31:139, May 3, 1970)

Cultivating the Good

GOODNESS REQUIRES EFFORT. Since evil infests our world and infects our minds and bodies, we mostly find it difficult to do the right thing. Hence, to become a genuinely good person requires sustained effort at self-cultivation. Aristotle writes that cultivating good character is like learning an art or a skill. If a person makes continual efforts to practice good deeds over a long period, he will form good habits. Good habits cultivated over many years leads to the formation of good character. The human spirit is like a field that must be sowed, cultivated and weeded every day if it is to bear a good crop.

If people do not attend to goodness but tolerate small faults, over time they will develop bad habits that become progressively more ingrained. Thus good begets good, while evil begets evil. Father Moon reminds us that because the propensity for evil is highly developed in fallen people, we must be actively engaged in efforts to do good; as even simple neglect can lead to our downfall.

1. Cultivating the Good through a Lifetime of Practice

Not to do any evil, to cultivate good, to purify one's mind—this is the teaching of the Buddhas.

Dhammapada 183 *(Buddhism)*

The virtues we acquire by first having actually practiced them, just as we do the arts. We learn an art or craft by doing the things that we shall have to do when we have learnt it: for instance, men become builders by building houses, harpers by playing on the harp. Similarly we become just by doing just acts, temperate by doing temperate acts, brave by doing brave acts.

Aristotle, Nicomachean Ethics 2.1.4 *(Hellenism)*

Carefully uphold the proper norms of conduct, and imitate them day and night so that there will not be a moment's neglect or cessation. After a time, we become familiar with them, and then we no longer need to imitate them but can make our own standard.

Chu Hsi *(Confucianism)*

Gain: The superior man, seeing what is good,
   imitates it;
Seeing what is bad, he corrects it in himself.

I Ching 42 *(Confucianism)*

Whatever you would make habitual, practice it; and if you would not make a thing habitual, do not practice it, but habituate yourself to something else.

Epictetus *(Hellenism)*

Engage in Torah and charity even with an ulterior motive, for the habit of right doing will lead also to right motivation.

Talmud, Pesahim 50b *(Judaism)*

By degrees, little by little, from time to time, a wise person should remove his own impurities as a smith removes the dross from silver.

Dhammapada 239 *(Buddhism)*

By sustained effort, earnestness, discipline, and self-control, let the wise man make for himself an island which no flood can overwhelm.

Dhammapada 25 *(Buddhism)*

Study of Torah leads to precision, precision to zeal, zeal to cleanliness, cleanliness to restraint, restraint to purity, purity to holiness, holiness to meekness, meekness to fear of sin, fear of sin to saintliness, saintliness to the holy spirit, and the holy spirit to life eternal.

Talmud, Aboda Zara 20b (Judaism)

This Atman, resplendent and pure, whom sinless disciples behold residing within the body, is attained by unceasing practice of truthfulness, austerity, right knowledge and continence.

Mundaka Upanishad 3.1.5 (Hinduism)

Make every effort to supplement your faith with virtue, and virtue with knowledge, and knowledge with self-control, and self-control with steadfastness, and steadfastness with godliness, and godliness with brotherly affection, and brotherly affection with love. For if these things are yours and abound, they keep you from being ineffective or unfruitful in the knowledge of our Lord Jesus Christ.

2 Peter 1.5-8

Maintaining your self-cultivation for a long time will gradually lead to a congenial spirit; a congenial spirit will find one tender, generous, amiable, and agreeable. Anyone who hopes for this must eliminate his ill feelings and break up his anger, and be free of the adversity which invites opposition and attracts indignation. Personal and thorough investigation for a long time will gradually lead to the clarification of principle; perfect understanding will find one able to passively influence others without openly criticizing them. Anyone who heeds this will be well-informed and influential, and free of the worry of rising up in contention and being rejected.

Even more must we actively observe the principles of things and deeply investigate our basic feelings; personally experience these things through your own faculties, carefully think about them through time—do these things and you will be free of the errors of bias and deceit. It is important that in all matters you always check your power of learning. If there should be any hindrances or irregularities probe deeply until you discover the malady and then root it out.

Chu Hsi (Confucianism)

"Listen! A sower went out to sow. And as he sowed, some seed fell along the path, and the birds came and devoured it. Other seed fell on rocky ground, where it had not much soil, and immediately it sprang up, since it had no depth of soil; and when the sun rose it was scorched, and since it had no root it withered away. Other seed fell among thorns and the thorns grew up and choked it, and it yielded no grain. And other seeds fell into good soil and brought forth grain, growing up and increasing and yielding thirtyfold and sixtyfold and a hundredfold."...

And he said to [his disciples], "Do you not understand this parable? The sower sows the word. And these are the ones along the path, where the word is sown; when they hear, Satan immediately comes and takes away the word which is sown in them. And these in like manner are the ones sown upon rocky ground, who, when they hear the word, immediately receive it with joy; and they have no root in themselves, but endure for a while; then, when tribulation or persecution arises on account of the word, immediately they fall away. And others are the ones sown among thorns; they are those who hear the word, but the cares of the world, and the delight in riches, and the desire for other things, enter in and choke the word, and it proves unfruitful. But those that were sown upon the good soil are the ones who hear the word and accept it and bear fruit, thirtyfold and sixtyfold and a hundredfold."

Mark 4.3-20

Teachings of Sun Myung Moon

Good and evil are not decided in the future, but in the present moment, every day. (*Way of God's Will* 1.1.2)

Whether you are good or evil is not determined by your thoughts. It is determined by your life. Just knowing in your head what is good does not put you in any relationship with the real world. (359:167, November 7, 2001)

You cannot just pick up a difficult textbook and study it unless you first know how to read. You need to practice reading and train over a long period to become a good reader. You cannot be a connoisseur of music just be listening to a few pieces. You need to train over many years to understand that music deeply and in every aspect. You cannot just stand at a podium and instantly be a great speaker; it requires training. It is the same with our thinking, attitude and behavior. We have to spend time training our minds and bodies. We can view meditation and prayer as ways of training the mind. (67:178, June 10, 1973)

Well-known violinists know the character of their own violin, having played it countless times, cleaning and caring for it for so long. They know how to make the best sound out of their instrument, and can play in total harmony with it. Therefore they make the most beautiful and even mysterious sounds. Just as a violinist makes special efforts to care for his instrument, you should make special efforts, through prayer, to cultivate your spirit. Wherever you go, you should raise your spiritual antenna and not be negligent even for a moment. (241:179, December 24, 1992)

How can we, who are fallen beings, return to the God of goodness? First, we have to cultivate our conscience; thus we begin to take after the goodness of our original self. Next, we have to act according to God's Word; thus we reflect the goodness of God and the value of His Word. After we have done these things, we will become people who realize goodness and appreciate the value of God's goodness. God can then rejoice, finding in us His ideal of goodness, for which He created all things and humankind. (131:170, May 1, 1984)

The spirit grows through give and take action between two types of nourishment: life elements of a yang type that come from God, and vitality elements of a yin type that come from the physical self. The spirit self… also returns an element to the physical self which we call the living spirit element…

Truth illuminates the innermost desires of the spirit mind. A person must first comprehend his spirit mind's deepest desire through the truth and then put this knowledge into action to fulfill his responsibility. Only then do the living spirit elements and vitality elements reciprocate within him, enabling him to progress toward goodness. The living spirit element and the vitality element have the relationship of internal nature and external form. Because all people have living spirit elements ever active within themselves, even an evil person's original mind inclines toward goodness. However, unless he actually leads a life of goodness, the living spirit elements cannot engage in proper give and take with the vitality elements, nor can they be infused into his physical self to make it wholesome. (*Exposition of the Divine Principle*, Creation 6.3.2)

You can attain heaven only if you have unity within yourself. Therefore, do not be arrogant. Be humble. Be a sacrifice. That is why we are taught to discipline the body through the path of religion. Although you dislike it, you should do fasting and make sacrifices for more than three years. (245:58, February 28, 1993)

2. Good Leads to More Good, while Neglecting the Good Leads to Evil

Make haste in doing good; check your mind from evil; for the mind of him who is slow in doing meritorious actions delights in evil.

Dhammapada 116 *(Buddhism)*

Run to do even a slight precept, and flee from transgression; for precept draws precept in its train, and transgression, transgression; for the recompense of a precept is a precept, and the recompense of a transgression is a transgression.

Mishnah, Avot 4.2 *(Judaism)*

Do not disregard evil, saying, "It will not come nigh unto me": by the falling of drops even a water jar is filled; likewise the fool, gathering little by little, fills himself with evil.

Do not disregard merit, saying "It will not come nigh unto me": by the falling of drops of water even a water jar is filled; likewise the wise man, gathering little by little, fills himself with good.

Dhammapada 121-22 *(Buddhism)*

For to him who has will more be given, and he will have abundance; but from him who has not, even what he has will be taken away.

Matthew 13.12

Truly, truly, I say to you, everyone who commits sin is a slave to sin.

John 8.34

Black goats must be caught early, before it is dark.

Igala Proverb *(African Traditional Religions)*

He who permits himself to tell a lie once, finds it much easier to do it a second and third time, till at length it becomes habitual; he tells lies without attending to it, and truths without the world's believing him.

Thomas Jefferson

Mencius said to Kau Tzu, "A trail through the mountains, if used, becomes a path in a short time, but, if unused, becomes blocked by grass in an equally short time. Now your heart is blocked by grass."

Mencius VII.B.21 *(Confucianism)*

It will be as when a man going on a journey called his servants and entrusted to them his property; to one he gave five talents, to another two, to another one, to each according to his ability. Then he went away. He who had received the five talents went at once and traded with them; and he made five talents more. So also, he who had the two talents made two talents more. But he who had received the one talent went and dug in the ground and hid his master's money. Now after a long time the master of those servants came and settled accounts with them. And he who had received five talents came forward, bringing five talents more, saying, "Master, you delivered to me five talents; here I have made five talents more." His master said to him, "Well done, good and faithful servant; you have been faithful over a little, I will set you over much; enter into the joy of your master." And he also who had the two talents came forward, saying, "Master, you delivered to me two talents; here I have made two talents more." His master said to him, "Well done, good and faithful servant; you have been faithful over a little, I will set you over much, enter into the joy of your master." He also who had received one talent came forward, saying, "Master, I knew you to be a hard man, reaping where you did not sow, and gathering where you did not winnow; so I was afraid, and I went and hid your talent in the ground. Here you have what is yours." But his master answered him, "You wicked and slothful servant! You knew that I reap where I have not sowed, and gather where I have not winnowed? Then you ought to have invested my money with the bankers, and at my coming I should have received what was my own with interest. So take the talent from him, and give it to him who has the ten talents. For to every one who has will more be given, and he will have abundance; but from him who has not, even what he has will be taken away. And cast the worthless servant into the outer darkness; there men will weep and gnash their teeth."

Matthew 25.14-30: Parable of the Talents

If good does not accumulate, it is not enough to make a name for a man. If evil does not accumulate, it is not enough to destroy a man. Therefore the inferior man thinks to himself, "Goodness in small things has no value," and so neglects it. He thinks, "Small sins do no harm," and so does not give them up. Thus his sins accumulate until they can no longer be covered up, and his guilt becomes so great that it can no longer be wiped out. In the I Ching it is said, "His neck is fastened in the wooden cangue, so that his ears are hidden. Misfortune."

I Ching, Great Commentary 2.5.7-8
(Confucianism)

Teachings of Sun Myung Moon

We can become good only if our body obediently follows our mind, which directs us towards goodness. All too often, however, our body rebels against the mind's direction, repeating by analogy Cain's murder of Abel. This is how evil grows within us. (*Exposition of the Divine Principle*, Foundation 1.2)

People who only go to church on Sunday without making any effort to pursue God's Will are very dull. They are too numb to know the difference between good and evil, even if others admonish them. They are used to taking each day for granted, just repeating the daily routine. Such people do not make spiritual progress; they remain in the same place.

After wasting their lives like this for 10 years or more, the day comes when they look back on their past with shame and regret, realizing, "My position is so far below what it could have been." (89:231-32, December 1, 1976)

People's original desire is to avoid evil and pursue goodness. Our [original] mind is always running to promote goodness and eliminate evil from our world; however, through personal experience, we are well aware of our evil mind, which strongly opposes or distorts the good mind. The stronger we uphold our good mind, to that degree we confront our evil mind.

Although our good mind prompts us to head toward a certain goal, it is often hard to see it clearly. Then our motivation falters. Feeling distant from the goal, there is nothing to stimulate our good mind to continue on the path. On the other hand, there is never any lack of stimulation for the evil mind. Each step on the road to evil links us to ever more evil. Considering this, people who have a mind to pursue a life of truth and goodness perforce find themselves isolated and beset with sorrows. (36:51-52, November 15, 1970)

Decision

THE MORAL LIFE IS A PURPOSEFUL LIFE; IT REQUIRES A DECISION. People do not become good automatically; those who just drift through life are liable to drown in its evil currents. At every turn we encounter two paths, the better and the worse, and it is our responsibility to choose between them. The scriptures describe it as a decision between life and death, between the narrow gate and the broad road, or between two masters.

Father Moon teaches that each person stands in the midway position, pulled in two directions by the opposing powers of good and evil. It is a contest between God, who speaks to us through the conscience, and Satan, who prompts us to satisfy our self-centered desires. Under these difficult circumstances, it is up to each of us to choose our path and keep to it.

Man always stands at the crossroads of good and evil.

Precepts 18 *(Perfect Liberty Kyodan)*

Both the good and the pleasant present themselves to a man. The calm soul examines them well and discriminates. Yea, he prefers the good to the pleasant; but the fool chooses the pleasant out of greed and avarice.

Katha Upanishad 1.2.2 *(Hinduism)*

Surely, the path that leads to worldly gain is one, and the path that leads to Nibbana is another; understanding this, the bhikkhu, the disciple of the Buddha, should not rejoice in worldly favors, but cultivate detachment.

Dhammapada 75 *(Buddhism)*

No one can serve two masters; for either he will hate the one and love the other, or he will be devoted to one and despise the other. You cannot serve God and mammon.

Matthew 6.24

God puts forth a parable: A man belonging to many partners at variance with each other, and a man belonging entirely to one master: are those two equal in comparison?

Qur'an 39.29

Behold, I [Moses] set before you this day a blessing and a curse: the blessing, if you obey the commandments of the LORD your God, which I command you this day, and the curse, if you do not obey the commandments of the LORD your God, but turn aside from the way which I command you this day, to go after other gods.

Deuteronomy 11.26-28

Hear with your ears that which is the sovereign good;
With a clear mind look upon the two sides
Between which each man must choose for himself,
Watchful beforehand that the great test may be accomplished in our favor.

Now at the beginning the twin spirits have declared their nature,
The better and the evil,
In thought and word and deed. And between the two
The wise ones choose well, not so the foolish.

Avesta, Yasna 30.2-3 *(Zoroastrianism)*

Enter by the narrow gate; for the gate is wide and the way is easy that leads to destruction, and those who enter by it are many. For the gate is narrow and the way is hard that leads to life, and those who find it are few.

Matthew 7.13-14

Evil and good are not equal, even though the abundance of evil may amaze you; so heed God, you men of wits, so that you may prosper!

Qur'an 5.100

Have We not given him two eyes,
and a tongue and two lips,
and pointed out to him the two conspicuous ways?
Yet he does not attempt the uphill path.
What will make you understand what the uphill path is?
It is to free a slave,
or to feed in a time of hunger an orphan near of kin or a poor man lying in the dust.
Then he is of those who believe, who exhort one another to patience, and exhort one another to mercy.

Qur'an 90.8-17

If by giving up a lesser happiness one may behold a greater one, let the wise man give up the lesser happiness in consideration of the greater happiness.

Dhammapada 290 *(Buddhism)*

The kingdom of Heaven is like treasure hidden in a field, which a man found and covered up; then in his joy he goes and sells all he has and buys that field.

The kingdom of Heaven is like a merchant in search of fine pearls, who, on finding one pearl of great price, went and sold all he had and bought it.

Matthew 13.44-46

Teachings of Sun Myung Moon

"I" am the crossing point of good and evil. (109:268, November 2, 1980)

We live in a world where good and evil confront each other. Good and evil each pulls our divided mind and body. Evil pulls us toward evil, and good pulls us toward good. Human beings stand midway between these two opposing forces; they become good or evil depending on which way they travel from the center line. You are wandering back and forth across this line. (36:55, November 15, 1970)

If the first human ancestors had not fallen but had reached perfection and become one in heart with God, then they would have lived relating only with God. However, due to their Fall, they joined in a kinship of blood with Satan, which compelled them to deal with him as well… they found themselves in the midway position—a position between God and Satan where they were relating with both. As a consequence, all their descendants are also in the midway position…

How does God separate Satan from fallen people who stand in the midway position? Satan relates with them on the basis of his connection with them through lineage. Therefore, until people make a condition through which God can claim them as His own, there is no way God can restore them to the heavenly side. On the other hand, Satan acknowledges that God is the Creator of human beings. Unless Satan finds some condition through which he can attack a fallen person, he also cannot arbitrarily claim him for his side. Therefore, a fallen person will go to God's side if he makes good conditions and to Satan's side if he makes evil conditions. (*Exposition of the Divine Principle,* Restoration 1.1)

How do we cross over the dividing line between good and evil? Good abides where we live for others and evil abides where we live centered on ourselves. If we look within, our [original] mind always tries to lead us towards good thought and a good direction. It says, "Serve others. Have an affectionate heart for others. Sacrifice for others. Live for others." Such is the path of goodness. (65:14, November 13, 1972)

If you act as your body desires, you are connected to hell. On the other hand, if you act as your mind wishes, you are connected to the Kingdom of Heaven. You alone are the dividing line between the Kingdom of Heaven and hell. (214:283, February 3, 1991)

Do you know what spiritual food is? Even when you are hungry, if you have to choose between spiritual food and physical food, you should feel that spiritual food is tastier than physical food. Then you can survive and stand on the side of God. Living your life based on spiritual power should be much more appetizing than the taste of life lived with physical power. (131:211, May 4, 1984)

Looking back at my youth, I remember how serious I was. I was at the point of deciding what to do with the rest of my life. At that crossroad, I knew that I should not let humanistic concerns determine my decision. Instead I concluded that I had to make my decision in accordance with God's Will. (211:134, December 30, 1990)

If I had not taken this path, surely I would be a powerful and respected man in some secular field. I would be recognized for my intelligence. I have the ability; I could have risen to leadership in my nation. Yet, instead, I chose a life filled with tears and sorrows. Ever since I came to know God, I have shed tears for Him.

Do you think I am not capable of avoiding persecution? Yet I endure and tolerate the persecution because I know God's situation—He has gone through far greater tribulations than mine. Do you think that when I was a young man I did not have any personal dreams and ambitions? I certainly had great ambition and dreams. But once I decided to go this way I cut them off, and ever since I have never nursed any personal ambition. That is how I could become who I am today. (*God's Will and the World*, May 1, 1977)

Good and Evil

HOW CAN ONE DISTINGUISH GOOD FROM EVIL? Are there universal indicators behind, within, or consequent upon an action by which one can determine whether it was a good or an evil act? What is the difference between a good person and an evil person?

Good and evil may be distinguished outwardly or inwardly. Some passages distinguish good and evil by their root in the self: good deeds are motivated by the conscience while evil deeds satisfy the body's desires. Other passages distinguish good and evil by the mind's purpose and intention. Discerning good and evil may be difficult, however, if we cannot fathom the mind's intention and there is no clear outward indication to go by. The end of an affair may take time to develop. Here there are passages calling for patience until the matter bears fruit, at which time good and evil will be evident.

Father Moon discusses these ways of distinguishing good and evil, but he mainly fixes on an objective standard: goodness is altruistic and seeks to benefit others, while evil is self-centered.

1. Goodness Is Selfless and Altruistic, while Evil Is to Gratify Selfish Desires

Every selfless act, Arjuna, is born from the eternal, infinite Godhead. God is present in every act of service. All life turns on this law, O Arjuna. Whoever violates it, indulging his senses for his own pleasure and ignoring the needs of others, has wasted his life.

Bhagavad-Gita 3.16 (Hinduism)

Every man must decide whether he will walk in the light of creative altruism or the darkness of destructive selfishness. This is the judgment. Life's most persistent and urgent question is, "What are you doing for others?"

Martin Luther King, Jr. (Christianity)

There are among them some who wrong their own souls; some who follow a middle course; and some who are, by Allah's leave, foremost in good deeds. That is the highest Grace.

Qur'an 35.32

Whosoever seeks, by whatever means, merely the happiness of cyclic existence for personal ends, he is to be understood as a mean person.

Whosoever reverses deeds done from base motives and turns back the happiness of worldly pleasures for the sake of his own liberation, that person is called middling.

Whosoever wishes to eliminate completely the sufferings of others through his own sufferings, that is the excellent person.

Bodhipathapradipa (Buddhism)

Four characters of men:
He who says, "What is mine is mine and what is yours is yours"—that is the average type: some say it is the character of Sodom.
He who says, "What is mine is yours and what is yours is mine" is undisciplined.
He who says, "What is mine is yours and what is yours is yours" is a saint.
He who says, "What is yours is mine and what is mine is mine" is wicked.

Mishnah, Avot 5.13 (Judaism)

If you, Rahula, are desirous of doing a deed with the body, you should reflect on that deed of your body, thus: "That deed that I am desirous of doing with the body is a deed of my body that might conduce to the harm of self and that might conduce to the harm of others and that might conduce to the harm of both; this deed of body is unskilled, its yield is anguish, its result is anguish." If you, Rahula, reflecting thus, should find it so, a deed of body like this, Rahula, is certainly not to be done by you.

Majjhima Nikaya 1.415 (Buddhism)

If, for my own sake, I cause harm to others,
I shall be tormented in hellish realms;
But if for the sake of others I cause harm to myself,
I shall acquire all that is magnificent.

By holding myself in high esteem
I shall find myself in unpleasant realms, ugly and stupid;
But should this [attitude] be shifted to others
I shall acquire honors in a joyful realm.

If I employ others for my own purposes
I myself shall experience servitude,
But if I use myself for the sake of others
I shall experience only lordliness.

Shantideva, Guide to the Bodhisattva's Way of Life 8.126-128 (Buddhism)

The gods and the demons, both having the Creator as their origin, were rivals of each other. So the demons, swollen with pride, said, "In what, pray, should we place the oblation?" And they proceeded to place the oblation in their own mouths. The gods then proceeded to place their oblations each in the mouth of one of his fellows. And the Creator gave Himself over to them.³

Satapatha Brahmana 5.1.1.1-2 *(Hinduism)*

It is the greatest happiness of the greatest number that is the measure of right and wrong.

Jeremy Bentham⁴ *(Humanism)*

Teachings of Sun Myung Moon

How do the directions of good and evil differ? Good always centers on God, the Absolute Being, or puts itself in the other person's shoes. Evil centers on the self, or puts itself in the subject position. What is good? It is to advance the purpose of the whole by sacrificing yourself. What is evil? It is to pull everything toward you. Thus, good and evil have different directions.

Your body wants to do everything it desires, while your mind tries to restrain you from acting to satisfy the body. Thus they also have different directions, one good and the other evil. (16:137, January 2, 1966)

For human beings, the most important thing is to be able to discern between good and evil. Yet until now, the standard for determining good and evil has been unclear. Evil is to present conditions that enable Satan to accuse human beings. What is sin? It is something that provides grounds for Satan to accuse. Christians more than anyone must know clearly what sin is, especially the root of sins.

Evil began at the Human Fall, when not only Satan but also Eve thought, "I will be the subject partner. I will be the center." God's Principle of Creation is to live for the sake of others, while the attitude of living for one's own sake is Satan's nature. You must know clearly the origin of good and evil.

An evil person tells others to live for his sake. God and Jesus work to subdue this kind of spirit, which is why they teach us not to be arrogant, to sacrifice for others and to serve others. (69:85, October 20, 1973)

How do we determine if someone is good or evil? It is whether he or she lives for a public purpose or for an individual purpose. That is the norm of human ethics.

A good person sacrifices him or herself for the sake of others while an evil person exploits others for his or her own benefit. This is my way of teaching about good and evil. (102:234, January 1, 1979)

There are two basic types of people in the world: those who think and act altruistically for the sake of the greater good, and those who think and act to benefit themselves.

Most people do not like to think about the world and act for its benefit. They prefer to think about themselves and act out of their self-centered thinking.

The altruistic person admires the saints who were dedicated to the welfare of the world, patriots who lived for their nation, and righteous leaders of the current era, taking them as role models for his own life. The self-centered person could care less about saints, patriots or today's leaders. He acts only to benefit himself.

Which type of person are you? Which type of person would you like as a friend?... You know the altruistic way is correct and a self-centered life is wrong, but what is your reality? You answer that you are altruistic, but your self-concept does not match your reality. The fact is, you are walking a self-centered path. You know the truth, but your reality does not match it. (117:214-15, March 7, 1982)

By the criterion of goodness, we can classify all people in the world into three groups: first, people who oppose goodness; second, people who know goodness but don't actively pursue it to make it their own (they end up living in the buffer zone between heaven and hell); and third, people who want to take responsibility for accomplishing goodness. It is people of this third group whom God needs to accomplish His will. (*Way of God's Will* 2.2)

What makes someone a good person? Someone who just takes a bite out of what he receives is an evil person, while someone who adds to what he receives and passes it on to others is a good person. This is why every parent wants their children to grow up to be better than themselves. (315:211, February 2, 2000)

Does the president of the United States think centering on himself or centering on the United States? Does he act for his next election or for the future of the nation? These matters determine good and evil.

To go one step further, if the president focuses only on the benefit of the United States, then he will only be a respected president within the United States. However, if he centers on the world and the benefit of the world, then the world will admire him as an American president who has worldwide influence. Otherwise, although he serves his nation's best interests, his actions will cause friction in the rest of the world.

All human beings are subject to this law and will be judged accordingly. What will ensnare you in the judgment? The main thing is the self-centered thinking. You will be judged for focusing on yourself. How can you confidently say that you will not be caught by this universal law? You will be liberated from the law when you become the type of person about whom people say, "He does not live for himself. He lives for the welfare of the world." (93:302, June 12, 1977)

2. Good or Evil Is Determined by the Intention of the Heart

Out of the heart come evil thoughts, murder, adultery, fornication, theft, false witness, slander. These are what defile a man.

       Matthew 15.19-20

How can activity be good or wicked? That which is performed with good intention is good; and that which is performed with evil intention is wicked... That which purifies the soul or by which the soul is purified, is merit—producing a happy feeling. That which keeps the soul away from good is demerit—producing an unhappy feeling.

    Pujyapada, Sarvarthasiddhi 6.3 (*Jainism*)

If a person has no wound in his hand, he may carry poison in it. Poison does not affect him, for he has no wound. There is no ill for him who acts without intent to do wrong.

      Dhammapada 124 (*Buddhism*)

Teachings of Sun Myung Moon

Originally good and evil started from one point; that one point is love. (26:282, November 10, 1969)

Analyze yourself: you have a dual structure. The conscience is in the position of good, while the body is in the position of evil. (227:46, February 10, 1992)

Good or evil can come to existence depending on the direction and the way of your mind. The direction and way of your mind will make the distinction between good and evil. (37:116, December 23, 1970)

A nation's constitution, which is inspired by its highest ideals, is the basis for determining right and wrong, good and evil within a nation. Likewise, as regards our own behavior, we need some basis or standard for distinguishing right from wrong. Think about it. How can someone who is always drunk determine whether his drinking is good or bad? He cannot be his own standard. This is the case for all of us. We find all kinds of justifications for everything we do, whether good or bad. How can we judge rightly?

Today throughout the world people do many evil things and justify them based on their own way of thinking. Hence, the world is in chaos. This state of affairs will continue as long as there is not a clear and accepted standard of good and evil. There should be one standard, and it should be absolute, unique, eternal and unchanging. (March 1, 1981)

3. Good or Evil Is Seen in a Person's Way of Life

You will know them by their fruits. Are grapes gathered from thorns, or figs from thistles? So, every sound tree bears good fruit, but the bad tree bears evil fruit. A sound tree cannot bear evil fruit, nor can a bad tree bear good fruit. Every tree that does not bear good fruit is cut down and thrown into the fire. Thus you will know them by their fruits.

Matthew 7.16-20

God enjoins justice, kindness, and charity to one's kindred, and forbids indecency, abomination, and oppression. He admonishes you so that you may take heed.

Qur'an 16.90

Now the works of the flesh are plain: fornication, impurity, licentiousness, idolatry, sorcery, enmity, strife, jealousy, anger, selfishness, dissension, party spirit, envy, drunkenness, carousing, and the like. I warn you, as I warned you before, that those who do such things shall not inherit the kingdom of God. But the fruit of the Spirit is love, joy, peace, patience, kindness, goodness, faithfulness, gentleness, self-control; against such there is no law.

Galatians 5.19-23

Worthless men live that they may eat and drink, whereas worthy men eat and drink that they may live.

Socrates[5] (Hellenism)

God's messenger said, "Do you know the thing which most commonly brings people into Paradise? It is fear to God and good character. Do you know what most commonly brings people into hell? It is the two hollow things: the mouth and the private parts."

Hadith of Tirmidhi and Ibn Majah (Islam)

"All who commit crimes, robbing, stealing, practicing villainy and treachery, and who kill men or violently assault them to take their property, being reckless and fearless of death—these are abhorred by all."

The king says, "O Feng, such great criminals are greatly abhorred, and how much more detestable are the unfilial and unbrotherly—as the son who does not reverently discharge his duty to his father, but greatly wounds his father's heart, and the father who can no longer love his son, but hates him; as the younger brother who does not think of the manifest will of Heaven, and refuses to respect his elder brother, and the elder brother who does not think of the toil of their parents in bringing up their children, and is very unfriendly to his junior. If we who are charged with government do not treat parties who proceed to such wickedness as offenders, the laws of our nature given by Heaven to our people will be thrown into great disorder and destroyed."

Book of History 5.9 (Confucianism)

Teachings of Sun Myung Moon

People who live self-centered lives cannot produce good seeds. Those who are trying to benefit themselves cannot bear good fruit. Simply speaking, people who want to use others for their benefit are evil. Good people, on the other hand, are willing to take other people's burdens. (41:91, February 12, 1971)

Good and evil are not determined by your beliefs. They are determined by your daily life. Whether you are destined for heaven and hell is not determined by your worldview, but by your daily life. (40:294-95, February 7, 1971)

Evil acts by using force. Its activity is not the natural way, but goes against nature. That is why it utilizes oppression, fear, intimidation and threats. (60:61, August 6, 1972)

Everything has its beginning and its end. Whether it is good or bad, once it begins, at some point it will reach its end. If it is a good thing, the result may take a long time to bear fruit but its record will remain in history. However, if it is a bad thing, its result will quickly appear. Good keeps step with eternity, while evil keeps step with the moment. A deed that quickly perishes is fascinated with the moment, while the deed that prospers is fascinated with eternity. (18:64, May 21, 1967)

Good is standing for a public purpose, and evil is standing for a personal purpose. By this standard a patriot and a faithful wife are good people. The greater cause they live for, the better they become. Evil is living for a selfish purpose. Since good is searching for something greater, it should at least be centered on the family rather than the individual. That is why a man and woman should marry and establish a family. Next, their family should be recognized and praised by their neighbors. After an individual establishes his family, he should go forth to benefit his tribe, his people, his nation and finally the world. (31:236, June 4, 1970)

Individual Responsibility

RESPONSIBILITY IS CENTRAL TO WHAT IT MEANS TO BE HUMAN. Other creatures have life, consciousness, and even intelligence, but only human beings are responsible to choose their manner of life and hence their destiny. Individual responsibility implies an attitude of self-criticism. We should not blame others for our own difficulties, but rather look for the cause within ourselves.

All the religions of the world emphasize, in one way or another, individual responsibility in matters of faith and practice, although the definition and limits differ. Buddhism and other non-theistic traditions regard the journey on the path to liberation as entirely the responsibility of the individual. Each individual is "a lamp unto himself"; each works out his own salvation alone and by himself. There is explicit rejection of reliance upon a savior from without, as both Buddha and Muhammad rejected characterizations of themselves as saviors.

On the other hand, in the monotheistic faiths, the context of individual responsibility is prevenient grace. As a person works out his own salvation, at the same time God is at work within. Salvation is a gift, yet it is our responsibility to receive it and not reject it. Father Moon characterizes this joint responsibility in numerical terms: 95 percent is God's responsibility and 5 percent is the human portion. In this view, responsibility ennobles human beings. It means that each of us has a role to play in our own perfection, and even an indispensable role in completing God's work of creation. This responsibility contains the gift of freedom. Several passages explore this teaching in light of the Human Fall and divine forbearance in not intervening to prevent it.

Many religions hold that an individual's destiny is at least partly determined by factors beyond his or her control: God's predestination, past karma, or the burden of inherited sin. Nevertheless, several texts reject the notion that such conditions impinge in any way on one's individual responsibility. Arguing against fatalism, they maintain that with every situation comes the opportunity to improve our lot by the exercise of responsibility. Father Moon goes one step further: he teaches that inasmuch as our individual selves are the results of many generations, fulfilling our responsibility benefits not only ourselves but countless ancestors as well.

1. Each Person Is Responsible for His or Her Own Self

O ye who believe! You have charge over your own souls.

Qur'an 5.105

If I am not for myself, who is for me? And when I am for myself, what am I? And if not now, when?

Mishnah, Avot 1.14 (Judaism)

By self do you censure yourself. By self do you examine yourself. Self-guarded and mindful, O bhikkhu, you will live happily.

Self, indeed, is the protector of self. Self, indeed, is one's refuge. Control, therefore, your own self as a merchant controls a noble steed.

Dhammapada 379-80 (Buddhism)

Whoever works righteousness benefits his own soul; whoever works evil, it is against his own soul: Your Lord is never unjust to His servants.

Qur'an 41.46

Work out your own salvation with fear and trembling.

Philippians 2.12

You must be lamps unto yourselves. Rely on yourselves, and do not rely on external help. Hold firm to the truth as a lamp and a refuge, and do not look for refuge to anything besides yourselves. A brother becomes his own lamp and refuge by continually looking on his body, feelings, perceptions, moods, and ideas in such a manner that he conquers the cravings and depressions of ordinary men and is always strenuous, self-possessed, and collected in mind. Whoever among my disciples does this, either now or when I am dead, if he is anxious to learn, will reach the summit.

Digha Nikaya 2.99-100 (Buddhism)

The LORD our God made a covenant with us in Horeb. Not with our fathers did the LORD make this covenant, but with us, who are all of us here alive this day.

Deuteronomy 5.2-3

Oneself, indeed, is one's savior, for what other savior could there be? With oneself well controlled one obtains a savior difficult to find.

Dhammapada 160 (Buddhism)

"Please, Man of Shakya," said Dhotaka, "free me from confusion!" "It is not in my practice to free anyone from confusion," said the Buddha.

"When you have understood the most valuable teachings, then you yourself will cross the ocean."

Sutta Nipata 1063-64 *(Buddhism)*

Not by traveling to the end of the world can one accomplish the end of ill. It is in this fathom-long carcass, friend, with its impressions and its ideas that, I declare, lies the world, and the cause of the world, and the cessation of the world, and the course of action that leads to the cessation of the world.

Samyutta Nikaya 1.62 *(Buddhism)*

[God to Adam]: "Adam, We give you no fixed place to live, no form that is peculiar to you, nor any function that is yours alone. According to your desires and judgment, you will have and possess whatever place to live, whatever form, and whatever functions you yourself choose. All other things have a limited and fixed nature... To you is granted the power of degrading yourself into the lower forms of life, the beasts, and to you is granted the power, contained in your intellect and judgment, to be reborn into the higher forms, the divine."

Pico della Mirandola[6] *(Humanism)*

Man's main task in life is to give birth to himself, to become what he potentially is. The most important product of his effort is his own personality.

Erich Fromm[7] *(Humanism)*

Teachings of Sun Myung Moon

In the life of faith, you absolutely cannot remain a bystander. You think you can follow me, Reverend Moon, but you cannot lead your life of faith through me; you must find it in yourself. Regardless of what others do, you have to keep on the path of faith by your own will. (153:136, November 15, 1963)

Even in the midst of the wilderness, you can build your dwelling. You must build it by yourself. No one can help you. Therefore, be self-sufficient, so you can help others. No matter how hard things may be, add something good to your daily life. Invest step by step. God also has been investing Himself and forgetting what He had invested: that is His tradition. (248:133, August 1, 1993)

You know what to do. You know better than I what needs to be done. This course is yours, not mine. (36:31, November 8, 1970)

Unless you develop yourself and arrive at maturity—the realm of God's direct dominion—you will not understand what love is. (137:100, December 24, 1985)

All things reach perfection after passing through the growing period (the realm of indirect dominion) by virtue of the autonomy and governance given by God's Principle. Human beings, however, are created in such a way that their growth requires the fulfillment of their own portion of responsibility, in addition to the guidance provided by the Principle. They must exercise this responsibility in order to pass successfully through the growing period and reach perfection. We can deduce from God's commandment to Adam and Eve (Gen. 2.17) that the first human ancestors were responsible to believe in the Word of God and not eat of the fruit. Whether or not they disobeyed God and fell depended not on God, but on them. Hence, whether or not human beings attain perfection does not depend only on God's power of creation; it also requires the fulfillment of human responsibility. In His capacity as the Creator, God created human beings in such a manner that they can pass through the growing period (the realm of indirect dominion) and attain perfection only when they have completed their own portion of responsibility. Because God Himself created human beings in this way, He does not interfere with human responsibility.

God endowed human beings with a portion of responsibility for the following reason. By fulfilling their given portion of responsibility—with which even God does not interfere—human beings are meant to inherit the creative nature of God and participate in God's great work of creation. God intends human beings to earn ownership and become worthy to rule over the creation as creators in their own right (Gen. 1.28), just as God governs over them as their Creator. This is the principal difference between human beings and the rest of creation. (*Exposition of the Divine Principle*, Creation 5.2.2)

> The path of life is not a way I go at another's urging,
> nor because someone leads me;
> I realize I can only walk this path if I cope with it by myself.
> It is a principle of nature:
> I feed myself when I am hungry
> and drink for myself when I am thirsty. (42:90, February 28, 1971)

2. Responsibility Is God's Gift and Provision to Human Beings

The LORD God took the man and put him in the Garden of Eden to till it and keep it. And the LORD God commanded the man, saying, "You may freely eat of every tree of the garden; but of the tree of the knowledge of good and evil you shall not eat, for in the day that you eat of it you shall die."

Genesis 2.15-17

For of course, no one would dare to believe or declare that it was beyond God's power to prevent the fall of either angel or man. But, in fact, God preferred not to use His own power, but to leave success or failure to the creature's choice.

Saint Augustine, City of God 14.27 (Christianity)

Rabbi Akiba said: Beloved is man, for he was created in the image of God. But it was by a special love that it was made known to him that he was created in the image of God; as it is taught, "For in the image of God made He man." (Gen. 9.6)[8]

Mishnah, Avot 3.18 (Judaism)

Everything is in the hand of Heaven except the fear of Heaven.

Talmud, Berakot 33b (Judaism)

Satan... came before me, saying, "Behold, here am I; send me, I will be Thy son, and I will redeem all mankind, that not one soul shall be lost. Surely I will do it; therefore give me my honor."

But my Beloved Son, who was my Beloved and Chosen from the beginning, said to me, "Father, Thy will be done, and the glory be Thine forever."

Therefore, because that Satan rebelled against me, and sought to destroy the agency of man, which I, the Lord God, had given him... I caused that he should be cast down; and he became Satan, yea, even the devil, the father of all lies, to deceive and to blind men, and to lead them captive at his will, even as many as would not hearken unto my voice.[9]

Pearl of Great Price, Moses 4.1-4
(Latter-day Saints)

Teachings of Sun Myung Moon

To bring about the perfection of humankind in true love, God required that human beings accomplish a condition of responsibility in order to reach unity with Him. For this purpose, God gave the Commandment to the first ancestors. God knew that they were in the growth period, as yet imperfect, so He established the Commandment as the condition for His children to inherit the most precious thing—true love. (277:197, April 16, 1996)

God gave human beings a portion of responsibility as the condition based on which He could love them more than any other being in creation. God's intention in giving this condition was to make them worthy to be the lords of creation by having them take after His creative nature. (*Exposition of the Divine Principle*, Predestination 4)

Because human beings have a portion of responsibility, they have supreme value, greater than any other creation. If Adam and Eve fulfilled their portion of responsibility, then there would be no such thing as bitterness in human life.[10] Had they fulfilled their portion of responsibility, then the human world, the angelic world, and the entire creation would have received God's governance with rejoicing and glory. That is the Principle. (63:320, October 22, 1972)

Why did God establish a portion of responsibility in our lives? As the omniscient and omnipotent Creator, God wanted to bequeath His omniscient and omnipotent creativity to us. As the Subject Partner of eternal and unchanging love, God wanted to establish us in a position where we could resemble Him as the Subject Partner of love. For these reasons, God gave us a portion of responsibility.

Hence, the human portion of responsibility is a condition for God's blessing. It is like the key to a treasure-chest which, when opened, gives us possession of everything. Yet it was this portion of responsibility that became an issue in bringing about the Human Fall. (20:210, June 9, 1968)

If God were to interfere with human actions during their growing period, it would be tantamount to ignoring the human portion of responsibility. In that case, God would be disregarding His own Principle of Creation... [For this reason,] God did not intervene in the acts that led the human beings to fall. (*Exposition of the Divine Principle*, Fall 6.1)

3. *A Responsible Person Digests Life's Circumstances without Complaint*

He who knows himself well never complains against others. He who knows his fate well never complains against Heaven. He who complains against others will find no way out. He who complains against Heaven will lose his will. The failure is caused by himself, yet he shifts blame to others. Is not such a man foolish?

Hsün Tzu (Confucianism)

Ambrosia can be extracted even from poison; elegant speech even from a child; good conduct even from an enemy, gold even from impurity.

Laws of Manu 2.239 (Hinduism)

The word of the LORD came to me again, "What do you mean by repeating this proverb concerning the land of Israel, 'The fathers have eaten sour grapes, and the children's teeth are set on edge'? As I live, says the Lord GOD, this proverb shall no more be used by you in Israel. Behold, all souls are mine; the soul of the father as well as the soul of the son is mine, the soul that sins shall die..."

Yet you say, "Why should not the son suffer for the iniquity of the father?" When the son has done what is lawful and right, and has been careful to observe all my statutes, he shall surely live. The soul that sins shall die. The son shall not suffer for the iniquity of the father, nor the father suffer for the iniquity of the son; the righteousness of the righteous shall be upon himself, and the wickedness of the wicked shall be upon himself... Therefore I will judge you, O house of Israel, every one according to his ways, says the Lord GOD.[11]

Ezekiel 18.1-30

There are certain recluses and brahmins who teach thus: Whatsoever weal or woe or neutral feeling is experienced, all is due to some previous action... Then I say to them, "So then, owing to a previous action, men will become murderers, thieves, unchaste, liars, slanderers, abusive, babblers, covetous, malicious, and perverse in view. Those who fall back on a former deed as the essential reason [for their behavior] there is neither desire nor effort nor necessity to do this deed or abstain from that deed. So then, the necessity for action or inaction not being found to exist in truth and verity, the term 'recluse' cannot reasonably be applied to yourselves, since you live in a state of bewilderment with faculties unguarded.

Others teach thus: Whatsoever weal or woe or neutral feeling is experienced, all that is due to the creation [predestination] of a Supreme Deity... Then I say to them, "So then, owing to the creation of a Supreme Deity, men will become murderers, thieves, unchaste... Those who fall back on the creation of a Supreme Deity as the essential reason [for their behavior] there is neither desire nor effort nor necessity to do this deed or abstain from that deed. So then, the necessity for action or inaction not being found to exist in truth and verity, the term 'recluse' cannot reasonably be applied to yourselves, since you live in a state of bewilderment with faculties unguarded.[12]

Anguttara Nikaya 1.173-74 (*Buddhism*)

Confucius remarked, "In the practice of archery we have something resembling the principle in a moral man's life. When the archer misses the center of the target, he turns round and seeks for the cause of his failure within himself."

Doctrine of the Mean 14 (*Confucianism*)

An individual natively desires to be cause.[13] He tries not to become a bad effect.

You try to help people and people try to help you because you and they want to be cause. When something bad happens, neither one wishes to be cause.

You want to be an effect. Then you find the effect bad. You try not to be an effect. And then you blame something or somebody.

Handbook for Preclears (*Scientology*)

Teachings of Sun Myung Moon

The problem here is myself, not anything else. Nevertheless, you complain about the world. When you say, "The world is going to ruin," it means you think, "I am not in trouble, but the world in which I live is in trouble." You blame the world for every problem while commending yourself for every good thing. This way of thinking is the problem. You do not understand what is wrong with you, yet you complain about what is wrong with the world. (140:25, February 1, 1986)

Regardless of whether a problem stemmed from your father or your grandfather, put them all on your list. Then, put your life on the line to save your ancestors, for it is Heaven's will that their problems have come to you. With that, get rid of all the blemishes from the past and build a bridge to the new heaven and earth. (310:126, June 15, 1999)

Hundreds of thousands of years of history are coalesced in you. You exist on the foundation of many countries and the sacrifices of billions of people. You are composed of all their resurrected cells; they exist in you. Therefore, if you fail to fulfill your responsibility, your ancestors and the world will suffer on your account. (124:78, January 23, 1983)

However, when you overcome all difficulties and become a victor, it polishes a glorious path for your descendants to follow because you, their ancestor, once walked it. (98:213, August 1, 1978)

As an individual, each one of us is a product of the history of the providence of restoration. Hence, the person who is to accomplish the purpose of history is none other than I, myself. I must take up the cross of history and accept responsibility to fulfill its calling. To this end, I must fulfill in my lifetime (horizontally), through my efforts, the indemnity conditions which have accumulated through the long course of the providence of restoration (vertically). Only by doing this can I stand proudly as the fruit of history, the one whom God has eagerly sought throughout His providence. (*Exposition of the Divine Principle*, Restoration 3)

4. Public Responsibility Begins with Personal Responsibility

If anyone sincerely considers the affairs of the world as their own personal responsibilities, they should start by righting the wrongs of the ruler's mind. If they wish to right the ruler's mind they should start with themselves.

Chu Hsi (Confucianism)

The ancients who wished to manifest their clear character to the world would first bring order to their states. Those who wished to bring order to their states would first regulate their families. Those who wished to regulate their families would first cultivate their personal lives. Those who wished to cultivate their personal lives would first rectify their minds. Those who wished to rectify their minds would first make their wills sincere...

From the Emperor down to the common people, all must regard cultivation of the personal life as the root or foundation. There is never a case when the root is in disorder and yet the branches are in order.

The Great Learning (Confucianism)

Now a bishop must be above reproach, the husband of one wife, temperate, sensible, dignified, hospitable, an apt teacher, no drunkard, not violent but gentle, not quarrelsome, and no lover of money. He must manage his own household well, keeping his children submissive and respectful in every way; for if a man does not know how to manage his own household, how can he care for God's church?

1 Timothy 3.2-5

Teachings of Sun Myung Moon

People who do not love their nation cannot love God. Those who do not love their parents cannot love their nation. Further, those who do not love themselves cannot love their parents. Therefore, to be able to love your parents, love your nation, love the world, and love God, you must first love yourself.

That is why I teach, "Before you desire to have dominion over the universe, you must first have dominion over yourself." You have to first establish that foundation in yourself to be a subject partner who can embody and give boundless love. Otherwise you are not adequate to love your family, your nation or the world; neither can you perfectly love God. That is what is meant by fully loving yourself. (22:97-98, January 26, 1969)

If you become responsible for an area, then you have to believe that all the hardship and struggle is your own, and without you, matters would not be resolved. You must be responsible for it all by yourself. (14:259, January 1, 1965)

Be a man who can respect his own character. You should be able to hold your head high before all things, knowing that they respect you. Then you can say, "Follow my example." (*Way of God's Will* 2.2)

Predestination

THE DOCTRINE OF PREDESTINATION PROVIDES an explanation for the fact that people have different fortunes, moral endowments, are born into different circumstances, and respond differently to religion. It ascribes these differences to the hand of God—who is omnipotent and controls all, and who is omniscient and sees the future. Someone who degenerates into a sinner does so because God eases him into sin. Someone who becomes a hero of faith can be so because God strengthens him. Absolute predestination holds that a person's eternal destiny—to salvation or damnation—is predetermined before his birth. It is already written down in God's ledger— along with the span of the person's life and the day of his death.

A believer who recognizes the hand of destiny never regards the occasions in life as accidental. Everything that happens, happens for a reason. An apparently chance meeting may have been decreed long ago. A sudden death or a stroke of good luck are not random events, but happen by God's decree. Since all human plans and designs only bear fruit if they are within God's will, Muslims commonly say, *inshallah*, "if it is the will of God." Day by day we can examine every event to discern the hand of God, and make every effort to conform our lives to the flow of His destined Will.

How is predestination reconciled with human free will? One answer that is consistent with absolute predestination counsels us to accept human ignorance as the context within which we strive in freedom. The omniscient God who knows everything through eternity already knows the outcome of our life, however as we can never possess such foreknowledge, we should still make our best effort. Then there are qualified doctrines of predestination, for which human freedom enters into the calculation of destiny. Such doctrines describe God as apportioning blessings and hardships as He wills, and then permitting us limited freedom to make the best of our lot. Father Moon, who rejects absolute predestination, teaches such a form of qualified predestination: God predestines everyone to salvation, but requires human responsibility as a necessary condition to realize that destiny.

1. God's Absolute Predestination

I will be gracious to whom I will be gracious,
and I will show mercy to whom I will show mercy.

Exodus 33.19

Lo! this is an admonishment, that whosoever will may choose a way unto his Lord; yet you will not, unless God wills. Lo! God is Knower, Wise. He makes whom He will to enter His mercy, and for evildoers has prepared a painful doom.

Qur'an 76.29-31

We know that in everything God works for good with those who love him, who are called according to his purpose. For those whom he foreknew he also predestined to be conformed to the image of his Son, in order that he might be the first-born among many brethren. Those whom He predestined He also called; and those whom He called He also justified; and those whom He justified He also glorified.

Romans 8.28-30

The Lord is the Doer, cause of all:
what avail man's designs?
As is the Lord's will, so it happens.
The Lord is Almighty, without impediment to
   His will.
All that is done is by His pleasure:
From each He is far, to each close.
All He considers, watches over, discriminates—
Himself He is sole and all.

Adi Granth, Gauri Sukhmani, M.5, p. 279
(Sikhism)

When Rebecca had conceived children by one man, our forefather Isaac, though they were not yet born and had done nothing either good or bad, in order that God's purpose of election might continue, not because of works but because of his call, she was told, "The elder will serve the younger." As it is written, "Jacob I loved, but Esau I hated."

Is there injustice on God's part? By no means! For he says to Moses, "I will have mercy on whom I have mercy, and I will have compassion on whom I have compassion." So it depends not upon man's will or exertion, but upon God's mercy. For the scripture says to Pharaoh, "I have raised you up for the very purpose of showing my power in you, so that my name may be proclaimed in all the earth." So then he has mercy upon whomever he wills, and he hardens the heart of whomever he wills.

Romans 9.10-16

Thou knowest me right well;
my frame was not hidden from thee,
when I was being made in secret,
intricately wrought in the depths of the earth.
Thy eyes beheld my unformed substance;
in thy book were written, every one of them,
the days that were formed for me,
when as yet there was none of them.

Psalm 139.15-16

Allah's Apostle, the true and truly inspired said, "Every one of you is collected in the womb of his mother for the first forty days, and then he becomes a clot for another forty days, and then a piece of flesh for another forty days. Then is sent to him the angel who breathes the soul into his body and is commanded to write down four words: his livelihood, his life span, his deeds, and whether he will be wretched or blessed (in religion). Verily, it may be that one of you will be performing the works of the people of Paradise, so that between him and Paradise there is the distance of only an arm's length, but then what is written for him overtakes him, and he begins to perform the works of the people of hell, into which he will go. Or maybe one of you will be performing the works of the people of hell, so that between him and hell there is the distance of only an arm's length, but then what is written for him overtakes him, and he will begin to perform the works of the people of Paradise, into which he will go.

Forty Hadith of an-Nawawi 4 (Islam)

Teachings of Sun Myung Moon

When God looks at a person, He sees the person's past, He penetrates his present mind, and based on these He foresees his future. (100:93, October 8, 1978)

Do you think that I was born to fulfill a certain purpose, which predetermined the way I grew up and what I have become? Or am I the product of my circumstances and the sum total of the things that happened to me as I went about my life? My life was predestined before I was born. Therefore even the features of my face[14] were predestined... I am not the man I am today because of things that happened to me in the course my life. I am the man whom I was predestined to become. I grew up holding on to the Principle; I did not go my own way unconnected to the Principle. (161:159, February 1, 1987)

God, being omniscient, foreknows who has the qualifications necessary to become a central figure in the providence of restoration. God predestines those whom He foreknows; then He calls upon them to fulfill the purpose of His providence. Calling the person is God's responsibility, but that alone does not entitle the person to be justified before God and be given glory. Only when the person completes his responsibility after being called by God is he justified and then glorified. God's predestination concerning an individual's glorification is thus contingent upon the completion of his portion of responsibility. Because the biblical verse does not mention the human portion of responsibility, people may misinterpret it to mean that all affairs are determined solely by God's absolute predestination. (*Exposition of the Divine Principle*, Predestination 4)

It is written that God loved Jacob and hated Esau even when they were still inside their mother's womb and had not done anything good or evil. God favored one and disfavored the other and told Rebecca that "the elder will serve the younger." (Romans 9.10-13) What was the reason for this favoritism? God favored one over the other in order to set up a certain course in the Providence of Restoration.

God gave Isaac twin sons, Esau and Jacob, with the intention of having them stand in the positions of Cain and Abel. They were to make the conditions of indemnity necessary for accomplishing His Will to recover the birthright of the elder brother, which was lost when Cain killed Abel in Adam's family. God intended to realize this Will by having Jacob (in the position of Abel) win over his elder brother Esau (in the position of Cain). Since Esau was in the position of Cain, he was "hated" by God. Since Jacob was in the position of Abel, he could receive God's love.

Nevertheless, whether God would in the end favor or disfavor them depended on whether or not they completed their given portions of responsibility. In fact, because Esau obediently submitted to Jacob, he was able to rise above his previous condition of being hated by God and receive the blessing of God's love equal to Jacob's. Conversely, even though Jacob was initially in the position to receive God's favor, he would have ceased to receive it had he failed in his responsibility. (*Exposition of the Divine Principle*, Predestination 4)

2. The Seemingly Chance Events of Life Are Actually the Workings of Destiny

No man bruises his finger here on earth unless it was so decreed against him in Heaven.

Talmud, Hullin 7b (Judaism)

Where you fall, there your God pushed you down.

Igbo Proverb (African Traditional Religions)

The order that God has arranged, mortal man cannot upset.

Akan Proverb (African Traditional Religions)

Whatever you do not wish to do because of
    your delusions,
You will do even against your will, bound by
    your karma.
The Lord, Arjuna, is present inside all beings,
Moving them like puppets by his magic power.

Bhagavad-Gita 18.60-61 (Hinduism)

Yüeh-cheng Tzu saw Mencius. "I mentioned you to the prince," said he, "and he was to have come to see you. Amongst his favorites is one Tsang who dissuaded him. That is why he failed to come."

"When a man goes forward," said Mencius, "there is something which urges him on; when he halts, there is something which holds him back. It is not in his power either to go forward or to halt. It is due to Heaven that I failed to meet the Marquis of Lu. How can this fellow Tsang be responsible for my failure?"

Mencius I.B.16

Do not say about anything, "I am going to do that tomorrow," without adding, "If God will." Remember your Lord whenever you forget, and say, "Perhaps my Lord will guide me even closer than this to proper conduct."

Qur'an 18.23-24

Come now, you who say, "Today or tomorrow we will go into such and such a town and spend a year there and trade and get gain;" whereas you do not know about tomorrow. What is your life? For you are a mist that appears for a little time and then vanishes. Instead you ought to say, "If the Lord wills, we shall live and we shall do this or that." As it is, you boast in your arrogance. All such boasting is evil.

James 4.13-16

For not of your will were you formed, and not of your own will were you born, and not of your will do you live, and not of your own will will you die, and not of your will are you to give account and reckoning before the Supreme King of kings, the Holy One, Blessed be He.

Mishnah, Avot 4.29 (Judaism)

Time is no one's friend and no one's enemy; when the effect of his acts in a former existence, by which his present existence is caused, has expired, he snatches a man away forcibly. A man will not die before his time has come, even though he has been pierced by a thousand shafts; he will not live after his time is out, even though he has only been touched by the point of a blade of grass. Neither drugs, nor magical formulas, nor burnt offerings, nor prayers will save a man who is in the bonds of death or old age. An impending evil cannot be averted even by a hundred precautions; what reason then for you to complain?

Institutes of Vishnu 20.43-46 (Hinduism)

Teachings of Sun Myung Moon

Our meeting together here is the unfolding of destiny through which God is weaving all things into one. This is not a chance encounter. The destiny that brought you here was formed over a long history. Among the multitudes of people of the world, why were you in particular able to come here?

Wherever you lived before you came here, Heaven checked your background [and determined that you had merit]. (November 4, 1990)

Despite all the difficulties and sufferings I endured after I came to America, I knew that I was destined to meet there with people who would appear out of the countless destined relationships[15] that composed America's history. It was my mission to guide them all to the path of God's blessings. Since I knew these things with certainty, I accepted every challenge and took it as my cross to bear, in order that in my lifetime I could give blessings to the people who represented such greatness.

I thought that I would meet some direct descendants of the Pilgrims, born of survivors among the 102 souls who endured such tribulations that half of them died either at sea or during that first winter. I thought about how fascinating it would be to meet them. The knowledge of what they went through encouraged me to overcome the obstacles in my path. No amount of rejection, persecution and cursing could weaken my determination to fulfill my responsibility to seek out and care for the descendants of the Pilgrims who came to my church through the working out of their destiny.

When I was released from the prison at Danbury, I did not want to return to Korea straight away. I preferred to stay in America one more week, even one more year, in hopes of meeting someone beloved of Heaven. I waited in America because still I sought to inherit her historical tradition. Even now, whenever I meet someone new, I think about how long his or her ancestors have waited for this moment. Since they waited, should I not also wait to receive them? Do you understand what I am saying?

When you have that kind of attitude throughout your life, you have no cause for complaint. If you bump into someone on the street, even a troublemaker who tries to pick a fight with you, you should think, "What is this situation going to bring me?" Instead of rejecting it, be open to the moment as an opportunity for the unfolding of destiny. Maybe you look around and suddenly see a long-lost relative, separated fifty years ago during the Korean War when you both had become refugees. What is the likelihood of such an "accidental" meeting? If that person had not bothered you on the street, you would have missed your only chance to meet your long-lost relative. Yet what was behind that incident? What made that man accost you? He may not know himself; he was playing a part in the unfolding of destiny.

When something like that happens, you should stop and think about your involvement in the encounter. If you did not keep an attitude to welcome destiny, it would have passed you by. Since a seemingly chance encounter may be fraught with destiny, you should not take anything casually.

You know the story of Joseph. His brothers put him in a well thinking to kill him, but they sold him instead and he was brought to Egypt as a slave. There the wife of his master Potiphar tried to seduce him, and when he would not be tempted she had him imprisoned. While in prison and waiting for the day of his execution, he interpreted Pharaoh's dream and was raised to the rank of Prime Minister of Egypt. How, in the midst of his misery, could Joseph have even imagined that such good fortune would befall him? Yet these things opened the way for him to save the Israelites. Who could have known that it would turn out that way? (November 4, 1990)

3. The Relationship between Destiny and Free Will

Rabbi Akiba says, Everything is foreseen, yet freedom of choice is given; the world is judged by grace, yet all is according to the preponderance of works.[16]

Mishnah, Avot 3.19 (Judaism)

No affliction befalls, except by the leave of God. Whoever believes in God, He will guide his heart. God has knowledge of everything.

Qur'an 64.11

O my servants, every one of you is in error, except the one I have guided, so ask guidance from Me and I will guide you. O my servants, every one of you is hungry, except him whom I have fed, so ask food of Me and I will feed you. O my servants, every one of you is naked except him whom I have clothed, so ask clothing of Me and I will clothe you. O my servants, you sin day and night, and I pardon your sins; so ask pardon of Me and I will pardon you.

Forty Hadith of an-Nawawi 24 (Islam)

All by Thee is accomplished, Thine is the might,
Thou watcheth Thy handiwork,
With chess pieces raw and ripe.
All that into the world have come, must depart hence—
All shall by turns go.
Why put out of mind the Lord, master of life and death?
By one's own hands is one's affairs set straight.[17]

Adi Granth, Asa-ki-Var, M.1, p. 473-74 (Sikhism)

Even though God foresees the free acts of the human will, freedom of choice remains, for God sees all time concurrently and through eternity.[18]

Boethius, The Consolation of Philosophy (Christianity)

Teachings of Sun Myung Moon

God is the absolute Being, unique, eternal and unchanging; therefore, the purpose of His creation must also be absolute, unique, eternal and unchanging... It follows that God's predestination of His Will—that the purpose of creation one day be fulfilled—must also be absolute, as it is written, "I have spoken, and I will bring it to pass; I have purposed, and I will do it." (Isa. 46.11) Since God predestines His Will absolutely, if the person who has been chosen to accomplish His Will fails, God must continue to carry on His providence until its fulfillment, even though it may require Him to choose another person to shoulder the mission.

For example, God willed that His purpose of creation be fulfilled through Adam. Although this did not come to pass, God's predestination of this providential will has remained absolute. Hence, God sent Jesus as the second Adam...

Although God's Will to realize the purpose of the providence of restoration is absolute, God predestines the process of its accomplishment conditionally, contingent upon the five percent responsibility of the central figure, which must be completed in addition to the ninety-five percent responsibility of God. The proportion of five percent is used to indicate that the human portion of responsibility is extremely small when compared to God's portion of responsibility. Yet for human beings, this five percent is equivalent to one hundred percent of our effort...

To what extent does God determine the fate of an individual? The fulfillment of God's Will through an individual absolutely requires that he complete his responsibility. Hence, even though God predestines someone for a particular mission, God's ninety-five percent responsibility and the person's five percent responsibility must be accomplished together before the person can complete his given mission and fulfill God's Will. If the person does not complete his responsibility, he cannot become the person God has purposed him to be. (*Exposition of the Divine Principle*, Predestination)

No matter what people may say or do, they are subject to the rhythm of heavenly fortune, which power flows throughout the universe. No one has the power to stand against it, so they are inclined to follow along with it. People who follow the right path in alignment with heavenly fortune grow and prosper along with it. Since they move with its rhythm as it pulses throughout the universe, they are bound to live forever. Nevertheless, many Western people want to be masters of their own destiny, but since they disregard the rhythm of heavenly fortune, things will not go as they want. Therefore, clever and wise Westerners will align themselves with the Principle that governs the universe...

No one wants to perish. No nation wants to perish. Nevertheless, today so many people are perishing, and nations are on the path of decline. Why are they perishing? It is not because of anything I do. But when the very universe opposes them, how can they stand against it? Only people who are aligned with heavenly fortune and who are obedient to the Principle that governs the universe can expect to survive and prosper. This has been the case for the heroes and saints throughout history. Wouldn't you like to become a hero or a saint? (94:19-20, June 19, 1977)

Synergy of Grace and Effort

THE RELATIONSHIP BETWEEN DIVINE GRACE AND HUMAN EFFORT is what Thomas Aquinas called synergy: effort calls forth grace, and grace prompts effort. A number of texts stress human initiative as calling forth grace—"God helps those who help themselves"; others describe God's grace as preceding and calling for our response.

Father Moon teaches that God's grace and power contribute some ninety-five percent towards the fulfillment of a work, leaving five percent as the human portion of responsibility. By leaving a small portion of the work unfinished as our portion, God provides a way for human beings to share in the work of creation and enjoy the glory of co-creators.

However, in the course of salvation history, the requirement that we human beings do our portion has sometimes been a cause of frustration to God when we fail or fall short; it means that God cannot unilaterally complete the task by Himself. God will reliably do His portion, but human beings are unreliable. Therefore, giving human beings a portion of responsibility means that God is essentially placing the fate of the universe in our hands.

Ask, and it will be given to you; seek, and you will find; knock, and it will be opened to you.

Matthew 7.7

He who conforms to the Way is gladly accepted by the Way;
he who conforms to virtue is gladly accepted by virtue;
he who conforms to loss is gladly accepted by loss.

Tao Te Ching 23 *(Taoism)*

If a man sanctify himself a little, he becomes much sanctified; if he sanctify himself below, he becomes sanctified from above; if he sanctify himself in this world, he becomes sanctified in the world to come.

Talmud, Yoma 39a *(Judaism)*

Work out your own salvation with fear and trembling; for God is at work in you, both to will and to work for his good pleasure.

Philippians 2.12-13

God changes not what is in a people, until they change what is in themselves.
Qur'an 13.11

Remembering me, you shall overcome all difficulties through my grace.
But if you will not heed me in your self-will, nothing will avail you.
Bhagavad-Gita 18.58 (Hinduism)

If you wish to find the true way,
Right action will lead you to it directly;
But if you do not strive for Buddhahood
You will grope in the dark and never find it.
Sutra of Hui Neng 2 (Buddhism)

Heaven helps the man who is devoted; men help the man who is true. The man who walks in truth and is devoted in his thinking, and furthermore reveres the worthy—he is blessed by Heaven.
I Ching, Great Commentary 1.12.1 (Confucianism)

God has declared: I am close to the thought that my servant has of Me, and I am with him whenever he recollects Me. If he remembers Me in himself, I remember him in Myself, and if he remembers Me in a gathering I remember him better than those in the gathering do, and if he approaches Me by as much as one hand's length, I approach him by a cubit... If he takes a step towards Me, I run towards him.
Hadith (Islam)

God gives each person a hook with which to pluck his fruit.
Igbo Proverb (African Traditional Religions)

Behold, I stand at the door and knock; if any one hears my voice and opens the door, I will come in to him and eat with him, and he with me.
Revelation 3.20

Prayer indeed is good, but while calling on the gods a man should himself lend a hand.
Hippocrates[19]

It is from below that the movement starts, and thereafter is all perfected. If the community of Israel failed to initiate the impulse, the one from above would also not move to go her. It is thus the yearning from below which brings about the completion above.
Zohar (Judaism)

All undertakings in this world depend both on the ordering of fate and on human exertion; but among these two the ways of fate are unfathomable; in the case of man's work action is possible.
Laws of Manu 7.205 (Hinduism)

Teachings of Sun Myung Moon

You must participate in God's great creative undertaking... Although God provides 95 percent of the ideal form necessary to reach perfection, human beings must still complete the remaining 5 percent by their own responsibility. God alone cannot bring about human perfection; each person has the responsibility to make a contribution in perfecting him or herself. (115:66, November 4, 1981)

The spirit grows through give and take action between two types of nourishment: life elements of a yang type that come from God and vitality elements of a yin type that come from the physical self. (*Exposition of the Divine Principle*, Creation 6.3.2)

As long as you complain and lament over your situation while just sitting in your chair, you will not make progress. God will not help you. God wants you to make new efforts each day. (327:48, July 24, 2000)

God creates to the level of 95 percent and then human beings should add their efforts in accordance with God's basic rules for creation in order to establish a value standard of 100 percent. In this way, God wants to give human beings the value of having participated in the completion of His Will. (130:19, December 11, 1983)

The proportion of five percent is used to indicate that the human portion of responsibility is extremely small when compared to God's portion of responsibility. Yet for human beings, this five percent is equivalent to one hundred percent of our effort...

We should recognize how minuscule the human portion of responsibility is in comparison to God's toil and grace, which is His portion of responsibility. On the other hand, when we consider the fact that over and over again central figures in the providence could not cope with their responsibility, we can appreciate how extremely difficult it was for them to fulfill even this comparatively small portion. (*Exposition of the Divine Principle*, Predestination 2)

No matter how great the saving grace of the cross of Christ, the salvation knocking at our door will be for naught unless we fortify our faith, which is our portion of responsibility. It was God's responsibility to grant the benefit of resurrection through the crucifixion of Jesus, but to believe or not to believe is strictly one's own portion of responsibility. (*Exposition of the Divine Principle*, Creation 5.2.2)

We are endowed with the nature to empathize with God. We should develop that nature; then when God rejoices we also will rejoice, and when God is sorrowful we also will be sorrowful. Unless you become a person who can intimately experience God's deep inner heart, you are in no position to become one with God and live in harmony with God, regardless of how much God loves you. (39:8-9, January 9, 1971)

God has borne all the responsibility for His sons and daughters on the road of restoration. But now surely the time has come when we should take on that responsibility. God has borne all that responsibility to help us, but now, by taking on Satan's attack, we can stand up as God's sons and daughters. (31:50, April 12, 1970)

Preparation and Making a Good Beginning

FOR ANY VENTURE TO SUCCEED, IT MUST BEGIN WELL. The Oriental proverb, "Well begun is half done," describes the theme of the passages in this section. A good beginning means, first of all, internal preparation. We should purify our heart, steel ourselves with firm resolution, and be clear about our philosophy and methods of proper action. Then we should take the measure of the task and gather sufficient resources to surmount the obstacles in our path. This is practical advice, but it applies especially to the spiritual aspirant. Those who regard life lightly and frivolously are liable to fall into straits worse than when they started.

Father Moon teaches that to become a person of significance, someone who makes a difference in the world, we need to prepare well. Without fixing our purpose, our life becomes ordinary and of no consequence, and without setting our determination and preparing a foundation of self-discipline, we are liable to be defeated by the challenges that await us. He provides the example of his own life, describing the preparations he made to take on the entire corrupt world-system.

1. Prepare Yourself for Life's Challenges

The superior man does not embark upon any affair until he has carefully planned the start.

I Ching 6: Conflict *(Confucianism)*

Success is the result of foresight and resolution; foresight depends upon deep thinking and planning to keep your secrets to yourself.

Nahjul Balagha, Saying 46 *(Shiite Islam)*

Check the edge of the axe before splitting wood.

Njak Proverb *(African Traditional Religions)*

The superior man gathers his weapons together in order to provide against the unforeseen.

I Ching 45: Gathering Together *(Confucianism)*

For which of you, desiring to build a tower, does not first sit down and count the cost, whether he has enough to complete it? Otherwise, when he has laid a foundation, and is not able to finish, all who see it begin to mock him, saying, "This man began to build, and was not able to finish." Or what king, going to encounter another king in war, will not sit down first and take counsel whether he is able with ten thousand to meet him who comes against him with twenty thousand?

Luke 14.28-31

Put on the whole armor of God, that you may be able to stand against the wiles of the devil... that you may be able to withstand the evil day.

Ephesians 6.10, 13

He who wants to expand the field of happiness, let him lay the foundation of it on the bottom of his heart.

Tract of the Quiet Way *(Taoism)*

Do you not know that in a race all the runners compete, but only one receives the prize? So run that you may obtain it. Every athlete exercises self-control in all things. They do it to receive a perishable wreath, but we an imperishable. Well, I do not run aimlessly, I do not box as one beating the air; but I pommel my body and subdue it, lest after preaching to others I myself should be disqualified.

1 Corinthians 9.24-27

A ship, which is not well prepared, in the ocean goes to destruction, together with its goods and merchants.
But when a ship is well prepared, and well joined together,
then it does not break up, and all the goods get to the other shore.
Just so a bodhisattva, exalted in faith,
but deficient in wisdom, swiftly comes to a failure in enlightenment.
But when he is well joined to wisdom, the foremost perfection,
he experiences, unharmed and uninjured, the enlightenment of the Jinas.

Verses on the Perfection of Wisdom which is the Storehouse of Precious Virtues 14.7-8 *(Buddhism)*

Teachings of Sun Myung Moon

To overcome a crisis you must have deep faith, plans made in detail, and the conviction to carry them out. (*Way of God's Will* 3.4)

Too many people today lack any sense of responsibility. They do not set goals or plan what they will do each day, they do not plan out the year, nor do they have a plan for their life. They just live moment by moment, doing whatever they please and grasping at whatever benefit comes their way. What will be the end result? Someday they will hit a stone wall and be shattered into pieces. (105:11, July 8, 1979)

You should have a definite sense of what kind of work you will do by the time you reach your twenties. You should be able to say with certainty, "This is what I will do," and fight to achieve it throughout your lifetime. That is the only way you can become an historic person, a person who contributes something to the world. If you only try to accommodate to circumstances and simply go with the flow, you will be carried away by the current and disappear.

After determining exactly what you will do, you will need a heart bold enough to continue fighting for your goal no matter what difficulties may arise. Instead of saying you don't like this or that, you must have the guts to digest whatever comes. (120:229, October 20, 1982)

Even if Heaven has prepared everything, it will not work unless we have prepared a corresponding foundation in our minds and bodies. (7:287, October 11, 1959)

Each morning when you go out into the fallen world, prepare your eyes, nose, ears, and every cell, even your mind, like armament ready for battle. (122:266, November 21, 1982)

To live is to compete. We cannot develop without competition. Losing a competition makes us miserable, but it can spur us to strive for the capability we need in order to win. To gain that capability, we need time to prepare and train…

A student studies to prepare. Especially adolescents should prepare, while carrying big dreams… By preparing intellectually, you can conquer the mental world. Then you are ready to act and utilize your well-honed capabilities to win in the competition. (*Blessing and Ideal Family* 7.5.5)

All of you want to be successful. How do you gain success? You have to prepare well. You should prepare, with enough material that you are able to digest the existing world, for upon it you are to erect your own new foundation. Your new foundation should exceed the old foundation; otherwise, you will not succeed in establishing it. This is a lesson of history. It is true in the path of our individual lives and in the life of our nation.

Look at the Unification Church: We face difficulties and persecution, yet in the midst of it all we are preparing for the future. Today I am fighting alone against America, a superpower with a population of 240 million that is feared the world over. Yet none of its leaders know of my work; none of them help me; none is my friend. In this situation, I cannot fight blindly. I prepare myself. I must prepare thoroughly and completely.

What preparation do I need? First, I must prepare mentally, to have an indomitable spirit that will never be defeated. Second, I must make more effort than anyone else in history to contribute to America's well being. Third, I must make concrete preparations for specific actions.

I must have a thoroughgoing and complete teaching, and then I need to strive. I cannot sit and rest with only a teaching. Having equipped myself with the truth, I must make limitless effort. Moreover, my effort cannot be self-centered. To generate the subjectivity required to surpass the existing system will require unending struggle. The guardians of the old order are not about to welcome a new system. Every new movement in history is tested in the crucible of conflict, where it either flourishes or perishes.

I try to find a way to overcome every difficulty. I proceed regardless of the price I must pay. It is an effort not to be absorbed by others, but to absorb them. Furthermore, I need a consistent praxis. As a religious leader, my method cannot involve violence. I work quietly. If others work eight hours a day, then I work twenty-four hours…

I cannot afford to lose! I must prepare myself, even with blood and tears. In the midst of tears, I must prepare! Though I am starving, I must prepare! Though I weep bitter tears, I must move forward! Though I may have to sleep on the streets, I must move forward! I do not believe that Heaven's victory is possible without making such a commitment. (133:217-226, July 19, 1984)

2. Taking the First Step

A big tree was once a small seed;
a nine-storey building started with a basket of earth;
a journey of a thousand miles begins with a first step.

Tao Te Ching 64

The way of the superior man may be compared to traveling to a distant place: one must start from the nearest stage. It may also be likened to ascending a height: one must begin with the lowest step.

Doctrine of the Mean 15

Teachings of Sun Myung Moon

After receiving the command of God which foretold that He would judge the earth after 120 years, Noah did not wait around, thinking, "So what if a year has passed; there are still 119 years left." God commands only once; it is up to each individual to commit to its great purpose. (19:237)

To achieve victory for the year, set your goals on New Year's Day. Then equip yourself with a fighting spirit and a driving power to pursue your goals and overcome the challenges for 365 days or more. If you do not do this, you are bound to be defeated before the year is over.

If you live one year like this, and then continue in this manner, it will eventually add up to 10 years, then 20 years, 30 years—and this becomes the path of a victorious life. (31:30, April 12, 1970)

Eternity does not start when we die. It begins at the moment we come to know God's will. Once we know it, if there is a gap of even one moment, eternity will be stopped.

Therefore, in pursuit of our life of faith, if we think, "I cannot make it this year, but I will do it next year" or "I cannot go in my adolescence, but I will go in my 20s," or "I cannot do it in my 20s, but surely I will in my 30s" or "I cannot in my 30s but I will in my 40s" or "I cannot in my 40s but I will in my 50s"… If we lived our whole life like this, we would never have lived even one day in accordance with God's Will. A person who lives like that cannot enter the Kingdom of Heaven when he dies. (37:219, December 27, 1970)

Perseverance and Patience

TO ACCOMPLISH ANYTHING TRULY WORTHWHILE requires perseverance and patience. Patience is not merely to wait for fate to intervene; rather it means to continue on one's path until the goal is achieved. Once the resolution is made and the task is begun, it should not be abandoned, for the result is often not decided until the very end. Perseverance requires long-suffering endurance of opposition, setbacks and delays, while maintaining steadfastly to one's original commitment. It requires forbearance, resisting the temptation to change course or take a shortcut that would violate one's principles. The scriptures express the virtue of perseverance through various metaphors: digging a well, boring to the pith of a tree, and water slowly but inexorably carving a hole in solid rock.

In this light, Father Moon speaks of God's forbearance as He has endured millennia of evils and sorrows, putting up with His fallen children's sins and rebellions out of love and hope for their ultimate liberation. Therefore, by demonstrating perseverance and patience, we take after God's perseverance and patience on our way to becoming God's sons and daughters. For the story of Job's patience in the midst of suffering, see Chapter 15: Testing.

1. Perseverance, Endurance and Forbearance

Though he be ever so tired by repeated failure, let him begin his operations again and again; for fortune greatly favors the man who perseveres in his undertakings.

Laws of Manu 9.300 (Hinduism)

Perseverance prevails even against Heaven.

Talmud, Sanhedrin 105a (Judaism)

Prosperity forsakes those who always dream of fate and favors those who persevere. One should therefore always be active and alert.

Matsya Purana 221.2 (Hinduism)

Once when the Master was standing by a stream, he said, "Could one but go on and on like this, never ceasing day or night!"

Analects 9.16 (Confucianism)

If fishermen, hunters, and farmers,
Thinking merely of their own livelihood,
Endure the sufferings of heat and cold,
Why am I not patient for the sake of the
　world's joy?

Shantideva, Guide to the Bodhisattva's
Way of Life 4.40 (Buddhism)

In the day of prosperity be joyful, and in the day of adversity consider; God made the one as well as the other, so that man may not find out anything that will be after him.

Ecclesiastes 7.14

You who believe, seek help through patience and prayer; God stands alongside the patient! We will test you with a bit of fear and hunger, and a shortage of wealth and souls and produce. Proclaim such to patient people who say, whenever disaster strikes them, "We are God's, and are returning to Him!" Such will be granted their prayers by their Lord as well as mercy. Those are guided!

Qur'an 2.153-57

Nanak, for man it is idle to ask for pleasure
　when suffering comes;
Pleasure and suffering are like robes which man
　must wear as they come.
Where arguing is of no avail, it is best to be
　contented.

Adi Granth, Var Majh, M.1, p. 149 (Sikhism)

Obstacles cannot crush me. Every obstacle yields to stern resolve. He who is fixed to a star does not change his mind.

Leonardo Da Vinci, *Notebooks* (Humanism)

One should preserve, without the slightest diminution, the faith which one had at the time of renunciation. One should not be swept away by the eddies of a mercurial mind.

Acarangasutra 1.36-37 (Jainism)

Rabbi Akiba, illiterate at forty, saw one day a stone's perforation where water fell from a spring, and having heard people say, "Waters wear stones," he thought, "If soft water can bore through a rock, surely iron-clad Torah should, by sheer persistence, penetrate a tender mind"; and he turned to study.

Talmud, Avot de Rabbi Nathan 6 (Judaism)

It matters not what you learn; but when you once learn a thing, you must never give it up until you have mastered it. It matters not what you inquire into, but when you inquire into a thing, you must never give it up until you have thoroughly understood it. It matters not what you try to think out, but when you once try to think out a thing you must never give it up until you have got what you want. It matters not what you try to sift out, but when you once try to sift out a thing, you must never give it up until you have sifted it out clearly and distinctly. It matters not what you try to carry out, but when you once try to carry out a thing you must never give it up until you have done it thoroughly and well. If another man succeed by one effort, you will use a hundred efforts. If another man succeed by ten efforts, you will use a thousand efforts. Let a man really proceed in this manner, and though dull, he will surely become intelligent; though weak, he will surely become strong.

Doctrine of the Mean 20 (Confucianism)

The LORD waits to be gracious to you;
therefore he exalts himself to show mercy to you.
For the LORD is a God of justice;
blessed are all those who wait for him.

Isaiah 30.18

Teachings of Sun Myung Moon

Look at the Chinese character meaning 'patience' or 'forbearance.' The top half is the character for sword, and the bottom half the character for heart.[20] From this, you can see that 'patience' means 'to set a sword over your heart.' If you are going to shoulder a large burden and accomplish a great task, your patience must be a hundredfold, a thousandfold, even infinite. (124:155-56, February 6, 1983)

The Chinese character for patience indicates that one should endure even under the threat of a knife to the heart. It is painful to have a knife stuck in your heart. Yet a person who endures that a thousand times can hope to triumph in a thousand battles. (93:320, June 12, 1977)

On your quest you will be hampered by innumerable foes, but you must fight them and fight them again, advance and advance again, clash and clash again. Thus supporting the altar of patience with your shoulders, feet, hands, torso and head, you must become a living offering who can climb over the hill of perseverance. (6:92, March 29, 1959)

A mature person makes effort to discover the sweet taste in all things bitter. That way, he knows their real taste. It is a law that things are sometimes up, sometimes down, as they go through their cycles. Likewise, sweet things leave a bitter taste, while bitter things have some sweetness in them. (98:205, August 1, 1978)

No matter how tired I may feel, once I think of the responsibility I have yet to fulfill, all that feeling of fatigue dissipates. (*Way of God's Will* 1.5)

The way of religion is prolonged endurance; the way of religion is continual sacrifice. When in faith we endure and sacrifice, we can find the world of great love that God has been working towards. This is definitely true. Therefore, when we say that God is love, we should understand that sacrifice and endurance dwell in it. (112:51, March 29, 1981)

Which is the good side? The good side waits for a long time, keeps patience for a long time and keeps hope for a long time. The evil side has no patience. If it is at a disadvantage, it will try to punch the other and jump to action at once. The good stays patient and endures even through struggle and frustration. Whatever comes, it maintains hope and does not fall into despair. A good person is patient and enduring not only for himself; he is also patient and enduring for those who are not patient. (93:112, May 21, 1977)

What was the secret of Jesus' victory over death? He lived for the sake of others and established a path of endurance through his own example. If in the Garden of Gethsemane he had said, "Father! Take this cup away from me! Please, I insist on it!" he would have lost everything. Yet instead he said, "Nevertheless, not my will, but Thy will be done." Because he endured and went on, he was victorious. That is his greatness. (76:227, March 2, 1975)

No torture or punishment could make me deviate from the heavenly path. Nor could six imprisonments stand in the way of the True Parent's search for His children. As I sat in a cold prison cell and watched drops of water fall from an eave, I pledged to myself, "Just as those droplets will eventually bore a hole through a boulder, the day will certainly come when these hot tears that fall from my eyes will melt God's heart that is frozen in grief and bring Him liberation and release." (May 1, 2004)

God has the mind to forbear with patience, in order to one day embrace the satanic world and even hell. That is why even the demons in hell will bow their heads before His presence. Therefore, if you desire to become champions at the last, the Father's sons and daughters at the last, then in your minds and bodies you must feel God's patience as your patience and God's endurance as your endurance. (4:243, May 18, 1958)

> Father, what Thou doest, we Thy children should do,
> and on the path Thou goest, we too must go—it is a destined way.
> Therefore, please do not allow us to become exhausted on the way,
> and give us unwavering hearts... to persevere and endure
> until the day we can receive the blessing,
> the day of Sabbath when Thou canst say,
> "You have won the victory, and you are Mine;
> all heaven and earth belong to you,
> My sons and daughters." (13:236, March 22, 1964)

2. Never Give Up, but Persevere to the Very End

Scripture credits with performance not him who begins a task, but him who completes it.
Talmud, Sota 13b (Judaism)

He who endures to the end will be saved.
Mark 13.13

But Lot's wife behind him looked back, and she became a pillar of salt.
Genesis 19.26

Let us not grow weary in well-doing, for in due season we shall reap, if we do not lose heart.
Galatians 6.9

You have crossed the great ocean; why do you halt so near the shore? Make haste to get on the other side, Gautama; be careful all the while!
Uttaradhyayana Sutra 10.34 (Jainism)

To try to achieve anything is like digging a well. You can dig a hole nine fathoms deep, but if you fail to reach the source of water, it is just an abandoned well.
Mencius VII.A.29 (Confucianism)

Suppose a man goes to the forest to get some of the pith that grows in the center of a tree and returns with a burden of branches and leaves, thinking that he has secured what he went after; would he not be foolish?

A person seeks a path that will lead him away from misery; and yet, he follows that path a little way, notices some little advance, and immediately becomes proud and conceited. He is like the man who sought pith and came back satisfied with a burden of branches and leaves.

Another man goes into the forest seeking pith and comes back with a load of branches. He is like the person on the path who becomes satisfied with the progress he has made by a little effort, and relaxes his effort and becomes proud and conceited.

Another man comes back carrying a load of bark instead of the pith he was looking for. He is like the person who finds that his mind is becoming calmer and his thoughts clearer, and then relaxes his effort and becomes proud and conceited.

Then another man brings back a load of the woody fiber of the tree instead of the pith. Like him is one who has gained a measure of intuitive insight, and then relaxes his effort. All of these seekers, who become easily satisfied after insufficient effort and become proud and overbearing, relax their efforts and easily fall into idleness. All these people will inevitably face suffering again.
Majjhima Nikaya 1.192-95: Simile of the Pith (Buddhism)

Master Tseng said, "The true Knight of the Way must perforce be both broad-shouldered and stout of heart; his burden is heavy and he has far to go. For Goodness is the burden he has taken upon himself; and must we not grant that it is a heavy one to bear? Only with death does his journey end; then must we not grant that he has far to go?"
Analects 8.7 (Confucianism)

Teachings of Sun Myung Moon

The Bible records… that in the Last Days even people with faith will find it hard to survive. Therefore, you must endure and forbear until the very end if you are to overcome this age of chaos and become victors. (4:237, May 18, 1958)

Our endurance should not end midway; it should go all the way. God has endured for six thousand years for this. Who is God? He is our Father. Because we inherited His flesh and blood and His virtues, we must be like Him. (44:28, May 4, 1971)

You cannot complete your life of faith in one morning or one day. It is a lifelong path. In a life of faith, the main issue is to maintain your dedication with a constant mind and heart with a view towards eternity, beyond death. Your center core must be unchanging. No matter how difficult, sorrowful or painful, it can never change. To follow the path of faith you must discover this core in yourself, something you can never deny. (59:234-35, July 23, 1972)

Even though you have forbearance, you may realize that it is far from the terminal point. Today many who have been supporting our church say that they are too tired to go on. You hear people say that the Unification Church is good, but its way is too difficult to follow... Indeed, it is hard to go this way. It is a path of tears—tears over what we see, tears over what we feel, and tears in the midst of struggle. Some think that now the time has come for the tears to stop, but it is not yet.

I know that the tears must continue; I know that the heart of God is waiting for more tears of forbearance, waiting for us, the plaintive ones. I cannot lift my face before Him even though I have endured thus far. Though I have endured from 1945 until today,[21] I have never thought about when I might reach the limit of patient forbearance.

I do not even wish for the days of endurance to end. It is a normal experience in the life of faith that once you start wishing for something to end you start looking after yourselves, and from that point on you feel anxious. (6:89, March 29, 1959)

God is eternal. Once He determines to do something, He never alters His course in the middle. What about you? You may be determined, but how long will you continue? For a month, a year, several years, ten years? Or will you continue for your entire lifetime? Your determination is bound to change. Sometimes you say to yourself, "If I like it, then I will do it. If I do not like it, I will not do it." However, truth is truth whether you live or die; it is eternal. Truth is beyond death, beyond changeability.

Therefore, in order to be a true person, with the steadfastness of unchanging truth, you have to be beyond death. To be beyond death, you first have to conquer death. This means there will be a collision at some point between your changeability and unchangeability. When they collide, your changeable elements will shatter and only your unchanging elements will remain. It will be a collision between life and death. At that time you must overcome death; then you will have life. It is reasonable that you must pass through this stage on the path to making a relationship with God.

When will the moment of truth come for you? It will be the time when there arises an opportunity to be unchanging and changing at the same time. Both life and death appear before you. That is when the truth emerges. (66:43, March 18, 1973)

CHAPTER 12

MORALITY

Self-Control

SELF-CONTROL IS THE BASIS OF ALL VIRTUES. Unruly thoughts, attractions of the senses, lustful desires, anger, covetousness, and avarice constantly arise in the mind of the person who has no mental discipline; and these impel him to do evil deeds. If a person cannot even direct his own thoughts, desires, and actions, how can he possibly have integrity in his relations with others? How can he keep his life on the path of truth? The philosopher John Locke said, "The discipline of desire is the background of character."

The passages in this section feature two nearly universal metaphors employed to describe self-control: military conquest and the horse and rider. The conquest of self is the most difficult of all conquests, yet the most important. Father Moon teaches that regardless of one's high-minded motives to change the world, all efforts are futile without the foundation of having mastered oneself. The task of gaining self-control is also likened to a rider on a wild horse. The higher mind or conscience, like an experienced rider, must gain control over the beast within. He may have to employ the bit and bridle of self-denial and asceticism, yet at all costs he must tame and subdue the lower self with its wanton desires.

1. Victory over the Self

Though one should conquer a million men on the battlefield, yet he, indeed, is the noblest victor who has conquered himself.

Dhammapada 103 *(Buddhism)*

He who is slow to anger is better than the mighty,
and he who rules his spirit than he who takes a city.

Proverbs 16.32

I count him braver who overcomes his desires than him who conquers his enemies; for the hardest victory is the victory over self.

Aristotle[1] *(Hellenism)*

Who is strong? He who controls his passions.

Mishnah, Avot 4.1 *(Judaism)*

He who conquers others has physical strength;
He who conquers himself is strong.

Tao Te Ching 33 *(Taoism)*

The Prophet declared, "We have returned from the lesser holy war (*al jihad al-asghar*) to the greater holy war (*al jihad al-akbar*)." They asked, "O Prophet of God, which is the greater war?" He replied, "Struggle against the lower self."[2]

Hadith *(Islam)*

Though a man should conquer thousands and thousands of valiant foes, greater will be his victory if he conquers nobody but himself.

Fight with yourself; why fight with external foes? He who conquers himself through himself will obtain happiness....

Difficult to conquer is oneself; but when that is conquered, everything is conquered.

Uttaradhyayana Sutra 9.34-36 (Jainism)

In the human soul there is a better and also a worse principle; and when the better has the worse under control, then a man is said to be master of himself; and this is a term of praise: but when, owing to evil education or association, the better principle, which is also the smaller, is overwhelmed by the greater mass of the worse—in this case he is blamed and is called the slave of self and unprincipled.

Plato, The Republic 9 (Hellenism)

Superior nature can be taught and inferior nature can be controlled.

Han Yu (Confucianism)

Man should discover his own reality
and not thwart himself.
For he has the self as his only friend,
or as his only enemy.
A person has the self as a friend
when he has conquered himself,
But if he rejects his own reality,
the self will war against him.

Bhagavad-Gita 6.5-6 (Hinduism)

Teachings of Sun Myung Moon

"Before you desire to have dominion over the universe, you must first have dominion over yourself": That is my motto. God's love, life and truth can be developed on the basis of self-mastery. (*Way of God's Will* 2.2)

Who is your enemy? The devil out there is not your enemy; you are your own enemy. Are your mind and body united as one in serving God? How difficult is it? Which is easier, to unite the world or to unite your own self? If you are united as an individual, then by extending that unity you can certainly unify the world. Then who is your enemy? Your own eyes are your enemy. Your own ears are your enemy. Your own nose is your enemy. Your own mouth is your enemy. Your own thoughts are your enemy. (91:285-86, February 27, 1977)

Because we are fallen, we have some elements to overcome. Therefore, I put forward the motto, "Before you desire to have dominion over the universe, you must first have dominion over yourself." The issue is not gaining worldly dominion. To have dominion over the self—this is the absolute goal of training. It is the purpose that religious people have pursued throughout history, and the important responsibility assigned to each of us today. Yet, we neglect this task. (82:281, February 1, 1976)

Stopping the mind and the body from fighting is more difficult than signing a truce to end a world war. (320:249, April 16, 2000)

2. Self-Discipline: Training the Unruly Beast Within

Be not like a horse or a mule, without
    understanding,
which must be curbed with bit and bridle, else
    it will not keep with you.

Psalm 32.9

Man makes a harness for his beast; all the more should he make one for the beast within himself, his evil desire.

Jerusalem Talmud, Sanhedrin 10.1 (Judaism)

Excellent are trained mules, so are thoroughbred horses of Sindh and noble tusked elephants; but far better is he who has trained himself.

Formerly this mind went wandering where it liked, as it wished and as it listed. Today with attentiveness I shall completely hold it in check, as a mahout controls an elephant in must.

Dhammapada 322, 326 (Buddhism)

Know that the Self is the rider, and the body the chariot; that the intellect is the charioteer, and the mind the reins. The senses, say the wise, are the horses; the roads they travel are the mazes of desire...

When a man lacks discrimination and his mind is uncontrolled, his senses are unmanageable, like the restive horses of a charioteer. But when a man has discrimination and his mind is controlled, his senses, like the well-broken horses of a charioteer, lightly obey the rein.

Katha Upanishad 1.3.3-6 (Hinduism)

The man of understanding... will regulate his bodily habit and training. Not yielding to brutal and irrational pleasures, he will regard even health as quite a secondary matter. His first aim will be not to be fair or strong or well, unless he is likely to gain temperance thereby, but to temper the body so as to preserve the harmony of the soul.

Plato, The Republic (Hellenism)

Irrigators lead the waters. Fletchers bend the shafts. Carpenters bend wood. The virtuous control themselves.[3]

Dhammapada 80 (Buddhism)

It is true that the mind is restless and difficult to control. But it can be conquered, Arjuna, through regular practice and detachment. Those who lack self-control will find it difficult to progress in meditation; but those who are self-controlled, striving earnestly through the right means, will attain the goal.

Bhagavad-Gita 6.35-36 (Hinduism)

What is meant by saying that cultivation of the personal life depends on the rectification of the mind is that when one is affected by wrath to any extent, his mind will not be correct. When one is affected by fear to any extent, his mind will not be correct. When he is affected by fondness to any extent, his mind will not be correct. When he is affected by worries and anxieties, his mind will not be correct. When the mind is not present, we look but do not see, listen but do not hear, and eat but do not know the taste of food. This is what is meant by saying that the cultivation of the personal life depends on the rectification of the mind.

Great Learning 7 (Confucianism)

That man is disciplined and happy
who can prevail over the turmoil
That springs from desire and anger,
here on earth, before he leaves his body.

Bhagavad-Gita 5.23 (Hinduism)

Teachings of Sun Myung Moon

The human conscience is the faculty of mind that represents God. It does not exist for your sake, but for the righteousness of Heaven. The conscience always strives for goodness. The body rebels against it. The body desires to be comfortable; it is selfish and insatiable to satisfy its instinctive needs. The conscience reproaches such a body and tries to bring it into submission. This is the reason why conflict and struggle arise continually within the self.

Therefore, religions throughout history have taught people methods to strike the body. Religions are training grounds to enable us to control our bodily desires and have the body to surrender to the mind. They train and guide fallen people to become the men and women God intended at the creation. (219:118, August 28, 1991)

"Before you desire to have dominion over the universe, you must first have dominion over yourself": I regard this as the most important matter. The three requisites for achieving this are to overcome the three enemies: food, sleep and sex. (366:287, January 17, 2002)

Despite every effort at self-cultivation, people are often caught by love. When they respond to the temptation of a handsome man or beautiful woman, they are caught. Human beings cannot claim to have attained self-mastery in matters of love. It is possible for people to control their sexual desire when they become one with God, but as long as they are self-centered they cannot overcome it. Even in movies, when a woman is being raped at first she fights, "No, no!" but once her passion is aroused she embraces the man. The power of love makes people give in to their enemies. (306:196, September 23, 1998)

Due to the Human Fall, love today is basically self-centered. That self-centered love does not originate from the mind, but rather is centered upon the body. The body is where Satan conducts his activities. The body is Satan's dance hall; it is Satan's mooring post. The mind represents God's dwelling place—the subject position. But the body, which should assume the object position, tries to make itself another subject. It continually asserts itself, alluring or deceiving the mind. In human life, it is crucial to correct this relationship.

Therefore, God established religion to restore fallen humans. Through religion God is teaching people how to strengthen their God-centered mind and reverse the body's dominion over their life and character. That is why religion requires fasting, sacrificial service, and a meek and humble attitude. These are methods to reduce the power of the body and make the body submit to the mind. Normally in religious life it takes about three to five years to overcome the habit of a body-centered life and create a new, spirit-centered way of life. (201:209, April 9, 1990)

When I put myself at the zero point and completely deny myself, at that point my mind and body can achieve perfect unity. (October 21, 2001)

Your goal is for the mind to be in control 100 percent. It is not enough for the mind and body to be 50-50. [After death] such a person will end up in the mid-level spirit world, in a buffer zone. If a person follows the body 60 percent of the time, he will undoubtedly go to hell... Always keep in mind that "I" am the womb that brings forth both good and evil. (37:122, December 23, 1970)

Are God's mind and body fighting?[4] No, they do not fight. How about you? If your mind and body do not become one, you can never enter the Kingdom of Heaven. (305:111, April 19, 1999)

Restraint

THE PATH TO SELF-CONTROL BEGINS WITH RESTRAINT. Restraint has several aspects. First, we should avoid situations that would tempt us to sin. This requires self-knowledge; since by knowing our weaknesses we can avoid compromising situations. Second, we should restrain ourselves from acting on the promptings of anger, arrogance and other momentary impulses. Thus Father Moon, knowing that he has a temper, says that he must make continual effort to restrain himself from exploding in anger because he recognizes the harm it would cause others. Third, religious teachings of non-violence and meekness, of preferring to be beaten than to harm others, train us in the discipline of restraint. Fourth, Father Moon teaches of God's restraint and forbearance in the face of constant insults and aggravations over thousands of years as an inspiring example for us as we strive to be people who restrain ourselves.

Be angry but do not sin; do not let the sun go down on your anger, and give no opportunity for the devil.[5]

Ephesians 4.26-27

Verily God forgives my people the evil promptings which arise within their hearts as long as they do not speak about them and did not act upon them.

Hadith of Muslim (Islam)

If an evil man, on hearing of what is good, comes and creates a disturbance, you should hold your peace. You must not angrily upbraid him; then he who has come to curse you will merely harm himself.

Sutra of Forty-two Sections 7 (Buddhism)

A single bangle does not make a sound.[6]

Igala Proverb (African Traditional Religions)

The anger of man does not work the righteousness of God.

James 1.20

Abu Huraira reported God's Messenger as saying, "The strong man is not the good wrestler; the strong man is only he who controls himself when he is angry."

Hadith of Bukhari and Muslim (Islam)

You have heard that it was said to the men of old, "You shall not kill; and whoever kills shall be liable to judgment." But I say to you that everyone who is angry with his brother shall be liable to judgment; whoever insults his brother shall be liable to the council, and whoever says "You fool!" shall be liable to the hell of fire.

Matthew 5.21-22

The very first principle of religion laid down by Lord Mahavira is *Ahimsa*—Non-injury to living beings—which must be observed very scrupulously and thoroughly, and behaving towards all living beings with proper restraint and control.

Dashavaikalika Sutra 6.9 (Jainism)

"Your cheeks are like halves of a pomegranate behind your veil" (Song 4.3): The emptiest of you are as well packed with religious observances as a pomegranate with seeds. For everyone who has the opportunity of committing a sin and escapes it and refrains from doing it performs a highly religious act. How much more, then, is this true of those "behind your veil," the modest and self-restrained among you!

Canticles Rabbah 4.4.3 (Judaism)

Whenever there is attachment in my mind
And whenever there is the desire to be angry,
I should not do anything nor say anything,
But remain like a piece of wood....

Whenever I am eager for praise
Or have the desire to blame others;
Whenever I have the wish to speak harshly and cause dispute;
At such times I should remain like a piece of wood.

Whenever I desire material gain, honor or fame;
Whenever I seek attendants or a circle of friends,
And when in my mind I wish to be served;
At these times I should remain like a piece of wood.

Whenever I have the wish to decrease or to stop working for others
And the desire to pursue my own welfare alone,
If [motivated by such thoughts] a wish to say something occurs,
At these times I should remain like a piece of wood.

Shantideva, Guide to the Bodhisattva's Way of Life 5.48-52 (*Buddhism*)

Teachings of Sun Myung Moon

Whenever you feel troubled, you should just let that feeling go. It is wrong to stand up in public and speak about this and that while you are still affected by bad feelings. (45:269, July 4, 1971)

When a person is powerful and capable, if he restrains himself, he gains the people's respect. But when people who do not have any power or authority show restraint, they are regarded as weak. I have a fiery temper, yet I restrain myself and endure. That is why people think I am a great man. (October 7, 1979)

Don't get angry. You who walk the path of believers in God will lose everything if you get angry centered on your own desire. (32:34, June 14, 1970)

I, Reverend Moon, am not originally a good-natured person. That is why I train myself, biting my tongue, controlling myself and saying to myself, "I must go this way!" (320:251, April 16, 2000)

If I were to lose my temper at someone, thinking, "That good-for nothing!" or if I were to nurse feelings of ill-will, "Just wait a few months and we'll see what happens to you…" in the end that person would be broken in pieces. That is why I bite my tongue and control myself. As the True Parent, I cannot use my mouth to curse others. Even as I hold back my words, Heaven releases me completely from my bitter feelings. When you see this, don't you think God loves me? (162:205, April 12, 1987)

In history those who strike first always lose. Look at the First and the Second World Wars: the side that struck first lost. In the Third World War also, the side striking first will lose.[7] This is why even in our individual lives we should persevere and restrain ourselves, for those who persevere will be blessed. Take the beating and persevere. Endure, and someday you will rise up. (7:222, November 13, 1959)

God is worthy of respect, for He has been restraining Himself in silence and with patience while enduring thousands of years of insults and suffering. When you truly realize what God has endured for your sake, you will feel deep in your heart, "Lord, you are truly my Father." As God's sons and daughters, should you not resolve to endure for His sake? It will take much endurance to become the core ancestors who embody the Father's tradition and bequeath it for thousands of generations to come. (363:254, December 25, 2001)

If we cannot forbear, then we cannot pay back the debt we owe to God and cannot resolve the grievances within His bosom. Because the fortune of heaven and earth moves along with God's providence, when we remain with God, sharing His bitterness, indignation and sorrow, then judgment can fall on the satanic world. This is the reason Heaven teaches us to restrain our anger, be gentle and modest, and persevere in our life of faith.

Satan will invade if we fall out of step with God and create a gap between God's providence and ourselves. Therefore, we who have the faith must unconditionally sacrifice and obey, following only the internal aspects of love. (1:113, June 10, 1956)

Integrity

INTEGRITY REFERS TO AN UNCHANGING CHARACTER. Regardless of the circumstances, a person of integrity maintains his purpose, keeps his promises, and does his duty. More than that, a person of integrity becomes the moral and spiritual center of his or her family and community. Others depend on him, trust him and rely on him. As Father Moon teaches, just as diamonds and gold are valued for their unchanging brilliance, a person of diamond-like value has an unchanging character.

One great test of integrity is duty; another is adversity. They place principle above expediency, as did Rama, the hero of the Hindu Ramayana who refused a kingdom rather than disobey his father's wishes. It is tempting to regard fulfilling a duty as an opportunity for wealth or personal advancement. It is a challenge to maintain a friendly disposition in adverse circumstances. It is even more difficult to fulfill one's obligations when to do so puts one at risk of life. However, a person of integrity disregards the circumstances and fulfills a duty for its own sake. Having taken on a task, he or she pursues it to the end with an unchanging mind.

1. A Life Based upon Principle

He who walks in integrity walks securely,
but he who perverts his ways will be found out.

Proverbs 10.9

When one follows unswervingly the path of virtue it is not to win advancement. When one invariably keeps one's word it is not to establish the rectitude of one's actions. A gentleman merely follows the norm and awaits his destiny.

Mencius VII.B.33 (Confucianism)

Virtue is the root; wealth is the result. If he makes the root his secondary object, and the result his primary, he will only wrangle with his people, and teach them rapine.

Great Learning 10.7-8 (Confucianism)

Not to be cheered by praise,
Not to be grieved by blame,
But to know thoroughly one's own virtues and powers
Are characteristics of an excellent man.

Precious Treasury of Elegant Sayings 29 (Buddhism)

If one's mind is sorrowless, stainless and secure, and is not disturbed when affected by worldly vicissitudes, this is the highest blessing.

Sutta Nipata 268 (Buddhism)

To gain a good reputation, be the kind of person that you want people to think you are.

Socrates (Hellenism)

Without goodness a man "cannot for long endure adversity; cannot for long endure prosperity." The good man rests content with goodness; he that is merely wise pursues goodness in the belief that it pays to do so.

Analects 4.2 (Confucianism)

Make [virtue] your first object. Give up money, give up fame, give up science, give up the earth itself and all it contains, rather than do an immoral act. And never suppose that in any possible situation, or under any circumstances, it is best for you to do a dishonorable thing. Whenever you are to do a thing, though it can never be known but to yourself, ask yourself how you would act were all the world looking at you, and act accordingly.

Thomas Jefferson

Teachings of Sun Myung Moon

When we call someone a person of character, we are not referring to appearance, education,[8] career or position. We look not at class or outward glory, but to what extent he or she is leading a principled life. A person with an unchanging mind to serve Heaven, who lives according to God's will with such a mind—that is a person of character. (19:285, March 10, 1968)

Does human character have bones? Have you ever seen the bone of character? Personality is what appears outwardly. That is the visible aspect; however, there is a hidden, bone-like foundation of character that is responsible for the visible aspect. It is the invisible cause of the visible personality. (177:315, May 22, 1988)

We should have this attitude: "I am inheriting God's undiluted tradition; therefore, I must always go the straight path. I have to win over all unrighteousness. Although it takes thousands of times more effort to subjugate force with something other than force, I will solve every problem and overcome any circumstance." In this way, we should establish our integrity as people loyal to Heaven. We should start with a pure mind and continue without faltering until we achieve the goal. (21:83, October 27, 1968)

We can never establish one unified world if we have a changing standard of goodness. A center must never move. The deeper it is, the calmer it should be. Look at the ocean: waves may rage on the surface because of a storm, but deep below the ocean is still. Let us learn from this. (*Way of God's Will* 2.2)

I want you to know that precious things, like diamonds, carry their own power and value. Others see that value and respect it and are moved by it. Who is the more precious person, one who is influenced by others or one who can influence others? What kind of person are you? Among those who influence others, the person having the best influence is the most precious person. (118:95, May 9, 1982)

The saints and sages who appeared in history are the best historical examples of true people. Why do we call them "true"? Something true is not only true in the present. It must be true in the past, true in the present and true in the future. Its truth transcends all circumstances. Therefore, a true person stands at the center of the past, the center of the present, and the center of the future.

Among the people in the world, who is nearest to being "true"? Is it a parent or a teacher you once had? Countless people have lived and died, but the person who should establish the basis of truth is none other than you yourself. Where, then, is your closest link to the truth? It is your conscience. We often say of a person, "He is conscientious. He has an upright mind." What does it mean for one's mind to be upright? It is upright in the past, it is upright in the present, and it will be upright in the future. (28:159, January 11, 1970)

March forward, trusting yourself. You should have the integrity to go forth absolutely alone. (*Way of God's Will* 1.4)

2. People of Integrity Fulfill Their Duty

Those who believe, and keep their duty, theirs are good tidings in the life of the world and in the Hereafter.

Qur'an 10.63-64

All a gentleman can do in starting an enterprise is to leave behind a tradition which can be carried on. Heaven alone can grant success.

Mencius I.B.14 (Confucianism)

The moral man conforms himself to his life circumstances; he does not desire anything outside his position. Finding himself in a position of wealth and honor, he lives as becomes one living in a position of wealth and honor. Finding himself in a position of poverty and humble circumstances, he lives as becomes one living in a position of poverty and humble circumstances. Finding himself in uncivilized countries, he lives as becomes one living in uncivilized countries. Finding himself in circumstances of danger and difficulty, he acts according to what is required of a man under such circumstances. In one word, the moral man can find himself in no situation in life in which he is not master of himself.

In high position he does not domineer over his subordinates. In a subordinate position he does not court the favors of his superiors. He puts in order his own personal conduct and seeks nothing from others; hence he has no complaint to make. He complains not against God, nor rails against men.

Thus it is that the moral man lives out the even tenor of his life, calmly waiting for the appointment of God, whereas the vulgar person takes to dangerous courses, expecting the uncertain chances of luck.

Doctrine of the Mean 14 (Confucianism)

He who does not fulfill his duty is not respected by honest men. It is how he acts that reveals the nobility or baseness of a man and distinguishes the honest or the dishonest person; otherwise the ignoble would resemble the noble, and he who is devoid of honor would resemble a man of integrity; he who is unworthy would be deemed worthy and he who is depraved would be considered to be a man of virtue. If, under the pretext of duty, I adopt this unrighteous course, calculated to produce the confusion of social roles, and do acts not recognized by the scriptures, I should, renouncing good, have to reap evil only![9] What sensible man, able to discern what is just and unjust, would respect me in this world, if I behaved viciously and dishonorably?... Why should I, Rama, not fulfill the command of my father, who was a devotee of truth? Neither ambition, forgetfulness, nor pride would cause me to destroy the bridge of morality!

    Ramayana, Ayodhya Kanda 109 *(Hinduism)*

Tzu-kao, Duke of She, who was being sent on a mission to Ch'i, consulted Confucius. "The king is sending me on a very important mission. Ch'i will probably treat me with great honor but will be in no hurry to do anything more. Even a commoner cannot be forced to act, much less one of the feudal lords. I am very worried about it…"

Confucius said, "In the world, there are two great decrees: one is fate and the other is duty. That a son should love his parent is fate—you cannot erase this from his heart. That a subject should serve his ruler is duty—there is no place he can go and be without his ruler, no place he can escape to between heaven and earth. These are called the great decrees. Therefore, to serve your parents and be content to follow them anywhere—this is the perfection of filial piety. To serve your ruler and be content to do anything for him—this is the peak of loyalty. And to serve your own mind so that sadness or joy do not sway or move it; to understand what you can do nothing about and be content with it as with fate—this is the perfection of virtue. As a subject and a son, you are bound to find things you cannot avoid. If you act in accordance with the state of affairs and forget about yourself, then what leisure will you have to love life and hate death?…

"Just go along with things and let your mind move freely. Resign yourself to what cannot be avoided and nourish what is within you—this is best. What more do you have to do to fulfill your mission? Nothing is as good as following orders—that is how difficult it is!"

    Chuang Tzu 4 *(Taoism)*

Teachings of Sun Myung Moon

A loyal subject and a treacherous subject originally belong to the same class of people. The only difference is that the former is obedient to the will of the king while the latter makes much of himself before everything else. A loyal subject always walks a straight line; the beginning and end of his works are the same. *(Way of God's Will 2.2)*

Because most people do not have an absolute center, they change their minds day and night. We cannot call them people of character. People of character keep their promises and have a high standard of righteousness. Once things are decided, they do not make any excuses. You should become people like that. Even if the laws of the universe were to change, you should never deviate from fulfilling what you have promised. (23:100, May 14, 1969)

By faithfully living according to Heaven's principles, we should find and establish our value. That value represents our original relationship with Heaven, our original relationship with people, and our original relationship with the universe.

Once you restore your eternally unchanging integrity before God's Will, you will be able to praise your own value. You can be proud of yourself as someone who eternally lives for the sake of others. This means that your day-to-day relationships with other people and all things will completely display the beauty of God's creation. Thus, the ultimate purpose of God's providence is to help human beings find the ultimate value of their life. (2:336-37, August 4, 1957)

Why does God need Reverend Moon? Because I am a handsome? No. For my worldly knowledge? No. Because I have power and wealth? No, I do not have any of those things. I am nothing. Yet God holds onto me because I know God's Will and devote all my life, day and night, to its fulfillment. That is the only reason God needs me.

Likewise, do I need you because I want to use you to make money? Do I want to use you to gain power? No. The reason why I need you more than any power or authority in America is because I sense your zeal for the Will of God. This connects us like a string, but it is stronger than anything else. (77:16, March 23, 1975)

3. People of Integrity Do Not Change according to the Circumstances

Once there lived a housewife named Vedehika who had a reputation for gentleness, modesty, and courtesy. She had a housemaid named Kali who was efficient and industrious and who managed her work well. Then it occurred to Kali the housemaid, "My mistress has a very good reputation; I wonder whether she is good by nature, or is good because my work, being well-managed, makes her surroundings pleasant. What if I were to test my mistress?"

The following morning Kali got up late. Then Vedehika shouted at her maid, "Hey, Kali!" "Yes, madam?" "Hey, what makes you get up late?" "Nothing in particular, madam." "Nothing in particular, eh, naughty maid, and you get up late?" And being angry and offended, she frowned.

Then it occurred to Kali, "Apparently, my mistress does have a temper inwardly, though she does not show it because my work is well-managed. What if I were to test her further?" Then she got up later. Thereupon Vedehika shouted at her maid, "Hey, Kali, why do you get up late?" "No particular reason, madam." "No particular reason, eh, and you are up late?" she angrily hurled at her words of indignation.

Then it occurred to Kali, "Apparently, my mistress does have a temper inwardly, though she does not show it because my work is well-managed. What if I were to test her still further?" She got up still later. Thereupon Vedehika shouted at her, "Hey, Kali, why do you get up late?" and she angrily took up the bolt of the door-bar and hit her on the head, cutting it. Thereupon Kali, with cut head and blood trickling down, denounced her mistress before the neighbors, saying, "Madam, look at the work of the gentle lady, madam, look at the action of the modest lady, madam, look at the action of the quiet lady. Why must she get angry and offended because I got up late and hit me, her only maid, cutting me on the head?" Thus the housewife lost her good reputation.

Analogously, brethren, a person here happens to be very gentle, very humble, and very quiet as long as unpleasant things do not touch him. It is only when unpleasant things happen to a person that it is known whether he is truly gentle, humble, and quiet.

Majjhima Nikaya 1.123-24 *(Buddhism)*

The well-taught noble disciple, when touched by a painful feeling, weeps not, wails not, knocks not on the breast, falls not into utter bewilderment. He feels the bodily feeling, but not the mental…

Moreover, he has no repugnance for painful feeling. As he has no repugnance for it, the lurking tendency to repugnance for painful feeling fastens not on him. He, when touched by painful feeling, delights not in sensual pleasure. Why so? Because, brethren, the well-taught noble disciple knows of a refuge from painful feeling apart from sensual ease. As he delights not in sensual ease, the lurking tendency to sensual ease fastens not on him…

If he feels a feeling that is pleasant, he feels it as one freed from bondage. If he feels a feeling that is painful, he feels it as one freed from bondage. If he feels a neutral feeling, he feels it as one freed from bondage.

Samyutta Nikaya 36.1.1.6 *(Buddhism)*

Teachings of Sun Myung Moon

Gold is valuable because its essence never changes, even in the fire. If your will changes whenever you are confronted with difficulties, what value do you have? You can never be called a person of character. (*Way of God's Will* 2.2)

Because your mind varies, your direction also varies, and because your direction varies, your purpose changes. You cannot fulfill one purpose when your mind is constantly changing. It is difficult enough to fulfill a goal with one mind; how much more difficult it is to fulfill it with two!

Therefore, in everything we do, we should have one mind. We must have the same mind in the morning, during the daytime and in the evening; the same mind in youth, middle age and old age. A person who starts a task with one mind, proceeds with one mind, and attains the result with one mind—his purpose will enlarge as he is able to maintain that one mind over longer periods.

We should have one mind. When we pursue a certain purpose, we need one mind. If we do not have one mind, we cannot fulfill the goal. From this, we deduce that God created this world with one mind, not with two minds. We have to begin with one mind and proceed in one direction in order to fulfill one goal. However, today, people are not able to keep one mind. (28:155, January 11, 1970)

Ever since the Human Fall, the form of our minds has been changing continually. If our minds were unchanging as they were supposed to be, we would all be holy people. Something can be holy if it is unique and unchanging. Thus, since white people always retain their white color, their white color is holy. Black people likewise keep their unique and unchanging black color; therefore it too is holy. But a worldly white person, whose mind and behavior constantly changes according to the circumstances, is on Satan's side. Regardless of his lofty social status, there is nothing holy about him…

The shape of a person's hands and face does not change. What changes is the mind. When a person's mind is changeable, it becomes Satan's dance floor. Is there any woman here who wants a changeable husband? Certainly not. Although she may not be perfect, she still prefers an unchanging man…

A holy couple, united in true love, does not change for eternity. The years follow that couple, not the other way around. Such a couple is the center of eternal life. (217:303-04, June 12, 1991)

Righteousness

RIGHTEOUSNESS MEANS A LIFE UPHOLDING HIGH PRINCIPLES and dedicated to public service. Righteous people are the spiritual and moral pillars of a society, bestowing its vision and setting its values. By their courage, moral rectitude, and devotion to public service they demonstrate the exemplary qualities of a good citizen. Righteousness is often demonstrated by concern for the greater good: for the community, the nation, even for the world. Father Moon calls this being a public person, living a public life. He teaches that we should strictly live with a mind to serve the greater good and never fall back into acting with selfish, greedy motives.

It is not easy to be a righteous person. Righteous people invariably place public duties ahead of personal gain. They are serious about the propriety of every action they take. When society is corrupt and decadent, such righteousness is not always welcomed, and righteous people face persecution. Yet the value of righteousness is so great that in the Old Testament story of Sodom and Gomorrah, God was willing to spare those sinful cities for the sake of 10 righteous men. Every community needs such people.

1. A Righteous Person Stands against Evil at the Cost to Himself

The Master said, "A gentleman in his dealings with the world has neither enmities nor affections; but wherever he sees Right he ranges himself behind it."

Analects 4.10 (Confucianism)

And if God had not repelled some men by others, the earth would have been corrupted.

Qur'an 2.251

Blessed are those who are persecuted for righteousness' sake, for theirs is the kingdom of heaven.

Matthew 5.10

Jesus went up to Jerusalem. In the temple he found those who were selling oxen and sheep and pigeons, and the moneychangers at their business. And making a whip of cords, he drove them all, with the sheep and oxen, out of the temple; and he poured out the coins of the moneychangers and overturned their tables. And he told those who sold the pigeons, "Take these things away; you shall not make my Father's house a house of trade."

John 2.13-16

They that are desirous of victory do not conquer by might and energy so much as by truth, compassion, righteousness, and spiritual discipline. Discriminating then between righteousness and unrighteousness, and understanding what is meant by covetousness, when there is recourse to exertion fight without arrogance, for victory is there where righteousness is. Under these conditions know, O king, that to us victory is certain in this battle. Indeed, where Krishna is, there is victory.

Mahabharata, Bhishma Parva 21 (Hinduism)

Neither let us be slandered from our duty by false accusations against us, nor frightened from it by menaces of destruction to the Government nor of dungeons to ourselves. Let us have faith that right makes might; and in that faith let us, to the end, dare to do our duty as we understand it.

Abraham Lincoln[10]

Teachings of Sun Myung Moon

The Chinese character for "righteousness," 義 (eui) is a combination of two characters: 羊 (yang) "sheep" and 我 (ah) "self."[11] In other words, when you put yourself in the position of a sacrificial lamb, you will create the condition for righteousness. (92:309, April 24, 1977)

Go and do something adventurous for the sake of the nation and God's righteousness. God will encourage you, "Go ahead and do it." Then you will meet with abuse. There will be a confrontation, but if you subjugate the evil on your own, then God will be pleased. It is the outcome God hopes for. Will God help you if you cower in fear, too afraid even to fight? Therefore, raise well-intentioned problems. (104:107, April 15, 1979)

You must be able to distinguish between good and evil, but how do you distinguish them? In the world good and evil are intermingled; however, the point where good and evil becomes distinguished is in yourself.

The world is evil; therefore, if you live without colliding with the world, you are an evil person. You live in a fallen realm; therefore, if you are living your life like a fish caught in a net, you are an evil person. If you just continue with your life instead of confronting the world's evils, you are an evil person. Since you know that the present-day world is an evil world, you must fight against it.

Why? It is because humans fell. Having fallen from our original position, you must climb back up, and in order to climb back up, you must struggle through it. It will not do to stay still. Otherwise, you will never be able to greet the new world that humankind desires. You will not leave a mark of goodness in history, and history will not be able to progress. That is why, as people who would advance the cause of goodness, you must fight. (33:42, August 1, 1970)

It is a principle that the side of justice grows stronger with persecution and difficulty. Therefore, when we are hit we will develop even more. (93:134, May 21, 1977)

When good people pursue a certain goal, they are often uncertain about their objective, and on the path they find little support to stimulate and strengthen their aspiration for goodness. On the other hand, evil people find help every step of the way and relationships to encourage them from the beginning to the end. Therefore, a person who is seeking truth inevitably finds him or herself in situations of loneliness and sorrow.

The path of the person who upholds goodness will not be a smooth one. Not many people welcome an individual who strives to cultivate a character of exceptional goodness, especially as he tries to assemble an environment that meets his standard. There will be opposition when that person tries to build a family of goodness, and even stronger evil forces will surround and oppose any attempt to build a tribe of goodness. (36:52, November 15, 1970)

> Father! I am going forward as a strong man,
> bold and magnanimous;
> I will not be put to shame.
> Please, watch over me on my path;
> I will make Thee proud of me. (134:142-43, February 25, 1985)

2. A Righteous Person Leads a Public Life and Identifies His Welfare with the Public Good

Do not be anxious, saying, 'What shall we eat?' or 'What shall we drink?' or 'What shall we wear?' For the Gentiles seek all these things; and your heavenly Father knows that you need them all. But seek first his kingdom and his righteousness, and all these things shall be yours as well.

Matthew 6.31-33

It is not righteousness that you turn your faces [in prayer] to the East and to the West. Righteousness is this:

to believe in God, and the Last Day, the angels, the Book, and the Prophets,

to give of one's substance, however cherished, to kinsmen, and orphans, the needy, the traveler, beggars, and to free the slave,

to perform the prayer and to pay the alms.

And they who fulfill their covenant, when they have engaged in a covenant, and endure with fortitude misfortune, hardship, and peril, these are they who are true in their faith, these are the truly God-fearing.

Qur'an 2.177

I delivered the poor who cried,
and the fatherless who had none to help him.

The blessing of him who was about to perish
   came upon me,
and I caused the widow's heart to sing for joy.
I put on righteousness, and it clothed me;
my justice was like a robe and a turban.
I was eyes to the blind,
and feet to the lame.
I was a father to the poor,
and I searched out the cause of him whom I
   did not know.
I broke the fangs of the unrighteous,
and made him drop his prey from his teeth.

Job 29.12-17

He will not cry or lift up his voice,
or make it heard in the street;
a bruised reed he will not break,
and a dimly burning wick he will not quench;
he will faithfully bring forth justice.
He will not fail or be discouraged
till he has established justice in the earth;
and the coastlands wait for his law.

Isaiah 42.2-4

Kung-sun Ch'ou asked Mencius, "May I ask what your strong points are?"

"I have an insight into words. I am good at cultivating my 'flood-like ch'i.'"

"May I ask what this 'flood-like ch'i' is?"

"It is difficult to explain. This is a *ch'i* (breath) which is, in the highest degree, vast and unyielding. Nourish it with integrity and place no obstacle in its path and it will fill the space between heaven and earth. It is a ch'i which unites righteousness and the Way. Deprive it of these and it will collapse. It is born of accumulated rightness and cannot be appropriated by anyone through a sporadic show of rightness. Whenever one acts in a way that falls below the standard set in one's heart, it will collapse… You must work at it and never let it out of your mind. At the same time, while you must never let it out of your mind, you must not forcibly help it grow either."

Mencius II.A.2 (*Confucianism*)

Teachings of Sun Myung Moon

Do you want to be blessed? Do you want to live eternally? Then, you should become a public person. (31:168, May 24, 1970)

When you make it your business to serve others and to touch others' hearts, you are going beyond the life of a private individual. (241:118, December 20, 1992)

A human being is not meant to live for his or her individual self. Yet, these days many worldly people say, "I work for myself." In other words, they live for the sake of themselves. How pitiful are these people? They are like orphans without parents or siblings. You should be able to say, "I live for the sake of all the people of the world." (24:21, June 22, 1969)

You should be able to declare, "I have tackled the most difficult problem in the nation." It is not enough to deal with problems within the church. Furthermore, you should be able to declare, "I have tackled the most difficult problem in the world." Unless you do it willingly, you will remain on a servant level and cannot reach the level of an adopted son.[12] You have to be willing to digest all the difficulties in the world—all the things that servants can do—with joy. (113:111, May 1, 1981)

There is no need to worry whether something will be done or not. The question is whether you did it or not. (308:209, January 5, 1999)

The public-minded person speaks from public-mindedness; he sees, hears, feels, thinks, eats and sleeps and does everything from the public-minded standpoint. When you look at the world with a public-minded eye, you come to love everything. (111:244, February 22, 1981)

Whether your work is small or big, regardless of the task, you should not relate to it personally. In other words, your mind should be intense. Your state of mind should be like a ball that is completely round after the air has been pumped in, with pressure. Your mind should keep that pressure like a completely round ball, and never go flat. If instead your mind is uneasy or self-centered, dominated by personal greed, it is like a sharp edge forming in that round, ball-like mind. (40:278-89, February 7, 1971)

3. Righteous People are the Guardians of a Nation

Then Abraham drew near, and said, "Wilt thou indeed destroy the righteous with the wicked? Suppose there are fifty righteous within the city; wilt thou then destroy the place and not spare it for the fifty righteous who are in it? Far be it from thee to do such a thing, to slay the righteous with the wicked, so that the righteous fare as the wicked! Far be that from thee! Shall not the Judge of all the earth do right?"

Genesis 18.23-25

Run to and fro through the streets of Jerusalem,
look and take note!
Search her squares to see
if you can find a man,
one who does justice
and seeks truth;
that I may pardon her...
O Lord, do not thy eyes look for truth?

Jeremiah 5.1-3

I will leave seven thousand in Israel, all the knees that have not bowed to Baal, and every mouth that has not kissed him.[13]

1 Kings 19.18

There are [always] thirty righteous men among the nations, by whose virtue the nations of the world continue to exist.[14]

Talmud, Hullin 92a (Judaism)

Teachings of Sun Myung Moon

Since I came to America I have been working as hard as I can, and also I am pushing Americans to go through many hardships. Nevertheless, if we can prosper, it can be a blessing to America, and an indemnity condition that can cover the failure of America to fulfill its God-given mission. Then, I can pray to God, "Heavenly Father, please have regard for these Thy children and forgive America for their sakes. Although America deserves to perish, because these children are devoted to Thee, please save this nation." It is similar to Abraham's prayer when he pleaded with God to spare Sodom and Gomorrah if ten righteous people could be found. (103:200, February 25, 1979)

Many people are patriots, but saints are rare. A saint is someone who sacrifices for the world. Do you think that I want you, the people whom I love, to be merely filial children, or patriots, or saints? I am pushing you to become saints. (111:141, February 8, 1981)

Sincerity and Authenticity

A PERSON'S INNER INTENTION GOES FAR TOWARDS DETERMINING the extent to which a particular action is good or evil, effective or ineffective. As Buddha so forcefully stated in the Dhammapada, action begins with the mind; it is created by the mind; it goes forth according to the inner state of the mind. In some of the passages gathered here, sincerity means the natural and spontaneous flow of the mind, devoid of all pretense and egoistic grasping. Other passages call for self-examination and self-cultivation in order to manifest true sincerity. Father Moon views the cultivation of sincerity, what he calls *jeongseong*, as fundamental to the spiritual life.

This section treats sincerity as a virtue in daily life. On the topic of sincerity in approaching God, see Chapter 16: *Devotion* and *Purity of Intention*.

1. Sincerity Flows Spontaneously out of the Heart's Affections

Mind is the forerunner of all evil states. Mind is chief; mind-made are they. If one speaks or acts with wicked mind, because of that suffering follows one, even as the wheel [of the cart] follows the hoof of the draught ox.

Mind is the forerunner of all good states. Mind is chief; mind-made are they. If one speaks or acts with pure mind, because of that happiness follows one, even as one's shadow that never leaves.

Dhammapada 1-2 (Buddhism)

The heart is like a king with his troops. If the king is a good one, then his troops will be good too, and if the king is wicked, his troops follow suit…

If a person's heart is healthy, his body will be at ease, and if a person's heart is malicious, the body will be malevolent.

Hadith (Islam)

Abu Huraira reported God's Messenger as saying, "God does not look at your forms and your possessions, but He looks at your hearts and your deeds."

Hadith of Muslim (Islam)

To the pure all things are pure, but to the corrupt and unbelieving nothing is pure; their very minds and consciences are corrupted.

Titus 1.15

If you do not perceive the sincerity within yourself and yet try to move forth, each movement will miss the mark.

Chuang Tzu 23 (Taoism)

Let love be genuine; hate what is evil, hold fast to what is good; love one another with brotherly affection; outdo one another in showing honor. Never flag in zeal, be aglow with the Spirit, serve the Lord.

Romans 12.9-10

Sincerity [Absolute Truth] is the Way of Heaven; the attainment of Sincerity is the Way of man. He who possesses Sincerity achieves what is right without effort, understands without thinking, and naturally and easily is centered on the Way. He is a sage.

Doctrine of the Mean 20.18 (Confucianism)

While there are no stirrings of pleasure, anger, sorrow, or joy, the mind may be said to be in a state of equilibrium (*chung*). When those feelings have been stirred, and they act in their due degree, there ensues what may be called the state of harmony (*ho*). This equilibrium is the great root from which grow all the human actings in the world, and this harmony is the universal path which they all should pursue. Let the states of equilibrium and harmony exist

in perfection, and a happy order will prevail throughout heaven and earth, and all things will be nourished and flourish.
Doctrine of the Mean 1.4-5 (Confucianism)

By the Truth I mean purity and sincerity in their highest degree. He who lacks purity and sincerity cannot move others. Therefore he who forces himself to lament, though he may sound sad, will awaken no grief. He who forces himself to be angry, though he may sound fierce, will arouse no awe. And he who forces himself to be affectionate, though he may smile, will create no air of harmony. True sadness need make no sound to awaken grief; true anger need not show itself to arouse awe; true affection need not smile to create harmony. When a man has the Truth within himself, his spirit may move among external things. That is why the Truth is to be prized!
Chuang Tzu 31 (Taoism)

Teachings of Sun Myung Moon

You should speak with your mind—your inmost self. If it resonates with God, you can become one with God and automatically know the truth of the universe. (102:34, November 19, 1978)

A good person can always embrace everything with his heart: whatever he sees, whomever he meets and wherever he goes. (*Way of God's Will* 2.3)

You cannot serve God with all your sincerity if you are simply following someone else's instructions, or because someone obliges you to. The heart of sincerity is something that automatically springs forth from within you. In that state, you do not need any education about loyalty, filial piety and fidelity. (*Way of God's Will* 2.3)

When I put my hands to do something, I think, "I was born for this task." You too should be able to say, "I was born for this; I was made for this." Then work on it with enjoyment. Doing things because we like it is love. The relationship of love enables us to cross over the hill of joy. Until we find a way to like a task, we should not put our hands to it. God blesses the world when we enjoy what we do. (308:214, January 5, 1999)

Blessed are those who have an unchanging internal standard of heart to worship Heaven, be harmonious with others, and love the earth. (*Way of God's Will* 2.3)

In order to attain the object of your sincerity, your mind must be unified. You must possess a single mind; you cannot have two minds. You must offer your sincerity with a single mind from the beginning to the end. Sincerity is not something you can lend to someone and then take back. Therefore, if your initial sincerity is not matched by equal sincerity in the middle and at the end, it cannot be called sincerity. (17:227-28, January 29, 1967)

We cannot overcome with tricks or by talent, but only with sincerity. (42:228, March 14, 1971)

2. Cultivate Sincerity before Taking Action

Keep your heart with all vigilance, for from it flow the springs of life.

Proverbs 4.23

The truly upright is that which flows out of your genuine innermost self as a result of the sincerity shown by the kami; on all occasions, you must exert this sincerity to the utmost, even in the most minor of your activities. Courtesy and ritual without this sincerity and honesty is mistaken and insufficient. It is like drawing a bow and merely releasing the string blindly without firming your hand, or like trying to move in a boat without an oar.

Moshimasa Hikita, Records of the Divine Wind
(Shinto)

Thoughts alone cause the round of births (samsara); let a man strive to purify his thoughts. What a man thinks, that he is: this is an old secret.

By the serenity of his thoughts a man blots out all actions, whether good or bad. Dwelling within his Self with serene thoughts, he obtains imperishable happiness.

If the thoughts of a man were so fixed on Brahman as they are on the things of this world, who would not then be freed from bondage?

The mind, it is said, is of two kinds, pure and impure: impure from the contact with lust, pure when free from lust.

When a man, having freed his mind from sloth, distraction, and vacillation, becomes as it were delivered from his mind, that is the highest point.

Maitri Upanishad 6.34.3-7 (Hinduism)

What is meant by "making the will sincere" is allowing no self-deception, as when we hate a bad smell or love a beautiful color. This is called satisfying oneself. Therefore the superior man will always be watchful over himself when alone.

When the inferior man is alone and leisurely, there is no limit to which he does not go in his evil deeds. Only when he sees a superior man does he then try to disguise himself, concealing his evil and showing off the good in him. But what is the use? For other people see him as if they see his very heart. This is what is meant by the saying that what is true in a man's heart will be shown in his outward appearance. Therefore the superior man will always be watchful over himself when alone.

Tseng Tzu said, "What ten eyes are beholding and what ten hands are pointing to—isn't it frightening?"

Wealth makes a house shining and virtue makes a person shining. When one's mind is broad and his heart generous, his body becomes big and is at ease. Therefore the superior man always makes his will sincere.[15]

Great Learning 6.1-4 (Confucianism)

We should examine ourselves and learn what is the affection and purpose of the heart, for in this way only can we learn what we honestly are.

Science and Health, p. 8 (Christian Science)

If, brethren, a woman or man or a young lad fond of self-adornment, on examining the reflection of his own face in a bright clean mirror or bowl of clear water, should see therein a stain or speck, he will strive to remove that stain or speck; and when he no longer sees it there he is pleased and satisfied, thinking, "A gain it is to me that I am clean." Likewise a monk's introspection is most fruitful in good conditions, thus: "Do I or do I not generally live covetous? Do I or do I not generally live malevolent in heart? Do I or do I not generally live possessed by sloth and torpor? Do I or do I not generally live excited in mind? Do I generally live in doubt and wavering, or have I crossed beyond it? Do I generally live wrathful or not? Do I generally live with soiled thoughts or clean thoughts? Do I generally live with body passionate or not? Do I generally live sluggish or full of energy? Do I generally live uncontrolled or well controlled?"

If on self-examination a monk finds thus: "I generally live covetous, malevolent in heart, possessed by sloth and torpor, excited in mind, doubtful and wavering, wrathful, with body passionate, sluggish, uncontrolled"—then that monk must put forth extra desire, effort, endeavor, exertion, impulse, mindfulness, and attention for the abandoning of those wicked, unprofitable states.

Anguttara Nikaya 5.66 *(Buddhism)*

Teachings of Sun Myung Moon

The saying, "Sincerity moves Heaven," like "Faith will move mountains," is a proverb in Korea, but truly it is also the natural order of things. The proverb, "Act with utmost sincerity," means act with all your efforts, inside and outside, heart and soul. The proverb, "Practice everything with sincerity in your words and deeds," means to completely unite your body and soul in a conscientious life. This means a life of dedication. We call it "utmost sincerity" or *jeongseong*. The Korean word *jeong* deals with the spirit, and *song* means the fulfillment of the Word. Thus *jeongseong* means fulfilling everything inwardly and outwardly and offering it.[16] If you do everything with *jeongseong* you can "move Heaven." (78:31, May 1, 1975)

Usually, what percentage of your feelings turns out to be true? You should analyze the process of your life and gauge the results. You cannot assess whether God or the Devil is with you unless you can connect with your internal environment and analyze what percentage of your feelings are right and what percentage are wrong. Develop this mindfulness in your life of faith.

If you develop such mindfulness, your feelings will accurately disclose what is coming your way. When you go out for a certain purpose, without even praying you will sense at your first step whether your journey will lead to something good or something bad. You will sense immediately whether it will make God happy or sad. You will be able to sense, "This pleases God" or "This pains God." Develop your faith through experiencing the feelings of God in your inner self. (40:288, February 7, 1971)

Do not bear a grudge, thinking, "This work is tiring, yet Reverend Moon never acknowledges me." Were I always to praise your efforts, it would block the flow of your love and sincerity. By staying quiet, your sincerity and love can flow. Like water and air, love flows when there is a hole to flow into. (308:205, January 5, 1999)

In your life of faith, do you have an explosive and stimulating power in the center of your heart which is moving unceasingly towards the world of God's Will? When you have that heart, it is evident that God is with you. On the other hand, if you don't have that power, it is evident that God is distant from you.

When your heart is pouring out love for humankind, and you have the mind to share your life with others limitlessly, it is clear that you belong to Heaven. But if after awhile you become proud of your great love, then your self-centered love and proud self-centered values are evidence that God has begun to leave you. Be careful! People like that are not headed for heaven. Their self-centeredness will take them so far, and they will reach their limit. The world of self-centered limitations is different from the world God desires. (32:21-22, June 14, 1970)

Therefore, you have to be able to empathize with Heaven and move God's heart. Whenever you are in a quandary, it is a time to offer more sincerity, live more for the sake of others, and love more. (308:203, January 5, 1999)

Human beings still affiliated with the fallen realm… must complete a revolution of conscience. This means that they must maintain a tradition of true love, true life, and true lineage in accordance with the predisposition of the original mind endowed in us by God. They must do this without even the smallest deviation, regardless of whatever worldly sovereignty or ideology they may encounter. They must live a life of "high noon settlement," where they do not leave any shadow or even a speck of shame in the presence of God or the creation. The revolution of conscience is completed when our lives reach a state of one mind, one body, and one thought, and so establish an eternal and unchanging tradition as the ground of our pure love and pure lineage. The age of unity and harmony will blossom from that point. (January 27, 2004)

Honesty

HONESTY INCLUDES TELLING THE TRUTH, speaking truthfully what is on our mind and heart, keeping promises, and acting in accordance to our words. Honesty before God requires confessing our sins and confronting our particular propensity to do evil, along with repentance and the pledge to reform. Thus, Father Moon teaches that our prayers should be honest reports to God about our thoughts, words and deeds, plus setting goals and making determination about how we shall think, speak and act in the future.

1. Speaking Truthfully to Others and to God

Let your conduct be marked by truthfulness in word, deed, and thought.
> Taittiriya Upanishad 1.11.1 *(Hinduism)*

Lying lips are an abomination to the LORD.
> Proverbs 12.22

Do not assert with your mouth what your heart denies.
> Tract of the Quiet Way *(Taoism)*

No man should talk one way with his lips and think another way in his heart.
> Talmud, Baba Metzia 49 *(Judaism)*

Putting away falsehood, let everyone speak the truth with his neighbor, for we are members one of another.
> Ephesians 4.25

Straightforwardness and honesty in the activities of one's body, speech, and mind lead to an auspicious path.
> Tattvarthasutra 6.23 *(Jainism)*

Lying does not mean that one could not be rich;
Treachery does not mean you may not live to old age;
But it is the day of death [judgment] about which one should be baffled.

If a lie runs for twenty years, it takes truth one day to catch up with it.

The truth got to market, but it was unsold; lying costs very little to buy.
> Yoruba Proverbs *(African Traditional Religions)*

One should speak the truth and speak it pleasingly; should not speak the truth in an unpleasant manner nor should one speak untruth because it is pleasing; this is the eternal law.
> Laws of Manu 4.138 *(Hinduism)*

A gentleman is ashamed to let his words outrun his deeds.

Analects 14.29 (Confucianism)

O you who believe, wherefore do you say what you do not?
Very hateful is it to God, that you say what you do not.

Qur'an 61.2-3

A speaker of falsehood reaches purgatory; and again so does one who, having done a misdeed, says, "I did not." Both of them, men of base deeds, become equal in the other world.

Dhammapada 306 (Buddhism)

If you plot and connive to deceive men, you may fool them for a while, and profit thereby, but you will without fail be visited by divine punishment. To be utterly honest may have the appearance of inflexibility and self-righteousness, but in the end, such a person will receive the blessings of sun and moon. Follow honesty without fail.

Oracle of Amaterasu at the Kotai Shrine (Shinto)

The Duke of She addressed Confucius saying, "In my country there was a man called Upright Kung. His father appropriated a sheep, and Kung bore witness against him." Confucius said, "In my country the upright men are of quite another sort. A father will screen his son, and a son his father—which incidentally does involve a sort of uprightness."

Analects 13.18 (Confucianism)

Teachings of Sun Myung Moon

Being truthful is an attribute of righteousness, and being dishonest is an attribute of unrighteousness. (364:226, January 3, 2000)

When walking a path toward enlightenment, there should be no tricks or devices between the teacher and the student. You should be honest with each other. It means you should face each other with utmost sincerity. (33:125, August 11, 1970)

Instead of clever patchwork to smooth over a situation in the moment, you should have a pure heart and patiently wait for God's blessings. (127:89, May 5, 1983)

Just as God is a unified being, your mind and the body should be one centering on Heaven. Your thoughts should flow from that unified point... In other words, your words and your deeds, your mind and your efforts, should be one. Only then are you protected. Only then will people testify to you and declare you a public person. (381:65, June 12, 2002)

People should be honest. Honesty enables us to pass through anything. If you admit honestly when you make a mistake, you will develop. Goodness cannot grow without going through this process. Can people always do well? People make mistakes, but they must be honest about them if they are to develop.

By honestly confessing and repenting for your mistakes you can make a new determination. Making a mistake is not bad; it can stimulate you to leap forward. A mistake can be a good thing if it motivates you to leap to the good side. For example, if you failed a test because you did not study, the shock and shame of failure can motivate you to become an honor student. The failing grade becomes an opportunity to change your direction towards the good.

Therefore, you should be honest. People who try to hide their mistakes cannot develop. On the other hand, honest people develop because the universe pushes them and supports them wherever they go. Whether in the East or the West, in the past, present or future, an honest person is everyone's friend. (100:87-88, October 8, 1978)

Be an honest believer. You should be able to report honestly about yourself to God and say, "Father, I will be honest with you, so treat me honestly. You were honest with me when I appeared before you in righteousness. Now that I stand before you carrying the burden of an unrighteous heart, will you treat me the same way? Regardless, I will face you with the reality of what is in my heart. Deal with me according to your righteous judgment." (45:242-43, July 4, 1971)

I teach honesty, purity, and sacrifice from the standpoint of the Principle. First, a person must be honest in the presence of God. The Unification Principle teaches that falsehood separates us from God. I emphasize to our members that they are God's emissaries and must identify themselves as my followers, even if it means they will be severely persecuted… Whoever does not have the courage to do so, we have no need of them. People who do not identify themselves out of fear of harassment will miss out on all the blessings that come as a result of persecution… I can understand that people who face constant harassment do such things, but I do not praise such behavior. (91:128, February 3, 1977)

2. Keeping Promises

When a man vows a vow to the LORD, or swears an oath to bind himself by a pledge, he shall not break his word; he shall do according to all that proceeds from his mouth.

Numbers 30.2

Fulfill the covenant of God once you have pledged it, and do not break any oaths once they have been sworn to. You have set up God as a Guarantee for yourselves; God knows everything you are doing.

Do not be like a woman who unravels her yarn after its strands are firmly spun. Nor take your oaths in order to snatch at advantages over one another, to make one party more numerous than the other. For God will test you by this.

Qur'an 16.91-92

When man appears before the Throne of Judgment, the first question he is asked is not, "Have you believed in God," or "Have you prayed and performed ritual acts," but "Have you dealt honorably, faithfully in all your dealings with your fellowman?"

Talmud, Shabbat 31a (Judaism)

Tzu-chang asked about getting on with people. The Master said, "Be loyal and true to your every word, serious and careful in all you do, and you will get on well enough even though you find yourself among barbarians. But if you are disloyal and untrustworthy in your speech, frivolous and careless in your acts, even though you are among your own neighbors, how can you hope to get on well?"

Analects 15.5 (Confucianism)

Teachings of Sun Myung Moon

Once you have promised to give something to a friend, you should fulfill it without fail. Breaking a promise will stain your character. (*Way of God's Will* 2.2)

Making excuses [for not fulfilling one's word] is not the way to have many virtuous friends, to be positively recognized by one's superiors, or to be trusted by one's subordinates. People who make excuses are generally losers. You should not make excuses whenever something unexpected happens. I never make excuses, even in the face of death. If confronted with the facts of the matter, I might wince with the answers, but I will never make excuses... Only honest people will survive and prevail over circumstances. We need to become honest believers more than anything else. (45:269, July 4, 1971)

A person of character fulfills his promises. If you say, "You forced me to make that promise, and therefore I do not have to keep it," then you are not a person of character. In the law, a contract is a promise made and agreed to in public. All the parties to the contract must keep their promises. After signing a contract, a person who does not fulfill his promise is punished by public regulations; hence keeping it is the responsibility of any law-abiding person. (31:13, April 8, 1970)

You should become a person who can be entrusted with a precious treasure. (*Way of God's Will* 2.2)

Caution and Vigilance

A PERSON WALKING THE ROAD OF LIFE MUST BE VIGILANT. It will not do to lead a carefree and casual existence. Moment by moment we face occasions to either do good or evil, either to remain faithful to principles or to violate them. There are snares and pitfalls along the way, and to fall into one could spell disaster. Hence we need caution, vigilance and mindfulness to survive and progress on the spiritual path.

Hence, the world's scripture call for vigilance, to be alert against any sin or diversion from a life lived in accordance with God's Will. The Christian Bible warns that the Lord comes "like a thief in the night" and encourages constant wakefulness through such passages as the Parable of the Wise and Foolish Maidens. Islam calls us to constantly remember (*zakara*) God, His commandments, and His mercies, and reminds us through the duty of daily prayer. The Jewish sages recommended interpreting commandments strictly to place "a fence around the law," so that there can be no possibility of transgression. The religions of the East promote meditative disciplines that train the aspirant to watch over his or her thoughts at all times. Father Moon affirms the need for vigilance at all times, and reminds us of the biblical figures of old who made serious mistakes due to momentary lapses in vigilance.

In fear and trembling,
With caution and care,
As though on the brink of a chasm,
As though treading thin ice.

                Analects 8.3 (Confucianism)

Work out your own salvation with fear and trembling.

                Philippians 2.12

A monk should step carefully in his walk, supposing everything to be a snare for him.

                Uttaradhyayana Sutra 4.7 (Jainism)

Even those who have much learning,
Faith, and willing perseverance
Will become defiled by a [moral] fall
Due to the mistake of lacking alertness.

                Shantideva, Guide to the Bodhisattva's
                Way of Life 5.26 (Buddhism)

The Master said, "Danger arises when a man feels secure in his position. Destruction threatens when a man seeks to preserve his worldly estate. Confusion develops when a man has put everything in order. Therefore the superior man does not forget danger in his security, nor ruin when he is well established, nor confusion when his affairs are in order. In this way he gains personal safety and is able to protect the empire. In the I Ching it is said: 'What if it should fail? What if it should fail?' In this way he ties it to a cluster of mulberry shoots [makes success certain]."

I Ching, Great Commentary 2.5.9 (*Confucianism*)

Misfortune is the root of good fortune;
Good fortune gives birth to misfortune.
Who knows where is the turning point?

Tao Te Ching 58 (*Taoism*)

What is lawful is obvious, and what is unlawful is obvious; and between them are matters which are ambiguous and of which many people are ignorant. Hence, he who is careful in regard to the ambiguous has justified himself in regard to his religion and his honor; but he who stumbles in the ambiguous has stumbled in the forbidden, as the shepherd pasturing around a sanctuary is on the verge of pasturing in it. Is it not true that every king has a sanctuary, and is not the sanctuary of God that which He has forbidden?

Forty Hadith of an-Nawawi 6 (*Islam*)

Rabbi Akiba said, "Laughter and levity accustom a man to immorality. Tradition is a fence for Torah. Tithes are a fence for riches. Vows are a fence for saintliness. A fence for wisdom is silence."

Mishnah, Avot 3.17 (*Judaism*)

Just as a wealthy merchant with only a small escort avoids a perilous route; just as one desiring to live avoids poison; even so should one shun evil things.

Dhammapada 123 (*Buddhism*)

I seek union with the Good Mind,
And I forbid all traffic with the wicked.

Avesta, Yasna 49.3 (*Zoroastrianism*)

Only when a man will not do some things is he capable of doing great things.

Mencius IV.B.8 (*Confucianism*)

Forsake the outward sin, and the inward; surely the earners of sin shall be recompensed for what they have earned.

Qur'an 6.120

Do only such actions as are blameless... If at any time there is doubt with regard to right conduct, follow the practice of great souls, who are guileless, of good judgment, and devoted to truth.

Taittiriya Upanishad 1.11.2, 4 (*Hinduism*)

Men of understanding [are] such as remember God, standing, sitting, and reclining.

Qur'an 3.190-91

Be mindful when you are alone, in the shadow of your coverlet.

Tract of the Quiet Way (*Taoism*)

If while going, standing, sitting or reclining when awake, a thought of sensuality, hatred or aggressiveness arises in a monk, and he tolerates it, does not reject, discard, and eliminate it, does not bring it to an end, that monk, who in such a manner is ever and again lacking in earnest endeavor and moral shame, is called indolent and void of energy.

If while going, standing, sitting, or reclining when awake, a thought of sensuality, hatred, or aggressiveness arises in a monk, and he does not tolerate it, but rejects, discards, and eliminates it, brings it to an end, that monk, who in such a manner ever and again shows earnest endeavor and moral shame, is called energetic and resolute.

Itivuttaka 110 (*Buddhism*)

The kingdom of Heaven shall be compared to ten maidens who took their lamps and went to meet the bridegroom. Five of them were foolish, and five were wise. For when the foolish took their lamps, they took no oil with them; but the wise took flasks of oil with their lamps. As the bridegroom was delayed, they all slumbered and slept. But at midnight there was a cry, "Behold, the bridegroom! Come out to meet him." Then all those maidens rose and trimmed their lamps. And the foolish said to the wise, "Give us some of your oil, for our lamps are going out." But the wise replied, "Perhaps there will not be enough for us and for you; go rather to the dealers and buy for yourselves." And while they went to buy, the bridegroom came, and those who were ready went in with him to the marriage feast; and the door was shut. Afterward the other maidens came also, saying, "Lord, lord, open to us." But he replied, "Truly, I say to you, I do not know you." Watch therefore, for you know neither the day nor the hour.

Matthew 25.1-13

Teachings of Sun Myung Moon

You, the young ones, are standing at the crossroads of good and evil. If you take one wrong step, you might fall into a steep and deep pit of death. Although it is difficult, take the step that will let you stand tall. Then you can be victorious princes and princesses who look out at the hope for a shining tomorrow that lies on the broad plane. Therefore, you need to watch each step. Be careful as you walk on the snow-covered road. (59:214, July 16, 1972)

The greater you become, the more you have to watch under your feet. The smaller you become, the more you have to look up to Heaven. (*Way of God's Will*)

Be careful about the words you speak, be careful about what your eyes see, and be careful about the words you hear. Do not listen to self-centered remarks; do not look at selfish deeds; do not even talk to the person who lives selfishly; and do not make excuses for yourself. (93:319, June 12, 1977)

To be public means to live for the whole, and to be private means to live for the self. When you calmly evaluate yourself, you may find yourself in a quandary over what is public and what is private. Therefore, religion teaches fasting, suffering, modesty and humility, in order to restrain the body, which is inclined to be self-centered. (149:271, November 27, 1986)

Think once, twice and three times before you act. (93:320, June 12, 1977)

An unwarranted or improper statement can ruin your entire life. Hearing one unrighteous word can ruin your entire life. One wrong action can also ruin your life. Making a wrong friend can also lead you to ruin your life. Hence, many saints and sages have taught that we should be cautious about what we hear, say, and do, and about whom we take for friends. East or West, past or present, this philosophy is true.

On the other hand, one righteous, good statement at the opportune time can bring total, dramatic success to a life. Hearing the right things at the right moment can lead to a decision that will make an entire life successful. One right action at the right time can bring great success. It is the same with making a friend; for example, a sister here could go out to the street, meet a good man and have one conversation. That could be enough to initiate a friendship that leads to him becoming her husband. (91:29-30, January 2, 1977)

The road to misfortune does not ordinarily start from a major crisis. More often it is a trivial matter that opens the door to great unhappiness. It is hard to overcome even a small difficulty as long as your thinking is self-centered. Therefore, you should think twice about what you are doing. In analyzing great mistakes or serious crimes we invariably find that if the person had thought of the impact his actions would have on the well-being of others, he probably would not have committed such a blunder…

Particularly when we are faced with making an important decision, you are liable to choose the path to misfortune unless you stop to think twice before you act, to check whether your thinking is public or self-centered. Those who reason from selfishness are truly their own worst enemy. (93:298, June 12, 1977)

The fall of Adam and Eve was not the result of a planned failure that took one year or ten years. Their failure was brought forth in one moment, and that failure of a moment became the base for the corruption of the Kingdom that had been in preparation for millions of years. When we think about this, we realize how fearful one moment is.

Due to the failure of a single moment, people walking the religious path in every age have had to pay a price of great suffering. Numerous secular people too have been ruined by a single misstep of a moment. All their subsequent suffering became part of a tremendous sacrificial offering, for indemnity. When we understand this, every hour that we ordinarily live so casually becomes fearful, even a single second within that hour, and we want to exert ourselves to make it a success.

Every hour in your daily life is fearful, even each minute of every hour. Know how to struggle for every moment. For apart from one moment, Heaven cannot exist. (37:219, December 27, 1970)

If only Noah had been more prudent in the days after the flood, he would not have become drunk and lain naked. Would he have done such a thing if he had thought it over a bit more? With just a little more prudence and patience, he would not have allowed himself to get drunk. We can definitely say his mission would have succeeded if he had continued to be prudent. Likewise, when Abraham was making his offering, why did he only divide two of the three offerings and neglect to cut the birds? He would not have made the mistake if he had thought more carefully as he was arranging the offering. (99:39, August 27, 1978)

When Jacob was receiving his trial from Heaven, he never relaxed his mental vigilance for a moment. (3:337, February 9, 1958)

Prudent Speech

A LOOSE OR MALICIOUS TONGUE can cause much suffering. Evil speech can destroy friendships, ruin reputations and generate needless prejudice. It can be argued that if Jesus hadn't been surrounded by rumors and gossip, he could have won far more acceptance by the people of his day. Since talk can cause damage to others and to oneself, one's words should be weighed carefully.

Therefore, before we speak, we should carefully consider whether our words will be edifying or damaging to others. Before we repeat a tale we have heard, we should first ascertain whether it is true. Before we talk about doing something, we should carefully consider if we are ready to do it ourselves. Therefore, a wise person is one of few words. Good parents train their children to be well mannered and not speak overly much at meals.

You shall not go up and down as a talebearer among your people.

Leviticus 19.16

If the ear does not hear malicious gossip, the heart is not grieved.

Yoruba Proverb (African Traditional Religions)

False words are not only evil in themselves, but they infect the soul with evil.

Plato, Phaedo (Hellenism)

Out of the abundance of the heart the mouth speaks. The good man out of his good treasure brings forth good, and the evil man out of his evil treasure brings forth evil. I tell you, on the day of judgment men will render account for every careless word they utter; for by your words you will be justified, and by your words you will be condemned.

Matthew 12.35-37

Let him who believes in Allah and the last day either speak good or be silent.

Forty Hadith of an-Nawawi 15 (Islam)

When words are many, transgression is not lacking,
but he who restrains his lips is prudent.

Proverbs 10.19

The Messenger of God... took hold of his tongue and said, "Restrain this." I said, "O Prophet of God, will what we say be held against us?" He said, "May your mother be bereaved of you, Mu'adah! Is there anything that topples people on their faces into hell-fire other than the harvests of their tongues?"

Forty Hadith of an-Nawawi 29 (Islam)

Speak not harshly to anyone. Those thus addressed will retort. Painful, indeed, is vindictive speech. Blows in exchange may bruise you.

Dhammapada 133 (Buddhism)

The tongue is an unrighteous world among our members, staining the whole body, setting on fire the cycle of nature, and set on fire by hell. For every kind of beast and bird, of reptile and sea creature, can be tamed and has been tamed by humankind, but no human being can tame the tongue—a restless evil, full of deadly poison. With it we bless the Lord and Father, and with it we curse men, who are made in the likeness of God.

James 3.6-9

The origin of all trouble
within this world
is a single word
spoken in haste.

Moritake Arakida, *One Hundred Poems about the World* (Shinto)

A noisy bird builds a bad nest.

Kanufi Proverb (African Traditional Religions)

To be always talking is against nature. For the same reason a hurricane never lasts a whole morning, nor a rainstorm all day. Who is it that makes the wind and rain? It is Heaven and earth. And if even Heaven and earth cannot blow or pour for long, how much less in his utterances should man?

Tao Te Ching 23 (Taoism)

The Master said, "Where disorder develops, words are the first steps. If the prince is not discreet, he loses his servant. If the servant is not discreet, he loses his life. If germinating things are not handled with discretion, the perfecting of them is impeded."

I Ching, Great Commentary 1.8.10 *(Confucianism)*

A person is born with an axe in his mouth. He whose speech is unwholesome cuts himself with his axe.

When a person praises someone who should be blamed, or attacks someone worthy of praise, then this man is accumulating evil with his mouth and this evil will not lead to happiness.

It is little harm if one loses money in gambling with dice, even losing everything, including oneself; but if one bears ill-will towards well-conducted ones it is greater harm indeed. Insulting men of real worth, bearing ill-will in thought and speech, leads to eons upon eons in the states of misery.

Sutta Nipata 657-60 *(Buddhism)*

You who believe, if some perverse man should come up to you with some piece of news, clear up the facts lest you afflict some folk out of ignorance and some morning feel regretful for what you may have done...

You who believe, do not let one folk ridicule another folk. Perhaps they are better than they are. Nor let women mistreat other women; perhaps they are better than themselves. Nor should you find fault with one another nor shout at one another using nicknames; it is bad to use a dirty name instead of one you can believe in. Those who do not turn away from it are wrongdoers.

You who believe, refrain from being overly suspicious: some suspicion is a crime. Do not spy on one another, nor yet any of you slander others. Would one of you like to eat his dead brother's flesh? You would loathe it! Heed God, for God is Relenting, Merciful.

Qur'an 49.6-12

Teachings of Sun Myung Moon

You must not bring harm to others by your words. (*Way of God's Will* 2.1)

If you mistakenly utter just one wrong word among your colleagues, that one wrong word can break the bond between you. With one wrong word, both you and the person who hears that word will suffer. (89:116, November 1, 1976)

Words are so powerful. One wrong word can damage many people and even destroy the world. A loving word only flourishes and develops. It may include some rough language, but as long as it is spoken out of love the whole universe rejoices.

A word can be a fearful thing. If I speak a word of truth, you might be caught in its judgment. Maybe you were laughing a second before, but immediately you become very serious. Then if I say, "I will forget and forgive everything you have done," you will feel a great weight off your shoulders by that one simple phrase. (91:91, January 30, 1977)

I had to pray for three weeks as a result of uttering one careless word. (*Way of God's Will* 2.2)

Satan's weapon is to create division by criticizing. Satan whispers, "That person has this and that bad point. Stay away from him." He creates divisions by continually whispering in your ears something bad about another person. Should you ignore these criticisms or gossip about them to others? If you gossip, you are on the side of Satan. (215:240, February 20, 1991)

When you are investing your effort, don't nag or complain. Close your mouth, be quiet, and just give. Your silence signifies that you are the owner. You will become the pole that can welcome the dawn's twilight and the morning sunshine.[17] Is not the dawn a time of tranquil silence? (325:117, June 30, 2000)

In the past, noble families trained their children not to speak carelessly, especially in the morning. They taught them to speak only when spoken to. Such manners are also required in our life of faith. (40:73-74, January 24, 1971)

If you work much and speak little, you will be a winner. But if you do little and speak much, you will be a loser. (*Way of God's Will* 2.2)

Moderation

MODERATION IS UNIVERSALLY REGARDED as a virtue. Excessive behavior of any kind—stinginess or profligacy, mortification of the flesh or licentiousness, self-righteousness or abject submissiveness—should be eschewed in favor of the Golden Mean or Middle Path.

However, each tradition has its distinctive emphasis. Aristotle's classic statement of the Golden Mean emphasizes the work of reason in finding the middle and keeping to it. The role of wisdom to know the mean is reflected in the popular Christian prayer, "God, grant me the serenity to accept what cannot be changed, the courage to change what should be changed, and the wisdom to know the difference." The Buddha's Middle Path defines the religious life as threading a line between grasping at being and taking refuge in nothingness. Throughout the history of Buddhism, philosophers and practitioners have sought to define this middle way between withdrawal from the world and social engagement, between effort at spiritual growth and attacking the pride that can arise with its attainment, and so on—an enduring dialectic. The Confucian mean is about personal balance, which is manifest in one's actions and in the harmony of one's relationships.

These traditional expressions of the mean are about individual behavior. Father Moon's description of the mean, on the other hand, has a global outlook. The mean is achieved when a person's individual balance is substantiated in harmonious relationships with others and then pursues actions in society to bring together high and low, rich and poor, black and white to form a level "horizon" of life.

Moral virtue is a mean... between two vices, the one involving excess, the other deficiency, and its character is to aim at what is intermediate in passions and in actions...

Hence also it is no easy task to be good. For in everything it is no easy task to find the middle. Just as to find the middle of a circle is not for everyone but for him who knows; so, too, anyone can get angry—that is easy—or to give or spend money; but to do this to the right person, to the right extent, at the right time, with the right aim, and in the right way, that is not for every one, nor is it easy.

Aristotle, Nicomachean Ethics II.9 (*Hellenism*)

The servants of the Most Gracious are... those who, when they spend, are not extravagant and not niggardly, but hold a just balance between those extremes.

Qur'an 25.67

Be not righteous overmuch, and do not make yourself overwise; why should you destroy yourself? Be not wicked overmuch, neither be a fool; why should you die before your time?

Ecclesiastes 7.16-17

In practicing the ordinary virtues and in the exercise of care in ordinary conversation, when there is deficiency, the superior man never fails to make further effort, and where there is excess, never dares to go to the limit.

        Doctrine of the Mean 13.4 *(Confucianism)*

With regard to honor and dishonor the mean is proper pride, the excess is known as a sort of empty vanity, and the deficiency undue humility.

        Aristotle, Nicomachean Ethics II.7 *(Hellenism)*

The master said, "'The Ospreys!' Pleasure not carried to the point of debauch; grief not carried to the point of self-injury."[18]

        Analects 3.20 *(Confucianism)*

Be generous but not extravagant; be frugal but not miserly.

        Nahjul Balagha, Saying 32 *(Shiite Islam)*

Remember, no human condition is ever permanent. Then you will not be overjoyed in good fortune nor too scornful in misfortune.

        Socrates *(Hellenism)*

That things have being, O Kaccana, constitutes one extreme of doctrine; that things have no being is the other extreme. These extremes have been avoided by the Tathagata, and it is a middle doctrine he teaches.[19]

        Samyutta Nikaya 22.90 *(Buddhism)*

However hungry you are, you do not eat with both hands.[20]

        Akan Proverb *(African Traditional Religions)*

Eat and drink, but waste not by excess: for God loves not the wasters.

        Qur'an 7.31

Give me neither poverty nor riches;
feed me with the food that is needful for me,
lest I be full, and deny thee,
and say, "Who is the LORD?"
or lest I be poor, and steal,
and profane the name of my God.

        Proverbs 30.8-9

Your fame or your person, which is dearer?
Your person or your goods, which is worth more?
Gain or loss, which is the greater bane?
That is why excessive meanness is sure to lead to great expense;
Too much store is sure to end in immense loss.
Know contentment, and you will suffer no disgrace;
Know when to stop, and you will meet with no danger.
You can then endure.

        Tao Te Ching 44 *(Taoism)*

While there are no stirrings of pleasure, anger, sorrow, or joy, the mind may be said to be in a state of equilibrium (*chung*). When those feelings have been stirred, and they act in their due degree, there ensues what may be called the state of harmony (*ho*). This equilibrium is the great root from which grow all the human actions in the world, and this harmony is the universal path which they all should pursue. Let the states of equilibrium and harmony exist in perfection, and a happy order will prevail throughout heaven and earth, and all things will be nourished and flourish.

        Doctrine of the Mean 1.4-5 *(Confucianism)*

Teachings of Sun Myung Moon

What does it mean to live by the norm? A person takes the middle path, seeking harmony by adopting the mean in all aspects of life. The middle path does not lean to one side in its affections. You can attain it when you do not have a preference for high or low, but proceed in harmony with all. Be a person who lives by the norm, by taking the middle path. (120:224, October 17, 1982)

Sin, destruction and evil arise from taking a personal standpoint. If a person's personal property exceeds a certain limit, it becomes evil. There is a limit to how much of a person's life should be devoted to personal affairs, and once a person transgresses that limit, his life becomes evil. Then he is bound to decline, sinning more and more. (31:165, May 24, 1970)

God gives each person a certain quota of material substance to consume here on earth. Suppose you were allocated a large amount, but you say, "No, I don't need that much. I will use as little of it as possible." In that case, all the rest of the material wealth that God allocated to you would be transferred to your children and your posterity. Any people or nation with this kind of attitude will prosper. (161:126, January 11, 1987)

A well-rounded person is one who fits the four directions. (*Way of God's Will* 2.2)

Let's say that the white race represents the day and black race represents the night. Then if white people don't like black people, it is like the day not liking the night. Can this situation continue? The cycle of day and night is balanced, half and half. Any people that goes against nature will perish.

Does one of your eyes look up and the other look down? No, they are at the same level. When you breathe through your nose, can one nostril point up and the other down? No. Everything on your face is in harmony and balance. Likewise, people who disregard the balance of the universe will disappear. Therefore, those WASPs who insist on white supremacy are scoffed at by young people throughout the world; they are in decline.

Likewise, American young people are dying and American families are breaking down because there is a fundamental imbalance between the individual and the family. (339:139-40, December 10, 2000)

Something new and great emerges from the union of the East and the West. For this reason, many of the children born from international couples are geniuses. (376:277, April 19, 2002)

Without a horizon, the equilibrium that is conducive to unity cannot last. Hence, we must preserve the horizon and keep it level. To establish a level horizon, we begin by finding balance in a subject-object relationship. Subject and object partners exist to make absolute balance.

Next, the balanced subject and object partners make their surrounding horizon level. We cannot make it level all at once. It requires balancing the high and the low, and making adjustments along the way.

After making our surroundings level, we attain the standard for eternal settlement. Unity emerges at this point, unity around the [subject and object partners] at the center.

Hence, you should understand that balance, the horizon, and unity form a trinity. Among these three where does God abide? He dwells in the unity. Yet unity requires a level horizon, and a level horizon requires balance. The world of balance, horizon and unity breaks apart if even one of them is lacking. (298:168-69, January 1, 1999)

Modesty

SCRIPTURE'S CONCERNS ABOUT MODEST DRESS and minimal use of makeup are for promoting a chaste inner life. One's outward appearance reflects one's mind. A painted face and immodest dress are advertisements for a wanton mind, while simple apparel and a natural, unadorned face are characteristic of a gentle and pure spirit.

Beauty can be divine or a cause of temptation—it depends upon the motivation. In this regard, Father Moon asks some revealing questions: "For whom do you put on makeup, for your husbands or for other men?" and "Do you adorn yourself to attract others to love you or to spread your love to others?"

1. Modesty in Dress

Women should adorn themselves modestly and sensibly in seemly apparel, not with braided hair or gold or pearls or costly attire but by good deeds, as befits women who profess religion.

1 Timothy 2.9-11

Tell the believing men to lower their gaze and be modest. That is purer for them. Lo! God is Aware of what they do.

And tell the believing women to lower their gaze and be modest, and to display of their adornment only that which is apparent, and to draw their veils over their bosoms, and not to reveal their adornment save to their own husbands or fathers... or children who know naught of women's nakedness. And let them not stamp their feet so as to reveal what they hide of their adornment. And turn unto God together, O believers, in order that ye may succeed.[21]

Qur'an 24.30-32

Let not yours be the outward adorning with braiding of hair, decoration of gold, and wearing of fine clothing, but let it be the hidden person of the heart with the imperishable jewel of a gentle and quiet spirit, which in God's sight is very precious. So once the holy women who hoped in God used to adorn themselves and were submissive to their husbands, as Sarah obeyed Abraham, calling him lord.

1 Peter 3.3-5

Woman, before decking yourself, make yourself
    acceptable to your Lord,
Lest He should visit not your couch, and your
    makeup be gone to waste.
In the woman finding acceptance with her
    Lord, lies beauty of her makeup.
Should her makeup be acceptable, shall she
    have love of her Lord.
Let her deck herself in fear of the Lord, joy in
    God her perfume,
Love her sustenance.
Dedicating body and mind to her Lord, let her
    in love to Him be united.

Adi Granth, Var Suhi, M.3, p. 788 (Sikhism)

In *The Book of Songs* it is said,

> Over her brocaded robe
> She wore a plain and simple dress,

In that way showing her dislike of the loudness of its color and magnificence. Thus the ways of the moral man are unobtrusive and yet they grow more and more in power and evidence; whereas the ways of the vulgar person are ostentatious, but lose more and more in influence until they perish and disappear.

The life of the moral man is plain, and yet not unattractive; it is simple, and yet full of grace; it is easy, and yet methodical. He knows that accomplishment of great things consists in doing little things well. He knows that great effects are produced by small causes. He knows the evidence and reality of what cannot be perceived by the senses. Thus he is enabled to enter into the world of ideas and morals.

Doctrine of the Mean 33 (Confucianism)

The body is impure, bad-smelling, and replete with various kinds of stench which trickle here and there. If one, possessed of such a body, thinks highly of him or herself and despises others, that is due to nothing other than lack of insight.[22]

Sutta Nipata 205-06 (Buddhism)

Teachings of Sun Myung Moon

One woman uses makeup to enhance her beauty; another is beautiful without makeup. Between the two, whose face is more in harmony when she smiles? Little children are beautiful. How would it be if you put makeup on their faces, lipstick and eye shadow? Think how ugly and unnatural they would look. From God's point of view, from the vantage point of His great age, you are younger than a new baby. When God sees us humans wearing makeup and enjoying it, I think He might feel far more displeased than we would on seeing a made-up baby lying in a crib. (97:49-50, February 26, 1978)

In the sight of God, fallen human beings are so ugly and dirty and distorted that He does not want to look at them. He does not want to smell them or get anywhere near them. Nevertheless, women believe that God would prefer to see them in church wearing makeup, jewelry and their best clothing. It is ridiculous and pathetic! (94:42, June 26, 1977)

Do you women put on makeup for your husbands, or to look attractive to other men? Generally, a husband does not like his wife's makeup. He might say that her manicured fingernails look like fox claws. Actually, they can be dangerous. Does a loving husband want to touch those claws? If he liked his wife's nail polish, he would ask her to put it on everyday. Have you ever heard of a husband who gives his wife manicures? I don't know of any. Women who put on makeup are not responding to their husbands; they responding to Satan's electrical waves. (201:104-05, March 11, 1990)

Women should always look beautiful, even if it requires using makeup and perfume. A wife should not be indebted to her husband in emotional life. She should always concern herself with her husband's body and clothes. If he comes home tired, she should prepare water for him to wash his face… A woman's smile is the flower of the family. To establish a harmonious family, a wife needs to be a first-class actress in both comedy and tragedy. Whether her husband is joyful or sad, she should have the ability to completely melt him all the time. (27:88, November 26, 1969)

Do you women put on makeup in front of the mirror, thinking, "I am going to attract the attention of a lot of men by looking beautiful"? Or do you think, "I want to look pretty in order to spread joy to others"? Which is it? You are thinking to look beautiful so others may think well of you and be attracted to you. That way of thinking is Satan's way.

Why are butterflies colorful and flowers beautiful? Their beauty spreads joy to the whole creation. It would be okay to wear makeup if you were thinking, "I am putting on makeup to make the world more beautiful, like a flower or a butterfly." It is not the makeup a woman wears but her motivation for wearing it that determines whether she is on the side of heaven or hell. (129:316-17, December 1, 1983)

2. Modesty in Manners and Deportment

Turn not your cheek in scorn toward folk, nor walk with pertness in the land. Lo! God loves not each braggart boaster. Be modest in your bearing and subdue your voice. Lo! the harshest of all voices is the voice of the ass.

Qur'an 31.18-19

Because the daughters of Zion are haughty
and walk with outstretched necks,
glancing wantonly with their eyes,
mincing along as they go,
tinkling with their feet;
the Lord will smite with a scab
the heads of the daughters of Zion,
and the Lord will lay bare their secret parts.

Isaiah 3.16-17

If you are handsome, do not go astray after lewdness, but honor your Creator, and fear Him, and praise Him with the beauty which He has given you.

Pesikta Rabbati 127a (Judaism)

He who beholds a beautiful woman should say, "Blessed be He who hath created such in His universe." But is even mere looking permitted? The following can surely be raised as an objection: "Thou shalt keep from every evil thing" [Deut. 23.10] implies that one should not look intently at a beautiful woman, even if she be unmarried, nor at a married woman, even if she be ugly, nor at a woman's gaudy garments, nor at male and female asses or at a pig and a sow or at fowls when they are mating.

Talmud, Avoda Zara 20ab (Judaism)

Easy is the life of a shameless one who is as impudent as a crow, back-biting, presumptuous, arrogant and corrupt.

Hard is the life of a modest one who seeks purity, is detached, humble, clean living and reflective.

Dhammapada 244-45 (Buddhism)

Teachings of Sun Myung Moon

We must uphold etiquette proper to the law of love. When your parents-in-law come to see you, can you tell them, "Father, mother, please wait until we finish kissing"? We must have modesty and observe proper etiquette. A man must keep the etiquette proper to a husband, and a wife the courtesy proper to a wife. (112:65, March 29, 1981)

Children in reputable families are raised to be prudent in all things. Every step taken, every word uttered, every action contemplated must be prudent. Manners are complex, and it's not easy to master them. What child likes to mind his manners?

In this age of permissiveness no one cares much about manners, yet they are critical. If we don't teach young people manners, it's our own ruination: our family has no future. Families with noble traditions contain many useful educational resources for teaching their children how to relate well with adults, with siblings, and with parents. (42:17, February 19, 1971)

Women chased Elvis Presley wherever he performed. They tried to touch him and grab him and even jump on him. If he had announced, "Any woman who likes me can come to see me tonight," undoubtedly there would be a long line of women at his door, many leaving their husbands behind.

Do singers like Elvis Presley and sports champions fulfill a good purpose or an evil purpose? Generally these superstars influence the world in a satanic way. Men and women who carefully groom their appearance and dress in the most elegant fashions generally have a satanic effect on the world. (122:263, November 21, 1982)

Chastity

CHASTITY IS TO CONTROL ONE'S SEXUAL DESIRE: to refrain from premarital sex and to have sexual relations only with one's spouse. Chastity requires the institution of marriage for its most joyful fulfillment. The extreme asceticism of a celibate monk or nun is a vocation only for the few, those who are willing to sacrifice continually the God-given desire to love and be loved. God created us to love, form families and raise children to propagate the human race. In this regard, sexuality within marriage is a wonderful gift, a joyful experience and a blessing of God.

However, as fallen human beings we do not naturally discipline our sexual desires to be employed in a faithful marriage bond. That requires training, and religions have traditionally served this purpose. Religions teach that adultery is among the most serious sins. They train the mind to subdue the desires of the flesh, and set boundaries on behavior to avoid temptation to sin. They lift up marriage as a holy institution. However, in today's secular society, people have forgotten the discipline of desire. Promiscuity and "free sex" are everywhere, promising instant happiness but yielding disappointment, heartbreak, and broken homes. Marriage is under attack, and many young people are cohabiting rather than marrying, largely because they no longer believe that they can make a lasting marriage. As the original standard of faithful marriage is forgotten, homosexuality and lesbianism are gaining acceptance as alternative lifestyles.

Father Moon speaks passionately and directly about this topic. Based upon his teaching that the Human Fall was an act of illicit love, he sees the misuse of love as the root of all sins, crimes, unhappiness and suffering in human life. (See Chapter 6) The Fall caused people to devalue love and use it wrongly. Therefore, he calls us to elevate love to its original, heavenly purpose as the linking point between human beings and God. Sex in marriage should be a holy act, what he calls 'absolute sex.' Love between husband and wife should have the same absoluteness as God's love for us. Anything less creates separation from God.

1. Refrain from Adultery, the Most Serious Sin

Neither fornicate, for whosoever does that shall
   meet the price of sin—
doubled shall be the chastisement for him on
   the Resurrection Day.

Qur'an 25.68-69

Let marriage be held in honor among all, and let the marriage bed be undefiled; for God will judge the immoral and the adulterous.

Hebrews 13.4

Whoever has illicit affairs with the wives of his relatives or friends, either by force or by mutual consent, he is to be known as an outcaste.

Sutta Nipata 123 (Buddhism)

But fornication and all impurity or covetousness must not even be named among you, as if fitting among saints. Let there be no filthiness, nor silly talk, nor levity,[23] which are not fitting; but instead let there be thanksgiving. Be sure of this, that no fornicator or impure man… has any inheritance in the kingdom of Christ and of God. Let no one deceive you with empty words, for it is because of these things that the wrath of God comes upon the sons of disobedience.

Ephesians 5.3-6

Approach not adultery: for it is a shameful deed and an evil, opening the road to other evils.

Qur'an 17.32

He who commits adultery is punished both here and hereafter; for his days in this world are cut short, and when dead he falls into hell.

Vishnu Purana 3.11 *(Hinduism)*

Now Joseph was handsome and good-looking. And after a time his master's wife cast her eyes upon Joseph, and said, "Lie with me." But he refused and said to his master's wife, "Lo, having me my master has no concern about anything in the house, and he has put everything that he has in my hand; he is not greater in this house than I am; nor has he kept back anything from me except yourself, because you are his wife; how then can I do this great wickedness, and sin against God?"

Genesis 39.6-9

Four misfortunes befall a careless man who commits adultery: acquisition of demerit, disturbed sleep, third, blame; and fourth, a state of woe. There is acquisition of demerit as well as evil destiny. Brief is the joy of the frightened man and woman. The king imposes a heavy punishment. Hence no man should frequent another man's wife.

Dhammapada 309-10 *(Buddhism)*

Drink water from your own cistern,
flowing water from your own well.
Should your springs be scattered abroad,
streams of water in the streets?
Let them be for yourself alone,
and not for strangers with you.
Let your fountain be blessed,
and rejoice in the wife of your youth,
a lovely hind, a graceful doe.
Let her affection fill you at all times with delight,
be infatuated always by her love.
Why should you be infatuated, my son, with a loose woman
and embrace the bosom of an adventuress?
For a man's ways are before the eyes of the LORD,
and he watches all his paths.
The iniquities of the wicked ensnare him,
and he is caught in the toils of his sin.
He dies for lack of discipline,
and because of his great folly he is lost.

Proverbs 5.15-23

For this is the will of God, your sanctification: that you abstain from unchastity; that each one of you know how to take a wife for himself in holiness and honor, not in the passion of lust like heathen who do not know God.

1 Thessalonians 4.3-5

The body is not meant for immorality, but for the Lord… Do you not know that your bodies are members of Christ? Shall I therefore take the members of Christ and make them members of a prostitute? Never! Do you not know that he who joins himself a prostitute becomes one body with her? For, as it is written, "The two shall become one flesh." But he who is united to the Lord becomes one spirit with him. Shun immorality. Every other sin which a man commits is outside the body; but the immoral man sins against his own body. Do you not know that your body is a temple of the Holy Spirit within you, which you have from God? You are not your own; you were bought with a price. So glorify God in your body.

1 Corinthians 6.13-20

Teachings of Sun Myung Moon

Violating and misusing love is the gravest of all sins. Men and women who have been victimized by love often want to commit suicide and throw away their lives. Hence, we should know that committing a sin against love is worse than murder. (92:79, March 20, 1977)

The critical point in life where Adam and Eve and innumerable heroes and spiritual masters throughout history have failed is the matter of the purity of their sexual love. It is a problem that no one today can solve, not the family, nor the school, the church or the government.

I teach the best plan to keep purity: 'absolute sex.' What is absolute sex? Once joined in marriage, your relationship to your spouse is eternal. You form an absolute love relationship that will never change under any circumstances. How can that be? It is because as husband and wife you love each other within God's eternal and absolute love.

Absolute sex is not an obligation only for women; it also applies to men. It is Heaven's principle that all men and women must keep. On the other hand, free sex is a wicked trend that should be completely eradicated from the planet earth. The things associated with free sex—drugs, violence, homosexuality, and HIV/AIDS—only drive humanity down the path to destruction. (288:283-84, November 30, 1997)

Free sex is like a poisonous snake. Its head is like a man's sexual organ and its open mouth is like a woman's sexual organ. One bite from this poisonous snake can spread HIV/AIDS. One bite forever cuts down the ideal world... How can people conquer this snake, employing only their conscience? Coming to their aid, the religions of the world have always taught how to subdue the flesh. They have always commanded, "Do not drink, smoke or engage in free sex!"

Only love that is absolute, unique, unchanging and eternal can eradicate free sex. The feeling you get from drugs or alcohol or free sex cannot compare to the absolute joy and stimulation of absolute sex. In absolute sex all the cells in the body and mind activate and connect to the one center. It is supreme ecstasy, far beyond the intoxication of alcohol or drugs. Within its essence lie absolute freedom, absolute happiness, absolute hope, and the absolute fulfillment of all one's dreams. This is true love...

Where is the place where all the cells want to unite? It is [the partner's] sexual organ. All creatures desire to arrive at their partner's sexual organ as their final destination. The sexual organs are the connecting point for love, life, lineage and conscience. [Depending on how they are used,] they are the beginning point of heaven or hell. (279:174-75, August 4, 1996)

Why do we say that one man must love only one woman? What's wrong with the American lifestyle of one-night stands? Why should we have only one love? Why should there be only one man for one woman? What's wrong with a man loving several different women and a woman loving several different men? It is wrong because it lacks true love. What is true love? A man's true love and a woman's true love is the same. True love does not belong to the man or the woman, but it is the one love that unites both. That is why every man asks his sweetheart, "Do you love me?" and every woman asks her man the same question. Everyone asks their partner, "How much do you love me?" and they answer each other, "I love you more than the universe." (118:291, June 20, 1982)

Some married men, when they see a pretty woman, think how nice it would be if she were their wife. Such a person has two minds. We call him a man with the mind of a thief. Satan started from two minds; thus it is right to call such a man with two minds "Satan." He is no different from Satan. (*Blessing and Ideal Family* 1.2.6)

The sexual organ is the most fearful of the senses, because love was the cause of the Human Fall. That is why religions treat adultery as the most serious sin. The free sex that we see in the modern world today is an extension of hell. It is hell on earth and hell in the spirit world. It will entirely perish. (261:303-04, July 24, 1994)

Love, life, and lineage want to attach themselves to the sexual organs of men and women. They are the place to connect with God. They are the place where the Original Parent of all human beings comes and visits us. The sexual organs are the palace of love, palace of life, palace of lineage, and the palace of conscience. They are the starting point. Without them, we cannot find love; without them, we cannot find life. Without them, there would be no way for the life in a man and the life in a woman to meet as one. They are where a man and a woman meet and where a lineage comes into being. Your conscience, too, must be in accord with your sexual organ or it cannot manifest correctly.

Each of us has love; each of us has life, and each of us has a lineage. Inquiring where they come from, we learn that they are linked to our parents' sexual organs. They are linked to the love that is in our parents' sexual organs. That is how precious these organs are. The core of all the ideal traditions of the universe flows through their gates. The living water of eternal life flows from them. To become eternal living water, there must be love. So love is the most important. That is how precious these organs are. In nature, precious things, treasures, do not lie in plain view. Instead, they are hidden. Is this not true of gold? It is hidden, distributed in layers of feldspar or other rocks.

However, as the result of the human fall, all this was turned upside down. Each woman now thinks that her sexual organ is her own, but it is not hers. A man can never perfect his love without his wife's sexual organ. Likewise, a woman cannot maintain her love forever unless she has her husband's sexual organ to bring love to her. As long as men and women regard their sexual organs as their own, they cannot realize eternal love. Rather, they must exchange their sexual organs. The owner of a man's organ is his wife, and the owner of a woman's organ is her husband...

Will a new key fit two different locks? These days some knuckleheaded professors talk about free sex, and say this represents the liberation of love, or the emancipation of sex. They are thieves, and this world has become hell on earth because of such thinking. (300:320-21, April 15, 1999)

2. Young People Should Be Abstinent before Marriage

How can a young man keep his way pure?
By guarding it according to thy word.
Psalm 119.9

So shun youthful passions and aim at righteousness, faith, love, and peace, along with those who call upon the Lord from a pure heart.
2 Timothy 2.22

Those who abstain from sex,
Except with those joined to them in the marriage bond...
These will be the heirs who will inherit Paradise.
Qur'an 23.5-11

Let those who cannot find the wherewithal for marriage keep themselves chaste, until God gives them means out of His grace...

Do not force your slave-girls into prostitution when they desire chastity, for your profit in worldly goods.

Qur'an 24.33

If any man takes a wife, and goes in to her, and then spurns her, and charges her with shameful conduct, and brings an evil name upon her, saying, "I took this woman, and when I came near her, I did not find in her the tokens of virginity," then the father of the young woman and her mother shall take and bring out the tokens of her virginity to the elders of the city in the gate... But if the thing is true, that the tokens of virginity were not found in the young woman, then they shall bring out the young woman to the door of her father's house, and the men of her city shall stone her to death with stones, because she has wrought folly in Israel by playing the harlot in her father's house; so you shall purge the evil from the midst of you.

Deuteronomy 22.13-21

The Buddha said, "Of all longings and desires, there is none stronger than sex. Sex as a desire has no equal. Rely on the Oneness. No one under heaven is able to become a follower of the Way if he accepts dualism."[24]

Sutra of Forty-two Sections 25 (Buddhism)

Teachings of Sun Myung Moon

When a girl grows up and becomes a young woman, she looks for a young man. But will she really find true love in him? Can a young man be confident that he can trust his girlfriend? Without true love, men and woman cannot trust each other. Why? They do not understand that a man and a woman exist for the sake of each other. Instead, they are accustomed to using their partners to serve themselves. People use the opposite sex as servants or slaves because they do not know the value of true love. One's first love should last eternally. (297:145, November 19, 1998)

When you are a young person nearing twenty, where do you take your clean and unstained purity, all wrapped up? You take it to the altar where God will be most happy to receive it. Then you join with your spouse, who has also guarded his or her purity. Then when God binds you together at the holy place [your sexual organs], you become a holy husband and wife.

Your purity should be your pride. Nevertheless, if you think that you can use your sexual organ freely in the manner of dogs or pigs, it would be better to cut it off or dig it out. (64:85, October 24, 1972)

You should not sully your innocence during adolescence. It is the precious period when you can overcome and indemnify the sorrow of Adam and Eve, who lost their innocence during their youth. You should preserve your innocence, precious and clean. You should have the integrity and resolution to say, "Even if I have to live alone for a thousand years, I will not allow anyone to violate my love."

My tradition and teaching is that you cannot hold your partner of love unless you have loved your people and your nation. You cannot hold you partner of love unless you have loved the world. You cannot hold your partner of love unless you have loved God. Once you have loved God, loved the world and loved the nation, then you can love your spouse. This is a fundamental rule. (37:108, December 22, 1970)

The time has come when men as well as women should keep their chastity. If a man takes a wrong step and loses his chastity, it is as if his entire clan committed a serious offense against God's Will.

The time has come when it is no longer acceptable for an elderly man to have a secret affair. A man's philandering will ruin his entire clan. Once you understand the Unification teaching, you cannot do that. (*Blessing and Ideal Family* 1.2.6)

I am thinking that your children should be married at an early age, because I want them to be certain of marrying their first love. If each of you had met your spouse during adolescence with your first love intact, you would be so happy. First love is so pure! You would approach your spouse like a pure child loving its mother and father. Such a loving man and woman create an ideal couple and give birth to wonderful children. (118:310, June 20, 1982)

3. Is Touching or Even Looking Permitted?

You shall not eat of the fruit… neither shall you touch it, lest you die.

Genesis 3.3

Offering presents to a woman, romping with her, touching her ornaments and dress, sitting with her on a bed, all these are considered adulterous acts.

Laws of Manu 8.357 (*Hinduism*)

You have heard that it was said, "You shall not commit adultery." But I say to you that every one who looks at a woman lustfully has already committed adultery with her in his heart.

Matthew 5.27-28

The adultery of the eye is the lustful look, and the adultery of the tongue is the licentious speech, and the heart desires and yearns, which the parts may or may not put into effect.

Hadith of Muslim (*Islam*)

It is true that you commit no actual crimes; but when you meet a beautiful woman in another's home and cannot banish her from your thoughts, you have committed adultery with her in your heart. Consider a moment! Would you have sufficient control over yourself to imitate the sage Lu Nan-tze if you were placed in a similar position? When he once found himself obliged to pass the night in a house whose only other occupant was a woman, he lighted a lamp and read aloud until morning to avoid exposing her to unjust suspicions.

Treatise on Response and Retribution, Appended Tales (*Taoism*)

The Buddha said, "Be careful not to look at women and do not talk with them. If you must speak with them, be properly mindful and think, 'I am a *shramana* living in a turbid world.[25] I should be like the lotus flower and not be defiled by the mud.' Regard old women the way you regard your mother. Regard those who are older than you the way you regard your elder sisters; regard those who are younger than you as your younger sisters, and regard children as your own. Bring forth thoughts to rescue them, and put an end to bad thoughts."

Sutra of Forty-two Sections 29 (*Buddhism*)

Teachings of Sun Myung Moon

In the Western world, men and women shake hands, hold hands and hug each other so casually that they do not feel any special sensation. In the East, however, men and women rarely have physical contact with each other. So if they happen to merely brush against each other, they feel an electric spark.

Which is better, for men and women to have frequent physical contact or to refrain from touching until they are fully mature? When the electricity sparks, would you rather it be 50 volts or 100 volts? Therefore, you should wait. What do you think? Should young men and women go on dates, hold hands and kiss each other before marriage? You should wait and refrain from touching until you are fully ripe, like an apple that has turned totally red. Then even at the touch of your partner's hand you will feel an exciting electrical spark. Yet most American women never experience the full sensation of first love, because having dissipated their electricity, the remaining charge is only at 50 volts or even 30 volts. Now what do you think of American style love?

Satan uses this and many other methods to invade the realm of high-intensity love. To a pure teenage boy, a girl is like a palace of mysteries. Likewise, to a pure teenage girl, a boy is like a palace of mysteries. But these days, where is the mystery? Boys and girls behave like animals. They love each other like cats and dogs, without any vertical love. (125:103, March 13, 1983)

The religious life is one in which your conscience tortures your body until it surrenders. Once the flesh is completely dead, your conscience should occupy it so it can never come back to life again. Thus, the mind must dominate the flesh.

Therefore, you should turn your habitual way of seeing inside out and see straight. Your eyes, which have been looking at things 180 degrees opposite the way they ought to, should now turn 180 degrees opposite their former way of seeing. Whereas, before, when you were on the satanic side you looked through the left eye, now you should look through the right eye. In other words, your eyes, which could not see properly because they were 180 degrees off, should be united with your conscience and return to their original place, coming back to the right side after having rotated 360 degrees. From that time on, your eyes are welcome to view anything because you see with the eyes of the original mind. (261:303-04, July 24, 1994)

4. Homosexuality—the Extreme of Free Sex

You shall not lie with a male as with a woman; it is an abomination.

Leviticus 18.22

The bodhisattva does not approach the five kinds of unmanly men in order to be friendly with or close to them.[26]

Lotus Sutra 14 (Buddhism)

And Lot said to his people, "You commit lewdness, such as no people in creation ever committed before you. Do you indeed come in unto males?"[27]

Qur'an 29.28-29

God gave them up to dishonorable passions. Their women exchanged natural relations for unnatural, and the men likewise gave up natural relations with women and were consumed with passion for one another, men committing shameless acts with men and receiving in their own persons the due penalty for their error.

Romans 1.26-27

Teachings of Sun Myung Moon

Free sex, homosexuality, the lesbian movement and the like destroy human rights and dignity. (*Way of Unification* 5.2.4.2)

Free sex is what Satan likes most. God is the opposite. God wants 'absolute sex.' Archangels do not have partners—that is why homosexuality and lesbianism has emerged. With God, on the other hand, there is absolute partnership.

Now is the Last Days, when we are harvesting the seeds of free sex that Adam and Eve sowed in the Garden of Eden. That is why free sex is rampant throughout the whole world, especially in America. That is why families are breaking down. These are the satanic fruits of the Last Days. In this world full of free sex, people say, "It's okay for men to marry each other" because they do not have an absolute partner of love. (282:27, February 16, 1997)

Satan has worked to break down the basis for lasting love; hence free sex, homosexuality and lesbianism are rampant. Homosexuality and lesbianism grew from the seeds of the archangel; that is why they do not have eternal love partners. Satan is making people around the world expose their bodies more and pulling them in the direction of death. Humanity is experiencing its ultimate fate as descendants of the archangel, who instigates death to all. (279:121, August 1, 1996)

Could homosexuality exist in a world that abides by Heaven's principles? Lesbianism, alcoholism and such exist because people suffer from emotional misalignment. They suffer in this world, which is hell on earth. We, on the other hand, strive to live in God's Kingdom, so our way of life is 180 degrees different from them. (243:191, January 10, 1993)

If you practiced homosexuality before joining the Unification Church and you have still not ended such relationships, you will go straight to hell. Once you are deeply moved by the truth, everything of that old lifestyle should flee away. You have been born again. Now, no matter how much you formerly enjoyed it, your heart says no. Therefore, you have nothing to do with it. If you cannot subjugate those feelings, you should repent and pray and wail with tears. (219:233, September 8, 1991)[28]

Sobriety and Temperance

LIQUOR, DRUGS AND GAMBLING MAY SEEM like pleasant diversions, yet they are the cause of countless people's downfall. They render a man's spirit blind to the light of truth and deaf to the promptings of conscience. They lead to addictions that destroy the body, anti-social behavior that breaks up families and damages careers, and even criminal acts. It is well known that many people use alcohol and drugs for their effect of reducing inhibitions as a prelude to casual sex. Even cigarettes can have this effect, as well as influence young people to try harder drugs. Despite some contemporary medical models of addiction that regard it as a disease, the world's religions affirm that people are responsible to live soberly and steer clear of alcohol, drugs and gambling.

Father Moon recognizes that people often turn to cigarettes, drugs and alcohol because they are dissatisfied with life and cannot find the love they crave. Yet they are poor substitutes. The solution to drinking and drugs is true love. Temporary drug-induced intoxication pales in comparison to the deep emotional satisfaction of true, godly love.

You who believe! Intoxicants and gambling... are an abomination—of Satan's handiwork: eschew such that you may prosper. Satan's plan is to stir up enmity and hatred among you by means of liquor and gambling, and to hinder you from the remembrance of God and from prayer. Will you not then abstain?

Qur'an 5.90-91

Do not get drunk with wine, for that is debauchery; but be filled with the Spirit.

Ephesians 5.18

To the addict, nothing is like his dope;
to the fish, nothing is like water:
But those immersed in the love of God feel
    love for all things.

Adi Granth, Wadhans, M.1, p. 557 (Sikhism)

Let the time that is past suffice for doing what the Gentiles like to do, living in licentiousness, passions, drunkenness, revels, carousing, and lawless idolatry. They are surprised that you do not now join them in the same wild profligacy, and they abuse you; but they will give account to him who is ready to judge the living and the dead.

1 Peter 4.3-5

Men who are grave and wise,
Though they drink, are mild and masters of
    themselves;
But those who are benighted and ignorant
Are devoted to drink, and more so daily.
Be careful, each of you, of your deportment—
What heaven confers, when once lost, is not
    regained.

Book of Songs, Ode 196 (Confucianism)

Woe to those who rise early in the morning,
that they may run after strong drink,
who tarry late into the evening
till wine inflames them!
They have lyre and harp,
timbrel and flute and wine at their feasts,
but they do not regard the deeds of the LORD,
or see the work of his hands.

Isaiah 5.11-12

What are the six channels for dissipating wealth? Taking intoxicants; loitering in the streets at unseemly hours; constantly visiting shows and fairs; addiction to gambling; association with evil companions; the habit of idleness...

Gambling and women, drink and dance and
    song,
Sleeping by day and prowling around by night,
Friendship with wicked men, hardness of heart,
These six causes bring ruin to a man.

Gambling and drinking, chasing after those
Women as dear as life to other men,
Following the fools, not the enlightened ones,
He wanes as the darker half of the moon.

The drunkard always poor and destitute;
Even while drinking, thirsty; haunting bars;
Sinks into debt as into water stone,
Soon robs his family of their good name.

One who habitually sleeps by day
And looks upon the night as time to rise
Licentious and a drunkard all the time,
He does not merit the rank of householder.

Digha Nikaya 3.182-85, Sigalovada Sutta
(Buddhism)

Who has woe? Who has sorrow?
Who has strife? Who has complaining?
Who has wounds without cause?
Who has redness of eyes?
Those who tarry long after wine,
those who go to try mixed wine.
Do not look at wine when it is red,
when it sparkles in the cup
and goes down smoothly.
At the last it bites like a serpent,
and stings like an adder.
Your eyes will see strange things,
and your mind utter perverse things.

You will be one who lies down in the midst of the [rolling] sea,
like one who totters to and fro like the top of a mast.
"They struck me," you will say, "but I was not hurt;
they beat me, but I did not feel it.
When shall I awake?
I will seek another drink."

Proverbs 23.29-35

Rabbi Isaac said, quoting Proverbs 23.31, "Wine makes the faces of the wicked red in this world, but pale in the world to come." Rabbi Me'ir said, "The tree of which Adam ate was a vine, for it is wine that brings lamentation to man."

Talmud, Sanhedrin 70ab (Judaism)

The Gambler:
These nuts that once tossed on tall trees in the wind
but now smartly roll over the board, how I love them!
As alluring as a draught of Soma on the mountain,
the lively dice have captured my heart.

My faithful wife never quarreled with me
or got angry; to me and my companions
she was always kind, yet I've driven her away
for the sake of the ill-fated throw of a die.

Chorus:
His wife's mother loathes him, his wife rejects him;
he implores people's aid but nowhere finds pity.
A luckless gambler is no more good
than an aged hack to be sold on the market.

Other men make free with the wife of a man
whose money and goods the eager dice have stolen.
His father and mother and brothers all say,
"He is nothing to us. Bind him, put him in jail!"

The Gambler:
I make a resolve that I will not go gaming.
So my friends depart and leave me behind.
But as soon as the brown nuts are rattled and thrown,
to meet them I run, like an amorous girl.

Chorus:
To the meeting place the gambler hastens.
"Shall I win?" he asks himself, hoping and trembling.
But the throws of the dice ruin his hopes,
giving the highest scores to his opponent.

Dice, believe me, are barbed: they prick and they trip,
they hurt and torment and cause grievous harm.
To the gambler they are like children's gifts, sweet as honey,
but they turn on the winner in rage and destroy him...

Abandoned, the wife of the gambler grieves.
Grieved too, is his mother as he wanders to nowhere.
Afraid and in debt, ever greedy for money,
he steals in the night to the home of another.

He is seized by remorse when he sees his wife's lot,
beside that of another with well-ordered home.
In the morning, however, he yokes the brown steeds
and at the evening falls stupid before the cold embers.

Rig Veda 10.34 (Hinduism)

Teachings of Sun Myung Moon

You know in your conscience that drinking, dissipation and gambling are wrong. That is also why society restricts these activities. They are what ruin the basis of life. Transgressions of love ruin the family, and gambling ruins the society. (320:135, April 1, 2000)

Satan deploys his weapons. First, he deploys his air weapon—tobacco. Next he deploys his liquid weapon—alcohol, and finally his solid weapon—drugs. With these weapons he rots people's spirits, rots their bodies, and through the nostrils he rots the lungs. Therefore, we do not drink alcohol. We do not smoke. We do not take drugs. These three are Satan's weapons to destroy humanity. They are fearsome weapons because they block the spirit from communicating with the divine Being. (126:71, April 10, 1983)

Tobacco is a weapon of temptation. When a woman asks a man for a cigarette, casual sex is the usual outcome. In the Orient the men smoke, but it is regarded as disreputable for a woman to smoke. A woman asking a man for a cigarette is inviting him, "Let's have sex!" The cigarette is the bait. A man inviting a woman to share a drink together is another way of asking for sex. It is the same with sharing drugs. Once they are intoxicated, the man does as he pleases with her, and she does whatever she wants with him. What do they do? They engage in free sex. (287:118-19, September 19, 1997)

A man may be a husband and a father with many responsibilities at home, yet he continually neglects his wife and children and goes off to the local bar, seeking only his own pleasure. Is that person more susceptible to Satan or to God?

While he is drinking, he may be very happy. He might even jump up on top of the bar and dance to express his joy. However, such joy can never last. It has no element of the future, of eternity. His happy moment of drunkenness passes, and before long his family and his world lie in ruins. (124:244, February 20, 1983)

In the Orient we have a saying, *Ju-saek-jab-ki*: "Liquor, women and gambling lead to mischief." Liquor, women and gambling are the causes of all the world's crimes. Is there a major criminal case where alcohol, drugs, women or gambling are not involved?

Drugs are simply a stronger form of liquor. In a drug-induced intoxication you have no control over anything, including your behavior with women. Drinking and drugs destroy any wholesome relationships between men and women. And at the gambling casino thousands of years of achievement can wash away overnight. (230:115-16, April 26, 1992)

When Chinese people gamble, they sometimes bet everything. If a man runs out of money, he may bet his house and even his wife. He may lose his wife! If a master gambles with his servant and loses to him, the master has no choice but to pay off the money he bet—even all his property. What does he do next? He quietly drinks poison and dies. Then his servant can claim his house, his wife, and all that he had. Gambling is that formidable. (124:157-58, February 6, 1983)

Do you have true love in your home? I do not sense much confidence in your answer. You say yes, but you have yellow tobacco stains on your fingers and the smell of alcohol on your breath. If you had true love, your body would be fragrant. (215:244, February 20, 1991)

In today's families, husbands and wives are quarreling, parents are quarreling, children are quarreling—all are at odds with each other. This inevitably leads to a world where people find joy only in free sex; all their higher emotions are impoverished. To rekindle their emotions, people resort to hallucinogens and heroin. First they stimulate themselves with marijuana, and to continue the stimulation they graduate to opium and narcotics. (243:251, January 17, 1993)

Love's intense power activates all the cells, stimulating them all with one vibration. At the moment when mind and body, man and woman, are completely engaged in giving and receiving… the power of love explodes one hundred percent. Love's intense electricity is so intoxicating; that is why love is good. It is far more stimulating than the artificial intoxication that comes from drinking alcohol or taking opium. (117:76, February 1, 1982)

Whether in America, England, Japan, Germany, or anywhere in developed world, people lack any direction in life; they don't know which way to go. Having lost vertical true love, people desperately seek love on this horizontal plane. Unable to find it, they end up resorting to free sex. Every human being has an antenna that picks up love's emotion. It could link them with the high-dimensional universe of true love, but that world has vanished. Therefore, to supplement the paltry stimulation of fallen love, people take drugs and engage in free sex.

However, drugs and free sex are no substitute for true love. The more people pursue them, the farther away they are from love. Accordingly, they find that having free sex is not satisfying. Then they turn to drugs, yearning to feel that moment of love's rapture. Through drug-induced hallucinations they can feel imaginary love, but the feeling lasts only until the drug wears off.

The stimulating effect of the strongest drug cannot be compared to true love. Even drugs lean on true love, we can see that. Love creates an electrical vibration between heaven and earth. The touch of love's vibration rings out through the universe as if through the speaker of a giant radio. [Connecting to the drug world is like turning on a broken radio and hearing a faint noise, but with true love we tune in to the clear signal.] When the true love loudspeaker booms, "Wah-ah," the whole world gets excited. Everybody in the universe stands up and dances to its music. You may think the Twist is an exciting dance, but in the true love dance you even fly! (247:126-27, May 1, 1993)

CHAPTER 13

LOVE

True Love

TRUE LOVE IS THE SUPREME LOVE. It is highly desired, yet rare in the world. These passages can only begin to describe this ideal love, whose various attributes will be treated at length in the following sections.

Most essentially, true love is grounded in divine love. Love or compassion, being the core of Ultimate Reality, is manifested by the saint who can rise above self-centered attachments and desires. As God created for the sake of His creatures, so true love is totally committed to the welfare of the beloved. As God is absolute, eternal and unchanging, true love never changes and cannot be defeated by the vicissitudes of life. As God is the Parent of all humanity and the creator of all things, so a person with true love is impartial and all-embracing. Therefore, true love is displayed to individuals who are deeply united with God and fulfill God's purpose for their life.

True love is beyond the reach of most people, who are caught up in self-centered pursuits. Yet it is not so far off, for everyone has within him or herself the potential for love. A parent who gives everything for the sake of his or her children has tasted it. Maybe he had habitually lived for his own pleasure, but with the birth of a child his life goes through a total reorientation—from self to the other, from taking to giving. Parental love is close to God's true love, and hence we call God our Father. This inborn potential is illustrated by the Chinese character for benevolence (仁), which contains elements signifying "two (二) people (人)"; the same elements that are combined to make the character for Heaven (天). Thus love is innate in our being, through love God dwells with us, and by loving we resemble God.

1. The Nature of True Love

If I speak in the tongues of men and of angels, but have not love, I am a noisy gong or a clanging cymbal. And if I have prophetic powers, and understand all mysteries and all knowledge, and if I have all faith, so as to remove mountains, but have not love, I am nothing. If I give away all I have, and if I deliver my body to be burned, but have not love, I gain nothing.

Love is patient and kind; love is not jealous or boastful; it is not arrogant or rude. Love does not insist on its own way; it is not irritable or resentful; it does not rejoice at wrong, but rejoices in the right. Love bears all things, believes all things, hopes all things, endures all things.

Love never ends; as for prophecies, they will pass away; as for tongues, they will cease; as for knowledge, it will pass away. For our knowledge is imperfect and our prophecy is imperfect; but when the perfect comes, the imperfect will pass away. When I was a child, I spoke like a child, I thought like a child, I reasoned like a child; when I became a man, I gave up childish ways. For now we see in a mirror dimly, but then face to face. Now I know in part; then I shall understand fully, even as I have been fully understood. So faith, hope, love abide, these three; but the greatest of these is love.

1 Corinthians 13

Beloved, let us love one another; for love is of God, and he who loves is born of God and knows God. He who does not love does not know God;

for God is love. In this the love of God was made manifest among us, that God sent his only Son into the world, so that we might live through him. In this is love, not that we loved God but that he loved us and sent his Son to be the expiation for our sins. Beloved, if God so loved us, we also ought to love one another. No man has ever seen God; if we love one another, God abides in us and his love is perfected in us...

There is no fear in love, but perfect love casts out fear. For fear has to do with punishment, and he who fears is not perfected in love. We love, because he first loved us. If anyone says, "I love God," and hates his brother, he is a liar; for he who does not love his brother whom he has seen, cannot love God whom he has not seen.

1 John 4.7-12, 18-20

The infinite joy of touching the Godhead is easily attained by those who are free from the burden of evil and established within themselves. They see the Self in every creature and all creation in the Self. With consciousness unified through meditation, they see everything with an equal eye.

I am ever present into those who have realized Me in every creature. Seeing all life as My manifestation, they are never separated from Me. They worship Me in the hearts of all, and all their actions proceed from Me. Wherever they may live, they abide in Me.

When a person responds to the joys and sorrows of others as if they were his own, he has attained the highest state of spiritual union.

Bhagavad-Gita 6.28-32 (Hinduism)

Teachings of Sun Myung Moon

What is a life of true love? True love is the spirit of public service. It brings the peace that is at the root of happiness. Selfish love is a mask for the desire to have one's partner exist for one's own sake; true love is free of that corruption. Rather, its essence is to give, to live for the sake of others and for the sake of the whole.

True love gives, forgets that it has given, and continues to give without ceasing. True love gives joyfully. We find it in the joyful and loving heart of a mother who cradles her baby in her arms and nurses it at her breast. True love is sacrificial love, as with a filial son who gains his greatest satisfaction in helping his parents. God created the universe out of just such love: absolute, unique, unchanging and eternal, investing everything without any expectation or condition of receiving something in return.

True love is the wellspring of the universe. Once a person possesses it, true love makes that person the center and the owner of the universe. True love is the root of God and a symbol of His will and power. When we are bound together in true love, we can be together forever, continually increasing in the joy of each other's company. The attraction of true love brings all things in the universe to our feet; even God will come to dwell with us. Nothing can compare to the value of true love. It has the power to dissipate the barriers fallen human beings created, including national boundaries and the barriers of race and even religion.

The main attributes of true love are that it is absolute, unique, unchanging and eternal, so whoever practices God's true love will live with God, share His happiness and enjoy the right to participate as an equal in His work. Therefore, a life lived for the sake of others, a life of true love, is the absolute prerequisite for entering the Kingdom of Heaven. (September 12, 2005)

First Corinthians 13 states, "faith, hope and love abide... but the greatest of these is love." But people do not understand what love is. What does it mean to love with your whole heart and mind and soul? It means that you love even risking your life. Have you experienced loving someone completely? Have you loved your husband or your wife completely? Have your loved your teacher completely as his disciple? Have you loved your nation completely? No one, not a single person, has loved completely.

Therefore, just as in a factory a single mold is used to cast thousands of parts, we need a model human being—a true person—from which to propagate true people throughout the world. That is why God promised to send the Messiah. (Way of Unification 8.4.1)

What is true love? It is God's love. What is the path to true love? To become the owner of true love, we must possess God and His attribute of eternity. It is as simple as that. Why? True love has the quality of eternity. Therefore, to meet the condition of [true] love, we should be eternal. We will have true love between us only when our love is eternal. Therefore, on the path to love it is obligatory that we become eternal and unchanging people. Thus, love is eternal. It is eternal, unchanging and unique. Therefore when we have that kind of eternal heart for Heaven, our path will lead us to true love, to love that is all in all. (123:328, January 9, 1983)

What is the holiest thing in the world? It is true love. True love begins from God. God desires the path of true love above all, not any other path. God wants to see, hear, eat, and touch through true love. Were you to receive a kiss from God, you would feel such joy and happiness as if your insides were about to explode. (*Blessing and Ideal Family* 1.3.8)

When God exercised His power as the Creator, He created everything centered on love. God relates to everything with true love. In the spirit world, the connection of true love makes you the leader of all things. You can create anything. Therefore, it is our aspiration to relate to everything in true love. Unless you make a connection with true love, everything you do will be in vain. (147:116, August 31, 1986)

Ultimately, the original source of love is not in human beings, but in the first causal Being, who is absolute and unchanging. That is why a family of love is a God-centered family. Such families are the basic units for the realization of the ideal in human society. Beginning with families that realize the highest ideal of absolute love, love can expand to the nation and the world. The world of unity that is formed in families that perfect and complete love will surely expand to bring about God's promise of an ideal world of eternal happiness. (89:227, November 27, 1976)

Suppose a husband and wife give birth to a child with a deformity. Do they terminate its life and say, "Well, we can try again"? Is that true love? No, of course not. By the same token, a husband cannot think that if his wife displeases him, he can simply divorce her and marry someone else. Rather, he should determine to stay with her through thick and thin, always compensating for her shortcomings and her faults. That is the proper course, and such love will pass muster in the spirit world where love is more visibly dominant than it is on earth. Such a person can be called a true husband. True love is not seen when it is easy to love. True love becomes evident when you love someone even though it is difficult.

The same principle of love applies in a student's relationship to a [difficult] teacher and vice-versa. It also applies in the relationship between a nation's president and its people. (117:292, April 11, 1982)

If God has a creation that He cherishes and thinks most valuable, does He intend to throw it away after spending just one day, 10 years or 100 years with it? Or did He create it to be with Him eternally? Surely this applies to human beings, whom God created to live with Him eternally. We are the object partners of the absolute God, who created us out of absolute love for His good pleasure.

Likewise, if a man takes pleasure in a woman for a few days, 10 years or 100 years, and then discards her, it is not love. If it were love, the more he loved her, the longer he would want to be with her.

There was once a man whose wife died young. He stayed single the rest of his life, always carrying her handkerchief. Nehru, the Prime Minister of India, always wore roses on his clothes because his wife had loved roses. (39:342-43, January 16, 1971)

True love is love that continues forever. It is love that does not change, whether in spring, summer, autumn, or winter. It does not diminish when a person is a child, middle-aged, a senior citizen, or has passed on to the eternal spirit world. True love does not change. (194:303, October 30, 1989)

2. Compassion and Benevolence

'Benevolence (仁)' means 'man (人).' When these two are conjoined, the result is 'the Way.'
            Mencius VII.B.16 (Confucianism)

Benevolence (仁) is simple undifferentiated gentleness. Its energy is the springtime of the universe, and its principle is the mind of living things in the universe.
            Chu Hsi (Confucianism)

Compassion is a mind that savors only mercy and love for all sentient beings.
            Nagarjuna, Precious Garland 437 (Buddhism)

Anas and 'Abdullah reported God's Messenger as saying, "All [human] creatures are God's children, and those dearest to God are those who treat His children kindly."
            Hadith of Baihaqi (Islam)

Those immersed in the love of God feel love for all things.[1]
            Adi Granth, Wadhans, M.1, p. 557 (Sikhism)

He who is skilled in welfare, who wishes to attain that calm state (Nibbana), should act thus: He should be able, upright, perfectly upright, of noble speech, gentle, and humble. Contented, easily supported, with few wants and simple tastes, with senses calmed, discreet, not impudent, not greedily attached to families...

[He should always hold this thought,] "May all beings be happy and secure, may their hearts be wholesome! Whatever living beings there be: feeble or strong, tall, stout or medium, short, small or large, without exception; seen or unseen, those dwelling far or near, those who are born or those yet unborn—may all beings be happy!"

Let none deceive another, nor despise any person whatsoever in any place. Let him not wish any harm to another out of anger or ill-will. Just as a mother would protect her only child at the risk of her own life, even so, let him cultivate a boundless heart towards all beings. Let his thoughts of boundless love pervade the whole world: above, below, and across without any obstruction, without any hatred, without any enmity. Whether he stands, walks, sits or lies down, as long as he is awake, he should develop this mindfulness. This, they say, is the noblest living here.[2]
            Sutta Nipata 143-151, Metta Sutta (Buddhism)

Now, I am jealous of no one,
Now that I have attained unto the Society of the Saints:
I am estranged with no one: nor is anyone a stranger to me,
Indeed, I am the friend of all.
All that God does, with that I am pleased;
This is the wisdom I have received from the saints.
Yea, the One God pervades all: and, seeing Him, I am wholly in bloom.

Adi Granth, Kanara, M.5, p. 129 (Sikhism)

If you step on a stranger's foot in the marketplace, you apologize at length for your carelessness. If you step on your older brother's foot, you give him an affectionate pat, and if you step on your parent's foot, you know you are already forgiven. So it is said, "Perfect ritual makes no distinction of persons; perfect righteousness takes no account of things [wealth]; perfect knowledge does not scheme; perfect benevolence knows no [partiality in] affection; perfect trust dispenses with gold."³

Chuang Tzu 23 (Taoism)

Teachings of Sun Myung Moon

Through many religions, God has taught us that we must love. The Buddha described it by the word compassion. Confucianism described it as benevolence and righteousness. Its teachings on benevolence, righteousness, propriety and wisdom indicate that there is no virtue unless love is included. The Chinese character for benevolence (仁) shows two (二) people (人). The Chinese character for Heaven (天) also contains two (二) people (人). (256:205, March 13, 1994)

Love cannot be true love if it is only for me. True love cannot be my individual possession. True love is for all people and for the whole universe. True love is what connects the family, the society, the nation, the world and universe. (*Blessing and Ideal Family* 1.3.8)

Even among fallen human beings, a parent's love for his or her children approximates original parental love. Parental love is absolute because it can transcend the parent's consciousness of his or her existence and activity. It is not comprehended by biological instinct, nor can it be constrained by a ruler's decree. Parental love transcends ideology. It transcends humanistic values. It can even transcend God's value. (8:273, February 7, 1969)

What is true love? It is God's love. Then, what is God's love? Jesus defined it as love that is capable of loving even an enemy...

Those who can unconditionally love everyone, including their enemies, must command the respect of others, whether they are black, white or yellow. This would be true in the past, in the present, and on into the future, even a million years from now. So this must be a universal truth.

Consider all the founders of religion—Jesus, Confucius and Mohammed. Throughout their lives they lived for the benefit of the world, loving humankind. (115:315-16, November 29, 1981)

How can we digest the evils of the world? With military power? With economic power? With the power of knowledge, or gold? No, we must digest this evil world with the power of love...

A small child climbs up on to the topknot on the head of his great grandfather, who is so old he is near death, and then slips off. As he sliding down, he urinates and defecates all over the old man, covering him from his head to his waist with urine and feces. Can such a thing be forgiven? The grandmother and grandfather will shout, "Oh, no!" and the mother and father will shout, "Oh, no" and make a tremendous fuss. But will the great grandfather shout, "This brat humiliated me! You must punish him for this!" No, he cannot. He will just laugh.

What great power and authority can do this? Only the unsurpassed power of love! Love is like a huge pot that melts everyone together and creates harmony. What a wonderful melting pot! (139:209-10, January 31, 1986)

3. Love's Circular Motion

Love works in a circle, for the beloved moves the lover by stamping a likeness, and the lover then goes out to hold the beloved in reality. Who first was the beginning now becomes the end of motion.

Thomas Aquinas, Summa Theologica[4] *(Christianity)*

Those who act kindly in this world will have kindness.

Qur'an 39.10

Blessed are the merciful, for they shall attain mercy.

Matthew 5.7

I love those who love me,
and those who seek me diligently find me.

Proverbs 8.17

Beloved, if God so loved us, we also ought to love one another. No man has ever seen God; if we love one another, God abides in us and his love is perfected in us...

God is love, and whoever abides in love abides in God, and God abides in him...

We love, because he first loved us.

1 John 4.11-12, 16, 19

In that day you will know that I am in my Father, and you in me, and I in you. He who has my commandments and keeps them, he it is who loves me; and he who loves me will be loved by my Father, and I will love him and manifest myself to him.

John 14.20-21

Believers, men and women, are protecting friends of one another.

Qur'an 9.71

Be subject to one another out of reverence for Christ. Wives, be subject to your husbands, as to the Lord.

Ephesians 5.21

True love is a love of beauty and order, temperate and harmonious.

Plato, The Republic *(Hellenism)*

Teachings of Sun Myung Moon

Absolute love is not forced. It circulates naturally. (196:134, December 31, 1989)

Love does not come from "me." It comes from my partner. Knowing this, we conclude that people were made to live for others. Every man was born for a woman, and every woman was born for a man. Only by living for the sake of the other can we find love and receive love. There is no true love when you ask others to live for your sake. (143:54, March 15, 1986)

Men and women were not created to live for their own sake, but for the sake of their partner of the opposite sex. A man is born for the sake of a woman. Likewise, whether or not a woman is beautiful, or even if she hates men, she was born for a man; just look at the way her body is shaped. God designed each sex to live for the sake of its opposite.

Likewise, when parents live for the sake of the children and the children live for the sake of the parents, there is circular motion. The more they live for each other's sake, they faster the motion becomes. This is the ideal form—not a square, but round and three-dimensional. Each member adds to the other's energy; hence the more we live for each other, the more dynamic our circular motion becomes. The family forms a sphere that can continue this way for eternity.

This is why circular forms are so widespread in the world. The face is circular. The eyes are round. They must engage in complete give and take. Veins and arteries also engage in give and take. Sickness occurs when the balance is broken, when there is giving but no way to receive. In sum, all beings that move must establish the principle of living for the sake of another. Otherwise, they cannot continue to exist. (69:83-84, October 20, 1973)

Love, especially true love, involves a spiral action. As two elements revolve, they penetrate each other and rise at the same time. Nearby objects are drawn into the swirl. The spiral action takes place due to the power of give and take action. This is how Jesus could say that he was in the Father and the Father in him. Through love, Jesus is in us and we are in him—it is entirely possible. God, Jesus and us combine in a great sphere. (124:51, January 23, 1983)

When something is rotating, its vertical and horizontal axes unite only at the most central point. When you and your partner come together at that central point, the entire universe resonates. You can even come to know the spirit world clearly. The world of love has no need for a system of education, nor does it need anyone to dominate and govern it. Love governs us. Doesn't even God completely submit to love? And if we are headed in the wrong direction, the world of love corrects our direction and sets us on the right way. We automatically know the way we should go. (214:233, February 2, 1991)

4. True Love Begins from Faith and Character

What is meant by saying that the regulation of the family depends on the cultivation of the personal life is this: Men are partial toward those for whom they have affection and whom they love, partial toward those whom they despise and dislike, partial toward those whom they fear and revere, partial toward those whom they pity and for whom they have compassion, and partial toward those whom they do not respect. Therefore there are few people in the world who know what is bad in those whom they love and what is good in those whom they dislike. Hence it is said, People do not know the faults of their sons and do not know [are not satisfied with] the bigness of their seedlings. This is what is meant by saying that if the personal life is not cultivated, one cannot regulate his family.[5]

Great Learning 8 (Confucianism)

He who does not love does not know God; for God is love.

1 John 4.8

It is not for the sake of the husband, my beloved, that the husband is dear, but for the sake of the Self.[6]

It is not for the sake of the wife, my beloved, that the wife is dear, but for the sake of the Self.

It is not for the sake of the children, my beloved, that the children are dear, but for the sake of the Self.

Brihadaranyaka Upanishad 2.4.4-5 (Hinduism)

The fruits of the Spirit are love, joy, peace, patience, kindness, goodness, faithfulness, gentleness, self-control; against such there is no law.

Galatians 5.23

What kind of love is this that to another can shift?
Says Nanak: True lovers are those who are forever absorbed in the Beloved.
Whoever discriminates between treatment held good or bad,
Is not a true lover—he rather is caught in calculations.

Adi Granth, Asa-ki-Var, M.2, p. 474 (Sikhism)

Wherefore let us exhort all men to piety, that we may avoid evil, and obtain the good, of which Love is to us the lord and minister; and let no one oppose him—he is the enemy of the gods who oppose him. For if we are friends of the God and at peace with him we shall find our own true loves, which rarely happens in this world at present...

My words... include men and women everywhere; and I believe that if our loves were perfectly accomplished, and each one returning to his primeval nature had his original true love, then our race would be happy.

Plato, Symposium (Hellenism)

Now tell me: can a man love anyone who hates himself? Can he be in harmony with someone else if he's divided in himself, or bring anyone pleasure if he's only a disagreeable nuisance to himself?

How necessary it is for a man to have a good opinion of himself, give himself a bit of a boost to win his own self-esteem before he can win that of others.

Erasmus, Praise of Folly (Humanism)

Teachings of Sun Myung Moon

People seek love with each other—horizontal love, while God's love is vertical love. If love is to be perfect, the horizontal and the vertical lines must be connected. (238:140, November 22, 1992)

It is a teaching of the Principle that God dwells in an individual whose mind and body are in oneness. Why does God dwell there? Love most certainly dwells where a person's mind and body are united. Love is the starting point of unity. The object partner's love brings God near, to dwell there.

It is said that human beings are temples of God. What kind of place is a holy temple? Is it a place of work? No, a temple is a place of rest and tranquility. Where can we rest? We can rest in the midst of God's love; that is the most ideal place. Don't you agree? So we can be God's temples when we can rest in God's love.

We aspire to have such a mind, with God's love and peace abiding within our inmost heart. Then we would dwell in what is called "the world of heart *(shimjung)*." That place is like an ever-flowing spring of the purest fresh water. Love and peace well up from within, never ceasing, never stagnating. It is endless because God dwells there.

Become that kind of person, a temple of God, and you can comfort those who are crying out in pain. (91:77, January 30, 1977)

True love moves at the zero point. The zero point is where the mind and body become one. There, every void is filled and every excess flattened. There the mind and body have perfect rest. At the zero point, only love has the power to move us. Nothing else works. At the zero point both the wife's mind and the husband's mind are at zero; therefore they can become one, they can become totally one. At the zero point, neither the wife nor the husband clings to their own concepts. Abiding there, they have no concept of "two," only "one." What does it mean? They are living for each other. That is the zero point. In that state they free in everything; wherever they go and whatever they do they are free. (230:103, April 26, 1992)

A person who does not love himself cannot love God. A person who does not love himself cannot love his parents. A person who does not love his parents cannot love his country. You must first love yourself to be able to love your parents, love your country, love the world, and love God. (22:97, January 26, 1969)

According to the ideal of love, all love relationships in the animal and plant kingdoms are for reproduction only. Human beings are the sole exception. Humankind enjoys freedom in the conjugal relationship of love. This is humanity's special privilege as the lord of all creation. God blessed His sons and daughters with the infinite joy of love.

However, the true freedom that God allowed requires human responsibility. If an individual were to insist upon and practice freedom of love without responsibility, how much confusion and destruction would take place! Achieving the highest ideal of human love is possible only when one takes responsibility for love.

We can think of this responsibility in three ways. The first responsibility is to become a master of true love—truly thanking God for the freedom of love and knowing how to cultivate and control ourselves. We do not take this responsibility for a love relationship merely because of law or social convention. Instead, a person should establish this responsibility through his own self-mastery and self-determination within a committed vertical relationship with God.

The second responsibility is toward our partner of love. By nature, people do not want their spouse's love to be shared with others. Horizontal conjugal love, which differs from the vertical love between parents and children, loses its potential for perfection the moment it is divided. This is because the Principle of Creation requires husband and wife to become one in absolute love. Each spouse has the responsibility to practice absolute love, living for the sake of the other.

The third responsibility of love is toward our children. The love of parents is the basis for children's pride and happiness. They would wish to be born through the total and harmonious unity of their parents in true love, and they would wish to be raised in that kind of love. The highest responsibility of parents is not only to rear their children externally, but also to offer them life elements of true love that can perfect their spirituality. This is why the family is so valuable. (277:201-02, April 16, 1996)

Living for Others

THE SPIRITUAL LIFE THAT BEGINS WITH FAITH AND DEVOTION to God finds its completion in deeds of loving-kindness and service to others: "We love, because he first loved us." (1 John 4.19) Living for the sake of others is love's fundamental ethic.

Living for others is a natural expression of a loving heart that flows spontaneously from a person's inner being. This is because human beings take after God, who from the moment of creation has continually been living for the sake of His creatures. Nevertheless, due to the fall, human nature became corrupted. Misunderstanding love as a matter of personal pleasure disconnected from the divine source, our minds, attitudes and habits became self-centered. Hence many people find it quite an effort to serve others without the expectation of some sort of payback. We have created a society of takers, not givers, leading inevitably to inequality, resentment and crime.

Passages from all the world's faiths recommend service and living to benefit others as the supreme way of life in this world. Jesus identifies service as the most authentic way of leadership, and exemplified it in his own life as one who came "not to be served, but to serve." Moreover, some texts, notably the Bhagavad-Gita and the Tao Te Ching, identify it as the fundamental principle by which God creates and sustains the universe. Every selfless act in the service of others is an act born of God. Father Moon has much to say on this topic, affirming the life of living for the sake of others as the lifestyle of the Kingdom.

1. Helping Others and Caring for Others Is the Fundamental Ethic of Human Life

Bear one another's burdens, and so fulfill the law of Christ.

Galatians 6.2

Rendering help to another is the function of all human beings.

Tattvarthasutra 5.21 (Jainism)

All men are responsible for one another.

Talmud, Sanhedrin 27b (Judaism)

The best of men are those who are useful to others.

Hadith of Bukhari (Islam)

Let no one seek his own good, but the good of his neighbor.

1 Corinthians 10.24

Above all hold unfailing your love for one another, since love covers a multitude of sins. Practice hospitality ungrudgingly to one another. As each has received a gift, employ it for one another, as good stewards of God's varied grace.

1 Peter 4.8-10

Be kind to parents, and the near kinsman, and to orphans, and to the needy, and to the neighbor who is of kin, and to the neighbor who is a stranger, and to the companion at your side, and to the traveler, and to [slaves] that your right hands own. Surely God loves not the proud and boastful such as are niggardly, and bid other men to be niggardly, and themselves conceal the bounty that God has given them.

Qur'an 4.36-47

Until now each and every one throughout the world has been concerned only with himself. How pitiful it is! You have no mind to help others, however hard you may think it over. Henceforth, ceaselessly strive to restore your mind! I, God (Tsukihi), request it from you all equally. If you ask what kind of mind it is, it is the mind to save single-heartedly all people of the world. Henceforth, if only all people of the world equally help each other on any and every matter, believe that I will accept your minds and will work any and every kind of salvation!

Ofudesaki 12.89-94 *(Tenrikyo)*

Do not seek to benefit only yourself, but think of other people also. If you yourself have abundance, do not say, "The others do not concern me, I need not bother about them!" If you were lucky in hunting, let others share it. Show them the favorable spots where there are many sea lions that can be easily slain. Let others have their share occasionally. If you want to amass everything for yourself, other people will stay away from you and no one will want to be with you. If you should one day fall ill, no one will visit you because, for your part, you did not formerly concern yourself about others. Grant other people something also. The Eskimo do not like a person who acts selfishly.

Yamana Eskimo Initiation *(Native American Religions)*

Teachings of Sun Myung Moon

The essence of love is to live for the sake of others instead of waiting for others to serve you. This is different from what passes for love in the secular world. Therefore, religion teaches to live for the sake of others—to be obedient, to serve and to sacrifice. (46:42, July 18, 1971)

Altruism—investing oneself for others, for the nation and for the world, living a life of sacrifice and service to others—may be considered by today's society to be a most foolish philosophy of life. As you come to understand the deepest truths, however, you will understand that altruism is the secret to living in eternal happiness and the way most beneficial to human beings. (198:163, February 1, 1990)

It is a principle that those who invest themselves for the sake of others and live for the sake of their partners will go to heaven. Because educational philosophies and cultural traditions throughout history have taught this idea, the planet Earth has been preserved at least to its current extent. (69:86, October 20, 1973)

The way of true love can never be found without a partner to live for. (398:284, December 15, 2002)

Live a broad and grand life on earth to be on the track to heaven. Live for others. Invest repeatedly and forget what you have invested. Love and forget, and continue to love infinitely because you were born to live for others. (306:215, September 23, 1998)

Who is a good person? Not someone who wishes that others would obey him. No, a good person is one who lives for the whole. Don't family members agree on who is the most promising and best-natured child in the family? From grandparents to cousins, if you ask them they will say, "Yes, that one gives the most." Undoubtedly that child is not the one who always asks his grandfather to please him. Rather, although he is a little child, he always considers how to behave and how to serve in order to make his grandfather happy. Day and night he tries to help all his family members, even cousins and in-laws. That child is undoubtedly a grandson on whom the family can place great hope. (174:11-12, February 23, 1988)

The universe was created by investing, based on love for the sake of others. Hence, when a person lives for the sake of others, he aligns himself with the original activity of creation, and this brings him into oneness with God. This person will not perish, because God will never perish. He will surely become an owner of the universe, because God is the Owner of the universe. Seen this way, it is clear that the person who lives for the sake of others becomes a central figure. (270:165, May 29, 1995)

I know that the American people respect individualism. However, individualism that lost sight of relationships between subject and object partners cannot endure. That is why America has reached a blind alley. How can we save America? We have to remind her of the essence of the Christian life, which is God's original way of life. There is no other way. In this sense, even though you do not welcome Reverend Moon, you need him. He teaches God's principle: You individuals should live for your families, families for your communities, communities for your nation, your nation for the world, and the world for God. (69:88, October 20, 1973)

2. Serve Others without Demanding Anything in Return

Jesus said, "You know that the rulers of the gentiles lord it over them, and their great men exercise authority over them. It shall not be so among you; but whoever would be great among you must be your servant, and whoever would be first among you must be your slave."

Matthew 20.25-27

Without selfless service are no objectives fulfilled;
In service lies the purest action.

Adi Granth, Maru, M.1, p. 992 (Sikhism)

One who serves and seeks no recompense
Finds union with the Lord.
Such a servant alone takes the Master's guidance, says Nanak,
As on him is divine grace.

Adi Granth, Sukhmani 18, M.5, pp. 286f. (Sikhism)

When you are in the service of your fellow beings you are only in the service of your God.

Book of Mormon, Mosiah 2.17 (Latter-day Saints)

The sage does not accumulate for himself.
The more he uses for others, the more he has himself.
The more he gives to others, the more he possesses of his own.
The Way of Heaven is to benefit others and not to injure.
The Way of the sage is to act but not to compete.

Tao Te Ching 81 (Taoism)

Unlike material possessions, goodness is not diminished when it is shared, either momentarily or permanently, with others, but expands and, in fact, the more heartily each of the lovers of goodness enjoys the possession the more does goodness grow. What is more, goodness is not merely a possession that no one can maintain who is unwilling to share it, but it is one that increases the more its possessor loves to share it."

Saint Augustine, City of God 15.5 (Christianity)

Do nothing from selfishness or conceit, but in humility count others better than yourselves. Let each of you look not only to his own interests, but also to the interests of others.

Philippians 2.3-4

Teachings of Sun Myung Moon

The blessing of all blessings is to give sacrificial love and service for the sake of others. (43:309, May 2, 1971)

Regardless of sex or age, everyone is longing for love. What kind of love? Love that is for the sake of others, not love that demands others love them. (211:206; December 30, 1990)

Do not think selfishly that you should receive love. A loving heart always seeks to sacrifice and yield to others, and after giving wants to give still more. That is God's heart.

For example, if I had one billion dollars and gave it all away to the poor on the streets, my mind would not be at ease. I would regret that I did not have more money to give away to help every human being in need. (133:180, July 10, 1984)

What is God's love? It is a love that is not satisfied with what it has given. It feels ashamed because it wanted to give more. If you give your utmost and still feel ashamed that you could not give more, then you are an owner of true love. A loving parent feels anxious that she could not buy better clothes for her children, so she supplements the deficiency with love. Therefore, love that was given in scarcity is returned in abundance. Love does not diminish when it is spent, but flourishes because it is supplemented by something bigger. Therefore, nothing prospers without love. Eternal life does not exist without love. (38:327-28, January 8, 1971)

What is the essence of love? It is living for others. It is giving to others—giving from a desire arising out of our own free will. Where did that love originate? It originated from God. God is the Subject of absolute love, and giving is the essence of His love.

We can see the essence of love in parental love. The child may spurn the parent, rebel and turn to evil, yet if the parent loves him even more than before, the child will repent. If the parent were to scold the child, saying, "I loved you so much, even breaking my back for you, you ungrateful brat!" then after three such scoldings the child might run away. But suppose that parent repents in tears, standing in front of the child and saying, "It is my fault for not loving you more." Don't you think that child would turn around? Greater love has the power to digest and unite lesser love. (48:182, September 12, 1971)

Let me explain with several illustrations why God made the principle of living for others. First, let me ask you a question. If someone truly loves you and sacrifices for you 100 percent, would you want to return only 50 percent, keeping the other 50 percent in your pocket? Or would you want to give more, even everything you have? Which is in accordance with your original conscience? The answer is, you would want to return more than you receive.

Here is Mr. Pak translating for me. If I give him 100 percent true love, and he knows this, then he will return more than 100 percent. So 100 percent is returned as 110 percent. After you receive 110 percent, in response to his sincerity, you would give again 120 percent. In this way the concept of eternity comes about. That's why God set up this principle—as the basis of eternity. It makes development and prosperity possible.

Second, if among five people in a family there is one who lives for the sake of the family, eventually he or she will become the center of that family. When he or she is established as the center, subject-object relationships are formed. This creates a realm of voluntary dominion. People today don't understand how happy it would be to be ruled by a subject who lives absolutely for his or her objects. You can never imagine how glorious it is to be under the direct dominion of God in the spirit world. This is the true subject-object relationship.

Third, we know that love and ideals are more precious than life itself, yet we tend to think we produced them and they belong to us. This is a big misunderstanding. Love and ideals come from your partner. Because they come from your object, the principle of living for others is necessary. God, the King of Wisdom, knows all of this, so He made this principle. (73:326-27, August 10, 1974)

3. In Creating the Universe, God Gave Everything for the Sake of His Creations

We love, because he first loved us.

1 John 4.19

Heaven is eternal and Earth everlasting.
They can be eternal and everlasting because
    they do not exist for themselves,
And for this reason can exist forever.
Therefore the sage places himself in the
    background,
but finds himself in the foreground.
He puts himself away, and yet he always
    remains.
Is it not because he has no personal interests?
This is the reason why his personal interests are
    fulfilled.

Tao Te Ching 7 (Taoism)

At the beginning, mankind and the obligation of selfless service were created together. "Through selfless service, you will always be fruitful and find the fulfillment of your desires": this is the promise of the Creator....

Every selfless act, Arjuna, is born from the eternal, infinite Godhead. God is present in every act of service. All life turns on this law, O Arjuna. Whoever violates it, indulging his senses for his own pleasure and ignoring the needs of others, has wasted his life. But those who realize the God within are always satisfied. Having found the source of joy and fulfillment, they no longer seek happiness from the external world. They have nothing to gain or lose by any action; neither people nor things can affect their security.

What the outstanding person does, others will try to do. The standards such people set will be followed by the whole world. There is nothing in the three worlds for Me to gain, Arjuna, nor is there anything I do not have; I continue to act, but I am not driven by any need of my own. If I ever refrained from continuous work, everyone would immediately follow my example. If I stopped working I would be the cause of cosmic chaos, and finally of the destruction of this world and these people.

Strive constantly to serve the welfare of the world; by devotion to selfless work one attains the supreme goal in life. Do your work with the welfare of others always in mind. It was by such work that Janaka attained perfection; others, too, have followed this path.

The ignorant work for their own profit, Arjuna; the wise work for the welfare of the world, without thought to themselves. By abstaining from work you will confuse the ignorant, who are engrossed in their actions. Perform all work carefully, guided by compassion.

Bhagavad-Gita 3.10-26 (Hinduism)

The threefold offspring of Prajapati—gods, men, and demons—dwelt with their father Prajapati as students of sacred knowledge.[7]

Having lived the life of a student of sacred knowledge, the gods said, "Speak to us, sir." To them then he spoke this syllable: "*Da.*" "Do you understand?" "We understand," said they. "You said to us, 'Restrain yourselves (*damyata*).'" "*Om,*" said he. "You do understand."

Then the men said to him, "Speak to us, sir." To them he spoke this syllable: "*Da.*" "Do you understand?" "We understand," said they. "You said to us, 'Give (*datta*).'" "*Om*," said he. "You do understand."

Then the demons said to him, "Speak to us, sir." To them he spoke this syllable: "*Da.*" "Do you understand?" "We understand," said they. "You said to us, 'Be compassionate (*dayadhvam*).'" "*Om*," said he. "You do understand."

The same thing does thunder, the divine voice, here repeat, "*Da! Da! Da!* Restrain yourselves. Give. Be compassionate." One should practice this same triad: self-restraint, giving and compassion.

Brihadaranyaka Upanishad 5.2.2:
The Voice of Thunder (Hinduism)

Teachings of Sun Myung Moon

What kind of being is God? God acts according to the law of priority of the universal and public. It requires that every being act to benefit the greater whole ahead of its own existence. Living by that law means to embody the spirit of sacrifice and service. (105:99, September 30, 1979)

Love is to invest oneself 100 percent. Out of love, when God created heaven and earth He invested Himself 100 percent. That is why true love starts from living for the sake of others. (189:202, April 6, 1989)

When God created humans beings as His partners of love, He was living for their sake. Therefore, human beings are meant to model after God and live for the sake of others. However, due to the Fall, we came to live for ourselves. The philosophy of living for the sake of others is based on the fact that all love comes from one's partner. (149:273, November 27, 1986)

Parents invest and forget for the sake of their children, a husband invests and forgets for the sake of his wife, and a wife invests and forgets for the sake of her husband. Siblings, too, invest and forget. God envisioned this standard of love at the beginning of creation, which He founded to manifest His ideal of love. (253:66, January 7, 1994)

God created the universe by investing Himself. Since God invested Himself completely, the complete result was guaranteed. As this is the principle of creation, we likewise should invest ourselves completely and sincerely. By giving sincerely you find your future object, build your foundation, and create the circumstances in which you can succeed. All this is impossible by merely receiving. The principle of creation is to live for others. (82:323, February 1, 1976)

God's act of creation required an investment of energy. The act of creating consumes energy. How much did God invest? You read the Bible, and you think that everything was created easily according to the Word of God, "Let there be... and it was." It was not that way. Rather, God completely invested His true life, true love, and true ideal in His creations.

Hence, there was a difference between the situation before the creation and after God finished His creation. Before the creation, the God only thought of Himself. After God created, He entered the age of existing for the sake of His object partners...

In this way, my existence is no longer for own benefit. Instead, I exist for the sake of my partner. Parents exist for the sake of their children. Because words such as "love" and "ideal" presume the existence of a counterpart, the origin of ideal existence does not begin at the position where we exist for our own sake but where we exist for the sake of our partner.

This is the reason God invested completely in creating His partner. God wanted to create an object partner of greater value, more complete and ideal. After creating Adam and Eve, God determined that He would exist for their sake. He made the transition from living for Himself to living for the sake of His partner.

For this reason, we cannot hope to attain our ideal as long as we put ourselves first. We can attain our ideal only by living for the sake of others, especially for the sake of our partner. This principle stems from the origin of the universe. (69:82-83, October 20, 1973)

Sacrificial Love

TRUE LOVE IS SACRIFICIAL LOVE. It calls forth self-sacrifice in the service of others. Love prompts us to get involved in the knotty problems of the world, gives us the strength to bear with the failings and weaknesses of others, and moves us to help others regardless of the cost. We have the example of Jesus Christ, who out of love, offered his life to redeem sinful humanity. Moses in his time, and Muhammad as well, endured persecution and exile, risking their lives to enlighten and liberate their people—all for the love of God and humanity.

Out of Buddhism comes the figure of the bodhisattva, who vows to devote himself to save all beings. He regards his own happiness as incidental to the happiness of others, and would rather not enjoy the fruits of his own spiritual progress before first liberating others.

On this topic, Father Moon describes the root of sacrificial love in God, who invested Himself endlessly at the creation to make a beautiful home for His children. God, who ever since the fall, has continuously and sorrowfully devoted Himself as would a loving Parent to rescue prodigal humanity from the pits of sin and grief. Such divine love is manifested every day in the human love of parents, who willingly sacrifice for their children's future.

1. Sacrificing Everything—Even Your Life—for the Sake of Those You Love

Greater love has no man than this, that a man lay down his life for his friends.

John 15.13

The Son of man came not to be served but to serve, and to give his life as a ransom for many.

Matthew 20.28

Therefore be imitators of God, as beloved children. And walk in love, as Christ loved us and gave himself up for us.

Ephesians 5.1-2

Love will make men dare to die for their beloved—love alone; and women as well as men. Of this, Alcestis, the daughter of Pelias, is a monument to all Hellas; for she was willing to lay down her life on behalf of her husband, when no one else would.[8]

Socrates, in Plato, Symposium *(Hellenism)*

By this we know love, that he [Christ] laid down his life for us; and we ought to lay down our lives for the brethren. But if any one has the world's goods and sees his brother in need, yet closes his heart against him, how does God's love abide in him? Little children, let us not love in word or speech but in deed and in truth.

1 John 3.16-18

We, truly, have come for your sakes, and have borne the misfortunes of the world for your salvation. Do you flee the one who has sacrificed his life that you may be quickened?... Do you imagine that he seeks his own interests, when he has, at all times, been threatened by the swords of the enemies; or that he seeks the vanities of the world, after he has been imprisoned in the most desolate of cities?...

Verily, he has consented to be sorely abased that you may attain glory, and yet, you are disporting yourselves in the vale of heedlessness. He, in truth, lives in the most desolate of abodes for your sakes, while you dwell in your palaces.

Tablets of Bahá'u'lláh Revealed after the Kitáb-i-Aqdas (Baha'i Faith)

Teachings of Sun Myung Moon

If I put my life on the line to subjugate evil, then the life-giving love of God will be bestowed upon me. (40:243, February 6, 1971)

A sacrificial spirit—where for the sake of a neighbor you can throw away your life as if it were a worthless piece of straw—is exactly true love. (224:254, December 7, 1991)

Love would not be possible if human beings did not have an original nature to sacrifice. We do not think of it as a sacrifice when we sacrifice for someone we love. We feel it is worthwhile, even as we sacrifice more and more. (63:25, October 1, 1972)

In the course of loving their children, parents will sacrifice. No matter how much they sacrifice for their children they do not take it as painful, because the heart of love is contained in their sacrifice. All the energy they expend returns to them as stimulating love. The more they give out, the more joy they feel. That is the power by which they can overcome the pain of sacrifice.

Likewise, husband and wife may make sacrifices for each other to the point of giving their lives, yet through it all, they feel joy. In love they can invest infinitely, and feel infinite joy in return.

Sacrifice in itself is consumptive; it is a minus force. How can one feel joy by becoming diminished? From a worldly viewpoint it is impossible. However, it is possible because of love.

Why did God pour out His love? Because without love, nothing returns. Through a relationship of love between subject and object partners, an eternal give and take action is set in motion which multiplies God's power. Therefore, we can conclude that love establishes eternity. That is why the Bible says that God is love.

According to the laws of mechanics, the output can never be greater than the input. If that were true where love is concerned, then when God loved it would drain out all His energy and nothing would return to Him. Therefore, He set up the ideal that in loving, the output is greater than the input.

Accordingly, true parent-child relationships, true husband-wife relationships, and true brotherly relationships are established through sacrificial love. The genuineness of those relationships depends upon keeping the standard of sacrifice.

Children know that their parents truly love them when they sacrifice themselves for them. Although the sacrificial position is a sorrowful one, when the children perfectly appreciate it and return love to the parents, the parents can feel more joy.

Likewise, a couple that sacrifices for each other finds their love constantly renewed, revived by the power of sacrifice. A husband and wife who share their suffering with each other can become one eternally. True friends also, are those who sacrifice themselves for each other. The position of love can be established when one sacrifices oneself and gives himself for others. Thus sacrifice accompanies love. (September 11, 1972)

Love embraces all. Love goes beyond the law. Because it goes beyond the law, not even death can stand in its way. Love can penetrate any wall, even a wall tens of thousands of years in the making. Though the wall is so strong that no army can invade, love can push its way through safely. The most formidable wall will crumble when you attack it with the weapons of self-sacrifice and investing everything, for the sake of love. (49:52, October 3, 1971)

You should sacrifice the person closest to you. What principle has God employed in His efforts to restore this world? To save this sinful world and all the wretched people of the earth, God sacrificed the person He loved most.

God sent His servants as offerings, and when the time came God offered up His only Son. This has always been the way of God's providence: He sacrifices the most beloved on His side for the sake of Satan's tribe. Can you possibly experience how God must feel, to sacrifice His beloved ones to liberate the followers of His worst enemy? Yet He perseveres in this providence for the sake of the world and for the sake of His enemies. Therefore, the entire human race should give God honor and glory. (33:298, August 21, 1970)

When an individual sacrifices him or herself for the sake of others, the others will recognize him as a virtuous person. If a certain family lives sacrificially for other families, those families will respect it as a virtuous family. If a community sacrifices itself for other communities and dedicates its full energy for them, then they will honor it as the most virtuous of communities. Likewise, if a nation seeks to sacrifice itself for all nations in the world, then the other nations will honor that nation as the most noble among nations.

This principle is God's Will, and God sent Jesus to establish it. Christianity is spread throughout the world. If Christians were living this way, sacrificing their own nations to save other nations, and giving everything they owned for the sake of saving humanity, then surely the churches would today be fulfilling the Will of the God of goodness. (69:86, October 20, 1973)

2. Enduring Life's Hardships and Sorrows to Help People in Need

The believer who participates in human life, exposing himself to its torments and suffering, is worth more than the one who distances himself from its suffering.

                  Hadith of Ibn Majah *(Islam)*

One who stays in the shade does not know the sun's heat.[9]

            Igala Proverb *(African Traditional Religions)*

A man should share in the distress of the community, for so we find that Moses, our teacher, shared in the distress of the community.

                  Talmud, Taanit 11a *(Judaism)*

And as he sat at table in the house, behold, many tax collectors and sinners came and sat down with Jesus and his disciples. And when the Pharisees saw this, they said to his disciples,

"Why does your teacher eat with tax collectors and sinners?" But when he heard it, he said, "Those who are well have no need of a physician, but those who are sick."

Matthew 9.10-12

If I have to be reborn I should wish to be born as an 'untouchable', so that I may share their sorrows, sufferings and the affronts leveled at them, in order that I may free myself and them from that miserable condition.

Mohandas K. Gandhi (*Hinduism*)

It is not always physical bravery that counts. One must have the courage to face life as it is, to go through sorrows and always sacrifice oneself for the sake of others.

Kipsigis Saying (*African Traditional Religions*)

We who are strong ought to bear with the failings of the weak, and not to please ourselves; let each of us please his neighbor for his good, to edify him. For Christ did not please himself; but, as it is written, "The reproaches of those who reproached thee fell on me."

Romans 15.1-3

Those who are morally well adjusted look after those who are not; those who are talented look after those who are not. That is why people are glad to have good fathers and elder brothers. If those who are morally well adjusted and talented abandon those who are not, then scarcely an inch will separate the good from the depraved.

Mencius IV.B.7 (*Confucianism*)

A bodhisattva resolves, "I take upon myself the burden of all suffering; I am resolved to do so; I will endure it. I do not turn or run away, do not tremble, am not terrified, nor afraid, do not turn back or despond.

"And why? At all costs I must bear the burdens of all beings. In that, I do not follow my own inclinations. I have made the vow to save all beings. All beings I must set free. The whole world of living beings I must rescue from the terrors of birth, of old age, of sickness, of death and rebirth, of all kinds of moral offense, of all states of woe... My endeavors do not merely aim at my own deliverance. For with the help of the boat of the thought of all-knowledge, I must rescue all these beings from the stream of Samsara, which is so difficult to cross... I myself must grapple with the whole mass of suffering of all beings. To the limit of my endurance I will experience in all the states of woe, found in any world system, all the abodes of suffering...

"And why? Because it is surely better that I alone should be in pain than that all these beings should fall into the states of woe. Therefore I must give myself away as a pawn through which the whole world is redeemed from the terrors of hells, of animal birth, of the world of Death, and with this my own body I must experience, for the sake of all beings, the whole mass of painful feelings. And on behalf of all beings I give surety for all beings, and in doing so I speak truthfully, am trustworthy, do not go back on my word. I must not abandon all beings."[10]

Sikshasamuccaya 280-81,
Vajradhvaja Sutra (*Buddhism*)

"I should be a hostel for all sentient beings, to let them escape from all painful things. I should be a protector for all sentient beings, to let them all be liberated from all afflictions. I should be a refuge for all sentient beings, to free them from all fears...

"I should accept all sufferings for the sake of sentient beings, and enable them to escape from the abyss of immeasurable woes of birth and death. I should accept all suffering for the sake of all sentient beings in all worlds, in all states of misery, forever and ever, and still always cultivate foundations of goodness for the sake of all beings. Why? I would rather take all this suffering on myself than to allow sentient beings to fall into hell. I should be a hostage to those perilous places—hells, animal realms, the nether world—as a ransom to rescue all sentient beings in states of woe and enable them to gain liberation.[11]

"I vow to protect all sentient beings and never abandon them. What I say is sincerely true, without falsehood. Why? Because I have set my mind on enlightenment in order to liberate all sentient beings; I do not seek the unexcelled Way for my own sake."

Garland Sutra 23 *(Buddhism)*

Teachings of Sun Myung Moon

To reach the Kingdom of Heaven, you must pass through hell. *(Way of God's Will* 1.8)

Love always requires sacrifice, and it also requires overcoming. (46:35, July 18, 1971)

In my student days, whenever I came home from school I would change my student uniform for a laborer's clothes and go out to do menial labor. It was not because I lacked for money, but because I wanted to experience the life of a laborer. I carried coal, worked on the docks and as a farmhand. I experienced every sort of job, to learn everything about suffering and joys of working people. I thought it my responsibility to liberate them all. (37:35-36, December 22, 1970)

To bring happiness to this unhappy, chaotic world, we should conquer a path of misery and unhappiness. That means we have to taste the bottom of human misery. The only way we can liberate the misery of the world is by leading an even more miserable life. If this way did not bring results, we would have to say that God does not exist.

I walked the path of abuse and persecution throughout my life for this very reason. I determined that I would walk this path throughout my life. How would you fare in such miserable circumstances? Are you someone who can stand, determined to do the will of God, and say, "Follow me! I am not discouraged, but full of joy"? If so, then you can bring real happiness to the people in that wretched place.

The people we respect as saints, heroes, patriots and exemplary women all became famous, historical figures only after enduring such circumstances. America's patriots tasted the misery of the nation's travails and fought bravely to establish the nation at the risk of their lives. All the saints of this world, and all God's sons and daughters, have done likewise. (91:287, February 27, 1977)

The law of priority of the universal and public upholds and protects people who sacrifice themselves for the whole. It eliminates people who only pursue their own benefit and hate to sacrifice. (105:91-92, September 30, 1979)

Some religious people pray, "Please let me go to the Kingdom of Heaven." Those people are frauds. The proper attitude is this: a wife thinks to send her husband to the Kingdom of Heaven first and follow him there later. It is wrong if she thinks she alone deserves to enter the Kingdom while abandoning her husband. Likewise, a son thinks to send his parents and siblings to the Kingdom of Heaven first and only afterwards to enter himself. A loyal citizen would not want to enter the Kingdom of Heaven until he has sent his entire nation there first, even all the people of the world. Those who would first liberate God before they enjoy the delights of the Kingdom of Heaven are people who resemble Jesus. Their desire is in line with the Messiah's responsibility.

The Messiah does not think, "I must quickly enter the Kingdom of Heaven." He works to send individuals, families, tribes, peoples, nations and the world to the Kingdom of Heaven. He even strives to liberate all the denizens of hell and send them to the Kingdom of Heaven, because he is determined to carry all the sadness of God on his shoulders.

The Messiah never dreams of living happily in the Kingdom of Heaven alone. He is willing to enter the Kingdom only after he has liberated all humankind on earth and all the inmates of hell, because he knows God's sorrow. God does not feel comfortable to see hell. By creating the Kingdom of Heaven on earth and in heaven, the Messiah will release God from having to see hell. Only when he knows that God can relax upon seeing the work of salvation completely finished, will the Messiah enter the Kingdom of Heaven. (188:283-84, March 1, 1989)

Universal Love

TRUE LOVE IS UNIVERSAL. IT HAS NO LIMITS. When we are immersed in the love of God, we can experience that everyone is our brother or sister. Here is a major distinction between absolute, true love and the relative love of fallen people: true love is impartial and universal, while fallen love is partial to kith and kin, to friends and compatriots. In the words of Martin Luther King, Jr., "An individual has not started living until he can rise above the narrow confines of his individualistic concerns to the broader concerns of all humanity."[12]

Yet is love for humanity enough? Not if we mean only a general sentiment that can be satisfied by acts of charity and political efforts to benefit the downtrodden. The real stage of love is actual relationships. How can we love strangers and people of faraway nations with the same intensity and concreteness as we love members of our own family? Here scripture speaks of extending to strangers the way we treat members of our own family. Father Moon is very clear on this score. To demonstrate universal love that transcends race, he recommends that we give one of our children in marriage to someone of another race. By digesting every difficulty in relating to our in-laws, we become people whose love truly goes beyond the racial barrier.

1. A Heart to Love All People

May good befall all,
May there be peace for all,
May all be fit for perfection, and
May all experience that which is auspicious.

Om, May all be happy.
May all be healthy.
May we all experience what is good and let no one suffer.
Om, Peace, Peace, Peace!
    The Universal Prayer (Hinduism)

He lets his mind pervade one quarter of the world with thoughts of love, and so the second, and so the third, and so the fourth. And thus the whole wide world, above, below, around, and everywhere, does he continue to pervade with the heart of love, far-reaching, exalted, beyond measure. Just as a mighty trumpeter makes himself heard—and that without difficulty—in all the four directions; even so of all things that have the shape of life there is not one that he passes by or leaves aside, but regards them all with mind set free, and deep-felt love. Verily this is the way to a state of union with Brahma.
    Digha Nikaya 13.76-77, Tevigga Sutta (Buddhism)

A man once asked the Prophet what was the best thing in Islam. He replied, "It is to feed the hungry and to give the greeting of peace both to those one knows and to those one does not know."
    Hadith of Bukhari (Islam)

Of the adage, Only a good man knows how to like people, knows how to dislike them, Confucius said, "He whose heart is in the smallest degree set upon Goodness will dislike no one."
    Analects 4.3-4 (Confucianism)

The sage has no fixed [personal] ideas.
He regards the people's ideas as his own.
I treat those who are good with goodness,
And I also treat those who are not good with goodness.
Thus goodness is attained.
I am honest with those who are honest,
And I am also honest with those who are dishonest.
Thus honesty is attained.

Tao Te Ching 49 (Taoism)

Teachings of Sun Myung Moon

The sages of old… taught us to love Heaven, to love the earth, and to love humankind. (19:285, March 10, 1968)

God's love is the original source of the universe, and it embraces the world. If such love had reached each and every person, wouldn't this world be a realm where love is everywhere, whether we go up or down?

In such a world, what would we value in a person? It would not be eloquence or good looks. We would value people of character, those who are faultless from any angle. Their fragrance would spread to everyone who knew them. Shouldn't you be like that? When you relate to others with the heart that each is a part of God and no one is unrelated to God, then everyone becomes your friend. (33:89-90, August 9, 1970)

A loving heart is the same whether it is for an enemy or a friend. It is universal. The whole is the same as one cell. The universe is formed like a human being, each composed of 400 trillion cells living in oneness. You can become one with God when you become the embodiment of love that can connect to all of these cells. (225:132, January 5, 1992)

God's love has no boundaries. Love transcends national borders. Love transcends race. In love there is no discrimination between black, white, and yellow.

Love is the greatest thing. Wherever love flows freely and without fear, the environment adapts to it; who or what would want to rebel? This way of thinking is pleasing to God. Distributing love everywhere is the only way to win God's favor. (164:93, April 26, 1987)

What is the character of God? God is a being who loves His object partner more than He loves Himself. God's activity of loving the object partner more than self brings unity; then together they can love an object partner of greater scope. Since this is the core of God's practice, God sends the person closest to Himself to the evil world, offering him as a sacrifice for humankind. This is God's way of thinking.

That is why the sages, saints and great men of history invariably taught, "Love all humankind." They did not restrict their love to only their family, but loved their country. They went beyond their country to love the world. They loved this way even though they were not welcomed, but rejected and sacrificed. (100:81, August 8, 1978)

2. Loving Others with the Same Heart as We Have for Our Own Family

As a mother protects her only child at the risk of her own life, let him cultivate a boundless heart towards all beings.
                 Khuddaka Patha, Metta Sutta *(Buddhism)*

It is to regard other people's countries as one's own; regard other people's families as one's own; regard other people's person as one's own.
                 Mo Tzu[13]

Lacking compassion for all beings,
Filial piety causes *samsara*.[14]
                 Milarepa *(Buddhism)*

Treat the aged of your own family in a manner befitting their venerable age and extend this treatment to the aged of other families; treat your own young in a manner befitting their tender age and extend this to the young of other families.
                 Mencius I.A.7 *(Confucianism)*

I should accommodate and serve all beings as attentively as I show filial respect to my parents, due respect to my teachers, to elders, and arhats, up to the Tathagatas, all in equality.
                 Gandavyuha Sutra, Vows of Samantabhadra *(Buddhism)*

The bodhisattva, the great being, having practiced compassion, sympathy, and joy, attains the stage of the best-loved only son. For example, the father and mother greatly rejoice as they see their son at peace. The same is the case with the bodhisattva who abides in this stage: he sees all beings just as the parents see their only son. He greatly rejoices when he sees them practicing goodness. So we call this stage the best-loved.

For example, the father and mother are worried at heart as they see their son ill. Commiseration poisons their heart; the mind cannot part with the illness. So it is with the bodhisattva, the great being, who abides in this stage. As he sees beings bound up in the illness of illusion, his heart aches. He is worried as in the case of an only son. Blood comes out from all pores of the skin. That is why we call this stage as that of an only son.

A child picks up earth, dirty things, tiles, stones, old bones, pieces of wood and puts them into his mouth, at which the father and mother, apprehensive of the harms that might arise thereby, take the child with the left hand and with the right take these out. The same goes with the bodhisattva: he sees that all beings are not grown up to the stage of law body and that non-good is done in body, speech, and mind. The bodhisattva sees, and with the hand of wisdom has it extracted. He does not wish that man should repeat birth and death, receiving thereby sorrow and worry.

When a father and mother part with their beloved son as the son dies, their hearts so ache that they feel that they themselves should die together with him. The same is the case with the bodhisattva: as he sees a benighted person fall into hell, he himself desires to be born there, too. [He thinks,] "Perhaps the man, as he experiences the pain, may gain a moment of repentance where I can speak to him of the Law in various ways and enable him to gain a thought of good."

For the father and mother of an only son, in sleep or while awake, or while walking, standing, sitting, or reclining, their minds always think of the son. If he does wrong, they give kindly advice and lead the boy that he does not do evil any more. The same is the case of the bodhisattva: as he sees beings fall into the realms of hell, hungry ghosts and animals, or sees them doing good and evil in the world of man and in heaven, his mind is ever upon them and not apart from them. He may see them doing all evil, yet he does not become angry or punish with evil intent.[15]
                 Mahaparinirvana Sutra 470-71 *(Buddhism)*

Teachings of Sun Myung Moon

Do not nurse only your own dear child, but try to be a mother who treats other children with the heart that they are yours as well. With that heart, the babies who suckle at your breast will certainly become great men and women. (31:168, May 24, 1970)

You can build the world of peace on this earth if you become people who act according to the Kingdom of Heaven's universal teaching to unfold the movement of God's love, life and truth. This means your parents are not only your biological parents; your siblings are not only your biological siblings, and your children are not only your biological children. When you become a person who regards all people as your parents, your siblings and your children, then as you look upon the multitudes of people suffering in this world of death, you cannot relate to them without tears. Looking at people your own age as your siblings, or younger people as your own children, you will feel a strong sense of responsibility to save them. You will make every effort, with tears. If you truly become this kind of person, then you will be a central pillar for building the Kingdom of Heaven. (2:144, March 17, 1957)

Jesus said, "A man's foes will be those of his own household." (Matt. 10.36) He meant that when you love your family members more than other people, they become your enemies that block you from entering the Kingdom of Heaven. (161:249, February 22, 1987)

Parents who praise their child for being filial to them cannot raise true filial children. Parents who want to raise true filial children should teach them, "My child, love your brothers and sisters even more than you love me. Love your neighbors and your nation more than you love me." I think that parent is qualified to have many filial children.

If there is a good king, that king should teach his loyal subjects, saying, "I appreciate that you give devotion and love for me, but first love your fellow citizens and God, and then love me." That is the good king who can rightly lead many loyal subjects.

Likewise, how does God lead the saints? God does not teach them, "Do your utmost duty to show your loyalty to Me." Instead He says, "Don't pay Me so much regard; first love the people. Liberate every being on this earth and all the spirit beings in the spirit world, and then love Me." Because God is that kind of being, He bears the name Jehovah, Lord of all beings.[16] (85:265, March 3, 1976)

Who is a son of filial piety? He discovers what his parents most want and completes it; thus he tries to align himself with his parents' desires. Whatever his eyes see, he sees through the eyes of his parents. Whatever his heart feels, he feels through the heart of his parents. Whatever words he hears, he thinks, "Would my parents like this kind of speech?" A filial son or daughter devotes all five senses to delighting in his or her parents' world.

The thing that filial sons and daughters, patriots, and saints have in common is their concern for others—their family, their nation and the world respectively. Then let us turn our eyes to God, the Center of the entire universe. If you were to love God in like manner, you would embrace heaven and earth with love. You would devote all your heart and mind to benefit all beings in the universe; to make them fit to receive God's love.[17] (161:132-33, January 18, 1987)

3. Love Especially the Stranger, the Foreigner, and Those Whom Society Despises

For the LORD your God is God of gods and Lord of lords, the great, the mighty, and the terrible God, who is not partial and takes no bribe. He executes justice for the fatherless and the widow, and loves the stranger, giving him food and clothing. Love the stranger therefore; for you were strangers in the land of Egypt.

Deuteronomy 10.17-20

A lawyer... said to Jesus, "Who is my neighbor?" Jesus replied, "A man was going down from Jerusalem to Jericho, and he fell among robbers, who stripped him and beat him, and departed, leaving him half-dead. Now by chance a priest was going down that road; and when he saw him he passed by on the other side. So likewise a Levite, when he came to the place and saw him, passed by on the other side. But a Samaritan, as he journeyed, came to where he was; and when he saw him, he had compassion, and went to him and bound up his wounds, pouring on oil and wine; then he set him on his own beast and brought him to an inn, and took care of him. And the next day he took out two denarii and gave them to the innkeeper, saying, 'Take care of him; and whatever you spend, I will repay you when I come back.' Which of these three, do you think, proved neighbor to the man who fell among the robbers?" He said, "The one who showed mercy on him." And Jesus said to him, "Go, and do likewise."[18]

Luke 10.25-37: Parable of the Good Samaritan

When Israel crossed the Red Sea, the angels were about to break forth in song, but the Holy One rebuked them, "My children are drowning, and you would sing?"

Talmud, Megilla 10b (Judaism)

The bodhisattva should adopt the same attitude towards all beings, his mind should be even towards all beings, he should not handle others with an uneven mind, but with a mind which is friendly, well-disposed, helpful, free from aversions avoiding harm and hurts, he should handle others as if they were his mother, father, son, or daughter. As a savior of all beings should a bodhisattva behave towards all beings. So should he train himself if he wants to know full enlightenment.

Perfection of Wisdom in Eight Thousand Lines 321-22 (Buddhism)

Teachings of Sun Myung Moon

You cannot enter the Kingdom of Heaven unless you love strangers more than you love your own brothers and sisters. You must love all people in the same way that you love God. (*Way of God's Will* 1.8)

Jesus Christ lived and worked with twelve difficult people. Each disciple represented a particular type of person and displayed the worst aspects of that personality type. On your path, you also should know twelve different types of people and deal with their fallen natures: people with personalities resembling January, February, March, etc., the twelve months of the year. (January 10, 1982)

You white people cannot say, "I only like white people. I can love white grandparents, but I cannot love black grandparents or Asian grandparents. I can love a well-dressed and cultured grandmother, but I cannot love those... primitives!" No, you should make extra effort to love elderly Africans as much as you love your own grandparents. That is the formula for training yourself to live properly on this earth. (130:274, February 5, 1984)

Suppose you have three sons. You could marry one to a German wife, one to a French wife, and one to an African wife, and take in all three couples to live in your home. You would have three daughters-in-law each from nations that have been enemies to each other. How could you create an atmosphere where they will not fight or quarrel?

Have everyone eat food out of the same pot. What if a morsel falls back into the pot from your African daughter-in-law's mouth? Are you going to clean it off, or not mind and keep on eating? Some of you would not like it in the beginning; you would rather not eat at all, but you must. Why? You cannot love African people without eating what they eat. When you can eat that spilt food without it bothering you, God will dwell in your home and God's love will dwell in your home. (99:134-35, September 10, 1978)

Americans should not say, "Only Americans," and Oriental people should not say, "Only Oriental people." No good comes from favoring family members, or the people of our tribe or nation. We have to digest the problem of racial discrimination with the love of Heaven. How do we prove we are doing it? By international and interracial marriage. (112:86, April 1, 1981)

Love Your Enemy

THE PRESCRIPTION TO LOVE YOUR ENEMY and to requite evil with good is sometimes thought of as an impractical and perfectionist ethic. But in fact, this doctrine is widely taught in the world's religions. It is in fact a fundamental principle for relating peaceably with others.

Many people seek recompense for wrongs done to them in the name of "justice." Yet if everyone demanded an eye for an eye, the whole world would be blind. Revenge only multiplies evil in the world; neither does it solve the fundamental root of evil, which lies in Satan's accusations against God and humanity. As Father Moon explains, only the unparalleled love of enemy can overcome evil at its root and lead to the advancement of God's Kingdom.

Several passages in this section describe Jesus' example of loving his enemies as he hung from the cross. We have also included quotations from two modern-day apostles of this doctrine: Mahatma Gandhi and Martin Luther King, Jr.

You have heard that it was said, "You shall love your neighbor and hate your enemy." But I say to you, Love your enemies and pray for those who persecute you, so that you may be sons of your Father who is in heaven; for he makes his sun rise on the evil and on the good, and sends rain on the just and on the unjust. For if you love those who love you, what reward have you? Do not even the tax collectors do the same? And if you salute only your brethren, what more are you doing than others? Do not even the Gentiles do the same? You, therefore, must be perfect, as your heavenly Father is perfect.

Matthew 5.43-48

God says, "Resemble Me; just as I repay good for evil so do you also repay good for evil."

Exodus Rabbah 26.2 (Judaism)

It may be that God will ordain love between you and those whom you hold as enemies. For God has power over all things; and God is Oft-forgiving, Most Merciful.

Qur'an 60.7

The Messenger of God said, "Shall I inform you of the best morals of this world and the hereafter? To forgive him who oppresses you, to make a bond with him who severs from you, to be kind to him who insults you, and to give to him who deprives you."

Hadith (Islam)

"He abused me, he beat me, he defeated me, he robbed me!" In those who harbor such thoughts hatred is not appeased.

"He abused me, he beat me, he defeated me, he robbed me!" In those who do not harbor such thoughts hatred is appeased.

Hatreds never cease through hatred in this world; through love alone they cease. This is an eternal law.

Dhammapada 3-5 (Buddhism)

When we look beneath the surface, beneath the impulsive evil deed, we see within our enemy-neighbor a measure of goodness and know that the viciousness and evilness of his acts are not quite representative of all that he is. We see him in a new light. We recognize that his hate grows out of fear, pride, ignorance, prejudice, and misunderstanding, but in spite of this, we know God's image is ineffably etched in his being. Then we love our enemies by realizing that they are not totally bad and that they are not beyond the reach of God's redemptive love.

Martin Luther King, Jr., *Strength to Love* (Christianity)

It is not nonviolence if we merely love those that love us. It is nonviolence only when we love those that hate us. I know how difficult it is to follow this grand law of love. But are not all great and good things difficult to do? Love of the hater is the most difficult of all. But by the grace of God even this most difficult thing becomes easy to accomplish if we want to do it.

Mohandas K. Gandhi, *All Men Are Brothers* (Hinduism)

Do good to him who has done you an injury.

Tao Te Ching 63 (Taoism)

The good deed and the evil deed are not alike. Repel the evil deed with one which is better, then lo!, he between whom and you there was enmity shall become as though he were a bosom friend.

But none is granted it save those who are steadfast, and none is granted it save a person of great good fortune.

Qur'an 41.34-35

If you meet your enemy's ox or his ass going astray, you shall bring it back to him. If you see the ass of one who hates you lying under its burden, you shall refrain from leaving him with it, you shall help him to lift it up.

Exodus 23.4-5

Aid an enemy before you aid a friend, to subdue hatred.

Tosefta, Baba Metzia 2.26 (Judaism)

It is easy enough to be friendly to one's friends. But to befriend the one who regards himself as your enemy is the quintessence of true religion. The other is mere business.

Mohandas K. Gandhi (Hinduism)

And when they came to the place which is called The Skull [Calvary], there they crucified him, and the criminals, one on the right and one on the left. And Jesus said, "Father, forgive them; for they know not what they do." And they cast lots to divide his garments.

Luke 23.33-34

Teachings of Sun Myung Moon

What kind of person can be close to God and attend Him in the Kingdom of Heaven? One who resembles God. Since the nature of God is to love His enemies, then the person who tries to love his or her enemies and invests him or herself completely for that purpose will be able to live near God's royal throne.

From this standpoint, the most precious education is to learn to love your enemies. The noblest training to cultivate your mind is to train yourself to always make effort to love your enemies. (124:155, February 6, 1983)

What is true love? It is God's love. What is God's love? In Jesus' words, it is to love your enemy. If white people love other white people, there is nothing special about that. When a white person loves a black person, however, that is close to true love. Loving your enemy is true love, without a doubt.

Why is loving your enemy true love? It is true because no one can criticize or complain about it. It is always round and can flow everywhere. Whether that love goes towards one side or the other, it is all good. Wherever it goes—into the eyes, into the nose, into the mouth—wherever it goes, it is good. (115:315-16, November 29, 1981)

What is the difference between love in the satanic world and love in the heavenly world? Satanic love repays evil for evil, while heavenly love repays evil with good. When we love even our enemy, Satan runs away.

That is why Jesus went a paradoxical way, and taught believers to walk a paradoxical way. They had no choice because everything is turned upside-down. West had become East, East had become West. South had become North, and North had become South.

Therefore, you cannot enter the Kingdom of Heaven unless you love your enemies—your individual enemies, your family's enemies, your clan's enemies, your nation's enemies, and your world's enemies. God likewise is in this situation. (130:161, January 8, 1984)

I am teaching you to love those who hate you. If you love them, sooner or later they will come to like you. If you return good three times for every time someone does you wrong, eventually that person will bow his head. Try it yourself and see if I am right or not. Everyone has a conscience. (39:302-04, January 16, 1971)

True love has influence on the enemy. If you overcome the first, second, third and fourth difficult situation with love, the enemy will disappear. Jesus loved his enemies knowing that love has such great power. (121:173, October 24, 1982)

Did you ever take pity on someone who opposed you and persecuted you? Did you ever think that he might be jealous of you on account of your many blessings? Did you ever think that the reason he persecutes you is because he is jealous of you? (105:31, July 8, 1979)

The reason why God does not punish an enemy, even though He would want to kill him, is that He is thinking of the enemy's parents, wife, sons and daughters who love him. God cannot bear to strike that enemy with His whip because He would experience the painful hearts of all those good people as they wept many tears out of their love for him. God's love is like that.

When you really feel this heart of God, could you take revenge on your enemy? If you really knew all the precious love connected with that person, instead of hitting him you would get someone to go and help him. Thus you come closer to the great way of the universal Principle, which instructs us to embrace everything with love. When you practice it, heaven and earth will shake and even God will cry out with tears, "You truly resemble Me. How happy I am!" This is how we should understand the teaching to love our enemies. Where can we find the power to love our enemies? The source is neither knowledge, nor money, nor earthly power. It is only true love. (201:150, March 30, 1990)

You should love your distant relations more than your immediate family. God gave His own Son, Jesus, to be killed because He was living for the benefit of Israel ahead of His own Son. Even though Israel had turned against His Son, God loved Israel more. Likewise, even on the cross Jesus loved his enemies. He interceded for the Roman soldier who pierced him with a spear, saying, "Father, forgive them, for they do not know what they do." He did not say this to make peace with Rome, but to find the peace of God and the peace of God's family. (235:224, September 20, 1992)

How much does God love His enemy? God's love is such that He sacrificed His own Son in order to save His enemy's children… If you can love your enemies more even than you love your own children, then Satan will surrender to you, exclaiming, "I could never do that. I could never be worthy to receive such love." At that point Satan will retreat. You should know that this is the path of Abel.

As Jesus was dying on the cross, he prayed for his enemies rather than for himself; he prayed that his sacrifice would become the source of their blessing. Can any being with a conscience not bow his head and yield to such great love? However vicious the enemy may be, he cannot help but bow down and surrender. By practicing this you can completely separate yourself from your enemy's wrath—and you will discover that you have no enemy.

Then Satan has no choice but to issue a certificate signed, "This son or daughter of God loved me, their enemy. Therefore I cannot stand in the way of God loving this person." Satan can no longer hold on to his grudge, but when he sees God embracing and loving the person, he must say, "Amen!" This is how you must clear your relationship with Satan. (118:172, May 30, 1982)

Why is God on my side? It is because I have tried to love even those who opposed me. I have not sought revenge on the enemies who stood against me. I do not want an eye for an eye, a tooth for a tooth, or a life for a life. I try to digest everything with love. (168:204, September 20, 1987)

> When I doubt people, I feel pain.
> When I judge people, it is unbearable.
> When I hate people, there is no value to my existence.
> Yet if I believe, I am deceived.
> If I love, I am betrayed.
> Suffering and grieving tonight, my head in my hands
> Am I wrong?
> Yes, I am wrong.
>
> Even though we are deceived, still believe.
> Though we are betrayed, still forgive.
> Love completely even those who hate you.
> Wipe your tears away and welcome with a smile
> Those who know nothing but deceit
> And those who betray without regret.
> Oh Master! The pain of loving!

Look at My hands.
Place your hand on My chest.
My heart is bursting, such agony!
But when I loved those who acted against Me
I brought victory.
If you have done the same thing,
I will give you the crown of glory. *(The Crown of Glory)*

Forgiveness

A LARGE-HEARTED ATTITUDE OF FORGIVENESS to those who have done us wrong is advocated in all the scriptures. Forgiveness is at the heart of Jesus' message; indeed according to The Lord's Prayer it is incumbent upon the Christian to forgive. God is most forgiving. It states in the Qur'an that people who seek to draw near to God should likewise be full of forgiveness. Forgiving is natural to a parent; therefore if we can take a parental heart towards others, akin to the heart of God our Father, we can forgive them. While it may be difficult to forgive people who do us grave injustice or injury, it is far preferable to holding a grudge, which would only fester and poison the spirit.

Yet how can we forgive? Forgiveness is not a natural thing. It will not do to simply forget a wrong or sweep it under the rug. Such easy or ritualistic forgiveness is phony and can mask deeper feelings of lasting resentment. As theologian Paul Tillich wrote, "Forgiving presupposes remembering. And it creates a forgetting not in the natural way we forget yesterday's weather, but in the way of the great 'in spite of' that says: I forget although I remember."[19] Father Moon teaches that we need to find a positive reason to forgive, a reason to make a new beginning in relating to that person in spite of the painful memory of previous wrongs. Thus he explores the reasons why God forgives us, and searches for that point of weakness and pathos in the wrongdoer that can evoke the heart of compassion.

Give us this day our daily bread;
And forgive us our debts,
As we also have forgiven our debtors.
Matthew 6.11-12

If you efface and overlook and forgive, then lo! God is forgiving, merciful.
Qur'an 64.14

Allah is All-Forgiving and loves the one who forgives others.
Algama' Alsaghair 2.1749 (Islam)

For if you forgive men their trespasses, your heavenly Father also will forgive you; but if you do not forgive men their trespasses, neither will your Father forgive your trespasses.
Matthew 6.14-15

Better and more rewarding is God's reward to those who believe... and when angry, even then forgive...

Let evil be rewarded by like evil, but he who forgives and seeks reconciliation shall be rewarded by God. He does not love the wrongdoers...

True constancy lies in forgiveness and patient forbearance.
Qur'an 42.36-37, 40, 43

Take heed to yourselves; if your brother sins, rebuke him, and if he repents, forgive him; and if he sins against you seven times in the day, and turns to you seven times, and says, "I repent," you must forgive him.
Luke 17.3-4

The best deed of a great man is to forgive and forget.

    Nahjul Balagha, Saying 201 (Shiite Islam)

The truly great man must forgive people without being forgiven by them.

    Chu Hsi (Confucianism)

Release: The superior man tends to forgive wrongs and deals leniently with crimes.

    I Ching 40 (Confucianism)

Moses son of Imran said, "My Lord, who is the greatest of Thy servants in Thy estimation?" and received the reply, "The one who forgives when he is in a position of power."[20]

    Hadith of Baihaqi (Islam)

The scribes and the Pharisees brought a woman who had been caught in adultery, and placing her in the midst they said to him, "Teacher, this woman has been caught in the act of adultery. Now in the law Moses commanded us to stone such. What do you say about her?" This they said to test him, that they might have some charge to bring against him. Jesus bent down and wrote with his finger on the ground. And as they continued to ask him, he stood up and said to them, "Let him who is without sin among you be the first to throw a stone at her." And once more he bent down and wrote with his finger on the ground. But when they heard it, they went away, one by one, beginning with the eldest, and Jesus was left alone with the woman standing before him. Jesus looked up and said to her, "Woman, where are they? Has no one condemned you?" She said, "No one, Lord." And Jesus said, "Neither do I condemn you; go, and do not sin again."

    John 8.3-11

Do not rejoice when your enemy falls,
and let not your heart be glad when he stumbles;
lest the LORD see it, and be displeased,
and turn away his anger from him.

    Proverbs 24.17-18

Who takes vengeance or bears a grudge acts like one who, having cut one hand while handling a knife, avenges himself by stabbing the other hand.

    Jerusalem Talmud, Nedarim 9.4 (Judaism)

Subvert anger by forgiveness.

    Samanasuttam 136 (Jainism)

Kuan Chung... could seize the fief of P'ien with its three hundred villages from its owner, the head of the Po family; yet Po, though he lived on coarse food to the end of his days, never uttered a single word of resentment. The Master said, "To be poor and not resent it is far harder than to be rich yet not presumptuous."

    Analects 14.11 (Confucianism)

Then Peter came up and said to him, "Lord, how often shall my brother sin against me, and I forgive him? As many as seven times?" Jesus said to him, "I do not say to you seven times, but seventy times seven."

    Matthew 18.21-22

Doing an injury puts you below your enemy;
Revenging one makes you but even with him;
Forgiving it sets you above him.

    Benjamin Franklin, Poor Richard's Almanack

Where there is forgiveness, there is God Himself.

    Adi Granth, Shalok Kabir, p. 1372 (Sikhism)

Teachings of Sun Myung Moon

Great forgiveness is possible when you have understood the other person's situation one hundred percent. Because God knows our situations, He forgives us. (2:220, May 26, 1957)

Joseph forgave his brothers, although they were his enemies who had sold him into slavery. Yet Joseph forgave them for his father's sake, because they were all his father's sons. Put yourself in Joseph's position. Like Joseph, we have many enemies, yet we have no choice but to forgive them because they are all the children of our Father, God. We forgive them for God's sake, because we believe in God. (146:125, June 8, 1986)

Among the countless people I have been leading, many have committed transgressions. I deal with them with the attitude, "I will forgive you one hundred times." This is the fatherly heart.

Suppose your own son were arrested as a robber and a murderer and was facing execution. Would you as a parent say, as you watched your son walking toward the execution chamber, "It is a good thing that you are about to die. You should be killed quickly"? No, you would look for every possible way to win him a pardon. That is the heart of a parent. You would forgive him, even a thousand or ten thousand times. (157:259-60, April 10, 1967)

You leaders who live with your members, if one of your members is wrong, do not tell him he is wrong to his face, but look for how you can forgive him. Look at his wife; is she worse than her husband? Look at his children; are they worse than their father? Then look at his mother and father; are they worse than their child? No, among his family some are good people.

Thus thinking of his family's good qualities and their love for him, you can find a way to love him. Then the blessings gathered in that family will be joined with you. If you live this way, you will not perish. Heaven will protect you. (308:208, January 5, 1999)

God does not strike someone who is defeated. Rather, God shows mercy to those who recognize their sin and repent. God exists; therefore anyone who raises a sword to strike a defeated person will bring ruin on his descendants. Instead, we should pray for him and give him guidance with the heart of a close friend. (25:333, October 12, 1969)

Among the Christian martyrs who were thrown to the lions in the coliseums of Rome, there were two kinds of people. One kind prayed, "God, take revenge upon my persecutors. Punish them! May they all perish!" Their mind was to resist the unjust Caesar up to the moment of death. The other kind prayed, "Forgive their sins! Forgive the Caesar! May Rome one day become God's nation on this earth!"

Compare the destinies of these two kinds of martyrs. Those who prayed for their enemies, for Rome and Caesar, are dwelling in an exalted realm among those who are victorious over Satan. But those who died with the self-centered desire to receive salvation and held a grudge against Rome are dwelling somewhere below the realm of Rome. (130:233, January 29, 1984)

When Jesus taught us to love our enemies, do you think he meant that we should forgive Satan? You should be clear about this question.

When someone asked him, "Lord, how often shall my brother sin against me, and I forgive him? As many as seven times?" Jesus answered, "I do not say to you seven times, but seventy times seven." If Jesus, the Son of God, could forgive people to that extent, should he not also forgive Satan? Yet he cannot do that; it is impossible.

When Jesus prayed for his enemies, the object of his prayers was not Satan but rather the people whom Satan invaded. Evil people are merely victims of God's enemy; therefore he forgave them and sought for them, as God was seeking for them. Yet, this does not mean that he should forgive Satan. (92:187, April 10, 1977)

O Source of all goodness! I earnestly pray that Thou wilt forgive through Thine infinite love and magnanimity the many religious believers of this nation for their past acts of persecution against the children of the Unification movement. [Because of their actions,] some who joined the movement for a time grew tired and lonely and fell away, unable to endure the persecution, unable to find even one person to console them on the lonely path. And I know that many who remain on the path are exhausted.

Thinking of how they ought to be bowing their heads and begging Thy forgiveness, my indignation against them is hard to bear, and I long to resolve the grudges in Thy heart. Still, thinking about Thy merciful path of restoration, as Thou seekest to recover the children of the enemy, I know that Thou canst not help but bless them again— and therefore I pray that Thou wilt forgive them.

Father, I earnestly ask Thee to please forgive and once again extend Thy grace to the pitiable churches that betrayed Thee. (27:301-02, December 28, 1969)

A Good Heart

LOVING-KINDNESS AND COMPASSION spring naturally from a good heart. Hence, cultivating a good heart ought to be a priority in life. A number of passages praise a loving heart as superior to faith, knowledge, dedication to the truth, and all other virtues.

A loving heart is rooted in God—what Father Moon call's God's heart (Korean: *shimjung*). Shimjung is God's irrepressible impulse to love—the very motivation for His creation. (See Chapter 1: *Divine Love and Compassion*) In human terms, it is closest to the heart of a mother, who cannot help but love her child. A good heart is impartial and all embracing, able to digest evil and unpleasant people as well as kind and virtuous people. Therefore, it is indispensable to reconciling opponents and resolving conflicts.

1. Loving-Kindness

Be kind to one another, tenderhearted, forgiving one another, as God in Christ forgave you.

Ephesians 4.32

May I look on all beings with the eye of friend! May we look on one another with the eye of friend!

Yajur Veda 36.18 (*Hinduism*)

He who can find no room for others lacks fellow feeling, and to him who lacks fellow feeling, all men are strangers.

Chuang Tzu 23 (*Taoism*)

Treat people in such a way and live amongst them in such a manner that if you die they will weep over you; alive they crave for your company.

Nahjul Balagha, Saying 9 (*Shiite Islam*)

Gentle character it is which enables the rope of life to stay unbroken in one's hand.

Yoruba Proverb (*African Traditional Religions*)

Monks, whatsoever grounds there be for good works undertaken with a view to [favorable] rebirth, all of them are not worth one-sixteenth part of that goodwill which is the heart's release; goodwill alone, which is the heart's release, shines and burns and flashes forth in surpassing them.

Itivuttaka 19 (*Buddhism*)

Even though it be the home of someone who has managed for long to avoid misfortune, we gods will not enter into the dwelling of a person with perverse disposition. Even though it be a dwelling where a man be in mourning for father and mother, if he be a man of compassion, we deities will enter in there.[21]

Oracle of the Kami of Kasuga (Shinto)

Rabbi Yohanan ben Zakkai said, "Go forth and see which is the good way to which a man should cleave." Rabbi Eliezar said, "A good eye"; Rabbi Joshua said, "A good friend"; Rabbi Jose said, "A good neighbor"; Rabbi Simeon said, "One who foresees the fruit of an action"; Rabbi Elazar said, "A good heart." Thereupon he said to them, "I approve the words of Elazar ben Arach, rather than your words, for in his words yours are included."

Mishnah, Avot 2.13 (Judaism)

Teachings of Sun Myung Moon

No matter that you plan to go another way; the heart of love for the sake of others will always point you in the right direction, as a compass always points north. (138:99, January 19, 1986)

Make a habit of liking people. Tell them that you like them even if they do not like you. It is training. (118:116, May 9, 1982)

Have you ever shed tears for others? It is easy for people to weep for themselves, but have you wept for others? There are two kinds of tears. A person who sheds tears for him or herself will go to hell, but a person who sheds tears for others will go to heaven. (96:172-73, January 3, 1978)

Respect all things as holy things. Treat them as sacred objects. Respect all people as holy people, each one the sacred body of God. Respect yourself as a holy person, with the thought that your mind is God's mind and your body is God's body. (102:113, November 27, 1978)

Do we say of someone who possesses much knowledge, "He is an outstanding person"? No. He must have a good heart. A good person has an innately good framework of life and original nature. Whether knowledgeable or not, a good person has a good heart. (39:315, January 16, 1971)

Your eyes should become more benevolent. Of course they shine when you look at a good person, but even when you see wicked people you should add extra effort to look at them with a heart of compassion and love. True love has the capacity to digest even evil things. It possesses such power. (123:225, January 2, 1983)

You may have beautiful eyes, but if they glow with the light of jealousy or personal ambition, seeking to take advantage of others or out for blood, those eyes are fearsome and ugly to behold. Yet even though your eyes may be unattractive and irregular-shaped, if they shine with the light of love, benevolence and peace, then those eyes will captivate people. They are charming and possess magnetic power. So when you act with love as the inner motivation, even wearing a mask cannot hide your beauty. (116:53-54, December 13, 1981)

2. A Loving Heart and Its Roots in God's Heart

Gentleness and goodness are the roots of humanity.

      Book of Ritual 38.18 (Confucianism)

To love is to know Me,
My innermost nature,
the truth that I am.

      Bhagavad-Gita 18.55 (Hinduism)

All men have this heart that, when they see another man suffer, they suffer, too... Take an example: a man looks out and sees a child about to fall into a well. No matter who the man is, his heart will flip, flop, and he will feel the child's predicament; and not because he expects to get something out of it from the child's parents, or because he wants praise from his neighbors, associates, or friends, or because he is afraid of a bad name, or anything like that.

      Mencius II.A.6 (Confucianism)

The Dwelling of the Tathagata is the great compassionate heart within all the living. The Robe of the Tathagata is the gentle and forbearing heart.[22]

      Lotus Sutra 10 (Buddhism)

As a mother protects her only child at the risk of her own life, let him cultivate a boundless heart towards all beings.

      Khuddaka Patha, Metta Sutta (Buddhism)

Allah is kind and loves whoever is kind;
Allah is clean and loves whoever is clean;
Allah is generous and loves whoever is generous.

      Hadith of Muslim 913.2 (Islam)

What sort of religion can it be without compassion?
You need to show compassion to all living beings.
Compassion is the root of all religious faiths.

      Basavanna, Vacana 247 (Hinduism)

Teachings of Sun Myung Moon

Because God is love, let us center our lives on heart *(shimjung)*, the essence of love.[23] We advance on the path by developing a character that springs from the heart. (84:123, February 22, 1976)

In the heart of love, everything becomes one. It is all-inclusive, not discriminating. Being all-inclusive, it is also embracing. Inclusiveness is the inner core that manifests outwardly as tolerance. Inner and outer engage in circular motion; thus tolerance promotes inclusiveness and inclusiveness promotes tolerance.
 Beyond that, love is mutually responsive. "Mutually responsive" means the grandfather is not always absolute. Nor are the grandchildren always absolute. At times, the grandfather may become a grandchild, and the grandchild may become the grandfather. This is what is meant by "mutually responsive." Therefore, anywhere that loving hearts and a loving atmosphere prevail, there is no opposition; everyone welcomes it. Neither knowledge nor power can create such a tolerant and embracing environment; only love can do it.
 When a hungry child is embraced in its mother's bosom, it can forget its hunger and go to sleep. What else could be as precious as love? Diamonds? Suppose your wife or child was ill and on the verge of dying. Would you refuse to take a diamond out of your jewelry box and sell it to cover the medical costs? Would that be love? Genuine love has the power to move anything. (139:196-97, January 31, 1986)

Due to the human fall, nothing about the human realm of heart entitles us to stand before God except for one condition that remains unchanged: parents' loving heart for their children. Children's love toward their parents cannot be the standard, because in the beginning we betrayed God from the position of children. Hence we lost the emotional basis to relate to God as His children. On the other hand, God loved Adam and Eve even at the moment of their Fall. That original nature remains in our hearts. It remains the basis for parents to act according to their original mind in loving their children. Therefore, among people living in the fallen realm, only parents' love toward their children remains as an original, prelapsarian standard of love. It shall remain as an eternal standard. (23:206, May 25, 1969)

If parents have a child with a handicap or birth defect, they are heart-broken yet make special efforts to take care of that child. The love of even worldly parents unmistakably reflects God's heart. That is why restoration is possible when you are filial toward your parents. (99:127-28, September 10, 1978)

Right now what we need most is the glow of love. God's love is like the guide rope of a net. That love should set its anchor in me. Where should we set the center of our character? Not in the truth, but rather in the heart *(shimjung)*. (33:68, August 8, 1970)

Good Deeds

GOOD DEEDS ARE A MANIFESTATION of a healthy spiritual life. Good deeds promote friendship and harmony in our dealings with people. Good deeds create merit for heaven and improve our relationship with God. While religions often emphasize faith as the key to salvation, all genuine faith is manifested outwardly in transformed behavior. Father Moon recommends unflagging efforts to do good deeds, whether they are appreciated or not, both to fulfill love in our hearts and as spiritual training to love more profoundly.

Many garlands can be made from a heap of flowers. Many good deeds should be done by one born a mortal.

Dhammapada 53 *(Buddhism)*

Be mindful of your duty [to God], and do good works; and again, be mindful of your duty, and believe; and once again: be mindful of your duty, and do right. God loves the doers of good.

Qur'an 5.93

For we are his workmanship, created in Christ Jesus for good works, which God prepared beforehand, that we should walk in them.

Ephesians 2.10

Every selfless act, Arjuna, is born from the eternal, infinite Godhead. God is present in every act of service. All life turns on this law.

Bhagavad-Gita 3.16 *(Hinduism)*

Every person's every joint must perform a charity every day the sun comes up: to act justly between two people is a charity; to help a man with his mount, lifting him onto it or hoisting up his belongings onto it is a charity; a good word is a charity; every step you take in prayers is a charity; and removing a harmful thing from the road is a charity.

Forty Hadith of an-Nawawi 26 *(Islam)*

Good deeds annul evil deeds. This is a reminder for the mindful.

Qur'an 11.114

Whoever, by a good deed, covers the evil done, such a one illumines this world like the moon freed from clouds.

Dhammapada 173 *(Buddhism)*

He who carries out one good deed acquires for himself one advocate in his own behalf, and he who commits one transgression acquires one accuser against himself. Repentance and good works are like a shield against calamity.

Mishnah, Avot 4.13 *(Judaism)*

Heaven is not attained without good deeds.

Adi Granth, Ramkali-ki-Var, M.1, p. 952 *(Sikhism)*

What does it profit, my brethren, if a man says he has faith but has not works? Can his faith save him? If a brother or sister is ill-clad and in lack of daily food, and one of you says to them, "Go in peace, be warmed and filled" without giving them the things needed for the body, what does it profit? So faith by itself, without works, is dead.

But someone will say, "You have faith and I have works." Show me your faith apart from your works, and I by my works will show you my faith. You believe that God is one; you do well. Even the demons believe—and shudder. Do you want to be shown, you shallow man, that faith apart from works is barren? Was not Abraham our father justified by works, when he offered his son Isaac upon the altar? You see that faith was active along with his works, and faith was completed by works, and the scripture was fulfilled which says, "Abraham believed God, and it was reckoned to him as righteousness"; and he was called the friend of God. You see that a man is justified by works and not by faith alone... For as the body apart from the spirit is dead, so faith apart from works is dead.[24]

James 2.14-26

Is there a "righteous man" who is good and a righteous man who is not good? He who is good to Heaven and good to man, he is a righteous man who is good; good to Heaven but not good to man, that is a righteous man who is evil.

Talmud, Kiddushin 40a *(Judaism)*

Teachings of Sun Myung Moon

A good person has both unwavering faith and accumulated good deeds. (73:116, August 16, 1974)

Pay attention to people and treat each one with a loving heart and with truth. Say at least three good and positive things each day. Along with your words, do three good deeds each day, no matter how small. When you greet someone, do not say words out of habit but with sincerity and genuineness. (99:142, September 10, 1978)

Do a good deed and forget about it. Although you forget, it remains in God's memory, connected to His goodness. (*Way of God's Will* 1.1.2)

Carry out the difficult tasks others avoid, while remaining detached from the things you like. Solve your parents' most difficult problems for them and take upon yourself all their outside difficulties as well. (17:338, April 30, 1967)

Good people are those who willingly take responsibility for other people's debts. (41:90, February 13, 1971)

Good or evil in the conduct of the physical self is the main determinant of whether the spirit self becomes good or evil. This is because the physical self provides a certain element, which we call the vitality element, to the spirit self. In our everyday experience, our mind rejoices when our physical self performs good deeds but feels anxiety after evil conduct. This is because vitality elements, which can be good or evil according to the deeds of the physical self, are infused into our spirit self. (*Exposition of the Divine Principle,* Creation 6.3.1)

Giving and Receiving

THE WISDOM OF GIVING is the topic of passages in this section. When we give to one another freely and without conditions, sharing our blessings with others and bearing each other's burdens, the giving multiplies. We receive far more than we gave. Even when there is no immediate prospect of return, Heaven keeps accounts of giving, and in the end blessing will return to the giver, multiplied many-fold. We must give first; to expect to receive without having given is to violate the universal law. (See Chapter 2: *Duality*) Conversely, giving with strings attached—in order to receive, to curry favor or to make a name for oneself—is condemnable.

Father Moon's extensive teachings about giving provide a philosophical basis for this universal moral wisdom. Giving is rooted in the nature of the Creator, who invested Himself utterly to create all things in heaven and earth. He goes on to explain several reasons for giving's paradoxical power to yield increase the more it is spent: first, because in giving we pattern our lives after the Creator; second, through the concept of give-and-take action as seen in the cycles of the natural world; and third, in the investment of parents in their children, with its joyful yield over the years—growth, prosperity and grandchildren. To encourage us to give without any conditions, he counsels us to "give and give and forget what you have given."

1. *The Way of Giving and Its Rewards*

It is more blessed to give than to receive.
    Acts 20.35

You will not attain piety until you expend of what you love; and whatever thing you expend, God knows of it.
    Qur'an 3.92

He who gives liberally goes straight to the gods; on the high ridge of heaven he stands exalted.
    Rig Veda 1.125.5 (*Hinduism*)

Give not with the thought to gain, and be patient unto thy Lord.
    Qur'an 74.6-7

One must pour cold water on the ground before he can tread on soft soil.[25]
    Yoruba Proverb (*African Traditional Religions*)

One man gives freely, yet grows all the richer; another withholds what he should give, and
    only suffers want.
A liberal man will be enriched,
and one who waters will himself be watered.
    Proverbs 11.24-25

Verily, misers go not to the celestial realms. Fools do not indeed praise liberality. The wise man rejoices in giving and thereby becomes happy thereafter.
    Dhammapada 177 (*Buddhism*)

The accumulation of wealth is the way to scatter the people, and the letting it be scattered among them is the way to collect the people.

Great Learning 10.9 *(Confucianism)*

He who sows sparingly will also reap sparingly, and he who sows bountifully will also reap bountifully. Each one must do as he has made up his mind, not reluctantly or under compulsion, for God loves a cheerful giver. And God is able to provide you with every blessing in abundance, so that you may always have enough of everything and may provide in abundance for every good work.

2 Corinthians 9.6-8

The Buddha said, "When you see someone practicing the Way of giving, aid him joyously, and you will obtain vast and great blessings." A novice asked, "Is there an end to those blessings?" The Buddha said, "Consider the flame of a single lamp. Though a hundred thousand people come and light their own lamps from it so that they can cook their food and ward off the darkness, the first lamp remains the same as before. Blessings are like this, too."

Sutra of Forty-two Sections 10 *(Buddhism)*

Teachings of Sun Myung Moon

True love begins from investing and forgetting. (225:15, January 1, 1992)

Is the essence of [ordinary] human love the same as the original essence God's love? Out of human love, people seek to receive; but when we embody God's original love, we seek to give. (130:118, January 1, 1984)

Goodness is the driving force that advances life. Therefore, we must give. What shall we give? We should give life. More than your life, you should give your love—the one love that is of God—parental love. That is why our motto is, "Go forth with the heart of the parent, in the shoes of a servant, shedding sweat for earth, tears for humanity, and blood for heaven." Do this, and you will not perish. Absolutely, you will not perish. (34:246, September 13, 1970)

The universe's motion began with an act of giving. I teach that all motion arises according to the principle of give-and-take action.[26] Does "give-and-take action" mean we first give and then take, or first take and then give? When you give first and then receive you feel good, but when you receive and cannot give you feel ashamed. (239:222, November 25, 1992)

In give-and-take action, does "give" come first, or "take?" Giving comes first. Do parents first give for the sake of their children, or children for the sake of their parents? Parents give first. Then it is logical that the act of giving began with the One who is the origin of all existence, and through the links of the chain of existence it has been passed down to us. (239:59, November 23, 1992)

Unity takes place where people invest creative energy—where there is giving. It does not happen where people mainly seek to receive. To receive can be good if after receiving, you add interest to it and give out more than you received. But even God dislikes the person who receives and only seeks to receive still more. No more will be given to him. (82:326, February 1, 1976)

Take an illustration of a good man and a bad man. Each begins with ten friends. The good man unselfishly serves his friends day in and day out, this year, next year, for ten years, for his whole life. All ten people say he is their very best friend. Since they like him, they introduce him to their mother and sisters and all their relatives.

The bad man thinks that his friends exist to serve him. By the time he tells them three times, "Hey you! Serve me!" every one of his friends would run away; they would want nothing more to do with him. Isn't that true? It is universally true: A self-centered way of life leads you down the road of self-destruction, to hell. But those who give, living their lives in service to others, will enter the Kingdom of Heaven. They are living in accordance with God's Principle. (69:86, October 20, 1973)

God created all creatures in heaven and earth by investing completely His heart of love. It means He gave. Because God has this nature, it is certain that a counterpart will come into being who also has such a heart. As a result, human beings can form a relationship with God, and through that relationship, to manifest God's love. By living this way, we can only prosper.

Our conscience does not understand this fact logically and with certainty, but nevertheless it tells us to love each other and live for the sake of each other. Similarly, religions teach us to sacrifice ourselves for the sake of others. Thus our conscience, in agreement with morality and ethics, tells us to live for the sake of others, sacrifice ourselves for the sake of others, and love others. (112:300, April 25, 1981)

2. The Virtuous Cycle of Giving and Receiving

Give, and it will be given to you… for the measure you give will be the measure you get back.

Luke 6.38

Blessed are the merciful, for they shall obtain mercy.

Matthew 5.7

Those who act kindly in this world will have kindness.

Qur'an 39.10

Who is honored? He who honors his fellowman.

Avot 4.1 (Judaism)

When a greeting is offered you, meet it with a greeting still more courteous, or at least of equal courtesy.

Qur'an 4.86

There was presented to me a papaya,
And I returned for it a beautiful *keu* gem;
Not as a return for it,
But that our friendship might be lasting.

There was presented to me a peach,
And I returned for it a beautiful *yaou* gem;
Not as a return for it,
But that our friendship might be lasting.

There was presented to me a plum,
And I returned for it a beautiful *kew* stone;
Not as a return for it,
But that our friendship might be lasting.[27]

Book of Songs, Ode 64 (Confucianism)

Teachings of Sun Myung Moon

The more you love God, the more of God's love you will receive. This is the principle for expanding the love of God in your life. You will receive God's love because you have loved God. (40:244, February 6, 1971)

The more you love, the more you receive love—not only from God but also from the people you love. Hence your investment yields a two-fold return, and even more. Your one effort at giving love yields a many-fold return, because it connects with multiple dimensions. (90:21, December 5, 1976)

A good person is someone who adds to what he receives and passes it on to others. For that reason, parents want their children to grow to be better than them. Likewise, a husband wants his wife to be better than him; a wife wants her husband to be better than her; an elder brother wants his younger brother to grow up to be better than him, and so on. (315:211, February 2, 2000)

Which is more joyful, the joy of owning something precious or the joy of giving your prized possession to someone else? Giving leads to multiplication. What you give with a sincere heart will be returned to you many-fold. You have initiated give-and-take action, a virtuous cycle of ever-increasing giving. It comes back to you, and the next time you want to give more. That is how giving expands. (248:96, August 1, 1993)

Look! When there is air at low pressure, a corresponding region of high pressure is created and circulation necessarily occurs. God is the king of wisdom. Why do you have to give and give and forget what you have given? It is because it guarantees circulation, which becomes an eternal circulation. This is the logic of the theory of eternal life. When you invest, invest, and invest more, the principle of eternal life operates. When you live for others, you do not perish. (204:107, July 1, 1990)

When flowing water comes to a depression, it must fill that depression before moving on. The same is true with air. Loves also flows, and if there is a depression, it works to fill that depression before moving on. (241:306, January 1, 1993)

The power of true love comes from investing. It is the power of giving, not just receiving. When we give totally, we ultimately reach a point where there is nothing left to give. That is the 'zero point,' where we become completely empty. Then we have the capacity to receive anything that comes to us. Whenever we give even more returns. By continuing in this way we generate a never-ending process of giving and receiving. This forms an eternal balance.

    A world where everyone lives for the sake of others centering on true love is perfected through countless such relationships of giving and receiving. (315:210, February 2, 2000)

Why does the person who gives flourish? Why do you grow larger when you give? It is because giving connects you with the origin—with God's principle by which He created the universe. God created by giving, and what was given kept on growing.

    You Americans will continue to prosper only if you change your concept of life to the way of giving. Then the universe will help you, since you will be living in accord with the Principle of Creation. But if you continue to take and take, your life will shrink.

The root of true love is the eternal cycle of giving. The power of giving multiplies; taking only makes things get smaller. It is a mysterious fact. In ordinary physics, energy dissipates when it is put to work, but the principle of love is that giving leads to increase. Everything you give moves in a cycle and ultimately comes back to you—with interest! For example, Abraham left his home as one man carrying a blessing, but after thousands or years it has multiplied to touch billions of people. (183:324, November 9, 1988)

Your partner is the foundation for your hopes, the foundation of your happiness, and the foundation for your everything. When God created heaven and earth, He created all things and human beings as His object partners. The principle of give-and-take action governs action, movement, and law in the universe. It states that nothing comes back until it has been given completely. Isn't that so? For a wife to love her husband completely, she first must feel that he loves her completely. Only then will she say, "I'm going to really love him." You begin to give back completely when you receive completely. That is the principle of heaven and earth… If you begin to return before you have received, then it will not come back to you in its entirety. (60:232, August 17, 1972)

3. Giving Without any Conditions or Concern for Past Slights

He who gives his wealth to purify himself,
and confers no favor on any man for
  recompense,
only seeking the Face of his Lord the Most
  High;
He shall surely be satisfied.

Qur'an 92.18-21

A gift is a gift of integrity
when it is given at the right place and time to
  the proper person,
To one who cannot be expected to return the
  gift—
and given merely because it should be given.

But what is given to get a gift in return,
or for the sake of some result,
Or unwillingly,
That is a gift in the sphere of passion.

A gift is called slothful when it is given
not at the right time and place,
Nor to a worthy person,
nor with proper ceremony, but with contempt.

Bhagavad-Gita 17.20-22 (Hinduism)

A man who is out to make a name for himself will be able to give away a state of a thousand chariots, but reluctance would be written all over his face if he had to give away a basketful of rice and a bowlful of soup when no such purpose was served.

Mencius VII.B.11 (Confucianism)

"If I give this, what shall I [have left to] enjoy?"
Such selfish thinking is the way of the ghosts;
"If I enjoy this, what shall I [have left to] give?"
Such selfless thinking is a quality of the gods.

Shantideva, Guide to the Bodhisattva's Way of Life 8.125 (Buddhism)

Teachings of Sun Myung Moon

True love is love that gives and forgets what it gave. Having forgotten what you gave, you want to give again and again. (162:239, April 12, 1987)

You give and then forget. You do not keep an account of what you gave, but forget it. When you give and forget, you are elevating your beloved above yourself. Give and forget—that's the idea. As soon as you remember what you gave, it breaks the circuit of giving.

Unity does not exist where there is self-assertion—where a husband asserts his rights or a wife asserts her rights. God created the universe by investing without limit. Therefore, when a man gives limitlessly for the sake of his wife, and the woman likewise gives limitlessly for her husband, they can achieve total unity. You couples can become completely one by giving and forgetting, following God's pattern. (267:301-02, February 5, 1995)

God desires a free, peaceful, and happy place where giving has no accusers and receiving has no conditions attached. God's purpose is to expand this place worldwide and bring all humankind to live there. (13:249, April 12, 1964)

Charity

CHARITY TO THE POOR AND THE NEEDY is a traditional virtue encouraged by all religions. Our relationship to the Highest Good creates a natural bond of family among all members of the community, rich and poor. We can experience God's love and compassion for all his children, and especially for those who suffer from poverty, disease, war, famine and natural disasters. Giving alms and charity is a concrete expression of this spiritual bond of love. Texts such as the Parable of the Sheep and the Goats from the New Testament liken helping a poor man to giving offerings to God or the highest saints. Charity is not excused even for the poorest giver, according to several texts.

Some passages describe the attitude one should take in giving charity. The dignity of the transaction should be upheld by all means. "Do not let your left hand know what your right hand is doing" describes the value of anonymity for both the donor and the recipient: for the donor to eliminate any occasion for boasting and for the recipient to preserve his dignity. An even higher form of charity, according to Maimonides, is to extend interest-free loans and other forms of aid to help the poor man get started in a business or trade and thus earn his own living. In a modern version of the adage, "Give a man a fish; you have fed him for today. Teach a man to fish; and you have fed him for a lifetime," Father Moon has been developing oceanic fishing enterprises with the intent to help the people of Africa become self-sufficient in food.

1. Charity in an Expression of God's Love and Draws Us Near to God

Blessed is he who considers the poor;
the LORD delivers him in the day of trouble.

Psalm 41.1

They feed with food the needy wretch, the orphan, and the prisoner, for love of Him, saying, "We wish for no reward nor thanks from you."

Qur'an 76.8-9

They sold their possessions and goods and distributed them to all, as any had need.

Acts 2.45

Charity—to be moved at the sight of the thirsty, the hungry, and the miserable and to offer relief to them out of pity—is the spring of virtue.

Kundakunda, Pancastikaya 137 (Jainism)

If there is among you a poor man, one of your brethren, in any of your towns within your land which the Lord your God gives you, you shall not harden your heart or shut your hand against your poor brother, but you shall open your hand to him, and lend him sufficient for his need, whatever it may be... You shall give to him freely, and your heart shall not be grudging when you give to him; because for this the Lord your God will bless you in all your work and in all that you undertake. For the poor will never cease out of the land; therefore I command you, You shall open wide your hand to your brother, to the needy and the poor, in the land.

Deuteronomy 15.7-11

When the Son of man comes in his glory, and all the angels with him, then he will sit on his glorious throne. Before him will be gathered all the nations, and he will separate them one from another as a shepherd separates the sheep from the goats, and he will place the sheep at his right hand, but the goats at his left. Then the King will say to those at his right hand, "Come, O blessed of my Father, inherit the kingdom prepared for you from the foundation of the world; for I was hungry and you gave me food, I was thirsty and you gave me drink, I was a stranger and you welcomed me, I was naked and you clothed me, I was sick and you visited me, I was in prison and you came to me." Then the righteous will answer him, "Lord, when did we see you hungry and feed you, or thirsty and give you drink? And when did we see you a stranger and welcome you, or naked and clothe you? And when did we see you sick or in prison and visit you?" And the King will answer them, "Truly, I say to you, as you did it to one of the least of these my brethren, you did it to me."

Matthew 25.31-40:
Parable of the Sheep and the Goats

On the Day of Judgment God Most High will say, "Son of Adam, I was sick and you did not visit me." He will reply, "My Lord, how could I visit Thee when Thou art the Lord of the Universe!" He will say, "Did you not know that my servant so-and-so was ill and yet you did not visit him? Did you not know that if you had visited him you soon would have found Me with him?"

Hadith of Muslim (Islam)

"Ye shall walk after the Lord your God" [Deut. 13.4]. But how can a man walk after God who is a devouring fire? [Deut. 4.24]. It means, walk after His attributes: clothe the naked, visit the sick, comfort the mourner, bury the dead.

Talmud, Sota 14a (Judaism)

When the Holy One loves a man, He sends him a present in the shape of a poor man, so that he should perform some good deed to him, through the merit of which he may draw to himself a cord of grace.

Zohar 1.104a (Judaism)

The gods have not ordained that humans die of
   hunger;
even to the well-fed man death comes in many
   shapes.
The wealth of the generous man never wastes
   away,
but the niggard has none to console him.

He who, possessed of food, hardens his heart
against the weak man, hungry and suffering,
who comes to him for help, though of old he
   helped him—
surely he finds none to console him.

He is liberal who gives to anyone who asks for
   alms,
to the homeless, distressed man who seeks
   food;
success comes to him in the challenge of battle,
and for future conflicts he makes an ally.

He is no friend who does not give to a friend,
to a comrade who comes imploring for food;
let him leave such a man—his is not a home—
and rather seek a stranger who brings him
   comfort.

Let the rich man satisfy one who seeks help;

and let him look upon the long view:
For wealth revolves like the wheels of a chariot,
coming now to one, now to another.

In vain does the mean man acquire food;
it is—I speak the truth—verily his death;
he who does not cherish a comrade or a friend,
who eats all alone, is all sin.

Rig Veda 10.117.1-6 (Hinduism)

Teachings of Sun Myung Moon

Parents suffer when one of their children are sick. When one of your siblings is hurt, you feel pain. When seeing people suffering from poverty or war, a saint feels their suffering more intensely than his own difficulties. Forgetting his own circumstances, he gives all he has to help them. This way has been bequeathed as the standard of morality the world over, in all ages and nations. It is the philanthropic spirit, the love for humanity. (186:74-75, January 29, 1989)

When you see gaunt children playing on the street, underfed and wearing tattered clothes, you should hug and embrace them as you would your own children. You should feel ashamed if you do not want to do that. You should feel more shameful than would a parent who abandoned her child feel should she catch a glimpse of him on the street. Seeing him as she passes by the town, where years before she had left him on a doorstep or perhaps in the care of a nanny, she cannot hold up her head. That is the bond of heart. If your own children were that gaunt, wouldn't you embrace them and shed tears until your bones melt? (46:281, August 17, 1971)

While walking on the street, if you see an old man with a hump in his back you should think, "My Father might have such an appearance when He visits me." When you see the rough and swollen hands of a laborer, you should think, "My Father who is searching for me might look worse than him." When you meet a beggar, you should be able to bow your head, thinking, "He is not a beggar, but actually my Father." Know that God's heart dwells in each of these miserable and pitiful looking people. You should love them, regardless of your situation and social position, shedding tears with the heart that each of them is your own father. Only then, can you meet God. (8:345-46, February 28, 1960)

At lunch time, if you should see an elderly person who is in distress because he does not have enough money to buy food, take him with you to the cafeteria and treat him to a good meal. Serve him as you would serve your grandparents. (215:109, February 6, 1991)

I cannot forget those who visited me when I was lonely in prison and comforted me in my miserable plight. I might forget about my family members or relatives, but never those who sought me because of the bonds of true love. (63:208, October 14, 1972)

Once I rescued a prostitute, a young girl who had fallen into that pitiful situation. I loved her as my own sister; I remember it as if it were yesterday. After listening to her story, I wept with her and truly uplifted her. That kind of deed is greater and more precious than prayer. (May 1, 1977)

I have studied the ocean industry because I know it is a way to feed the starving people of Africa. For twenty years, steadfast, without letting up, I have worked hard to pave this road. I made my own nets, built boats in my own factories, and created my own methods of fishing. The waters off Africa have an abundance of fish. If only the people of Africa could harvest them, they would have food to spare. How then could they possibly die of starvation?...

Sixty thousand people starve to death every year, mostly in Africa. Ask your own conscience. These people are starving due to the want of food, whereas here in America you eat so much that you become as plump as a cow and then have to work hard dieting and exercising to reduce that weight. Should you not be punished by God? (261:307, July 24, 1994)

2. The Manner of Giving Charity

A kind word with forgiveness is better than charity followed by injury; God is Self-sufficient, Forbearing.

O you who believe, do not make your charity worthless by reproach and injury, like him who spends his wealth to be seen by men.

Qur'an 2.263-64

One should give even from a scanty store to him who asks.

Dhammapada 224 (*Buddhism*)

Even a poor man who himself subsists on charity should give charity.

Talmud, Gittin 7b (*Judaism*)

He who has two coats, let him share with him who has none; and he who has food, let him do likewise.

Luke 3.11

When you give alms, do not let your left hand know what your right hand is doing, so that your alms may be in secret; and your Father who sees in secret will reward you.

Matthew 6.3-4

Enlightening beings are magnanimous givers, bestowing whatever they have with equanimity, without regret, without hoping for reward, without seeking honor, without coveting material benefits, but only to rescue and safeguard all living beings.

Garland Sutra 21 (*Buddhism*)

O you who believe, give of the good things which you have earned, and of the fruits of the earth which We have produced for you, and do not aim at getting anything bad for the purpose of giving it away, when you would not take it for yourselves save with disdain...

If you publish your almsgiving, it is well, but if you hide it and give it to the poor, it will be better for you, and will atone for some of your ill-deeds. God is Informed of what you do...

[Alms are] for the poor who are straitened for the cause of God, who cannot travel in the land [for trade]. The unthinking man accounts them free from want because of their restraint. You shall know them by their mark: They do not beg of men with importunity. And whatever good things you give, surely God knows it.

Qur'an 2.267-73

And in their wealth and possessions they remembered the right of those [needy] who asked and those who [for some reason] were prevented from asking.

Qur'an 51.19

The highest degree of charity—above which there is no higher—is he who strengthens the hand of his poor fellow Jew and gives him a gift or [interest-free] loan or enters into a business partnership with the poor person. By this partnership the poor man is really being strengthened as the Torah commands in order to strengthen him till he is able to be independent and no longer dependent on the public purse. It is thus written, "Strengthen him [the poor person] so that he does not fall and become dependent on others" (Leviticus 25:35).

A lower standard of charity is one in which the benefactor has no knowledge of the recipient and the latter has no knowledge of the individual source of charity—"giving in secret." This is practicing the mitzvah of charity for the sake of the mitzvah.[28] Such charity is like the courtyard in the [ancient] Temple where the righteous used to place their donations secretly and the poor would benefit from them in secret. Similar to this secret courtyard is the act of one who puts his money into the charity box.

Below this rank is the case where the recipient is known to the benefactor but the latter is unaware of the source of the charity. This is what the sages used to do when they would go in secret and place their gifts at the door of the poor. It is fitting to do this and meritorious in those cases where the officials in charge of the communal charity do not behave righteously.

Where the recipient is aware of the source of the charity but the giver does not know to whom the money is being given, the degree is lower. Yet, there is merit since the poor are saved from direct shame.

Of less merit is charity where both are known to each other but the gift is made before the poor asks for it.

Of lower degree is where one gives charity after being asked for it. Lower still is one who gives less than what is fitting but with good grace, and least of all is one who gives unwillingly.

Maimonides, Mishneh Torah:
The 8 Degrees of Charity (Judaism)

Teachings of Sun Myung Moon

When you meet a poor person and give him alms out of sympathy, never say, "Hey, you are a young fellow who can work. What's the matter with you?" I suggest you say to him, "Though it is but a small token, if you revere it highly you will receive many blessings in the future."[29] You can say this to everyone to whom you give alms. (127:89, May 5, 1983)

When you offer your substance to build the Kingdom of Heaven, do not think that you are offering what belongs to you; think that your offering already belongs to Heaven.

Likewise, when you give to others, do not think that you are giving to them out of your own pocket. Give with the mind that it comes from the treasury of Heaven. The person receiving it will know your mind; thus he will recognize that he is actually receiving from God. Then God will take note and return it to you ten times over. (102:119-20, November 27, 1978)

The most excellent giving is to give generously to others although you yourself are in want. (*Way of God's Will* 2.2)

Our mind urges our body to help the poor and sacrifice for others, even though we may be going through hardships of our own. (41:60, February 13, 1971)

It is said, "Do not let your left hand know what your right hand is doing." If you lend ten thousand dollars to someone and then remember it with added interest, you cannot be an owner of the Kingdom of God. You should forget about the money you lent. When parents raise children, do they remember how much money they spent for their care? Do they tally up a bill and present it to their grown children, demanding payment with interest? No, a parent's heart is to forgive and forget it all. Moreover, after forgetting what they have given, parents are anxious that they could not have given something better. (36:85, November 15, 1970)

When I was a student in Seoul, my home was outside the city, in Huk Suk Dong. For a nickel I could ride a streetcar to school. The ride took only a short time, while on foot the journey took over an hour. Every day I walked, in order to save that nickel to give to some needy person on the street. By the time I came home, the nickel was gone, not to the train conductor but to a needy person. (244:25, January 29, 1993)

I observed the beggars closely; there were many on the street by the Noryangjin Station and the Hwasin Department Store. As I walked, I would quickly distinguish the old ones from the young ones. I would not give to the young ones; I only gave to those who were handicapped, blind or elderly. Likewise when you give alms, give to those who truly need it. (50:308, November 8, 1971)

Hospitality

HOSPITALITY TO GUESTS, ESPECIALLY TO TRAVELERS seeking food and rest, is a traditional virtue from ancient times. Abraham was exemplary in his hospitality to strangers, three of whom turned out to be angels. Father Moon describes the custom in his parents' home, where hospitality to strangers was a rule firmly enforced by his father. The best families create such a loving atmosphere in their home that it attracts people and even animals from miles around.

Even families of little means should give their best hospitality to guests regardless of the hardship it might cause them; this is illustrated by three texts lauding exemplary hospitality *in extremis,* by Lot who defended his guests against molestation by the people of Sodom, by a companion of Muhammad who gave his last morsel to a guest of the Prophet, and by a Hindu householder who preferred to die of thirst rather than withhold drink from a thirsty stranger.

Do not neglect to show hospitality to strangers, for thereby some have entertained angels unawares.[30]

Hebrews 13.1

See to it that whoever enters your house obtains something to eat, however little you may have. Such food will be a source of death to you if you withhold it.

A Winnebago Father's Precepts
(Native American Religions)

Let him who believes in Allah and the Last Day be generous to his neighbor, and let him who believes in Allah and the Last Day be generous to his guest.

Forty Hadith of an-Nawawi 15 *(Islam)*

The husband and wife of the house should not turn away any who comes at eating time and asks for food. If food is not available, a place to rest, water for refreshing one's self, a reed mat to lay one's self on, and pleasing words entertaining the guest—these at least never fail in the houses of the good.

Apastamba Dharma Sutra 8.2 *(Hinduism)*

The two... came to Sodom in the evening; and Lot was sitting in the gate of Sodom. When Lot saw them, he rose to meet them, and bowed himself with his face to the earth, and said, "My lords, turn aside, I pray you, to your servant's house and spend the night, and wash your feet; then you may rise up early and go on your way."[31] They said, "No; we will spend the night in the street." But he urged them strongly; so they turned aside to him and entered his house; and he made them a feast, and baked unleavened bread, and they ate. But before they lay down, the men of the city, the men of Sodom, both young and old, all the people to the last man, surrounded the house; and they called to Lot, "Where are the men who came to you tonight? Bring them out to us, that we may know them." Lot went out of the door to the men, shut the door after him, and said, "I beg you, my brothers, do not act so wickedly. Behold, I have two daughters who have not known man; let me bring them out to you, and do to them as you please; only do nothing to these men, for they have come under the shelter of my roof."

Genesis 19.1-8

A man came to find the Prophet and the latter asked his wives for something to give him to eat. "We have absolutely nothing," they replied, "except water." "Who wants to share his meal with this man?" asked the Prophet. A man of the Companions then said, "I." Then he led this man to his wife and said to her, "Treat generously the guest of the Messenger of God." She replied, "We have nothing except our children's supper." "Oh, well," he replied, "get your meal ready, light your lamp, and when your children want supper, put them to bed." So the woman prepared the meal, lit the lamp, put the children to bed, then, getting up as if to trim the lamp, she extinguished it. The Companion and his wife then made as if to eat, but in fact they spent the night with empty stomachs. The next day when the Companion went to find the Messenger of God, the latter said to him, "This night God smiled." It was then that God revealed these words, "and they prefer the others before themselves, although there be indigence among them" [Qur'an 59.9].

Hadith of Bukhari *(Islam)*

The fame of Rantideva is sung in this and the other world, Rantideva, who, though himself hungry, was in the habit of giving away his wealth as it came, while trusting in God to provide his needs. Even in time of famine, Rantideva continued his generosity though his family was reduced to poverty.

For forty-eight days he and his family were starving; a little liquid, and that enough for only one, was all that remained. As he was about to drink it, an outcaste came begging for water. Rantideva was moved at the sight and said, "I do not desire from God the great state attended by divine powers or even deliverance from rebirth. Establishing myself in the hearts of all beings, I take on myself their suffering so that they may be rid of their misery." So saying, the compassionate king gave that little liquid to the outcaste, though he himself was dying of thirst.

Srimad Bhagavatam 9 *(Hinduism)*

Teachings of Sun Myung Moon

A household that is always prepared to welcome noble guests will receive blessings. (100:259, October 22, 1978)

Treat people who come to visit you as kings. Serve them as kings and attend them like kings. (89:290, December 4, 1976)

Make hospitality to friends and visitors your family custom. Care for them so well that they say, "Your house is better than mine. This meal is more delicious than the food at my house. Can I stay here one more night?" When you make your house a place where every guest or friend wants to come and stay, even ignoring their own families, you have the Kingdom of Heaven in your family. (16:328, July 31, 1966)

The more people you invite into your home to eat and sleep there, whether they stay in a guestroom or in the attic, the more blessed your family will be. The time will come when families will compete in the practice of hospitality. Families will want to become famous for hosting guests from the neighborhood, the county, from around the nation and from overseas. People do not practice hospitality because they are materially wealthy; they practice hospitality because they are wealthy in heart and love. There is happiness in hosting others, even though you may be eating hard bread. (244:49, January 29, 1993)

Your home should be a place where passing beggars want to sleep or even lean against your doorstep to take shelter from the cold. Even the neighborhood dogs want to lie down there, and birds want to take shelter. There should be bird-droppings on your doorstep from the birds that nest in your eaves. When you make your home like that, you will flourish and God will be with you. Why? Because the place where God's love dwells attracts all living things; it is a place of peaceful Sabbath rest for all beings. (100:299, October 22, 1978)

My family had a tradition: Nobody passing by our house left with an empty stomach. Our home was widely known to every beggar in the district; they all visited and received our hospitality. When my mother served our grandparents their dinner, she also served the beggars. [It was a heavy physical ordeal for my mother. Yet on one occasion when she neglected to feed a beggar, my father took his own meal and gave it to him. Thenceforth my mother had to feed the beggars or else my father would go hungry.][32]

   I am grateful to my mother, who did not complain though she labored to feed these strangers. It became a motive for a person like me to lead a movement to feed the world. (130:276, February 5, 1984)

All the beggars that lived in or near our district used to visit our house. Our house was like a meeting place for beggars. There were always a few of them sleeping in the guestroom. There was an old mill in our village where beggars would congregate. I made friends with many of them. When our family made rice cakes I always took pity on them and brought them some.[33] When a beggar left our house in the morning, I thought, "Who will give them lunch?" Since there was no one, I often fed them. Without asking my mother for anything, I took the food she had set aside for my lunch and shared it with the beggars. It was a good deed. Thinking about it now, I think I did well. (127:111, May 5, 1983)

The Great Commandment

AS A CONCISE SUMMATION OF THE LAW OF LOVE, Jesus' Great Commandment is without parallel. It links together love's two dimensions: vertical love for God and horizontal love for other people. In this brief section, we give several examples of Father Moon's commentary on this verse.

You shall love the Lord your God with all your heart, and with all your soul, and with all your mind. This is the great and first commandment. And a second is like it, You shall love your neighbor as yourself. On these two commandments depend all the law and the prophets.

Matthew 22.37-39

And behold, a lawyer stood up to put him to the test, saying, "Teacher, what shall I do to inherit eternal life?" [Jesus] said to him, "What is written in the law? How do you read?" And he answered, "You shall love the Lord your God with all your heart, and with all your soul, and with all your strength, and with all your mind; and your neighbor as yourself." And he said to him, "You have answered right; do this, and you will live." But he, desiring to justify himself, said to Jesus, "And who is my neighbor?"

Luke 10.25-29

Teachings of Sun Myung Moon
God gave us a commandment: "You shall love the Lord your God with all your heart, and with all your soul, and with all your mind. This is the great and first commandment." (Matt. 22.37-38) You should remember that God kept this commandment before humankind did…

When listening to the commandment, if you think that it starts with you, you are seriously mistaken. God is the Subject of human life, love and ideals. Before He brought this commandment to humankind, God first went through a historical course of exerting his entire mind and will for the sake of humankind. In other words, before any human being loved God with all his heart and soul and mind, God loved humankind with all His heart and soul and mind. God could give us this commandment because God first kept it Himself. (4:304, October 5, 1958)

True love has two axes: the vertical and the horizontal. True love on the vertical axis means that God is the Creator; He is the source of true love, and He loves His creation. Human beings, as the supreme creation of God, are the recipients of God's true love and return love and beauty to Him.

True love on the horizontal axis means that our actions are motivated by love for the sake of others, and we give our love to others in a way that will be genuinely beneficial to them. Within a family, the husband may energetically pursue the Will of God, even running far ahead of his wife. But if his motivation is for the sake of his family, all the members of that family will feel united in love. We can see, therefore, that the true concept of unification emerges when we act from the motivation of sacrificially loving others.

All creation is an effort of giving. It is a universal law that the giver prospers and grows. When a person only takes from others in order to satisfy his desires, that selfish action is not love, and it ultimately creates enemies. He will become more isolated and decline. But a person who gives of himself to benefit others creates friends who will in turn help him. He will inevitably receive more than he gave, and he will prosper. Therefore, the person of true love lives for the highest purpose, and then gives of himself. These two axes of true love are the principle behind Jesus' great commandment. "You shall love the Lord your God with all your heart, and with all your soul, and with all your mind" teaches the vertical axis of true love, and "You shall love your neighbor as yourself" teaches the horizontal axis of true love. (November 25, 1988)

While on earth we must attend God in a way that brings Him joy. So what should be our standard of attendance? By making offerings that meet with God's desire we develop a character that matches with God's heart. That is the meaning of Jesus' first commandment, "You must love the Lord your God with all your heart, all your soul and all your strength."

Once you love God with all your heart, all your soul and all your strength, what happens next? God then manifests His love through you to relate with all people. Since you have become one with God's love, you are able to love all people. Hence in your family, you give your utmost love to your father and mother, and then you give your utmost love to your brothers and sisters. That family will be a happy family.

God wants to dwell in the family whose members love the Lord their God with all their heart, all their soul and all their strength, and then love their brothers and sisters in the same manner, even more than they love [God] their Father. If we establish our family like that, God cannot help but dwell there. (101:153-54, October 29, 1978)

The second commandment is to love the people of the world like your own self. Just as you should love God by offering even your whole life, you should love your neighbors even by sacrificing your life. Just like you stake your life to protect yourself, you should become a person who can risk his or her life to love and protect all people. (143:137, March 17, 1986)

Jesus said, "Love your neighbor as you love yourself," but what does it mean? Specifically, it means that when you go into the world, you should love elderly people as your own grandparents, middle-aged people as your own parents, and youth as your own children. You love the people in all these positions: above and below, right and left, and front and rear. (128:23, May 29, 1983)

Who is your neighbor? Are your neighbors only those who also believe in Jesus? No. Your neighbors include people at the ends of the earth. Even the people in the bosom of the Devil are your neighbors. When Jesus said to love your enemies, he included the Roman soldiers. Actually, you should not think of your neighbors as neighbors, but as your older brothers. It is a principle of the Unification Church that you have to restore Cain. Every Cain-type person is actually your older brother. (138:187, January 21, 1986)

CHAPTER 14

WISDOM

The Primary Ends of Education

WHAT ARE THE PURPOSES OF EDUCATION? Classical education in all cultures of the world was concerned primarily with cultivating virtue. Education was about cultivating the soul, developing a civilized character and forming good citizens. However, in today's schooling the focus is on technical knowledge and the skills needed for the complex modern workplace. Character and values get short shrift. Theodore Roosevelt is said to have warned, "To educate a man in mind and not in morals is to educate a menace to society."[1] Study of the world's scriptures leads us back to consider education's primary ends.

Father Moon distinguishes three levels of education: first, education of heart cultivates the emotional basis for unselfish love; second, education of norm deals with the morality of good relationships; third, academic and technical education follow on these two foundations. Much of the first two levels of education is done at home as the responsibility of parents. Yet schools can also play a part, particularly by providing character education and marriage education. Given that deficiencies in character and marital problems can detract from performance in the workplace, educating for these ends need not be seen as in contradiction to the career orientation of modern schooling.

1. The Primary Purpose of Education: to Cultivate Virtue

Knowledge is the food of the soul.
     Plato, Protagoras (Hellenism)

True learning induces in the mind service of mankind.
     Adi Granth, Asa, M.1, p. 356 (Sikhism)

The end and aim of wisdom is repentance and good deeds.
     Talmud, Berakot 17 (Judaism)

A faithful study of the liberal arts humanizes character and permits it not to be cruel.
     Ovid (Hellenism)

Confucius said, "The superior man extensively studies literature and restrains himself with the rules of propriety. Thus he will not violate the Way."
     Analects 6.25 (Confucianism)

The parents of a child are but his enemies when they fail to educate him properly in his boyhood... Knowledge makes a man honest, virtuous, and endearing to society. It is learning alone that enables a man to better the condition of his friends and relations. Knowledge is the holiest of holies, the god of the gods, and commands respect of crowned heads; shorn of it a man is but an animal. The fixtures and furniture of one's house may be stolen by thieves; but knowledge, the highest treasure, is above all stealing.
     Garuda Purana (Hinduism)

As soon as a child can understand what is said, nurse, mother, tutor, and the father himself vie with each other to make the child as good as possible, instructing him through everything he does or says, pointing out, "This is right and that is wrong, this honorable and that disgraceful, this holy and that impious; do this, don't do that." If he is obedient, well and good. If not, they straighten him with threats and beatings, like a warped and twisted plank.

Later on when they send the children to school, their instructions to the teachers lay much more emphasis on good behavior than on letters or music. The teachers take good care of this, and when the boys have learned their letters... they set the works of good poets before them on their desks to read and make them learn them by heart, poems containing much admonition and many stories, eulogies, and panegyrics of the good men of old, so that the child may be inspired to imitate them and long to be like them.

Plato, Protagoras 325c-e (Hellenism)

When things are investigated, knowledge is extended; when knowledge is extended, the will becomes sincere; when the will is sincere, the mind is rectified; when the mind is rectified, the personal life is cultivated; when the personal life is cultivated, the family will be regulated; when the family is regulated, the state will be in order; when the state is in order, there will be peace throughout the world.

The Great Learning (Confucianism)

Because perfect wisdom tames and transforms him, wrath and conceit he does not increase. Neither enmity nor ill-will take hold of him, nor is there even a tendency towards them. He will be mindful and friendly... It is wonderful how this perfection of wisdom has been set up for the control and training of the Bodhisattvas.

Perfection of Wisdom in Eight Thousand Lines
3.51-54 (Buddhism)

You shall therefore lay up these words of mine in your heart and in your soul; and you shall bind them as a sign upon your hand, and they shall be as frontlets between your eyes. And you shall teach them to your children, talking of them when you are sitting in your house, and when you are walking by the way, and when you lie down, and when you rise.

Deuteronomy 11.18-19

Does not wisdom call,
does not understanding raise her voice?
On the heights beside the way,
in the paths she takes her stand;
beside the gates of the town,
at the entrance of the portals she cries aloud,
"To you, O men, I call,
and my cry is to the sons of men.
O simple ones, learn prudence;
O foolish men, pay attention.
Hear, for I will speak noble things,
and from my lips will come what is right;
for my mouth will utter truth;
wickedness is an abomination to my lips.
All the words of my mouth are righteous;
there is nothing twisted or crooked in them.
They are all straight to him who understands
and right to those who find knowledge.
Take my instruction instead of silver,
and knowledge rather than choice gold;
for wisdom is better than jewels,
and all that you may desire cannot compare
   with her."

Proverbs 8.1-11

Teachings of Sun Myung Moon

Moral education teaches the norm that people should place the public good ahead of self-interest. (24:212, August 17, 1969)

All people live with a desire for goodness. Therefore education should teach: "Before you love God, you must love human beings." "Live for all humankind." "Love people and live for their sake." "You were born for the sake of others, not for yourself." (64:20, October 22, 1972)

We have a general idea that people who are good-hearted and sacrificial lead a better life. Moral education everywhere in the world aims at the cultivation of character to this end. Why? In their condition of fallenness, people aspire to rise to a higher state. Yet since Heaven cannot instruct each person one at a time in detail, it resorts to implicit teachings using symbols and metaphors. Despite the diversity of human cultures, the result of Heaven's work is that all moral instruction today tells people to do right and accumulate virtuous deeds. (65:118-19, November 5, 1972)

One does not need any education to become an evil person. If a person wants to do evil or become evil, he will do it whether you teach him or not; so what is the point of educating him? No one teaches him to do evil; still he becomes evil without thinking about it. On the other hand, it is not easy to become a good person. To become a good person, someone capable of practicing goodness throughout a lifetime, education is indispensable. How nice it would be if we could walk that road easily! However, since good and evil travel in exactly opposite directions, the path to goodness is not easy at all. (39:23, January 9, 1971)

Conventional schools do not teach about marriage, even though it is a very significant matter. Marriage education is not given much space in the curriculum compared to the seriousness of its problems. There is a lack of education about the needs and aspirations of the opposite sex. There is a lack of education concerning the issues that typically arise after marriage. The schools disregard questions of how to build happy marriages or how to properly educate children. Instead, they focus on teaching science and mathematics. This is certainly an aberration. (*Tongil Segye* 108, March 9, 1978)

Let us create children's educational materials about keeping purity before marriage.[2] Let us create educational materials on how to make good fraternal and peer relationships, educational materials on marriage and on parenting, and educational materials on developing ideal families, extended families and clans. (233:336, August 2, 1992)

The family is the school of love; it is the most important school in life. Within the family, children cultivate the depth and breadth of their heart to love others.[3] It is education of love and emotion that only parents can provide, and it becomes the foundation stone to form the children's character. The family is also the school teaching virtues, norms and manners. It is the way of Heaven that people receive academic education, physical education and technical education on the foundation of this primary education of heart and norm. (271:80, August 22, 1995)

Children surely need to be educated about love. They do not necessarily need their parents to educate them in knowledge, but their parents are essential to educate them about love. Are they providing an education about love when the mother and father fight? Parents should teach by example how two people can become one with each other. Hence, the mother and father should be pleasing to Heaven; the father should be pleasing to the mother and the mother pleasing to the father. They should like each other and be parents whom the children like. Likewise, both parents should like all their children—it should not be the case that the father likes only some children and not others…

That is why we must receive an education about love in the presence of God and centering on God's love. This education does not begin with human beings. God is their Heavenly Parent, so God should educate human beings about love. God would want to continue this education until people can fully grasp all the values of their Heavenly Parent; at that point they can be said to have reached maturity.

But is it recorded in the Bible that Adam and Eve grew up receiving God's love? There is nothing about their receiving love; instead the Bible begins with an unpleasant story about their Fall. (51:172-73, November 21, 1971)

Koreans know well how to face death because they have been well educated about it. Teaching people how to conclude their lives well is the essence of education. (25:158, October 3, 1969)

2. Education Broadens the Mind and Opens New Possibilities for Advancement

A good, all-round education, appreciation of the arts, a highly trained discipline and pleasant speech; this is the highest blessing.

       Sutta Nipata 261 *(Buddhism)*

There is no greater wealth than wisdom; no greater poverty than ignorance; no greater heritage than culture.

     Nahjul Balagha, Saying 52 *(Shiite Islam)*

Confucius said, "By nature men are pretty much alike; it is learning and practice that set them apart."

       Analects 17.2 *(Confucianism)*

The truth will make you free.

          John 8.32

No man is free, but he who labors in the [study of] Torah.

       Mishnah, Avot 6.2 *(Judaism)*

Teachings of Sun Myung Moon

People do not enjoy studying in the beginning. They might enjoy sleeping, but not studying—at least not at first. But after awhile people enjoy studying, because they see that through study their area of activity is widened. (36:120, November 22, 1970)

Everyone wants to have a fine son. How should you educate him to make him great? Some people think it lies in the quality of schooling, from kindergarten to college. However, education is for a lifetime. Therefore, you should devote yourselves diligently to educate your children with proper values. Having done that, when one day he takes your place at the head of the family, he will represent you, having the same mind as you and following in your footsteps. (24:257, August 24, 1969)

Parents think, "To get my children into good universities I have to make them study. Studying leads to success in life." I do not agree. They tell their children, "You have to have knowledge to be successful." That is not true. The most precious thing is how much you love your country and how much you love God—not know Him but *love* Him. (144:130, April 12, 1986)

Educational systems in every nation of the world place too much stress on the value of competition and reward only the winners. They mold people for a life of "survival of the fittest." This has been a plague undermining the healthy human endeavor to lead humankind into a world of peaceful interdependence. Now some intellectuals are questioning this emphasis on competition. They should understand that the emphasis in education needs to shift to cooperation, as it is vital for human survival. In light of this, the goals and philosophies of education will have to undergo a profound transformation. (74:109, November 21, 1974)

The Search for Knowledge

THE SEARCH FOR KNOWLEDGE is incumbent upon everyone. Education and diligent study elevates and ennobles the human person. Several aspects of the search are developed in these passages. First, the search for truth is a religious obligation, and the search takes us back to the Source of the universe from whence comes all truth. Second, an important aspect of learning is to examine oneself. This includes recognizing the extent of our ignorance—how little we know. Third, knowledge is not handed to us, but requires us to comprehend a topic and make it our own. Therefore the student makes thorough efforts to understand the matter from all angles. Fourth, the search should be broad, embracing all religions and cultures, including all the sciences.

Several of Father Moon's remarks in this section were addressed to gatherings of academics and scientists. Others describe his personal search for truth.

1. God and His Principles Are the Starting-point for Understanding

The fear of the LORD is the beginning of wisdom.

Proverbs 9.11

Understanding is the reward of faith. Therefore do not seek understanding that you may believe, but believe that you may understand, as was said, "Except ye believe, ye shall not understand" (Isaiah 7.9).

Saint Augustine, On the Gospel of John 29.6
(Christianity)

Without faith there is no knowledge, without knowledge there is no virtuous conduct, without virtues there is no deliverance, and without deliverance there is no perfection [Nirvana].

Uttaradhyayana Sutra 28.30 (Jainism)

If any of you lacks wisdom, let him ask God, who gives to all men generously and without reproaching, and it will be given him.

James 1.5

Yet among the mature we do impart wisdom, although it is not a wisdom of this age or of the rulers of this age, who are doomed to pass away. But we impart a secret and hidden wisdom of God, which God decreed before the ages for our glorification.

1 Corinthians 2.4-7

Carefully ponder moral principles and cultivate their source.

Chu Hsi (Confucianism)

Truth is the way; truth is the goal of life, Reached by sages who are free from self-will.

Mundaka Upanishad 3.1.6 (Hinduism)

A disciple in training will comprehend this earth, the realm of death and the realm of the gods. A disciple in training will investigate the well-taught Path of Virtue, even as an expert garland-maker picks flowers.

Dhammapada 45 (Buddhism)

Teachings of Sun Myung Moon

To reach the goal of philosophy, to know the ultimate truth, it is necessary to posit a transcendent or absolute Being. Why is this? Apart from the Absolute Being, one cannot understand the origin of existence or its meaning. Therefore, when facing serious difficulties, people have sought solutions through making a relationship with the Absolute Being and the truth of that Being. (24:318, September 14, 1969)

The truth is one, and it is the principle that rules both the natural world and the human world. In nature this principle is the root and source of all things of the universe. For human beings this principle is the absolute value of true love, which guides us to complete our personalities through harmonizing our spirituality and physicality and to realize truth, goodness, and beauty.

I do not believe that the claims of theism, humanism, and materialism are in irreconcilable conflict. I think, rather, that they were incomplete and one-sided expressions of the one principle of absolute values. In order to fundamentally solve various human problems of the modem world, we should find this one principle, the absolute value—which can cope with the whole, beyond any existing ideologies and claims.

The search for absolute value leads us ultimately to the fundamental question of God. To accept that God exists is to recognize that there exists a universal principle which operates consistently in nature and the human world. On this foundation, values that appear to be relative can be understood as interrelated with each other when viewed from the viewpoint of the absolute value. (170:268-70, November 27, 1987)

2. Know Thyself

An unexamined life is not worth living.
Socrates, in Plato, Apology 38 (Hellenism)

He who knows others is wise;
He who knows himself is enlightened.
Tao Te Ching 33 (Taoism)

Mencius said, "A gentleman steeps himself in the Way because he wishes to find it in himself."
Mencius IV.B.14 (Confucianism)

Too late did I love Thee, O Beauty so ancient and yet so new! Too late did I love Thee! For behold, Thou wert within, and I without, and there I was seeking Thee—I, unlovely, rushed heedlessly among the things of beauty Thou didst make. Thou wert with me, but I was not with Thee. Those things kept me far from Thee, things which would not be had they not been in Thee.
Saint Augustine, Confessions 10.27 (Christianity)

What thing I am I do not know.
I wander secluded, burdened by my mind.
When the Firstborn of Truth has come to me
I receive a share of that selfsame Word.
Rig Veda 1.164.37 (Hinduism)

God gives wisdom to whom He will, and he to whom wisdom is given has truly received abundant good. But none remember except men of understanding.
Qur'an 2.269

I know nothing except the fact of my ignorance.
Socrates (Hellenism)

To know when one does not know is best.
To think one knows when one does not know is a dire disease.

Tao Te Ching 71 (Taoism)

The fool who knows that he is a fool is for that very reason a wise man; the fool who thinks he is wise is called a fool indeed.

Dhammapada 63 (Buddhism)

Teachings of Sun Myung Moon

If you do not know your present position, you are like a person sailing on the ocean without knowing his latitude and longitude. You must know where you are now before you can set your proper course. (120:303, October 20, 1982)

In today's world, quite a few people attempt to commit suicide, taking overdoses of sleeping pills... Why do they take their own lives? It is because they do not know the purpose of their life. When studying philosophy, the first question you ask is: "What is life?" The next question is: "What is the purpose of our life?" (222:70)

What is the origin of the evil mind that incites evil desires in opposition to the original mind? What is the root cause of the contradiction that brings people to ruin? In order to ward off evil desires and follow good desires, we must overcome this ignorance and gain the ability to distinguish clearly between good and evil. Then we can take the path to the good life the original mind seeks. (Exposition of the Divine Principle, *Introduction*)

How can we find the truth by which to judge what is good and what is bad in this evil world? You have to get rid of your self-centered mind and take the lowest position. The Bible says, "Every one who exalts himself will be humbled, but he who humbles himself will be exalted."[4] (2:138, March 17, 1957)

If you know yourself, you will say, "I am inadequate in many areas." This is a good gift to have. (*Way of God's Will* 1.3)

3. Comprehend the Truth Not Merely on the Authority of a Teacher, but from One's Own Extensive Study and Research

Do not be misled by reports, or tradition, or hearsay. Be not led by the authority of religious texts, nor by mere logic or inference, nor by considering appearances, nor by the delight in speculative opinions, nor by seeming possibilities, nor by the idea: "This is our teacher." But when you know for yourselves that certain things are unwholesome and wrong, and bad, then give them up... And when you know for yourselves that certain things are wholesome and good, then accept them and follow them.

Anguttara Nikaya 1.190-91 (Buddhism)

The search for knowledge is an obligation laid on every Muslim.

Hadith of Ibn Majah and Baihaqi (Islam)

Thinking is like drilling a well; if we are persistent we will reach clear water. At first it must be muddied, but by gradually scraping away it will naturally become clear.

Chu Hsi (Confucianism)

He who devotes himself to the study of the law
   of the Most High
will seek out the wisdom of all the ancients,
and will be concerned with prophecies;
he will preserve the discourse of notable men
and penetrate the subtleties of parables;
he will seek out the hidden meanings of
   proverbs
and be at home with the obscurities of parables.
He will serve among great men and appear
   before rulers;
he will travel through the lands of foreign
   nations,
for he tests the good and the evil among men.

Ecclesiasticus 39.1-4 (Christianity)

By collecting contrasting divergent opinions I hope to provoke young readers to push themselves to the limit in the search for truth, so that their wits may be sharpened by their investigation. It is by doubting that we come to investigate, and by investigating that we recognize the truth.

Peter Abelard, Inquiry into Divergent Views of the
Church Fathers (Christianity)

The most useful piece of learning for the uses of life is to unlearn what is untrue.

Antisthenes [5] (Hellenism)

Freethinkers are those who are willing to use their minds without prejudice and without fearing to understand things that clash with their own customs, privileges, or beliefs. This state of mind is not common, but it is essential for right thinking; where it is absent, discussion is apt to become worse than useless.

Leo Tolstoy (Humanism)

Teachings of Sun Myung Moon

The ultimate purpose of religion can be attained only when one first believes it in one's heart and then puts it into practice. However, without first understanding, beliefs do not take hold. (*Exposition of the Divine Principle*, Introduction)

Do not recklessly make a move when you are given a vague teaching. Do not make a move unless the direction is established in clear truth. Even if someone propounds a new teaching with great persuasiveness, do not simply believe it. First discuss it with someone who is more Abel-like[6] than you. (3:212, November 1, 1957)

Although you have joined the Unification Church, if it does not answer all your questions, then pack up and leave. (150:110, September 4, 1960)

Philosophers, saints and sages set out to pave the way of goodness for the people of their times. Yet so many of their accomplishments have become added spiritual burdens for the people of today.
   Consider this objectively. Has any philosopher ever arrived at the knowledge that could solve humanity's deepest anguish? Has any sage ever clearly illuminated the path by resolving all the fundamental questions of human life and the universe? Have not their teachings and philosophies raised more unsettled questions, thus giving rise to skepticism?...
   If we are created in such a way that we cannot live apart from God, then surely our ignorance of God consigns us to walk miserable paths. Though we may diligently study the Bible, can we really say that we know clearly the reality of God? Can we ever grasp the heart of God? (*Exposition of the Divine Principle*, Introduction)

Before I began my path of life, I asked the question, "Does God exist?" Only after I could give a clear answer, "Definitely, God exists," did I begin my course. (13:201, March 15, 1964)

When searching for truth, it is not enough to just accept what you read in the Bible. We need to be able to measure the truth with precision. I searched for truth like a researcher who does experiment after experiment to prove his results. The Divine Principle contains many such well-tested discoveries. (May 1, 1977)

What did God teach me when I was a boy? Do you know what a hard time God gave me? Step by step I had to verify for myself the two fundamental axioms: love passes through the shortest distance, and the origin of the universe is the father-son relationship. Then from these two truths I had to work out everything else.

I had to elucidate the truths of the world of the principle from this new starting-point—the original father-son relationship that has nothing to do with the lineage of the secular world. Hence, I could not understand anything without knowing the particulars of the Human Fall. Now I have uncovered the origin, and from it, I have revealed the law of the universe, the heavenly law. (376:315, April 29, 2002)

Once I started seriously questioning a certain passage in the Bible, I would strive continually even for three years to solve the mystery of it. Until I could shout, "Eureka!" I would push myself to penetrate the root of the problem. (35:38, September 27, 1970)

4. Investigate All Sides of a Subject

A gentleman can see a question from all sides without bias. The small man is biased and can see a question only from one side.

Analects 2.14 (Confucianism)

I am not biased in favor of Mahavira, nor averse to Kapila or other teachers. I am committed to the preaching that is truly rational.

Haribhadra, Loktattvanirnaya 38 (Jainism)

There are three things that occasion sorrow to a superior man [who is devoted to learning]: If there be any subject of which he has not heard, and he cannot get to hear of it; if he hear of it, and cannot get to learn it; if he have learned it, and cannot get to carry it out in practice.

Book of Ritual 18.2.2.20 (Confucianism)

Ben Zoma said, Who is wise? He who learns from every person, as it is taught, "From all my teachers I have acquired wisdom." [Psalm 119.99]

Mishnah, Avot 4.1 (Judaism)[7]

The Buddha says, "To be attached to a certain view and to look down upon others' views as inferior—this the wise men call a fetter."

Sutta Nipata 798 (Buddhism)

Comprehend one philosophical view through comprehensive study of another one.

Acarangasutra 5.113 (Jainism)

I intend to make a careful study of my own religion and, as far as I can, of other religions as well.

Mohandas K. Gandhi (Hinduism)

Science without religion is lame, religion without science is blind.

Albert Einstein, The World as I See It

Teachings of Sun Myung Moon

In order to become a great scholar, you should absorb the great teachings of the many great men and women of the past. As you go through kindergarten, elementary, middle and high school, college and graduate school, you should be absorbing all the knowledge of the world's prominent thinkers. You need to digest them and synthesize their thoughts into your own understanding. You can appear as a new, extraordinary thinker as you add your originality to the elements they provide. That is the way to become a world-class scholar.

The same applies on the path to fulfilling the Will of goodness. (35:327, November 1, 1970)

It is sad to see that, although knowledge in various fields of study does interrelate, all too often scholars prefer to concentrate only on their own field of study. Extreme specialization provides knowledge that may mean little to anyone other than the individual who pursues it. The joy of discovery should inspire a scholar to communicate his findings to others in terms they can understand. We should all be willing to listen, lest our knowledge be superficial and imprecise.

Religious people have felt threatened by the development of science—especially since the time of the Renaissance. Yet how can a religious person be concerned with salvation without being concerned with developing the knowledge and techniques necessary to solve the problems of hunger, disease, old age, and inadequate housing and clothing? Certainly science has contributed much towards these ends.

Furthermore, in contemplating the mystery and wonder of man and the universe, religion and science through inspiration, logic and observation both seek to explain, or at least point to, the cause that brought into existence the universe and humankind. Such contemplation of our origin and purpose is certainly one of the things that distinguish us as human beings. It provides us with never-ending sources of energy. In this regard, twentieth century cosmologists and biologists concern themselves with matters related to the concerns of theologians and philosophers. (95:202-03, November 25, 1977)

In a world of many cultures, religions and social systems, where can we find a transcendent ideal and public purpose that can harmonize them all? To avoid being misled by partial values that favor one nation, culture, religion, race, or social system over another, we invite scientists and scholars representing every nationality, culture, religion, race and social system in a common search for truth. This truth should regard both the spiritual and physical aspects of human beings, that is, the needs of physical well-being within a comfortable and productive environment, as well as the spiritual needs—regard for personal virtue, promotion of morality and religious faith, and respect for the traditions of every culture. We must lift up the absolute value which will create the basis for constructive cooperation in every aspect of human existence. (November 25, 1988)

Tradition

TRADITION CONTAINS THE ACCUMULATED WISDOM of the generations. It is bequeathed through the study of history, the recitation of proverbs and folklore, in public ceremonies and at home. Some of its best teaching material consists of the lives of great men and women, as well as ordinary citizens who lived lives of exemplary goodness and self-sacrifice. Tradition can be hard to find in today's culture of celebrity and instant fame, yet its importance can hardly be overlooked.

Family lies at the heart of tradition. Parents pass on their values and morals to their children through teaching and example. Good parents encourage their children to keep their ways and even surpass them. A stable family structure maintains and strengthens tradition, passing on its wisdom to succeeding generations.

Tradition endures.
> Akan Proverb *(African Traditional Religions)*

Stand by the roads, and look,
and ask for the ancient paths,
where the good way is; and walk in it,
and find rest for your souls.
> Jeremiah 6.16

Taming Power of the Great:
The superior man acquaints himself with many sayings of antiquity
and many deeds of the past,
in order to strengthen his character thereby.
> I Ching 26 *(Confucianism)*

The teachers... put into his hands the works of great poets, and make him read and learn them by heart, sitting on his bench at school. These are full of instruction and of tales and praises of famous men of old, and the aim is that the boy may admire and imitate and be eager to become like them.
> Plato, Protagoras 325e *(Hellenism)*

On Thee alone we ever meditate,
And ponder over the teachings of the loving mind,
As well as the acts of the holy men,
Whose souls accord most perfectly with truth.
> Avesta, Yasna 34.2 *(Zoroastrianism)*

The virtues of what the ancients had to say, when perfectly digested and thoroughly penetrated, will all be useful for self-cultivation, and they can daily be put into practice and carried out thoroughly and steadfastly.
> Chu Hsi *(Confucianism)*

Without proverbs [traditional wisdom], the language would be but a skeleton without flesh, a body without a soul.
> Zulu Proverb *(African Traditional Religions)*

Employ your time in improving yourself by other men's writings so that you shall come easily by what others have labored hard for.
> Socrates *(Hellenism)*

If I have seen further than others, it is by standing upon the shoulders of giants.
> Isaac Newton

He established a testimony in Jacob,
and appointed a law in Israel,
which he commanded our fathers
to teach to their children;
that the next generation might know them,
the children yet unborn,
and arise and tell them to their children,
so that they should set their hope in God,
and not forget the works of God,
but keep his commandments.
> Psalm 78.5-7

Hear, O sons, a father's instruction,
and be attentive, that you may gain insight;
for I give you good precepts:
do not forsake my teaching.

When I was a son with my father,
tender, the only one in the sight of my mother,
he taught me, and said to me,

"Let your heart hold fast my words;
keep my commandments, and live;
do not forget, and do not turn away from the words of my mouth.
Get wisdom; get insight.
Do not forsake her, and she will keep you;
love her, and she will guard you."

Proverbs 4.1-6

Teachings of Sun Myung Moon

Goodness is not realized instantly. If we are to be good people, we have to inherit from the past. This is why we need education. We need to go to a school and learn. What should we learn? Throughout history, those who have sacrificed to pave the way for goodness did not have an easy life. We should inherit the spirit of those who made sacrifices in the past. (50:101, November 6, 1971)

For a nation to prosper, it should preserve the inheritance of history. Young children absorb stories from the elderly and enjoy folktales. Like the new buds that receive sap from the tree, children should inherit all the historical essence of their culture.

Though children may be crying with runny noses, if you say you will tell them a fairy tale, they immediately stop crying and wait for the story to begin. They truly enjoy listening to it. Why? It is because they desire to inherit history. It is a principle of heaven and earth. (28:188, January 11, 1970)

What should each nation's history textbook contain to properly educate its citizens? It should gather accounts of the lives of those citizens who sacrificed the most for their nation. The people discussed in the textbook should be the rulers and good people who sacrificed and suffered for the sake of the people. Among them should be some who gave their lives. (65:216, November 19, 1972)

There are many traditions that bind together families and nations, but only a tradition based on love can unite them eternally. It can even unite the world. What kind of love? It must be a love that longs for eternity. In the family, this is none other than parental love. Parental love is not the love of the moment. It becomes an eternal inheritance of children, from generation to generation.

Don't parents want to pass on their tradition completely and see it develop? Hence when parents educate their children, they tell them, "You should be better than me." They say, "Become a better person! You should be better than me in at least one thing."

Parents even compel their children to strive in this way, and there is nothing wrong in it. They constantly pay attention to their children and encourage them to fulfill that expectation. They do not let their children do whatever they please. Not at all! They push them to go in directions not of their own choosing, for their benefit. They make sacrifices for them so that children will turn out to be better than they are. (95:49, October 23, 1977)

You are inheriting as a free gift all the foundations I have fought to establish throughout my life. However, that is not enough. You should inherit my tradition of practice. You should inherit my way of dying and living as your tradition.

Not only that, you should also teach this tradition to others. Teach it to your children, your husbands and your wives. For example, it is my tradition that husbands and wives should respect and praise each other, saying, "My husband is a great person; my wife is a great person." A married couple that practices this tradition will educate their children to do the same. (113:303-04, May 10, 1981)

Scripture and Interpretation

SCRIPTURE IS THE BEDROCK OF RELIGIOUS KNOWLEDGE. All the higher religions are founded on inspired teachings or divine truths revealed by their founders and codified as scripture. Thus, scripture is the basis upon which believers lead their lives. It is also the enduring standard for evaluating new ideas and theological innovation. Regular study of scripture is recommended for gaining wisdom and finding guidance for daily life.

Nevertheless, the proper interpretation of scripture is not simple. The many disagreements of the meaning of scripture have created lasting disputes and fractures in communities of faith. One reason for this confusion is that the scriptures were written using parables and veiled language. Understanding the meaning of these symbols and parables requires spiritual discernment, even the assistance of the Holy Spirit.

Another issue is the problem of the letter and the spirit. Religious traditions always have to balance fidelity to the letter of a text with openness to new spiritual insights. Where scripture is meant to be a "raft," in Buddha's terms, which takes us across the sea of troubles that we might walk free on that blessed other shore, fixation on the words of scripture can be a burden to further spiritual advancement. Old interpretations need to give way to new ones or the scripture itself can become an impediment—a situation that occurred in Jesus' day.

The section closes with passages on the limitations of scripture as finite expressions of God's infinite truth. Jesus, Buddha and other Founders lived in circumstances where they could only teach a part of what they knew of God's truth, according to the level that their disciples could receive it. Father Moon affirms the value of all scriptures as expressions of the truth of God, given at various times and places to elevate humanity for the fulfillment of God's purpose. Nevertheless, since there is still much of God's Word yet to be revealed, the world is due for a new expression of truth fit for this scientific age.

1. Take Instruction from Regular Study of Scripture

O how I love thy law! It is my meditation all the day.

         Psalm 119.97

But as for you, continue in what you have learned and have firmly believed, knowing from whom you learned it and how from childhood you have been acquainted with the sacred writings which are able to instruct you for salvation through faith in Christ Jesus.

All scripture is inspired by God and profitable for teaching, for reproof, for correction, and for training in righteousness, that the man of God may be complete, equipped for every good work.

         2 Timothy 3.14-17

The work which the sages saw in the sacred sayings
Are manifestly spread forth in the triad of the Vedas.
Follow them constantly, you lovers of truth!
This is your path to the world of good deeds.

     Mundaka Upanishad 1.2.1 *(Hinduism)*

And these words which I [Moses] teach you shall be upon your heart; and you shall teach them diligently to your children, and shall talk of them when you sit in your house, and when you walk by the way, and when you lie down, and when you rise. And you shall bind them for a sign upon your hand, and they shall be as frontlets between your eyes. And you shall write them upon the doorposts of your house and on your gates.[8]

Deuteronomy 6.6-9

We have sent down the Qur'an in Truth, and in Truth has it descended: and We sent you [Muhammad] but to give glad tidings and to warn sinners. It is a Qur'an which We have divided into parts from time to time, in order that you might recite it to men at intervals; We have revealed it by stages. Say: Whether you believe in it or not, it is true that those who were given prior insight, when it is recited to them, fall down on their faces in humble prostration, and say: "Glory to our Lord! Truly has the promise of our Lord been fulfilled!" They fall down on their faces in tears, and it increases their earnest humility.

Qur'an 17.105-9

Know that he who reads and recites the Law-flower Sutra—that man has adorned himself with the adornment of the Buddha, and so is carried by the Tathagata on his shoulder.

Lotus Sutra 10 *(Buddhism)*

I am leaving you a trust. So long as you cling to it you can't go wrong. That is the rope God has extended from heaven to earth. That is the Qur'an.

Hadith of Darimi 1 *(Islam)*

Absorbed in the scriptures and their purport, he transcends the cycle of birth and death.

Acarangasutra 5.122

The holy Word is the Preceptor; by devoted meditation on it am I its disciple.
By absorbing the discourse of the Inexpressible I remain free from the taint of illusion.[9]

Adi Granth, Ramkali Siddha Goshti, M.1, p. 943 *(Sikhism)*

Whosoever labors in the Torah for its own sake merits many things; and not only so, but the whole world is indebted to him: he is called friend, beloved, a lover of the All-present, a lover of mankind; it clothes him in meekness and reverence; it fits him to become just, pious, upright, and faithful; it keeps him far from sin, and brings him near to virtue.

Mishnah, Avot 6.1 *(Judaism)*

And when a company meets together in one of the houses of God to pore over the Book of God and to study it together among themselves, the Shekhinah comes down to them and mercy overshadows them, the angels surround them, and God remembers them among them that are His.

Forty Hadith of an-Nawawi 36 *(Islam)*

If two sit together and the words between them are of Torah, then the Shekhinah is in their midst.

Mishnah, Avot 3.2 *(Judaism)*

Where two or three are gathered in my name, there am I in the midst of them.

Matthew 18.20

Teachings of Sun Myung Moon

The ultimate purpose of religion can be attained only when one first believes it in one's heart and then puts it into practice. However, without first understanding, beliefs do not take hold. It is in order to understand the truth and thereby solidify our beliefs that we study the Holy Scriptures. (*Exposition of the Divine Principle*, Introduction)

It is God's responsibility to give us His Word and guidance, and it is our responsibility to believe and practice it in order to fulfill the providence. (*Exposition of the Divine Principle*, Resurrection 2.1)

Jesus instructed the people, "Truly, truly, I say to you, he who hears my word and believes has passed from death to life." (John 5:24) Why are we judged when we do not believe in God's Word? In the Garden of Eden the first human ancestors disbelieved in God's Word and fell. To be restored to life we must believe in God's Word with greater faith than our disbelieving ancestors. We cannot be restored unless our faith is stronger than their will to rebellion. (69:128, October 23, 1973)

When you read the Bible, you should look at the saddest things. Not the sections about heaven or the Book of Revelation, but the saddest contents. To become someone's close friend, don't you need to empathize with the most painful moments in his life? It is the same principle for us who would reconnect with God as His sons and daughters: we have to understand God's most painful moments.

Then when you listen to God's Word, you will feel deep, bottomless sorrow in the core of your soul. You will weep your eyes out with heart-felt grief without understanding why. You may not be able to stop weeping after ten days, a hundred days, even a thousand days—you will want to weep endlessly. Only when you understand God's Word in this light will you begin to understand the core of God's heart. (10:137, September 18, 1960)

Wherever you go in the world, you should gather and study the message God revealed to us; it is called *Hoondokhwe*, the education that pleases God.[10] When you enter a new town, you should regard setting up a gathering to read God's word as more important than introducing yourself. Those who enjoy gathering and reading the *hoondok* scriptures will enter the Kingdom of Heaven.

God dwells with us where we read His words. When we diligently keep *hoondokhwe*, the spirits in the spirit world descend and participate with us, thereby receiving the benefit of returning resurrection. Thus, keeping *hoondokhwe* is the way to mobilize the heavenly spirit world. Through keeping *hoondokhwe* you will make your family a true family. You will revive the church through the works of the Holy Spirit. The purpose of studying God's word is to resemble God and True Parents, the original forms of the Word. Keeping *hoondokhwe* unites the True Family; likewise, by keeping *hoondokhwe* your family may become one with the True Family. (321:32, February 14, 2000)

2. Scripture Teaches in Parables

We have put forth for men in this Qur'an every kind of parable, in order that they may receive admonition.

Qur'an 39.27

Knowing that all the living have many and various desires deep-rooted in their minds, I have, according to their capacity, expounded the various laws by which these [desires] could be overcome with various reasonings, parabolic expressions, and expedients.

Lotus Sutra 2 (*Buddhism*)

And when Jesus was alone, those who were about him with the Twelve asked concerning the parables. And he said to them, "To you has been given the secret of the kingdom of God, but for those outside everything is in parables;

so they may indeed see but not perceive, and may indeed hear but not understand; lest they should turn again, and be forgiven."

Mark 4.10-12

He who does not know that indestructible Being of the Rig Veda, that highest ether-like Self wherein all the gods reside, of what use is the Rig Veda to him? Those only who know It rest contented.

Svetasvatara Upanishad 4.8 *(Hinduism)*

The biblical tales are only the Torah's outer garments, and woe to him who regards these as being the Torah itself!

Zohar, Numbers 152a *(Judaism)*

It is He who sent down upon you the Book, wherein are verses clear that are the Essence of the Book, and others ambiguous. As for those in whose hearts is swerving, they follow the ambiguous part, desiring dissension and desiring its interpretation; and none knows its interpretation, save only God.[11] And those firmly rooted in knowledge say, "We believe in it; all is from our Lord"; yet none remembers, but men possessed of minds.

Qur'an 3.7

First of all you must understand this, that no prophecy of scripture is a matter of one's own interpretation, because no prophecy ever came by the impulse of man, but men moved by the Holy Spirit spoke from God.

2 Peter 1.20-21

Were you to cleanse the mirror of your heart from the dust of malice, you would apprehend the meaning of the symbolic terms revealed by the all-embracing Word of God made manifest in every dispensation, and would discover the mysteries of divine knowledge.

Book of Certitude 68-69 *(Baha'i Faith)*

Teachings of Sun Myung Moon

God reveals well in advance all the essential matters of His Will in parables and symbols, in order that people living in any age can understand the demands of the providence for their time and for the future according to the level of their intellect and spirituality. The fact that God used parables and symbols in the Bible has inevitably resulted in many divergent interpretations. This is a major reason why the churches have become divided. In interpreting the Bible, therefore, the most important matter is to find the right perspective. (*Exposition of the Divine Principle*, Second Advent 2.1)

The Bible is like a love-letter written by a bridegroom searching for his bride and containing many secret codes. Why does God write in code? It is because God is a God of heart. Not everyone is meant to decipher the Bible; only the bride and bridegroom should be able to decipher it. In other words, only those who have prepared themselves to attend the Lord with a heart akin to God's heart can decipher the Bible; to anyone else it is an impenetrable mystery.

The Bible has a code. It is like a key that opens the gate to allow the bridegroom to enter. What is that key? It is heart. The heart of a parent does not change, whether the child is feeding on its mother's breast or has grown old and gray. There is no difference in that heart.

So we need to search for the original source of all the hearts hidden in the Bible. Finding it does not require a Ph.D. Theologians have been analyzing the Bible for centuries, but their theories just come and go. Heart cannot be controlled by logic. It cannot be experienced through theories. No systematic analysis can comprehend it. Why? Because heart flows with the heavenly law and with nature.

It does not matter how well you know theology. You cannot understand the Bible unless you interpret it by the flow and feeling of heart. The current theological trend will pass away, but the world of heart remains forever. It is the alpha and omega, the first and the last, the beginning and the end. (8:305-06, February 14, 1960)

Some prayerful people consider nature to be the number one Bible. It does not take second place. The Bible that describes the history of Israel does not always give a clear message. Do you know how much I shook my head as I read it? It can be very ambiguous; people understand what they want from it, as if it were a fortune-teller telling their fortune. For some it is a way to escape from reality. So the natural world created by God is better than the Bible at carrying out the hard task of judging the facts and clarifying everything from beginning to end. (20:270, July 7, 1968)

Why does the Bible sometimes seem to be leading us toward the Kingdom of Heaven and sometimes not? The present world is not the Kingdom of Heaven. It is encircled by the satanic world... God's champions today, like the prophets and sages of Israel and the saints of the early Christian church whom we know from the Bible, are like God's secret agents sent on missions in the satanic world.

When the CIA and the KGB send their agents into enemy territory, they take pains not to reveal their plans to the enemy. The CIA bureau chief notifies his agents about their missions using a secret code that he alone knows. Likewise, the Bible contains God's most important directives to His operatives, but as coded messages that God alone understands. For example, in describing the Last Days Jesus said, "But of that day and hour no one knows, not even the angels of heaven, nor the Son, but the Father only." (Matt. 24.36) Hence it stands to reason that when the Last Days arrive, God will send another prophet to decipher the code, as it is written in Amos 3.7, "Surely the LORD God does nothing without revealing His secret to His servants the prophets."

To have that secret revealed to you, you must directly connect with God. That is why it is said that you should go into your secret chamber, anoint your head with oil, and have a show-down prayer with God. Now that we know the Bible contains coded messages, it is evident that we will be judged if we interpret its symbols and parables carelessly. (73:207-08, September 18, 1974)

3. Do Not Get Caught up in the Letter of the Scriptures; the Letter Is but a Gateway to the Spirit

The written code kills, but the Spirit gives life.
2 Corinthians 3.6

Lord Mahavira said to Gautama, "When Dharma is not seen by the seer directly it is seen through the wire mesh of words. Conjecture is the wire mesh that covers that window. Multiple sects and systems result from such an indirect observation. The path suggested to you, Gautama, is the direct path of the seer. Be vigilant and a seer of Dharma."
Uttaradhyayana Sutra 10.31 (Jainism)

Mahamati, let the son or daughter of a good family take good heed not to get attached to words as being in perfect conformity with meaning, because truth is not of the letter. Be not like the one who looks at the fingertip. When a man with his fingertip points out something to somebody, the fingertip may be taken wrongly for the thing pointed at. In like manner, simple and ignorant people are unable even unto their death to abandon the idea that in the fingertip of words there is the meaning itself, and will not grasp ultimate reality because of their intent clinging to words, which are no more than the fingertip.... Be not like one who, grasping his own fingertip, sees the meaning there. You should rather energetically discipline yourself to get at the meaning itself.
Lankavatara Sutra 76 (Buddhism)

The fish trap exists because of the fish; once you've gotten the fish, you can forget the trap. The rabbit snare exists because of the rabbit; once you've gotten the rabbit, you can forget the snare. Words exist because of meaning; once you've gotten the meaning, you can forget the words. Where can I find a man who has forgotten words so I can have a word with him?

Chuang Tzu 26 (Taoism)

O monks, a man is on a journey. He comes to a vast stretch of water. On this side the shore is dangerous, but on the other it is safe and without danger. No boat goes to the other shore which is safe and without danger, nor is there any bridge for crossing over. He says to himself, 'This sea of water is vast, and the shore on this side is full of danger; but on the other shore it is safe and without danger. No boat goes to the other side, nor is there a bridge for crossing over. It would be good therefore if I would gather grass, wood, branches, and leaves to make a raft, and with the help of the raft cross over safely to the other side, exerting myself with my hands and feet.' Then that man gathers grass, wood, branches, and leaves and makes a raft, and with the help of that raft crosses over safely to the other side, exerting himself with his hands and feet. Having crossed over and got ten to the other side, he thinks, "This raft was of great help to me. With its aid I have crossed safely over to this side, exerting myself with my hands and feet. It would be good if I carry this raft on my head or on my back wherever I go."

What do you think, O monks: if he acted in this way would that man be acting properly with regard to the raft? [No, Sir.] In which way, then, would he be acting properly with regard to the raft?

Having crossed and gone over to the other side, suppose that man should think, "This raft was a great help to me. With its aid I have crossed safely over to this side, exerting myself with my hands and feet. It would be good if I beached this raft on the shore, or moored it and left it afloat, and then went on my way wherever it may be." Acting in this way would that man act properly with regard to the raft.

In the same manner, O monks, I have taught a doctrine similar to a raft—it is for crossing over, and not for carrying. You who understand that the teaching is similar to a raft, should give up attachment to even the good Dhamma; how much more then should you give up evil things.

Majjhima Nikaya 1.134-35:
Parable of the Raft (Buddhism)

Teachings of Sun Myung Moon

Fallen people's spiritual sensibility is extremely dull. Hence, they generally tend to adhere strictly to the letter of the truth in their efforts to follow God's providence. Such people cannot readily adjust themselves to the dispensation of the new age, even though the providence of restoration is moving toward it. They are generally too strongly attached to the outdated perspective provided by the doctrines of the old age. This is well illustrated by the case of the Jewish people of Jesus' day who were so attached to the Old Testament that they could not respond to Jesus' call to open a new chapter of the providence. On the other hand, those believers who receive divine inspiration through prayer are able to grasp spiritually the providence of the new age. Even though this may put them at odds with the doctrines of the old age, they will still respond to the promptings of the spirit and follow the calling of the new providence. (*Exposition of the Divine Principle,* Eschatology 5.2)

4. Scriptures Teach Only a Finite Portion of Heaven's Truth

And if all the trees in the earth were pens, and the sea, with seven more seas to help it [were ink], the words of God could not be spent. Lo! God is Mighty, Wise.

Qur'an 31.27

All the Scriptures mean as much—no more, no less—
to the discerning spiritual man
As a water tank
in a universal flood.

Bhagavad-Gita 2.45-46 (Hinduism)

The water from the ocean contained in a pot can neither be called an ocean nor non-ocean, but it can be called only part of the ocean. Similarly, a doctrine, though arising from the Absolute Truth, is neither the Truth nor not the Truth.

Vidyanandi, Tattvarthaslokavartika 116 (Jainism)

The Word is measured in four quarters.
The wise who possess insight know these four divisions.
Three quarters, concealed in secret, cause no movement.
The fourth is the quarter that is spoken by men.

Rig Veda 1.164.45 (Hinduism)

The Torah we have is the incomplete form of heavenly wisdom.

Genesis Rabbah 17.5 (Judaism)

I have yet many things to say to you, but you cannot bear them now. When the Spirit of truth comes, he will guide you into all the truth.[12]

John 16.12-13

Every term has a Book. God blots out, and He establishes whatsoever He will; and with Him is the Essence of the Book.
Whether We show you a part of that We promise them, or We call you unto Us, it is you only to deliver the message, and Ours is the reckoning.[13]

Qur'an 13.39-40

Now it happened to the venerable Malunkyaputta, being in seclusion and plunged in meditation, that a consideration presented itself to his mind: "These theories which the Blessed One has left unelucidated, has set aside and rejected—that the world is eternal, that the world is not eternal, that the world is finite, that the world is infinite, that the soul and the body are identical, that the soul is one thing and the body another, that the saint exists after death, that the saint does not exist after death... these the Blessed One does not elucidate to me. And the fact that the Blessed One does not elucidate them to me does not please me..."

[The Buddha]: "If, Malunkyaputta, a man had been wounded by an arrow thickly smeared with poison, and his friends and companions, relatives and kinsfolk, were to procure for him a physician or surgeon; and the sick man were to say, 'I will not have this arrow taken out until I have learnt whether the man who wounded me belonged to the warrior caste, or the brahmin caste, or to the farmers' caste, or to the menial caste.'

"Or again he were to say, 'I will not have this arrow taken out until I have learnt the name of the man who wounded me, and to what clan he belongs.'

"Or again he were to say, 'I will not have this arrow taken out until I have learnt whether the man who wounded me was tall, or short, or of middle height.'

"Or again he were to say, 'I will not have this arrow taken out until I have learnt whether the man who wounded me was black, or dusky, or of a yellow skin.'

"Or again he were to say, 'I will not have this arrow taken out until I have learnt whether the man who wounded me was from this or that village, town, or city.'... That man would die, Malunkyaputta, without ever having learnt this.

"In exactly the same way, Malunkyaputta, any one who should say, 'I will not lead the religious life under the Blessed One until the Blessed One shall elucidate to me either that the world is eternal or that the world is not eternal, etc.'—that person would die before the Tathagata had ever elucidated this to him.

"The religious life does not depend on the dogma that the world is eternal; nor does the religious life depend on the dogma that the world is not eternal. Whether the dogma obtain, that the world is eternal, or that the world is not eternal, there still remain birth, old age, death, sorrow, lamentation, misery, grief, despair, for the extinction of which in the present life I am prescribing... This profits not, nor has to do with the fundamentals of religion, nor tends to aversion, absence of passion, cessation, quiescence, the supernatural faculties, supreme wisdom, and Nirvana; therefore have I not elucidated it."

Majjhima Nikaya 1.426-31 *(Buddhism)*

Teachings of Sun Myung Moon

Spirit and truth are unique, eternal and unchanging. However, the degree and scope of their teaching and the means of their expression will vary from one age to another as they restore humankind from a state of utter ignorance. For example, in the age prior to the Old Testament, when people were still unenlightened and could not directly receive the Word of truth, God commanded them to make sacrificial offerings as a substitute for the Word. In the course of time, the spirituality and intellect of human beings were elevated to the point when, in Moses' day, God granted them the Law, and at the time of Jesus He gave the Gospel. Jesus made it clear that his words were not the truth itself; rather, he declared that he himself was "the way, the truth, and the life." (John 14:6) Jesus was the incarnation of the truth. His words were just a means by which he expressed himself. Thus, the scope and depth of Jesus' words and the method of his teaching varied according to whom he was speaking.

In this sense, we must understand that the verses in the Bible are only one means of expressing the truth and are not the truth itself. The New Testament is but an interim textbook given to enlighten the people of two thousand years ago, whose spiritual and intellectual levels were far lower than today. The modern, scientific-minded thirst for the truth cannot be satisfied by expressions of truth which are limited in scope and couched in symbols and parables aimed specifically at instructing the people of an earlier age. For modern, intellectual people to be enlightened in the truth, there must appear another textbook of higher and richer content, with a more scientific method of expression. (*Exposition of the Divine Principle*, Eschatology 5.1)

Intellectual Knowledge and Spiritual Wisdom

THERE IS A HUGE DIFFERENCE BETWEEN INTELLECTUAL knowledge and the spiritual truth that is conducive to salvation and enlightenment. Intellectual and conceptual knowledge, for all its utility in the world, does not always profit the spiritual seeker, and too much of it may even impede higher realization. There is a gulf between Athens and Jerusalem—between the conceptual systems of secular philosophy and the scriptural truth of religion. Scriptures call us to check our priorities, as we live in an age that pushes secular learning.

A second topic of this section concerns ways of knowing. While intellectual knowledge is gained through empirical perception of sense data and rational formulation of theories, spiritually minded people employ intuition and sensitivity to the inner dimensions of reality. Reliance upon reason can be an impediment to the spiritual path; hence much religious practice, such as Zen Buddhism, is aimed at blocking the intellect. For instance the Zen koan, "Has a dog the Buddha nature?" only leads the questioner into a welter of mental confusion until he realizes that the way out is beyond any conceptual understanding whatsoever. Nevertheless, Father Moon regards both the paths of rationality and spirituality as having their place in the Kingdom, and seeks for a balance.

The final texts return to the opposition between secular knowledge and divine knowledge, focusing particularly on the damage caused by science and technology when it is not restrained or directed by spiritual wisdom. Ultimately science and all secular knowledge needs to be guided by what Father Moon calls "absolute values,"—the true love of God that seeks to benefit humanity and the whole creation.

1. Intellectual Knowledge Does Not Profit for Salvation

What has Athens to do with Jerusalem?
      Tertullian *(Christianity)*

Knowledge puffs up, but love builds up. If any one imagines that he knows something, he does not yet know as he ought to know. But if one loves God, one is known by Him.
      1 Corinthians 8.1-3

My now-deceased mother really scolded me. She said, "Go away somewhere into the wilderness, since all you seem to do is look at books. For all the days to come you will be pitiful because the book blocks your path. Never will anything be revealed to you in a vision, for you live like a white man."
      Delaware Testimony *(Native American Religions)*

Of making many books there is no end, and much study is a weariness of the flesh.
      Ecclesiastes 12.12

A thousand and hundred thousand feats of intellect shall not accompany man in the hereafter.
      Adi Granth, Japuji 1, M.1, p. 1 *(Sikhism)*

This is true knowledge: to seek the Self as the true end of wisdom always. To seek anything else is ignorance.
      Bhagavad-Gita 13.11 *(Hinduism)*

Though I reach a high rung of knowledge, I know that not a single letter of the teachings is within me, and I have not taken a single step in the service of God.
      The Baal Shem Tov *(Judaism)*

True words are not fine-sounding;
Fine-sounding words are not true.
The good man does not prove by argument;
And he who proves by argument is not good.
True wisdom is different from much learning;
Much learning means little wisdom.
      Tao Te Ching 81 *(Taoism)*

Of all things seen in the world
Only mind is the host;
By grasping forms according to interpretation
It becomes deluded, not true to reality.

All philosophies in the world
Are mental fabrications;
There has never been a single doctrine
By which one could enter the true essence of things.
      Garland Sutra 10 *(Buddhism)*

Where is the wise man? Where is the scribe? Where is the debater of this age? Has not God made foolish the wisdom of the world? For since, in the wisdom of God, the world did not know God through wisdom, it pleased God through the folly of what we preach to save those who believe. For the Jews demand signs and the Greeks seek wisdom, but we preach Christ crucified, a stumbling block to Jews and folly to Gentiles, but to those who are called, both Jews and Greeks, Christ the power of God and the wisdom of God. For the foolishness of God is wiser than men, and the weakness of God is stronger than men.

1 Corinthians 1.20-25

Rabbi Eleazar Hisma said, "Offerings of birds and purifications of women, these, yea these, are the essential precepts. Astronomy and geometry are but fringes to wisdom."[14]

Mishnah, Avot 3.23 (Judaism)

It was necessary for human salvation that certain truths which exceed human reason should be made known to him by divine revelation. Even as regards those truths about God which human reason could have discovered, it was necessary that humans be taught by a divine revelation; because the truth about God such as reason could discover would only be known by a few, and that after a long time, and with the admixture of many errors. Whereas humankind's whole salvation, which is in God, depends upon the knowledge of this truth. Therefore, in order that human salvation might be brought about more fitly and more surely, it was necessary that they be taught divine truths by divine revelation. Therefore, besides philosophical science built up by reason, there necessarily should be a sacred science learned through revelation.

Thomas Aquinas, Summa Theologica 1.1.1 (Christianity)

The whole object of the Prophets and the Sages was to declare that a limit is set to human reason where it must halt.[15]

Maimonides, Guide of the Perplexed 1.32 (Judaism)

Human philosophy has made God manlike. Christian Science makes man Godlike. The first is error; the latter is truth. Metaphysics is above physics, and matter does not enter into metaphysical premises or conclusions. The categories of metaphysics rest on one basis, the divine Mind.

Science and Health, 269 (Christian Science)

Teachings of Sun Myung Moon

The ideal world will not be realized based upon the human brain but upon God's love. (*Way of God's Will* 1.8)

Philosophy and religion have different starting-points. Philosophy [at its best] is a human quest in search of God, but religion is the path laid out for us to meet God and begin to live with God. (187:70, March 19, 1989)

Extensive reading of sacred texts and philosophy books that line library shelves does not enable you to achieve unity of mind and body. (May 1, 2004)

Know that no amount of knowledge will enable you to fulfill the ideal of creation. Neither knowledge, nor power, nor money avail us to fulfill God's ideal of creation. Only with love can we fulfill it. The same goes for the purpose of our life—only with love can we accomplish it. Therefore, parents who push their children to study all day long [thinking that it is the only way to success], are making a serious mistake. (144:130, April 12, 1986)

Do not boast because you attend a first-rank university. I do not regard it as such a great thing. Maybe you study seven hours per day—that amounts to about 2,000 hours in a year, but if you divide it by 24 hours it is not that many days. It is nothing to brag about.
    Love is far more precious, and it cannot be learned so quickly. Love is absolute and eternal, so you cannot master it even in your whole lifetime. You can receive a Ph.D. after studying a field of

secular knowledge for a few years, but you cannot get the diploma of love even after 30 or 40 years, because the field of love is without limit. Love keeps expanding, only to circle around and return to the starting-point. You can spend an infinite amount of time studying love. Nevertheless, you never grow tired of it. It is just fun, filled with more happiness, gratitude and dignity than anything else in the world. (113:324-25, May 10, 1981)

If you are so cocksure of your intellectual prowess, go ahead and see where it leads you. The story of your demise will simply become another cautionary tale in the textbook for raising true sons and daughters. (60:75, August 6, 1972)

Absolute value relates to love and emotion, not intellect. Love is the highest value, containing the purpose of existence and the perfection of existence. True love is such that both the giver and the recipient are happy. Love is not something to be learned. It should sprout and be experienced directly in a person's original mind.

The world of intellect develops through cognition, but the world of emotion does not. Therefore, absolute value remains in the dimension of absolute love, not intellect. From this perspective, the First Cause cannot be found within the sphere of our cognition but is experienced in an emotional dimension.

Values lacking love do not last forever; they are changeable and someday will vanish. Philosophies and teachings up to the present time have been helpful to humankind in some respects, but in other respects they have misled the development of thought and the progress of history. Hence, it is inevitable that we re-evaluate our value systems. (102:59, November 25, 1978)

2. Attaining Spiritual Wisdom

The kami-faith is caught, not taught.
                                Shinto Proverb

A monk asked Joshu, "Has a dog the Buddha nature?"

Joshu answered, "Mu [Emptiness]."

Mumon's comment: To attain this subtle realization, you must completely cut off the way of thinking.[16]
                                Mumonkan 1 (*Buddhism*)

Pure Knowing has nothing to do with hearing much.
                                Wang Yangming (*Confucianism*)

God is spirit, and those who worship Him must worship in spirit and truth.
                                John 4.24-25

Now we have received not the spirit of the world, but the Spirit which is from God, that we might understand the gifts bestowed on us by God. And we impart this in words not taught by human wisdom but taught by the Spirit, interpreting spiritual truths to those who possess the Spirit. The unspiritual man does not receive the gifts of the Spirit of God, for they are folly to him, and he is not able to understand them because they are spiritually discerned. The spiritual man judges all things, but is himself to be judged by no one. "For who has known the mind of the Lord so as to instruct him?" But we have the mind of Christ.
                                1 Corinthians 2.12-16

In the heart of the enlightened man there is a window opening on the realities of the spiritual world, so that he knows, not by hearsay or traditional belief, but by actual experience, what produces wretchedness or happiness in the soul just as clearly and decidedly as the physician knows what produces sickness or health in the body. He recognizes that knowledge of God and worship are medicinal, and that ignorance and sin are deadly poisons for the soul. Many even so-called "learned" men, from blindly following others' opinions, have no real certainty in their beliefs regarding the happiness or misery of souls in the next world, but he who will attend to the matter with a mind unbiased by prejudice will arrive at clear convictions on this matter.

Al-Ghazzali, *The Alchemy of Happiness* (Islam)

Knowledge is of five kinds, namely: sensory knowledge, scriptural knowledge, clairvoyance, telepathy, and omniscience. These five kinds of knowledge are of two types: the first two kinds are indirect knowledge and the remaining three constitute direct knowledge. In sensory knowledge... there is only the apprehension of indistinct things... But clairvoyance, telepathy, and omniscience is direct knowledge; it is perceived by the soul in a vivid manner without the intermediary of the senses or the scriptures.

Tattvarthasutra 1.19-29 (Jainism)

Teachings of Sun Myung Moon

We should cultivate the heart of true love through experience. True love cannot be learned through the spoken or written word, or through general education. This is how it was in the beginning. Adam and Eve, who were created as infants, were to grow and experience love at each stage of life, perfecting in turn the heart of true children, the heart of true brother and sister, and the heart of true parents. Only by experiencing each of these kinds of love, can we become ideal people who fulfill the purpose of creation. (282:209, March 13, 1997)

There are generally two types of people: the intellectual type and the spiritual type. When intellectual type people search for an answer, if their research coincides with their reasoning they accept it, but if it does not they reject it. Spiritual type people are more intuitive, making decisions based on intuition more than reason. People of the spiritual type feel from inside and apply it to the outside, while the intellectual type experience the outside and apply it in the inside. One type is extroverted and the other, introverted.

Intellectual type people usually do not like to pray. They resist praying and question the need for it. They do not feel comfortable calling out, "Heavenly Father!" They do not feel that it is real. Prayer, God, etc. appear to them like superstition. Since they don't believe in prayer, they feel to pray would be to deny their integrity. They judge the truth of something by whether it agrees with their theoretical model of the world. Spiritual type people, on the other hand, love saying the words, "Heavenly Father" from birth. They delight in prayer, and do not need any explanation.

Intellectual type people cannot launch a revolutionary spiritual movement. In the world of faith, those who can do something extraordinary are not intellectuals, but are rather uninformed and simple-minded people who are spiritual. They do what comes to them, disregarding what the world says. Believing that God told them to do it, they just go ahead and do it. After doing it, they find that what they did turned out to be right. Great persons can appear from among such spiritual people.

The apostle Paul was an intellectual type person. Nevertheless, after having a spiritual experience on the road to Damascus, he totally changed. Having felt something explosive from inside that was greater than anything he had experienced from external investigation, he came to deny everything he had been taught and accepted his new experience as the truth. Hence, he could become the pioneer of a new revolutionary religion, Christianity.

You should know which type of person you are. In general, spiritual people are thick in spirit but pointy in intellect. Therefore, although they may be solid in the beginning, they will not be consistent all the way, and after a time their works often fail. By the same token, although a person of truth may be strong, if his spirituality is weak his works will also eventually fall short. Therefore, whichever type of person we are, we need to balance these two aspects.

There is a saying, "Worship God in spirit and truth." (John 4.23) It means that people should make these two sides parallel and find harmony between them. We should be able to control both the spirit world and the physical world. Standing in the center of spirituality and rationality, we should be able to make adjustments between the right and the left. Otherwise, we cannot reach perfection. (76:136-37, February 2, 1975)

Fallen people have been overcoming their internal ignorance by enlightening their spirituality and intellect with "spirit and truth" (John 4:23)...

"Spirit" in this context denotes the inspiration of Heaven. Cognition of a spiritual reality begins when it is perceived through the five senses of the spirit self. These perceptions resonate through the five physical senses and are felt physiologically. Cognition of truth, on the other hand, arises from the knowledge gleaned from the physical world as it is perceived directly through our physiological sense organs. Cognition thus takes place through both spiritual and physical processes.

Human beings become complete only when their spirit self and physical self are unified. Hence, the experience of divine inspiration gained through spiritual cognition and the knowledge of truth obtained through physical cognition should become fully harmonized and awaken the spirituality and intellect together. It is only when the spiritual and physical dimensions of cognition resonate together that we can thoroughly comprehend God and the universe. (*Exposition of the Divine Principle*, Eschatology 5.1)

3. The Danger of Highly-Developed Knowledge When Spiritual Wisdom Is Lacking

The intuitive mind is a sacred gift and the rational mind is a faithful servant. We have created a society that honors the servant and has forgotten the gift.

Albert Einstein

Who is wise and understanding among you? By his good life let him show his works in the meekness of wisdom. But if you have bitter jealousy and selfish ambition in your hearts, do not boast and be false to the truth. This wisdom is not such as comes down from above, but is earthly, unspiritual, devilish. For where jealousy and selfish ambition exist, there will be disorder and every vile practice. But wisdom from above is first pure, then peaceable, gentle, open to reason, full of mercy and good fruits, without uncertainty or insincerity.

James 3.13-17

Love without wisdom means love without discrimination. Wisdom without humanity means knowledge not translated into action. Therefore, humanity is to love mankind and wisdom is to remove its evil.

Tung Chung-Shu (*Confucianism*)

Science is one thing; wisdom is another. Science is an edged tool, with which men play like children, and cut their own fingers.

Sir Arthur Eddington

Know verily that knowledge is of two kinds: divine and satanic. The one wells out from the fountain of divine inspiration; the other is but a reflection of vain and obscure thoughts. The source of the former is God Himself; the motive force of the latter the whisperings of selfish desire. The one is guided by the principle: "Fear God; God will teach you"; the other is but a confirmation of the truth: "Knowledge is the most grievous veil between man and his Creator." The former brings forth the fruit of patience, of longing desire, of true understanding, and love; while the latter can yield naught but arrogance, vainglory, and conceit.

Book of Certitude 69 (Baha'i Faith)

As long as men in high places covet knowledge and are without the Way, the world will be in great confusion. How do I know this is so? Knowledge enables men to fashion bows, crossbows, nets, stringed arrows, and like contraptions, but when this happens the birds flee in confusion to the sky. Knowledge enables men to fashion fishhooks, lures, seines, dragnets, trawls, and weirs, but when this happens the fish flee in confusion to the depths of the water. Knowledge enables men to fashion pitfalls, snares, cages, traps, and gins, but when this happens the beasts flee in confusion to the swamps. And the flood of rhetoric that enables men to invent wily schemes and poisonous slanders, the glib gabble of "hard" and "white," the foul fustian of "same" and "different," bewilder the understanding of common men. So the world is dulled and darkened by great confusion. The blame lies in the coveting of knowledge.

In the world everyone knows enough to pursue what he does not know, but no one knows enough to pursue what he already knows. Everyone knows enough to condemn what he takes to be no good, but no one knows enough to condemn what he has already taken to be good. This is how the great confusion comes about, blotting out the brightness of sun and moon above, searing the vigor of hills and streams below, overturning the round of the four seasons in between. There is no insect that creeps and crawls, no creature that flutters and flies, that has not lost its inborn nature. So great is the confusion of the world that comes from coveting knowledge!

Chuang Tzu 10 (Taoism)

The unleashed power of the atom has changed everything save our modes of thinking, and we thus drift towards unparalleled catastrophes.

Albert Einstein

Teachings of Sun Myung Moon

We should admit that the various sciences and philosophies today have failed in solving the world's problems. The grand promise of natural science has too often been used for evil purposes instead of for the true happiness of humanity. The social sciences have been corrupted due to the influence of partisan political interests and thus have played a dysfunctional role on many occasions. Philosophy has become a lifeless study, having given up the great pursuit of the ultimate ideals of human beings. This trend is becoming more serious because of the passive attitude of many scholars.

I think that scholars should not be satisfied only with carrying on their own research. They should respond to the call of the world, which is in need of active guidance. The world demands responsible action by scholars who enlist their capabilities for the good of mankind in accordance with a right value perspective. (170:268-70, November 27, 1987)

Human beings are creations of God, created to lead life with a definite value perspective in accordance with the purpose of creation. Yet people have disregarded this value perspective and taken science as a panacea, believing it to be omnipotent. Consequently, technology has become a source of increasing damage.

In human life, science can only be a means; it cannot be an end. The purpose of human life is to realize God's purpose of creation. A human being is a unified being of both physical and spiritual entities. Hence, on the foundation of physical life, he is to lead a life of value—a life of love, truth, goodness and beauty. Technology is needed only for the convenience of physical life, which will allow physical life to become a proper basis for spiritual life. Therefore science that disregards or fails to emphasize the life of value actually brings about the destruction of humanity's value perspective, leading to today's reality of fear and insecurity. Only searching for and discovering the true value perspective can achieve the deliverance of humankind from this unfortunate reality. Science, in turn, must be in accord with this value perspective, which, needless to say, must be based on absolute value.

Where can the absolute value be found? It can only be found in God's love. Truth, goodness and beauty, when they are based on God's love, are elevated to the absolute value itself. In the end, human beings can only avoid the harm that misuse of science and technology brings when science itself recognizes God and people use technology in accordance with God's love. (106:53, November 23, 1979)

In the library at the University of Cambridge, I saw tens of thousands of rare books in cases. I looked around to see who was studying them, but there was no one; only the librarian was there. This showed me that the age had passed when knowledge ruled the world and the pen was mightier than the sword. Money controls the world now.

Money is the element through which Satan rules the world today. Yet Satan rules the world through knowledge as well. As people seek knowledge of the external world through science, they forget about God, and in the end they lose God. Meanwhile, philosophy, which should form the backbone of knowledge, extols materialism and holds that God does not exist. Theology, which should be the head of knowledge, claims that God is dead...

Instead of believing that human beings are descended from God, intellectuals now believe that humankind is descended from the apes. Does that make God happy? Not at all. Because of ideas like that, God would sometimes like to smash the walls of the universities. (99:103-104, September 1, 1978)

The Teacher

TEACHERS SHOULD SET A GOOD EXAMPLE of integrity in their own teachings and impart moral teachings in accord with their own high standard of conduct. They should have mature faith, rich experience, and discernment to treat each student in the way that best suits the student's individual temperament and interests. They should regard their task as not merely to impart knowledge, but also to motivate and inspire their students with a vision for their lives. Most of all, the best teachers have the heart of a parent, training their students as they would their own children.

The ability to teach is a gift from God, and teachers are in a sense partners with God the divine Teacher. Therefore, good teachers show God's unconditional love by devoting themselves to all who wish to learn regardless of their ability to pay. When they lecture, they are mindful that God may wish to use them as His mouthpiece. The final passages thus describe teaching as a divine calling. These include examples of Father Moon's advice to pastors about delivering a sermon.

1. Qualities of a Good Teacher

Teachers train the pupil in what they have been trained; they make him hold fast to moral precepts; they thoroughly instruct him in the lore of every subject; they speak well of him among his friends and companions; they counsel him for his safety and benefit.

Digha Nikaya 3.185-91, Sigalovada Sutta *(Buddhism)*

Set the believers an example in speech and conduct, in love, in faith, in purity. Till I come, attend to the public reading of scripture, to preaching, to teaching. Do not neglect the gift you have, which was given you by prophetic utterance when the council of elders laid their hands upon you. Practice these duties, devote yourself to them, so that all may see your progress. Take heed to yourself and to your teaching; hold to that, for by so doing you will save both yourself and your hearers.[17]

1 Timothy 4.12-16

The teacher, brethren, should regard the pupil as his son. The pupil should regard the teacher as his father. Thus these two, by mutual reverence and deference joined, dwelling in community of life, will win increase, growth, progress in this Norm-discipline.

Vinaya Pitaka, Mahavagga 3.1 *(Buddhism)*

As in the sky flies the white-clothed crane,
Keeping its mind behind,
In its heart continually remembering its young ones;
So the true Guru keeps the disciple absorbed in the love of God,
And also keeps him in his heart.

Adi Granth, Gauri, M.4 *(Sikhism)*

When, therefore, anyone takes the name of Abbot he should govern his disciples by a twofold teaching; namely, he should show them all that is good and holy by his deeds more than by his words; explain the commandments of God to intelligent disciples by words, but show the divine precepts to the dull and simple by his works.

Saint Benedict of Nursia, The Benedictine Rule 2 *(Christianity)*

Harun ar-Rashid said to his son's tutor, "I have delivered to you my own blood and the treasure of my soul. You have authority over him and he has to obey you, so be worthy of the trust that the Caliph of all Muslims has placed in you. Let him recite the Qur'an, teach him history and read him poetry. Teach him the traditions of the Messenger and politeness of speech, and not to laugh except when it is appropriate. Let no hour pass without teaching him something that will benefit him, but do not hurt him, as this may quash his thoughts, causing him to love idleness and become familiar with it. Correct him with kindness and compassion. Only if he refuses to obey can you use punishment and force."

Ibn Khaldun,[18] *Raising Children in Islam (Islam)*

Confucius said, "The thought that,

I have left my moral power untended,
My learning unperfected;
I have heard of righteous men, but have been unable to go to them,
I have heard of evil men, but have been unable to reform them.

—it is these thoughts that disquiet me."

Analects 7.3 *(Confucianism)*

Teachings of Sun Myung Moon

Professors should inculcate in their students strong determination and clear values for meeting the challenges of the times. In this sense, professors and religious leaders share a common task. More than merely transmitting knowledge and publishing the results of their research, they should inspire their students to live a life of responsibility. (130:16, December 18, 1983)

Everyone should meet at least one mentor in his life on whom he can totally depend, to whom he can offer himself unconditionally, whom he can trust never to violate his heart, and to whom he can entrust everything he has and feel totally at ease. In this way he can understand the heart of God. He can taste the heart of a true child in relation to his Heavenly Father. (4:168, April 6, 1958)

Teachers, you should protect your school as you would your own home, with a sense of ownership. You should teach your students as you would your own children, with the heart of a father or mother.[19] (203:308, June 27, 1990)

Teachers should educate their students with love, standing in the place of parents (*in loco parentis*). They should teach with love that is eternal, building ties with their students that last beyond their school days. They should make such efforts to form such deep, loving relationships with their students that they never forget them for the rest of their lives.

True teachers imbue their teaching with love. They do not teach just to earn a living; they teach out of an irrepressible love and desire to teach, even at great personal cost. Teachers and students should have such a relationship that, night or day, the teachers long to meet them and convey their knowledge—always with love, and the students are eager to receive it. (127:17, May 1, 1983)

Schoolteachers who care for their nation's destiny dedicate themselves to inculcate their students with the proper values. Holding their hands and with tears in their eyes they tell their students, "More than you have obeyed me, be loyal to your nation." Students who receive such teaching will fulfill their teachers' hopes. When dedicated teachers regard the nation and the world as more precious than themselves, and when parents raise their children with sincerity while upholding the nation and world above their families, they will educate those young people to become the future pillars of the nation. (25:98, September 30, 1969)

Teachers and professors have a great deal of influence on young people. However, their parents influence them even more. It is the family that exerts the most influence on the formation of an individual's character.

The family is the school of love, the most important school in life. In the family, children expand the capacity of their hearts through education in love and emotions that only parents can provide. This becomes the cornerstone to form the children's character. Further, the family is the school teaching virtues and norms. Education in academics, sports, technology, etc., should be given on the foundation of this primary education in heart and norms; this is the heaven-designed way.

Hence, just as parents should become true parents and give their children true love, they also should become true teachers and educate their children properly in heart and norms. Though children may not be aware of their parents' role as true teachers, inevitably they learn from them and come to resemble them. The role of parents is that important. (271:80-81, August 22, 1995)

2. Teachers that Value Their Students

Confucius said, "From the very poorest upwards—beginning even with the man who could bring no better present than a bundle of dried flesh—none has ever come to me without receiving instruction."

Analects 7.7 *(Confucianism)*

I teach young children, and I treat the children of the poor exactly the same as the children of the rich. Those that cannot afford to pay, I teach without charge. Since I am also a fisherman, to encourage those who do not wish to come and learn I give them each a fish to take home.

Talmud, Taanit 24a *(Judaism)*

And he told this parable: "A man had a fig tree planted in his vineyard; and he came seeking fruit on it and found none. And he said to the vinedresser, 'Lo, these three years I have come seeking fruit on this fig tree, and I find none. Cut it down; why should it use up the ground?' And he answered him, 'Let it alone, sir, this year also, till I dig about it and put on manure. And if it bears fruit next year, well and good; but if not, you can cut it down.'"

Luke 13.6-9

The sage always excels in saving people, and so abandons no one;
Always excels in saving things, and so abandons nothing.
This is called following one's discernment.
Hence the good man is the teacher the bad learns from;
And the bad man is the material the good works on.
Not to value the teacher
Nor to love the material
Though it seems clever, betrays great bewilderment.

Tao Te Ching 27 *(Taoism)*

There are four types of men:
The man who has knowledge and is aware of it is a scholar—follow him.
The man who has a great deal of knowledge but is not aware of what he has is asleep—wake him up.
The man who knows nothing and is aware that he knows nothing is ignorant—teach him.
The man who knows nothing but is not aware that he knows nothing is a devil—avoid him.

Al-Ghazzali, Ihia' Ulum el-Din 59.1 *(Islam)*

The Master said, "Only one who bursts with eagerness do I instruct; only one who bubbles with enthusiasm do I enlighten. If I hold up one corner and a man cannot come back to me with the other three, I do not continue the lesson."

Analects 7.8 *(Confucianism)*

Socrates to Ischomachus: "Does teaching consist in putting questions?"

[Ischomachus replies]: "Indeed, the secret of your system has just this instant dawned upon me. I seem to see the principle in which you put your questions. You lead me through the field of my own knowledge, and then by pointing out analogies to what I know, persuade me that I really know some things which hitherto, as I believed, I had no knowledge of."

Socrates, in Xenophon, *Oeconomicus* *(Hellenism)*

Much Torah have I learned from my teachers, more from my colleagues, but from my students most of all.

Talmud, Taanit 7a *(Judaism)*

Even when walking in a party of no more than three I can always be certain of learning from those I am with. There will be good qualities that I can select for imitation and bad ones that will teach me what requires correction in myself.

Analects 7.21 *(Confucianism)*

That which gives a sage his sageliness is fondness for learning and inquiry from inferiors. Take Shun: From the time when he plowed and sowed, exercised the potter's art, and was a fisherman, until he became emperor, there was no time when he was not learning from others how to practice goodness.

Chu Hsi (Confucianism)

Teachings of Sun Myung Moon

God does not demand that you exist for Him; rather, He says that He exists for you, His creations. Who are true parents: those who want their children to live for them, or those who live for their children? Likewise, who is a true teacher, the one who tells his students that they come to class only so he can earn a salary, or the one who says, "Even though you cannot afford to pay tuition, I will still teach you." A true teacher loves his pupils regardless, and would even sell his own suit to get money for a student's tuition. (104:210, May 6, 1979)

When you meet someone, do not treat him casually. Always consider whether he or she can teach you something. Have a hungry mind, eager to learn something new from him or her. You should discern right away whether to relate to that person as your subject partner or as your object partner. By attending to this point, you are always ready to learn. (76:132, February 2, 1975)

When a teacher gives an exam, he usually asks a few questions that he thinks the students do not know. If he has a class of 50, he gives a very tough problem to pick out which of his students is truly the best. The professor will make a special relationship with the student who solves that difficult problem. From then on, he will greet that student warmly and encourage him. If he puts forth a problem to you that nobody else was ever able to answer before and you find a way solve it, it becomes the basis for you to become his successor. (66:45, March 18, 1973)

God has been merciless to me. God opposed me every step of the way as I climbed up from the very bottom. Yet I endured it all because I knew that without me, God would be all alone. I passed all the tests, and now God believes in me.

It is the same with you. If a doctoral candidate writes an excellent dissertation, then his professor will say, "You have taught me something new; now you are my teacher." The professor and all his colleagues will approve of you and even boast about you. Will you do likewise, so I will be able to praise you through all the ages? (320:250, April 16, 2000)

3. Co-Teaching with God

This will be a time for you to bear testimony. Settle it therefore in your minds, not to meditate beforehand how to answer; for I will give you a mouth and wisdom, which none of your adversaries will be able to withstand or contradict.

Luke 21.13-15

I planted, Apollos watered, but God gave the growth. So neither he who plants nor he who waters is anything, but only God who gives the growth. He who plants and he who waters are equal, and each shall receive his wages according to his labor. For we are God's fellow workers; you are God's field.

1 Corinthians 3.6-8

He who sees through the eye tells proverbs.[20]

Igala Proverb *(African Traditional Religions)*

To many it is not given to hear of the Self. Many, though they hear of it, do not understand it. Wonderful is he who speaks of it. Intelligent is he who learns of it. Blessed is he who, taught by a good teacher, is able to understand it.

The truth of the Self cannot be fully understood when taught by an ignorant man, for opinions regarding it, not founded in knowledge, vary one from another. Subtler than the subtlest is this Self, and beyond all logic. Taught by a teacher who knows the Self and Brahman as one, a man leaves vain theory behind and attains to truth...

Words cannot reveal Him. Mind cannot reach Him. Eyes do not see Him. How then can He be comprehended, save when taught by those seers who indeed have known Him?

Katha Upanishad 1.2.7-8; 2.6.12 *(Hinduism)*

Teachings of Sun Myung Moon

God is the true teacher, who teaches with true love. (203:237, June 26, 1990)

When you stand at the podium to teach, believe that God is standing beside you. When you lecture, speak representing Jesus and all the founders of religion, and represent the president of the nation and its people. Believe that through your teaching, you can bring your students to a place where they can live with God. (148:277, June 5, 1977)

Through a life of prayer you can feel indescribable joy, even the joy [of anticipation] that God felt in His heart prior to creating all things. If you have a sincere, dedicated prayer life, you can reach the spiritual state where you know, "This is it!" That is the very position in which God stood when He was creating all things. In that mystical state of creating through the Word, you should proclaim the Word. Then people will definitely be touched by the Word. (29:321, March 13, 1970)

Had there been no Human Fall, we would have had God as our best parent and best teacher. Since God is full of love and knowledge, who could teach anything better? Yet in this fallen world, Satan says, "Go to the best university! Find a lover!" to capture young people for himself. Does American-style love have anything to do with God?

God still wants to teach us two things: "I am your True Teacher, and I am your True Parent." If we could only learn that, we would know everything. (102:233, January 1, 1979)

Discipleship

A STUDENT SHOULD SEEK OUT a good teacher to receive instruction and submit to discipline. He becomes more than merely a recipient of knowledge; he becomes a disciple. Discipling is a valuable part of education. It recognizes that a good education engages a student's entire being, to be molded and shaped by a course of training and instruction.

The relationship between teacher and disciple is typical of Eastern religions, which conceive of truth as embodiment more than as words. But we also find it in medicine and any field where learning requires mastering an art through a long apprenticeship.

This section concludes with passages that recognize the variable capacities of students to receive the truth. Again, this is not a matter of intelligence but rather of the heart. God tries to fill us with new wine, but if our wineskins are old they will burst. He wants to plant His seed in our hearts, but if our hearts are rocky soil, it will not take root. Therefore, a major task for the student of any spiritual path is to clear away the debris and make his or her heart ready to receive and respond to spiritual truth.

1. Apprenticing to a Good Teacher

If at any time there is doubt with regard to right conduct, follow the practice of great souls, who are guileless, of good judgment, and devoted to truth.

Taittiriya Upanishad 1.11.4 (Hinduism)

Let your house be a place of meeting for the wise, and dust yourself with the dust of their feet, and drink their words with thirst.

Mishnah, Avot 1.4 (Judaism)

One not knowing a land asks of one who knows it,
he goes forward instructed by the knowing one.
Such, indeed, is the blessing of instruction,
one finds a path that leads him straight onward.

Rig Veda 10.32.7 (Hinduism)

Approach someone who has realized the purpose of life and question him with reverence and devotion; he will instruct you in this wisdom. Once you attain it, you will never be deluded.

Bhagavad-Gita 4.34-35 (Hinduism)

Should one see a wise man, who, like a revealer of treasure, points out faults and reproves; let one associate with such a wise person; it will be better, not worse, for him who associates with such a one.

Let him advise, instruct, and dissuade one from evil; truly pleasing is he to the good, displeasing is he to the bad.

Dhammapada 76-77 (Buddhism)

I will follow the examples of the Buddhas from thought to thought. Even though the void of space has end, and the worlds of beings, the karmas of beings, the sorrows of beings all have end, yet my practice and following the examples of the Buddhas will not be ended. Thought succeeds thought without interruption, and in deeds of body, speech, and mind, without weariness.

Gandavyuha Sutra, Vows of Samantabhadra (Buddhism)

Arise! Awake! Approach the great and learn. Like the sharp edge of a razor is that path—so the wise say—hard to tread and difficult to cross.

Katha Upanishad 1.3.14 (Hinduism)

One man is much the same as another, and that he is best who is trained in the severest school.

Thucydides, The Peloponnesian War 1.84 (Hellenism)

Yen Hui said with a deep sigh, "The more I strain my gaze up towards it, the higher it soars. The deeper I bore down into it, the harder it becomes. I see it in front; but suddenly it is behind. Step by step the Master skillfully lures one on. He has broadened me with culture, restrained me with ritual. Even if I wanted to stop, I could not. Just when I feel that I have exhausted every resource, something seems to rise up, standing out sharp and clear. Yet though I long to pursue it, I can find no way of getting to it at all."²¹

Analects 9.10 *(Confucianism)*

When your view is the same as your teacher's, you destroy half your teacher's merit; when your view surpasses your teacher's, you are worthy to succeed him.²²

Mumonkan 17 *(Buddhism)*

Teachings of Sun Myung Moon

Do you know an earthly person with the character of God? Someone with the pure disposition of Jesus? Find that person and make him your friend. If you know a person of noble character, please follow him. If you know someone with a God-like disposition who brings harmony wherever he goes, follow him and attend him. Then you will surely gain the path of life. (2:318, July 7, 1957)

There is no life apart from the heart. The path through the valley of life is difficult and grim. When you seek a teacher, seek a teacher of the heart, not a teacher of knowledge. If you dig into the valley of the heart, the more you dig, the more tears you shed and the more your "self" disappears. (9:81, April 16, 1960)

Maybe you are someone with a talent for writing. After you write a particularly fine poem or essay, do you ever think, "I'm grateful to my teachers who taught me how to write well"? Do you ever miss your teachers and wonder how they were doing? Do you remember a teacher who made a striking impression on you with something he wrote on the blackboard? Truly, they made great efforts to educate you. Sometimes you resented a strict teacher who chastised you and gave you a hard time, but now you recognize that his training has made you a better writer. (104:278-79, June 1, 1979)

My idea is to give you an extremely hard time, in order to make you into filial children of God and loyal patriots in the service of your nation and the world. Should I strike you if you do not go this way? In the relation between father and child, elder brother and younger brother, or teacher and disciple, one should say firmly, "Father, please cut off my bone!" "Elder brother, please cut off my bone!" "Teacher, please cut off my bone!" It is true love to make someone overcome his present difficulties by kicking him with your foot. (49:304, October 17, 1971)

A teacher who tells you, "You don't need to study hard. Just take it easy," is a fake. Why do your teachers push you to study hard? It is not for the sake of the present, but for the future. They want you to prepare for the future. If you do as they say, your future will expand without a doubt. (93:232, June 5, 1977)

President Eu was my disciple; he went through a lot of suffering for my sake. For instance, he was deeply concerned about me when I was in the prison. When I think about him, I reflect on when I was lying in prison. I was pulled by his love. It made me want to see him. Whenever I sent him a note on a scrap of paper, he regarded it as precious as his life. (33:83 August 9, 1970)

2. Understanding Does Not Take Root without Properly Cultivating the Self

Jesus said to them, No one puts new wine into old wineskins; if he does, the new wine will burst the skins and will be spilled, and the skins will be destroyed. But new wine must be put into fresh wineskins.[23]

Luke 5.37-38

First take up the words,
Ponder their meaning,
Then the fixed rules reveal themselves.
But if you are not the right man,
The meaning will not manifest itself to you.

I Ching, Great Commentary 2.8.4 (Confucianism)

If there is no host on the inside to receive it [the Tao], it will not stay; if there is no mark on the outside to guide it, it will not go. If what is brought forth from the inside is not received on the outside, then the sage will not bring it forth. If what is taken in from the outside is not received by a host on the inside, the sage will not entrust it.

Chuang Tzu 14 (Taoism)

There is the man who sees but has not seen
   Speech [the words of the Vedas];
there is the man who hears but has not
   heard Her,
but to another She reveals her lovely form
like a loving wife, finely robed, to her husband.

Rig Veda 10.71.4 (Hinduism)

Hear then the parable of the sower. When any one hears the word of the kingdom and does not understand it, the evil one comes and snatches away what is sown in his heart; this is what was sown along the path. As for what was sown on rocky ground, this is he who hears the word and immediately receives it with joy; yet he has no root in himself, but endures for a while, and when tribulation or persecution arises on account of the word, immediately he falls away. As for what was sown among thorns, this is he who hears the word, but the cares of the world and the delight in riches choke the word, and it proves unfruitful. As for what was sown on good soil, this is he who hears the word and understands it; he indeed bears fruit, and yields, in one case a hundredfold, in another sixty, and in another thirty.

Matthew 13.18-23: Parable of the Sower

When the man of highest capacities hears the
   Tao
He does his best to put it into practice.
When the man of middling capacity hears the
   Tao
He is in two minds about it.
When the man of low capacity hears Tao
He laughs loudly at it.
If he did not laugh, it would not be worth the
   name of Tao.

Tao Te Ching 41 (Taoism)

Teachings of Sun Myung Moon

Why did God send me into situations that were very difficult to tolerate, like prison? Looking back on it, I know it was to broaden my heart. Why should you broaden your heart? God wants to enter and live in you. He tries to step in with his [right] foot, but your heart is closed and He cannot put it in. Then He kicks you with His left foot again and again to enlarge your mind. God keeps on kicking until He can fit one foot inside; then two feet. Next He would put His hands inside, and then put His head in. [Bending over to demonstrate.] God can enter because your heart has enlarged. Eventually, it can become really big.

    I observe True Mother[24] when she becomes pregnant. In the beginning her belly is small, but as time goes by it grows bigger and bigger. It increases until the baby is born; then it decreases again. It is the same with her womb: it starts out small, but look how it expands! A ten-pound baby can grow within its watery bag. I thought, "How much can her womb stretch? The sac of my heart should stretch even more."

Ladies, have you ever thought that the baby in your womb might die because your womb could not stretch enough to accommodate it? Then what about your heart? When God's seed is planted in the sac of your heart and starts to grow, it should grow to be as big as God Himself. But what if the sac of your heart cannot expand enough to contain God in all His immensity? What would happen to God, who is growing inside? If something goes wrong with the baby in your womb, you have a miscarriage after three months. Would God like to go into the sac of your heart if He thought it would miscarry in the middle of His growth? Would God want to plant His seed there? (110:325-26, January 4, 1987)

Learning and Practice

WHEN A TRUTH IS LEARNED IT MUST BE PRACTICED. Indeed, knowledge that is not put into practice is not truly learned; it soon fades away like a mirage. True knowledge arises when the conceptual becomes experiential. This applies particularly to religious and moral teachings, whose practice may be difficult. The hypocrite is someone who claims to be wise and devout but never acts accordingly. Unity of word and deed is a central quality of authentic personhood.

Likewise, a teacher should first practice what he preaches. An Oriental virtue is to be reserved and taciturn, in order that one not display knowledge that he has not mastered in practice. The same wisdom applies to leaders in business or any field. A leader who in his youth has experienced all the hard jobs will easily win the respect and loyalty of his people, because he knows what he is asking of them.

Be doers of the word, and not hearers only, deceiving yourselves. For if any one is a hearer of the word and not a doer, he is like a man who observes his natural face in a mirror; for he observes himself and goes away and at once forgets what he was like.[25]

James 1.22-24

Though he recites many a scriptural text, but does not act accordingly, that heedless man is like a cowherd who counts others' cattle. He has no share in the fruits of the religious life.

Though he can recite few scriptural texts, but acts in accordance with the teaching, forsaking lust, hatred, and ignorance, with right awareness and mind well emancipated, not clinging to anything here or in the next life, he shares the fruits of the religious life.

Dhammapada 19-20 (Buddhism)

That knowledge is very superficial which remains only on your tongue: the intrinsic merit and value of knowledge is that you act up to it.

Nahjul Balaga, Saying 90 (Shiite Islam)

Not study is the chief thing, but action; and whoso multiplies words, multiplies sin.

Mishnah, Avot 1.17 (Judaism)

Every one then who hears these words of mine and does them will be like a wise man who built his house upon the rock; and the rain fell, and the floods came, and the winds blew and beat upon that house, but it did not fall, because it had been founded on the rock. And every one who hears these words of mine and does not do them will be like a foolish man who built his house upon the sand; and the rain fell, and the floods came, and the winds blew and beat against that house, and it fell; and great was the fall of it.

Matthew 7.24-27

The one who would have the worst position in God's sight on the Day of Resurrection would be a learned man who did not profit from his learning.

Hadith of Darimi (Islam)

No one who really has knowledge fails to practice it. Knowledge without practice should be interpreted as lack of knowledge... No one should be described as understanding filial piety and respectfulness, unless he has actually practiced filial piety toward his parents and respect toward his elder brother. Knowing how to converse about filial piety and respectfulness is not sufficient to warrant anybody's being described as understanding them. Or it may be compared to one's understanding of pain. A person certainly must have experienced pain before he can know what it is. Likewise to understand cold one must first have endured cold; and to understand hunger one must have been hungry.

How, then, can knowledge and practice be separated? It is their original nature [to be in accord] before selfish aims separated them.

Wang Yang-Ming, Instructions for Practical Living (Confucianism)

Vainly understanding without practice is understanding that has no use. It is nothing but empty understanding. Vainly practicing without understanding is practice that has no direction. It is nothing but misguided practice.

Knowledge and action always need each other. It is like a person who has eyes but no legs and so cannot walk, or who has legs but no eyes and so cannot see. With respect to priority, knowledge comes first. With respect to import, action carries more weight.

When you know something but have not yet acted on it, then your knowledge is still shallow. Once you personally experience something, then your knowledge will become increasingly clearer, and its import will be different than before.

Chu Hsi (Confucianism)

Tzu-kung asked about the true gentleman. The Master said, "He does not preach what he practices until he has practiced what he preaches."

Analects 2.13 (Confucianism)

Just as a man or a woman has known what is truth, so he or she should practice that truth with zeal, and should teach it those persons who should practice it so, as it is!

Avesta, Yasna 35.6 (Zoroastrianism)

The Master said, "Do not be to ready to speak of it, lest the doing of it should prove to be beyond your powers."

Analects 14.21 (Confucianism)

Teachings of Sun Myung Moon

Whatever you conceive in your head, you should practice. It is not enough to only think it. Why do you need to act? When your actions are in accord with your words it creates a center, a place of unity between word and deed, and of unity between mind and body.[26] (248:89, August 1, 1993)

Whatever you learn you must practice. You must practice it in all dimensions: in your vertical relationships, in your horizontal relationships, and in all four directions, widely and deeply.[27] By so training yourself in this world, you will become adept when you go to the spirit world. (248:166, August 1, 1993)

Human beings… cannot become the object partners who inspire God with joy unless they understand His will and make effort to live accordingly. Hence, human beings are endowed with emotional sensitivity to the heart of God, intuition and reason to comprehend His will, and the requisite abilities to practice it. *(Exposition of the Divine Principle*, Eschatology 1.1)

I do not have the right to teach you anything unless I have first practiced it. (134:203, July 20, 1985)

Teaching is not just a matter of repeating what you have heard. You have to speak from experience; then the knowledge becomes real. (205:130, July 9, 1990)

I believe that anyone who would become a world-level leader, in charge of many people, should first have many life experiences before the age of thirty. You should acquire unforgettable stories from having gone through many challenging life experiences. That is my conclusion after experiencing it all.

Then, when you ask your people to do manual labor, you can appeal to them with the heart you felt while you were a laborer. For example, suppose you once worked at a job where you carried loads of clay across a narrow bridge using poles to balance yourself. When you tell your story about that job and the dangers you faced, your workers will become serious.

An expert is someone who explains and teaches everything on the basis of his or her own experience. (65:302-03, March 4, 1973)

This teaching is not just a theory. I tested everything through my own experience, which involved all kinds of suffering. I have put this teaching to the test and applied it in practice. (133:83, July 8, 1984)

Chapter 15

Faith

Faith

IN THIS WORLD AFFLICTED WITH SIN, most people are not in touch with their true selves. God cannot easily be felt or experienced. Truth cannot easily be understood or practiced. Relying on ourselves, we wander aimlessly in a sea of vain desires and false conceptions. Human beings need a star to guide them through the darkness, a map by which to navigate in uncharted waters. This is faith.

Faith begins with belief in the tenets of religion and effort to orient our life in accord with God's commandments. A religion's creed may be only a few words, yet those few words can rightly guide us into a relationship with God.

As we go deeper, we realize that our faith itself is a gift of God. It is the way God provides out of His love to reconnect with fallen human beings, who are in no condition to save themselves. Here is St. Paul's distinction between faith and works. A similar doctrine was taught by Shinran, the Japanese Buddhist saint who placed his faith in the 'Power of Another.' This is pure faith, uncontaminated by self-seeking. There are no grounds for pride, even in one's ability to have faith. Father Moon affirms that as all people are contaminated by sin and stem from a sinful lineage, no one can possibly pay off the debt of sin by his own efforts. Hence the only proper basis for a relationship with God is to rely on God's gracious love for us, His children.

Faith matures into a mutual relationship with God, characterized by trust and faithfulness (Heb., *emunah*). As we strive to live the way that God would have us live, we can overcome adversity knowing that God is faithful to us. Yet as we relate to God as our Subject of faith, we can ask whether God can equally count on our faithfulness to Him. People are so double-minded, vacillating between faithfulness and faithlessness from one day to the next. To become the sort of person whom God can trust to remain faithful through any adversity requires absolute integrity and self-mastery (see Chapter 12). God searches out such people, to whom He assigns great missions.

Father Moon calls us to "absolute faith." This is the unshakable faith that remains firm despite the vicissitudes of life. It is not compromised by the believer's personal preferences. Opposition, tragedy and loss can shake a person of weak faith. The pleas of family and loved ones cannot turn back absolute faith. Like Peter, who denied his lord, in a crisis the person of weak faith runs away or even loses faith altogether. But with absolute faith we can move mountains, overcome any adversity, and even triumph over death.

1. Belief—the Starting-point of Faith

For God so loved the world that He gave His only Son, that whoever believes in Him should not perish but have eternal life.

    John 3.16

Faith... is to believe in Allah, His angels, His books, His messengers, and the Last Day, and to believe in divine destiny, both the good and the evil thereof.

    Forty Hadith of an-Nawawi 2 (*Islam*)

Trembling with fear, [the jailer] fell down before Paul and Silas, and brought them out and said, "Men, what must I do to be saved?" And they said, "Believe in the Lord Jesus, and you will be saved, you and your household."

Acts 16.29-31

O mankind, I am the Messenger of God to you all, of Him to whom belongs the sovereignty of the heavens and the earth. There is no God but He. He gives life, and He makes to die. So believe in God, and His messenger, the Prophet who can neither read nor write, who believes in God and in His words, and follow him that haply you may be led aright.

Qur'an 7.158

He who does not understand the will of Heaven cannot be regarded as a gentleman.

Analects 20.3.1 (Confucianism)

He [Abraham] believed the LORD, and he reckoned it to him as righteousness.

Genesis 15.6

Who therefore shrinks from the religion of Abraham, except he be foolish-minded? Indeed, We chose him in the present world, and in the world to come he shall be among the righteous. When his Lord said to him, "Surrender," he said, "I have surrendered myself to the Lord of all Being." And Abraham charged his sons with this and Jacob likewise, "My sons, God has chosen for you the religion; see that you die not save in surrender." Why, were you witnesses when death came to Jacob? When he said to his sons, "What will you serve after me?" They said, "We will serve your God and the God of your fathers Abraham, Ishmael and Isaac, One God; to Him we surrender." That is a nation that has passed away; there awaits them that they have earned, and there awaits you what you have earned; you shall not be questioned concerning the things they did. And they say, "Be Jews or Christians and you shall be guided." Say, "Nay, rather the creed of Abraham, a man of pure faith; he was no idolater." Say you, "We believe in God, and in that which has been sent down on us and sent down on Abraham, Ishmael, Isaac and Jacob, and the Tribes, and that which was given to Moses and Jesus and the Prophets; of their Lord; we make no division between any of them, and to Him we surrender."[1]

Qur'an 2.130-36

By faith you shall be free and go beyond the world of death.

Sutta Nipata 1146 (Buddhism)

Faith is composed of the heart's intention.
Light comes through faith.
Through faith men come to prayer,
Faith in the morning, faith at noon and at the setting of the sun.
O Faith, give us faith!

Rig Veda 10.151.4-5 (Hinduism)

There are four kinds of faith. The first is the faith in the Ultimate Source. Because of this faith a man comes to meditate with joy on the principle of Suchness. The second is the faith in the numberless excellent qualities of the Buddhas. Because of this faith a man comes to meditate on them always, to draw near to them in fellowship, to honor them, and to respect them, developing his capacity for goodness and seeking after the all-embracing knowledge. The third is the faith in the great benefits of the Dharma. Because of this faith a man comes constantly to remember and practice the various disciplines leading to enlightenment. The fourth is faith in the Sangha, whose members are able to devote themselves to the practice of benefiting both themselves and others. Because of this faith a man comes to approach the assembly of Bodhisattvas constantly and with joy to seek instruction from them in the correct practice.[2]

Awakening of Faith in Mahayana (Buddhism)

Inexpressible is the state of faith;
Whoever attempts to describe it shall in the end regret his rashness.
This state pen and paper cannot record,
Nor cogitation penetrate its secret.
The great, immaculate Name of God
May only be realized by one
Whose mind is firmly fixed in faith.

Through faith the mind and intellect find concentration;
And to the seeker are revealed all the stages of enlightenment.
Through faith one will not receive blows in the Hereafter,
Nor be subjected to death's terror.
The great, immaculate Name of God
May only be realized by one
Whose mind is firmly fixed in faith.

Through faith man meets no obstacle on the Path,
And shall proceed to his abode with God with his honor universally proclaimed.
One with faith shall not stray into sects and byways,
But be fixed in true religion.
The great, immaculate Name of God
May only be realized by one
Whose mind is firmly fixed in faith.

Adi Granth, Japuji 12-14, M.1, p. 3 (Sikhism)

Teachings of Sun Myung Moon

Faith is the path each person must walk in search of God. Faith should be nurtured through a direct vertical relationship between God and each individual. (*Exposition of the Divine Principle*, Preparation 1)

Why do we lead a life of faith? It is to invest a higher form of energy that transcends our individual selves. Its direction is toward the world of higher realm, not the fallen world in which we now live. That is why theories that deny God's existence are groundless. (89:76, July 11, 1976)

The measure of the life of faith is not money or any glory in this world... The center of infinite value is God alone; therefore, we should make God the standard of our life of faith. We should not pay attention to anything besides God. (68:130-31, July 29, 1973)

The primary thing is to have a firm faith in the Center. Unless you have firm faith, all your willpower and zeal is of no use. Ask yourself, "What will happen to my faith if some calamity befalls me along the way?" What would be your answer? (27:114, November 30, 1969)

Why did Adam fall? He fell because he lacked faith. Faithlessness was the first cause of the Fall... Consequently, we must go the way of faith. Through our faith, we should reverse the effects of our ancestors' fall due to their lack of faith. Then we can go upward. To go upward, even above the point where our ancestors fell, we must have absolute faith. (126:35, April 10, 1983)

To go the way of restoration you need the Messiah. Fulfilling the condition of faith, with its three aspects—the central figure, the object for the condition, and the period of indemnity—is like recovering from an illness. To be healed, you need a doctor, the prescribed remedy, and a period of time. The doctor tells you, "Take this medicine for three days" or "I have to give you this medical treatment each day for a week." In the same way, a sin-sick person must keep faith in the Messiah, the Lord. He is your Physician. You must believe his word more than your own ideas. (63:183-84, October 14, 1972)

In our life of faith, the most critical issue is God, the object of our faith. At the same time, God, as the Subject of faith, has human beings as His objects. While we human beings place God as the object of our faith, God treats us as the objects of His faith. This intersection forms the gateway in which we stand. Therefore, we should uphold God's essential teaching, sharing life and death with Him. And at the same time, we should uphold the value of people, sharing life and death with them. (59:237-38, July 23, 1972)

People make a great mistake when they think that all they have to do is "just believe" in God and Jesus in order to receive God's overflowing blessings. They believe they can have everything they want, without doing anything in return. That attitude of faith is like that of a thief, who takes things without earning them.

Why did Jesus undergo the way of suffering? He did it to save the world. The Bible says, "For God so loved the world..." God needed Jesus to undergo his difficult course in order to prepare an environment in which God could love the people of His nation, and through them to love the world. Shouldn't we who believe in Jesus join with Jesus in taking responsibility for this? (124:296, March 1, 1983)

What does Heaven long for? Not for believers, but for those who practice and substantiate their faith in their daily life. (6:84, March 29, 1959)

You cannot go this path having an old-fashioned faith, just believing and expecting everything will be solved and accomplished by itself. We must go forward with the right attitude of faith—with determination to survive and neutralize the powers of death that may confront us. Passion, faith, endeavor and endurance—all these are necessary to receive the first level of inheritance from Heaven. (6:131, March 29, 1959)

2. Faith is a Gift of God, Not a Human Work

For by grace you have been saved through faith; and this is not your own doing, it is the gift of God—not because of works, lest any man should boast. For we are His workmanship, created in Christ Jesus for good works, which God prepared beforehand, that we should walk in them.

Ephesians 2.8-10

God has endeared the Faith to you, and has made it beautiful in your hearts, and He has made hateful to you unbelief, wickedness, and rebellion: such indeed are those who walk in righteousness—a grace and favor from God.

Qur'an 49.7

No one can come to me unless it is granted him by the Father.

John 6.65

He it is who sent down peace of reassurance into the hearts of the believers, that they might add faith to their faith.

Qur'an 48.4

Abandon all supports and look to me for protection. I shall purify you from the sins of the past; do not grieve.

Bhagavad-Gita 18.66 (Hinduism)

Did you receive the Spirit by works of the law, or by hearing with faith? Are you so foolish? Having begun with the Spirit, are you now ending with the flesh? Did you experience so many things in vain?—if it really is in vain. Does he who supplies the Spirit to you and works miracles among you do so by works of the law, or by hearing with faith? Thus Abraham "believed God, and it was reckoned to him as righteousness." So you see that it is men of faith who are sons of Abraham…

Now it is evident that no man is justified before God by the law; for "He who through faith is righteous shall live."

Galatians 3.2-7, 11

"If even a good man can be reborn in the Pure Land, how much more so a wicked man!" People generally think, however, that if even a wicked man can be reborn in the Pure Land, how much more so a good man! This latter view may at first sight seem reasonable, but it is not in accord with the purpose of the Original Vow [of Amida Buddha], with faith in the Power of Another. The reason for this is that he who, relying on his own power, undertakes to perform meritorious deeds, has no intention of relying on the Power of Another and is not the object of the Original Vow of Amida. Should he, however, abandon his reliance on his own power and put his trust in the Power of Another, he can be born in the True Land of Recompense. We who are caught in the net of our own passions cannot free ourselves from bondage to birth and death, no matter what kind of austerities or good deeds we try to perform. Seeing this and pitying our condition, Amida made his Vow with the intention of bringing wicked men to Buddhahood. Therefore the wicked man who depends on the Power of Another is the prime object of salvation.[3]

Shinran, Tannisho (Buddhism)

One of the crowd said [to Jesus], "Teacher, I brought my son to you, for he has a dumb spirit; and whenever it seizes him, it dashes him down; and he foams and grinds his teeth and becomes rigid… have pity on us and help us." And Jesus said to him, "If you can! All things are possible to him who believes." Immediately the father of the child cried out and said, "I believe; help my unbelief!"

Mark 9.17-24

Teachings of Sun Myung Moon

How can we explain the relationship our Father has with us, considering that we are all descendants of the sinful lineage? We cannot escape the bondage of sinful history. We live within the realm of sin, unable to overcome it. Because we cannot relate well with the Father even by our best efforts, we are taught to believe with all our heart. This is the message of the Gospel of Jesus Christ, which teaches us to approach the Father not through any other way but by believing in our hearts. (7:52-53, July 12, 1959)

How will you be justified by Heaven? You cannot take pride in your merits and efforts for Heaven. These things do not acquit you at the judgment. Only by your experience of God's heart and Jesus' heart within you, bearing fruit—a relationship that even God and Jesus cannot break—will establish the condition for eternal life. (4:107, March 16, 1958)

As you live your life of faith, do you have an explosive and stimulating power in the center of your heart, which moves unceasingly towards the world of God's Will? When you have that heart, then it is evident that God is with you. On the other hand, if you do not have that power, it is evident that God is separate from you. When your heart is pouring out love for people, and you have the heart to share your life limitlessly with others, it is clear that you belong to Heaven.

You must know that self-centered love and arrogant, self-centered values are evidence that God is already leaving you. (32:21-22, June 14, 1970)

God created humankind and has believed in us unfailingly. God has maintained that standard throughout history, no matter how often people betrayed His trust. Fallen parents in this world believe in their children, even though they are not trustworthy. They continue to believe in their children even after being deceived and lied to again and again. This is the very heart of God...

What happens when you believe in someone who cannot be believed, love someone who is unlovable, and stay by the side of someone you cannot live with? Even though they may leave you, once they realize your love for them, it will move their heart and they will return. God has been walking the providence of restoration with that heart. (*Way of Unification* 8.4.8)

With what heart did God create this world? God created this world with a heart that longed for all things to become worthy of His infinite trust. He longed for human beings to become worthy of His infinite trust...

God tried to believe in people, believing that they could be in such oneness as to not even be conscious of the word 'faith.' With this heart God sought for people of eternal faith. Yet due to the human Fall this heart of God has remained unfulfilled. (4:71, March 9, 1959)

> We know we appear unworthy.
> When we critique and analyze ourselves
> we know we do not measure up as beings able to offer something to Thee.
> Yet let us not forget that we are already Thy children.
> It is our destined relationship,
> which cannot be broken whatever we do. (24:245, August 24, 1969)

3. To Trust in God and Live by Faith in Him

Put your trust on the Exalted in Might, the Merciful—who sees you standing forth in prayer, and your movements among those who prostrate themselves. For it is He who hears and sees all things.

Qur'an 26.218-20

Trust in the LORD with all your heart,
and do not rely on your own insight.
In all your ways acknowledge Him
and he will make straight your paths.

Proverbs 3.5-6

The righteous shall live by being faithful.

Habakkuk 2.4

Rabbi Simlai said, "Six hundred and thirteen commandments were given to Moses, 365 negative commandments, answering to the number of the days of the year, and 248 positive commandments, answering to the number of a man's members. Then David came and reduced them to eleven [Psalm 15]. Then came Isaiah, and reduced them to six [Isaiah 63.15]. Then came Micah, and reduced them to three [Micah 6.8]. Then Isaiah came again, and reduced them to two, as it is said, 'Keep ye judgment and do righteousness.' Then came Amos, and reduced them to one, as it is said, 'Seek me and live.' Or one may say, then came Habakkuk [2.4], and reduced them to one, as it is said, 'The righteous shall live by his faith.'"⁴

Talmud, Makkot 23b-24a *(Judaism)*

Not every one who says to me, "Lord, Lord," shall enter the kingdom of Heaven, but he who does the will of my Father who is in heaven.

Matthew 7.21

What does it profit, my brethren, if a man says he has faith but has not works? Can his faith save him? If a brother or sister is ill-clad and in lack of daily food, and one of you says to them, "Go in peace, be warmed and filled," without giving them the things needed for the body, what does it profit? So faith by itself, if it has no works, is dead.

James 2.14-17

I do as I talk
and live up to my words in deed;
take a balance and weights in your hands
O my Lord!
If my words and deeds
should differ slightly
by even a barley grain,
you kick me and go,
O Lord Kudala Sangama!

Basavanna, Vacana 440 *(Hinduism)*

Teachings of Sun Myung Moon

What kind of faith does God desire? When Jesus said, "Believe in me," he meant we should believe in him as he believed in God. Jesus could say, "I am God's Son, and I believe in God," because as His Son, he was certain that God trusted him just as he trusted God his Father. (5:180, January 18, 1959)

Although you believe in Jesus as your Lord and the subject of your faith, it is not good if you just believe in Jesus and stop there. Believing in Jesus is just the first step on the walk of faith with Jesus, on whom you stake your eternal life. Once you have developed a living relationship of faith with Jesus, it becomes the basis to experience God as a living reality. If you genuinely believe in Jesus, then you can accomplish these things. (3:19, September 8, 1957)

When you declare that you believe in Jesus, does it mean that you only have to believe in the things that Jesus likes? Or do you also have to reject the things that Jesus hates? Surely, just as you have to do what Jesus likes, you must also reject what Jesus hates. What are the things that Jesus hates? They are, simply, Satan and sin. (124:294, March 1, 1983)

Unless you feel in your heart that God loves you, and unless you are so proud of these great words of God as to be eager to declare them throughout the universe, you cannot stand tall as God's son or daughter. You must have absolute confidence that comes by trusting completely in God's authority. (22:205, February 4, 1969)

Although we believe that God is our Heavenly Father, we should strive for the day when Heavenly Father, our Subject Partner, trusts us, His object partners, one hundred percent. We should take God's purpose as our clear goal, and dash forward to reach it with one hundred percent conviction. This is the last significant problem that people of this era have to solve…

You know very well that the first human ancestors fell because they did not trust God. They fell because they did not have faith. (6:209-10, May 17, 1959)

Among people of faith, which of these three will God side with: The person who believes but does nothing? The person who has the conviction to act but acts negligently? Or the person translates his faith 100 percent into action, even courageously dedicating his life? Which type of person do you want to be? (92:312-13, April 24, 1977)

What is the most important experience in a life of faith? It is to feel that you are living a subject-object relationship with God. You experience that God exists, that He loves you. Then, honoring God as your Subject of faith, you become very serious to act in ways that make God take notice of you and support what you are doing. You must feel God's presence with you so much that whenever you pray you feel gratitude to Him. Then indeed He is with you. You may not experience this in the beginning, but when you reach a certain level in your life of faith, you will feel it naturally. (58:312, June 25, 1972)

You have to remain faithful and keep your integrity towards Heaven even though you live in the satanic world. Have you ever regarded the children you are raising as God's children? Have you ever thought that you and your spouse belong to God? Have you ever considered that your parents, your ancestors, your people, and your country all belong to God? Ignorant people on this earth are not aware that Heaven is moving the world towards this standard. (8:85, November 8, 1959)

> May we gathered here today become people about whom Thou art able to say:
> "You are the person I have hoped for.
> You are someone I can trust and someone I can love." (1:101, June 6, 1956)

4. Absolute Faith—Untainted by Personal Desires and Unaffected by Circumstances

For truly, I say to you, if you have faith as a grain of mustard seed, you will move this mountain, "Move from here to there," and it will move; and nothing will be impossible to you.

Matthew 17.20

He who has in his heart faith equal to a single grain of mustard seed will not enter hell, and he who has in his heart as much pride as a grain of mustard seed will not enter Paradise.

Hadith of Muslim (Islam)

[Jesus] said, "Follow me." But he said, "Lord, let me first go and bury my father." But he said to him, "Leave the dead to bury their own dead; but as for you, go and proclaim the kingdom of God." Another said, "I will follow you, Lord; but let me first say farewell to those at my home." Jesus said to him, "No one who puts his hand to the plow and looks back is fit for the kingdom of God."

Luke 9.59-62

Those journeying to heaven do not look back; they ascend the heaven, the two worlds.

Satapatha Brahmana 9.2.3.27 (Hinduism)

But Lot's wife behind him looked back, and she became a pillar of salt.

Genesis 19.26

"My clothes are torn, I shall soon go naked," or "I shall get a new suit": a monk should not entertain such thoughts. At one time he will have no clothes, at another time he will have some. Knowing this to be a salutary rule, a wise monk should not complain about it.

Uttaradhyayana Sutra 2.12-13 (Jainism)

For I am sure that neither death, nor life, nor angels, nor principalities, nor things present, nor things to come, nor powers, nor height, nor depth, nor anything else in all creation, will be able to separate us from the love of God in Christ Jesus our Lord.

Romans 8.38-39

Say: Lo! My worship and my sacrifice and my living and my dying are for Allah, the Lord of the Worlds.

Qur'an 6.162

Though the fig tree do not blossom,
nor fruit be on the vines,
the produce of the olive fail
and the fields yield no food,
the flock be cut off from the fold
and there be no herd in the stalls,
yet I will rejoice in the LORD,
I will exult in the God of my salvation.

Habakkuk 3.17-18

Teachings of Sun Myung Moon

When you pray, be aware of your privilege as a glorious son or daughter of God. Then when you pray, "O Lord, please grant me my wish; I truly want it to be done," God will grant your request. Thus you will discover the living God. You will see that God is alive and working on your behalf.

By harnessing the power of God in this way, you can heal your members when they become sick. When you go through difficult times, you will find that God is directly helping you. Live this way, and you will have many realizations. You will gain the confidence and conviction to overcome every obstacle. You will know with certainty that God is on your side. (65:286, January 1, 1973)

On the way of our faith there should be no self-assertion or self-concept. Absolute faith means there is no concept of self at all. If I say I believe absolutely, it means there should be no opposition to that within myself. When you say you are united with God, there should be no ego. You have to unite completely with the Subject, leaving no trace of self. In the life of faith there is no place for egoism. (46:82, July 25, 1971)

When God called Noah, He did not instruct him to do something that corresponds with common sense. He said, "Noah, build an ark on the heights of a mountain." God could have told Noah to build the ark near the seashore or by a river, but instead He gave Noah instructions that seemed completely implausible. Nevertheless, Noah carried out God's command in faith, and persevered in doing so for 120 years. God always conducts His providence in ways that ordinary people cannot understand. (70:64, February 8, 1974)

If you follow the secular environment and try to pursue a life of faith at the same time, you cannot attain absolute faith. Most people live routine lives and think, "I am acceptable in God's sight." However, regarding the fundamental problem—how to enter the Kingdom of God—living a routine life in this fallen world does not suffice... Why is it, that without an absolute standard of faith, we cannot establish the Kingdom of God? It is because Satan dwells there. (46:79-80, July 25, 1971)

When you walk with absolute faith, even if your nation comes against you, you must never yield. Although your family may oppose you, with absolute faith you should not be defeated. Even if your loving spouse persecutes you, you must hold on to the attitude of absolute faith. Why do we live our life with an attitude of absolute faith? Quite simply, the way to goodness requires that we overcome the evil environment. (29:206)

The purest and most trustworthy person does as God does: although belief seems impossible he never stops believing, although loving is difficult he never stops loving, and although he cannot stand living with his partner he continues to live together with her. That kind of person will definitely become a victor over any circumstances. (*Way of Unification* 8.4.8)

How serious are you, as you stand before God's tremendous Providence which He has been conducting through history? How much are you united with God's Will? Are you leading a life of absolute faith, centered on God's Will? You should be able to say, "Though winds and tempest blow, and though I may perish, my conviction is firm. I could be wrong, but God's Will can never be wrong." You should have such a rock-solid conviction. It is folly to desire for the Kingdom of God when your faith is ever changing from morning to evening. (46:74, July 25, 1971)

Where do we connect to love? It is at the point where we become absolutely zero, where there is no trace of self. To find perfect love, there is no place for "me." It is the same with faith. As God's object partner I believe in my Subject absolutely, and God as my Subject partner believes in me as His object partner absolutely. In faith, there is no self. In absolute faith, there is no place for "me." Faith is absolute at the zero point.

When you unite with your partner in absolute love, there is no "I." Likewise, when you unite with your partner in absolute faith, there is no "I." This is how two become one. Follow this way, and you will become completely one. (279:146, August 4, 1996)

At the time of creation, God created with absolute faith. When God spoke, He determined according to His Word that created beings would become His object partners. In other words, He spoke based on absolute faith. Furthermore, the objects that God created by His absolute faith were for the sake of His absolute love. (273:298, October 29, 1995)

5. Faith in the Face of Adversity

Father, if it be possible, let this cup pass from me; nevertheless not as I will, but as thou wilt.

Matthew 26.39

Now there was a day when [Job's] sons and daughters were eating and drinking wine in their eldest brother's house; and there came a messenger to Job, and said, "The oxen were plowing and the asses feeding beside them; and the Sabeans fell upon them and took them, and slew the servants with the edge of the sword; and I alone have escaped to tell you." While he was yet speaking, there came another, and said, "The fire of God fell from heaven and burned up the sheep and the servants, and consumed them; and I alone have escaped to tell you." While he was yet speaking, there came another, and said, "The Chaldeans formed three companies, and made a raid upon the camels and took them, and slew the servants with the edge of the sword;

and I alone have escaped to tell you." While he was yet speaking, there came another, and said, "Your sons and daughters were eating and drinking wine in their eldest brother's house; and behold, a great wind came across the wilderness, and struck the four corners of the house, and it fell upon the young people, and they are dead; and I alone have escaped to tell you."

Then Job arose, and rent his robe, and shaved his head, and fell upon the ground, and worshipped. And he said, "Naked I came from my mother's womb, and naked shall I return; the LORD gave, and the LORD has taken away; blessed be the name of the LORD."

In all this, Job did not sin or charge God with wrong.

Job 1.13-22

Saul said to David, "You are not able to go against this Philistine to fight with him; for you are but a youth, and he has been a man of war from his youth." But David said to Saul, "Your servant used to keep sheep for his father; and when there came a lion, or a bear, and took a lamb from the flock, I went after him and smote him and delivered it out of his mouth; and if he arose against me, I caught him by his beard, and smote him and killed him. Your servant has killed both lions and bears; and this uncircumcised Philistine shall be like one of them, seeing he has defied the armies of the living God."

1 Samuel 17.33-36

When a surah comes down, enjoining them to believe in God and to strive and fight along with His Apostle, those with wealth and influence among them ask you for an exemption, saying, "Leave us behind; we would be with those who sit." They prefer to be with the women who remain behind; their hearts are sealed and so they understand not.

But the Apostle, and those who believe with him, strive and fight with their wealth and their persons; for them are all good things, and it is they who will prosper.

Qur'an 9.86-88

And as Peter was below in the courtyard, one of the maids of the high priest came; and seeing Peter warming himself, she looked at him, and said, "You also were with the Nazarene, Jesus." But he denied it, saying, "I neither know nor understand what you mean." And he went out into the gateway. And the maid saw him, and began again to say to the bystanders, "This man is one of them." But again he denied it. And after a little while again the bystanders said to Peter, "Certainly you are one of them; for you are a Galilean." But he began to invoke a curse on himself and to swear, "I do not know this man of whom you speak." And immediately the cock crowed a second time. And Peter remembered how Jesus had said to him, "Before the cock crows twice, you will deny me three times." And he broke down and wept.

Mark 14.66-72

Teachings of Sun Myung Moon

Suppose you have been married for some time and are deeply in love, but suddenly your spouse dies. You feel as if all of heaven and earth were crumbling. At that moment you could curse God for taking your loved one away, but instead you should think: What could be the reason this has happened? You should recall that God often takes away something precious in order to give something more precious. Such is the heart of a parent.

You should think about your situation in light of the principle of restoration through indemnity, remembering that on the path of restoration, indemnity is something to be grateful for. Then you can appreciate it, saying, "God chose me to suffer this loss because He knows I am the only one strong enough to go this indemnity course." And then, if you come before God with a settled spirit and pray, "What's next?" God will be amazed. When you look at the long view, your suffering today will accrue as blessings to your descendants 100 years, 1,000 years in the future. (104:106, April 15, 1979)

Absolute faith! It is the subject of my prayer these days. Not the faith of Peter, but absolute faith. Absolute faith!... With absolute faith, you can go on even though you are dying. Prison is nothing; not even death can stop you from continuing on the path. Jesus prayed, "My Father, if it is possible let this cup pass from me. Nevertheless, not as I will, but as Thou wilt." Even though he died away from home, he died not for himself, but for the sake of the Father. He became a glorious offering.

Do you understand what your limitations are? You have to be courageous even in the face of death. Then a leap will occur—a leap. When you have made up your mind to die and go forward—even at the most difficult point where you cannot escape either down into the earth or up into the sky—God will surely appear. Hence, I am not bothered by the question of whether or not God exists. I experience so many of His works—works like in dreams. God always works as He desires for His people of absolute faith. (126:238, *Unification Family Life* 3.3.2)

Because our first ancestors fell due to disbelief, to go forward we have to overcome disbelief. We can go over the line where our first ancestors fell when we act out of absolute faith. What is the meaning of absolute faith? It means to go forward in the face of death, go forward even though you are dying, and continue even after you are dead. (126:35, April 10, 1983)

Today throughout the world Christianity appears to be fading. Even the United States, this gigantic nation, seems to be sinking. What kind of people does God, the unchanging Subject, look for to be His object partners? He cannot work with people who dance to the world's tune and accommodate themselves to it. People change and the world changes, yet God looks for people who determine never to change, who say, "Even though the world may perish, we will not change." God is expecting us to be such people, who stand on firm ground and who demonstrate both faith and zealous deeds. (66:47, March 18, 1973)

You call upon God, you cry out for God's Will, you seek after God's truth, and you fight for God's glory. What is the purpose of such a life of faith? First, its purpose is to make you absolutely firm and resolute. God cannot trust you unless you have the conviction that no suffering can overpower you, and no historical sorrow can defeat you, for the foundation laid in your mind and body is unshakable. Unless God can trust you, He cannot use you to bring an end to the evil state of affairs of your generation. (12:304, August 11, 1963)

Witness

MOST RELIGIONS ENCOURAGE EVANGELISM, sharing the truth with others with the aim of leading them to salvation. The religious mandate to bear witness to the truth grows out of love—concern for that person's eternal life, based upon the conviction that the truth of religion is liberating and will bring out that person's higher potential. Witness begins by example, to "let your light so shine before men." Through good deeds and a compassionate heart the believer demonstrates living faith that is attractive to others. Next comes preaching and teaching the doctrine. Although evangelism sometimes meets with opposition, nevertheless it should be carried out with a pure mind and upright conduct while always trusting in God's guidance.

All authority in heaven and on earth has been given to me. Go therefore and make disciples of all nations, baptizing them in the name of the Father and of the Son and of the Holy Spirit, teaching them to observe all that I have commanded you; and lo, I am with you always, even to the close of the age.

    Matthew 28.18-20: The Great Commission

Call to the way of your Lord with wisdom and kindly exhortation. Reason with them in the most courteous manner. Your Lord knows best those who stray from His path and those who are rightly guided.

    Qur'an 16.125

The Exalted One said... "Go you forth, brethren, on your journey, for the profit of the many, for the bliss of the many, out of compassion for the world, for the welfare, the profit, the bliss of devas and mankind!

"Go not any two together. Proclaim, brethren, the Norm, goodly in its beginning, goodly in its middle, goodly in its ending. Both in the spirit and in the letter make known the all-perfected, utterly pure righteous life. There are beings with but little dust of passion on their eyes. They are perishing through not hearing the Norm. There will be some who will understand."

    Vinaya 1.21 (Buddhism)

Lords of light, fill me with the sweetness of the bee-honey, so I may speak the glorious Word to the masses of the people.

    Atharva Veda 6.69.2 (Hinduism)

Hillel said, "Be of the disciples of Aaron—one that loves peace, that loves mankind and brings them nigh to the Law."

    Mishnah, Avot 1.12 (Judaism)

Those who teach this supreme truth of the Gita to all who love me perform the greatest act of love; they will undoubtedly come to me. No one can render me more devoted service; no one on earth can be more dear to me.

    Bhagavad-Gita 18.68-69 (Hinduism)

Understand that through saving others you shall also be saved.

    Ofudesaki 3.47 (Tenrikyo)

You are the light of the world. A city set on a hill cannot be hid. Nor do men light a lamp and put it under a bushel, but on a stand, and it gives light to all in the house. Let your light so shine before men, that they may see your good works and give glory to your Father who is in heaven.

    Matthew 5.14-16

I should be a lamp for the world
Replete with the virtues of Buddhahood,
Their ten powers, their omniscience.
All sentient beings
Burn with greed, anger, and folly;
I should save and free them,
Have them extinguish the pains of the states
    of woe.

    Garland Sutra 36 (Buddhism)

We are ambassadors for Christ, God making His appeal through us. We beseech you on behalf of Christ, be reconciled to God... We put no obstacle in anyone's way, so that no fault may be found with our ministry, but as servants of God we commend ourselves in every way: through great endurance, in afflictions, hardships, calamities, beatings, imprisonments, tumults, labors, watching, hunger; by purity, knowledge, forbearance, kindness, the Holy Spirit, genuine love, truthful speech, and the power of God; with the weapons of righteousness for the right hand and for the left; in honor and dishonor, in ill repute and good repute. We are treated as impostors, and yet are true; as unknown, and yet well known; as dying, and behold we live; as punished, and yet not killed; as sorrowful, yet always rejoicing; as poor, yet making many rich; as having nothing, and yet possessing everything.

Our mouth is open to you, Corinthians; our heart is wide. You are not restricted by us, but you are restricted in your own affections. In return—I speak as to children—widen your hearts also.

2 Corinthians 5.20-6.13

If you are aware of a certain truth, if you possess a jewel, of which others are deprived, share it with them in a language of utmost kindliness and goodwill. If it be accepted, if it fulfill its purpose, your object is attained. If anyone should refuse it, leave him unto himself, and beseech God to guide them. Beware lest you deal unkindly with him.

Epistle to the Son of the Wolf 15 *(Baha'i Faith)*

These twelve Jesus sent out, charging them, "Go nowhere among the Gentiles, and enter no town of the Samaritans, but go rather to the lost sheep of the house of Israel. And preach as you go, saying, 'The kingdom of Heaven is at hand.' Heal the sick, raise the dead, cleanse lepers, cast out demons. You received without paying, give without pay. Take no gold, nor silver, nor copper in your belts, no bag for your journey, nor two tunics, nor sandals, nor a staff; for the laborer deserves his food. And whatever town or village you enter, find out who is worthy in it, and stay with him until you depart. As you enter the house, salute it. And if the house is worthy, let your peace come upon it; but if it is not worthy, let your peace return to you. And if any one will not receive you or listen to your words, shake off the dust from your feet as you leave that house or town. Truly, I say to you, it shall be more tolerable on the day of judgment for the land of Sodom and Gomorrah than for that town.

"Behold, I send you out as sheep in the midst of wolves; so be wise as serpents and innocent as doves. Beware of men; for they will deliver you up to councils, and flog you in their synagogues, and you will be dragged before governors and kings for my sake, to bear testimony before them and the Gentiles. When they deliver you up, do not be anxious how you are to speak or what you are to say; for what you are to say will be given to you in that hour; for it is not you who speak, but the Spirit of your Father speaking through you...

"So have no fear of them; for nothing is covered that will not be revealed, or hidden that will not be known. What I tell you in the dark, utter in the light; and what you hear whispered, proclaim upon the housetops."

Matthew 10.5-28

Monks, there are these two gifts, the carnal and the spiritual. Of these two gifts the spiritual gift is preeminent. Monks, there are two sharings together, the sharing of the carnal and the sharing of the spiritual. Of these two sharings together the sharing of the spiritual is preeminent.

Itivuttaka 98 *(Buddhism)*

There is a traffic in speakers of fine words;
Persons of grave demeanor are accepted as gifts;
Even the bad let slip no opportunity to acquire them.
Therefore on the day of an emperor's enthronement
Or at the installation of the three officers of state,
Rather than send a team of four horses, preceded by a disc of jade,
Better were it, as can be done without moving from one's seat, to send this Tao.
For what did the ancients say of this Tao, how did they prize it?
"Pursuing, they [who have Tao] shall catch; pursued, they shall escape"?
They thought it, indeed, the most precious of all things under heaven.

Tao Te Ching 62 *(Taoism)*

Teachings of Sun Myung Moon

By witnessing through the Divine Principle, we are carrying out a movement to revive love. [We are building] the world of heart, which transcends time and space. Our words and our prayers are ultimately for the sake of love. Let us realize the ideal of love—that is perfection. (33:69, August 8, 1970)

God rejoices when we testify to Him with an earnest heart. God desires to work through good people to save every human soul from the world of death. God would not withhold anything from people who understand this deep wish of Heaven—and who take it upon themselves to resolve the grief in God's heart by shouldering the burden in God's place, fighting to save people, and declaring God's heart to the world. (8:259, January 17, 1960)

Witnessing means inducing people to leave the satanic world with a smile and follow the heavenly path. It is guiding them to the Kingdom of Heaven. You cannot force people to come; people are spiritual beings… Give your utmost love to them and cry with painful heart in order to raise them one by one and persuade them to follow the path of God's providence. (50:279, November 8, 1971)

Witness with the heart of Heavenly Father looking for His lost child. (10:219, October 14, 1960)

Witnessing is about loving someone else's child more than your own children and loving people who are not of your community more than your own people. You love them as you would your siblings and your children, more than anyone else in the fallen world would. You are Abel, and your victory in loving Cain—loving him according to Abel's standard of faith—brings Cain to heaven. You should think to receive your blessings after he does. (93:281, May 19, 1994)

Loving your brothers like God loves them opens the way to the Kingdom of God. You are trying to follow True Father. With such a mind, help your brothers follow me. From this viewpoint, the one who teaches the highest, quickest and best way to go to the Kingdom of God is neither God nor True Father, but your brother. (66:125, April 18, 1973)

Although God loves you, if you are not so proud of God's words that you want to shout them out to the cosmos, then you cannot really stand as a child of God. (22:205, February 4, 1969)

Before we can educate others about God, eternal life and true love, we should know them ourselves. Then, no matter what others say, we can speak of them from our own experience. We should speak from the facts that we know, and not merely repeat what others have said. That is how we can come closer to God and become central figures. We need to obtain this, if we are to bring many others to participate in the heavenly world and digest the remnants of the satanic world. (205:130-31, July 29, 1990)

May all those who follow Thy heart be as candles lighting the five continents, lighthouses on the great sea. May we become witnesses—knowing the mission we shoulder, ready to testify to Thy deep heart, and going forward as incarnations of Thy love. (86:91, March 7, 1976)

Jesus shed tears of compassion for the people on earth, even after suffering injustice and mistreatment at their hands. In the Last Days there must emerge many believers who will do the same.

When you meet a good person, love and serve him well. When you make the acquaintance of bad people, be worried and anxious for their sake. Go forward bearing a cross for each of them, for the sake of creating heavenly families, a heavenly society and world. Persevere while embodying the heart of Jesus Christ, and be victorious in fulfilling the Will of God. (1:254-55, November 25, 1956)

Let God lead your way. Then you will feel the heart of God in front of you, leading you always. In such a state you can teach a crowd, no matter how large. God will coach you, and you will speak in spite of yourself. You hear what you are saying, but at the same time you marvel at what you say. In that state of mind, everything happens spontaneously. Every movement of your body and every facial expression is natural and in sync with your spoken words. Continue to have such experiences, and a life-giving movement will arise from your labors. (96:168, January 3, 1978)

Sometimes you feel a spiritual connection to a person passing by. You feel something familiar about him even though you see him for the first time. You think, "Have I met that man before?" Do not miss this opportunity. Approach him and make a connection. That person is absolutely necessary for you. Speak to him with your utmost sincerity; invest your heart for him more than you ever did for God, and do not let go of him. Then you will form an inseparable relationship. By this method, you will expand the base of love that bonds all of your companions. If you do this often, you will become a bearer of grace and draw near to the Kingdom of Heaven. (308:213, January 5, 1999)

When you experience the living God, you will go out witnessing even if people tell you not to do so. It is because witnessing produces the most stimulating and new results. If you carry on a sincere conversation with ten people, all ten will become new people. After that, go to church and pray. See what happens: when they make progress, you will also advance. (30:154, March 21, 1970)

As you wake at dawn, pray and shed tears for the people of your district... You will find yourself shedding tears, because you realize that when God looks down upon that village, He too is weeping, knowing that everyone there is heading toward hell. When you enter a state of resonance with God's sorrowful heart, then the whole spirit world will be mobilized to help you. (96:282, February 13, 1978)

> May we awaken this people which is asleep,
> that they may become Thy sons and daughters.
> We appeal to Thee:
> May we save all the people of the world,
> being swallowed by the darkness. (2:335, August 4, 1957)

Hope

HOPE IS INTEGRAL TO FAITH in God. A hopeful view of the world's future follows from faith in the God of history who is moving forward to fulfill His promises. God has promised an end to violence and oppression, poverty and sorrows. Even though people do not always see the realization of their hopes in this world, they can still hope for a future beyond death, a new life in the eternal world. Therefore, God created human beings to hope, and by keeping hope alive we can draw closer to God.

Father Moon teaches that in the religious life we should keep a positive and hopeful attitude, ever maintaining our vision and our hopes regardless of the circumstances. We should keep our minds fixed on eternity, with a hope that transcends even death. We should carry the torch of hope, following in the footsteps of Abraham, Isaac, Jacob, Moses and others who, in the words of the Letter to the Hebrews, possessed "the conviction of things unseen, assurance of things hoped for." Above all, we should hope for the fulfillment of God's Kingdom, especially in these days of the advent of the True Parents.

Where there is no vision, the people perish.

Proverbs 29.18

Youths may faint and be weary,
and young men may fall, exhausted;
but they who hope in the LORD shall renew
    their strength.

Isaiah 40.30

Behold, the eye of the LORD is on those who
    fear him,
on those who hope in his steadfast love,
that he may deliver their soul from death,
and keep them alive in famine.

Our soul waits for the LORD;
he is our help and shield.
Yea, our heart is glad in him,
because we trust in his holy name.
Let thy steadfast love, O LORD, be upon us,
even as we hope in thee.

Psalm 33.18-22

Let him who hopes for the encounter with his Lord work righteousness, and not associate with his Lord's service anyone.

Qur'an 18.110

Now faith is the assurance of things hoped for, the conviction of things not seen. For by it men of old received divine approval.

By faith we understand that the world was created by the word of God, so that what is seen was made out of things which do not appear.

By faith Abel offered to God a more acceptable sacrifice than Cain, through which he received approval as righteous, God bearing witness by accepting his gifts; he died, but through his faith he is still speaking. By faith Enoch was taken up so that he should not see death; he was not found, because God had taken him. Now before he was taken he was attested as having pleased God. And without faith it is impossible to please him. For whoever would draw near to God must believe that he exists and that he rewards those who seek him.

By faith Noah, being warned by God concerning events as yet unseen, took heed and constructed an ark for the saving of his household; by this he condemned the world and became an heir of the righteousness which comes by faith.

By faith Abraham obeyed when he was called to go out to a place which he was to receive as an inheritance; and he went out, not knowing where he was to go. By faith he sojourned in the land of promise, as in a foreign land, living in tents with Isaac and Jacob, heirs with him of the same promise. For he looked forward to the city which has foundations, whose builder and maker is God. By faith Sarah herself received power to conceive, even when she was past the age, since she considered him faithful who had promised. Therefore from one man, and him as good as dead, were born descendants as many as the stars of heaven and as the innumerable grains of sand by the seashore.

These all died in faith, not having received what was promised, but having seen it and greeted it from afar, and having acknowledged that they were strangers and exiles on the earth. For people who speak thus make it clear that they are seeking a homeland. If they had been thinking of that land from which they had gone out, they would have had opportunity to return. But as it is, they desire a better country, that is, a heavenly one...

Therefore, since we are surrounded by so great a cloud of witnesses, let us also lay aside every weight, and sin which clings so closely, and let us run with perseverance the race that is set before us, looking to Jesus the pioneer and perfecter of our faith, who for the joy that was set before him endured the cross, despising the shame, and is seated at the right hand of the throne of God.

Hebrews 11.1-16, 12.1-2

What more shall we be than we are? Listen to John the evangelist: "It is not yet apparent what we shall be: [but] we know that, when He shall appear, we shall be like Him." How? "For we shall see Him as He is." A great promise, but the reward of faith... If you believe, ask for the reward of faith; but if you believe not, with what face can you seek the reward of faith?

Saint Augustine, On the Gospel of John 40.9 (Christianity)

We therefore hope in Thee, O Lord our God, that we shall soon behold the triumph of Thy might, idolatry will be uprooted from the earth, and falsehood be utterly destroyed.

We hope for the day when the world will be perfected under the dominion of the Almighty and all mankind learn to revere Thy name; when all the wicked of the earth will be drawn in penitence unto Thee.

O may all the inhabitants of the world recognize that unto Thee every knee must bend, every tongue pledge loyalty. Before Thee, O Lord our God, may they bow in worship, and give honor to Thy glorious name.

May they all acknowledge Thy kingdom, and may Thy dominion be established over them speedily and forevermore. For sovereignty is Thine, and to all eternity Thou wilt reign in glory.

Daily Prayer Book, Alenu (Judaism)

Difficult and painful as it is, we must walk on in the days ahead with an audacious faith in the future. When our days become dreary with low-hovering clouds of despair, and when our nights become darker than a thousand midnights, let us remember that there is a creative force in this universe, working to pull down the gigantic mountains of evil, a power that is able to make a way out of no way and transform dark yesterdays into bright tomorrows. Let us realize the arc of the moral universe is long, but it bends toward justice.

Martin Luther King, Jr.[5] (Christianity)

Teachings of Sun Myung Moon

Hope brings with it revival, development, victory and prosperity (64:311, November 12, 1972)

The highest hope of a human being is to reconnect with God.[6] (68:131, July 29, 1973)

Because God continues to have eternal hope, today we too continue to cherish an eternal hope. (1:99, June 6, 1956)

God works through the person who lives for the future, studies for the future, fights for the future, hopes for the future, and goes forward to make a new future. (97:241-42, March 19, 1973)

A person entertains all kinds of hope in his life. However, in the end he runs into death. He passes away having left behind all the hopes he had fostered. Although he wandered through life seeking new hope, wishing to live today and tomorrow, when he runs into death he goes the last path in despair.

Self-centered people may seem to have hope, but they lack the hope that can carry them over the hill of death. As they approach the time of their death, they lose all hope and just fade away. Shall we die in this manner? Or shall we find the one hope by which we can go beyond death, scoffing at death and even delighting in it? This is the most crucial question for human beings living on earth today.

Heaven has made limitless efforts to equip earthly people with a hope that transcends death, in order that they might live with their eyes fixed on the eternal world. Therefore, people who lead a religious life should not live embracing earthly hopes, but should live entertaining the hope of transcending death. They should dream of a world where hope springs eternal. (6:45, March 22, 1959)

While enduring suffering and hardship, we keep a hopeful spirit. We get down on our knees and pray, "O God, please let our hope be realized." We inherited this spirit from our forebears, and we will pass it down to our descendants. We are not like ordinary people, who when facing the same circumstances, would easily blame God saying, "If God exists, why does He let His people suffer?" (168:52, September 1, 1987)

May we go forth with a bold and vibrant attitude as God's hopeful sons and daughters, going towards the nation of peace, the peace of the Kingdom of Heaven. (33:273, August 16, 1970)

Today is the day of the proclamation of the True Parents. Although this is a world without hope, where people do not believe in anything or hope for anything, one sprout of hope is blossoming—the True Parents. (202: 341, May 27, 1990)

> Snow and cold wind of the bitter dark night,
> lift off the weight of your cold ruthless hand.
> Spring breeze will chase you and bring flowery fragrances,
> breathing new life to the suffocated hills.
>
> Though you most ruthless of winter winds blow,
> doomed in a moment you too shall be calmed.
> Spring breeze will chase you and bring flowery fragrances,
> breathing new life to the suffocated hills.
>
> Butterfly awake and you meadow lark of spring,
> our land has suffered this nightmare too long.
> Spring breeze will chase you and bring flowery fragrances,
> breathing new life to the suffocated hills.[7] (*Song of the Spring Breeze*)

Assurance

A PERSON WITH CONFIDENCE IN GOD'S PROVISION need not bother about worldly cares. God is in control and will perform His purpose regardless of what people may do. Why should we be anxious about money or having life's necessities, when at any moment God can provide what we need? Why should we be anxious about the results of our efforts, when God is the Shaper of destinies? Even the prospect of death is of little import from the standpoint of eternal life. Jesus tells us that God who provides for the birds of the air and lilies of the field will provide for us as well, as long as we "seek His Kingdom and His righteousness." In other words, the key to experiencing the peace of God is to have a selfless mind-set and live utterly for His sake.

Father Moon's particular understanding of God's provision adds the dimension of mutuality: As God provides for human needs, He longs to find people who will comfort Him by concerning themselves about His needs and His situation. Thus, Father Moon experienced God calling him to share in His suffering. When through such experiences we experience God's bitter heart, we recognize that our sadness and worry over our personal situation pales in comparison to God's sadness and worry over us. Our greatest satisfaction, then, is to comfort God even in the midst of our own suffering. In such times, we can feel assurance and support coming from God's deepest heart.

Do not be anxious about your life, what you shall eat or what you shall drink, nor about your body, what you shall put on. Is not life more than food and clothing? Look at the birds of the air: they neither sow nor reap nor gather into barns, and yet your heavenly Father feeds them. Are you not of more value than they? And which of you by being anxious can add one cubit to his span of life? And why are you anxious about clothing? Consider the lilies of the field, how they grow; they neither toil nor spin; yet I tell you, even Solomon in all his glory was not arrayed like one of these. But if God so clothes the grass of the field, which today is alive and tomorrow is thrown into the oven, will he not much more clothe you, O men of little faith? Therefore do not be anxious, saying "What shall we eat?" or "What shall we wear?" For the gentiles seek all these things; and your heavenly Father knows that you need them all. But seek first his kingdom and his righteousness, and all these things shall be yours as well.

Matthew 6.25-33

How many animals do not carry their own provision! God provides for them and for you. He is Alert, Aware.

Qur'an 29.60

In the Changes it is said, "If a man is agitated in mind, and his thoughts go hither and thither, only those friends on whom he fixes his conscious thoughts will follow" [Hexagram 31: Influence].

The Master said, "What need has nature of thought and care? In nature all things return to their common source and are distributed along different paths; through one action, the fruits of a hundred thoughts are realized. What need has nature of thought, of care?"

I Ching, Great Commentary 2.5.1 (Confucianism)

My Lord, boundless as
The sun and moon
Lighting heaven and earth;
How then can I have concerns
About what is to be?

Manyoshu 20 (Shinto)

Not that I complain of want; for I have learned, in whatever state I am, to be content. I know how to be abased, and I know how to abound; in any and all circumstances I have learned the secret of facing plenty and hunger, abundance and want. I can do all things in Him who strengthens me.

Philippians 4.11-13

Those who surrender to God all selfish attachments are like the leaf of a lotus floating clean and dry in water. Sin cannot touch them. Renouncing their selfish attachments, those who follow the path of service work with body, senses, and mind for the sake of self-purification. Those whose consciousness is unified abandon all attachment to the results of action and attain supreme peace.

Bhagavad-Gita 5.10-12 *(Hinduism)*

The Exalted One said to Bhaddiya, "Bhaddiya, what motive have you, who are wont to resort to forest-dwelling, to the roots of trees, to lonely spots, in exclaiming, 'Ah! 'tis bliss! Ah! 'tis bliss!'?"

"Formerly, sir, when I enjoyed the bliss of royalty as a householder, within my palace guards were set and outside my palace guards were set. So also in the district and outside. Thus, sir, though guarded and protected, I dwelt fearful, anxious, trembling, and afraid. But now, sir, as I resort to forest-dwelling, to the roots of trees, to lonely spots, though alone, I am fearless, assured, confident, and unafraid. I live at ease, unstartled, lightsome, with heart like that of some wild creature. This, sir, was the motive I have for exclaiming, 'Ah! 'tis bliss! Ah! 'tis bliss!'"

Udana 19-20 *(Buddhism)*

We know that in everything God works for good with those who love Him, who are called according to His purpose.

Romans 8.28

Unless the LORD builds the house,
those who build it labor in vain.
Unless the LORD watches over the city,
the watchman stays awake in vain.
It is in vain that you rise up early and go late
 to rest,
eating the bread of anxious toil;
for he gives His beloved sleep.

Psalm 127.1-2

One who has a true hold on life, when he walks on land does not meet tigers or wild buffaloes; in battle weapons of war do not touch him. Indeed, a buffalo that attacked him would find nothing for his horns to butt, a tiger would find nothing for its claws to tear, a weapon would find no place for its blade to lodge. Why? Because such men have no "death-spot" in them.

Tao Te Ching 50 *(Taoism)*

Not by might, nor by power, but by my Spirit, says the LORD of hosts.

Zechariah 4.6

Should the lord bestow His might on the
 tiny ant,
Hordes million-strong it may destroy.
Whomsoever He Himself sends not to death,
He guards by the strength of His arm.
Despite all his efforts,
All man's endeavors turn fruitless.
None other is savior or destroyer:
He Himself is guardian of all beings.
Thou man! why all this anxiety?
Says Nanak, Contemplate Him who is beyond
 thy understanding,
Who is so wonderful.

Adi Granth, Gauri Sukhmani 17,
M.5, p. 285-86 *(Sikhism)*

The man who has had his feet cut off in punishment discards his fancy clothes—because praise and blame no longer touch him. The chained convict climbs the highest peak without fear—because he has abandoned all thought of life and death. These two are submissive and unashamed because they have forgotten other men, and by forgetting other men they have become men of Heaven. You may treat such men with respect and they will not be pleased; you may treat them with contumely and they will not be angry. Only because they are one with the Heavenly Harmony can they be like this.[8]

Chuang Tzu 23 *(Taoism)*

When a drunken man falls from a carriage, though the carriage may be going very fast, he won't be killed. He has bones and joints the same as other men, and yet he is not injured as they would be, because his spirit is whole. He didn't know he was riding, and he doesn't know he has fallen out. Life and death, alarm and terror do not enter his breast, and so he can bang against things without fear of injury. If he can keep himself whole like this by means of wine, how much more can a man keep himself whole by means of Heaven! The sage hides himself in Heaven—hence there is nothing that can do him harm.[9]

Chuang Tzu 19 *(Taoism)*

Teachings of Sun Myung Moon

People in the everyday world can purchase a home, appliances, furniture, and live a comfortable life just by working eight hours a day. We Unificationists work 24 hours a day, yet we do not own our own homes and barely have enough money to live on… Yet under these circumstances, are we in despair? No, we live in hope. That is our pride. It is the same with me, Reverend Moon. What do you think I am proud of? It is that I am afraid of nothing. There is nothing in heaven or on earth that I am afraid of, because my efforts are entirely for [God's Will]. How bold! (107:83, April 6, 1980)

Do not do anything for the sake of yourself, but think how to live for the sake of God, heaven and earth, your nation, your tribe, your family and your spouse. If you live for others, you will be elevated into the perfect world. Even if you try to escape and retreat because you think you have been too self-centered, you will be dragged into heaven. How peaceful! How trouble-free!

If you live your life centered on yourself, you are anxious about everything, saying, "Alas, I failed! I failed!" However, if you live for the sake of others for ten and twenty years, everyone will be your friend. If you live for the sake of others, your heart will become empty, and the truth will come to you. (203:102, June 17, 1990)

God teaches you when your spirit is joyful and shining like daylight. That is why you should strive to have a bright spirit. Always be grateful. Whenever something is troubling you, it is best to resolve it right away.

Why should you make this effort? It is to reduce the gap between God and yourself. Therefore, rather than lamenting over your difficulties by yourself, it is better to have a religion. Report your problems to Heaven: "O God, please take my situation under Thy care. Thou knowest my situation, so deal with the matter as Thou wilt." With this prayer, you can release all your cares. That is the life of a religious person. Try to live this way, and you can have many hours in communion with God. Then, regardless of your present situation, you can always find hope. (91:272-73, February 27, 1977)

> Where people gather together with others,
> though they try to resolve matters things become complicated again.
> But where people gather centered on Heaven,
> the matters that have formed knots in people's minds are solved. (7:13, July 5, 1959)

When you are raising funds or witnessing, or whatever you do, if you do it with prayer and a heart of devotion, you will be shown in advance what kind of person you will meet. You set out to go somewhere, but you mysteriously desire to go to a place you had not intended to go. There you meet a person whom God loves. Having these experiences, can you possibly say that God does not exist? (69:288, January 1, 1974)

[When I was beaten in prison] I lost so much blood that I was more dead than alive. How did I survive? I did not pray to God asking, "Father, please let me live." I was determined not to show weakness even at the point of death. I am not a common weakling. I prayed, "Father, even if I die, I die for Thee. Do not worry about me." Not even once did I pray asking God to deliver me from suffering. God already knew my suffering. (93:321, June 12, 1977)

Gratitude and Indebtedness

A GRATEFUL HEART is essential to living faith. Sincere believers keep ever in mind that God's power and grace sustains them, and for that they are grateful. Children first learn gratitude when the family says grace at meals, in the simple act of thanking God for the food on the table. As we recognize God's grace everywhere, guiding our path and helping us in our weakness, we find more to be grateful for. When we encounter difficult situations, we can take the challenges as opportunities for growth and as God's gifts intended to push us to higher peaks of love and service. Gratitude is the way to live with God, living in time with His rhythm. There is no room for complaint. Complaining is poison to the spirit, automatically separating us from God and blinding us to His good will.

Our gratitude increases when we recall our indebtedness to all those who have loved and invested themselves on our behalf—parents and teachers, siblings, spouse—and to all those we depend on for sustenance and protection—the soil and its produce, the workers who prepare and deliver food to our table, make the appliances we use and the cars we drive, the police and firemen who protect us, the doctors and hospitals who treat us when we are sick—the list is endless. Ultimately we are indebted to God, the Source of our life and the Author of our salvation. How can we possibly repay all these debts? At least we can be grateful; then we also can give to others.

1. Gratitude and Thanksgiving for God's Gifts

O you who believe! Eat of the good things that We have provided for you, and be grateful to God, if it is Him that you worship.

Qur'an 2.172

God created foods to be received with thanksgiving by those who believe and know the truth. For everything created by God is good, and nothing is to be rejected if it is received with thanksgiving; for then it is consecrated by the word of God and prayer.

1 Timothy 4.3-5

Abraham caused God's name to be mentioned by all the travelers whom he entertained. For after they had eaten and drunk, and when they arose to bless Abraham, he said to them, "Is it of mine that you have eaten? Surely it is of what belongs to God that you have eaten. So praise and bless Him by whose word the world was created."

Talmud, Sota 10b (Judaism)

It is God who has made the night for you, that you may rest therein, and the day, as that which helps you to see. Verily God is full of grace and bounty to men, yet most men give no thanks.

It is God who has made for you the earth as a resting place, and the sky as a canopy, and has given you shape—and made your shapes beautiful—and has provided for you sustenance of things pure and good; such is God, your Lord. So glory to God, the Lord of the Worlds!

Qur'an 40.61, 64

Ah, children—
Be not arrogant, but
Assist the deities of
Marvelous spirit power
In their work.

Even the grains, and the
Teeming grass and trees—
Even these are favored with
Blessings from Amaterasu,
Great Goddess of the Sun.

Morning and evening,
At each meal you take,
Consider the blessings of
Toyouke-no-kami,
You people of the world.

The blessings of the
Gods of heaven and earth—
Without these,
How could we exist,
Even for a day, even for a night?

Forget not the grace
Of generations of ancestors;

From age to age, the ancestors
Are our own *ujigami*,
Gods of our families.[10]

Norinaga Motoori, *One Hundred Poems on the Jeweled Spear* (Shinto)

The unworthy man is ungrateful, forgetful of benefits [done to him]. This ingratitude, this forgetfulness is congenial to mean people... But the worthy person is grateful and mindful of benefits done to him. This gratitude, this mindfulness, is congenial to the best people.

Anguttara Nikaya 1.61 (Buddhism)

One upon whom We bestow kindness
But will not express gratitude,
Is worse than a robber
Who carries away our belongings.

Yoruba Proverb (African Traditional Religions)

Be not like those who honor their gods in prosperity and curse them in adversity. In pleasure or pain, give thanks!

Mekilta to Exodus 20.20 (Judaism)

Teachings of Sun Myung Moon

Before eating food, good men and women first remember the bounties of Heaven, then the earth, and then humankind. (*Way of God's Will* 1.1.2)

What is the essence of a life of faith? It is a heart of gratitude to God. That heart is the basis by which we can transcend the relationship ordinary fallen people have with God and enter a higher relationship with God—that of oneness. Should we thank God only when we are prospering? No. Did God care for us only when things were going well for Him? No. The more difficult the situation, the more firm was God's determination, regardless of the suffering, to labor and struggle on our behalf. Therefore, today, to properly serve God as our Father, we should demonstrate our gratitude to Him when we are going through difficult situations rather than easy ones. When you understand this principle, you will be able to give gratitude to God even when your path requires you to bear a very heavy cross. (29:338, February 16, 1970)

> Let us become people who at the morning breakfast table ask ourselves
> what we are going to do after we eat this food;
> who at the lunch table feel
> ashamed and remorseful over what we have left unfinished;
> and who at the dinner table reflect
> whether we have spent the day well and concluded it without lack.

Father, may we be Thy children who ask ourselves
whether we start the day as Thine,
and having arrived at this moment, are Thine.
Yet have we spent this day with worldly minds?
When we remember Thy concern for us,
we know we must spend this day valuably.
When we lay down in bed, exhausted,
do we have any regrets of things left undone?
May we not go to bed until we have repented with tears…

Though my body is exhausted,
at the point when I can hold on no more,
I must think that in Thy longing for me:
Thou hast overcome suffering harsher than mine.
I recognize that only by overcoming this suffering
can I become a son or daughter who can comfort Thy sorrowful past;
therefore I shall purify myself on the path to becoming Thy child,
and offer myself completely as a sacrifice before Thee.

To live with gratitude—there is nothing else.
If some of us were given wives who are inadequate, still we can be grateful
that Thou has given us such wives, for we can serve them throughout our life.
If our children become the cross of our life, still we can be grateful
that through them Thou provideth us a way to bear a cross.
Though circumstances drive us to the pits of despair in situations we cannot control,
though we may collapse, let it be reckoned as an opportunity
to reaffirm our gratitude to Thee as Thy sons and daughters. (29:238, March 14, 1970)

Father! Please enable me to feel grateful for all the grace Thou hast given,
that a day could come when I could meet Thee—a day like today. (39:78, January 9, 1971)

Although you have nothing with you, you are happy because you are eating with the most wonderful Person. (*Way of God's Will* 1.8)

Even as we endure and bear up under difficulty, we should be thankful and sing hymns. God may be on His way to visit us, but if He sees that we are enduring not thankfully but with bitterness, He will turn back.

With what do we need to endure? A thankful spirit! Without a thankful spirit, we cannot endure. And even if we do endure, if we do not have a thankful heart, God cannot be with us. (44:28-29, May 4, 1971)

What was the Fall? [The archangel] compared himself to everyone from a self-centered viewpoint; this led to complaint. Complaint led to rebellion. Therefore, complaint is not permissible for believers….

To complain is essentially to attack God. But as we human beings have to repay God, complaining to God is absolutely unacceptable. My life up until now has been like that. I could never be a complainer, even though I was put in prison and tortured to the point of vomiting blood. Even though the entire world opposes me, I am grateful, knowing that it is severing my relationship with Satan's realm.

It is natural that we receive opposition as long as the enemy's realm exists. Therefore, let us not complain. Let us be grateful for everything and every circumstance, and let us go our way in silence. (September 11, 1972)

Today God is examining us, looking at whether our hearts are truly thankful. It is like in a courtroom: when a criminal is being sentenced, if he or she accepts the sentence with gratitude, the judge and even the prosecutor will want to show mercy and reduce the penalty. (104:279, June 1, 1979)

2. Our Debt to God, to Nature and to Our Forbearers, Which We Repay by Helping Others

All human bodies are things lent by God. With what thought are you using them?

Ofudesaki 3.41 (Tenrikyo)

When a man is born, whoever he may be, there is born simultaneously a debt to the gods, to the sages, to the ancestors, and to men.

When he performs sacrifice it is the debt to the gods which is concerned. It is on their behalf, therefore, that he is taking action when he sacrifices or makes an oblation.

And when he recites the Vedas it is the debt to the sages which is concerned. It is on their behalf, therefore, that he is taking action, for it is said of one who has recited the Vedas that he is the guardian of the treasure store of the sages.

And when he desires offspring, it is the debt to the ancestors which is concerned. It is on their behalf, therefore, that he is taking action, so that their offspring may continue, without interruption.

And when he entertains guests, it is the debt to man which is concerned. It is on their behalf, therefore, that he is taking action if he entertains guests and gives them food and drink. The man who does all these things has performed a true work; he has obtained all, conquered all.

Satapatha Brahmana 1.7.2.1-5 (Hinduism)

The kingdom of Heaven may be compared to a king who wished to settle accounts with his servants. When he began the reckoning, one was brought to him who owed him ten thousand talents; and as he could not pay, the lord ordered him to be sold, and his wife and children and all that he had, and payment to be made. So the servant fell on his knees, imploring him, "Lord, have patience with me, and I will pay you everything." And out of pity for him the lord of that servant released him and forgave him the debt. But that same servant, as he went out, came upon one of his fellow servants who owed him a hundred denarii; and seizing him by the throat he said, "Pay what you owe." So his fellow servant fell down and besought him, "Have patience with me, and I will pay you." He refused and went and put him in prison till he should pay the debt. When his fellow servants saw what had taken place, they were greatly distressed, and they went and reported to their lord all that had taken place. Then his lord summoned him and said to him, "You wicked servant! I forgave you all that debt because you besought me; and should not you have had mercy on your fellow servant, as I had mercy on you?" And in anger his lord delivered him to the jailers, till he should pay all his debt.

Matthew 18.23-34

Teachings of Sun Myung Moon

Where did your life come from originally? From your parents, who invested themselves in you, and from nature, which gave you the food to make your flesh, blood and bones. If you were to repay everything that they have lent you, you would have nothing left. Furthermore, you are indebted to God who originally gave you life. What, then, do you have left? God, your parents and nature invested themselves in you; therefore, you are a chunk of indebtedness.

Have you paid these debts? Are you even trying to pay them? At least, a debtor can be thankful.

Your creditors are not asking you to pay your debt. In fact they are not even claiming that you owe them. How thankful you ought to be!

Jesus told a parable about a cruel servant. His lord had generously forgiven him a debt he could not pay, but he turned around and threw a man into jail who was indebted to him. On hearing of it, his lord spoke angrily to him for being so cruel after he himself had received mercy.[11] We have nothing that is inherently ours. God gave us life unconditionally, without requiring us to sign any contract or pay interest on his loan or repay the principal within a fixed number of years. The only way we can repay Him and show our gratitude is by giving to others. (93:193, May 29, 1977)

The attitude of a believer must always be that of a debtor. Have you paid your debts? If you have no worldly debts, why not incur some debts as a form of training? You should experience the hardships of being in debt. It is truly miserable. If you owe even a penny, your creditor can grab you by the lapels and treat you like dirt. In the same way, since you owe a debt to God, it is not proper for you to assert yourself. (43:108, April 25, 1971)

God must be so exhausted, coping with the billions of fallen people in the world. How tired must God be as He strives to fulfill His Will! So if you pray, "Heavenly Father, don't worry. I will do it!" even if it is just words, God would approve. When you pray in such a way, God says, "Wow! That person is a great guy. He has a future." (93:22, May 8, 1977)

What can you pay in return for receiving the grace of God? You have to say, "I will pay for it with my filial love." (*Way of God's Will*)

> We may be anxious,
> we may be lonely,
> our situation may be miserable,
> but when we recall that Thou, O Father, art even more miserable than we,
> we understand that we must become sacrifices
> and comfort Thee, our pitiful Father. (25:38, September 28, 1969)

The Fear of God

THE FEAR OF GOD IS A POSITIVE emotion because it directs us away from harmful things and propels us to do what is right. People who lack the fear of God more readily commit sin, as they do not fear God's punishment. Having denied the existence of God they justify themselves, often with one of the modern ideologies which says that the moral rules of religion are fetters to be broken in the name of individual freedom. Yet as Father Moon explains, ever since the Human Fall fear has become a negative emotion, one that can lead to all kinds of self-centered behavior when it dominates our thinking.

The higher dimensions of holy fear—reverence and awe—should pervade our worship and guide our steps in life. They keep us mindful that our life and the purpose of our existence is not our own doing, but from God. They also contribute to our sense of meaning and value, as servants of the King and hence partakers in His glory.

1. The Fear of God as a Prod to Moral Behavior

The fear of the LORD is the beginning of wisdom.

Proverbs 9.11

O you who believe! Fear God as He should be feared, and die not except in a state of submission.[12]

Qur'an 3.102

May your fear of Heaven be as strong as your fear of man!

Talmud, Berakot 28b (Judaism)

Do not call conspiracy all that this people call conspiracy, and do not fear what they fear, nor be in dread. But the LORD of hosts, him you shall regard as holy; let him be your fear, and let him be your dread.

Isaiah 8.12-13[13]

God has revealed the fairest of statements, a Scripture consistent, [with promises of reward] paired [with threats of punishment], at which creeps the flesh of those who fear their Lord, so that their flesh and their hearts soften to God's reminder. Such is God's guidance, with which He guides whom He will.

Qur'an 39.23

Monks, two bright things guard the world: shame and fear of blame. If these two bright things did not guard the world... the world would fall into promiscuity, as is the case with goats, sheep, poultry, pigs, dogs, and jackals.

Itivuttaka 36 (Buddhism)

Fear God and give him glory, for the hour of his judgment has come.

Revelation 14.7

When the Israelites saw the Egyptians lying dead on the seashore, and saw the great power which the LORD had put forth against Egypt, the people were in awe of the LORD and put their faith in him and in Moses his servant.

Exodus 14.30-31

"Their mouth is full of curses and bitterness. Their feet are swift to shed blood, in their paths are ruin and misery, and the way of peace they do not know. There is no fear of God before their eyes." Now we know that whatever the law says it speaks to those who are under the law, so that every mouth may be stopped, and the whole world may be held accountable to God.

Romans 3.14-19

Teachings of Sun Myung Moon

The reason why people who believe in God continue to commit sins is because their faith in God has been merely conceptual. It has not touched their innermost feelings. Who among them would ever dare to commit sin if they experienced God in the depths of their being? Would they not tremble if they felt the reality of the heavenly law that those who commit crimes cannot escape the destiny of hell? (*Exposition of the Divine Principle*, Introduction)

Today, we are reaping the consequences of the Fall: Immorality is rampant. Teenagers, in particular, are the victims of widespread sexual degradation. The advanced nations are little different from Sodom and Gomorrah of biblical times. God abhors this immoral behavior. We must fear the wrath of God. His punishment is imminent. (201:206-07, April 19, 1990)

[After she fell] Eve realized that according to God's heavenly law, Adam was supposed to be her husband. Thus she thought then if she returned to Adam's bosom, she could escape the fear of God. Centering on Satan's love, fear and independence conspired together to bring Adam to his knees. Fear and self-insistence has continued ever since to dominate the fallen human race. Now in the last days, the way of individualism has become dominant throughout the world and is ruining the world. (256:230, March 13, 1994)

At least Adam and Eve in the Garden of Eden felt shame enough to conceal their naked bodies with fig leaves, but American young people these days feel no shame, doing all manner of indecent behavior even outdoors in city parks. Because Adam and Eve felt a sense of shame over what they did, they could repent. But these young people are shameless; they are far from repentful. (95:149, November 11, 1977)

2. Reverence and Awe

The LORD is in his holy temple;
let all the earth keep silence before him.

Habakkuk 2.20

The fire of hell has been forbidden to these two eyes: the eye that remained sleepless through watching in the ways of God, and the eye that wept with spirit trembling at the fear of God.

Hadith of Darimi *(Islam)*

Divine things,
Proceeding from the mind
Of the unseen kami—
How awesome, and
Not to be taken lightly!

Norinaga Motoori, *One Hundred Poems on the Jeweled Spear* (Shinto)

The true believers are those whose hearts are filled with awe at the mention of God, and whose faith grows stronger as they listen to His revelations. They put their trust in their Lord, pray steadfastly, and give in alms of that which We have given them. Such are the true believers. They shall be exalted and forgiven by their Lord, and a generous provision shall be made for them.

Qur'an 8.2-4

The fear of God is mighty and of great weight.
Egoism is worthless and just vociferous.
Walk under the weight of such great fear;
And through Divine grace obtain knowledge of God.

None crosses the ocean of existence unless he bear fear;
Through fear the fear-directed life is beautified with divine love.
Through fear of God, the fire of fear blazes in the human frame.
Through fear of God and love is molded spiritual beauty.
Without fear of God all that is uttered is misshapen and worthless—
The mold and the shaping stroke both blind...

Through fear of God vanish worldly fears.
The fear of God which eliminates all other fear—how may it be called fear?
No other resting place is except Thee;
All that happens is Thy will.
One might be afraid of it if anything other than God held any fear—
To be shaken with such fears is sheer perturbation of mind.

Adi Granth, Gauri, M.1. p. 151 *(Sikhism)*

Teachings of Sun Myung Moon

Father! Our hearts are filled with fear as we recollect Thy sorrowful historical course. Knowing Thy difficult labors, whenever we approach Thy majesty, our minds are struck with awe. (6:328, June 28, 1959)

Give reverence and honor to God, who has restrained Himself, silently enduring the path of suffering for thousands of years. Have the heart that God is your true Father. Make a determination that regardless of the suffering you may endure, you will become the central ancestors who will leave behind the Father's tradition for tens of thousands of years. (363:254, December 25, 2001)

Although I have a mouth, I keep silent. Not because I do not know how to speak, but because I am cautious that by misspeaking I might go against Heaven's law. Not because I do not know how to complain, but because of God. (67:316, July 22, 1973)

Most people curse Heaven, living with resentment and despair; few are the people who pledge their loyalty to God. Since we are among that loyal few, God treats us with seriousness. Nevertheless, think about God's heart and His situation: How wretched it is that He has such a small group of insignificant people as us with which to restore the world. (93:217, June 1, 1977)

> O Father, Thy sons and daughters gathered here feel fearful
> that we might not be adequate to become sons and daughters
> who can receive everything Thou wouldst give us,
> and who can give everything to Thee.
> We fear that we may not be able to represent
> the world, history and the cosmos,
> when to us Thou wouldst express Thy heart,
> the heart Thou hast always wanted to give us. (35:288, October 25, 1970)

Doubt

FAITH IN THE INTANGIBLE IS INEVITABLY MET BY DOUBT. Doubts arise from faith's unrealistic claims, from the challenges that living a life of faith entails, and from the skepticism that abounds in today's secular environment. Unresolved doubts can weigh down and even sink a believer sailing on the voyage of faith, as symbolized by Peter's unsuccessful attempt to walk on water.

Every believer is responsible to confront and overcome his or her doubts. Intellectually, we can find answers to satisfy our unresolved questions. Ultimately, we should graduate from the level of belief to attain knowledge of God based upon lived experience.

Now Thomas, one of the twelve, called the Twin, was not with them when Jesus came. So the other disciples told him, "We have seen the Lord." But he said to them, "Unless I see in his hands the print of the nails, and place my finger in the mark of the nails, and place my hand in his side, I will not believe." Eight days later, his disciples were again in the house, and Thomas was with them. The doors were shut, but Jesus came and stood among them, and said, "Peace be with you." Then he said to Thomas, "Put your finger here, and see my hands; and put out your hand, and place it in my side; do not be faithless, but believing." Thomas answered him, "My Lord and my God!" Jesus said to him, "Have you believed because you have seen me? Blessed are those who have not seen and yet believed."

John 20.24-29

The boat was many furlongs distant from the land, beaten by the waves... And in the fourth watch of the night he [Jesus] came to them, walking on the sea. But when the disciples saw him walking on the sea, they were terrified, saying, "It is a ghost!" And they cried out in fear. But immediately he spoke to them, saying, "Take heart, it is I; have no fear."

And Peter answered him, "Lord, if it is you, bid me come to you on the water." He said, "Come." So Peter got out of the boat and walked on the water and came to Jesus; but when he saw the wind, he was afraid, and beginning to sink he cried out, "Lord, save me." Jesus reached out his hand and caught him, saying to him, "O man of little faith, why did you doubt?"

Matthew 14.24-31

Whatever monk has doubts about the Teacher, is perplexed, is not convinced, is not sure, his mind does not incline to ardor, to continual application, to perseverance, to striving. This is the first mental barrenness that thus comes not to be got rid of by him whose mind does not incline to ardor, to continual application, to perseverance, to striving.

And again, this monk has doubts about the Dhamma... has doubts about the Order... has doubts about the training... If these mental barrennesses are not rooted out, that he should come to growth, expansion, and maturity in this Dhamma and discipline—such a situation does not occur.

Majjhima Nikaya 1.101 (*Buddhism*)

If any of you lacks wisdom, let him ask God, who gives to all men generously and without reproaching, and it will be given him. But let him ask in faith, with no doubting, for he who doubts is like a wave of the sea that is driven and tossed by the wind. For that person must not suppose that a double-minded man, unstable in all his ways, will receive anything from the Lord.

James 1.5-7

If you are in any doubt concerning what We have sent down to you, then question those who have read the Book before you; Truth has come to you from your Lord, so do not be a waverer; do not be someone who rejects God's signs, so you be a loser.

Qur'an 10.94-95

Out of the element of participation follows the certainty of faith; out of the element of separation follows the doubt in faith. And each is essential for the nature of faith. Sometimes certainty conquers doubt, but it cannot eliminate doubt. The conquered of today may become the conqueror of tomorrow. Sometimes doubt conquers faith, but it still contains faith. Otherwise it would be indifference...

The fundamental symbol of our ultimate concern is God. It is always present in any act of faith, even if the act of faith includes the denial of God... Atheism, consequently, can only mean the attempt to remove any ultimate concern—to remain unconcerned about the meaning of one's existence. Indifference toward the ultimate question is the only imaginable form of atheism...

Doubt is not the opposite of faith; it is one element of faith.

Paul Tillich (Christianity)

Teachings of Sun Myung Moon

Do you believe in God, or do you *know* God? You say you know Him; then, do you believe in His love, or do you *know* it? You say God is alive; do you believe He is alive, or do you *know* it? By the same token, you say you are of God's lineage, but do you just believe you are of His lineage, or do you *know* it?

What is faith? According to Hebrews chapter 11, "Faith is the assurance of things hoped for, the conviction of things not seen." It is something provisional, not connected to the reality we experience. (359:87, 011106)

Compare faith and observable reality. Faith looks intangible and unreal, but is in fact eternal and substantial. The reality of this world is vivid and evident to our senses, but it cannot be trusted; it is ephemeral and inconstant. Life grounded in faith in God has the quality of constancy. (66:49, March 18, 1973)

When your faith is big, reality seems small. But when your faith is small, reality looms overwhelmingly before you. (*Way of God's Will* 3.4)

The world around us fills us with doubts. You should confess them before the Father and pray, "Father, please remove these doubts from my mind and body." Have the courage to fully entrust yourself, and your enslavement by sin, to the Father, the Subject of your faith. At least establish this mind-set at the center of your heart; it is the only way to walk the path of faith.

When God comes seeking us, the condition He requires of us is faith. We must use faith to forget all about the self, destroy the world of doubt, and create a world that promotes faith. In this way we can bring order to this sinful environment, create an environment of goodness, demolish the environment of death, and build an environment of life...

Take all your doubts off your chest and bravely hand them over to God. Say, "God, I have come with all the doubts of the universe. Since Thou hast made a heavenly relationship with me, I trust that Thou wilt not abandon me. Please accept this confession of my doubts and resolve them all for me."...

We must truthfully confess all our doubts to the Subject of our faith. The act of confession is a sacred thing. With utmost sincerity, challenge the limits of conventional thinking and call out, "Father! Father!" Then your Father will surely respond. God is responsible to deal with people like you…

The reason Adam and Eve fell was because they doubted. Hence, during the process of restoration, whenever we have any doubts we should clarify them. A doubt that is allowed to grow large will preoccupy the mind. Therefore, you must have the courage and determination, even the audacity, to get clarification from God for any question you have. (3:11-13, September 8, 1957)

We who believe in the existence of God should be able to see real evidence of His existence in our daily life. We should be able to demonstrate the reality of God beyond any doubt to this unbelieving world. (120:100, October 5, 1982)

Hypocrisy

WHEREVER PEOPLE SUBSCRIBE TO A RELIGION or doctrine of moral excellence, there is always the danger of hypocrisy. The hypocrite wishes to enjoy the approval of his peers and even the benefits of a religious office by appearing outwardly moral or religious, while inwardly he is not. Where religion makes serious demands upon people's lives, such as Jesus' call to love your enemy, Islam's call to jihad or Buddhism's strict precepts of monastic discipline, the hypocrite tries to circumvent these demands while appearing outwardly righteous. The hypocrite does not pay the price of commitment to the religious life and hence does not reap its spiritual benefits; hence he remains at a low state.

Furthermore, when hypocrisy becomes prevalent and lowers the standards expected of religious people, it brings religion itself into disrepute. In Father Moon's survey of history, he teaches that the decline of the Christian spirit, accompanied by hypocrisy of the rich who tolerated and justified widespread poverty and racism, was the direct cause for the spread of materialistic ideologies in the 19th and 20th centuries. (See Chapter 8: *Christianity*) Only by recovering the true godly spirit of religion, Father Moon teaches, can we establish a spiritual civilization that can bring lasting peace to this planet.

Woe to you, scribes and Pharisees, hypocrites! For you are like whitewashed tombs, which outwardly appear beautiful, but within they are full of dead men's bones and all uncleanness. So you also outwardly appear righteous to men, but within you are full of hypocrisy and iniquity.

Matthew 23.27-28

He who has the character of a sinner, though he lays great stress on the outward signs of his religious calling as a means of living, he who does not control himself though he pretends to do so, will come to grief for a long time.

Uttaradhyayana Sutra 20.43 (*Jainism*)

Whoever derives a profit for himself from the words of the Torah is helping on his own destruction.

Mishnah, Avot 4.7 (*Judaism*)

Better to swallow a red-hot iron ball like a flame of fire than to be an immoral and uncontrolled person feeding on the alms offered by the devout.

Dhammapada 307 (*Buddhism*)

Many are the gurus who rob the disciple of his wealth; but rare is the guru who removes the disciple's afflictions.

Kularnava Tantra 13 (*Hinduism*)

Just as kusa grass cuts the hand when wrongly grasped, even so monkhood wrongly handled drags one to a woeful state. Any loose act, any corrupt practice, a life of dubious holiness—none of these is of much fruit.

Dhammapada 311-12 *(Buddhism)*

Woe to those who pray
and are heedless of their prayers,
to those who make display
and refuse charity.

Qur'an 107.4-7

Prayers to the Deity accompanied by monetary gifts secured by injustice are sure not to be granted. Pray in all righteousness and the Deity will be pleased to listen to your supplication. Foolish is he who, in impatient eagerness and without following the path of righteousness, hopes to obtain divine protection.

Shinto-Uden-Futsujosho *(Shinto)*

Beware of practicing your piety before men in order to be seen by them; for then you have no reward from your Father who is in heaven.

Matthew 6.1

O believers, void not your freewill offerings with reproach and injury, as one who expends of his substance to show off to men and believes not in God and the Last Day. The likeness of him is as the likeness of a smooth rock on which is soil, and a torrent smites it, and leaves it barren. They have no power over anything that they have earned. God guides not the people of the unbelievers.

Qur'an 2.264

The man of superior "righteousness" takes action,
and has an ulterior motive to do so.
The man of superior "propriety" takes action,
and when people do not respond to it, he will stretch his arms and force it on them.

Tao Te Ching 38 *(Taoism)*

Physician, heal thyself.

Luke 4.23

What is the use of your matted hair, O witless man? What is the use of your antelope skin garment? Within, you are full of passions; without, you embellish yourself [with the paraphernalia of an ascetic].

Dhammapada 394 *(Buddhism)*

And of mankind are some who say, "We believe in God and the Last Day," when they believe not. They think to beguile God and those who believe, and they beguile none save themselves; but they perceive not. In their hearts is a disease, and God increases their disease. A painful doom is theirs because they lie. And when it is said to them, "Make not mischief on the earth," they say, "We are only peacemakers." Behold they are indeed the mischief-makers but they perceive not.[14]

Qur'an 2.8-12

Teachings of Sun Myung Moon

If you convey God's words to someone only with the intention to use him or her in some way, you will never be able to establish the standard of the Way. Give what you have to others with a sincere heart. *(Way of God's Will 3.3)*

Satan is clever and smart. Using his cunning, he manipulates God's methods to put himself at the center. Likewise, people who act on their selfish desires cause the worst harm within the world of religion. They will speak about the will of God or the advancement of their nation, but actually they are doing things only to benefit themselves. Ignoring the fact that God is the starting-point of everything, they act only for themselves. Anyone who collects believers' money for the greater purpose of God and uses that money unscrupulously for himself is a thief. The same applies to anyone who takes church property for his own use without getting permission. Such people will be destroyed from within. (*God's Will and the World,* April 3, 1983)

What is the purpose of religion? It is to clean out Satan's den within my body that causes me to struggle. All of us need to do this, and that is why we need religion. Yet many believers only try to discern evils in the world out there while they cover up their own faults. They think that they will attain goodness when they get to heaven. However, this does not make any sense. (131:23, March 11, 1984)

It is time to overcome the hypocritical faith in God's name that lacks true love, and abandon all selfish works that violate original human rights and result in injustice. (400:95, December 27, 2002)

Although Christian doctrine teaches that all humanity descended from the same parents, many citizens of Christian nations who profess this doctrine will not even sit together with their brothers and sisters of different skin colors. (*Exposition of the Divine Principle,* Introduction)

As religious people, we should feel responsible for the shaky spiritual foundation of this generation, and should deeply repent. Throughout the long history of religion, we have not made a convincing witness for the living God. We have been negligent in the practice of love. As a result, we have allowed atheism to prevail and communism to flourish throughout the world. As religious people, we should take responsibility for this.
  Today God is calling us. All religious people, standing on the internal foundation of deep self-reflection, should challenge the evils of our world and work creatively in order to realize God's Will on earth. The living God does not want to relate with us not merely in the context of scriptures and rituals. He wants to dwell in the hearts of people who keep God's Will in their minds and live it twenty-four hours a day. (135:222, November 16, 1985)

Heresy

THE MOST INSIDIOUS CAUSE OF DEVIATION from the religious path is the lure of false teaching, or heresy. The scriptures of every major religion warn against it. "Heresy" means opinion, and the wisdom of God's revelation to the founding saint of the religion is not something to be altered or revised on the basis of someone else's opinion.
  It is true that every genuine religion at its birth was branded a heresy by the leaders of the orthodox establishment. Yet in addition, heretical offshoots of these new religions usually sprang up within a generation of the Founder's passing, or even in the Founder's lifetime. Yet by the Will of God, the mainstream religions became established while the heresies that beset them did not. Nowhere do we find that a heresy ever defeated a major religion's line of orthodox development. Despite their theological attraction, there must be good reasons why heresies were branded as such.
  A number of the passages gathered here attack false prophets and heretics for having base motives: they are hypocrites using religion for worldly gain (although orthodox teachers could have the same flaw). Some attribute these false teachings to the work of demons and evil spirits. Others point to their rotten fruits: licen-

tious living, greed, and the sowing of dissension. On the other hand, some heresies deceive through advocating a standard of conduct even more austere or a faith even more extreme than what is called for in the correct path—Devadatta being a prime example. Still other passages attack heretics for fomenting schism and breaking down the unity of the faith.

Beware of false prophets, who come to you in sheep's clothing but inwardly are ravenous wolves. You will know them by their fruits.
Matthew 7.15-16

God's Messenger is reported as saying, "In the last times men will come forth who will fraudulently use religion for worldly ends and wear sheepskins in public to display meekness. Their tongues will be sweeter than sugar, but their hearts will be the hearts of wolves. God will say, 'Are they trying to deceive Me, or are they acting presumptuously towards Me? I swear by Myself that I shall send trial upon those people which will leave the intelligent men among them confounded.'"
Hadith of Tirmidhi (Islam)

There will be false teachers among you, who will secretly bring in destructive heresies, even denying the Master who brought them, bringing upon themselves swift destruction. And many will follow their licentiousness, and because of them the way of truth will be reviled. And in their greed they will exploit you with false words; from of old their condemnation has not been idle, and their destruction has not been asleep.
2 Peter 2.1-3

In later times some will depart from the faith by giving heed to deceitful spirits and doctrines of demons, through the pretensions of liars whose consciences are seared.
1 Timothy 4.1-2

Thus have We appointed unto every Prophet an adversary—devils of humankind and jinn—who inspire in one another plausible discourse through guile.
Qur'an 6.112

Mara the Evil One will expound to the bodhisattva a counterfeit of the Path.
Large Sutra on Perfect Wisdom 382 (Buddhism)

Even Satan disguises himself as an angel of light.
2 Corinthians 11.14

For the time is coming when people will not endure sound teaching, but having itching ears they will accumulate for themselves teachers to suit their own likings, and will turn away from listening to the truth and wander into myths.
2 Timothy 4.3-4

Had falsehood been allowed to show separately from truth, seekers of truth would have easily discerned it, and would have kept away from falsehood. And had truth been allowed to appear distinct from falsehood, people would not have found [it] easy to criticize religion. But unfortunately men started mixing parts of truth with falsehood, and Satan exploited this situation, and got complete control over the minds of its followers. Only such persons can escape its trap, who have advanced with the help of God towards sober and rational ways of meditation.
Nahjul Balagha, Khutba 55 (Shiite Islam)

Mara, the Evil One, may come along in the guise of a teacher, and say, "Give up what you have heard up to now!... What you have heard just now, that is not the word of the Buddha. It is poetry, the work of poets. But what I here teach to you, that is the teaching of the Buddha, that is the word of the Buddha." If, on hearing that, a Bodhisattva wavers and is put out, then one should know that he has not been predicted by the Tathagata, that he is not fixed on full enlightenment. But... a monk whose outflows are dried up does not go by someone else whom he puts his trust in, for he has placed the nature of Dharma directly before his own eyes.

Perfection of Wisdom in Eight Thousand Lines 17.2 (Buddhism)

Then if any one says to you, "Lo, here is the Christ!" or "There he is!" do not believe it. For false Christs and false prophets will arise and show great signs and wonders, so as to lead astray, if possible, even the elect.

Matthew 24.23-24

Be not those who split up their religion and become schismatics, each sect exulting in its tenets.[15]

Qur'an 30.32

I am astonished that you are so quickly deserting him who called you in the grace of Christ and turning to a different gospel—not that there is another gospel, but there are some who trouble you and want to pervert the gospel of Christ. But even if we, or an angel from heaven, should preach to you a gospel contrary to that which we preached to you, let him be accursed. As we have said before, so now I say again: If any one is preaching to you a gospel contrary to that which you received, let him be accursed.

Galatians 1.6-9

One thing, when it comes to pass, does so to the loss, to the unhappiness of many folk… to the misery of the gods and humankind. What is that one thing? Schism in the order of monks. When the order is broken there are mutual quarrels, mutual abuse, mutual exclusiveness, and mutual betrayals. Thereupon those who are at variance are not reconciled, and between some of those who were at one there arises some difference.

Itivuttaka 11 (Buddhism)

Devadatta appealed to some friends of his, saying, "Come, we will approach the Lord and ask for five policies, saying, 'Lord, the Lord in many a figure speaks in praise of desiring little, of being contented, of expunging evil, of being punctilious, etc. Lord, the following five policies are conducive thereto: Monks must be forest dwellers for as long as they live; whoever should abide in a village, sin would besmirch him. They must be beggars for alms; whoever should accept an invitation to a meal would commit sin. They should wear rags; whoever accepts a robe given by a householder, commits sin. They should dwell at the root of a tree; whoever should go under cover commits sin. They should never eat fish and flesh; whoever eats fish or flesh commits sin.' The recluse Gotama will not allow these five policies, but we will win the people over to them."

Devadatta's friends replied, "It is possible, with these five policies, to make a schism in the recluse Gotama's Order, a breaking of the concord. For, your reverence, people esteem austerity."

Devadatta and his friends approached the Lord, and put the matter of these five policies before him.

"Enough, Devadatta," he said. "Whoever wishes, let him be a forest dweller, whoever wishes, let him stay in a village; whoever wishes, let him be a beggar for alms; whoever wishes, let him accept an invitation; whoever wishes, let him wear rags; whoever wishes, let him accept robes given by a householder…"

Devadatta was joyful and elated that the Lord did not accept his five policies. He entered Rajagaha and taught them to the people, and such people as were of little faith thought that Devadatta and his friends were punctilious while Gotama was permissive of profligacy. But the people who had faith and were believing complained to the monks that Devadatta was creating a schism, and the monks told the Lord. He said to Devadatta, who acknowledged the truth of the complaint,

"Do not let there be a schism in the Order, for a schism in the Order is a serious matter, Devadatta. He who splits an Order that is united sets up demerit that endures for an eon and he is boiled in hell for an eon. But he who unites an Order that is split sets up sublime merit and rejoices in heaven for an eon."

Vinaya Pitaka 2.192-98 *(Buddhism)*

Teachings of Sun Myung Moon

Enemies will certainly appear on the path you travel. Enemies will appear challenging your faith and your finances. Furthermore, some members of our Unification Church will become each other's enemies. Satan will seize the moment when you make a small mistake and drive you to the path of Cain.

How should you lead your life to defeat these enemies and not stand in the position of Cain? Do not live for your own comfort, but live a life of sacrifice for the sake of the whole. (3:212, November 1, 1957)

Some people, after they learned the Divine Principle taught in the Unification Church, use it to advance their own interests. Such people are swindlers and thieves. They use the Principle that I brought to build a comfortable domain for themselves inside the realm of Unificationism. They steal the Word, the Divine Principle, although it does not belong to them but belongs to Heaven. Pretending as if it was their own teaching, they use it for their own purposes. They create devious groups, which use guile to snatch up followers whom they swindle [with a counterfeit of the truth]. Their bodies are like the skeletons in the valley of dry bones. They appear to be alive, but their spirits are dead. (June 21, 2001)

Since a fallen person stands in the midway position between God and Satan and relates with both of them, the works of a good spirit may be accompanied by the subtle influences of an evil spirit... In the present era, spiritual phenomena are becoming ever more prevalent. Unless religious leaders can correctly distinguish the works of good spirits from the works of evil spirits, they cannot properly instruct and guide those who experience spiritual phenomena. (*Exposition of the Divine Principle*, Fall 4.4)

The Last Days is the time when people return to the spiritual level reached by the first human ancestors just prior to the Fall. Today, being the Last Days, is the time when people throughout the world are reaching this level. Just as Adam and Eve prior to the Fall were able to converse directly with God, today many people on earth can communicate with the spirit world. The prophecy that in the Last Days, "I will pour out my Spirit upon all flesh, and your sons and daughters shall prophesy, and your young men shall see visions, and your old men shall dream dreams" (Acts 2.17), may be explained based on this insight from the Principle. In the Last Days, many people will receive the revelation, "You are the Lord." Often these people will be misled into believing that they are the Second Coming of Christ. Why do they stray from the right path?

Upon creating human beings, God gave them the mandate to rule over the universe. (Gen. 1:28) Yet due to the Fall, they have been unable to fulfill this blessing. When fallen people are spiritually restored through the providence of restoration to the top of the growth stage, they will reach the level of heart comparable to that of Adam and Eve just before their Fall. God gives certain people who are at this stage the revelation that they are the Lord, in recognition that they have reached the level of maturity at which He had once blessed human beings with dominion over the universe.

Believers in the Last Days whose devout faith entitles them to receive the revelation that they are "the Lord" stand in a position similar to that of John the Baptist. John the Baptist came with the mission to make straight the way of Jesus. (John 1:23) In the same way, these people of faith are given the mission to prepare, in their particular areas of responsibility, the way for Christ at the Second Advent. Since they are to act as the Lord's representatives in their respective fields, God gives them the revelation that they are the Lord.

When someone who is gifted with spiritual communication receives the revelation that he is the Lord, he should understand this phenomenon through the teachings of the Principle. He should not act wrongly, mistaking himself for Christ at the Second Advent. Otherwise, he may end up playing the role of an antichrist. For this reason, the Bible contains prophecies that in the Last Days there will appear many antichrists...

People who contribute to the providence of restoration usually are responsible for only a part of the providence. Focusing only on their vertical relationship with God, they are often not sensitive to their proper horizontal relationship with other spiritually attuned people. Strife can break out among them, as each thinks that the Will of God which he serves is different from that which the others are serving. Their conflicts are aggravated when each of them receives the revelation that he is the best. Yet God offers such encouragement to spur each on to do his very best in carrying out his particular mission within the greater providence. God also gives such revelations because each is, in truth, the one best suited for his respective area of mission. (*Exposition of the Divine Principle*, Resurrection 2.2.6)

God did not create denominations or religious sects. In fact, religion itself is a byproduct of the Fall. It is Satan who fosters denominational schisms and religious divisions. In heaven there are no walls between nations, denominations or religions. It is a world composed of one huge family. (May 8, 2001)

Arguing with God

SINCE WE CAN EXPERIENCE GOD AS A REAL PERSON, who loves and cares for human beings as His children, it is not enough to respond only with simple devotion and blind faith. Having questions we cannot answer, struggling by ourselves and making no headway, we stop and demand that God give us the answer. With our feet firmly planted we take a stand, questioning the way things are and arguing that they can be better. The prophets and sages who disputed with God were neither doubters nor atheists, nor were they complainers of little faith. Rather, they dared to stand up and confront God, motivated by a burning desire for deeper insight into Gods' truth and the experience of His Presence.

Abraham argued with God; he challenged God to be merciful on the cities of Sodom and Gomorrah. Moses pleaded with God; he took the blame upon himself for the Israelites' apostasy when they made the golden calf. Muhammad argued with God to reduce the number of obligatory prayers from fifty down to five. Job argued with God because conventional wisdom said that his suffering must be the just punishment for his sins, yet he knew himself to be innocent. The Talmudic sages argued with God to uphold the value of human free will.

In all these encounters, the prophets and sages of old showed the way to relate to God while upholding their personal integrity. They argued based upon righteousness and deeply held beliefs. They stood before God with a clean conscience and took their life in their hands to challenge the conventional doctrines, because they knew that God transcended the limited human teachings about Him.

The LORD said, "Because the outcry against Sodom and Gomorrah is great and their sin is very grave, I will go down to see whether they have done altogether according to the outcry which has come to me; and if not, I will know."

So the men turned from there, and went toward Sodom; but Abraham still stood before the LORD. Then Abraham drew near, and said, "Will you indeed destroy the righteous with the wicked? Suppose there are fifty righteous within the city; will you still destroy the place and not spare it for the fifty righteous who are in it? Far be it from you to do such a thing, to slay the righteous with the wicked, so that the righteous fare as the wicked! Far be that from you! Shall not the Judge of all the earth do right?"

Genesis 19.20-25

At the end of forty days and forty nights the LORD gave me [Moses] the two tables of stone, the tables of the covenant. Then the LORD said to me, "Arise, go down quickly from here; for your people whom you have brought from Egypt have acted corruptly; they have turned aside quickly out of the way which I commanded them; they have made themselves a molten image... Let me alone, that I may destroy them and blot out their name from under heaven; and I will make of you a nation mightier and greater than they."...

Then I lay prostrate before the LORD as before, forty days and forty nights; I neither ate bread nor drank water, because of all the sin which you have committed... because the LORD had said that he would destroy you. And I prayed to the LORD, "O LORD God, destroy not your people and your heritage, whom you have redeemed through your greatness, whom you have brought out of Egypt with a mighty hand. Remember your servants, Abraham, Isaac, and Jacob; do not regard the stubbornness of this people, or their wickedness, or their sin, lest the land from which you brought us say, 'Because the LORD was not able to bring them into the land which he promised them, and because he hated them, he has brought them out to slay them in the wilderness.' For they are your people and your heritage, whom you brought out by your great power and by your outstretched arm."

Deuteronomy 9.11-29

"When the angel raised me [through the heavens]," said the Prophet, "then God prescribed for my people fifty prayers [a day]. As I came back with this regulation, I passed near Moses. 'What has God prescribed for your people?' he asked. 'He has prescribed fifty prayers,' I replied. 'Go back to the Lord,' said Moses, 'for your people will not be strong enough to endure that.' So I went back into the presence of God, who reduced the number by half. Then when I came near Moses, I said to him, 'They have been reduced by half.' 'Go back to the Lord,' he said, 'for your people will not be strong enough to endure that.' I went back into the presence of God, who reduced the number again by half. Coming back to Moses, I told him of this new reduction. 'Go back to the Lord,' he replied, 'for your people will not have the strength to endure that.' I went back into the presence of God and He said to me, 'There will be five prayers then, but they will be worth fifty in my eyes, for nothing can be changed of what has been spoken in My presence.' I went back to Moses, who said to me again, 'Go back to the Lord.' 'I am ashamed before the Lord,' I replied."[16]

Hadith of Bukhari (Islam)

God said, "When I conquer, I lose. When I am conquered, I gain. I conquered the generation of the flood. But did I not lose, for I destroyed my world? So, too, with the generation of the Tower of Babel. So, too, with the men of Sodom. But at the sin of the golden calf I was conquered; Moses prevailed over me [to forgive their sin], and I gained, in that I did not destroy Israel."

Pesikta Rabbati 32b-33a (Judaism)

I will take my flesh in my teeth,
and put my life in my hand.
Behold, he will slay me; I have no hope;
yet I will defend my ways to his face.
This will be my salvation,
that a godless man shall not come before him.
Listen carefully to my words,
and let my declaration be in thy ears.
Behold, I have prepared my case;
I know that I shall be vindicated.
Who is there that will contend with me?
For then I would be silent and die.
Only grant two things to me,
then I will not hide myself from thy face:
withdraw thy hand far from me,
and let not dread of thee terrify me.
Then call, and I will answer;
or let me speak, and do thou reply to me.
How many are my iniquities, and my sins?
Make me know my transgression and my sin.
Why dost thou hide thy face,
and count me as thy enemy?

Job 13.14-24

Rabbi Eliezer brought forward all of the arguments in the world [in favor of his position on a certain matter of ritual cleanliness], but his colleagues did not accept them from him.

He said to them, "If the law agrees with me, let this carob tree prove it." The carob tree leaped a hundred cubits from its place in the garden. The sages replied, "No proof can be brought from a carob tree."

He said to them, "If the law agrees with me, let this stream of water prove it." The stream of water began to flow backwards. The sages replied, "No proof can be brought from a stream of water."

Again he said to them, "If the law agrees with me, let the walls of this schoolhouse prove it." The walls began to shake and incline to fall. Rabbi Joshua leaped up and rebuked the walls saying, "When disciples of sages engage in a legal dispute what is your relevance?" In honor of Rabbi Joshua the walls did not tumble. In honor of Rabbi Eliezer they did not right themselves, and are still inclined even to this day.

Again Rabbi Eliezer said to the sages, "If the law agrees with me, let it be proved from Heaven." A divine voice came forth and said, "Why do you dispute with Rabbi Eliezer, for in all matters the law agrees with him!" But Rabbi Joshua rose to his feet again and exclaimed, "'It is not in heaven.' [Deut. 30.12]"

Some time later, Rabbi Nathan met the prophet Elijah and asked him, "What did the Holy One, blessed be He, do when rebuked by Rabbi Joshua?" Elijah replied, "He laughed with joy, saying, 'My children have defeated me, my children have defeated me.'"[17]

Talmud, Baba Metzia 59ab (Judaism)

Teachings of Sun Myung Moon

When Moses faced the truth that the Israelites had fallen away, he did not immediately chastise them; instead, he appealed to God, blaming himself and his inadequacy. He went again up Mount Sinai and fasted for 40 days. He prayed, "Father, why can't these people enter the Promised Land even when they see it before their eyes? Who is responsible for that? It is my responsibility." He appealed to God to take him as an offering and turn aside from destroying his people. (1:144, July 1, 1956)

If you work at witnessing 10 hours a day and cannot find even one receptive person, then try working 15 hours a day. If you still cannot find someone, then double your investment to 20 hours. If that still does not work, add 4 more hours and work 24 hours a day. If that still does not work, call on God seriously, saying, "Father, shouldn't Thou be helping me? This work is Thy Will as well as mine. Thou didst promise that if I ask, I shall receive, and if I seek, I shall find, and if I knock, it shall be opened." (54:325, March 31, 1972)

Didn't Adam and Eve betray God? To restore that history through indemnity, you should ask God to betray you. Make such a determination and declare, "God, You can say to me, 'I do not know you.' Although You do not recognize me, I will fulfill the duty of a filial child up to the last moment of the struggle. I will not deviate from this course." (31:49, April 12, 1970)

In the late Middle Ages, man's original mind was repressed, its free development blocked by the social environment of feudalism and the secularization and corruption of the Roman church. Faith is the path each person must walk in search of God. Faith should be nurtured through a direct vertical relationship between God and each individual. Yet in that age, the papacy and the clergy, with their rituals and dogmas, constrained the people's devotional life...

According to the Principle of Creation, we are created to attain perfection by fulfilling our given responsibility of our own free will, without God's direct assistance. We are then to attain oneness with God and acquire true autonomy. Therefore, it is the calling of our original nature to pursue freedom and autonomy...

[Believers] protested the medieval view that faith required unquestioning obedience to the dictates of the Church in all areas of life, which denied them the right to worship God according to the dictates of conscience based on their own reading of the Bible. They also questioned the otherworldly and ascetic monastic ideal which devalued the natural world, science and the practical affairs of life. Out of these grievances, many medieval Christians... called for the revival of the spirit of early Christianity, when believers zealously lived for the Will of God, guided by the words of Jesus and the apostles. This medieval movement... exploded in the Protestant Reformation. (*Exposition of the Divine Principle*, Preparation 1)

Those believers who receive divine inspiration through prayer are able to grasp spiritually the providence of the new age. Even though this may put them at odds with the doctrines of the old age, they will still respond to the promptings of the spirit and follow the calling of the new providence. Among the disciples of Jesus, there was not one who was overly attached to the Old Testament Scriptures. Rather, they all responded to the spiritual experiences which they could sense through their inner minds. In the Last Days, people who lead an ardent life of prayer or who live by their conscience will feel intense anxiety in their hearts. This is because in their hearts they vaguely sense a spiritual calling and want to follow the providence of the new age, yet they have not come in contact with the new truth which can guide them to act accordingly. (*Exposition of the Divine Principle*, Eschatology 5.2)

Testing

EVERYONE ON THE PATH OF FAITH WILL BE TESTED. Scripture records that the great people of faith were tested many times. Abraham endured ten trials of faith. Satan tested Job with loss of family and property. Muhammad had to overcome many obstacles as he struggled to proclaim the message to the idolators of Mecca. Jesus was tempted in the wilderness and tested again on the way to the cross. Hindu and Buddhist saints as well faced life-and-death trials, and with absolute faith overcame them.

Overcoming tests gives us strength and toughness of character. Testing also accompanies grace, either before or afterwards, to qualify us to receive the grace and retain it.

Father Moon explains the reason why people of faith encounter testing by referring to the Book of Job's account of the bargaining between Satan and God. Since human beings fell away from oneness with God, God accedes to Satan, "the Accuser," the right to test human beings in order to prove whether they are indeed worthy of returning to God's realm. Satan ruthlessly looks for any hint of selfishness that would disqualify them and give him a claim over them. Only the most faithful and selfless people can pass his tests.

Sometimes a test requires us to deal with an inconceivable situation. The famous Qur'anic passage of Moses and *al-Khidr*, the "Green Man," presents a trial where Moses must believe in things entirely contrary to common sense; but he cannot. In the Hindu Ramayana, Sita the wife of Rama proves her fidelity by jumping into a blazing pyre, and in a Buddhist sutra a seeker throws himself off a cliff to certain death; both pass the test and are unharmed. And how inconceivable was it to Abraham that God would ask him to sacrifice his son? We include accounts of several of the tests in Father Moon's life.

1. Satan Tests People of Faith

Now there was a day when the sons of God[18] came to present themselves before the LORD, and Satan also came among them. The LORD said to Satan, "Whence have you come?" Satan answered the LORD, "From going to and fro on the earth, and from walking up and down on it." And the LORD said to Satan, "Have you considered my servant Job, that there is none like him on the earth, a blameless and upright man, who fears God and turns away from evil?" Then Satan answered the LORD, "Does Job fear God for nought? Hast thou not put a hedge about him and his house and all that he has, on every side? Thou hast blessed the work of his hands, and his possessions have increased in the land. But put forth thy hand now, and touch all that he has, and he will curse thee to thy face." And the LORD said to Satan, "Behold, all that he has is in your power; only upon himself do not put forth your hand." So Satan went forth from the presence of the LORD.

Now there was a day when his sons and daughters were eating and drinking wine in their eldest brother's house; and there came a messenger to Job, and said... "Your sons and daughters were eating and drinking wine in their eldest brother's house; and behold, a great wind came across the wilderness, and struck the four corners of the house, and it fell upon the young people, and they are dead; and I alone have escaped to tell you."

Then Job arose, and rent his robe, and shaved his head, and fell upon the ground, and worshiped. And he said, "Naked I came from my mother's womb, and naked shall I return; the LORD gave, and the LORD has taken away; blessed be the name of the LORD."

In all this Job did not sin or charge God with wrong.

Again there was a day when the sons of God came to present themselves before the LORD, and Satan also came among them to present himself before the LORD. And the LORD said to Satan, "Whence have you come?" Satan answered the LORD, "From going to and fro on the earth, and from walking up and down on it." And the LORD said to Satan, "Have you considered my servant Job, that there is none like him on the earth, a blameless and upright man, who fears God and turns away from evil? He still holds fast his integrity, although you moved me against him, to destroy him without cause." Then Satan answered the LORD, "Skin for skin! All that a man has he will give for his life. But put forth thy hand now, and touch his bone and his flesh, and he will curse thee to thy face." And the LORD said to Satan, "Behold, he is in your power; only spare his life."

Satan went forth from the presence of the LORD, and afflicted Job with loathsome sores from the sole of his foot to the crown of his head. And he took a potsherd with which to scrape himself, and sat among the ashes. Then his wife said to him, "Do you still hold fast to your integrity? Curse God, and die." But he said to her, "You speak as one of the foolish women would speak. Shall we receive good at the hand of God, and shall we not receive evil?"

Job 1.6-2.10

Jesus was led up by the Spirit into the wilderness to be tempted by the devil. And he fasted forty days and forty nights, and afterward he was hungry. And the tempter came and said to him, "If you are the Son of God, command these stones to become loaves of bread." But he answered, "It is written,

> 'Man shall not live by bread alone,
> but by every word that proceeds from the mouth of God.'"

Matthew 4.1-4

Once there was a person who sought the True Path in the Himalayas. He cared nothing for all the treasures of the earth or even for all the delights of heaven, but he sought the teaching that would remove all mental delusions. The gods were impressed by the man's earnestness and sincerity and decided to test his mind. So one of the gods disguised himself as a demon and appeared in the Himalayas, singing,

> Everything changes,
> Everything appears and disappears.

The seeker heard this song which pleased him so, as if he had found a spring of cool water for his thirst or as if he were a slave unexpectedly set free. He thought, "At last I have found the true teaching that I have sought for so long." He followed the voice and at last came upon the frightful demon. With an uneasy mind he approached the demon and said, "Was it you who sang the holy song that I have just heard? If it was you, please sing more of it." The demon replied, "Yes, it was my song, but I can not sing more of it until I have had something to eat; I am starving." The man begged him in earnest, saying, "It has a sacred meaning to me and I have sought its teaching for a long time. I have only heard a part of it; please let me hear more." The demon said again, "I am starving, but if I can taste the warm flesh and blood of a man, I will finish the song." The man, in his eagerness to hear the teaching, promised the demon that he could have his body after he had heard the teaching. Then the demon sang the complete song,

> Everything changes,
> Everything appears and disappears,
> There is perfect tranquility
> When one transcends both life and
>   extinction.

Hearing this, the man, after he wrote the poem on rocks and trees around, quietly climbed a tree and hurled himself to the feet of the demon, but the demon had disappeared and, instead, a radiant god received the body of the man unharmed.

Mahaparinirvana Sutra 424-33 (Buddhism)

When the future Buddha sat down at the foot of the Bodhi tree with his soul fully resolved to obtain the highest knowledge, the whole world rejoiced; but Mara, the enemy of good law, was afraid. He whom they call the God of Pleasure, the owner of various weapons, the flower-arrowed, the lord of the course of desire—it is he whom they also style Mara, the enemy of liberation. His three sons, Confusion, Gaiety, and Pride, and his three daughters, Lust, Delight, and Craving, asked him the reason for his despondency, and thus he answered them,

"This sage, wearing the armor of resolution, and having drawn the arrow of wisdom with the barb of truth, sits yonder intending to conquer my realms—hence my mind is despondent. If he succeeds in overcoming me and proclaims to the world the path of final bliss, all this my realm will today become empty…"

Then, seizing his flower-made bow and his five arrows of infatuation, the Great Disturber of the minds of living beings, together with his children, approached the root of the Bodhi tree. Placing his left hand on the end of the barb and playing with the arrow, Mara addressed the calm seer as he sat on his seat preparing to cross to the further side of the ocean of existence,

"Up, up, O Kshatriya, afraid of death! Follow your own duty [as member of the warrior caste] and abandon this path of liberation. Conquer the lower worlds by force of arms, and gain the higher worlds as well! That is a glorious path to travel, which has been followed by leaders of men for generations. This mendicant life is ill-suited for one born of royalty to follow…"

But even when thus addressed, the Shakya saint, unheeding, did not change his posture. Mara then discharged his arrow of love at him and set in front of him his daughters Lust, Delight, and Craving, and his sons Confusion, Gaiety, and Pride. Still he gave no heed and swerved not from his firmness. Mara, beholding him thus, sank down, and slowly pondered,

"He does not even notice the arrow… Can he be devoid of all feeling? He is not worthy of my flower-shaft, nor my arrow Gladdener, nor even my sending my daughter Rati to tempt him. He deserves the terrors, attacks, and blows from all the gathered hosts of the demons."

Then Mara called to mind his own army, mustering them for the overthrow the Shakya saint. His followers swarmed around, wearing different forms and carrying arrows, trees, darts, clubs, and swords in their hands; with faces of boars, fishes, horses, asses, and camels, of tigers, bears, lions, and elephants—one-eyed, many-faced, three-headed… One of them, his eyes rolling wildly, lifted a club against him; but his arm was instantly paralyzed… Another hurled upon him a mass of blazing straw as big as a mountain peak…. Despite all these various scorching assaults on his body and his mind, and all these missiles showered down upon him, the Shakya saint did not in the least degree move from his posture nor deviate from his firm resolution…

Then some being of invisible shape, but of preeminent glory, standing in the heavens and beholding Mara thus malevolent against the seer, addressed him in a loud voice unruffled by enmity, "Take not on yourself, O Mara, this vain labor; throw aside your malevolence and retire to your home; this sage cannot be shaken."

Ashvaghosha, Buddhacarita 13[19] (Buddhism)

Teachings of Sun Myung Moon

Due to the Human Fall, Satan tramples upon human beings and dominates the whole earth. To turn this situation around, we need to employ the principle of indemnity. Since Satan treated human beings with contempt, human beings should win Satan's respect and deference. They should do this by themselves, without the help of Jesus, the Holy Spirit, or God. Whatever sinful condition Satan presents them with, they should be able to overcome it. Only then can human beings become God's victorious sons and daughters.

On your path you will encounter many trials from Satan. Especially if you become open to communicate with the spirit world, you will face many trials. If you fail Satan's tests, Satan will accuse you, saying, "You are not qualified," and block your way. (3:210, November 1, 1957)

Consider the suffering of Job. First, his happy life vanished when he lost his possessions and children. Then he was cast into a situation where his friends scorned him and his wife accused him, and where his whole body was covered with wounds and itched so that he had to scratch it with tiles. Yet through it all, he never held a grudge against God. Instead, in silence and contemplation he overcame the pain, and through his illness he experienced something of God's love. Because Job was that kind of man, Heaven could bless him with possessions and children even more than before. (2:114-15, March 10, 1957)

Satan originally belonged to God. Therefore, he knows the original way he should go, and through which the universe becomes one. Yet why did he become Satan? It was because he was self-centered. Instead of centering upon God with true love, he set himself up apart from God and lived with selfish love. Satan knows that God is entitled to claim every person who has true love. Therefore, when a person of true love appears, Satan will give him back to God, saying, "He does not belong to me; he belongs to You."

But for love to be true love, it has to transcend every barrier, whether in the individual, family, tribe, nation or world. If you want to become a true person who possesses true love, you must go beyond all these levels and connect with the cosmos. That is the principle. Therefore Satan says to God, "You may choose Your man, but he still lives in my world. Before You can count him as belonging to Your nation, he has to overcome all kinds of persecution, even beyond the national level, in order to prove himself worthy of Heaven."

When Satan gave this condition to God, God had to answer, "You are correct." Satan continued, "Anyone who is dedicated to the greatest, universal purpose, and who consistently lives for the sake of others with God's love, belongs to Your nation. Nevertheless, I will be there to claim him as my own if I find any evidence of self-centeredness or attachments to the things of my realm." (124:65-65, January 23, 1983)

Satan sometimes tests you based on the original content of creation. The question is whether or not you have become a person of the original standard. If you resist, Satan will say, "God, this person has the wrong concept and does not meet the original standard. To prove it, give him to me and let me thrust him into hell. I am sure he will fall." Job was tested ten times, yet still he was grateful and said, "Naked I came from my mother's womb, and naked I shall return; the Lord gave, and the Lord has taken away." Job always went to zero. Thus he fulfilled the formula.

Because of this, Job received new blessings a hundred-fold and a thousand-fold. He was a model of a victorious person during the age of restoration. Although he was struck ten times, he always kept a grateful heart, remained at the zero point, and held on to absolute faith in God. Therefore Satan drew back from Job, and Job could be revived and granted all his desires. (246:20-21, March 23, 1993)

Satan tempted Jesus three times. First, while he was fasting for forty days, Satan tempted him with food. He appeared before Jesus and asked him to change a stone into bread. This would be good news to a starving person, but Jesus refused. He clearly stated, "Man does not live on bread alone, but on every word that comes from the mouth of God." This means that Jesus refused to yield any conditions to Satan pertaining to the necessities of life.[20] (3:121, October 13, 1957)

Throughout my life I experienced tribulation. Satan came against me with all his power, using the cruelest methods. Just as in the story of Job in the Bible, Satan told God, "He is only able to achieve something because You blessed him. I demand to test him by taking everything away from him; then I will see if he is so strong." Satan made that demand concerning me several times, and God had to push me into life-threatening situations.

Likewise, you must face the fact that God will not help you directly. Instead, you will encounter terrible difficulties and feel completely helpless. You will think that although you deserve God's help, God is nowhere near you and does not help you at all. However, if you overcome that trial, God's help will surely arrive—although indirectly. (117:160-61, February 28, 1982)

Although Reverend Moon may be a person of some importance, and although God loves him, he is not exempt from the course that human beings must go through during which they are to take responsibility to indemnify sin without God's help. In other words, I had to overcome Satan on my own. In the beginning, Adam was given his appointed task to subjugate Satan and Satan's world in order to establish the realm of God's ideal. Therefore, I should likewise overcome my environment to reach the realm of God's ideal. Do you understand?

To pay my portion of indemnity, I had to be driven out, stripped of my clothes and chased out into the cold. Therefore, I discarded my coat and gave away my meager portion of food. I willingly paid that price, to the point that even Satan took pity on me and had someone offer me a coat. That was a wonderful moment, when Satan gave me that coat. It meant that no one in the satanic world would ever take away my clothes ever again…

We all have to go through such a battle. We go through hardship and persecution, are stripped of our clothes and beaten, but then people on Satan's side appear who will dress us and bind up our wounds. By going through such a course, people will come to our side. (124:303-04, March 1, 1983)

Satan said, "I will see how strong Reverend Moon's love really is," and tested me by taking my son Heung Jin. Satan tested me in this: in this moment of grief, who would I love more, God and humankind, or my own son? I could not seek revenge against Satan. I would not give him an opening. I only devoted my efforts to liberate the nations… I determined to make Heung Jin's passing an offering to mobilize the spirit world and lay a victorious foundation for Heaven to advance the work on earth…

I understood one principle: the priest who offers a sacrifice to God does not shed tears. Through the offering he should glorify Heaven, support humankind and strive to establish the conditions to restore everything in the satanic world. Therefore, there were no tears on my face as I offered up my beloved son and laid him to rest. I stood proudly in my public position. When Satan saw this, he could not help but respect me. He had to acknowledge, "Reverend Moon, you are indeed a man of Heaven." Hence, even though the realm of death struck the life of Heaven, I made up for the loss and went beyond it with the power of love. (130:162-63, January 8, 1984)

No matter how Satan tries to test you and jump on you, if you sacrifice yourself there will not be any problem. If you make excuses for yourself, however, Satan will overpower you. (*Way of God's Will* 3.4)

2. Trials Are to Prove that We Belong to God

And verily We shall try you until We know those of you who really strive and are steadfast, and until We test your record.

Qur'an 47.31

Prove me, O LORD, and try me;
test my heart and my mind.
For thy steadfast love is before my eyes,
and I walk in faithfulness to thee.

Psalm 26.2-3

We will test you with a bit of fear and hunger, and a shortage of wealth and souls and produce. Proclaim such to patient people who say, whenever disaster strikes them, "We are God's, and are returning to Him!" Such will be granted their prayers by their Lord as well as mercy. Those are guided!

Qur'an 2.154-57

Blessed is the man that endures temptation: for when he is tried, he shall receive the crown of life, which the Lord hath promised to them that love him.

James 1.12

Every soul must taste of death, and We try you with evil and with good, for ordeal. And unto Us you will be returned.

Qur'an 21.35

With ten trials Abraham our father was tried, and he bore them all, to make known how great was the love of Abraham our father.

Mishnah, Avot 5.4 (Judaism)

After these things God tested Abraham, and said to him, "Abraham!" And he said, "Here am I." He said, "Take your son, your only son Isaac, whom you love, and go to the land of Moriah, and offer him there as a burnt offering upon one of the mountains of which I shall tell you."

Genesis 22.1-2

And Jacob was left alone; and a man wrestled with him until the breaking of the day. When the man saw that he did not prevail against Jacob, he touched the hollow of his thigh; and Jacob's thigh was put out of joint as he wrestled with him. Then he said, "Let me go, for the day is breaking." But Jacob said, "I will not let you go, unless you bless me." And he said to him, "What is your name?" "Jacob." "Your name shall no more be called Jacob, but Israel, for you have striven with God and with men, and have prevailed." Then Jacob asked him, "Tell me, I pray, your name." But he said, "Why is it that you ask my name?" And there he blessed him. So Jacob called the name of the place Peniel, saying, "For I have seen God face to face, and yet my life is preserved."

Genesis 32.24-30

After the death of Ravana, Rama sent for Sita... When Sita eagerly arrived, after her months of loneliness and suffering, her husband received her in full view of a vast public. But she could not understand why her lord seemed preoccupied and moody and cold. Rama suddenly said, "My task is done. I have now freed you. I have fulfilled my mission. All this effort has been not to attain personal satisfaction for you or me. It was to vindicate the honor of the Ikshvahu race and to honor our ancestors' codes and values. After all this, I must tell you that it is not customary to admit back to the normal married fold a woman who has resided all alone in a stranger's house. There can be no question of our living together again. I leave you free to go where you please and to choose any place to live in. I do not restrict you in any manner."

On hearing this, Sita broke down. "My trials are not ended yet," she cried. "I thought with your victory our troubles were at an end...! So be it." She beckoned to Lakshmana and ordered, "Light a fire at once, on this very spot."

Lakshmana hesitated and looked at his brother, wondering whether he would countermand the order. But Rama seemed passive and acquiescent. Lakshmana gathered faggots and got ready a roaring pyre within a short time. The entire crowd watched, stunned, while the flames rose higher and higher. Still Rama made no comment. He watched. Sita approached the fire, prostrated herself before it, and said, "O Agni, great god of fire, be my witness." She jumped into the fire.

From the heart of the flame rose the god of fire, bearing Sita, and presented her to Rama with words of blessing. Rama, now satisfied that he had established his wife's integrity in the presence of the world, welcomed Sita back to his arms.[21]

Ramayana, Yuddha Kanda 118-20 (*Hinduism*)

Teachings of Sun Myung Moon

Three years after a person learns the Will of God, he will face a big trial. This is to individually indemnify the position of Peter, who followed Jesus for three years and then denied him. (*Way of God's Will* 3.4)

As a year consists of four seasons, in your life there is a spring-like period in which you receive a blessing, a summer-like period in which the blessing grows, an autumn-like period in which you bear the fruit of the blessing, and then a winter-like period of trial. Be grateful for trials. They come from the love of God, to separate us from Satan. If you endure and overcome them, a spring-like period of new blessing will follow. (*Way of God's Will* 3.4)

When God is about to give grace, He puts the person through a test, either before or after the grace, to prevent Satan's accusation. Moses' course provides examples of this. God granted Moses the grace... to depart from Egypt only after he had completed the test of living in the wilderness of Midian for forty years. Only after giving the test in which God tried to kill Moses did He grant the three signs and ten plagues. Only after giving the test of the three-day course did God grant the pillars of cloud and fire. Only after giving the test of crossing the Red Sea did God give the grace of manna and quail. After giving the test of the battle with the Amalekites, God granted the grace of the tablets of stone, the Tabernacle, and the Ark of the Covenant. (*Exposition of the Divine Principle*, Moses and Jesus 2.3)

The first human beings should have been absolutely determined to keep God's commandment not to eat of the fruit, yet they fell at the risk of their lives when the Archangel tempted them. Accordingly, for Jacob to... restore the foundation to receive the Messiah, he had to triumph in a fight at the risk of his life with an angel, representing Satan. Jacob was desperate to overcome this trial as he wrestled with the angel at the ford of Jabbok. He triumphed and received the name "Israel." In this trial, it was God who tested Jacob by putting the angel in the position of Satan. God's purpose in doing this was not to make Jacob miserable, but to help him secure the position of Abel and complete the restoration of his family by winning the qualification to rule the angel. (*Exposition of the Divine Principle*, Moses and Jesus 1.2)

It was nerve-wracking for God to watch Jacob in that battle. Since the angel was fighting on behalf of Satan, God did not want Jacob to give up, but He could not say anything to Jacob. Imagine how anxious God must have been to watch each moment ticking during the battle between the two?

Jacob did not give up even to the last moment. He would not let go of the angel no matter how desperately the angel tried to shake him off. At that point, God publicly acknowledged Jacob's victory, and the angel, as Satan's representative, had to acknowledge it as well. Hence he blessed Jacob with the name "Israel." At that moment, all the hosts of heaven shouted for joy. They deeply exhaled, now that anxiety over the outcome was relieved. (20:229-30, June 9, 1968)

Even God Himself kicked Reverend Moon to test him. He said, "Reverend Moon, you are a heretic. I don't know you!" Yet no matter how strangely God treated me, I had already grabbed onto God's coattails. I told Him, "Heavenly Father, no matter how Thou dost treat me, Thou canst not dissuade me from my path."

This dispute dragged on for forty days. Since God opposed me, Jesus, Buddha, Mohammed, and all the saints in spirit world also joined in, "Reverend Moon, you are a heretic! We will not accept you until you change your teachings." Yet throughout those forty days, I did not change one iota. I was steadfast as a rock. They all saw that I would not change even if they persisted for 400 years.

After 40 days the atmosphere cleared; the showdown had to end. God had to resolve the dispute and issue a decree. He stepped forward and said, "I have been testing Reverend Moon during these 40 days… and I can now declare before heaven and earth that he is the greatest victor in all of history." (161:41-42, January 1, 1987)

3. Trials Forge Character and Build Unshakable Faith

And you shall remember all the way which the LORD your God has led you these forty years in the wilderness, that he might humble you, testing you to know what was in your heart, whether you would keep his commandments, or not. And he humbled you and let you hunger and fed you with manna, which you did not know, nor did your fathers know; that he might make you know that man does not live by bread alone, but that man lives by everything that proceeds out of the mouth of the LORD. Your clothing did not wear out upon you, and your foot did not swell, these forty years. Know then in your heart that, as a man disciplines his son, the LORD your God disciplines you.

Deuteronomy 8.2-5

Mencius said, "Shun rose from the fields; Fu Yüeh was raised to office from among the builders; Chiao Ke from amid the fish and salt; Kuan Chung from the hands of the prison officer; Sun Shu-ao from the sea and Po-li Hsi from the market. That is why Heaven, when it is about to place a great burden on a man, always first tests his resolution, exhausts his frame, makes him suffer starvation and hardship, and frustrates his efforts so as to shake him from his mental lassitude, toughen his nature and make good his deficiencies."

Mencius VI.B.15 *(Confucianism)*

And to keep me from being too elated by the abundance of revelations, a thorn was given me in the flesh, a messenger of Satan, to harass me, to keep me from being too elated. Three times I [Paul] besought the Lord about this, that it should leave me; but he said to me, "My grace is sufficient for you, for my power is made perfect in weakness." I will all the more gladly boast of my weaknesses, that the power of Christ may rest upon me. For the sake of Christ, then, I am content with weaknesses, insults, hardships, persecutions, and calamities; for when I am weak, then I am strong.

2 Corinthians 12.7-10

Life is like a hill.
Mawu the Creator made it steep and slippery,
To right and left deep waters surround it,
You cannot turn back once you start to climb.
You must climb with a load on your head.
A man's arms will not help him, for it's a trial,
The world is a place of trial.

Fon Song (African Traditional Religions)

Moses... found one of our servants to whom We had given mercy from Ourselves and taught him knowledge from Our very presence. Moses said to him, "May I follow you so you may teach me some of the common sense you have been taught?" He said, "You will never have any patience with me! How can you show any patience with something that is beyond your experience?"

He said, "You will find me patient, if God so wishes. I will not disobey you in any matter." He said, "If you follow me, do not ask me about anything until I tell you something to remember it by."

So they both started out until, as they boarded a ship, he bored a hole in her. [Moses] said, "Have you scuttled her to drown her crew? You have done such a weird thing!" He said, "Didn't I say that you would not manage to show any patience with me?" He said, "Do not take me to task for what I have forgotten, nor weigh me down by making my case too difficult for me."

They journeyed on and when they met a youth, he killed him. Moses said, "Have you killed an innocent soul, who himself had not murdered another? You have committed such a horrible deed!" He said, "Did I not tell you that you would never manage to have any patience with me?" He said, "If I ever ask you about anything after this, do not let me accompany you. You have found an excuse so far as I am concerned."

They both proceeded further till when they came to the people of a town, they asked its inhabitants for some food, and they refused to treat either of them hospitably. They found a wall there which was about to tumble down, so he set it straight. Moses said, "If you had wished, you might have accepted some payment for it." He said, "This means a parting between you and me. Yet I shall inform you about the interpretation of what you had no patience for.

"As for the ship, it belonged to some poor men who worked at sea. I wanted to damage it because there was a king behind them seizing every ship by force. The young man's parents were believers, and we dreaded lest he would burden them with arrogation and disbelief. We wanted the Lord to replace him for them with someone better than him in purity and nearer to tenderness. The wall belonged to two orphan boys in the city, and a treasure of theirs lay underneath it. Their father had been honorable, so your Lord wanted them to come of age and claim their treasure as a mercy from your Lord. That is the interpretation of what you showed no patience for."[22]

Qur'an 18.65-82

If the Holy One is pleased with a man, He crushes him with painful sufferings. For it is said, "And the LORD was pleased with him, hence He crushed him by disease" (Isaiah 53.10). Now, you might think that this is so even if he did not accept them with love. Therefore it is said, "To see if his soul would offer itself in restitution." Even as the trespass-offering must be brought by consent, so also the sufferings must be endured with consent. And if he did accept them, what is his reward? "He will see his seed, prolong his days." And more than that, his knowledge [of Torah] will endure with him. For it is said, "The purpose of the LORD will prosper in his hand."[23]

Talmud, Berakot 5a (Judaism)

Teachings of Sun Myung Moon

Undergoing many trials in your life of faith, lay the foundation of victory and make yourself a solid rock which God can trust. (*Way of God's Will* 3.4)

God is with you only after you win over your environment. (*Way of God's Will* 3.2)

You should have a mind to test whether you qualify as God's good object partners, whether you are living in one accord with Him. How can find out whether you have the qualifications? You should throw yourself into situations of suffering and hardship. Sometimes you may think that you cannot survive the ordeal. However, these tests are the means by which you can prove your worth and establish your value. (66:45, March 18, 1973)

As we walk on and on, shall we say our way is steep? We cannot compare our anguished hearts with the anguish of Thy heart, or compare how we are mistreated with the footprints Thou didst leave in Satan's realm, where Thou wast blocked at every turn. Even as we go along this steep way, may a sense of mission well up in our hearts to take responsibility for the Will of Heaven. (4:293-94, September 14, 1958)

God is unchanging. However, in order to create unchanging people, He tests you by appearing as a changeable, capricious God. But God's capriciousness is only from your viewpoint. God appears to contradict Himself when He sometimes says, "Do this!" and later says, "No, do that!" First He says, "Go!" and then He says, "No, come!" God tests you by appearing to change from one moment to the next in order to find whether you are a person whose faith in Him will never change. (66:46, March 18, 1973)

During the Korean War that broke out on June 25th, 1950, I would see mothers carrying their young children on their backs, refugees on the road to the South. Yet the children were too young to know that they are traveling as refugees to escape from war. A child, having been told that he and his family are going somewhere, is at first happy to go and even hums. Then the mother who has been carrying him on her back loses strength along the way and makes the child walk. After a while the child says, "Mommy, no. I'm not going if you don't carry me on your back. Carry me on your back, carry me!"

What should a loving parent do in such a situation? She ought to carry the child, but if she carries him, both of them will die. What, then, should she do? She should make him walk. If he refuses to walk, she must threaten him and even slap his face to make him walk. By all means, they must reach their place of refuge.

What would you do if you were the mother? Would you leave him behind to die, or would you drag him by force? Which is the best way? Leave him behind to die? You do not like either alternative, but what will you do? You have to take him, no matter what. You have to drag him mercilessly, even by tearing and pulling his ears, or by making a hole in his nose and pulling him by a leash. Under the circumstances, that is real love. (32:256, July 19, 1970)

> Makest Thy cruel winds whip the faces of these young people;
> stir up the storm-wind and hurricane to push them and drive them back.
> In the midst of wind and frost they will remain honorable,
> become rock-hard young men and women,
> and emerge as victors. (121:187, October 24, 1982)

Chapter 16

Prayer and Worship

Prayer

PRAYER LIES AT THE CORE OF THE RELIGIOUS LIFE in most religions. The passages collected here discuss the efficacy of prayer and give guidance on how to pray. Through prayer, we develop a relationship with God, exposing our inner life to Him and receiving His grace. In prayer we repent for our sins, ask God for help, and receive God's guidance. We learn to trust in God to fulfill our prayers, and to follow His guidance for what we should do to progress in our life of faith. Conversely, God can begin to trust us as we declare our intention in prayer to do good, and then strive to fulfill it. Thus, prayer life can develop into a living relationship with God, as substantial as with a friend or indeed, with our own parents.

Prayer directs our heart to God and purifies it, providing a natural defense against temptations and the evil promptings of our fallen self. As we cultivate a taste for prayer, it nourishes our spirit and brightens our entire life. We receive divine energy in our conscience to do what is right, strength of character to endure hardships, and comfort in our heart as we seek to love.

Some of these texts give instruction on how to pray. Prayer should be done constantly, sometimes with vigils far into the night. Prayer should be honest; it is quiet and sincere conversation from the heart. Prayer should be accompanied by deeds; the prayer of the hypocrite is without effect. Among the best prayers are those that put the welfare of others ahead of oneself and, as Father Moon teaches, prayers to comfort God's heart. Some representative prayers can be found in the Invocation which opens this anthology.

1. God Answers Prayer

Your Lord says, "Call on Me; I will answer your prayer."

Qur'an 40.60

The LORD is near to all who call upon him, to all who call upon him in truth.

Psalm 145.18

When My servants ask you concerning Me, I am indeed Close to them. I listen to the prayer of every suppliant when he calls on Me.[1]

Qur'an 2.186

Cast your burden on the Lord, and he will sustain you.

Psalm 55.22

Lord of creation! No one other than Thee pervades all these that have come into being. May that be ours for which our prayers rise, may we be masters of many treasures!

Rig Veda 10.121.10 (Hinduism)

Therefore I tell you, whatever you ask in prayer, believe that you have received it, and it will be yours.

Mark 11.24

Is any one among you suffering? Let him pray. Is any cheerful? Let him sing praise. Is any among you sick? Let him call for the elders of the church, and let them pray over him, anointing him with oil in the name of the Lord; and the prayer of faith will save the sick man, and the Lord will raise him up; and if he has committed sins, he will be forgiven. Therefore confess your sins to one another, and pray for one another, that you may be healed. The prayer of a righteous man has great power in its effects. Elijah was a man of like nature with ourselves and he prayed fervently that it might not rain, and for three years and six months it did not rain on the earth. Then he prayed again and heaven gave rain, and the earth brought forth its fruit.

James 5.13-18

You must always pray unto the Father in my name; and whatsoever you shall ask the Father in my name, which is right, believing you shall receive, behold it shall be given unto you. Pray in your families unto the Father, always in my name, that your wives and your children may be blessed.

Book of Mormon, 3 Nephi 18.19-21
(Latter-day Saints)

Teachings of Sun Myung Moon

Prayer is calling to God and conversing with Him. (270:17, May 3, 1995)

Prayer is a covenant between man and God; it is a pledge. Whatever you pray about, you have to practice.

There is no need to pray for the same thing day after day. You only need to pray for it once with genuine sincerity. Then seek and long for it with a prayerful heart even if it takes ten or twenty years to be fulfilled. (40:299, February 7, 1971)

Prayer is making a wish. By making a wish, you place yourself in an object position to God, the Subject. You set up a subject-object relationship of love.

Having unfulfilled wishes and longings is good, because they motivate us to make this relationship. Because we lack confidence to fulfill them ourselves, we pray... clinging to God. (112:54, March 29, 1981)

Through prayer you receive strength. Through prayer you are given wisdom to know how situations will develop in the future. You will be taught how to deal with every work. The wisdom gained through prayer can equip you for a great mission. Prayer is indispensable if you are pioneering a such a path. (104:111, April 15, 1979)

[In times of difficulty], pray and ask God for His power to sustain you on the path. Declare your determination: "Father, although I might die for this work, I will do it. Though I suffer from hunger and thirst, I will cling to Thee, my God." Thus, your prayer is a pledge and a proclamation.

Once you have made that proclamation, then on your own, decide your course and determine to accomplish it. Practice love; then surely God will listen and encourage you to go forward. Once you have prayed, as long as you practice what you have prayed about, overcoming obstacles one by one, then God will approve of you and recognize you as a trustworthy person. (112:54, March 29, 1981)

Test the power of your prayer. Pray every day for one person [without telling him]. Pray tearfully for his well-being, and see what happens. Amazingly, he will feel a magnetic attraction to you. He will feel drawn to you, but he won't know why. (104:113, April 15, 1979)

When you make a request in prayer, it passes through several stages before it is answered. And when it is answered, the answer may come in an unexpected way. Furthermore, when you pray for a blessing, depending on your condition, you may receive a certain amount of blessing, only to have something else taken away...

We are also praying for the world. When your personal devotions and efforts at spreading the Word do not go well, do not worry that your prayers are ineffective. Continue praying, and far away something in the communist world crumbles. Yet it takes time. So pray for something that will not come to pass in your lifetime but thousands of years from now. I am praying such prayers; therefore the work of God will continue to flourish for thousands of years after I am gone, until my prayers are fully answered. (104:110, April 15, 1979)

2. Prayer Protects Against Evil

Prayer restrains one from shameful and unjust deeds; and remembrance of God is the greatest thing in life, without doubt.

Qur'an 29.45

Beings possessed by carnal passions, anger, or infatuation have but to revere and remember the Bodhisattva Kuan Shih Yin and they will be set free from their passions.[2]

Lotus Sutra 25 (Buddhism)

What lies between a man and infidelity is the abandonment of prayer.

Hadith of Muslim (Islam)

Establish regular prayers at the two ends of the day and at the approaches of the night: for those things that are good remove those that are evil. This is a word of remembrance to those who remember.[3]

Qur'an 11.114

In the name of God, the Beneficent, the Merciful.
Say, "I take refuge in the Lord of mankind,
the King of mankind,
the God of mankind,
from the evil of the sneaking whisperer
who whispers in the hearts of mankind,
of the jinn and of mankind."[4]

Qur'an 114

Teachings of Sun Myung Moon

Prayer is needed to purify the mind and spirit. It is necessary training to purify the mind and to focus the mind on God. (181:325, October 3, 1988)

When we are going the wrong way, prayer guides us to the right direction. (45:247, July 4, 1971)

Those who pray do not make serious mistakes; they know what to do.

Once you develop the habit of prayer and relish its taste, you will find it tastier than food and more interesting than listening to music or watching a movie. Moreover, you will find that you are better able to distinguish between good and evil and make the correct choices in life. (128:172, June 12, 1983)

Through prayer you should know the invisible enemy and discern the enemy's manifest works.[5] (19:146, January 1, 1968)

Through prayer, your mind should completely subjugate your body. Through prayer, your conscience will receive energy and become one with God vertically; then Satan will surely flee away. Through a life of prayer, you cultivate the path for uniting mind and body and for connecting with God, becoming one with Him. Then God will be within you, and Satan will have no choice but to run away. (229:7, April 9, 1992)

3. Prayer from the Heart

There is a polish for everything that becomes rusty, and the polish for the heart is the remembrance of God.

                        Hadith of Tirmidhi *(Islam)*

"To serve the LORD your God with all your heart" [Deut. 11.13]. What is a service with the heart? It is prayer.

                        Sifre Deuteronomy 41 *(Judaism)*

Set me free, I entreat Thee from my heart;
If I do not pray to Thee with my heart,
Thou hearest me not.
If I pray to Thee with my heart,
Thou knowest it and art gracious unto me.

           Boran Prayer (African Traditional Religions)

Let the words of my mouth
and the meditation of my heart
be acceptable in thy sight, O LORD,
my rock and my redeemer.

                                  Psalm 19.14

Always let a man test himself: if he can direct his heart, let him pray; if he cannot, let him not pray.

                      Talmud, Berakot 30b *(Judaism)*

Of all the prayers of the heart, the best prayer is the prayer to the Master to be given the grace of properly praising the Lord.

    Adi Granth, Maru Ashtpadi, M.5, p. 1018 *(Sikhism)*

Behold, thou desirest truth in the inward being;
therefore teach me wisdom in my secret heart…

Create in me a clean heart, O God,
and put a new and right spirit within me.
Cast me not away from thy presence,
and take not thy Holy Spirit from me.
Restore to me the joy of thy salvation,
and uphold me with a willing spirit.
Then I will teach transgressors thy ways,
and sinners will return to thee…

The sacrifice acceptable to God is a broken spirit;
a broken and contrite heart, O God, thou wilt not despise.

                                 Psalm 51.6-17

People are granted birth into this world by the kami. Accordingly, the mind of a person is something which communes with the will of the kami, and one must thus avoid doing anything which would impair that mind. To be visited with the blessings of the kami, one must first direct one's mind wholeheartedly to prayer; to be granted the protection of the kami, one must make a foundation of honesty. In this way, the person's pristine, undefiled mind will be awakened to the original, profound way.

    Records of the Enshrinement of the Two Imperial Deities at Ise *(Shinto)*

Prayer is an act of daring. How else could a mortal utter a prayer before the Kings of Kings?

                        Nachman of Breslov *(Judaism)*

Teachings of Sun Myung Moon

Do not pray casually, but ask your original mind. Do not pray looking up into the sky, but look into your mind. Open the door of your mind. (308:16, November 21, 1998)

When you pray, your heart should be as desperate as a baby crying for mother's milk. (18:185, June 6, 1967)

When you pray, do not think that God is up in the sky. God is right behind your mind. First you have to battle to focus your mind. As your mind and body become more and more united they rise up, connecting to the realm of resonance. (306:255: September 23, 1998)

Do not pray when you are in a fickle mood. Rather, you should pray when you are in the most profound and heavenly state of mind. Your mind should abide at the center of your heart, not near the borderline.
    When you want to pray about an important matter in your life, first purify yourself. Make sure your environment is free from worldly distractions and your inner state is far removed from the borderline; then pray. (123:80, December 12, 1982)

Pray with all sincerity, never wavering... "Heavenly Father, how can I best attend Thee? How sincerely have I attended Thee? Have I properly represented my family, my community, my tribe and my nation before Thee?" You can know the answer at once, and knowing it, you shed tears. Fallen people cannot attend Heavenly Father without tears of repentance. Without cleansing we cannot re-create our environment, which having been lost sorely needs re-creation...
    Do you weep when thinking about your nation? Do you wail in repentance when thinking about the world? Since Heavenly Father is weeping for them, and the Lord [Christ] is also weeping for them, you people on earth should be doing the same. When you stand with God and Christ, you can participate in their life. (171:19, December 5, 1987)

Whether I am in the east or the west, prayer helps me to move in a circular orbit around the Axis. I can then participate in the realm of life where God dwells. However, people usually do not live centered on the Axis. They live a casual life, as they want... Prayer is what tunes me to the center point. (171:14, December 5, 1987)

How does one make a true prayer? By overcoming obstacles with patience, love and sacrifice. People who live this way see their prayers fulfilled. They do not even need to pray, since they are already advancing to fulfill it. (112:52, March 29, 1981)

4. How to Pray

Call on your Lord with humility and in private.
    Qur'an 7.55

When you pray, go into your room and shut the door and pray to your Father who is in secret; and your Father who sees in secret will reward you.
    And in praying do not heap up empty phrases as the Gentiles do; for they think that they will be heard for their many words. Do not

be like them, for your Father knows what you need before you ask him.

Matthew 6.7-8

O believers, when you stand up to pray wash your faces, and your hands up to the elbows, and wipe your heads, and your feet up to the ankles. If you are defiled, purify yourselves; but if you are sick or on a journey, or if any of you comes from the privy, or have touched women, and you can find no water, then have recourse to wholesome dust and wipe your faces and hands with it. God does not desire to make any impediment for you; but He desires to purify you, and that He may complete His blessing upon you; haply you will be thankful.

Qur'an 5.6

Prayer should not be recited as if a man were reading a document.

Jerusalem Talmud, Berakot 4.3 (Judaism)

It is better in prayer to have a heart without words than words without a heart.

Mohandas K. Gandhi[6] (Hinduism)

The Great Spirit is everywhere; He hears whatever is in our minds and hearts, and it is not necessary to speak to Him in a loud voice.

Black Elk (Native American Religions)

Teachings of Sun Myung Moon

When you pray, you should shed tears and sweat. (112:54, March 29, 1981)

What prayer position do you prefer? The best is to kneel and lower your head. You have to restrict your body. You will feel pain and discomfort, but you must be serious to overcome it. Then God will accept you as His. (104:110, April 15, 1979)

Prayer is powerful. It is a pledge, an oath and a proclamation to Heaven. (240:35, December 11, 1992)

The way of righteousness requires that we declare our intentions and then report what we do. First declare in your prayer, "Father, I will do such and such today," and later on report, "I have accomplished those things today." (308:211, January 5, 1999)

Prayer is to honestly report your situation to God; then you draw closer to Him. Since you are not just saying idle words but reporting what you have practiced, your report remains as a record. Because your report remains as a record, God acts to give blessings. That is why a person who prays is powerful. Though he prays quietly, he is a powerful person. (233:105, July 30, 1992)

The Tao—the spiritual path—begins with prayer. Traditionally, people pray in the mountains. They pray in the mountain fastness, alone and solitary. In such a place you should cultivate yourself. (157:13, February 1, 1967)

5. Pray Constantly, Day and Night

Pray constantly.
1 Thessalonians 5.17

Celebrate constantly the praises of your Lord, before the rising of the sun and before its setting; yea, celebrate them for part of the hours of the night, and the sides of the day: that you may have spiritual joy.
Qur'an 20.130

I bless the LORD who gives me counsel;
in the night also my heart instructs me.
Psalm 16.7

The truest vision comes a little before daybreak.
Hadith of Tirmidhi and Darimi (Islam)

Rabbi Johanan said, "Would that man could pray all day, for a prayer never loses its value."
Jerusalem Talmud, Berakot 1.1 (Judaism)

O you wrapped up in your raiment!
Keep vigil the night long, save a little—
A half thereof, or abate a little thereof
Or add [a little] thereto and chant the Qur'an in measure,
For We shall charge you with a word of weight.
Lo! The vigil of the night is when impression is more keen and speech more certain.
Lo! You have by day a chain of business.
So remember the name of thy Lord and devote thyself with complete devotion.
Qur'an 73.1-8

Teachings of Sun Myung Moon

In the Bible we read that we should pray constantly. Why is it a crucial teaching to live by? Satan controls this fallen world. He lures us every which way and continually afflicts us with pain and suffering. The only way God's power can reach us is in the perpendicular direction of the Spirit. (201:208, April 9, 1990)

When you pray for public things all day and all night, your prayer becomes a living prayer. Then every few years the level of your prayer will advance, with different topics for the prayer. (104:112, April 15, 1979)

Pray often to touch limitless spiritual power. That power should become the main spring of your life. (*Way of God's Will* 2.2)

Indescribable joy comes from a life of prayer. You enter the state of God's thought at the time of creation. (29:321, March 13, 1970)

Pray a lot. Although you may live alone, if you pray hard you will never be lonely. Prayer is like breathing. If you pray a lot, you will become spiritually bright. You will become very sensitive and acquire the ability to discern good and evil. Effective prayer requires sacrifices and special devotions. (30:283, April 4, 1970)

Prayer supplies the warehouse of the heart. If you do not have time to pray, pray through the work you do. (27:89, October 26, 1969)

When you become a person of complete character, your life becomes a prayer. (*Way of God's Will* 2.2)

6. Unselfish Prayer

He who prays for his fellowman, while he himself has the same need, will be answered first.
     Talmud, Baba Kamma 92a (Judaism)

The pure whom you have found worthy for
 their righteousness and their good mind,
Fulfil their desire, O Wise Lord, let them attain it!
I know that words of prayer which serve a good end
Are successful before you.
     Avesta, Yasna 28.10 (Zoroastrianism)

Sitting cross-legged,
They should wish that all beings
Have firm and strong roots of goodness
And attain the state of immovability.

Cultivating concentration,
They should wish that all beings
Conquer their minds by concentration
Ultimately, with no remainder.

When practicing contemplation,
They should wish that all beings
See truth as it is
And be forever free of opposition and contention.
     Garland Sutra 11 (Buddhism)

Teachings of Sun Myung Moon

Your prayers will definitely be realized if they are not for selfish ends but in accordance with God's Will and righteousness. (104:109, April 15, 1979)

Instead of praying to receive a blessing, pray that you can offer devotion for God's sake. To pray out of a desire to receive a blessing is a selfish prayer. It is better to pray asking God's blessing on the nation and the world. (126:339, May 1, 1983)

My teaching is this: Do not pray for yourself. Pray for the fulfillment of your mission, pray for others, and offer your prayer as words of comfort to God. (91:117, February 3, 1977)

People who are experienced in the spiritual life know to pray for themselves at the very last. If you enter into the realm of the holy, the realm of the spiritual, you will naturally pray for God first. And the moment you meet the Lord, you want to invoke blessings upon Him.
 By praying for God's sake, you can know God's heart throughout history. Next you should pray for Jesus; then you will understand his heart when he walked the earth. Then you should pray representing the multitudes of saints in Christendom who have fought for the great Will of the dispensation, putting yourself in their places. Following in the footsteps of all the prophets and saints who walked the path of faith since the fall of Adam and Eve, you should pray in tears, "Please allow me to become an offering to cleanse all their sorrows." After you have finished that prayer, you may pray for your beloved children, and lastly for yourself. That is the order, according to heavenly law. (7:328, October 18, 1959)

When in prayer we pledge before God to advance the foundation of Heaven's victory at the cost of sacrificing ourselves, God takes responsibility and fulfills our prayer. To fulfill the content of our prayers, God does not walk an easy path. He goes through many courses to arrive at the place to meet our requests. When you stand in the most miserable situation akin to God's, then God can directly take action; otherwise God cannot act. As long as we stand in a sacrificial and sorrowful situation, and our true heart corresponds with God's desire, then God will recognize us and be merciful to us. (18:269, June 12, 1967)

Meditation

MEDITATION CLEANSES THE MIND OF ALL OBSTRUCTIONS and opens the door to Ultimate Reality that lies within. The various techniques of meditation all have in common the restricting of the body and sense stimuli, controlling the mind's wandering thoughts and feelings, and finally attaining a pure state of stillness where the true Self-nature can reveal itself.

While most of our scriptural sources on meditation describe its practice in the Eastern religion, meditation is also widespread in Christianity, Islam and Judaism. Mystics, monastics, Sufis and Kabbalists all developed meditative techniques to raise practitioners to a higher state of communion with the Spirit of God. Silent meditation is often employed as preparation for prayer, as a time of quiet when the mind is calmed and clarified and its spiritual senses heightened before communing with God. Father Moon values meditation in this context. He sometimes calls it "prayer," but what he means is a meditative, stilling technique that is an element of effective prayer.

The topic of meditation is vast, and one can practice it for a lifetime without getting to the end of it. Some aspects presented here include: quieting one's thoughts, focusing on the breath, developing intense concentration, the discipline of "mindfulness" of one's body, feelings, and thoughts, visualization of a divine image, and the shamanistic quest for a supernatural vision.

1. One-Pointed Concentration

Concentration is unafflicted one-pointedness.

Nagarjuna, Precious Garland 437 (Buddhism)

Within the lotus of the heart He dwells, where the nerves meet like the spokes of a wheel at its hub. Meditate on Him as OM. Easily may you cross the sea of darkness.

Mundaka Upanishad 2.2.6 (Hinduism)

Can you keep the unquiet physical soul from straying, hold fast to the Unity, and never quit it?
Can you, when concentrating your breath, make it soft like that of a little child?
Can you wipe and cleanse your vision of the Mystery till all is without blur?

Tao Te Ching 10 (Taoism)

On one occasion a certain monk was seated not far from the Buddha in cross-legged posture, holding his body upright, enduring pain that was the fruit born of former action, pain racking, sharp, and bitter; but he was mindful, composed, and uncomplaining. Seeing the monk so seated and so employed, the Buddha gave this utterance:

For the monk who has left behind all karma,
And shaken off the dust aforetime gathered,
Who stands fast without thought of "I" or "mine"—
For such there is no need to talk to people.

Udana 20, Nanda sutta (Buddhism)

Arouse your entire body with its three hundred and sixty bones and joints and its eighty-four thousand pores of skin; summon up a spirit of great doubt and concentrate on the word "mu" [nothingness]. Carry it continually day and night. Do not form a nihilistic conception of vacancy, or a relative conception of "has" or "has not." It will be just as if you swallowed a red-hot iron ball, which you cannot spit out even if you try. All the illusory ideas and delusive thoughts accumulated up to the present will be exterminated, and when the time comes, internal and external will be spontaneously united. You will know this, but for yourself only, like a dumb man who has had a dream. Then all of a sudden an explosive conversion will occur, and you will astonish the heavens and shake the earth.[7]

Mumonkan 1 (Buddhism)

As long as I am seated in this meditation, I shall patiently suffer all calamities that might befall me, be they caused by an animal, a human being or a god.

I renounce, for the duration of this meditation, my body, all food, and all passions. Attachment, aversion, fear, sorrow, joy, anxiety, self-pity... all these I abandon with body, mind, and speech. I further renounce all delight and all repulsion of a sexual nature.

Whether it is life or death, whether gain or loss, whether defeat or victory, whether meeting or separation, whether friend or enemy, whether pleasure or pain, I have equanimity towards all.

In [attaining] knowledge, insight, and proper conduct, [the cause] is invariably nothing but my own soul. Similarly, my soul is cause for both the influx of karmas and the stopping of that influx.

One and eternal is my soul, characterized by intuition and knowledge; all other states that I undergo are external to me, for they are formed by associations. Because of these associations my soul has suffered the chains of misery; therefore I renounce with body, mind, and speech, all relationships based on such associations.

Thus have I attained to equanimity and to my own self-nature. May this state of equanimity be with me until I attain salvation.[8]

Samayika Patha (Jainism)

Teachings of Sun Myung Moon

There is a reason why people on the path to enlightenment go off to meditate in the mountains. We cultivate external determination based on our internal determination—the confidence that we will not deviate from our course no matter what obstacles we encounter. We must have the conviction that even if we fall to the bottom, we will support our minds and bodies. Without this conviction, there is no way we can run the race, or even enter the stadium. Each of us is a racer who is competing in some event; therefore we should train ourselves with unchanging conviction in order to reach the goal. The attitude of a devout believer—the attitude of a person walking the path to enlightenment—is like that of a racer competing in a race. You must have this attitude. Whether awake or asleep, you should have a burning desire to accomplish your goal. (7:135, August 9, 1959)

2. Breathing to the Rhythm of the Cosmic Breath

Undivided I am,
undivided my soul,
undivided my sight,
undivided my hearing;
undivided my in-breathing,
undivided my out-breathing,
undivided my diffusive breath;
undivided the whole of me.

Atharva Veda 19.51.1 (Hinduism)

Pure spirit reaches in the four directions, flows now this way, now that—there is no place it does not extend to. Above, it brushes heaven; below, it coils on the earth. It transforms and nurses the ten thousand things, but no one can make out its form. Its name is called One-with-Heaven. The way to purity and whiteness is to guard the spirit, this alone; guard it and never lose it, and you will become one with spirit, one with its pure essence, which communicates and mingles with the Heavenly Order.[9]

Chuang Tzu 15 (Taoism)

Holding the body steady, with the three upper parts erect,
And causing the senses with the mind to enter into the heart,
A wise man with the Brahma-boat should cross over
All the fear-bringing streams.

Having repressed his breathings here in the body, and having his movements checked,
One should breathe through his nostrils with diminished breath.
Like that chariot yoked with vicious horses,
His mind the wise man should restrain undistractedly.

Svetasvatara Upanishad 2.8-9 (Hinduism)

Teachings of Sun Myung Moon

Get up early in the morning and pray. When praying, listen to the sound of your heart. Think of the origin of your heart, imagining that the harmony of heaven and earth is flowing through your arteries and veins. Then, your health will improve. (27:85, November 26, 1969)

How can we experience the heart of God, when He rejoiced upon creating all things? Meditate on Him from morning till evening sunset while sitting in a garden or a mountain meadow. Be so immersed in your meditation that you lose track of time. Breathe in deeply, and the air of the universe will come to you with life force. Live along with the life force of the universe. Exhale, and all beings will come alive anew. If you enter a state of deep relaxation, all things will harmonize with you. You will attain the position of an absolute being that can have dominion over all creations...

Exhale, and all things receive; inhale, and all things give out. If you reciprocate with the creation centered on love, all things in the universe will interact with each other. Keep on relating with them and become their center of harmony. Thus you will become a being who resembles nature in all its beauty, like the universe itself. Once you dwell in that state, you will become a center of harmony for the whole universe. (29:133, February 26, 1970)

What does the nose symbolize? With its two nostrils, it represents Adam and Eve, male and female. The right nostril symbolizes the male and the left nostril the female. God breathes through these holes. What does God breathe? He breathes the air of love. The atmosphere of the spirit world is love. Man and woman were created as partners of love, to be trained in love here on earth and then breathe love in the spirit world. When you have a cold and can only breathe through one nostril, it is like a divorce. When you can only breathe through your mouth, it is as if God can only breathe through the things of creation but not through man and woman, whom He needs to breathe properly. (118:111, May 9, 1982)

3. Quiet the Mind and Enter a Calm State, Empty of Self

When all the senses are stilled, when the mind is at rest, when the intellect wavers not—then, say the wise, is reached the highest state.

Katha Upanishad 2.6.10 (Hinduism)

Wherever the mind wanders, restless and diffuse in its search for satisfaction without, lead it within; train it to rest in the Self. Abiding joy comes to those who still the mind. Freeing themselves from the taint of self-will, with their consciousness unified, they become one with God.

Bhagavad-Gita 6.26-27 (Hinduism)

The wise man should surrender his words to his mind;
and this he should surrender to the Knowing Self;
and the Knowing Self he should surrender to the Great Self;
and that he should surrender to the Peaceful Self.[10]

Katha Upanishad 3.13 (Hinduism)

Be still, and know that I am God.

Psalm 46.10

Block the passages,
Shut the doors,
Let all sharpness be blunted,
All tangles untied,
All glare tempered,
All dust smoothed.
This is called mysterious leveling.

Tao Te Ching 56 (Taoism)

Attain utmost vacuity;
Hold fast to quietude.
While the myriad things are stirring together,
I see only their return.
For luxuriantly as they grow,
Each of them will return to its root.
To return to the root is called quietude,
Which is also said to be reversion to one's destiny.
This reversion belongs with the eternal:
To know the eternal is enlightenment.

Tao Te Ching 16 (Taoism)

The Self-existent pierced sense openings outward;
therefore a man looks out, not in.
But a certain wise man, in search of immortality,
turned his gaze inward and saw the Self within.[11]

Katha Upanishad 4.1 (Hinduism)

The wise, self-controlled, and tranquil souls, who are contented in spirit, and who practice austerity and meditation in solitude and silence, are freed from all impurity, and attain by the path of liberation the immortal, the truly existing, the changeless Self.

Mundaka Upanishad 1.2.7-11 (Hinduism)

Only after knowing what to abide in can one be calm. Only after having been calm can one be tranquil. Only after having achieved tranquility can one have peaceful repose. Only after having peaceful repose can one begin to deliberate. Only after deliberation can the end be attained. Things have their roots and their branches. Affairs have their beginnings and their ends. To know what is first and what is last will lead one near the Way.[12]

Great Learning (Confucianism)

Commune with your own heart upon your bed, and be silent.

Psalm 4.4

Teachings of Sun Myung Moon

We need training in the way we think and the way we use our mind. Meditation and prayer are methods for cultivating the mind. (67:178, June 10, 1973)

Zen meditation brings your mind to a level place on the horizontal line. There you lose consciousness of self. Consciousness is formed through resonance; in that horizontal state it can resonate with wavelengths coming from the vertical world. (296:203, November 9, 1998)

When we pray or meditate, as when Buddhists practice Zen, we are seeking a state that is void of self. What is our goal in seeking this state? It is to awaken the elements that can become the nucleus of the mind. If you set that one standard and establish the center of your mind, you will see, hear and cognize everything in accord with the principles of Heaven. Then you can offer a full bow before God and return Him glory. (2:193, May 19, 1957)

We seek the deep ravine of the world of mind. Buddhists who meditate also ask, "What is mind?" and enter the deep ravine of the mind. When you enter the deep ravine of the mind and journey to the state of the original mind before the Human Fall, you will be connected to Heaven. Indeed, without entering the world of the mind, you cannot make a relationship with Heaven.

As long as we are holding on to the world, we cannot contact or attend Heaven. Human beings are composed of mind and body, yet because spirit and flesh are in opposition, we are unable to attain the original world of the mind in a state of mind-body unity. Instead, the journey to the world of the mind requires that we deny the world of body—deny it one hundred percent. We have to remove all that the body desires and isolate ourselves from the world. We have to separate from the world and put it behind us. This is the religious path; it is opposite the ways of the world. It seeks that original point to which we should return. (21:37-38, September 1, 1968)

Make your mind taut like a round air-filled balloon. If you are insecure or self-centered, or if you are approaching things from a personal viewpoint, then your mind is not round but wrinkled and jagged. Therefore, you need to stretch your mind and make it round.

When your mind rolls like a ball, it makes smooth contact with a flat plane. But if it is jagged, only the points make contact. In that case, it will not smoothly stimulate anything but will act against everything. That is when we feel conscience-stricken, and if we continue this way gradually the standard of our conscience will decline.

Therefore, you need to keep your mind taut like a round balloon. Then upon receiving a stimulus, the whole of it will resonate. Take two tuning forks and strike one; the other will vibrate with the same frequency. A well-rounded mind makes a good resonating vessel. It has the sensitivity to feel the spiritual vibration coming from the Subject Being. Therefore, when living a life of faith, you need to take time to meditate. Meditate while longing for goodness. When you meditate, open the door of your mind completely and make your mind round.

Then, God's original nature and your original nature will resonate together. The individual qualities of your mind [e.g., your spring-like personality] will resonate completely with those same qualities of God, uniting you in a complete relationship with the Subject Being. In that state, when you go out to pursue your desired purpose, God will certainly be with you. (40:278, February 7, 1971)

4. Mindfulness—Awareness of All Thoughts and Feelings

There is this one way, monks, for the purification of beings, for the overcoming of sorrow and misery, for the destruction of pain and grief, for winning the right path, for the attainment of Nibbana, namely the Four Arousings of Mindfulness. What are these four?

Here a monk lives contemplating the body in the body... contemplating feelings in feelings... contemplating consciousness in consciousness... and contemplating mental objects in mental objects, ardent, clearly conscious and mindful, having overcome in this world, covetousness and dejection.

And how, monks, does a monk live contemplating body in the body?

Here a monk, having gone to the forest, sits down cross-legged keeping his body erect and setting up mindfulness in front of him. Mindful he breathes in, mindful he breathes out. Breathing in long, he knows, "I breathe in long." Breathing out long, he knows, "I breathe out long." Breathing in short, he knows, "I breathe in short." Breathing out short, he knows, "I breathe out short." "Experiencing the whole body I shall breathe out," thus he trains himself...

And further, a monk knows when he is going, "I am going"; he knows when he is standing, "I am standing"; he knows when he is sitting, "I am sitting"; he knows when he is lying down, "I am lying down"; or just as the body is disposed so he knows it...

And further, a monk reflects on this very body enveloped by the skin and full of manifold impurity from the soles up and from the crown of the head down, thinking, "There are in this body: hair of the head, hair of the body, nails, teeth, skin, flesh, sinews, bones, marrow, kidney, heart, liver, membranes, spleen, lungs, bowels, intestines, mesentery, feces, bile, phlegm, pus, blood, sweat, fat, saliva, mucus, synovic fluid, urine."... And seeing a body dead for one day, or two or three, swollen, discolored, decomposing, thrown aside in the cemetery, he applies this perception to his own body, "Truly, this body of mine, too, is of the same nature, it will become like that and will not escape it."...

And how, monks, does a monk live contemplating feelings in feelings?

Here a monk when experiencing a pleasant feeling knows, "I experience a pleasant feeling"; when experiencing a painful feeling knows, "I experience a painful feeling"; when experiencing a feeling that is neither pleasant nor painful knows, "I experience a neither pleasant nor painful feeling."...

And how does a monk live contemplating consciousness in consciousness?

Here, monks, a monk knows the consciousness with craving as with craving; the consciousness without craving as without craving; the consciousness with anger as with anger; the consciousness without anger as without anger; the consciousness with ignorance as with ignorance; the consciousness without ignorance as without ignorance...

And how does a monk live contemplating mental objects in mental objects?

Here, monks, a monk lives contemplating mental objects in the mental objects of the five hindrances. When sense desire is present, a monk knows, "There is sense desire in me," or when sense desire is not present he knows, "There is no sense desire in me."... When anger is present, he knows... when sloth and torpor is present, he knows... when restlessness and worry are present, he knows... when doubt is present, he knows...

Truly, monks, whoever practices these Four Settings up of Mindfulness for seven years, then one of two results may be expected by him: highest knowledge here and now or, if some remainder of clinging is yet present, the state of non-returning.[13]

Majjhima Nikaya 1.55-63, Satipatthana Sutta
(Buddhism)

Leave behind all phenomenal distinctions and awaken the thought of the Consummation of Incomparable Enlightenment by not allowing the mind to depend upon notions evoked by the sensible world—by not allowing the mind to depend upon notions evoked by sounds, odors, flavors, touch-contacts, or any qualities. The mind should be kept independent of any thoughts which arise within it. If the mind depends upon anything it has no sure haven.

Diamond Sutra 14 *(Buddhism)*

Man's feelings are the evil aspect of his nature. If one realizes they are evil, then this evil will not exist in the first place. If the mind is in the state of absolute quiet and inactivity, depraved thoughts will cease of themselves.

Li Ao *(Confucianism)*

Teachings of Sun Myung Moon

In the mind there is a door, called the door to the mind. God enters through that door. That door does not open only to one direction. Since the mind is in motion, the door is also in motion. For God (plus) to enter through this door, we should relate to Him as a minus (object partner). Yet if our direction is slightly off, even by just a degree, the door will not open.

There indeed exists a door to the mind of each human being. You can discern it in your prayers. The feeling you get when you pray changes depending upon the time of day. Praying at 1:00 a.m. has a different feeling than praying at 3:00 a.m. Try it yourself, and you will sense the difference. If you pray in a deep mysterious state, you will feel different depending upon what time you are praying. The feelings of your prayers in the morning, in the afternoon and in the evening are all different.

The same is with the state of our mind. Our emotions change with the seasons, our feelings towards our loved ones change; in such ways the world of the mind is constantly changing. That is why we need to discover the best time to pray. You need to pray when your spiritual senses are keen, so your sensitivity to God will be high. As you enter deeper and deeper into a state of feeling connected to God, you will eventually reach the door to the mind.

The door to your mind connects with the door to God's mind. Once it opens, the way unfolds to experience God's feelings.

What should you do to enter such a state? You should cultivate your mind. First, examine the state of your mind. It was originally to be at the zero point, but because of the Fall its direction has deviated by 180 degrees. Although your mind is supposed to rest at the zero point, because of the Fall it behaves randomly and unpredictably. Your first task is to return it to the original point.

Since we are 180 degrees opposite the zero point, we should struggle to turn around in a clockwise direction. As we move in this direction seeking the zero point, we will feel a minus-like sensation. Nevertheless, most people are inclined to go counterclockwise. Yet going in that direction they will not succeed, even if they continue for a thousand years. Everyone must return to the zero point…

If your mind is deviated from the path by a certain angle, you should adjust your mind's direction by the opposite angle and return it to the proper course… Each of us has a good mind and an evil mind. You may think that your mind is always good, it is not so. As a result of the Fall, human beings are contaminated by Satan's realm of evil minds. We struggle to remain in the realm of good minds.

For this reason, what is most important is to find the zero point and reach the door to the mind. Learning how to do this is crucial in our life of faith. Therefore, you should learn to discern when is the right moment to open the door to your mind and how to match it to the door of God's mind. (76:127-129, February 2, 1975)

5. Visualizations and Visions

Fog, smoke, sun, fire, wind,
Fireflies, lightning, a crystal, a moon—
These are the preliminary appearances,
Which produce the manifestation of Brahman
    in yoga.

    Svetasvatara Upanishad 2.11 *(Hinduism)*

Buddha then replied to Vaidehi, "You and all other beings besides ought to make it their only aim, with concentrated thought, to get a perception of the Western Quarter. You will ask how that perception is to be formed. I will explain it now. All beings, if not blind from birth, are uniformly possessed of sight, and they all see the setting sun. You should sit down properly, looking in the western direction, and prepare your thought for a close meditation on the sun; cause your mind to be firmly fixed on it so as to have an unwavering perception by the exclusive application of your thought, and gaze upon it when it is about to set and looks like a suspended drum.

"After you have thus seen the sun, let that image remain clear and fixed, whether your eyes be shut or open—such is the perception of the sun, which is the First Meditation.

"Next you should form the perception of water; gaze on the water clear and pure, and let [this image] also remain clear and fixed; never allow your thought to be scattered or lost.

"When you have thus seen the water you should form the perception of ice. As you see the ice shining and transparent, you should imagine the appearance of lapis lazuli.

"After that has been done, you will see the ground consisting of lapis lazuli, transparent and shining both within and without. Beneath this ground of lapis lazuli there will be seen a golden banner with the seven jewels, diamonds and the rest, supporting the ground. It extends to the eight points of the compass, and thus the eight corners [of the ground] are perfectly filled up. Every side of the eight quarters consists of a hundred jewels, every jewel has a thousand rays, and every ray has eighty-four thousand colors which, when reflected in the ground of lapis lazuli, look like one hundred thousand million suns, and it is difficult to see them all one by one... Lodged high up in the open sky these rays form a tower of rays, whose stories and galleries are ten millions in number and built of a hundred jewels. Both sides of the tower have each ten thousand million flowery banners furnished and decked with innumerable musical instruments. Eight kinds of cool breezes proceed from the brilliant rays. When those musical instruments are played, they emit the sounds 'suffering,' 'non-existence,' 'impermanence,' and 'non-self'—such is the perception of the water, which is the Second Meditation...

"Make the images as clear as possible, so that they may never be scattered or lost, whether your eyes be shut or open. Except only during the time of your sleep, you should always keep this in your mind. One who has reached this stage of perception is said to have dimly seen the Land of Highest Happiness (Sukhavati).

"One who has obtained samadhi is able to see the Land clearly and distinctly: this state is too much to be explained fully—such is the perception of the Land, and it is the Third Meditation."[14]

    Meditation on Buddha Amitayus 9-11 *(Buddhism)*

Before I could go on my vision quest, I had to purify myself in the *oinikaga* tipi, the *inipi*, the sweat lodge... With the buffalo-horn ladle, Good Lance poured ice-cold water over the red-glowing stones. There was a tremendous hiss as we were instantly enveloped in a cloud of searing white steam... Good Lance prayed. He used ancient words, "This steam is the holy breath of the universe. Hokshila, boy, you are in your mother's womb again. You are going to be reborn." They all sang two songs, very ancient songs, going way back to the days when we Sioux roamed the prairie. Suddenly I felt wise with the wisdom of generations. These men, my relatives, sang loud and vigorously... The little hut was shaken as if in the grip of a giant hand. It was trembling as a leaf trembles in the wind. Beneath us the earth seemed to move. "Grandfather is here," said Good Lance. "The spirits are here; the Eagle's wisdom is here." We believed it; we knew it. The pipe was passed... Four times we smoked. After the last time, Good Lance told me, "Hokshila, you have been purified; you are no longer a child; you are ready now and made strong to go up there and cry for a dream."...

Our vision pit was an L-shaped hole dug into the ground, first straight down and then a short horizontal passage deep under the roots of the trees. You sit at the end of that passage and do your fasting, anywhere from one to four days... in my case, it was decided that I should stay there alone without food or water for two days and two nights...

The first hours were the hardest. It was pitch dark and deathly still. I sat there without moving. My arms and legs went asleep. I could neither hear nor see nor feel. I became almost disembodied, a thing with a heart and wild thoughts but no flesh or bones. Would I ever be able to see and hear again?... I don't know how long I sat there. All sense of time had left me long ago. I didn't know whether it was day or night, had not even a way to find out. I prayed and prayed, tears streaming down my cheeks. I wanted water but kept praying. Toward evening of the second day—and this time is only a wild guess—I saw wheels before my eyes forming up into one fiery hoop and then separating again into bright, many-colored circles, dancing before my eyes and again contracting into one big circle, a circle with a mouth and two eyes.

Suddenly, I heard a voice. It seemed to come from within the bundle that was me, a voice from the dark. It was hard to tell exactly where it came from. It was not a human voice; it sounded like a bird speaking like a man. My hackles rose... "Remember the hoop," said the voice, "this night we will teach you." And I heard many feet walking around in my small vision pit. Suddenly I was out of my hole, in another world, standing in front of a sweat bath on a prairie covered with wildflowers, covered with herds of elk and buffalo.

I saw a man coming toward me; he seemed to have no feet; he just floated toward me out of a mist, holding two rattles in his hand. He said, "Boy, whatever you tell your people, do not exaggerate; always do what your vision tells you. Never pretend." The man was wearing an old-fashioned buckskin outfit decorated with quillwork. I stretched out my hands to touch him, when suddenly I was back inside my star quilt, clutching my medicine bundle of stones and tobacco ties. I still heard the voice, "Remember the hoop; remember the pipe; be its spokesman." I was no longer afraid; whoever was talking to me meant no harm.

Suddenly before me stretched a coal-black cloud with lightning coming out of it. The cloud spread and spread; it grew wings; it became an eagle. The eagle talked to me: "I give you a power, not to use for yourself, but for your people. It does not belong to you; it belongs to the common folks." I saw a rider on a gray horse coming toward me, he held in his one hand a hoop made of sage. He held it high... and again everything dissolved into blackness. Again out of the mist came a strange creature floating up, covered with hair, pale, formless. He wanted to take my medicine away from me, but I wrestled with him, defended it. He did not get my medicine. He, too, disappeared.

Suddenly somebody shook me by the shoulder. "Wake up, boy." My father and my uncle had come for me. The two days and two nights were over.

Leonard Crow Dog, Sioux Vision Quest
(*Native American Religions*)

Teachings of Sun Myung Moon

As you become one with all beings, what phenomena will occur? You will feel something multi-dimensional that you have never felt before. It will come mysteriously...

Once you enter the door to your mind, you will have intuitions and premonitions. Maybe as you walk down the street you see a bird flying. All of sudden, you feel the door to your mind opening. You do not realize what is happening, but suddenly you receive a heavenly inspiration that teaches you some lesson. Maybe the inspiration will hit you when you hear someone talking. The more you practice, the more often you will experience such incidents.

The next stage is to enter a dream-like state, not a dream in deep sleep but a state half dreaming and half waking. The Apostle Paul experienced three levels of heaven in that state, when he did not know whether it was a dream or reality...

Do not let such experiences pass casually. Collect them, analyze them logically, and figure out the direction that God is leading you. Keep a record of your experiences every day and you will see that your most unforgettable visions actually came true; their predictions were one hundred percent accurate.

Maybe in that dream-like state you were talking with someone about certain things, and later on you actually talk with that person and the things you discussed actually happen. Maybe in your dream you and a friend were singing a certain song. Later on that person actually sings it. Such phenomena can take place. What do they mean? You entered a spiritual realm, and there your mind was resonating with everything in that realm. Your mind was like a tuning fork, resonating with the vibrations of the cosmos. If you have such an experience, treasure it as precious...

Where does God appear to us? Not in the sky, but in the [original] mind. For this reason, we know that our self and our original mind are two different entities.[15] If you do not feel it, it is because your original mind has not fully established its existence. Being often dragged about by the body, it cannot stand. Therefore, once your mind is established in its existence and subjectivity, things will change.

Once you reach a higher state, during prayer you can communicate with your original mind. Your prayer will resonate with your mind, and you will hear yourself in your mind. At this stage you will receive messages or warnings about events in your daily life. Religious people should keep a record of these experiences.

Whenever you relate with someone, do not be careless or indifferent. Think, "What can this person teach me?" Have a hungry mind, eager to learn something new from him or her. Also, you should discern right away whether to relate to him or her as your subject partner or as your object partner... Then your mind will be happy and will be automatically attracted to that person.

This is due to the influence of mind waves. Do you believe that every mind emits mind waves? When you meet a butcher, don't you smell meat? When you meet a fabric merchant, don't you smell fabric? Just as you can smell a person's unique body odor, you can also smell the mind's odor. Such phenomena happen.

In our body, we have a special sense which strives to reach out to everything. It sends out invisible energy waves to locate its object partners. It is true. Even if our mind wants to go its own way, it cannot. As the pole of a magnet is attracted to the opposite pole, minus is attracted to plus, and plus is attracted to minus.[16]

Therefore, the attitude of believers should be that all beings are related to us. Why? Due to the Human Fall we lost all relationships—with God, among human beings and with nature, all were entirely severed. In order for us to reconnect our relationships, we should always strive to make these connections ourselves. If we do not have the attitude to make connections with others, we cannot improve the environment in which we live.

For this reason, you should all have a mind to anticipate new things. When praying in the morning, you should feel, "Today, something good will happen." But do not just think that good things will just happen. You have to seek for them. This attitude of seeking should be your life of faith. Experience and continual practice bring relationships to life. Yet it all stems from cultivating a dream-like state in meditation.[17] (76:129-133, February 2, 1975)

Sometimes we hold all-night prayer vigils, focusing on God and leaving all worldly matters aside. We do not sleep, but try to enter a state beyond sleep. As we cultivate the mind and repress our consciousness, remnants of our flesh mind sink down and our spirit rises to the surface like pure water. Then although we are tired, we reach a state beyond sleep—a state where we are half sleeping and half awake. We can hear sounds, but not precisely; we can see things, but not clearly. Dream-like phenomena unfold, and God can instruct us.

We hold prayer vigils to disconnect from carnal desires and unify the spirit. Your spirit will be elevated to the point where God may give you a glimpse of your future. After many of these vigils, you will arrive at a state where in prayer you see visions and hear voices. Your eyes see events both spiritual and earthly; your ears hear sounds both spiritual and earthly. Then you can direct events in the spirit world and on earth. (91:275, February 27, 1977)

At the next level, we can receive oral directions or symbolic visions. Visions require careful analysis. Directions are directly given, but visions require interpretation, and this is where we meet with problems. Heaven often teaches us by words, but sometimes it is through a vision. For example, you have a vision of a beautiful spring-like day; a pair of deer drinks at a stream and then looks far off at the mountains. That vision is a very good sign, and you can expect that something good will happen.

This is not a coincidence. God is working to cultivate the field of your mind. Why so? The field of your mind is not flat like glass. It is rough and uneven. It may appear flat, but look closer and you see that its surface is rough. When the light of Heaven hits a rough surface, it is not reflected, but scatters in all directions. That is why revelations are received and interpreted differently. Therefore, to properly discern Heaven's guidance, we need to cultivate the various aspects of our mind, piece by piece. This requires our effort.

Beyond the stage of revelations as oral directions or symbolic visions, we arrive at the stage of direct revelations in silence. Like John in the Book of Revelation, you can have spiritual experiences all day long, journeying into the other world and exploring its mysteries. Eventually, everyone is to be connected to the spirit world, reaching the realm of God's heart and feelings.

Unless you experience such things in your life of faith, you cannot carry out God's great Will on the stage of your own life. Therefore, I do not trust believers who have not had actual spiritual experiences. Please understand how important it is for you to have these spiritual experiences for cultivating your life of faith…

God works when you pray, sending His spiritual power like electricity. But since this high-voltage energy is stronger than your consciousness, it will lift your consciousness to feel the supernatural.

However, when supernatural and divine emotions come inside you, your body, imbedded with fallen nature, rebels against God's original divinity. Fallen people do not naturally harmonize with God's divine energy, no matter how strongly it tries to penetrate. As a result, the energy does not come all at once. Like alternating plus and minus energies, like a spreading sound wave that is sometimes strong and sometimes gentle, the energy comes as a series of vibrations. They overwhelm your conscious mind and display their spiritual power. That is how God performs His work.

When God is working with you all the time like this, what happens? Your body-centered fallen nature is gradually purified, and eventually it will accept God's indwelling activity naturally and 100 percent. Then, when God ceases sending His spiritual power in this way, your own spirituality will exceed God's work in you. At that point God will be with you, and He will teach you without your realizing it.

You should reach this level of total purification, after going through all these stages: the dream-like state, oral directions, revelations, and so on. At this level, your mind will fully direct you. You may want to chastise someone, but your mind will stop you. You may want to say something sweet, but instead you say words of admonishment. Such phenomena can seem incomprehensible. You need to learn how to adjust to them, otherwise, you could be regarded as an insane person.

You must absolutely experience something like this in your life of faith. People who experience these things in their life of faith, always testing and experimenting, will become strong. They have first-hand knowledge and do not need to believe what others tell them. Experience and practice are the most necessary elements in our life of faith. (76:133-136, February 2, 1975)

Praise

WORSHIP SHOULD BE ARDENT AND EMOTIONAL; and there is no better way to generate emotional power than by praising God in songs and chants. Praise is a natural expression of our love for Him. Hymns and psalms give poetic and heartfelt voice to the word, penetrating the soul more deeply than any theological discourse. Singing can elevate us into an exalted spiritual state where we experience the mystic glories of heavenly choirs of angels. Chanting a sacred syllable or repeating the Lord's holy names attunes our mind to Ultimate Reality and call forth its mystic power.

1. On the Value of Praise

He is the Living One; there is no god but He: call upon Him, giving Him sincere devotion. Praise be to God, Lord of the Worlds!

    Qur'an 40.65

I know that my greatest good is to worship
The Wise Lord and those that have been and are.[18]
By their names will I worship them
And come before them with praise.

    Avesta, Yasna 51.22 (Zoroastrianism)

Enthusiasm: The ancient kings made music in order to honor merit, and offered it with splendor to the Supreme Deity,
inviting their ancestors to be present.

    I Ching 16: Enthusiasm (Confucianism)

The words dearest to God are four: Glory be to God, Praise be to God, There is no god but God, and God is most great.[19]

    Hadith of Muslim (Islam)

The word which all the Vedas extol,
Toward which all asceticism points,
In quest of which men live disciplined lives,
That will I tell you, that is "OM."

This syllable, indeed, is imperishable Brahman;
This syllable, indeed, is the End supreme.
The one who knows this selfsame syllable
Will surely obtain whatever he desires.[20]

Katha Upanishad 1.2.15-16 (Hinduism)

The elements of word OM are fourths, the elements: the letter A, the letter U, the letter M. The waking state, the common-to-all-men, is the letter A... the dreaming state, the Brilliant, is the letter U... the deep-sleep state, the Cognitional, is the letter M... The fourth is without an element, with which there can be no dealing, the cessation of phenomena, benign, without a second. This AUM is the Self indeed.[21]

Mandukya Upanishad (Hinduism)

All Buddhas in the universe throughout past, present, and future invariably attain Buddhahood with the seed of the five characters of "Namu Myo Ho Renge Kyo."[22]

Nichiren (Buddhism)

If man, with constant endeavor, praise the Lord of the Universe, the unlimited Supreme Being, with His Thousand Names,[23] if he worships daily and with devotion the same imperishable Being, meditating on Him, praising Him, bowing to Him, and making offerings to Him, if he sings daily the praise of Vishnu, the Great Lord of the whole universe who has neither beginning nor end and presides over the world, he overcomes all unhappiness.

Mahabharata, Anusasana Parva 254 (Hinduism)

When, indeed the Holy Spirit saw the human race was guided only with difficulty toward virtue, and that, because of our inclination toward pleasure, we were neglectful of an upright life, what did He do? The delight of melody He mingled with the doctrines so that by the pleasantness and softness of the sound heard we might receive without perceiving it, the benefit of the words... A psalm implies serenity of the soul; it is the author of peace, which calms bewildering and seething thoughts. For, it softens the wrath of the soul, and what is unbridled it chastens. As psalm forms friendships, unites those separated, conciliates those at enmity. Who, indeed, can still consider him an enemy with whom he has uttered the same prayer to God? So that psalmody, bringing about choral singing, a bond, as it were, toward unity, and joining the people into a harmonious union of one choir, produces also the greatest of blessings, charity.

Saint Basil (Christianity)

Teachings of Sun Myung Moon

Song is the material basis for harmonizing with God. That is why when you sing you should be intoxicated with joy. (16:289, July 31, 1966)

Hymns sung with deep emotion are the best form of entreaty and spirit-filled prayer. If you look into the eyes of people singing and praying, you will see something moving in them. You feel, "Ah, from here, God's work begins!" (17:21, November 6, 1966)

Prayer is a time to be in harmony with God. From this perspective, prayer by singing can be more moving than prayer in words. When singing hymns, you can quickly experience the feeling of being drawn into a world of mystery. (270:19, May 3, 1995)

Buddhist monks chant and beat the wood block. We listen to sermons and sing hymns. They are all conditions. (January 5, 1999)

All creation praises God: even the insects, birds, fish and beasts praise Him. (269:171, April 17, 1995)

May we become Thy sons and daughters who sing songs of Thy love, after fulfilling all Thy hopes and all Thy Will!...

May we become true children who comfort our Father with songs of joy and glory, who have accomplished Thy hope, Thy work and Thy thought, and who forever live with Thee! (5:280, February 22, 1958)

2. Hymns and Psalms of Praise

Make a joyful noise to the LORD, all the lands!
Serve the LORD with gladness!
Come into his presence with singing!
Know that the LORD is God!
It is he that made us, and we are his;
we are his people, and the sheep of his pasture.
Enter his gates with thanksgiving,
and his courts with praise!
Give thanks to him, bless his name!
For the LORD is good;
his steadfast love endures forever,
and his faithfulness to all generations.

Psalm 100

Sing you all, and sing aloud!
Devotees, sing your songs.
Let children, too, sing. Sing to Him
who is like a mighty fortress.
Let the viol send down its strains,
the lute raise its voice around,
the bow string strike its echoing sound:
to Indra is our hymn upraised.

Rig Veda 8.69.8-9 (Hinduism)

I will extol thee, my God and my King,
and bless thy name for ever and ever.
Every day I will bless thee,
and praise thy name for ever and ever.
Great is the LORD, and greatly to be praised,
and his greatness is unsearchable.
One generation shall laud thy works to
    another,
and shall declare thy mighty acts.
On the glorious splendor of thy majesty,
and on thy wondrous works, I will meditate.
Men shall proclaim the might of thy terrible
    acts,
and I will declare thy greatness.
They shall pour forth the fame of thy abundant
    goodness,
and shall sing aloud of thy righteousness.

Psalm 145.1-7

He is God, there is no god but He.
He is the knower of the Unseen and the
    Visible;
He is the All-merciful, the All-compassionate.

He is God, there is no God but He.
He is the King, the All-holy, the All-peaceable,
The All-faithful, the All-preserver,
The All-mighty, the All-compeller, the
    All-sublime.
Glory be to God, above that they associate!

He is God, the Creator, the Maker, the Shaper.
To Him belong the Names Most Beautiful.
All that is in the heavens and the earth magnifies Him;
He is the All-mighty, the All-wise.[24]

Qur'an 59.22-24

Come together, you all, with the power of spirit,
to the Lord of heaven, who is One, the Guest of the people.
He, the ancient, desires to come to the new.
To Him all pathways turn; verily He is One.

We all here are Thine, O Indra, praised by many,
We who go about, attached to Thee, Lord of wealth!
O Lover of song, none but Thee receives our songs.
Love these our words as the earth loves her creatures.

Loud songs have sounded to the bounteous Indra,
One worthy of praise, the Supporter of mankind,
to the much invoked, waxing strong with lovely hymns,
and the immortal One who is sung day by day.

Towards Indra have all our loving songs, joined to the heavenly light, proceeded in unison;
as a wife embraces her husband, comely bridegroom,
so they encompass the bounteous One for His grace.

Sama Veda 372-375 (Hinduism)

Teachings of Sun Myung Moon

    Grace filling me with golden light, measureless blessing divine;
    God gives eternal life to me, perfect rejoicing is mine.
    Glorious the song ringing in my heart for my Father above;
    Gratefully I give offering to Him, triumph and glorious love.

    Joy surging like an ocean wave, flowing so deep in my soul;
    Hope rises as I go in praise, knowing that man will be whole.
    Glorious the song ringing in my heart for my Father above;
    Gratefully I give offering to Him, triumph and glorious love.

    High, limitless eternal life, touching the top of the sky;
    Praise filling every part of me, blessing that never will die.
    Glorious the song ringing in my heart for my Father above;
    Gratefully I give offering to Him, triumph and glorious love.

    You've chosen me to do Your will, thankful, I vow to be true;
    I'm pledging in my heart of hearts, "Father, my life is for You."
    Glorious the song ringing in my heart for my Father above;
    Gratefully I give offering to Him, triumph and glorious love. *(Grace of the Holy Garden)* [25]

    Now the light of glory arises like the sun that shines on high;
    Now awaken into freedom, O revive, you spirits, O revive!
    Wake the mountains and the valleys; bring alive the springs of the earth.
    Light the world forever with the Light of your rebirth.
    Light the world forever with the Light of your rebirth.

    We are called to bring back the glory to the life of God above;
    Now the Lord in His greatness fills the universe with tender love,

Ever seeking souls awakened, ever calling them to be free.
How shall I attend Him who is calling to me?
How shall I attend Him who is calling to me?

From the dark of death I awaken and rejoice to live in grace;
When the One who came to save me holds me tenderly in His embrace;
How can I return the blessing? Though in all my life I will try.
I can never stop feeling how unworthy am I.
I can never stop feeling how unworthy am I! *(Blessing of Glory)*

Devotion

DEVOTION MEANS TO WORSHIP GOD OUT OF LOVE. Love can be volitional, expressed in acts of dedication and sacrifice, as in the biblical commandment, "Love God with all your heart, with all your soul and with all your mind." In the Abrahamic faiths, devotion is primarily expressed in acts of loyalty and dedication to God's will.

Love for God can also be an emotional experience. Devotional worship is expressed in joyful and emotional outpourings of praise and song and in the constant longing for God's sweet presence. This powerful mode of religious consciousness is particularly manifest in the Hindu and Sikh bhakti tradition, the dancing and song of Sufi Muslims and Hassidic Jews, and in the outpourings of the Holy Spirit in Pentecostal Christianity.

Many passages of scripture describe this mystical emotion as a transfigured sublime love of a bride for her beloved, as in the Song of Solomon in the Bible, in the loves of Radha and Krishna or Sita and Rama in the Hindu tradition, and in the devotion of Mary Magdalene to Jesus. Father Moon teaches that there is a fundamental link between the love of man and woman and the joining of heaven and earth.

Father Moon also adds a new, minor key to this longing to experience God's love by bringing in the element of God's suffering heart. If God's real circumstances are full of suffering and pain, then the longing for emotional unity with God should also take us into the experience of divine sorrow. His prayers are full of tears, commiserating with God. Knowing that God is in pain also motivates us to act in this world to alleviate His suffering by saving our brothers and sisters from sin, oppression and despair. At this deep level, heart and action become one.

1. Deeds of Devotion to God and His Will

Whatever you do, do all to the glory of God.
1 Corinthians 10.31

Let all your deeds be done for the sake of Heaven.
Mishnah, Avot 2.17 (Judaism)

The most excellent action is love for God's sake and hatred for God's sake.
Hadith of Abu Dawud (Islam)

He is the Living One; there is no god but He: call upon Him, giving Him sincere devotion.
Qur'an 40.65

You shall love the LORD your God with all your heart, with all your soul, and with all your might. And these words which I command you this day shall be upon your heart; and you shall teach them diligently to your children, and shall talk of them when you sit in your house, and when you walk by the way, and when you lie down, and when you rise. And you shall bind them as a sign upon your hand, and they shall be as frontlets between your eyes. And you shall write them upon the doorposts of your house and upon your gates.

Deuteronomy 6.5-9

Whatever I am offered in devotion with a pure heart—a leaf, a flower, fruit, or water—I partake of that love offering. Whatever you do, make it an offering to me—the food that you eat, the sacrifices that you make, the help you give, even your suffering. In this way you will be freed from the bondage of karma.

Bhagavad-Gita 9.26-27 (Hinduism)

Holy is the man of devotion;
Through thoughts and words and deed
And through his conscience he increases
    Righteousness;
The Wise Lord as Good Mind gives the dominion.
For this good reward I pray.

Avesta, Yasna 51.21 (Zoroastrianism)

Teachings of Sun Myung Moon

The spirit of loyalty, filial piety and integrity, which stands as straight as the pine or bamboo, will be the central thought and spirit of the Kingdom of God on earth that is to be established. We must be loyal to heaven because heaven is God's country. We must offer eternal filial devotion to God because He is the Father of humankind. (100:253, October 19, 1978)

You are doing things on behalf of God, so you must know God's circumstances and what He is doing right now. In order to be God's representatives, you should make sure that you represent God's point of view, follow the path of His Will, and know where He would have you go. (70:257, February 13, 1974)

What shall we do in order to receive God's love? Since God has total love for us, we should also invest totally. The saying, "Sincerity moves Heaven," like "Faith will move mountains," is a proverb in Korea, but truly it is also the natural order of things. The proverb, "Act with utmost sincerity," means act with all your efforts, inside and outside, heart and soul. The saying, "Practice everything with sincerity in your words and deeds," means to completely unite your body and soul in a conscientious life. This means a life of dedication. We call it "utmost sincerity" or *jeongseong*. The Korean word *jeong* deals with the spirit, and *song* means the fulfillment of the Word. Thus *jeongseong* means fulfilling everything inwardly and outwardly and offering it.[26] If you do everything with *jeongseong* you can "move heaven."

When Heaven moves, what happens? Since God has regard for such people, He makes His love dwell with them. Love wants to be with them. Love naturally dwells with people whose thoughts are for God and all His creatures. Therefore, when you offer *jeongseong*, you stand in a position to receive God's love. As God loves all humankind, if you offer everything with *jeongseong* for the sake of God you will feel God's love from the very first moment, and as a result you can love God.

Due to the Fall, we cannot truly love God. Therefore, by offering *jeongseong* for God, God's love that has been searching for us can find us, and through that love we can come to know God and to love God. (78:31-32, May 1, 1975)

Without a heart of utmost sincerity (*jeongseong*) and love, it is absolutely impossible to root out Satan's lineage. How else can we completely pull out the root that was planted when Adam and Eve fell, that extends deep into God's heart and torments God as He deals with the world's sorrowful history? If we are to succeed in pulling out that root, we have to dig beneath it. That means we must go to a place of suffering more intense than the pain of God. If God is sleeping, we should be awake. We should willingly stand in a position hundreds of times more painful than what God's heart experienced at the time of the Fall; only then can we pull out Satan's root. Our heart of devotion should go that deep. (308:208, January 5, 1999)

2. Love and Longing for God

The supreme Lord who pervades all existence, the true Self of all creatures, may be realized through undivided love.

Bhagavad-Gita 8.22 (Hinduism)

Those who remember the Lord with every breath, each morsel,
And in whose mind ever abides the spell of the Lord's Name—
Says Nanak, are blessed, perfect devotees.

Adi Granth, Var Gauri, M.5, p. 319 (Sikhism)

The Chakora bird longs for the moonlight,[27]
The lotus longs for sunrise,
The bee longs to drink the flower's nectar,
Even so my heart anxiously longs for Thee, O Lord.

Basavanna, Vacana 364 (Hinduism)

As a hart longs for flowing streams,
so longs my soul for thee, O God.
My soul thirsts for God,
for the living God.
When shall I come and behold
the face of God?
My tears have been my food
day and night.

Psalm 42.1-3

Beloved, what more shall I say to you?
In life and in death, in birth after birth
you are the lord of my life.
A noose of love binds
my heart to your feet.
My mind is fixed on you alone, I have offered you everything;
in truth, I have become your slave.
In this family, in that house, who is really mine?
Whom can I call my own?
It was bitter cold, and I took refuge
at your lotus feet.
While my eyes blink, and I do not see you,
I feel the heart within me die.

A touchstone I have threaded, and wear upon my throat, says Chandidasa.[28]

Chandidasa (Hinduism)

Once, while Yasoda was holding the baby Krishna on her lap, she set him down suddenly to attend to some milk that was boiling over on the oven. At this the child was much vexed. In his anger he broke a pot containing curdled milk, went to a dark corner of the room taking some cheese with him, smeared it over his face, and began feeding a monkey with the crumbs. When his mother returned and saw him, she scolded him. As a punishment, she decided to tie him with a rope to a wooden mortar. But to her surprise the rope, although long enough, seemed too short. She took more rope, but still it was too short. Then she used all the ropes she could find, but still Krishna could not be tied. This greatly mystified Yasoda. Krishna smiled within himself, but now, seeing that his mother was completely tired out and perplexed, he gently allowed himself to be bound.

He who has neither beginning, nor middle, nor end, who is all-pervading, infinite, and omnipotent, allowed himself to be bound by Yasoda only because of her great love. He is the Lord omnipotent, the Lord of all beings, the controller of all; yet he permits himself to be controlled by those who love him.[29]

Srimad Bhagavatam 10.3 *(Hinduism)*

Teachings of Sun Myung Moon

How much do you adore and yearn for God? What is at stake in this question is whether you are prepared to completely forget about your own situation and offer everything for God; in other words, whether or not you can become a perfect minus before the perfect Plus. When you can stand before the absolute Plus as an absolute minus, then the perfect Plus will rush straight toward you. (36:100, November 22, 1970)

Many are the believers who grasp the doctrine, but few are the believers who know the Real Being whom the doctrine describes. Few are the believers who can say, "Lord, Thy mind is my mind and my mind is Thine. Thy sorrow is my sorrow."

Have you ever felt God's heart of grief, a heart in fetters, a heart so sorrowful it feels as if your bones are melting? Understand that wherever Jesus went during his thirty-odd years on the earth, he had such an intense heart that he was constantly on the verge of losing consciousness and fainting. (4:126, March 23, 1958)

Today, we have to go beyond just the word "faith" and substantiate our faith in our daily life. That is, we must become people who live our lives with Heaven… God taught the way of faith to countless numbers of our ancestors throughout history. Nevertheless, more than just be believers, God longed that they would become people who could live together with Him. This is what Heaven is longing for us to become.

God is longing for you to become people who can willingly sacrifice, die and be resurrected for the sake of your faith. God longs for you to relate to Him as your Father, to overcome death and rejoice in your resurrection to the realm of life, and to sing His praises in the eternal ideal world. God dearly misses each one of you. He has persevered to find you and meet you. (6:84, March 29, 1959)

Do you call out to God, "Father!" with the heart to liberate His heart, which is immersed in the sorrow that pervades the 6,000 years of history? If you cling to the distressed heart of the Father and call on Him, with just that one word you can reunite heaven and earth. That was how Jesus clung to God when he called, "Abba." Unless you can attain the same level, the sorrow of God will never leave you. (3:58, September 22, 1957)

> My misery is not from hunger;
> my sorrow is not from being mistreated.
> Oh loving Father, I did not realize that
> no sorrow is worse than being apart from Thee.
>
> No matter how lacking a place may be,
> if Thou art there it has everything.
> Even in the center of hell,
> if Thou art there it becomes heaven.
> Father, whether I live or die, my place is only with Thee. (43:135, April 25, 1971)

3. Devotion to God as a Bride for Her Bridegroom

Upon my bed by night
I sought him whom my soul loves;
I sought him, but found him not;
I called him, but he gave no answer.
"I will rise now and go about the city,
in the streets and in the squares;
I will seek him whom my soul loves."
I sought him, but found him not.
The watchmen found me,
as they went about the city.
"Have you seen him whom my soul loves?"
Scarcely had I passed them,
when I found him whom my soul loves.
I held him, and would not let him go
until I had brought him into my mother's
   house,
and into the chamber of her that conceived
   me.[30]

      Song of Solomon 3.1-4

As the mirror to my hand,
the flowers to my hair,
kohl to my eyes,
tambul to my mouth,
musk to my breast,
necklace to my throat,
ecstasy to my flesh,
heart to my home—

As wing to bird,
water to fish,
life to the living—
so you are to me.
But tell me,
Madhava, beloved,
who are you?
Who are you really?

Vidyapati says, They are one another.[31]

      Vidyapati (Hinduism)

How may I live, Mother, without the Lord?
Glory to Thee, Lord of the Universe!
To praise Thee I seek;
Never without the Lord may I live.

The Bride is athirst for the Lord;
All night is she awake lying in wait for Him.
The Lord has captured my heart;
He alone knows my agony:
Without the Lord the soul is in travail and pain—
Seeking His Word and the touch of His feet.
Show Thy grace, Lord; immerse me in Thyself.

    Adi Granth, Sarang, M.1, p. 1232 *(Sikhism)*

My beloved speaks and says to me:
"Arise, my love, my fair one,
and come away;
for lo, the winter is past,
the rain is over and gone.
The flowers appear on the earth,
the time of singing has come,
and the voice of the turtledove
is heard in our land.
The fig tree puts forth its figs,
and the vines are in blossom;
they give forth fragrance.
Arise, my love, my fair one,
and come away.
O my dove, in the clefts of the rock,
in the covert of the cliff,
let me see your face,
let me hear your voice,
for your voice is sweet,
and your face is comely."

      Song of Solomon 2.10-14

Now when Jesus was at Bethany in the house of Simon the leper, as he sat at table, a woman[32] came with an alabaster flask of ointment of pure nard, very costly, and she broke the flask and poured it over his head. But there were some who said to themselves indignantly, "Why was the ointment thus wasted? For this ointment might have been sold for more than three hundred denarii, and given to the poor." And they reproached her. But Jesus said, "Let her alone; why do you trouble her? She has done a beautiful thing to me. For you always have the poor with you, and whenever you will, you can do good to them; but you will not always have me. She has done what she could; she has anointed my body beforehand for burying. And truly, I say to you, wherever the gospel is preached in the whole world, what she has done will be told in memory of her."

Mark 14.3-9

O Rama… I wish to be with thee! I shall experience no fatigue in following thee, even if I may no longer rest near thee on a luxurious couch. The harsh grass, the reeds, the rushes and thorny briars on the way, in thy company, will seem as soft as lawns or antelope skins! The dust raised by the tempest that covers me will resemble rare sandalwood paste, O my dear Lord. When, in the dense forest, I sleep beside thee on a grassy couch, soft as a woolen coverlet, what could be more pleasant to me? Leaves, roots, fruits, whatever it may be, little or much, that thou hast gathered with thine own hand to give to me, will taste of ambrosia!… To be with thee is heaven, to be without thee is hell; this is the truth![33]

Ramayana, Ayodhya Kanda 30 (Hinduism)

Teachings of Sun Myung Moon

God is the eternal Lord of our bodies and the eternal Lord of our hearts. Consider the most loving couple in the original world: The wife will not resent the husband for loving God more than he loves her. Likewise, the wife may love God more than she loves her husband, but the husband will not complain, "Why do you love God more than you love me?" The Kingdom of Heaven is the world where both husband and wife rejoice to see such a thing. God is our Subject Partner, transcending any earthly love. He is the eternal Lord of our bodies. As long as God embraces us in His bosom, as long as we dwell within His garden, we do not mind if we die right there. Since our hearts are united with their eternal Lord, what more could we ask for? (7:255, September 20, 1959)

If a woman feels about a man, "If I could be with that man, I wouldn't care if I died," and she is joined with that man, she wants nothing else under heaven. She doesn't care if she eats well or poorly. She doesn't care if she cries. She doesn't care if she even dies. There is nothing greater for her. In the same way, as human beings, our highest ambition is to take possession of God's love. When we do, we become the lords of the universe and possess the authority of a king, even a king of kings.

God endowed everyone, whether handsome or unattractive, with such ambition. It is God's original ideal that all people have this desire in common, so that everyone will naturally arrive at this destination.

The oneness of God and human beings through love: How can God and human beings, one vertical and the other horizontal, become one? God's love is perpendicular to human love. For this reason, God sent the Holy Spirit after Jesus ascended into heaven. The Holy Spirit is the love of the mother…

The Kingdom of God on Earth, the messianic ideal, is for realizing God's vertical love on the horizontal plane. After God sends the returning Lord to this earth and establishes him in the center, he develops God's domain horizontally. It is accomplished in two ways. First, mind and body are no longer two, but become one. Second, man (representing mind) and woman (body) establish a mutual relationship and become the radiating center for the harmony of heaven and earth. (252:119, November 14, 1993)

The Fall was not the failure to consider God's circumstances. It was the failure to consider His heart. As God seeks fallen humanity, He has the heart that is capable of relating with His lost sons and daughters, but He does not have people with whom to share this heart. Therefore, God has worked to find and establish such people. You need to clearly know that this has been the providence of salvation and the purpose for sending the Savior.

Before we wish for the Kingdom of Heaven, we should desire for God's heart; and before we wish for God's heart, we should first reflect on how we should live or lives. First of all, we should have a heart of attendance. It is the original character of human beings to long for what is exalted and precious, and on finding it, to bow our heads before it. We human beings fell, but we were created with a heart that desires to relate with the exalted and precious heart of Heaven. We learn how to communicate at this level of heart through a life of attendance.[34] Therefore, anyone who has never experienced a life of attendance does not have even the slightest connection with the Kingdom of Heaven. (8:291, February 14, 1960)

> Father! Today please let our bodies move, our minds move
> and our thoughts move in the garden of Thy heart.
> We realize Thy heart is a heart of infinite love,
> a heart of infinite sorrow pierced with an infinity of wounds…
>
> Exceedingly sorrowful Father;
> Thou hast worked exceedingly hard,
> and still even now Thy heart feels exceedingly anxious!…
> May we become sons and daughters who offer our full devotion,
> giving our entire minds and bodies,
> until we can be recognized as having no inadequacies before Thy heart.
>
> We do not want Heaven to give us anything material,
> we do not want Heaven to understand our situation,
> and we do not want Heaven to give us grace—
> only allow us to know Thine innermost heart. (8:262, February 7, 1960)

Purity of Intention

SINCE THE ESSENCE OF WORSHIP is the disposition of the heart, the intention we bring to an act of worship determines its value. Even when the outward form of an act expresses faith and obedience, a person's inner intentions become manifest in the end. Progress on the path to God requires purity of heart and sincerity of mind.

Intention begins our life in the world. When the Israelites approached the Temple and sung the psalm, "Who shall ascend the hill of the LORD?" they were declaring that in their daily lives they had been obedient to God's commandments to live ethically and justly. From that pure starting-point, we can cultivate a mind conducive to worship by placing our practical concerns in second place to the affairs of Heaven. As we glorify God in our minds and dedicate our bodies to His service, our sincere intention opens the door to an authentic relationship. For the antithesis of sincerity, see Chapter 15: *Hypocrisy*. For more on the role of sincerity in everyday life, see Chapter 12: *Sincerity and Authenticity*.

1. Purity and Sincerity of Heart

Blessed are the pure in heart, for they shall see God.

Matthew 5.8

A man becomes pure through sincerity of intellect; thereupon, in meditation, he beholds Him who is without parts.

Mundaka Upanishad 3.1.8 (Hinduism)

Who shall ascend the hill of the LORD?
and who shall stand in his holy place?
He who has clean hands and a pure heart,
who does not lift up his soul to what is false,
and does not swear deceitfully.
He will receive blessing from the LORD,
and vindication from the God of his salvation.
Such is the generation of those who seek thee,
who seek the face of the God of Jacob.[35]

Psalm 24.3-6

All you who come before me, hoping to attain the accomplishment of your desires, pray with hearts pure from falsehood, clean within and without, reflecting the truth like a mirror.[36]

Oracle of Temmangu (Shinto)

Though I had nothing to eat but a red-hot ball of iron, I will never accept even the most savory food offered by a person with an impure mind.

Though I were sitting upon a blazing fire hot enough to melt copper, I will never go to visit the place of a person with a polluted mind.[37]

Oracle of the Kami Hachiman (Shinto)

O my brother! A pure heart is as a mirror; cleanse it with the burnish of love and severance from all save God, that the true sun may shine within it and the eternal morning dawn.

Seven Valleys and the Four Valleys 21 (Baha'i Faith)

Sincerity (*ihsan*): You should worship God as if you saw Him; for although you do not see Him, He sees you.

Forty Hadith of an-Nawawi 2 (Islam)

Sincerity (*makoto*) is the mind of the kami. Accordingly, when serving the kami in worship, if one has a mind of sincerity, the kami will surely respond.

Ekken Kiabara, Divine Injunctions (Shinto)

A man who makes efforts to cleave to God has no time to think of unimportant matters; when he constantly serves the Creator he has no time to be vain.[38]

Israel Baal Shem Tov (Judaism)

I know your works: you are neither cold nor hot. Would that you were cold or hot! So, because you are lukewarm, and neither cold nor hot, I will spew you out of my mouth.[39]

Revelation 3.15-16

Teachings of Sun Myung Moon

God does not work where utmost sincerity is lacking. (*Way of God's Will* 1.1.1)

God's heart is the home of eternal blessing. Prepare within yourself a place where God's heart can abide; then His blessing will flow through you. (*Way of God's Will* 2.3)

Guide us not to be sons and daughters who live for ourselves and keep Christ at a distance. (2:300, June 30, 1957)

We cannot overcome with tricks or by talent, but only with a sincere heart. The question is how much sincerity you invest in loving and serving God, with how much sincerity you long for Him, with how much sincerity you seek to know His inmost feelings, and through these experiences how much you can restore a father-son relationship with Him. (42:228, March 14, 1971)

Regardless of whether anyone is watching, you should fulfill your responsibility. You should keep your promise with God. (104:112, April 15, 1979)

True sons and daughters should show sincerity, not mainly about the practical things of everyday life, but rather sincerity of hope in God, sincerity to glorify God, sincerity in their filial piety to our Heavenly Father, and sincerity in submission to God's will. If you practice all these forms of sincerity, then heaven will become your heaven and Heavenly Father will become your Heavenly Father. (17:245, January 29, 1967)

Some people forsake everything for a doctrine or abandon their own views for the sake of an ideology, but if they are not doing it to find the truth that can elevate their minds, then they cannot make a worthy relationship with Heaven. What must we do to enter the nucleus of the divine mind and cleanse our defiled minds that have inherited our ancestors' lineage of sin from the beginning of history? We must give our utmost; as Jesus said, "Love the Lord God with all your heart, and with all your soul, and with all your mind." (2:194, May 19, 1957)

2. Sincerity as the Measure of Worship

Like a clear mirror
Reflecting images according to the forms,
So from Buddha's field of blessings
Rewards are obtained according to one's heart.
Garland Sutra 10 (Buddhism)

When the monks assembled before the midday meal to listen to his lecture, the great Hogen of Seiryo pointed at the bamboo blinds. Two monks simultaneously went and rolled them up. Hogen said, "One gain, one loss."

Mumon's comment, "Tell me, who gained and who lost? If you have an eye to penetrate the secret, you will see where their teacher failed. However, I warn you strongly against discussing gain and loss."
Mumonkan 26 (Buddhism)

Actions are but by intention and every man shall have but that which he intended. Thus he whose migration was for Allah and His messenger, his migration was for Allah and His messenger, and he whose migration was to achieve some worldly benefit or to take some woman in marriage, his migration was for that for which he migrated.[40]
Forty Hadith of an-Nawawi 1 (Islam)

God revealed this to David: "There is no more unjust man among My slaves than he who serves Me for the sake of Paradise or for fear of Hell. Would I have been unworthy to be served if I had not created the Paradise and Hell?"
As-Sharani[41] (Islam)

O God, if I worship Thee for fear of Hell, burn me in Hell,
And if I worship Thee in hope of Paradise,
Exclude me from Paradise.
But if I worship Thee for Thine own sake,
Grudge me not Thine everlasting Beauty.
Rabi'a[42] (Islam)

The Dharma is without taint and free of defilement. He who is attached to anything, even to liberation, is not interested in the Dharma but is interested in the taint of desire. The Dharma is not an object. He who pursues [the Dharma as an] object is not interested in the Dharma but is interested in objects... The Dharma is not a secure refuge. He who enjoys [it as] a secure refuge is not interested in the Dharma but is interested in a secure refuge... The Dharma is not a society. He who seeks to associate with the Dharma is not interested in the Dharma but is interested in association.

Holy Teaching of Vimalakirti 6 (*Buddhism*)

Teachings of Sun Myung Moon

Why did you come and sit in this room this morning? Are you sitting here and listening to my good message so that you can become a great person? Or are you sitting here and listening to my message because you want to make the church prosper and make America great? Which is your reason for being here, the former or the latter? After listening to me now, those of you who came with the first motivation have converted to the second. You prove that by your laughter! (118:45, May 2, 1982)

People who believe in religion for their own benefit stop believing when they receive blessings, because their goal of faith was to receive blessings. After enjoying their blessings for a time, they fall away from God. You should be different. The goal of your faith in God should be to bless the world, because that is what God wants from you. (127:27, May 1, 1983)

When I visited the spirit world, I saw that the martyrs who died in order to enter heaven did not enter heaven. Rather, those martyrs who died with a grateful heart entered and dwell there. They went the way of martyrdom with this heart: "God walked a suffering path to find me; He shed His blood for me. I will go anywhere and do anything to repay God for His grace."

For whom did they die? Did they die for their own sake? No, they died for the sake of heaven and earth. On the other hand, those martyrs who thought, "I will die like this because it is the path to heaven," for whom did they die? They died for themselves. As fallen people, we can never enter the Kingdom of God by insisting on ourselves. (41:355, February 18, 1971)

When you offer sincere devotion,[43] you must not offer it merely for your own work. Do you realize this? If your devotion is merely for your own work, it turns out to be just that; it is like asking God, who makes His sunlight shine over all the earth, not to shine it equally on everyone but to shine it only on you.

Hence, you must have the presence of mind that you are praying as a representative of all humanity, even representing God. When you pray representing God, when you offer your sincere devotion representing God, you must try to imagine how much sincere devotion God Himself has been offering throughout providential history and continues to offer even now. (308:200-201, January 5, 1999)

God's sorrow is that He has no one who will suffer with Him when He suffers and be sorrowful with Him when He is sorrowful. Though God has embraced humankind for thousands of years, He has suffered alone. He suffered injustice alone, and suffered sorrow alone. When He suffered hardship, He had no one with whom to share the hardship. When He was sorrowful, there was no one to share His sorrow. That is why God's suffering has been so great, and His sorrow so great. (11:95, February 12, 1961)

Father, make Thy heart and mind my heart and mind,
Thy situation my situation,
Thy hope my hope,
Thine enemy my enemy
and Thy battle my battle.
May we be Thy victorious offerings,
sons and daughters who make Thy dream come true. (5:213, February 1, 1959)

Offerings and Tithes

OFFERINGS ARE MATERIAL EXPRESSIONS of faith and devotion. The animal sacrifices of ancient times long ago gave way to monetary donations and tithes, as well as gifts to mendicant monks. Every offering, regardless of its kind, represents an outward expression of a devoted heart. Essentially, an offering is a substitute for the self. Therefore, scripture instructs us to offer up the things that are dearest, willingly and without any reservations or lingering attachments. The biblical standard for offerings is the tithe—ten percent of one's income.

1. Offerings—Out of a Pure and Devoted Heart

You will not attain piety until you expend of what you love; and whatever thing you expend, God knows of it.

Qur'an 3.92

Every sacrifice is a boat to heaven.

Satapatha Brahmana 4.2.5.10 (Hinduism)

The spirit that eats a man's offering, pays him back with life.

Yoruba Proverb (African Traditional Religions)

And the beasts of sacrifice—We have appointed them for you as among God's waymarks; therein is good for you. So mention God's name over them, standing in ranks; then, when their flanks collapse, eat of them and feed the beggar and the suppliant. So We have subjected them to you; haply you will be thankful.[44]

The flesh of them shall not reach God, neither their blood, but godliness from you shall reach Him. So He has subjected them to you, that you may magnify God for that He has guided you.

Qur'an 22.36-37

Weeds are the bane of fields; lust is the bane of mankind. Hence what is given to those without lust yields abundant fruit.

Weeds are the bane of fields; hatred is the bane of mankind. Hence what is given to those rid of hatred yields abundant fruit.

Weeds are the bane of fields; delusion is the bane of mankind. Hence what is given to those rid of delusion yields abundant fruit.

Weeds are the bane of fields; craving is the bane of mankind. Hence what is given to those rid of craving yields abundant fruit.

Dhammapada 356-59 (Buddhism)

The dedication of the offering is God; that which is offered is God; God offers it on God's fire. God is attained by those who concentrate on God's work.

Some aspirants offer material sacrifices; others offer selfless service upon the altar of God. Some renounce all enjoyment of the senses, sacrificing them in the fire of asceticism. Others partake of sense objects but offer them in service through the fire of the senses. Some offer the workings of the senses and the vital forces through the fire of self-control, kindled in the path of knowledge.

Some offer wealth; others offer asceticism and suffering. Some take vows and offer knowledge and study of the scriptures; and some make the offering of meditation. Some offer the forces of vitality, regulating their inhalation and exhalation, offering their life-breath as they breathe in and breathe out. Others offer the forces of vitality by fasting. All these understand the meaning of sacrifice and will be cleansed of their impurities.

Bhagavad-Gita 4.24-30 (Hinduism)

Of the saying, "The word 'sacrifice' is like the word 'present'; one should sacrifice to a spirit as though the spirit were present," Confucius said, "If I am not present at the sacrifice, it is as though there were no sacrifice."

Analects 3.12 (Confucianism)

Rabbi Meir was once asked, "Why do the scriptures tell us in some passages that sacrifice is very pleasant unto the Lord, while in others it is said that God dislikes sacrifices?" He answered, "It depends whether a man's heart is sacrificed at the time he brings the sacrifice."

Baraita Kallah 8 (Judaism)

And [Jesus] sat down opposite the treasury [of the Temple], and watched the multitude putting money into the treasury. Many rich people put in large sums. And a poor widow came, and put in two copper coins, which make a penny. And he called his disciples to him and said to them, "Truly, I say to you, this poor widow has put in more than all those who are contributing to the treasury. For they all contributed out of their abundance, but she out of her poverty has put in everything she had, her whole living."

Mark 12.41-44

Whatever is given should be given with faith, not without faith—with joy, with modesty, with fear, with kindness.

Taittiriya Upanishad 1.11.3 (Hinduism)

"Make your offering," said the Master. "As you make it be pleased in mind. Make your mind completely calm and contented. Focus and fill the offering-mind with the giving. From this secure position you can be free from ill will."

Sutta Nipata 506 (Buddhism)

When a man goes to sacrifice he must remain peaceful, without a hot heart. He must stay thus for at least a day. If he quarrels on that day or is hot in his heart he becomes sick and destroys the words of the lineage and of the sacrifice.

Luhya Saying (African Traditional Religions)

The word of the LORD came by Haggai the prophet, "Is it a time for you yourselves to dwell in your paneled houses, while this temple lies in ruins? Now therefore thus says the LORD of Hosts: 'Consider how you have fared. You have sown much, and harvested little; you eat, but you never have enough; you drink, but you never have your fill; you clothe yourselves, but no one is warm; and he who earns wages earns wages to put them in a bag with holes... Go up to the hills, and bring wood and build the temple, that I may take pleasure in it and that I may appear in my glory', says the LORD."[45]

Haggai 1.3-8

Now the company of those who believed were of one heart and soul, and no one said that any of the things which he possessed was his own, but they had everything in common. And with great power the apostles gave their testimony to the resurrection of the Lord Jesus, and great grace was upon them all. There was not a needy person among them, for as many as were possessors of lands or houses sold them, and brought the proceeds of what was sold and laid it at the apostles' feet; and distribution was made to each as any had need. Thus Joseph who was surnamed by the apostles Barnabas (which means, Son of encouragement), a Levite, a native of Cyprus, sold a field which belonged to him, and brought the money and laid it at the apostles' feet.

But a man named Ananias with his wife Sapphira sold a piece of property, and with his wife's knowledge he kept back some of the proceeds, and brought only a part and laid it at the apostles' feet. But Peter said, "Ananias, why has Satan filled your heart to lie to the Holy Spirit and to keep back part of the proceeds of the land? While it remained unsold, did it not remain your own? And after it was sold, was it not at your disposal? How is it that you have contrived this deed in your heart? You have not lied to men but to God." When Ananias heard these words, he fell down and died.

Acts 4.32-5.5

Teachings of Sun Myung Moon

People present offerings because they want to be saved and return to God. The offering they give is in place of their bodies. When it is done properly, the three—the person making the offering, the offering, and God—become one. No gap should exist there. (274:199-200, November 3, 1995)

Restoration through indemnity is the guiding principle of our walk of faith. Every act of indemnity requires an offering. The offering serves as a conditional object given in place of ourselves. In other words, the offering is an object external to ourselves, and we are the internal counterpart of the object. We must be united with our offering to advance in our life of faith. (67:113, May 27, 1973)

There should be no separation between the offering and the person offering it. They should be united in heart. In other words, when you make an offering, you should give something you love. It will not do to offer something you do not care about. You should regard the sacrificial offering as representing your very blood and flesh. Therefore, you should offer the most valuable thing you own. If you own something very precious, it will make a good offering. (47:285, August 30, 1971)

Instead of offering a lamb, have this conviction: "Like a lamb that obediently goes to the slaughter, I will absolutely obey Thee, O Lord." Instead of offering a cow, think, "Like a cow that offers its whole self, I will be an absolute sacrifice for Thy will." Instead of offering a dove with an earnest heart, think, "With this heart I will love Thee absolutely." (97:289, March 26, 1978)

Suppose you have some precious treasure or property. Would you think it wonderful if God's order comes to offer all of it for the sake of the world? Do you yearn for the day when you can offer it? People who think like that will be blessed. If you really want to give it, then God will bless you and add to your abundance before that time comes. (308:206, January 5, 1999)

God originally intended that human beings possess all things of creation on the basis of true love. When you can rightly proclaim that you are the inheritors of all things because you embody true love while Satan does not, then Satan cannot accuse you. Therefore, you must love material things more than Satan loves them. Taking back the tithe from the satanic world and offering it to Heaven… is the condition to demonstrate that you are better than Satan in loving humankind, loving the world, and loving God. (128:101, June 5, 1983)

Do you know the story of Ananias and Sapphira in the Bible? After selling their property to offer it to the church, they hid some of the proceeds and donated only half, claiming that it was everything. For this, they were punished. When it comes to making an offering, "everything" means everything. If you hold something back, you will pay a price for it and be punished. You are not permitted to have a lingering attachment to the offering or think of it as your own possession. If you have such an attitude, you should clean it up before the time of judgment arrives. (122:22-23, October 31, 1982)

When you make a donation at church, you should not use money left over after buying something to eat. That money is defiled. God is not present with donations given out of the change you received after buying things at the market. (48:86, September 5, 1971)

I hear that in some Christian churches, those who make large donations are chosen to be elders and deacons. We should not have such motives. We should give our donations in the spirit of giving our lives for the sake of our nation and the world, and [confirm them] by loving our nation and the world. (166:71, May 25, 1987)

Today in Christian churches they circulate baskets for the donation. What would you call this way of collecting donations? Are they beggars? Shall we also receive donations in this fashion? The congregation should make donations in a donation box placed at the entrance door as an expression of sincere gratitude for having offered their utmost devotion and received grace from God. (166:319, June 14, 1987)

2. Tithes

All the tithe of the land, whether of the seed of the land or of the fruit of the trees, is the LORD's; it is holy to the LORD.[46]

Leviticus 27.30

Then Jacob made a vow, saying, "If God will be with me, and will keep me in this way that I go, and will give me bread to eat and clothing to wear, so that I come again to my father's house in peace, then the LORD shall be my God, and this stone, which I have set up for a pillar, shall be God's house; and of all that thou givest me I will give the tenth to thee."

Genesis 28.20-22

All the tithe of herds and flocks, every tenth animal of all that pass under the herdsman's staff, shall be holy to the LORD. A man shall not inquire whether it is good or bad, neither shall he exchange it; and if he exchanges it, then both it and that for which it is exchanged shall be holy; it shall not be redeemed.

Leviticus 27.32-33

Will man rob God? Yet you are robbing me. But you say, "How are we robbing thee?" In your tithes and offerings. You are cursed with a curse, for you are robbing me; the whole nation of you. Bring the full tithes into the storehouse, that there may be food in my house; and thereby put me to the test, says the LORD of hosts, if I will not open the windows of heaven for you and pour down for you an overflowing blessing.

Malachi 3.8-10

"A son honors his father, and a servant his master. If then I am a father, where is my honor? And if I am a master, where is my fear?" says the LORD of hosts to you, O priests, who despise my name. "You say, 'How have we despised thy name?' By offering polluted food upon my altar. And you say, 'How have we polluted it?' By thinking that the LORD's table may be despised. When you offer blind animals in sacrifice, is that no evil? And when you offer those that are lame or sick, is that no evil? Present that to your governor; will he be pleased with you or show you favor?... Oh, that there were one among you who would shut the doors, that you might not kindle fire upon my altar in vain! I have no pleasure in you," says the LORD of hosts, "and I will not accept an offering from your hand."

Malachi 1.6-11

Teachings of Sun Myung Moon

By offering a tithe from your possessions, it is as if you offered all that you have. Although you do not offer everything, offering one tenth with all of your heart and mind has the value of the whole. By offering one part, the other nine parts also come to be considered holy.

The person who tithes will never perish. As days go by, his storeroom will fill with more material blessings. (31:240, June 4, 1970)

You should give a tithe of everything you possess, even a tithe of your time. (150:219, April 15, 1961)

Just as you pay taxes to your nation, you should pay tithes to Heaven. (150:219, April 15, 1961)

Tithing applies in every aspect of life. Even in school, one of ten classrooms should be used for less fortunate children to give them classes free of charge. (166:319)

Whenever you raise funds from others, add something of your own; then your offering will be acceptable to God. Do not set aside a portion of the proceeds for yourself; instead, add a tithe from your own possessions. If you earned nine, add one-tenth to make it ten and offer it; then the offering will be accepted. To scrape up the money you can sell your clothes, your watch or even your schoolbooks. Since you and your family are a central family collecting money from the community, nation and world to offer to God, you need to set the example by collecting money from your own possessions. (116:145, December 27, 1981)

When you tithe, your offering should be the first and the purest thing, which you have invested with your most sincere heart and mind. Suppose you are going to offer one of your sons. Would you offer a son whom you dislike or who is hopeless? That son is not qualified to be an offering. Rather, you should offer your best son, the one whom you love most. Why? The offering represents your very self. (48:85, September 5, 1971)

Offering a fixed portion of your income for the maintenance of the church sounds extremely good, but I think it is extremely bad. Making an offering to God should the first priority in life, before thinking of your life or your possessions. By thinking that it is enough to offer only a small percentage of your income, you are cultivating the habit of putting your life first and putting God second. If you put God in second place, eventually He will end up in last place. (96:101, January 2, 1978)

Ritual

FATHER MOON TEACHES THAT GOD INSTITUTED RITUALS in every faith as a means by which people might approach Him. All rituals, therefore, have value. When performed with pure intention and following precisely their prescribed form, ritual offers respect to heaven and establishes for the believer a "foundation of faith."

There is no way to do justice in this book to the wide variety of rituals and rites by which the peoples of the world worship God and show their respect to Heaven. Some of the types of rituals included here are: keeping a sacred time—the Sabbath, the Eucharist or sacred meal, circumcision, baptism, worship at holy places, worship by images and symbols, and dietary laws.

1. Liturgy and Worship

Where two or three are gathered in my name, there am I in the midst of them.

Matthew 18.20

Ascribe to the LORD, O families of the peoples, ascribe to the LORD glory and strength!
Ascribe to the LORD the glory due his name; bring an offering, and come into his courts!
Worship the LORD in holy array; tremble before him, all the earth!

Psalm 96.7-9

Those who, knowing my true nature, worship me steadfastly are my true devotees. Worship me in the symbols and images which remind you of me, and also in the hearts of my devotees, where I am most manifest... Observe the forms and rituals set forth in the scriptures, without losing sight of their inner spirit.

Srimad Bhagavatam 11.5 (Hinduism)

The LORD is in his holy temple; let all the earth keep silence before him.

Habakkuk 2.20

Let us do it
the way it is usually done
so that we may have the usual result.

Yoruba chant (African Traditional Religions)

All the Islamic worship practices aim at morality: Prayer restrains from shameful and unjust deeds; giving alms takes from the wealthy to purify their souls from greed; the fast is a lesson in patience and will; and the pilgrimage is a training course in bearing difficulties and hardships, in equality among all creatures, and in cultivating the roots of peace within the human soul.

Al-Ghazzali, Ihia' Ulum el-Din 130.1 (Islam)

Wang-sun Chia asked about the saying,

> Better pay court to the stove
> Than pay court to the shrine.

Confucius said, "It is not true. He who has put himself in the wrong with Heaven has no means of expiation left."

Analects 3.13 (Confucianism)

Teachings of Sun Myung Moon

The worship service is the time when we make an offering. It is the time when we report to Heaven what we have done and repent for our mistakes. Therefore, it is a most serious time, when we are not free to do as we like. (11:163, June 24, 1961)

We earnestly pray that Thou wilt allow this place, where we bow to Thee with hearts rejoicing and which is guarded by angels and the heavenly hosts, to become an altar of wondrous blessing that can lead our whole lives to victory. (7:12, July 5, 1959)

Please let this place become a holy sanctuary where we become one with Thy mind. Please allow it to become a holy place where only Thou canst take dominion, and where we can be close to Thy heart, be moved to tears by Thy situation, and be in harmony with Thy hope. (21:132, November 17, 1968)

2. The Sabbath

And the LORD said to Moses, "Say to the people of Israel, You shall keep my Sabbaths, for this is a sign between me and you throughout your generations, that you may know that I, the LORD, sanctify you. You shall keep the Sabbath, because it is holy for you; everyone who profanes it shall be put to death; whoever does any work on it, that soul shall be cut off from among his people. Six days shall work be done, but the seventh day is a Sabbath of solemn rest, holy to the LORD; whoever does any work on the Sabbath day shall be put to death. Therefore the people of Israel shall keep the Sabbath throughout their generations, as a perpetual covenant. It is a sign for ever between me and the people of Israel that in six days the LORD made heaven and earth, and on the seventh day he rested, and was refreshed."[47]

Exodus 31.12-17

The function of lighting the Sabbath candles has been entrusted to the women of the holy people... This tabernacle of peace [the divine *Shekhinah*] is the Matron of the world, and the souls which are the celestial lamp abide in her. Hence it behooves the matron of the house to kindle the lights, because thereby she is attaching herself to her rightful place and performing her rightful function. A woman should kindle the Sabbath lights with zest and gladness, because it is a great honor for her, and further, she qualifies herself thereby to become the mother of holy offspring who will grow to be shining lights of learning and piety and will spread peace in the world, and she also procures long life for her husband. Hence she should be very careful to observe this ceremony.[48]

Zohar 1.48b (Judaism)

Teachings of Sun Myung Moon

The Sabbath day is the day when we return glory to God. (21:76, October 20, 1968)

The Sabbath is not a day to rest comfortably and sleep all day. Rather, it is a day to become one with God and rejoice to participate in God's joy. Then you will be able to enter into God's eternal Sabbath when you go to the Kingdom of Heaven in the spirit world. You will rejoice in God's eternal love, in the eternal Sabbath of the eternal God. Yet because of the Human Fall, neither God nor humankind could enjoy this Sabbath. (20:330, July 14, 1968)

Once a week Unification church members offer bows and recite the Pledge. That day is a holy day. The breakfast we eat on that holy day is a holy meal. We have to dissolve God's pain and sorrow caused by the Fall. Because they fell, Adam's family could not attend God and could not share a sacred meal with Him. This became a source of God's pain and grief. To dissolve this pain, we bow and recite the Pledge and eat the meal with a heart to praise and honor God. (280:289, February 13, 1997)

3. The Eucharist

For I received from the Lord what I also delivered to you, that the Lord Jesus on the night when he was betrayed took bread, and when he had given thanks, he broke it, and said, "This is my body which is [broken] for you. Do this in remembrance of me." In the same way also the cup, after supper, saying, "This cup is the new covenant in my blood. Do this, as often as you drink it, in remembrance of me."

1 Corinthians 11.23-25

Whoever, therefore, eats the bread or drinks the cup of the Lord in an unworthy manner will be guilty of profaning the body and blood of the Lord. Let a man examine himself, and so eat of the bread and drink of the cup. For any one who drinks without discerning the body eats and drinks judgment upon himself.

1 Corinthians 11.27-29

Teachings of Sun Myung Moon

Christianity is based upon the blood of Jesus, which connects us to his lineage. What is the sacrament of the Eucharist for? The wine represents Jesus' blood and the bread, his body. Partaking of them joins us to his blood and body—to his lineage. But having inherited it, we should love our enemies. Unless you love your enemies, you are not truly of Jesus' lineage. (May 21, 2000)

The Holy Wine Ceremony in the Unification Church has the same meaning as the Christian Holy Communion has for receiving Jesus. At the Holy Communion, you eat bread and drink wine symbolizing Jesus' flesh and blood. Its meaning is this: since human beings are fallen, they should receive a new body. The Holy Wine Ceremony has a similar significance: Through this rite fallen people reverse the process of the Fall. (*Blessing and Ideal Family* 4.4.2)

4. Circumcision

This is my covenant, which you shall keep, between me and you and your descendants after you: Every male among you shall be circumcised. You shall be circumcised in the flesh of your foreskins, and it shall be a sign of the covenant between me and you. He that is eight days old among you shall be circumcised; every male throughout your generations, whether born in your house or bought with your money from any foreigner who is not of your offspring... shall be circumcised. So shall my covenant be in your flesh an everlasting covenant.

Genesis 17.10-14

Teachings of Sun Myung Moon

At the time of Adam the blood lineage was stained. That is the reason for the Jewish rite of circumcision. Circumcision is drawing blood from the male sexual organ—the organ through which Satan's blood lineage was transmitted at the Fall. It is cut to indemnify Satan's invasion of the male sexual organ at the time of Adam. (277:264, April 18, 1996)

God gave the Israelites the commandment that all their males be circumcised. Circumcision is done by cutting the tip of the male organ and letting out some blood. Thus sanctified, the Israelites could live in the realm of Abraham's blessing. Sin infiltrated humankind through the male organ, so circumcision, by letting blood from the male organ, restored the sin by indemnity. It fulfilled the law of indemnity as it was practiced in the Old Testament Age, that is, "an eye for an eye, a tooth for a tooth, a wound for a wound." Thus, circumcision established the condition to return to God. Now you know why circumcision was necessary: to separate human beings from the blood relationship that was made at the Fall. (54:143, March 22, 1972)

5. Baptism and Purification by Ritual Bathing

Wash away, Waters, whatever
sin is in me, what wrong I have done,
what imprecation I have uttered,
and what untruth I have spoken.[49]

Rig Veda 10.9.8 (Hinduism)

Repent, and be baptized every one of you in the name of Jesus Christ for the forgiveness of your sins; and you shall receive the gift of the Holy Spirit.

Acts 2.38

Do you not know that all of us who have been baptized into Christ Jesus were baptized into his death? We were buried therefore with him by baptism into death, so that as Christ was raised from the dead by the glory of the Father, we too might walk in newness of life. For if we have been united with him in a death like his, we shall certainly be united with him in a resurrection like his. We know that our old self was crucified with him so that the sinful body might be destroyed, and we might no longer be enslaved to sin. For he who has died is freed from sin. But if we have died with Christ, we believe that we shall also live with him. For we know that Christ being raised from the dead will never die again; death no longer has dominion over him. The death he died he died to sin, once for all, but the life he lives he lives to God. So you also must consider yourselves dead to sin and alive to God in Christ Jesus.

Romans 6.3-11

Teachings of Sun Myung Moon

By making the indemnity condition of baptism by water, we can be spiritually born anew through Jesus and the Holy Spirit. Furthermore, by taking a piece of bread and a cup of wine at the sacrament of Holy Communion, we receive the precious grace of partaking in Jesus' body and blood. All these are examples of conditions of lesser indemnity. *(Exposition of the Divine Principle, Restoration 1.1)*

Baptism with water is for purifying the body, soiled by sin. It is the next stage after purifying the sexual organ by circumcision. Yet the issue remains, how to connect the people purified in this way to the path of love. (277:265, April 18, 1996)

Holy water is the water of victory, the water of sanctification. Its sanctifying power removes Satan's blood and introduces Heaven's lineage. (215:347, March 1, 1991)[50]

6. Pilgrimage and Holy Places

Three times a year all your males shall appear before the LORD your God at the place which he will choose: at the feast of unleavened bread, at the feast of weeks, and at the feast of booths.[51] They shall not appear before the LORD empty-handed; every man shall give as he is able, according to the blessing of the LORD your God which he has given you.

Deuteronomy 16.16-17

In those days and in that time, says the LORD, the people of Israel and the people of Judah shall come together, weeping as they come; and they shall seek the LORD their God. They shall ask the way to Zion, with faces turned toward it, saying, "Come, let us join ourselves to the LORD in an everlasting covenant which will never be forgotten."[52]

Jeremiah 50.4-5

And when We settled for Abraham the place of the House, "You shall not associate with Me anything. And do purify My house for those that shall go about it and those that stand, for those that bow and prostrate themselves;

"And proclaim among men the Pilgrimage, and they shall come unto you on foot and upon every lean beast, they shall come from every deep ravine, that they may witness things profitable to them and mention God's name on days well-known over such beasts of the flocks as He has provided them, 'So eat thereof, and feed the wretched poor.' Let them then finish with their self-neglect and let them fulfill their vows, and go about the Ancient House."[53]

Qur'an 22.26-29

Pilgrimage falls during known months. Anyone who undertakes the Pilgrimage during them should commit no sexual intercourse, immorality or quarreling during the Pilgrimage. God knows any good you do. Make provision; yet the best provision is heedfulness.

Qur'an 2.197

Though the poorest of mankind come here once for worship, I will surely grant their heart's desire.

Oracle of Itsukushima in Aki (Shinto)

Teachings of Sun Myung Moon

Suppose you die amidst tears and suffering… while devoting your life for God. Then even if your grave is at the top of the Himalayas, people from all over the world will visit your tomb and weep in memory of you. The locals might want to discourage them from coming, but no one can stop them. Isn't it true? When Jesus was being led to his death on Golgotha, he prayed as the Son of God. Who knows what actually took place? Yet that awesome event [has inspired millions to visit Jerusalem.] (97:104, March 1, 1978)

My hometown is Jeongju in North Korea. Would you like to visit there? Why would you like to go there? When we go there, there are many stories that I would like to tell you. I have many anecdotes about my childhood. Therefore, you should visit there at least once in your lifetime. If you do not, it will be your shame in the spirit world. In the future, Unificationists will regard it as Mecca for Muslims or as Jerusalem for Christians. (*Way of Unification* 8.3.4.3)

7. Symbols, Images and Relics

Worship me in the symbols and images which remind you of me.
Srimad Bhagavatam 11.5 (Hinduism)

Then the Sun Goddess Amaterasu imparted unto the first emperor the myriad Maga-tama beads and the mirror which had been used to lure her out of the cave as well as the sword Kusa-nagi... and said, "This mirror—have it with you as my spirit, and worship it just as you would worship in my very presence."[54]
Kojiki 39.2-3 (Shinto)

In due time they purified the bones of the deceased Saint with the finest water, and, placing them in golden pitchers in the city of Mallas, they chanted hymns of praise, "The jars hold great relics, full of virtue, like the jeweled ore of a great mountain, and the relics are unharmed by fire, just as the sphere of Brahma in heaven is unharmed [though the whole earth be burned up]. These bones, pervaded with universal benevolence, and not liable to burning by the fire of passion, are preserved under the influence of devotion; though they are cold, they still warm our hearts."

The wise know the virtues of the Buddha to be such that, given equal purity of mind, the same fruit will be won either by reverencing the Seer during his worldly existence or by doing obeisance to his relics after his passing into Nirvana.
Ashvaghosha, Buddhacarita 28.69 (Buddhism)

With a love for the happiness of different beings Shiva Puja shall be performed—so say the wise men. The pedestal represents Shiva's consort Parvati and his phallic emblem represents the sentient being. Just as lord Shiva remains ever in close embrace of the Goddess Parvati, so also the phallic emblem holds on to the pedestal forever... The devotee shall install the phallic emblem and worship it with the sixteen prescribed types of homage and services: invocation, offering the seat, water offering, washing the feet, water for rinsing the mouth as a mystical rite, oil bath, offering of cloth, scents, flowers, incense, lamps, and food, waving of lights, betel leaves, obeisance, and mystical discharge and conclusion... Everywhere Shiva accords benefit as befitting the endeavor put in.[55]
Shiva Purana, Vidyeshvarasamhita 11.22-35
(Hinduism)

Teachings of Sun Myung Moon

Just as among sinful humanity there are filial children who love their parents, there should be sons and daughters of Heaven who come forward to break away from the history of sin. To demonstrate their dedication people need an object partner representing Heaven; that is why they set up an altar, arrange a place to pray, or erect a statue of Buddha.

Even when you are by yourself, you need to make offerings and to set up an altar or a sacred image where you can offer your devotions. Then, whenever you meet with good fortune, upon your return you should look at the sacred image and present an offering of sincerity in front of Heaven, saying, "I am grateful for today's good fortune. I offer this gift before Thee, Heavenly Father, as a token of it." (123:189, January 1, 1983)

In Buddhism today, many people pray for blessings in front of the Buddha's statue. The external difference between the worshipper as the object partner and the statue as the subject partner is enormous. However, in the world of the heart, there is no difference. When people believe and relate to the statue as God, moved by the feelings it inspires in them, then God inspires their minds and fulfills their wishes. (6:342, June 28, 1959)

By wearing a cross around their neck, people show themselves to be Christians. If you carry a picture of True Parents, it symbolizes that you are their son or daughter. It begins with a symbol, then image, and finally substance. [People who carry the picture] enter the realm of the formation stage—the first of the three stages of formation, growth and completion; hence they are protected. Therefore, as tribal messiahs, you should give True Parents' pictures to everyone in your clan. (212:109, January 2, 1991)

8. Dietary Laws—to Sanctify the Food We Eat

You shall not eat any abominable thing. These are the animals you may eat: the ox, the sheep, the goat, the hart, the gazelle, the roebuck, the wild goat, the ibex, the antelope, and the mountain sheep. Every animal that parts the hoof and chews the cud, among the animals, you may eat. Yet of those that chew the cud or have the hoof cloven you shall not eat these: the camel, the hare, the rock badger, because they chew the cud but do not part the hoof, are unclean to you. And the swine, because it parts the hoof but does not chew the cud, is unclean for you. Their flesh you shall not eat, and their carcasses you shall not touch.

Of all that are in the waters you may eat these: whatever has fins and scales you may eat. And whatever does not have fins and scales you shall not eat; it is unclean for you.

You shall not eat anything that dies of itself; you may give it to the alien who is within your towns, that he may eat it, or you may sell it to a foreigner; for you are a people holy to the LORD your God…

You shall not boil a kid in its mother's milk.[56]

Deuteronomy 14.3-21

What does God care whether a man kills an animal in the proper way and eats it, or whether he strangles the animal and eats it? Or what does God care whether a man eats unclean animals or clean animals? "If you are wise, for yourself you are wise, but if you scorn, you alone shall bear it" [Proverbs 9.12]. So you learn that the Commandments were given only to purify God's creatures, as it says, "God's word is purified, it is a protection to those who trust in Him." [2 Samuel 22.31][57]

Tanhuma Leviticus, Shemini 15b (Judaism)

O mankind! Eat of that which is lawful and wholesome in the earth… Allah hath forbidden you only carrion, and blood, and swine's flesh, and that which has been sacrificed to anything other than Allah. But he who is driven by necessity, neither craving nor transgressing, it is no sin for him. Lo! Allah is Forgiving, Merciful.[58]

Qur'an 2.168, 173

Teachings of Sun Myung Moon

When we eat, we should first offer our food to heaven and then eat. Likewise, when we sit, we should first sanctify the place and then sit. (236:338, November 9, 1992)

When you sit at the table you may enjoy the food, saying, "These are wonderful dishes you prepared today." It tastes good, so you eat it. You think you know enough, but you do not know how it was prepared. There could be many stories behind the scenes. You do not know whether the rice was stolen, or from whom was it brought, or what kind of people grew it and prepared it. Maybe the farmer who grew the rice once slept with your wife. Maybe the machinery used to cultivate it was made by a gang of your enemies. If you knew these things, you would not be able to eat.

God knows it all; therefore He instructs us to purify the things we eat. Without cleansing and purifying the things we eat, we who yearn for Heaven while living in the midst of Satan's world cannot reach Heaven. (138:183, January 21, 1986)

We use Holy Salt to sanctify what we eat and wear. Since the land we live in is not God's nation, God's sons and daughters should not eat the harvest of the land without first sanctifying it. Would that we lived in a land where we could eat freely of its fruits without needing to sanctify them! (48:252, September 19, 1971)

Beyond Ritual

WHEN RITUAL IS OVERLY RELIED UPON, it may imbue an aura of sanctity not matched by deeds or wisdom. Ritual is no substitute for authentic piety, love of one's neighbor and personal realization of God. Nearly every religion has its own internal critique of ritualism. Even when the founder of one religion is apparently criticizing the ritualism of another religion, the passage was originally a prophetic word to his own people.

Father Moon concurs in these critiques, and adds two more: First, ritual can create a barrier between different denominations and faiths, which runs contrary to the will of God for religious unity. In this time of coming together, the barriers of ritual should be transcended. Second, acts of pious devotion to God and Jesus do not often grant the inner knowledge to know their heart and will. For example, many Christians revere the cross as the sign of salvation, when for Jesus it was the accursed instrument of his death and the source of millennia of grief and frustration that he could not have lived to complete his mission to build God's Kingdom on earth.

Chief among the religious rituals in ancient times was animal sacrifice, yet, with a few exceptions, animal sacrifice is rare in religion today. Religions have come to regard acts of devotion, study, and charity the essence of the ancient ritual sacrifices that are required by scripture but no longer practiced. Thus, the Talmud regards charity to one's neighbor as the equivalent of sacrificing a lamb as a sin offering. In a similar vein, the Buddha criticizes animal sacrifice as creating evil karma by killing life, and instead teaches a spiritual meaning of sacrifice as fulfilled in honoring parents, caring for family, and giving charity to monks.

1. Better than Ritual Is a Loving Heart and Righteous Deeds

With what shall I come before the LORD?
and bow myself before God on high?
Shall I come before him with burnt offerings,
with calves a year old?
Will the LORD be pleased with thousands of rams,
with ten thousands of rivers of oil?
Shall I give my first-born for my transgression,
the fruit of my body for the sin of my soul?
He has showed you, O man, what is good;
and what does the LORD require of you
but to do justice, and to love kindness,
and to walk humbly with your God?

Micah 6.6-8

Even three times a day to offer
Three hundred cooking pots of food
Does not match a portion of the merit
Acquired in one instant of love.

Nagarjuna, Precious Garland 283 *(Buddhism)*

One sabbath [Jesus] was going through the grainfields; and as they made their way his disciples began to pluck heads of grain. And the Pharisees said to him, "Look, why are they doing what is not lawful on the sabbath?" And he said to them, "Have you never read what David did, when he was in need and was hungry, he and those who were with him: how he entered the house of God, when Abiathar was high priest, and ate the bread of the Presence, which it is not lawful for any but the priests to eat, and also gave it to those who were with him?" And he said to them, "The sabbath was made for man, not man for the sabbath; so the Son of man is lord even of the sabbath."

Mark 2.23-28

Of old, one of the ancestral gods was roaming through the land of his descendant gods, and he came to Mount Fuji in the province of Suruga, just as it was becoming evening, so he went to the home of the gods of Mount Fuji and begged to be provided with a place to stay for the night. The god of Mount Fuji, however, replied, "Unfortunately, today is the day that the first fruits are being offered to the gods, and all of my family are under taboos of purification and abstinence. As a result, it would not be fitting for us to put up an unknown stranger. On this day of all days, please excuse me from being more courteous to you."

With this, the other deity was filled with resentment, and said, "I am your ancestor! Even so, will you not put me up? For this I will make it snow both winter and summer on this very mountain in which you live, cover it with mist and cold the year long, so that no person may climb it to give you offerings!"

And with these words, he ascended instead Mount Tsukuba in the province of Hitachi, and begged there for a place to stay the night. The god of Tsukuba replied, "Tonight we are keeping the abstinence of the first fruits, but we cannot refuse your request." And so he respectfully provided the visiting deity with food and a place to stay.

Thereupon, the ancestor deity was filled with joy, and said, "How dear, my child, you are to me, and how majestic your shrine. Here, may you prosper forever with the heavens and earth, with the sun and moon, and may people gather here forever to present you with food offerings, so that your generations continue in ease without end."

As a result, Mount Fuji became covered with snow year-round so that it could not be climbed. Mount Tsukuba, on the other hand, is a gathering place for many people, who enjoy themselves with singing and dancing to this day.[59]

Hitachi Fudoki *(Shinto)*

The Master said: A man who is not humane, what can he have to do with ritual?

Analects 3.3 *(Confucianism)*

Not by sacred water is one pure, although
  many folk bathe in it.
In whom is truth and dhamma, he is pure; he is
  a brahmin.

Udana 6 *(Buddhism)*

The evildoers who pursue Devotion held
  sacred by thine initiate,
because they have no part in the Good Mind,
  O Lord,
from them she shrinks back, with Righteousness,
as far as the wild beasts of prey shrink back
  from us!

Avesta, Yasna 34.9 *(Zoroastrianism)*

People under delusion accumulate tainted merits but do not tread the Path. They are under the impression that to accumulate merits and to tread the Path are one and the same thing. Though their merits from alms-giving and offerings are infinite, they do not realize that the ultimate source of sin lies in the three poisons within their own mind.[60]

Sutra of Hui Neng 6 *(Buddhism)*

Undiscerning men, theologians
preoccupied with scriptural lore,
Who claim there is nothing else,
utter words with ephemeral results.
Their words promise better births through
    cultic acts,
dwell at length on various rites,
And aim at pleasure and power.

These men are full of desire, zealous for heaven.
They cling to pleasures and power
and are fooled by their own discourses.
They have no knowledge consisting in
    commitment,
fixed in concentration.[61]

Bhagavad-Gita 2.42-44 (Hinduism)

Teachings of Sun Myung Moon

The living God wants to relate with us not merely in the context of scriptures and rituals, but rather dwelling in the hearts of people who keep God's will in their minds and live it in daily life. (135:222, November 16, 1985)

You may gaze adoringly at Jesus' face and even touch it. You may walk with Jesus and live with Jesus, as you think he would want you to live. But unless your heart is connected with Jesus' heart, it is of no use. You have to touch Jesus through the connection of heart, and live with Jesus through the heart. (10:200, October 2, 1960)

> Many people worship Heaven,
> but few say they will take responsibility for Heaven's sake.
> Many people know that the way of Heaven is good,
> but want to avoid the thorny path that lies along the way.
> Father, you have toiled for our sake through countless ages,
> but humankind wants to avoid the path of toil
> which must be traversed along the true way, the way of Heaven.
> They even think to entrust the sorrow and suffering of humanity to Thee—
> Please pardon them. (16:15, December 26, 1965)

2. With the Changing of the Age, Old Rituals Are Replaced by Purer Forms of Devotion

Once, as Rabbi Yohanan ben Zakkai was coming forth from Jerusalem, Rabbi Joshua followed after him and beheld the Temple in ruins. "Woe unto us," Rabbi Joshua cried, "that this, the place where the iniquities of Israel were atoned for, is laid waste!"

"My son," Rabbi Yohanan said to him, "be not grieved. We have another atonement as effective as this. And what is it? It is acts of loving-kindness, as it is said, 'For I desire mercy and not sacrifice' [Hosea 6.6]."

Talmud, Abot de Rabbi Nathan 6 (Judaism)

Once, when the Exalted One dwelt near Savatthi in Anathapindika's Park at Jeta Grove, a great sacrifice was being prepared for brahmin Uggatasarira: five hundred bulls, five hundred steers, and as many heifers, goats, and rams were brought to the post for sacrifice. Now brahmin Uggatasarira went and visited the Exalted One, greeted him, exchanged the usual polite talk and sat down at one side. He said, "I have heard that the laying of the fire and the setting up of the pillar are very fruitful, very advantageous... I am indeed anxious, Master Gotama, to lay the fire, to set up the pillar;

let Master Gotama counsel and instruct me for my happiness and welfare for many a day."

"Brahmin, even before the sacrifice, a man who lays the fire, who sets up the pillar, sets up three swords, evil, ill in yield, ill in fruit. Even before the sacrifice, a man laying a fire, setting up a pillar, causes to rise such thoughts as, 'Let there be slain for the sacrifice so many bulls, steers, heifers, goats, rams!' Thinking to make merit, he makes demerit; thinking to do good, he does evil; thinking he seeks a way of happy going, he seeks a way of ill going. He sets up firstly this thought-sword, which is evil, ill in yield, ill in fruit. Again, brahmin, even before the sacrifice...he speaks such words as, 'Let there be slain so many bulls, steers, heifers, goats, rams!'... He sets up secondly this word-sword... Moreover, brahmin, even before the sacrifice, he himself first sets foot on the business, saying, 'Let them slay.'... He sets up thirdly this deed-sword...

"Brahmin, these three fires, when esteemed, revered, venerated, respected, must bring best happiness. What three? The fires of the venerable, the householder, the gift-worthy. And what is the fire of the venerable? Consider the man who honors his father and mother—this is called the fire of the venerable... Consider, brahmin, the man who honors his sons, womenfolk, slaves, messengers, workmen—this is called the fire of the householder... Consider, brahmin, those recluses and godly men who abstain from pride and indolence, who bear things patiently and meekly, each taming self, each calming self, each cooling self—this is called the fire of the gift-worthy... These three fires, when esteemed, revered, venerated, respected, must bring the best happiness."[62]

Anguttara Nikaya 4.41-45:
The Great Sacrifice (Buddhism)

Thus says the LORD of hosts, the God of Israel: "Add your burnt offerings to your sacrifices, and eat the flesh. For in the day that I brought them out of the land of Egypt, I did not speak to your fathers or command them concerning burnt offerings and sacrifices. But this command I gave them, 'Obey my voice, and I will be your God, and you shall be my people; and walk in all the way that I command you, that it may be well with you.' But they did not obey or incline their ear, but walked in their own counsels and the stubbornness of their evil hearts, and went backward and not forward."[63]

Jeremiah 7.21-24

"And in every place offerings are burnt and presented unto My name" [Malachi 1.11]. "'In every place!' Is this possible?" Rabbi Samuel ben Nahmai said in the name of Rabbi Jonathan, "This refers to the scholars who devote themselves to the study of the Torah in whatever place they are: [God says], 'I account it to them as though they burned and presented offerings to My name.'..."

"Bless the LORD, all you servants of the LORD, who stand in the house of the LORD in the night seasons" [Psalm 134.1]. "What is the meaning of 'in the night seasons'?" Rabbi Johanan said, "This refers to the scholars who devote themselves to the study of the Torah at nights: Holy Writ accounts it to them as though they were occupied with the Temple service."[64]

Talmud, Menahot 110a (Judaism)

But when Christ appeared as a high priest of the good things that have come, then through the greater and more perfect tent (not made with hands, that is, not of this creation) he entered once for all into the Holy Place, taking not the blood of goats and calves but his own blood, thus securing an eternal redemption. For if the sprinkling of defiled persons with the blood of goats and bulls and with the ashes of a heifer sanctifies for the purification of the flesh, how much more shall the blood of Christ, who through the eternal Spirit offered himself without blemish to God, purify your conscience from dead works to serve the living God...

And every priest stands daily at his service, offering repeatedly the same sacrifices, which can never take away sins. But when Christ had offered for all time a single sacrifice for sins, he sat down at the right hand of God, then to wait until his enemies should be made a stool for his feet. For by a single offering he has perfected for all time those who are sanctified. And the Holy Spirit also bears witness to us; for after saying, "This is the covenant that I will make with them after those days, says the Lord: I will put my laws on their hearts, and write them on their minds," then he adds, "I will remember their sins and their misdeeds no more." Where there is forgiveness of these, there is no longer any offering for sin.

Hebrews 9.11-14, 10.11-18

There are five great sacrifices, namely, the great ritual services: the sacrifice to all beings, sacrifice to men, sacrifice to the ancestors, sacrifice to the gods, sacrifice to Brahman. Day by day a man offers sustenance to creatures; that is the sacrifice to beings. Day by day a man gives hospitality to guests, including a glass of water; that is the sacrifice to men. Day by day a man makes funerary offerings, including a glass of water; that is the sacrifice to the ancestors. Day by day a man makes offerings to the gods, including wood for burning; that is the sacrifice to the gods. And the sacrifice to Brahman? The sacrifice to Brahman consists of sacred study.[65]

Satapatha Brahmana 11.5.6.1-3 (Hinduism)

Teachings of Sun Myung Moon

If people commit sin, they must cleanse themselves of sin with a degree of intensity equal to the sin. To wash off the stains of sin, people must put in their personal effort and offer of their possessions. In particular, people need to make an offering in order to pay indemnity. People of every age have made such offerings, even though they did not clearly understand their function as objects by which to make indemnity conditions. Based on their level of understanding, primitive people sacrificed animals and even human beings as offerings. That was why they did these horrible things. All the earth's creatures should be embraced in God's love and live harmoniously together with God, yet because of the Fall they had to shed blood. They had to shed blood! Because false love, false life and false lineage came into this world, the things of creation had to shed blood. (374:21, April 4, 2002)

In prayer, we offer our mind and body before God. Rather than offering material things [animals] before God, we offer our time of devotion, dedicating our mind and my body completely, in prayer. (28:25, January 1, 1970)

Symbolic offerings [animal sacrifices] were objects for the condition made necessary as substitutes for the Word, because after the first human ancestors lost God's Word at the Fall, people were not able to receive God's Word directly. Hence, during the Age of the Providence to Lay the Foundation for Restoration (the age from Adam to Abraham), sacrifices had been offered as objects for the condition in laying the foundation of faith. However, by Moses' time that age had come to a close. Humanity had entered a new era, the Age of the Providence of Restoration (Old Testament Age), when they could once again receive God's Word directly. Thus, there was no longer any need of a symbolic offering in laying the foundation of faith. (*Exposition of the Divine Principle*, Moses and Jesus 2.1.1.2)[66]

[In this age] it is a problem that Christianity has so many denominations. It is time for Christians to start a movement to burn their denominational identities, take down their denominational signboards, and remove all their crosses. (399:100-01, December 21, 2002)

Chapter 17

Obedience and Sacrifice

Call and Mission

WHEN SAINT PAUL WAS STRUCK BY SPIRITUAL LIGHTNING ON THE ROAD to Damascus, he experienced the demanding presence of God deep in his soul. This was not simply a conversion to the new Christian faith. More than that, Paul received a mission to preach Christ to the Gentiles. That sense of mission burned in his heart and motivated him to strive for the rest of his life to plant churches throughout the Greco-Roman world. Thenceforth he devoted himself as a "living sacrifice" in obedience to God's call.

Throughout history, God has commissioned saints and righteous people like Paul to be His instruments. God needs people of faith who will take up various missions and fulfill them in His name. The prophets of Israel, the disciples of Jesus, the Companions of Muhammad and countless believers ever since have answered the call to mission. Obedient to their calling, their lives have been challenging and difficult. Yet because they cherished that divine purpose in their hearts and felt a strong sense of responsibility to fulfill it, they persevered.

1. God's Call and Our Sense of Mission

Now the LORD said to Abram, "Go from your country and your kindred and your father's house to the land that I will show you."

Genesis 12.1

Believers, be God's helpers. When Jesus the son of Mary said to the disciples, "Who will help me on the way to God?" they replied, "We are God's helpers."

Qur'an 61.14

I am the LORD, I have called you in
  righteousness,
I have taken you by the hand and kept you;
I have given you as a covenant to the peoples,
a light to the nations,
To open the eyes that are blind,
to bring out the prisoners from the dungeon,
from the prison those who sit in darkness.

Isaiah 42.6-7

Now as he journeyed he approached Damascus, and suddenly a light from heaven flashed about him. And he fell to the ground and heard a voice saying to him, "Saul, Saul, why do you persecute me?" And he said, "Who are you, Lord?" And he said, "I am Jesus, whom you are persecuting; but rise and enter the city, and you will be told what you are to do." The men who were traveling with him stood speechless, hearing the voice but seeing no one. Saul arose from the ground; and when his eyes were opened, he could see nothing; so they led him by the hand and brought him into Damascus. And for three days he was without sight, and neither ate nor drank.

Now there was a disciple at Damascus named Ananias. The Lord said to him in a vision, "Ananias." And he said, "Here I am, Lord." And the Lord said to him, "Rise and go to the street called Straight, and inquire in the house of Judas for a man of Tarsus named Saul; for behold, he is praying... for he is a chosen instrument of mine to carry my name before the Gentiles and kings and the sons of Israel; for I will show him how much he must suffer for the sake of my name." So Ananias departed and entered the house. And laying his hands on him he said, "Brother Saul, the Lord Jesus who appeared to you on the road by which you came, has sent me that you may regain your sight and be filled with the Holy Spirit." And immediately something like scales fell from his eyes and he regained his sight. Then he rose and was baptized.

Acts 9.3-18

I, an idle bard, by Thee am a task assigned:
In primal time I was commanded night and day
   to praise Thee.
The bard was summoned by the Master to the
   Eternal Mansion,
and honored with the robe of divine laudation
   and praise.
On the holy Name ambrosial he was feasted.
As by the Master's guidance on this he has
   feasted, has felt blessed,
the bard has spread and proclaimed divine
   praise by the holy Word.

Adi Granth, Var Majh, M.1, p. 150 (Sikhism)

Teachings of Sun Myung Moon

God's plan is to call good individuals out of the sinful world and have them... accomplish His work. Thus did God call Abraham out of the sinful world to be the standard-bearer of goodness and blessed him with descendants who would uphold the Will of God. (*Exposition of the Divine Principle*, Parallels 7.1)

God's providence of salvation—a work of re-creation—cannot be completed in an instant. It begins from one point and gradually expands to cover the whole. Therefore, in the providence of salvation, God first predestines one person to be the central figure and then calls him to a mission...

   God, being omniscient, foreknows who has the qualifications necessary to become a central figure in the providence of restoration. God predestines those whom He foreknows; then He calls upon him to fulfill the purpose of the providence. Calling the person is God's responsibility, but that alone does not entitle the person to be justified before God and given glory. Only when the person completes his responsibility after being called by God is he justified and then glorified. (*Exposition of the Divine Principle*, Predestination 3-4)

Fallen people's spiritual sensibility is extremely dull. Hence, they generally tend to adhere strictly to the letter of the truth in their efforts to follow God's providence. Such people cannot readily adjust themselves to the dispensation of the new age, even though the providence of restoration is moving toward it. They are generally too strongly attached to the outdated perspective provided by the doctrines of the old age. This is well illustrated by the case of the Jewish people of Jesus' day who were so attached to the Old Testament that they could not respond to Jesus' call to open a new chapter of the providence. On the other hand, those believers who receive divine inspiration through prayer are able to grasp spiritually the providence of the new age. Even though this may put them at odds with the doctrines of the old age, they will still respond to the promptings of the Spirit and follow the calling of the new dispensation. (*Exposition of the Divine Principle*, Eschatology 5.2)

Ten years ago God sent me to America, the representative nation of the free world, and directed me to speak His message to all Americans. If people ask me, "Reverend Moon, what is your purpose here?" I would tell them, "When people are sick, they send out for a doctor. Since the American people are sick, I came from the East as a doctor to heal America. America is burning. I am the firefighter who will put out the flames." This is what I am fulfilling. (123:320, January 9, 1983)

Each of us should think: "God has expectations for me; He tells me to build a new world. He commissioned me with the responsibility to resolve all the complicated problems of the past. Then, what is my position? I am not an ordinary individual who is perishing; now I belong to humankind, the world, and my Heavenly Father."

Our hearts should be awe-struck over the fact that we have been called, although we are an unworthy people and an unworthy lot. While countless others who volunteered themselves in service of their nation were not chosen, God chose us and made us His children. For this we should have grateful minds and reverent hearts. (9:344, January 30, 1960)

What more could I ask for, that in these historical Last Days, I could be appointed as an object partner to my lonely God? Is there anything more I could ask for? Even if I die, my bones crushed into powder and dispersed in the wind, could I hold any resentment? The world will always have plenty of worthless lives, people who die like pigs and dogs. (62:140, September 17, 1972)

2. Efforts and Hardships of the Mission

I saw the LORD sitting upon a throne, high and lifted up; and his train filled the temple. Above him stood the seraphim; each had six wings: with two he covered his face, and with two he covered his feet, and with two he flew. And one called to another and said:

"Holy, holy, holy is the LORD of hosts;
the whole earth is full of his glory."

And the foundations of the thresholds shook at the voice of him who called, and the house was filled with smoke. And I said: "Woe is me! For I am lost; for I am a man of unclean lips, and I dwell in the midst of a people of unclean lips; for my eyes have seen the King, the LORD of hosts!"

Then flew one of the seraphim to me, having in his hand a burning coal which he had taken with tongs from the altar. And he touched my mouth, and said: "Behold, this has touched your lips; your guilt is taken away, and your sin forgiven." And I heard the voice of the LORD saying, "Whom shall I send, and who will go for us?" Then I said, "Here am I! Send me." And he said, "Go, and say to this people:

'Hear and hear, but do not understand;
see and see, but do not perceive.'
Make the heart of this people fat,
and their ears heavy,
and shut their eyes;
lest they see with their eyes,
and hear with their ears,
and understand with their hearts,
and turn and be healed."

Isaiah 6.1-10

O LORD, thou knowest;
remember me and visit me,
and take vengeance for me on my persecutors.
In thy forbearance take me not away;
know that for thy sake I bear reproach.
Thy words were found, and I ate them,
and thy words became to me a joy
and the delight of my heart;
for I am called by thy name,
O LORD, God of hosts.

I did not sit in the company of merrymakers,
nor did I rejoice;
I sat alone, because thy hand was upon me,
for thou hadst filled me with indignation.
Why is my pain unceasing,
my wound incurable,
refusing to be healed?
Wilt thou be to me like a deceitful brook,
like waters that fail?

Jeremiah 15.15-18

The Thaqif... stirred up their louts and slaves to insult [Muhammad] and cry after him until a crowd came together, and compelled him to take refuge in an orchard...

When the Apostle reached safety he said, so I am told, "O God, to Thee I complain of my weakness, little resource, and lowliness before men. O Most Merciful, Thou art the Lord of the weak, and Thou art my Lord. To whom wilt Thou confide me? To one afar who will misuse me? Or to an enemy to whom Thou hast given power over me? If Thou art not angry with me I care not. Thy favor is wider for me. I take refuge in the light of Thy countenance by which the darkness is illumined, and the things of this world and the next are rightly ordered, lest Thy anger descend upon me or Thy wrath light upon me. It is for Thee to be satisfied until Thou art well pleased. There is no power and no might save in Thee."

Ibn Ishaq, Sirat Rasul Allah (Islam)

If any other man thinks he has reason for confidence in the flesh, I have more: circumcised on the eighth day, of the people of Israel... as to righteousness under the law blameless. But whatever gain I had, I counted as loss for the sake of Christ. Indeed I count everything as loss because of the surpassing worth of knowing Christ Jesus my Lord. For his sake I have suffered the loss of all things, and count them as refuse, in order that I may gain Christ and be found in him, not having a righteousness of my own, based on law, but that which is through faith in Christ, the righteousness from God that depends on faith; that I may know him and the power of his resurrection, and may share his sufferings, becoming like him in his death, that if possible I may attain the resurrection from the dead.

Not that I have already obtained this or am already perfect; but I press on to make it my own, because Christ Jesus has made me his own. Brethren, I do not consider that I have made it my own; but one thing I do, forgetting what lies behind and straining forward to what lies ahead, I press on toward the goal for the prize of the upward call of God in Christ Jesus. Let those of us who are mature be thus minded; and if in anything you are otherwise minded, God will reveal that also to you.

Philippians 3.4-15

Teachings of Sun Myung Moon

Living a life of faith presents many challenges. No doubt you received a call, but the question is: are you following it? It is hard to follow your call. It is even harder to be loyal and filial to God. (40:86, January 24, 1971)

When following the path of God's calling, you will surely face internal struggles. You who are called must be skillful in sorting them out. Since you are responsible for many people, if you make a misstep a large number may perish and you will have created a huge problem. Therefore, you should not act hastily or carelessly. Do not be overly joyful when you see something good, and do not grieve too much when you see something bad. You should always straighten your mind, sort out right from wrong, and move forward with care. (40:98-99, January 24, 1971)

May we may be intoxicated with our sense of mission, that we might receive Heaven's commands and fulfill our responsibilities completely.

To establish Heaven's Will on earth, let us become sons and daughters who know only to fight without resting or deviating, who know the laws of Heaven and the laws of this cosmic battle, and who will represent the unchanging Center, until the glory of restoration and the ideal of the eternal God are revealed in all things of creation. (2:180, April 14, 1957)

After receiving the call to walk the way of God's Will, you should always search with sincerity for the objective you are meant to fulfill. I am moving forward with the entire problem of the providence of restoration; that path is not peaceful. I have to surmount many disturbing and ever-changing situations, beyond anything I could have imagined when I started.

As you walk this way, purge your mind of greed and rid your heart of pride. It is impossible to succeed with the mind of "I am going to try this; I am going to attempt that." Even if your plan succeeds, it may contradict the Providence since it was planned from a human perspective. (40:77, January 24, 1971)

Father! Thou knowest the direction that we, Thy sons and daughters, should go; Thou knowest the path we shall have to walk. Our minds do not begin from within ourselves, for we have been chosen as Thy helpers, not for ourselves. Since it is for others and for Thee, Father, we pray Thou wilt take dominion over our hearts and not let them change to the very end. (6:62, March 29, 1959)

Obedience and Submission

OBEDIENCE IS NECESSARY AS LONG AS secular goals and worldly lifestyles continue to deviate from God's will and God's standards of conduct. Ever since God commanded Adam not to eat the fruit in the Garden of Eden, God has repeatedly set forth commandments that conflict with self-centered and humanistic desires. Therefore, relating with God requires submitting to God's will and denying self-will. This is an especially prominent theme in Islam, whose name, *islam*, means "submission."

Obedience requires sacrifice. When Jesus prayed, "Not my will, but Thy will be done," he was practicing the way of obedience even to the point of giving his life. Obedience is not about doing God's will when it is convenient or agreeable to our one's way of thinking. As Abraham found out when God ordered him to sacrifice his son, obedience can require doing something inconceivably difficult.

Nevertheless, the hardships of obedience and submission are ultimately for our good. God lays out commands to guide humankind on the path of growing to perfection; don't all parents require their children to follow rules so that they might grow up to be mature and well-adjusted adults? God had that loving purpose in mind when He gave the commandment to Adam and Eve, and that same loving purpose lies within His commandments to us today.

1. Obedience to God's Will and God's Commandments

Whosoever submits his will to God, while doing good, his wage is with his Lord, and no fear shall be upon them, neither shall they sorrow.

Qur'an 2.112

And now, Israel, what does the LORD your God require of you, but to fear the LORD your God with all your heart and with all your soul, and to keep the commandments and statutes of the LORD, which I [Moses] command you this day for your good?

Deuteronomy 10.12-13

Has the LORD as great delight in burnt offerings and sacrifices
as in obeying the voice of the LORD?
Behold, to obey is better than sacrifice,
and to hearken to the fat of rams.

1 Samuel 15.22

Ritual purification, though million-fold, may not purify the mind.
Nor may absorption in trance still it, however long and continuous.
Possessing worlds multiple quenches not the rage of avarice and desire.
A thousand million feats of intellect bring not emancipation.

How then to become true to the Creator?
How to demolish the wall of illusion?
Through obedience to His Ordinance and Will.

Adi Granth, Japuji 1, M.1, p. 1 (Sikhism)

Do you not know that if you yield yourselves to any one as obedient slaves, you are slaves of the one whom you obey, either of sin, which leads to death, or of obedience, which leads to righteousness? But thanks be to God, that you who were once slaves of sin have become obedient from the heart to the standard of teaching to which you were committed, and, having been set free from sin, have become slaves of righteousness. I am speaking in human terms, because of your natural limitations. For just as you once yielded your members to impurity and to greater and greater iniquity, so now yield your members to righteousness for sanctification.

When you were slaves of sin, you were free in regard to righteousness. But then what return did you get from the things of which you are now ashamed? The end of those things is death. But now that you have been set free from sin and have become slaves of God, the return you get is sanctification and its end, eternal life. For the wages of sin is death, but the free gift of God is eternal life in Christ Jesus our Lord.

Romans 6.16-23

Teachings of Sun Myung Moon

You should establish the heavenly law in yourself by absolutely obeying in your appointed duties, in your daily life, and regarding matters of the heart. (45:88, June 13, 1971)

I am not the origin. My origin must be the Being who transcends me, and my purpose must be transcendent of myself. If it were not the case, how could I stand in a position to confront this world?

My life did not begin from my parents, my society, tribe or nation, but from one transcendent Origin—God, the Absolute Being. My will must be firmly connected to His transcendent, absolute Will. My motivation must not be tainted by any relative factors stemming from history, my circumstances or the society in which I live.

Only when a person's origin is linked to the transcendent Cause, the transcendent Purpose, can he or she leap, transcend and extricate him or herself from worldly circumstances. (36:64, November 15, 1970)

When you are working in a company, what would happen to you if you took the attitude, "This work is inane. I will do what I want to do"? Living in America, suppose you took the attitude, "This country has too many laws that restrict what people can do. I will simply ignore them!" What would happen to you? No good can come from denying the rules of work or the laws of your nation. Likewise, no good can come from denying the tenets of religion.

Everyone must come under the rule of law and the regulations of the workplace, but the laws we follow in the religious life are different. The former are promulgated in this world, but the laws of the religion originate from the other world. The religious life is actually to live in two worlds. Do you understand? You are actually living in two worlds. (92:298, April 24, 1977)

When you go to the hospital, two beings know your condition well. One is the germ—that is Satan's position. The other is the doctor—he represents God. Should you relate with the germ (Satan)? No, you should team up with the doctor (God). Then, you have to do what the doctor says. You must absolutely obey; that is the only way. What if you said to the doctor, "I'll do whatever I want"? You would have to pay a price. (189:49, March 12, 1989)

> Father! We face the reality that we are far too distant from Thee—
> sublime, majestic, dwelling at the center of the universe, Lord of the ideal, Center of love.
> To span this great distance we know the path that lies before us:
> not the original, natural path but a path going the opposite way—
> the grief-filled course of restoration. (110:65-66, November 9, 1980)

2. Striving for Absolute Obedience—to Make My Will as God's Will

A sacrificial vessel:
The superior man, taking his stance as righteousness requires, adheres firmly to Heaven's decrees.

I Ching 50 (Confucianism)

Make [God's] will as your will,
so that He may make your will as His will;
make naught your will before His will,
so that He may make naught the will of others before your will.

Mishnah, Avot 2.4 (Judaism)

O you who believe! Be mindful of your duty to God, and seek the way to approach unto Him, and strive in His way in order that you may succeed.

Qur'an 5.35

Be not like the servants who minister to their Master upon condition of receiving a reward; but be like servants who minister to their Master without the condition of receiving a reward; and let the fear of Heaven be upon you.

Mishnah, Avot 1.3 (Judaism)

We sent not an Apostle but to be obeyed, in accordance with the Will of God. If they had only, when they were unjust to themselves, come unto thee and asked God's forgiveness... But no, by thy Lord, they can have no real faith until they make thee judge in all disputes between them, and find in themselves no resistance against thy decision, but accept them with the fullest conviction.

If We had ordered them to sacrifice their lives or to leave their homes, very few of them would have done it; but if they had done what they were told, it would have been best for them, and would have gone furthest to strengthen their faith.[1]

All who obey God and the Apostle are in the company of those on whom is the grace of God: of the Prophets, the Saints, the Martyrs and the Righteous. Ah! What a beautiful fellowship!

Qur'an 4.64-69

I have come down from heaven, not to do my own will, but the will of Him who sent me.

John 6.38

"Father, if thou art willing, remove this cup from me; nevertheless not my will, but thine, be done."

Luke 22.42

By one man's disobedience many were made sinners, so by one man's obedience many will be made righteous.

Romans 5.19

In the days of his flesh, Jesus offered up prayers and supplications, with loud cries and tears, to him who was able to save him from death, and was heard for his godly fear. Although he was a Son, he learned obedience through what he suffered; and being made perfect he became the source of eternal salvation to all who obey him.

Hebrews 5.7-8

Teachings of Sun Myung Moon

Complete obedience means that a person has no sense of self in front of his Subject Partner. (271:118, August 23, 1995)

Everyone should practice obedience. However, while anyone can obey, not everyone can totally surrender him or herself. Only through total surrender can we fulfill the indemnity condition. (18:188, June 7, 1967)

Why does God require of us obedience? It is not to please God, but for us—for our joy. God puts us in the position of His ideal object partners and gives us responsibility to complete the purpose of re-creation. Therefore, we must push away and overcome the elements of the Fall. Because the Fall originated from disobedience, God commands us to have absolute obedience as the necessary condition to restore it. Therefore, in our religious way of life we should not complain. Nor should we make excuses. We must have absolute obedience.

Absolute obedience requires hard work, but the purpose of that hard work is to set conditions that enable us to stand in the perfected position and achieve God's original goal of creation. Therefore, if we sacrifice and work hard, we can enter the realm of perfection. We must go this way because there is no other way. Hence religion cannot emphasize enough the necessity of hard work, undertaken in faith.

On the path of restoration, complaint is absolutely prohibited. The path of restoration is a tear-stained path of total sacrifice. Nevertheless, we should go joyfully and hopefully. It is the path of re-creation, which is hopeful for us, and we should rejoice in that hope. We are walking in faith, so we must not despair. Why, then, should we go the way of obedience? Sacrifice and hard work are the means by which we give everything and gain everything. (*God's Will and the World*, September 11, 1972)

Jesus showed us obedience and complete submission. Obedience is following an order when the circumstances allow, and complete submission is obeying even in impossible circumstances. Jesus taught the dutiful way of obedience and complete submission to the disbelieving people. By this he showed us the way to block Satan's basic nature and life elements.

The satanic world incessantly tries to exploit and take advantage of human beings and the creation, but Jesus took the opposite direction. Jesus lived a life that Satan could not live—he was meek and humble, he practiced obedience and complete submission, and he lived a life of sacrifice and service. Because he lived with these qualities, Satan had to surrender. Jesus is the representative of all human beings. Likewise, unless you can live as Jesus taught in your daily life, being meek and humble, practicing obedience and complete submission, and ever sacrificing and serving others, know that you still belong to Satan's tribe. (3:188-89, October 27, 1957)

Throughout the long eons of history, God has been carrying out a providence to set up ways by which people ignorant of the human portion of responsibility could claim that they have fulfilled their portions of responsibility. This has always required absolute obedience. The original portion of responsibility was not fulfilled because Adam and Eve failed to obey God's commandment. Obeying God's Word is the first condition to complete the human portion of responsibility. For Adam and Eve, they could have completed their portion of responsibility by absolutely obeying God's command, "Do not eat of the fruit."

Therefore, those seeking the way of restoration must absolutely obey God's words. You should not just obey to some extent. You should say you will obey even at the cost of your life. Step forward on the path of obedience and climb over the summit of the satanic world. That is what Jesus meant when he said, "He who loves father or mother more than me is not worthy of me; and he who loves son or daughter more than me is not worthy of me." (139:255-56, January 31, 1986)

Self-Sacrifice

SELF-SACRIFICE IS TO OFFER ONE'S ENTIRE SELF—body, mind and spirit—to the service of God and the fulfillment of His will. In times of oppression, self-sacrifice may mean literally to give up one's life as a martyr. In times of relative ease, self-sacrifice means to be a "living sacrifice," dedicating every action to the divine purpose.

Jesus offers a model of self-sacrifice in his death on the cross, and teaches the same by the commandment he gave his followers—"take up your cross and follow me." As individuals, each of us has a cross to bear, maybe several, and religion commends that we deal with our burdens with an attitude of submission and self-sacrifice. However, Father Moon, like other great saints before him, takes up public crosses, putting his life on the line to save others and confront the evils of the world. This is the noblest way of life.

1. Offering Oneself as a Living Sacrifice

I appeal to you therefore, brethren, by the mercies of God, to present your bodies as a living sacrifice, holy and acceptable to God, which is your spiritual worship.

Romans 12.1

To Thee as a sacrifice Zarathustra offers the very life and being of his self;
He dedicates the first fruits of his loving thoughts to Ahura Mazda;

He offers the best of his words and deeds
and willing obedience to the Divine Law.

                        Avesta, Yasna 33.14 (Zoroastrianism)

I have been crucified with Christ; it is no longer I who live, but Christ who lives in me; and the life I now live in the flesh I live by faith in the Son of God, who loved me and gave himself for me.

                        Galatians 2.20

O Son of Man! If you love Me, turn away from yourself; and if you seek My pleasure, regard not your own; that you may die in Me and I may eternally live in you.

                        Hidden Words of Bahá'u'lláh, Arabic 7 (Baha'i Faith)

Man, in truth, is himself a sacrifice.

                        Chandogya Upanishad 3.16.1 (Hinduism)

Would that I were an offering,
Taken up in the kami's hand,
Drawn near to my god,
Drawn near to my god.

                        Kagura-Uta (Shinto)

Teachings of Sun Myung Moon

Human beings should present themselves as living offerings before God and become the fruits of goodness who can demonstrate Heavenly Father's internal heart. (2:77, March 3, 1957)

An offering should not have any concept of possession. A person who would be an offering should sacrifice for his people; he should move forward for the purpose of the whole, not for his own purpose. As an offering, you should set a public goal and exert yourself for that, not for a private goal. As an offering, you should become a foundation, or good soil, upon which God can destroy evil and establish the way of goodness. (14:10, April 19, 1964)

The Chinese character for "righteousness," 義 (*eui* in Korean), is a combination of two Chinese characters, 羊 (*yang*) meaning "sheep" and 我 (*ah*) meaning "self." [In other words, when you put yourself in the position of a lamb, you will create the condition for righteousness.] (92:309, April 24, 1977)

All human beings have to travel a course of re-creation and restoration, and this requires that we walk the path of sacrifice. We cannot re-create ourselves by ourselves; we must walk a path by which God invests His energy to create our ideal selves. That is why we must sacrifice. We sacrifice so that God has room to re-create us as His partners. This is the original standard of the Principle. Therefore, a religion that seeks human perfection or the ideal world must inspire its followers to make extraordinary efforts. We sacrifice our self-centeredness, and in proportion to that sacrifice God restores our original nature. This course is necessary because we are products of the Fall. Accordingly, all religious people must walk a path of effort and endure hardships. It is the fundamental point of re-creation. (*God's Will and the World*, September 11, 1972)

To reach the ideal of perfection is not easy. It requires a state of absolute self-denial. We cannot do this if we insist on our own viewpoint. (*God's Will and the World*, April 3, 1983)

The God of goodness is the God of sacrifice and love. Love cannot exist apart from sacrifice. Love is the essence of sacrifice. If you sacrifice yourself for someone you love, you do not consider that sacrifice to be a sacrifice. The more you sacrifice yourself, the more fulfilled you feel. Love has this paradoxical nature. The size of one's love always becomes apparent in the degree of sacrifice. That is what determines whether a love is great or small. The greater the sacrifice, the greater is the love. A small sacrifice only demonstrates a lowly love. (63:25, October 1, 1972)

When you see things with the mind of love, you do not think of yourself but deny yourself and go the way of sacrifice. You must become a perfect minus in front of a perfect plus. When a perfect minus appears in front of a perfect plus, another plus is attracted to it. For example, if I am a perfect minus before a nation, the ultimate plus, God, will be attracted... This is a principle of heaven and earth.

Therefore, the tradition of patriots is one of blood, sweat and tears. The tradition of filial piety is one of blood, sweat and tears. It is the same with the way of virtuous women, virtuous men, patriots and saints. This is the mainstream tradition: only through sacrificing our blood, sweat and tears are we connected with the Kingdom of Heaven, the world of unity. This is an infallible truth. (113:118, May 1, 1981)

> Many people worship Thee hoping for Heaven's blessing;
> others make devotions to become Thy children;
> but today, even after six thousand years have passed,
> it is difficult to find devoted people, Thy true sons and daughters,
> who want to be offerings to Thee. (5:8, November 9, 1958)

2. Taking up the Cross—Sacrifice unto Death

Jesus told his disciples, "If any man would come after me, let him deny himself and take up his cross and follow me. For whoever would save his life will lose it, and whoever loses his life for my sake will find it."[2]

Matthew 16.24-25

In accepting the true Dharma, may I abandon body, life, and property, and uphold the true Dharma.

Lion's Roar of Queen Srimala 3 (Buddhism)

Jesus has many lovers of his kingdom of heaven, but he has few bearers of his Cross. Many desire his consolation, but few desire his tribulation. He finds many comrades in eating and drinking, but he finds few who will be with him in his abstinence and fasting. All men would joy with Christ, but few will suffer anything for Christ. Many follow him to the breaking of his bread, for their bodily refreshment, but few will follow him to drink a draft of the chalice of his Passion. Many honor his miracles, but few will follow the shame of his Cross and his other ignominies.

Thomas á Kempis, *Imitation of Christ* 2.11 (Christianity)

It is better to suffer for doing right, if that is God's will, than for doing wrong.

1 Peter 3.17

The Master said, "The determined scholar and the man of virtue will not seek to live at the expense of injuring their virtue. They will even sacrifice their lives to preserve their virtue complete."

Analects 15.8 (Confucianism)

Fish is what I want; bear's palm is also what I want. If I cannot have both, I would rather take the bear's palm than fish. Life is what I want; dutifulness is also what I want. If I cannot have both, I would rather take dutifulness than life.

On the one hand, though life is what I want, there is something I want more than life. That is why I do not cling to life at all costs. On the other hand, though death is what I loathe, there is something I loathe more than death. That is why there are troubles I do not avoid. If there is nothing a man wants more than life, then why should he have scruples about any means, so long as it will serve to keep him alive? If there is nothing a man loathes more than death, then why should he have scruples about any means, so long as it helps him to avoid trouble? Yet there are ways of remaining alive and ways of avoiding death to which a man will not resort. In other words, there are things a man wants more than life and there are also things he loathes more than death. This is an attitude not confined to the moral man but common to all men. The moral man simply never loses it.

Mencius VI.A.10 *(Confucianism)*

Teachings of Sun Myung Moon

Jesus sacrificed himself in order to make the people worthy of receiving God's love, that the world might be lovable to God. Even in death, he remained completely faithful to his mission. If a religion arises that inspires its believers to voluntarily walk the path of death that Jesus walked, that religion will build the final foundation to defeat Satan's realm and save the world. Jesus willingly bore the cross to his death, out of love for the world. A worldwide religion that is willing to walk the same path of sacrifice will become God's hope and Jesus' hope. (124:299, March 1, 1983)

> A complaining person cannot go this way;
> a person who makes excuses cannot go this way;
> a person who puffs himself up will retreat from this way.
> It is the way of the cross that Jesus trod, shedding blood;
> the prolongation of Golgotha. (6:125, April 12, 1959)

What is a religious life? Religious people base their lives on a different philosophy from other people. They approach life with the attitude: "Regardless of my circumstances, I will not take the road to hell by acting for my personal benefit, for that is the devil Satan's foundation. Instead, I will take the public road to heaven, no matter what sacrifices it may entail."

We seek to act as God acts and live for the sake of the public good. For the sake of the public good, God sacrifices His own family, sacrifices His own nation, and even sacrifices His own world. Although God has all authority, He has endured immeasurable sorrow and suffering as He journeyed through history alone, ever seeking the public good—the welfare of humanity. Yet He accepted it all, never blaming anyone else or making excuses for Himself. We need to understand that God stands in such a position because He is absolutely public-minded. He does not boast about what He has done. He does not boast that He has worked to benefit others. Working quietly to the end, God devotes Himself entirely to public tasks until the day the public world is completed. (101:146-47, October 29, 1978)

The more difficult the task, the more blessings come. Right now what I miss the most is being tortured in prison and vomiting blood.

Your bodies should resonate with God's vibration, but they cannot because they are stuck to Satan's stony rock. You must be shaken loose from that rock if you are to be free to resonate with God. That is why religion teaches us to sacrifice. Practice asceticism and do penance! Why? It is to cut off all satanic attachment and become God's resonant counterpart. (102:35, November 19, 1978)

So far the basic error of religious teaching has been this: though religion has taught the basic value of sacrifice and service, it has valued sacrifice mainly for the purpose of receiving salvation. The purpose of self-sacrifice ought to be to liberate God and humankind; people have been ignorant of this truth. Instead of sacrificing for the selfish purpose of attaining a high place in heaven, we should sacrifice for God and humankind. The purpose of sacrifice determines whether a believer's religious path ends up being good or evil. (102:234, January 1, 1979)

This is our motto: "Let us go forth with the heart of a parent in the shoes of a servant, shedding sweat for the earth, tears for humankind, and blood for heaven." Why do we need this motto?... The eternal God has been weeping countless tears as He seeks to eradicate the path of pain, path of sorrows, and the path of death. As God has shed His sweat, tears, and blood first, today we should take up that task in His place. (14:244, January 1, 1965)

I worked to accomplish this task oblivious to rain and snow. Nightfall was like dawn, and I would even forget to eat. I could not take things lightly because I knew God and felt the serious responsibility that comes with knowing God. More than anybody else, I knew how sorrowful God was. Thus, even if my body were torn apart, crumbled into dust and blown away, all those scattered cells could still cry out as God's cells. I grappled with this path of death, accepting it as a worthy death for a man. (137:178, January 1, 1986)

War against Evil

LIVING FAITH IS ROBUST AND UNCOMPROMISING in the fight against evil. Goodness requires striving in the ways of God—what Islam calls *jihad*. One level of striving is the inner struggle against demons and selfish desires—what Christians term "spiritual warfare" and Islam calls the "greater jihad." Yet as long as society is filled with injustice and peace is threatened by aggressors, the world will need fighters who will stand up for a righteous cause. Indeed, in many traditions passivity in the face of injustice is regarded as sin, whereas love calls us to fight to defend the weak and stop the oppressor from doing wrong.

Some situations call for guns, notably for self-defense and to defeat an aggressor. However, there are better ways to fight for goodness than by taking up arms. A spiritual view of the warrior's task sees the struggle for justice in the world as primarily a spiritual battle. Behind the hostility of earthly enemies lie the "powers and principalities" of the Devil. Defeating an opponent physically does not necessarily overcome his inner hostility; it can rather exacerbate it, particularly if the victors are vindictive or uncaring. On the other hand, once we win over our opponents' hearts and minds, the Devil is defeated and flees away. Even if the enemy is hostile and must be defeated by force of arms, the real victory is not secure until we have educated them to realize God's Will.

Therefore, the way of the spiritual warrior is to practice the maxim, "love your enemy." This means we should sacrifice ourselves and live for our enemy's sake, even though they reject, ridicule and persecute us. Our love for the enemy only becomes apparent in sacrifice. Death is no problem if in dying we can touch our enemy's heart—as Jesus did on the cross. (See Chapter 13: *Love Your Enemy*) It takes a great deal of courage and fortitude to fight this kind of war, for it is as dangerous as any military engagement. Father Moon's statements about the fighting spirit mainly describe fighting in the way of such a spiritual warrior.

1. The Warrior for Righteousness

He is the true hero who fights to protect the helpless.

        Adi Granth, Shalok, Kabir, p. 1412 *(Sikhism)*

For a warrior, nothing is higher than a war against evil. The warrior confronted with such a war should be pleased, Arjuna, for it comes as an open gate to heaven. But if you do not participate in this battle against evil, you will incur sin, violating your dharma and your honor…

Death means the attainment of heaven; victory means the enjoyment of the earth. Therefore rise up, Arjuna, resolved to fight! Having made yourself alike in pain and pleasure, profit and loss, victory and defeat, engage in this great battle and you will be freed from sin.

        Bhagavad-Gita 2.31-38 *(Hinduism)*

O Prophet! Exhort the believers to fight. If there be of you twenty steadfast they shall overcome two hundred, and if there be a hundred steadfast they shall overcome a thousand of those who disbelieve, because they [the disbelievers] are a people without intelligence.

        Qur'an 8.65

Share in suffering as a good soldier of Christ Jesus. No soldier on service gets entangled in civilian pursuits, since his aim is to satisfy the one who enlisted him.

        2 Timothy 2.3-4

Those are the future saviors of the peoples
Who through Good Mind strive in their deeds
To carry out the judgment which Thou has
   decreed, O Wise One, as righteousness.
For they were created the foes of Fury.

        Avesta, Yasna 48.12 *(Zoroastrianism)*

The LORD said to Joshua… "Be strong and very courageous, being careful to do according to all the law which Moses my servant commanded you; turn not from it to the right hand or to the left, that you may have good success wherever you go. This book of the law shall not depart out of your mouth, but you shall meditate on it day and night, that you may be careful to do all that is written in it; for then you shall make your way prosperous, and then you shall have good success. Have I not commanded you? Be strong and of good courage; be not frightened, neither be dismayed, for the LORD your God is with you wherever you go."

        Joshua 1.7-9

They that are desirous of victory do not conquer by might and energy so much as by truth, compassion, righteousness, and spiritual discipline. Discriminating then between righteousness and unrighteousness, and understanding what is meant by covetousness, when there is recourse to exertion fight without arrogance, for victory is there where righteousness is. Under these conditions know, O king, that to us victory is certain in this battle. Indeed, where Krishna is, there is victory.

        Mahabharata, Bhishma Parva 21 *(Hinduism)*

O my Father, Great Elder,
I have no words to thank you,
But with your deep wisdom
I am sure that you can see
How I value your glorious gifts.
O my Father, when I look upon your greatness,
I am confounded with awe.
O Great Elder,
Ruler of all things earthly and heavenly,
I am your warrior,
Ready to act in accordance with your will.

        Kikuya Prayer *(African Traditional Religions)*

There came out of the camp of the Philistines a champion named Goliath, of Gath, whose height was six cubits and a span. He had a helmet of bronze on his head, and he was armed with a coat of mail, and the weight of the coat was five thousand shekels of bronze. And he had greaves of bronze upon his legs, and a javelin of bronze slung between his shoulders. And the shaft of his spear was like a weaver's beam, and his spear's head weighed six hundred shekels of iron; and his shield-bearer went before him. He stood and shouted to the ranks of Israel, "Why have you come out to draw up for battle? Am I not a Philistine, and are you not servants of Saul? Choose a man for yourselves, and let him come down to me. If he is able to fight with me and kill me, then we will be your servants; but if I prevail against him, then you shall be our servants and serve us." And the Philistine said, "I defy the ranks of Israel this day; give me a man, that we may fight together." When Saul and all Israel heard these words of the Philistine, they were dismayed and greatly afraid...

David said to Saul, "Let no man's heart fail because of him; your servant will go and fight with this Philistine." And Saul said to David, "You are not able to go against this Philistine to fight with him; for you are but a youth, and he has been a man of war from his youth." But David said to Saul, "Your servant used to keep sheep for his father; and when there came a lion, or a bear, and took a lamb from the flock, I went after him and smote him and delivered it out of his mouth; and if he arose against me, I caught him by his beard, and smote him and killed him. Your servant has killed both lions and bears; and this uncircumcised Philistine shall be like one of them, seeing he has defied the armies of the living God."...

When the Philistine looked, and saw David, he disdained him; for he was but a youth, ruddy and comely in appearance. And the Philistine said to David, "Am I a dog, that you come to me with sticks?" And the Philistine cursed David by his gods. The Philistine said to David, "Come to me, and I will give your flesh to the birds of the air and to the beasts of the field."

Then David said to the Philistine, "You come to me with a sword and with a spear and with a javelin; but I come to you in the name of the LORD of hosts, the God of the armies of Israel, whom you have defied. This day the LORD will deliver you into my hand, and I will strike you down, and cut off your head; and I will give the dead bodies of the host of the Philistines this day to the birds of the air and to the wild beasts of the earth; that all the earth may know that there is a God in Israel, and that all this assembly may know that the LORD saves not with sword and spear; for the battle is the LORD's and he will give you into our hand."

When the Philistine arose and came and drew near to meet David, David ran quickly toward the battle line to meet the Philistine. And David put his hand in his bag and took out a stone, and slung it, and struck the Philistine on his forehead; the stone sank into his forehead, and he fell on his face to the ground... Then David ran and stood over the Philistine, and took his sword and drew it out of its sheath, and killed him, and cut off his head with it.

1 Samuel 17.4-51

Teachings of Sun Myung Moon

From morning until night you must be strong warriors. No matter how big the obstacles are in front of you, you must have conviction that you can overcome them. Set your determination: "I will break through the barrier, though my fist be mangled and my body crushed." Never forget that God has made you His instruments to complete the mission for the sake of humanity's future. By joining this fight you can become God's princes and princesses, who resurrect the people of the past, liberate the present, and give hope to future generations. (73:106, August 4, 1974)

"I will become God's true soldier. No matter how terrible this battlefield for God may be, I will join the front line." That is my spirit. I never once complained to God even when the world's persecution swarmed about me—even when I was in a position of utter loneliness due to persecution and suffering. This is what I can take pride in. (193:73, August 20, 1989)

I did not pray to God asking Him to save me even when I collapsed under torture. When people were pursuing me, I did not pray to God asking Him to protect me on my path or to save me from my pursuers. As a man of character, I have my own reserve of strength. I have the spirit and inner strength to fight. I say to my self, "God will probably save me if I collapse unconscious due to lack of strength. But before that, with my own power…" I know that God is waiting, preparing things in advance before I go. (138:358, January 24, 1986)

Each of you should pledge, "I will win God's victory." What is your attitude? Is it, "When the battle is joined, I will be the first to volunteer. When a Goliath appears, I will be David"? (118:129, May 9, 1982)

Twelve men representing the twelve tribes were sent to spy on Canaan. All except Joshua and Caleb reported that they would not be able to defeat seven tribes of Canaan. While the Israelites had lowered their flag to half-mast, Joshua and Caleb proclaimed, "God is alive. Believe in Him, who parted the Red Sea for us and kept us alive thus far." They proclaimed that the only way for Israel to survive was to believe in God, who does wonders for His people. Know that it was on the basis of Joshua and Caleb's faith that God opened the way for Israel. (19:240, January 15, 1968)

Our situation is analogous to David and Goliath's. We don't have weapons and we didn't receive any military training. We are like the humble shepherd David, a mere child, who had no armor but wore only patched-up rags. His only weapon was a sling; ours is the Word of God.
    Whether in America, Korea, the Middle East or Russia, we will clash with Satan's forces and keep fighting until we win. We are training and focusing our strength for the battles to come. Although my forehead is crushed, my eyeballs pop out and my lifeblood drains out, I have to go this path for the sake of God's work.
    United Nations soldiers from sixteen nations fought and died for the sake of Korea. Perhaps Unification Church members throughout the world may have to shed more blood in the fight against communism than those United Nations soldiers did in the Korean War. Regardless, we must go forward. If we retreat from the challenge, then God will lose any basis for hope in this world. Therefore we march forward, knowing that the destiny of heaven and earth is in our hands. (88:323-33, October 3, 1976)

"With the forceful and courageous sound of my pledge, the sound of my youthful heart beating, and the uproar of the corps running towards the enemy camp, I hold on to the thought, 'Everything depends on this moment!'"—if you have this attitude, billions of spirits in spirit world who have been waiting for this moment will welcome you with applause. Even the spirits in hell will say, "Please, please be victorious. We will help you even if we have to crawl."
    In a few years, such a breathtaking moment when all heaven and earth are mobilized will come to this land. Then you should fight courageously, even if you fall down on the battlefield and vomit blood. Fight to the end for the cause of righteousness. If in the battle you must offer your life as a loyal subject of Heaven, your sacrifice will resolve countless sins. On that battlefield will begin a new history.

We have been preparing ourselves for that final, critical moment, always maintaining a righteous and courageous standard and cherishing the desire to secure the final unification. Have we not willingly endured rejection by our own family, our own nation, and numerous religious denominations? God, history, and all humanity have been waiting for that final day. For its sake have we not suffered the sacrifice of many loved ones, wishing that they too could realize that solemn and magnificent victory? Now, when everything can be consummated by the stroke of my sword and by my own words and deeds, is this not a moment unprecedented in history? To fight on the actual battlefield, witnessing it with my own eyes and feeling it with my senses—what life can be more fruitful than this? (57:352, June 5, 1972)

2. Spiritual Warfare

Though we live in the world we are not carrying on a worldly war, for the weapons of our warfare are not worldly but have divine power to destroy strongholds. We destroy arguments and every proud obstacle to the knowledge of God, and take every thought captive to obey Christ.

2 Corinthians 10.3-5

Humility is my mace;
To become the dust under everyone's feet is my dagger.
These weapons no evildoer dare withstand.

Adi Granth, Sorath, M.5, p. 628 *(Sikhism)*

Be strong in the Lord and in the strength of his might. Put on the whole armor of God, that you may be able to stand against the wiles of the devil. For we are not contending against flesh and blood, but against the principalities, against the powers, against the world rulers of this present darkness, against the spiritual hosts of wickedness in the heavenly places. Therefore take the whole armor of God, that you may be able to withstand the evil day, and having done all, to stand. Stand therefore, having girded your loins with truth, and having put on the breastplate of righteousness, and having shod your feet with the equipment of the gospel of peace; besides all these, taking the shield of faith, with which you can quench all the flaming darts of the evil one. And take the helmet of salvation, and the sword of the Spirit, which is the word of God.

Ephesians 6.10-17

Invincible is the army of the Saints.
Great warriors are they; humility is their breastplate;
The songs of the Lord's glory are their weapons;
The word of the Guru is their buckler.
They ride the horses, chariots, and elephants
Of the understanding of the Divine Path.
Without fear, they advance towards the enemy.
They ride into battle singing the Lord's praise.
By conquering those five robber chiefs, the vices,
They find that they have also conquered the whole world.

Adi Granth, Slok Sehskriti, M.5, p. 1356 *(Sikhism)*

Teachings of Sun Myung Moon

We can stand on God's side if we have the heart to love the enemy. (52:87, December 22, 1971)

You can expect fierce battles, but you must love your enemies whenever you encounter them. If you possess this spirit, someday victory will be yours. (March 12, 2000)

The enemy we must fight against is not a certain person on the earth, but rather Satan, who grasped the height of authority, raised the banner of rebellion against God, and has been accusing God throughout the course history. (3:180, October 27, 1957)

The kind of fighting we are involved in is more intense than physical fighting with guns. We are using ammunition of love, while Satan is shooting arrows of jealousy and slander. My determination is this: the more the forces of evil shoot at us, the more intensely we have to return volleys of love. Our love must be greater than the enemy's opposition. Their weapons are ineffective against us; their bullets they just bounce off us. In contrast, our bullets are extremely powerful; whomever they strike are melted in love and born anew.

The more people harass me, the more progress I make. The more they pursue me, the more I advance. Look at this court case: the United States government versus Reverend Moon, a religious leader. Its absurdity has become apparent to almost everyone. The government's arrogance makes the contest more dramatic—like David versus Goliath. (119:111-12, July 4, 1982)

God works through one good person to make ten evil people surrender. It is God's will for evil to surrender voluntarily. When evil obeys goodness absolutely and without any reservations: that is a real victory. Therefore, God requires us to go through such difficulties that even evil people will take pity on us. God is still searching for such sons and daughters whose determination to gain victory on this earth is such that they will induce the evil side to surrender before the good side. (41:115, February 14, 1971)

In order to build the ideal world, there should appear people on God's side who are stronger than any individual, family, tribe, people or nation, stronger even than the entire fallen world. God and Satan are fighting over human beings, who stand in the midway position. Even though a person may be on God's side, he cannot remain if he can be broken when someone on Satan's side strikes him. But if a person overcomes no matter how much he is oppressed, persecuted and driven to the point of death, then Satan himself will testify, "He is a person on God's side," and God also will acknowledge him. Sons and daughters should emerge who are victorious in this battle, overcoming Satan, the angels, and any person who comes against them. (54:36-37, March 10, 1972)

Father! We have gone through the exhausting historical age of indemnity, and a new age is before our eyes. We see that all our enemies, who were once so powerful, who carried such authority when they took the offensive against us, approach the setting of their sun. However, we should not wish them to quickly perish.

We now realize that Heaven left them in their positions in order to save everything at once, to expand the domain of the Providence, and to establish the standard to divide good from evil in this age by which every sin can be liquidated. Therefore, we will have to open a way for even them to live.

As Jesus, while he was dying on the cross, asked for blessings on the Roman soldiers who nailed him to the cross, we pledge anew to take upon ourselves the mission of the Savior, who saves people in their actual situations. (75:244-45, January 5, 1975)

3. Situations When War is Justified [3]

And if God had not repelled some men by others, the earth would have been corrupted.
Qur'an 2.251

War is an evil thing; but to submit to the dictation of other states is worse... Freedom, if we hold fast to it, will ultimately restore our losses, but submission will mean permanent loss of all that we value... To you who call yourselves men of peace, I say: You are not safe unless you have men of action on your side.
Thucydides, History of the Peloponnesian War (Hellenism)

Let those fight in the way of God who sell the life of this world for the next. Whoso fights in the way of God, be he slain or be he victorious, on him we shall bestow a vast reward.

How should you not fight for the cause of God, and of the feeble among men and women and children who are crying, "Our Lord! Bring us forth from out of this town whose people are oppressors! Give us from Thy presence some protecting friend! Give us from Thy presence some defender!"

Those who believe do battle for the cause of God; and those who disbelieve do battle for the cause of idols. So fight the minions of the devil. Lo! The devil's strategy is ever weak.
Qur'an 4.74-76

Hear, O Israel; you are to pass over the Jordan this day, to go in to dispossess nations greater and mightier than yourselves, cities great and fortified up to heaven, a people great and tall... Know therefore this day that he who goes over before you as a devouring fire is the LORD your God; he will destroy them and subdue them before you; so you shall drive them out, and make them perish quickly, as the LORD has promised you.

Do not say in your heart, after the LORD your God has thrust them out before you, "It is because of my righteousness that the LORD has brought me in to possess this land"; whereas it is because of the wickedness of these nations that the LORD is driving them out before you.
Deuteronomy 9.1-4

When the Prophet assigned a leader to an expedition squadron, he would enjoin them... saying, "Fight in the name of Allah and in the way of Allah. Fight those who disbelieve in God. Do not use treacherous means, do not plunder and do not mutilate. Do not kill children or hermits and do not set fire to date palms or drown them with water. Do not cut down fruit-bearing trees and do not burn crops, for you never know when you might be in need of them. Do not slay animals whose meat is edible except what is necessary for you to eat.

If you should meet an enemy to the Muslims, then invite them to one of three things; if they respond to you accordingly then accept them and refrain from any action. Call them to Islam... invite them to emigrate to the lands of Islam... or call them to pay the *jizyah* from their wealth and in a state of submission."
Hadith (Islam)

Revolution: Water and fire extinguish each other, behaving as two women who live together but whose wills conflict—such is the nature of revolution. "Faith is not reposed in it until the day of its completion" means that revolution must come first, after which public faith will be established. A civilized and enlightened attitude brings joy; great success makes it possible to put all things to rights. Upon the achievement of a necessary revolution, regret vanishes. The renovating activities of the celestial and terrestrial forces produce the progress of the four seasons. T'ang and Wu rebelled in accordance with Heaven's decree, and the people responded to them.
I Ching 49 (Confucianism)

King T'ang said, "Come, you multitudes of the people, listen all to my words. It is not I, the Little

Child, who dare to undertake a rebellious enterprise; Heaven has given the charge to destroy the sovereign of Hsia for his many crimes.

"Now, you multitudes, you are saying, 'Our prince is not compassionate to us but is calling us away from our husbandry to attack and punish Hsia.' I have indeed heard these your words. But the sovereign of Hsia is guilty and, as I fear God, I dare not but punish him.

"Now you are saying, 'What are the crimes of Hsia to us?' The king of Hsia in every way exhausts the strength of his people and exercises oppression in the cities of Hsia. His people have all become idle and will not assist him. They are saying, 'When wilt thou, O sun, expire? We will all perish with thee.' Such is the course of the sovereign of Hsia. And now I must go punish him. I pray you assist me, the One Man, to carry out the punishment appointed by Heaven."

Book of History 4.1 *(Confucianism)*

Teachings of Sun Myung Moon

Not many people on this earth welcome an individual who pursues a different kind of goodness. When a good individual works to form a family of goodness, the surrounding people do not welcome him. When that good family strives to expand into a tribe of goodness, the tribulations besetting his path become even more difficult. And when that good tribe tries to form a nation of goodness, certainly an even greater evil power will rise in rebellion to block its way. Moreover, when that good nation pursues a world of goodness, the nations of the existing world, which is not good, will oppose it in every way possible.

Evil tribes rose and fought against the way of the good tribe. All nations opposed the good nation; none welcomed it even though it had long been the hope of humanity. A nation of goodness must survive this confrontation with the evil nations and prevail in the battle of good versus evil. We know well that this is why history developed through this kind of struggle. (36:52-53, November 15, 1970)

It is an error brought about by ignorance of the fundamental providence of God to regard the cause of struggles and wars as mere conflicts of interests and contests between ideologies. Humankind has suffered through a sinful history ever since the first human ancestors fell under the subjugation of Satan. However, as long as God's purpose of creation still stands, the purpose of this history must be to cut out ties with Satan and restore God's kingdom. If there were no wars or divisions in this fallen world, then the sovereignty of evil would continue forever and the world would never be restored. Therefore, God has worked His providence to restore the heavenly sovereignty by degrees. He sends prophets and saints to the fallen world to found religions and raise the level of morality. He establishes governments with higher standards of goodness which come to oppose and destroy regimes with lower standards of goodness. To fulfill the providence of restoration, therefore, conflicts and wars are unavoidable...

Although there have been times when evil seemed to prevail, in the end the relatively evil social and political forces declined and were absorbed by the more godly forces. The wars which have shaped the rise and fall of nations are thus unavoidable during the course of the providence to re-establish the reign of good.

For example, in the Bible God ordered the Israelites to destroy the seven tribes of Canaan. When Saul disobeyed Him, leaving some of the Amalekites alive with their cattle, God severely punished him. (1 Sam. 15.18-23) While on that occasion God commanded the Israelites to destroy the Gentiles, at another time, when the Israelites of the northern kingdom turned to evil, God delivered them into the hands of the Assyrians. (2 Kgs. 17.23) We must understand that God's only intention by these events was to obliterate the sovereignty of evil and restore the sovereignty of good. Therefore, fights between individuals within the same good sovereignty on the side of God are evil, because they can weaken and even cause the disintegration of the good sovereignty itself. On the other hand, wars conducted by a good sovereignty to destroy an evil sovereignty are good in that they further the fulfillment of the providence of restoration. (*Exposition of the Divine Principle*, Eschatology 4.2)

Do you respect King David? Did he do a good deed when he killed Goliath? Or was he no better than a common street fighter? From God's point of view, David did well. For by that one deed he saved the foundation of Israel's nationhood that God had labored for 3,000 years to build. (103:181-82, February 25, 1979)

Persecution

SACRIFICE IS OFTEN THRUST UPON A MAN OR WOMAN in the form of persecution. Few desire to be mistreated, misunderstood, slandered, ostracized and harassed. Yet persecution often follows righteous believers like a shadow. Persecution is of no value if it crushes us. However, those who can persevere with faith and digest these troubles without complaint or resentment can attain the highest goal of fellowship with Heaven.

Persecution can be a blessing, because it pushes us into the realm of total self-sacrifice and self-denial. Its circumstances allow us to attain an unsurpassed degree of selflessness beyond what we could achieve by our own efforts. In view of the beatification which comes through sacrifice, it is not surprising that people who are persecuted in faith often lose any negative feelings of hate or vengefulness toward their persecutors and even develop compassion for them. Selflessness begets holiness and relatedness to the divine. Hence the paradoxical fact of history that religions thrive in times of persecution.

Father Moon also teaches that God and Satan have, as it were, a contract between them: If Satan unrighteously persecutes innocent believers, God has a right to claim compensation for damages. In this way, throughout history goodness at first suffers attack but triumphs in the end. God takes this principle to its logical application: Believers should welcome maltreatment and even consciously embark on a course leading to persecution as a way to advance the divine purpose.

Blessed are you when men revile you and persecute you and utter all kinds of evil against you falsely on my account. Rejoice and be glad, for your reward is great in heaven, for so men persecuted the prophets who were before you.

Matthew 5.11-12

As the elephant in the battlefield withstands the arrows shot from a bow, even so will I endure abuse; verily most people are lacking in virtue.

Dhammapada 320 (*Buddhism*)

Assuredly you will be tried in your property and in your persons, and you will hear much wrong from those who were given the Scripture before you and from the idolators. But if you persevere and ward off [evil], then that is the steadfast heart of things.

Qur'an 3.186

In Ch'en, supplies ran short and his followers became so weak that they could not drag themselves onto their feet. Tzu-lu came to the Master and said indignantly, "Is it right that even gentlemen should be reduced to such straits?" The Master said, "A gentleman can withstand hardships; it is only the small man who, when submitted to them, is swept off his feet."

Analects 15.1 (Confucianism)

We rejoice in our sufferings, knowing that suffering produces endurance, and endurance produces character, and character produces hope, and hope does not disappoint us, because God's love has been poured into our hearts.

Romans 5.3-5

Do men imagine that they will be left at ease because they say, "We believe," and will not be tested with affliction? Lo! We tested those who were before you. Thus God knows those who are sincere, and knows those who feign.

Qur'an 29.2-3

If the world hates you, know that it has hated me before it hated you. If you were of the world, the world would love its own; but because you are not of the world, but I chose you out of the world, therefore the world hates you. Remember the word that I said to you, "A servant is not greater than his master."

John 15.18-20

The Israelites do not return to righteousness except through suffering.

Talmud, Menahot 53b (Judaism)

The right attitude for the seeker of truth on this lofty Path is, "Let my people look askance; let my wife and children forsake me; let men deride; let kings punish; but I shall be steadfast, O Supreme Deity; I shall serve and ever serve Thee with mind, speech, body, and act; I shall not leave Thy Law."

Kularnava Tantra 2 (Hinduism)

Who shall separate us from the love of Christ? Shall tribulation, or distress, or persecution, or famine, or nakedness, or peril, or sword? As it is written,

For thy sake we are being killed all the day long;
we are regarded as sheep to be slaughtered.

No, in all these things we are more than conquerors through him who loved us.

Romans 8.35-37

Or do you think that you shall enter the Garden without such trials as came to those who passed away before you? They encountered suffering and adversity, and were so shaken in spirit that even the Apostle and those of faith who were with him cried, "When will come the help of God?" Ah! Verily the help of God is always near!

Qur'an 2.214

They will lay their hands on you and persecute you, delivering you up to the synagogues and prisons, and you will be brought before kings and governors for my name's sake. This will be a time for you to bear testimony. Settle it therefore in your minds, not to meditate beforehand how to answer; for I will give you a mouth and wisdom, which none of your adversaries will be able to withstand or contradict. You will be delivered up even by parents and brothers and kinsmen and friends, and some of you they will put to death; you will be hated by all for my name's sake.

Luke 21.12-17

Monks, this is the meanest of callings, this of an almsman. A term of abuse in the world is this, to say "You scrap-gatherer! With bowl in hand you roam about!" Yet this is the calling entered on by those clansmen who are bent on the good because of good, not led thereto by fear.

Itivuttaka 89 (Buddhism)

After the Buddha's extinction,
In the last dread evil age,
We will proclaim this sutra.
Though many ignorant men
Will with evil mouth abuse us,

And beat us with swords and staves,
We will endure it all.
Monks in that evil age,
Heretical, warped, suspicious,
Crying "attained" when they have not,
Will have minds full of arrogance…

Abounding in fear and dread,
Devils will take possession of them
To curse, abuse, and insult us.
But we, reverently believing Buddha,
Will wear the armor of long-suffering;
For the sake of preaching this sutra
Every hard thing we will endure.
We will not love body nor life,
But care only for the Supreme Way.[4]

Lotus Sutra 13 (Buddhism)

The Lord GOD has given me
the tongue of those who are taught,
that I may know how to sustain with a word
him that is weary.
Morning by morning he wakens,
he wakens my ear
to hear as those who are taught.
The Lord GOD has opened my ear,
and I was not rebellious,
I turned not backward.
I gave my back to the smiters,
and my cheeks to those who pulled out the beard;
I hid not my face
from shame and spitting.

For the Lord GOD helps me;
therefore I have not been confounded;
therefore I have set my face like a flint,
and I know that I shall not be put to shame;
he who vindicates me is near.
Who will contend with me?
Let us stand up together.
Who is my adversary?
Let him come near to me.
Behold, the Lord GOD helps me;
who will declare me guilty?
Behold, all of them will wear out like a garment;
the moth will eat them up.

Isaiah 50.4-9

King Nebuchadnezzar made an image of gold, whose height was sixty cubits and its breadth six cubits… [At] the dedication of the image… the herald proclaimed aloud, "You are commanded, O peoples, nations, and languagues, that when you hear the sound of the horn, pipe, lyre, trigon, harp, bagpipe, and every kind of music, you are to fall down and worship the golden image that King Nebuchadnezzar has set up; and whoever does not fall down and worship shall immediately be cast into a burning fiery furnace." Therefore, as soon as all the peoples heard the sound of the horn, pipe, lyre, trigon, harp, bagpipe, and every kind of music, all the peoples, nations, and languages fell down and worshipped the golden image which King Nebuchadnezzar had set up.

At that time certain Chaldeans came forward and maliciously accused the Jews. They said to King Nebuchadnezzar, "O king, live for ever!… There are certain Jews whom you have appointed over the affairs of the province of Babylon: Shadrach, Meshach, and Abednego. These men, O king, pay no heed to you; they do not serve your gods or worship the golden image which you have set up."

Then Nebuchadnezzar in furious rage commanded that Shadrach, Meshach, and Abednego be brought. Then they brought these men before the king. Nebuchadnezzar said to them, "Is it true, O Shadrach, Meshach, and Abednego, that you do not serve my gods or worship the golden image which I have set up? Now if you are ready when you hear the sound of the horn, pipe, lyre, trigon, harp, bagpipe, and every kind of music, to fall down and worship the image which I have made, well and good; but if you do not worship, you shall immediately be cast into a burning fiery furnace; and who is the god that will deliver you out of my hands?"

Shadrach, Meshach, and Abednego answered the king, "O Nebuchadnezzar, we have no need to answer you in this matter. If it be so, our God whom we serve is able to deliver us from the burning fiery furnace; and he will deliver us out of your hand, O king. But if not, be it known to you, O king, that we will not serve your gods or worship the golden image which you have set up."

Then Nebuchadnezzar was full of fury, and the expression of his face was changed against Shadrach, Meshach, and Abednego. He ordered the furnace heated seven times more than it was wont to be heated. And he ordered certain mighty men of his army to bind Shadrach, Meshach, and Abednego, and to cast them into the burning fiery furnace. These men bound them in their mantles, their tunics, their hats, and their other garments, and cast them into the burning fiery furnace. Because the king's order was strict and the furnace very hot, the flame of the fire slew those men who took up Shadrach, Meshach, and Abednego. And these three men, Shadrach, Meshach, and Abednego, fell bound into the burning fiery furnace.

Then King Nebuchadnezzar was astonished and rose up in haste. He said to his counselors, "Did we not cast three men bound into the fire?" They answered the king, "True, O king." He answered, "But I see four men loose, walking in the midst of the fire, and they are not hurt; and the appearance of the fourth is like a son of the gods."

Then Nebuchadnezzar came near to the door of the burning fiery furnace and said, "Shadrach, Meshach, and Abednego, servants of the Most High God, come forth, and come here!" Then Shadrach, Meshach, and Abednego came out from the fire. And the satraps, the prefects, the governors, and the king's counselors gathered together and saw that the fire had not had any power over the bodies of those men; the hair of their heads was not singed, their mantles were not harmed, and no smell of the fire had come upon them. Nebuchadnezzar said, "Blessed be the God of Shadrach, Meshach, and Abednego, who has sent his angel and delivered his servants, who trusted in him, and set at nought the king's command, and yielded up their bodies rather than serve and worship any god except their own God."

Daniel 3.1-28

Teachings of Sun Myung Moon

You have to pass through hell in order to reach the Kingdom of Heaven. (*Way of God's Will* 1.8)

Persecution is God's strategic expedient to recover the ownership of the satanic world. If you understand this principle, it becomes self-evident why true religions prosper under persecution. The founders of the major religions of the world—Jesus, Buddha, Confucius, and Mohammed—all were persecuted. Yet, because of this principle, these persecuted people became saints. History progresses following this principle; therefore, with the flow of time they were naturally destined to become the victors. (189:205-06, April 6, 1989)

Human history has been a history of struggle—a fight between God and Satan, or good and evil, over humanity standing in the middle. Because human history started with the Fall, evil got a head start. Therefore, throughout history the evil side has always taken the offensive and been the aggressor. Good has been passive and defensive; yet, God is on the side of good. In the end, the good side always wins the victory. The good side always begins as the underdog; yet, it comes out victorious and expands. (88:209, September 18, 1976)

God's strategy is to be struck and then be compensated, including an additional amount for damages, while Satan's strategy is to strike first, for which he must pay compensation in the end. That is why Satan falls after striking, while God is struck and yet prospers. By following that strategy and taking up the course of persecution, I could continue to prosper and build an ever-stronger foundation of victories. (249:105, October 8, 1993)

Just as religions developed the most when they struggled under the threat of martyrdom, we are free of corruption when under persecution. (*Way of God's Will* 3.4)

As long as your thinking is self-centered, Satan, the second subject, is your lord. That is why religions require complete self-denial. You cannot sever your relationship with Satan if you insist on yourself.

How does God create the circumstances where we can fulfill the condition of self-denial? We cannot do it by ourselves. Certainly, religions teach people to deny themselves and lead a life of self-denial, but in the end, we cannot do it by ourselves. The standard of self-denial must be created within reciprocal relationships. If someone else pushes you into the position of being negated, it is equivalent to self-denial. In this way, God creates the sphere of denial for religious people by arranging for everyone to oppose them. This is the motive behind persecution.

When a person comes to believe in God and religion, he or she is often opposed by the people closest to him—his parents and loved ones. It is a case of Satan, the second subject, attacking God, the first subject. When someone strikes a righteous person unjustly, it sets a condition that must be repaid. Because of this repayment, the development of religion is secured. (*God's Will and the World*, April 3, 1983)

True people of faith accept persecution and trials as nutrition for their spiritual growth, rather than as a source of resentment against those who persecute them. (129:303, November 25, 1983)

Bear every cross. Willingly be the first to be hit by the stones thrown by people in the villages. Be the foremost target of all their curses and accusations, and the first to receive their beatings. (96:123, January 2, 1978)

Does true love break when hit with a fist? Which would break, true love or the fist? The bones of the fist would break. If it hits again and again, it will disintegrate. That is why God permits Satan to keep striking. Every time true love is struck, the one who strikes it is weakened.

Why does God not stop persecution? Why doesn't He remove the persecutors? Because He knows that the more they strike, the faster they will decline. In this way, the persecution will completely cease. Then it becomes fertilizer. Once it rots, it will become good soil. (230:131, May 1, 1992)

You should experience many tears. The underside of revolutionary history is always filled with blood and tears. It is full of accusations, persecutions, abuses and beatings. It is the path that I, Reverend Moon, also have walked. Yet no matter how many tears you weep, God's sorrow is millions of times greater than your sorrow. A human being's two-dimensional sorrow cannot be compared to God's three-dimensional sorrow. (11:227, September 20, 1961)

> Running my course ever grateful to Thee,
> I am nearly 70, having reached old age.
> In the prime of my life when I was healthy and strong
> I burned up all my passion attending Heaven;

now gone is the time to return glory to Thee.
Since the day I was driven out as one rejected by the people, a rebel against humanity,
I endured in silence while the Unification Church was struck.
Yet I thank Thee because it could endure and progress
through the heavenly principle of being struck and taking back what was lost…

Father! Thou art love.
Thou didst put me behind steel bars to prepare for me the measure of joyful circumstances,
to place me in the position to inherit, to give me blessings.
Now that it is over, I see that everything was love,
and the touch of Thy expansive generosity.
Recalling it now, I can only thank Thee. (164:334, April 17, 1987)

Martyrdom

WHEN PEOPLE OF FAITH ENCOUNTER HOSTILE AUTHORITIES who feel threatened by their convictions and values, some may pay the ultimate price. Father Moon explains from a spiritual viewpoint that whenever goodness advances, Satan exacts his toll. That is why it is often the best people who are sacrificed.

The word "martyr" means witness. In their steadfastness in the face of death, the martyrs bear testimony to their faith and to God who inspires such faith. The example of the martyr, who places God above his or her own life, is powerful and inspiring. Martyrdom, therefore, strengthens the community of faith, deepening its roots and furthering its growth. Tertullian famously wrote, "The blood of the martyrs is the seed of the church."

Today some regard fighters who die in the course of offensive operations that take innocent lives, e.g., suicide bombers, as martyrs. If that is martyrdom, it is the weakest form. The highest form of martyrdom stands on the foundation of goodness and mercy, even as Jesus blessed the Roman soldiers who nailed him to the cross.

Precious in the sight of the Lord is the death of his saints.

    Psalm 116.15

Then they will deliver you up to tribulation, and put you to death; and you will be hated by all nations for my name's sake.

    Matthew 24.9

Surely, the gates of Paradise are beneath the shadow of swords.[5]

    Hadith of Muslim (Islam)

Count not those who were slain in God's way as dead, but rather living with their Lord, by Him provided, rejoicing in the bounty that God has given them, and joyful in those who remain behind and have not joined them, because no fear shall be upon them, neither shall they sorrow, joyful in the blessing and bounty from God, and that God leaves not to waste the wage of the believers. And those who answered God and the Messenger after the wound had smitten them—to all those of them who did good and feared God—shall be a mighty wage.

    Qur'an 3.169-71

Holy is the death of heroic men,
Who lay down their lives in an approved cause.
Such alone may be called heroes, as at the
   Divine Portal obtain true honor:
Obtaining honor at the Divine Portal, with
   honor they depart,
And in the hereafter they suffer not.
Such reward they shall obtain if on the Sole
   Lord they meditate,
Whose service drives away all fears.
They utter not aloud their suffering; they bear
   all in their minds—
The Lord himself knows all.
Holy is the death of heroic men,
Who lay down their lives in an approved cause.

*Adi Granth, Wadhans, Alahaniyan Dirges,
M.1, pp. 579f. (Sikhism)*

When Rabbi Akiba was taken out for execution, it was the hour for the recital of the Shema, and while they combed his flesh with iron combs, he was accepting upon himself the kingship of heaven [by reciting the Shema]. His disciples said to him, "Our teacher, even to this point?" He said to them, "All my days I have been troubled over this verse, 'with all your soul' [Deut. 6.5], which I interpret 'even if He takes your soul.' When shall I have the opportunity of fulfilling this? Now that I have the opportunity, shall I not fulfill it?" He prolonged the last word [of the Shema] until he expired while saying it.[6]

Talmud, Berakot 61b (Judaism)

When the Rajah of Kalinga mutilated my body, I was at that time free from the idea of an ego-identity, a personality, a being, and a separated individuality. Wherefore? Because then when my limbs were cut away piece by piece, had I been bound by the distinctions aforesaid, feelings of anger and hatred would have been aroused within me.

Diamond Sutra 14 (Buddhism)

Stephen, full of grace and power, did great wonders and signs among the people. Then some of those who belonged to the congregation of the Freedmen [as it was called], and some of the Cyrenians, the Alexandrians, and those from Cilicia and Asia, arose and disputed with Stephen. But they could not withstand the wisdom and the spirit with which he spoke. Then they secretly instigated men, who said, "We have heard him speak blasphemous words against Moses and God." And they stirred up the people and the elders and the scribes, and they came upon him and seized him and brought him before the council, and set up false witnesses who said, "This man never ceases to speak words against this holy place and the Law; for we have heard him say that this Jesus of Nazareth will destroy this place [the temple], and will change the customs which Moses delivered to us." And gazing at him, all who sat in the council saw that his face was like the face of an angel. And the high priest said, "Is this so?" And Stephen said, "Brethren and fathers, hear me...

Now when they heard these things they were enraged, and they ground their teeth against him. But he, full of the Holy Spirit, gazed into heaven and saw the glory of God, and Jesus standing at the right hand of God; and he said, "Behold, I see the heavens opened, and the Son of man standing at the right hand of God." But they cried out with a loud voice and stopped their ears and rushed together against him. Then they cast him out of the city and stoned him; and the witnesses laid down their garments at the feet of a young man named Saul. And as they were stoning Stephen, he prayed, "Lord Jesus, receive my spirit." And he knelt down and cried with a loud voice, "Lord, do not hold this sin against them." And when he had said this, he died.

Acts 6.8-7.2, 7.54-60

To seal the testimony of this book and the Book of Mormon, we announce the martyrdom of Joseph Smith the Prophet, and Hyrum Smith the Patriarch. They were shot in Carthage jail, on the 27th of June, 1844, about five o'clock p.m., by an armed mob—painted black—of from 150 to 200 persons. Hyrum was shot first and fell calmly, exclaiming: "I am a dead man!" Joseph leaped from the window, and was shot dead in the attempt, exclaiming, "O Lord my God!" They were both shot after they were dead, and both received four balls.

Doctrine and Covenants 135.1 *(Latter-day Saints)*

If physical death is the price that I must pay to free my white brothers and sisters from a permanent death of the spirit, then nothing can be more redemptive.[7]

Martin Luther King, Jr. *(Christianity)*

Teachings of Sun Myung Moon

Great religions were born and grew up in the soil of persecution and martyrdom. They stand on a foundation of the precious traditions of their founders. Therefore, we must not avoid sacrifices as we recover the original honor of our religions. (271:72, August 21, 1995)

Throughout history religions have taught the value of sacrifice, ultimately to guide people in approaching God. The stairway to Heaven has thousands of steps. For each step God must triumph and Satan must be defeated, but each time Satan demands his maximum price—a sacrifice. Satan does not like to be defeated. That is why so many martyrs appeared in Christian history.

Christianity has produced more martyrs than any other religion because it is the central religion of the providence. To human eyes, each martyr's death looked like a setback, yet in fact it was a victory for God. The martyrs are the reason Christianity kept advancing victoriously despite opposition and persecution. At every step, Satan demanded a huge sacrifice as the price for his defeat. (130:283)

Christianity today is proud of its history of martyrdom. In every place and in every age, wherever Christianity spread its martyrs have shed blood. The blood they shed laid the foundation for Christian missions. However, we should not just reflect on the miserable sacrifices suffered by individuals, families, or groups. Know that God, in guiding them, walked a path more tragic than theirs. (13:220-21, March 22, 1964)

Have you ever thought that you might be defeated or fall away? Never allow it to happen, even at the point of death! You should not waver even in the face of execution by a firing squad or the torture of having each knuckle of your fingers severed. Live your entire life this way and you will have transcended life and death. Then you can be a friend of God, because He is transcendent of life and death. Though you may be killed, since you transcend life and death, you will live on as a friend of God. (66:317, May 17, 1973)

No matter what pain, sorrow, and sufferings they may face, those who know that their position based upon the Universal Teaching are not shaken; they shall overcome those hills. Those who think, "I am a person who can tolerate this suffering, and I will not surrender even on this hill of death," are successful in the course of life. Those who think, "I will not change the direction of my life, no matter what hills of persecution and death come to me. I have a value that cannot be replaced with anything under the sun," are citizens of Heaven. Whether on earth they live or die, they still belong to Heaven. (9:166, May 8, 1960)

Many people were martyred in the two thousand years of Christian history. You should be ready to follow in their footsteps, saying, "I offer my life for Heaven. My death will lay the foundation to liberate all the people." Then you will surely create that foundation. When the time comes, instead of ten thousand people dying, God will fulfill His promise to you and save the important people in your family and tribe. Your sacrifice is that important. As long as your foundation remains, future generations will stand on that foundation and rise up. (218:236, August 19, 1991)

At the time of Jesus' death, Israel and Rome were his enemies, but rather than curse these enemies Jesus loved them and taught his disciples to love them. He resolved, "Rome may be my enemy today, but in the future Rome will surely be blessed through my followers." That blessing was more than enough to save Rome. Jesus wanted more than anything to give Rome this blessing. Thinking of Rome's future, he forgave the Roman soldiers and blessed them. (101:151, October 29, 1978)

A person who becomes a martyr in order to enter heaven will fall down to hell. However, a person who is willing to go into hell in order to send the whole world to heaven will be brought into the Kingdom of Heaven, even if he protests. (39:197, January 10, 1971)

CHAPTER 18

HUMILITY AND SELF-DENIAL

Humility

AN ATTITUDE OF HUMILITY IS ESSENTIAL ON THE PATH to God. Any self-conceit, whether nurtured by superior intelligence, wealth, high status, or the praise of others, is an obstacle blocking our way. Genuine humility requires a constant willingness to deny oneself, to be critical of oneself, to endure hardship without complaint, and to be open to Heaven's guidance even when it differs from one's preconceived concepts.

Humility requires sincerity and honesty; thus some passages liken the humble person to a little child, whose natural spontaneity and acceptance of life is the antithesis of the often-complicated personality of the adult with its many masks, hidden resentments, and prejudices. Other scriptures teach us to cultivate humility by meditating on the insignificance and transience of the human being, who is nothing but a puff of wind, a bag of excrement, food for worms.

Here, too, is the paradoxical wisdom that the humble and self-effacing person ultimately prospers and wins more respect from others than the person who is arrogant and powerful. We have the example of Jesus, who took the path of humility to triumph over the Devil's most deadly attack. Father Moon explains this in terms of the principle that humility, being in accord with the original way of life in Eden, aligns us with God and His creative power, while arrogance places us in Satan's camp—ultimately a losing cause. In another passage, he alludes to the natural cycle of rise and fall, where arrogance places us at the peak of the cycle where the only way forward is to decline, while humility places us at the bottom where all roads lead upward.

1. Blessed Are the Meek

Blessed are the meek, for they shall inherit the earth.

Matthew 5.5

Successful indeed are the believers
who are humble in their prayers,
and who shun vain conversation,
and who are payers of the poor-due,
and who guard their modesty.

Qur'an 23.1-5

If you desire to obtain help, put away pride. Even a hair of pride shuts you off, as if by a great cloud.

Oracle of Kasuga (Shinto)

Turn not your cheek in scorn toward folk, nor walk with pertness in the land. Lo! God loves not each braggart boaster. Be modest in your bearing and subdue your voice. Lo, the harshest of all voices is the voice of the ass.

Qur'an 31.18-19

This is the man to whom I will look:
he that is humble and contrite in spirit,
and trembles at my word.

Isaiah 66.2

Now, in exile, the Holy Spirit comes upon us more easily than at the time the Temple was still standing. A king was driven from his realm and forced to become a wayfarer. When in the course of his wanderings, he came to the house of poor people, where he was given modest food and shelter, but received as a king, his heart grew light and he chatted with his hosts as intimately as he had done at court with his high courtiers. Now that He is in exile, God does the same.[1]

Dov Baer of Mezirech (Judaism)

Be humble, be harmless,
Have no pretension,
Be upright, forbearing;
Serve your teacher in true obedience,
Keeping the mind and body in cleanness,
Tranquil, steadfast, master of ego,
Standing apart from the things of the senses,
Free from self;
Aware of the weakness in mortal nature.

Bhagavad-Gita 13.7-8 (Hinduism)

All men are children of Adam, and Adam was created from soil.

Hadith of Tirmidhi (Islam)

Be of an exceedingly humble spirit, for the end of man is the worm.

Mishnah, Avot 4.4 (Judaism)

O Lord, what is man, that thou dost regard him,
or the son of man, that thou dost think of him?
Man is like a breath,
his days are like a passing shadow.

Psalm 144.3-4

Reflect upon three things, and you will not come within the power of sin: know from where you came, to where you are going, and before whom you will in future have to give account and reckoning. From where you came—from a fetid drop; to where are you going—to a place of dust, worms, and maggots; and before whom you will in future have to give account and reckoning—before the Supreme King of kings, the Holy One, blessed be He.

Mishnah, Avot 3.1 (Judaism)

The Prophet said, "Have I not taught you how the inhabitants of Paradise will be all the humble and the weak, whose oaths God will accept when they swear to be faithful? Have I not taught you how the inhabitants of hell will be all the cruel beings, strong of body and arrogant?"

Hadith of Bukhari (Islam)

It is humble people whom God protects and liberates; it is the humble whom He loves and consoles. To the humble He turns and upon them bestows great grace, that after their humiliation He may raise them up to glory. He reveals His secrets to the humble, and with kind invitation bids them come to Him. Thus, humble people enjoy peace in the midst of many vexations, because their trust is in God, not in the world. Hence, you must not think that you have made any progress until you look upon yourself as inferior to all others.

Thomas á Kempis, Imitation of Christ 1.2 (Christianity)

Teachings of Sun Myung Moon

God's love dwells upon the foundations of meekness, humility, fasting, sacrifice and even martyrdom. (282:227, March 26, 1997)

The higher the religion, the less it stresses the self and the more it stresses meekness, humility, and one step further, sacrifice and service. Why must it do that? Those are the laws of the original homeland. People are like wanderers searching for their original homeland. To train people in the laws of that homeland, the higher religions teach the way of sacrifice. (77:190, April 6, 1995)

Satan's basic nature is arrogance and wrath. That is the way he deals with people in the world. Jesus, on the other hand, came before the people with meekness and humility. Satan ultimately acknowledged Jesus because he knew that humility is in accord with the heavenly law. When you act with gentleness and humility, the satanic world naturally surrenders. Jesus knew this principle, and therefore he assumed the posture of gentleness and humility. You, too, can open up a new way to reach God… when you remain always gentle and humble. Examine yourself: are you living by Jesus' teachings of gentleness and humility, meekness and obedience, and sacrifice and service? If you are not practicing these teachings in your daily life, know that you still belong to Satan's tribe. (3:187, October 27, 1957)

I examined the Book of Life in heaven. I saw that the people whose names are recorded in that book were all simple and lowly. Millionaires, famous preachers and politicians are not found there. (107:21, February 21, 1980)

The Garden of Eden is not a world filled with disputes. It is not a world where people promote themselves, but a world full of humility and love. (98:31, April 8, 1978)

How can we hold on to individualism? There is not one part of us that we can claim as our very own. When we were conceived from our parents' love and grew beginning from our mother's ovum, 99.999 percent of our being was our mother's bone, blood and flesh, and the other 0.001 percent was added from our father's sperm. No one at the time of their birth has the concept, "I belong to myself." (299:113, February 7, 1999)

At the Fall evil began first and rose up, so we must carry out a strategy to push evil down and pull goodness up. How shall we carry this out? First, we must take control of our arrogance. The Fall occurred when the archangel Lucifer and human beings pushed God aside and attempted to elevate themselves. Arrogance was Satan's original nature. Arrogance is the desire to elevate oneself without regard to law, discipline, obligations, or the affect on the surrounding environment. It is the desire to live unconstrained by justice or law.

How do we describe a person who lives in accordance with the law? Do we say he is arrogant? No, we say he or she is as an honest person… We must put a stop to behavior that ignores the law and disregards one's position and surroundings. We must suppress arrogance and take on the quality of humility. (37:112, December 23, 1970)

When you are in a high position, there is no way to unite your mind and body. It is better to let yourself be stepped on. God has trampled on me for forty years, lest I get above myself. As you are stepped on, those elements in you that want to exalt themselves are smashed and brought back to unity. Do you understand this?

You should be cursed, trampled on and mistreated, just like the vagrant Bamboo Hat Kim. Regardless of how you are treated, you should discover the self that can accept all these tribulations gratefully. (144:231, April 25, 1986)

I never asked for blessings in my prayers. I never said, "God, please give me some money." I thought, "I need to suffer more since I have not undergone enough hardships." God likes such thinking. (102:314, February 21, 1979)

2. A Simple and Lowly Heart, Like that of a Child

At that time the disciples came to Jesus, saying, "Who is the greatest in the kingdom of heaven?" And calling to him a child, he put him in the midst of them, and said, "Truly, I say to you, unless you turn and become like children, you will never enter the kingdom of heaven."[2]

Matthew 18.1-3

For the natural man is an enemy to God, and has been from the fall of Adam, and will be, forever and ever, unless he yields to the enticings of the Holy Spirit, and puts off the natural man and becomes a saint through the atonement of Christ the Lord, and becomes as a child, submissive, meek, humble, patient, full of love, willing to submit to all things which the Lord sees fit to inflict upon him, even as a child submits to his father.

Book of Mormon, Mosiah 3.19 (Latter-day Saints)

The great man is he who does not lose his child's heart.

Mencius IV.B.12 (Confucianism)

Within the world
the palace pillar is broad,
but the human heart
should be modest.

Moritake Arakida, One Hundred Poems about the World (Shinto)

Teachings of Sun Myung Moon

What kind of person does God choose to carry out His works? There are eminent and powerful people who are ambitious to influence the world, but God does not choose them. He selects ordinary people, even laggards. God does not choose the people on top, but people on the bottom. (102:300, January 21, 1979)

Jesus said, "I thank thee, Father, Lord of heaven and earth, that thou hast hidden these things from the wise and understanding, and revealed them to babes." (Matt. 11.25) He was lamenting over the spiritual ignorance of the Jewish leadership of his time, while on the other hand, he was grateful that God bestowed grace upon pure and uneducated believers by revealing His providence to them. In today's Korean Christianity, at a time parallel to Jesus' day, similar phenomena are taking place, albeit in more complex ways. Through pure and innocent lay believers, God has been revealing many heavenly secrets concerning the Last Days. However, because they would be chastised as heretics if they were to proclaim them in public, they are keeping these truths to themselves. Meanwhile, like the priests, rabbis and scribes of Jesus' time, many Christian clergy take pride in their knowledge of the Bible and their ability to interpret it. They take pleasure in the reverence they receive from their followers; they are content to carry on the imposing duties of their offices; yet, to God's grief, they are entirely ignorant of God's providence in the Last Days. (*Exposition of the Divine Principle*, Second Advent 3.3.4)

> May we lay down before Thee, Father, all the rituals, ideologies and concepts of the world.
> We ask that Thou dost grant us meek, humble minds like those of children.
> May we have humble minds that can be molded as Thou wouldst mold us. (7:7, July 5, 1959)

> Father! Allow us to open our hearts, and to have hearts that long for Thee,
> like hungry babes longing for their mothers' milk. (20:7, March 31, 1968)

3. Taking a Humble Position and Placing Others above Oneself

Do nothing from selfishness or conceit, but in humility count others better than yourselves.

Philippians 2.3

Whoever proclaims himself good,
know, goodness approaches him not.
He whose heart becomes dust of the feet of all,
Saith Nanak, pure shall his repute be.

Adi Granth, Gauri Sukhmani 12, M.5, p. 278 (Sikhism)

A gentleman does not grieve that people do not recognize his merits; he grieves at his own incapacities.

Analects 14.32 (Confucianism)

Two men went up to the temple to pray, one a Pharisee and the other a tax collector. The Pharisee stood and prayed thus with himself, "God, I thank thee that I am not like other men, extortioners, unjust, adulterers, or even like this tax collector. I fast twice a week, I give tithes of all that I get." But the tax collector, standing far off, would not even lift up his eyes to heaven, but beat his breast, saying, "God, be merciful to me a sinner!" I tell you, this man went down to his house justified rather than the other; for every one who exalts himself will be humbled, but he who humbles himself will be exalted.

Luke 18.10-14

He does not show himself; therefore he is luminous.
He does not justify himself; therefore he becomes prominent.
He does not boast of himself; therefore he is given credit.
He does not brag; therefore he can endure for long.
It is precisely because he does not compete that the world cannot compete with him.
Is the ancient saying, "To yield is to be preserved whole" empty words?
Truly he will be preserved, and all will come to him.

Tao Te Ching 22 (Taoism)

He who knows the masculine but keeps to the feminine,
Becomes the ravine of the world.
Being the ravine of the world,
He dwells in constant virtue,
He returns to the state of the babe.
He who knows the white but keeps to the black,
Becomes the model of the world.
Being the model of the world,
He rests in constant virtue,
He returns to the infinite.

He who knows glory but keeps to disgrace,
Becomes the valley of the world.
Being the valley of the world,
He finds contentment in constant virtue,
He returns to the Uncarved Block.[3]

Tao Te Ching 28 (Taoism)

In the barren north, there is a sea, the Celestial Lake. In it there is a fish, several thousand *li* in width, and no one knows how many li in length. It is called the leviathan. There is also a bird, called the roc, with a back like Mount T'ai and wings like clouds across the sky. Upon a whirlwind it soars up to a height of ninety thousand li. Beyond the clouds and atmosphere, with only the blue sky above it, it then turns south to the southern ocean.

A quail laughs at it, saying, "Where is that bird trying to go? I spurt up with a bound, and I drop after rising a few yards. I just flutter about among the brushwood and the bushes. This is also the perfection of flying. Where is that bird trying to go?" This is the difference between the great and the small.

Similarly, there are some men whose knowledge is sufficient for the duties of some office. There are some men whose conduct will benefit some district. There are some men whose virtue befits him for a ruler. There are some men whose ability wins credit in the country. In their opinion of themselves, they are just like what is mentioned above.

Chuang Tzu 1 *(Taoism)*

Teachings of Sun Myung Moon

If you stay in a low position and try to put everyone else in a higher position, no walls will block your way. (230:35, April 15, 1992)

Goodness is quiet when evil is active because it cannot act in conjunction with evil. Goodness emerges only after the evil departs. (*Way of God's Will* 1.1.2)

Evil started from one being who was arrogant and put himself in a high position. The opposite of arrogance is humility. Our first task is to be humble. We must take the position opposite to what Satan takes delight in, or else we cannot succeed. Instead of being arrogant, we must put ourselves in the position to sacrifice and do things at the cost of our lives. (52:302, January 9, 1972)

People who justify themselves cannot enter the Kingdom of God. The position of absolute faith is not a place to justify yourself. Rather, someone else should defend you while you keep silent. In the Kingdom of Heaven, you cannot be proud of your achievements. What you thought was one hundred percent might from God's viewpoint be only one percent. Therefore, a self-centered person cannot enter the Kingdom of Heaven.

The Kingdom of God starts from absolute faith. When you live by absolute faith, you cannot insist on your own opinion... Instead, you must rely on other people who defend you and declare that you are correct. That is the only way to establish the correctness of your opinion according to the standard of absolute faith. If you are not living this way, than you had better change and live by the absolute standard; only this way can you establish the Kingdom of Heaven. (46:79-80, July 25, 1971)

If you are clinging to God, it is okay to boast that God is helping you. God likes to hear people proclaiming His works. However, if you boast about your own doings, everything you did will be shattered. (342:11, December 29, 2000)

What kind of being is God? Does He say, "I am God Almighty! I created you to serve Me. Love Me and sacrifice everything for Me!"? A being who says such a thing is not the true God. God has set the tradition of sacrifice and service by changing babies' soiled diapers and cleaning up after feeble and doddering parents. God wants you to live by this tradition and be His textbooks for education in meekness and humility. (116:68, December 20, 1981)

Some people follow God's Will for a time but then abandon it. Some people when they learn of God's Will do not want to separate from the secular world; they may go back and forth for a time but end up living no differently than secular people. Some people think that they are living for God's Will, but whenever they do something good they brag about it. Finally, there are people who sacrifice for God's Will yet still feel ashamed that they did not do more. They are always looking at things from the perspective of God's Will, not from their own perspective. Among these four categories of people, only those in the last category will last all the way to the end. (89:232, December 1, 1976)

America emerged as the fruit of history, but now she must go back and connect with the Cause of history. In other words, she must rediscover God.

America is the most powerful nation in the West, but on its way back should it continue increasing? Or should it decrease? This is a question. In seeking for God, America should lower itself.

Why do arrogant people need to learn humility? It is to return to the Cause. However, you [who are returning to the Cause] should not only be humble. Sometimes you need to assert yourselves. You cannot just be humble all the time. Powerfully march forward! This means advance to the result. (117:93, February 14, 1982)

Turn the Other Cheek

JESUS TEACHES US TO TURN THE OTHER CHEEK—to bear insults and abuse without complaint and putting aside all thoughts of revenge. The discipline of non-resistance, even to the point of death, has great value for self-conquest. If we respond to evil in kind, the evil can attach itself to us and can dominate us. The hatred of our attacker only feeds our resentment at being a victim, and as a result we lose our balance and spiritual strength. But by bearing with insults and abuse without diminution of our own goodwill and mental concentration, we can digest the enemy's hatred and preserve a foundation of spiritual independence and subjectivity. Ultimately, it is only by preserving our spiritual subjectivity in the midst of the insults that we can have the strength to love our enemy and win him over.

Although some question how an ethic of non-resistance can be reconciled with justice, scriptures affirm that God vindicates those who turn the other cheek. Father Moon cites Jesus' crucifixion as a prime instance of how one man's submission to the cruelest torture and death can yield a tremendous historical victory. Yet at the same time, Father Moon teaches that even God must turn the other cheek and bear with countless insults, and for the same reasons as human beings. God must also uphold His absoluteness in the face of insult by continuing to love even the unlovable archangel who turned against him. God, too, seeks His justice, but only through the principle of love—overcoming evil with God.

You have heard that it was said, "An eye for an eye and a tooth for a tooth." But I say to you, Do not resist one who is evil. But if any one strikes you on the right cheek, turn to him the other also; and if any one would sue you and take your coat, let him have your cloak as well; and if any one forces you to go one mile, go with him two miles.[4]

Matthew 5.38-41

Those who beat you with fists,
Do not pay them in the same coin,
But go to their house and kiss their feet.

Adi Granth, Shalok, Farid, p. 1378 *(Sikhism)*

Those who are insulted but do not insult others in revenge, who hear themselves reproached without replying, who perform good work out of the love of the LORD and rejoice in their sufferings… are "as the sun when it goes forth in its might."

Talmud, Yoma 23a *(Judaism)*

Brethren, if outsiders should speak against me, or against the Doctrine, or against the Order, you should not on that account either bear malice, or suffer resentment, or feel ill will. If you, on that account, should feel angry and hurt, that would stand in the way of your own self-conquest.

Digha Nikaya 1.3 *(Buddhism)*

There should be neither harming nor reciprocating harm.

Forty Hadith of an-Nawawi 32 (Islam)

Victory breeds hatred, for the defeated live in pain. Happily live the peaceful, giving up victory and defeat.

Dhammapada 201 (Buddhism)

He who, without anger, endures reproach, flogging and punishments, whose power and potent army is patience—him I call a Brahmin.

Dhammapada 399 (Buddhism)

No one is more patient over injury which he hears than God.

Hadith of Bukhari and Muslim (Islam)

The Lord... is forbearing toward you, not wishing that any should perish, but that all should reach repentance.

2 Peter 3.9

Monks, even as low-down thieves might be carving you limb from limb with a two-handled saw, even then whoever sets his mind at enmity is not a doer of my teaching. Monks, you should train yourselves thus, "Our minds shall not be perverted, we will not utter evil words, we shall abide cherishing thoughts of good, with minds full of goodwill and with no hatred in our heart. Beginning with that thief, we shall abide suffusing the whole world with thoughts of goodwill that are extensive, exalted, and immeasurable, without hostility and malevolence."

If you, monks, were to attend repeatedly to this exhortation on the parable of the saw, would you see any form of ridicule, subtle or gross, that you could not endure?

Majjhima Nikaya 1.129 (Buddhism)

Beloved, never avenge yourselves, but leave it to the wrath of God; for it is written, "Vengeance is mine, I will repay, says the Lord." No, "if your enemy is hungry, feed him; if he is thirsty, give him drink; for by doing so you will heap burning coals upon his head."[5]

Romans 12.19-20

If an evil man, on hearing of what is good, comes and creates a disturbance, you should hold your peace. You must not angrily upbraid him; then he who has come to curse you will merely harm himself.

Sutra of Forty-two Sections 7 (Buddhism)

To our most bitter opponents we say, "We shall match your capacity to inflict suffering by our capacity to endure suffering. We shall meet your physical force with soul force. Do to us what you will, and we shall continue to love you... Throw us in jail, and we shall still love you. Send your hooded perpetrators of violence into our community at the midnight hour and beat us and leave us half dead, and we shall still love you... We shall so appeal to your heart and conscience that we shall win you in the process, and our victory will be a double victory."

Martin Luther King, Jr., Strength to Love (Christianity)

Teachings of Sun Myung Moon

When two boys are fighting, one yields to the other with a heart of tolerance. Though he may want to fight to the finish out of anger, he yields because he thinks that someday they might become friends. If God were to judge between the two boys, He would decide in favor of the boy who forgives and embraces the other with tolerance. (100:84, October 8, 1978)

Among the saints and great people of history, are there any who were not mistreated or persecuted during their earthly life? All the great figures of history encountered opposition, but those who defended themselves as being right are not reckoned among the saints.

Jesus was condemned; he carried with him all of history's pain and injustice; yet he went his way in silence. Nevertheless, he reappeared as the historical victor. Why? It is because he did not fight with the evil. (80:34, October 4, 1975)

Jesus said, "But if any one strikes you on the right cheek, turn to him the other also," (Matt. 5.39) because when giving totally it is necessary to go that far. If you give completely, everything will come back to you—this is Heaven's principle. Jesus blessed the Roman soldiers who nailed him to the cross and pierced his chest with a spear because he had determined to give himself completely before he passed on. He knew that by doing so, even the country of his enemies would return to him. And indeed, the Roman Empire eventually became a Christian kingdom. (69:88, October 20, 1973)

The person who wins by striking someone three times will be subjugated by the person who yields ten times. Jesus followed this principle; isn't it true in today's world as well? Good people yield and sacrifice themselves. Those who use their fists well are not good people. The person who tries to win another over with love even as he is being beaten, who endures without complaint or regret, and who loves even at the sacrifice of his family—this is a good person.

Why is that? It is because God is that way. The One who is the center of the universe follows this path; therefore it is the standard of goodness. We take this path as we journey toward the world of goodness. (101:68, October 28, 1978)

Never pray like this: "O Lord, send a legion of angels to attack the people opposing me, so they cannot oppose me anymore." You should rather pray, "O Lord, please save my enemies, for they are in need of Thy mercy and Thy blessings." Why? They are in the position of Cain, and as Abel it is your responsibility to love and embrace Cain. Once you achieve oneness between Cain and Abel, you will prosper and not decline.[6]

The New York Times and *The Washington Post* oppose me and slander me, yet whenever I need to take out a newspaper advertisement I instruct my people to give them my advertising dollars. It may seem strange, but I always maintain the magnanimous position of Abel.

We do not really have enemies. Even though people insult us, we patiently endure them and keep advancing. We have no need to avenge ourselves, because God will take care of everything. (89:114, October 4, 1976)

Without maintaining the standard of eternal love, God would have no basis to someday exercise His authority over Satan. Therefore, God had to set up the condition of loving Satan no matter how viciously Satan opposed God.

Thus, God's philosophy is one of non-resistance. Why is that? Until the world of heavenly ideal is fulfilled on this earth, God must love the archangel, who became Satan, regardless of the circumstances. (316:79, February 10, 2000)

God has the power to sweep away all satans in an instant. Yet what would happen then? God's omnipotence would be broken. That is why, in order not to be invaded by Satan, God always retreats when Satan shoots arrows at Him. God is omnipotent, but only by patient endurance can God eventually subjugate Satan and set him under His dominion, where Satan cannot escape no matter how much he tries with all of his power. Only then can God secure His position and His omnipotence.

What would happen if God were to say, "I can't take it any more!" and turn everything upside down? The universe would be gone. God would become unthinkably miserable. Now can you appreciate the incredible value of patience?

In this aspect, patience can be the incentive for renewal and re-creation. In other words, by enduring our enemy's insults, we can forgive him. In doing so, we can gain dominion over him. Always. (76:219-20, March 2, 1975)

Repentance

REPENTANCE IS THE FIRST STEP on the road to recovering our relationship with God and realizing our original self. Sins, attachments, and mistaken views must be acknowledged as such; then it is possible to turn away from the old life and set out on the new path of faith. Since accumulated sins and delusions form a barrier obscuring the presence of God, repentance is a condition for God to forgive the sin and eradicate illusion, that the divine Presence may once again grace the penitent's life.

Repentance begins with words of contrition uttered in prayer—heart-felt and accompanied by tears. The forgiveness, release and insight that follow should awaken the will to make amends for previous wrongdoing and lead to changing the direction of one's life.

Father Moon teaches that repentance goes beyond expressing remorse for one's individual sins. People are more than just individuals; each human being contains within him or herself the fruit of history, and furthermore each represents his or her society, nation and world. Therefore we should repent for more than just our individual selves; we should repent for our ancestors' sins, our nation's sins, and the world's sins. Going deeper still, when we recognize how distant we are from the divine ideal, and how much God suffers, longing to embrace us in His bosom but unable to reach our hearts, we can repent for that as well. Thus, repentance becomes a journey of self-discovery that penetrates ever deeper into the depths of the soul.

1. Recognizing Sin, Confessing Sin, and Tearful Repentance for Sin

Repent, for the kingdom of heaven is at hand.[7]
Matthew 3.2

Truly, God loves those who repent, and He loves those who cleanse themselves.
Qur'an 2.222

The sacrifice acceptable to God is a broken spirit;
a broken and contrite heart, O God, thou wilt not despise.
Psalm 51.17

If one hides the evil, it adds and grows. If one bares it and repents, the sin dies out. Therefore all Buddhas say that the wise do not hide sin.
Mahaparinirvana Sutra (Buddhism)

Concern over remorse and humiliation depends on the borderline. The urge to blamelessness depends on remorse.[8]
I Ching, Great Commentary 1.3.4 (Confucianism)

All our righteousnesses are as filthy rags.[9]
Isaiah 64.6

As was the will of God, so I ought to have
    thought;
As was the will of God, so I ought to have
    spoken;
As was the will of God, so I ought to have acted.
If I have not so thought, so spoken, so acted,
Then do I repent for the sin,
Do I repent by my thought, word, and deed.
Do I repent with all my heart and conscience.

Patet 6 (Zoroastrianism)

Our transgressions are past counting,
There is no end to our sins,
Be merciful, forgive us, O Lord;
We are great sinners and wrongdoers.
There is no hope of our redemption.
O Lord, dear Lord, our deeds weighed in the
    balance
Would get us no place in Thy court!
Forgive us and make us one with Thyself
Through the grace of the Guru.

Adi Granth, Shalok Vadhik, M.3, p. 1416 (Sikhism)

I question myself on my sin, O Varuna,
desirous to know it. I seek out the wise
to ask them; the sages all give me this answer,
"The God, great Varuna, is angry with you."
What, then, O God, is my greatest transgression
for which you would ruin your singer, your friend?
Tell me, O God who knows all and lacks nothing,
so that, quickly prostrating, I may sinless crave
    pardon.

Rig Veda 7.86.3-4 (Hinduism)

Though I seek my refuge in the true faith of
    the Pure Land,
Yet my heart has not been truly sincere.
Deceit and untruth are in my flesh,
And in my soul is no clear shining.
In their outward seeming all men are diligent
    and truth speaking,
But in their souls are greed and anger and
    unjust deceitfulness,
And in their flesh do lying and cunning triumph.
Too strong for me is the evil of my heart.
I cannot overcome it.
Therefore my soul is like unto the poison of
    serpents;
Even my righteous deeds, being mingled with
    this poison,
Must be named deeds of deceitfulness.
Shameless though I be and having no truth in
    my soul,
Yet the virtue of the Holy Name, the gift of
    Him that is enlightened,
Is spread throughout the world through my
    words,
Although I am as I am.
There is no mercy in my soul.
The good of my fellow man is not dear in my eyes.
If it were not for the Ark of Mercy,
The divine promise of the Infinite Wisdom,
How should I cross the Ocean of Misery?
I, whose mind is filled with cunning and deceit
    as the poison of reptiles,
Am impotent to practice righteous deeds.
If I sought not refuge in the gift of our Father,
I should die the death of the shameless.[10]

Shinran (Buddhism)

Teachings of Sun Myung Moon

Jesus' very first teaching was, "Repent, for the Kingdom of Heaven is at hand." What should we repent for? Very simply, we should repent for all those actions which violate the rule stating that we should live by sacrifice and service to others. (105:92, September 30, 1979)

We should repent. Our first assignment is to repent. Before a criminal is released from prison, he must pay the price for his crime. Likewise, under whatever name, unless we make a condition to liquidate our crimes, we cannot be released. All people today are faced with this situation. (99:75, September 1, 1978)

It is a normal fact of life—when a child hurts or offends his mother or father, he has to apologize with tears before the parent will forgive him. It does not matter what country you live in—crime leads to punishment, and punishment, whether by inflicting pain or physical restraint, causes suffering. What is the purpose for giving punishment? Repentance.

Therefore, when you repent you have to shed tears. You should feel much pain in those tears. Your repentance is not genuine unless you feel more pain over your mistakes and sins than if someone were giving you a beating as punishment. (99:76, September 1, 1978)

Have you repented? How can you help others unless you have thoroughly repented, and God has accepted your repentance? How can you save others? Can you become the judge of others' sins if you have not yet been forgiven of your own sins? Have you ever deeply experienced that you are a sinner?

You do not just carry your own sins. You must understand that you carry the sins of history, sins committed by past generations. Also, you should understand that you are responsible for the sins of the present world. Furthermore, you should recognize your responsibility for the sins of the future. You bear these three levels of sin [on top of your own]. (99:90, September 1, 1978)

People go to the church and pray, "Father, I committed such and such sins. I repent of them and pray for Thy forgiveness." We should rather pray, "Father, please forgive me for having destroyed the heavenly order, for having violated the original relationship with Thee, for having violated relationships with other people, for damaging the creation, and for all other sins that I personally committed, especially violations of the heart."

If you make such repentance, receive God's forgiveness, bring victory and gain God's approval, then everything will be solved. Heaven is looking for the individuals who make such repentance...

You should understand that there is no sin greater than having violated someone's heart. Today, fathoming God's heart, you should understand that you are sinners who violated God's heart of love, sinners who rejected the heart of all creation, and obstructionists who blocked the fulfillment of the world of heart. I hope you understand this and repent from your hearts. (9:160, May 8, 1960)

In American society you have a strong sense of freedom. You interpret the meaning of freedom to mean, "I can do whatever I please; why should I feel ashamed or feel pangs of conscience?"

Yet suppose your father was a thief or a traitor, would you still be able to hold up your head? Suppose your father was a felon, would you still be proud? What if you were the offspring of an adulterer? If you were to face your own sin, and also realize that you are descendants of sinners, could you still proudly say, "I am free; I can do whatever I please"?

The answer is only too clear. Before enjoying your freedom, you proud people had better die and be resurrected. You had better first cleanse yourselves by atoning for these sins, going the reverse way, so that you may be forgiven. (66:14, March 11, 1973)

> Inadequate as we are, how dare we show ourselves before Thee?
> How can we raise our heads before Heaven?
> Even if we died ten million times,
> it would be a deserved penalty.
> We are held prisoner by the chains of sin,

and deserve to go through the suffering of the judgment.
Therefore, we bow ourselves with souls bared,
hoping for Thy merciful love and grace. (2:168, April 14, 1957)

2. Repentance for National Sins

If my people who are called by my name humble themselves, and pray and seek my face, and turn from their wicked ways, then I will hear from heaven, and will forgive their sin and heal their land.

2 Chronicles 7.14

Jonah arose and went to Nineveh, according to the word of the LORD. Now Nineveh was an exceedingly great city, three days' journey in breadth. Jonah began to go into the city, going a day's journey. And he cried, "Yet forty days, and Nineveh shall be overthrown!" And the people of Nineveh proclaimed a fast, and put on sackcloth, from the greatest of them to the least of them. Then tidings reached the king of Nineveh, and he arose from his throne, removed his robe, and covered himself with sackcloth, and sat in ashes. And he made proclamation and published through Nineveh, "By the decree of the king and his nobles: Let neither man nor beast, herd nor flock, taste anything; let them not feed, or drink water, but let man and beast be covered with sackcloth, and let them cry mightily to God; yea, let every one turn from his evil way and from the violence which is in his hands. Who knows, God may yet repent and turn from his fierce anger, so that we perish not?" When God saw what they did, how they turned from their evil way, God repented of the evil which he had said he would do to them; and he did not do it.[11]

Jonah 3.3-10

Teachings of Sun Myung Moon

Religions, especially Christianity, have focused on repentance for personal sins, but not for social and national sins. Look, however, at Jesus and the saints and prophets; they did not focus on repenting their own personal sins but rather on social and national sins. (99:75, September 1, 1978)

Have you repented? Are you shedding tears to repent for your own sins? Are you repenting for your ancestors' sins? Beyond that, are you shedding tears to save the nation and the world?
    There are two kinds of tears. The first kind of tears we shed for our own forgiveness; the second kind of tears we shed to save others and bring them to repentance. You should shed both kinds of tears. Only then can there be complete repentance. (99:75, September 1, 1978)

As God proceeded with the providence, in what did He inspire people to believe? What was the first thing He caused people to experience? It was not joy. First, He caused us to grieve for ourselves. Next, he inspired in us a heart to mourn over the situation of our family, society, tribe, nation and world, and then over how distant we were from Him. God set up this basic attitude to open the way by which we could stand before Him. (4:51, March 2, 1958)

3. Genuine Repentance Requires Changing Behavior

And whosoever repents and does good, he verily repents towards God with true repentance.

Qur'an 25.71 (Islam)

If a man finds that he has made a mistake, then he must not be afraid of admitting the fact and amending his ways.

Analects 1.8.4 (Confucianism)

Whosoever looks upon his wrongdoing as wrongdoing, makes amends by confessing it as such, and abstains from it in the future, will progress according to the Law.

Digha Nikaya 1.85 (Buddhism)

How is one proved a repentant sinner? Rab Judah said, "If the object which caused his original transgression comes before him on two occasions, and he keeps away from it."

Rabbi Jose ben Judah said, "If a man commits a transgression, the first, second, and third time he is forgiven; the fourth time he is not forgiven."

Talmud, Yoma 86b (Judaism)

He who has committed a sin and has repented, is freed from that sin, but he is purified only by resolving to cease: "I will do so no more."...

He who, having either unintentionally or intentionally committed a reprehensible deed, desires to be freed from it, must not commit it a second time.

If his mind be uneasy with respect to any deed, let him repeat the penances prescribed for it until they fully satisfy his conscience.

Laws of Manu 11.231-34 (Hinduism)

Expiation and repentance, to a man who continues to commit sinful acts, knowing them to be harmful, are of no avail. Futile is it to bathe an elephant if he is straightway to roll again in the mud.

Srimad Bhagavatam 6.1 (Hinduism)

Say, O My slaves who have been prodigal to their own hurt! Despair not of the mercy of God, who forgives all sins. Lo! He is the Forgiving, the Merciful. Turn to Him repentant, and surrender unto Him, before there can come upon you the doom, when you cannot be helped. And follow the better of that which has been revealed unto you from your Lord, before the doom comes on you suddenly when you know not. Lest any soul should say, "Alas, my grief that I was unmindful of God, and I was indeed among the scoffers!" Or should say, "If God had but guided me, I should have been among the dutiful!" Or should say, when it sees the doom, "Oh, that I had but a second chance, that I might be among the righteous!"

Qur'an 39.53-58

Do not procrastinate the day of your repentance until the end; for after this day of life, which is given us to prepare for eternity, behold, if we do not improve our time while in this life, then comes the night of darkness wherein there can be no labor performed. You cannot say, when you are brought to that awful crisis, that I will repent, that I will return to my God. Nay, you cannot say this; for that same spirit which possesses your bodies at the time that you go out of this life, that same spirit will have power to possess your body in that eternal world. For behold, if you have procrastinated the day of your repentance even until death, behold, you have become subjected to the spirit of the devil, and he has sealed you his.

Book of Mormon, Alma 34.33-35 (Latter-day Saints)

Teachings of Sun Myung Moon

We are people who recognize that we are in a disordered and diseased state, and we have come to this place to be repaired. We have individual problems, family problems, national-level problems, and global problems, all of which need fixing…

How then can you prove that you are completely healed? You are in good shape when you feel disgust for your old self and your former way of life. Do you still have fond memories of those days? Do you sometimes dream of the good times you used to have? If so, it means you have not yet fully recovered from your illness.

Again, you meet a handsome man who whispers in your ear, "You are so beautiful! Why don't you forget about that difficult husband of yours and come live with me?" If such a temptation pulls you in the slightest, it means you have not yet fully recovered from your illness. You are cured when you have become immune to such temptations, when they do not affect you at all. (May 1, 1978)

Most people's lives vacillate back and forth between good and evil, between a public life and a self-centered life. They often end up falling into a self-centered life. But if they continue that way, they are destined to perish. Therefore, from time to time they repent of their self-centered past and strive once again to live a public life, biting their teeth. Nevertheless, they do not endure it for long and again fall back into self-centeredness… In such a way, people vacillate back and forth. Eventually, they are inclined to live a private life, distant from the standard of public goodness. Most people's lives of faith have been like that. This is why people who lead private lives need to continually repent. (31:242, June 4, 1970)

Although God joyfully receives you this day, you should nevertheless have a tearful heart of thorough repentance. Question yourself: "Why did I not know Heavenly Father sooner? And why did I not understand the standpoint of God, who is so worried over humankind?" When you think of your former ignorance, you should wail with indignation. God will sympathize with you if you have a heart of repentance over the past. If you lack a heart of repentance, you have no business participating in God's work. (13:330, April 14, 1964)

Until the last moment of your life you should be repenting. You must not leave the earth without doing it. (99:110, September 1, 1978)

Judge Not

SCRIPTURE CAUTIONS US NOT TO JUDGE another person's faults, even when they are evident, because neither are we perfect and free from error. Scriptures of all faiths echo Jesus' teaching, not to regard the speck in your neighbor's eye before removing the log from your own eye. Father Moon teaches the rule of three: before criticizing another person once, criticize yourself three times. Furthermore, before we correct another person, we should first invest in loving and helping them.

Judge not, that you be not judged. For with the judgment that you pronounce you will be judged, and the measure you give will be the measure you get. Why do you see the speck that is in your brother's eye, but do not notice the log that is in your own eye? Or how can you say to your brother, "Let me take the speck out of your eye," when there is the log in your own eye? You hypocrite, first take the log out of your own eye, and then you will see clearly to take the speck out of your brother's eye.

Matthew 7.1-5

Easily seen are others' faults, hard indeed to see are one's own. Like chaff one winnows others' faults, but one's own one hides, as a crafty fowler conceals himself by camouflage.

He who sees others' faults is ever irritable—his corruptions grow. He is far from the destruction of the corruptions.

Dhammapada 252-53 (Buddhism)

The vile are ever prone to detect the faults of others, though they be as small as mustard seeds, and persistently shut their eyes against their own, though they be as large as vilva fruit.

Garuda Purana 112 (Hinduism)

Do not judge your comrade until you have stood in his place.[12]

Mishnah, Avot 2.5 (Judaism)

A man holding a basket of eggs does not dance on stones.

Buji Proverb (African Traditional Religions)

Confucius said, "The gentleman calls attention to the good points in others; he does not call attention to their defects. The small man does just the reverse of this."

Analects 12.16 (Confucianism)

Why do you pass judgment on your brother? Or you, why do you despise your brother? For we shall all stand before the judgment seat of God; as it is written,

> As I live, says the Lord, every knee shall bow to me
> and every tongue shall confess to God.

So each of us shall give account of himself to God.

Romans 14.10-12

The scribes and the Pharisees brought a woman who had been caught in adultery, and placing her in the midst they said to him, "Teacher, this woman has been caught in the act of adultery. Now in the Law Moses commanded us to stone such. What do you say about her?" This they said to test him, that they might have some charge to bring against him. Jesus bent down and wrote with his finger on the ground. And as they continued to ask him, he stood up and said to them, "Let him who is without sin among you be the first to throw a stone at her." And once more he bent down and wrote with his finger on the ground. But when they heard it, they went away, one by one, beginning with the eldest, and Jesus was left alone with the woman standing before him. Jesus looked up and said to her, "Woman, where are they? Has no one condemned you?" She said, "No one, Lord." And Jesus said, "Neither do I condemn you; go, and do not sin again."[13]

John 8.3-11

He who treads the Path in earnest
Sees not the mistakes of the world;
If we find fault with others
We ourselves are also in the wrong.
When other people are in the wrong, we
    should ignore it,
For it is wrong for us to find fault.
By getting rid of this habit of fault-finding
We cut off a source of defilement.
When neither hatred nor love disturb our mind
Serenely we sleep.

Sutra of Hui Neng 2 (Buddhism)

Censuring others and praising himself, concealing good qualities present in others and proclaiming noble qualities absent in himself, he causes them to have low status. Disparaging himself and praising others, proclaiming qualities which are present in others and not proclaiming those that are absent in himself, with humility and modesty he lifts them to high status. No obstacle should be created in the [spiritual] development of others.

Tattvarthasutra 6.25-27 *(Jainism)*

Teachings of Sun Myung Moon

Before judging someone, study him for at least three years. *(Way of God's Will 2.2)*

Do not criticize others; the problem is within you. A weak point of young people is that their minds are stretched out in all directions, like tree branches. Do you know what I mean? They are perceptive and quick; after one glance they are quick to make comments. However, they tend to overlook themselves.

Therefore, before you criticize someone, you should first find three points to criticize in yourself. Be only one-third as critical of that person as you are of yourself. (25:93-94, September 30, 1969)

Do not judge anyone in your heart. You yourself are a sinner, a priest who failed to complete your responsibility; so how can you judge others? (89:268, December 4, 1976)

When you receive God's grace, you should use it to fight Satan on behalf of God, with the heart of Heaven's indignation. You should not judge other people based on your opinions. To enjoy the grace you received [while passing judgment on others who received less] is not the right attitude of faith. If you do so, you will not be able to walk the path acceptable to God. (2:200-01, May 19, 1957)

If you are deficient in your character, listen to other people's testimonies to make up for it. Listen to them, absorb their experiences as your own, and strengthen your character thereby. You should learn from many people's experiences.

Do not criticize their testimonies after hearing them. To criticize means to set yourself up as determining whether it is on the side of Satan or God. But in so doing, it is you who are split to be either on Satan's side or God's side. Therefore, criticism is like cancer to your growth. (76:141, February 2, 1975)

Examine yourself. Before you speak ill of another, you should look at whether you have that problem. Before you point the finger at another, you should first point it at yourself. Only when you can give yourself a perfect score on every point are you in a position to judge others as you wish.

Jesus taught this when he encountered the men who were about to stone to death a woman who had committed adultery. He said to them, "Let he who is without sin cast the first stone," and they all ran away.

Doesn't this also apply to you? You women should not praise your own offspring while criticizing other people's children. Rather, you should regard yourself as representing all womankind, and love every mother's child as your own. It is the same with you men. (118:245, June 6, 1982)

Self-Denial

PEOPLE ARE BLIND TO THEIR OWN SELF-CENTEREDNESS. We know that selfish and greedy people are far from goodness; yet, everyone is tainted by selfishness to some extent. This self-centeredness needs to be exposed and beaten mercilessly; otherwise our goodness is superficial and ephemeral. Therefore, we should deny ourselves.

A life of self-affirmation and pleasure seeking leads, in the end, to emptiness and loss. Self-denial seems to lead to death and loss, but in fact it leads to abundant life with God. Thus we encounter the paradoxical truth, in the words of Jesus, "whoever would save his life would lose it; and whoever loses his life will save it." These teachings are common to all the world-level religions.

Father Moon affirms the value of self-denial. He explains why human beings should have to travel such a paradoxical and unnatural course to reach the goal of life based upon his insights on the Human Fall. Although God created humans to manifest the character of love and altruism, because of the Fall we are infected by Satan, whose nature is pure self-centeredness. Hence, we face the predicament that in order to restore our original selves we must first deny our existing selves that are stained by satanic elements.

If any man would come after me, let him deny himself and take up his cross and follow me. For whoever would save his life will lose it; and whoever loses his life for my sake and the gospel's will save it.

Mark 8.34-36

He who has no thought of "I" and "mine" whatever towards his mind and body, he who grieves not for that which he has not, he is, indeed, called a bhikkhu.

Dhammapada 367 (Buddhism)

They are forever free who renounce all selfish desires and break away from the ego-cage of "I," "me," and "mine" to be united with the Lord. Attain to this, and pass from death to immortality.

Bhagavad-Gita 2.71 (Hinduism)

The Man of the Way wins no fame,
The highest virtue wins no gain,
The Great Man has no self.

Chuang Tzu 17 (Taoism)

Where egoism exists, You are not experienced,
Where You are, is not egoism.

You learned ones: expound in your mind
this inexpressible proposition.

Adi Granth, Maru-ki-Var, M.1, p. 1092 (Sikhism)

Torah abides only with him who regards himself as nothing.

Talmud, Sota 21b (Judaism)

"Subhuti, what do you think? Does a holy one say within himself, 'I have obtained Perfective Enlightenment'?"

Subhuti replied, "No, World-honored One... If a holy one of Perfective Enlightenment said to himself, 'Such am I,' he would necessarily partake of the idea of an ego-identity, a personality, a being, a separated individuality."

Diamond Sutra 9 (Buddhism)

Truly, truly, I say to you, unless a grain of wheat falls into the earth and dies, it remains alone; but if it dies, it bears much fruit. He who loves his life loses it, and he who hates his life in this world will keep it for eternal life.

John 12.24-25

Remember, those who fear death shall not escape it, and those who aspire to immortality shall not achieve it.

Nahjul Balagha, Khutba 43 (Shiite Islam)

O Son of Man! If you love me, turn away from yourself; and if you seek my pleasure, regard not your own; that you may die in me and I may eternally live in you.

Hidden Words of Bahá'u'lláh, Arabic 7 (Baha'i Faith)

You, who sit on the top of a hundred-foot pole, although you have entered the Way you are not yet genuine. Proceed on from the top of the pole, and you will show your whole body in the ten directions.

Mumon's Comment: If you go on further and turn your body about, no place is left where you are not the master. But even so, tell me, how will you go on further from the top of a hundred-foot pole? Eh?[14]

Mumonkan 46 (Buddhism)

If, like a cracked gong, you silence yourself, you have already attained Nibbana: no vindictiveness will be found in you.

Dhammapada 134 (Buddhism)

Yen Yüan asked about perfect virtue. The Master said, "To subdue one's self and return to propriety is perfect virtue. If a man can for one day subdue himself and return to propriety, all under heaven will ascribe perfect virtue to him."

Analects 12.1.1 (Confucianism)

Knowing that this body is like foam, and comprehending that it is as unsubstantial as a mirage, one should destroy the flower-tipped shafts of sensual passions [Mara], and pass beyond the sight of the King of death.

Dhammapada 46 (Buddhism)

Teachings of Sun Myung Moon

Absolute faith is not the place of self-affirmation, but of self-negation. (*Way of God's Will* 3.2)

What is the most serious obstacle to entering the Kingdom of Heaven? An enemy called "I" is lurking about. "I" am the enemy. The reason why we pray and put effort into our life of faith is ultimately to be victorious over "me." Our goal is to achieve the victory whereby we no longer face Satan's accusation, but as long as "I" exists, it is impossible to completely break away from that condition.

We should be able to deny this "I" in the name of God. We must totally deny ourselves. Only by total self-denial can we cut all the strings by which Satan has been pulling us. We should understand that something like the silk threads of a spider web connect us to Satan, who uses them to pull us. We have to cut them all with a razor. (122:13, April 26, 1982)

Jesus came to this earth to teach us that before we desire to live, to be a ruler of others, or to be happy, we should first be willing to die. Since human history was ruined due to selfishness and self-centered thinking, the only way to save it is to go in the opposite direction. That is what Jesus meant by the paradoxical words, "Those who desire to live shall die, and those who are willing to die shall live."

With those words he set up the teaching to abolish this world of self-seeking, in which everyone regards him or herself, not the whole, as most important. In the world where everyone thinks, "I am number one," everyone is divided. No one likes arrogant people. Conversely, everyone likes individuals who willingly live for others and lift them up. (67:182, June 3, 1973)

The Fall was the beginning of the consciousness of "myself." Therefore, you should deny yourself, especially your body. Get rid of Satan, that narcissistic being, by denying yourself. Return to God by always living for the sake of others. Know clearly that this is the path laid out by religion to seek after enlightenment and the method to attain unity through the way of love. (214:65, February 1, 1991)

Satan exists nowhere else than in "myself." Since ego exists, suspicion, jealousy, excessive desire and anger come about. Therefore, kill your ego. Everything that has to do with "I" is Satan. Scoff at yourself and judge yourself. Satan always invades through someone close to you or the things you like most. (*Way of God's Will* 3.4)

Living for the self ends with the self, but living for others continues forever. Therefore, for goodness to continue, you should live for your counterpart—the greater whole. This is particularly the case when you are in a position of leadership...

Therefore, the public road begins with denying the self. Denying the self does not mean the self disappears. Goodness begins when you try to find yourself in another and value that relationship. This is the principle law and way for goodness to develop. (57:63, May 28, 1972)

The religions of Asia traditionally taught self-denial and rejection of material possessions. Conversely, Western people seek to raise themselves up and gain material prosperity. The end result of such a self-centered life is material wealth but emptiness of spirit. (97:67, February 26, 1978)

As long as you insist on keeping to the ways you grew up with, you can never unite with people of other societies and nations and who have different ways of thinking. The simple way to unite with them is to forget totally about yourself. By completely denying yourself you can make relationships everywhere. (360:192, November 16, 2001)

Subduing the Desires of the Flesh

ALL RELIGIONS AGREE THAT THE SEEKER of Ultimate Reality must restrain his or her desires and subdue the passions of the flesh. Striking and weakening the body through rigorous self-control, fasting, sitting hours at meditation, etc. are all commendable ways to struggle against the flesh's desires and ultimately to dominate them.

For most people, the most challenging of them all is sexual desire. Jesus taught that we should be ruthless, "If your eye causes you to sin, pluck it out…" to which we add a Buddhist story of a nun who did just that—to quench her counterpart's sin, not her own. Buddhism promotes the technique of meditating on "the loathsomeness of the body" as a bag of fluids, lymph, bile and feces to help men curb their desire for the opposite sex. Father Moon also recommends summoning up an attitude of disgust for the body, calling it "Satan's dance-hall."

Related passages on self-conquest are found in Chapter 12: *Self-Control;* yet perfect self-control is nearly impossible to attain. Father Moon explains this predicament as a consequence of humanity's impaired condition after the Fall. Extreme and forceful practice is required to do what does not come naturally. Therefore, religions developed to teach the path of intense and unrelenting efforts at striking at the body and subduing its desires. In some religions these practices became organized into monasticism; nevertheless people in every walk of life should be making efforts in this direction.

1. Extinguishing the Desires of the Body

Beloved, I beseech you…to abstain from the passions of the flesh that wage war against your soul.

1 Peter 2.11

Through the abandonment of desire the Deathless is realized.

Samyutta Nikaya 47.37 (Buddhism)

Put to death what is earthly in you: fornication, impurity, passion, evil desire, and covetousness, which is idolatry. On account of these the wrath of God is coming. In these you once walked, when you lived in them. But now put them all away: anger, wrath, malice, slander, and foul talk from your mouth.

Colossians 3.5-8

Is he who relies on a clear proof from his Lord like those for whom the evil that they do seems pleasing while they follow their own lusts?

Qur'an 47.14

Only on complete obliteration of sensuality can one forsake violence.

Acarangasutra 4.45 (Jainism)

Manifest plainness,
Embrace simplicity,
Reduce selfishness,
Have few desires.

Tao Te Ching 19 (Taoism)

When all the desires that surge in the heart
Are renounced, the mortal becomes immortal.
When all the knots that strangle the heart
Are loosened, the mortal becomes immortal,
Here in this very life.

Brihadaranyaka Upanishad 4.4.7 (Hinduism)

Realizing that pleasure and pain are personal affairs, one should subjugate his mind and senses.

Acarangasutra 2.78 (Jainism)

Confucius said, "There are three things against which a gentleman is on his guard. In his youth, before his blood and vital humors have settled down, he is on his guard against lust. Having reached his prime, when the blood and vital humors have finally hardened, he is on his guard against strife. Having reached old age, when the blood and vital humors are already decaying, he is on his guard against avarice."

Analects 16.7 (Confucianism)

Monks, there are these three feelings. What three? Pleasant feeling, painful feeling, and feeling that is neither painful nor pleasant. Pleasant feeling, monks, should be looked upon as pain, painful feeling should be looked upon as a barb, feeling that is neither painful nor pleasant should be looked upon as impermanent. When these three feelings are looked upon in these ways by a monk, that monk is called "rightly seeing."

Itivuttaka 47 (Buddhism)

Teachings of Sun Myung Moon

The true religious life starts from denying all relationships with the body. If you read the scriptures, can you find any guidance about eating good food and leading an easy life? It is impossible to find such guidance. Religion teaches you to serve, sacrifice, be gentle and humble. Therefore religious people pray for the sake of others even at the risk of their lives. The body by itself cannot do this. In this way you can knock down your body.

The mind and body fight when they have the same amount of strength. So you should make effort to weaken your body. When your mind can subdue your weakened body for several months, then even after the body regains its strength it will follow the mind out of habit. When you reach such a level, you will find that your plans turn out well, having support from Heaven. Then it will be difficult to lead the life you led in the past. You will gravitate towards living an upright life according to your conscience. This is the purpose of the religious life. (38:272, January 8, 1971)

Religions present teachings on how to conquer the body. They instruct us: Be forceful in restricting your body. Do not give in to what the body wants to do. For this reason, religions direct us not to go to theatres or walk through red-light districts. They command men not to chase after women, and advise women to consider men as thieves and to avoid paying attention to them.

Can you ladies in the Unification Church date? No, you cannot. Can you men date? No, you cannot. Do I use force to keep you from dating? No. Go ahead, try dating if you want to, but you will find you cannot do it. If someone was stopping you by force, you would do it all the more. Go ahead and try it, and fall on your own back.

What should you do with your body? You should subdue it. Seeking for goodness requires you to subjugate your body. That is why I am asking you to twist the neck of your bodily desires. The body likes to be arrogant. It demands that others serve it. Its philosophy is: "Mine is mine, and yours is mine." (39:193, January 10, 1971)

You young men should cut off your desire to have every attractive woman you see. You should cut off the music you enjoy listening to—everything the world delights in. Religions direct you to strike the body. The highest religions advocate denying the flesh completely. Throughout history, religions have taught asceticism and sacrificial service. Why? There is a reason for it. To enter the Kingdom of Heaven, we have to realize heaven in this hellish human world.

Is this world a place of misery or of happiness? It is a world of misery. Can this world of misery and turmoil ever become a world of happiness if everyone keeps on eating, playing, drinking and dancing? No, the world will only become more miserable. Therefore, anyone seeking the world of happiness should go to a place of misery and there make a break-through. The way forward can only be found in a place of misery. If it is not there, then God does not exist. (91:286-87, January 30, 1977)

We strike the body to eliminate Satan's influence. We strike the body to allow the Holy Spirit to take control. To strike our body is to strike Satan. When we strike Satan, the Holy Spirit can occupy what Satan had previously ruled. (1:126, June 27, 1956)

2. Feeling Revulsion for the Body and the Corrupt Senses

If your hand causes you to sin, cut it off; it is better for you to enter life maimed than with two hands to go to hell, to the unquenchable fire. And if your foot causes you to sin, cut it off; it is better for you to enter life lame than with two feet to be thrown into hell. And if your eye causes you to sin, pluck it out; it is better for you to enter the kingdom of God with one eye than with two eyes to be thrown into hell.

Mark 9.43-47

In Jivaka's pleasant wood walked the nun Subha. A gallant met her there and barred the way. Subha said to him, "What have I done to offend you, that you stand obstructing me? For it is not fitting, sir, that a man should touch a sister in orders..."

"You are young, a maiden, and faultless—what do you seek in the holy life? Cast off that yellow robe and come! In the blossoming woodland let us seek our pleasure... If you will do my bidding, come where the joys of the sheltered life await you; dwell in a house of verandas and terraces…"

"What so infatuates you about this carcass, filled with carrion, to fill a grave, so fragile, that it seems to warrant such words?"

"Eyes you have like a gazelle's, like an elf's in the heart of the mountains—'tis those eyes of yours, sight of which feeds the depth of my passion. Shrined in your dazzling, immaculate face as in the calyx of a lotus, 'tis those eye of yours, sight of which feeds the strength of my passion…"

"O you are blind! You chase a sham… What is this eye but a little ball lodged in the fork of a hollow tree, bubble of film, anointed with tear-brine, exuding slime-drops, compost wrought in the shape of an eye of manifold aspects?"

Forthwith the maiden so lovely tore out her eye and gave it to him. "Here, then! Take your eye!" Her heart unattached, she sinned not.

Straightaway the lust in him ceased and he begged her pardon. "O pure and holy maid, would that you might recover your sight! Never again will I do such a thing. You have sore smitten my sin; blazing flames have I clasped to my bosom; a poisonous snake I have handled—but O, be healed and forgive me!"

Freed from molesting, the nun went on her way to the Buddha, chief of the Awakened. There in his presence, seeing those features born of utmost merit, her eye was restored.

Therigatha 366-99 (*Buddhism*)

The body, brethren, is not the self. If body were the self, this body would not be subject to sickness, and one could say of body, "Let my body be thus; let my body not be thus." But inasmuch as body is not the self, that is why body is subject to sickness, and one cannot say of body, "Let my body be thus; let my body not be thus."…

Now what do you think, brethren, is body permanent or impermanent? [Impermanent, Lord.] And is the impermanent painful or pleasant? [Painful, Lord.] Then what is impermanent, painful, and unstable by nature, is it fitting to consider as, "this is mine, this am I, this is my self"? [Surely not, Lord.]…

Therefore, brethren, every body whatever, be it past, future, or present, be it inward or outward, gross or subtle, lowly or eminent, far or near—every body should be thus regarded, as it really is, by right insight—"this is not mine; this am not I; this is not my self."

Samyutta Nikaya 3.68 (*Buddhism*)

He who delights in subduing evil thoughts, who meditates on the loathsomeness of the body, who is ever mindful—it is he who will make an end of craving. He will sever Mara's bond.

Dhammapada 350 (*Buddhism*)

The mouth is a vessel filled with foul
Saliva and filth between the teeth,
The nose with fluids, snot, and mucus,
The eyes with their own filth and tears.

The body is a vessel filled
With excrement, urine, lungs, and liver;
He whose vision is obscured and does not see
A woman thus, lusts for her body.

This filthy city of a body,
With protruding holes for the elements
Is called by stupid beings
An object of pleasure.

Why should you lust desirously for this
While recognizing it as a filthy form
Produced by a seed whose essence is filth,
A mixture of blood and semen?

He who lies on the filthy mass
Covered by skin moistened with
Those fluids, merely lies
On top of a woman's bladder.[15]

Nagarjuna, Precious Garland 149-57 (*Buddhism*)

Get back, I hate you!
Don't hold my sari, you fool!
A she-buffalo is worried of its life,
And the butcher, of its killing!
The pious think of virtues,

And the wicked, of vices;
I am worried of my soul,
And you, of lust…

Fie on this body!
Why do you damn yourself
In love of it—this pot of excrement,
The vessel of urine, the frame of bones,
This stench of purulence!
Think of Lord Shiva,
You fool![16]

          Akkamahadevi, Vacana 15 and 33 *(Hinduism)*

Teachings of Sun Myung Moon

Your eyes, nose, ears, mouth, and hands are in contact with two roads. When your eyes see for "me" they become the Devil's eyes; when your nose smells for "me" it becomes the Devil's nose, and when your ears hear for "me" they become Devil's ears. You should rather see with eyes that care for others, care for the nation, the world, and heaven and earth—in other words, you should see with God's eyes. Those eyes of yours do not exist for your successful career… they exist for the sake of others—to save the nation and liberate humankind. (214:65, February 1, 1991)

When you come home at night and wash your face, look at the mirror and say, "Eyes, nose, ears, hands and feet; you are always a problem." Ask them, "Did you do anything sinful today?" You should reflect upon what you have seen with your eyes, what you have said with your mouth, how you have acted, and everything you have done by your own power. Then you should go the opposite way. (122:264, November 21, 1982)

Who is your enemy? Your own eyes and ears, your nose, mouth, your thoughts—those are your enemies. You must make your eyes God's eyes, your ears God's ears, your nose God's nose, your mouth God's mouth, and your hands and feet God's hands and feet. By doing so, you should find the "I" that can live entirely for the world.

    That is your revolution. The borderline between heaven and hell is within your own self. If you move to the right you end up in the Kingdom of God; if you move to the left you end up in hell. Some people stay on the borderline, shifting sometimes to the right, sometimes to the left, back and forth. Others go to the left; they are headed for hell… Still others keep pushing themselves to live for God and His Will their whole life long… Among those three types of people, which are you? Even Unification Church members are divided among these three types. Some are A, some are B and some are C. Which type do you want to be? "A!" Oh, you people are ambitious! But you will face many difficulties…

    You young men, when you see an attractive young woman, do you want to flirt with her? You must cut off that thought. You must cut off all the messages [about love] that you hear every day. You must cut off all the things the world says are good. You must cut off all of them. That is why religion commands us to strike our own body. The higher the religion, the more sacrifice it demands. Is that the correct thing to do, or not? It is correct. All the religions throughout history have taught people to live an ascetic life, to sacrifice and serve. There is a purpose for it. (91:285, February 27, 1977)

Do you women realize how much you are tempting men? If you are attractive, you should think, "I don't want to have a pretty face." (116:18, December 1, 1981)

You must deplore the reality that your body is the Devil's dance hall. Your body is the Devil's love nest. Having been defiled by the Devil's love, your body inherited the Devil's blood lineage.

You should recognize that based on this blood relationship, Satan's realm of power is controlling you in order to trample upon your original character. Furthermore, Satan desires through this lineage to dominate you for millions of years to come.

What can you do about this alarming fact? Your country cannot remove Satan for you. You have to do it yourself. (214:285, February 3, 1991)

Satan's blood flows in my veins. Satan's greed and Satan's selfishness are in me. Recognize this fact, and always consider that Satan's love, Satan's greed, and Satan himself occupy your very self. Pull out this Satan! Pull out Satan's blood lineage, Satan's desires, and all self-centered satanic elements.

With what can you pull them out? For this purpose God set up religions and has been leading the providence of restoration and salvation. (115:42, October 28, 1982)

There are two types of love: love that is pleasing to Satan and love that is pleasing to God… But if you are going about seeking temporary love, you will arrive at death. Whenever you feel an urge for temporary love, you should whip yourself and pray single-mindedly to strive only for eternal life, while thinking of the darkness of death that awaits you if you gratify that urge. (*Blessing and Ideal Family* 1.4.3)

Many times Eve was left alone. When she made a fuss, crying out loud under the shade of a tree, the archangel was there to comfort her. Sometimes he carried her on his back. Sometimes he sat her on his lap. When she was sitting on his lap face-to-face, his sexual organ would almost be touching hers. They had often seen animals mating and knew it was how they came to have their young. Under those circumstances, all the archangel had to do was push his organ into hers, and she would feel, "I like it!" Man and woman feel pleasure when their sexual organs touch. The thing was bound to happen sooner or later, and that is exactly how the Fall took place.

You men, if a woman comes to you, sits naked on your lap, and touches your sexual organ, would you accept it? Suppose she were very attractive; when she touches your organ, would it be erect, or not? Your love organ should not be hard and erect. No, it should remain limp. If you ever face such a temptation, know that it is an opportunity to restore through indemnity the action of the Fall. Therefore, even if a very attractive woman tries to force your organ into hers, you should push her away with such force that she tumbles to the ground, and chase her away to a far off place where you will never see her again. (285:201, May 4, 1997)

Non-Attachment to Wealth and Possessions

WEALTH AND POSSESSIONS ARE SHACKLES that chain us to the fallen world. They promote greed and avarice, increasing self-centered desire. The love of money has been called "the root of all evil," and materialism has become a great obstacle to humanity's spiritual progress.

Traditionally, the path to God has required renunciation of wealth and attachment to material goods. Monks and nuns typically take formal vows of poverty. Yet ordinary people may live free from possessiveness, sacrificing wealth for the sake of a greater good. Some contribute generously to charities; others forgo lucrative careers to care for a sick family member or to go on a mission to help people in need. They find peace of mind and great satisfaction having given up the anxiety of keeping and amassing material things for a life of giving and service.

Father Moon links the religious teaching of non-attachment with his philosophy of true love. He explains that God's love begins from the foundation of non-possessiveness, while people who are attached to possessions find that their possessions get in the way of expressing love. This principle applies not only to our relationship with God and in daily life with our loved ones, but also to the well-being of nations and this planet Earth.

1. Money as a Cause of Downfall

The love of money is the root of all evils.
1 Timothy 6.10

Woe is he... who has gathered riches and counted them over, thinking his riches have made him immortal!
Qur'an 104.1-3

Do not race after riches, do not risk your life for success, or you will let slip the Heaven within you.
Chuang Tzu 29 *(Taoism)*

Man shall not live by bread alone, but by every word that proceeds from the mouth of God.
Deuteronomy 8.3, Matthew 4.4

No one can serve two masters; for either he will hate the one and love the other, or he will be devoted to the one and despise the other. You cannot serve God and mammon.
Matthew 6.24

Riches ruin the foolish, but not those in quest of the Beyond. Through craving for riches the ignorant man ruins himself as he does others.
Dhammapada 355 *(Buddhism)*

"I got this today," they say; "tomorrow I shall get that. This wealth is mine, and that will be mine too. I have destroyed my enemies. I shall destroy others too! Am I not like God? I enjoy what I want. I am successful. I am powerful. I am happy. I am rich and well-born. Who is equal to me? I will perform sacrifices and give gifts, and rejoice in my own generosity." This is how they go on, deluded by ignorance.

Bound by their greed and entangled in a web of delusion, whirled about by a fragmented mind, they fall into a dark hell.
Bhagavad-Gita 16.13-16 *(Hinduism)*

When they see merchandise or diversion they scatter off to it, and they leave you standing. Say, "What is with God is better than diversion and merchandise. God is the best of providers."
Qur'an 62.11

He who loves money will not be satisfied with money; nor he who loves wealth, with gain: this also is vanity.

When goods increase, they increase who eat them; and what gain has their owner but to see them with his eyes?

Sweet is the sleep of a laborer, whether he eats little or much; but the surfeit of the rich will not let him sleep.

There is a grievous evil which I have seen under the sun: riches were kept by their owner to his hurt, and those riches were lost in a bad venture; and he is father of a son, but he has nothing in his hand.

As he came from his mother's womb he shall go again, naked as he came, and shall take nothing for his toil, which he may carry away in his hand.
Ecclesiastes 5.10-15

The life of moneymaking is one undertaken under compulsion, and wealth is evidently not the good we are seeking; for it is merely useful for the sake of something else.
Aristotle, Nicomachean Ethics I.5 *(Hellenism)*

You have the right to work, but never to the fruit of work. You should never engage in action for the sake of reward, nor should you long for inaction. Perform work in this world, Arjuna, as a man established within himself—without selfish attachments, and alike in success and defeat. For discipline is perfect evenness of mind.

Seek refuge in the attitude of detachment and you will amass the wealth of spiritual awareness. Those who are motivated only by desire for the fruits of action are miserable, for they are constantly anxious about the results of what they do. When consciousness is unified, however, all vain anxiety is left behind. There is no cause for worry, whether things go well or ill.

Bhagavad-Gita 2.47-50 (Hinduism)

The impulse "I want" and the impulse "I'll have"—lose them! That is where most people get stuck; without those, you can use your eyes to guide you through this suffering state.

Sutta Nipata 706 (Buddhism)

Busy not yourself with this world, for with fire we test gold, and with gold we test our servants.

Hidden Words of Bahá'u'lláh,
Arabic 54 (Bahá'í Faith)

Teachings of Sun Myung Moon

Money can be ugly. It can be filthier than dung. People do not become evil because they are soiled with dung, but people who misuse money become wicked—filthier than dung. So I try not to use money for myself. I try to give all of it to others. (381:304, June 17, 2002)

Money can provide you with the things you desire: women, food, good clothes, and a fine house. Certainly we need money, yet money also can be a problem. When you have money, do you want to employ it to love others, or employ it to amass power? We need money, but it should be used to benefit the whole and to realize love. (116:18, December 1, 1981)

Power, wealth and knowledge, which worldly people ordinarily desire, are not the necessary and sufficient conditions for peace and happiness. True happiness is not proportional to how much property you own, nor is it obtained by multiplying external comforts. The only sure way to obtain genuine peace and limitless happiness is to live for others and give to others with true love; when those deeds go around they will return to you. (294:68, June 11, 1998)

In creating the world as His object partner, God had no concept of possession. If a person has the concept that he owns things, then he cannot give more than he has. If he owns things worth one hundred dollars, he cannot give more than one hundred dollars' worth of things. On the contrary, God creates by investing and forgetting, investing and forgetting. God can invest infinitely because he has no concept of self. Do you understand this principle? A person cannot be conscious of self when investing for his or her counterpart. To think, "This money is for me to use. This is my portion," is Satan's way of thinking. (287:265, 971005)

Humankind longs for a world of peace, free from war and suffering. Yet it is difficult to be hopeful when the traditional authority of national leaders and religions are supplanted by a "money solves all" mentality, which is utterly insufficient in the face of youth decline, family breakdown, drugs and AIDS. 294:61, June 11, 1998)

The world's developed nations, while seeking for the ultimate material civilization, have fallen into its trap. Obsession for material wealth dominates the mind and spirit; the human soul has become the slave of matter. The result is a collapse of true love. Although cities are lined with skyscrapers and the people enjoy material abundance, the lives of city-dwellers have become like a barren desert. In such desolation, an oasis of true love is nowhere to be found. Without true love, our society is a breeding-ground for selfishness.

The most grievous victim of this selfishness is nature. The natural environment is devastated, the water and air are polluted, and even the ozone layer, which has been protecting humanity, is damaged. If this situation continues unchecked, humanity will reach the point where it cannot escape self-destruction, all due to the material civilization it has erected for itself.

The twenty-first century is the time to return to the original world that God desires. The age of material civilization will give way to an era of spiritual civilization, where spirit and mind are ascendant. The twenty-first century will arrive in just five years. At this juncture it is my earnest desire that developing countries do not repeat the same mistake of developed nations and fall into the trap of material civilization, but take a lesson from them and dash into a world where the mind and spirit rule. (271:95-96, August 23, 1995)

2. Giving Away One's Wealth and Finding Contentment with Little

Jesus said to [the rich young man], "If you would be perfect, go, sell what you possess and give to the poor, and you will have treasure in heaven; and come, follow me." When the young man heard this he went away sorrowful; for he had great possessions.

And Jesus said to his disciples, "Truly, I say to you, it will by hard for a rich man to enter the kingdom of Heaven. Again I tell you, it is easier for a camel to go through the eye of a needle than for a rich man to enter the kingdom of God."

Matthew 19.21-24

If beings knew, as I know, the fruit of sharing gifts, they would not enjoy their use without sharing them, nor would the taint of stinginess obsess the heart and stay there. Even if it were their last bit, their last morsel of food, they would not enjoy its use without sharing it, if there were anyone to receive it.

Itivuttaka 18 (Buddhism)

Who is rich? He that rejoices in his portion.[17]

Mishnah, Avot 4.1 (Judaism)

Other people live to eat, but I eat to live.

Socrates[18] (Hellenism)

The Great Man—his face and form blend with the Great Unity, the Great Unity which is selfless. Being selfless, how can he look upon possession as possession?

Chuang Tzu 11 (Taoism)

Having the fewest wants, I am nearest to the gods.

Socrates (Hellenism)

Not that I complain of want; for I have learned, in whatever state I am, to be content. I know how to be abased, and I know how to abound; in any and all circumstances I have learned the secret of facing plenty and hunger, abundance and want. I can do all things in him who strengthens me.

Philippians 4.11-13

And he [Jesus] called to him the twelve, and began to send them out two by two... He charged them to take nothing for their journey except a staff; no bread, no bag, no money in their belts.

Mark 6.7-9

This is the way of Torah: A morsel with salt shall you eat and water by measure shall you drink; and you shall lie upon the earth, and you shall live a life of hardship, and labor in the Torah. If you do thus, happy shall you be and it shall be well with you.

Mishnah, Avot 6.4 (Judaism)

The Master said, "Incomparable was Hui! A handful of rice to eat, a gourdful of water to drink, living on a mean street—others would have found it unendurably depressing, but to Hui's cheerfulness it made no difference at all. Incomparable indeed was Hui!"

Analects 6.9 (Confucianism)

Brothers should appropriate neither house, nor place, nor anything for themselves; and they should go confidently after alms, serving God in poverty and humility, as pilgrims and strangers in this world. Nor should they feel ashamed, for God made Himself poor in this world for us. This is that peak of the highest poverty which has made you, my dearest brothers, heirs and kings of the kingdom of heaven, poor in things but rich in virtues. Let this be your portion. It leads into the land of the living and, adhering totally to it, for the sake of our Lord Jesus Christ wish never to have anything else in this world, beloved brothers.

Rule of Saint Francis (Christianity)

When we were sitting with God's Messenger in the mosque, Musab ibn Umair came to us wearing only a cloak of his patched with fur. When God's Messenger saw him he wept to think of his former affluence. He then said, "How will it be with you when one of you goes out in the morning wearing a mantle and goes out in the evening wearing another, when one dish is placed before him and another removed, and you cover your houses as the Kaaba is covered?" On receiving the reply, "Messenger of God, we shall then be better than we are today, having leisure for worship and possessing all we require," he said, "No, you are better today than you will be at that time."

Hadith of Tirmidhi (Islam)

Teachings of Sun Myung Moon

The wealth we have belongs to Heaven. It belongs to God. It belongs to those who are living for the sake of others. Therefore, let us not use our wealth for personal benefit. Otherwise, we shall perish. (399:18, December 18, 2002)

Is that handkerchief in your pocket yours? No, it does not belong to you. You think it belongs to you, but you are mistaken. You are mistaken if you think that your house belongs to you, and the land under your name. You are mistaken if you think that husband, wife, sons and daughters are your husband, your wife, and your children, and therefore you may treat them as you please. That concept of ownership is an evil way of thinking, which arose after the Human Fall. We did not know it, but behind the scenes, God has been working for thousands of years to straighten it out. Therefore, for our part, we have to deny ownership. We should give up the idea that we own anything of God's creation. (293:172, May 26, 1998)

You should be willing to offer [to God] all your possessions without any reservation. You should be willing to burn them all, and then burn even the altar as a burnt offering. You should not feel that you are qualified to own even your personal belongings. Then, after you finish fulfilling the role of a high priest, you will reap the fruits of all your offerings. Heaven will prepare them for you.[19] (342:227, January 12, 2001)

God will remember and love the person who would gather up all of America's wealth and give it to Africa. (91:24, January 16, 1977)

When you amass wealth, do not think about using it to benefit your children. Before bequeathing it to your children, you should devote it for the sake of the world. After all, your children should live for the sake of the world. Therefore, your first priority should be to offer your wealth to the world; then you can provide for your children. God will bless you and your family if you have a heart to provide for your family members only after offering your wealth to your people and nation. Do not worry that your children will go without; God will feed them and care for them. (26:52-53, October 18, 1969)

Money is the result. Yet everyone is concerned about money without looking behind it at its cause. Why do we need money? We do not need it just to eat and live; we need it to connect with the purpose of the cause, and to connect with the world. Nevertheless, people do not have such a concept. Although they are resultant beings, people do not recognize that their purpose, and the purpose of their money, is to make the Causal Being happy. If they did, they would understand that they should use their money to serve their parents, to share with their siblings and relatives, and to benefit their nation and the world. This is a universal law.

If your nation is pleased that you are wealthy, and if your parents and siblings are pleased as well, then you can freely enjoy your wealth. Wherever you go, everyone will be pleased. But if others are resentful of your money while you alone are pleased with it, then you are bound to decline. From this perspective, business conglomerates that operate based on pragmatism, amassing great profits on the backs of their workers, will surely decline. They will be punished by Heaven. (117:101-02, February 14, 1982)

Moses lived in the opulent palace of the Pharaoh, but he belittled it, saying, "So what?" and thought more of his people. Therefore, he could become the leader of his people. (*Way of God's Will* 1.3)

People in the everyday world can purchase a home, appliances, furniture, and live a comfortable life just by working eight hours a day. We Unificationists work 24 hours a day, yet we do not own our own homes and barely have enough money to live on. My goodness! We are like beggars. Do you realize that we are different from the world? We are 180 degrees different. Yet under these circumstances, are we in despair? No, we live in hope. That is our pride. (107:83, April 6, 1980)

Separation from Family

ALTHOUGH GOD'S PURPOSE FOR HUMAN LIFE IS FULFILLED in loving families, people on the spiritual quest often leave home and family behind. Sometimes it comes at the command of God, as when Abraham was called to leave his home and journey to an unknown land. Initiation into the ranks of monastic life likewise requires a painful separation from loved ones.

In other cases, aspirants may encounter opposition from possessive family members, who would drag them away from the path. Thus Jesus warned his disciples to expect opposition from their loving parents and spouses, and warned them of the cost of discipleship: "He who loves father or mother more than me is not worthy of me." Father Moon explains that separating from family and friends is necessary in the course of restoration, which requires a fundamental reorientation of the self from the customary fallen love of the world to the higher love of God.

Do not think that I have come to bring peace on earth; I have come not to bring peace, but a sword. For I have come to set a man against his father, and a daughter against her mother, and a daughter-in-law against her mother-in-law; and a man's foes will be those of his own household. He who loves father or mother more than me is not worthy of me; and he who loves son or daughter more than me is not worthy of me.

Matthew 10.34-37

O believers, take not your fathers and brothers to be your friends, if they prefer unbelief to belief; whosoever of you takes them for friends, those—they are the evildoers.

Say, "If your fathers, your sons, your brothers, your wives, your clan, your possessions that you have gained, commerce you fear may slacken, dwellings you love—if these are dearer to you than God and His Messenger, and to struggle in His way, then wait till God brings His command: God guides not the people of the ungodly."

Qur'an 9.23-24

Consort not with those that are dear, neither with those that are not dear; for not seeing those that are dear and seeing those that are not dear are both painful.

Dhammapada 210 (Buddhism)

Put no trust in a neighbor,
have no confidence in a friend;
guard the doors of your mouth
from her who lies in your bosom;
for the son treats the father with contempt,
the daughter rises up against her mother,
the daughter-in-law against her mother-in-law;
a man's enemies are the men of his own house.
But as for me, I will look to the LORD,
I will wait for the God of my salvation;
my God will hear me.

Micah 7.5-7

God has made up a parable about those who disbelieve: Noah's wife and Lot's wife were both married to two of our honest servants; and they betrayed them both. Neither had any help at all from them as far as God was concerned. It was said, "Enter the Fire along with others who are entering it."

God has made up a parable about those who believe: the wife of Pharaoh[20] when she said, "My Lord, build a house for me in Paradise with you, and save me from Pharaoh and his doings. Save me from such wrongdoing folk!"

Qur'an 66.10-11

Now the LORD said to Abram, "Go from your country and your kindred and your father's house to the land that I will show you."

Genesis 12.1

Every one who has left houses or brothers or sisters or father or mother or children or lands, for my name's sake, will receive a hundredfold, and inherit eternal life.

Matthew 19.29

He who forsakes his home in the cause of God, finds in the earth many a refuge, wide and spacious; should he die as a refugee from home for God and His Apostle, his reward becomes due and sure with God: and God is Oft-forgiving, Most Merciful.

Qur'an 4.100

If any one comes to me and does not hate his own father and mother and wife and children and brothers and sisters, yes, and even his own life, he cannot be my disciple.

Luke 14.26

Even your brothers and the house of your
   father,
even they have dealt treacherously with you;

they are in full cry after you;
believe them not,
though they speak fair words to you.

Jeremiah 12.6

One day she who was formerly the mate of the venerable Sangamaji came towards him, drew near and said, "Recluse, support me with our little child." At these words the venerable Sangamaji was silent. So a second time and yet a third time his former wife repeated her words, and still the venerable Sangamaji was silent. Thereupon she set down the child in front of him and went away, saying, "Here is your child, recluse! Support him!" But the venerable Sangamaji neither looked at the child nor spoke to him. When from a distance she saw this, she thought to herself, "This recluse needs not even his own child." So she turned back, took up the child and went away.

Udana 5-6 (Buddhism)

Give up your wealth and your wife; you have entered the state of the houseless; do not, as it were, return to your vomit. Gautama, be careful all the while!

Leave your friends and relations, the large fortune you have amassed; do not desire them a second time; Gautama, be careful all the while...

Now you have entered on the path from which the thorns have been cleared, the great path; walk in the right path, Gautama, be careful all the while!

Uttaradhyayana Sutra 10.29-32 (Jainism)

How could I be diligent, good Shariputta, when there are my parents to support, my wife and children to support, my slaves, servants and work-people to support, when there are services to perform for friends and acquaintances, services to perform for kith and kin, services to perform for guests, rites to perform for the ancestors, rites to perform for the gods, duties to perform for the king—and this body too must be satisfied and looked after!

What do you think, Dhananjani? Suppose someone failed to live the holy life because of his parents, his wife, and so on; because of this failure...the guardians of Niraya hell might drag him off to their hell. Would he gain anything by saying, "I failed to live the holy life because of my parents?"

Majjhima Nikaya 2.186-87 (Buddhism)

He who is kind toward much-beloved friends loses his own good from his mind, becoming partial; observing such danger in friendship, let one walk alone like a rhinoceros.

As a spreading bush of bamboo is entangled in various ways, so is the longing for children and wives: not clinging to these, even like a bamboo just sprouting forth, let one walk alone like a rhinoceros...

If one lives in the midst of company, love of amusement and desire arises; strong attachment for children arises; let therefore one who dislikes separation, which must happen sooner or later from these beloved, walk alone like a rhinoceros...

Having abandoned the different kinds of desire, founded on child, wife, father, mother, wealth, corn, relations, let one walk alone like a rhinoceros.

Let a wise man, having discovered that such is attachment, that there is in it but little happiness, that it is but insipid, that there is more affliction in it than comfort, that it is a fishhook, walk alone like a rhinoceros.

Having cast off the bonds, like a fish which breaks the net in the water, like a fire that returns not to the spot already burned up, let one walk alone like a rhinoceros.

Sutta Nipata 37-62: Rhinoceros Discourse (Buddhism)

Teachings of Sun Myung Moon

Jesus said, "He who loves father or mother more than me is not worthy of me; and he who loves son or daughter more than me is not worthy of me." This is a formula on the path to God. The deeper the loving attachments you had in the satanic world, the more intensely will those very people try to dissuade you from going on the heavenly way. Know, therefore, that it is a universal truth that you will have enemies among the members of your own family. (92:207, April 10, 1977)

Jesus said, "Anyone who loves his father or mother more than me is not worthy of me; and anyone who loves his son or daughter more than me is not worthy of me." (Matt. 10:37) That is one of the reasons why he was severely opposed.

Why did he speak like that? It was to sever the original sin. Satan's blood is mixed in fallen humans and must be extracted. He continued: "Your own family members are your enemies." How can such a saying make sense? Because the original sin remains in fallen human beings. He was right. As long as people continue to love one another while carrying the original sin, the original sin cannot be removed. This is undeniable. While we continue to love our family members, we cannot overcome this pivotal barrier. That is why Jesus called them enemies.

Blood lineage is transferred through love; therefore love—parental love, conjugal love and children's love—should be reversed 180 degrees. We should think: "I do not need anything but God. God is above all." There is no other way to remove the original sin. (79:160, July 20, 1975)

"I think my husband is the best, my wife is the best, and my sons and daughters are the best." But what good is being the best of a lineage inherited from Satan? This is what you should deny.

To possess God's love you must deny your husband's love, your wife's love and your children's love. God originally intended human beings to relate with Him alone. If there are any traces of Satan's play on your bodies, the original ideal of love cannot take root. (140:24, February 1, 1986)

On the path to God, you cannot make progress without experiencing the state of heavenly love that is higher than the first love you knew in worldly life… A couple may have married after falling madly in love and felt that only death could part them, but once the two of them come to know God's will they should find that higher realm of love [to which their marriage seems pale in comparison]; then they will abandon their marriage within a week. (102:20, November 19, 1978)

How do we restore this world? We plant ourselves as individuals by going in the opposite direction, and then we can pull others to go forward. This is why in high-level religions such as Buddhism those on the path must leave their homes. They are not permitted to love their father and mother, older sister or brother. The words in the Bible, "Anyone who does not hate his own father and mother and wife and children and brothers and sisters… cannot be my disciple," seem paradoxical, but they must be accepted as a rational theory to guide us to the path of Heaven. (181:212-13, October 3, 1988)

If I know that I am self-centered and full of evil thoughts, should I continue to enjoy my habitual way of relating to people close to me? No, I should feel revulsion at the way I treat them. Feeling that way, I would want to be alone.

Thus, a person of conscience may isolate himself and tell others not to come near him. Eventually, others will recognize that person; even the universe will protect him as he strives for oneness. On the contrary, the universe will attempt to expel the person who constantly creates problems and who pollutes his surroundings by his evil actions. He will quickly travel down the road to destruction.

Nature knows that human beings are evil. Therefore, do you think it will be sympathetic to the person who lives as he pleases, not caring about how he affects others? Or to the person who lives a solitary life over concern that he might be polluted by human relationships?

Have you ever had a friend whom you disliked and wished would never come around, but who visited you constantly? Maybe the first few times you would talk to him, but if he came repeatedly you would slam the door in his face... It is out of these considerations that asceticism emerged in the religious life. People seeking solitude would go deep in the mountains and live as hermits, desiring to sever any relationships with other human beings. We can view the emergence of such asceticism as a natural thing... Nature finds something hopeful in such people. (November 4, 1990)

It is extremely difficult to leave your beloved children behind to follow the lonely path of Heaven, where no one welcomes you, but that is my life story. When I went to North Korea, I abandoned my wife and infant child. I did not go because I wanted to. I went at Heaven's command, because God required it. I resisted and agonized for about a day or two, but because I knew God's situation was worse than my troubles, I went. (64:148, October 29, 1972)

You have struggled over your attachment to your family. Everyone loves his or her own sons and daughters. So do dogs and pigs, and people as dull as trees and stones. Reverend Moon is no different. It is not that I lack the heart to love my children; my love for them is as strong and sensitive as any parent.

Towards my mother I am very sentimental. I loved her dearly. However, when my mother visited me in prison, I glared at her fiercely and shouted, "I am not your son." My mother is no longer alive. When I learned that she had passed away, I felt I had been an undutiful son.

However, that son worked for God's Will and to uphold the heavenly law. He worked for the sake of the nation and the world instead of working for himself and the happiness of his clan. (168:148, September 13, 1987)

Separation from the World

A WORLDLY LIFE IS INCOMPATIBLE with the path to God. To seek after pleasure, wealth, fame and material comforts inevitably distracts from pursuing a spiritual purpose. More than harmless distractions, such worldly passions and attachments drag the soul to hell. Hence, scriptures contain numerous admonitions to avoid conforming to the world and its values.

Wise men and women regard worldly achievement as an illusion. They do not delight in worldly pleasures, but devote themselves to God's will. At all times they seek to remain detached from worldly thoughts and sense impressions. They measure achievement by spiritual progress, rather than by the standards of worldly success.

In some religions, separation from the world is achieved by physical isolation in a monastic community. More often the boundaries are invisible, enforced by moral suasion and church discipline. For people who are "in the world but not of the world," their lives may appear outwardly ordinary, yet the inner content of their lives is quite different, without attachment to the world's prevailing values.

1. Not Conforming to the Ways of the World

Do not be conformed to this world, but be transformed by the renewal of your mind, that you may prove what is the will of God, what is good and acceptable and perfect.

Romans 12.2

As a sweet-smelling, lovely lotus may grow upon a heap of rubbish thrown by the highway, even so a disciple of the Fully Enlightened One outshines the ignorant worldly people in wisdom.

Dhammapada 58-59 (Buddhism)

For what is a man profited, if he shall gain the whole world and lose his own soul? Or what shall a man give in exchange for his soul?

Matthew 16.26

A man came to the Prophet and said, "O Messenger of Allah, direct me to an act which, if I do it, will cause Allah to love me and people to love me." He said, "Renounce the world and Allah will love you; renounce what people possess and people will love you."

Forty Hadith of an-Nawawi 31 (Islam)

Do not serve mean ends. Do not live in heedlessness. Do not embrace false views. Do not be one who upholds the world.

Dhammapada 167 (Buddhism)

I have given them thy word; and the world has hated them because they are not of the world, even as I am not of the world. I do not pray that thou shouldst take them out of the world, but that thou shouldst keep them from the evil one. They are not of the world, even as I am not of the world. Sanctify them in truth; thy word is truth. As thou didst send me into the world, so I have sent them into the world.

John 17.14-18

A complete disregard for all worldly things, perfect contentment, abandonment of hope of every kind, and patience—these constitute the highest good of one who has subjugated his senses and acquired knowledge of Self.

No need of attaching yourself to things of this world. Attachment to worldly objects is productive of evil.

Mahabharata, Santi Parva 329 (Hinduism)

Stagnation: To conserve his stock of virtue, the superior man withdraws into himself and thus escapes from the evil influences around him. He declines all temptations of honor and riches.

I Ching 12 (Confucianism)

The sage patterns himself on Heaven, prizes the Truth, and does not allow himself to be cramped by the vulgar. The stupid man does the opposite of this. He is unable to pattern himself on Heaven and instead frets over human concerns. He does not know enough to prize the Truth but instead, plodding along with the crowd, he allows himself to be changed by vulgar ways, and so is never content.

Chuang Tzu 31 (Taoism)

He who has found the Mother [Tao]
And thereby understands her sons [things of the world],
And having understood the sons,
Still keeps to its Mother,
Will be free from danger throughout his lifetime.
Close the mouth,
Shut the doors [of cunning and desire],
And to the end of life there will be peace without toil.
Open the mouth,
Meddle with affairs,
And to the end of life there will be no salvation.[21]

Tao Te Ching 52 (Taoism)

Vimalakirti wore the white clothes of a layman, yet lived impeccably like a religious devotee. He lived at home, but remained aloof from the realm of desire, the realm of pure matter, and the immaterial realm. He had a son, a wife, and female attendants, yet always maintained continence. He appeared to be surrounded by servants, yet lived in solitude. He appeared to be adorned with ornaments, yet always was endowed with the auspicious signs and marks. He seemed to eat and drink, yet always took nourishment from the taste of meditation. He made his appearance at the fields of sports and in the casinos, but his aim was always to mature those people who were attached to games and gambling... He engaged in all sorts of businesses, yet had no interest in profit or possessions. To train living beings, he would appear at crossroads and on street corners, and to protect them he participated in government.

Holy Teaching of Vimalakirti 2 (Buddhism)

Teachings of Sun Myung Moon

If you still carry relationships with the self-centered, fallen world, you cannot walk the way of God's purpose and Will. (21:102, November 17, 1968)

The secular world covets wealth, knowledge and power as the most important things. However, these three things cannot connect you to God. What connects you to God? True love. (270:308, July 23, 1995)

In this world, what people most admire are fakes. Therefore, the genuine article does not come before you straightforwardly. It may appear to you as upside-down... Would you welcome a person who walked on his hands with his feet in the air? Maybe so, but at least he is whole. Would you still welcome him if he were really malformed?

Therefore, the Bible teaches that those who seek to die will live and those who seek to live will die. It means that those who seek to perish will succeed and those who seek to succeed will perish; those who think they are foolish are eminent and those who think they are eminent are foolish; those who seek to live a difficult life will be wealthy and those who seek to live a wealthy life will be beset by difficulties. (102:251, January 14, 1979)

You should possess an earnest heart, rooted in the eternal world beyond time and space. With such a heart, you should be able to endure, overcoming worldly labors, hardships, and even the fear of death. To gain victory on your individual path, you should be able to deny all attachments, despise all pain, and walk forward with dignity. (7:97, July 19, 1959)

We will not trade our commitment to God for any amount of gold or all the power in the world. We will not sell ourselves for money, power or women. We are not so cheap. Rather than lead a treacherous life on a worldly throne, I prefer to be unchanging and live as a beggar. (124:253, February 20, 1983)

Give up your desire for material possessions, your hopes for your children, your love for your spouse, and even your self-love. Do not hold on to these attachments; then you can go beyond the world. Only when you cut off every element within yourself that is conducive to ambition and to human attachments can you become an offering for the sake of the world. (2:118, March 10, 1957)

Those who cherish their worldly situation and relationships cannot avoid the judgment of the Last Days. To avoid the judgment, you must turn away from the world and escape its ways. You should not follow worldly trends. For this reason, religions teach: "Abandon the world!" "Cut off all relationships with the world!" "Do not associate with the world!" "Don't compromise with the world!" "Cut yourself off from the world!" "Deny the world and seek higher awareness!" Only people who follow this path will see the dawning of a new ideal. By not compromising with the world, religion cultivates the determination to go beyond the mistakes of the past, press forward in the present, and break through to a new future. (21:136-37, November 17, 1968)

People who have inherited the satanic lineage characteristically put themselves first. America these days, despite its Christian cultural roots, has become a nation of individualism. With so-called secular humanism, people are confused about their direction in life and seek happiness by external stimulation. What are the consequences? They fall off the cliff as lepers. Men and women love and cuddle with each other day and night, but they are bound to acquire AIDS, wither, and fall. (187:241, February 11, 1989)

2. Denial of Worldly Comforts and Pleasures

Come behold this world, which is like unto an ornamented royal chariot, wherein fools flounder, but for the wise there is no attachment.

Dhammapada 171 (Buddhism)

Pleasure lies in gold, silver, women, and delectable objects;
Pleasure lies in mounts, soft beds, mansions, and attractions of the palate.
With all such pleasures, how may the Name find place in the mind?

Adi Granth, Sri Raga, M.1, p. 25 (Sikhism)

Hillel used to say, "More flesh, more worms; more wealth more care; more women more witchcraft; more maidservants more lewdness; more menservants more thieving; more Torah more life; more assiduity more wisdom; more counsel more understanding; more charity more peace."

Mishnah, Avot 2.8 (Judaism)

The streams of this world are dirty and its springs are turbid. Its window dressing and its show is beautiful but destructive. It is a quickly ending deception, a speedily fading light, a hurrying shade, and a weak and unreliable protection. It is so deceptive that it waits till those who abhor it start taking interest in it, and those who do not know its deception are attracted by it, and are satisfied with it, then it shows scanty regard for them, it snares and captivates them, and tying the rope of death round their necks drags them to their graves.

Nahjul Balagha, Khutba 86 (Shiite Islam)

From endearment springs grief, from endearment springs fear; for him who is wholly free from endearment there is no grief, much less fear.

From affection springs grief, from affection springs fear; for him who is wholly free from affection there is no grief, much less fear.

From attachment springs grief, from attachment springs fear; for him who is wholly free from attachment there is no grief, much less fear.

From lust springs grief, from lust springs fear; for him who is wholly free from lust there is no grief, much less fear.

From craving springs grief, from craving springs fear; for him who is wholly free from craving there is no grief, much less fear.

Dhammapada 212-16 (Buddhism)

But fornication and all impurity or covetousness must not even be named among you, as is fitting among saints. Let there be no filthiness, nor silly talk, nor levity, which are not fitting; but instead let there be thanksgiving. Be sure of this, that no fornicator or impure man, or one who is covetous (that is, an idolater), has any inheritance in the kingdom of Christ and of God. Let no one deceive you with empty words, for it is because of these things that the wrath of God comes upon the sons of disobedience. Therefore do not associate with them.

Ephesians 5.3-7

"And ye shall be holy unto me, for I, the LORD, am holy" [Leviticus 20.26]. Even as I am holy, so be you holy. As I am separate, so you be separate. And "I have severed you from the other peoples that you should be mine" [idem.]. If you sever yourselves from the other peoples, then you belong to me; but if not, then you belong to Nebuchadnezzar and his fellows." Rabbi Eliezer said, "How can we know that a man must not say, 'I have no desire to eat pig, I have no desire to have intercourse with a woman whom I may not marry'; but he must say, 'Yes, I would like to do these acts, but what can I do? My Father who is in heaven has forbidden them.' Because it says, 'I have severed you from among the nations to be mine.' He who is separated from iniquity receives to himself the Kingdom of Heaven."

Sifra 93d (Judaism)

Teachings of Sun Myung Moon

The things of this evil world do not lead us to the gate of happiness; rather they drive us into the snares of death. (47:49, August 19, 1971)

Heaven's emotions are in contradiction with humanistic emotions. God does not dwell where people are comfortable, and people must negate themselves to be in accord with Heaven. This is a fact. Therefore, a religion that accommodates itself to the world does not last long. (51:187, November 21, 1971)

In this world where good and evil are ever in opposition, your body pulls you to become evil while your mind pulls you to be good. Hence your mind cannot completely control the body, and you are caught in the middle, constantly going back and forth. You are better off following a religion that places God's will as absolute; then you can go to a place that is separated from the satanic world. Leave this world beset by the opposition of good and evil, and live a life of putting goodness first in a separated realm. If you practice such a life, then you will live eternally in the good sovereignty in the spirit world. (36:82, November 15, 1970)

In order to accomplish your responsibility, you should stand firm, denying everything that has an emotional connection with Satan—Satan's love, Satan's recognition, and Satan's lineage. Why? When Adam was walking the course to fulfill his portion of responsibility, he carried with him all of Satan's emotions. That is why he failed. What about you? In seeking to accomplish your portion of responsibility, have you cut off all your emotional attachments to Satan's world? No, you have not been able to cut them off. Can you accomplish your responsibility without cutting them off? No, you cannot. That is why you must deny yourself. (139:250, January 31, 1986)

Pioneers and people who move history do not seek worldly pleasures. They have the spirit of an explorer who strives to overcome every obstacle on the way to his goal, the promised destination. (7:87, July 19, 1959)

We should be eternally different from the satanic world. We should be 180 degrees opposite. We should have nothing to do with alcohol, drugs, free sex, and homosexuality. Instead, we should be indignant that Satan has destroyed countless good people through these evils, utilizing false love to leave a trail of sorrow through history. We should be indignant that Satan has compelled Heaven to make countless sacrifices. (244:148-49, February 1, 1993)

Many American parents encourage their children to date and worry about them if they do not. On the other hand, I teach, "Do not date! Do not touch women!" Whose teaching is more in line with Heaven? (122:263, November 21, 1982)

Asceticism, Monasticism and Celibacy

ASPIRANTS WHO WISH TO COMPLETELY SEVER themselves from worldly life may adopt the secluded and sometimes solitary life of a monk or nun. In Buddhism and Jainism, and in Roman Catholic and Orthodox Christianity, the highest religious vocations require celibacy—monks, nuns and priests. Asceticism also abounds in Hinduism, where in addition to life-long ascetics, there is the tradition that brahmins would spend the last years of their lives as solitary ascetics devoting themselves to the goal of liberation. Christian monasticism took institutional form in order to provide a supportive setting for those who wished to take vows of poverty and chastity, who valued the love of Christ which surpasses the love of women.

There is no monasticism in Islam. Nevertheless, Muslims practice asceticism on a wide scale with the month-long fast of Ramadan. Fasting and all-night prayer vigils attack the body's desire for food and sleep. They are examples of ascetic practices within everyone's reach, unlike traditional monasticism which is practiced only by a spiritual elite. In Thailand and Sri Lanka, Buddhist young men usually devote six months to monastic training before embarking on family life.

In line with his teaching on subduing the desires of the body, Father Moon praises monasticism for its devotion to attaining mind-body unity. Nevertheless, a tension exists between the path of the celibate priest and the family ideal that God purposed at the creation. Hence, at the end of this section are passages critical of the monastic life; such are found in nearly every tradition where it is practiced: asceticism can lead to an overly severe personality devoid of compassion; monasticism is incompatible with the generative and productive life of the world which is ordained by God.

Father Moon's teaching points to the deeper problem that led God to institute the path of celibacy and asceticism in the first place: the corruption of marriage at the Human Fall. In the final passages, he describes the dawning of a new age in which marriage is restored to its original estate and there is no more need for the discipline of celibacy. While celibacy was a true and noble path in past ages, the time has come for religion to exalt marriage above the celibate life. Indicative of this sea-change is the decline of monasticism and celibacy that is being felt all over the religious world.

1. The Ascetic Life of a Monk or Nun

The blue-necked peacock which flies through the air never approaches the speed of the swan. Similarly, the householder can never resemble the monk who is endowed with the qualities of the sage, who meditates, aloof, in the jungle.

Sutta Nipata 221 (Buddhism)

Go on the begging tour, stay in a forest, eat but a little, speak only measured words, put up with misery, conquer sleep, practice friendship with all and non-attachment in an excellent manner.

Vattakera, Mulacara 981 (Jainism)

"Revile not, harm not, live by rule restrained;
Of food take little; sleep and sit alone;
Keep thy mind bent upon the higher thought."
Such is the message of awakened ones.

Udana 43 (Buddhism)

The first degree of humility is obedience without delay. This becomes those who, on account of the holy subjection which they have promised, or of the fear of hell, or the glory of life everlasting, hold nothing dearer than Christ. As soon as anything has been commanded by the Superior they permit no delay in the execution, as if the matter had been commanded by God Himself...

Let permission to speak be seldom given... If anything must be asked of the Superior, let it be asked with all humility and respectful submission. But coarse jests, and idle words or speech provoking laughter, we condemn everywhere to eternal exclusion; and for such speech we do not permit the disciple to open his lips...

The vice of personal ownership must by all means be cut out in the monastery by the very root, so that no one may presume to give or receive anything without the command of the Abbot; nor to have anything whatever as his own, neither a book, nor a writing tablet, nor a pen, nor anything else whatsoever, since monks are allowed to have neither their bodies nor their wills in their own power. Everything that is necessary, however, they must look for from the Father of the monastery; and let it not be allowed for anyone to have anything which the Abbot did not give or permit him to have. Let all things be common to all.

Rule of Saint Benedict (Christianity)

Let him always wander alone, without any companion, in order to attain [final liberation], fully understanding that the solitary man, who neither forsakes nor is forsaken, gains his end.

He shall neither possess a fire, nor a dwelling; he may go to a village for his food, indifferent to everything, firm in purpose, meditating and concentrating his mind on God.

A potsherd [for an alms-bowl], the roots of trees [for a dwelling], coarse worn-out garments, life in solitude, and indifference towards everything are the marks of one who has attained liberation.

Let him not desire to die, let him not desire to live; let him wait for [his appointed] time, as a servant for the payment of his wages.

Let him put down his foot purified by his sight [i.e., watching not to step on any creature], let him drink water purified by straining with a cloth [so as not to swallow any creature], let him utter speech purified by truth, let him keep his heart pure.

Let him patiently bear hard words, let him not insult anybody, and let him not become anybody's enemy for the sake of his body.

Against an angry man let him not in return show anger, let him bless when he is cursed, and let him not other speech, devoid of truth, scattered at the seven gates.

Delighted in what refers to the Soul, sitting [in yoga postures], independent, entirely abstaining from sensual enjoyments, with himself for his only companion, he shall live in this world, desiring the bliss [of liberation]…

Let him go to beg once a day, let him not be eager to obtain a large quantity of alms; for an ascetic who eagerly seeks alms attaches himself also to sensual enjoyments…

By eating little, and by standing and sitting in solitude, let him restrain his sense, if they are attracted to sensual objects.

By the restraint of his senses, by the destruction of love and hatred, and by the abstention from injuring the creatures, he becomes fit for immortality.

Laws of Manu 6.37-60 (Hinduism)

Teachings of Sun Myung Moon

What are we trying to restrain? We are trying to deaden the body. That is why religions teach us to fast, do prayer vigils all night without sleep, be celibate and live as a hermit. In the Catholic Church the highest vocation is to be a priest or a nun; they do not marry for their entire life. In Buddhism also, most monks are celibate.

Compare these disciplines with the lifestyle of American youth. It is quite the opposite of that of religious people who make it their chief aim to conquer the body. As a result, they are living a hellish existence, constantly besieged by the temptations of the satanic world. The youth of America should realize this; they should understand that the way they are living is contrary to God's Will. Instead of pursuing the body's pleasure, we should torment our body. Why? Because [due to the Fall] our body has become Satan's dance floor. (215:236, February 20, 1991)

Christians in the Middle Ages practiced asceticism and placed great hardship on their bodies. However, in modern times many churches became disparaging of the ascetic life; they have lost sight of the fact that the body dominates the conscience unless one takes active measures to stop it. Not knowing this principle, they turned away from a central aspect of the Christian tradition. Now that you know clearly that the enemy lives in your physical body, you must treat it as an enemy. You must continue on the ascetic path until the body is suppressed. (254:222, February 13, 1994)

Two pluses repel each other. God is in the position of a plus, but Satan also tries to stand in this plus position, although [as a servant of God] he should be in the minus position—such is Satan. Why does the path of self-cultivation call us to asceticism? Its purpose is to strike Satan's realm within each of us, that plus side that belongs to evil, in order to switch it over to the minus position. (4:23, February 16, 1958)

The path of religion is one of denial. On that path we should deny the desire for food, sleep, sex, and all the things that we like. Give up your sexual desire! Go without food and sleep! Originally, a human being should eat, sleep, and enjoy things. However, as these desires of the body lead us to death, we must reject them.

Burst a nuclear bomb in your body! Break and completely subjugate your body! The body wants to be respected and live in comfort. It dislikes harsh conditions and likes what is easy, soft and plump. But we should despise all that the body likes. We should love what is difficult, hard and rough. The body likes a high position. It is happy to eat well, even by taking someone else's money. It does not care about anyone but itself. We have to destroy such a nature. We have to bring the body down to be humble, to serve and to sacrifice. (18:66, May 21, 1967)

2. Fasting

On the tenth day of this seventh month is the Day of Atonement; it shall be for you a time of holy convocation, and you shall afflict yourselves [by fasting].

Leviticus 23.27

O believers, prescribed for you is the Fast, even as it was prescribed for those that were before you—haply you will be god-fearing—for days numbered... the month of Ramadan, wherein the Qur'an was sent down to be a guidance to the people, and as clear signs of the Guidance and the Salvation. So let those of you, who are present at the month, fast it; and if any of you be sick, or if he be on a journey, then a number of other days; God desires ease for you, and desires not hardship for you; and that you fulfill the number, and magnify God that He has guided you, and haply you will be thankful.

Qur'an 2.183-85

My son, you ought to be of some help to your fellow men, and for that reason I counsel you to fast. Our grandfather who stands in our midst sends forth all kinds of blessings. Try then and obtain one of these. Try to have one of our grandfathers, one of the War Chiefs, pity you. Then some day as you travel along the road [of life], you will know what to do and encounter no obstacles. Without any trouble you will then be able to seek the prize you desire. Then the honor will be yours to glory in, for without any exertion have you obtained it. All the war power that exists has been donated to our grandfathers who are in control of warfare, and, if, reverently, you thirst yourself to death, then they will bestow blessings upon you. Now if you do not wear out your feet, if you do not blacken your face with charcoal, it will be for naught that you inflict suffering upon yourself. These blessings are not obtainable without effort. Try to have one of all the spirits created by Earthmaker take pity upon you. Whatever he says will come about. If you do not possess a spirit to strengthen you, you will be of no consequence and the people will show you little respect.

A Winnebago Father's Precepts
(*Native American Religions*)

And when you fast, do not look dismal, like the hypocrites, for they disfigure their faces that their fasting may be seen by men. Truly, I say to you, they have received their reward. But when you fast, anoint your head and wash your face, that your fasting may not be seen by men but by your Father who is in secret; and your Father who sees in secret will reward you.

Matthew 6.16-18

Teachings of Sun Myung Moon

What does the body desire? It likes to be comfortable; that is why we are told to walk the path of suffering. Next, the body likes to eat good food; that is why religion tells us to fast. You must do the opposite of what the body desires. (40:24, February 1, 1986)

Going hungry for many days is among the most miserable and painful experiences. Yet we should transcend our hunger and yearn for God more than food.

Unification Church members are obliged to fast for seven days. Who among you has done a seven-day fast? There are many of you! Think back on your own experience: when the seventh day arrived were you watching the clock for the moment you could eat again? Were you counting down the minutes and the seconds? When the clock struck midnight, did you think, "Hooray! At last it is time to eat!"? Or at that moment did you lift your heart to God, longing for Him? Which did you crave more, God or food? Most of you probably craved for food. But actually, when you fast you should long for God more than for food.

During my thirties, I was hungry every single day. Do you know how much I longed to eat some food? If I even overheard someone talking about food, my mouth would involuntarily drop open and I would start to drool. Whenever that happened, I would say out loud, "G-o-d" rather than "F-o-o-d." You should all have such experiences. Unless you fast and conquer hunger, its power will block God's love from coming to you. (94:293, October 9, 1977)

What is required to engraft the love of God into our lives? What I fear most is the physical body. The body is the enemy. It has three supreme truths: The first is to eat. Eating when you are hungry is a truth. The problem arises when eating takes control of your life. Therefore, you should overcome the desire for food. You should establish that you love God more than eating, more than your body craves food when it is hungry. By doing so, you tap into a higher love and gain power to control your body. This is why people fast. Even Jesus fasted for forty days. All the prophets and founders of religion fasted…

The second truth is sleep. You should win over sleep. How can you find God's love by overcoming sleep? The test comes when you are getting sleepy; then you can show that you love God more than you like to sleep. Many prophets and saints exerted themselves to the utmost fighting against sleep. They would do all kinds of things to stay awake, even stab their legs with a knife, because they regarded sleep as the enemy. You, too, should adore God in a place where you overcome sleep. I slept less than two hours a day every day for more than seven years. God's love can approach you when you go over the boundary line of hunger and desire to sleep…

The third truth is sex… (94:275, October 9, 1977)

3. Celibacy

[Jesus] said to them, "Not all men can receive this saying, but only those to whom it is given. For there are eunuchs who have been so from birth, and there are eunuchs who have been made eunuchs by men, and there are eunuchs who have made themselves eunuchs for the sake of the kingdom of Heaven. He who is able to receive this, let him receive it."

Matthew 19.12

For in the resurrection they neither marry nor are given in marriage, but are like angels in heaven.

Matthew 22.30

Both learning and the practice of the Teaching are lost to him who is given to sexual intercourse. He employs himself wrongly. That is what is ignoble in him.

Sutta Nipata 815 (Buddhism)

The unmarried man is anxious about the Lord, how to please the Lord; but the married man is anxious about worldly affairs, how to please his wife, and his interests are divided. And the unmarried woman or virgin is anxious about the affairs of the Lord, how to be holy in body and spirit; but the married woman is anxious about worldly affairs, how to please her husband. I say this for your own benefit, not to lay any restraint upon you, but to promote good order and to secure your undivided devotion to the Lord.

1 Corinthians 7.32-35

Free from selfish attachment, they do not get compulsively entangled even in home and family... Enjoying solitude and not following the crowd, they seek only me.

Bhagavad-Gita 13.9-10 (Hinduism)

I renounce all sexual pleasures, either with gods or men or animals. I shall not give way to sensuality, nor cause others to give way to it, nor consent to their giving way to it, as long as I live.

Acarangasutra 24 (Jainism)

Having abandoned the different kinds of desire, founded on child, wife, father, mother, wealth, corn, relations, let one walk alone like a rhinoceros.

Sutta Nipata 60 (Buddhism)

Teachings of Sun Myung Moon

[Due to the Fall,] the human ancestors were caught in the enemy's trap. Can God publicly recognize families formed in this realm? This is why religions have emphasized celibacy. Some of you gathered here have many sons and daughters, but you also should have led celibate lives. This is not just my word; is it not taught in Buddhism and Catholicism? Do you know why? It brings people closer to God.

The first ancestors of humankind were unable to have their proper wedding ceremony before God. In that sense, none of us human beings have truly been born; how then can we have weddings? As descendants of the Fall, we must first go the path of restoration and receive the grace of salvation. (21:45-46, September 1, 1968)

In order to uphold the heavenly ideal of love, God had no choice but to form religions that exalted the celibate life. Men and women are meant to follow true love and become husbands and wives who meet the heavenly standard, but because of our ancestors' mistake that betrayed Heaven's love, they cannot. Therefore, God set up the way of celibacy, so that at least single persons could receive the love of God by following the celibate way of life. (*Blessing and Ideal Family* 2.2.4)

From the perspective of the Divine Principle, all men and women in this world are offspring of the archangel.[22] Therefore, they are not qualified to marry. For this reason, God encouraged people to live a life of celibacy. God could not marry the first parents. How then can He approve of marriages between impure, slovenly people who have fallen into a puddle of sewage? Such love is unprincipled. This is why the higher religions emphasize celibacy. (25:203, October 4, 1969)

Do angels have spouses? No. That is why religions so far have encouraged the celibate life. The Buddha's original standard that monks and nuns should not marry is in accord with the Principle. These days some Buddhist monks and nuns marry, but by doing so they fall short of the standard. In fact, married Protestant clergy also fall short. (*Blessing and Ideal Family* 2.2.4)

Archangels are not yet qualified to marry. In the Bible, the Sadducees asked Jesus, "There were seven brothers; the first married, and died, and having no children left his wife to his brother. So too the second and the third, down to the seventh. After them all, the woman died. In the resurrection to which of the seven will she be wife? For they all had her." Jesus answered, "In the resurrection they neither marry nor are given in marriage, but are like angels in heaven." (Matt. 22:25-30) Jesus answered that way because it was still the age of restoring the archangelic realm, a realm where people cannot yet have a marriage partner. Because religion has been in the archangelic realm, it could not exalt marriage.[23] This is the reason higher religions have emphasized the celibate life. (50:193, November 7, 1971)

4. The Problem with Asceticism—Lack of Love

If I give away all I have, and if I deliver my body to be burned, but have not love, I gain nothing.

1 Corinthians 13.2-3

If a man should go naked…feed on potherbs, wild rice, or Nivara seeds…wear coarse hempen cloth, or carry out any other [ascetic] practices…yet the state of blissful attainment in conduct, in heart, in intellect, have not been practiced by him, realized by him, then he is far from shramanaship, far from brahminship. But from the time, O Kassapa, when a monk has cultivated the heart of love that knows no anger, that knows no ill will—from the time when, by the destruction of the deadly intoxications, he dwells in that emancipation of heart, that emancipation of mind, that is free from those intoxications, and that he, while yet in this visible world, has come to realize and know—from that time, O Kassapa, is it that the monk is called a shramana, is called a brahmin!

Digha Nikaya 1.167 (*Buddhism*)

Some invent harsh penances. Motivated by hypocrisy and egoism, they torture their innocent bodies and Me who dwells within. Blinded by their strength and passion, they act and think like demons.[24]

Bhagavad-Gita 17.5-6

O brother, wither away your sensuality, passions, and egotism. There is no benefit in emaciating this gross body [through penances]. We will never praise you merely because of your withered body.

Nisitha-bhasya 3758 (*Jainism*)

Should one perform a million ritual acts and of these be proud,
they leave him only fatigued, and are of little avail.
One who performs innumerable austerities and for these bears pride,
shall remain caught in transmigration, moving between heaven and hell.
With all a man's effort, should his self not turn compassionate,
How may he have access to the Divine Portal?

Adi Granth, Gauri Sukhmani 12, M.5, p. 278 (*Sikhism*)

There was a great seer of strict vows, foremost of those wise in the law, the learned ascetic

Mandapala. He followed the path of the seers who held up their seed [in chastity], austere and master of his senses. After he had abandoned his body, he attained to the world of the ancestors. Yet he failed to find the fruit of his acts there. Finding his worlds without reward, although he had won them with his asceticism, he questioned the celestials: "Why are these worlds that I won with my austerities closed to me? Where did I fail that this should be the results of my acts?" They said, "Men are born indebted to rites, to the study of the Veda, and to offspring, doubt it not. You are an ascetic and a sacrificer, but you have no offspring; these worlds are closed to you because of this matter of offspring. A son saves his father from the hell called *Put*, Hermit. Therefore, O brahmin, strive for the continuity of children!"[25]

Mahabharata 1.220 (Hinduism)

We sent Jesus son of Mary, and gave him the Gospel, and placed compassion and mercy in the hearts of those who followed him. But monasticism they invented—We ordained it not for them—only seeking God's pleasure, and they observed it not with right observance. We give those who believe their reward, but many of them are evil-livers.[26]

Qur'an 57.27

Then the disciples of John came to him, saying, "Why do we and the Pharisees fast, but your disciples do not fast?" And Jesus said to them, "Can the wedding guests mourn as long as the bridegroom is with them?"

Matthew 9.14-15

Let us rejoice and exult and give him the glory, for the marriage of the Lamb has come, and his Bride has made herself ready; it was granted her to be clothed with fine linen, bright and pure—
for the fine linen is the righteous deeds of the saints.

Revelation 19.7-8

Teachings of Sun Myung Moon

Can celibacy as taught by Catholicism and Buddhism be the basis of human happiness? No. Yet no religion on earth has demonstrated what the basis of happiness is. Religions did not uphold the family as the basis because no family had appeared that was worthy of that position. However, sensing that one day such a family would appear, they emphasized celibacy. It was the foundation for people to form a pure and correct family. (*Blessing and Ideal Family* 2.2.4)

God intended man and woman to live in perfect love and perfect eternity, without the slightest separation. God is perfect and eternal; the position of children is perfect and eternal, and therefore God wanted the positions of husband and wife to be perfect and eternal. Is passionate lovemaking divine or sinful? After the Fall, human love became dirty and stained. Has humankind ever seen perfect love under God, manifesting the purpose of God?

Who has really known the purpose of religion and salvation? Many religious people feel that the world is filled with filthiness; therefore they separate themselves from it and live a solitary life. It is often thought that a religious, divine life is a solitary life, but we must realize that the Kingdom of God in heaven and on earth has been ready for a long, long time, from the very beginning of creation, and it is just waiting to be occupied. The problem has been to find occupants fit for that kingdom. (99:225, April 17, 1977)

We enter the Kingdom of Heaven as married couples, as families, as clans extending out to third cousins, and as whole nations. Ultimately the entire world will be Heaven. This is the way of the

Unification Church. Its goal is not individual salvation. Consistent with this principle, the church holds mass weddings. Today these mass weddings are objects of mockery and curiosity, but to anyone who knows their content, they are amazing phenomena.

Marriage was not recognized during the religious age of the archangel. But we are now entering the age of marriage, and marriage in the Kingdom of Heaven as well. The time has come when the married Buddhist priest will win over the Buddhist monk. In the Roman Catholic Church the priests and nuns are fast disappearing; if Catholic priests and nuns remain single, they will end up in hell. Now, when universal fortune seeks the bond of bride and bridegroom, Catholic priests and nuns must get married; otherwise, they will perish. (50:31, October 3, 1971)

If I, Reverend Moon, do not encourage celibate Buddhist monks and Catholic priests and nuns to marry now, monasteries will very soon become arenas of free sex. Flirtations and illicit affairs will cause many to fall away. When the Buddhist and Catholic religions bring millions of monks and nuns to receive the Marriage Blessing, then they will come alive. Otherwise, they will die out.

Some priests are having illicit affairs. Others are getting married despite their vows. Why is that? Since the time has come, their minds are pulled in that direction. When the high tide comes in, you have to move with the tide and walk back to the shore; otherwise you will drown. Now the tide is coming in, and those priests who were used to standing up at low tide are being forced to turn around and marry in order to keep from swallowing water. (246:24, March 23, 1993)

The internal reason why the higher religions have advocated celibacy is because the True Parents of humankind had not yet come and instituted marriage before God. But now the Unification Church has appeared as the first religion in history to promote marriages approved by God, and it began to hold mass weddings. Hence, from now on Buddhism will have more married monks. The same is happening in the Catholic Church. The reason why the Catholic Church faces problems today is because it still does not permit its priests to marry. If it continues this way, they will all leave the church.

These problems arose particularly after 1960, the year the True Parents were married. From that year, everything began to change. This change permeated the non-religious world as well, and it entered the era of free sex. In the non-religious world the family is being destroyed through free sex, while the sphere of religion is entering the age of marriage. (244:148, February 1, 1993)

PART FOUR

FAMILY AND SOCIETY

CHAPTER 19

Family

The Basic Form of Life

THE FAMILY IS THE BASIC FORM OF LIFE. Its relations constitute the environment where people are reared, molding their character, values and identities. People sometimes try to set up alternatives to the traditional family, but these fail to persist beyond one or two generations. There is a "form" to the family; not in the sense of a precise set of roles, but rather a general principle that even single-parent families, childless families and families blended with stepparents and other relations take after as best they can. What is the "form" of the family? Outwardly, it consists of the pattern of relationships linking parents and children, husband and wife, and siblings; inwardly, it is the true, godly love that governs these relationships.

There is another sense in which the family is the basic form of life: it is the "textbook" for relationships in the larger society. Good family relations are productive of good citizens, who apply the lessons of relating with elder, same-age and younger family members to their relations with superiors, peers and subordinates.

Father Moon teaches extensively about both aspects of the family's form. He characterizes its structural pattern as the "four-position foundation," a notable teaching because it brings God into the family as a veritable member. He also describes the family spatially as extending in six directions. In either case, the form is spherical and characterized by equality of all positions. This is possible when the dynamic in all the family relations is true love. Each family member lives for the sake of the others, creating a virtuous circle of giving that generates energy and equalizes all. Such families are the building-blocks of virtuous societies.

1. The Family Ideal

He who loves his wife as himself; who honors her more than himself; who rears his children in the right path, and who marries them off at the proper time of their life, concerning him it is written: "And you will know that your home is at peace."

Talmud, Yebamot 62 (Judaism)

Supporting one's father and mother, cherishing wife and children and a peaceful occupation; this is the greatest blessing.

Sutta Nipata 262 (Buddhism)

There are five relations of utmost importance under Heaven... between prince and minister; between father and son; between husband and wife; between elder and younger brothers; and between friends.[1]

Doctrine of the Mean 20.8 (Confucianism)

What are "the things which men consider right"? Kindness on the part of the father, and filial duty on that of the son; gentleness on the part of the elder brother, and obedience on that of the younger; righteousness on the part of the husband, and submission on that of the wife; kindness on the part of elders, and deference on that of juniors; with benevolence on the part of the ruler, and loyalty on that of the minister; —these ten are the things which men consider to be right.

Book of Ritual 7.2.19 (Confucianism)

May in this family discipline overcome indiscipline, peace discord, charity miserliness, devotion arrogance, the truth-spoken word the false spoken word which destroys the holy order.

Avesta, Yasna 60.5 (Zoroastrianism)

Natural mildness should be there in the family. Observance of the vows leads to mildness... Right belief should there be amongst family members. Crookedness and deception cause unhappiness in the family. Straightforwardness and honesty in one's body, speech, and mental activities lead the family to an auspicious path. Purity, reverence, ceaseless pursuit of knowledge, charity, removal of obstacles that threaten equanimity, service to others—these make the family happy.

Tattvarthasutra 6.18-24 (Jainism)

When father, mother, sons, elder and younger brothers all act in a manner suited to their various positions within the family, when husbands play their proper role and wives are truly wifely, the way of that family runs straight. It is by the proper regulation of each family that the whole world is stabilized.

I Ching 37 (Confucianism)

The union of hearts and minds and freedom from hate I'll bring you.
Love one another as the cow loves the calf that she has borne.
Let son be loyal to father, and of one mind with his mother;
let wife speak to husband words that are honey-sweet and gentle.

Let not a brother hate a brother, nor a sister hate a sister;
unanimous, united in aims, speak you words with friendliness.
I will make the prayer for that concord among men at home
by which the gods do not separate, nor ever hate one another.

Be not parted—growing old, taking thought,
thriving together, moving under a common yoke,
come speaking sweetly to one another;
I'll make you have one aim and be of one mind.

Common be your water-store, common your share of food;
I bind you together to a common yoke.
United, gather round the sacrificial fire
like spokes around the nave of a wheel.

With your common desire I'll make you all have one aim,
be of one mind, following one leader,
like the gods who preserve their immortality.
Morn and eve may there be the loving heart in you.[2]

Atharva Veda 3.30 (Hinduism)

Teachings of Sun Myung Moon

Human beings have a basic need to feel and connect with each other. For this, we need wives and husbands; we need young people and old people. This is why, regardless of the world's opinion, we have worked to establish the family as a universal form. (21:120, November 17, 1968)

A family should have both a father and a mother, and both sons and daughters. Only then can it be the complete foundation for happiness... when all the varieties of heart are present in the family. (32:197, July 15, 1970)

Neither men nor women were created for their own sakes, but for the sake of their partners of the opposite sex. Let us say that there is a beautiful woman who hates men. Yet when you look at her figure, it is clear that God gave her beauty for the sake of a man. God designed each sex to live for the sake of its opposite.

Likewise, when parents live for the sake of the children and the children for the sake of the parents, taking good care of each other, they revolve around each other. The more they live for each other, they faster they revolve. This is the ideal form—not a square, but round and three-dimensional. Each adds to the other's energy; hence the more we live for each other the faster our circular motion becomes. The family forms a sphere and can continue that way for eternity. (69:83-84, October 20, 1973)

The family is the smallest unit where we can practice and perfect the Four Great Loves—the Four Great Hearts: true parental love, true brotherly and sisterly love, true conjugal love, and true filial love. A true family is the foundation of its members' true love and true happiness. It is where true life and true lineage sprouts. A true family is the training ground and school to achieve true love and true character. (294:65-66, June 11, 1998)

God's love abides where parents, husband and wife, and children are united in love. Where these three kinds of love come together, God dwells absolutely and for eternity. This family is God's dwelling-place. Wherever there is unchanging parental love, unchanging conjugal love, and unchanging children's love, God is always present. (131:112, April 22, 1984)

What is an ideal family? Some might say, "It is a family whose members all trust each other." Some might say, "It is a family whose members know each other well." These descriptions fall short. An ideal family is a family whose members are connected with an inseparable bond of heart. It is a family whose members feel each other's pain as their own, or even more deeply than their own pain. Hence they willingly sacrifice themselves to carry the others' burden. Such a family can be called an ideal family. (228:46, March 3, 1992)

Human beings are born from love and should walk the path of love. Even at the point of death, they should die for love. From this perspective, love is more valuable than life itself; it even precedes life. That is why people willingly give their lives for love.

Love is eternal. Eternal, unchanging love is celebrated in poetry, novels and great literature. These prompt us to desire eternal and unchanging love, not momentary love.

A newborn baby automatically searches for its mother's breast, following the vibrations of her love. The infant does not care whether she is beautiful or ugly; all that matters is that she is its mother. An infant nursing at its mother's breast is a sacred scene, manifested in limitless variety.

Thus, we are born from love, and we grow by receiving love. Each of us is the fruit of our parents' love and the manifestation of their love. Our parents love us because we are the fruit of their love. Parental love can expand infinitely, producing innumerable fruits. It is the starting point on the road to individual love, family love, love for the tribe, love of country, love for the world, love for the universe and love for God.

After we are born, our parents take responsibility to raise us to become good people for our sojourn on earth. Our parents provide for us and teach us, acting not only on behalf of the family, but also on behalf of the nation and the world. They provide us with physical sustenance and education until we reach the age of individual maturity. That is when we should link to the horizontal foundation of love, which is marriage.

Parents take care of us until we marry. In marriage we inherit the love our mother and father have shared in their life together. When we give birth to our own children and start rearing them, we finally begin to understand how much our parents loved us, and thus we inherit parental love. Through this process, we develop into people who can fully give and receive love. This is how each of us matures as a perfected man or woman.

From infancy to the time of maturity, we grow in the love of our parents—a vertical love. Then the time comes to experience conjugal love—a mutual, horizontal love. In this way we enter the integrated realm of love. Heaven and earth together form a spherical world, covering all the dimensions of top and bottom, left and right, and front and back. When the vertical and horizontal love relationships are linked, they interact, revolve, become integrated, and finally merge into a single center of harmony.

The vertical axis of love links Heaven and earth. Once it is firmly secured, there arises the need for horizontal love. This takes place during adolescence. (298:298, March 19, 1999)

When a husband and wife truly love each other and build a family, it symbolizes the planting of God. In the original world, the parents represent God, with husband and wife each embodying a different side of God. Each of their sons and daughters represents another small God. Since God is the original entity of true love, by embodying true love each member of the family becomes one with God. Parents are the living embodiments of God and thus represent Him [to their children]. Husband and wife each represent God [to each other], and the children represent Him as well. Thus three generations, centering on true love, are at the level of God.

This is why all the family members—parents, husbands and wives, and children—need true love. A family formed in this way, centering on true love, is the foundation for the Kingdom of Heaven. Unless we first make such a foundation, the Kingdom of Heaven can never be established. This is the formula... God, the Parent of the entire universe, abides in the center of these manifold relationships of love. (298:307, March 19, 1999)

2. The Family as the School of Love and Virtue

Lord, give us joy in our wives and children, and make us models for the God-fearing.

Qur'an 25.74

The moral life of man may be likened to traveling to a distant place: one must start from the s stage. It may also be likened to ascending a height [of public responsibility]: one must begin from the lowest step [one's family].

Doctrine of the Mean 15.2 (Confucianism)

If a man does not know how to manage his own household, how can he care for God's church?

1 Timothy 3.5

What is meant by saying that "in order to establish moral order in his state, one must first guide his family properly" is this: One cannot convince others of what he cannot convince the members of his own family. Therefore the wise governor does not need to go beyond his family in order to find the principles needed for governing his state. Here he finds his own son's respectful obedience to his father, with which a governor should be served; affection for one's relatives, with which higher officials should be treated; and paternal kindness, with which all people should be regarded.

Great Learning 9.1 (Confucianism)

When the family declines, ancient traditions are destroyed. With them are lost the spiritual foundations for life, and the family loses its sense of unity. Where there is no sense of unity, the women of the family become corrupt; and with the corruption of its women, society is plunged into chaos. Social chaos is hell for the family and for those who have destroyed the family as well.

Bhagavad-Gita 1.40-41 (Hinduism)

Teachings of Sun Myung Moon

The family is the most important school in human life, for it is the school of love. (271:80, August 22, 1995)

The family is the training ground of the heart. You are trained in brotherly and sisterly love, so treat your classmates in school with that same heart and your fellow citizens in the nation with that same heart. Hence, the education your parents give you to be loving brothers and sisters is for the sake of the school, the community and the nation.

Parents should bequeath their heart and sensibility to their children and descendants. As parents you are role models, but this involves more than teaching by example. By your love you are laying the emotional foundation for your children, so that they are able to live for the family, the community and the nation. (180:131, August 22, 1988)

The ideal family is a school; it is also a textbook. The husband and wife are its joint authors. When their children can live by the lessons from that textbook, they can make it anywhere in the world. This is a formula. (131:112, April 22, 1984)

The family is the textbook for attaining the Kingdom of Heaven. God prepared it for human beings as an instruction manual for connecting with Him. If you take its lessons and apply them to the nation, you become patriots; apply them to the world and you become saints; apply them to heaven and earth and you become the divine sons and daughters of God. (137:78, December 18, 1985)

Morals are the universal virtues acquired by training in the family. The Chinese character for virtue (德) contains the character 十, ten, with the shape of a cross whose vertical and horizontal lines symbolize heaven and earth—hence the entire universe, as well as man and woman—two beings. Next it has the character 四, four, which represents the four-position foundation; then 一, one, and 心, mind or heart. It means that virtues (德) are established when the four (四) parties of the four-position foundation of heaven and earth (十) become one (一) in heart (心). Since the character 十 means ten and also two, it symbolizes twelve entities: grandfather, grandmother, husband, wife, son and daughter, six people each composed of mind and body. When these twelve become one, they indicate virtue. (375:59, April 13, 2002)

All around the world today, the family is changing, and the traditional family structure is being challenged in many ways. With increasing industrialization and modernization, humanity's value systems are crumbling, and our standards of ethics and morality are in flux. In addition, selfish individualism, hedonism, and the worship of money are robbing us of our humanity, and increasingly free sex and immorality are furthering the destruction of the family.

How tragic it is that we are faced with such trends! If nothing is done, in the future humanity will not have any hope. No matter how social conditions may change, the importance of the relationship between parents and children is unshakable. The value of the family does not change. I repeat—love is the source of people's happiness and joy, and the family is the foundation for happiness and peace. (271:80-81, August 22, 1995)

These days, when we prevent families from breaking down and teenagers from falling, we liberate God's sorrowful heart. It brings God the happiness that He could not experience in the Garden of Eden, where He could not intervene [to stop the Fall]. (305:273, August 21, 1998)

3. A Complete Family Has a Spherical Form

Thus I have heard, the Buddha was once staying near Rajagaha in the Bamboo Wood at the Squirrels' Feeding Ground. Now at this time young Sigala, a householder's son, rising betimes, went forth from Rajagaha, and with wet hair and wet garments and clasped hands uplifted, paid worship to the several quarters of the earth and sky: to the east, south, west, and north, to the nadir and the zenith.

And the Exalted One early that morning dressed himself, took bowl and robe and entered Rajagaha seeking alms. Now he saw young Sigala worshipping and spoke to him thus,

"Why, young householder, do you worship the several quarters of earth and sky?"

"Sir, my father, when he was dying, said to me: 'Dear son, you should worship the quarters of the earth and sky.' So I, sir, honoring my father's word, rise and worship in this way."

"But in the religion of an educated man, the six quarters should not be worshipped thus."

"How then, sir, in the religion of an educated man, should the six quarters be worshipped? It would be an excellent thing if the Exalted One would so teach me the correct way…"

"How, O young householder, does the educated man serve the six quarters? The following should be looked upon as the six quarters: parents as the east, teachers as the south, wife and children as the west, friends and companions as the north, servants as the nadir, and religious leaders as the zenith.

"In five ways should a child minister to his parents as the eastern quarter: 'Once supported by them, I will now be their support; I will perform duties incumbent on them; I will keep up the lineage and tradition of my family; I will make myself worthy of my heritage.'

"In five ways parents thus ministered to, as the eastern quarter, by their child, show their love for him: They restrain him from vice, they exhort him to virtue, they train him to a profession, they contract a suitable marriage for him, and in due time they hand over to him his inheritance. Thus is the eastern quarter protected by him and made safe and secure.

"In five ways should pupils minister to their teachers as the southern quarter: by respectfully greeting them, by waiting upon them, by eagerness to learn, by personal service, and by attentiveness to their teaching.

"In five ways do teachers, thus ministered to as the southern quarter by their pupils, love their pupil: They train him in what they have been trained; they make him hold fast to moral precepts; they thoroughly instruct him in the lore of every subject; they speak well of him among his friends and companions; they counsel him for his safety and benefit. Thus is the southern quarter protected by him and made safe and secure.

"In five ways should a wife as western quarter be ministered to by her husband: by respect, by courtesy, by faithfulness, by handing over authority to her, by providing her with adornment.

"In five ways does the wife, ministered to by her husband as the western quarter, love him:

Her duties are well performed, she is hospitable to their relatives, she is faithful, she watches over the wages and goods which he brings home, she discharges all her business with skill and industry. Thus is the western quarter protected by him and made safe and secure.

"In five ways should one minister to his friends and companions as the northern quarter: by generosity, courtesy, and benevolence, by treating them as he treats himself, and by being as good as his word.

"In five ways do his friends and familiars, thus ministered to as the northern quarter, love him: They protect him when he is off his guard, and on occasions guard his property; they become a refuge in danger; they do not forsake him in his troubles; and they show consideration for his family. Thus is the northern quarter protected by him and made safe and secure.

"In five ways does a noble master minister to his servants and employees as the nadir: by assigning them work according to their strength, by supplying them with food and wages, by tending them in sickness, by sharing with them unusual delicacies, by granting them leave at times.

"In five ways, thus ministered to by their master, do servants and employees love him: They rise before him, they lie down to rest after him, they are content with their wages, they do their work well, and they carry about his praise and good fame. Thus is the nadir by him protected and made safe and secure.

"In five ways should the layman minister to saints, priests, and religious leaders as the zenith: by affection in act and speech and mind, by keeping open house to them, and by supplying their temporal needs.

"Ministered to as the zenith, monks, priests, and religious leaders show their love for the layman in six ways: They restrain him from evil, they exhort him to good, they love him with kindly thoughts, they teach him what he has not heard, they correct and purify what he has heard, they reveal to him the way of heaven. Thus by him is the zenith protected and made safe and secure."

Digha Nikaya 3.185-91, Sigalovada Sutta
(Buddhism)

Teachings of Sun Myung Moon

To exist in the spatial dimension, human beings need to stand in relation to what is above and below, right and left, front and back... Centering on the individual, in the family there are parents and children, husband and wife, and brothers and sisters. Similarly, in the nation, centering on the leader, families should embrace all the civilizations of East and West and all the civilizations of North and South. Then they can embrace all people of the world as brothers and sisters. Ultimately we will form a global family at every level.

Thus, the core concept of the universe is the concept of the family. Heaven represents parents. Earth represents children. East symbolizes man, West symbolizes woman. That is why, when a woman gets married, she usually follows wherever her husband goes. Nevertheless, they have equal value—when the west reflects the sunlight, it has the same value as the east. The relationship of brothers is the same. When the older brother works on some task, the younger brothers naturally help him.

Therefore, human beings should exist within relationships of parents and children, husband and wife, and elder and younger siblings. And these three relationships meet at one central point. There can be only one center. Above and below, right and left, and front and back should not have different centers. If the central point is different, then the balance of the relationships between above and below, right and left, and front and back will be broken. Eventually, above, below, right, left, front, back and the central point all together comprise seven positions. In a harmonious and unified family these seven form a perfect sphere; they constitute a God-centered family with all elements united in perfect true love. (*True Family and World Peace*, June 16, 1997)

An ideal family is one whose family members are united as one centered on their parents and in attendance to God.

Conjugal love is a horizontal relationship; therefore a husband and wife should align their love on the vertical axis of God's love. God is the owner of parental love, children's love, husband's love and wife's love. God's love is the ideal love. Since God is the subject of love, if we become one with God, we can always embody God's love. Then we can create an ideal family that will never break apart for eternity. It is logical.

Parental love is focused on children and children's love is connected to parents. A husband's love is connected to his wife, and a wife's love is connected to her husband. These different types of love cannot become one by themselves. The subjective force that can unify them is God's love. Once the Subject dwells in them, they all automatically become one. Conversely, without God, human love is self-centered and cannot bring unity.

Although the family members have diverse relationships with each other, when they are united in love, they are equally close to one another. Hence there is equality among them. Why? They participate in a unified entity with a spherical form. The cause and result become one; and the vertical and the horizontal become one; God and the family members become one. In the world that runs on the power of love, there is nothing but love. Whatever they do, there is nothing but love. Such is the ideal world. When families on earth reach that state, they create the Kingdom of Heaven on earth. This is the ideal of God.

Based on this principle, I teach you to respect your parents as God. Husbands should respect their wives as God, and wives should regard their husbands as God. Parents should value their children as God. Likewise, you should experience God as your Parent, your Wife, your Husband, and your Child. This is the path to the Kingdom of God. (89:154-55, November 7, 1976)

Why does a wife weep when her husband dies? Why are people sorrowful if they have no sons or daughters? The fundamental principle of the universe is that we have to possess all the directions of the compass.

Ideal relationships generate the very power that enables the universe to exist. Therefore, everything engages in give and take. The North Pole and the South Pole engage in give and take; the stars have give and take with each other. In sum, everything exists in relationship to a counterpart.

The ideal for any existing being is to engage in complete give and take, and thereby gain the support of the universe. We say that it has the support of 'heavenly fortune.' This is the universe's supporting power that surrounds the existing being and maintains its existence forever. All existence cooperates with it.

Therefore, it will not do if a family has no children. These days in the West, many people think that children are unnecessary. But just let them wait until they go to the spirit world; then they will see whether what I say is true. Wherever a person stands, there is always an above (parents) and a below (children). Everyone needs to pass through the number 3, that is, through these three stages. (70:76-77, February 8, 1974)

The family is the smallest unit that connects the past, the present and the future. A family is like a microcosm of the world. Within it the past, the present and the future are linked together—this refers to the interdependence of grandfather, father and son. When a son has children and becomes a father, at the same moment the father becomes a grandfather. These three generations—representing the past, the present and the future—should be united as one. Such a family can establish a base for lasting happiness. It has the power to repulse Satan's attacks, regardless of the turmoil in the world. (28:162, January 11, 1970)

Filial Piety

FILIAL PIETY IS THE AGE-OLD MORAL PRINCIPLE that children show respect and honor to their parents. It is the parents' due, for they have sacrificed and labored for their children's sake, giving them birth, feeding them and providing them with a good start in life. Therefore, filial children do not regard it as an imposition to care for their parents in their old age. Ideally this is not regarded as a matter of duty, but as the spontaneous and natural prompting of a grateful heart.

Among Father Moon's extensive teachings about filial piety are these: Filial should be encouraged as an enduring tradition that links the generations in an unbroken chain of lineage. Filial piety is perfected in a mature unselfish mind of the adult child who sympathizes with his parents' difficulties and sufferings and recognizes them to be more serious then his or her own small problems. Most importantly, filial piety is a doorway to a deeper relationship with God, our divine Parent.

1. Filial Piety as the Root of Virtue

Honor your father and your mother, that your days may be long in the land which the LORD your God gives you.

Exodus 20.12

There are three partners in man, God, father, and mother. When a man honors his father and mother, God says, "I regard it as though I had dwelt among them and they had honored me."

Talmud, Kiddushin 30b (Judaism)

Do not neglect the sacrificial works due to the gods and the fathers! Let your mother be to you like unto a god! Let your father be to you like unto a god! Let your teacher be to you like unto a god!

Taittiriyaka Upanishad 1.11.2 (Hinduism)

Thy Lord has decreed... that you be kind to parents. Whether one or both of them attain old age in your lifetime, do not say to them a word of contempt, nor repel them, but address them in terms of honor. And, out of kindness, lower to them the wing of humility, and say, "My Lord! Bestow on them Thy mercy even as they cherished me in childhood."

Qur'an 17.23

The superior man works upon the trunk. When that is firmly set up, the Way grows. And surely proper behavior towards parents and elder brothers is the trunk of Goodness?

Analects 1.2 (Confucianism)

Those who wish to be born in [the Pure Land] of Buddha... should act filially towards their parents and support them, and should serve and respect their teachers and elders.

Meditation on Buddha Amitayus 27 (Buddhism)

This do I ask, O Lord; reveal to me the truth. Who fashioned piety in addition to dominion? Who made a son respectful and attentive to his father?

Avesta, Yasna 44.7 (Zoroastrianism)

Now filial piety is the root of all virtue, and the stem out of which grows all moral teaching... Our bodies—to every hair and bit of skin—are received by us from our parents, and we must not presume to injure or wound them: this is the beginning of filial piety. When we have established our character by the practice of the filial course, so as to make our name famous in future ages, and thereby glorify our parents: this is the end of filial piety. It commences with the service of parents; it proceeds to the service of the ruler; it is completed by the establishment of [good] character.

Classic on Filial Piety 1 *(Confucianism)*

If your parents take care of you up to the time you cut your teeth, you take care of them when they lose theirs.

Akan Proverb *(African Traditional Religions)*

Teachings of Sun Myung Moon

Filial piety cannot be practiced with a self-centered attitude. (62:37, September 10, 1972)

Who is a filial child? He or she always thinks of what his or her parents want most and then acts upon it, taking the position of their object partner. The eyes of a filial child see the things his or her parents would like to see. The ears of a filial child hear the sounds his or her parents would like to hear. The heart of a filial child has feelings his or her parents would like to feel. In other words, filial children love centered on their parents' five senses, always yearning for the realm of their parents' heart. They only want what is good for their parents, never anything bad. And when their parents have something good, they try to make it even better. (161:132, January 18, 1987)

A son or daughter who worries more about his or her parents' cares and difficulties than about his or her own can be called a filial son or daughter. On the other hand, a son who always expects his parents to worry about his troubles, never concerned that they have their own difficulties, is not truly united with his parents.

According to the principle of filial piety, the child who habitually ignores his parents' situation will fail to properly respond to his parents at the crucial moment when they desperately need his help. Though the son clings to his parents, continually imploring them to recognize and resolve his difficulties, at the crucial moment he will be a treacherous son. We experience this in our daily life.

Filial piety starts when a child worries about his parents' difficulties more than his own, adding theirs to his own, and accepts this as a matter of course. On the other hand, when the child ignores his parents' difficulties, a breach occurs in the relationship. The way of impiety starts there. (62:187, September 25, 1972)

A filial son takes responsibility for his parents' sorrow. He goes to difficult places in order to resolve their sorrow, that they might rejoice. If his parents work ten hours and the son works fifteen, the parents will feel joy corresponding to the extra five. Thus, a filial son considers how to supplement what is missing. He serves his parents, trying his best. (24:261, August 24, 1969)

What should you do in order to become a filial son or daughter? You should always keep your mind and heart in line with the direction of your parents' heart. A child who walks the path of filial piety does not act apart from his parents. If his parents go east, he goes east, and if his parents go west, he goes west. Should his parents suddenly turn back, he turns back without dissent. Even if they change their direction ten times, he still follows them.

If you resist and complain, "Father and mother, I don't like this. What kind of parents are you, changing your minds so impulsively?" then you will not be able to keep the way of filial piety all the way to the end. Even when your parents do something that seems crazy, you should still follow your parents' direction. It might seem that they are mad, but your parents know what they are doing and why they are doing it.

Sometimes parents act capriciously to test their children, to pick the most filial child from among them... Therefore, you should take your parents' follies as your vocation. (62:32-33, December 18, 1985)

When educating children, parents should not teach them only to love their parents. They should explain to their children, "I am a loyal patriot who loves this nation. I'm not a mother first, but a patriotic mother; I'm not only a father, but a loyal citizen." In order to teach filial piety, parents should behave with filial piety themselves.[3] Otherwise, their children will fall like autumn leaves. (26:296, November 10, 1969)

People have traditionally brought up their children to put the benefit of their own families first, but this is upside-down. Rather, we should train our children first to please Heaven, then please the world, then please the nation and the community, and after that, to please our family. That is the original principle. But our way of life has become upside-down due to the Human Fall. (8:105, November 22, 1959)

2. The Inseparable Bond between Parents and Children

We have enjoined on man kindness to his parents: In pain did his mother bear him, and in pain did she give him birth. The carrying of the child to his weaning is thirty months. At length, when he reaches the age of full strength and attains forty years, he says, "O my Lord! Grant me that I may be grateful for Your favor which You have bestowed upon me, and upon both my parents, and that I may work righteousness such as You may approve; and be gracious to me in my issue. Truly have I turned to You and truly do I bow to You in Islam."

Such are they from whom We shall accept the best of their deeds and pass by their ill deeds: they shall be among the Companions of the Garden: a promise of truth, which was made to them. Paradise, holding the true promise which has been given them.

Qur'an 46.15-16

Brethren, one can never repay two persons, I declare. What two? Mother and father. Even if one should carry about his mother on one shoulder and his father on the other, and so doing should live a hundred years; and if he should support them, anointing them with unguents, kneading and rubbing their limbs, and they meanwhile should even void their excrements upon him—even so could he not repay his parents. Moreover, if he should establish his parents in supreme authority, in the absolute rule over this mighty earth abounding in the seven treasures—not even thus could he repay his parents. Why not? Brethren, parents do much for their children; they bring them up, they nourish them, they introduce them to this world.

However, brethren, whoso incites his unbelieving parents, settles and establishes them in the faith; whoso incites his immoral parents, settles and establishes them in morality; whoso incites his stingy parents, settles and establishes them in liberality; whoso incites his foolish parents, settles and establishes them in wisdom—such a one, just by so doing, does repay, does more than repay what is due to his parents.

Anguttara Nikaya 1.61 (Buddhism)

One companion asked, "O Apostle of God! Who is the person worthiest of my consideration?" He replied, "Your mother." He asked again, "And second to my mother?" The Prophet said, "Your mother." The companion insisted, "And then?" The Messenger of God said, "After your mother, your father."

Hadith of Bukhari and Muslim (Islam)

Son, why do you quarrel with your father,
Due to him you have grown to this age?
It is a sin to argue with him.

Adi Granth, Sarang, M.4, p. 1200 (Sikhism)

Hearken to your father who begot you,
and do not despise your mother when she is old.
Buy truth, and do not sell it;
buy wisdom, instruction, and understanding.
The father of the righteous will greatly rejoice;
he who begets a wise son will be glad in him.
Let your father and mother be glad,
let her who bore you rejoice.

Proverbs 23.22-25

My father, thank you for petting me;
My mother, thank you for making me comfortable;
Thank you for robing me with wisdom, which is more important than robing me with clothes.
Slaves will minister unto you;
Servants will be your helpers.
Children whom I shall bear will minister unto you.

Yoruba Nuptial Chant (African Traditional Religions)

Teachings of Sun Myung Moon

No one can change the relationship between parents and children. It cannot be rationalized away. No amount of force can destroy it; nor can the lure of knowledge, power, and money. The relationship between a child and his or her parents is undeniable; it is destiny. It is inalienable, no matter how much people may try to break it.

Since this relationship, which is derived from love, life and lineage, is eternal, it can enable us to unite with God for eternity. (206:235, October 14, 1990)

Parents and children form an inseparable relationship—especially mother and child. Can you argue with that? Although this is a fallen world, nothing can change the love between a mother and her child. Neither education nor political revolution can touch this bond. It is so even in the animal world, in the way of a mother bear loving her cubs. It will continue for billions of years, eternally, never changing. Motherhood is an unchanging principle. The entire universe revolves around motherhood. (143:52, March 15, 1986)

To whom do you belong? You belong to your parents and to your children. Then, to whom do your parents belong? They belong to their children and to God. So, you should first belong to God, then to your parents, then to your children, and finally to yourself.

Therefore, can you attain perfection by yourself? You cannot. That is why moral laws and traditional customs the world over instruct us to respect and attend our parents. That is why these teachings remain and guide our lives to this day. Know that this is the reason we should honor and serve our parents and love our children. (18:209-210, June 8, 1967)

Since parents give life to their children, children should be willing to give their lives for their parents. Life came from love. Hence, it is logical that we sacrifice life for love. There is no contradiction here. (137:76, December 18, 1985)

Children should pay back their parents for the love their parents gave them. When food was scarce their parents fed them, even while they went about with empty stomachs. They loved them at such a cost in order to raise children who will do the same for them.

Parents, you should first go the path of toilsome work and difficulties. Then, with that as a foundation, your children will also go the path of toilsome work and difficulties that can bring comfort to you. Moreover, because you have been filial to your parents, your children will develop filial piety towards you. And by raising such children, you can bequeath a good lineage to future generations. However, if you live only for yourself and neglect your parents, you cannot expect that your children will be filial towards you.

Who is a filial child? He loves his parents as his parents loved him. A person who lives this way has a foundation to relate with God… The principle of give and take action states that only when a reciprocal base is formed can there be some return. God comes and abides only upon such a foundation. It is a necessary foundation for establishing the Kingdom of Heaven.

Therefore, sons and daughters who can live in the Kingdom of Heaven are those who willingly paid back the debt of their parents' love. When your parents became old and senile, you should willingly and gladly attend them. You can think about how when you were an infant your parents changed your diapers and wiped you clean. You should not feel anything difficult in doing this; it is natural for a filial child. (35:241-42, October 19, 1970)

Your parents tell you to be filial. Why? They want you to participate in the same path of love that they walked, a path that centers on the parents. Yet there is more: The path of parents' true love leads to a relationship with the invisible God. Unity with your parents connects you with both realms of heart—invisible as well as visible, vertical history as well as horizontal history. That is why your parents teach you to become a filial child.

Yet today many people question, "Why should I live a life of filial piety?" Especially, people in America think that way. They even wonder, "Did our parents ever think of giving birth to me? Or did they just happen to conceive me while making love?" They do not know this principle.

The vertical standard must be set before a horizontal standard can be set. For instance, when we construct a building, we first make sure that the beams are vertically straight and then we align them horizontally. Otherwise, the building will fall down. Therefore, while living in the world, we should connect to the vertical standard. (136:203, December 29, 1985)

Yet these days, children are denying their parents. From that starting point, they go on to flaunt basic human ethics and morality. This negation of morality is a sign that we are living in the Last Days. Unification Church members: do not dance to the rhythm of this present trend. Instead, uphold a firm and true connection with your elders. Parents must establish it, children must establish it, and educators must establish it. (21:121, November 17, 1968)

Sibling Love

LOVE AND HARMONY AMONG SIBLINGS is essential for peace in the family. Few matters cause parents more anxiety than quarrels among their children. Yet with the common propensity for sibling rivalry, harmony is not easily kept.

Sibling relations are grounded in parental love. Siblings mirror their parents; hence when parents set a good example in caring for their children, the siblings can readily follow in caring for one another. Furthermore, sibling relations are a young person's first step to relations in the wider world, with friends and peers. In God's family, all people are brothers and sisters. Therefore, sibling love should extend to love for all people. Hence scripture's words about forgiving and reconciling with one's "brother" apply not only to siblings in the same family, but to brothers and sisters in the family of faith, and ultimately to all men and women in the world.

Behold, how good and pleasant it is
when brothers dwell in unity!
It is like the precious oil upon the head,
running down upon the beard,
upon the beard of Aaron,
running down on the collar of his robes!
It is like the dew of Hermon,
which falls on the mountains of Zion!
For there the LORD has commanded the blessing,
life for evermore.

Psalm 133

Set things right between your two brothers, and fear God; haply so you will find mercy.

Qur'an 49.10

Surely proper behavior towards parents and elder brothers is the trunk of Goodness.

Analects 1.2 (Confucianism)

The Book of Songs says,

> When wives and children and their sires are one,
> 'Tis like the harp and lute in unison.
> When brothers live in concord and at peace
> The strain of harmony shall never cease.
> The lamp of happy union lights the home,
> And bright days follow when the children come.

Confucius, commenting on the above, remarked, "In such a state of things what more satisfaction can parents have?"

Doctrine of the Mean 15.3 (Confucianism)

You have heard that it was said to the men of old, "You shall not kill; and whoever kills shall be liable to judgment." But I say to you that every one who is angry with his brother shall be liable to judgment; whoever insults his brother shall be liable to the council, and whoever says, "You fool!" shall be liable to the hell of fire. So if you are offering your gift at the altar, and there remember that your brother has something against you, leave your gift there before the altar and go; first be reconciled to your brother, and then come and offer your gift.

Matthew 5.21-24

Teachings of Sun Myung Moon

How should brothers and sisters love each other? What should be their standard of love? They should love each other as their parents love them. Children learn love from their parents.

Children can begin to inherit their parents' love by relating with their siblings. A boy can love his older sister as he would love his mother; a girl can love her older brother as she would her father.

The eldest son should love his younger brothers as his father loves him, and the eldest daughter should love her younger sisters as her mother loves her. (66:121, April 18, 1973)

Do filial sons and daughters bring their parents presents, saying, "I love you Daddy and Mommy," while always fighting with their brothers and sisters? No, such children are not filial. Any mother would think that a good son or daughter is one who loves his or her brothers and sisters more than her. This principle applies not only in the family, but in the family of humankind. If we live by this principle, then we can make the Kingdom of Heaven on earth. (95:189, November 13, 1977)

Suppose the president of a nation has a younger brother in his family who is a mere laborer. He should not say to his younger brother, "You are a mere laborer, so you should work for me." If he were a true brother, he would be sad that his younger brother's position was so far beneath his, and he would want to do whatever he could to elevate his brother. Such is brotherly heart and love. (7:38, July 5, 1959)

When you regard your brother's difficulties as less important than your own, the brotherhood relationship becomes distant. (62:188, September 25, 1972)

In a family, when brothers fight, whom do the parents side with? No parent will side with the one who hit first, or who fights for a selfish purpose. The reason why they do so is because they want their child to grow up to be good. This is consistent with moral education throughout history. (31:235, June 4, 1970)

People who have good relationships with their own siblings will be more likely to get along with their neighbors and friends when they go out into society. They are also bound to have wholesome relationships with friends of the opposite sex. They will not relate to the opposite sex with sensual or unhealthy feelings, but rather with brotherly or sisterly feelings. (*Tongil Segye* 194, p. 16)

If in the past you fought with your sisters or brothers, give them a feast to make them happy and apologize for your past behavior. Be reconciled with them and love them again as you love your mother and father. If you do this, how beautiful it would be! Then after your parents pass away, your brothers and sisters will help, serve, and love each other with the same regard as they had for their parents. From such a mind and heart, the Kingdom of Heaven starts to become a reality.

You can also see aspects of your mother and father in your aunts and uncles and cousins. Your aunts and uncles display aspects of your father and mother, grandfather and grandmother. You should regard them as gifts to show God. You should love them with your life. The Kingdom of Heaven is where everyone lives together and loves one another. Everyone!

From this point of view, the world is an expanded family. There are people in the community of the same age as your grandparents, aunts and uncles, parents, and brothers and sisters…

In the sight of God, all people in the world are His sons and daughters. Therefore, we should love all the people of the world as our brothers and sisters. If you see a poor beggar who is about your father's age, you should care for him as if he were your father. How beautiful! Is God happy to see His children fighting? It is the principle of family relationships applied to the whole of humanity, who are the children of God's family. (184:65-66, November 13, 1988)

Cain and Abel must never be divided. They are like the right hand and the left hand. Everyone should believe that my God is also my brother's God; that the God who loves me also loves my brother. (3:207, November 1, 1957)

Friendship

THE LESSONS LEARNED IN RELATING TO SIBLINGS find immediate application in making and keeping friends. Friendship is the natural extension of sibling love. Strong friendships are built on an emotional connection of empathy and shared experiences, but friendship also has an ethical component: The good friend is honest, faithful and true, and always seeks to benefit his friends, while the bad friend uses his friends for his own benefit. The scriptures admonish people to choose their friends carefully, lest they be misled or find themselves abandoned in times of adversity.

1. True Friends and False Friends

Greater love has no man than this, that a man lay down his life for his friends.

John 15.13

And the believers, men and women, are protecting friends one of another; they enjoin the right and forbid the wrong, and they establish worship and pay the poor-due, and they obey God and His messenger.

Qur'an 9.71

The gentleman by his culture collects friends about him, and through these friends promotes goodness.

Analects 12.24 (Confucianism)

I am distressed for you, my brother Jonathan;
very pleasant have you been to me;
your love to me was wonderful,
passing the love of women.[4]

2 Samuel 1:26

The dog says, "If you fall down, and I fall down, the play will be enjoyable."[5]

Nupe Proverb (African Traditional Religions)

It is because one antelope will blow the dust from the other's eye that two antelopes walk together.[6]

Akan Proverb (African Traditional Religions)

Fellowship with Men:
Men bound in fellowship first weep and lament,
But afterward they laugh.

The Master said,
"Life leads the thoughtful man on a path of many windings.
Now the course is checked, now it runs straight again.
Here winged thoughts may pour freely forth in words,
There the heavy burden of knowledge must be shut away in silence.
But when two people are at one in their inmost hearts,
They shatter even the strength of iron or of bronze.
And when two people understand each other in their inmost hearts,
Their words are sweet and strong, like the fragrance of orchids."

I Ching, Great Commentary 1.8.6 (Confucianism)

There are three sorts of friend that are profitable, and three sorts that are harmful. Friendship with the upright, with the true-to-death, and with those who have heard much is profitable. Friendship with the obsequious, friendship with those who are good at accommodating their principles, friendship with those who are clever at talk is harmful.

Analects 16.4 (Confucianism)

The friend who always seeks his benefit,
The friend whose words are other than his deeds,
The friend who flatters just to make you pleased,
The friend who keeps you company in wrong,
These four the wise regard as enemies:
Shun them from afar as paths of danger.

The friend who is a helper all the time,
The friend in happiness and sorrow both,
The friend who gives advice that's always good,
The friend who has full sympathy with you,
These four the wise see as good-hearted friends
And with devotion cherish such as these
As does a mother cherish her own child.

Digha Nikaya 3.187, Sigalovada Sutta (Buddhism)

Only few people act in our interest in our absence,
When we are not around.
But in our presence, every Dick and Harry, slaves and freeborn,
Display their love for us.

Yoruba Verse (African Traditional Religions)

Teachings of Sun Myung Moon

Do you have a best friend, someone with whom you have an unbreakable bond? Someone you treasure more than anyone else in the world, including your wife? A relationship with a best friend cannot be broken by an angry word or a day's quarrel. You cannot abandon him even at the risk of your life.

You do not feel this way about your friend out of sympathy, but because you are connected from the bottom of your heart, which is the source of goodness. A relationship that is connected to the goodness in your original mind can never be broken. (42:218, March 14, 1971)

Who is a true friend? A true friend lives for her friends; she does not regard her friends as existing for her benefit. Suppose among ten friends, one of them lived his or her life for the sake of the other nine. If you ask them, "Who is your best friend?" they will all pick the friend who lived for the others. (70:72, February 8, 1974)

As we cultivate our relationship with another person—a friend or family member, over time we connect a part of our life to that person's life and also connect emotionally. What may have begun as a professional or formal relationship expands to fill more aspects of our life. Our friend's presence grows ever larger in our heart, and in time he or she becomes someone whom we cannot live without. (59:296, July 30, 1972)

Happy is the man who has friends who commiserate with his mishaps and sorrows. Happy is the man who, when he is in pain, has friends or children who are willing to take any pains and even risk their lives on his behalf. (150:196, February 15, 1961)

When you visit an acquaintance whose face you barely know, you do not feel at ease; instead you feel awkward. But when you visit a friend to whom you have strong emotional ties, you feel at ease. You feel free to interfere in your friend's affairs, and your friend can step into your personal life as well. A strong friendship is bound with ties of emotional affection. Friends can cope with any external difficulty on the strength of their bond of heart. (33:133, August 11, 1970)

If you want to be someone's best friend, you should understand his agony and suffering, and comfort him in his misfortune. If you have a relationship with him through heart and love, you will move him, and he will move you. (7:306, October 11, 1959)

2. Wisdom in Choosing Friends

Associate not with evil friends, associate not with dishonorable people;
Associate with good friends, associate with noble people.

Dhammapada 78 (Buddhism)

Bad company ruins good morals.

1 Corinthians 15.33

What is attached to the defiled will be defiled; and what is attached to the pure will be pure.

Mishnah, Kelim 12.2 (Judaism)

Those that are good, seek for friends; that will help you to practice virtue with body and soul. Those that are wicked, keep at a distance; it will prevent evil from approaching you.

Tract of the Quiet Way (Taoism)

Sit in the assembly of the honest; join with those that are good and virtuous; nay, seek out a noble enemy where enmity cannot be helped and have nothing to do with the wicked and the unrighteous. Even in bondage you should live with the virtuous, the erudite, and the truthful; but not for a kingdom should you stay with the wicked and the malicious.

Garuda Purana 112 (Hinduism)

As the man one makes his friend,
As the one he follows,
Such does he himself become;
he is like unto his mate.
Follower and following,
Toucher and touched alike,
As a shaft with poison is smeared
Poisons all the bunch unsmeared,

Both are fouled. A man inspired
In the fear of being soiled
Should not company with rogues.

Itivuttaka 68 (Buddhism)

It is by dealing with a man that his virtue is to be known, and that too after a long time; not by one who gives it a passing thought or no thought at all; by a wise man, not by a fool. It is by association that a man's integrity is to be known... It is in times of trouble that his fortitude is to be known... It is by conversing with him, that a man's wisdom is to be known, and that too after a long time; not by one who gives it a passing thought or no thought at all; by a wise man, not by a fool.

Udana 65-66 (Buddhism)

When you gain a friend, gain him through testing,
and do not trust him hastily.
For there is a friend who is such at his own convenience,
but will not stand by you in your day of trouble.
And there is a friend who changes into an enemy,
and will disclose a quarrel to your disgrace.
And there is a friend who is a table companion,
but will not stand by you in your day of trouble.
In your prosperity he will make himself your equal,
and be bold with your servants;
but if you are brought low he will turn against you,
and will hide himself from your presence.
A faithful friend is a sturdy shelter:
he that has found one has found a treasure.

There is nothing so precious as a faithful friend,
and no scales can measure his excellence.
A faithful friend is an elixir of life;
and those who fear the Lord will find him.
Whoever fears the Lord directs his friendship
aright,
for as he is, so is his neighbor also.

Sirach 6.7-17 (*Christianity*)

Teachings of Sun Myung Moon

Keeping company with bad friends can ruin your entire life. Therefore, from ancient times people have been taught to be careful in selecting friends. This wisdom applies across the ages and countries of the world.

No one finds it easy to be considerate of others when he finds himself in a difficult circumstance. This is common to everyone. When people are in bad straits, and to avoid more suffering, they may take advantage of their friends. Catching their friends unawares, they may deceive them and use them, to their hurt.

Considered in this light, who on earth can you trust? It is difficult to find a friend with genuine integrity, on whom you can rely. Although you believe a person to be your good friend, he might step on you and take advantage of you if his circumstances press on him. For this reason, selecting your close friends, and choosing who to build a good relationship with, is a most difficult question. (91:29-30, January 2, 1977)

When you make a friend, is he someone who works and aspires for a better future? Or does he live only for today, without any ambition? Friends who lack ambition will cause you to decline as time goes by. Therefore, make relationships with better friends in order to build up your future. (32:14, June 14, 1970)

Do any of you want a friend who is strongly inclined to self-indulgence? Is a friend who always cares about only him or herself a good friend or a bad friend? Why bad? That kind of person sows divisions and discord. He separates his friends from their families, clans, and networks of relationships. That kind of person blocks relationships, just like a pulling down a window-shade blocks the view out of a window. You should clearly understand why such a friend is bad. Evil connects with self-indulgence…

You want a good friend, right? You do not want bad friends, do you? Is a friend who says, "Skip your meal and forget about school! Come out and play!" a good friend? Rather, a good friend would feed you if you did not eat at mealtime, and a good friend would encourage you to go to school even if you do not want to go. That is a good friend; he is in every way the opposite of a bad friend. Here we distinguish the good from the evil. (36:69, November 15, 1970)

Analyze each of your friends—one friend is like this and another is like that. Study and compare your friends of different types. Is this one calm, or arrogant, or strong, or indecisive? Select three or four of them and verify whether your judgment of them was correct. (54:177, March 24, 1972)

Conjugal Love

THE MARRIAGE BOND IS DIVINELY SANCTIONED; it carries with it the promise of God's blessing. The joys of conjugal love are a gift of God. Through bearing the fruits of conjugal love—children—we participate as co-creators with God. More than that, conjugal love can be a place to meet God and know God's love in a most intimate and real way.

Father Moon teaches extensively on this topic: God created human beings to become complete through marriage. He offers much practical advice on how spouses can strengthen and renew their love. Yet, the mutual affection between husband and wife is only the half of it; more fundamental is the vertical link between God's love and human love that is created through the blessing of marriage. The God of love created the human love between man and woman to mirror divine love. Hence it should be absolute, unchanging and unique: spouses should be as faithful to each other as God is to each of us as individuals. These days, when many people are questioning the value of marriage, people would do well to heed the voices of religion which lift up the place of marriage within the divine plan of life.

Several scripture passages ground marriage in the original plan which God instituted in the Garden of Eden. Here is Father Moon's unique contribution: he explains how this original conjugal love was damaged by the Human Fall. As a result, conventional human love inevitably deviates from divine love, putting the ideal of marriage out of reach. A central purpose of Father Moon's mission is to restore conjugal love to its original blessed state through the Holy Blessing Ceremony which he offers to all humankind.

1. Love and Affection between Husband and Wife

Sweet be the glances we exchange,
our faces showing true concord.
Enshrine me in your heart and let
one spirit dwell within us.

I wrap around you this my robe
which came to me from Manu,
so that you may be wholly mine
and never seek another.

                Atharva Veda 7.36-37 *(Hinduism)*

Not those are true husband and wife that with each other [merely] consort:
Truly wedded are those that in two frames, are as one light.

         Adi Granth, Var-Suhi-Ki, M.3, p. 788 *(Sikhism)*

Among His signs is that He created spouses for you among yourselves that you may console yourselves with them. He has planted affection and mercy between you.

                          Qur'an 30.21

Set me as a seal upon your heart,
as a seal upon your arm;
For love is strong as death,
jealousy is cruel as the grave.
Its flashes are flashes of fire,
a most vehement flame.
Many waters cannot quench love,
neither can floods drown it.
If a man offered for love
all the wealth of his house,
it would be utterly scorned.

                       Song of Solomon 8.6-7

O that you would kiss me with the kisses of your mouth!
For your love is better than wine,
your anointing oils are fragrant,
your name is oil poured out;
therefore the maidens love you.
Draw me after you, let us make haste.
The king has brought me into his chambers.

We will exult and rejoice in you;
we will extol your love more than wine;
rightly do they love you. [7]

     Song of Solomon 1.2-4

Behold the comely forms of Surya!
her border-cloth and her headwear,
and her garment triply parted,
these the priest has sanctified.

I take your hand for good fortune, that you
may attain old age with me, your husband. The
 solar deities—
Bhaga, Aryaman, Savitri, Purandhi—
have given you to me to be mistress of my
 household.

Pushan, arouse her, the most blissful one;
through whom a new generation will spring to
 life.
She, in the ardor of her love, will meet me,
and I, ardently loving, will meet her…

Live you two here, be not parted,
enjoy the full length of life,
sporting with your sons and grandsons,
rejoicing in your own abode.

May Prajapati bring forth children of us, may
Aryaman unite us together till old age,
Not inauspicious, enter your husband's house,
be gracious to our people and animals.

Come, not with fierce looks, not harming your
 husband,
good to animals, kind-hearted and glorious,
a mother of heroes, loving the gods,
pleasant, gracious to humans and to animals.

Make her, thou bounteous Indra,
a good mother of sons; grant her
good fortune; give her ten sons
and make her husband the eleventh.

Be a queen to your father-in-law,
a queen to your mother-in-law,
a queen to your husband's sisters,
and a queen to your husband's brothers.

May the universal Devas
and Apas join our hearts together;
so may Matarisvan, Dhatri,
and Dveshtri unite us both.[8]

    Rig Veda 10.85.35-47 *(Hinduism)*

Kwan-kwan go the ospreys,
On the islet in the river.
The modest, retiring, virtuous, young lady—
For our prince a good mate is she.

Here long, there short, is the duckweed,
To the left, to the right, borne about by the
 current.
The modest, retiring, virtuous, young lady—
Waking and sleeping, he sought her.

He sought her and found her not,
And waking and sleeping he thought about her.
Long he thought; oh! long and anxiously;
On his side, on his back, he turned, and back
 again.

Here long, there short, is the duckweed;
On the left, on the right, we gather it.
The modest, retiring, virtuous, young lady—
With lutes, small and large, let us give her
 friendly welcome.

Here long, there short, is the duckweed;
On the left, on the right, we cook and present it.
The modest, retiring, virtuous, young lady—
With bells and drums let us show delight in her.[9]

    Book of Songs, Ode 1 *(Confucianism)*

Kaen-kwan went the axle ends of my carriage,
As I thought of the young beauty, and went to
 fetch her.
It was not that I was hungry or thirsty,
But I longed for one of such virtuous fame to
 come and be with me.
Although no good friends be with us, we will
 feast and be glad.

Dense is that forest in the plain,
And there sit the long-tailed pheasants.
In her proper season that well-grown lady,

With her admirable virtue, is come to instruct me.
We will feast, and I will praise her:
"I love you, and will never be weary of you."

Although I have no good spirits,
We will drink, and perhaps be satisfied.
Although I have no good viands,
We will eat, and perhaps be satisfied.
Although I have no virtue to impart to you,
We will sing and dance.

I ascend that lofty ridge,
And split the branches of the oaks for firewood.
I split the branches of the oaks for firewood
Amid the luxuriance of their leaves.
I see you whose match is seldom to be seen,
And my whole heart is satisfied.

Book of Songs, Ode 218 *(Confucianism)*

Teachings of Sun Myung Moon

Man and woman are God's masterpieces. When they love each other centered on God, it is supreme, transcendental love, not worldly love. They feel that their love is the best of all loves; the most beautiful love, shining forever. Where can they experience and fulfill such love? Only in the family. (26:154, October 25, 1969)

A husband and wife love each other without conditions. Their love is unconditional. Their love is absolute, eternal love. (112:294, April 25, 1981)

When a husband and wife love each other, the man does not block his wife from entering deep into his heart. The woman likewise does not resist her husband. Even if impenetrable walls surround their hearts, love has no difficulty surmounting them. (49:52, October 3, 1971)

When you love your spouse, you feel your body's desire to unite with your beloved. When husband and wife become one flesh in true love, they become inseparable. They can live in unity, loving each other forever. (187:47, January 6, 1989)

Why is marriage so important? It is the path to finding love. It is the path to knowing what love is. It teaches about life.
    Marriage joins the life of a woman and the life of a man. In time [through children], it joins the lineage of the man and the lineage of the woman. It thus begins a history, a nation, the world and the Kingdom of Heaven on earth. (279:114-15, August 1, 1996)

What is the Kingdom of Heaven as a couple? It is the state of matrimony where a man and woman are totally united as one. It is not like a typical marriage where in the beginning you tell your spouse, "I love you," but after a few years you say good-bye and divorce… A heavenly couple is inseparable; they could lose their legs by exploding dynamite but still keep embracing with their upper bodies! That is possible only with true love. To achieve that kind of love, your mind and body must be completely united. Then you can attain the Kingdom of Heaven as a couple. (96:29, January 1, 1978)

The purpose of marriage is to synchronize the man's heart and the woman's heart to perfect their love. The wedding ceremony is a proclamation of the couple's commitment and determination toward that goal. If you start with the goal to perfect your love and heart through your married life, you are on the way to fulfilling the ideal of family. If you actually fulfill it, upon your death you will certainly go to heaven, because your lives will be heaven. (97:277, March 26, 1978)

A man's wife represents his mother; she contains elements of his mother as well. At the same time, she contains elements of his elder sisters, younger sisters, and indeed all the women in the world. When he loves his wife, who contains all these elements, he is loving his mother, his elder sisters and younger sisters, and indeed all the women in the world.

Likewise, to woman, her husband represents and contains elements of her father, elder brothers, younger brothers and all the men in the world. In loving him, she loves her father, her brothers, and all the men in the world. This is the ideal of the family. (*God's Will and the World*, September 21, 1978)

We marry for the sake of our partner. Therefore, the man should have the attitude that even if he finds some aspects of his wife unattractive, he will love her even more than if she were beautiful. This is the principled way of thinking. (97:321, April 1, 1978)

What is the solution for unity? It is the heart to love each other. Love can come from pity as well as from liking. Few couples love each other from the start.[10] Love grows with time. A woman marries a man who is absolutely stubborn, and thinks the man is totally unlovable. Then the woman takes pity on him for the many obstacles that he must confront because of the stubbornness. Then, when her pity turns to love, the man can find solace in her. The woman might even find her husband's stubbornness useful because she is not stubborn enough herself, and this way, turns his stubbornness to mutual advantage. So, love's affection can bloom even from pity, and eventually lead to unity. (41:332-33, February 18, 1971)

Families that live in hardship are not necessarily unhappy. Sharing a single piece of bread, when the husband feeds his wife even though he does not eat, or the wife feeds her husband even though she goes hungry—how deep is the love in that family! (216:270, April 7, 1991)

A woman is better off taking a wild and rough man for a husband rather than one who is delicate and fine-featured. The husband-wife relationship brings together opposites. Therefore, a woman who takes a wild and tough man as her opposite partner will live happily. The wife who receives the love of such a husband is a happy wife. You women should not forget this, and encourage your husbands to be rough and tough.

It is the law of love that the strength of a man becomes like a gentle spring breeze in front of a woman. Among men matters are determined by the strongest fist, but in front of a beloved woman that fist becomes as soft as cotton. Therefore, a woman should not be afraid of a man who is wild and rough. Rather she should think that the stronger a man is, the more worthy he is to receive her love. (*Blessing and Ideal Family* 4.1.6)

Do you wish to become a loving couple that shines like the moon and even like the sun? Try to dig out all the beautiful points in your spouse. It may take a lifetime of digging, and still you cannot fathom them all. Finally when you arrive in the spirit world, you can plumb love's deepest core.

Therefore, wives, study your husbands. You may think he is one way, but then you should discover another side of him. Study him from every possible angle, and you can see the whole universe in him. Then you can think he is more amazing than God! When you married him you saw him only through a small lens, from one direction, not from all directions. As long as you continue to regard him only from that narrow perspective, you cannot find ideal love. Over the years of living together you need to study him from every direction.

Do you have an unforgettable memory of your husband at his most charming? What is it? It is his body. So observe his entire body. After a fight, you glance at your husband and you will see his eyes blink. They blink just as your eyes blink. Observe carefully his breathing, his eyes, nose, lips and emotions—all these parts of him are just like you. The man you love exists for you, so you can never let him go.

If your heart never gets old, your love will never grow old either. Your life will never be boring and your lineage will endure forever. True love never grows old. It becomes more beautiful the older it gets. With such a heart you will always see your husband as the best-looking man in the world, and he will look at you as the most beautiful woman in the world.

It doesn't matter that your wife looks unattractive; through the eyes of love, she is the most beautiful woman. Regardless of her form on earth, in the spirit world she will appear young and pretty, transfigured by the light of love that is brighter than any earthly light. A woman who places great store in her beauty is dismayed to see it fade as she grows old, and when she passes on to the other world she takes on an ugly appearance. On the other hand, a woman who shares a lifetime of love with her husband becomes beautiful in the other world. Her husband becomes the most handsome man.

The light of love is the highest form of light. Because it is the highest, it has the power to beautify anything. Therefore, think that the wife whom you love is the very light of heaven and earth. She is your love, your dream, your happiness, your freedom and your peace. Then when you go out of town, should you meet an alluring vixen you will not be tempted in the least. That temptress would appear like rotten fish in your eyes. There is no other way to beauty than by the love and light of God. (297:168-70, November 19, 1998)

A husband and wife are like partners. Just as people have different faces, they have different destinies. If a man has a bad fortune, but he marries a woman whose fortune is good, his fortune can change for the better. Conversely, if a wife's fortune is bad but her husband's is good, her fortune can change for the better.

Over time, the husband and wife balance their destinies, as if they are leveling a mountain and filling in a valley to make a plain. After leveling the ground, the husband and wife can do many things together, such as plowing the fields and cultivating diverse crops and trees. (*God's Will and the World*, September 22, 1978)

Heaven starts in the family. Unless you can find God in your spouse, you cannot enter the Kingdom of Heaven. (*Way of God's Will* 1.8)

2. Marriage Makes a Man or a Woman Complete

He that has not got a wife
is not yet a complete man.

                Benjamin Franklin, *Poor Richard's Almanack*

The unmarried person lives without joy, without blessing, without good.

                Talmud, Yebamot 62b *(Judaism)*

Then the LORD God said, "It is not good that the man should be alone; I will make him a helper fit for him." So out of the ground the LORD God formed every beast of the field and every bird of the air, and brought them to the man to see what he would call them; and whatever the man called every living creature, that was its name. The man gave names to all cattle, and to the birds of the air, and to every beast of the field; but for the man there was not found a helper fit for him. So the LORD God caused a deep sleep to fall upon the man, and while he slept took one of his ribs and closed up its place with flesh; and the rib which the LORD God had taken from the man he made into a woman and brought her to the man. Then the man said, "This at last is bone of my bones and flesh of my flesh; she shall be called Woman, because she was taken out of Man." Therefore a man leaves his father and his mother and cleaves to his wife, and they become one flesh.[11]

                Genesis 2.18-24

In the beginning there was only the Self, one only... He found no joy; so even today, one who is all alone finds no joy. He yearned for a second. He became as large as a man and a woman locked in close embrace. This self he split into two; hence arose husband and wife. Therefore, as Yajnavalkya used to observe, "Oneself is like half of a split pea." That is why this void is filled by woman. He was united with her, and thence were born human beings.

              Brihadaranyaka Upanishad 1.4.17 and 1.4.3
                            (Hinduism)

The righteous cannot flourish save when they are male and female together, like Abraham and Sarai.

                Zohar 1.82a *(Judaism)*

He is only a perfect man who consists (of three persons united): his wife, himself and his offspring; thus says the Veda, and learned brahmins propound this maxim likewise, "The husband is declared to be one with his wife."

                Laws of Manu 9.45 *(Hinduism)*

Teachings of Sun Myung Moon

A man by himself or a woman by herself is only one half. They marry to become complete. The love that you should perfect in your marriage is not egoistic love based on the belief that you live to gratify yourself. That kind of love is temporary and false. You should think that you are not born for your own sake but for the sake of your partner. Then you should give and forget, give and forget. True love begins from that point. (262:67-68, July 23, 1994)

Living for others is the basic rule of the existing world; all things are created for others and nothing was created for itself. Hence, man was not born for man; he was born for woman. Woman was not born for woman, but for man.

    Whether beautiful or ugly, every woman exists for the sake of a man. All the characteristics and emotions of man and woman are designed for each other, not for themselves. When the partners in a marriage say to each other, "I was born for you, I will live for you, and I will die for you," they are considered an ideal, happy couple. This is, indeed, correct from the perspective of the basic rule of the existing world. This is the starting-point for true love. (135:234, December 11, 1985)

Young men and women aspire to become great individuals. They want to build a good family and become good parents. Yet at the same time, they feel that they are lacking something within themselves. That is why, whether man or woman, they desire to have a good partner in their life. For the same reason, people wish to have children who are better than themselves. How wonderful it would be if we could complement our weaknesses through our counterpart! All people, when they love each other, carry such a desire deep in their hearts. (26:147, October 25, 1969)

Woman has a feminine nature and man has a masculine nature; God made them as divided embodiments of Himself. How can they come together as one? Through love. Having formerly been divided, when they come together they will experience how strong the love is that God had been holding within Himself. Otherwise, they would never know God's love.

You have love within you, but by yourself you cannot know it. You can experience it when you embrace your spouse. When you love your spouse, you feel all the love that was inside you from the beginning. (185:187, January 8, 1989)

A husband needs his wife more than any other person in the world. The wife needs her husband more than any other person in the world. A husband and wife should be each other's walking stick, companions who are ever advising each other. (27:87, November 26, 1969)

Husbands, the woman standing before you is God's daughter. Also, before she is your wife, she is humanity's daughter. If you can love her as God's beloved daughter and a woman whom all humanity loves, then you are qualified to be her husband. Men who do not respect their wives are not true husbands. Do you have such regard for your wife? If not, you should change, even now.

Wives, you should not think that your husband only belongs to you. First, he is a son of God; next, he represents all the men in the world. You should become a woman who can love this man more than all humanity can, and love him more than God loves him...

When a woman marries, she should be willing to become like her husband's left foot, walking in step with him on their family's path of love for God and all humanity. The husband is like the right foot and the wife is like the left foot. You should not go through life crippled; therefore you should marry. Your couple should not walk with a limp; both the right foot and the left foot should be healthy and strong. If it can walk straight, your couple is destined to live a harmonious married life. (88:318, October 3, 1976)

Many women think it is okay not to marry if they do not want to. Yet if a woman does not marry, her physical body will not be able to function as a woman, and she will eventually get sick. A woman's body is built with marriage as its normal life state. For a woman to live a single life and never marry a man is not normal, and to think that it is all right not to marry is not normal thinking. (238:71-72, November 19, 1992)

3. True Conjugal Love Unites a Man, a Woman and God

When a man is at home, the foundation of his house is the wife, for it is on account of her that the *Shekhinah* (divine Presence) does not depart from the house. So our teachers have understood the verse, "And Isaac brought her into his mother Sarah's tent" (Genesis 24.67), to mean that the Shekhinah came into Isaac's house along with Rebecca. Esoterically speaking, the supernal Mother is together with the male only when the house is in readiness and at the time the male and female are conjoined. At such time blessings are showered forth by the supernal Mother upon them.[12]

Zohar 1.50a (Judaism)

Woman, O Gautama, is the sacrificial fire, her sexual organ is the fuel, the hairs the smoke, the vulva the flame, sexual intercourse the cinders, enjoyment the sparks. In this fire the gods offer semen as a libation. Out of this offering a new person is born.

Brihadaranyaka Upanishad 6.2.13 (Hinduism)

The Originator of the heavens and the earth; He has appointed for you of yourselves spouses, and pairs also of the cattle, by means of which He multiplies you.

Qur'an 42.11

See now, when desire brings man and woman together, there issues from their union a son in whom both their forms are combined, because God has fashioned him in a mold partaking of both. Therefore a man should sanctify himself at such time, in order that the form may be as perfect as possible.

Zohar, Genesis 90b (Judaism)

When a man begins to consecrate himself before intercourse with his wife with a sacred intention, a holy spirit is aroused above him, composed of both male and female. And the Holy One, blessed be He, directs an emissary who is in charge of human embryos, and assigns to him this particular spirit, and indicates to it the place to which it should be entrusted. This is the meaning of, "The night said, a man-child has been conceived" (Job 3:3)... Then the spirit descends together with the image,[13] the one in whose likeness the spirit existed above. With this image the man grows; with this image he moves through the world.

Zohar 3.104b (Judaism)

By the first nuptial circumambulation the Lord shows you His ordinance for the daily duties of wedded life. The scriptures are the Word of the Lord, learn righteousness through them, and the Lord will free you from sin...

By the second nuptial circumambulation you are to understand that the Lord has caused you to meet the true Guru; the fear in your hearts has departed; the filth of selfishness in your minds is washed away...

By the third nuptial circumambulation there is longing for the Lord and detachment from the world...

By the fourth nuptial circumambulation the mind reaches to knowledge of the Divine and God is inwardly grasped. Through the grace of the Guru we have attained with ease to the Lord; the sweetness of the Beloved pervades us, body and soul. Dear and pleasing is the Lord to us; night and day our minds are fixed on Him. By exalting the Lord we have attained the Lord: the fruit our hearts desired, for He has arranged these nuptials. The soul, the spouse, delights in the Beloved's Name. The Lord God is united with His Holy Bride; the heart of the Bride flowers with His Name.[14]

Adi Granth, Raga Suhi, M. 4, p. 773-74:
the Laavaan (Sikhism)

Teachings of Sun Myung Moon

A man is born to find a woman, and a woman is born to find a man. We are created as man and woman to reach a higher level of God's love through our union. As single people we cannot reach the fullness of God's love—true love. We may touch God's love, but it will only be one-dimensional love. As single people we cannot experience God's three-dimensional and spherical love.

    Therefore, a man and woman marry in order to reach that higher realm of love. In God's original world before the Fall, when a husband and wife united they would form a mighty center, creating a sphere. The stronger the horizontal bond between them, the more they would connect to the vertical power of love. Their minds and bodies would revel in it and totally become one. (109:275, November 2, 1980)

When husband and wife are one in heart, they should become one in body. When they are one in heart and body, then they become one with God.

    The husband and wife become one in the center of love's shimmering light as God covers the place where the man and woman are joined. The light embraces them and transforms them by its mysterious power. It transports them to an inexplicable, wondrous state. (296:33, October 11, 1998)

God first created Adam as His incarnation. At the same time that Adam is God's Son, he is also God Himself, wearing God's body. Next, God created Eve as Adam's partner in order to perfect horizontal love as the ideal love of husband and wife. At the same time that Eve is God's Daughter, she is also the Bride who perfects God's horizontal ideal of love in substantial form.

    Where Adam and Eve reach perfection, marry with God's blessing, and consummate their first love, this is precisely the place where God receives His bride in substantial form. This is because God's ideal absolute love descends vertically and participates in the ideal conjugal love flowing horizontally between Adam and Eve. The true love of God and the true love of human beings—one vertical and the other horizontal—join, reach perfection and bear fruit at a single point. (277:198-99, April 16, 1996)

What is the purpose of marriage? It is to fulfill God's ideal of creation. An individual by him or herself cannot fulfill it. It requires that we form a couple whose hearts are united with the heart of God, the Subject of all creation. Thus, when He moves, we move, and when He is still, we are still. That is how the inner and outer become one. Unless we set the standard as a couple through which we can harmonize with God, we cannot fulfill His purpose of creation. (35:321, October 19, 1970)

4. Marriage Is a Sacred Partnership, Aligning Two Human Beings with the Divine Image

I am He, you are She;
I am Song, you are Verse,
I am Heaven, you are Earth.
We two shall here together dwell,
becoming parents of children.

    Atharva Veda 14.2.71 (Hinduism)

Representing heaven and earth, I have created husband and wife. This is the beginning of the world.

    Mikagura-uta (Tenrikyo)

From the beginning of creation, "God made them male and female." "For this reason a man shall leave his father and mother and be joined to his wife, and the two shall become one flesh." So they are no longer two but one flesh. What therefore God has joined together, let not man put asunder.

Mark 10.6-9

Blessed art Thou, O LORD our God, King of the universe, who created humankind in His image, in the image of the likeness of His form, and has prepared for him from His very own person an eternal building. Blessed art Thou, O LORD, Creator of man...

May Thou make joyful these beloved companions, just as Thou gladdened Thy creatures in the Garden of Eden in primordial times. Blessed art Thou, O LORD, who makes bridegroom and bride to rejoice.

Blessed art Thou, O LORD, King of the universe, who created mirth and joy, bridegroom and bride, gladness, jubilation, dancing and delight, love and brotherhood, peace and fellowship. Quickly, O LORD our God, may the sound of mirth and joy be heard in the streets of Judah and Jerusalem, the voice of bridegroom and bride, jubilant voices of bridegrooms from their canopies and youths from the feasts of song. Blessed art Thou, O LORD, who makes the bridegroom rejoice with the bride.[15]

Talmud, Ketubot 8a (Judaism)

The gospel of Love... presents the unity of male and female as no longer two wedded individuals, but as two individual natures in one; and this compounded spiritual individuality reflects God as Father-Mother, not as a corporeal being. In this divinely united spiritual consciousness, there is no impediment to eternal bliss—to the perfectibility of God's creation.

Science and Health (Christian Science)

All the souls in the world, which are the fruit of the handiwork of the Almighty, are all mystically one, but when they descend to this world they are separated into male and female, though these are still conjoined. When they first issue forth, they issue as male and female together. Subsequently, when they descend to this world they separate, one to one side and the other to the other. Afterwards God mates them—God and no other, He alone knowing the mate proper to each. Happy is the man who is upright in his works and walks in the way of truth, so that his soul may find its original mate, for then he becomes indeed perfect.

Zohar 1.85b (Judaism)

The sacred partnership of true marriage is constituted both by the will of God and the will of man. From God comes the very institution of marriage, the ends for which it was instituted, the laws that govern it, the blessings that flow from it; while man, through generous surrender of his own person made to another for the whole span of life, becomes, with the help and cooperation of God, the author of each particular marriage, with the duties and blessings annexed hereto from divine institution...

That mutual familiar intercourse between the spouses themselves, if the blessing of conjugal faith is to shine with becoming splendor, must be distinguished by chastity so that husband and wife bear themselves in all things with the law of God and of nature, and endeavor always to follow the will of their most wise and holy Creator with the greatest reverence towards the work of God...

The love of which We are speaking is not that based on the passing lust of the moment, nor does it consist in pleasing words only, but in the deep attachment of the heart which is expressed in action, since love is proved by deeds. This outward expression of love in the home demands not only mutual help but must go further; must have as its primary purpose that man and wife help each other day by day in forming and perfecting themselves in the interior life, so that through their partnership in life they may advance ever more and more in virtue, and above all that they may grow in true love towards God and their neighbor.

Pope Pius XI, Casti Connubi (Christianity)

In the celestial glory there are three heavens or degrees; and in order to obtain the highest, a man must enter into this order of the priesthood (meaning the new and everlasting covenant of marriage); and if he does not, he cannot obtain it.

And again, verily I say unto you, if a man marry a wife by my word, which is my law, and by the new and everlasting covenant, and is sealed unto them by the Holy Spirit of promise, by him who is anointed, unto whom I have appointed this power and the keys of this priesthood; and it shall be said unto them—Ye shall come forth in the first resurrection... which glory shall be a fullness and a continuation of the seeds forever and ever.[16]

Doctrine and Covenants 131.1-3, 132.19
(Latter-day Saints)

Teachings of Sun Myung Moon

We can solve the fundamental problems of family life by strengthening marriage. Although some religious people regard marriage as sinful, we proclaim it the holiest of states.

God instituted marriage as the only proper way for a man and a woman to love each other. Furthermore, when a man and a woman become one in marriage, whom do they come to resemble? They resemble God. Indeed, it is only when a man and woman unite in matrimony that they can fully resemble God, who created us in His image male and female. Only then can God dwell with us. (70:76, February 8, 1974)

If you only love as a single person, and do not embark on the path of loving as a husband and wife, your life will end in ruin. Love among single people inevitably breaks apart. It is a lifestyle that damages society and even the world. (111:257, February 22, 1981)

Commonly people think that love is what a man and a woman enjoy together. Yet that kind of love has no root in the past or outlook toward the future; it is merely a phenomenon with no direction. It is selfish love. Selfish love cannot be the source of peace, the basis of unity or the basis for freedom. How can there be peace, unity or freedom where people love each other one day and separate the next? There is no happiness there, only regret; no freedom there, only more obstacles; no unity there, only loneliness. That kind of love leads only to destruction.

I want you to understand that Satan employs such love as a weapon to destroy the ideals of human life. Using this kind of love as a weapon, Satan is robbing us of true freedom, true peace and true unity. From this perspective, the satanic expression of love is truly God's adversary. It is a most dreadful sin, a most hated enemy. (104:141, April 29, 1979)

Why do we marry? It is to resemble God. God is the harmonious being of dual characteristics. Man and woman are the divided manifestations of God's dual characteristics. They have to unite as one body, becoming like a seed, in order to enter God's original dwelling place.

To yield good seed, you have to go the way of love. This means that you must be born in love, set love as your goal while growing, make love your aim in life, and walk the path of love. Then you will return to love. (138:99, January 19, 1986)

Why do you have to marry? It is because God exists with dual characteristics. A man and a woman each reflect one of these aspects of divinity. Therefore, they must come together and unite to manifest the fullness of God's image. That is why marriage is the essential condition for your complete growth in the ideal of human love.

Marriage blends men and women into the semblance of the divine unity, so that human beings might fully become the image of God. God created human beings and all things for the purpose of consummating His love. Where do you consummate that love? It is while you live on earth, in the relationship between husband and wife, in the family. That is why your wedding day is the most joyful day in your lives. (123:217, January 2, 1983)

We do not marry for ourselves, but for the sake of another. What do I mean in saying that marriage is for the other rather than for ourselves? Heaven and earth abide in a relationship between subject and object. By this principle, marriage between a man and a woman participates in the joining of heaven and earth.

With the man on the right side and the woman on the left side, their marriage symbolizes the fulfillment of all the horizontal relationships in the universe. Since the man as the subject partner is above, and the woman as the object partner is below, their marriage represents the fulfillment of the vertical relationship between God and human beings. Therefore, marriage is not mainly for the man, nor mainly for the woman. It is rather to accord with heavenly law. This is also the reason why men and women were created differently; they were born to accord with heavenly law. (101:38-39, October 28, 1978)

When a man and a woman embrace in perfect love, they bring perfection to the universe. Were their love to shatter, it would shatter the order of the universe and bring chaos to the vertical world. (118:32, April 26, 1982)

Look at this world: The mineral kingdom has positive and negative ions, the plant kingdom has stamen and pistil, and the animal kingdom has male and female. Scientists have found that even germs are male and female. God created all things so that they can become one at their particular level centering on love. Seeing this universe of pairs, we understand that they are that way so that all can be linked to the love of a man and a woman, who come together representing heaven and earth. Thus all things celebrate the love of human beings.

Just as we lay a foundation before building a house, God created the entire pair system as the foundation for human beings to love. Doesn't human love have many qualities in common with the love of animals? For instance, if a male and female are going along together and the female is attacked, the male will risk its life to defend the female. When they have offspring, they will risk their lives to defend them. Human love is that way because the foundation on which it was created is that way. (222:123, October 28, 1991)

Marriage is the union of all virtues of heaven and earth. Encompassing vertical and horizontal, left and right, and front and back, it is the completion of the whole. Marriage is where we perfect the ideals of children, siblings, husband and wife, and parents. For this reason, had Adam and Eve become a true husband and wife, they would have been the parents most beloved of God. They would have stood in the position of the second creators, inheriting everything that God experienced as the First Creator. Through raising their children, they would have developed the heart of love as God's representatives. After attaining that heart through direct experience, they would profoundly understand and empathize with their children as they in turn traversed the positions of children, siblings, husbands and wives, and parents.

Their marriage and conjugal love as husband and wife was to be the origin and starting-point of God's love, life and lineage in human beings. It was to be the starting-point for fulfilling God's ideal, the Kingdom of God on earth and in heaven.

God is the root of love, root of life, root of lineage, and the root of the Kingdom of Heaven on earth and in heaven. At the marriage of Adam and Eve, God would enter into their hearts and experience with them the love of their conjugal union. Then God would be the vertical True Parent, and Adam and Eve the horizontal True Parents. Because each of us would be born with the blood and flesh of these two sets of parents, our minds would be aligned with the vertical and our bodies with the horizontal.[17]

This would form the realm of the harmonious oneness of God and human beings in love. In that realm, people who perfect their love both in mind and body would become God's sons and daughters. We would enter into a parent-child relationship with God, become God's princes and princesses, and inherit the entirety of His world. Then, when we perfect husband-wife unity centering on true love, we would form a family that lives in attendance to God. Our family would be the base of peace and of God's ideal. As man and woman, each being a half of the whole, we would come together to form one body; and as God's partners we would perfect the ideal of divine love. (254:106, February 1, 1994)

The first union of love between Adam and Eve was to have signified the perfection of God's own love. It was to have been a continual feast of happiness where God, Adam and Eve, and all creatures in the universe would be intoxicated with joy and blessings. Their marriage would most certainly have been the joyful ceremony to establish the originating point of God's love, life, and lineage among human beings. This was Adam and Eve's original destiny. Yet instead they covered their lower parts, hid themselves among the trees, and trembled in fear, because they had formed an immoral relationship that set the origin for false love, false life, and false lineage contrary to the heavenly way. (288:127, November 26, 1997)

The issue here is that God's true love and human beings' love must start out from the same point and become one as subject and object partners. Otherwise, human love will have different directions and purposes than God's true love. It then becomes impossible to establish the absolute ideal world that both God and human beings desire.

This purpose of God—to start God's true love and human true love from the same point—was interrupted and blocked by the Fall. False parents came into being as a result of Satan's love, and human beings as descendants of those false parents inherited false love, false life, and false lineage. These false elements take them to hell. (275:55, October 31, 1995)

The International Holy Blessing Ceremony is the ceremony of resurrection that enables us to uproot and restore completely all that was defiled in our families because of the Fall, especially the false love, false life and false lineage we received from the false parents... Through the Blessing Ceremony we receive the enormous grace of being engrafted with the seeds of true love, true life and true lineage, by which God and human beings can become one through love. I sincerely hope that all humanity throughout the world will receive this enormous blessing, change to become heavenly families, and be registered in the Kingdom of Heaven on earth. (275:59, October 31, 1995)

Ethics of Married Life

LOVE IN MARRIAGE is not unfettered emotion; it survives and thrives through the discipline of married life. The path of marriage holds special challenges to a couple committed to a lifetime together. It serves as a crucible for refining character and a school for perfecting love.

Scriptures spell out some of the traditional ethical rules that have informed marriages through the ages. They spell out different but complementary roles in the household. Husbands should honor their wives and wives should obey their husbands. Both spouses should be faithful, sharing everything together and never contemplating divorce. While occasionally these traditional roles have been made to justify a double standard, when rightly understood they describe reciprocal and mutual responsibilities. (See Chapter 20: *Women's Rights* for a discussion of equality between the sexes in the larger society.) Father Moon teaches that the ideal of marriage is when the spouses live for the sake of each other, the husband respecting his wife as God's daughter and the wife respecting her husband as God's son. Love is the ultimate basis of the equality of husband and wife.

1. The Core Ethic of Conjugal Love: Spouses Are Subject to Each Other

Be subject to one another out of reverence for Christ. Wives, be subject to your husbands, as to the Lord. For the husband is the head of the wife as Christ is the head of the church, his body, and is himself its Savior. As the church is subject to Christ, so let wives also be subject in everything to their husbands.

Husbands, love your wives, as Christ loved the church and gave himself up for her, the he might sanctify her, having cleansed her by the washing of water with the word, that he might present the church to himself in splendor, without spot or wrinkle or any such thing, that she might be holy and without blemish. Even so husbands should love their wives as their own bodies. He who loves his wife loves himself. For no man ever hates his own flesh, but nourishes it and cherishes it, as Christ does the church, because we are members of his body. "For this reason a man shall leave his father and mother and be joined to his wife, and the two shall become one flesh." This mystery is a profound one, and I am saying that it refers to Christ and the church; however, let each one of you love his wife as himself, and let the wife see that she respects her husband.

Ephesians 5.21-33

You wives, be submissive to your husbands, so that some, though they do not obey the Word, may be won without a word by the behavior of their wives, when they see your reverent and chaste behavior...

Likewise you husbands, live considerately with your wives, bestowing honor on the woman as the weaker sex, since you are joint heirs of the grace of life.

1 Peter 3.1-2, 7

The husband should give to his wife her conjugal rights, and likewise the wife to her husband. For the wife does not rule over her own body, but the husband does; likewise the husband does not rule over his own body, but the wife does.

1 Corinthians 7.3-4

Your wife has rights over you.

Hadith of Bukhari (Islam)

A man is forbidden to compel his wife to her marital duty.

Talmud, Erubin 100b (Judaism)

Your wives are as a tilth to you: so approach your tilth when or how you will; but do some good act for your souls beforehand, and fear God.

Qur'an 2.223

Teachings of Sun Myung Moon

The way of love is to exalt your spouse a thousand times above yourself. God went through a course of absolute obedience to humanity to reach the realm where He could love us as His object partners. A husband and wife married in God's love desire to practice just such a high standard of love—the standard of love that God desires from His object partners. Each partner gives the other absolute obedience. Each continually gives and forgets what he or she has given. From that practice, the flower of love blooms between the husband and wife. (288:68-69, October 31, 1997)

You who were born as a woman should have the attitude that you will love your husband as God and as the representative of all humanity. Unless you love him more than anyone in the world, you cannot enter the Kingdom of Heaven. Likewise, you men should know that unless you love only one woman, and love her as God and the representative of all humanity, you cannot love God or humanity. (97:321-22, April 1, 1978)

A wife who lives with true love attends her husband as God. Moreover, she attends him as she would attend Christ, the Lord. Christ is the King of kings; therefore she attends her husband like a king. When she rejoices in her husband as if she were beholding the Lord, she is lifted up to the value of God's partner; and as God's partner, she would manifest the value of God.

Likewise, a husband with true love attends his wife as God, as the Bride of Christ, and as a queen. (March 9, 1978)

You should have absolute obedience, absolute sacrifice, and absolute love for God. But before practicing all this for God, first practice it for your wife or for your husband. (97:312, March 26, 1978)

What is the most valuable part of the human body? It is the love organ. What is the love organ? It is the reproductive organ. Does your reproductive organ belong to you? No, it belongs to your spouse. Who decided that? God. It is the way God created heaven and earth.

Everything in creation was created for love. Therefore, no creature has its reproductive organ for its own sake. Each achieves love by offering its reproductive organ to its partner. Connecting with your partner is the only way to complete love. This is the heavenly law.

True love is absolute, unique and unchanging. Do you need true love? Only when you are connected to true love can you become an owner of love who is absolute, unique, unchanging.

What does this mean? It means that a man alone cannot be an owner of true love. He can perfect his love only through connecting with his counterpart, who is the owner of his reproductive organ. A woman can perfect her love only when she connects to true love; this means when she takes ownership of her husband's reproductive organ, and her husband takes ownership of hers. (297:156, November 19, 1998)

A husband holds the key to his wife's holy place, and a wife holds the key to her husband's holy place. No one can enter it without that key, which is conferred by marriage.

Does a man's sexual organ belong to the man, or to his wife? It was not created for the man, but for the woman. Do you understand? Since the male organ was created for a woman, it belongs to the woman. Therefore, you men cannot use it as you wish. Only your wife can use your organ as she wishes. This is the heavenly law. (130:126, January 1, 1984)

When all men and women recognize that their sexual organ belongs to their spouse and not to themselves, they will bow their heads and become humble when they receive their spouse's love. Love comes to you only from your partner. If you do not live for the sake of your partner, what you are doing is not love. (279:123, August 1, 1996)

There is etiquette between husband and wife. A wife should not just walk about the house naked out of a desire to entice her husband. She should first ask him, "Is it okay if I do this?" Likewise, if his wife is fast asleep, a husband should not wake her up saying, "Honey, come here!" Even in bed the couple should be courteous and respectful of each other. (225:160, January 12, 1992)

2. Relations between the Sexes: Different Responsibilities but Equality in Love

Men are the protectors and maintainers of women, because God has given the one more strength than the other, and because they support them from their means. Therefore the righteous women are devoutly obedient, and guard in the husband's absence what God would have them guard.

Qur'an 4.34

In the family women's appropriate place is within; men's, without. When men and women keep their proper places they act in accord with Heaven's great norm.

I Ching 37 (Confucianism)

All of you are guardians and are responsible for your wards. The ruler is a guardian; the man is a guardian of his family; the lady is a guardian and is responsible for her husband's house and his offspring; and so all of you are guardians and are responsible for your wards.

Hadith of Bukhari (Islam)

So the LORD God caused a deep sleep to fall upon the man, and while he slept took one of his ribs and closed up its place with flesh; and the rib which the LORD God had taken from the man he made into a woman and brought her to the man. Then the man said, "This at last is bone of my bones and flesh of my flesh; she shall be called Woman, because she was taken out of Man."

Genesis 2.21-23

It was right for woman to be made from a rib of man. First, to signify the social union of man and woman, for the woman should neither use authority over man, and so she was not made from his head; nor was it right for her to be subject to man's contempt as his slave, and so she was not made from his feet.

Saint Thomas Aquinas, Summa Theologica 1.1.92.3 (Christianity)

Woman is as much the creation of God as man is. If she was made from man, this was to show her oneness with him; and if she was, this was to prefigure the oneness of Christ and the Church.

Saint Augustine, The City of God 22 (Christianity)

The husband who wedded her with sacred texts always gives happiness to his wife, both in season or out of season.

He may be destitute of virtue, or seek his pleasure elsewhere, or devoid of good qualities, yet a faithful wife must constantly revere her husband as a god.

Women need perform no sacrifice, no vow, no fast; if she obeys her husband, she will for that reason alone be exalted in heaven...

She who, controlling her thoughts, words, and deeds, never slights her lord, resides after death with her husband in heaven, and is called a virtuous wife.

Laws of Manu 5.153-65 (Hinduism)

Do not abuse your wife. Women are sacred. If you make your wife suffer, you will die in a short time. Our grandmother, Earth, is a woman, and in abusing your wife you are abusing her. By thus abusing our grandmother, who takes care of us, by your action you will be practically killing yourself.

A Winnebago Father's Precepts
(Native American Religions)

Teachings of Sun Myung Moon

The equality of the sexes originates from the relationship of love. Is a woman a match for her husband in physical strength? Can she equal him in jumping? Externally, a man is better than a woman in many respects. Yet a woman is better in expressing love; this makes them equal. There is equality between the sexes—between woman and man—only through love. (209:208, November 29, 1990)

Can a woman win over her husband in a fistfight? She cannot. Can she defeat him by using force? If she uses force, she will be defeated every time. However, even force is under the dominion of love. When a woman embraces her husband with love, he may pull her and push her, but then he lifts her up and they spin round and round.

    For example, I can hold True Mother in my arms and spin her round and round. She says, "I'm so dizzy!" but she is happy. Maybe I will kick her playfully, but even as she complains, "Why are you lifting me up and spinning me around?" she is joyful. We pay no attention to the movements of our feet and our bodies as we spin around in the bosom of love; it is pure ecstasy. (137:217, January 3, 1986)

When you couples begin your families, it is good if the husband leads a public life and the wife is in charge of the home.[18] (*Blessing and Ideal Family* 7.3.3)

A wife should be obedient and supportive of her husband. Of course, for this to work, the husband should fulfill his responsibility [toward her]. (*Blessing and Ideal Family* 7.1.6)

Wives, do you resent your loving husband for being in a higher position than you? Husbands, do some of you dislike your beloved wife because she is better than you? The two of you are one. One! Once you become one, you can freely go wherever you want: you can come up from below, come down from above, or stay in the middle. There are no obstacles. (91:141, February 6, 1977)

In your family, do you respect your father but regard your mother as insignificant? Do you celebrate your father's birthday magnificently but do not even remember your mother's birthday? Even non-believers know that the relationship between husband and wife should be harmonious like heaven and earth.

Harmony arises when opposites come together. There is harmony among your eyes, nose, ears and lips because opposites come together. Likewise, only when a father and mother come together can they embrace everything in the world. The father alone cannot do it; it is impossible.

These days the world puts the man first. Therefore we must promote a movement for women's liberation, one that deals with the fundamental issue. In the Principle perspective, the husband should obey his wife for the first three years of marriage. That is the proper course of restoration. Since Adam and Eve fell together, they must climb up together through a path of re-creation. (21:194, November 20, 1968)

3. The Good and the Bad in Husbands and Wives

A good wife who can find?
She is far more precious than jewels.
The heart of her husband trusts in her,
and he will have no lack of gain.
She does him good, and not harm,
all the days of her life.
She seeks wool and flax,
and works with willing hands.
She is like the ships of the merchant,
she brings her food from afar.
She rises while it is yet night
and provides food for her household
and tasks for her maidens.
She considers a field and buys it;
with the fruit of her hands she plants a vineyard.
She girds her loins with strength
and makes her arms strong.
She perceives that her merchandise is profitable.
Her lamp does not go out at night.
She puts her hands to the distaff,
and her hands hold the spindle…
She opens her mouth with wisdom,
and the teaching of kindness is on her tongue.
She looks well to the ways of her household,
and does not eat the bread of idleness.
Her children rise up and call her blessed;
her husband also, and he praises her,
"Many women have done excellently,
but you surpass them all."
Charm is deceitful, and beauty is vain,
but a woman who fears the Lord is to be praised.
Give her of the fruit of her hands,
and let her works praise her in the gates.

Proverbs 31.10-31

Socrates' wife Xanthippe would first abuse him and then throw water at him. He once joked, "Did I not say that Xanthippe was thundering now, and would soon rain?" When Alcibiades said to him, "The abusive temper of Xanthippe is intolerable," he replied, "But I am used to it, just as I should be if I were always hearing the noise of a pulley, and you yourself endure to hear geese cackling." To which Alcibiades answered, "Yes, but they bring me eggs and goslings." "Well," rejoined Socrates, "and Xanthippe brings me children." Once, she attacked him in the market-place and tore his cloak off; his friends advised him to fight her off with his hands. "Yes?" said he, "And while we are boxing, you may all cry out, 'Well done, Socrates! Well done, Xanthippe!'?" Socrates used to say, "A man ought to live with a restive woman. A horseman who can handle violent-tempered horses is easily able to handle all the others. Likewise, after handling Xanthippe, I can live easily with anyone."

Socrates (Hellenism)

Sujata, the young wife of an eldest son of a rich merchant, Anathapindika, was arrogant, did not respect others and did not listen to the instruction of her husband and his parents. Consequently, some discord arose in the family. One day the Blessed One came to visit Anathapindika and noticed this state of affairs. He called the young wife, Sujata, to Him and spoke to her kindly, saying, "Sujata, there are seven types of wives:

A wife who is pitiless, corrupt in mind,
Neglecting husband and unamiable,
Inflamed by other men, a prostitute bent on murder,
Call that wife a slayer!

A wife who would rob her husband of his gains—
Though little be the profit that he makes,
Whether by craftsmanship, or from his trade, or by the plough—
Call that wife a robber!

The slothful glutton, bent on doing nothing,
A gossip and a shrew with strident voice,
Who brings to low account her husband's zeal and industry—
Call that wife a master!

Who with loving sympathy,
Just as a mother for her only son,
For husband cares, and over his stored-up wealth keeps watch and ward—
Call that wife a mother!

Who holds her husband in the same regard
As younger sister holds the elder born,
The meek in heart, who in his every wish her husband serves—
Call that wife a sister!

And she who is as glad her lord to see
As boon companions long apart to meet,
A gracious character of gentle birth, a fond helpmate—
Call that wife a friend!

If fearless of the lash and stick, unmoved,
All things enduring, calm, and pure in heart,
She bear obedience to her husband's word, from anger free—
Call that wife a handmaid!

Now she who's called: a mistress, slayer, thief,
Who's harsh, immoral, lacking in respect, when death comes—
Will wander in the miseries of hell.

But mother, sister or companion, slave,
In precept long established and restrained, when death comes—
Will wander in the happy heaven world.

These, Sujata, are the seven kinds of wives a man may have; and which of them are you?" "Lord," said Sujata, "let the Exalted One think of me as a handmaid from this day forth."

Anguttara Nikaya 4.91, Sujata Sutta *(Buddhism)*

If you marry a man and you want to be certain of always retaining him, work for him. With work you will always be able to retain your hold on men. If you do your work to the satisfaction of your husband, he will never leave you.

Remain faithful to your husband. Do not act as though you are married to a number of men at the same time. Lead a chaste life. If you do not listen to what I am telling you and you are unfaithful to your husband, all the men will jeer at you. They will say whatever they wish [and no one will interfere].

Do not act haughty to your husband. Whatever he tells you to do, do it. Kindness will be returned to you if you obey your husband, for he will treat you in the same manner.

A Winnebago Elder's Instructions
(Native American Religions)

Teachings of Sun Myung Moon

What is the problem with families today? Isn't it that both the husband and wife are insisting, "Live for my sake" and "You must love only me"? Such a selfish attitude is the characteristic of Satan, so God will leave such a family. Once Satan enters a family, it breaks down. The parents raise the children, insisting, "You must live for us." The children tell their parents, "Father, mother, live for me." They each want the other to live for their sake, so the family breaks apart. (69:87, October 20, 1973)

Wives often lie to their husbands, and husbands to their wives, in order to hide things from each other. Each tries to possess a realm over which they have sole control. If your family is like this, you are still connected with Satan's world. (396:257, November 10, 2002)

When a wife suggests to her husband, "Please do this," he answers, "Yes." When the husband suggests to his wife, "Please do this," she answers, "Yes." Is it right when a husband and wife obey each other like that?... Should the central point of a marriage be the husband, the wife, or their love? It should be love. (91:220, February 20, 1977)

It is not easy being a husband. Although you come home tired from work, you still have responsibilities toward your wife. Although your work was full of difficulties and aggravations, you still have responsibilities toward your wife. The greater the difficulties, the greater are your responsibilities toward your wife. The fact that you are tired is no excuse.

The same is true for you wives. It does not matter whether you like your husband or do not like your husband; you still have responsibilities toward him. The basic rule is joint responsibility.

Your spouse stands before you as God's representative on earth. He or she is in a unique position as God's representative, more than any other person in the nation or any other person on earth. Husbands and wives who have thoughts other than this while they live on earth will go to a fearful hell.

Likewise, as parents, you have to be careful that you never cause your children to say, "Our mother and father are always fighting." If your children see you like that, then regardless of how well you do otherwise, you will end up in hell. Rather, you should act in such a way that your children say, "Our father represents God. He is God in our home. Our father is our home's president. Our father is our home's saint." They should say the same things about their mother. The sages of old had a saying, "All is well when there is harmony at home." In the Unification Church, we go a step further and call for "harmony with Heaven." We must create harmony with Heaven everywhere in the cosmos. (101:41-42, October 28, 1978)

A woman who sometimes gets hysterical, crying, "Eeek!" needs a mate who can comprehend her ways. When she gets upset at her husband, calling, "John!" he should calmly reply, "Oh, yes?" He should not snap back at her, "What do you want now?" Instead he should take his time, slowly turn to face her, and say, "Yessss?" [making a face].

The rockiest and steepest mountain has the loudest and strongest echo. When you shout at it, "Bee!" the mountain answers with a resounding "Boo-oom." A husband should give that kind of echo to his wife. When his wife nags him, "Ng, ng, ng," he responds, "umm, umm, ummmm." A true man has such a nature, something that is mysterious to his wife. He should be different from her and not just react to whatever she says. (118:225-26, June 6, 1982)

When a husband and wife have separate bank accounts and say, "This is my money and that is your money," is that perfect love? Perfect love goes beyond this and says, "My money is as much yours as it is mine."

Would you want to set preconditions on your partner before you get married, or would you ask only for love? Does a person who requires his or her partner to sign a prenuptial agreement really trying to love or just pretending to love? Perhaps he or she is using love.

That is not our way; we should live for love. Marriage means gathering together all your power, knowledge, money, and yourself, and putting everything in one package to present to your husband, asking only for his love in return. (92:192, April 10, 1977)

When a true husband or true wife encounters difficulties, he or she does not weep and complain, "Because of that terrible husband…" or "because of that terrible wife, I am ruined." Instead, they weep repentant tears, saying, "Because I was lacking in devotion, I could not make my husband happy," or "I could not make my wife happy." The husband and wife who live together in this manner are a true husband and a true wife. (204:41, June 29, 1990)

Who is a true wife? A true wife determines that she was born for her husband, lives for him and would die for him. Only in that place, can she be a true wife.

Who is a true husband? A true husband determines that he was born for his wife, lives for her and would die for her. The ideal of God's creation lies in this, though most people don't realize it.

As we practice this, we come to understand the principle: We exist to live for the sake of others. Only by living in this manner can we find true love. Since God set up this principle, it is the only path for humans to find happiness and hope. (77:293, April 25, 1975)

4. Divorce is Hateful to God; Spouses Should Be Faithful 'Till Death and Beyond

The lawful thing which God hates most is divorce.[19]

Hadith of Abu Dawud (Islam)

Some Pharisees came up to him and tested him by asking, "Is it lawful to divorce one's wife for any cause?" He answered, "Have you not read that he who made them from the beginning made them male and female, and said, 'For this reason a man shall leave his father and mother and be joined to his wife, and the two shall become one flesh'? So they are no longer two but one. What therefore God has joined together, let not man put asunder." They said to him, "Why then did Moses command one to give a certificate of divorce, and to put her away?" He said to them, "For your hardness of heart Moses allowed you to divorce your wives, but from the beginning it was not so. And I say to you: whoever divorces his wife, except for unchastity, and marries another, commits adultery."

Matthew 19.3-9

The LORD is the witness between you and the wife of your youth, because you have broken faith with her, though she is your partner, the wife of your marriage covenant. Has not the LORD made them one? In flesh and spirit they are his. And why one? Because he was seeking godly offspring. So guard yourself in your spirit, and do not break faith with the wife of your youth. For I hate divorce, says the LORD God of Israel.

Malachi 2.14-16

God has indeed heard (and accepted) the statement of the woman who pleads with you concerning her husband and carries her complaint to God; and God hears the arguments between both sides among you. Surely God is Hearing, Seeing.

If any men among you divorce their wives by *zihar*, calling them their mothers, they are not their mothers; none can be their mothers except those who gave them birth. They utter words iniquitous and false.[20]

Qur'an 58.1-2

The husband receives his wife from the gods; he does not wed her according to his own will; doing what is agreeable to the gods, he must always support her while she is faithful.

"Let mutual fidelity continue until death"; this may be considered as a summary of the highest law for husband and wife.[21]

Laws of Manu 9.95, 9.101 (Hinduism)

They continue by legislation to attack the indissolubility of the marriage bond, proclaiming that the lawfulness of divorce must be recognized, and that the antiquated laws should give place to a new and more humane legislation. Many and varied are the grounds put forward for divorce, some arising from the wickedness and the guilt of the persons concerned, others arising from the circumstances of the case... in a word, whatever might make married life hard or unpleasant... Opposed to all these reckless opinions stands the unalterable law of God, fully confirmed by Christ, a law that can never be deprived of its force by the decrees of men, the ideas of a people or the will of any legislator: "What God hath joined together, let no man put asunder."

Pope Pius XI, Casti Connubi (Christianity)

It floats about, that boat of cypress wood,
There in the middle of the Ho.
With his two tufts of hair falling over his
    forehead,
He was my mate;
And I swear that till death I will have no other.
O mother, O Heaven,
Why will you not understand me?

It floats about, that boat of cypress wood,
There by the side of the Ho.
With his two tufts of hair falling over his
    forehead,
He was my only one;
And I swear that till death I will not do the evil
    thing.
O mother, O Heaven,
Why will you not understand me?[22]

Book of Songs, Ode 45 (Confucianism)

A virtuous wife who, after the death of her husband, constantly remains chaste even though she have no son, will reach heaven just as do men living a life of renunciation.

Laws of Manu 5.160 (Hinduism)

Teachings of Sun Myung Moon

When man and woman became husband and wife, their relationship should be eternal. If the beginning was good, the end also should be good. It should remain constant. If you were happy in the beginning, you should be happy at the end. (86:109, March 14, 1976)

Children who grow up in a loving home become anxious and distressed if hear that their parents want to divorce. Good children will claim, "I am your child, the union of both of you. You should make any kind of compromise for me. Please be the great parents I know you are. I need you." We should teach young people that this claim is just: their parents have no right to divorce due to their parental responsibility for their children.

Because of their love for their children, parents do not have any right to even contemplate divorce. Young people in this country should assert their rights and launch an anti-divorce movement. (October 23, 1977)[23]

Young people: do not think that if you do not like their spouse you can choose to divorce her. The universe is not made that way. If you value yourself, you should value love just as much. Therefore once you are bound together as husband and wife, you have to maintain that relationship for eternity. All human beings are destined to walk this path. That is where the value of a human being lies. (117:292, April 11, 1982)

God is the absolute being. God is one, not two. Adam and Eve had the characteristics of God, so they were also absolute beings. Adam was created with God's male characteristics, and Eve was created with God's female characteristics—these characteristics are absolute. The love that can unite the inner [male] and outer [female] characteristics is absolute love; even God obeys it absolutely.

Therefore love regards each husband and wife as the one and only couple in the universe. They are absolute, eternal and unchanging. Yet because couples do not understand this principle, they divorce. As long as you maintain your foundation in this principle, you can never divorce. (226:171, February 4, 1992)

Why do a husband and wife fight? They fight because they each want to receive love. Couples who only want to receive love will not last. A family whose members only want to receive love will fall apart. But a family whose members are determined to give love to each other will not break down. It will survive, even if others wish it ill. Love that prompts us to live for each other is eternal love. (36:76, November 15, 1970)

If a wife is boastful and despises her husband, she puts herself in hell. What is hell? It is the universe's trash can [for people who lack love]. However, even if a wife is on the verge of plunging into the deepest hell, if she has a righteous husband who holds on to her hand, saying, "I will stay with you, no matter what," then she will not go to hell. The same is true when a wife does that for her husband. This is the gospel of all gospels. (161:324, March 8, 1987)

When a bride-to-be or husband-to-be is asked, "How long will you love your spouse?" If he or she answers, "As long as my spouse is young," would their partner be happy with that? Rather, the answer should be, "I will love my spouse until death, and further, for eternity." Eternity encompasses the future and beyond. When you say that you will love your spouse until your death, it means that you will love and give everything you have to him. Am I right? The term, "eternity" covers all, and "until death" means to love everything about your spouse. We can be satisfied with nothing less. (37:24, December 22, 1970)

5. The Trouble with Polygamy

The possession of many wives undermines a man's moral nature.
      Srimad Bhagavatam 11.3 *(Hinduism)*

You will not be able to deal equally between your wives, however much you wish to do so.[24]
      Qur'an 4.129

Whoever has many wives will have troubles in surfeit.
He will be deceitful, he will lie, he will betray to have them together;
It is not certain that he can have peace to pray well.
      Yoruba Poem *(African Traditional Religions)*

Teachings of Sun Myung Moon

When a woman marries a man, should she have relationships with only one man, or with hundreds? There must be only one man in her life. Why only one? It is for true love. In order to achieve absolute true love, we marry only one person. (122:234, November 14, 1982)

There is only one person in the universe whom you are meant to marry. Therefore, consider that you and your spouse are the only two people in the universe. You should abide in that first love, which only one man and one woman can share. Then God will abide with you. (265:251, November 23, 1994)

Parental Love

BEING A PARENT CALLS FORTH THE NOBLEST and most unselfish emotions in ordinary people. Rare is the parent who would not sacrifice his or her life for the sake of their child. Having children is a life-altering experience, calling forth moral strength to end destructive lifestyles and become responsible role models to their children. Parenting challenges people as nothing else to be sacrificial, patient, forgiving—in short, to develop a love that more closely resembles the love of God.

Parental love is the highest stage in the family school of love. To enter into that stage, couples have a duty to have children; it is a duty to love and to their own perfection. Furthermore, parents are responsible to educate their children in the most basic matters of life—what Father Moon calls education in heart and norm. This education has three aspects, each treated in turn: moral instruction, discipline, and setting an example. Scriptural wisdom regards discipline to be an essential duty of parents, when done out of love and concern for their proper growth. Failure to discipline children, on the other hand, is a form of abuse, because it leads to rotten character. A parent's example in particular concerns the parents' example of faith and devotion to God; it is key to the children developing their own faith. Next, parents are guardians, protecting their children from harm. Anyone who has had a teenage daughter knows of the sleepless nights spent worried about her and thinking about how to keep her safe. The final group of passages speaks about the heart of parents to unconditionally love their children, forgiving them when they fall short and wanting the very best for them.

1. The Essential Value of Children

God blessed them, and God said to them, "Be fruitful and multiply, and fill the earth."
Genesis 1.28

He who refrains from procreation is as though he impaired the divine image.
Genesis Rabbah 34.14 (Judaism)

Lo, children are a heritage from the LORD,
the fruit of the womb a reward...
Happy is the man who has his quiver full of them!
Psalm 127.3-5

Children are the clothes of a man.[25]
Yoruba Proverb (African Traditional Religions)

The whole future of the race depends upon its attitude toward children; and a race which specializes in women for "menial purposes" or which believes that the contest of the sexes in the spheres of business and politics is a worthier endeavor than the creation of tomorrow's generation, is a race which is dying.
L. Ron Hubbard, Science of Survival (Scientology)

Teachings of Sun Myung Moon

Once we marry, we should have children. Some may think that it does not matter whether or not we bear children. But that is not the case. Unless we bear children, we cannot fulfill the will of love.

There are four directions of love: east, west, north and south, around the center. When love is centered, its root can spread in all four directions and support the tree. (214:12, February 1, 1991)

Why do we need children? It is to know God's love, His love as our Parent. We need children to know how to attend [God] as our Parent... So we should not only give orders to our children, we should attend them and live for them [as God lives for us]. Only then can we comprehend God's love.

We need our children as a textbook. Without children, we are incomplete. We cannot know God's love because we cannot know how much God loves human beings, His children. Just as we cannot know the love of a husband or wife unless we become a husband or a wife, we cannot know parental love for children until we become parents. God created us so that we can learn to love by relating with each other. Hence if we do not have children, we cannot become true parents. (133:138-39, July 10, 1984)

Mothers and fathers cannot achieve unity without children. Why do parents prefer their children's love? They cannot help it. Mother and father love each other as they love their children together, not just individually. It forms a rope of love that binds mother and father into one. A chain made of iron will eventually rust and break, but the rope of love lasts forever. Neither money nor food can bind parents and children. Only love can bind them. (18:329, August 13, 1967)

What is marriage for? It is to establish a family with children. If you do not have children, your relationship may begin to deteriorate. Only after giving birth to children can your family be secure. Even if a husband might want to divorce his wife out of resentment, if his wife gives him a son, he cannot easily divorce. He feels committed to keep his family intact. For the sake of our families, we should have children. (23:25, May 11, 1969)

You should love your children more than you love your spouse. (130:163, January 8, 1984)

If you women are asked, "Who do you like better, your husband or your children?" the correct answer should be, "My children." You can divorce your husband, but you cannot separate from your children. Even if you were to disown them and have their names removed from the record of your family tree, you would still be connected to them in lineage. After divorcing your husband, you might forget him. Yet if you were separated from your children, as time goes by you would miss them more and more. Anyone who has children can understand this. (18:112, May 28, 1967)

Parents want their children to be better than themselves. No parent wants his children to be inferior to him. A good-looking man and a beautiful woman married each other and bore a homely child. Yet if you say to them, "Your child is better looking than you are," they are happy. It is true. No parent would take offense at that statement. (77:102, April 1, 1975)

True Mother[26] gave birth to thirteen children. She once remarked, "Nothing in the world has given me more pleasure than giving birth to my babies and nursing them at my breast. Now that I have grown old, I look back on those times as the most pleasurable of my life." (44:199, May 7, 1971)

There is no multiplication in the spirit world. The multiplication of children happens only on earth. The earth is the only place where the citizens of the Heavenly Kingdom can be multiplied. That is why on earth, you should give birth to many children, centering on God's true love. (218:200, July 28, 1991)

2. Raising Children with Firmness and Love

Train up a child in the way he should go,
and when he is old he will not depart from it.

Proverbs 22.6

Fathers, do not provoke your children to anger, but bring them up in the discipline and instruction of the Lord.

Ephesians 6.4

He who spares the rod hates his son,
but he who loves him is diligent to discipline him.

Proverbs 13.24

You can only coil a fish when it is fresh.[27]

Nupe Proverb (African Traditional Religions)

What son is there whom his father does not discipline? If you are left without discipline, in which all have participated, then you are illegitimate children and not sons. Besides this, we have had earthly fathers to discipline us and we respected them... For the moment all discipline seems painful rather than pleasant; later it yields the peaceful fruit of righteousness to those who have been trained by it.

Hebrews 12.7-11

A child picks up earth, dirty things, tiles, stones, old bones, pieces of wood and puts them into his mouth, at which the father and mother, apprehensive of the harms that might arise thereby, take the child with the left hand and with the right take these out...

For the father and mother of an only son, in sleep or while awake, or while walking, standing, sitting or reclining, their minds always think of the son. If he does wrong, they give kindly advice and lead the boy that he does not do evil any more.

Mahaparinirvana Sutra 471 (Buddhism)

As the child, according to its natural disposition, commits thousands of faults,
the father instructs and slights, but again hugs him to his bosom.

Adi Granth, Sorath, M.5 (Sikhism)

[The prodigal son] arose and came to his father. But while he was yet at a distance, his father saw him and had compassion, and ran and embraced him and kissed him. And the son said to him, "Father, I have sinned against heaven and before you; I am no longer worthy to be called your son." But the father said to his servants, "Bring quickly the best robe, and put it on him; and put a ring on his hand, and shoes on his feet; and bring the fatted calf and kill it, and let us eat and make merry; for this my son was dead, and is alive again; he was lost, and is found."

Luke 15.20-24

A daughter keeps her father secretly wakeful,
and worry over her robs him of sleep;
when she is young, lest she do not marry,
or if married, lest she be hated;
while a virgin, lest she be defiled
or become pregnant in her father's house;
or having a husband, lest she prove unfaithful,
or, though married, lest she be barren.

Ecclesiasticus 42.9-10 (Christianity)

Teachings of Sun Myung Moon

Children do not like it if you criticize them repeatedly. Rather, they are happy if you accept and praise them even when they do wrong. Immature children need to be appeased in this way, to encourage them with praise. Nevertheless, children are self-centered. When they see something they like, they want to have it right away. Therefore, they need education. (36:73, November 15, 1970)

Sometimes parents push their children hard, and even spank them on occasion, but it is for their sake. Then after pushing them like that, the father and mother pray for their children in tears, unable to sleep at night. That is true love. (102:253-54, January 14, 1979)

Do you know what true parental love is? A true parent never thinks, "Now I am investing in my children's future, but someday I will receive it all back with interest." Parental love is to sacrifice day and night in loving their children, giving and giving more without ceasing. Thus, a mother keeps her children in mind even when she goes to the market, thinking that she would like to buy something more for them. That sort of parental love is close to the original love that God implanted in us. Because love has this origin, there is a basis to save humankind. (142:35, March 3, 1986)

Parents want to give their child the most valuable thing they own. Nevertheless, as long as the child is unable to manage it properly, they cannot give it. Were they to receive it when they were not ready, it could harm them. For example, a sharp knife is dangerous for a child, and no parent lets his child play with one, no matter how much he wants it. (29:108, February 25, 1970)

There is a Korean proverb, "Give a piece of cake to a person you hate, but a spank to the one you love." It makes sense. When our parents scold us, we need to understand their loving heart, and when they hit us with a rod, we need to feel the pain they are going through and shed tears with them. Then we can inherit the proper tradition to continue in the next generation. (95:81, October 23, 1977)

Parents who raise their fists and strike their children in anger should immediately repent. The mother who does not hit her children, but rather sheds tears of compassion and love, is a more effective parent. The mother who disciplines this way will never be dominated by her children. She will always be successful at inducing her children to submit to her guidance. Were she to hit them, she would get poorer results. (41:332, February 18, 1971)

You and your spouse should never fight in front of your children. Never. Promise that you will never do it. This is the case in my own family. Because my wife and I have kept that promise, our children grew up secure in the belief that their parents never quarrel and love each other more than any other parents in the world. Thus you should educate your children, that they can regard their parents as their source of hope… If you have a son, he should say, "I want to become like my Dad." Your daughter should say, "I want to become like my Mom." That is the right way to educate them. (90:123, October 21, 1976)

Parents can give a general direction to their children and let them solve the detailed problems by themselves. I was a self-supporting student. Tigers let their cubs experience severe trials and harsh discipline in order to rear them to be the kings of the mountain by developing their wild nature. Iron gets stronger by heating. This is an important lesson to think about when educating children. (*Blessing and Ideal Family* 7.5.5)

No matter how painful a situation your children put you through, when they come to you with tears in their eyes and ask your forgiveness, you must forget all the bad memories and once again put on a happy face. (23:182, May 18, 1969)

What is the essence of love? It is living for others. It is giving what we have to others. Where does love originate? It originates from God. Since God is the Subject of absolute love, He desires to give. That is the essence of His love. When viewed from this perspective, parental love is the closest to the essence of love.

Parental love always strives to give. Although a child turns to wickedness and refuses to listen to his parents, if the parents continue to love him even more than before, the child will repent. Were the parent to reproach the child, saying, "You still don't recognize my love for you, even though I have invested so much for you that my back is bent!" and strike him with a stick, after three times the child would pack and run away. However, if the parent weeps in front of the child, saying, "Your problems are all because I could not love you enough. It is my fault for not loving you more," and showers him with still more love, the child's heart will melt and he will return to the parent. A greater love has the subjective ability to embrace and digest a lesser love. (48:182-83, September 12, 1971)

According to spiritual law, the worst crime is for a parent to neglect or abuse his or her children, driving them into the dungeons of hell. There is no forgiveness for such acts... God could never treat His children that way, so He cannot forgive those who do.

On the other hand, God is moved to see parents who are willing and ready to die for their children. He will say, "You resemble Me; that is the way I have been living, sacrificing everything for My children." Thus, parents who would die for their children can enter heaven. (93:335, June 17, 1977)

3. Educating Children in Their Parents' Tradition

The LORD said, "Shall I hide from Abraham what I am about to do, seeing that Abraham shall become a great and mighty nation, and all the nations of the earth shall bless themselves by him? No, for I have chosen him, that he may charge his children and his household after him to keep the way of the LORD by doing righteousness and justice; so that the LORD may bring to Abraham what he has promised him."

Genesis 18.17-20

And remember when Luqman said to his son by way of instruction, "O my dear son! Establish worship and enjoin kindness and forbid iniquity, and persevere, whatever may befall you. Lo! That is the steadfast heart of things."

Qur'an 31.17

What any man should provide for his children as a legacy is learning. Other things are not real wealth.

Naladiyar 134 (Jainism)

You shall therefore lay up these words of mine in your heart and in your soul; and you shall bind them as a sign upon your hand, and they shall be as frontlets between your eyes. And you shall teach them to your children, talking of them when you are sitting in your house, and when you are walking by the way, and when you lie down, and when you rise.

Deuteronomy 11.18-19

My son, keep your father's commandment,
and forsake not your mother's teaching.
Bind them upon your heart always;
tie them about your neck.
When you walk, they will lead you;
when you lie down, they will watch over you;
and when you awake, they will talk with you.
For the commandment is a lamp and the teaching a light,
and the reproofs of discipline are the way of life.

Proverbs 6.20-23

One should not promise a child to give him something and then not give it to him, because he will thereby teach the child to tell lies.

Talmud, Sukkah 46b (Judaism)

I am reminded of your sincere faith, a faith that dwelt first in your grandmother Lois and your mother Eunice and now, I am sure, dwells in you.

2 Timothy 1.5

Teachings of Sun Myung Moon

Bequeath to your children a good tradition that they will continue to follow throughout their lives. (71:19, March 24, 1974)

Parents usually tell their children, "You should become this or that kind of person, and you should do this or that kind of work." But it is far better to tell them, "You should be a person who knows God." (11:308, March 5, 1962)

The family is the school of love; it is the most important school in life. The family is where children cultivate the depth and breadth of their heart *(shimjung)* by receiving an education in love and emotion that only parents can provide. This becomes the foundation stone for building the children's character. The family is also the school teaching virtues, norms and manners. It is the way of Heaven that academic education, physical education and technical education should be given on the foundation of this primary education of heart and norm.

    Parents should be true parents, showering their children with true love. At the same time they should also be true teachers, properly educating their children in heart and moral norms. Though some parents may not be aware their role as teachers, their children still learn from them by imitation. The role of parents is that important. Children develop their character of love and their spiritual nature when they are nurtured by their parents' true love and when they emulate their parents' lives of love. (271:80-81, August 22, 1995)

A father should be his child's best friend. When he comes home, his child should run to him, even if he was playing with a friend. A father should become his child's best teacher. And he should be the center of heart. (57:282, June 4, 1972)

As parents you should set the right example by your devoted service to God's Will, and in your daily life of faith and service… By doing so, you are raising children who will respect their parents and not talk back to them, and who will honor their parents by obeying whatever you ask them to do. (31:268, June 4, 1970)

Even a father who lives a life of crime does not tell his children, "I am a robber and a murderer, and you should follow in my footsteps." No, however evil they may be, parents do not teach their children to be evil. When parents say to their children, "At least you should not be bad," it implies that they themselves were bad; when they say, "At least you should do well," it means they themselves did not do well.

It is right that parents invest everything completely for their children; that way they can leave a legacy behind. This is an age-old principle of education. It would be even better if the parents left such an excellent legacy that it should be bequeathed to the society and to the world. If parents act like that, no one will say they are bad parents.

A while ago, I read that some parents left their children in an orphanage to travel around the world. That kind of neglect causes children to become bad. If the parents are always with their children, watching over them and correcting them, they will not become bad. (36:73, November 15, 1970)

Do you want to be blessed? Do you want to live eternally? Then, you should become a public person. When educating your children, do not love them only as your own children. Love them with the heart to offer them for the people of the world. When nursing your child in your bosom, consider yourself the representative of all mothers on this planet earth, and regard your baby as the representative of all humankind. Do not nurse your baby with the heart to love only your child. Rather, be a mother who loves other babies as if they were also yours. Babies nourished with the milk of such a mother will definitely become great people. And if your children do not attain such greatness, it will be a descendant one or two generations later who turns out to be someone who can lead the world. This is a formula. (31:168, 700524)

When you die, there are three things you should leave behind: First, that you lived by the path of the Principle, following God's Will. Second, that you raised good offspring. Third, that you imparted education to your children that will enable them to achieve greatness in the world. (101:200, October 30, 1978)

The Love of Grandparents

GRANDPARENTS GRACE A FAMILY WITH WISDOM, experience, and delightful love for their grandchildren. In traditional cultures where three generations live under one roof, children honor their grandparents and care for them in their infirmity as a part of daily life, learning lessons of love and respect in the process. Grandparents are moral anchors. There are too many cases where parents are corrupted by drugs or crime and rendered unfit to care for their children; then the grandparents step in to the breach to take over the parenting role. Father Moon decries the loss of the three-generation family in urbanized, industrialized society as contributing to selfishness and a coarsening of morality.

In many traditions, the honor given parents and grandparents is linked to the honor given the ancestors and the gods in one vertical chain of devotion. In this light, Father Moon speaks of grandparents as representatives of God in the home. Honoring them is a way of honoring God, the greatest Grandparent of all.

You shall rise up before the hoary head, and honor the face of an old man, and you shall fear your God: I am the LORD.

Leviticus 19.32

The feeling of grandparents for their grandchildren can be expressed this way: "Our children are dear to us; but when we have grandchildren, they seem to be dearer than our children were." You might say that the grandmother falls all over herself to try to show her appreciation for her grandchild. It goes right back to those wishes that were made for them when they were little girls: the wish that they would live to become grandmothers someday. So when the time comes and they reach grandmotherhood, they do extra little duties to show their appreciation.

Henry Old Coyote (Native American Religion)

Do not neglect the sacrificial works due to the gods and the fathers! Let your mother be to you like unto a god! Let your father be to you like unto a god! Let your teacher be to you like unto a god! Let your guest be to you like unto a god!

Taittiriya Upanishad 1.11.2 (Hinduism)

Father and mother
Are gods of the family;
Even so, honor them as gods with
Heartfelt service,
All of you of human birth.

Norinaga Motoori, One Hundred Poems on the Jeweled Spear (Shinto)

O son, help your father in his old age,
and do not grieve him as long as he lives;
even if his mind fails, be considerate with him;
in all your strength do not despise him.
For a kindness to a father will not be forgotten,
and against your sins it will be credited to you.

Ecclesiasticus 3.12-14 (Christianity)

My father sent for me; I saw he was dying. I buried him in that beautiful valley of winding waters. I love that land more than all the rest of the world. A man who would not love his father's grave is worse than a wild animal.

Nez Perce Tradition (Native American Religions)

Teachings of Sun Myung Moon

As children, you are destined to inherit the fortune of your grandparents and parents. Why do you need grandparents? They represent the past—they embody the living history of the past. Parents represent the present age and children represent the future. Thus, the family connects the past, present and future, as well as East, West, North and South. Grandparents, parents, children and God—the center of them all is true love. Think about whether it is this way in your family. By loving and respecting your grandfather and grandmother, you inherit everything from the past and learn from the past. From your father and mother you learn about the present. By loving and cherishing your children, you learn about the future… The three-generation family is like the entire universe. It is like a textbook to learn how to love the universe. Hence, if there isn't a grandmother or a grandfather in your family, you may feel insecure. (162:140, April 5, 1987)

[In a traditional family] the grandfather and grandmother, the bride's mother-in-law, father-in-law, and sister-in-law, and the grandchildren should all live together. What is the center? God. Centering on God, three generations are settled—formation, growth and completion. Hence, children need to know how to love not just their father and mother, but also their grandfather and grandmother. They should honor their grandfather and grandmother with a higher status than their father and mother. Loving them is the way for the children to love God. (128:18, May 29, 1983)

Grandparents represent God in heaven; their position is like Heaven. As the elders in the family, our grandparents bring Heaven to us. That is why you need to attend them as the representatives of God. Think of them as representatives of the King of Heaven and serve them as you would serve God. This teaching is one of the traditions of the ideal family. (251:219, October 17, 1993)

If the husband and wife fight, the grandfather and grandmother will say, "Now, now. Don't do that!" When the children fight or the grandchildren fight, they say, "Now, now. Don't do that!" In this way, with love, they play the role of a servant. They live for the sake of the other members of the family, telling each of them, "You are in a high position. You are wonderful." Grandparents play the role of the servant of love to the greatest extent… The greatest, most amazing and most powerful person in the universe is the person who walks the way of the servant of love. (135:121-22, October 4, 1985)

It is wonderful when a daughter-in-law loves her grandmother and grandfather so much that she always buys better things for them than for her husband. She may be good-looking, and the old grandfather and grandmother may be all wrinkled, yet whenever she goes shopping she looks to buy something for them, something finer than what she buys for her husband, and she does it with a more joyful heart. What a wonderful scene! If she does that, then the grandfather and grandmother will give her everything they had hidden away—everything having to do with love.

Who is the oldest being in the world? It is God. Therefore, you learn from loving your grandfather how to love God and live for His sake. When you learn this tradition, you can receive all the treasures of love stored in Grandfather God's secret warehouse. It is wonderful! (107:329, June 8, 1980)

It is true that many grandchildren and daughters-in-law hate to see the cane their grandfather carries about.[28] Perhaps they wish the grandfather an early death? Rather, good grandchildren and daughters-in-law who have loving hearts would think, "Oh God, when the cane disappears someday, I will be drenched in tears." (184:270, January 1, 1989)

If the people of a nation hold the elderly in contempt, eventually that nation will lose its national character. A person who doesn't like old people is selling out the character and tradition of his nation. (21:120, November 17, 1968)

CHAPTER 20

SOCIETY

Family as the Cornerstone of Society

SOCIETY IS AN ORGANISM WITH FAMILIES as its cells. Let these building-blocks be healthy, and society will be healthy. On the other hand, when families break down, society cannot but be in turmoil. The prevalence of family breakdown in our time is a worrying trend, boding no good for a nation's future.

Nevertheless, it would be a mistake to construe "family values" as family-centered. The attitude that "my home is my castle" would only be another form of selfishness. The lessons learned in the family "school of love" (See Chapter 19: *The Basic Form of Life*) are meant to be applied at every level of social organization. Thus, Confucian ethics regards the norm of filial piety as the basis for the ethic of public service: serving parents at home is training to serve the nation. Likewise, the ways of love for siblings, parents, and children are to be extended to caring for one's neighbors who are our peers, our parents' age, and our children's age. In this way, loving relationships in the individual family extend to encompass the universal family of humankind.

1. Healthy Families Make for a Strong Nation

The Way lies at hand yet it is sought afar off; the thing lies in the easy yet it is sought in the difficult. If only everyone loved his parents and treated his elders with deference, the Empire would be at peace.

Mencius IV.A.11 (*Confucianism*)

The natural family, stable and monogamous—as fashioned by God and sanctified by Christianity—in which different generations live together, helping each other to acquire greater wisdom and to harmonize personal rights with other social needs, is the basis of society.

Pope Paul VI, Populorum Progressio (*Christianity*)

When a family declines, ancient traditions are destroyed. With them are lost the spiritual foundations for life, and the family loses its sense of unity. Where there is no sense of unity, the women of the family become corrupt; and with the corruption of its women, society is plunged into chaos. Social chaos is hell for the family and for those who have destroyed the family as well.

Bhagavad-Gita 1.40-42 (*Hinduism*)

As history testifies, the prosperity of the State and the temporal happiness of its citizens cannot remain safe and sound where the foundation on which they are established, which is the moral order, is weakened and where the very fountainhead from which the State draws its life, namely, wedlock and family, is obstructed by the vices of its citizens.

Pope Pius XI, Casti Connubi (*Christianity*)

Teachings of Sun Myung Moon

The strongest foundation for the unity of humanity is the universal and essential love generated through the ideal of the true family. (330:252, August 18, 2000)

Family education determines the future destiny of the entire nation. When there are many families living by the principle of public service, the nation will flourish; when there are many families living with a private standard, the nation will perish. (31:243, June 4, 1970)

Unrest among today's youth has created problems throughout the world.[1] The cause of this unrest almost always has to do with emotional issues that result from not having sound parents and brothers and sisters, and from unhealthy man-woman relationships. Considering this fact, where do we look for the clue to correct these destructive problems? It is in the family. (23:13, May 11, 1969)

All juvenile problems originate in the family. Most of these children have parents, but the parents' heart is not deeply implanted in their children's hearts. In other words, these children did not experience parental love down to their bones. The generation gap arose from that point. (25:60, September 28, 1969)

The most serious problem besetting humankind is the destruction of family values due to immorality and moral decadence. Moral decadence is truly the original sin that pushes people into the abyss of suffering and despair. Whether the world of the future will resemble heaven or hell will be determined by whether we can establish a moral code that sustains the purity of the family and protects family values. (288:140, November 26, 1997)

America is bound to decline, like Rome in ancient times. Rome was not defeated by foreign invasions. It perished from within, after moral corruption undermined the people's values of love and family. Today America is vulnerable for the same reason. It is declining from within; it will not continue for long. Despite its developed civilization, America is beset by confusion over sex. The developing countries are too; [they take their lead from America.] Unless we can restore discipline and a strong moral fiber, America and the world will have no hope for a better future. (118:296, June 20, 1982)

2. Virtues Learned in the Family Are the Basis of Public Virtue

Treat the aged of your own family in a manner befitting their venerable age and extend this treatment to the aged of other families; treat your own young in a manner befitting their tender age and extend this to the young of other families, and you can roll the empire on your palm. *The Book of Songs* says,

> He set an example for his consort
> And also for his brothers,
> And so ruled over the family and the state.

In other words, all you have to do is take this very heart here and apply it to what is over there. Hence one who extends his bounty can bring peace to the Four Seas; one who does not cannot bring peace even to his own family. There is just one thing in which the Ancients greatly surpassed others, and that is the way they extended what they did.

Mencius I.A.7 *(Confucianism)*

Do not rebuke an older man but exhort him as you would a father; treat younger men like brothers, older women like mothers, younger women like sisters, all in purity.

1 Timothy 5.1-2

Regard old women the way you regard your mother. Regard those who are older than you the way you regard your elder sisters; regard those who are younger than you as your younger sisters, and regard children as your own. Bring forth thoughts to rescue them, and put an end to bad thoughts.

Sutra of Forty-two Sections 29 (Buddhism)

From affection for parents came the honoring of the ancestors; from the honoring of the ancestors came the respect and attention shown to the Heads of the families. By the respect and attention shown the Heads all the members of the clan were united. Through their unity came the dignity of the ancestral temple. From that dignity arose the importance attached to the altars of the land and grain. From that importance there ensued the love all the people with their hundred surnames. From that love came the right administration of punishments and penalties. Through that administration the people had the feeling of repose. Through that restfulness all resources for expenditure became sufficient. Through the sufficiency of these, what all desired was realized. That realization led to all courteous usages and good customs, and from these, in fine, came all happiness and enjoyment.

Book of Rites 14, The Great Treatise (Confucianism)

Filial piety is the constant method of heaven, the righteousness of earth, and the practical duty of man. Heaven and earth invariably pursue the course of filial piety, and the people take it as their pattern. The ancients imitated the brilliant luminaries of heaven, and acted in accordance with the advantages afforded by the earth, so that they were in accord with all under Heaven; and in consequence their teachings, without being severe, were successful, and their government, without being severe, secured perfect order.

Classic of Filial Piety 7 (Confucianism)

Teachings of Sun Myung Moon

The family, comprised of father and mother, husband and wife, and children, is a microcosm of the world. You should understand that the path of humankind is to love all kinds of people, expanding from the love you have for the members of your own family. You should love elderly people as your grandparents, middle-aged people as your parents, people a few years older than you as your elder brothers and sisters, and people [a few years] younger than you as your younger brothers and sisters. (105:106, September 30, 1979)

Love your neighbors' parents as you love your own parents, love your neighbors' grandparents as you love your own grandparents, and love your neighbors' children as you love your own children. This is how you expand vertical and horizontal relationships and extend front and back relationships. Do you understand this principle? You must expand these relationships for the vertical standard of heart to take root and the Way of Heaven to appear. (70:152, February 9, 1974)

And when you fight with someone, fight carrying the heart of a parent towards your opponent. That is, even though he may be an enemy, ultimately he is like your child. That is why our motto is, "Let us go forth with the heart of a parent and the body of a servant, shedding sweat for earth, tears for humankind, and blood for Heaven." This is the only way to complete restoration. (17:338-39, April 30, 1967)

Your parents represent everyone who gives you love: your teachers, your friends, and the Subject Partner [God]. Hence, you can take them as representing all people. Therefore, serving your parents is the way to serve all people and receive the love of all people. This is the meaning of the traditional [Confucian] teaching that virtuous sons and daughters serve their parents with filial piety. (105:108, September 30, 1979)

True parents do not teach their children that it is enough to have filial piety while ignoring the needs of their country. They teach them, "Go the way of patriots and serve your nation, even at the sacrifice of your family. Go the way of saints and live for the sake of the world, even at the sacrifice of your nation. Seek the welfare of Heaven and earth, even if you must give up the world; and even if you have to give up heaven and earth, seek for God." Just as an individual does his filial duty by putting his family's welfare ahead of himself, to become a patriot he must put the welfare of the nation ahead of his family. To become a saint, he must put the salvation of the world ahead of his own nation, and to become a divine son, he must establish God's Kingdom in heaven and on earth even at the sacrifice of everything in the world. (May 3, 1997)

The Moral Foundations of Society

A GOOD SOCIETY IS BUILT ON SPIRITUAL AND MORAL foundations. In this technological and materialistic age, Father Moon joins many contemporary spiritual leaders in warning us that the steady decline of morality and spiritual values poses a looming threat to social peace. Among these neglected foundations are: first, morality and virtue, which forms people into upright citizens; second, education—especially character education, which can give young people a sense of purpose and direction and empower them to shun the hedonistic lifestyle of sex and drugs; and third, religion. With its message of peace and conciliation, religion can tame the raging battles and self-aggrandizing attitudes of partisan politicians; and by calling on God, religion can procure divine blessings for the nation.

In particular, America's Founding Fathers were explicit about the role of morality and religion in securing the nation's liberties and preserving its prosperity. During Father Moon's long ministry in the United States, he frequently spoke out, calling for America to return to God and honor His will.

1. The Foundation of Morality

The earth is upheld by the veracity of those who have subdued their passions, and, following righteous practices, are never contaminated by desire, covetousness, and wrath.

Vishnu Purana 3.12 *(Hinduism)*

No individual is lost and no nation is refused prosperity and success if foundations of their thoughts and actions rest upon piety and godliness, and upon truth and justice.

Nahjul Balagha, Khutba 21 *(Shiite Islam)*

The world stands upon three things: upon the Law, upon worship, and upon showing kindness.

Mishnah, Avot 1.2 *(Judaism)*

When people submit to force they do so not willingly but because they are not strong enough. When people submit to the transforming influence of morality they do so sincerely, with admiration in their hearts.

Mencius II.A.3 *(Confucianism)*

We have no government armed with power capable of contending with human passions unbridled by morality and religion. Our Constitution was made only for a moral and religious people. It is wholly inadequate to the government of any other.

John Adams

Of all the dispositions and habits which lead to political prosperity, religion and morality are indispensable supports. In vain would that man claim the tribute of patriotism, who should labor to subvert these great pillars of human happiness, these firmest props of the duties of men and citizens.

George Washington, Farewell Address

When the personal life is cultivated, the family will be regulated; when the family is regulated, the state will be in order; when the state is in order, there will be peace throughout the world. From the Son of Heaven down to the common people, all must regard cultivation of the personal life as the root or foundation. There is never a case when the root is in disorder and yet the branches are in order.

The Great Learning (Confucianism)

Let there arise out of you a group of people, inviting to all that is good, enjoining what is right and forbidding what is wrong; they are the ones to attain happiness and prosperity.

Qur'an 3.104

In *The Book of Songs* it is said,

> He makes no show of his moral worth,
> Yet all the princes follow in his steps.

Hence the moral man, by living a life of simple truth and earnestness, alone can help to bring peace and order in the world.

Doctrine of the Mean 33 (Confucianism)

Where, after all, do universal rights begin? In small places, close to home—so close and so small they cannot be seen on any maps of the world. Yet they are the world of the individual persons; the neighborhoods; the school or college; the factory, farm or office. Such are the places where every man, woman and child seeks equal justice, equal opportunity, equal dignity without discrimination. Unless their rights have meaning there, they have little meaning anywhere. Without concerned citizen action to uphold them close to home, we shall look in vain for progress in the larger world.

Eleanor Roosevelt[2]

Teachings of Sun Myung Moon

The Bible teaches about the nine fruits of the Holy Spirit: love, joy, peace, patience, benevolence, goodness, loyalty, gentleness and self-control. (Gal. 5:22-23) These nine fruits of the Spirit are the standards of the nation that God proposes and intends to establish. They comprise that society's way of life. (4:112, March 16, 1958)

Good citizenship does not appear automatically, but arises out of a person's character and family. It flows from character, heart and education through family life. These are the bases for noble deeds by which people can advance to positions of responsibility and enhance their country's prestige. Build these foundations and become someone your country needs. If you do not build them, you may end up becoming a corrupt official. (34:19, August 29, 1970)

Peace and happiness depend on people's moral and spiritual development. This is because a nation, even the world, is only as peaceful as individuals and families that comprise it. Science and technology can be used for good—for the improvement of human life—when they are utilized by good people.

Throughout history, saints and great teachers have devoted themselves to guiding families, societies and nations toward a peaceful and happy world. To take on the challenges of the twenty-first century, humanity needs true parents, true teachers and true owners who can raise leaders of mature morality and spirituality. (271:74, August 22, 1995)

An ideal society is characterized by universally shared values. This means that everyone practices true love, observing universal ethics and morality. All members of society pursue a life of goodness and righteousness. To establish that ideal, we aim to build a society rooted in moral principles, whereby all people live moral lives in keeping with the absolute value of God's true love.

An ideal world presupposes ideal families and mature individuals. An ideal family requires the harmony of ideal parents, ideal husband and wife, and ideal sons and daughters in true love. An individual can be called mature when his or her mind and body function in harmony through true love. When people at that level of maturity practice goodness and righteousness in their family, they create the foundation for true love. When they practice it in society, which is the extension of the family, they build the world of supreme love, the world that operates in accordance with the Way of Heaven. This indeed is the ideal world. (271:78, August 22, 1995)

2. The Foundation of Education

Rabbi Assi and Rabbi Ammi, on an educational inspection tour, came to a town and asked for its guardians. The councilmen appeared, but the rabbis said, "These are not guardians, but wreckers of a town! The guardians are the teachers of the young, and instructors of the old, as is written: 'Except the LORD keep the city, the watchman wakes but in vain' [Psalm 127.1]."

Lamentations Rabbah (Judaism)

When Confucius was going to Wei, Jan Ch'iu drove him. The Master said, "What a dense population!" Jan Ch'iu said, "When the people have multiplied, what next should be done for them?" The Master said, "Enrich them." Jan Ch'iu said, "When one has enriched them, what next should be done for them?" The Master said, "Instruct them."

Analects 13.9 (Confucianism)

The source and root of all the evils which affect individuals, people and nations with a kind of poison, and confuse the minds of many is this: ignorance of the truth and not only ignorance, but at times a contempt for, and a deliberate turning away from it.

It is therefore necessary to confront evil and erroneous writing with what is right and sound: against broadcasts, motion pictures, and television shows which incite to error or the attractions of vice, must be projected those which uphold truth and strive to preserve wholesome morality.

Pope John XXIII, Ad Petri Cathedram *(Christianity)*

Teachings of Sun Myung Moon

Democracy has produced secular humanism, which is expelling God from society. Secular humanism is driving out the morality and justice taught by the saints and holy men, and is spurring on the trend towards free sex. Humanity is altogether unaware that it is diving headlong into the abyss… We have the mission of preventing this tragedy. (193:306, October 8, 1989)

This world stands at a crossroads leading either to the kingdom of Heaven or the kingdom of hell. Which way it goes depends chiefly on whether it protects family values—the ethical norms that preserve the purity of the family. Is there any nation on earth that has solved humanity's common plight: corruption of youth and their continual abuse of drugs, family breakdown and skyrocketing divorce, the AIDS epidemic, sexual crimes and political oppression? Conventional education, even religious teachings, cannot meet the challenge.

What meaning is it for a society to enjoy economic prosperity and political freedom when its families suffer in agony, with no solution in sight? Therefore, people have come to the point where they are seeking educational material and methods to protect and promote family values. Promoting family values is the fundamental issue in this age after the end of the Cold War. (288:140, November 26, 1997)

3. The Foundation of God and Religion

Unless the LORD watches over the city,
the watchman stays awake in vain.
Psalm 127.1

Every assembly which is for the sake of Heaven will in the end be established, and every assembly which is not for the sake of Heaven will in the end not be established.
Mishnah, Avot 4.14 (Judaism)

God who gave us life gave us liberty. And can the liberties of a nation be thought secure when we have removed their only firm basis, a conviction in the minds of the people that these liberties are of the gift of God? That they are not to be violated but with His wrath? Indeed, I tremble for my country when I reflect that God is just; that His justice cannot sleep forever.
Thomas Jefferson

We must divide all the children of Adam into two classes; the first belong to the kingdom of God, the second to the kingdom of the world… The one to produce piety, the other to bring about external peace and prevent evil deeds; neither is sufficient in the world without the other.
Martin Luther, Secular Authority (Christianity)

This erring race of human beings dreams always of perfecting its environment by the machinery of government and society, but it is only by the perfection of the soul within that the outer environment can be perfected. "What thou art within, that outside thee thou shalt enjoy"; no machinery can rescue you from the law of your being.
Sri Aurobindo (Hinduism)

The fundamental basis of this nation's laws was given to Moses on the Mount. The fundamental basis of our Bill of Rights comes from the teachings we get from Exodus and Saint Matthew, from Isaiah and Saint Paul. I don't think we emphasize that enough these days. If we don't have a proper fundamental moral background, we will finally end up with a totalitarian government which does not believe in rights for anybody except the State!
Harry S. Truman

To exclude the Church, founded by God Himself, from life, from laws, from the education of youth, from domestic society, is a grave and fatal error. A state from which religion is banished can never be well regulated.
Pope Leo XIII, Immortale Dei (Christianity)

Teachings of Sun Myung Moon

This land can revive only if people appear who will open their eyes anew and look towards Heaven. That, we believe, is the purpose of this movement. Therefore, we earnestly pray, may we become the people who can take responsibility for the world's revival.[3] (5:278, February 15, 1959)

It will be difficult to preserve social prosperity and maintain a peaceful order in the world as long as political sovereignty operates apart from moral and spiritual values. (359:143, November 6, 2001)

God blesses those nations that lift up religious values to lead politics, just as each citizen strives for oneness between his or her mind and body. Only by doing so will nations come to practice the principle of living for the sake of others. Yet politicians still look only to the earth, blind to Heaven's authority. Communist leaders tried for seventy years to establish prosperity without God, and now their nations are bankrupt. Likewise, the West is plagued by recession, crime and social decay; its problems will not be solved until its leaders open their eyes and discover their true cause. (234:225, August 20, 1992)

There have been many dictators in history. Many politicians have taken advantage of their position to benefit themselves and their family, and some have even attempted to control the world—all to satisfy selfish desires so huge as to exceed what their tribe or nation could give them. Nations have traditionally led their people with political power. They defined what was good for their people as political strength. They used their power to conquer the weak, add to their territory and expand the scope of their control.

On the other hand, the central theme of religions down through history is philanthropy. Religions are, broadly speaking, on the side of God. Therefore they teach such virtues as love, benevolence, righteousness and goodness. Their purpose is not self-aggrandizement. Rather, religions invest all their efforts for the benefit of others and strive for the welfare of the world. They work to transform this evil world into Heaven's world by promoting a spirit of reconciliation. (213:7, January 13, 1991)

We should recognize that our present crisis stems from our neglect or denial of God. Communism failed because it denied the existence of God. America, likewise, will suffer greatly if she does not reclaim her spiritual heritage. Even Christianity, when it loses sight of God, will be powerless to stop the world's decline. Diverse fields such as philosophy, economics, politics and the arts can attain their true potential for human betterment only when they realize their purpose in the light of God. Thus, the key to solving today's problems is to find God. Only a comprehensive understanding of God's Will and Providence can illuminate the solution to the crisis we are facing today. (262:234-35, July 26, 1994)

Now the time has come for America to awaken once again. It is time to develop a new movement of nation-building by seeking for God-centered true parents, true families, true nations and a true world. God is about to leave America, and only sincere efforts to attend God[4] will keep Him from departing. God prepared for six thousand years before He settled on America. He does not really want to leave America; where else would He go?

When America properly attends God, all its problems—family breakdown, corrupt ethics, immorality among youth, and racial conflict—will be solved of their own accord. America is the land where all five races should be living together in harmony. It is supposed to be the model for the Kingdom of God on earth. (*True Family and World Peace*, January 22, 2000)

Patriotism and Public Service

CITIZENSHIP, PATRIOTISM, PUBLIC SERVICE: these words define the arena of ethical conduct beyond the level of family and friends. Society functions well when its citizens are active participants, volunteering for public duties and taking responsibility to solve problems in their neighborhoods and communities. Particularly in a democracy, which is government "of the people and by the people," an attitude of public service is the defining characteristic of good citizens.

In times of peril, love of country calls forth sacrifice. Patriots are proud to offer themselves—their lives if necessary—in the service of their country. The biblical Esther pleads for her people at the risk of her life to save them from destruction. The Psalmist poignantly expresses love of the land in his lament "By the waters of Babylon." We include a medieval Korean poem that pledges absolute loyalty to the sovereign; it is familiar to Unificationists who have adapted it as a hymn of dedication to God's will. Here we supplement scripture with memorable words by modern patriots who set the example of sacrifice and dedication to their nations' welfare and who led their people to victory in the face of tyranny. Among the heroes in that pantheon, Father Moon pays particular tribute to Yu Gwansoon, a young Korean girl whose death at the hands of the Japanese police inaugurated the Korean independence movement.

Father Moon teaches that a nation has three aspects: people, land and sovereignty. In a number of scripture passages, the requirement of submission to government authority even includes counsel to patiently endure tyrants, for the sake of the order and public safety their regimes maintain. However, Father Moon links loyalty and respect for the ruler with the prophetic duty to admonish and guide him to rule according to God's will. Father Moon teaches that love of country is one stage on the ladder of public love that begins with love of family and ends with love of humanity, the universe and God (see below, World Citizenship). He views these loves as in alignment, not in conflict, and tells parents to inculcate patriotism in the young.

1. The Duty of Citizens to Serve Their Country

There is not one of us but has his appointed position, and we are verily ranged in ranks [for service].

Qur'an 37.164-65

Your people will rebuild the ancient ruins
and will raise up the age-old foundations;
you will be called Repairer of Broken Walls,
Restorer of Streets with Dwellings.

Isaiah 58.12

Among the actions and good deeds for which a believer will continue to receive reward after his death are knowledge which he taught and spread, a good son whom he left behind, or a copy of the Qur'an which he left as a legacy, or a mosque which he built, or a house which he built for the traveler, or a stream which he caused to flow, or a contribution which he gave from his property when he was alive and well, for which he will continue to receive reward after his death.

Hadith of Ibn Majah (Islam)

Strive constantly to serve the welfare of the world; by devotion to selfless work one attains the supreme goal in life. Do your work with the welfare of others always in mind...

The ignorant work for their own profit, Arjuna; the wise work for the welfare of the world, without thought to themselves.

Bhagavad Gita 3.23-25 (Hinduism)

If liberty and equality, as is thought by some, are chiefly to be found in democracy, they will be best attained when all persons alike share in the government to the utmost.

Aristotle, Politics (Hellenism)

When you cease to make a contribution, you begin to die.

Eleanor Roosevelt

And so, my fellow Americans, ask not what your country can do for you; ask what you can do for your country. My fellow citizens of the world, ask not what America will do for you, but what together we can do for the freedom of man.

John Fitzgerald Kennedy[5]

Teachings of Sun Myung Moon

When you belong to a nation, you must know how to love all its citizens. (1:336, December 30, 1956)

What kind of person is a patriot? A patriot wants his country only to flourish. He would rather that his country not have any problems to be concerned about. But since he has a loving mind towards his country, when he sees a problem he takes full responsibility in dealing with it. (161:133, January 18, 1987)

People who silently do public duties and serve their community and nation become its owners, wherever they may go. (5:16, November 9, 1958)

Be ready to do the most painful, unpleasant work. When you see the filthiest place in your neighborhood, think, "I should be cleaning it up." (284:154, August 1, 1993)

Take on the most difficult task for your nation; take on the most difficult task for your church; and take on the most difficult task for the world: If you don't go this way willingly, you remain as a servant and cannot reach the realm of an adopted son. You have to be willing to digest all these tasks with joy. (113:111, May 1, 1981)

Individuals should not take advantage of their nation; on the contrary, individuals should willingly let their nation take advantage of them, offering themselves for their nation's benefit. That is our duty as citizens. We should encourage all the people of our nation to take this direction. (24:20-21, June 22, 1969)

We must eliminate the basis of evil—including greed, decadence, distrust and false love—from society at every level—family, community, nation, world and universe—through practicing sacrifice, service, honesty, and true love centering on God. (167:100, June 30, 1987)

2. A Patriot's Sacrifice for King, People and Country

I only regret that I have but one life to lose for my country.

                                    Nathan Hale[6]

Though this frame should die and die,
though I die a hundred times,
My bleached bones all turn to dust,
my very soul exist or not—
What can change the undivided heart
that glows with faith toward my lord?[7]

              Chong Mongju, Tan Shim Ga *(Confucianism)*

The name of peace is sweet, and the thing itself is beneficial, but there is a great difference between peace and servitude. Peace is freedom in tranquility; servitude is the worst of all evils, to be resisted not only by war, but even by death.

                    Marcus Tullius Cicero[8] *(Hellenism)*

Is life so dear, or peace so sweet, as to be purchased at the price of chains and slavery? Forbid it, almighty God! I know not what course others may take, but as for me, give me liberty or give me death!

                                 Patrick Henry[9]

Let us therefore brace ourselves to our duties, and so bear ourselves that if the British Empire and its Commonwealth last for a thousand years, men will still say, "This was their finest hour."

                           Sir Winston Churchill [10]

By the waters of Babylon,
there we sat down and wept,
when we remembered Zion.
On the willows there
we hung up our lyres.
For there our captors
required of us songs,
and our tormentors, mirth, saying,
"Sing us one of the songs of Zion!"
How shall we sing the LORD's song
in a foreign land?
If I forget you, O Jerusalem,
let my right hand wither!
Let my tongue cleave to the roof of my mouth,
if I do not remember you,
if I do not set Jerusalem
above my highest joy!

                                   Psalm 137.1-6

Mordecai told him... the exact sum of money that Haman had promised to pay into the king's treasuries for the destruction of the Jews... and charged Esther to go to the king to make supplication to him and entreat him for her people...

Then Esther... [sent] a message to Mordecai, saying, "All the king's servants and the people of the king's provinces know that if any man or woman goes to the king inside the inner court without being called, there is but one law; all alike are to be put to death, except the one to whom the king holds out the golden scepter that he may live. And I have not been called to come in to the king these thirty days." And they told Mordecai what Esther had said.

Then Mordecai told them to return answer to Esther, "Think not that in the king's palace you will escape any more than all the other Jews. For if you keep silence at such a time as this, relief and deliverance will rise for the Jews from another quarter, but you and your father's house will perish. And who knows whether you have not come to the kingdom for such a time as this?"

Then Esther told them to reply to Mordecai, "Go, gather all the Jews to be found in Susa, and hold a fast on my behalf, and neither eat nor drink for three days, night or day. I and my maids will also fast as you do. Then I will go to the king, though it is against the law; and if I perish, I perish."

                                   Esther 4.7-16

Teachings of Sun Myung Moon

A nation needs patriots. Patriotism—love of country—is the tow-line that moves a nation forward. A patriot cannot abandon his nation; even if he leaves, he vows to return one day.[11] So strong is that tow-line that, for the sake of the suffering people of his land, a patriot will spurn personal success and does not mind enduring hardships. The power of love makes this possible. (175:204, April 17, 1988)

Out of love for their land and their nation, patriots fought against all conditions of oppression. They hoped for the day of victory and had unshakable faith that such a day would surely come. That is how they could resist the oppressors and carry on their struggle. (5:321, March 1, 1959)

Why do the Korean people revere Yu Gwansoon as a patriot? Was she merely a young girl who died miserably at the hands of the Japanese police? It is because for the sake of her nation she accounted her life worthless; she loved her nation and her people more than her life. (141:293, March 2, 1986)

A patriot might live in poverty and eat nothing but salt soup and barley rice, but when a foreigner comes to visit he prepares the finest meal. He thinks that he must not expose his poverty, out of concern for his nation's honor. We too should not behave lightly, exposing our petty squabbles while forgetting our nation's honor. Be patriots, who strive to present their nation in a beautiful light. (26:136, October 19, 1969)

Patriots should love three things: the sovereign, the land and the people. These are the three elements that comprise a nation. A patriot should love all three with true love. To do so, he must invest his family, devoting it for the welfare of the nation...

By no logic in the universe can you become a patriot by putting your family first. Love always strives to connect with something greater. (207:251, November 11, 1990)

True love is the starting point of all ideals; its action continues for eternity. When young people possess it, they will possess a power stronger than life itself. With true love, they will acquire a new outlook on their country. When young people acquire such a new outlook, their country will discover new possibilities for advancement. When diverse interest groups in the nation adopt an attitude based on true love, they will be able to rise above their conflicting interests and create a society of cooperation, harmony and progress.

True love of country manifests as sacrificial and patriotic loyalty. This is the primary force that moves a country forward. Each of the numerous national heroes whom we respect today exemplified a life of patriotic sacrifice rooted in true love. (288:201, November 28, 1997)

3. Respect for the Governing Authorities

Render unto Caesar the things that are Caesar's, and to God the things that are God's.

Mark 12.17

Pray for the welfare of the empire, because were it not for the fear it inspires, every man would swallow his neighbor alive.[12]

Mishnah, Avot 3.2 (Judaism)

The sultan is God's shade on earth to which each one of his servants who is wronged repairs. When he is just he will have a reward, and it is the duty of the common people to be grateful; but when he acts tyrannically the burden rests on him, and it is the duty of the common people to show endurance.

Hadith of Baihaqi (Islam)

Let every person be subject to the governing authorities. For there is no authority except from God, and those that exist have been instituted by God. Therefore he who resists the authorities resists what God has appointed, and those who resist will incur judgment. For rulers are not a terror to good conduct, but to bad. Would you have no fear of him who is in authority? Then do what is good, and you will receive his approval, for he is God's servant for your good. But if you do wrong, be afraid, for he does not bear the sword in vain; he is the servant of God to execute his wrath on the wrongdoer. Therefore one must be subject, not only to avoid God's wrath but also for the sake of conscience. For the same reason you also pay taxes, for the authorities are ministers of God, attending to this very thing. Pay all of them their dues, taxes to whom taxes are due, revenue to whom revenue is due, respect to whom respect is due, honor to whom honor is due.

Romans 13.1-7

Hearing and obeying [those in government] are the duty of a Muslim both regarding what he likes and what he dislikes, as long as he is not commanded to perform an act of disobedience to God, in which case he must neither hear nor obey.

Hadith of Bukhari and Muslim (Islam)

Teachings of Sun Myung Moon

Although each of us as an individual is as precious as heaven and earth put together, we should serve our family. Then, just as we place our family above ourselves, we should place the community above our family and the nation above the community. (10:328, November 27, 1960)

Serve the president of your nation as you would attend your parents and teachers, serve your parents as you would attend your teachers and the president of your nation, and serve your teachers as you would attend your parents and the president of your nation. This is the teaching of the Three Subjects Thought.[13] Its central focus is true love. (212:28, January 1, 1991)

When I speak to American young people about patriotism, they blink their eyes in perplexity and retort, "How should I love my country?" The problem is: no one has properly educated them about love. They see that their parents' relationship is entirely carnal, and they experience relationships with their siblings and friends that are entirely carnal. They see everyone practicing animalistic love—love below the level of animals.

People say, "What do you mean, love my country? I express my patriotism by paying my taxes." With that attitude, how can they learn love of country? Love of country starts from love taught in the family. How do parents teach patriotism? They teach their children how to love their siblings and how to love their parents. At the same time, they tell them, "We love our nation just as we love you, so you should love our nation too." When children are taught like that, they understand right away from experience what patriotism is about. That is the best education. If people were raised with that tradition, instead of wondering, "What is American patriotism?" they would understand immediately and bow their heads in respect. No other explanation would be needed…

Patriots regard the words of the President as superior to their father's words. Therefore, parents should educate their children that love of country is higher than filial love. They should teach, "You and I must be loyal to our country when it is in peril, and even offer our lives for our country." That is the tradition thoughtful people should pass on to the next generation; it will correct the course of our nation's history. (95:51-52, October 23, 1977)

Labor

THE PRIMARY WAY THAT MOST PEOPLE CONTRIBUTE to society is through their labor. We spend our adult lives working to provide for our families and ourselves; yet before we receive any benefit, our labor adds to the overall wealth of the nation. Furthermore, labor is one way by which we take after God, the Maker of heaven and earth. God created us to find satisfaction in our labor and to enjoy its fruits. By our work we become co-creators with Him.

No society can be prosperous unless its members are educated to have a work ethic and have the opportunity to better themselves through their labor. A practical function of religion is to encourage the virtues that make for economic success: industry, thrift, dependability, responsibility and integrity in the workplace, and the love of one's job.

Although certain religious traditions exalt a life of poverty and mendicancy above a productive life of work, most traditions promote honest work and self-sufficiency, even for members of the clergy. Although most religions reject a life devoted solely to worldly profit, they value work as having divine approval when its gains are spent appropriately—in serving others, charity and proper worship.

1. All Work Is Sacred and in the Service of Heaven

Work is worship.
Virashaiva Proverb (Hinduism)

Great is labor; it confers honor on the laborer.
Talmud, Nedarim 49b (Judaism)

Abu Hurayrah said, "While we were with the Prophet a young man appeared. We said, 'This young man should sacrifice his youth, energy and strength to worship Allah.' The Prophet heard what we had said and replied, 'Nothing is in the way of Allah except that a man be slain in the way of Allah, or a man feed his parents, or a man feed his family, or a man strive to support himself. These are in the way of Allah.'"
Hadith of al-Soyouti[14] (Islam)

How can he become wise who handles the plow...
the smith sitting by the anvil...
[or] the potter sitting at his work?...
All these rely upon their hands,
and each is skillful in his own work.
Without them a city cannot be established,
and men can neither sojourn or live there.
Although they are not sought out for the
    council of the people,
nor attain eminence in the public assembly...
They keep stable the fabric of the world,
and their prayer is in the practice of their trade.
Ecclesiasticus 38.25-34 (Christianity)

A favorite saying of the rabbis of Yavneh was: I am God's creature and my peasant neighbor is God's creature. My work is in the town and his work is in the country. I rise early for my work and he rises early for his work. Just as he does not presume to do my work, so I do not presume to do his work. Will you say, I do much and he does little? We have learned, "One may do much or one may do little; it is all the same, provided he directs his heart to Heaven."
Talmud, Berakot 17a (Judaism)

All appointments are from Heaven, even that of a janitor.

      Talmud, Baba Batra 91b *(Judaism)*

Love work and hate lordship.

      Mishnah, Avot 1.10 *(Judaism)*

The LORD said to Moses, "See, I have called by name Bezalel the son of Uri, son of Hur, of the tribe of Judah: and I have filled him with the Spirit of God, with ability and intelligence, with knowledge and all craftsmanship, to devise artistic designs, to work in gold, silver, and bronze, in cutting stones for setting, and in carving wood, for work in every craft… And I have given to all able men ability, that they may make all that I have commanded you: the tent of meeting, and the ark of the testimony, and the mercy seat that is thereon, and all the furnishings of the tent."

      Exodus 31.1-8

Teachings of Sun Myung Moon

Whatever I do on earth, even working in a factory, is material to enrich my eternal life. (216:127-28, March 9, 1991)

You should not be halfhearted about your work. If you are, you will never amount to more than an errand boy, and an errand boy can never establish himself. So, when you work, you should invest all of your heart in it.

Think that you were born for the work, as if it were your eternal spouse.[15] In order to make the relationship with your spouse absolute and eternal, it requires investing and forgetting, investing and forgetting. Likewise, only by your investment will you form an absolute relationship with your work. (330:117-18, August 14, 2000)

Economic activity sets up a relationship between the worker and the materials he works with. You should love the things you make and sell; they are your object partners. By doing business with them and loving them, you impute to them a value equal to yourself. Thus, if you are worth 100, then each product of your business will also be worth 100. If you are worth 1,000, then your product—even a small, inexpensive pocketbook—will be worth 1,000. Why does a fountain pen that once belonged to a famous person sell for thousands of dollars at auction? Even though it was for his casual use, it holds that person's love as his object partner, which imputes to it his great value. (102:126, November 27, 1978)

Rather than regarding an industry as important, we should place greater value on the people who work in that industry. Rather than regarding science as important, we should place greater value on the scientists. Rather than regarding art as important, we should place greater value on the artists.

But, what is the current trend? An industry is valued, but not its workers; science is valued, but not its scientists; art is valued, but not artists; diplomacy is valued, but not diplomats. The human beings in each field are devalued. What happened to the people? They have been devalued. (99:116; September 10, 1978)

This morning at the opening of the Washington, D.C. church, [its director] Col. Bo Hi Pak was probably happy, but I was not. Why? It is because we purchased a church building that had been built by others. It would have been better if we ourselves had built this church from scratch. The Mormons who built this church cut slabs of marble from mountains more than 9,000 feet high and carried them here. You worked for about two months repairing and painting the building, but it took the Mormons three years when they first built it. I wish that you would have invested greater love and effort than the Mormons, but as it is, how can you compare your devotion to this building to theirs? You who worked refurbishing the building, do you think you are better than them? You say yes, but are you confident that God, who knows the building's history, would agree with you?

I had another thought when I walked into the building. The Mormons built this building with lots of energy and hard work, but then they sold it. They abandoned it and then went out and built a new temple. The important question is: did they put more heart, tears and sweat into building their new and bigger temple than their forbearers did for this church long ago, or did they just put up money and give the plans to a contractor to build it? Did they build it with their money, or with their heart, sweat and labor? That is an important question, though they do not know it.

Put yourself in the position of God. Would He rather dwell in a big new marble temple or in a small and humble temple that was built by the members' labor and devotion? To God, the size of the building means nothing. Whether it is beautiful or plain means nothing. From this perspective, God would rather be in this building than in the newly built Mormon Temple. If you Unification Church members are more sincere and dedicated than the present-day Mormons, if you are actively taking responsibility to save this city, then surely God will continue dwelling in this place that has a tradition of dedicated believers—the Mormons of old—who worshiped Him here with rejoicing. With this in mind, I entered this building. (95:254-55, December 4, 1977)

2. The Virtues of Industry, Hard Work and Self-Reliance

Let one practice here good industry; let one make the needy prosperous.

Avesta, Visparad 15.1 *(Zoroastrianism)*

When the prayer is finished, scatter in the land and seek God's bounty, and remember God frequently, that you may prosper.

Qur'an 62.10

Idleness is the enemy of the soul.

The Benedictine Rule *(Christianity)*

Go to the ant, O sluggard;
consider her ways, and be wise.
Without having any chief,
officer, or ruler,
she prepares her food in summer,
and gathers her sustenance in harvest.
How long will you lie there, O sluggard?
When will you rise from your sleep?

A little sleep, a little slumber,
a little folding of the hands to rest,
and poverty will come upon you like a vagabond,
and want like an armed man.

Proverbs 6.6-11

Weeping is not the answer to poverty; a lazy man who is hungry has no one to blame but himself.

There is no place where one cannot achieve greatness; only the lazy prospers nowhere. There is no place that does not suit me, O Divinity!

Yoruba Proverbs *(African Traditional Religion)*

He who says, "It is too hot, too cold, too late!"
Leaving the waiting work unfinished still,
Lets pass all opportunities for good.
But he who reckons heat and cold as straws
And like a man does all that's to be done,
He never falls away from happiness.

Digha Nikaya 3.185 *(Buddhism)*

Life is sweet for the self-reliant worker.

Ecclesiasticus 40.18 (Christianity)

When you eat the fruit of the labor of your hands; you shall be happy, and it shall be well with you.

Psalm 128.2

We were not idle when we were with you, we did not eat anyone's bread without paying, but with toil and labor we worked night and day, that we might not burden any of you. It was not because we have not that right, but to give you in our conduct an example to imitate. For even when we were with you, we gave you this command: If any one will not work, let him not eat. For we hear that some of you are living in idleness, mere busybodies, not doing any work. Now such persons we command and exhort in the Lord Jesus Christ to do their work in quietness and to earn their own living.

2 Thessalonians 3.8-12

The little that one produces [oneself] with a broken hoe is better than the plenty that another gives you.

Buji Proverb (African Traditional Religion)

One who claims to be a saint
And goes about begging—
Touch not his feet!

He whose livelihood is earned through work,
And part given away in charity—
Such a one, Nanak, truly knows the way to God.

Adi Granth, Var Sarang, M.1, p. 1245 (Sikhism)

The person who extends a loan to the needy is greater than the one who gives charity, and one who associates a poor person with him in business enabling him to earn for himself is greater than all the others.

Talmud, Shabbat 63a (Judaism)

A clansman has wealth acquired by energetic striving, amassed by strength of arm, won by sweat, lawful and lawfully gotten. At the thought, "Wealth is mine acquired by energetic striving, amassed by strength of arm, won by sweat, lawful and lawfully gotten," bliss comes to him, satisfaction comes to him. This is called "the bliss of ownership."

A clansman by means of wealth acquired by energetic striving... both enjoys his wealth and does meritorious deeds therewith. At the thought, "By means of wealth acquired... I both enjoy my wealth and do meritorious deeds," bliss comes to him, satisfaction comes to him. This is called "the bliss of wealth."

Anguttara Nikaya 2.68 (Buddhism)

Teachings of Sun Myung Moon

"You wealthy families, I see you drinking and dancing, enjoying yourself like the grasshopper in the fable. In the meantime, I will work so hard that my waistline will shrink like that of the ant. Go ahead, you grasshoppers! Keep singing, dancing and joking around! I will be the ant who keeps digging until I have built my own house and produced enough dirt to cover your graves." If this is your attitude and way of life, you will revive the souls in hell and become kings and queens of the Heavenly Kingdom. (339:146, December 10, 2000)

Hard labor relieves insomnia and stress; it is especially good for people who spend their time only thinking. If you office workers were to do even a day's labor at the construction site, it would relieve all your stress. If you cannot sleep because of stress, I recommend you go down into a tunnel and work there digging the tunnel for several days. Then you will have no problem sleeping. (230:168, May 1, 1992)

If you are a large tree, many birds will build their nests in your branches. Therefore, when you walk around soiled with dung, you should keep your internal dignity. Be a superb person who can dance pleasantly to the rhythm of the universe. (*Way of God's Will* 2.2)

We should experience fun in everything that we do. Farming should be fun; plowing with sweat running down our faces should be fun; carrying heavy things should be fun, too. I did all kinds of labor. As long as we are in harmony with nature and deal with every situation and relationship we face, we can succeed at just about anything. (355:96, October 3, 2001)

You need money to succeed in your mission. No one will give it to you; you have to make it with your own hands. I built the worldwide foundation for this movement with my own hands; no one did it for me. Even if I were a castaway on a deserted island I could survive. I know what mushrooms are edible, which herbs are good to eat and which are poisonous. If I have a string and a hook, I can make a fishing pole and catch as many fish as I need. I know how to be self-sufficient wherever I go. My educational philosophy is that before your reach your thirties you should be trained to be as self-sufficient as I am. (117:24-25, January 30, 1982)

There is no work that I, Sun Myung Moon, cannot do. In a mine, I become a miner and endure the hardships there. It may be difficult, but I think that even in that mine I have to fulfill God's Will. I once lived among thieves deep in the mountains. I did not participate in their thievery, but I found a way to survive there. On the ocean, I am a fisherman's fisherman. In the field, I am a farmer's farmer. Wherever I may be on this planet earth, I am a man who is capable of making a solid foundation within three weeks with my bare hands. (273:305, October 29, 1995)

Those who want to live off the government's welfare benefits will never prosper, no matter how many years may pass. People who are indebted to others can never be more than servants. Rather, you should spend your life on earth helping others. If you have helped others in this life, then when you cross over to the next world you will arrive at a high realm. However, those who live for their own sake, who prefer to receive rather than to give, and who are in debt to others, will end up in the dark regions of hell. (248:98, August 1, 1993)

Freedom

THE ASPIRATION FOR FREEDOM HAS BEEN A POWERFUL FORCE in human history. God signaled His love of freedom to a band of Israelite slaves in Egypt, and by liberating them set the example for freedom-loving people everywhere. People everywhere aspire for freedom because God created us to be free. God respects human freedom to the degree that He does not interfere with our wrong choices, even when they lead to sin and misery.

Nevertheless, God grants human beings freedom for a purpose—that we might attain our full perfection as His ideal partners. Hence, freedom is not an end in itself, but a means to greater ends: true love, true community, the Kingdom of God. Furthermore, freedom is only meaningful and efficacious when it is conducive to God's plan for human life. Freedom when used wrongly as an occasion to sin can lead to bondage. Therefore, God created us with a conscience as the inner compass to guide our free will in a good direction, and wants to provide every child with loving parents to educate them in the proper use of freedom.

The issues surrounding freedom are basic to democracy; hence we include several passages by its seminal political theorists. Critiques of secular democratic notions of freedom, particularly from the Catholic Church, are echoed in some of Father Moon's negative judgments on the excessive value given to freedom and its widespread abuse in Western democracies.

Finally, we include several passages describing Father Moon's unique teaching that God is not free, and that He is in need of liberation more than anyone.

1. The Basis for Freedom in God and God's Creation

Now the Lord is the Spirit, and where the Spirit of the Lord is, there is freedom.

2 Corinthians 3.17

I have seen the affliction of my people who are in Egypt, and have heard their cry because of their taskmasters; I know their sufferings, and I have come down to deliver them out of the hand of the Egyptians, and to bring them up out of that land to a good and broad land, a land flowing with milk and honey.

Exodus 3.7-8

Proclaim liberty throughout the land to all its inhabitants.[16]

Leviticus 25.10

The Spirit of the LORD God is upon me,
because the LORD has anointed me
to bring good tidings to the afflicted;
he has sent me to bind up the brokenhearted,
to proclaim liberty to the captives,
and the opening of the prison to those who are bound;
to proclaim the year of the LORD's favor.[17]

Isaiah 61.1-2

O ye who believe! You have charge over your own souls.

Qur'an 5.105

We hold these truths to be self-evident, that all men are created equal; that they are endowed by their Creator with certain inalienable rights; that among these are life, liberty, and the pursuit of happiness.

The U.S. Declaration of Independence

You will know the truth, and the truth will make you free.

John 8.32

Our quest for self-determination, justice, freedom and peace in our Homelands and our Territories… is a renewal of what we enjoyed before the coming of our White Brothers from across the sea. We lived contentedly under the *Gai Eneshah Go' Nah*, The Great Law of Peace. We were instructed to create societies based on the principles of Peace, Equity, Justice, and the Power of Good Minds.

Our societies are based upon great democratic principles of the authority of the people and equal responsibilities for the men and the women. This was a great way of life across this Great Turtle Island and freedom with respect was everywhere. Our leaders were instructed to be men of vision and to make every decision on behalf of the seventh generation to come; to have compassion and love for those generations yet unborn.

We were instructed to give thanks for All That Sustains Us. Thus, we created great ceremonies of Thanksgiving for the life-giving forces of the Natural World, as long as we carried out our ceremonies, life would continue. We were told that "The Seed is the Law." Indeed, it is The Law of Life. It is The Law of Regeneration. Within the seed is the mysterious force of life and creation. Our mothers nurture and guard that seed and we respect and love them for that. Just as we love our Mother Earth, for the same spiritual work and mystery.

Chief Oren Lyons[18] *(Native American Religion)*

The denial or limitation of human rights—as for example the right to religious freedom, the right to share in the building of society, the freedom to organize and to form unions, or to take initiatives in economic matters—do these not impoverish the human person as much as, if not more than, the deprivation of material goods?

Pope John Paul II, Sollicitudo Rei Socialis
(Christianity)

Teachings of Sun Myung Moon

Freedom is truly one of the Creator's most precious gifts to humanity. God created human beings to exercise freedom as spiritual beings. (133:289, November 19, 1984)

People of the world... without exception, all wish to be free. They want to live in a free society, a free nation, and a free world. Without peace and freedom in our minds, there is no true happiness... Today, although we strongly pursue freedom, we must admit that we still do not experience the condition of true freedom, coming from the heart. (7:14-15, July 5, 1959)

In truth, human beings lost their freedom as a result of the Fall. Yet even fallen people possess intact a seed of their original nature which seeks freedom, and this makes it possible for God to carry on the providence to restore it. With the progress of history, people have been ever more zealously aspiring for freedom, even at the cost of their lives. This is evidence that we are in the process of restoring our freedom, long lost due to Satan. The purpose of our search for freedom is to facilitate the accomplishment of our God-given responsibility, which is essential for fulfilling our purpose of creation. (*Exposition of the Divine Principle*, Fall 5.2)

Heavenly Father, who observes the universe from the highest heaven, wants human beings to lead. He doesn't want people to merely obey as if drawn around by the neck. That is what the mind desires, right? Your mind wants to be completely free. Ask anyone: no one wants to be controlled. You will enjoy complete freedom once you attain the status of a person of true love. Then you can travel anywhere, even to the throne of God. You can meet God anytime you like. You can become God's friend! (Earthly Life and the Spirit World 1.5.3.2)

Freedom originates in true love; without true love freedom has no root. Furthermore, without first planting this root of freedom, we cannot complete our ideal world. A wife whose husband loves her is totally free. A husband whose wife loves him regardless of how he behaves is totally free. He can touch her and even jab her, knowing that she enjoys it. She can run around the house naked, knowing that he will not object. What greater freedom is there? Why does that woman disrobe and walk about naked—to assert her freedom or out of love? Out of love, she expresses her freedom. (203:10, June 10, 1990)

The best freedom is to live well, protected by nature. Your freedom is guaranteed when you can live in accord with universal law, without any conflict or contradiction. Then you will enjoy the nature's protection. There is nothing better. (117:290-91, April 11, 1982)

Examine your motivation in searching for freedom. Does your heart truly seek for the freedom that can bring harmony to all creation? If you can put yourself in God's position and share His heart for freedom, your heart would seek the standard of freedom that all people can enjoy together. (4:318, October 12, 1958)

Democracy has been promoting the freedom and liberation of human beings. However, we should now promote the freedom and liberation of God. If this matter is resolved, the liberation of human beings, not to mention their freedom, will automatically be achieved. (344:54, June 26, 2001)

2. Freedom Starts by Becoming Master of Oneself in Accordance with the Moral Law

No man is free who is not master of himself.
Epictetus, Discourses 2.10 (Hellenism)

Truly, truly, I say to you, everyone who commits sin is a slave to sin.
John 8.34

For freedom Christ has set us free; stand fast therefore, and do not submit again to a yoke of slavery.
Galatians 5.1

For you were called to freedom, brethren; only do not use your freedom as an opportunity for the flesh, but through love be servants of one another.
Galatians 5.13

The quest for pleasure brings nothing but torment abounding;
Man thus makes of his evil desires only a shackle about the neck.
Thou seeker of false delights, liberation comes only through the love of God.
Adi Granth: Gauri Ashtpadi, M.1, p. 222 (Sikhism)

What then? Are we to sin because we are not under law but under grace? By no means! Do you not know that if you yield yourselves to any one as obedient slaves, you are slaves of the one whom you obey, either of sin, which leads to death, or of obedience, which leads to righteousness? But thanks be to God, that you who were once slaves of sin have become obedient from the heart to the standard of teaching to which you were committed, and, having been set free from sin, have become slaves of righteousness.
Romans 6.15-18

Teachings of Sun Myung Moon

God created human beings to exercise freedom as spiritual beings. At the same time, God also required human beings to be responsible for how they use their freedom. This is because freedom requires self-discipline and self-control. Freedom exists within the law, not apart from the law.

There are physical and spiritual laws at work in the universe; they are the ultimate limits to freedom. For example, you are free to jump off the top of the New Otani Hotel. That is your freedom, but your free act will bring your own destruction because you are going against the laws of nature. You are free to go into the ocean and breathe water instead of air, but the laws of nature work at that moment too. Your lungs cannot bear it and you will die.

Spiritual laws, however, are not so obvious. Yet they are as absolute as the laws of nature. To recognize spiritual laws, we must recognize that humans are spiritual beings, created by God. God, being the Creator, alone predetermined the purpose of creation and set up its spiritual laws. All value begins with God. He determined the purpose of human life and how people are to achieve that purpose. That is the foundation of absolute value. From this absolute foundation emerge moral principles, which comprise spiritual law. Human beings, created as spiritual beings, are bound by this spiritual law.

The fundamental purpose of human life is what the Creator purposed us to be, and we exist on this earth to achieve this purpose. Therefore, our spiritual happiness is realized when we accomplish our responsibility in accordance with God's moral law. Should we violate this law, it will result in self-destruction, just as surely as if we were to disregard the laws of nature. (133:289-90, November 19, 1984)

The freedom that God grants us is premised on responsibility. If everyone insisted on the freedom to love as they wished without taking responsibility for their actions, how great would be the resulting chaos and destruction! Human perfection, the attainment of the sublime ideal of love, is only possible when we take responsibility for love. (277:201, April 16, 1996)

You begin to truly experience freedom when you are completely pervaded by love. Your body wants to act freely, but it is impossible unless it embodies true love.

The American concept of freedom is so wrong. Historically, the most difficult person to deal with is your own self. This is why you must be merciless to yourself. Do you understand? Unless you become such a person, you cannot be free. (203:23-24, June 10, 1990)

Americans have made a mockery of freedom with their pursuit of trashy love. Isn't that so? Americans have no right to speak of freedom. How can they justify the freedom to party and seek pleasure everywhere while their children are weeping, their husbands and wives are suffering, and their families are breaking down? Rather than pursuing vain freedom, we should seek for true love. When we find true love, we will find true freedom as well. (203:12-13, June 10, 1990)

Freedom that departs from the Principle is not true freedom. Freedom that avoids responsibility is not true freedom. Freedom that produces no results is not true freedom. Thus, any act of freedom must be within the Principle. It must carry responsibility and produce results. A person who seeks freedom without these conditions is naturally far removed from the heavenly way. (4:318-319, October 12, 1958)

3. Freedom Requires Social Solidarity within an Orderly Social System; It Is Far Removed from Individualism

You can only protect your liberties in this world by protecting the other man's freedom. You can only be free if I am free.

Clarence Darrow[19]

The natural liberty of man is to be free from any superior power on earth, and not to be under the will or legislative authority of man, but to have only the law of Nature for his rule. The liberty of man in society is to be under no other legislative power but that established by consent in the commonwealth, nor under the dominion of any will, or restraint of any law, but what that legislative shall enact according to the trust put in it. Freedom, then, is not… liberty for every one to do what he lists, to live as he pleases, and not to be tied by any laws, but freedom of men under government is to have a standing rule to live by, common to every one of that society, and made by the legislative power erected in it.

John Locke, *Two Treatises on Government* (Humanism)

What man loses by the social contract is his natural liberty and an unlimited right to everything he tries to get and succeeds in getting; what he gains is civil liberty and the proprietorship of all he possesses.

Jean-Jacques Rousseau, *The Social Contract* (Humanism)

The roots of the contradiction between the solemn affirmation of human rights and their tragic denial in practice lies in a notion of freedom which exalts the isolated individual in an absolute way, and gives no place to solidarity, to openness to others and service to them. While it is true that the taking of life not yet born or in its final stages is sometimes marked by a mistaken sense of altruism and human compassion, it cannot be denied that such a culture of death, taken as a whole, betrays a completely individualistic concept of freedom, which ends up becoming "the freedom of the strong against the weak," who have no choice but to submit.

It is precisely in this sense that Cain's answer to the Lord's question, "Where is Abel your brother?" can be interpreted: "I do not know; am I my brother's keeper?" (Gen. 4:9). Yes, every man is his "brother's keeper," because God entrusts us to one another. And it is also in view of this entrusting that God gives everyone freedom, a freedom which possesses an inherently relational dimension. This is a great gift of the Creator, placed as it is at the service of the person… but when freedom is made absolute in an individualistic way, it is emptied of its original content, and its very meaning and dignity are contradicted.

There is an even more profound aspect which needs to be emphasized: freedom negates and destroys itself, and becomes a factor leading to the destruction of others, when it no longer recognizes and respects its essential link with the truth. When freedom, out of a desire to emancipate itself from all forms of tradition and authority, shuts out even the most obvious evidence of an objective and universal truth, which is the foundation of personal and social life, then the person ends up by no longer ends up taking as the sole and indisputable point of reference for his own choices the truth about good and evil, but only his subjective and changeable opinion or, indeed, his selfish interest and whim.

This view of freedom leads to a serious distortion of life in society. If the promotion of the self is understood in terms of absolute autonomy, people inevitably reach the point of rejecting one another. Everyone else is considered an enemy… society becomes a mass of individuals placed side by side, but without any mutual bonds… social life ventures on to the shifting sands of complete relativism. Everything is negotiable, everything is open to bargaining: even the first of the fundamental rights, the right to life.

Pope John Paul II, Evangelium Vitae (Christianity)

Teachings of Sun Myung Moon

Liberty exists where everyone lives for others and honors others. When we live for others, we are liberated as well. Living for others is intrinsically liberating. That is why I tell you to live for the sake of others. (323:73, May 31, 2000)

What people today mean by freedom is the right to assert oneself. Their freedom is merely a shield for their self-centered lifestyle. When ten people each assert their freedom, they erect ten walls around themselves, and within those walls their personalities and interests diverge to such an extent that they cannot get along together…

Today the Western world exalts freedom. Yet you should regard the word "freedom" as a fearful word. What is true freedom? If people take freedom as the opportunity to lift up God and the world, it is well and good. This is freedom that everyone can enjoy. But if people are self-centered and put everyone down, then where can there be freedom? (107:272-74, June 1, 1980)

Historically the pursuit of freedom was born out of the desire to lift up society to a higher dimension. It was not born to break down and destroy the social order. Yet today's young people say, "We want the freedom to drink, dance and enjoy rock music." Crying out, "freedom!" they flaunt social norms, break down the social order and ruin the foundations of society. This freedom is nothing but self-indulgence. It is one of Satan's destructive strategies. (116:102, December 27, 1981)

The greater the freedom, the greater is the need to maintain discipline and respect for law and order. The greater the precision of a piece of machinery, the more exactly its vertical and horizontal motion must accord with the principles of its design. Freedom yields abundant fruit as long as laws are obeyed. This truth cannot be denied, particularly in today's advanced social system and scientific civilization.

Can human beings enjoy freedom while ignoring the social system? No, the social system exists for the benefit of human beings. Therefore, people need to align themselves to the laws, organization and structure of their social system and prepare themselves to function within it. They should even take on leadership roles and protect it. People who fulfill this role can have no dealings with self-indulgent freedom.

To travel anywhere, we need a road. We require a direction. Today's free societies are lacking direction. How can they have direction, when everyone does as they please? Yet is there such a thing as a mind without direction? It is the mindset of ruin. (49:190-93, October 10, 1971)

The freedom that most people seek for is not what they can enjoy eternally, nor does it touch the core of their original mind. Instead, the pursuit of freedom drives people to extreme individualism and leaves them more and more isolated.

As long as people do not uphold Heaven's principles, do not pursue their relationship with God, and do not lift up the concept of freedom that is perfect and unchanging, the freedom that people seek for on earth will not be aligned with the freedom Heaven is seeking. Therefore, as the prevailing trend demonstrates, the more aggressively people pursue freedom, the farther away they are from it. (4:318, October 12, 1958)

The democratic world seeks to live by Christian teachings, but its way of life is permeated by individualism, bolstered by scientific technology. Hence, the freedom people pursue in today's democratic societies is fundamentally opposed to Christian teaching.

Christianity teaches freedom for the entire cosmos, liberation for the whole, and unity in the heart of God. Christian freedom is a state where we can rejoice together with God and the entire world. However, most people in the democratic world today insist on an individualistic concept of freedom. As a result, they deny their nation, their society, their community, and even their family and the relationship of husband and wife. Eventually, they come to deny the very Center of their mind [God].

What do they have left? Loneliness. When their loneliness reaches the extreme and explodes, they no longer trust others or even themselves. Their feeling of loneliness and distrust becomes an all-encompassing fear and depression, which leads to self-destructive behavior, even suicide. This trend is ever more evident in contemporary times.

Hence, if we really want freedom, we should not cry out for the irresponsible freedom that people sought in the past or are seeking today, but we should seek for the true freedom that accompanies the ideal of God's love. (4:319-20, October 12, 1958)

Equality

SCRIPTURES OF ALL FAITHS PROCLAIM THE EQUALITY of all people: rich and poor, black and white, men and women, from the East and from the West. Yet this lofty ideal is rarely matched in practice. Operating from our limited cultural perspectives, we are prone to treat people who seem alien or different with discrimination and prejudice. Even in democratic societies that proclaim equality as a central principle, racial and cultural prejudices are still widespread.

What is the basis of equality? First, the Abrahamic faiths ground equality in our common origin in God the creator and in our common parentage from Adam and Eve. Next, there are ethical and legal provisions to treat all people equally. Third is recognition that all people regardless of their race or class are equally capable of achieving enlightenment and self-realization. In Father Moon's view, however, none of these are sufficient for the attainment of true equality. True equality must be grounded in divine love and its practice by living for the sake of others. His ultimate prescription for bridging the gulf between races and cultures: interracial and intercultural marriage, where all prejudices are burned up in the fire of love.

1. The Basis of Equality in Descent from Common Parents, Common Humanity, and Potential for Divinity

Have we not all one Father? Has not one God created us?

Malachi 2.10

O Mankind, fear your Lord, who created you of
  a single soul,
and from it created its mate,
and from the pair of them scattered abroad
many men and women

Qur'an 4.1

But a single man [Adam] was created for the sake of peace among mankind, that none should say to his fellow, "My father was greater than your father."

Mishnah, Sanhedrin 4.5 (Judaism)

It is beyond the shadow of a doubt that every real man... however unusual to us may be the shape of his body, or the color of his skin, or the way he walks, or the sound of his voice, and whatever the strength, portion or quality of his natural endowments, is descended from the single first-created man.

Saint Augustine, City of God 15.8 (Christianity)

There is neither Jew nor Greek, there is neither slave nor free, there is neither male nor female, for you are all one in Christ Jesus.

Galatians 3.28

I look upon all creatures equally; none are less dear to me and none more dear.

Bhagavad-Gita 9.29 (Hinduism)

The souls of all people are equal, whether they live on the high mountains or at the bottoms of the valleys.[20]

Ofudesaki 13.45 *(Tenrikyo)*

Confucius said, "In education there are no class distinctions."

Analects 15.38 *(Confucianism)*

All those who take refuge in me, whatever their birth, race, sex, or caste, will attain the supreme goal; this realization can be attained even by those whom society scorns.

Bhagavad-Gita 9.32-33 *(Hinduism)*

I do not call him a brahmin merely because he is born of a brahmin womb or sprung from a brahmin mother. Being with impediments, he should address others as "sir." But he who is free from impediments, free from clinging—him I call a brahmin.[21]

Dhammapada 396 *(Buddhism)*

"You are a native of Kwangtung, a barbarian. How can you expect to be a Buddha?" asked the Patriarch.

Hui Neng replied, "Although there are northern men and southern men, north and south make no difference to their Buddha-nature. A barbarian is different from Your Holiness physically, but there is no difference in our Buddha-nature."

Sutra of Hui Neng 1 *(Buddhism)*

Teachings of Sun Myung Moon

Whether American, British or German, whether black, white or yellow, we are all from one. (132:130, May 27, 1984)

Every person wants to participate equally in God's love. The way to that equality is through establishing God's family. (97:265, March 19, 1978)

The world of heart is a world where everyone is equal. The Kingdom of Heaven, which is the expansion of one family, is the world of brotherhood. (*Way of God's Will* 2.3)

A mother cares for all her children with the same love, regardless of their ability and character. She gives birth to each one and raises them on the same bowl of soup. Isn't that so? All people are equal in this respect: they grew up by entrusting their precious lives to the hands of their parents. In the parental heart, there cannot be any discrimination. (33:164, August 11, 1970)

People in general have a desire to be equal and want the same things. Yet people are all different and live in different circumstances. What is the substance that can create equality among everyone despite their differences? It is love.

Consider little babies: they have nothing, they cannot talk, and they don't have anything to offer. Yet they are so cute! When we look at them we love them; we just want to put our cheek against theirs and kiss them. Even puppies come and lick them. In that love, there is no high or low. Love brings everyone to the same level. (254:208, February 13, 1994)

Don't the things that make Westerners weep also make Easterners weep? They do. Why do Koreans weep at the same scenes that also make their enemies the Japanese weep? The world is united in emotional responses. Is there any difference between Korean parents and Japanese parents in their love for their children? No, there is not. (41:331, February 18, 1971)

2. Racial Equality

Have you not seen how that God sends down water from the sky, and therewith We bring forth with it fruits of diverse hues? And in the mountains are streaks white and red, of diverse hues, and pitch black.

Men too, and beasts and cattle are of diverse colors. Even so only those of His servants who have understanding fear God.

Qur'an 35.27-28

I dream of the day when all Americans will be judged, not by the color of their skin but by the content of their character.

Martin Luther King, Jr. *(Christianity)*

Ethiopia will quickly stretch out her hands to God.

Psalm 68.31

"Are you not like the Ethiopians to me,
O people of Israel?" says the LORD.
"Did I not bring up Israel from the land of Egypt, and the Philistines from Caphtor and the
    Syrians from Kir?"[22]

Amos 9.7

The Prophet said to Abu Thur, "Look Abu Thur, you are not favored over a black man or a red man unless you are more righteous than they."

Algama' Alsaghair 3.2740 *(Islam)*

Lord God of glory is He to whom both the Aryans and the outcastes belong.[23]

Rig Veda 8.51.9 *(Hinduism)*

They approach me in a half-hesitant sort of way, eye me curiously or compassionately, and then, instead of saying directly, "How does it feel to be a problem?" they say, "I know an excellent colored man in my town"; or, "I fought at Mechanicsville"; or, "Do not these Southern outrages make your blood boil?" At these I smile, or am interested, or reduce the boiling to a simmer, as the occasion may require. To the real question, How does it feel to be a problem? I answer seldom a word.

And yet, being a problem is a strange experience, —peculiar even for one who has never been anything else, save perhaps in babyhood and in Europe. It is in the early days of rollicking boyhood that the revelation first bursts upon one, all in a day, as it were. I remember well when the shadow swept across me... In a wee wooden schoolhouse, something put it into the boys' and girls' heads to buy gorgeous visiting-cards—ten cents a package—and exchange. The exchange was merry, till one girl, a tall newcomer, refused my card,—refused it peremptorily, with a glance. Then it dawned upon me with a certain suddenness that I was different from the others; or like, mayhap, in heart and life and longing, but shut out from their world by a vast veil.

W. E. B. Du Bois[24]

Among four-footed animals, whatever the size, you can see that they are of different kinds and species. Now look at the creatures that crawl on their bellies... at the fish and water life, the birds and the breeds that fly—you can see they are of different kinds and species. Yet there is not among men differences in kind or species in the manner that they are found among other species.

Unlike in other species there is not among men differences with regard to their eyes, ears, mouths, noses, lips, eyebrows and even their hair—all are the same type. From the neck to the groin, from the shoulder to the hip, from the back to the chest—is it all of one kind with men. Hands, feet, fingers, nails, calves and thighs are all standard… they do not have the variety of inherited features that other creatures have. Differences among human beings are differences only by convention.

Sutta Nipata 603-611 *(Buddhism)*

Teachings of Sun Myung Moon

What is the color of true love? Does true love have a color? In love there is no color. Anyone who is color-conscious can never attain true love. Anyone who sees color is not a person of true love. (161:22, January 1, 1987)

In the sight of God, there is no difference between black people, white people and yellow people. Love makes God color-blind. He does not see the color of people's skin. The color of the heart is much more intense and vibrant than skin color. (258:122, March 17, 1994)

What would be God's ideal art project? You answer, "People," but how could people become God's masterpiece when blacks and whites fight? A world of only white people would be like God painting a picture all in white. You try drawing a picture all in white. Why doesn't it work? Hence, God needs black and other colors as well.

White does not show up against a white background. No artist paints on a white background; he needs to use various colors. Likewise, God needs people of diverse colors to create His masterpiece. It should be a three-dimensional masterpiece in which every part is harmonious and united. (96:220, January 22, 1978)

I wish that you mothers could bear twins—one black and one yellow. Especially, if a white mother could do it, how amazing it would be! All three races would come together at one time. Do you think God would be displeased and say, "How insane"? When He sees a white mother nursing a black child and a yellow child, would He say, "How disgusting"? No. He would say, "Wow, it is marvelous! Amen!"

Listen. If yellow butterflies were to fly only to yellow flowers, it would be dull. When white and black ones also come, that is beautiful. (130:102-03, January 1, 1984)

When Jesus stumbled while carrying his cross to Calvary, a black person, Simon of Cyrene, took up Jesus' burden. That act signifies that in the Last Days, God will raise up black people. (91:219, February 20, 1977)

When a white person takes a black person's hand, it is a much greater thing than simply the meeting of two individuals. In holding that hand, he is holding the hand of all black people and their history of tears. In hearing him, he is listening to the black race's woeful stories. Their clasped hands represent the reunion of heaven and earth, which had been separated for so long. (95:140, November 6, 1977)

Differences in skin color are nothing more than the result of our ancestors having had to adapt to different climates and environments in different parts of the globe. In areas with large amounts of snowfall, we find mainly white people living. In places such as Africa where the rays of the sun are particularly bright, we find mainly black people. Fundamentally, though, people are the same. The color of our blood is the same. Our flesh and bones look the same. We all have the capacity to love. Thus, there should be no discrimination based on race.

This is why... in accordance with the natural principles, more and more people will marry interracially. When a black person and a white person marry, it is like the North Pole and the South Pole coming together. When a yellow person and a black person marry and have children, both parents contribute their good attributes and their descendants are better as a result. (315:212, February 2, 2000)

The universe is built to be in natural balance... God gave white people blue or light-colored eyes, as a charming complement to their white skin. See how the blue of the iris blurs the white of the eye. This is as it should be, emphasizing the pupil and de-emphasizing the white of the eye.

On the other hand, in black and Oriental people, who have very dark or black irises, the contrast with the white of the eye is an attractive feature. For people with dark complexions, the black iris makes the whites of their eyes stand out beautifully. If their pupils were blue, it would blur the whites of the eyes and make their eyes weak-looking.

Also, when black people smile, their teeth are sensational. You black people, smile and see. Your tongue is very red, to show better against your white teeth. This is why you have thicker lips, too—to better show your teeth. Everything about black person's face is fascinating!

Today this civilization is mostly trying to destroy or downplay certain original qualities in people instead of trying to enhance them. But I foresee the time when white people will be crazy about blacks. White women in particular will prefer the dramatic appearance of black men.

Blacks are identified mostly with ghettos such as Harlem, which seem to accumulate the trash of humanity. They are like the valley that collects all the soil and debris that wash down from the hills; there they decay and smell, like rotting manure. But this is not bad; it makes for the most fertile soil, where life can germinate most abundantly. In America, black people shed their sweat and blood, becoming the fertilizer to create a new society for white people. You must know that American civilization was built on the backs of black people.

Yet life germinates powerfully in that manure. It is no accident that black people are passionate and strong, and have an explosive sense of love. Also, they tend to trust people, as they represent the valley, accepting everything that washes down.

White people, on the other hand, are like the high mountain top. Nothing accumulates on its rocky surface, and it is very cold. Hence, white people and not very trusting, and they tend to be cold-hearted. In the past, when white people traveled on horses, if a horse broke a leg they would kill the animal and move on. That is not right; it is not in accord with nature. Oriental people would not do that, and neither would black people. White people have a tradition of dueling for love, in which one man dies and the woman goes with the winner. Love cannot come through destruction of life; life must be protected so that it can give love.

This is how we search out the principle to understand and correct all customs and cultural values to be in accord with the original form. (107:308-09, June 8, 1980)

3. There Are No Races or Class Distinctions in Heaven

As men, we are all equal in the presence of death.

Publius Syrus[25] *(Hellenism)*

One fate comes to all, to the righteous and the wicked, to the good and the evil, to the clean and the unclean... One fate comes to all.

Ecclesiastes 9.2-3

There will be tribulation and distress for every human being who does evil, the Jew first and also the Greek, but glory and honor and peace for every one who does good, the Jew first and also the Greek. For God shows no partiality.

Romans 2.9-11

Know all human beings to be repositories of Divine Light;
Stop not to inquire about their caste;
In the hereafter there are no castes.

Adi Granth, Asa, M.1, p. 349 *(Sikhism)*

Teachings of Sun Myung Moon

In heaven there is no color. Everyone there shines so brightly that they appear to be silver—a silvery color so brilliant and radiant that it takes on a purple sheen. (293:224, May 26, 1998)

It is very possible that when white people go to the spirit world and try to enter the gate to heaven, they will be met by a black security guard. Conversely, black people will be met by a white security guard. Under those circumstances, would you back away, saying, "I don't really need to be here; I will go somewhere else"? Suppose the guard stopped you, and then started cursing and kicking you. Would you grab his legs and beg his forgiveness, saying, "I deserve whatever punishment you give me, for on earth I was an ignorant racist. Please forgive me"? Or would you run away? (116:110, December 27, 1981)

4. Living by the Standard of Equality

You shall have one law for the sojourner and for the native; for I am the LORD your God.

Leviticus 24.21-23

When a stranger sojourns with you in your land, you shall not do him wrong. The stranger who sojourns with you shall be to you as the native among you, and you shall love him as yourself; for you were strangers in the land of Egypt.

Leviticus 19.33-34

Once a prince attacked a shepherd, slapping him on his face. When the shepherd complained to Umar bin al-Khattab, Umar's judgment was that he should slap the prince back in the same way. The prince said, "How he can slap me while I am a prince and he is just a commoner?" Umar replied, "In Islam you are both equal."

Muhammad Ahmad al-Maula,[26]
Arab Stories 126.2 *(Islam)*

If the brahmin, kshatriya, etc. initiated into my holy order of equality still subscribe to castes and exult therein, they behave like unregenerate beings.

Sutrakritanga 1.13.10-11 *(Jainism)*

For the white to lord it over the black, the Arab over the non-Arab, the rich over the poor, the strong over the weak or men over women is out of place and wrong.

Hadith of Ibn Majah *(Islam)*

Please reflect that the man you call your slave was born of the same seed, has the same good sky above him, breathes as you do, lives as you do, dies as you do! You may see him free, he may see you a slave—the odds are level.

Seneca, Moral Epistles 47 *(Hellenism)*

Slaves, be obedient to those who are your earthly masters, with fear and trembling, in singleness of heart, as to Christ; not in the way of eye-service, as men-pleasers, but as servants of Christ, doing the will of God from the heart, rendering service with a good will as to the Lord and not to men, knowing that whatever good any one does, he will receive the same again from the Lord, whether he is a slave or free.

Masters, do the same to them, and forbear threatening, knowing that he who is both their Master and yours is in heaven, and that there is no partiality with him.

Ephesians 6.5-9

The Merciful demands that your servant be your equal. You should not eat white bread, and he black bread; you should not drink old wine, and he new wine; you should not sleep on a feather bed and he on straw. Hence it was said, "Whoever acquires a Hebrew slave acquires a master."

Talmud, Kiddushin 20a *(Judaism)*

Nearly eighty years ago we began by declaring, "All men are created equal"; but now from that beginning we have run down to the other declaration that for some men to enslave others is a "sacred right of self-government." These principles cannot stand together. They are as opposite as God and mammon, and whoever holds to the one must despise the other.

Abraham Lincoln[27]

Teachings of Sun Myung Moon

In the world of love there is no discrimination between above and below. (*Way of God's Will* 1.8)

In the world of true love… everyone has the right to equal position, equal participation, and equal inheritance. (294:65, June 11, 1998)

Do not violate human rights by discriminating in hiring, promoting and firing your personnel. Whether a woman or man, black or white, everyone is equal. One must not discriminate, for to do so would violate their human rights. (342:298, January 13, 2001)

When everyone lives for the sake of others centered on love, equality emerges among their relations. (107:152, April 20, 1980)

Racial discrimination, religious struggle, and selfish nationalism give rise to situations resulting in the violation of human rights. The age when people could be ruled by force has passed. The twenty-first century is an age when people live together, transcending races, nations, and religions. This means that the age of ruling through true love has begun. (369:221, February 24, 2002)

The strategy for creating a realm of equality—as there has never been one—is to sacrifice ourselves for others, wish them good fortune, win the hearts of those who strike you, and give them in return blessing equal to your own. This is the way to open the perfect realm of equality. (56:335, May 18, 1972)

The way to create equality between the upper class and the lower class is for upper class people to embrace lower class people and elevate them toward the upper class. This can only happen if there is a center of absolute value. That is God's love.

God's love embraces people of high class and low class alike. It is never one-directional or one-sided. Its energy flows in spherical motion, moving freely from the top to the bottom. All welcome it wherever it appears.

God's love holds absolute value, whenever and wherever. In God's love we feel happy, satisfied and secure. Although you may be a poor working man, you are totally free to love those in high places. Although you are accustomed to life in the highest position, you can freely love the people at the bottom. People dwelling in God's love are welcome wherever they go. (115:172-73, November 10, 1981)

Just because you are a white person, you should not say, "I only like whites. When it comes to the elderly, I will care for white seniors, but not blacks and Asians. I will care for those who are neat and well-dressed, but not those who are unkempt and wearing rags." No, you should love them all as you would love your own grandparents in your home. (130:274, February 5, 1984)

Wherever I go, when I am assigning people to a mission, I do not discriminate against blacks or those who did not complete college. If you possess true love and practice love for the sake of others, then you will uphold human rights correctly. This is the mainstream. The creation of heaven and earth began from this point. I cannot forgive the act of diluting and squandering this main current of my teaching…

You should not neglect your younger brother merely because he is handicapped. You should not disregard in-laws or relatives. The world tends to treat everyone with disrespect, doesn't it? If you who graduated from a university disrespect those who only completed high school, you are violating their human rights. (342:298, January 13, 2001)

The day before yesterday I took a group of about twenty people to a seafood restaurant… When we were about to place our order, the waiter told us that we all had to wear ties to be seated, and he offered to lend us all ties. But the thing displeased me; I said, "No thank you," and walked out of the restaurant with my group. The restaurant staff saw me as I was driven away in a fancy car. They must have wondered, "Why does a rich person like him object to wearing a tie?" They probably realized they had missed a great opportunity, but I will not visit that place again. They should not discriminate against people for not wearing ties. Even if they offer to make an exception for me, I will not give them my business. If they treat me like that, how will they treat black people? I want to stand up for you, because I know you are going through hardships. (*God's Will and the World*, May 1, 1977)[28]

The democratic world will never enjoy true equality until true love is engrafted to it. With true love, men and women can be equal, and all people can be free. With true love, we can establish democracy in the true sense. (230:87-88, April 26, 1992)

In the future, the five races will become one. Love is one. Although people differ according to whether they come from the East, West, North or South, and according to their different social ranks, the axle on which they turn is one. The flowers that bloom from the heart of red, passionate love are varieties of the same flower—the flower of God's love... Hence, these days many people believe that it is okay to marry interracially. (101:74-75, October 28, 1978)

Women's Rights

THE MOVEMENT FOR WOMEN'S RIGHTS and equality of the sexes that began in the last century is a major force for human betterment. Yet amidst the profusion of feminist ideas and trends, can scriptures instruct us to discern what is best and most enduring? This section deals specifically with women's rights in society. The more fundamental man-woman relationship is marriage, and there the matter of sex roles and equality of the sexes comes up with special force—see Chapter 19: *Ethics of Married Life*.

Against the persistent mistreatment of women, scriptures affirm the essential equality and dignity of both man and woman before God. Scriptures also affirm the right of women to an education and to seek the highest goal of faith—an outstanding Buddhist passage praises the resolve of a nun who defeats the Devil's whispering that women are not fit for enlightenment. On the other hand, the scriptures encourage the traditional womanly role of childbearing as the basis of female dignity. Further, there is scriptural warrant for the subordination of women as a consequence of the Fall and the first woman's sin—a theme to which Father Moon adds a unique twist when he attributes women's subordination at least in part to the degradation of men to the level of "archangels."

It is undeniable that men and women are distinctly unequal in their physical stature and abilities. A Buddhist text ridicules the notion that such external differences have any meaning, based on its perspective that Mind is the only reality. That won't do for Father Moon, who affirms the reality of the created world. Rather, he teaches that love is the basis of the equality of men and women. He supports the traditional value of childbearing, calling it God's special gift to women, but at the same time he applauds women who aspire to leadership positions in society and he encourages his women followers to take on traditional male roles. In this respect his thought resonates with the dreams of the pioneering American feminist Susan B. Anthony, who is quoted here.

1. The Basis of Equality between Men and Women

God created man in his own image, in the image of God he created him; male and female he created them.

Genesis 1.27

And their Lord answers them, "I waste not the labor of any that labors among you, be you male or female—the one of you is as the other."

Qur'an 3.195

When women are honored, there the gods are pleased; but where they are not honored, no sacred rite yields rewards.

When the female relations live in grief, the family soon wholly perishes; but that family where they are not unhappy ever prospers.

Laws of Manu 3.56-57 (*Hinduism*)

My dear sisters the women, you have had a hard life to live in this world, yet without you this world would not be what it is. Wakan Tanka intends that you should bear much sorrow—comfort others in time of sorrow.[29] By your hands the family moves.

Sioux Tradition of the Sacred Pipe
(*Native American Religion*)

The sister Soma... when she was returning from her alms-round, after her meal, entered Dark Wood for noonday rest, and plunging into its depths sat down under a certain tree. Then Mara the Evil One, desirous of arousing fear, wavering and dread in her, desirous of making her desist from concentrated thought, went up to her and addressed her in verse,

> That opportunity [for arahantship] the sages may attain
> is hard to win. But with her two-finger wit that may no woman ever hope to achieve.

Then Soma thought, "Who now is this, human or non-human, that speaks verse? Surely it is Mara the Evil One who speaks verse, desirous of arousing in me fear, wavering and dread..." The sister replied in verses:

> What should the woman's nature signify when consciousness is tense and firmly set, when knowledge rolls ever on, when she by insight rightly comprehends the Dhamma?
> To one for whom the question arises: Am I a woman [in these matters], or am I a man, or what not am I then?
> To such a one is Mara fit to talk.

Then Mara the Evil One thought, "Sister Soma recognizes me!" and sad and sorrowful he vanished.

Samyutta Nikaya 1.128, Suttas of Sisters *(Buddhism)*

Thou art woman, Thou art man; Thou art youth and maiden... it is Thou alone who, when born, assumes diverse forms.

Svetasvatara Upanishad 4.3 *(Hinduism)*

Shariputra, "Goddess, what prevents you from transforming yourself out of your female state, by nature filthy and an unfit vessel?"

Goddess, "Although I have sought my 'female state' for these twelve years, I have not yet found it. Reverend Shariputra, if a magician were to incarnate a woman by magic, would you ask her, 'What prevents you from transforming yourself out of your female state?'"

Shariputra, "No! Such a woman would not really exist, so what would there be to transform?"

"Just so, Reverend Shariputra, all things do not really exist. Now, would you think, "What prevents one whose nature is that of a magical incarnation from transforming herself out of her female state?" Thereupon, the goddess employed her magical power to cause the elder Shariputra to appear in her form and to cause herself to appear in his form. Then the goddess, transformed into Shariputra, said to Shariputra, transformed into a goddess, "Reverend Shariputra, what prevents you from transforming yourself out of your female state?"

And Shariputra, transformed into a goddess, replied, "I no longer appear in the form of a male! My body has changed into the body of a woman! I do not know what to transform!"

The goddess continued, "If the elder could again change out of the female state, then all women could also change out of their female states. All women appear in the form of women in just the same way as the elder appears in the form of a woman. While they are not women in reality, they appear in the form of women. With this in mind, the Buddha said, 'In all things, there is neither male nor female.'"[30]

Holy Teaching of Vimalakirti 7 *(Buddhism)*

Teachings of Sun Myung Moon

Even in America, where the women's rights movement has been promoting equality between the sexes, men today still have more privileges than women. Although American women may be somewhat better off, generally speaking women throughout the world live their lives dominated by men and carry resentment that they were born as women. The United States has laws granting equality between men and women. Nevertheless, in a fight, a man has the strength to defeat even two women combined! Don't many women still think, "I wish I were born a man"?

Throughout history, while men have enjoyed good fortune, a woman's lot has been miserable. Is it mainly women who assault and violate men, or men who violate women? Men violate women. It has been this way throughout history. In case of criminal assault against the opposite sex, over ninety percent are committed against women. For this reason, women have been holding a grudge against men and pursue women's rights.

Why doesn't God solve this problem and establish equality among the sexes? Why doesn't He make those malicious men surrender, but instead just allow them to continue? This is the issue. (243:268, January 28, 1993)

How are you going to assure equal rights? By force? External laws? Emotional persuasion? It is through love. It is through love that women can be equal to men. Through love, a mother can be equal to her son, even though he may be the president of a nation. Where there is love, everything can be equal. In this sense, we have to understand that the central core of equality lies in men and women who hope for a peaceful family centered on true love.

A husband wants to return to his wife's bosom and a wife wants to return to her husband's bosom and become one. There, nothing is high or low. They are indeed experiencing equality. Can there be equality in any other place? Equal rights for men and women exist only in a peaceful family (129:51-52, October 1, 1983)

Equality is born from the concept of "we." It does not exist when "I" am the center. The center must be "we." You must understand this. Equality arises from "we"-centeredness, in the love among "we." It cannot arise from self-centeredness.

Unfortunately, most feminists have an "I"-centered concept, and most men who believe in traditional male superiority think the same way. They are both wrong; the correct viewpoint is to advocate human rights for all people. To seek equality by putting women first does not make sense. The only sensible way to seek equality is to uphold the rights of everyone, centered on love.

I don't favor either the feminist movement or the tradition of male superiority. Men should live for the sake of women, and women should live for the sake of men. (131:109, April 22, 1984)

Just as human beings want to see God during their lifetime, God also wants to see true individuals. Yet if God called for either the man first or the woman first, the one who was not picked would complain.

Therefore, God cannot help but make love supreme. In that way, both the man and the woman can see God together, touch God together, and share God together.

If the most precious thing in the world were some material thing, surely the man and woman would fight over it; but once they understand that it is love, they will become one and possess it together, by caring for each other. (*True Family and World Peace*, March 14, 1999)

2. The Human Fall as the Cause of Male Domination

The man said, "The woman whom thou gavest to be with me, she gave me fruit of the tree, and I ate." Then the LORD God said to the woman, "What is this that you have done?" The woman said, "The serpent beguiled me, and I ate." The LORD God said... to the woman,

> "I will greatly multiply your pain in childbearing;
> in pain you shall bring forth children,
> yet your desire shall be for your husband,
> and he shall rule over you."[31]

Genesis 3.12-16

Let a woman show deference, not being a slave to her husband; let her show she is ready to be guided, not coerced. She is not worthy of wedlock who is worthy of chiding. Let the husband too, manage his wife like a steersman, pay honor to her as his life partner, share with her as the co-heir of grace...

Those temptations are most severe which are brought about through women. Indeed, through Eve Adam was deceived, and thus did it come about that he departed from the divine commands. When he learned his mistake and was conscious of the sin within himself, he wished to hide but could not. And so God said to him, "Adam, where art thou?... You desired to leave the Lord your God for one woman, and you are fleeing the One whom formerly you wished to behold. With one woman you have preferred to hide yourself, to abandon the Mirror of the world, the abode of paradise, the grace of Christ."[32] Should I go on to tell of how Jezebel severely persecuted Elijah, and Herodias caused John the Baptist to be put to death?

Ambrose of Milan, Letters 59, 60 (Christianity)

I want you to understand that the head of every man is Christ, the head of a woman is her husband, and the head of Christ is God. Any man who prays or prophesies with his head covered dishonors his head, but any woman who prays or prophesies with her head unveiled dishonors her head... For a man ought not to cover his head, since he is the image and glory of God; but woman is the glory of man. (For man was not made from woman, but woman from man. Neither was man created for woman, but woman for man.) That is why a woman ought to have a veil on her head, because of the angels.[33]

1 Corinthians 11.3-11

I looked into Paradise and found that the majority of its dwellers were the poor people, and I looked into the (Hell) Fire and found that the majority of its dwellers were women.

Hadith of Bukhari 8.76.554 (Islam)

Teachings of Sun Myung Moon

Until now, it was mainly women who were required to keep their chastity, wasn't it? Who lost their chastity in the Garden of Eden? Was it the woman or the man? The woman, you say? The man also lost it. The man who was the center of Eden also lost it. Adam became involved with Eve, and by his action the original root was cut off.

Nevertheless, it was the woman—Eve—who caused the man—Adam—to fall. Hence, to indemnify this, women have been mistreated by men. Isn't that so? I am carrying out a movement for equality of the sexes and the liberation of women. This must be done for the sake of future generations. (26:334-35, October 3, 1969)

To this day, have women been mistreated or honored? Have they been punished for being seductive? Yes, but that was not the chief reason. The reason women suffer is because their husbands are not their true husbands. Fallen men are in the position of archangels, and angels are not supposed to have a spouse. This is why higher religions have encouraged people to remain single. Men are archangel figures, like the archangel Lucifer at the Fall who seduced a woman when he was not supposed to have a wife. For this reason, women do not have proper husbands. (39:214, January 10, 1971)

Because Eve drove a nail into God's heart, archangelic men have been driving many nails into women's hearts. (302:232, June 14, 1999)

Eve was created as God's princess, and at the same time as God's future partner. God created her to become His beloved partner, even God's wife.
　Why is this? To share love, God needs a body, a form. God has no form in the spirit world. Light like that of the sun stays in the sky twenty-four hours a day; thus does the incorporeal God manage everything from above. But it is not possible for an incorporeal being to become the love partner of human beings who have bodily form.
　For this reason, the incorporeal God created Adam and Eve each with a body. They were His absolute works, created for the ideal of love, as His partners. Whose form does God take? God takes the form of both Adam and Eve. God is the internal Father embodied in Adam the external father; God is the internal Mother embodied in Eve the external mother. (199:361, February 21, 1990)

3. Striving for Equality of the Sexes

Learning is incumbent upon every believer, man and woman.

Sunnan of Ibn Majah 224 (Islam)

Women should have equal pay for equal work and they should be considered equally eligible to the offices of principal and superintendent, professor and president. So you must insist that qualifications, not sex, shall govern appointments and salaries.

Susan B. Anthony

Husband and wife are also equal. Their differences should be respected but not used to justify the domination of one by the other. In collaboration with society, the Church must collectively affirm and defend the rights of women.

Pope John Paul II[34] (Christianity)

In the Lord woman is not independent of man nor man of woman; for as woman was made from man, so man is now born of woman.[35] And all things are from God.

1 Corinthians 11.11-12

Women naturally have important roles to play in peacemaking. Nearly all of us receive our first lessons in peaceful living from our mothers because our need for love is the very foundation for human existence. From the earliest stages of our growth, we are completely dependent on our mother's care and it is very important that she expresses her love… If children do not receive the proper affection, in later life they will find it harder to love others. This is how a mother's love has a bearing on peace.

Tenzin Gyatso, The Fourteenth Dalai Lama (Buddhism)

The day will come when man will recognize woman as his peer, not only at the fireside but in the councils of the nation. Then, and not until then, will there be the perfect comradeship, the ideal union, between the sexes that shall result in the highest development of the race.

Susan B. Anthony

Teachings of Sun Myung Moon

Man is woman's teacher and woman is man's teacher. Men and women learn from each other. (247:174, May 2, 1993)

When a woman shares in her husband's work, or a man shares in his wife's work, they will better know each other. Then they can do anything.[36] (116:183, January 1, 1982)

I am going to make you ladies into fishing captains. You will take well-educated men, even Ivy League graduates, out to sea. They will become your crew. Do you women want to do it? Can you answer "yes" with a strong voice? "Yes!" That's what I want to hear! You must learn to have guts.

To become a great woman captain, you must be trained to take charge in the midst of a storm. When the men of your crew are scared to death, you will command them, even by using your fists. How will you feel when those men obey your orders? You will feel good! (95:97-98, November 1, 1977)

How can women claim equality with men? A man eats two portions of food to a woman's one. Men work at heavy labor while women follow timidly behind. Is that equality? What about wrestling? Have you ever seen a woman and a man wrestle each other? How, then, can a woman be equal to a man? Only in love are men and women equal; that is how it is meant to be.

How does God love women, when He appointed men to do the hard work and fighting? Nowadays we can purchase rice and cook it, but in the old days men had to go into the mountains or the fields and hunt for game to put on the table while fighting off lions and tigers. On the other hand, women have one ability that gives them standing before men: the ability to bear a child. I believe that God gave women the privilege of childbearing as a condition to maintain some measure of equality with men. The Creator made women to bear children in order to balance their weaknesses in other respects. But lately women are refusing to have children... (103:273, March 11, 1979)

There is an old saying, "Women are weak, but mothers are strong." A woman by herself may be weak, but if as a mother she assumes the position of the subject of love, or as a wife or a daughter she takes up the role as the center of love, then she becomes the strongest of all. How can this be? When a woman—as a mother, wife or daughter—assumes the position of the subject of love and then gives one hundred percent to her object partners, God's love comes in to fill up the vacuum that is left after she has given everything. That is when the power of God's love starts working. So even though she is a woman, by resembling God and assuming the position of the subject of love, she generates tremendous force. The power of that love will give life to the family, give life to the nation, and give life to the world. (*True Family and World Peace*, May 11, 1992)

The age of women has arrived. Now we women throughout the world should create a movement for the practice of true love. It begins by embracing our husbands and properly educating our children... and it expands as we women take up leadership roles in the political arena, in business, in culture and the arts, in society and so on, to work for world peace.

Let us remember our forbearers, Rebecca, Tamar and Mary, who went through difficult trials as they fulfilled the major responsibilities of women in God's providence of salvation. Let us inherit their strong spirit and willpower by which they overcame life-threatening dangers and obstacles and opened the way for us to make a relationship with Heaven. Let us also cultivate our families and make them into havens where true parents, true couples and true children dwell. In these ways, let us arise and join in the holy cause of changing this evil world into the heavenly world. (April 10, 1992)

Justice

INJUSTICE AND OPPRESSION CAUSE OFFENSE to God and humanity. People everywhere will fight for justice, but believers who know God's all-encompassing love have a special responsibility to use their influence to promote justice. Scriptures admonish people of faith not to sit idly by and not assist the downtrodden in obtaining the justice that is their due. Long before oppressed people in frustration take up arms to revolt against their oppressive circumstances, religious people should strive as society's conscience to prompt the authorities to give justice to those who have long been denied it.

Father Moon himself often tasted injustice, but he never seeks to avenge himself upon his persecutors. Instead, he always chooses the method of love and forbearance, firm in his conviction that the way of service and sacrifice is the surest way to overcome injustice on all sides.

Thus says the LORD, "Do justice and righteousness, and deliver from the hand of the oppressor him who has been robbed. And do no wrong or violence to the alien, the fatherless, and the widow, nor shed innocent blood."

Jeremiah 22.3

O ye who believe! Stand out firmly for justice, as witnesses to God, even as against yourselves, or your parents, or your kin, and whether it concerns rich or poor: for God can best protect both. Follow not the lusts of your hearts lest you swerve, and if you distort justice or decline to do justice, verily God is well acquainted with all that you do.[37]

Qur'an 4.135

Take away from me the noise of your songs;
To the melody of your harps I will not listen.
But let justice roll down like waters,
and righteousness like an ever-flowing stream.

Amos 5.23-24

Beware of the plea of the oppressed, for he asks God Most High only for his due, and God does not keep the one who has a right from receiving what is due.

Hadith of Baihaqi (Islam)

God said, "O My servants, I have forbidden wickedness for Myself and have made it forbidden among you, so do not do injustice to one another."

Forty Hadith of an-Nawawi 24 (Islam)

The LORD said to Moses, "Go in to Pharaoh and say to him, 'Thus says the LORD, Let my people go.'"

Exodus 8.1

Whoever of you sees something of which God disapproves, then let him change it with his hand; and if he is not able to do so, then with his tongue; and if he is not able to do so, then with his heart; and that is faith of the weakest kind.

Forty Hadith of an-Nawawi 34 (Islam)

All that is necessary for evil to triumph is for good people to do nothing.

Edmund Burke[38]

To come to the relief of the distressed and to help the oppressed, act as amends and expiation of many sins.

Nahjul Balagha, Saying 22 (Shiite Islam)

If you are neutral in a situation of injustice, you have chosen the side of the oppressor. If an elephant has his tail on the foot of a mouse, and you say you are neutral, the mouse will not appreciate your neutrality.

Desmond Tutu (Christianity)

Upon seeing someone else committing a sin or following a way which is not good, it is a commandment to return him to doing good and to make it known to him that he is sinning against himself, for it is written, "You shall definitely rebuke your fellow." When rebuking someone, whether in matters between him and others or between him and God, one should do so in private, speak to him in repose and soft tones, and make sure that he understands that one is speaking to him for his own good, and [thereby] to bring him to life in the World to Come.

Maimonides, *Mishneh Torah* (Judaism)

Justice is conscience, not a personal conscience but the conscience of the whole of humanity. Those who clearly recognize the voice of their own conscience usually recognize also the voice of justice.

Alexander Solzhenitsyn [39]

Someone said, "What do you say concerning the principle that injury should be recompensed with kindness?" The Master said, "With what will you then recompense kindness? Recompense injury with justice, and recompense kindness with kindness."[40]

Analects 14.36 (Confucianism)

According to Anas ibn Malik, the Prophet said, "Help your brother whether he is oppressor or oppressed." Anas replied to him, "O Messenger of God, a man who is oppressed I am ready to help, but how does one help an oppressor?" "By hindering him doing wrong," he said.

Hadith of Bukhari (Islam)

No man can put a chain around the ankle of his fellow man without at last finding the other end fastened about his own neck.

Frederick Douglass[41]

While women weep, as they do now, I will fight. While men go to prison, in and out, in and out, as they do now, I will fight. While there is a drunkard left, where there is a poor lost girl upon the streets, where there remains one dark and without the light of God, I'll fight. I'll fight to the very end.[42]

William Booth (Christianity)

Teachings of Sun Myung Moon

God is calling to us to challenge worldly unrighteousness, evil, sins and crimes, and practice true love. (234:273, August 26, 1992)

I believe that we people of faith should feel responsible for the lawlessness and injustice of this age, and we should be the first to assess our role in permitting it. God is calling upon leaders, especially us religious leaders, to stand against the world's injustices and evils and to bestow His true love upon the world. (330:247, August 18, 2000)

Before dreaming of eternity, religious people should first work with God in their daily life to eradicate evil. They should be fighters for goodness. (37:219, December 27, 1970)

He who sees unrighteousness but leaves it alone is not a man of conscience. (*Way of God's Will* 2.2)

Who possesses the central and highest conscience in the universe? God. When a man of conscience sees injustice, does he sit still? No, he explodes in righteous indignation. Is God's conscience any weaker? After seeing six thousand years of injustice His indignation grows hot; He prepares to do battle. God cannot stand by when sees people committing wickedness—damaging the world for their own selfish benefit or for their own family's or tribe's benefit. He reserves a day to strike them down.

Consider the Roman Empire. For four hundred years Rome had dominated the world, but when she persecuted Christianity, God punished her. Less than four hundred years after Jesus' death, Rome surrendered. (51:44, November 4, 1971)

I have endured, thinking that justice does not win by fighting, but wins by enduring. There were times when I was so indignant that my whole body was numb. But I endured, accounting myself an inadequate and unworthy son and thinking, "God has endured far more indignation than me." (74:252, December 31, 1974)

When young people dedicate themselves to sacrifice and service with God's true love, they will find the key to solving world poverty and hunger. They will be able to heal the feelings of animosity and hatred caused by differences between rich and poor and by different historical backgrounds and experiences.

Only based on love that loves the unlovable, can we find a clear direction to overcome the intractable conflicts that plague our age. We can even find common ground to meet the ideological divide between the advocates of freedom and the advocates of equality. (288:201-02, November 28, 1997)

Once true love is perfected in the human world, what possible political, economic, cultural, or environmental problems could persist? In the world of true love, every problem can be solved. It is the world of freedom, peace and happiness, replete with joy. It is the world of God's ideal. It is the world where joy and happiness are magnified infinitely and eternally, and where everyone has the right to equal position, equal participation, and equal inheritance. (294:65, June 11, 1998)

Economic Justice

AS LONG AS A SOCIETY TOLERATES GREAT DISPARITIES in living standards between rich and poor, it cannot be regarded as a just society. Such disparities weaken the bonds of solidarity between citizens, and generate class distinctions and their accompanying prejudices. Furthermore, equality of opportunity and equal justice under the law is a fiction in a society where the wealthy have every advantage over the poor. Visionaries of every age have sought for economic democracy to accompany political democracy. Socialisms of various stripes have arisen in response to this perennial desire of the original mind.

Economic justice begins with the commandment not to steal. Thieves are not only those who steal from other people, but also and more damagingly, those in a position of authority who rob from the public trough. This leads to the question of what is 'public' and what is 'private.' God created the earth, with its air, water and mineral resources, and in biblical Israel, all the land belonged to God with the people as its stewards. This scriptural viewpoint challenges the capitalist concept of private property, and suggests that a just economic system should involve some notion of shared ownership.

Furthermore, from God's perspective, all people are members of one family. How, then, can the wealthy sleep in good conscience while some of their brothers and sisters go hungry? The early Christians held all property in common, a tradition that has persisted in utopian socialist experiments to this day. The key to successful socialism, according to Father Moon, is God's love, which is the fount of the impulse to charity and brotherly love. It can prompt the wealthy to share their blessings, creating a virtuous cycle of giving. (See Chapter 13: *Charity*)

Communism, on the other hand, sought to institutionalize common ownership through a state mechanism that took from the rich to distribute to the poor. It utilized proletarian resentment to justify what was essentially stealing, enforced with great brutality. It took this despicable strategy, in Father Moon's view, because of its atheism and hostility to religion.

Instead of looking to the state to redress economic imbalances, we can look to ourselves. We can cease to strive only for our individual profit and instead regard each other as brothers and sisters, members of God's family. Then, just as family members apportion income and expenses when making their monthly budget, people of each village or neighborhood would meet on a regular basis and voluntarily apportion income and share expenses to promote fairness and equality. By the same token, employers and factory owners should pay their workers a decent wage, not only to encourage their good industry but also out of regard for their value as human beings. Likewise, in the family of nations, wealthy nations would voluntarily offer aid and technological assistance to developing nations, with the goal that all people on the planet would have comparable standards of living. Supporting this, we should promote a culture that honors people more for their charity than for their wealth. Father Moon envisions this as a practical way to achieve economic justice.

1. Stealing and Misappropriating Public Property

You shall not steal.

Exodus 20.15

Whoever steals what is considered to belong to others, whether it be situated in villages or the forest, he is to be known as an outcast.

Whoever having contracted debts defaults when asked to pay, retorts, "I am not indebted to you!" he is to be known as an outcast.

Whoever is desirous of stealing even a trifle and mugs a person going along the road in order to take it, he is to be known as an outcast.

Sutta Nipata 119-21 (Buddhism)

Lo! those who devour the wealth of orphans wrongfully, they do but swallow fire into their bellies, and they will be exposed to burning flame.

Qur'an 4.10

As for the thief, both male and female, cut off their hands. It is the reward for their own deeds, and an exemplary punishment from God.[43]

Qur'an 5.38

Woe unto the defrauders,
Those who when they take the measure from mankind demand it full,
But if they measure unto them or weigh for them, they cause them loss.

Qur'an 83.1-3

These acts are included in stealing: prompting another to steal, receiving stolen goods, creating confusion to overcharge or underpay, using false weights and measures, and deceiving others with artificial or imitation goods.

Akalanka, Tattvartharajavartika 7.27 (Jainism)

Because what is yours is not yours, how then can you regard what is not yours as yours?[44]

Talmud, Derek Eretz Zuta 2.5 (Judaism)

Nature has poured forth all things for the common use of all men. And God has ordained that all things should be produced that there might be food in common for all, and that the earth should be the common possession of all. Nature created common rights, but usurpation has transformed them into private rights.

Ambrose of Milan, *On the Duties of the Clergy* 1.132 (Christianity)

Private property does not constitute for anyone an absolute and unconditional right. No one is justified in keeping for his exclusive use what he does not need, when others lack necessities.

Pope Paul VI, *Populorum Progressio* (Christianity)

Metals and natural resources as petrol, sulfur, and iron are [public property] the same as water, grass and salt; therefore no governor is allowed to give some men exclusive possession of them, and if he does then his acts are false.

Muhammad ibn Idris ash-Shafi'i 346.5 *(Islam)*

Teachings of Sun Myung Moon

Religion teaches people to deny and reject everything that our body desires. Our body tells us to steal food when it is hungry, but Heaven teaches us always to say, "No" to that impulse. (131:25, March 11, 1984)

What is wrong with stealing? The item you steal is the result of someone's sacrifice and service; hence it has public value. When you take it without paying anything for it, you negate that public value. That is a sin. (105:92-92, September 30, 1979)

The Fall took place when the archangel, rather than respecting Adam and serving him sacrificially, instead manipulated the situation to swindle Adam. Then he looted God's creation. Looting, destroying and swindling followed upon hatred and deception. If you take part in any of these, you will go to hell. (310:199, June 15, 1999)

When using public funds, you should have a more anxious heart than I [about using the money correctly]. You should feel that taking even one penny for your personal use is as painful as amputating one of your limbs. If you are casual about public funds, you will inevitably decline. The sin will come around and bite you. You may be swindled, robbed or even killed. (360:321, November 18, 2001)

All events in history are the expansion of the deeds of individuals. What means and methods have successful people used to rise to the top? To reach their goal, they take advantage of other people or embezzle from organizations. This has been the tradition throughout history.

Ever since the Human Fall, when human beings received the blood of Satan, they unconsciously became arrogant and started using others to satisfy their own needs. That has been the direction of human history, is the result of the seeds sown at the Fall. (46:141, August 8, 1971)

Suppose while walking down the street, you find a golden nugget that fell from somewhere. Do not take it for yourself; if you do, it is as if you were committing a theft. Such found money is public money; therefore you should not use it for yourself.

Do you understand the meaning of public money? If you make an offering to the church with an ulterior motive, I Reverend Moon will not accept it. Even if you give it to True Mother [seeking to have her influence me], I do not touch it. Misusing public money is more fearful than taking poison. You will surely be caught and made to pay when you arrive in the spirit world. (January 13, 2001)

If you value your personal property more than public property, you are violating the way of Heaven. If you value your personal integrity more than public integrity, you are contrary to the way of Heaven. (51:291, November 28, 1971)

The things that you own, your material possessions, are not truly your own; you are their temporary steward. (23:334, June 15, 1969)

One of the main teachings of the Unification Church is: What is mine is yours, yours is the nation's, the nation's is the world's, the world's is God's, and God's is mine. (57:272, June 4, 1972)

2. Allocating a Community's Wealth to Provide Economic Security for All

When you reap the harvest of your land, you shall not reap your field to its very border, neither shall you gather the gleanings after your harvest. And you shall not strip your vineyard bare, neither shall you gather the fallen grapes of your vineyard; you shall leave them for the poor and for the sojourner: I am the LORD your God.

Leviticus 19.9-10

At the end of every seven years you shall grant a release. And this is the manner of the release: every creditor shall release what he has lent to his neighbor; he shall not exact it of his neighbor, his brother, because the LORD's release has been proclaimed... For there will be no poor among you, for the LORD will bless you in the land which the LORD your God gives you for an inheritance to possess, if only you will obey the voice of the LORD your God, being careful to do all this commandment.[45]

Deuteronomy 15.1-5

And you shall hallow the fiftieth year, and proclaim liberty throughout the land to all its inhabitants; it shall be a jubilee for you, when each of you shall return to his property and each of you shall return to his family...[46]

If your brother becomes poor, and sells part of his property, then his next of kin shall come and redeem what his brother has sold. But if he has not sufficient means to get it back for himself, then what he sold shall remain in the hand of him who bought it until the year of jubilee; in the jubilee it shall be released, and he shall return to his property...

And if your brother becomes poor, and cannot maintain himself with you, you shall help him; like a stranger and a sojourner, that he may live with you. Take no usury or interest from him, but fear your God; that your brother may live beside you. You shall not lend him your money at interest, nor sell him your food at a profit.

And if your brother becomes poor beside you, and sells himself to you, you shall not make him serve as a slave: he shall be with you as a hired servant and as a sojourner. He shall serve with you until the year of the jubilee; then he shall go out from you, he and his children with him, and go back to his own family, and return to the possession of his fathers. For they are my servants, whom I brought forth out of the land of Egypt; they shall not be sold as slaves. You shall not rule over him with harshness, but shall fear your God.

Leviticus 25.10-43

The Duke sent Pi Chan to ask about the "well-field" system. "Your prince, "said Mencius, "is going to practice benevolent government... It must begin with land demarcation. When boundaries are not properly drawn, the division of land according to the well-field system and the yield of grain used for paying officials cannot be equitable. Despotic rulers and corrupt officials always neglect the boundaries. But once boundaries are correctly fixed, there will be no difficulty in settling the distribution of land and determining fair taxes... I suggest that in the country the tax should be one part in nine, using the method of a fixed share of the produce...

A section measuring one *li* square is divided into nine plots. The central plot of 100 *mu* is public land, while the other eight plots of 100 *mu* each are held by eight families who share the duty of cultivating the public field. Only when the work on the public field is finished do they turn to their own work.[47]

Mencius III.A.3 (Confucianism)

Thus it is manifest that the best political community is formed by citizens of the middle class, and that those states are likely to be well-administered in which the middle class is large, and stronger if possible than both the other classes.

Aristotle, Politics 4.11 (Hellenism)

Now the company of those who believed were of one heart and soul, and no one said that any of the things which he possessed was his own, but they had everything in common. And with great power the apostles gave their testimony to the resurrection of the Lord Jesus, and great grace was upon them all. There was not a needy person among them, for as many as were possessors of lands or houses sold them, and brought the proceeds of what was sold and laid it at the apostles' feet; and distribution was made to each as any had need.

Acts 4.32-36

As long as there is any property, and while money is the standard of all other things, I cannot think that a nation can be governed either justly or happily: not justly, because the best things will fall to the share of the worst men; nor happily, because all things will be divided among a few (and even these are not in all respects happy), the rest being left to be absolutely miserable...

I reflect on the wise and good constitution of the Utopians, among whom all things are so well governed and with so few laws, where virtue hath its due reward, and yet there is such an equality that every man lives in plenty...

No man may live idle, but every one follows his trade diligently: yet they do not wear themselves out with perpetual toil from morning to night as if they were beasts of burden... but dividing the day and night into twenty-four hours, they appoint six of these for work—three before dinner and three after. They then sup, and at eight o'clock, counting from noon, go to bed and sleep eight hours. The rest of their time besides that taken up in work, eating and sleeping is left to every man's discretion; yet they are not to abuse that interval to luxury and idleness...

And thus, since they are all employed in some useful labor, and since they content themselves with fewer things, it falls out that there is a great abundance of all things among them: so that it frequently happens that, for want of other work, vast numbers are sent out to mend the highways. But when no public undertaking is to be performed, the hours of working are lessened. The magistrates never engage the people in unnecessary labor, since the chief end of the constitution is to regulate labor by the necessities of the public, and to allow all the people as much time as is necessary for the improvement of their minds, in which they think the happiness of life consists.

Sir Thomas More, Utopia (Humanism)

Teachings of Sun Myung Moon

In the ideal world, all of life's activities and labors will be expressed in the practice of joyful service for the sake of others based on a heart of love. Therefore, there will be equality in standards of living. (269:156, April 3, 1995)

Your financial life should not be centered only on the needs and desires of your own family. You should live with the others in the community in mind—some of whom are wealthy, some middle-class, and others poor—and place yourself in the middle range. Your community should have a monthly meeting to determine the range of the top, middle and bottom third of people's incomes, and what are each family's living expenses. Then through discussion, they should determine the following month's budget, which every family should observe. If we live by this principle, our way of life will be guaranteed.

When you receive your monthly salary, you will compare your living expenses with the average of people better off and worse off than yourselves, and based on whether you are in the top, middle or bottom third, you will give a certain proportion of your salary to help those in need. You will make this your consistent practice. If you do not, your life can be invaded by the spirit world. The spirit world operates this way.

You cannot live just accumulating money, as in the world of capitalism. I do not have money stored up.

In the future, when your children are living with you, they should not live better than your neighbor's children. If you have only three children while the average number of children per family in your neighborhood is four or five, you should willingly help other families to equalize their standard of living with yours. Families with fewer children should offer financial help to the families with more children. Since you are all brothers and sisters [in God's family], you should think of your neighbors' children as your nephews and nieces. The children should marry each other, strengthening the bonds between those who offer help and those who receive help. Such relationships expand the foundation of peace. (324:254-56, July 24, 2000)

The direction of politics should be oriented to true love, centered on the ideal of family. Economics and all activities of culture should likewise be centered on true love. If they continue as they have been, things will go wrong again and again. The world should inevitably become one, and do so centering on economy, not on politics. Political systems are based upon a governing class and a governed class. The world of peace and unification can only be realized when such things disappear, and the world moves to a system of management based on economic relations...

Once the world adopts the paradigm of global family, we will enter the era of equalization. Arriving at a single standard of living, and the peace that flows from it, is a task for the economy... We should leave behind systems of governance based on the concept of struggle or notions of superiority and inferiority. Things should develop through relationships based on love. (303:192-93, August 25, 1999)

In the ideal world established by people who have perfected God's love, the purpose of the whole and purpose of the individual will be in natural harmony. Because human beings have desire and a natural inclination towards love, God permits us to have individual ownership and pursue our individual purposes. Even so, we would not pursue unlimited wealth or go after deviant purposes that might harm the purpose of the whole. Perfected human beings would only hold on to property for their individual possession according to their status in agreement with their conscience and original nature.

Especially, people who have become true owners would pursue all their economic activity in the spirit of love and gratitude. Hence, there could be no greed or corruption. Neither would they insist on the interests of the nation or region inconsistent with the purpose of the whole. The aim of economic activity is the welfare of everyone, rather than the mere pursuit of individual profit. This is the way of mutual prosperity, based on God's true love. Through mutual participation, political life would realize the ideals of freedom, equality and happiness. (271:77, August 22, 1995)

The system in the spirit world is organized based on life. There is no politics. It is a world where the family ideal is expanded centered on the direct love of God. Politicians bend according to which way the wind blows and hold to the concept of struggle. Hence they do not hesitate to use any means to accomplish their goals. However, such a thing does not exist in the spirit world. The spirit world's main concern is how to improve the caliber of human life, based on an economy that promotes an equal standard of living for all. We should establish such a system on earth as well.

True love transcends politics and economics. True love goes beyond power, money, knowledge or anything else. How do we live when we center on true love? We help everyone to have an equal standard of living. We should not accomplish this by political means, through enlarging the power of government. We do it by expanding the scope of our life for the betterment of others. That is the Kingdom of Heaven on earth. (303:193-94, August 25, 1999)

3. The Rich Should Spread Their Wealth among the People

The state flourishes when wealth is more equally spread.

Francis Bacon[48] (Humanism)

Workman and employer should, as a rule, make free agreements, and in particular should freely agree to wages; nevertheless, there underlies a dictate of natural justice more imperious and ancient than any bargain between man and man, namely, that remuneration ought to be sufficient to support a frugal and well-behaved wage-earner... to maintain himself, his wife, and his children in reasonable comfort.

Pope Leo XIII, Rerum Novarum (Christianity)

To share your bread with the hungry,
and bring the homeless poor into your house;
when you see the naked, to cover him,
and not to hide yourself from your own flesh—
Then shall your light break forth like the dawn,
and your healing shall spring up speedily;
your righteousness shall go forth before you,
the glory of the LORD shall be your rear guard.

Isaiah 58.7-8

Alms are for the poor and the needy,
and for those employed to administer them,
and for those whose hearts have been reconciled,
for those in bondage and in debt,
those in the cause of God, and for the wayfarer:
this is ordained by God, and God is full of knowledge and wisdom.[49]

Qur'an 9.60

If I have withheld anything that the poor desired,
or have caused the eyes of the widow to fail,
or have eaten my morsel alone,
and the fatherless has not eaten of it...
if I have seen any one perish for lack of clothing,
or a poor man without covering...
Then I could not have faced His majesty.

Job 31.16-23

When the wicked are prosperous and the righteous are not,
if the situation continues for long the righteous become frustrated.
Like a small needle, that is how one first starts the act of falsehood.
The day it becomes as big as a hoe,
It kills.

Yoruba Song (African Traditional Religion)

The highest degree of charity—above which there is no higher—is he who strengthens the hand of his poor fellow Jew and gives him a gift or [interest-free] loan or enters into a business partnership with the poor person. By this partnership the poor man is really being strengthened as the Torah commands in order to strengthen him till he is able to be independent and no longer dependent on the public purse. It is thus written, "Strengthen him [the poor person] so that he does not fall and become dependent on others" (Leviticus 25:35).

Maimonides, *Mishneh Torah* (Judaism)

Teachings of Sun Myung Moon

The issue is the management of money: who eats better and who owns better possessions. If we are in positions of leadership, we should not seek to own the best things. If we desire to have below-average things, giving [our better things to others] for the sake of the whole, then equalization will be realized naturally. (324:253-54, June 24, 2000)

Everything should circulate like water. What is warm must become cool. What is cool must become warm. By "Warm" I mean the rich and by "cool" I mean the poor; hence the rich should extend themselves to help the poor. This must happen naturally. If the wealthy people willingly take responsibility for the poor in their community, everyone will be able to live together in harmony. If this becomes a community tradition, all the people will help one another. They will strive not to be indebted to one another. By helping one another, they will all become prosperous together—naturally. (253:238, January 30, 1994)

To bring unity between the people of the upper and lower classes, we must enable the people of the upper class to harmonize with the people of the lower class and raise the people of the lower class to the level of the upper class. To accomplish this requires a central point of absolute value. That central point is God's love. Then what is God's love like? God's love can be with both the people of the upper class and the people of the lower class. God's love is never one-directional; it moves in a spherical motion. It can move around freely from the highest point to the lowest. Wherever God's love appears, it is welcomed by all people everywhere, and it creates harmony everywhere, at all times. God's love always possesses absolute value whenever and wherever it may be. If we have God's love, we are happy; we feel filled and secure. Though a person may be at the very bottom, with God's love he can love those on top, and with God's love the people on top can love those at the bottom. (115:172, November 10, 1981)

Problems in labor relations can be solved by practicing parental love. The owner of the company is in the role of parent, and his employees are in the position of children. The owner should care for his employees as parents care for their children. Don't parents save money to bequeath it to their children? The owner should likewise think that his purpose is to bequeath his company's wealth to his employees. (116:121, December 27, 1981)

Let me tell you a way to solve labor disputes. Just as there are labor unions, a company's owners should form an owners or shareholders' union.[50] Then the two unions can get together and discuss the situation: "We laborers need to support our families, and you shareholders want to see production increase over last year. Instead of fighting each other and competing for a bigger slice of the pie, we should work together." They can agree that for three years instead of the profits going to the owners, they will put it in one pot. If the labor union members worked harder, then a higher percentage of the proceeds should go to them, but if the owners' union members worked harder, then a higher percentage of the profits should be given to them. Instead of fighting, let them compete. (342:288-89, January 13, 2001)

The twenty-first century shall be a century of righteousness. It will be a century of spirit and soul, when wealth will not be the dominating factor. It will be a century when God and human beings live together as one. A new awareness will come to every person—that living for the sake of others has eternal value, far greater than living for oneself. In the twenty-first century, selfishness will decline. The altruistic values of interdependence, mutual prosperity and universally shared values will be triumphant. (219:120, August 28, 1991)

4. The Virtues of Market Capitalism: Incentives to Honest Labor and the "Invisible Hand" that Enriches the Whole

It is not from the benevolence of the butcher, the brewer, or the baker, that we expect our dinner, but from their regard to their own interest. We address ourselves, not to their humanity but to their self-love, and never talk to them of our necessities but of their advantages.

Adam Smith, *The Wealth of Nations*

Every individual necessarily labors to render the annual revenue of the society as great as he can. He generally, indeed, neither intends to promote the public interest, nor knows how much he is promoting it... He intends only his own gain, and he is in this, as in many other cases, led by an invisible hand to promote an end which was no part of his intention.

Adam Smith, *The Wealth of Nations*

I take it that it is best to leave each man free to acquire property as fast as he can. Some will get wealthy. I don't believe in a law to prevent a man from getting rich; it would do more harm than good... I want every man to have the chance—and I believe the black man is entitled to it—in which he can better his condition; when he may look forward and hope to be a hired laborer this year and the next, work for himself afterward, and finally to hire men to work for him!

Abraham Lincoln[51]

Teachings of Sun Myung Moon

When I am making money, it is not for myself. Nor am I doing it for my parents. I am doing it for the world... Such is the way we all should live. (113:52, April 26, 1981)

How powerful it is to have money! How wonderful it is to have money! But who else likes the fact that you have money? If money had true love in it, then everyone would rejoice that you have it. If a person with true love has power, we think it a good thing. Why? Because he uses that power to protect the world and the cosmos. Likewise, we appreciate knowledge in the hands of a person with true love, because he uses it to make our world more comfortable and a better place in which to live. It is the same with money. With true love, we want to use our money for the sake of the world, not for ourselves. All the world's problems will be solved once we center on true love. (161:300-01, March 1, 1987)

The gap between North and South, and between whites and blacks, is largely a problem of wealth versus poverty. White people are well-off and black people are poor. There must be some extraordinary movement in which white people sell their possessions and use the money to help the poor black people of the world. If such a movement becomes strong, it will change the whole world. At the same time, there should be a movement among blacks to no longer blame whites for their poverty, but to say, "It is our fault, not the whites' fault, that we are in poverty. We should work hard to overtake white people." (161:19, January 1, 1987)

5. Communism and Its Errors

The history of all hitherto existing society is the history of class struggles...

The theory of the Communists may be summed up in the single sentence: Abolition of private property...

Let the ruling classes tremble at a communist revolution. The proletarians have nothing to lose but their chains. They have a world to win. Workers of the world, unite!

    Karl Marx, *The Communist Manifesto*

In a higher phase of communist society... only then can the narrow horizon of bourgeois right be fully left behind and society inscribe on its banners: from each according to his ability, to each according to his needs.

    Karl Marx, *Critique of the Gotha Program*

Communism is completely opposed to the natural law itself, and its establishment would entail the complete destruction of all property and even human society.

    Pope Pius IX[52] (*Christianity*)

The mission of the proletariat is an article of faith. Marxism is not only a science and politics; it is also a faith, a religion. And upon this its strength is based.

    Nicolas Berdyaev, *The Origin of Russian Communism* (*Christianity*)

The Christian who wants to live his faith in political action conceived as service cannot, without contradicting himself, adhere to ideological systems that are radically, or in substantial points, opposed to his faith and the concepts of man—neither to the ideology of Marxism, its atheistic materialism, its dialectics of violence and the way it absorbs any transcendental character of man and his personal and collective history; nor to the ideology of liberalism, which tends to exalt individual freedom without any limitation.

    Pope Paul VI (*Christianity*)

Socialism... is drifting toward truth which the Christian tradition has always supported. Indeed, it cannot be denied that its progress often comes close to the just demands of Christian reformers.[53]

    Pope Pius XI, Quadragesimo Anno (*Christianity*)

Teachings of Sun Myung Moon

Since the beginning of history, people have sought to diminish the gap between the upper and lower classes. Communism is the strongest example of this trend. The ideal of communism is to eliminate exploitation between the classes in human societies and to construct a classless society. However, the biggest problem with communism is its atheism, and the fact that it seeks to create an ideal world on a foundation which denies God. It is also a problem that communist states in practice carry out their programs according to the private will of a few dictators. (115:169-70, November 10, 1981)

In one aspect the communist world is better than the democratic world: It lifts up laborers and farmers as the heroes of society. God could take this as a reason to preserve the communist world even if the democratic world were to collapse. However, communism's problem is that it is atheistic. (130:103, January 1, 1984)

Today we hear the communist battle cry: "Liberate the workers and peasants from capitalist oppression!" However, does that cry for liberation accord with the liberation sought by the religion of God? Is it in accord with the hopes of people of faith who are working to liberate all people, even God Himself? Does that cry seek to make God the complete Subject of goodness forevermore? The answer is no.

Communism's hope is based on a materialist conception of reality. Communism rejects God, calls religion "the opiate of the people," and is devoted to stamping out religion. In theory also, it contradicts its own claim of liberation. It is undoubtedly a liberation scheme against God. Communism is in fact the flag bearer of the Devil, and is mounting a full-scale offensive against the flag bearer of God's own church. (85:230-31, March 3, 1976)

The Communist Party has the motto, "Workers of the world, unite!" Our motto is, "All people with conscience, unite!" The Communist Party denies middle and upper class people, but we the people of conscience will unite all three classes. We include all the races—black, white and yellow—everyone. (52:136, December 26, 1971)

The philosophers who came up with the law of the dialectic, Hegel and Engels in particular, saw a conflicting, confronting nature within universal law. Unless we successfully resolve the question of the dialectic within the universe, we cannot find the true formula for the ideal world. We cannot discover the way to establish peace and harmony within organizations that have a hierarchical structure. We must explain the errors of such theories as "survival of the fittest," "the strong eat the weak," and "power causes progress." Otherwise, people will think that mistreating others is not a sin. (132:142, May 31, 1984)

The communist system is for the state, and democracy is for the individual. To bridge this gap we should find a middle way. The nation that develops that middle way will have the ideal economic system. (52:263, January 2, 1972)

6. Globalization and the Equalization of Capital

The solidarity which binds all men together as members of a common family makes it impossible for wealthy nations to look with indifference upon the hunger, misery and poverty of other nations whose citizens are unable to enjoy even elementary human rights. The nations of the world are becoming more and more dependent on one another, and it will not be possible to preserve lasting peace so long as glaring economic and social imbalances persist.

Justice and humanity demand that those countries which produce consumer goods, especially farm products, in excess of their own needs should come to the assistance of those other countries where large sections of the population are suffering from want and hunger. It is nothing less than an outrage to justice and humanity to destroy or to squander goods that other people need for their very lives.

Of itself, however, emergency aid will not go far in relieving want and famine when these are caused—as they so often are—by the primitive state of a nation's economy. The only permanent remedy for this is to make use of every possible means of providing these citizens with the scientific, technical, and professional training they need, and to put at their disposal the necessary capital for speeding up their economic development with the help of modern methods...

The developing nations, obviously, have certain unmistakable characteristics of their own... time-honored traditions and customs. In helping these nations, therefore, the more advanced communities must recognize and respect this individuality. They must beware of making the assistance they give an excuse for forcing these people into their own national mold.

There is also a further temptation which the economically developed nations must resist: that of giving technical and financial aid with a view to gaining control over the political situation in the poorer countries... a new form of colonialism—cleverly disguised, no doubt, but actually reflecting that older, outdated type from which many nations have recently emerged. Such action would, moreover, have a harmful impact on international relations, and constitute a menace to world peace.

Necessity, therefore, and justice demand that all such technical and financial aid be given without thought of domination, but rather for the purpose of helping the less developed nations to achieve their own economic and social growth.

Pope John XXIII, Mater et Magistra *(Christianity)*

Trade relations can no longer be based solely on the principle of free, unchecked competition, for it very often creates an economic dictatorship. Free trade can be called just only when it conforms to the demands of social justice... competition should not be eliminated from trade transactions; but it must be kept within limits so that it operates justly and fairly, and thus becomes a truly human endeavor.

Now in trade relations between the developing and highly developed economies there is a great disparity in their overall situation and in their freedom of action. In order that international trade be human and moral, social justice requires that it restore to the participants a certain equality of opportunity... International agreements on a broad scale... could establish general norms for regulating prices, promoting production facilities, and favoring certain infant industries. Isn't it plain to everyone that such attempts to establish greater justice in international trade would be of great benefit to the developing nations, and that they would produce lasting results?

Pope Paul VI, Populorum Progressio *(Christianity)*

Teachings of Sun Myung Moon

Advanced countries have lots of money. But whose is it? It is God's. Whose is the power? It is God's. Whose knowledge is it? It is God's as well. God is the Parent of humankind. Therefore, everything that belongs to God—material, power, knowledge and such—belongs to humankind. For this purpose democracy appeared in modern days.

In democracy, sovereignty belongs to the people—to all humankind. That is why it is believed that sovereignty should be under control of the people. Yet, in reality, it is in the hands of conglomerates. At the present time, America is wealthy, but she alone should not be wealthy. She should distribute her wealth among other nations; that is the heavenly way. America must aid other nations financially, otherwise she cannot continue being wealthy. What belongs to America does not belong to America alone, but belongs to the world. (13:27, October 16, 1963)

How did America become a nation that is respected throughout the world? It is because after World War II, she financially helped all the enemy nations that she had defeated. Since she gave it on behalf of God, her position was elevated. Yet, when she reduced her giving, her position gradually declined. (26:53, October 18, 1969)

When a famine occurs in one part of the world, then the parts of the world where food is abundant should rush more food into the hungry areas. We have to build this kind of world. Presently, 20 million people are dying of starvation every year, while America is wasting too much food. This is a violation of the universal law. (247:94, April 25, 1993)

A nation that promotes only its own interests will perish. A nation that exploits other nations, using them as its foothold for its own prosperity, will perish in the end. The reason why America is being accused is because after she provides other nations with some financial aid, she attempts to make money off of them. (26:294, November 10, 1969)

When offering aid to less fortunate nations, America should offer it with parental heart, shedding tears for them and taking the role of a servant. When giving to those unfortunates who have shed many tears, she should also shed many tears for them. America should not look down on them from the height of authority and power, as she does now. Otherwise, her giving will only foment rebellion and discontent. The first to shed tears should be the donor, not the recipient. Why? The donor is in the position of a parent. Therefore, when the donor offers aid, she should do so with tears. If she gives while belittling the recipients, she will perish…

Nevertheless, there is no excuse for the Republic of Korea to say, "Well, America, you are bragging that you used to provide us with financial aid. Someday we will teach you a lesson." (13:27-28, October 16, 1963)

We can never have world peace until those nations which have been blessed with material and technological advantages willingly share them with the other nations of the world. The blessings of science and technology are meant for all humankind, and they should be shared. Every nation should have an equal chance to utilize technology for the people's well being, just as all nations' athletes should enjoy high quality coaching and ultimately compete on a level playing field. Otherwise, the advanced nations will be resented and hated by those who are deprived. The Unification Movement is committed to helping them share the blessings of technology with all nations, and to helping developing nations establish their own industrial base as the key to economic independence. (November 25, 1988)

In this world poverty is rampant. Hunger and poverty are deep-seated problems. Religious believers have a serious responsibility to deal with this situation. Over the past 20 years or so, I have been endeavoring to develop the resources of the ocean, personally fishing and investing substantial amount of funds. As a result, I succeeded in inventing high-potency protein powder… a nutritional supplement for health that is being effectively distributed to Africa and other parts of the world.

In order to eliminate the tragedy of starvation on the earth, I am putting my resolution into practice. I understand that all religions should unite and cooperate with one another in producing foods through agricultural development and ocean industries to help underdeveloped countries. If religions lead the way in practicing true love through the investment of human resources and materials, I believe it will be a great hope to the world. (271:71-72, August 21, 1995)

The U.S. administration insists that all trade barriers should be dismantled and excess farm products should be free to go to any country and be sold at the market price. This is known as the Uruguay Round. It calls for the poor countries with subsistence agriculture to open up their gates and be flooded with farm products from wealthy nations. However, I am suggesting that, like farm products, the population of the world should be allowed to flow back and forth anywhere it wants to go. That is, all national boundaries should be dismantled. (261:309, July 24, 1994)

Unity and Community

EACH RELIGION HAS A VISION OF UNITY—for its own believers. Today we cherish a greater vision of the unity of the whole human race—encompassing people of every race, religion and nationality. Nevertheless, the principles for forming community remain the same. Scriptures provide guidance, because every religion began as a movement of unity bringing together disparate groups to join together in a new society around a universal teaching. Father Moon teaches that this unity has to penetrate every family, for the family is the basis for all greater levels of social unity.

Several passages use the metaphor of the human body, whose various organs perform their functions in a coordinated way, to depict the varieties of social roles that should mutually support each other in a harmonious community. The body depends on the proper functioning of all its parts, from the lowest to the highest. Likewise in a true community, everyone has a place of honor.[54]

1. Unity as God's People and God's Family

Behold, how good and pleasant it is
when brothers dwell in unity!

Psalm 133.1

The believers indeed are brothers; so set things right between your two brothers, and fear God; haply so you will find mercy.

Qur'an 49.10

And the Lord called his people Zion, because they were of one heart and one mind, and dwelt in righteousness; and there was no poor among them.

Pearl of Great Price, Moses 7.18
(Latter-day Saints)

I do not pray for these only, but also for those who believe in me through their word, that they may all be one; even as thou, Father, art in me, and I in thee, that they also may be in us, so that the world may believe that thou hast sent me.

John 17.20-22

Hold fast, all together, to God's rope, and be not divided among yourselves. Remember with gratitude God's favor on you, for you were enemies and He joined your hearts in love, so that by His grace you became brethren. You were on the brink of the fiery Pit, and He saved you from it. Thus does God make His signs clear to you, that you may be guided.

Let there arise out of you one community, inviting to all that is good, enjoining what is right, and forbidding what is wrong: those will be prosperous. Be not like those who are divided amongst themselves and fall into disputations after receiving clear signs: for them is a dreadful penalty.[55]

Qur'an 3.103-5

Meet together, speak together,
let your minds be of one accord,
as the gods of old, being of one mind,
accepted their share of the sacrifice.

May your counsel be common, your assembly common,
common the mind, and the thoughts of these united.
A common purpose do I lay before you,
and worship with your common oblation.

Let your aims be common,
and your hearts of one accord,
and all of you be of one mind,
so you may live well together.

Rig Veda 10.191.2-4 (Hinduism)

There is neither Jew nor Greek, there is neither slave nor free, there is neither male nor female; for you are all one in Christ Jesus.

Galatians 3.28

Our Essence is not bound to any place;
The vigor of our wine is not contained
In any bowl; Chinese and Indian
Alike the shard that constitutes our jar,
Turkish and Syrian alike the clay
Forming our body; neither is our heart
Of India, or Syria, or Rum,
Nor any fatherland do we profess
Except Islam.

Muhammad Iqbal, *The Mysteries of Selflessness* (Islam)

All humans are caught in an inescapable network of mutuality, tied in a single garment of destiny. Whatever affects one directly, affects all indirectly. I can never be what I ought to be until you are what you ought to be, and you can never be what you ought to be until I am what I ought to be.

Martin Luther King, Jr. (Christianity)

Teachings of Sun Myung Moon

God's greatest desire is that all humankind, all five colors, would wish to unite and live together with God eternally. (93:15-16, May 8, 1977)

More than outward agreement, the important thing is to achieve inward unity, unity of heart. (60:34, August 1, 1972)

To accomplish the gigantic task of unification, we need to find a gigantic power. This is none other than the power of supreme love, love that does not become the circumstantial victim of society. Supreme love transcends every national, racial, and cultural barrier. Ordinary human love is limited; down through history it has shown itself unable to overcome these barriers. Therefore, we must center on the love and heart of God... People from the East and West rejoice to meet here today because around that axis, the heart of God is linking us together as one. (*God's Will and the World*, September 11, 1977)

In the future, four families will live together sharing the same house. I would like to build condominiums where a Korean family, a Japanese family, an American family and a German family would live together in the same apartment, sharing one living room and one dining room. They would become as one family. This oneness is the way to build the Kingdom of Heaven. (131:244, May 4, 1984)

Imagine two enemy families who have cursed each other throughout their lives, people who would never dream of living together. What would happen if these families joined together by wedding their children in a Holy Marriage Blessing? A son from one family and a daughter from the other family become husband and wife, love each other and build a happy home. Would the parents in each family curse their own children? When their son loves this beautiful daughter of a hated enemy, and she as their daughter-in-law gives birth to Heaven's grandchildren as pure and clear as crystal, the grandparents would smile with pleasure. In time the two lineages that were once soaked with enmity will be transformed.

What method other than cross-cultural marriage will empower Whites and Blacks, Jews and Muslims, Orientals and Westerners, and people of all races to live as one human family? The ideal family is the model for living together in peace. The ideal family is the nest where we live and learn to become one. There we have the foundation of love and respect between parents and children, shared trust and love between husband and wife, and mutual support among siblings. For this fundamental reason, you should receive the Holy Marriage Blessing from the True Parents and establish Heaven's tradition of ideal families, even if it means risking your very life. (September 21, 2005)

2. Unity against a Common Enemy

Every kingdom divided against itself is laid waste, and no city or house divided against itself will stand.

Matthew 12.25

We must, indeed, all hang together or, most assuredly, we shall all hang separately.[56]

Benjamin Franklin

"A house divided against itself cannot stand." I believe this government cannot endure permanently half slave and half free. I do not expect the Union to be dissolved – I do not expect the house to fall – but I do expect it will cease to be divided. It will become all one thing or all the other. Either the opponents of slavery will arrest the further spread of it and place it where the public mind shall rest in the belief that it is in course of ultimate extinction; or its advocates will push it forward till it become alike lawful in all the states, old as well as new, North as well as South.

Abraham Lincoln[57]

When the Nazis came for the communists,
I remained silent;
I was not a communist.

When they locked up the social democrats,
I remained silent;
I was not a social democrat.

When they came for the trade unionists,
I did not speak out;
I was not a trade unionist.

When they came for me,
there was no one left to speak out.[58]

Martin Niemöller (Christianity)

My children, war, fear, and disunity have brought you from your villages to this sacred council fire. Facing a common danger, and fearing for the lives of your families, you have yet drifted apart, each tribe thinking and acting only for itself. Remember how I took you from one small band and nursed you into many nations. You must reunite now and act as one. No tribe alone can withstand our savage enemies, who care nothing about the eternal law, who sweep upon us like the storms of winter, spreading death and destruction everywhere.

My children, listen well. Remember that you are brothers, that the downfall of one means the downfall of all. You must have one fire, one pipe, one war club.[59]

Tekanawita (Native American Religion)

Teachings of Sun Myung Moon

Today, you and I stand together facing a common destiny… I know to my bones that people who advocate righteousness in this evil world can be eliminated easily if they lack a substantial foundation. Therefore, professors and students, together with Christians and believers of all religions, should stand together. (129:304, November 25, 1983)

Why did God place Israel as a colony of the evil Roman Empire? It was so the Jews would unite internally around a movement for independence, so that they would make the foundation to stand against the Roman Empire. God often uses a providential strategy of raising a strong enemy to unite His people. If you visit the Catacombs in Rome and see the Christians' underground dwellings, you can witness how strongly united those Christians were in the face of terrible persecution from Rome. Like the Jews who faced Roman power, God put the Christians in the same situation in order to make them unite. (105:124-25, October 4, 1979)

3. Interdependence on the Model of the Human Body

Just as the body is one and has many members, and all the members of the body, though many, are one body, so it is with Christ. For by one Spirit we were all baptized into one body—Jews or Greeks, slaves or free—and all were made to drink of one Spirit.

For the body does not consist of one member but of many. If the foot should say, "Because I am not a hand, I do not belong to the body," that would not make it any less a part of the body. And if the ear should say, "Because I am not an eye, I do not belong to the body," that would not make it any less a part of the body. If the whole body were an eye, where would be the hearing? If the whole body were an ear, where would be the sense of smell? But as it is, God arranged the organs in the body, each one of them, as he chose. If all were a single organ, where would the body be? As it is, there are many parts, yet one body. They eye cannot say to the hand, "I have no need of you," nor again the head to the feet, "I have no need of you." On the contrary, the parts of the body which seem to be weaker are indispensable, and those parts of the body which we think less honorable we invest with the greater honor, and our unpresentable parts are treated with greater modesty, which are more presentable parts do not require. But God has so adjusted the body, giving the greater honor to the inferior part, that there may be no discord in the body, but that the members may have the same care for one another. If one member suffers, all suffer together; if one member is honored, all rejoice together.

1 Corinthians 12.12-26

Abu Musa reported the Prophet as saying, "Believers are to one another like a building whose parts support one another." He then interlaced his fingers.

Hadith of Bukhari and Muslim *(Islam)*

Beware lest the desires of the flesh and of a corrupt inclination provoke divisions among you. Be ye as the fingers of one hand, the members of one body. Thus counsels you the Pen of Revelation, if ye be of them that believe.

Gleanings from the Writings of Baha'u'llah 72 *(Baha'i Faith)*

When one finger is sore you do not cut it off.[60]

Njak Proverb *(African Traditional Religion)*

Teachings of Sun Myung Moon

To create the ideal world, we must have an overall model or blueprint. An important Unification image is that of a mature or perfected person, with mind and body united. Ideals and purposes spring from the mental and spiritual life of a God-centered person. The nervous system transmits the resulting directives of the mind to the cells, and relays information from the body back to the brain. When this exchange occurs smoothly we say that the individual is in harmony.

The mental and spiritual life of humanity can be likened to the mind of an individual, and the economic and socio-political life of humanity to the body of an individual. The spiritual ideals, aspirations, and love of God are manifested through religion, around which theology, philosophy, art, and all culture revolve. Religious leaders and theological and philosophical thinkers, then, function as the central nervous system, transmitting, interpreting, and developing messages from God for the whole body, humanity. (133:272, August 13, 1984)

Blood circulates throughout your whole body, from the head down to the soles of your feet. When that blood that went to the feet comes to the head, can the head say, "Don't come near me"? In the same way, as we circulate through the entire universe, there cannot be any discrimination between black, white and yellow people. The parts of the body are variously colored. Are brown eyes prejudiced against black hair? Do white nails say to yellow skin, "You are of a different kind"? There is no way the body can be segregated by color. (91:280, February 27, 1977)

In the human body, the lungs, heart and stomach maintain harmonious interaction in accord with the directions of the brain, transmitted through the spinal cord and the peripheral nervous system. By analogy, the three branches of government in the ideal world—the legislative, judicial and executive branches—will interact in harmonious and principled relationships when they follow God's guidance as conveyed through Christ and people of God. Just as the four limbs of the body move according to the commands of the brain for the welfare of the individual as a whole, the economic institutions of the ideal world, corresponding to the limbs, will uphold the desire of God and promote the welfare of the entire world. Just as the liver stores nourishment for the entire body, in the ideal world there will always be a certain reserve to be tapped as needed for the public good.

Since every part of the human body has a vertical relationship with the brain, horizontal relationships are naturally established between the different organs to form an integrated organism. Likewise, in the ideal world, because people's horizontal relationships with each other are rooted in their vertical relationship with God, they will form one integrated and interdependent society in which they share all their joys and sorrows. In this society, to hurt someone else will be experienced as hurting one's own self. Hence, its citizens simply will not want to commit crime. (*Exposition of the Divine Principle*, Preparation 3.2)

World Citizenship

THE WORLD SEEMS TO BE MOVING INEXORABLY towards unity, yet centrifugal forces threaten to blow it apart. Trends towards globalization in communications, education, transportation and trade are tying nations together into an interdependent network of mutual benefit. Nevertheless, the path to world unity cannot be forged only on the basis of trade. As long as the world agenda is dictated by the dominant economic powers, there will be peoples in the developing world who feel the juggernaut of globalization as a mortal threat. Proud peoples with a glorious history will seek alternative ways to assert their pride of place—the rise of Islamicism being one example. Therefore, economics does not hold the key to world unity. That key, that central element, is religion.

Certainly, religious teachings can be divisive. Yet each religion contains teachings that lift up the ideal of world unity, rooted in God who is the Parent of all humankind. God sees all human beings as His children; therefore the world is destined to be one family. Religious teachings demarcate the path to make this unity a reality, for example Father Moon's promotion of international, interracial and interfaith marriage.

Consider the family of humankind one.

Jinasena, Adipurana *(Jainism)*

O mankind! We created you from a single pair of a male and a female and made you into nations and tribes, that you might know each other [not that you might despise each other]. Verily the most honored among you in the sight of God is he who is the most righteous.

Qur'an 49.13

All the people of the whole world are equally brothers and sisters. There is no one who is an utter stranger. There is no one who has known the truth of this origin. It is the very cause of the regret of *Tsukihi* (God).

Ofudesaki 13.43-44 *(Tenrikyo)*

Let all mankind be thy sect.

Adi Granth, Japuji 28, M.1, p. 6 *(Sikhism)*

I am not an Athenian or a Greek, but a citizen of the world.

Socrates[61] *(Hellenism)*

You are a citizen of the world, and a part of it; not a subservient but a principal part. You are capable of comprehending the divine order, and of considering the connections of things. What then does the character of a citizen promise? To hold no private interest, to deliberate about nothing as a separate individual but, like the hand and foot, which, if they had reason and understood the constitution of nature, would never pursue or desire anything without reference to the whole being.

Epictetus, Discourses 2.10 *(Hellenism)*

When you see the Earth from space, you don't see any divisions of nation-states there. This may be the symbol of the new mythology to come; this is the country we will celebrate, and these are the people we are one with.

Joseph Campbell, *The Power of Myth*

From the viewpoint of absolute truth, what we feel and experience in our ordinary daily life is all delusion. Of all the various delusions, the sense of discrimination between oneself and others is the worst form, as it creates nothing but unpleasantness for both sides. If we can realize and meditate on ultimate truth, it will cleanse our impurities of mind and thus eradicate the sense of discrimination. This will help to create true love for one another.

Tenzin Gyatso, the Fourteenth Dalai Lama *(Buddhism)*

O contending peoples and kindreds of the earth! Set your faces towards unity, and let the radiance of its light shine upon you. Gather ye together, and for the sake of God resolve to root out whatever is the source of contention among you. Then will the effulgence of the world's great Luminary envelop the whole earth, and its inhabitants become the citizens of one city, and the occupants of one and the same throne.

Gleanings from the Writings of Baha'u'llah 111 (Baha'i Faith)

If love and agreement are manifest in a single family, that family will advance, become illumined and spiritual; but if enmity and hatred exist within it, destruction and dispersion are inevitable. This is likewise true of a city. If those who dwell within it manifest a spirit of accord and fellowship, it will progress steadily and human conditions become brighter, whereas through enmity and strife it will be degraded and its inhabitants scattered. In the same way the people of a nation develop and advance toward civilization and enlightenment through love and accord, and are disintegrated by war and strife. Finally, this is true of humanity itself in the aggregate. When love is realized and the ideal spiritual bonds unite the hearts of men, the whole human race will be uplifted, the world will continually grow more spiritual and radiant, and the happiness and tranquility of mankind be immeasurably increased. Warfare and strife will be uprooted, disagreement and dissension pass away, and Universal Peace unite the nations and peoples of the world. All mankind will dwell together as one family, blend as the waves of one sea, shine as stars of one firmament, and appear as fruits of the same tree. This is the happiness and felicity of humankind. This is the illumination of man, the glory eternal and life everlasting; this is the divine bestowal.

'Abdu'l-Baha, The Promulgation of Universal Peace (Baha'i Faith)

Teachings of Sun Myung Moon

Everyone longs to live in one unified world that transcends nationality. This longing springs from the inner world of the heart. It calls out from the ideal and heart of true human beings. It is also the heart and hope of God. (115:177, November 10, 1981)

We have to transcend nationalism. A people should emerge whose hearts transcend ethnic loyalties, which loves other peoples more than its own people. (34:337, September 20, 1970)

From this time on, the definition of "my country" will need to expand. Although everyone has their home country where they were born and live, in a larger sense, the entire world that God, our Father, created is "my country." (219:121, August 28, 1991)

In the events of history, people strive for the sake of their nation. That is the human way of thinking, but how does God think? If God were to say, "I only love America!" then He would be the God of only America. In that case, when it comes time for America to perish, God would also perish. But God never thinks that way. His thoughts are far above human thoughts. He would promote the way of thinking that we ought to live by placing the world's welfare above the welfare of our nation or our family. (95:53, October 23, 1977)

The reason God established America was for America to save the world. Yet Americans do not know that America must save the world. Only once in world history did a single nation become the center and unify the entire world religiously and culturally. Was that not America, when it occupied the whole world at the end of World War II? President Kennedy understood this, and he encouraged America to help all the struggling nations of the world. (215:200-01, February 17, 1991)

In accordance with my cosmic teaching, we should make the world into one household. A home has a father and a mother; in this household Heaven is our father and the earth is our mother. A home also has brothers and sisters; all human beings are our brothers and sisters. (36:296, December 13, 1970)

We are all part of one world family… This is the significance of the words [from the Family Pledge], "Our family… pledges to build the universal family encompassing heaven and earth and perfect the world of freedom, peace, unity and happiness."[62] It is not about my personal freedom, peace, unity and happiness, but rather the freedom, peace, happiness and freedom of everyone in the universal family. The whole world is our family.

When you arrive in heaven, you will not find people separated by national borders. People of all nationalities are assembled together. Are you prepared to live that way? Do you have such a universal viewpoint that you can embrace all people from the past, present and future? (260:191-93, May 8, 1994)

You can enter the Kingdom of Heaven only when you have lived with people of seven different nationalities. (*Way of God's Will* 1.8)

Every being is situated in space relative to what is above and below, right and left, front and back. In the family, each person stands in relation to above and below, right and left, and front and back. This same pattern applies to the nation and the world. Thus in the family, each individual should have a loving relationship with parents above and children below, husband on the right and wife on the left, and elder siblings in front and younger siblings in back. Similarly in the nation, each family, beginning with the President, should embrace families from all regions, and then embrace all people of the world, East and West, and North and South, as their brothers and sisters. We are ultimately responsible to create the model in our own family, which can be replicated on every level. (*True Family and World Peace*, July 18, 1997)[63]

Through this, we can finally build the providential house of God's desire. That house will be our nation, our world, and our heaven and earth. People of all five races will dwell there. Americans, Germans, French, Italians, British and Japanese—all former enemies—will gather there. Yet despite their past history as enemies, they will be unable to feel any enmity towards each other no matter how hard they try. Love will unite them, as they live for the sake of others. (106:83, December 9, 1979)

A religion which puts its own nation and people first will never be able to realize God's Will on the world level. We must go beyond our ethnicity and our nation, beyond our national traditions, cultures and social conventions. We must seek a society that embraces all the world's peoples and a world which can be in accord with God's Will. For this to happen, all people should be united in heart and live together as one. Unless the religions of the world work decisively to unite their concepts of the good life and the [ideal] world, religion will not endure.

Therefore, as a church, we should not take delight in the idea that our church should be supreme in the world; rather, we should delight in lifting up the world. When we look at the course of history centered on religion, this present age is at a turning point. A concept which puts me first, a concept which puts my family first, my nation first—with such concepts globalism is impossible. (27:179, December 14, 1969)

Human history has been moving toward one unified world. Therefore, anything that limits your purpose to the individual, family, tribe or nation will pass away. (12:45, September 10, 1962)

A new era has begun, the era of *Cheon Il Guk,* the Kingdom of Heaven on earth. All people—in the spirit world and in the physical world, on the right and on the left, and Muslims and Christians—will live together as one family. This is the meaning of *Cheon Il Guk.* World peace can be realized only when there are no barriers or borders dividing religions.

Our children can build a world of peace through inter-religious and international marriages. When Jews and Muslims have their children marry each other, and when communists and people from the free world have their children marry each other, we will eventually become the members of one family...

We must establish one global family under God. The simplest way to accomplish this is through cross-cultural marriages between Jews and Muslims, and between communists and democrats. For instance, if the children of North Korean leader Kim Jong-il and the children of South Korean president Roh were to marry each other, the enmity between their two nations would dissipate. Then world peace would radiate outwards from the Korean peninsula.

I, Reverend Moon, am the champion of interreligious, interracial, international marriage. If the United Nations were to invite me to give such marriage blessings to all humanity, it would not take even one week to restore the entire world. I am proclaiming that the solution to the world's problems is not far away; it is right here. (March 2, 2003)

Chapter 21

Leadership and Government

God-Fearing Leadership

GOD IS SOVEREIGN OVER ALL HUMAN INSTITUTIONS. Hence, the first principle of leadership is that governments should operate in conformity with heavenly law. Leaders should fear God and govern their people in a way that is acceptable to Him. Leadership is not only a public trust; it is also a position of God's vicegerent. Therefore, God would wish that a country's leaders be imbued with spiritual values. Kings and presidents should recognize that they are accountable to God, who is not slow to punish those who violate His trust. They are also accountable to rule according to the higher Law by which God intends to order human affairs.

The God of Israel has spoken,
the Rock of Israel has said to me:[1]
When one rules justly over men,
ruling in the fear of God,
He dawns on them like the morning light,
like the sun shining forth upon a cloudless morning,
like rain that makes grass to sprout from the earth.

2 Samuel 23.3-4

O David! We indeed set you as a vicegerent on earth;
therefore judge aright between men.
Do not follow not the lusts of your heart,
for they will mislead you from the path of God.

Qur'an 38.26

Heaven hears and sees as our people hear and see; Heaven brightly approves and displays its terrors as our people brightly approve and would fear; such connection is there between the upper and lower worlds. How reverent ought the masters of the earth to be!

Book of History 2.3.3, Counsels of Kao Yao (Confucianism)

If [a ruler] enjoins fear of God, the Exalted and Glorious, and dispenses justice, there will be great reward for him; and if he enjoins otherwise, it redounds on him.

Hadith of Muslim (Islam)

Revere the anger of Heaven,
And presume not to make sport or be idle.
Revere the changing moods of Heaven,
And presume not to drive about at your pleasure.
Great Heaven is intelligent,
And is with you in all your goings.
Great Heaven is clear-seeing,
And is with you in your wanderings and indulgences.[2]

Book of Songs, Ode 254 (Confucianism)

Neither cities nor States nor individuals will ever attain perfection until the small class of philosophers whom we termed useless but not corrupt are providentially compelled, whether they will or not, to take care of the State, and until a like necessity be laid on the State to obey them; or until kings, or if not kings, the sons of kings or princes, are divinely inspired with a true love of true philosophy.

Plato, The Republic 6 (Hellenism)

Step beyond what is human,
elect for the Divine Word,
and establish your leadership.

                Atharva Veda 7.105 *(Hinduism)*

If your kingdom exists for the doctrine
and not for fame or desire,
then it will be extremely fruitful.
If not, its fruit will be misfortune.

        Nagarjuna, Precious Garland 327 *(Buddhism)*

When you set a king over you... When he sits on the throne of his kingdom, he shall write for himself in a book a copy of this law, from that which is in charge of the Levitical priests, and it shall be with him, and he shall read in it all the days of his life, that he may learn to fear the LORD his God, by keeping all the words of this law and these statutes, and doing them; that his heart may not be lifted up above his brethren, and that he may not turn aside from the commandment, either to the right hand or to the left; so that he may continue long in his kingdom, he and his children, in Israel.

                    Deuteronomy 17.14-20

You, leaning on the Dhamma, honoring, respecting, and revering it, doing homage to it, hallowing it, being yourself a banner of the Dhamma, a signal of the Dhamma, having the Dhamma as your master, should provide the right watch, ward, and protection for your own people, for the army, for the nobles, for vassals, for brahmins, and householders, for town and country dwellers, for the religious world, and for beasts and birds. Throughout your kingdom let no wrongdoing prevail. And whosoever in your kingdom is poor, to him let wealth be given.

                    Digha Nikaya 3.60-61,
Chakkavatti-sihanada Suttanta *(Buddhism)*

Teachings of Sun Myung Moon

A true leader is one who wants, on behalf of God, to establish God's Will and heavenly law on this earth. (11:172, July 9, 1961)

We should be like God's shadow. Only when we become completely one with God as His object partner, like His shadow, can we lead others in any situation. Only then can we lift our heads and speak with authority. (237:144, November 13, 1992)

It is difficult to maintain order in the world and protect public prosperity and peace as long as political leaders conduct affairs while ignoring moral and spiritual values. No political power or earthly authority should stand above God and the heavenly law. (359:323, November 8, 2001)

Ideally, the president and representatives in Congress should all have Christian values. They should all pass that test. Does God approve of the separation of religion from politics? Is God only the God of religion? If the Christian nations continue to separate religion from politics, in the future they will face certain doom. Yet even now it is not too late for a movement to break down the barriers between denominations, in order that Christians may speak as one strong voice to the political leadership. Then the world will have a path to a bright future. The United Nations and the United States should be governed with the support of people with Christian values. Christians should also be at the forefront of the movement for world unity. (93:81-82, May 15, 1977)

Now the time has come for religious people to demonstrate their leadership. It cannot be leadership from blind faith, narrow-mindedness, arrogance, or self-righteousness. True leadership is altruistic and based upon God's Will. We religious people should reflect deeply and recognize that we are responsible for many of the absurdities and problems in this age. We have not become exemplary in practicing love. We need to repent that we have not exerted ourselves for world salvation because we have been preoccupied with saving ourselves or benefiting our tribe. Now, truly, not only should we have faith, we also need to practice love. (234:273, August 26, 1992)

Who decides whether a policy is good or bad? What standard can you use to assess it? It is not for the leader of the free world or the leader of the communist world to make that judgment. It can only be made by the Owner who rules history and moves heaven and earth—by whatever name you call Him. (104:206, May 6, 1979)

Righteous Leadership

AMONG THE REQUISITE QUALITIES OF A LEADER is righteousness. Righteousness is defined as dedication to the public welfare regardless of the cost to oneself. A righteous leader does not shrink from facing difficult problems. He is committed to public justice and fights to establish it, overcoming any obstacles along the way. Moreover, he knows that a great task requires sacrifice, not only from himself, but also from his subordinates. He never takes their suffering for granted and has the greatest solicitude for the hardships they must endure, yet he perseveres despite these difficulties. He keeps to the task for the sake of future generations.

On the personal level, a righteous leader has integrity. He does not seek to profit from his office, and he never misuses public funds for his own benefit. Any corruption is toxic, to be avoided at all costs.

1. A Passion for Justice and a Fierce Love for the People

I have sworn upon the altar of God, eternal hostility against every form of tyranny over the mind of man.

Thomas Jefferson[3]

And if God had not repelled some men by others, the earth would have been corrupted.

Qur'an 2.251

Then the LORD said to Moses, "Go in to Pharaoh and say to him, 'Thus says the LORD, Let my people go, that they may serve me.'"

Exodus 8.1

Jesus went up to Jerusalem. In the temple he found those who were selling oxen and sheep and pigeons, and the money-changers at their business. And making a whip of cords, he drove them all, with the sheep and oxen, out of the temple; and he poured out the coins of the money-changers and overturned their tables. And he told those who sold the pigeons, "Take these things away; you shall not make my Father's house a house of trade."

John 2.13-16

Whoever of you sees something of which God disapproves, then let him change it with his hand; and if he is not able to do so, then with his tongue; and if he is not able to do so, then with his heart; and that is faith of the weakest kind.

Forty Hadith of an-Nawawi 34 (Islam)

Those are the future saviors of the peoples
Who through Good Mind strive in their deeds

To carry out the judgment which Thou has decreed, O Wise One, as righteousness.
For they were created the foes of Fury.

Avesta, Yasna 48.12 (Zoroastrianism)

My mission, today, is the same as it was at the time of the Prophet. I shall strive till I eradicate impiety and injustice, and till I establish a rule of justice and truth, a humane and heavenly regime.

By God! Have the Quraysh given up realizing who or what I am? I have fought against them and defeated them when they were infidels, and now I will fight against them to remove their tyrannous, unjust, and impious rule. Today I am as much their well-wisher as I was during the lifetime of the Holy Prophet, and my courage and determination have not diminished.[4]

Nahjul Balagha, Sermon 38 (Shiite Islam)

How can he be said truly to love, who exacts no effort from the objects of his love? How can he be said to be truly loyal, who refrains from admonishing the object of his loyalty?

Analects 14.8 (Confucianism)

I have nothing to offer but blood, toil, tears and sweat.

Sir Winston Churchill

A man should share in the distress of the community, for so we find that Moses, our teacher, shared in the distress of the community.

Talmud, Taanit 11a (Judaism)

And I [Moses] looked, and behold, you had sinned against the LORD your God; you had made yourselves a molten calf; you had turned aside quickly from the way which the LORD had commanded you. So I took hold of the two tables, and cast them out of my two hands, and broke them before your eyes. Then I lay prostrate before the LORD as before, forty days and forty nights; I neither ate bread nor drank water, because of all the sin which you have committed, in doing what was evil in the sight of the LORD, to provoke him to anger. For I was afraid of the anger and hot displeasure which the LORD bore against you, so that he was ready to destroy you.

Deuteronomy 9.16-19

Teachings of Sun Myung Moon

What kind of person is a true leader? He is able to deal with every difficult situation. Misery and hunger do not dissuade him. Though he encounters tragedy and weeps bitter tears, he never thinks of turning back. Even in the face of death, he continues to push forward. He does not mind suffering losses in the present as long as his actions will benefit future generations and advance the purpose of God. (118:41, May 2, 1982)

Don't be pulled by your circumstances. You yourself must pull your circumstances. (*Way of God's Will* 1.3)

The path of a person who upholds goodness is not smooth. Not many people welcome an individual who strives to cultivate a character of exceptional goodness, especially as he tries to separate the evil environment from his surroundings. There is opposition when he tries to build a family of goodness, and even stronger evil forces surround and oppose any attempt to build a tribe of goodness.

If he were to lead that tribe of goodness to expand to a nation of goodness, tremendous evil forces would no doubt raise their flag against him and try to block his way. And if he were to try and lead that nation of goodness to establish a world of goodness, then evil nations, rather than helping the nation of goodness on its way, would no doubt oppose it in every way possible. (36:52, November 15, 1970)

In order to become a person capable of carrying a great responsibility:
You must establish the foundation that you can master your circumstances and build upon them.
You must be the most outstanding in advancing the Will of God.
You must be foremost in considering the whole purpose.
You must be concerned about your subordinates and pray for them before you eat or sleep.
You must think that you exist for them, not they for you.
You must want to add your effort to whatever gifts God has given you. (*Way of God's Will* 1.3)

Jesus visited his disciples after his resurrection because, although they betrayed him, he could not betray the pledge he made to them. A leader cannot be at ease until he carries out his pledges. (*Way of God's Will* 1.3)

Does anyone respect a leader who thinks only about the present and not the future? I don't believe that any leader of a nation is like that. A great leader has a vision of the future and inspires the people to endure suffering for the sake of the future. (97:88, March 1, 1978)

Leaders can never lead without tears. True leaders are those who foresee that their nation will face trials and train their people before the tribulations come by driving them into suffering and hardship. (*Way of God's Will* 1.3)

2. A Leader Acts on Principle and at the Sacrifice of Himself

Confucius said: Those rulers whose measures are dictated by mere expediency will arouse continual discontent.

Analects 4.12 (*Confucianism*)

Anyone who is to be prime minister must prepare his one heart and two eyes. When the eyes are clear then one can know the honest and the dishonest. When the heart is impartial then one can advance the honest and retire the dishonest.

Chu Hsi (*Confucianism*)

Duke Ching of Ch'i asked Confucius about government. Confucius replied saying, "Let the prince be a prince, the minister a minister, the father a father, and the son a son." The Duke said, "How true! For indeed, when the prince is not a prince, the minister not a minister, the father not a father, the son not a son, one may have a dish of millet in front of one and yet not know if one will live to eat it."[5]

Analects 12.11 (*Confucianism*)

The closest to Allah and most loved by Him in the hereafter is the just governor, and the farthest from Allah and most hated by Him is the aggressive and unjust governor.

Tuhafit al-Ahuazi 1327 (*Islam*)

The gentleman weighs his abilities before entering office, rather than the other way around.

Chu Hsi (*Confucianism*)

Your Majesty, what is the point of mentioning the word 'profit'? All that matters is that there should be benevolence and rightness. If Your Majesty says, "How can I profit my state?" and the counselors say, "How can I profit my family?" and the officials and commoners say, "How can I profit my person?" then those above and those below will be trying to profit at the expense of one another and the state will be imperiled. When regicide is committed in a state of ten thousand chariots, it is certain to be by a vassal with a thousand chariots, and when it is committed in a state of a thousand chariots, it is certain to be by a vassal with a hundred chariots. A share of a thousand in ten thousand or a hundred in a thousand is by no means insignificant, yet if profit is put before rightness, there is no satisfaction short of total usurpation. No benevolent man ever abandons his parents, and no dutiful man ever puts his prince last. Perhaps you will now endorse what I have said: "All that matters is that there should be benevolence and rightness. What is the point of mentioning the word 'profit'?"

Mencius I.A.1 *(Confucianism)*

The king Wu Ting appointed Yueh prime minister. He gave Yueh his instructions:

Morning and evening, send in your reprimands, and so help me to patch up my personal virtue. Imagine that I am a steel weapon; I will use you for a whetstone. Imagine I have to cross a big river; I will use you for a boat and oars. Imagine I am a year of record drought; I will use you as a copious rain...

You, yes you, teach me what should be my aims. You be the malt that works up the brew. Imagine we are making a good soup, you be the salt and prunes.[6]

Book of History 4.8.1-3 *(Confucianism)*

Teachings of Sun Myung Moon

Who is a man of character? He is a man who can stand in the central position in society. When there is a man of character in the village, he plays the central role in the material and spiritual lives of the village people. For this reason he is an object of respect. A nation likewise centers on a man of character; he is its representative. Society forms as the people make mutual relationships centering on him. Likewise, the world also requires a man of character as the center. (29:125, February 26, 1970)

The taller a tree grows, the deeper its roots go down into the soil. If its root is exposed, the tree will either wither away or be uprooted by a strong wind. A leader is like that root. *(Way of God's Will* 1.3)

Looking back on your life, you should be able to say, "I took responsibility for the most difficult problem in my church. I took responsibility for the most difficult problem in my nation. More than that, I took responsibility for the most difficult problem in the world." (113:111, May 1, 1981)

Those who sacrifice positively become central figures. Among the children in a family, the one who sacrifices the most is respected as the filial child. A nation chooses patriots for its leaders because they sacrifice more than ordinary citizens. Among saints also, the one who sacrifices more than others becomes the saint of saints. This is a heavenly principle. (113:326, May 10, 1981)

Make up for your leader's shortcomings and help him grow. He who judges his leader stands in the position of Cain. But he who conceals his leader's faults and tries to take responsibility for him will stand in Abel's position someday.[7] *(Way of God's Will* 1.3)

The biggest obstacle [to good government] is politics. Politicians should not misuse the political process to enrich themselves. They should submit to a system of management. They need to follow the rule of law. Mismanagement of public funds wreaks injustice in society. The fundamental problem is politicians' desire for inordinate wealth. No one in a position of power should seek to be wealthier than ordinary people. Instead, they should give the best things to others for the sake of the whole. If leaders are content to live with a below-average income, then equalization will be come automatically. Otherwise, the misuse of public money is the biggest threat to a prosperous future.

The second problem is personnel management—to change people's positions unfairly and arbitrarily. Democracies and other regimes as well divide into and perpetuate factions—ruling and opposition parties, and their leaders grant position and status based upon party loyalty. This causes tremendous damage. Experienced and capable people who were settled into their jobs are crushed and removed—or at least blocked from rising higher so they can offer greater service. Left out of favor, they flounder about and cannot improve their status. Such misuse of politics will have to disappear. A new management system must be instituted that provides equal opportunity to all and rewards people fairly based on their merit. Once again, this requires that public money is distributed fairly and equitably. (324:253-54, June 24, 2000)

3. The Righteous Leader Keeps Away from Corruption

There is no vice more detestable than avarice, more especially in great men and such as bear sway in the government of a state.

Cicero (Hellenism)

He who receives office in order to profit from it is like an adulterer, who gets his pleasure from a woman's body. God says, "I am called holy, you are called holy; if you have not all the qualities which I have, you should not accept leadership."

Pesikta Rabbati 111a (Judaism)

Do not ask for the position of authority, for if you are granted this position as a result of your asking for it, you will be left to discharge it yourself; but if you are given it without asking you will be helped [by God].

Hadith of Muslim (Islam)

By God, any official who takes anything from the public funds without justification will meet his Lord carrying it on himself on the Day of Judgment.

Hadith of Muslim (Islam)

Bribery is the door through which come all manner of sins. Those who live by bribery cut off their mother's breasts.

Somadeva, Nitivakyamrita 17.184 (Jainism)

The great Way is easy, yet people prefer bypaths:
The court is corrupt,
The fields are overgrown with weeds,
The granaries are empty;
Yet there are those dressed in fineries,
With swords at their sides,
Filled with food and drink,
And possessed of too much wealth.
This is known as taking the lead in robbery.
Far indeed is this from the Way.

Tao Te Ching 53 (Taoism)

Teachings of Sun Myung Moon

Whether religious leaders or politicians, their greatest weakness is selfishness. (299:105, February 6, 1999)

Among two people, the one who willingly works for the sake of others—for something greater transcending himself—stands on the side of good, while the other who does whatever is expedient for his own self-interest is evil. Government officials should live for the sake of the nation. If instead they use their office only to benefit their own families, they are evil. (170:175-76, November 15, 1987)

Do not rob from your organization's funds for your personal use. It is destroying the public environment and every bit as unlawful as robbing the state. Anyone who does such things, no matter how they try to live a good life, will not succeed. (347:85, July 3, 2001)

If you value your personal property more than public property, you are violating heavenly law. If you value your private life more than your public responsibility, you are violating God's will. (51:291, November 28, 1971)

When you [leaders] arrive in the spirit world, what will be reckoned as the most serious sins you committed on earth? The first is misusing public funds; the second, not doing your very best for your public mission; the third, violating the Principle. These are the three major sins.[8] (97:155-56, March 12, 1978)

You ministers, be careful. Using the church for your selfish purpose is the same as using God. Therefore, when guests visit your church or when you are out evangelizing, you should never occupy your mind with the question, "Would this person donate a lot of money?" (33:164, August 11, 1970)

Exemplary Leadership

THE BEST LEADERS ARE THEMSELVES EXAMPLES of virtue and righteousness. A society will be blessed when its elite members—politicians, business leaders, professors, celebrities and sports heroes—recognize their duty to be examples of honesty, integrity and morality. When they become role models, the common people will naturally follow their example.

We can identify three aspects of exemplary leadership. First, it begins in the family. The manner in which a leader cares for his or her spouse and children and manages the household is the starting point for his or her work in the wider spheres of government and social responsibility.

Second, it is leadership that governs by educating hearts and minds. In China, Confucius and his followers set forth the ideal of exemplary leadership against the views of Legalists who taught that leadership flowed from law and its vigorous enforcement— "power by the barrel of the gun" as Mao Zedong would later put it. Confucius countered that all the state's power would not banish discontent if the leaders were corrupt; on the contrary, the people would only learn violence and oppression.

Third, we have examples of exemplary leadership in the saints and religious teachers whom God sent to this earth. Jesus of Nazareth did not just teach through the words of his sermons, but also by his practice of sacrificial love. The Christian who walks in the footsteps of Jesus asks, "What would Jesus do," and does likewise. Jesus loved his enemies on the cross—a difficult example to follow—thus laying the basis for Christians ever since to love their enemies and pray for their persecutors. When the political leaders follow these saints' examples, they can establish world peace without doubt.

These qualities of exemplary leadership are summarized in Father Moon's teaching called the *Three Subjects Thought*. The standard of leadership is to be a "true parent, true teacher and true owner." Such leaders partake of the nature of God, our Heavenly Father, who superintends this world as its Owner, cares for all its creatures with deep parental love, and continually educates us to the true way of life.

1. An Exemplary and Virtuous Personal Life

If a ruler himself is upright, all will go well even though he does not give orders. But if he himself is not upright, even though he gives orders, they will not be obeyed.

Analects 13.6 (Confucianism)

When the king is deceitful, who will not be deceitful? When the king is unrighteous, who will not be unrighteous?

Somadeva, Nitivakyamrita 17.183 (Jainism)

Concerned alone with the upholding of the world,
You should act.
Whatever the best man does,
others do that also.
The world follows
the standard he sets for himself.

Bhagavad-Gita 3.20-21 (Hinduism)

When cattle are crossing, if the old bull swerves,
They all go swerving, following his lead.
So among men, if he who's reckoned best
Lives not aright, much more do other folk.
If the ruler be unrighteous, the whole land
dwells in woe.

When cattle are crossing, if the bull goes straight,
They all go straight because his course is straight.
So among men, if he who's reckoned best
Lives righteously, the others do so too.
The whole land dwells in happiness if the ruler
lives aright.

Anguttara Nikaya 2.75 (Buddhism)

When the righteous man is in the town, he is its luster, its majesty, and its glory. When he leaves it, its luster, its majesty, and its glory depart.

Genesis Rabbah 68.6 (Judaism)

Guide them by edicts, keep them in line with punishments, and the common people will stay out of trouble but will have no sense of shame. Guide them by virtue, keep them in line with the rites, and they will, besides having a sense of shame, reform themselves.[9]

Analects 2.3 (Confucianism)

Chi K'ang-tzu asked Confucius about government, saying, "Suppose I were to slay those who have not the Way in order to help those who have the Way, what would you think of it?" Confucius replied, saying, "If you desire what is good, the people will at once be good. The essence of the gentleman is that of wind; the essence of small people is that of grass. And when a wind passes over the grass, it cannot choose but bend."

Analects 12.19 (Confucianism)

If you have a good heart, you naturally become the object of others' respect, but if you have a selfish motive, though you may receive respect to your face, behind your back people will ask, "What use is his being a lama, guru, etc.?" Since they are free to speak they will do so, which may not be undeserved. Similarly, when a leader is strongly motivated by selfishness, though people may show respect and shower praises on him in his presence, later on if he meets with problems they will rejoice, which is natural.

Tenzin Gyatso, The Fourteenth Dalai Lama (Buddhism)

The Book of Songs says,

> How profound was King Wen!
> He maintained his brilliant virtue without interruptions
> And regarded with reverence that which he abided.

As a ruler, he abided in benevolence *(jen)*. As a minister, he abided in reverence. As a son, he abided in filial piety. As a father, he abided in deep love. And in dealing with the people of the country, he abided in faithfulness.

The Book of Songs says,

> Look at that curve in the Ch'i River.
> How luxuriant and green are the bamboo
>   trees there!
> Here is our elegant and accomplished prince.
> His personal life is cultivated
> As a thing is cut and filed
> And as a thing is carved and polished.
> How grave and dignified!
> How majestic and accomplished!
> Here is our elegant and accomplished prince.
> We can never forget him.

"As a thing is cut and filed" refers to the pursuit of learning. "As a thing is carved and polished" refers to self-cultivation. "How grave and how dignified" indicates precaution. "How majestic and distinguished" expresses awe-inspiring appearance. "Here is our elegant and accomplished prince. We can never forget him" means that the people cannot forget his eminent character and perfect virtue.

Great Learning 3.3-4 (Confucianism)

Verily in the Messenger of God you have a good example for him who looks unto God and the Last Day, and remembers God much.

Qur'an 33.21

When [Jesus] had washed their feet, and taken his garments, and resumed his place, he said to them, "Do you know what I have done to you? You call me Teacher and Lord; and you are right, for so I am. If I then, your Lord and Teacher, have washed your feet, you also ought to wash one another's feet. For I have given you an example, that you also should do as I have done to you."

John 13.12-15

For to this you have been called, because Christ also suffered for you, leaving you an example, that you should follow in his steps.

1 Peter 2.21

Teachings of Sun Myung Moon

People who live for the sake of the whole should be exemplary in all aspects of living: work, speech, and behavior. Then they will be automatically respected as elders. (318:147, May 5, 2000)

What is goodness? It is to discard what is evil and seek what is good. This means you should embody goodness and practice it. You should become that kind of leader.
    What is a leader? He is the model and standard for others to follow. Although he is in the central position, he does not isolate himself from the people. Rather, he cares for the people, protects them and guides them towards goodness. That is why the people want to take him as their model and emulate him. (118:38, May 2, 1982)

Be a man who can respect his own character. You should be able to hold your head high before all things, knowing that they respect you. Then you can say, "Follow my example." (*Way of God's Will* 2.2)

To become a leader, first, you should be able to solve economic difficulties. Second, you should have skill at diplomacy. Third, you should be an eloquent speaker who can persuade the masses. (85:263, March 3, 1976)

What was God's purpose in sending saints and prophets to this earth? It was to educate all people about the meaning of God's true love by demonstrating the character and exemplary life that God desires. (219:110, August 27, 1991)

2. A Leader Strives to Be a True Parent, a True Teacher and a True Owner

Now a bishop must be above reproach, the husband of one wife, temperate, sensible, dignified, hospitable, an apt teacher, no drunkard, not violent but gentle, not quarrelsome, and no lover of money. He must manage his own household well, keeping his children submissive and respectful in every way; for if a man does not know how to manage his own household, how can he care for God's church?

1 Timothy 3.2-5

Heaven and Earth are the father and mother of all things. Men are the sensibility of all things. It is telling the truth, thinking well, and seeing things clearly that make the principal ruler. The principal ruler is father and mother to the common people.

Book of History 5.1.1: The Great Declaration (Confucianism)

What is meant by saying that "in order to establish moral order in his state, one must first guide his family properly" is this: One cannot convince others of what he cannot convince the members of his own family. Therefore the wise governor does not need to go beyond his family in order to find the principles needed for governing his state. Here he finds his own son's respectful obedience to his father, with which a governor should be served; affection for one's relatives, with which higher officials should be treated; and paternal kindness, with which all people should be regarded.[10]

Great Learning 9.1 (Confucianism)

Heaven, earth and man are the basis of all creatures. Heaven gives them birth, earth nourishes them, and man brings them to completion…

The enlightened and worthy ruler, being of good faith, is strictly attentive to the three bases.

His sacrifices are conducted with utmost reverence; he makes offerings to and serves his ancestors; he advances brotherly affection and encourages filial conduct. In this way he serves the basis of Heaven.

He personally grasps the plough handle and ploughs a furrow, plucks the mulberry himself and feeds the silkworms, breaks new ground to increase the grain supply and opens the way for a sufficiency of clothing and food. In this way he serves the basis of earth.

He sets up schools for the nobles and in the towns and villages to teach filial piety and brotherly affection, reverence and humility. He enlightens the people with education and moves them with rites and music. Thus he serves the basis of man.

Tung Chung-shu, Luxuriant Gems of the Spring and Autumn Annals (Confucianism)

Those who in ancient times invented writing drew three lines and connected them through the middle, calling the character "king" (王). The three lines are Heaven, earth and man, and that which passes through the middle joins the principles of all three. Occupying the center of Heaven, earth and man, passing through and joining all three—if he is not a king, who can do this?

Thus the king is but the executor of Heaven… He patterns his actions on its commands and causes the people to follow them… The highest humanity rests with Heaven, for Heaven is humaneness itself. It shelters and sustains all creatures, transforms them and brings them to birth, nourishes them and completes them…

Since man receives his life from Heaven, he must also take from Heaven its humaneness and himself be humane. Therefore he reveres Heaven and knows the affections of father and son, brother and brother; he has a heart of trust and faithfulness, compassion and mercy; he is capable of acts of decorum and righteousness, modesty and humility; he can judge between right and wrong, between what accords with and what violates duty. His sense of moral order is brilliant and deep, his understanding is great, encompassing all things.

Only the way of man can form a triad with Heaven. Heaven's will is constantly to love and benefit, its business to nourish and bring to age, and spring and autumn, winter and summer are the instruments of its will. The will of the king is likewise to love and benefit the world, and his business to bring peace and joy to his time; and his love and hate, his joy and anger, are his instruments... Therefore the great concern of the ruler lies in diligently watching over and guarding his heart, that his loves and hates, his angers and joys may be displayed in accordance with right, as the mild and cool, the cold and hot weather come forth in proper season.

Tung Chung-shu, Luxuriant Gems of the Spring and Autumn Annals (Confucianism)

Teachings of Sun Myung Moon

Our three great wishes are, first, to become a true parent; second, to become a true teacher; and third, to become a true leader. Do you want to be successful and become a governor or even the President of the United States? First, you must become the head of your own household. To become the head of your household, you must inherit the family tradition and stand in the position of the head who can represent God and your ancestors. By doing so, all families in the nation will come to respect you. (205:20, July 15, 1990)

Among all parents, those who live more for the sake of their children are true parents. Teachers who do more for the sake of their students are true teachers, and the president who sacrifices more for the nation is a true president. (285:226, May 19, 1997)

A leader must take responsibility for his people. More than that, he must protect them. And not only protect them, but also raise them. (210:98, December 1, 1990)

Everyone here has parents and teachers, and you also have the leader of your nation. Everyone undeniably needs such people. However, when compared to the true standard of parenthood, parents are at many different levels. What level of parent do you want to attain? Likewise, the standard of a true teacher is not measured by whether someone is a professor at an Ivy League university such as Harvard, Yale or Columbia in the United States, or Oxford and Cambridge in England. Also, leaders of nations are at different levels compared to the true standard of leadership. Even if someone is the president of a superpower such as the United States, does this mean he or she is a true president?

In fact, today in the family, children do not trust parents. In school, students do not trust their teachers. Citizens do not trust the leaders of their nation. Whose responsibility is it that children do not trust their parents? Since their father and mother are not united as one, not trusting each other fully, the children cannot trust them. Neither can they trust their siblings.

Family relationships have reached the breaking-point. From this perspective, how can we possibly attain the true standard of even one of these three subject positions—either as a parent, teacher or leader? (285:214-15, May 3, 1997)

The principle of true parent-child relationships applies to the philosophy of management. The relationship between an employer and his employees should be viewed in this way, not as a conflict relationship... in the manner of Communism. Problems in labor relations can be solved by practicing parental love. The owner of the company is in the role of parent, and his employees are in the position of children. The owner should care for his employees as parents care for their children. Don't parents save money to bequeath it to their children? The owner should likewise think that his purpose is to bequeath his company's wealth to his employees. (116:121, December 27, 1981)

God expects you to become a true parent, a true teacher and a true leader. What do you think is the highest standard and absolute model for those three positions? It is God. God is the True Parent among parents, True Teacher among teachers, and True King among kings. God is the Eternal True Parent, Eternal True Teacher, Eternal True Leader and King. If we are children of God, we need to become a true parent first, just like God. We should also follow the way of a true teacher, just like God. And we need to follow the way of a true leader, just like God. The ultimate model for the three subject positions is God. (285:224, May 3, 1997)

Government for the People

THE WELFARE OF ITS CITIZENS SHOULD BE THE CHIEF CONCERN of government. The scriptures affirm that a ruler should put the people's needs ahead of his own. This is signified by his titles: the prophets of Israel called their rulers "shepherds," Jesus called rulers of the Kingdom "servants," and Chinese tradition regarded the emperor as "the father and mother of the people."

A leader can show consideration to his followers by personal kindness, forgiving their mistakes, and believing the best about them even when he knows they are likely to fall short. He can demonstrate solidarity with their difficulties by forgoing the pomp and ostentation of high office and living simply as one of the people. Moreover, scriptures encourage benevolent government policies, including reducing taxes in times of economic recession, investing in the people to create jobs, empowering them to have ownership over their work, and providing for the welfare of the poor and destitute. (See also Chapter 20: *Economic Justice*)

The precepts of governance that make for a benevolent rule are universal, which is why scriptures written in ancient times, when all governments were monarchies, remain relevant today. Nevertheless, this section also includes some texts on democracy, because in modern times a government "of the people and by the people" has proven to be the surest way to have a government "for the people." Yet democracy has also produced its share of monstrosities; the French Revolution is but one example. More than just free elections and a representative government, the animating spirit behind democracy can make all the difference between the blessings of liberty and totalitarian terror. Hence in the Western experience, democracies built upon Christian values have done better than those based on materialism. Yet even American democracy with its emphasis on individual freedom is deficient in many ways, according to Father Moon. A better underpinning for democracy, he declares, is the spirit of true love.[11]

1. Servant Leadership

In the happiness of his subjects lies a king's happiness; in their welfare his welfare; whatever pleases him he shall not consider as good, but whatever pleases his subjects he shall consider as good.

Kautilya, Artha-shastra 1.19 (Hinduism)

When loss is above and gain below, the people's joy is boundless. When those above exhibit no pride to the ones below them, their virtue is brightly illumined.

I Ching 42 (Confucianism)

Desiring to rule over the people,
One must, in one's words, humble oneself
  before them;
And, desiring to lead the people,
One must, in one's person, follow behind them.
Therefore the sage takes his place over the
  people yet is no burden;
Takes his place ahead of the people yet causes
  no obstruction.
That is why the empire supports him joyfully
  and never tires of doing so.

Tao Te Ching 66 (Taoism)

Governing a large state is like boiling a small fish.

Tao Te Ching 60 (Taoism)

Lay no burden on the public which the majority cannot bear.

Talmud, Baba Batra 60b (Judaism)

To demand much from oneself and little from others is the way for a ruler to banish discontent.

Analects 15.14 (Confucianism)

The man of perfect virtue, wishing to be established himself, seeks also to establish others; wishing to be enlarged himself, he seeks also to enlarge others.

Analects 6.28 (Confucianism)

The highest duty of a ruler is to protect his subjects; the ruler who enjoys the rewards of his position is bound to that duty.

Laws of Manu 7.144 (Hinduism)

The Caliph is a shepherd over the people and shall be questioned about his subjects.

Hadith of Bukhari and Muslim (Islam)

Jesus said, "You know that the rulers of the Gentiles lord it over them, and their great men exercise authority over them. It shall not be so among you; but whoever would be great among you must be your servant, and whoever would be first among you must be your slave; even as the Son of man came not to be served but to serve, and to give his life as a ransom for many."

Matthew 20.25-28

Public men are proud to be the servants of the State and would be ashamed to be its masters.

Sir Winston Churchill[12]

It was by the mercy of God that you were lenient with them (O Muhammad), for if you had been stern and hard-hearted they would have deserted you. So pardon them and ask forgiveness for them and consult with them about the conduct of affairs.

Qur'an 3.159

Moses son of Imran said, "My Lord, who is the greatest of Thy servants in Thy estimation?" and received the reply, "The one who forgives when he is in a position of power."

Hadith of Baihaqi (Islam)

Guardianship is not to give an order but to give one's self.

Nyika Proverb (African Traditional Religion)

Teachings of Sun Myung Moon

If you want to rule others, first be ruled by them. (*Way of God's Will* 1.3)

Leaders are people who let others use them, yet they do not perish. Come, let yourself be used by all the people of the world for the sake of God. Then they will come under your influence. (*Way of God's Will* 1.3)

The leader who commands his followers when they are not willing to obey will perish. (*Way of God's Will* 1.3)

If you want to become someone of high status, you should be able to take good care of the people under you. (34:250, September 13, 1970)

A sovereign should become one with his people. He should think that all that he owns is not for himself, but for his country. If that happens, the country will prosper. (30:88, March 17, 1970)

The larger-minded person can embrace and manage smaller-minded people. Can you be a person of such breadth of character that people of every nationality will admire you and want you to lead them? (102:139, December 10, 1978)

We should live for the sake of others. A leader who lives a self-centered life invites discontent and leads others to disobey the heavenly way. Living for the sake of others is the way to resemble God. When you inherit God's true love and practice it to love your family, society, nation, and world, you are living in accordance with the basic order of universe. Only through practicing true love can you become a true person of perfected character, and hence become a true parent, true teacher, and true owner. You become a peacemaker. When you live your life for the sake of others, you are headed towards the first gate of peace. (356:276, October 20, 2001)

A self-centered person cannot be a leader. It doesn't matter that he has a college degree or even that he is a professor. Rather, a leader needs to have a mind to live for the sake of the whole and be equipped in all areas. A person with such qualifications will climb to the top. At election time, people will not vote for a candidate whom they perceive is self-centered. They will choose the candidate who lives for the sake of the whole, who will benefit them. This formula for leadership has been constant throughout history.

Be a wise leader who embraces his people twice after chastising them once. Let them feel, "He scolded us for our own good"; otherwise, they will scorn you and oppose you, and in the end Satan will invade (54:207, March 24, 1972)

When a person whom you work with for the first time makes a mistake, remember how little you have given him and invested in him. Then despite his mistake, you can forgive him. As the leader, greet him with a delightful heart before you expect him to do so to you. If you expect him to greet you with a bright face when you yourself do not, then you are a thief. (81:305, December 29, 1975)

If one of your people does something wrong, do not take action against him right away. Even if he did something very wrong, try to find a way to have him do something good to improve the situation. Although that small good condition is far outweighed by the evil he did earlier, on account of it you can have room to reserve judgment until you can deal properly and comprehensively with the situation. (72:313, July 14, 1974)

A responsible person even when he knows the truth lets himself be deceived. (324:202, June 24, 2000)

Use clear judgment in handling affairs in your daily life. Then your heart should follow. To be clear about affairs means to act in accordance with reason. You should never act on a matter when you are confused or uncertain about it. Analyze well how to handle relationships with those above you and below you, on your right and on your left, in front of you and behind you. Once that is clear, you can cultivate affectionate feelings to embrace them all. The cloth of affection can wrap up everyone: grandfathers, grandmothers, babies, everyone.

The cloth of intellect is one-sided, while the cloth of affection is all-embracing. Look at me: I love even 80-year-old grandmothers, and they flock to my place. Grandmothers and tiny infants all rejoice to be wrapped in the cloth of love. They hug each other, the infants resting in the old ladies' arms, never wanting to leave. With the cloth of love you can create that kind of place. (81:328, December 29, 1975)

2. Consideration for the Poor

The government is the guardian of those who have no guardian.
        Hadith *(Islam)*

All those who are weary, disabled, crippled and infirm, who are orphan, childless, widowers, and widows are my brothers who totter and falter with no one to turn to. When the gentleman rules the government he must support such people.
       Chu Hsi *(Confucianism)*

If the chief has many breasts they are sucked by the people.
    Akan Proverb *(African Traditional Religion)*

When there is a question of defending the rights of individuals, the poor and the helpless have a claim to especial consideration. Those of the richer class have many ways of shielding themselves, and stand less in need of help from the State; whereas those who are badly off have no resources of their own to fall back upon, and must chiefly depend upon the assistance of the State. And it stands to reason that wage-earners, who are undoubtedly among the weak and necessitous, should be specially cared for and protected by the Government.
    Pope Leo XIII, Rerum Novarum *(Christianity)*

Give me your tired, your poor,
Your huddled masses yearning to breathe free,
The wretched refuse of your teeming shore.
Send these, the homeless, tempest-tossed to me,
I lift my lamp beside the golden door!
        Emma Lazarus[13]

Emperor Nintoku climbed up a high mountain and, viewing the lands of the four quarters, said, "There is no smoke rising from fireplaces in the land. The entire land is impoverished. For a period of three years the people are released from all taxes and conscription." For this reason, the palace became dilapidated; although the rain leaked in everywhere, no repairs were made. The dripping rain was caught in vessels, and the inhabitants moved around to places where it did not leak.

Later, when he viewed the land again, the entire land was filled with smoke. Therefore, realizing that the people were now rich, he reinstated taxes and conscription. For this reason, the common people flourished and did not suffer from his conscription. Thus his reign is praised as being the reign of a saintly ruler.

Kojiki 110 (Shinto)

Ho, shepherds of Israel who have been feeding yourselves! Should not shepherds feed the sheep? You eat the fat, you clothe yourselves with the wool, you slaughter the fatlings; but you do not feed the sheep. The weak you have not strengthened, the sick you have not healed, the crippled you have not bound up, the strayed you have not brought back, the lost you have not sought, and with force and harshness you have ruled them. So they were scattered, because there was no shepherd; and they became food for all the wild beasts… Therefore, you shepherds, hear the word of the LORD: Thus says the Lord GOD, "Behold, I am against the shepherds; and I will require my sheep at their hand, and put a stop to their feeding the sheep; no longer shall the shepherds feed themselves. I will rescue my sheep from their mouths, that they may not be food for them."

Ezekiel 34.2-10

If you take away from the midst of you the yoke,
the pointing of the finger, and speaking
   wickedness,
if you pour yourself out for the hungry
and satisfy the desire of the afflicted,
then shall your light rise in the darkness
and your gloom be as the noonday.

Isaiah 58.9-10

Give the king thy justice, O God,
and thy righteousness to the royal son!
May he judge thy people with righteousness,
and thy poor with justice…

For he delivers the needy when he calls,
the poor and him who has no helper.
He has pity on the weak and the needy,
and saves the lives of the needy.
From oppression and violence he redeems their
   life;
and precious is their blood in his sight.

Psalm 72

Teachings of Sun Myung Moon

A leader who, when he sees miserable people living on the street, feels shocked and finds himself sobbing, unable to control his body as he grabs on to a utility pole for balance—such a leader will naturally develop. (160:197, May 12, 1969)

Rather than building a lavish presidential palace, the president would do better if he lived in a flimsy mud hut that will hardly last until the end of his term before it must be torn down, and instead invested the nation's revenues for the next generation. His country would prosper, and he would be known as a leader who lives for his people.
   And yet, God lives for the sake of humankind even more than that. (382:149-50, June 21, 2002)

Living for the self ends with the self, but living for others continues forever. Therefore, for goodness to continue, you should live for your counterpart—the greater whole. This is particularly the case when you are in a position of leadership. Hence, anyone who aspires to become a world-level figure should live for the sake of the world. If he practices this, he may even become a world leader. On the other hand, a world leader who tramples upon those beneath him cannot remain. A world leader should be a leader who lights up the world. (57:63, May 28, 1972)

In the future, politics will be mainly a matter of good management. There will be no place for politicians to manipulate policies for unrighteous ends, as all people follow the Principle way and live for the sake of peace. The government will provide an exemplary model of management that serves to benefit the entire people.

The function of government will be to help people with economic difficulties and provide a way for everyone to eat and live. People will be categorized into three levels according to their standard of living—top, middle and bottom—and the average standard of living will be determined. Then the government will set up an administrative mechanism to equalize people's living standards to the middle level...

This administrative mechanism will incorporate the ethics of a single household planning the family budget, in which everyone takes responsibility for each other. Family members who are spending too much try to lower their expenses, while those in need receive more, in order that everyone in the family is at an equal level in the middle.[14] Likewise in society, those who are blessed with more will contribute to lift up others. (324:253-54, June 24, 2000)

Today, the industrialized North must reach out to help liberate the South from pervasive impoverishment. The developed nations must lend a helping hand to the support the development of the developing countries and the new democracies. Each nation's attitude must be changed from a selfish one to an unselfish one. That in itself will be a revolution. Nations can do this when their leaders think of themselves in the role of parents. From that perspective, nations will regard each other as brother and sister nations. Then a fresh new vision will emerge and new opportunities will open up before of us. (219:120, August 28, 1991)

3. Democracy

We hold these truths to be self-evident, that all men are created equal, that they are endowed by their Creator with certain unalienable rights, that among these are Life, Liberty and the pursuit of Happiness. —That to secure these rights, governments are instituted among men, deriving their just powers from the consent of the governed.

U.S. Declaration of Independence

I know no safe depository of the ultimate a powers of society but the people themselves; and if we think them not enlightened enough to exercise their control with a wholesome discretion, the remedy is not to take it from them, but to inform their discretion by education.

Thomas Jefferson

The ruler who submits to democratic ideals,
His rule is lasting.

Adi Granth, Maru, M.1 (Sikhism)

I sought for the greatness and genius of America in her commodious harbors and her ample rivers—and it was not there, in her fertile fields and trackless forests—and it was not there, in her rich mines and vast world commerce—and it was not there, in her democratic Congress and her matchless Constitution—and it was not there. Not until I went to the churches of America and heard her pulpits aflame with righteousness did I understand the secret of her genius and power. America is great because she is good, and if America ever ceases to be good, America will cease to be great.

Alexis de Tocqueville, *Democracy in America*

Few things help an individual more than to place responsibility on him, and to let him know that you trust him.

Booker T. Washington

The king's country, Sire, is harassed and harried. There are dacoits abroad who pillage the villages and townships and who make the roads unsafe. Were the king, so long as that is so, to levy a fresh tax, verily his majesty would be acting wrongly. Perchance his majesty might think, "I'll soon put a stop to these scoundrels' game by punishments and banishment, fines and bonds and death!" But their license cannot be satisfactorily put a stop to by such a course. The remnant left unpunished would still go on harassing the realm.

Now there is one method to adopt to put a thorough end to this disorder. Whosoever there be in the king's realm who devote themselves to keeping cattle and the farm, to them let his majesty give food and seed corn. Whosoever there be in the king's realm who devote themselves to trade, to them let his majesty give capital. Whosoever there be in the king's realm who devote themselves to government service, to them let his majesty give wages and food. Then those men, following each his own business, will no longer harass the realm; the king's revenue will go up; the country will be quiet and at peace; and the populace, pleased with one another and happy, dancing their children in their arms, will dwell with open doors.

Digha Nikaya 1.135: Kutadanta Sutta (Buddhism)

Teachings of Sun Myung Moon

In these last days of human history, heavenly law has descended upon the earth in the name of democracy, bringing an end to the long phase of history in which people sought to obtain happiness by seizing property, land and people. (*Exposition of the Divine Principle*, Eschatology 2.3)

At the time of Jesus, people's lives were as insignificant as flies to the persons in power. The system of laws into which Jesus was born was just like a world without laws. If the administrators or persons of power wanted to have him killed, it could be done as easily as killing a fly. Jesus' proclamation of a fundamental human revolution could not be permitted or accepted under the system of that society. We can say that the fact that Jesus was nailed to the cross was an almost unavoidable occurrence under the system of those days. God, who knows this so well, knows that one of the most necessary things for the days of the second advent of the Messiah is a system of laws in which a person cannot be killed just because it is someone else's will. The system which God prepared for the last two thousand years is democracy.

Democracy is the system which respects human rights. Democracy is the system in which a minority group can survive in the midst of a majority group. Democracy is the system which guarantees freedom of speech, freedom of association, freedom of press, and freedom of assembly. If we consider the Constitution of America, which can be regarded as the representative nation of democracy, the most absolute freedom among all freedoms is the freedom of religion. It is stated in the Constitution that the American Congress and Government shall not make any laws which can restrict religions. (October 19, 1978)

The French Revolution established democracy with the proclamation of the Declaration of the Rights of Man. Nonetheless, the democracy born out of the French Revolution was a Cain-type democracy. Although it destroyed absolutism... the leading thinkers behind the French Revolution were Enlightenment figures such as Denis Diderot (1713-1784) and Jean Le Rond D'Alembert (1717-1783), who adhered to atheism or materialism. Furthermore, despite its ideals of individual freedom and equality, the actual course of French democracy in the years of the revolution and afterward tended toward totalitarianism....

From their very origins, the democracies which emerged in England and the United States were different from the democracy born out of the French Revolution... The English and American democracies were founded by sincere Christians, the fruits of the Abel-type view of life, and were born out of their victorious fight with absolutism to win religious freedom. Hence, these are Abel-type democracies. (*Exposition of the Divine Principle*, Preparation 3.1)

Democracy is the ideology of brotherhood. It promotes equality by upholding freedom. But is freedom alone enough to secure happiness? No. To secure happiness, love must be the highest value. (201:73, March 1, 1990)

If democracy were to use love as its basis, then the world would become one. That kind of democracy could become world-level democracy. Even communism, if it were centered on true love, could also make one world. Where there is love, the word "purge" cannot exist. (90:311-12, January 15, 1977)

While much in America seems attractive, if you dig deeper you will find some disagreeable aspects. There is always a taint of racism. People live as isolated individuals and have not become as one community. The law is not always in agreement with human rights. (90:304, January 15, 1977)

If a black person wanted to run for the presidency, would white Americans support him? What do you think? Would they elect a capable black candidate? ...As long as blacks and whites are fighting over their rights, are there truly human rights?

The democratic world is a world of individualism. It takes no account of relationships, such as husband and wife. Each individual is his or her own center. Yet in reality, people cannot exist without relationships. Everything exists in the context of relationships. A society that valued relationships above all else would encourage everyone to make relationships with their counterparts, for that is the very nucleus from which the world will become one. First, families become one; then they build relationships with their neighbors and unify their neighborhood. Based upon this principle, people would assemble themselves into a single structure, connecting everyone throughout the world. (228:8, March 1, 1992)

Law and Punishments

GOVERNMENTS ENACT AND ENFORCE LAWS to protect their citizens, restrain evildoers, and promote the general welfare. God is the origin of law; He created this universe to function according to the laws of science and implanted a conscience within each human heart to know right from wrong. The constitutions and statutes that constitute a nation's laws approximate the heavenly law; that is why we they usually are in agreement with the dictates of conscience.

Laws are needed to restrain wickedness. People who do not follow the dictates of conscience, by which they ought to govern themselves to do right and avoid wickedness, are restrained by the law's sharp distinctions between right and wrong, what is permitted and what is prohibited. In this sense, people who cultivate their character to become people of conscience do not need the law and are unlikely to run afoul of the law.

Laws prescribe punishment as a deterrent to crime and to establish justice. The government in meting out punishments is a co-worker with God, who is the final dispenser of justice. Indeed, one can regard hell as a vast prison in the spirit world to restrain evildoers from trampling on heaven's domains. Punishment can serve as 'indemnity,' an opportunity for the criminal to pay the debt of sin.

On the other hand, there should always be an element of mercy in the criminal justice system, should the criminal repent with sincerity and turn his life around. Father Moon teaches that the chief purpose of prison should be education and rehabilitation. This was, in fact, the core idea of the twentieth century movement to convert prisons where inmates languished in cells into 'penitentiaries' where they could be rehabilitated through work and education. The two poles of justice and mercy form the perspective from which to view ethical issues such as the death penalty.

1. The Law's Noble Purpose

When Marduk commissioned me to guide the people aright and to direct the land, I established law and justice in the language of the land in order to promote the welfare of the people.

The Code of Hammurabi[15]

The Creator… projected that excellent form, Law. This law is the controller of the ruler; therefore, there is nothing higher. So even a weak man hopes to defeat a stronger man through the law, as one does with the help of a king.

Brihadaranyaka Upanishad 1.4.14 (Hinduism)

As ruler and president… you must in everything reverence the statutes and proceed by them to the happy rule of the people. They were the reverence of King Wen and his caution; in proceeding by them to the happy rule of the people, say, "If I can only attain to them."

Book of History 5.9.3.8 (Confucianism)

Laws are partly framed for the sake of good men, in order to instruct them how they might live on friendly terms with one another, and partly for the sake of those who refuse to be instructed, whose spirit cannot be subdued, or softened, or hindered from plunging into evil.

Plato, Laws 9 (Hellenism)

He who renders true judgments is a co-worker with God.

Mekilta, Exodus 18.13 (Judaism)

By justice a king gives stability to the land.

Proverbs 29.4

If punishment is properly inflicted after due consideration, it makes all people happy; but inflicted without consideration, it destroys everything.

If the ruler did not, without tiring, inflict punishment on those worthy to be punished, the stronger would roast the weaker, like fish on a spit. All barriers would be broken through, and all men would rage against each other in consequence of mistakes with respect to punishment.

But where Punishment, with a black hue and red eyes, stalks about, destroying sinners, there the subjects are not disturbed, provided he who inflicts it discerns well.

Laws of Manu 7.20-25 (Hinduism)

He who distinguishes good deeds from evil,
Who shows the results of karma—he is called
   a king.
Ordained by the host of gods, the gods delight
   in him.
For the sake of himself or others, to preserve
   the righteousness of his land,
And to put down the rogues and criminals in
   his domains,
Such a king would give up, if need be, his life
   and his kingdom.[16]

Golden Light Sutra 12 (Buddhism)

Every one had better be ruled by divine wisdom dwelling within him; or, if this be impossible, then by an external authority, in order that we may be all, as far as possible, under the same government, friends and equals.

And this is clearly seen to be the intention of the law, which is the ally of the whole city; and is seen also in the authority which we exercise over children, and the refusal to let them be free until we have established in them a principle analogous to the constitution of a state, and by cultivation of this higher element have set up in their hearts a guardian and ruler like our own, and when this is done they may go their ways...

What shall he profit, if his injustice be undetected and unpunished? He who is undetected only gets worse, whereas he who is detected and punished has the brutal part of his nature silenced and humanized; the gentler element in him is liberated, and his whole soul is perfected and ennobled by the acquirement of justice and temperance and wisdom.

Plato, The Republic 9 *(Hellenism)*

Teachings of Sun Myung Moon

What are laws? Laws exist to prevent the destruction of things that are worthy of protection. There is a natural law that protects the universe from destruction. Likewise, nations have laws to protect society from destruction. Once we understand the purpose of laws, we can appreciate the importance of obeying them. (118:198, June 1, 1982)

Every country has its laws, whose purpose is to maintain goodness. After all, a nation's constitution and the laws enacted by its legislature function to protect the general welfare, not destroy it. What about people who violate the law? All countries have prisons to punish them. Yet the standards of what is allowed and what is prohibited differ from one country to another according to the system of government and the views of its leaders. (216:306, April 15, 1991)

A nation enacts laws to enhance the public way of life. It places restrictions on people who live only to satisfy selfish desires and the desires of the body. The law sets limits on such self-centered activities; the more self-centered they are, the narrower are the limits the law sets. (105:15-16, July 8, 1979)

Human laws today are based on Roman laws, and Roman laws are the foundation of world culture. However, human morals are based on the conscience. Conscience precedes law...

Society needs laws, because its members seek a social order that is in agreement with the untainted conscience. In the end, where do human laws have their basis? Their basis is in heavenly law. (33:44, August 2, 1970)

The law should set up a bright line distinguishing right from wrong. Doesn't American law based on its Constitution set up a standard of right and wrong? The law does not punish people for serving the public. You can do infinite amounts of public service, and it is always welcomed. But many kinds of self-centered activities are prohibited. Whenever your self-centered actions damage the public, the law gets in the way. Hence, using violence to harm people or destroy property is illegal. Vandalizing public buildings is illegal.

From this perspective, when someone speaks harsh, vituperative words that hurt others, He also violates the [heavenly] law. (111:239, February 22, 1981)

Why should you obey the laws of your nation? You may think, "That's a bad law. I know that some crooked congressman introduced the bill and got it passed, so I'm not going to obey that law. I will follow my own laws." Nevertheless, laws are made to preserve the freedom of the nation as a whole, and the nation's freedom is a higher good than the preferences of particular individuals or groups. From this perspective, it is right to obey the law. By the same token, God's law protects the freedom and integrity of the entire universe, above and beyond the desires of any of its creatures. (May 1, 1982)[17]

At the Human Fall evil started first, ahead of goodness. Hence we must make effort to suppress evil and elevate goodness. What strategy shall we use? First, we must take control over our arrogance. The Fall occurred when human beings exalted themselves and pushed God aside. That was the beginning of Satan's nature. Arrogance is the desire to elevate oneself without regard to law and discipline or to how it may affect the surrounding environment or the social order. An arrogant person has no regard for duty or law.

How do we describe a person who lives in accordance with the law? Do we say He is arrogant? No, we say he or she is as an honest person. The Korean word for honesty (*jeongjik*) is composed of two Chinese characters, 正 meaning "right" and 直 meaning "straight." The law establishes what is straight. With the law we separate good from evil and distinguish between right and wrong.

An arrogant person ignores the law. We must put a stop to behavior that ignores the law and violates the norms expected according to one's position and circumstances. (37:112, December 23, 1970)

What will be the constitution of the Kingdom of Heaven? It will establish the power of love and foster the life force of love. All laws in the Kingdom of Heaven will be for protecting love. (111:171, February 15, 1981)

2. The Administration of Justice

Whenever you judge between people, you should do so with justice. How superbly God instructs you to do so; God is Alert, Observant!

Qur'an 4.58

Hear the cases between your brethren, and judge righteously between a man and his brother or the alien that is with him. You shall not be partial in judgment; you shall hear the small and the great alike; you shall not be afraid of the face of man, for the judgment is God's.

Deuteronomy 1.16-17

He is not thereby just because he hastily arbitrates cases. The wise man should investigate both right and wrong.

The intelligent person who leads others not falsely but lawfully and impartially, who is a guardian of the law, is called one who abides by righteousness.

Dhammapada 256-57 (*Buddhism*)

A thief shall, running, approach the king, with flying hair, confessing that theft, saying, "Thus I have done, punish me."

Whether he is punished or pardoned [after confessing], the thief is freed from the guilt of theft; but the king, if he punishes not, takes upon himself the guilt of the thief.

Laws of Manu 8.314, 316 (*Hinduism*)

What destroyed your predecessors was just that when a person of rank among them committed a theft they left him alone, but when a weak one of their number committed a theft they inflicted the prescribed punishment on him. I swear by God that even if my daughter Fatima should steal, I would have her hand cut off.

Hadith of Bukhari and Muslim *(Islam)*

If the thief steals something he takes an oath to decide his fate, but if the oath steals something what will it take?

Igala Proverb *(African Traditional Religions)*

You shall not bear false witness against your neighbor.

Exodus 20.16

Whoever commits a delinquency or crime, then throws it upon the innocent, has burdened himself with falsehood and a flagrant crime.

Qur'an 4.112

A single witness shall not prevail against a man for any crime or for any wrong in connection with any offense that he has committed; only on the evidence of two witnesses, or of three witnesses, shall a charge be sustained. If a malicious witness rises against any man to accuse him of wrongdoing, then both parties to the dispute shall appear before the LORD, before the priests and the judges who are in office in those days; the judges shall inquire diligently, and if the witness is a false witness and has accused his brother falsely, then you shall do to him as he had meant to do to his brother; so you shall purge the evil from the midst of you.

Deuteronomy 19.15-20

Teachings of Sun Myung Moon

A nation's laws impose punishment on criminals for the purpose of setting the indemnity conditions necessary for maintaining order in society. (*Exposition of the Divine Principle*, Restoration 1.1)

I cannot bend the law even for True Mother. The law rules her, as it rules me. (180:115, August 7, 1988)

You cannot have freedom without principle or law; you cannot have freedom without order… When there is no law and order, freedom brings only destruction. When you violate the law of a nation, you have to go to prison.

Yet if America is really a free country, why does it need prisons? Shouldn't we just close them down and let everyone do whatever they want? Shouldn't people be free to do whatever they want, even run down the street stark naked? Today in America people do that, even practice prostitution and homosexuality, and they regard it as their right to be free. Can we dispense with prison? Well then, should John Hinckley be able to get away with shooting President Reagan and insist that he not be arrested?

Certainly we need to incarcerate those who do not abide by the nation's laws. Even in the spirit world there are prisons for those who do not abide by the laws of the spirit world. Schools need a room for detention, and families need a punishing spot. (112:73-74, April 1, 1981)

If a prosecutor or malicious person obtains the execution of an innocent man for personal motives, then according to the heavenly law he himself shall be sentenced to death. The person who was killed unfairly shall receive a reward, while the person who caused his death shall be punished. (93:111, May 21, 1977)

3. Just and Merciful Punishments

Human punishment is execrable even when just.

     Pope Sixtus (Christianity)

A sovereign should not inflict excessive punishment.

     Matsya Purana 220.10 (Hinduism)

The superior man gives careful thought to his judgments and is tardy in sentencing people to death.

     I Ching 61 (Confucianism)

Whoever strikes a man so that he dies shall be put to death. But if he did not lie in wait for him, but God let him fall into his hand, then I will appoint for you a place to which he may flee. But if a man willfully attacks another to kill him treacherously, you shall take him from my altar, that he may die.

     Exodus 21.12-14

O you who believe! Equal recompense is prescribed for you in cases of murder: a freeman for a freeman, a slave for a slave, a woman for a woman.[18] But if any remission is made by the brother of the slain, then grant any reasonable demand and compensate him with handsome gratitude. This is a concession and a mercy from your Lord.

     Qur'an 1.178

Should I [Imam Ali] be killed, see that there is no widespread retaliation. Do not roam about with a drawn sword... and do not start a massacre of my opponents and enemies. See that only one man, that is my murderer, is killed in punishment for the crime of murder, and that nobody else is molested or harmed or harassed. The punishment to the man who attempted the murder shall take place only when I die of the wound delivered by him, and this punishment shall be only one stroke of the sword to end his life. He should not be tortured before his death; his hands and feet should not be cut off, because I have heard the Holy Prophet saying, "Do not cut off the hands and feet of anybody, even a biting dog."

     Nahjul Balagha, Letter 47 (Shiite Islam)

O king, through compassion you should always
Generate an attitude of help
Even for those embodied beings
Who have committed appalling sins.

Especially generate compassion
For those murderers, whose sins are horrible;
Those of fallen nature are receptacles
Of compassion from those whose nature is great.

Free the weaker prisoners
After a day or five days;
Do not think the others
Are never to be freed...

As long as the prisoners are not freed,
They should be made comfortable
With barbers, baths, food, drink,
Medicine and clothing.

Just as unworthy sons are punished
Out of a wish to make them worthy,
So punishment should be enforced with
 compassion
And not through hatred or desire for wealth.

Once you have analyzed the angry
Murderers and recognized them well,
You should banish them without
Killing or tormenting them.

     Nagarjuna, Precious Garland 331-37 (Buddhism)

Teachings of Sun Myung Moon

When the state executes someone who committed a capital crime, it is not thereby guilty of the crime of killing a human being. Why not? The government carried out the execution under public statutes enacted for the benefit of society. Being sanctioned by laws that were enacted to benefit the nation and the world, the execution may be justified. (88:298, October 3, 1976)

I envision the day when all nations are united under a world government like the United Nations and agree on a world standard of law. A person who commits a crime will receive swift punishment; he or she will be sent away to a facility near the North Pole or the South Pole. There convicts are quarantined like patients with leprosy or SARS and provided with food to last only one year. In that hellish environment they are trained to survive; and through suffering hardships they are educated in the heavenly way. That education elevates their character and restores them to people who will abide by the law for the rest of their lives.[19] (May 17, 2003)

The American legal system has a provision for criminals to be pardoned. How about in the ideal universal legal system: can a convicted criminal receive pardon? Yes it is possible, but to be entitled to receive it, he should sacrifice and serve. In that case the law shows mercy, and the person can make a new start down the path of a reformed life. (105:92, September 30, 1979)

4. The End of the Law

He who loves his neighbor has fulfilled the law. The commandments, "You shall not commit adultery, You shall not kill, You shall not steal, You shall not covet," and any other commandment, are summed up in this sentence, "You shall love your neighbor as yourself." Love does no wrong to a neighbor; therefore love is the fulfilling of the law.

Romans 13.8-10

The wise man is always free; he is always held in honor; he is always master of the laws. The law is not made for the just, but for the unjust. The just man is a law unto himself and he does not need to summon the law from afar, for he carries it enclosed in his heart, having the law [of God] written on the tablets of his heart...

The wise man is free, since one who does as he wishes is free. Not every wish is good, but the wise man wishes only that which is good; he hates evil for he chooses what is good. Because he chooses what is good he is master of his choice, and because he chooses his work he is free.

Saint Ambrose of Milan, Letter 54 (Christianity)

Teachings of Sun Myung Moon

Every country has its laws, whose purpose is to maintain goodness... At the same time, everyone is endowed with a conscience. Even without an education, the conscience knows what is right and urges us to act accordingly. Through the conscience, every person can know right from wrong and has the ability to regulate him or herself, quite apart from the law. (216:306, April 15, 1991)

The law is an instrument to regulate people who would take advantage of the society and world for personal gain. The law is needed to deter self-centered people and groups from transgressing the line of what is permitted. How should we live in order not to transgress the law? Those who live for the sake of others do not require laws to deter them from doing wrong. We need to reach that level, where we are liberated from the law.

How shall you live if you want to be confident not to be caught in the net of the world's laws? If you live for your own selfish purposes, you are liable to be caught wherever you go. Instead, cultivate a life of living for the greater good of society. Then you will be liberated from the law. (93:301, June 12, 1977)

Would that the world was filled with true families! It would be a world governed by the heavenly way and heavenly laws, with no need for lawyers, prosecutors or even judges. (April 10, 2006)

Prophets and Messengers

FOR AS LONG AS THE KINGDOMS OF THIS WORLD have fallen short of the standards of God's kingdom, God has raised up prophets and messengers to represent Heaven's righteousness and call worldly leaders to account. These men and women put their lives at risk to speak out for justice and proclaim a higher vision of community. They stepped forward believing that they could prick the consciences of the powerful, that they might listen and turn away from evil, that their nation might avoid disaster.

The role of prophet is not limited to those rare founders of religion who were especially chosen to bring God's revelation into the world, though some like Muhammad are called such. People taking up the prophetic mantle include saints and righteous people of every age and in every culture, who dared to remind the rulers of their day of truths that were first revealed long ago. Often they must recast Heaven's message into contemporary terms. In their number we include Socrates and Mencius, and if space permitted we would add modern figures such as St. Francis of Assisi, Martin Luther, Nichiren, Mahatma Gandhi and Martin Luther King, Jr., to name but a few. In that sense, Father Moon has been called a prophet, and some of his prophecies are included here.

The prophets spoke challenging words that made powerful people uncomfortable; therefore they were persecuted, ridiculed and put to death. Some, like Nathan and Mencius, sought to protect themselves by couching the truth in parables in order to catch the ruler's conscience. But most were unable to keep in their ruler's good graces. The prophet Jeremiah, for example, was jailed several times. He revealed his inner struggle as he proceeded on his dangerous course.

An attribute of prophecy is the ability to predict the future. Yet prophets are no mere fortunetellers. Their gift gives them confidence to speak with authority on affairs of state. The prophet's predictions are accurate because of his or her close relationship with God, in whose hand lies the destinies of the nations.

1. The Mission of a Prophet

Every nation has its messenger. Once their messenger comes, judgment will be passed upon them in all fairness and they will not be wronged. They will say, "When will this promise be, if you have been telling the truth?" Say, "I possess no harm nor any advantage by myself, except concerning whatever God may wish. Every nation has a term; whenever their term comes, they will not postpone it for an hour nor advance it."

Qur'an 10.47-49

Now the word of the LORD came to me [Jeremiah], saying,

> "Before I formed you in the womb I knew you,
> and before you were born I consecrated you;
> I appointed you a prophet to the nations."

Then I said, "Ah, Lord GOD! Behold, I do not know how to speak, for I am only a youth." But the LORD said to me,

> "Do not say, 'I am only a youth';
> for to all to whom I send you you shall go,
> and whatever I command you you shall speak.
> Be not afraid of them,
> for I am with you to deliver you, says the LORD."

Then the LORD put forth his hand and touched my mouth; and the LORD said to me,

> "Behold, I have put my words in your mouth.
> See, I have set you this day over nations and over kingdoms,
> to pluck up and to break down,
> to destroy and to overthrow,
> to build and to plant."

Jeremiah 1.4-10

I am that gadfly which God has attached to the state, and all day long and in all places am always fastening upon you, arousing and persuading and reproaching you.

Socrates, in Plato, Apology (Hellenism)

The word of the LORD came to me, "Son of man, I have made you a watchman for the house of Israel; whenever you hear a word from my mouth, you shall give them warning from me. If I say to the wicked, 'You shall surely die,' and you give him no warning, nor speak to warn the wicked from his wicked way, in order to save his life, that wicked man shall die in his iniquity; but his blood I will require at your hand. But if you warn the wicked, and he does not turn from his wickedness or from his wicked way, he shall die in his iniquity; but you will have saved your life."[20]

Ezekiel 3.16-19

I cannot and will not recant anything, for to go against conscience is neither right nor safe. Here I stand, I can do no other, so help me God. Amen.

Martin Luther (Christianity)[21]

Teachings of Sun Myung Moon

What was God's purpose in sending saints and prophets to this earth? It was to educate all people about the meaning of God's true love by demonstrating the character and exemplary life that God desires. Especially God wanted them to educate the political leadership, and other leaders also, that they might practice the ways of God. Together they were to realize harmony between the world of the mind [religion] and the world of body [politics and economy] centered on God's true love.[22]

However, as the body often does not follow what the conscience requires, many rulers did not recognize the prophets and holy men who came to them. They refused their teachings and ignored their warnings.

Who can take responsibility to solve the tragedies and evils in contemporary society: confusion of values, moral corruption, drug addiction, terrorism, racial discrimination, and so on? Can politicians completely solve them with their political power? Politicians carry a great responsibility and burden in the decisions and choices they make. Especially in this age, when societies are more pluralistic than ever and nations are linked in a network of interdependence, it is crucial for leaders to take responsibility for making right judgments and decisions! Therefore, when leaders are about to make important decisions, I urge them to listen humbly to the voice coming from Heaven and look for solutions through following the heavenly way. (219:110, August 27, 1991)

This world needs prophets, not philosophers. You can't deny it. Did democratic thought originate with philosophers or prophets? Who were its primary exponents? We need to analyze it and come up with a clear answer. How about communism? It was put forward by philosophers. People of the world today follow what philosophers advocate, but we cannot completely accept their theories. From this viewpoint, the theories of the philosophers will pass away while the words of the prophets will endure.

Where are philosophers? They are at universities. Where are prophets? They are among religious believers. Do people give more respect to religion or to universities? They prefer the universities. All right then, where can we find hope, in universities or in religion? Clearly, in religion. We can find hope in a nameless religion, rather than at world-famous Harvard, Cambridge, or Oxford.

Among the prophets, were many of them scholars, or were they mostly uneducated people? They were mostly uneducated people. Yet conventionally, people put more trust in scholars than in the uneducated people we call prophets. From this viewpoint, we can conclude that the world is headed in the wrong direction. (79:334, September 28, 1975)

Churches must educate families, tribes and nations to go the right path. They are like the prophets in the past, who admonished their kings, especially when they were on the wrong track, and guided them to do right. Likewise, God is utilizing churches as the womb to give birth to families, tribes and peoples who will lead the future world. (106:35, November 11, 1979)

2. Speaking Truth to Power

The most excellent jihad is the uttering of truth in the presence of an unjust ruler.
            Hadith of Tirmidhi *(Islam)*

And the Lord sent Nathan to David. He came to him, and said to him, "There were two men in a certain city, the one rich and the other poor. The rich man had very many flocks and herds; but the poor man had nothing but one little ewe lamb, which he had bought. And he brought it up, and it grew up with him and with his children; it used to eat of his morsel, and drink from his cup, and lie in his bosom, and it was like a daughter to him. Now there came a traveler to the rich man, and he was unwilling to take one of his own flock or herd to prepare for the wayfarer who had come to him, but he took the poor man's lamb, and prepared it for the man who had come to him." Then David's anger was greatly kindled against the man; and he said to Nathan, "As the Lord lives, the man who has done this deserves to die; and he shall restore the lamb fourfold, because he did this thing, and because he had no pity."

Nathan said to David, "You are the man. Thus says the LORD, the God of Israel, 'I anointed you king over Israel, and I delivered you out of the hand of Saul; and I gave you your master's wives into your bosom, and gave you the house of Israel and Judah; and if this were too little, I would add to you as much more. Why have you despised the word of the LORD, to do what is evil in his sight? You have smitten Uriah the Hittite with the sword, and have taken his wife to be your wife, and have slain him with the sword of the Ammonites. Now therefore the sword shall never depart from your house, because you have despised me, and have taken the wife of Uriah the Hittite to be your wife.'"[23]

2 Samuel 12.1-10

Mencius went to P'ing Lu. "Would you or would you not," said he to the governor, "dismiss a lancer who has failed three times in one day to report for duty?"

"I would not wait for the third time."

"But you yourself have failed to report for duty many times. In years of famine close to a thousand of your people suffered, the old and the young being abandoned in the gutter, the able-bodied scattered in all directions."

"It was not within my power to do anything about this."

"Supposing a man were entrusted with the care of cattle and sheep. Surely he ought to seek pasturage and fodder for the animals. If he found that this could not be done, should he return his charge to the owner or should he stand by and watch the animals die?"

"In this I am at fault."

Mencius II.B.4 *(Confucianism)*

Amaziah the priest of Bethel sent to Jeroboam king of Israel, saying, "Amos has conspired against you in the midst of the house of Israel; the land is not able to bear all his words. For thus Amos has said,

'Jeroboam shall die by the sword,
and Israel must go into exile away from his land.' "

And Amaziah said to Amos, "O seer, go flee away to the land of Judah, and eat bread there, and prophesy there; but never again prophesy at Bethel, for it is the king's sanctuary, and it is a temple of the kingdom."

Then Amos answered Amaziah, "I am no prophet, nor one of the sons of the prophets; but I am a herdsman, and a dresser of sycamore trees, and the LORD took me from following the flock, and the LORD said to me, 'Go, prophesy to my people Israel.'

"Now therefore hear the word of the LORD.[24] You say, 'Do not prophesy against Israel, and do not preach against the house of Isaac.' Therefore thus says the LORD:
'Your wife shall be a harlot in the city, and your sons and daughters shall fall by the sword,
and your land shall be parceled out by line; you yourself shall die in an unclean land, and Israel shall surely go into exile away from its land.' "

Amos 7.10-17

Has not the history of those before you reached you: the folk of Noah, and 'Ad and Thamud, and those after them? None save God knows them. Their messengers came to them with clear proofs, but they thrust their hands into their mouths, and said, "Lo! we disbelieve in that with which you have been sent, and lo! we are in grave doubt concerning that to which you call us." Their messengers said, "Can there be doubt concerning God, the Creator of the heavens and the earth? He calls you that He may forgive you your sins and reprieve you until an appointed term." They said, "You are but mortals like us, who would fain turn us away from what our fathers used to worship. Then bring us some clear warrant." Their messengers said to them, "We are but mortals like you, but God gives grace to whom He will of His slaves. It is not ours to bring you a warrant unless by the permission of God. In God let believers put their trust! How should we not put our trust in God when He has shown us His ways? We surely will endure that hurt you do to us. In God let the trusting put their trust!" And those who disbelieved said to their messengers, "Verily we will drive you out from our land, unless you return to our religion." Then their Lord inspired them, "Verily we shall destroy the wrongdoers, and verily We shall make you to dwell in the land after them. This is for him who fears My Majesty and fears My threats." And they sought help from their

Lord, and every froward potentate was brought to naught.[25]

Qur'an 14.9-15

A king who does what is not righteous
and not suitable is mostly praised
by his subjects, for it is hard to know
what he will or will not tolerate;
therefore it is hard to know
what is useful or not to say.

If useful but unpleasant words
are hard to speak to someone else,
what could I, a monk, say to a king
who is a lord of the great earth?

But because of my affection for you
and through my compassion for all beings,
I tell you without hesitation
that which is useful but unpleasant.

O steadfast one, if true words
are spoken without anger,
one should take them as fit to be
heard, like water fit for bathing.

Realize that I am telling you
what is useful here and later.
Act on it so as to help
yourself and also others.

Nagarjuna, Precious Garland 301-6 (Buddhism)

Teachings of Sun Myung Moon

The time will come when religious leaders who speak for the Will of God will rise to prominence. Religious leaders are prophets. They must stand up fearlessly, declare God's Will, and point the way for humanity to go. (January 22, 2000)

In the period of the divided kingdoms of north and south, whenever the Israelites violated their covenant with God, straying from the ideal of the Temple, God sent many prophets—such as Elijah, Isaiah and Jeremiah—to admonish them and move them to repentance and internal reform. However, because the kings and the people did not heed the warnings of the prophets and did not repent, God chastised them externally by sending gentile nations such as Syria, Assyria and Babylon to attack them.

During the parallel period of the divided kingdoms of east and west, the papacy was corrupt. God sent prominent monks such as St. Thomas Aquinas and St. Francis of Assisi to admonish the papacy and promote internal reform in the Church. (*Exposition of the Divine Principle,* Parallels 4)

The truth of God never changes; it is the same in the past, the present and the future. In Old Testament times, whenever the rulers of Israel acted wickedly, God raised up prophets to admonish them. If the rulers heeded the prophets, obeyed God's word, and ruled the nation according to His word, then the nation would prosper. The Christian era was no different. In evil times God sent prophets to awaken the rulers of their age and warn them to follow God. If a ruler heeded their words, the land would revive and become prosperous.

This method worked rather well until the end of the Middle Ages. But then came the modern period with the doctrine of separation of church and state, the belief that religious leaders should have nothing to do with politics. This was an omen of the nation's downfall. It deprived society of the channel of communication between civil authorities and God. From that time on, Satan began to sharpen his daggers.

Today, I am speaking out against the mistakes of the American government. When the Carter administration made mistakes, I criticized them, saying "This is wrong." I shook hands with President Nixon, cooperating with him not because I needed him, but to introduce God's word to the American people. If Nixon had listened to me, America would not have declined as it did and Vietnam would not have fallen.

In 1974, I met President Thieu of Vietnam and strongly warned him that his country was on the path of ruin unless it changed direction. I told that he would have to inspire the people of his nation to sacrifice and put up a determined fight, and that his policy of relying on America would fail.

God's way is the same throughout history. He always raises a prophet or messenger to educate the rulers and civil authorities. I did not come to America to be active in politics. I want to educate the politicians to go in the right direction. This is my way of life.

Do you think I came to America to get rich? Do you think I came here to receive abuse? I am not so foolish. I am doing this work for the sake of God's name. God told me plainly, "Go to America and speak out. If the leaders of the nation will not listen to you, then the young people who will become its future leaders will listen to you." That is how you come to be here listening to me now. (93:83-84, May 15, 1977)

3. A Prophet Endures Rejection and Persecution

Elijah said [to the LORD], "I have been very jealous for the LORD, the God of hosts; for the people of Israel have forsaken thy covenant, thrown down thy altars, and slain thy prophets with the sword; and I, even I only, am left; and they seek my life, to take it away."

1 Kings 19.14

"Do not preach"—thus they preach—
"one should not preach of such things;
disgrace will not overtake us."
Should this be said, O house of Jacob?
Is the Spirit of the LORD impatient?
Are these his doings?
Do not my words do good
to him who walks uprightly?
But you rise against my people as an enemy;
you strip the robe from the peaceful,
from those who pass by trustingly with no
    thought of war...
If a man should go about and utter wind and lies,
saying, "I will preach to you of wine and strong
    drink,"
he would be the preacher for this people!

Micah 2.6-11

Jeremiah stood in the court of the temple of the LORD, and said to all the people, "Thus says the LORD of hosts, the God of Israel, Behold, I am bringing upon this city and upon all its towns all the evil that I have pronounced against it, because they have stiffened their neck, refusing to heed my words." Now Pashhur the priest, the son of Immer, who was chief officer in the temple of the LORD, heard Jeremiah prophesying these things. Then Pashhur beat Jeremiah the prophet and put him in the stocks that were in the upper Benjamin Gate of the temple...

O LORD, thou hast deceived me,
and I was deceived;
thou art stronger than I,
and thou hast prevailed.
I have become a laughingstock all the day;
everyone mocks me.
For whenever I speak, I cry out,
I shout, "Violence and destruction!"
For the word of the LORD has become for me
a reproach and derision all day long.
If I say, "I will not mention him,
or speak any more in his name,"
there is in my heart as it were a burning fire
shut up in my bones,
and I am weary with holding it in,
and I cannot.
For I hear many whispering.

Terror is on every side!
"Denounce him! Let us denounce him!"
say all my familiar friends,
watching for my fall.
"Perhaps he will be deceived,
then we can overcome him,
and take our revenge on him."
But the LORD is with me as a dread warrior;
therefore my persecutors will stumble,
they will not overcome me.
They will be greatly shamed,
for they will not succeed.
Their eternal dishonor
will never be forgotten.

O LORD of hosts, who triest the righteous,
who seest the heart and the mind,
let me see thy vengeance upon them,
for to thee have I committed my cause.

Jeremiah 19.14-20.2, 7-12

[The prophets] suffered mocking and scourging, and even chains and imprisonment. They were stoned, they were sawn in two, they were killed with the sword; they went about in skins of sheep and goats, destitute, afflicted, ill-treated—of whom the world was not worthy—wandering over deserts and mountains and in dens and caves of the earth.

Hebrews 11.36-38

Teachings of Sun Myung Moon

All prophets are unusual. It takes an unusual person to walk the path of Abel in search of the way of God's Will. Whenever a prophet appears, he acts in ways that are bizarre and out of the ordinary. All the prophets in the Old Testament and [the saints with prophetic missions] in the New Testament Age were unusual people. That is why they were ridiculed, opposed and persecuted. (89:129, November 1, 1976)

If you are in complete accord with truth and justice, then heavenly fortune will protect you completely. Heavenly fortune will strike any power that opposes you. Hence, if I truly become an object partner to God and dwell in a place of complete harmony with Him, then even a country such as America, or even the Soviet Union, will be struck down if it opposes me. It is because I understand this principle that I can be so bold. (214:194, February 2, 1991)

In the history of God's providence, prophets had to exercise their divine office while in the position of servants to the king. Therefore, when they spoke out the rulers attacked them, and many lost their lives. The Lord at the Second Coming comes as the fruit of all their sacrifices; he represents all the prophets of history as he stands in the Abel position before the world's rulers. Therefore, I, as the True Parent cannot be a petty person. Think about the difficult course of all the prophets of history, who shed their blood and had their heads cut off. I am to harvest that fruit. Therefore, I will speak the truth regardless. Like the prophets I also went to prison—six times in fact. Like them I always stand on the front line. (343:263, February 17, 2001)

I have been experiencing Thy reality of sorrow,
feeling the heart with which Thou dost face this world of enemies.
I know the sorrow of my Father who cannot come out and live in the sunshine;
the situation of my Father who has worked in the shadows.
I have pressed on in this way of life
anxious that I might become a child who resents his Father
or contradicts his Father at some point.

I know that when Thou didst find me,
Thou wert anxious about it also...

I have determined not to despair or disappoint Thee;
though I am pursued and driven out,
imprisoned with both my hands in handcuffs,
though I experience the lot of a slave or the lot of a servant.
I thank Thee for Thy grace of preserving my life
and letting me remain in Thy presence
from the day I determined to go forth until now.

How much hast Thou worked, Father,
in order to establish someone like me?
How much hast Thou sacrificed
for the sake of the path I must go...

Realizing [the extent of] Thy toil...
each time I wake from sleep I cannot but beg Thee
to forgive me as though I were a sinner.
While eating, I cannot help but put down my spoon
and with tears ask forgiveness for my past wrongs,
and each time I lay down, not being able to control my tired body,
I cannot help but scold myself
for not having a mind concerned about Thee...

Thou art a being to be pitied.
However much we might say that fellow named Moon of the Unification Church is to be pitied,
it is nothing. (30:270, March 29, 1970)

4. A Prophet Is Given True Visions of the Future

Surely the LORD God does nothing,
without revealing his secret to his servants the prophets.

Amos 3.7

Write the vision;
make it plain upon tablets,
so that he may run who reads it.
For still the vision awaits its time;
it hastens to the end—it will not lie.
If it seem slow, wait for it;
it will surely come, it will not delay.

Habakkuk 2.2-3

O Lord, your power is greater than all powers.
Under your leadership we cannot fear anything.
It is you who has given us prophetic power,
And has enabled us to foresee and interpret everything.

Dinka Prayer (African Traditional Religion)

It is an attribute of the possession of the absolute true self to be able to foreknow. When a nation or family is about to flourish, there are sure to be lucky omens. When a nation or family is about to perish, there are sure to be signs and prodigies. These things manifest themselves in the instruments of divination and in the agitation of the human body. When happiness or calamity is about to come, it can be known beforehand. When it is good, it can be known beforehand. When it is evil, it can be known beforehand. Therefore he who has realized his true self is like a celestial spirit.

Doctrine of the Mean 24 (Confucianism)

Nanak, sitting in this city of corpses, sings the Lord's praise
And enunciates this principle:
He who raised this creation and in manifold pleasures engaged it,
Sits apart, watching it.
Holy is the Lord, holy His justice;
True shall be the judgment He has pronounced.
As will its body's vesture be torn to shreds,
India shall remember my word.
In '78 they come; in '97 they depart—
Another hero shall someday arise.
Nanak utters the word of truth—
Truth he utters; truth the hour calls for.[26]

Adi Granth, Telang, M.1, p. 722f. (Sikhism)

Teachings of Sun Myung Moon

Fifty years ago I spoke visionary words, for example, that the in the future people could travel the world in a single day. People then ridiculed me as a madman, but they all fell away; some even went crazy. For the past fifty years and throughout my life, I prophesied the rise and fall of the world. I am today's representative prophet, representative educator and representative loving parent; and I am rising to the position of representative owner. (397:154, November 17, 2002)

I can predict the future of America and the future of Asia. Because we have been doing things that are needed for the distant future, it has been difficult for you to follow, to believe and to act. But with every passing year you are gaining a new understanding of the value of what we do. For decades the Korean people attacked me and persecuted me, but the time that I had been working for has now arrived. Hence, now the Korean people have changed their attitude. (103:110, February 11, 1979)

I predicted that communism could not last beyond 73 years, [and that is precisely what happened]. The disappearance of communism from the face of the earth is not the end of war, however. The more difficult struggle is the struggle between religions. I have been warning more about the danger of religious war—between Islam, Judaism and Christianity. I predicted it more than fifty years ago. (225:19, January 1, 1992)

Chapter 22

PEACE

The Peace of God

GOD IS THE SOURCE OF PEACE. When we look around us and see only conflict and war, when we despair of finding peace on earth, we turn to God, the King of Peace. When God comes to us, He soothes the anger in our breasts and lets us see our enemy from a different perspective, as a brother or sister. God is love; therefore with God we gain the power to love even our enemy. (See Chapter 13: *Love Your Enemy*) Therefore, the key to peace is to live with God, and to manifest God's love.

Father Moon adds an additional insight: since God's love dwells especially in the thick relationships of marriage and family, the God-centered, peaceful family is the actual building block of a peaceful society, nation and world.

Glory to God in the highest, and on earth peace, good will toward men![1]

Luke 2.14

May the LORD lift up his countenance upon you, and give you peace.

Numbers 6.26

God is peace, his name is peace, and all is bound together in peace.[2]

Zohar 3.10b (Judaism)

Peace I leave with you; my peace I give to you; not as the world gives do I give to you.

John 14.27

Allah summons to the abode of Peace, and leads whom He will to a straight path.

Qur'an 10.25

The whole of the Torah is for the purpose of promoting peace.

Talmud, Gittin 59b (Judaism)

Thou dost keep him in perfect peace, whose mind is stayed on thee, because he trusts in thee.

Isaiah 26.3

Our Father, it is thy universe, it is thy will:
Let us be at peace, let the souls of the people be cool.
Thou art our Father, remove all evil from our path.

Nuer Prayer (African Traditional Religions)

A man is a true Muslim when no other Muslim has to fear anything from either his tongue or his hand.

Hadith of Bukhari (Islam)

Tao invariably takes no action, and yet there is nothing left undone.
If kings and barons can keep it, all things will transform spontaneously.
If, after transformation, they should desire to be active,

1075

I would restrain them with simplicity, which has no name.
Simplicity, which has no name, is free of desires.
Being free of desires, it is tranquil.
And the world will be at peace of its own accord.

Tao Te Ching 37 *(Taoism)*

Teachings of Sun Myung Moon

God is the King of love, the King of peace and happiness and the Core of the ideal. Therefore, when human beings are blocked in their search after such things, there is no other way except through God. (72:11, May 7, 1974)

If people are quarreling and God appears in their midst, they change and want to help each other. (330:267, August 20, 2000)

True peace, true happiness and true freedom do not originate from human beings, but from the true God. Therefore, we can expect that people who are not living in accordance with God's Will, or who are entangled in sinful circumstances, cannot attain true peace, true happiness or true freedom. (78:103, May 6, 1975)

People have pursued peace throughout history. Nevertheless, this world is filled with distrust, treachery and hate; our efforts to establish a world of peace are at an impasse. Therefore, we are led to think that to attain our hope we must rely on an absolute and unchanging Being beyond time and space. That being must be God. We believe that God must be the Subject of all ideals—love, happiness and peace.

Nevertheless, God cannot establish happiness, love and peace by Himself. God needs relationships with object partners, human beings, to establish these ideals. God needs us to complete His love, His ideal, His joy and His peace. (74:46-47, November 27, 1974)

Why is fighting evil? It is because God cannot dwell amidst fighting. God is the King of peace, unification, unity, and supreme goodness. Therefore, He just cannot dwell in places of struggle. This world became evil due to the departure of God. (61:291, July 24, 1994)

When people say "peace," what are they talking about? They are not talking about peace itself, but a mutual relationship. There has to be love there. There can be no peace unless there is love. (175:196, April 17, 1988)

The Chinese characters for peace (平和 *pyeonghwa*) signify "horizontal" (平 *pyeong*) and "harmony" (和 *hwa*). This means that when a partner goes around, the center wants to go around along with it. This is possible only when there is harmony—not conflict—between the center and his partners.[3] (82:133, January 4, 1976)

The landing-place for peace among humankind can only be prepared by people who are grateful to God as their Center and who establish a unified realm of love. It would be a spherical realm, with love flowing equally in all directions, north, south, east and west. (357:131, October 29, 2001)

What educational materials will God employ to teach people how to realize peace on earth? He will use materials on love. Since love is invisible, God will find a man and a woman who love each other. Observing them, we learn that the source of peace in their relationship is love. Only love has the power to make peace possible. (193:153, October 3, 1989)

The basic unit of a peaceful world is not a peaceful nation but a peaceful family. A man and a woman, each with mind and body in harmony, who wed with God's Blessing and make a family—this is the basic unit of a peaceful world. These peaceful families are the families that have received God's Blessing through the True Parents—a blessing available for the first time in history. They structure their lives with true love and establish harmonious oneness. As these families prosper, they bring peace to their clans, to their communities, to their nations, and to the world. (December 27, 2002)

Human beings were created as temples of God. The Spirit of God was to be dwelling with them every moment of every day. In that situation, could people possibly make war on each other?

In the original world of creation, fighting among human beings would be as if your right hand were fighting your left hand, or as if your hand were trying to pull out your eye. In other words, in the ideal world of God's creation, war would be impossible. People would only be able to love each other and live in harmony. Their only challenge would be to compete in ways of glorifying their Creator.

In such a world there could be no conflict, no misunderstanding. There would only be harmony, cooperation and mutual assistance. People would be united in the pursuit of truth, goodness and beauty. It would truly be the world of peace that humanity has been seeking. This world would reflect the nature of God, whose primary characteristic is unselfishness, unselfish love, and unselfish peace. In religious terms it is called the Kingdom of God on earth. (219:116, August 28, 1991)

Inner Peace

PEACE BEGINS WITH PEACEFUL INDIVIDUALS. People who attain inner peace radiate peace to others. They possess inner strength, clarity and compassion with which to treat others peacefully, even in the face of hostility. By cultivating what Father Moon calls unity of mind and body, people can become vessels fit to receive God's abundant love, with which to share with others.

Cultivating inner peace must be the starting-point for all peacemaking efforts in the outer world. No political or economic program can produce a just and equitable peace if the people it seeks to help are full of hatred and violence in their hearts.

Just as a deep lake is clear and still, even so, on hearing the teachings and realizing them, the wise become exceedingly peaceful.

Dhammapada 82 *(Buddhism)*

Men do not mirror themselves in running water—they mirror themselves in still water. Only what is still can still the stillness of other things.[4]

Chuang Tzu 5 *(Taoism)*

As rivers flow into the ocean but cannot make the vast ocean overflow, so flow the streams of the sense-world into the sea of peace that is the sage.

Bhagavad-Gita 2.70 (Hinduism)

If a person's heart is peaceful, his body will be at ease, and if a person's heart is malicious, the body will be malevolent.

Hadith (Islam)

The Lord lives in the heart of every creature. He turns them round and round upon the wheel of his Maya. Take refuge utterly in Him. By His grace you will find supreme peace, and the state which is beyond all change.

Bhagavad-Gita 18.61-62 (Hinduism)

All this is full. All That is full.
From fullness, fullness comes.
When fullness is taken from fullness,
Fullness still remains.
Om. Peace, peace, peace.[5]

Isa Upanishad: Peace Chant (Hinduism)

The monk looks for peace within himself, and not in any other place. For when a person is inwardly quiet, there is nowhere a self can be found; where, then, could a non-self be found?

There are no waves in the depths of the sea; it is still, unbroken. It is the same with the monk. He is still, without any quiver of desire, without a remnant on which to build pride and desire.

Sutta Nipata 919-20 (Buddhism)

What causes wars, and what causes fighting among you? Is it not your passions that are at war in your members? You desire and do not have; so you kill. And you covet and cannot obtain; so you fight and wage war. You do not have, because you do not ask. You ask and do not receive, because you ask wrongly, to spend it on your passions.

James 4.1-3

Whence come wars, and fighting, and factions? Where but from the body and the lusts of the body? For wars are occasioned by the love of money, and money has to be acquired for the sake and in the service of the body.

Socrates, in Plato, Phaedo (Hellenism)

Once the good are perfectly good, there can be no war between them. This much is true, however, that while a good man is still on the way to perfection, one part of him can be at war with another of his parts; because of this rebellious element, two good men can be at war with each other. The fact is that in everyone "the flesh lusts against the spirit, and the spirit against the flesh." (Gal. 5.17)

Thus, the spiritual longing of one good man can be at war with the fleshly passion of another just as fleshly passion in one man can resist spiritual tendencies in another. And the war here is much like that between good and wicked men. So, too, a good deal like the war of the wicked against the wicked is the rivalry of fleshly desires in two good men, and this will continue until grace wins the ultimate victory of soundness over sickness in both of them.

Saint Augustine, City of God 15.5 (Christianity)

Wage jihad against the desires of your selves, and your hearts will be occupied by wisdom.

The best jihad is to ensure that one does not even consider transgressing against others.

Hadith (Islam)

Only when a man invites insult will others insult him. Only when a family invites destruction will others destroy it. Only when a state invites invasion will others invade it. The *T'ai Chia* says,

> When Heaven sends down calamities,
> There is hope of weathering them;
> When man brings them upon himself,
> There is no hope of escape.

Mencius IV.A.8 (Confucianism)

Mental violence has no potency and injures only the person whose thoughts are violent. It is otherwise with mental non-violence. It has potency which the world does not yet know.

Mohandas K. Gandhi (Hinduism)

Teachings of Sun Myung Moon

Can you find peace if your mind and body are fighting? How can you find happiness and peace when your mind and body are not one? (242:60, December 27, 1992)

Before we complain about the world's conflicts and the absence of world peace, we should reflect on ourselves and consider whether our minds and bodies are united into one, whether we are the starting-points of peace, and whether God is at the center of our endeavors for peace. (140:17-18, February 1, 1986)

From time immemorial, when saints and sages sought for the Kingdom of Heaven, they did not seek it by vying with their enemies, expressing wrath and anger, full of fury.

Rather, we understand that they forgot themselves even in front of their enemies' swords. They sought the Kingdom while quietly longing for God, worshipping God, and feeling peaceful embrace in God's bosom, while transcending the circumstances of the battle. (25:38-39, September 28, 1969)

We commonly say that the human body is the temple of God, but what is a holy temple? Is it a place to work for a living? Is it a factory or an office? When we think of a holy temple, we visualize a tranquil place of rest.

Where can we take rest? It should be amidst love. A holy temple is a tranquil place filled with God's love. If we wish to be God's temples, we should have this same quality: inwardly tranquil and filled with God's love. We want to elevate our inner selves to this high level. As people of God's love, we become participants in the world of heart. That means our love is like a well that never runs dry; you can draw water from it all you want yet it never runs out. The reason it never runs out is because God is there. (91:78, January 30, 1977)

What is peace? When your mind and body become one and you have a peaceful family, then there can be a peaceful nation and a peaceful world. Peace cannot come based on some man-made ideology. You have to make a foundation for peace in your mind and body, and then in your family among husband and wife, and parents and children, centering on God's original heart. Such families are the cornerstones of peace. Even if your family were immersed in a universe of peace, it would still have to receive direction from the root. (305:203, July 14, 1998)

The United Nations at its founding proclaimed a movement for world peace, and for sixty years it has dedicated itself to this task; yet world peace still remains far distant. Peace among nations can never come when those entrusted with the task have not resolved the Cain-Abel relationship between their own mind and body. (March 25, 2006)

The question is how I can turn the war going on inside of me into peace. This is extremely important. If I cannot accomplish this, then even though the world might be at peace, to me it will still be hell. (131:34, March 11, 1984)

Reconciliation and Peacemaking

JESUS CALLED PEACEMAKERS GOD'S SONS AND DAUGHTERS. Indeed, reconciling parties in conflict is to participate in the work of God, who desires that all the members of His family live in peace with one another. Yet the work of a peacemaker can be difficult. Even though he or she tries to be even-handed, demonstrating concern and empathy for both sides, the peacemaker is liable to be attacked and blamed by one side or the other. A peacemaker must therefore be willing to make sacrifices and take risks for peace—even to the extent of sacrificing his life.

Reconciliation requires much of the quarreling parties. Beyond a temporary truce, it requires genuine forgiveness. Ultimately, it should lead to bonds of love and solidarity between the former enemies. Father Moon teaches us to apply the scriptural ethic to love our enemy (See Chapter 13: *Love Your Enemy*), to reconciling with enemy nations and enemy religions.

1. Reconciliation

If you are offering your gift at the altar, and there remember that your brother has something against you, leave your gift there before the altar and go; first be reconciled to your brother, and then come and offer your gift.[6]

                              Matthew 5.23-24

Let us have concord with our own people,
and concord with people who are strangers to us;
The Divine Twins create between us and the
    strangers a unity of hearts.[7]

May we unite in our minds, unite in our purposes,
and not fight against the divine spirit within us.
nor the arrows of the War-god fall with the
    break of day.

                        Atharva Veda 7.52.1-2 *(Hinduism)*

Better and more rewarding is God's reward to those who believe and put their trust in Him: who avoid gross sins and indecencies and, when angered, are willing to forgive... Let evil be rewarded by like evil, but he who forgives and seeks reconciliation shall be rewarded by God...

True constancy lies in forgiveness and patient forbearance.[8]

                              Qur'an 42.36-43

If they (the enemy) incline to peace, you incline to it also, and trust in God.

                                  Qur'an 8.61

The Messenger of God said, "Shall I inform you of the best morals of this world and the hereafter? To forgive him who oppresses you, to make a bond with him who severs from you, to be kind to him who insults you, and to give to him who deprives you."

                                  Hadith *(Islam)*

With malice toward none; with charity for all; with firmness in the right, as God gives us to see the right, let us strive on to finish the work we are in; to bind up the nation's wounds; to care for him who shall have borne the battle, and for his widow, and his orphan—to do all which may achieve and cherish a just and lasting peace among ourselves, and with all nations.

                Abraham Lincoln, Second Inaugural Address

Teachings of Sun Myung Moon

You should offer your devotions in peaceful surroundings and with a peaceful heart. You should not worship where there is discord, because God is not present where there is discord. Your act of worship can bear fruit when there is goodness, with all evils having surrendered. It cannot bear fruit where there is conflict and complaint. That is why when there is a falling out among brothers, they should first reconcile before making an offering table for their ancestors.⁹ (286:209-10, August 11, 1997)

If each side insists, "I exist for myself," they can never be reconciled. To achieve the goal of peace, people on both sides need to take the stance, "I exist for you." Then they can come to the point of consoling one another. Peace can arise only when we say to our opponent, "I am here for you." (60:21, August 1, 1972)

Thus far, nations tried to expand their territory by invading others. However, from now on we should follow the principle that to reach the world we should deny ourselves. In order for your beloved nation to lead the world, it must go beyond national self-interest. If your nation cannot do this, it does not have the philosophy that can unify the world. (26:294, November 10, 1969)

What kind of world would it be if each nation thought, "God is on my side," while it treated other nations as the enemy? It would be a world of continual wars and conflicts.

To become God's sons and daughters, you have to love the way God loves. You have to love humanity. I know that God wants enemy nations to reconcile, become friendly, connect with each other and unite into one. That is why I work to encourage nations to think beyond their borders and form a united world. (83:312, February 25, 1976)

2. Peacemaking

Blessed are the peacemakers, for they shall be called sons of God.

Matthew 5.9

If two parties of believers fall to fighting, then make peace between them. And if one party of them does wrong to the other, fight that wrong-doer until it returns to the ordinance of God; then, if it returns, make peace between them justly, and act equitably. Lo! God loves the equitable.

Qur'an 49.9

He brings together those who are divided, he encourages those who are friendly; he is a peacemaker, a lover of peace, impassioned for peace, a speaker of words that make for peace.

Digha Nikaya 13.75, Tevigga Sutta (Buddhism)

During the short eons of swords,
They meditate on love,
Introducing to nonviolence
Hundreds of millions of living beings.

In the midst of great battles
They remain impartial to both sides;
For bodhisattvas of great strength
Delight in reconciliation of conflict.

Holy Teaching of Vimalakirti 8 (Buddhism)

Rabbi Baruqa of Huza often went to the marketplace at Lapet. One day, the prophet Elijah appeared to him there, and Rabbi Baruqa asked him, "Is there anyone among all these people who will have a share in the World to Come?" Elijah answered… "Those two will have a share in the World to Come!" Rabbi Baruqa asked the newcomers, "What is your occupation?"

They replied, "We are clowns. When we see someone who is sad, we cheer him up. When we see two people quarreling, we try to make peace between them."

Talmud, Ta'anit 22a (Judaism)

After all the kings had been seated and perfect silence had ensued, Krishna, possessing fine teeth and having a voice as deep as that of a drum, began to speak, "In order that, O Bharata, peace may be established between the Kurus and the Pandavas without a slaughter of the heroes, I have come hither. Besides this, O king, I have no other beneficial words to utter... Know, O thou of Kuru's race, that those wicked sons of thine, headed by Duryodhana, abandoning both virtue and profit, disregarding morality, and deprived of their senses by avarice, are now acting most unrighteously towards their foremost kinsmen. The terrible danger [of universal slaughter thus] has its origin in the conduct of the Kurus. If you become indifferent to it, it will then produce a universal slaughter. If, O Bharata, you are willing, you may be able to allay that danger even yet, for peace, I think, is not difficult of acquisition. The establishment of peace, O king, depends on you and me. Set right your sons, and I will set the Pandavas right."[10]

Mahabharata, Udyoga Parva 95 (Hinduism)

I have nothing new to teach the world. Truth and Non-violence are as old as the hills. All I have done is to try experiments in both on as vast a scale as I could.

Mohandas K. Gandhi (Hinduism)

We are asking the nations of Europe between whom rivers of blood have flowed to forget the feuds of a thousand years.

Winston Churchill[11]

Teachings of Sun Myung Moon

Antagonism has no place in God's love, only unity and harmony. In light of this, you can understand what the Bible means in saying that peacemakers will be called sons of God. (*Way of God's Will* 3.2)

How patient is God, who has been enduring for millions of years? We, too, need to possess His patience. I'm not saying we that should never fight. But there is a right time to fight: when we can fight for the benefit of both sides. We should not fight those who oppose us seeking their destruction. We should fight to educate both sides and bring them together in harmony. We should educate each side to no longer regard the other as the enemy. (104:33, March 25, 1979)

To bring about a united, peaceful world we must overcome the many challenges arising from differences in region, race, religion, culture, custom, language and nationality. If we view the world from the perspective of the Creator—through God's eyes of true love—we see that despite all these differences, the world is one.

When young people inspired by God's true love dedicate themselves to sacrifice and service, they can begin to solve poverty and hunger throughout the world. They can begin to heal the wounds caused by differences between rich and poor. They can help people overcome the animosities and hatreds arising from different historical experiences.

True love means to love that which cannot be loved. From this definition we can acquire a clear sense of direction for overcoming relationships of enmity and conflict. (288:201-02, November 28, 1997)

I have the mission to prevent racial conflict and make peace between the races, especially between blacks and whites. The best way to accomplish this is to inspire white people to humble themselves voluntarily and serve black people. (124:275, February 27, 1983)

Black people in America walked the path of slavery, taking the role of Abel as their part in the restoration of the heavenly side. It was black people who established America, not white people. Black people were sacrificed to build this nation; also the Indians were sacrificed. You should know that if there were ever a racial war, black people would want revenge, and neither would the other colored races leave the white race alone. Why do you think I, Reverend Moon, came to America? Indians are like my cousins. We are brothers. They are all perishing, and I have to prevent it. I didn't come here for revenge, but to save. I am here to help the races reconcile with each other.

Who can reconcile whites and blacks? Can a white person or a black person do it? No, it won't work. Blacks won't listen to a white person, and whites won't follow a black person. But black people can listen to someone of the yellow race. Yellow people were also the victims of the white establishment. If yellow people take the lead in forgiving their enemies—white Americans—and tell blacks to do the same, they will listen. A yellow man can teach black people to forgive, because their enemy, and the Indians' enemy, is also my enemy. Representing all minorities, I will take the lead in forgiving. I explain to them that they are Abel, and this is Abel's historical path. (106:241, December 30, 1979)

Responsible Christian leaders could not resolve the problems in the Persian Gulf, so as a safeguard [against a full-scale religious war] I am convening a dialogue between prominent Christian and Muslim leaders. Most Koreans would say, "What has it got to do with me if Iraqis die or a nuclear bomb falls there?" But I know humanity's dismal path, and I want to steer the world to avoid its hidden reefs. Hence, even though I am insulted and ridiculed, I am striving to save humanity through diplomatic efforts, even spending my own money. I am trying to get America and the Soviet Union aligned for this purpose. I have also worked for reconciliation between China and Taiwan, and recently I began efforts to reconcile Israel and the Arab world. (211:13, December 30, 1990)

I have reached the advanced age of eighty-five, by the Korean way of counting. But I will continue to work harder than anyone else until the day the Earth overflows with God's true families, guns in the Middle East fall silent and give way to fireworks of peace and joy, and shouts of "Mansei" celebrating the unification of my homeland Korea echo across the Pacific and are heard in America. (March 23, 2004)

3. Jesus' Sacrificial Love as a Model for Peacemaking

And when they came to the place which is called The Skull [Calvary], there they crucified him, and the criminals, one on the right and one on the left. And Jesus said, "Father, forgive them; for they know not what they do."

Luke 23.33-34

But now in Christ Jesus you who once were far off have been brought near in the blood of Christ. For he is our peace, who has made us both one, and has broken down the dividing wall of hostility…that he might reconcile us both to God in one body through the cross, thereby bringing the hostility to an end.

Ephesians 2.13-16

From now on, therefore, we regard no one from a human point of view; even though we once regarded Christ from a human point of view, we regard him thus no longer. Therefore, if any one is in Christ, he is a new creation; the old has passed away, behold, the new has come. All this is from God, who through Christ reconciled us to himself and gave us the ministry of reconciliation; that is, in Christ God was reconciling the world to himself, not counting their trespasses against them, and entrusting to us the message of reconciliation.

2 Corinthians 5.16-19

Teachings of Sun Myung Moon

Jesus presented a new direction for this conflict-ridden world. Oppressor nations and oppressed nations, such as Rome and Israel, viewed each other as enemies, thus creating high walls between them. Jesus' philosophy was that these walls needed to be demolished. He thought, "You Romans want to conquer me by force, but I will conquer you in the opposite way—with love." That is why he even sought blessings for his enemies as he was hanging on the cross.

His plea for the Roman soldiers, "Father, forgive them, for they know not what they do," expressed this amazing philosophy. By making this plea, Jesus became the model and the archetype for all nations of the world to overcome the conventional way of seeing each other as enemies. He became the example of someone who has no regard for national borders. (March 9, 2000)

Jesus' saying, "Love your enemies" is God's strategy to make evil surrender voluntarily. This is an amazing truth, full of grace. These simple-sounding words mark the boundary between victory and defeat in the battle between God and Satan. (316:81, February 10, 2000)

Jesus taught, "Love your enemy," but we are extending it even to loving enemy nations. After loving our personal enemies, we should leap over national boundaries to love and even save nations that attacked our nation in the past. This is the ideology of the Messiah. (93:160, May 22, 1977)

The Bible says, "Blessed are the peacemakers, they shall be called sons of God." Because I knew God's Will to establish the Kingdom of Heaven, I work to reconcile humankind. If either side throws a spear, I should be the first one to be hit. In order to bring reconciliation and save the two that are fighting, you shouldn't mind if you get bloodied first. (211:13, December 30, 1990)

Restitution

PEACE FLOURISHES WHERE THERE IS JUSTICE. While justice may not appear the same to people on opposing sides of a conflict, steps should be taken to right wrongs, pay back debts, and restore trust when it has been violated. Usually it is not enough to repent for having wronged one's neighbor; repentance should be accompanied by restitution.

Restitution is most effective when it is given freely by the guilty party to his victims, not exacted from him as the price of defeat. Compare the war reparations that Germany was forced to pay to France and England at the end of World War I by the Treaty of Versailles with the restitution Germany paid after World War II to

Jews and other victims of the Nazis. In the former instance where the reparations were forced upon Germany, it created massive German resentment and fueled calls for revenge that led directly to the rise of Hitler. In the second instance where Germany felt sincere repentance for its Nazi crimes, the restitution has served to foster good will between Germany and its former enemies.

Thus it is a principle of peacemaking that we should offer restitution willingly to those we have harmed, accompanied by genuine repentance for the wrongs we committed. There are also the sins we commit without knowing, or debts we inherit from the past, or wrongs for which we are collectively responsible; we can also make restitution for these. Father Moon has developed this concept into a teaching called 'restoration through indemnity.' He teaches that 'indemnity' is not a fixed amount, like an insurance claim, but rather a matter of giving whatever is required to assuage the other party's aggrieved heart. It can be small if the other party has a mind to forgive; or it can be great if the relationship has been strained by years of treachery and mistrust.

The phrase, "an eye for and eye and a tooth for a tooth" can be taken in its original biblical meaning as a legal formula for making restitution; and it is so understood in Judaism. People know innately that they should pay back the full amount of their debt. The phrase is often cited wrongly, however, as a justification for revenge. That is a completely different matter. Revenge by the aggrieved party is a kind of rough justice, but it is not conducive to peace. It only furthers the cycle of violence. The scriptures teach that it is better to forgive.

O dweller in the body, make reparation for whatever you have done!

Garuda Purana 2.35 (Hinduism)

The Day of Atonement atones for sins against God, not for sins against man, unless the injured person has been appeased.

Mishnah, Yoma 8.9 (Judaism)

Sama'a asked Imam 'Ali about whether there is a way to repentance for one who commits premeditated murder. He said, "No, not unless he pays the blood money to the murdered man's relatives, frees a slave, fasts for two consecutive months, asks God's forgiveness and offers voluntary prayers. If he does this then I would hope that his repentance would be accepted." Sama'a asked, "And if he has no money?" He said, "Then he should ask the Muslims for money so that he can pay the restitution to the blood-relatives."

Hadith (Shiite Islam)

If any harm follows, then you shall give life for life, eye for eye, tooth for tooth, hand for hand, foot for foot, burn for burn, wound for wound, stripe for stripe.[12]

Exodus 21.23-25

And We prescribed for them: "A life for a life, an eye for an eye, a nose for a nose, an ear for an ear, a tooth for a tooth, and for wounds retaliation." But whoever foregoes it in the way of charity, it shall be expiation for him.

Qur'an 5.45

In reconciling a great injury,
Some injury is sure to remain.
How can this be good?
Therefore the sage holds the left-hand tally
    [obligation] of a contract;
He does not blame others.
The person of virtue attends to the obligation;
The person without virtue attends to the
    exactions.

Tao Te Ching 79 (Taoism)

Whoever, by a good deed, covers the evil done, such a one illumines this world like the moon freed from clouds.

Dhammapada 173 (Buddhism)

If one has, indeed, done deeds of wickedness, but afterwards alters his way and repents, resolved not to do anything wicked, but to practice reverently all that is good, he is sure in the long run to obtain good fortune—this is called changing calamity into blessing.

Treatise on Response and Retribution 5 (Taoism)

Again, though I say to the wicked, "You shall surely die," yet if he turns from his sin and does what is lawful and right, if the wicked restores the pledge, gives back what he has taken by robbery, and walks in the statutes of life, committing no iniquity; he shall surely live, he shall not die. None of the sins that he has committed shall be remembered against him; he has done what is lawful and right, he shall surely live.

Ezekiel 33.14-16

There was a rich man named Zacchaeus; he was a chief tax collector, and rich... And Zacchaeus stood and said to the Lord, "Behold, Lord, the half of my goods I give to the poor, and if I have defrauded anyone of anything, I restore it fourfold." And Jesus said to him, "Today salvation has come to this house."

Luke 19.2, 8-9

Teachings of Sun Myung Moon

It is God's formula that the providence of restoration requires paying restitution, or indemnity. Indemnity cleanses the past and opens up a new opportunity for development. Why do we need to make restitution? It is necessary to clear up past sins and at the same time to separate from Satan, who accuses people day and night based on past sins.

This formula applies not only to ourselves as individuals, but also includes the wholes of which we are a part. Each of us is not only an individual living in the present moment but also a descendant who has inherited the fruits of history. Each of us stands before divine Providence not just as an individual but as a representative of the entire world. (99:164-65, September 18, 1978)

Restoration of indemnity means to restore what was lost to its original status. If you lose your health and become ill, it means to recover from illness to health. That is why the Old Testament teaches restitution according to the formula, "an eye for an eye and a tooth for a tooth." (252:128, November 14, 1993)

In a courtroom, a criminal who shows true repentance and willingness to make restitution for his crime wins mercy from the judge and prosecutor... No matter what kind of wrong he committed, if he makes a conscientious effort to extricate himself and give restitution he can win forgiveness. But if that person is hardheaded and claims he did no wrong, he has no way to be forgiven. (104:279, June 1, 1979)

Among friends, if you say something or do something accidentally that offends your friend, it can damage the friendship. This also applies to a married couple, where even a small slight may become a reason for divorce. If you find yourself in that situation, clarify what the error was, discuss the problem with your spouse, and whoever was in the wrong should make amends. You cannot just ignore the matter and bury it, or it will remain a sticking point between you forever.

Likewise, after a war between nations there should be some judgment as to which nation was in the wrong. The nation in the wrong should willingly compensate the nations that it aggressed against in order to resolve their lingering hostility. (89:116-17, November 1, 1976)

In the Bible, a king forgave the debts of his servant, but then the servant went and demanded payment from those who owed him money. On seeing this, the king demanded that the servant repay him the debt that he had forgiven, with interest. This is cause and effect. The Bible also teaches that giving even a glass of water to the least person will not be for nothing. These are lessons about how we should repay our debts. (85:35, March 2, 1976)

If you owe something to someone, you have to become his servant; otherwise, you will perish. You can establish your position only when others cannot accuse it, however much they may want to do so. (*Way of God's Will* 3.4)

The vengeful legalism that says "a life for a life, an eye for an eye, a tooth for a tooth, a hand for a hand, a foot for a foot, a burn for a burn, a wound for a wound, and a stripe for a stripe" cannot stem from the character of the Creator God. God is the God of love and forgiveness.[13] (124:202, February 15, 1983)

God supports me because I loved even those who opposed me. I did not seek revenge against my enemies. I did not requite an eye for an eye and a tooth for a tooth, a life for a life. I took all the blows and tried to digest them with love. (168:204, September 20, 1987)

The Futility of War

WAR DOES NOT BRING PEACE, BUT ONLY BEGETS MORE WAR. World War I was billed the war to end all wars, yet less than thirty years later Europe was engulfed by World War II. Understanding this truth, the greatest saints taught the doctrine of non-violence. They willingly suffered blows without retaliating in kind. This is the highest teaching for establishing a peaceful world. The ideal of God's Kingdom cannot be built in any other way.

Nevertheless, in the vicissitudes of history, when people encounter cruel aggressors, God permits them to defend themselves. Between the two parties in such a conflict, God aligns Himself on the side of the defender and against the aggressor. Hence through history, the aggressor who initiated war thinking he will win ended the loser. This again shows the futility of war as an instrument of national policy.

1. The Path of Non-Violence

Then they came up and laid hands upon Jesus and seized him. And behold, one of those who were with Jesus stretched out his hand, and drew his sword, and struck the slave of the high priest, and cut off his ear. Then Jesus said to him, "Put your sword back into its place; for all who take the sword will perish by the sword."

Matthew 26.51-52

Do not resist one who is evil. But if any one strikes you on the right cheek, turn to him the other also; and if any one would sue you and take your coat, let him have your cloak as well; and if any one forces you to go one mile, go with him two miles.

Matthew 5.39-41

Victory breeds hatred, for the defeated live in pain. Happily live the peaceful, giving up victory and defeat.

Dhammapada 201 (*Buddhism*)

For behold, they had rather sacrifice their lives than even to take the life of their enemy; and they have buried their weapons of war deep in the earth, because of their love towards their brethren.

    Book of Mormon, Alma 26.32 *(Latter-day Saints)*

How do you pray that sinners die? Rather pray that they should repent, and thus there will be no more wickedness.

    Talmud, Berakot 10a *(Judaism)*

The force of arms cannot do what peace does. If you can gain your desired end with sugar, why use poison?

    Somadeva, Nitivaktyamrita 344 *(Jainism)*

Abruptly King Hsiang asked me, "Through what can the Empire be settled?"
"Through unity," I said.
"Who can unite it?"
"One who is not fond of killing can unite it," I said.

    Mencius I.A.6 *(Confucianism)*

Through violence you may murder a murderer, but you can't murder murder. Through violence you may murder a liar, but you can't establish truth. Through violence you may murder a hater, but you can't murder hate. Darkness cannot put out darkness. Only light can do that.

    Martin Luther King, Jr., *Where Do We Go from Here: Chaos or Community?* *(Christianity)*

Some children were playing beside a river. They made castles of sand, and each child defended his castle and said, "This one is mine." They kept their castles separate and would not allow any mistakes about which was whose. When the castles were all finished, one child kicked over someone else's castle and completely destroyed it. The owner of the castle flew into a rage, pulled the other child's hair, struck him with his fist and bawled out, "He has spoiled my castle! Come along all of you and help me to punish him as he deserves." The others all came to his help. They beat the child with a stick and then stamped on him as he lay on the ground… Then they went on playing in their sand castles, each saying, "This is mine; no one else may have it. Keep away! Don't touch my castle!" But evening came, it was getting dark and they all thought they ought to be going home. No one now cared what became of his castle. One child stamped on his, another pushed his over with both hands. Then they turned away and went back, each to his home.[14]

    Yogacara Bhumi Sutra 4 *(Buddhism)*

Anger and hatred cannot bring harmony. The noble task of arms control and disarmament cannot be accomplished by confrontation and condemnation.

    Tenzin Gyatso, The Fourteenth Dalai Lama *(Buddhism)*

They shall beat their swords into ploughshares,
and their spears into pruning hooks;
Nation shall not lift up sword against nation,
neither shall they learn war any more.

    Isaiah 2.4

Teachings of Sun Myung Moon

God certainly does not want to unite the world with weapons, and neither do I. Weapons are instruments of power, but God is thinking how to unite the world with love. (103:184, February 25, 1979)

Among the historical great figures of the past…those who met opposition by defending themselves as being in the right cannot join the ranks of the saints. The people of Jesus' day condemned him to death. Although it grieved him, he endured his path in silence. Even so, he re-emerged as an historical victor. Why? Because he did not fight with those who condemned him. (80:34, October 4, 1975)

Why don't religious believers fight back when they are attacked? Why don't we teach people to fight with those in power? If humanity could find hope through violence, our way would be foolish. The original way of life in the Garden of Eden has nothing to do with violence or revenge. God's ideal of creation is not like that.

We cannot realize the ideal world by the sword. The original Garden of Eden is not a place of conflict. Its inhabitants are humble and full of love; they do not compete to exalt themselves. Yet up to the present, God had no choice but to coach with believers who were accustomed to fighting and struggling for power.

Now that we know how it is to live in the original world, we can clearly see that people who are self-centered and arrogant have nothing to do with God. True religion does not teach people to fight, exploit others and dominate others. We should live with "love" as our motto...

We cannot fight, because we have to live as we would in the original world. There we would be humble, and being humble, we would live for the sake of others and love others. We who pursue the heavenly nation should live by these three values. Then, although we may face all manner of opposition, we will gradually expand the realm where people practice this way of life. (98:33, April 8, 1978)

2. The Immorality and Futility of Aggressive War

In wars to gain land, the dead fill the plains; in wars to gain cities, the dead fill the cities. This is known as showing the land the way to devour human flesh. Death is too light a punishment for such men who wage war. Hence those skilled in war should suffer the most severe punishments.

Mencius IV.A.14 *(Confucianism)*

Fine weapons are instruments of evil.
They are hated by men.
Therefore those who possess Tao turn away from them...

Weapons are instruments of evil, not the instruments of a good ruler.
When he uses them unavoidably, he regards calm restraint as the best principle.
Even when he is victorious, he does not regard it as praiseworthy,
For to praise victory is to delight in the slaughter of men.
He who delights in the slaughter of men will not succeed in the empire...
For the slaughter of the multitude, let us weep with sorrow and grief.
For a victory, let us observe the occasion with funeral ceremonies.

Tao Te Ching 31 *(Taoism)*

If possible, so far as it depends upon you, live peaceably with all. Beloved, never avenge yourselves, but leave it to the wrath of God; for it is written, "Vengeance is mine, I will repay, says the Lord." No, "if your enemy is hungry, feed him; if he is thirsty, give him drink; for by so doing you will heap burning coals upon his head." Do not be overcome by evil, but overcome evil with good.

Romans 12.18-21

Refrain from anger, and forsake wrath!
Fret not yourself; it tends only to evil.
For the wicked shall be cut off;
but those who wait for the LORD shall possess the land.

Yet a little while, and the wicked will be no more;
though you look well at his place, he will not be there.
But the meek shall possess the land,
and delight themselves in abundant prosperity.

The wicked plots against the righteous,
and gnashes his teeth at him;
but the LORD laughs at the wicked,
for he sees that his day is coming.
The wicked draw the sword and bend their bows,
to bring down the poor and needy,
to slay those who walk uprightly;
their sword shall enter their own heart,
and their bows shall be broken.

Psalm 37.8-15

Imam 'Ali found a letter in the scabbard of the Messenger of God's sword on which was written, "The worst of people in the sight of God is the killer of one who does not fight him, and he who beats one who does not beat him...for he has committed the crime of *kufr* (disbelief) in what God has sent down upon Muhammad.

Hadith *(Shiite Islam)*

Do not fight the people until they initiate fighting, for then by the grace of God you will have justification, and leaving them alone until they initiate fighting is yet another justification. Then if you defeat them, do not kill the one who is fleeing, and do not finish off the wounded or expose nakedness or mutilate the dead.

Amir-ul-Mu'mineen 'Ali, *Da'aim al-Islam (Islam)*

Teachings of Sun Myung Moon

Think of how much money the world is wasting on war. Humanity needs to realize that we are committing fearful sins in the presence of history and our descendants. Let us take one example. How much money has the United States spent on the war in Iraq during the past three years? It is approaching $200 billion...

In this age, war is a most primitive and destructive means of resolving conflict, and will never lead to lasting peace. Now is the time, as the prophet Isaiah taught, to beat our swords into ploughshares and spears into pruning hooks. Humankind should end the perverse cycle of war, which only sacrifices our children's lives and squanders astronomical sums of money. The time has come for the countries of the world to pool their resources[15] and advance toward the world of peace desired by God, the Master of this great universe. (September 21, 2005)

God will not forgive a nation if it utilizes only for its own benefit the scientific technology it was given as a means to bring peace for all humankind. God granted science and technology to humanity for the happiness of all. It should not be monopolized only for the white race. Nor should it be used to create weapons, disregarding the realization of world peace. (190:178, June 19, 1986)

In a war, how do you distinguish between the good side and the evil side? The evil side strikes while the other side is at ease. That is why when two students are fighting, the teacher asks them, "Who started it?" and takes the side of the student who was attacked. The student who attacks first always loses, because the teacher takes the side of the one who was attacked. Likewise, throughout history, God takes the side of the defender.

Why is it wrong to attack first? Originally, goodness should have taken the lead in the universe, but instead evil took the initiative. At the Human Fall, Adam and Eve were struck when they were doing nothing wrong. God was attacked when He was doing nothing wrong. Thus, a characteristic of evil is aggression. When an attacker inflicts harm, he should pay for the violation. The person whom he attacked may request compensation for damages.

God knows this principle. Do you think He initiates wars? No, God's strategy is to be the defender, not the aggressor. Likewise, people on God's side receive blows; they do not attack.

They are not aggressors because God is not an aggressor, and they strive to follow God's example. God's people take the beating and endure, never giving up. Then they have the right to seek for compensation.

Satan is the king of aggressors. He is the father of all aggressors and evil people. God is the king of defenseless people who take beatings. The more a person is beaten, the more he can shorten the length of the indemnity period according to the principle of restoration through indemnity.

We can recognize this pattern throughout history: Satan attacks first and loses, while God is attacked but gains in the end. Look at the example of World War I: Germany started that war, but they lost. The Germans thought they could win the war; otherwise they would not have started it. Satan always thinks he can win; that is why his forces start wars. But no one can win by violating heavenly law. Look at World War II: Germany and Japan started the war, but they lost. God, the Supreme Judge, admonished the aggressors, "You are in the wrong." (91:243-44, February 23, 1977)

The Rise and Fall of Nations

GOD IS ACTIVE IN HISTORY AND GUIDES THE COURSE OF NATIONS: this was a first principle of God's revelation to Israel. The prophets of Israel recognized that God dispensed blessings and punishments to the nation according to whether they were faithful to God's will. Confucianism speaks of the Mandate of Heaven as a higher power that supports righteous rulers and causes the downfall of corrupt dynasties. The Qur'an likewise discerns the judgments of a righteous God in the history of the rise and fall of mighty nations, which left evidence of their former greatness in the ruins dotting the Arabian and Egyptian deserts. The downfall of the once mighty Roman Empire is further evidence that godlessness and moral decay lead to ruin. Father Moon continues this scriptural tradition in his warnings to America and the Western nations that they are liable to suffer the same fate. Nevertheless, he holds out hope that their impending downfall can be reversed, if only their people will turn to God.

I went down to the potter's house, and there he was working at his wheel. And the vessel he was making of clay was spoiled in the potter's hand, and he reworked it into another vessel, as it seemed good to the potter to do. Then the word of the LORD came to me, "O house of Israel, can I not do with you as this potter has done? says the LORD. Behold, like the clay in the potter's hand, so are you in my hand, O people of Israel. If at any time I declare concerning a nation or a kingdom, that I will pluck up and break down and destroy it, and if that nation, concerning which I have spoken, turns from this evil, I will repent of the evil that I intended to do it. And if at any time I declare concerning a nation or a kingdom that I will build and plant it, and if it does evil in my sight, not listening to my voice, then I will repent of the good, which I had intended to do to it. Now, therefore, say to the men of Judah and the inhabitants of Jerusalem: 'Thus says the LORD, Behold, I am shaping evil against you and devising a plan against you. Return, every one from his evil way, and amend your ways and your doings.'"

Jeremiah 18.3-11

Dishonesty about spoil has not appeared among a people without God casting terror into their hearts; fornication does not become widespread among a people without death being prevalent among them; people do not give short measure and weight without having their provision cut off; people do not judge unjustly without bloodshed becoming widespread among them; and people are not treacherous about a covenant without the enemy being given authority over them.

Hadith of Malik (Islam)

The Three Dynasties won the empire through benevolence and lost it through cruelty. This is true of the rise and fall, survival and collapse, of states as well. An emperor cannot keep the empire within the Four Seas unless he is benevolent; a feudal lord cannot preserve the altars to the gods of earth and grain unless he is benevolent; a minister or a counselor cannot preserve his ancestral temple unless he is benevolent; a gentleman or a commoner cannot preserve his four limbs unless he is benevolent.

Mencius IV.A.3 (Confucianism)

The Thirty-three great gods grow angry in their
    palaces
When the king disregards the evil done in his
    kingdom.
Then the land is afflicted with fierce and
    terrible crime,
And it perishes and falls into the power of the
    enemy.
Then property, families, and hoarded wealth all
    vanish,
And with varied deeds of deceit men ruin one
    another.

Whatever his reasons, if a king does not do his duty
He ruins his kingdom, as a great elephant a bed
    of lotuses.
Harsh winds blow, and rain falls out of season,
Planets and stars are unpropitious, as are the
    moon and sun,
Corn, flowers, and fruit and seed do not ripen
    properly,
And there is famine, when the king is
    negligent...

Then all the kings of the gods say to one another,
"This king is unrighteous; he has taken the side
    of unrighteousness!"
Such a king will not for long anger the gods;
From the wrath of the gods his kingdom will perish.

Golden Light Sutra 12 (Buddhism)

Have they not traveled in the land to see the nature of the consequence for those who disbelieved before them? They were mightier than those in power [today] and in the traces which they left behind them in the earth.[16] Yet God seized them for their sins, and they had no protector from God.

That was because their messengers kept bringing them clear proofs of God's sovereignty but they disbelieved; so God seized them. Lo! He is Strong, Severe in punishment.

Qur'an 40.21-22

Have you not seen how your Lord dealt with
    the people of Ad,
With the city of Iram, with lofty pillars,
The like of which were not produced in all the
    land?
And with the people of Thamud, who cut out
    huge rocks in the valley?
And with Pharaoh, Lord of Stakes?
All these transgressed beyond bounds in the lands
And heaped therein mischief on mischief.
Therefore did your Lord pour on them a
    scourge of diverse chastisements:
For your Lord is as a guardian on a watchtower.

Qur'an 89.6-14

The Duke of Chou said, "I make an announcement to all Yin and managers of affairs. Oh, august Heaven, the Lord-on-High, has changed his principal son [the ruler] and this great state Yin's mandate. Now that the king has received the mandate, unbounded is the grace, but also unbounded is the solicitude. Oh, how can he be but careful!

"Heaven has removed and made an end to the great state Yin's mandate. There were many former wise kings of Yin in Heaven, and the later kings and people here managed their mandate. But in the end [under the last king] wise and good men lived in misery so that, leading their wives and carrying their children, wailing and calling to Heaven, they went to where no one could come and seize them. Oh, Heaven had pity on the people of the four quarters, and looking with affection and giving its mandate, it employed the zealous ones [the leaders of the Chou]. May the [new] king now urgently pay careful attention to his virtue."

Book of History 5.12.2, Announcement of the Duke of Chou *(Confucianism)*

Great is the appointment of Heaven!
There were the descendants of Shang—
The descendants of the sovereigns of Shang
Were in number more than hundreds of thousands;
But when God gave the command,
They became subject to Chou.

They became subject to Chou;
The appointment of Heaven is not constant...
Before Yin lost the multitudes,
Its kings were the assessors of God.
Look to Yin as a beacon;
The great appointment is not easily preserved.

The appointment is not easily preserved;
Do not cause your own extinction.
Display and make bright your righteousness and name,
And look at the fate of Yin in the light of Heaven.[17]

Book of Songs, Ode 235 *(Confucianism)*

If there is an evil-minded king who practices wrong teachings, interferes with the disciples of the Buddha, slanders them, speaks ill of them, hurts them with sticks and swords, robs them of their daily necessities, and bothers those who support them, the king of Brahma Heaven and Indra will immediately send foreign armies to attack him. Also his evil acts will cause several sufferings: civil wars, famines, unseasonable storms, fighting, and lawsuits in his country. They will also cause him to lose his country before long.

Great Collection of Sutras *(Buddhism)*

In the land of softly lapping waves, the
Heart of the kami has turned hard.
Leaving the capital in ruins, which
I see, and feel how sad.

Man'yoshu I *(Shinto)*

The Lord protected Khorasan from Babur's invasion
And on Hindustan let loose terror.
The Lord Himself punishes not:
So He sent down the Mughal Babur, dealing death as Yama.
As the people wailed in their agony of suffering,
Didst Thou feel no compassion for them?
Thou who art Creator of all—
Should a powerful foe molest one equally powerful,
Little would the mind be grieved;
But when a ferocious tiger falls upon a herd of kine,
Then must the Master be called to account.
These dogs that despoiled the jewels [India's resources] and wasted them,
Now shameful will be their end.
Thou alone dost join and unjoin—
Such is the greatness of Thy might.
Whoever arrogates to himself greatness,
Tasting all pleasures to satiety,
In the eyes of the Lord is only a worm picking grain.

Adi Granth, Asa, M.1, p. 360 *(Sikhism)*

Thus says the LORD,
"For three transgressions of Israel,
and for four, I will not revoke the punishment;
because they sell the righteous for silver,
and the needy for a pair of shoes—
they trample the head of the poor into the dust of the earth,
and turn aside the way of the afflicted;
a man and his father go in to the same maiden,
so that my holy name is profaned;[18]
they lay themselves down beside every altar
upon garments taken in pledge;
and in the house of their God they drink
the wine of those who have been fined.

"Yet I destroyed the Amorite before them,
whose height was like the height of the cedars,
and who was as strong as the oaks;
I destroyed his fruit above,
and his roots beneath.

Also I brought you up out of the land of Egypt,
and led you forty years in the wilderness,
to possess the land of the Amorite.
And I raised up some of your sons for prophets,
and some of your young men for Nazirites.[19]
Is this not indeed so, O people of Israel?" says
    the LORD.

"But you made the Nazirites drink wine,
and commanded the prophets,
saying, 'You shall not prophesy.'

"Behold, I will press you down in your place,
as a cart full of sheaves presses down.
Flight shall perish from the swift,
and the strong shall not retain his strength,
nor shall the mighty save his life;
he who handles the bow shall not stand,
and he who is swift of foot shall not save himself,
nor shall he who rides the horse save his life;
and he who is stout of heart among the mighty
shall flee away naked in that day," says the LORD.

Amos 2.6-16

A few more moons, a few more winters, and not one of the descendants of the mighty hosts that once moved over this broad land or lived in happy homes, protected by the Great Spirit, will remain to mourn over the graves of a people once more powerful and hopeful than yours. But why should I mourn at the untimely fate of my people? Tribe follows tribe, and nation follows nation, like the waves of the sea. It is the order of nature, and regret is useless. Your time of decay may be distant, but it will surely come, for even the White Man whose God walked and talked with him as friend to friend, cannot be exempt from the common destiny. We may be brothers after all. We will see.

Chief Seattle[20] *(Native American Religion)*

On us shall descend some awful curse,
Like the curse that descended in far-off times.
Thus speaks the Creator of men,
But the men refuse to listen.
On us shall descend some awful curse,
Like the curse that descended in far-off times:
We have but one word to say:
Idle about! Sink in sloth!
Men of such kind will gain nothing from the
    Father,
For they know not His voice.
He is the one who loves man.

Dinka Prayer *(African Traditional Religion)*

Teachings of Sun Myung Moon

History does not progress by itself. God, working in the background, intervenes and leads its development over certain times and periods. (4:191, April 20, 1958)

Many civilizations rose and fell throughout history. Once-great cultures are now ruined and forgotten. Sometimes they declined due to external causes like weather, disease, or natural disasters, but mostly the cause was internal corruption, especially decline of religion or morality. (343:155, January 27, 2001)

A nation rises or falls depending on whether its drive for unification and preeminence is self-centered or for the peace of the entire world. (369:178, February 14, 2002)

Is there any country in the world today that says it will sacrifice itself for the sake of saving the world? America prospered when it worked together with other countries for their sake. But it has been declining ever since it began to say, "We have to hang on to just our country." (69:87, October 20, 1973)

Throughout human history there have been many great civilizations. Why did they perish? As their civilizations developed, rather than living for the sake of the world they became self-centered and devoured the rest of the world to satisfy their appetites. Do you think America is an exception?

America is the leading nation of the world; especially its culture moves the whole world. Yet America has become arrogant and discriminatory. If she continues this way, she will inevitably decline. Despite her worldwide fame, internally her children are being struck. Children are a nation's most precious possession and hope for the future, but they are being struck. (97:322, April 1, 1978)

At one time, Great Britain unified the world under the banner of Christianity. Yet the British thought the world existed for the sake of Britain. They did not understand that Great Britain was given its empire for the sake of the world. For that reason, Britain lost its empire. Today the United States is the worldwide power, but Americans should never think that the world exists to serve America's interests. America should serve the interests of the world. Otherwise America, like Britain before her, will decline. (247:111, April 25, 1993)

History goes around in cycles. People that were oppressed come to rule their former oppressors. Once they develop a superior ideology or way of life, they come to rule those who once ruled them… It is inevitable—a principle in this fallen world. (95:105-06, November 1, 1977)

As the historian Spengler pointed out, civilizations, like the four seasons of the year, repeatedly rise and fall. Today the age of the Atlantic civilization is passing, and the age of the Pacific civilization is emerging. (115:171, November 10, 1981)

When there is a low pressure, there is also a high pressure. Does the high pressure tell the low pressure to go away? High pressure will automatically feed the low pressure without asking permission. This is the natural law. Likewise, when water is high here and low there, it cannot remain still but seeks the same level.

Does this occur in today's fallen world? One nation is very rich and another is very poor; does this disparity create a flow like water and air to bring equity? Who, then, is going against the law of nature? Advanced nations are. If they go against God's law, they will eventually be destroyed. One way that God is punishing and warning these advanced nations is through AIDS and drug problems. He permits unlawful things like homosexuality and free sex, things that Satan loves.

Therefore, to prevent America's destruction, it should permit leveling to occur. Therefore, I will encourage the American people to fast occasionally and with the excess food help the starving people in the poor nations. Like the natural world, the human world has to come into balance and harmony under the natural law. (260:192, May 8, 1994)

We learn from history that even the powerful Roman Empire collapsed from within because of its sexual immorality. Ancient Pompeii was wiped out by a volcano, and when it was excavated centuries later it was clear why the city was destroyed—its people were focused on sex, drinking and sensual pleasure.

Whenever a society becomes morally corrupt it faces a quick downfall. This is not my opinion, but the lesson of history. It doesn't matter whether you are black, white or yellow, this rule applies to everyone. Moral corruption usually infects nations that have much money, power and knowledge.

America today is in the same position as the Roman Empire. You think it is the greatest country with its money, power and knowledge, but its moral standard is worse than in underdeveloped countries. Internally it has an incurable disease. Once a nation catches this disease, it inevitably declines. It cannot maintain its culture. Young people lose any discipline in their lives, families break down, churches lose their authority, and the social order breaks down. Is it or is it not the reality in America? Looking at the proud American people, I wonder how long their time of prosperity can last. (103:97-98, February 11, 1979)

Today's climate of free sex leads young people to kiss and sleep around with whomever they please. It is the path of destruction. America, Great Britain, France, Italy and the whole world have no defense. And since this is the trend in the advanced nations, the developing nations want to follow.

To protect the world from further harm, God would want to hasten the decline of these advanced nations. God would do this to protect the rest of the world, especially the relatively unstained third world nations, from this moral contagion. Don't you think God is in this situation? Thoughtful people will be searching for a new direction. (117:201-02, March 7, 1982)

God blessed America, but what did God have in mind? It is God's Will to save all humankind. God wanted America to become good and strong to be a foundation for world peace and the liberation of humanity according to God's Will. God wanted America to use its strength to chase out Satan and liberate this hell on earth.

When you go about in your fine clothes, do you remember that countless people left their blood-stained tracks on history, people who went through valleys of misery and wept bitter tears? Do you realize as you put on your clothes that you owe a debt to these people? Likewise, the house you live in and the environment you enjoy represent your indebtedness to all humanity.

You Americans were not given these blessings because you are a superior people. Would that you viewed these things according to God's Will, God's heart and God's ideal for the world, and think of the heavenly responsibility that comes with them. But since you do not, but just enjoy your blessings without realizing why you have them, they will surely be taken away. God will give them to another people who live more for the sake of the world.

Consider the countless American Indians whom your forbearers killed and drove off their land. Did they just disappear, or are they dwelling in the spirit world and nursing a desire for revenge? In addition to American Indians, white people invaded and looted many small and weak nations. Still, America has done better than Europe in serving God's Will. America surpassed even England in sending missionaries to the world. America came to Europe's aid in the World Wars and afterwards...

Having colonies would not be a bad thing if America served the people of her colonies more than she serves her own people. God would encourage America to spend more of its treasure to help the impoverished people of Asia. No one would oppose Americans if they served them, if they even sold their houses to raise the funds to help them. In that case, the people of the colonies would welcome Americans. They would say, "Thank you, America," and follow the American people as they would follow God. By such service to the needy of the world, the world could have become one. That was God's desire. Yet it didn't happen that way. Americans took the wealth for themselves and trampled upon the people. America rebelled against God's work in history. From that point on, things started to go wrong. (202:332-33, May 27, 1990)

Spiritually attuned people throughout the world are saying that the world is undergoing a sudden and dramatic change. Where is the world headed? Ordinary people think the dangers will only grow worse and the world will deteriorate into hopelessness. Only a very small number of people believe that the world will reach a place of hope. People have been predicting the decline of Western civilization; many think the world is headed into an age of darkness. As you know, Christianity has been the backbone of Western civilization, giving strength to its families, communities and nations. But now it is crumbling.

Young people in particular are pessimistic about the future. Still, we believe that almighty God will not leave His people without hope. He has prepared a path of hope that leads to a new world. (103:39-40, February 2, 1979)

I am not the only one talking about the decline of America. Intelligent people, politicians, scholars and religious leaders confirm what I am saying. What can cure America's ills? Can the American military do it? Can the knowledge of science that sends men to the moon cure this illness? Neither economists nor politicians nor scientists can do it. It is impossible to heal it without God. That is why God sent me to America. (93:122, May 21, 1977)

World Peace

IN THE NEW MILLENNIUM, with the world facing the global problems of environmental degradation, competition for scarce natural resources, terrorism and the proliferation of nuclear weapons, the time calls out for the establishment of world peace. What was formerly only a distant dream of prophets and visionaries must now become a reality—for humanity's very survival. As this circumstance has only arisen in modern times, we have supplemented texts from scriptures with statements by significant religious figures and visionaries of the last century.

God has inspired Father Moon to present numerous practical proposals for world peace. This modern-day prophet has quite a different view from the secular apostles of peace in our time, who held that through scientific and technological advances humanity would create a world of shared affluence in which the old prejudices of religion and culture would yield to secular democratic values and the freedom of the marketplace. Instead, Father Moon teaches that peace must be founded in God, and religion and spirituality must play a central role to move the peoples of the world towards one global family. As optimistic hope in progress towards a secular utopia has faded, and people are reconsidering the importance of religion and the internal foundations necessary for world peace, his words have taken on new cogency.

Father Moon has some rather specific proposals for building world peace, including reforming the United Nations to add a spiritual dimension, the demise of national borders, the joining of cultures through intercultural marriages, and an international highway linking all the world's cities. They are each an expression of his fundamental belief that world peace is built through the practice of true love.

1. God is the Basis of World Peace

Come, let us go up to the mountain of the LORD,
to the house of the God of Jacob;
That he may teach us his ways
and that we may walk in his paths.
For out of Zion shall go forth the law,
and the word of the LORD from Jerusalem.
He shall judge between the nations,
and shall decide for many peoples;
They shall beat their swords into ploughshares,
and their spears into pruning hooks;
Nation shall not lift up sword against nation,
neither shall they learn war any more.

Isaiah 2.2-4

I see no hope for permanent world peace. We have tried and failed miserably. Unless the world has a spiritual rebirth, civilization is doomed.

Dag Hammarskjöld

The wolf shall dwell with the lamb,
and the leopard shall lie down with the kid...[21]
They shall not hurt or destroy
in all my holy mountain;
for the earth shall be full of the knowledge of
the LORD
as the waters cover the sea.

Isaiah 11.6-9

Our hope is that the world's religious leaders and the rulers thereof will unitedly arise for the reformation of this age and the rehabilitation of its fortunes. Let them, after meditating on its needs, take counsel together and, through anxious and full deliberation, administer to a diseased and sorely afflicted world the remedy it requires.

Gleanings from the Writings of Bahá'u'lláh 110
(Baha'i Faith)

Teachings of Sun Myung Moon

When the Cold War ended, the world had a brief moment of celebration, as if peace had arrived. But humanity soon realized that the end of the Cold War did not automatically mean the advent of an era of world peace. Fierce battles continued. Even at this moment, brutal massacres are occuring in numerous places. This is the reality.

Conflicts arise for many reasons. But one of the primary factors contributing to their emergence is the deep-rooted disharmony that exists among the world's religions. Therefore, we should recognize how critically important it is that the religions dialogue with one another, learn to accept one another, and harmonize with each other.

In the modern age, in most nations, religious ideals have come to hold a place wholly separate from the centers of secular political power, and most people have come to accept this reality as the way things ought to be. I believe, however, that it is time for the international organizations whose purpose is to support the ideal of world peace to reconsider their relationship with the great religious traditions of the world...

At their root, human problems are not entirely social or political, and so social and political approaches will always be of limited effectiveness. Although secular authorities rule most human societies, religion lies at the heart of most national and cultural identities. In fact, religious faith and devotion have far greater importance in most peoples' hearts than do political loyalties.

The time has come for religion to renew itself and manifest true leadership in the world. People of faith should feel responsibility for the plight, suffering and injustices experienced by the world's peoples. Religious people have not been good examples in the practice of love and living for the sake of others and for this reason should engage in deep self-reflection. It is time for religious people to repent for their preoccupation with individual salvation and narrow denominational interests. Such practices have prevented religious bodies from giving their utmost to the cause of world salvation. Our age more than any other demands that we go beyond our faiths, and the interests of particular religions, and put our love and ideals into practice for the sake of the world.

In particular, God calls upon us leaders, especially religious leaders, in hope that we will stand against the injustices and evils of the world, and bestow His true love upon the world. Hence, all people of faith must become one in heart in order to give full expression, both in words and actions, to God's passionate desire for humanity's restoration and peace. (332:245-47, August 18, 2000)

From the viewpoint of God's historical dispensation, humankind is one large family that is to live by attending God as the True Parent, transcending national boundaries and racial and religious differences. Humankind is destined to cooperate as a global family and become as a single community. We live in an age when we can no longer feel that we have nothing to do with the problems of our neighbors or the suffering of other countries. We cannot ignore the reality of humanity ravaged by war, crime, drug abuse, pollution, the destruction of ecosystems, moral corruption and the scourge of AIDS.

Today, with the eyes of history upon us, we must answer to God. How can humankind, whose mandate is the realization of complete harmony and unity, overcome the unfortunate reality and greet the coming millennium with hope? How can we realize a peaceful world, in which everyone lives for and trusts others irrespective of personal and national interests? What is the new value system by which we shall attain this ideal? Rather than riding the chariot of science and technology pulled by the horses of secular humanism, we must humbly seek the answers within our original mind. If we cannot find the solution on earth, we must find it through listening to the voice of Heaven. (279:211-12, August 20, 1996)

2. The United Nations and Global Governance

We the peoples of the United Nations, determined
to save succeeding generations from the scourge of war, which twice in our lifetime has brought untold sorrow to mankind, and
to reaffirm faith in fundamental human rights, in the dignity and worth of the human person, in the equal rights of men and women and of nations large and small, and
to establish conditions under which justice and respect for the obligations arising from treaties and other sources of international law can be maintained, and
to promote social progress and better standards of life in larger freedom,

And for these ends—
to practice tolerance and live together in peace with one another as good neighbors, and
to unite our strength to maintain international peace and security, and
to ensure, by the acceptance of principles and the institution of methods, that armed force shall not be used, save in the common interest, and
to employ international machinery for the promotion of the economic and social advancement of all peoples
—have resolved to combine our efforts to accomplish these aims.

Accordingly, our respective governments, through representatives assembled in the city of San Francisco, who have exhibited their full powers found to be in good and due form, have agreed to the present charter of the United Nations and do hereby establish an international organization to be known as the United Nations.

            Preamble of the United Nations Charter

Now is the gracious Lord's ordinance
    promulgated,
No one shall cause another pain or injury;
All mankind shall live in peace together,
Under a shield of administrative benevolence.

            Adi Granth, Sri Raga, M.5, p. 74 *(Sikhism)*

In times past, one would be justified in feeling that the public authorities of the different political communities might be in a position to provide for the universal common good, either through normal diplomatic channels or through top-level meetings, by making use of juridical instruments such as conventions and treaties...

Today the universal common good presents us with problems which are worldwide in their dimensions; problems, therefore, which cannot be solved except by a public authority with power, organization and means co-extensive with these problems, and with a world-wide sphere of activity. Consequently the moral order itself demands the establishment of some such general form of public authority...set up by common accord and not imposed by force...

By the principle of subsidiarity...the public authority of the world community is not intended to limit the sphere of action of the public authority of the individual political community, much less to take its place. On the contrary, its purpose is to create, on a world basis, an environment in which the public authorities of each political community, its citizens and intermediate associations, can carry out their tasks, fulfill their duties and exercise their rights with greater security...

It is Our earnest wish that the United Nations Organization—in its structure and in its means—may become ever more equal to the magnitude and nobility of its tasks... This is all the more to be hoped for since all human beings...are becoming more consciously aware that they are living members of a universal family of humankind.

            Pope John XXIII, Pacem in Terris *(Christianity)*

Teachings of Sun Myung Moon

The biblical account of Cain and Abel reveals the beginnings of human conflict right in Adam's family. It provides the archetype for humankind's unending history of struggle, war and conflict. We are conflicted on many levels, beginning with the war between body and mind within each individual and extending to wars between nations and even to the global conflict between materialism and theism.

    Who can untie this ancient knot of Cain and Abel? It has been tightened for thousands of years and grows ever more tangled. Do you think the United Nations can do it? The U.N. at its founding proclaimed a movement for world peace, and for sixty years it has dedicated itself to this task; yet world peace still remains far distant. Peace among nations can never come when those entrusted with the task have not resolved the Cain-Abel relationship between their own mind and body. Therefore, the time has come to launch the Abel-type sovereignty for the peaceful, ideal world that will set its course according to God's Will.[22] (September 21, 2005)

World peace can be fully accomplished only when the wisdom and efforts of the world's religious leaders, who represent the internal concerns of the mind and conscience, work cooperatively and respectfully with national leaders who have much practical wisdom and worldly experience about the external reality or "body." In this light, it is time for us to give serious consideration even to the prospect of restructuring the United Nations. For example, perhaps it is possible to envision the United Nations as a bicameral institution.

The existing United Nations structure, composed of national representatives, may be regarded as a congress where the interests of each member nation are represented. However, I submit that serious consideration should be given to forming a religious assembly, or council of religious representatives within the structure of the United Nations. This assembly or council would consist of respected spiritual leaders in fields such as religion, culture and education. Of course, the members of this interreligious assembly will need to have demonstrated an ability to transcend the limited interests of individual nations and to speak for the concerns of the entire world and humanity at large.

The two chambers, working together in mutual respect and cooperation, will be able to make great advances in ushering in a world of peace. The wisdom and vision of great religious leaders will substantially supplement the political insight, experience and skill of the world's political leaders. (August 18, 2000)

3. Building a Culture of Peace that Unites the Peoples of the Earth as One

O mankind! We created you from a single pair of a male and a female and made you into nations and tribes, that you might know each other [not that you might despise each other].

Qur'an 49.13

For the development of a peaceful, friendly human family of nations with a rich variety of faith and political and economic systems, each of us has the responsibility to strive towards such harmony. There is no alternative.

Tenzin Gyatso, The Fourteenth Dalai Lama
(Buddhism)

Since wars begin in the minds of men, it is in the minds of men that the defenses of peace must be constructed;

That ignorance of each other's ways and lives has been a common cause, throughout the history of mankind, of that suspicion and mistrust between the peoples of the world through which their differences have all too often broken into war…

That a peace based exclusively upon the political and economic arrangements of governments would not be a peace which could secure the unanimous, lasting and sincere support of the peoples of the world, and that the peace must therefore be founded, if it is not to fail, upon the intellectual and moral solidarity of mankind.

Preamble to the Constitution of UNESCO

Peace is not something that you and I or a few great souls can create at once, by command. Even a million Christs or Krishnas could not do it. Try as he would, Lord Krishna could not prevent the great war between the Pandavas and Kauravas which is described in the Mahabharata. All humanity has to become Christ-like to bring peace on earth. When each one of us shapes his life according to the wisdom and example of a Christ, a Krishna, a Buddha, we can have peace here; not before…

So long as God's children differentiate, "We are Indians and you are Americans; we are Germans, you are English," so long will they be bound by delusion and the world divided. Much war and suffering and destruction will be prevented if we cease to emphasize differences and learn to love all without distinction or prejudice. Be more proud that you are made in the image of God than that you are of a certain nationality; for "American" and "Indian" and all the other nationalities are just outer coats, which in time will be discarded. But you are a child of God throughout eternity. Isn't it better to teach that ideal to your children? It is the only way to peace: Establish the true ideals of peace in the schools, and live peace in your own life.

Paramahansa Yogananda (Hinduism)

Let there be a small country with a few inhabitants. Though there be labor-saving contrivances, the people would not use them. Let the people mind death and not migrate far. Though there be boats and carriages, there would be no occasion to ride in them. Though there be armor and weapons, there would be no occasion to display them.

Let people revert to the practice of knotting ropes [instead of writing], and be contented with their food, pleased with their clothing, satisfied with their houses, and happy with their customs. Though there be a neighboring country in sight, and the people hear each other's cocks crowing and dogs barking, they would grow old and die without having anything to do with each other.[23]

Tao Te Ching 80 (Taoism)

When the eighty-four thousand kings of the eighty-four thousand cities of India are contented with their own territories and with their own kingly state and their own hoards of treasure, they will not attack one another or raise mutual strife. They will gain their thrones by the due accumulation of the merit of their former deeds; they will be satisfied with their own royal state, and will not destroy one another nor show their mettle by laying waste whole provinces. When all the eighty-four thousand kings of the eighty-four thousand capital cities of India think of their mutual welfare and feel mutual affection and joy...contented in their own domains... India will be prosperous, well-fed, pleasant, and populous.

Golden Light Sutra (Buddhism)

World peace is inconceivable unless the world's leaders come to recognize the interdependence in itself demands the abandonment of the politics of blocs, the sacrifice of all forms of economic, military or political imperialism, and the transformation of mutual distrust into collaboration. This is precisely the act proper to solidarity among individuals and nations.

Pope John Paul II, Sollicitudo Rei Socialis (Christianity)

In that day there will be a highway from Egypt to Assyria, and the Assyrian will come into Egypt, and the Egyptian into Assyria, and the Egyptians will worship with the Assyrians. In that day Israel will be the third with Egypt and Assyria, a blessing in the midst of the earth, whom the LORD of hosts has blessed, saying, "Blessed be Egypt my people, and Assyria the work of my hands, and Israel my heritage."

Isaiah 19.23-25

Teachings of Sun Myung Moon

In the 21st century, people will not be able to exercise dominion on the earth, or even exist there, while disregarding the ultimate principle of the Creator. The future of humanity will require closer relationships among people. In the future people will have no choice but to live very closely together, transcending their region, nationality and race. In other words, the vision of global family will become a reality. People will not only have to understand others who have different religions, cultures, traditions and lifestyles; they will have to accept them and interrelate with them. No individual or group will be able to selfishly maintain its own sanctuary. (219:9, August 24, 1991)

Today, on every level, boundaries cause division and conflict. If we can eliminate all the boundaries in this world, a world of peace would inevitably come about. We must recognize who owns those boundaries. Clearly, it is not God. It was the devil, Satan, who first created boundaries. Wherever a boundary exists, there is always the devil and his cohorts.

This is a result of the Human Fall, when the first human ancestors switched their lineage, and good and evil began to diverge from each other. When we look at the division between the East and the West, we see that different cultural spheres have led to antagonism at their boundaries and that the devil is encamped there. It was Satan, not God, who created boundaries, by digging all sorts of traps and enmeshing people in racial discrimination and evil cultures, histories, and traditions.

God's desire is for a world of goodness and unity—a world of oneness in which all humanity lives as one great family. Boundaries have no place in such a world. In a world without boundaries, there can be no enemies. The concept of "enemy" entails the existence of boundaries.

When we love our enemies and make oneness with them, the boundaries between us will collapse. That is why God's strategy and tactic has always been "Love your enemy." There can be no greater strategy for peace than this. Throughout history, this incredible fact has escaped humanity's understanding, and it has yet to be grasped even in modern times. (October 3, 2003)

The spirit world does not acknowledge national borders; it transcends them. We were given the responsibility to lead this dispensation on earth; hence, we all have to go beyond national boundaries... We bring Asian people to live in the West and Western people to the Orient. By virtue of this work, Oriental spirits are able to live in the West and Western spirits can move to the East. Muslim spirits can visit the Christian world and Christian spirits can visit the Islamic world. Before [this work was done] they were separated from one another, but now they can come and go anywhere they want.

Movements to make external unity have come into being, like the European Union that permits Europeans to travel freely throughout Europe. No power can succeed in blocking this trend. The world can have a future only when people are free to move about and live anywhere on earth. Yet still America restricts immigration and the communists prevent their people from leaving. That is not our way in the Unification Church. We don't say only Whites can join or that Blacks are not welcome. I come from Asia, but I don't say that anyone who is not an Asian should leave. We are colorblind and recognize no borders. (101:331-32, November 12, 1978)

Once true love is perfected in the human world, what possible political, economic, cultural, or environmental problems could persist? In the world of true love, every problem can be solved. It is a world of freedom, peace and happiness, replete with joy. It is the world of God's ideal. It is a world where joy and happiness are magnified infinitely and eternally, and where everyone has the right to equal position, equal participation, and equal inheritance. (294:65, June 11, 1998)

In the future there will be no fighting. Up to now we have had useless fights centering on the self. People fought to rob each other. In the unified world under God's sovereignty where people live for the sake of others, there will be no need for wars. Brothers do not need to rob each other; rather a needy person will have to run away as others try to give him more than he can use...

Laws will all disappear. When all people govern themselves by love, they will observe the law automatically. If all people practice love for the sake of others, there will be no crime. Higher and lower become one, and front and back, left and right, all become one. (224:173, November 24, 1991)

When minorities can receive equal benefit from the system, and when advanced nations supply the less advanced nations with technology in the spirit of helping them become economically independent, instead of exploiting them and their resources, then humankind will eliminate war and starvation. Then the conditions will be right for God's love to blossom and open the hearts of all humankind to establish the world of peace.

We should go beyond racism and even overcome the whole world with this thought. In the future, the five races should become one. Because God's love is one, and because God beholds beauty in oneness, God's interest and affection cannot differ among the lands He created. Interracial marriage is a symbol of God's love and will. Even the secular world recognizes that love does not respect national borders. How much more is it true in God's dominion? God's love is fundamentally different from the tragic bonds of love formed in a world historically dominated by power and authority. God's love does not just seek individual security and self-interest. It is the way of dedication for the benefit of God, the world and all humankind. (*Blessing and Ideal Family* 6.4.3)

For the sake of peace and human welfare, I propose that we build a passage for transit across the Bering Strait, where Satan has historically divided East and West, and North and South, and where the North American and Russian land masses are separated. This passage, which I call the "World Peace King Bridge and Tunnel," will link an International Highway System that will allow people to travel on land from Africa's Cape of Good Hope to Santiago, Chile, and from London to New York, across the Bering Strait, connecting the world as a single community.

God is warning that He will no longer tolerate separation and division. Carrying out this project will bind the world together as one village. It will tear down the manmade walls of race, culture, religion and country, and establish the world of peace that has been God's cherished desire.

The United States and Russia can become as one. The European Union, China, India, Japan, Brazil and all nations, and also the world's religions, can combine their energies to succeed in this project. The success of this project will be decisive in establishing the kingdom of the peaceful, ideal world, where people will no longer make war with each other.[24] (September 12, 2005)

Notes

Preface

1. 172:143, January 10, 1988. Father Moon's teachings are conventionally cited by the volume and page number according to where the passage appears in the Korean collection, *Moon Sun Myung Seonsaeng Malseum Seonjip [Selections from Rev. Sun Myung Moon's Words]*, 400+ volumes (Seoul: HSA-UWC, 1984-), as well as by date.

2. Although all translations were based on published Korean texts, much text-critical work remains to establish a reliable and accurate original text. The existing Korean text was made from transcriptions of speeches where the audio was sometimes indistinct. Then it was edited to cope with the problems of rendering oral language into written form. Furthermore, Father Moon often uses the blackboard to illustrate his sermons, and at those moments the words recorded on tape convey little of what he was writing on the board. Then, on occasions when he would lecture in Japanese or English, the Korean text was created by translating the words back into Korean. A precise and accurate foundational text of Father Moon's words, along with photographic records of his diagrams, is greatly to be desired.

Invocation

1. **Matthew 6.9-13:** The Lord's Prayer is not only a supplication; it includes a pledge to live up to the ideals of a Christian, specifically, to forgive. God only forgives us if we forgive others.

2. **Qur'an 1:** The Fatihah is the chief Muslim prayer; it is recited with prostrations five times a day.

3. **The Kaddish**: This is a most important Jewish prayer, recited at every sacred occasion and especially in remembrance of the dead. It is a source for The Lord's Prayer (above).

4. **Rig Veda 3.62.10:** The opening syllable OM is the cosmic sound of Being. When it is chanted it resonates in oneness with the divine Source. English translations cannot do justice to mantras which, when recited in the original language, call forth spiritual energies through the very sounds themselves. See Chapter 16, note 21.

5. **Khuddaka Patha:** The Three Refuges from this suffering world are the Buddha (the Teacher), the Dhamma (the Teaching), and the Sangha (the Taught). These three are also called the Three Jewels. Invocations and mantras beginning with the words 'Homage,' 'Obeisance' or 'All hail' are common in the Eastern religions.

6. **The Family Pledge:** The eight clauses of this prayer lay out a blueprint for becoming a true family of God's love. Reciting this pledge and then striving each day to fulfill it guides the family on a trajectory of spiritual growth. The word 'Cheon Il Guk,' Korean for 'The Nation of Cosmic Peace and Unity,' refers to the Kingdom of God on earth. The first clause speaks to creating a good environment and home; the second clause describes the vertical axis of service to the greater good; the third clause describes in the term "Four Great Realms of Heart" the intimate relations within the family of child's love, sibling love, marital love and parental love; the fourth clause signifies the family's role in building the global human family; and the fifth clause describes the family's influence as extending even to the spirit world. The sixth, seventh and eighth clauses describe the family as a fount of blessings, a creator of godly culture, and an incarnation of the divine.

Chapter 1

1. Geddes Mac Gregor, "God Beyond Doubt," in *The Living Pulpit* 6/1, p. 23.

2. Blaise Pascal, *Pensees* (1670), in John Gross, *The Oxford Book of Aphorisms* (New York: Oxford University Press, 1983), p. 11.

3. **Psalm 19.1-4**: There are slight differences in versification among the various Christian and Jewish Bibles. This anthology has adopted the versification of English-language Protestant Christian Bibles. In Catholic and Jewish Bibles, this passage is Psalm 19.2-5.

4. **Tao Te Ching 21**: The word essence (*ching*) also means spirit, intelligence, life force. 'Through this' in the last line can mean through intuition.

5. **John 1.18**: For Christianity, the book of nature and a person's own spiritual experience give only partial knowledge of Ultimate Reality. Only through the special revelation of God in Jesus Christ is the fullness of God's nature made manifest in the world.

6. **Deuteronomy 6.4**: The Shema is the Jewish confession of faith. The word "Lord" when written in small caps signifies the holy name of God, written in the Hebrew Bible (Old Testament) as "YHWH" but never spoken by observant Jews. Some Protestants call the name "Jehovah."

7. **Lankavatara Sutra**: This sutra teaches that the existing world is created by mind. The world of appearances, which is characterized by suffering, is rooted in the seeds of defilements that are accumulated in the subconscious mind. True Reality is what is realized when all defilements have been removed and the mind operates with Perfect Wisdom. The Suchness of existence is thus identical with the essence of Mind.

8. **January 16, 1971**: The Korean word for God, *Hananim*, includes *hana*, "the One" and *nim*, "exalted."

9. **November 25, 1982**: 'all phenomena,' lit. 'all dharmas' (諸法); in Chinese and Korean Buddhism, 'dharma' means a phenomenon or a constituent of existence, while 'Suchness' (眞如) is the true reality behind all dharmas (see the Lankavatara Sutra, above). Father Moon employs these technical Buddhist terms.

10. **Brihadaranyaka Upanishad 4.5.15**: This is the classic statement of the via negativa, as the seeker gradually strips away all relative phenomena to eventually attain the Absolute. Father Moon calls it the search for the 'zero point'; see Chapter 7, *Emptiness-Nirvana*.

11. **Katha Upanishad 2.3.7-8**: The specific meanings of these successive levels of reality are in some dispute. The mind is the seat of emotion, perceptions, and consciousness. The intellect (*budhi*) is a finer faculty of enlightened discrimination. The Great Atman is understood by some as the God within, by others as the collective consciousness of all minds. The Unmanifest is either the undifferentiated consciousness of reality or Brahman in his attribute as the seed of the causal realm. The Person (*Purusha*) is Brahman or the Supreme Being.

12. **Garland Sutra 37**: The teachings in this sutra are: (1) all beings equally possess Buddha nature when viewed from the standpoint of the Ultimate Truth; (2) all phenomena come into being due to their interdependence with other phenomena; (3) each experience contains all experience due to their interdependent relationship.

13. **January 29, 2001**: "Excruciating pain" or "deep pain and sadness" are inadequate ways to render into English the meaning of the Korean word *han*.

14. **Book of Songs, Ode 254**: This is a classic statement of the teaching that rulers must pay regard to the Mandate of Heaven, without which their reign becomes untenable.

15. **Zephaniah 1.14-18**: 'A day of wrath...' These are the opening words of the description of the Last Judgment in a famous musical sequence of the Roman Catholic requiem Mass: *Dies iræ, dies illa/ Solvet sæclum in favilla/ Teste David cum Sibylla*.

16. **Qur'an 2.115**: This has been interpreted by Muslims to mean that God appears to people of every culture and religion, east and west. God, who is one Unity (*tawhid*), embraces every one of his creatures.

17. **Sutra of Hui Neng 6**: 'Essence of Mind' as Hui Neng uses the term denotes the original mind which is intrinsically the same as Buddha nature.

But 'Essence of Mind' is *Tathata*, which can also be translated Essence of all things. These indeed are not different, as the essence of things can be grasped only by mind.

18. **1 Kings 19.11-12**: God is manifest in his Word, communicated to the heart. He is not in the storm or the earthquake or other manifestations of power in nature. This is a radical critique of nature-religion as it was practiced by the Canaanites.

19. **Exodus 3.13-15**: This passage, from Moses' encounter with God at the burning bush, gives the traditional etymology of the name of God, the Tetragrammaton YHWH, as The Eternal, 'I Am.' Here is also the foundation of Christian and Jewish theological discussion of God's unchangeability and eternity.

20. **Diamond Sutra 29**: 'Tathagata' is a title given to the Buddha, often in his cosmic manifestation as the being who has passed beyond this world into the realm of Nirvana that is neither here nor there. It means "Comes thus far," i.e., the one who has arrived at the goal of enlightenment.

21. **Bhagavad-Gita 8.17-21**: This is a description of the Day of Brahman, the ever-repeating cycle of cosmic time, measured in myriads of years, between the creation of one universe and its dissolution. In some cosmologies the Day of Brahman is divided into the four *yugas*, of which the Kali Yuga is the final period before the next cosmic dissolution.

22. **Diamond Sutra 32:** This is the fundamental stance of Buddhism towards worldly phenomena. It lies at the heart of Buddhism's ethic of nonattachment and it is comforting counsel to those who are suffering from pain, loss, or bereavement.

23. **Udana 80**: The Buddha only describes this condition negatively; he refuses to speculate on the nature of Being itself.

24. **Tao Te Ching 79**: By 'favoritism' is meant the perquisites the world gives to the rich and powerful.

25. **Mahaparinirvana Sutra 259**: Buddhist compassion is close to the Western concept of *agape* love. It is not desire seeking fulfillment, but rather the unconditional offering of love, like that of parents to their children.

26. **Adi Granth, Japuji 16**: The underlying source of the laws of creation, the 'Bull of Dharma,' is the divine mind, specifically divine compassion. The world's pain and suffering is a heavy burden.

27. **Hosea 11.9-11**: The prophet Hosea uttered these words of divine pathos while prophesying against the corruption of Ephraim, the northern kingdom of Israel. He recalls God's motherly love for Israel as a child, when God brought Israel forth from the land of Egypt and raised her as an infant. Admah and Zeboiim were towns destroyed alongside Sodom and Gomorrah.

28. Rudolph Bultmann, *Primitive Christianity in Its Contemporary Setting* (London: Thames and Hudson, 1956), p. 18.

29. **Genesis 1**: The six 'days' or stages of creation have been compared to the epochs of geologic time, since "with the Lord a thousand years is as a day" (2 Peter 3.8). Thus we have the big bang (first day), the ordering of the cosmos (second day), the solidification of the earth (third day), the clearing of its atmosphere so that the stars can be seen (fourth day), the beginnings of life in the oceans (fifth day), the emergence of land animals, and finally, man (sixth day). Yet even though the general account of the stages of creation may be shown to correspond with the account of creation put forward by modern science, the Bible was revealed to people who held to an ancient cosmology in which the earth was at the center and a solid dome, the firmament, formed the sky above and held back its waters.

30. **Qur'an 32.4-7**: The Qur'an, like the Bible, affirms that God made all things good. These verses describe God finishing the creation in six days and then ascending the throne to rest. God then directs affairs from heaven, until the coming Day of Judgment, when all will be dissolved and return to him.

31. **Tao Te Ching 51**: The passage continues that humans should act likewise in exercising dominion, whether over nature or over other people. 'Power' (*te*) means the force of virtue which arises from unity with cosmic law.

32. **Genesis Rabbah 9.2:** Some physicists conjecture that the reason why this universe is so perfectly fit for human beings is that it is one of a myriad of universes. While the atheists among them thinks that this would avoid the notion of an Intelligent Designer, scripture allows that even the divine

Designer may have worked by repeated experimentation until He got it right. This passage also points up the effort involved in creation.

33. **Maru Sohale:** The formless God, who exists without attributes beyond time and space, assumes attributes as He creates, "assumes might," according to the Sikh scriptures. In creating the human being as his dwelling, God dwells in the mind beyond the "nine abodes" of sensation, in the Tenth, the superconscious mind.

34. **Rig Veda 10.129**: In this account of the formation of cosmos out of chaos (represented by the Waters), 'that One,' *tad ekam*, is void of reality prior to the creation. The appearance of mind precedes creation; its motive is 'Love,' the desire of the One to find fulfillment with a partner. The first act of creation, dividing being from non-being, resembles the first day of creation in Genesis 1, when God divided the light from the darkness. The 'bearers of seed' and 'mighty forces' are the female and male principles respectively. Yet ultimately the miracle of creation remains a mystery: even the Vedic gods are ignorant of their origin, since they emerged after Being differentiated itself.

35. **Rig Veda 10.90.6-10,13-16**: The theme of this well-known hymn is sacrifice as the method of creation. The world comes into being through the sacrifice and dismemberment of the primordial *Purusha* (Supreme Being). According to one commentator, God allowed his absoluteness to be sacrificed so that He could be manifested in the world of space and time. The fruits of sacrifice were the four Vedas, which represent God's Word, and after them the physical world and humankind.

36. Naomi Tutu, *The Words of Desmond Tutu*, quoted in *The Living Pulpit* 6/1 (January-March 1997): 7.

37. **Lotus Sutra 3:** The image of existence as burning goes back to the Buddha himself, to his Fire Sermon (see Chapter 6, *Suffering*). The Buddha is our parent by virtue of his limitless compassion.

38. **Oracle of the Kami of Atsuta:** Shinto's sense of community and respect for nature is based on the bonds that tie people together with the kami and things of nature in one universal family. Atsuta is a shrine near Nagoya.

39. **August 30, 1959:** Although God exists in the fallen world, without love there is no true existence. Now God finds meaning to His existence for the first time.

Chapter 2

1. **John 1.1-5:** In Greek philosophy, the Word is the *logos* or plan by which God created the universe. The Bible asserts that Christ is himself the Word, the model and plan for creation.

2. **Proverbs 8.22-31:** "Little child" is sometimes translated "master workman," but the former better fits the context.

3. **January 27, 2004:** Certainly the thought crossed God's mind after the Human Fall dashed His hopes.

4. **Ambrose of Milan:** Flight from the World 3.15.

5. **October 29, 1972:** Parental love "downward" to children nurtures their hearts and induces a sense of obligation, which matures into filial piety, "children loving their parents." This passage describes several types of relationships and associated "aspects" of morality, alluding to Father Moon's teaching of the Four Great Realms of Heart and love: children's love, sibling love, conjugal love and parental love.

6. **Leviticus 19.18:** Quoted by Jesus in Matthew 22.36-40.

7. **Exodus 20.1-17:** There is some variation as to how the commandments should be divided. In the Jewish tradition the verse "I am the LORD your God, who brought you out of the land of Egypt, the house of bondage" is regarded as the first commandment, but Christians regard it as a prologue. Most Protestants and Orthodox Christians reckon "You shall have no other gods before me" as the first commandment and the prohibition of images as the second commandment. For Jews the second commandment includes both "You shall have no other gods" and the prohibition of graven images. Roman Catholics and some Lutherans likewise regard "You shall have no other gods" and the prohibition of graven images as constituting a single commandment, but reckon it the first commandment; they then divide the verse against covetousness into two commandments to make up the ten.

8. **Sanhedrin 56a**: Since the children of Noah are the ancestors of all humankind, the rabbis have traditionally interpreted the laws given by God to Noah after the flood in Genesis 9.3-7, as moral legislation binding upon all nations. By obeying these laws, Gentiles may be accounted righteous before God.

9. **Laws of Manu 10.63**: This list of universally applicable dharma for all castes and stages of life is called *sadharan* or *samanya dharma*. It is the universal foundation upon which are erected specific dharmas for different castes. It is a least common denominator by which Hindu society, for all its variety of castes, roles, and traditions, maintains an ethical consensus.

10. **July 9, 1959**: The 'Three Bonds' in traditional Korean Confucianism are: filial piety (of a son to his father), fidelity (of a wife to her husband), and loyalty (of a subordinate to his superior). The 'Five Moral Disciplines' are the 'five universal ways' in the above passage from the Doctrine of the Mean.

11. **Kularnava Tantra 3**: This "pulsation" is manifest in the breath, inhaling and exhaling.

12. **Bhagavad-Gita 13.19-22, 26**: The cosmos is formed by the polarity of *Purusha*—mind, consciousness, divinity—and *prakriti*—matter, energy, the world of nature. However, in monistic Vedanta, the duality of Purusha and prakriti is not at all benign or supportive of enlightenment, it is rather a fetter to be transcended.

13. **Thomas Aquinas**: Summa Theologica I-II, Q 26, art. 2.

14. **I Ching, Great Commentary 2.5.2-3**: The philosophy of the I Ching describes the constant dynamic interchange of yang and yin as every action engenders its opposite. One should understand the principles of change and use them to advantage. Hence the example: he who wishes to create and expand must first look within and concentrate the self.

15. **I Ching, Great Commentary 1.1.1-5**: The philosophy of Change finds its concrete form in the system of divination of the I Ching, with its 64 hexagrams, each composed of two trigrams. Each of the six lines of the hexagram may be yang or yin, firm or yielding. The lines change into each other according to rule: firm yang becoming yielding yin, firm yin becoming yielding yang. Thus the hexagrams denote a fortune that has potential for change. This passage is a commentary on two paradigmatic hexagrams: the Creative (*ch'ien*) composed of all six yang lines and the Receptive (*k'un*) composed of all six yin lines.

16. **Tao Te Ching 11**: The usefulness of the wheel, the vessel, and the house is through the empty space, or 'non-being,' contained in them. Utility comes through the reciprocal process of coming to be and ceasing to be, making a complete circuit of the Tao.

17. **November 23, 1992**: For giving and receiving as a principle of human relationships, see Chapter 13: *Giving and Receiving*.

18. **February 10, 1992**: This term, *cheon un*, is often translated as "heavenly fortune." See note 20, below.

19. **Lankavatara Sutra 78**: As all things are interdependent, mutually influencing one another through cause and effect, this concatenation must also include the observer. It is an illusion to think that there could exist a separate ego, which can stand outside of it. However, Buddhist insight can allow one to see the transcendent reality of no-birth, which is established in the mind when it rests in the state of Nirvana.

20. **January 31, 1993**: "Heavenly fortune," *cheon-un*, describes the result of the action of a universal power, all-pervading and at work throughout the universe, to prosper the way of all things that are in accord with the laws of Heaven.

21. **Pao-p'u Tzu**: Written by Ko Hung (253-333), the Pao-p'u Tzu is a classic of religious Taoism. It expounds belief in the Taoist Immortals, the doctrine of retribution, and the use of alchemical means to prolong life.

22. **Brihadaranyaka Upanishad 4.4.5-6**: This classic text describes the principle by which karma determines the site of reincarnation.

23. **Udana 1.1**: Dependent Origination (Skt. *paticcasamuppada*) describes the situation of human bondage; hence it could be compared to Paul's statement that 'through the law comes knowledge of sin' (Romans 3.20). Yet for the Buddhist, only by a proper knowledge of this law can bondage be overcome, by reversing the chain of causation: "If this is not, that does not come to be; from the stopping of this, that is stopped." See Chapter 7: *Reversal and Restoration*.

Chapter 3

1. **Genesis 1.26**: The plural has been variously understood as the persons of the Trinity, God speaking to his angels, or the plural of majesty.

2. **Tevigga Sutta**: The Buddha did not himself maintain the existence of Brahma as the supreme God; for no supreme God can be found in Emptiness. Yet the principle at issue is affirmed: the monk who has attained the goal of Nirvana is in the image of Ultimate Reality since his own being is empty. This argument is an example of the Buddha's 'skill in means,' expressing the truth of Buddhism in terms suitable to a Hindu who believes in Brahma.

3. **Galatians 2.20**: With the advent of Christ, divinity entered humanity and humanity became deified. For Christians of the Orthodox faith, the highest goal is divinization, oneness with Christ, as St. Athanasius taught: In Jesus Christ, God became man that man might be drawn back into the divine harmony.

4. **Vacana 820**: Indian temples are traditionally built in the image of the human body, which is the primordial blueprint of the cosmos. In Lingayat Shaivism, which seeks to overcome the formalization of temple worship, the body itself becomes a temple of Shiva in private worship.

5. **Sunnan ibn Majah** by Muhammad bin Zayed, a modern Islamic commentator, is considered one of the most important books on the Prophet's Sayings.

6. **Doctrine and Covenants 93.29-35**: While the human person is essentially spirit or Intelligence, matter and the body also have a positive role. As in the Christian tradition generally, scriptures of the Latter-day Saints teach that Spirit must be enfleshed to produce God's temple, and in order that humans may realize their full purpose.

7. **Ch'ang A-han Ching**: The first words attributed to the Buddha after his birth in the Mahayana tradition.

8. **Pope John Paul II**: Letter to the American Bishops, 1979.

9. **February 23, 1977**: This was Father Moon's criticism of the administration of President Carter, which trumpeted human rights while allowing communism to expand to its greatest extent.

10. **April 26, 1992**: This text does not deal with abortion in cases of rape or extra-marital affairs. It is helpful to distinguish between the potentiality of a human being and its actuality, and Unificationism concurs with the widespread Protestant belief that only when the infant draws its first breath does the spirit self enter the body (viz., Genesis 2.7), and it becomes a complete person composed of spirit and flesh. Hence Father Moon's condemnation of abortion is not based on the view that abortion is the equivalent of murder; rather abortion is a sin because it frustrates God's creation and denies the potential value inherent in that fetus to become a human being in the image of God.

11. **Luke 17.21**: This passage has been interpreted in various ways. The words 'within you' can also be translated 'in the midst of you,' in which case the passage means that the people should regard Jesus and his community which dwells among them as the incipient kingdom. But the more mystical meaning of the passage is that the kingdom is within the minds and hearts of believers.

12. **Romans 2.14-16**: The conscience is that universal attribute of man that allows everyone regardless of their beliefs to recognize the truth—and their own sin.

13. **Mencius II.A.6**: Mencius lists the four Confucian virtues: benevolence (*jen*), dutifulness or concern for the public good (*i*), observance of proper social and religious forms (*li*), and education (*chih*). The seeds of these virtues originate in human nature, which is essentially good.

14. **September 14, 1969**: The word "true" (Korean *ch'am*) is an adjective describing the nature of a thing as true and genuine. In relation to human beings, to be "true" is to embody the truth. We should distinguish it from the Korean word for "truth" in the sense of a propositional truth, *chilli*.

15. **January 16, 1971**: See September 14, 1969, above.

Chapter 4

1. **Man'yoshu I**: 'Smoke' and 'sea gulls' suggest the plentitude and harmony among man and nature.

2. **Jataka**: Mountains, pristine and full of natural beauty, have always been the preferred environment for ascetics, where they may most readily strive to penetrate the Absolute. In Asia, Buddhist monasteries and temples are often associated with nature preserves.

3. **December 10, 2000:** Literally, "10 li." A li is a Korean measure of distance, approximately 429 yards or 393 meters in length.

4. **Rig Veda 6.28**: This special regard for cows as sacred animals has persisted in India from Vedic times till today.

5. **Francis Bacon:** Letters, To Trinity College, Cambridge.

6. **Book of Ritual 7.3.1**: The 'dual forces in nature' are the yang and the yin. The 'Five Elements'—earth, air, water, fire and metal—are the basic constituents of all matter. The Chinese philosophy of changes combines yin-yang and five-element theory, viewing the balance between them and changes among them as active in nature, in shaping history and destiny, in the health of the human body, and in art and culture. Note also the connection to music, with its pentatonic scale.

7. **Aitareya Upanishad 1.1-3.12**: The *Purusha* formed at the beginning of creation is the macrocosmic Person; His parts are then invested in man, the microcosm. Likewise, Hindu temples are built on the pattern of the human body.

8. **Aitareya Upanishad 1.1-3.12**: The fontanel on the top of the skull is the place of the Crown charka and the doorway by which the spirit exits and ascends to heaven; See December 19, 1998 in Chapter 5: *The Passage Beyond.*

9. **October 25, 1959**: In other words, each person is a microcosm not only in space but also in time.

10. **February 27, 1977:** See 1 Corinthians 12.12-26 in Chapter 20: *Unity and Community.*

11. **Qur'an 33.72**: The 'Trust' means the responsibility to choose good and reject evil, to live by God's purposes. Among all created beings, only humans have free will and the responsibility it confers. Yet we have abused it.

12. **Yasna 29.1-9:** In this dialogue in heaven, the soul of the ox complains that he is oppressed by the wicked. He asks for justice from his creator, but the reply comes that there is no one. The soul of the ox and his mate pray again to God, who replies that the ox has been put in the power of man. But He also decrees laws of reciprocal service by which the oxen and mankind can live in harmony. The ox, not satisfied, asks for a righteous protector who will practice these laws. He is told he must make do with Zarathustra, who however lacks the power to actualize the teaching. When, the ox asks, will that teaching prevail, that he may be saved? Zoroastrianism in fact abolished the ritual slaughter of oxen which was practiced among the Vedic Aryans.

13. **Pacittiya 11:** This monastic rule refers to monks living in forest dwellings. It is interpreted to mean that monks should never cut down large trees to clear the land; they may only clear underbrush.

14. **Isaiah 11.6-9:** This image of the Peaceable Kingdom describes the harmony among all creatures in the Garden of Eden, as well as the world of God's kingdom in which this original harmony is restored. Another interpretation of the passage takes the "wolf" and "lamb" as metaphors for people: cruel oppressors (wolves) and humble believers (lambs).

15. **Paracelsus:** A physician "walks over the leaves" of the Book of Nature through years of experience in diagnosis and treatment. Both the good and the bad outcomes are teaching material.

16. **June 30, 2000:** 'right side...left side': literally, 'east...west.'

Chapter 5

1. **Hebrews 8.1-5:** The sacrifice which Jesus the high priest offers for the forgiveness of sins in the heavenly tabernacle is said to be in every way superior to sacrifices at the Jerusalem temple which were offered to atone for sins according to the Law. This teaching is rooted in neo-Platonism, which regards the spiritual realm, the realm of forms, as Reality, while the earthly realm is but its copy, shadow, and reflection. Hebrews quotes Exodus 25.40 as supporting this view: God instructed Moses to construct the tabernacle according to the pattern of the heavenly tabernacle that he saw on Mount Sinai.

2. **1 Corinthians 15.40-41:** Celestial bodies are those spirits who soar in divine love and grace; terrestrial bodies are earth-bound spirits who remain attached to worldly desires, but who may be lifted up through the ministrations of angels and higher beings.

3. **Doctrine and Covenants 76.54-93:** This is a visionary interpretation of the preceding passage which describes three spiritual realms. Latter-day Saints and their families who are members of the priesthood and who make active witness to the gospel may become celestial spirits. Honorable and conscientious Christians may become terrestrial spirits, and non-Christians, providing they do not blaspheme the Holy Spirit or commit gross crimes, may become telestial spirits.

4. **Doctrine and Covenants 88.36-40:** This teaches that people ascend to a 'kingdom' that suits their level of intelligence, virtue, light, mercy, and justice.

5. **February 27, 1977:** For the full passage, see Chapter 4: *Microcosm and Macrocosm*.

6. **Nectarean Shower of Holy Doctrines:** As in popular Japanese Buddhism, the scripture of this new religion contrasts the realm of appearances and sense impressions with the realm of Reality. The body belongs to the realm of appearances, but the spiritual life belongs to the order of Reality.

7. **Bhagavad-Gita 2.19-25:** The Self—the Atman or all-pervasive Spirit—preexists its incarnation in the physical body, and will continue to exist through eternity, clothed in body after body.

8. **On the Republic 6.14:** Excerpted from "Scipio's dream," a short representative statement of Stoic philosophy.

9. **Akan Proverb:** 'Onyame' is the most common Akan name for the Supreme Being. It means, roughly, 'the One who gives fullness.'

10. **I Ching 54:** As a bride-to-be prepares herself for a life-long marriage, human relationships are likely to be successful only if they are grounded in the perspective of eternity.

11. **June 22, 1969:** On 'Heavenly fortune,' see Chapter 2, note 20.

12. **Matthew 18.18:** Jesus gives the authority to bind and loose to his disciples, and hence to the church; compare Matthew 16.19, where that authority is given only to Peter. For Catholics, this passage refers mainly to the discipline and grace dispensed by the church, which, when determined on earth, endures in heaven. But for Protestants, who reject the mediation of a priesthood, the blessings of Christ are freely available to every believer as he avails himself of them through the sacraments, prayer, and good deeds. Hence ultimately it is the individual's own binding or loosing, while on earth, that will bind or liberate in heaven.

13. **May 1, 2004:** Literally, "pay indemnity conditions."

14. **February 2, 1975:** However, in other speeches, *mookshi* (묵시) may refer to the final stage (below) when God is fully present in the mind.

15. **December 19, 1998:** The fontanel is a soft spot on an infant's head that closes up by age 2. This may be an analogous organ on the newly-ascended spirit body. See Aitareya Upanishad 1.1-3.12 in Chapter 4: *Microcosm and Macrocosm*.

16. **Bhagavad-Gita 8.5-13:** This teaches that one's prayer and attitude at the time of death is all-important for the soul's subsequent journey. Regardless of the quality of one's life, just remembering God at the time of death can lead to liberation. Yet since death may come suddenly, and may be accompanied by much pain and distraction, the habit of remembering God should be nurtured throughout life. Some Hindus name their children with divine names in order that, at the time of death, the nat-

ural human desire to think of one's children will cause them to meditate on the divine name and thus win beatitude.

17. **March 29, 1968**: Children's love is not only the receptive love of a small child, but also includes filial piety—devotion to parents even to the point of caring for them in their old age.

18. **Rig Veda 10.154.5**: This is a prayer to Yama, the Indic god who governs the world of the dead, to allow the deceased to enter the higher realms. In the Vedas, Yama presides over the bright realms and is the object of offerings and supplications for the benefit of the departed.

19. **November 17, 1990**: Literally: "with what level of respect you should relate to the person." A complex ranking of levels of respect is inherent in the Korean language, and using them properly is a matter of common courtesy in Korean society. Without a formal introduction, for instance, knowing the person's age relative to one's own, a Korean may make a serious breach of etiquette when speaking.

20. **Hadith of Bukhari**: This is an episode from Muhammad's Night Journey (*Mi'raj*), where he was transported from Mecca to Jerusalem and then taken on a tour of the seven heavens, even to the throne of God.

21. **Garuda Purana 3.49-71**: Regarding the last verse: the Eastern conception of hell in Hinduism, Buddhism, and Jainism is analogous to the Christian concept of Purgatory. There is no eternal damnation; hell is a place to expiate evil karma with the end that the purified soul can again advance to a higher plane of existence.

22. **1 Peter 3:18-19**: This passage is usually interpreted to mean that Jesus preached to the spirits in hell and brought salvation to many, the "harrowing of hell."

23. **Qur'an 11.106-08**: Based on these verses, some Muslim theologians have deduced that the penalties in hell are not eternal, for "as long as the heavens and the earth endure, except as your Lord wills" may have a limit; while the duration of paradise in the next verse is explicitly stated to be without end.

24. **Qur'an 55.14-15**: The Jinn are spiritual beings; some may be lower-grade angels. Some are good and others are evil; see Qur'an 72.1-15 below.

25. **Gandavyuha Sutra**: The great bodhisattvas who are worshipped in popular Buddhism embody and symbolize different aspects of the Buddha. Samantabhadra, which means Universally Good, is the embodiment of the Buddha's vows and practices. Manjusri embodies the Buddha's wisdom. Avalokitesvara (Chinese: *Kuan Yin*) embodies the Buddha's compassion for beings in distress.

26. **Qur'an 53.4-10**: This passage describes Muhammad's vision of the archangel Gabriel on Mount Hira. The last line clarifies that the angel is not speaking for himself, but rather conveys God's revelation to "his [God's] slave."

27. **Tract of the Quiet Way**: In popular Taoism the great officials and emperors of old have ascended to heaven and become blessed spirits. Lord Scripture Glory (*Wen Chang*) is one of the chief Taoist deities.

28. **March 9, 1997**: Father Moon is talking about earthly men—men, because the archangel was a male being. Before marriage, men should relate to women as good archangels and not act the part of the fallen archangel Lucifer. See Chapter 6: *The Human Fall*.

29. **Shabbat 88b-89a**: This is an argument between God and the angels over the status of human beings: are they higher or lower than angels? God prefers human beings, and has Moses act as His spokesman. The passage is a midrash on Psalm 8 (see Chapter 1: *The Lord of Creation*), which proclaims the dominion of humankind (according to the Hebrew text, which is followed by the RSV). The angels quote verse 2 of the psalm to argue that God's glory belongs in the heavens, but after Moses' arguments, they concede that the psalm concludes in verse 10 with God's name found only in the earth. The point seems to be responsibility, which humans alone possess.

30. *Exposition of the Divine Principle,* **Fall 3.2**: The 'commandment' refers to Genesis 2:16-17. See Chapter 6: *The Human Fall.*

31. **Qur'an 2.154**: This refers specifically to the martyrs, those killed in the struggle for God.

32. **Kagura-Uta**: The branches of the *sakaki* tree, called *tamagushi*, are sacred in Shinto rites, and worshippers attach to them their offerings of hemp and paper streamers containing the prayers and fortunes of loved ones. The branches symbolize

the spirit of the kami bestowing blessings to the world. Shinto worship incorporates ritual dances (*kagura*) which seek to bring about harmony in the universe.

33. **Yanomami Shaman's Instruction**: This is a conversation between an experienced shaman and his apprentice. Note how the shaman is trained to become sensitive to faint odors, sounds, and touch which indicate the presence of spirits.

34. **Chief Seattle**: Treaty Oration (1854).

35. **Doctrine and Covenants 128.18**: The baptism for the dead is an important rite of the Latter-day Saints, bringing salvation to those who have passed away in ignorance—'those who have died in the gospel' are Christians ignorant of the new dispensation—and bringing wholeness and complete salvation to the cosmos. Notice the Bible references to Malachi 4.6 and Hebrews 11.39-40.

36. **April 19, 1964**: The opportunity occasioned by the second advent of Christ in our time.

37. **February 5, 1976**: For more on the Cain-Abel paradigm of conflict and reconciliation, see Chapter 6: *Cain and Abel*.

Chapter 6

1. **Myth of Pandora's Box**: The "box" can quite naturally be taken as a symbol for the female sexual organ; thus one can draw a parallel to the forbidden fruit in the Genesis story.

2. **Hutu Tradition**: Jumping inside the woman's mouth is a transparent symbol for sexual intercourse.

3. **Kojiki 4-6**: The deities Izanagi and Izanami represent the union of yang and yin, which is the source of all life, divine and human. However, these deities at first erred in the ritual of conjugal intercourse by which they were to create the land and all things. Their mistake was in allowing the woman to take initiative—a parallel to Eve's haste to eat the fruit in the Genesis story. The 'leech-child' (*piru-go*) was a monstrosity who was allowed to die of exposure. Izanami, too, would eventually die in childbirth (Kojiki 7.22); compare the curses in Genesis 3.3 and 3.16.

   The Japanese philosopher Nishida regards this myth as the Shinto version of Original Sin. According to Nishida, as Izanagi and Izanami were brother and sister, everything in the universe originated from an incestuous marriage. The procession around the heavenly pillar was a ritual designed to overcome the incest taboo, but the error in carrying out this ritual nullified its effect. Hence all humanity is the result of incest. The death of Izanami, the symbolic death of their daughter Amaterasu-omi-kami (Kojiki 15) and the expulsion of their son Susanoo (Kojiki 17.25) were punishments endured by the Shinto gods to atone for this original mistake.

4. **Ekottara Agama 34 and Ch'i-shih Ching**: These are both texts from the Chinese Tripitaka. The Ekkotara Agama is the Chinese translation of portions of the Anguttara Nikaya of the Pali scriptures. In the case of this text, however, the parallel Pali version is found in Digha Nikaya 3.27, the Aggana Suttanta.

5. **Zohar 1.36b**: This is a midrash on the Genesis story of Cain and Abel. It is typical of midrashic exegesis to deduce hidden significance to an unusual detail of the biblical text. In this case, Cain's request to Abel, "Let us go out into the field," are missing from the text of the Hebrew Bible (the Christian Bible inserts them from the Septuagint translation), and Jewish exegetes have long wondered at the reason for their absence. This midrash deduces that the missing words are a divine 'hint' pointing to Cain having an unspoken motive. Samael is a Jewish name for Lucifer.

6. Address, November 7, 1972, *Osservatore Romano* and *N.Y. Times* report

7. **Pearl of Great Price, Moses 4.1-4**: Satan's request to God contained two errors: he wanted to claim all the glory and credit for man's salvation when credit is due only to God, and he would save humanity by compulsion—'not one soul shall be lost,' without regard for man's free agency. Christ, the Beloved Son, correctly offers to God the credit for salvation. God then ordered Christ to cast Satan down to the earth, where he continues to seek to enslave humankind.

8. **Sutta Nipata 1103**: 'Mara' is the Buddhist name for the Devil.
9. **Job 1.6-12**: Satan gains power over human beings by accusing them before God. God, who is just, must listen to these accusations and deliver the guilty sinners into Satan's power. Yet who is without sin? Since Satan had corrupted humanity in the first place, he can capture everyone by this means. Were not for God's mercy, Satan would win every time.

   In the book of Job, however, the Devil is not fundamentally evil and opposed to God, but is rather the one whom God allows to test Job's integrity. In proving Job, Satan is serving a divine purpose.
10. **Yasna 30.3-5**: Zoroastrianism demands a decision, to choose either the good or the evil spirit which rage in conflict both within the self and throughout the cosmos.
11. **January 1, 2001**: Elsewhere, Heung Jin Moon explains that every earthly person has evil spirits living in his or her body. They are the spirits of people who long ago suffered on earth by the hand of one of his or her ancestors. Their goal is to get revenge by plaguing this descendant with negative thinking, pain and disease. Many more of these evil spirits have come down to lodge themselves in people's bodies since the 1980s.
12. **January 13, 2001**: The full passage is found in Chapter 2: *The Ten Commandments*.
13. **Qur'an 12.53**: Not even Muhammad, the best of men, regarded himself blameless.
14. **Bhagavad Gita 18.40**: The three *gunas* or qualities of matter are goodness or purity (*sattva*), energy or passion (*rajas*), and darkness or inertia (*tamas*). Every person contains all three qualities in different proportions, as all light is a mixture of the three primary colors. As forces operating within the world of matter (*prakriti*), the gunas condition human existence and obscure the way to the Self.
15. **Analects 4.6**: The last sentence means that it is the will, not the way, that is wanting.
16. **Psalm 51.5**: Protestants and Catholics have generally regarded the act of procreation as instrumental in transmitting original sin from one generation to the next. But this does not make the act itself sinful. According to Vatican II, *Gaudium et Spes*, conjugal love is a means of grace in Christian marriage.
17. **Scientology 0-8**: 'Engrams' bear the traces of attitudes and behaviors from past lives.
18. **Samyutta Nikaya 56.11**: This is the second of the Four Noble Truths, taken from the Buddha's first sermon called "Setting in Motion the Wheel of Truth." 'Craving for non-existence' refers to those ascetics who struggle mightily for Nirvana out of their desire for spiritual glory.
19. **Vacana 91**: This Shaivite passage opposes the tendency to despise women as responsible for men's downfall. Rather, men are at fault for their self-begotten lusts. Guheswara is a name of Shiva.
20. **Adi Granth, Sorath, M.3**: Sikhism describes the evil within the mind through the doctrine of the Five Robbers.
21. **Mahabharata**: These words were spoken by the evil King Duryodhana when he broke his promise to the five Pandava brothers to allow them to return from their exile in the forest to claim five villages. The 'divine spirit' is really an evil spirit that affirms his evil intentions.
22. **Hadith**: This is an important Sufi tradition. Muhammad is said to have uttered it at the end of his life, after defeating the pagans and marching victoriously into Mecca. The 'lesser jihad' being finished, the Muslims could reorient their struggle inwardly against the lower self.
23. **Fang Tradition**: This selection is taken from a creation story, and describes the rebellion of primal man as springing from a false sense of God's remoteness and man's independence.
24. **Tao Te Ching 38**: This passage hearkens back to the ancient golden age of the Great Tao, or Grand Unity, when people naturally lived in harmony with the Way. As society degenerated and became more artificial, teachings and doctrines arose to try and guide people on the path of goodness, which no longer came naturally. Formalism replaced genuineness. The lowest of these is 'propriety'; rules of decorum such as children observe towards their parents, or subjects towards their ruler.
25. **Psalm 115.3-8**: The Bible has a number of satires on idols as human creations, mere objects unable to do anything—for example Isaiah 44.9-20 and Jeremiah 10.1-10. Passages such as this have

fostered a general disdain for visual representations of the divine in Judaism, Christianity, and Islam. Such satires are perhaps uncomprehending of genuine image-worship, in which the image is understood only as a representation of transcendent Reality and a means to focus the mind on God, who is beyond form. Yet veneration of images may become idolatry when the images are themselves regarded as having magical powers.

26. **Samyutta Nikaya 56.11**: This is the first of the Four Noble Truths, taken from the Buddha's first sermon, called "Setting in Motion the Wheel of Truth." The 'five aggregates,' or *skandhas*, are the elements of the personality to which we cling in our vain craving for existence. They are: body-form, feeling, perception, activities that make karma, and consciousness.

27. **Genesis 6.5-6**: This passage introduces the story of the Deluge. It has given rise to numerous reflections on God's sorrow, illustrated by the next selection.

28. **Pearl of Great Price, Moses 7.28-37**: This is a conversation between God and Enoch—who lived prior to the Flood and who according to tradition was taken up alive into heaven—shortly before God sent the Flood upon the earth.

29. **Ofudesaki 17.64-70**: In Tenrikyo, sin is not intrinsic to human beings; rather it is the dust that collects on intrinsically pure minds and which needs to be swept away.

30. **Dinka Song**: Deng is the ancestor of the Dinka people and the chief deity, identified with Divinity as a whole and manifest in the fertilizing rain. Abuk is the first woman, earth, and the female principle. This song refers to the tradition of the separation of heaven and earth at the origin of humanity.

31. **Upasaka Sila Sutra**: The Enlightened One is the all-pervading cosmic Buddha (*Dharmakaya*), as well as the historical Sakyamuni.

32. **November 12, 1972**: Referring to the Christian martyrs in particular, as well as the persecuted of all faiths.

33. **Jeremiah 8.18-9.1**: The prophet Jeremiah laments heartsick over his people's suffering, ignorance, and unbelief. At the same time, the prophet speaks representing God and expressing the divine pathos.

34. **Israel Baal Shem Tov**: The Baal Shem Tov, a title which means "Master of the Good Name," was the founder of the Hasidic movement.

Chapter 7

1. **Book of Mormon, Alma 12.25**: The 'plan of redemption' refers to the inevitable Last Judgment and eschatological redemption of the righteous. The ultimate justice of God is founded upon his Word, which was declared before the creation of the world.

2. **Way of God's Will**: 'Will,' Korean 뜻, means God's original and unchanging purpose established at the time of creation.

3. **Luke 15.11-32**: The Parable of the Prodigal Son speaks not only of God's grace and forgiveness (represented by the father), but also of the ethic that righteousness be accompanied by forgiveness and compassion for sinners (represented by the father's admonishment to the elder brother).

4. **Lotus Sutra 4**: In the Buddhist Parable of the Prodigal Son, the rich elder represents the Buddha and the son is the ordinary person. The Buddha cannot show his grace directly, so in compassion he resorts to an expedient in order to reach his low-minded son. God has resorted to similar expedients to raise up fallen human beings, who began very distant from Him, to recognize their status first as servants of God, and ultimately as God's own sons and daughters.

5. **Ephesians 1.7-8**: This passage speaks of the blood of Christ, shed on the cross for the forgiveness of sins.

6. **Meditation on Buddha Amitayus**: In Pure Land Buddhism, compassion reaches to the nethermost hell. The grace of Buddha Amitayus, the Buddha of Infinite Life, or Buddha Amitabha (Jap. Amida), the Buddha of Infinite Light (who are one in the same), is sufficient to save even the most reprobate sinner. In the Amida Buddha's original vow, he pledged to save all sentient beings who would repeat his name ten times.

7. **Rig Veda 1.97**: This is a litany for the fire ritual. Agni, deity embodied in fire, symbolically burns away sin and mental pollution through the ritual fire.

8. **Engishiki 8**: This is a traditional litany for purification, recited at Shinto shrines.

9. **Leviticus 16.6-30**: This is the ancient ritual for the Day of Atonement. The high priest (Aaron) purified the altar and holy place with blood from the bull and goat that had been sacrificed, and placed the sins of the congregation upon the head of a remaining goat (the 'scapegoat') that was led into the wilderness. In modern Judaism the Day of Atonement (Yom Kippur) is observed with solemn fasting and the "sacrifice of prayer."

10. **Isaiah 53:4-6:** Christianity regards this prophecy of the suffering servant as applying uniquely to Jesus Christ and his atoning death on the cross. On the other hand, Jewish interpretation holds the servant to be Israel, or the righteous in Israel, whose suffering of exile and persecution is atonement for the sins of the nations—especially polytheism. Inasmuch as the church as the body of Christ also suffers and sacrifices to bring salvation to the world, Christians can also draw a second sense of this passage as enunciating this wider application to all believers.

11. **May 8, 1960:** "Saints" includes in particular Jesus, Buddha, Confucius and Muhammad, whom Koreans call "the Four Great Saints."

12. **Hebrews 9.11-14**: This passage compares the sacrifice of Christ, who shed his blood on the cross for the forgiveness of sins, with the above ritual of the Day of Atonement. It emphasizes that Christ's sacrifice was 'once and for all,' 'securing an eternal redemption,' while the atoning rites of the Old Testament were only temporary and had to be repeated every year. Since Hebrews was written after the Temple had been destroyed (in 70 A.D.) and its rites had ceased, the implication is that Christ's sacrifice is the only effective means of atonement. Other rituals of purification from the Old Testament, such as the rite of the red heifer (Numbers 19.1-10) are also mentioned in the comparison.

13. **Qur'an 24.35:** Islamic mystics since al-Ghazzali have interpreted these verses as expressing God's inner illumination of the human soul. The Niche, Glass, Lamp, Tree and Oil correspond to the five faculties of the soul: 1) the senses, 2) the imagination, 3) the discriminative intellect, 4) reason, the faculty capable of abstract knowledge, and 5) the transcendent prophetic spirit that can apprehend divine truth. The soul is thus a graded succession of lights, "Light upon light," whose source is God.

14. **Mumonkan 23**: This incident, when Hui Neng the Sixth Patriarch was fleeing from the followers of his rival Shen Hsiu, is also recounted in the Sutra of Hui Neng. In Zen, Enlightenment frequently occurs in such a manner: a sudden realization grows from an experience of crisis and extreme desperation. When it comes, one no longer depends on cognition or knowledge or secret lore. The authentic self shines forth.

15. **Dhammapada 93**: The invisible path refers to the fact that the liberated do not leave a trail of karma. This is because whatever he does is done with detachment, without a sense of "I," without any desire for reward.

16. **Luke 4.16-21:** Jesus is reading from the Old Testament, Isaiah 61.1-2. Historically, Isaiah was proclaiming to his impoverished community of Jews the dawn of liberation from oppression, captivity, and indebtedness—of a new time when God will once again favor Israel with abundance. But Jesus read the passage as a proclamation of all-encompassing liberation: release to those captive to sin and enlightenment to the spiritually blind as well as liberty to those suffering external oppression. With liberation comes the fulfillment of all creation, the "acceptable year of the Lord."

17. **Israel Baal Shem Tov:** The Kabbalistic doctrine of the "shattering of the vessels" holds that all in the beginning was God, that in creating God emanated Himself into all things, but that the creation shattered into fragments, imprisoning the divine sparks that are portions of God within "shells" of matter. The work of liberating these sparks to return to the Godhead is called *tikkun olam*, repair of the world.

18. **February 5, 1989**: 'People' means the population of an ethnic group within a nation.

19. **Anguttara Nikaya 5.322**: Nirvana is the Ultimate Good because it is the complete end of all the impulses and passions that produce evil.

20. **Sutta Nipata 1072-76**: This describes the freedom that comes from absence of self.

21. **Chuang Tzu 6**: Nü Yü is a female Taoist sage.
22. **Seng Ts'an**: Seng Ts'an was the Third Patriarch of the line of Chinese Ch'an (Zen) Buddhism. He gives us a quintessential statement of Zen enlightenment.
23. **Mundaka Upanishad 2.2.1**: The Self is the Atman, or divine mind.
24. **Goseigen**: Mahikari is a Japanese new religion known for its healing practices.
25. **Mahaparinirvana Sutra 575-76**: Healing King Ajatasatru shows the Buddha's great benevolence to even those most undeserving of grace. For King Ajatasatru (Pali *Ajatasattu*) was no friend of the Buddha, being a patron of the heretic Devadatta, and having killed his father the pious King Bimbisara and imprisoned his mother Queen Vaidehi. It is said that the king at last repented and learned the Teaching.
26. **Matthew 12.22-24**: Jesus performed many miracles for the people. Yet to the skeptical leaders they proved nothing; the devil can also do miracles.
27. **December 17, 2002**: Father Moon instituted a Burning Ceremony as a rite to symbolically cleanse people of all attachment to wealth and material things. Typically, the worshipper burns a precious article of clothing while regarding it as representing everything he or she owns. In another version of the ceremony, the worshipper writes his or her name on a piece of paper.
28. **Treasury of Elegant Sayings**: Subhashita Ratna Nidhi
29. **Qur'an 33.9-11, 25**: This surah describes the Battle of the Trench (A.H. 5), when a confederacy of opponents, with a force of ten thousand men, besieged the Muslims in Medina for more than two weeks.
30. **Exodus 15.1-11**: These verses are taken from the victory song which Moses and the Israelites sung at the Red Sea, at the great manifestation of God's power on which the biblical nation of Israel was founded.
31. **Lotus Sutra 25:** Kuan Yin (Jpn. *Kannon*) is the Bodhisattva Avalokitesvara, The One who Hears Cries, and represents the divine attribute of grace and help to people in distress. In Chinese Buddhism Kuan Yin is a female—the Goddess of Mercy—and this passage is recited to invoke her aid and offer her worship. Thus is she depicted in the Lotus Sutra, although in the Sanskrit original Avalokitesvara is male.
32. **February 2, 1969**: Literally, '30 li.'
33. **1 Samuel 2.4-9**: This is the Song of Hannah.
34. **Majjhima Nikaya 2.32**: This is a short formula for the doctrine of Dependent Origination (Pali: *paticcasamuppada*. A more complete formulation follows.
35. **Samyutta Nikaya 22.90**: This enumerates all twelve links in the chain of Dependent Origination, first forwards to show the origin of ill, then backwards to show its cessation.
36. **Tao Te Ching 41**: Note the pun on "the way out," which is the Way (*Tao*).
37. **1 Corinthians 15.21-22**: This and the Jewish passages that follow describe salvation as a reversal of the primordial Human Fall, which brought death and sin into the world.
38. **Shabbat 145b-146a**: The Israelites who stood at Mount Sinai are understood to include all Jews whenever and wherever they live.
39. **John 3.1-7**: To be 'born of water and the Spirit' refers to baptism with water, through which one receives the gift of the Holy Spirit.
40. **Itivuttaka 101**: In traditional Hinduism, the term 'twice-born' applied only to those who undertook instruction from a brahmin. Sakyamuni Buddha was not a brahmin in the conventional meaning; his caste was kshatriya. But as the Enlightened One, he declares himself to be a brahmin in the true sense of one who has attained Brahman. Thus he is qualified to initiate his followers into the Buddha doctrine and give them a second birth. The words 'born of my mouth' is an allusion to the Vedic myth of the creation of the castes (Rig Veda 10.90.11-12) in which the brahmins were born out of the mouth of the Supreme Being. Buddha is abolishing the caste system by declaring that all his followers are, as it were, brahmins, born out of the mouth of the Buddha by virtue of receiving his instruction.
41. *Exposition of the Divine Principle,* Resurrection 1.3: While this is not specifically a passage about rebirth, it conveys the notion of a step-wise process of spiritual growth that can comprehend these texts about "rebirth" in other religions. For more of this passage, see the section *Resurrection* (below).

42. **Ezekiel 37.1-14**: This passage is traditionally understood to be a prophecy of the resurrection of the dead. In its literal, historical sense it speaks figuratively of the reconstitution of the nation of Israel after years of exile in Babylon.

43. **Niyamasara 176-77**: In Jainism there is no pre-existent Supreme Being, but rather the state of eternal Godhood (*Paramatman*), which is humanity's goal and highest good.

44. **Luke 9.60**: Jesus uses two different meanings for the word 'dead' in this proverb. The first 'dead' are those that are physically alive but spiritually dead, in contrast to the true follower of Jesus who shares in eternal life.

45. **Yasna 34.3**: The passage asks that these prayers to God cause all creatures, not just the "man of insight," to achieve their destiny in God's Kingdom.

46. **Amos 9.7**: The prophet Amos warns Israel not to be overly proud of its status as the chosen people. God has been working to save even Israel's worst enemies, the Philistines and the Syrians, through their own dispensations.

47. **Isaiah 42.1-4**: This 'servant song' is understood differently by Jews and Christians. Jews interpret the servant to be Israel, and view the passage as a statement of Israel's vocation to be a light to the world. Christians understand the fuller meaning of the servant as realized in Jesus Christ. Either way, it indicates God's intention that His Servant should liberate everyone on earth.

48. **Larger Sukhavativyuha Sutra 9.1-5**: This is one of the chief hymns of Pure Land Buddhism. One should not interpret this passage as speaking of God's love in the western sense of the divine Being's love for his creatures. Rather, the ideal of the bodhisattva illustrates the Mahayana Buddhist principle that Ultimate Reality is itself all-embracing, inclusive of every living being and of the nature of compassion. One who truly understands this principle cannot help but feel suffering as long as there is even one individual who suffers, for that unfortunate individual is one's very self. This is the essence of the Bodhisattva Vow.

Chapter 8

1. **Tract of the Quiet Way**: Religion in China is syncretic, combining the Three Teachings (*san chiao*): Confucianism, Taoism, and Buddhism. Although the Tract of the Quiet Way is a Taoist scripture, the commentator P'an Ch'ung-Mou is a Confucian, and he calls for reverence of Buddhist sutras.

2. **Qur'an 5.44-48**: The Qur'an states that it is a trustworthy standard of truth, a 'watcher' over other revelations by which their beliefs can be tested and evaluated. Orthodox Islam goes further and regards the path laid down in the Qur'an to be the one sole path. Where the Jewish and Christian scriptures differ from the testimony of the Qur'an, the error is laid to the interpolations made by corrupt Jewish and Christian divines. But this interpretation goes beyond the letter of the Qur'an, which prohibits such disputes between religions. Each is held responsible only to the truth as found in its own scripture. Any contest between religious communities should be carried out on the field of good works. The question of reconciling different doctrines is left to God.

3. **Revelation of Amaterasu**: Amaterasu-omi-kami is the Sun Goddess and chief Shinto deity; here she proclaims her identity with Vairocana, the Buddha of the Sun. This edict proclaims the equivalence of Buddhist and Shinto worship.

4. **Qur'an 5.82-83**: Those Christians of the time of Muhammad exemplified an attitude that is ever essential to interreligious understanding: they were open to recognize the truth in another's religion and rejoice in it.

5. **Udana 68-69**: We give a version of this well-known Indian tale from the Buddhist canon, but some assert it is of Jain origin. It does illustrate well the Jain doctrine of *Anekanta*, the many-sidedness of things.

6. **Qur'an 29.46**: Muhammad regarded the "People of the Book" as including Jews, Christians and Zoroastrians, people of monotheistic religions with a written scripture.

7. **Acts 5.34-39:** The liberal attitude of Rabbi Gamaliel swayed the council to allow Peter and the Apostles freedom to preach the Christian gospel in Jerusalem. Christians use this passage to argue for toleration of unconventional sects and opinions. Gamaliel's dictum, that undertakings of men will fail but those of God cannot be defeated, is consistent with Jewish teaching: cf. Avot 4.14 in Chapter 20: *The Moral Foundations of Society*.

8. **July 19, 1984:** Freedom requires constant vigilance and sacrifices to maintain it. Father Moon spoke these words the day before he entered Danbury Prison for 13 months in a tax case that was widely viewed as thinly disguised government persecution of a new religion.

9. **Nihon Shoki 22:** The kami indwell the whole of life, and the divine can be seen within all the manifestations of nature—mountains, streams, forests, etc. Hence respect for nature and respect for the gods are one in the same.

10. **Invocation of the Mountain Spirit:** As the mountain is a symbol of strength and power, Sansang the mountain god is also the god of great generals, and is personified by the famous general Chae Yong of the Shilla Dynasty. He is also often symbolized by a tiger, which in legend inhabits the mountain recesses. When the shamaness *(mudang)* sings this song, she wears a general's costume and a hat with tiger's fur, and holds flags and a sword. The mountain god is one of twelve spirits invoked in turn during the shamanist ritual, called a *kut*.

11. **Igbo Invocation at a Trial:** Ala is the earth goddess, Chukwu is the Igbo name for God, the Creator; and Njoku is the yam deity. The Ofo and Aro are ritual sticks of wood or iron, specially consecrated, that create a channel for the spirits to operate in this world. Through their mediation, the gods can ferret out an evil-doer or a person who gives false testimony and punish him with misfortune.

12. **Shiva Purana, Rudrasamhita 18:** Worship of Ganesha is popular among contemporary Hindus. He is depicted with an elephant head and a human body. This passage is from his foundation legend, which recounts how Ganesha had been decapitated in battle, and to restore him to life the head of an elephant was affixed to his body. He is given blessings and is offered to humanity to be worshipped as "the remover of all obstacles"—a role suitable to the symbolism of an elephant.

13. **Srimad Bhagavatam 11.20:** The Sanskrit word "deva" means a deity, but interestingly it is the etymological root of the English word "devil."

14. **Dhammapada 393, etc.:** Among the problems in India that Buddhism came to address was the caste system, which was in essence a system of religiously sanctioned racial discrimination and apartheid. The highest caste was the Brahmin caste, whose members often functioned as priests. The Buddha rejected the idea that birth conferred any special status; instead he taught that one's status is commensurate with one's spiritual attainment.

15. **April 24, 1986:** "Subject and object relationships": Central to Buddhist doctrine is its teaching on causality and the interdependence of all phenomena. See Samyutta Nikaya 2.25, below, and teachings on Dependent Origination in Chapter 7: *Reversal and Restoration*. On "to reform the society of India," see the previous note on the caste system.

16. **November 21, 1990:** '*Sarvadharma*' (일체법, 一切法): Father Moon is using a Buddhist technical term, which means the oneness of all things, all laws, all states of existence.

17. **November 6, 1971:** 'Law sutras' (법문, 法文). Thus the Dhammapada means "Way of the Law" and the Lotus Sutra's full name is "Lotus of the Wonderful Law."

18. **Digha Nikaya 2.15:** The first words attributed to the Buddha after his birth.

19. **May 19, 1957:** 'No-self' (무아, 無我), is a Buddhist term that means a state without any ego. Elsewhere Father Moon speaks of it as the 'zero point.'

20. **July 10, 1984:** 'Self-nature' (자성, 自性): Father Moon employs a Buddhist term. It is sometimes translated 'Buddha-nature.'

21. **Diamond Sutra 21:** This and all the Perfection of Wisdom sutras teach a truth that is based in emptiness. Therefore, any attempt to speak the truth in words is no more than an expedient way to reach emptiness; no teaching or doctrine has any lasting value in itself.

22. **Classic on Filial Piety 1:** See Chapter 20: *The Family as the Cornerstone of Society*.

23. **November 10, 1998**: This is a quotation of the first sentence of the Four-Letter 'Small Teaching' (*Sohak*, 소학), a standard Korean Confucian school text. It draws a correspondence between growth in nature with its four seasons and human character with its four virtues. Thus the stage of sprouting in Spring corresponds to the virtue of benevolence; summer growth, to righteousness; autumn harvest, to propriety; and winter storage, to wisdom.

24. **August 28, 1998**: Three Bonds and Five Moral Disciplines (삼강오륜) is a traditional Korean term that summarizes Confucian ethics.

25. **Book of Songs, Ode 254:** The rulers of China owe their leadership to the Mandate of Heaven. If Heaven shows displeasure at a ruler by sending down calamities, it meant that he and sometimes even his dynasty had forfeited the Mandate and could justly be replaced.

26. **January 8, 1971:** Thus some Confucians regard "heaven" as the principle of nature or natural law, while others regard heaven as a higher power governing human destiny.

27. **November 17, 1986:** The "spiritual victory over the fallen angelic realm" was the accomplishment of their ancestor Jacob. See April 18, 1977 in Chapter 9: *Jacob*.

28. **Isaiah 53.6:** On this Jewish interpretation of the Suffering Servant, see Chapter 7, note 10.

29. **December 28, 1975:** "A homogeneous people": Korean people in particular admire this quality of the Jews, as they also have maintained the purity of their nation despite centuries of foreign invasions.

30. **Qur'an 17.104:** This refers to the dispersion of the Jews to many nations and their subsequent return to the Land of Israel in the Last Days, as Moses prophesied in Deuteronomy 30.1-5. From the perspective that we are now living in the Last Days, it is a message to Muslims that they should regard the establishment of the modern Jewish state as within God's plan.

31. **November 20, 1990:** The remarkable conjunction of Israel's independence and Korea's independence in the years following World War II is evidence that the mission of Christ at his Second Advent includes bringing to completion everything left unfulfilled in the former dispensations of the Old and New Testaments. Hence, just as Father Moon is working to resolve the conflict on the Korean peninsula, he is also working for peace in the Middle East.

32. **Acts 2.42-47:** "Breaking bread in their homes": This is the early Christian model for the cell church.

33. **Matthew 16:18-19:** Peter, *Petros*, means rock (*petra*) in Greek. This verse is the basis for the Roman Catholic Church's claim to be the one true church, based upon continuous apostolic succession back to Peter. Yet the early church was not so organized. In fact, supremacy of the Bishop of Rome was only established in the West after Emperor Constantine christianized the Roman Empire.

34. **October 21, 1973:** "Any nation in the Old World," literally, "nations governed by the Catholic Church." Although England was a Protestant country in 1620, it was still a country that enforced a single state religion—the Church of England—in the manner of the former Catholic system. The magisterial reformation that led much of northern Europe to adopt Protestant forms of the state religion was still mired in monarchic ways of thinking and was not thoroughgoing enough to create the conditions for democracy. It was the radical reformation, led by sects like the Puritans and the Plymouth Brethren, which led to the norm of religious freedom necessary for genuine democracy.

35. **Qur'an 2.136:** The word *Islam* means Submission or 'the Surrender.'

36. **Qur'an 5.13:** The Jews are accused of misusing their scripture, or conveniently forgetting parts of its message, or inventing novel interpretations (if the word 'treachery' is read as 'deceits'; otherwise the last line refers to the actions of the Jews of Medina who broke their agreements with the Muslims).

37. **Qur'an 5.14:** This is most likely a critique of sectarianism and denominationalism that plagues Christianity to this day. However, many Muslims believe the "neglected portion" was the prophecy (John 15.26) of the Comforter, which in Arabic (*Ahmad*) can be interpreted as a prophecy of the coming of Muhammad.

38. **Qur'an 5.116:** The Qur'an is condemning Mariolatry, not the Trinity per se.

39. **Qur'an 9:29**: This is the *jizya*, a tax levied upon all who did not accept Islam but were obliged to accept the protection of a Muslim state.

40. **June 21, 2001**: Father Moon is describing the attitude of many white American members of his church at the time.

Chapter 9

1. **Bhagavad-Gita 4.7-8**: Here God (Vishnu) is speaking of Himself in the first person. This is the classic verse on the doctrine of avatars. Each avatar comes for a specific mission to save the world and establish righteousness (*dharma*), according to the scriptures. The classical avatars of Vishnu include Rama and Krishna, but also the Buddha and the Kalkin who is to come in the Last Days.

2. **Chuang Tzu 33**: This chapter of the Chuang Tzu describes sages of various schools—Taoists, Mohists, Legalists, Confucianists—who wandered about China during the Chou dynasty, preaching their visions of peace and harmony.

3. **December 30, 1979**: This aptly describes Jesus' ministry; see Luke 14:16-24. Yet Buddha and Muhammad faced similar difficulties.

4. **Matthew 5.17-18**: Jesus fulfills the prophecies of the Old Testament prophets. Furthermore, the Gospel is the fulfillment of the Jewish Torah and Jesus is its preeminent interpreter. In truth, many of Jesus' teachings in the Sermon on the Mount are identical to the best sayings of the rabbis, particularly those in the Mishnah, tractate Avot (below).

5. **Avot 1.1**: 'Torah' means not only the words written in the first five books of the Bible. This passage speaks of an 'oral Torah' which was transmitted through the chain of succession to the rabbis. Its practical clarifications and inner teachings define the way of life which is true to the written commandments. The rabbis wrote the Mishnah and the Talmud as codifications of this oral Torah.

6. **Book of Ritual 7.1.2**: Confucius modeled his teachings on the example of these sage-kings of antiquity.

7. **Lotus Sutra 2**: Sakyamuni is speaking of his own gradual progress to perfect enlightenment over countless past lives, following the Buddhas of the past who had already achieved enlightenment.

8. **February 15, 1967**: 'Devote ourselves': this is the important Korean term *jeongseong* (정성), which means to offer sincere devotion through prayer, fasting, offerings and sincere efforts at loving God and neighbor.

9. **February 10, 1972**: The term of 120 years is based upon Genesis 6.3: "The LORD said, 'My spirit shall not abide in man for ever, for he is flesh, but his days shall be a hundred and twenty years.'" While some exegetes take this verse to mean a shortening of the human life-span, Father Moon follows the Christian exegetical tradition that understands this verse to be part of God's message to Noah, revealing to him that the flood would come in 120 years.

10. **Qur'an 21.51-71**: Though this episode is not found in the Bible, it is well attested in Jewish and Christian traditions.

11. **September 13, 1959**: Father Moon uses the term "Satan's world" broadly, not for an especially wicked people, but rather to mean the entire fallen world of humanity, which ever since the Human Fall has existed under Satan's dominion. He contrasts it with the chosen people, whom God raised up as His special possession as the only group and nation under His authority.

12. **Qur'an 14.35-37**: The Qur'an affirms the ancient Arab tradition that among the lands where Abraham journeyed, he went to Mecca, consecrated and restored the Kaaba to pure worship, and settled Hagar and Ishmael there.

13. ***Exposition of the Divine Principle,* Foundation 3.2**: For more on how Abraham's family fulfilled the restoration of Abel and Cain, see December 24, 1978 and December 30, 1979 in Chapter 9: *Jacob*.

14. **Genesis 22.1-18**: The binding of Isaac, the *Akedah*, was Abraham's ultimate test of faith. Isaac was his only son by his wife Sarah, born miraculously by God's hand after she was long past child-bearing age; furthermore, he was the one by whom God's promise of numerous descendants was to be fulfilled. Such was the love and attachment that

Abraham had for his son. Yet at God's command, he willingly offered him up, though it was more difficult than to sacrifice his own life. Isaac's self-sacrifice is sometimes compared to Jesus' crucifixion, where God the Father offers up His only Son.

15. **Genesis Rabbah 56**: Isaac is quite aware that he is about to be sacrificed, and his faith is tested as much as is Abraham's.

16. **Qur'an 37.101-107**: Islamic tradition affirms that Abraham's son of the sacrifice was Ishmael, not Isaac. Yet the Qur'an does not directly name Ishmael in this ambiguous passage. Muslims regard mention of Isaac's birth after the sacrifice as proof enough that the sacrifice had to be Ishmael the firstborn. In order to be consistent with the Bible, one would have to interpret this notice of Isaac's birth as a parallel passage not chronologically linked to the preceding verses. As a "gentle son" the description fits Isaac, who is characterized as "meek" in the Bible. In that case the blessing of Abraham and Isaac would be the reward for participating in the sacrifice.

17. **Genesis 25.8-9**: The peace that existed between Isaac and Ishmael when they together buried their father Abraham points to the peace that should arrive between Jews and Arabs in the Middle East when they put aside their differences to honor God their Parent, and honor the memory of Abraham in places like Hebron, where Abraham was buried.

18. *Exposition of the Divine Principle*, **Foundation 3.1.2.2**: The failure of the symbolic offering refers to the offering of animals recounted in Genesis 15.7-15, when Abraham neglected to cut the birds in half. See Foundation 3.1.2, above.

19. *Exposition of the Divine Principle*, **Foundation 3.1.2.3**: "Satan had invaded" Abraham not in any obvious way; what it means is that due to his previous mistake Abraham was liable to be attacked and fail to accomplish his mission to be the ancestor of the chosen people. Yet God gave him another chance to separate himself from Satan's accusation through the test of sacrificing Isaac. Thus the sacrifice of Isaac was a life-and-death matter, not only for Isaac but for the entire dispensation.

20. **December 24, 1978**: For Rebecca's crucial role in this affair, see *Women of the Bible*, below.

21. **December 24, 1978**: As Esau is called Edom (Gen. 25.30, above), in Jewish tradition Edom is identified with Rome.

22. **Genesis 32.24-30**: The struggle of Jacob is usually interpreted as not against a demon, but against an angel whom God was using to test Jacob. Father Moon's interpretation is that the angel was indeed sent by God, but for the purposes of this condition he represents Satan.

23. **December 30, 1979**: "The position of Abel" is the brother favored by God, whom the person in the Cain position should acknowledge and follow to restore Cain's failure to do so in the beginning of human history.

24. **Qur'an 12.22-32**: In the Bible's version of the story of Joseph and Potiphar's wife (Gen. 39.6-20), Potiphar immediately accepts his wife's allegations and throws Joseph into prison. The Qur'an adds the detail about the evidentiary meaning of the tear on the front or the back of the shirt and the wife's subsequent effort to justify herself.

25. **August 20, 1987**: People on 'Satan's side' are not egregious criminals but ordinary people who live by conventional standards and hence easily become Satan's tools. See note 11, above.

26. *Exposition of the Divine Principle*, **Foundation 3.1.2.1**: Abraham and Sarah in Egypt went through a course to restore the triangular relationship between Adam, Eve and the Archangel. It goes like this: Sarah begins as Abraham's sister (as Eve was Adam's sister); then she becomes Pharaoh's wife (as Eve first loved Lucifer); and finally she returns to Abraham as his acknowledged wife (as Eve returned to Adam as her rightful husband). This same course is repeated several times in the history of the Providence, for example with David, Bathsheba and Uriah (below).

27. **February 14, 1993**: Adam did not consummate his first love with the pure Eve as God intended, but instead united with fallen Eve; Jacob reversed this sequence by first loving Leah in fallen Eve's position and then receiving his first love, Rachel.

28. **February 14, 1993**: Besides being Jacob's mother, Rebecca was Laban's sister and Leah and Rachel's aunt.

29. **February 14, 1993**: Although Bilhah was legally Rachel's maidservant, as time went on she came

under the first wife Leah's authority, a situation also promoted by Jacob's continued favor to Rachel alone. This becomes evident in the situation of Joseph and his brothers. The 10 sons of Leah and the two maids are united in their dislike of Joseph the favorite.

30. **Genesis 38.6-30:** By the Levirate law, when a husband dies childless, the next of kin had the obligation marry his wife and have a son by her to perpetuate her first husband's lineage. In the book of Ruth, Boaz fulfills the Levirate law for Ruth's first husband and her mother-in-law. Onan's refusal to observe this law was motivated by the desire not to have to divide his inheritance with his brother's child.

31. **Sefer Peli'ah:** This Kabbalistic explanation of the providential reason for David's action is remarkably similar to Father Moon's. Like all the women in Jesus' lineage, Bathsheba represented Eve in a triangular relationship with two male beings: Adam and the Serpent. Her change of husbands thus served a restorational purpose: see note 26 and the two April 18, 1977 passages in relation to Tamar (above) and Mary (below).

    The Kabbalah's concept of transmigration (*gilgul*) is a type of reincarnation but always for a restorational purpose. And like Father Moon's teaching on returning resurrection, *gilgul* is conceived among some Kabbalists as a conjoining of the transmigrating soul with the soul of the earthly person, who maintains his or her distinct identity.

32. **October 13, 1970:** Although David had many wives, this term refers to Bathsheba's two marriages, first with Uriah and then with David. Likewise, fallen Eve was a "second wife," having had two relationships—her intended marriage to Adam and her actual marriage to Lucifer. Hence in restoration, women in the position of second wives—whether a wife to a second husband as was Bathsheba or a second wife of one husband as was Rachel—often play pivotal roles. For other triangular relationships, compare the relationship between Sarah, Abraham and the Pharaoh in Egypt; see note 26.

33. **Wolli Wonbon 242-43:** This passage is taken from *Wolli Wonbon*, the unpublished manuscript that Father Moon wrote in Pusan in 1951. It was his first draft of a systematic presentation of his teachings, which guided his church in the early years.

34. **October 29, 1978:** Buddha also had to overcome Satan's temptation: see Chapter 15: *Testing*.

35. **Buddhacarita 14:** This is an abbreviated form of the chain of dependent origination; see Chapter 7: *Reversal and Restoration*.

36. **Digha Nikaya 2.15:** These are the first words attributed to the Buddha after his birth.

37. **August 28, 1998:** Father Moon teaches that Confucianism, as well as Buddhism and other movements of mind and spirit of the "Axial Age" (fifth and sixth centuries B.C.), were intended to prepare the entire world to join with Jesus—had he been received in his lifetime—and build the worldwide Kingdom of God. Thus they laid a worldwide foundation corresponding to the direct foundation of Judaism. When Jesus was rejected and went to the cross, that opportunity was lost, and Confucianism continued to develop as a world religion in its own sphere. See below, *Exposition of the Divine Principle*, Parallels 6, in Jesus, Worldwide Preparation for His Advent.

38. **March 10: 1972:** 'Attending' (*moshida*) is an important Korean term describing an advanced stage of faith and devotion. To attend the Messiah means to serve him, love him, participate in his work of salvation, learn from him, and inherit everything from him, just as a filial son loves, serves and inherits everything from his father.

39. **February 21, 1972:** The purification of Jesus' lineage was largely the work of Mary and her foremothers; see April 18, 1977 and April 16, 1996 in Chapter 9: *Women of the Bible*.

40. **Mark 1.2-6**: "Locusts," probably locust beans or carob.

41. **Mark 6.30-44:** Of all the miracles of Jesus, the feeding of the 5,000 is the only one attested in all four gospels; it is even in the Qur'an (below).

42. **Qur'an 5.112-115:** This account conflates the feeding of the 5,000 with Peter's vision of the table spread in Acts 10.9-16.

43. **John 6.25-67:** This extended discussion about food follows John's version of the miracle of feeding the 5,000.

44. **Philippians 2.6-11:** This is the well-known hymn of Christ's *kenosis*, or self-emptying. By grasping at nothing and denying himself totally,

Jesus laid the condition to be totally vindicated and exalted by God.

45. **March 25, 1972:** Had Israel received Jesus, he would have led them into the New Testament Age. The teachings of Jesus, or New Testament, would have been revered by all Jews as orthodox scripture—a natural extension of the Torah, rather than as the scripture of a different religion as Christianity became.

46. **September 18, 1974:** By 'resurrection' Father Moon is referring to the resurrection of humanity that began with the spiritual rebirth at Pentecost when the disciples received the Holy Spirit. This is in line with the meaning of resurrection in the Divine Principle, the spiritual transformation from death into life. He is not speaking of Christ's resurrection, a unique phenomenon when he walked the earth for 40 days.

47. **Qur'an 33.40:** When a document is sealed, it is complete and there can be no further addition. As 'the Seal of the Prophets' Muhammad is regarded as the last prophet, completing for all time the testimony of God's revelation. For Islam, God's teaching will continue in later ages through reformers, sages, and saints, but no more through a Prophet.

48. **Sirat Rasul Allah:** Khadija was Muhammad's first wife and the first to recognize his divine mission. Marriage to first cousins is common in Arab society.

Chapter 10

1. **Lotus Sutra 13:** Nichiren, Japan's foremost exponent of the Lotus Sutra, believed his own time to be the Age of Degeneration of the Law (Jap. *Mappo*, Skt. *Saddharma-vipralopa*), which demands a restoration at its end. Hence many have expected the coming of the Maitreya Buddha, the 'Restorer,' who will inaugurate a new age. Some sects of Nichiren Buddhism such as Soka Gakkai and Risshoko Sekai identify Nichiren himself as the Restorer.

2. **August 1, 1996:** As there are no female angels, angels do not live as couples, according to Father Moon.

3. **Blessing and Ideal Family 5.1.2:** There are three stages of growth: formation, growth and completion. Each stage is subdivided into three levels: formation, growth and completion. This makes a total of nine levels. The Human Fall took place at the "completion level of the growth stage," which is the sixth level, prior to the "completion stage," which consists of levels seven through nine.

4. **Revelation 9.1-11:** This plague of locusts with the stings of scorpions is seen here as metaphorical for the outpouring of demons and evil spirits from hell, the "bottomless pit." They do not devour vegetation, but rather consume the human soul. The star that had fallen from heaven to earth symbolizes Satan, who increases his activities on earth in the Last Days.

5. **April 3, 1972:** Contemporary outbreaks of ethnic violence, as in Bosnia and Rwanda, often have spiritual causes, carried over from the piled up resentments of the dead who had previously fought the same enemies. Coming to earth, they can whip up war hysteria.

6. **Revelation 13.1-18:** The Beast represents human pretension to universal power, and imperial powers in every age have been identified as fulfilling this prophecy. Originally as written, the beast referred specifically to the Roman Empire. The pretensions of the Roman emperor to be a human god, whom all the world worshipped, were seen as a parody of Christ's true kingship. The 'seven heads' probably represent Rome with its seven hills; other features of the Beast: the ten horns, parts like a leopard, a bear, and a lion, resemble the four separate beasts in Daniel 7.2-7. Some scholars identify the miraculous healing of the wounded head to a legend which grew up around Emperor Nero, that he miraculously reappeared after his suicide in 68 A.D. The number 666 is the total numerical value of the letters "Nero Caesar" in the Aramaic language. Unbelievers and lapsed Christians worshipped the emperor; thus they were marked with the number of the Beast.

7. **June 16, 1957:** The original Satan has with him a host of small satans. These are evil spirits and evil people who oppose God's will.

8. **Qur'an 5.48**: This is the conclusion of a longer passage (see Chapter 8: *One Truth, Many Paths*.) affirming the divine source of each of the Abrahamic faiths and discouraging disputations over doctrinal differences. It offers a tantalizing hint that in the Last Days, God will reveal His word concerning these disputed teachings.

9. **Qur'an 16.101-102**: This does not refer to the inner-Muslim controversies over changes in the Qur'an, abrogated verses, etc., but rather the Qur'an as a new revelation adding to the older revelations of the Gospel and the Old Testament Law. "Who have surrendered," e.g. Muslims.

10. **Book of Certitude, 33-41**: In the Baha'i Faith, the Last Judgment is interpreted as the end of the old dispensations of religion and the beginning of the new dispensation centered on God's messenger Bahá'u'lláh.

11. **Hadith of Muslim**: In this tradition, Christ will appear in the flesh as a Muslim Imam. Yet most people will not heed.

12. **Sanhedrin 98a**: Rabbinic Judaism, faced with the seemingly never-ending delay of the Bible's messianic promises and purged of political ambition after the disastrous defeats in the Jewish War (68-70 C.E.) and the Bar Kochba Rebellion (132 C.E.), transformed the historical promise of the coming of the Messiah into a personal encounter of faith. Elijah is a heavenly interpreter of God's secrets.

13. **March 17, 1957**: Otherwise Satan would have a condition to accuse God, as in the book of Job, that his chosen ones were given the truth without proving themselves worthy to receive it.

14. **Qur'an 43.61**: Based on these words, many Muslims await the Second Coming of Christ, who will come to herald the Last Judgment.

15. **Digha Nikaya 3.76**: The Maitreya [Pali *Metteya*] is predicted to be the future Buddha in the scriptures of both Theravada and Mahayana Buddhism. Many regard him as the future leader who will usher in the new age of bliss and consummation.

16. **Hadith of Muslim**: See note 11, above.

17. **Doctrine of the Mean 31-32**: These chapters express the ideal of the Kingly Man who is to come. To a certain extent they apply to Confucius, and many hold that these verses were written in praise of him. On the other hand, Confucius did not receive honor in his lifetime; therefore these verses more properly anticipate one who has yet to make his appearance in the world.

18. **1 John 3.2**: That is, we shall all become perfect and Christ-like at the Second Coming of Christ. Thomas Aquinas described this Beatific Vision as "the ultimate goal for the redeemed."

19. **Pesikta Rabbati 162b-63a**: This rabbinic conception of a future suffering Messiah who will take upon himself the sins of Israel stands alongside the older belief that the Messiah will come as a conquering king. This is undoubtedly a midrash on Isaiah 53. Compare the standard Christian interpretation of that prophecy.

20. **Jeremiah 23.5-8**: 'Branch' is a messianic title, based on the prophecy in Isaiah 11.1, "There shall come forth a shoot from the stump of Jesse, and a branch shall grow out of his roots."

21. **Sanhedrin 99a**: This was said in the context of a rabbinical discussion where others were imagining supernatural delights, grapes the size of watermelons, and so on. Yet for most Jews throughout the last 2000 years this has been their central hope for the Messiah: to bring an end Israel's long exile and re-establish the Jewish homeland.

22. **Hadith of Bukhari 3.656**: The *jizya* is a tax levied by Muslim leaders on Christians and Jews who live in their countries. Supposedly for protection, the tax is demeaning and signifies their status as second-class citizens. Likewise, Christians have employed the cross as a sign of conquest in their battles with Muslims.

23. **Chong Gam Nok**: This Korean book of prophecy appeared in the 16th century. The passage quoted here follows a remarkably detailed prediction of the course of the Korean War, including allusions to Gen. Douglas MacArthur's landing at Inchon and the intervention of the People's Republic of China.

24. **Chong Gam Nok**: Ever since the mid-1980s, Father Moon has been promoting thousands of marriages between Japanese and Koreans.

25. **Chong Gam Nok**: It was at the International Blessing Ceremony of 36,000 couples in August 1992 that Father and Mother Moon were publicly proclaimed as the Messiah, Second Coming and True Parents—precisely in accordance with this prophecy.

26. **April 3, 1995:** "Interdependence" refers to economic relationships; "mutual prosperity" refers to the ethic of good government that transcends partisanship, and "universally shared values" refers to the common ground among all religions and philosophies of life. These are three essential characteristics of the social life in the Kingdom.

27. **Matthew 22.1-13:** The 'wedding garment' refers to the guest's character of righteousness and purity, as in Rev. 22.14: "Blessed are those who wash their robes, that they may have the right to the tree of life and that they may enter the city by the gates." Lacking the mark of good character, he does not belong at the feast.

Chapter 11

1. **Mark 4.26-29:** This parable represents the growth of the Kingdom of Heaven—interpreted either corporately or within the heart of the individual believer—as a natural process that occurs mysteriously and gradually, enlivened by God's fertilizing grace. It is likened to the growth of grain in three stages of formation—'the blade', growth—'the ear', and maturity—'the full grain', followed by a fourth stage of returning to God—'the harvest'.

2. **November 19, 1998:** 'Horizontal' here probably means the range of human relationships, as distinct from the 'vertical' relationship with God.

3. **Satapatha Brahmana 5.1.1.1-2:** The chief difference between demons and gods in this well-known story is that the demons are self-centered while the gods are generous and share with others.

4. **Jeremy Bentham:** *Introduction to Principles of Morals and Legislation* (1789).

5. **Socrates:** Quoted by Plutarch, *How a Young Man Ought to Hear Poems*.

6. **Pico della Mirandola:** *The Dignity of Man* (1587).

7. **Erich Fromm:** *Man for Himself* (1947).

8. **Avot 3.18:** To be created in the image of God implies that humans should live by the ethical commandments that enable them to conform to God's goodness and holiness. By making this known to us, God was giving us a responsibility to uphold this glorious purpose.

9. **Pearl of Great Price, Moses 4.1-4:** This passage, also given in Chapter 6, *The Devil and His Activities*, points to a central tenet of Latter-day Saints' teaching: the value of human freedom as God's special gift. Satan offered to save humanity by compulsion—'not one soul shall be lost,' without regard for human free agency and hence responsibility.

10. **October 22, 1972:** "Bitterness" translates the Korean word *han*. Sometimes incorrectly translated "grudge" or "resentment," *han* contains no jealousy and is not aimed at revenge. Rather, the pain of *han* is digested with faith and endurance.

11. **Ezekiel 18:** This important passage was uttered by the prophet Ezekiel to counter the fatalism which was prevalent among the Jews who had been exiled to Babylon and who blamed their lot on the sins of previous generations. In denying a determining role for inherited sin and stressing individual responsibility, he restored a measure of their faith and self-respect. In the Christian era, Jews have utilized this passage in arguments against the Christian doctrines of Original Sin and the vicarious Atonement of Christ.

12. **Anguttara Nikaya 1.173-74:** Shakyamuni Buddha argues against fatalism based on belief in karma or predestination. A person's accumulated karma or the predestination of God are only minor factors, conditioning but not determining the value and course of his or her life. There is still always room to apply oneself, gain merit, and advance on the path towards the ultimate goal. Elsewhere, the Buddha also argues against the easy belief that through reincarnation people will have many and frequent chances at life in this world.

13. **Handbook for Preclears:** In Scientology, to "be cause" means to take responsibility for one's actions and for all events that impinge on oneself. To reach the state of Clear means to fully be a cause, never blaming others when things go poorly but always taking responsibility oneself.

14. **February 1, 1987:** Literally, "the horizon above my eyes," a term from physiognomy describing the shape of the eyebrows and forehead and implying a certain fortune.

15. **November 4, 1990:** "Destined relationships" (*inyun*): The significant events in people's lives do not happen by accident. There is a destiny joining people together, linking them in time and space. Reverend Moon sees people's significance in terms of a history that flowed through their ancestry. Each is a link in a long chain of destined relationships extending into the past. Their meeting with Father Moon is fraught with significance, as it completes that chain.

16. **Avot 3.19:** This passage juxtaposes two pairs of contraries: divine foreknowledge and human freedom, and the divine attributes of mercy and justice.

17. **Asa-ki-Var, M.1:** The image of God in heaven moving chess pieces which determine man's destiny on earth is evocative of absolute predestination. Yet that is all the more reason to be mindful of God, Master of the game; for who knows on what basis He decides His moves, or whether He will not choose to move the pieces again?

18. **Boethius:** In other words, our free will is only apparent, based upon our human perspective with its limited knowledge. Nevertheless, this is no excuse for fatalism. We should act responsibly in freedom, knowing that God foresees these free acts of ours.

19. **Hippocrates:** *Regimen in Acute Diseases.*

20. **February 6, 1983:** 'heart,' Korean *ma-eum*, 마음, often translated 'mind,' can mean either mind or heart. In Korean, the mind includes emotion, intellect and will, while in English the word 'mind' mainly denotes the intellect, while the emotional function of mind is best rendered in English by 'heart.'

21. **March 29, 1959:** The text says "from the liberation of Korea," which happened in 1945. In that year Father Moon began his public ministry.

Chapter 12

1. **Aristotle:** Quoted in Stobaeus, *Floritegium*.
2. **Hadith:** This is an important Sufi tradition. The 'lesser jihad' is jihad in the ordinary sense: the war against external foes. The 'greater jihad' is the spiritual war, whose battleground is the soul.
3. **Dhammapada 80:** Self-control is as necessary to the inner life as skill in shaping wood, metal, or water is required for good industry. Spiritual training is the counterpart to learning a secular trade.
4. **April 19, 1999:** God has no form. By God's 'body,' Father Moon means His body-aspect, manifested through His creations and acts in history.
5. **Ephesians 4.26-27:** To practice this teaching by resolving each day's quarrels and meditating to digest each day's resentments before going to bed each night is a valuable spiritual exercise. For when anger is stored up day after day, it becomes much harder to eradicate.
6. **Igala Proverb:** Don't respond to provocation, but stay out of a quarrel.
7. **November 13, 1959:** The 'Third World War' refers to the Cold War. This is an early prediction of the defeat of communism.
8. **March 10, 1968:** 'Education': literally 'Academic clique'; in Korean society, the university a person graduated from gives him a certain status, cemented by the bonds among fellow alumni from the same class.
9. **Ramayana:** Rama is rejecting his friends' arguments that he should seize the throne and abrogate the command of his father, that he withdraw from the kingdom to live as an ascetic in the forest. He regards the duty of a filial son to obey his father's wishes to be more precious than a kingdom.
10. **Abraham Lincoln:** Address at New York City, February 27, 1860.
11. **April 24, 1977:** The Korean pronunciations are given here.
12. **May 1, 1981:** Father Moon describes the relationship with God in terms of levels of heart. The 'servant' level regards a right relationship with God in terms of keeping the laws of the covenant and fulfilling his duty. The 'adopted son' has a more inward relationship with God; he feels that God is his Father and willingly acts to fulfill God's Will, inspired by God's love. The distinction corresponds roughly to the Christian distinction

between justification by works and justification through faith—the latter being founded upon the experience of rebirth and leading to a life of dedication and walking with Christ.

13. **1 Kings 19.18:** In God's message to the prophet Elijah on Mount Sinai, we have mention of a righteous remnant that will be spared when God judges Israel. The concept of the remnant is found throughout the prophets: see Isaiah 6.13; 7.3-4; 10.20-23; Amos 5.15.

14. **Hullin 92a:** God destroyed Sodom and Gomorrah for want of ten righteous men; see Genesis 18.20-33.

15. **Great Learning 6.1-4:** This Confucian passage and the following Buddhist text describe an active and mindful type of sincerity, one requiring constant effort at practice and self-examination. It is quite a different concept from that of the Taoist and Sikh passages just given.

16. **May 1, 1975:** *Jeongseong* includes devotional acts such as prayers, prostrations, fasting and penances, as well as charity and service to others, all done with a sincere mind to love and serve God.

17. **June 30, 2000:** Traditional Korean villages often have a pair of carved poles stationed at the entrance.

18. **Analects 3.20:** 'The Ospreys!' refers to Ode 1 of the Book of Songs (See Chapter 19, *Conjugal Love*). Confucius interprets this ode as describing a model of conduct according to the Golden Mean: faithfulness in both joy and affliction.

19. **Samyutta Nikaya 22.90:** In practice, the 'middle doctrine' (*madhyamaka*) means avoiding both the extremes of worldliness ('things have being') and total renunciation ('things have no being').

20. **Akan Proverb:** This proverb means that as you restrain yourself when eating to stay within the bounds of good manners, you should also in all things resist temptation and act within the bounds of propriety.

21. **Qur'an 24.30-32:** Wearing the veil by Muslim women was instituted in the Qur'an as a practical protection against the temptation to adultery.

22. **Sutta Nipata 205-06:** The many Buddhist meditations on the body as filthy and worthless are mainly to cultivate an attitude of detachment from sense desires and bodily pleasures.

23. **Ephesians 5.3-6:** 'Levity' of a licentious nature.

24. **Sutra of Forty-two Sections:** This may be a criticism of Tantric rites, with their "secret yoga" of sexual union as a way to enlightenment.

25. **Sutra of Forty-two Sections 29:** A *shramana* (Sanskrit) is a wandering monk in the ascetic traditions of Indian Buddhism and Jainism.

26. **Lotus Sutra 14:** The 'five kinds of unmanly men' includes homosexuals, hermaphrodites, eunuchs, and those suffering from various kinds of impotence. The Sangha did not want anyone to join the order as an escape; it likewise barred from membership debtors who wanted to renege on their debts and young novices who did not have their parents' permission.

27. **Qur'an 29.28-29:** This passage refers to the story of Sodom and Gomorrah. According to the Bible (Genesis 19.4-11), when two angels came to Lot's home to warn him of the city's impending destruction, the mob demanded that Lot give the men over to them, that they might rape and sodomize them. Lot defended them and offered his daughters instead; at which point the mob sought to lay hands on Lot, but the angels rescued him.

28. **September 18, 1991:** Father Moon teaches that genuine spiritual rebirth can enable former homosexuals to put away that lifestyle and become new people. Through the power of the Spirit, they can control their former feelings and re-train themselves to love their heterosexual spouse. Nevertheless, the seemingly intractability of homosexual tendencies needs explanation. Psychologists beginning with Sigmund Freud regarded homosexuality as a disorder resulting from early childhood experience. Here is Freud's view of the problem:

"In all our male homosexuals there was very intense erotic attachment to a feminine person, as a rule to the mother, which was manifest in the very first period of childhood and later entirely forgotten by the individual. This attachment was produced or favored by too much love from the mother herself, but was also furthered by the retirement or absence of the father during the childhood period... Following this primary stage, a transformation takes place whose mechanism we know but whose motive forces we have not yet grasped.

"The love of the mother cannot continue to develop consciously so that it merges into repression. The boy represses the love for the mother by putting himself in her place, by identifying himself with her, and by taking his own person as a model through the similarity of which he is guided in the selection of his love-object. He thus becomes homosexual; as a matter of fact he returns to the stage of autoeroticism, for the boys whom the growing adult now loves are only substitute persons or revivals of his own childish person, whom he loves in the same way as his mother loved him. We say that he finds his love-object on the road to narcissism." (Sigmund Freud, *Leonardo da Vinci* [1909]).

Chapter 13

1. **Wadhans**: This is a good test of whether an emotion is godly love or ordinary love. Godly love is all-embracing, while ordinary love focuses on one object exclusively, thereby inciting jealousy. Godly love seeks to benefit others, while ordinary love is tinged with selfish desire.

2. **Metta Sutta**: This is the classic Buddhist teaching on loving-kindness.

3. **Chuang Tzu 23**: Perfect action is spontaneous, heartfelt, trusting, and intimate; it dispenses with formalities. It can only exist where there is true love.

4. **Thomas Aquinas, Summa Theologica**: I-II, q. 26, art. 2

5. **Great Learning 8**: Confucianism teaches that one should be partial towards one's own family and relatives—yet only as the starting point for a social ethic which is an expansion of family relations. To counter the tendency of partiality to become corrupt, another aspect to Confucian teaching is the search for a universal objective basis for action in the world: the cultivation of personal virtue. Each person should have a foundation of benevolence within himself or herself in order that love—both to family and to strangers—may be correct.

6. **Brihadaranyaka Upanishad 2.4.4-5**: The "Self" is Atman, or the God within. It is the seat of eternity, and entirely different from the individual ego. It is related to the Unification concept of the original mind or heart.

7. **Brihadaranyaka Upanishad 5.2.2**: Prajapati is the Hindu creator (Brahma). As he is instructing his students, this passage instructs us about the Creator's character and way of life.

8. **Socrates**: The story, immortalized by Euripides in his play *Alcestis*, was thus: prince Admetus was stricken with a fatal illness, but the fates decreed that he would recover if someone would die as his substitute. None of his servants was willing to volunteer; even his aged parents refused. Only his young bride Alcestis agreed to take his place. When she was about to expire, Hercules intervened and rescued her from the hand of Death to be joyfully reunited with her husband.

9. **Igala Proverb**: A criticism of those who, enjoying luxuries, forget that others are suffering.

10. **Sikshasamuccaya 280-81**: This is a statement of the Bodhisattva Vow, a central theme of Mahayana Buddhism. It describes the practice of dedicating one's merits, won through years of effort at spiritual discipline and selfless deeds, for the benefit of others. To regard one's own suffering in solidarity with the suffering of others empties one's suffering of self-hood. Hence the pride of suffering and pride in one's own spiritual accomplishment is overcome.

11. **Garland Sutra 23**: This is another statement of the Bodhisattva Vow. Here the emphasis is on saving others, not enjoying one's own enlightenment but making oneself a "hostage" for others who are suffering.

12. *The Words of Martin Luther King, Jr.*, selected by Coretta Scott King (New York: Newmarket Press, 1983).

13. **Mo Tzu**: Mo Tzu was a Chinese teacher and contemporary of Confucius. He taught an ethic of universal love in contrast to Confucius' view that love operates from the closest stage—family—outward to society.

14. **Milarepa**: Many Buddhists have the same criticism of Confucian ethics as Mo Tzu, that love of family members leads us to treat them preferentially and thus makes our love partial. Such love is neither

universal nor true; hence it is not conducive to liberation from the endless cycle of birth-and-death (*samsara*).

15. **Mahaparinirvana Sutra 470-71**: The love of a mother for her only child, as developed in this Mahayana text as the way of the bodhisattva, is similar to the Theravada concept of compassion as set forth in the Metta Sutta (above).

16. **March 3, 1976**: The biblical epithet "Jehovah, LORD of hosts" refers mainly to the armies of heaven, but Father Moon's term refers to all beings in heaven and on earth.

17. **January 18, 1987**: As God is the Father of the multitudes, by extending the ethic of filial piety to God our Heavenly Father, we can completely overcome any partiality and unite with the Father's universal love.

18. **Luke 10.25-37**: The bite of this story is that the Jews to whom Jesus was speaking looked down on Samaritans as inferiors of mixed blood and questionable religion. A second aspect of the story has to do with why the priest and Levite refused to help the injured man: they were afraid of incurring ritual uncleanness according to their strict interpretation of Jewish law. Hence in two ways the parable is an oblique criticism of people who put religious dogmatism above love for their fellow human beings.

19. Paul Tillich, "Forgetting and Being Forgotten," *The Eternal Now* (New York: Scribner's, 1963).

20. **Hadith of Baihaqi**: Muhammad attributes this teaching to Moses.

21. **Oracle of the Kami of Kasuga**: Shinto regards a dwelling where such mourning is going on to be polluted by death, normally a state which the gods would strictly avoid.

22. **Lotus Sutra 10**: 'Tathagata' means "Comes thus far," i.e., the one who has arrived at the goal of enlightenment. It is a title given to the Buddha, often in his cosmic manifestation as the Ultimate Reality. The 'Dwelling of the Tathagata' means his temple, and the 'Robe' is his authority as a master of the dharma.

23. **February 22, 1976**: 'Heart,' Korean *shimjung*, is the emotional core of God's being that is continually giving love and seeking to love. Each human being, framed in the image of God, has an original heart bearing the same nature.

24. **James 2.14-26**: This argument for good deeds to demonstrate faith relies on the example of Abraham, for it comes as a counterpoint to Galatians 3.1-11 (see Chapter 15: A *Gift of God*). Paul's teaching, that we are saved through faith and not by deeds according to the law, had been misinterpreted by some Christians as advocating antinomianism, the license to do most anything as long as it is not harmful, under the cover of faith. James corrects this misconception by asserting that faith, if it is true, will be substantiated and confirmed by good works.

25. **Yoruba Proverb**: In other words, be kind and generous to others if you expect others to help you.

26. **November 25, 1992**: Sometimes called "give-and-receive action."

27. **Book of Songs, Ode 64**: It is commonplace for people to give gifts with the intention of securing a favor in return. In such calculations, the gift and its return would be of roughly equal value. To return a gift of immensely greater value might burden the recipient with a feeling of indebtedness. This passage, however, describes an exchange of gifts with a purer motive: friendship that goes beyond the calculations of obligation.

28. **Maimonides, *Mishneh Torah***: A *mitzvah* is both a divine commandment and the blessing that accrues from fulfilling it.

29. **May 5, 1983**: Just as the giver of charity should not insult the recipient, the recipient of charity can learn to value the gift. Practicing this turns a moment of charity into a teaching moment. By valuing the gift as if it were from God, the recipient can align himself with God and receive blessings.

30. **Hebrews 13.1**: This refers to Abraham, who entertained angels at his home in Hebron (Genesis 18), and to Lot, who welcomed the angels into his house in Sodom (Genesis 19, below).

31. **Genesis 19.1-8**: Although the Bible identifies the two men as angels, we presume that Lot did not know it, but was treating them as he would any guest.

32. **February 5, 1984**: Found in the English text though absent in the Korean text; this sentence is probably authentic.

33. **May 5, 1983**: Rice cakes are an oriental dessert served on special occasions.

Chapter 14

1. August Kerber, *Quotable Quotes on Education* (Detroit: Wayne State University, 1968), p. 138.

2. **August 2, 1992**: Literally, "centering on Adam and Eve."

3. **August 22, 1995**: "Heart to love others": Korean, *shimjung*.

4. **March 17, 1957**: Luke 14.11.

5. **Antisthenes**: Antisthenes (c. 445-365 B.C.) was the founder of the Cynic school of Greek philosophy.

6. **November 1, 1957**: 'Abel-like,' i.e., with a better standard of faith.

7. **Avot 4.1**: Benjamin Franklin quoted this aphorism in the *Poor Richard's Almanack*.

8. **Deuteronomy 6.5-9**: This is a portion of the central text of the Torah (Deut. 6.4-9), known as the Shema. Devout Jews observe this commandment of teaching and study by reciting these verses three times a day at prayers and devoting many hours each weak to Torah study. In addition, it is the basis for ritual use of passages of the Torah wrapped inside the phylacteries worn on the forehead and the arm at times of prayer, and inside the *mezuzah* affixed to the doorframes of every home.

9. **Ramkali Siddha Goshti**: Veneration and reading of the Adi Granth, the Sikh scripture, is central to Sikh piety. Sikhism was originally founded on the model of guru-disciple, but from the decree of Gobind Singh, the tenth and last Guru, Sikhs have relied on Scripture as the embodiment of the guru's wisdom. Hence the Adi Granth is called the Guru Granth.

10. **February 14, 2000**: *Hoondokhwe* means "gathering for reading and learning." The Unification tradition is to gather every morning as a family and with neighbors to read selections from Father Moon's teachings, supplemented with words from other scriptures.

11. **Qur'an 3.7**: This verse distinguishes between verses that are plain, and verses that are ambiguous, or allegorical, and thus subject to a variety of interpretations. There is dispute among exegetes about whether there should be a period at this point (as translated here)—in which case only God knows the hidden meaning. Otherwise it states that "those who are firmly rooted in knowledge" know the hidden meaning. If the former is correct, then the Qur'an will ever be open to interpretation; but if the latter is correct, then the scholars (*ulama*) are the final authority on all meanings of the Qur'an.

12. **John 16.12-13**: Jesus only had three years to teach his disciples, and many truths of heaven were left unrevealed.

13. **Qur'an 13.38-40**: The 'Essence of the Book' is the fullness of truth known only to God; what is revealed in the Qur'an and in the previous scriptures may only be a part of this fulness of truth. How is Muhammad or any of the prophets, who are but mortals, to know?

14. **Avot 3.23**: Offerings and purity laws are God's commandments in scripture, while the sciences are knowledge of human devising.

15. **Maimonides, *Guide of the Perplexed***: For Maimonides, the proper arena for rational investigation concerns questions of philosophy. The limit concerned the commandments of the Law, the *halakhah*, that regulates Jewish life.

16. **Mumonkan 1**: 'Mu' means emptiness, but emptiness cannot be realized conceptually. Proper meditation requires complete denial of the intellect.

17. **1 Timothy 4.12-16**: The teaching positions in the church: bishop, priest, and deacon, are endowed in a ceremony of the laying of hands.

18. **Ibn Khaldun**: Philosopher and historian (1332 – 1406 A.D.), a founder of Arabic history, philosophy and social science.

19. **June 27, 1990**: This passage expresses Father Moon's doctrine of Three Subjects Thought, connecting the three roles of parent, teacher and owner. Here it is from the perspective of the teacher. See Chapter 21: *Exemplary Leadership*.

20. **Igala Proverb**: Only one with much life experience, who sees with the eye of wisdom, is qualified to instruct others.

21. **Analects 9.10**: Yen Hui was Confucius' favorite disciple, and he excelled all the others. Yet he more than anyone was aware of how far away he was from the standard of his master.

22. **Mumonkan 17**: The place of the teacher is important in Zen Buddhism, but straight imitation is not.
23. **Luke 5.37-38**: Since Jesus' words were challenging to the conventional wisdom, they could hardly be received by people bound to the traditions of the past.
24. **January 4, 1987**: 'True Mother' is the title of Father Moon's wife.
25. **James 1.22-24**: If a teaching is not put into practice, it may readily be forgotten. This frequently happens to sensitive people who receive spiritual revelations; if not acted upon they rapidly slip away.
26. **August 1, 1993**: Unity between mind and body is the standard of perfection; see Chapter 3: *Perfection*.
27. **August 1, 1993**: Vertical relationships are inter-generational with parents and grandparents; horizontal relationships are with peers.

CHAPTER 15

1. **Qur'an 2.130-36**: Islam takes its name from the word "surrender" (in Arabic, *islam*). As one who surrendered his will to God, Abraham's faith is exemplary for the Muslim, just as for the Jew and the Christian. Therefore Judaism, Christianity, and Islam are called the Abrahamic religions.
2. **Awakening of Faith in Mahayana**: This description of the four faiths includes faith in the traditional Three Treasures—the Buddha, the Dharma, and the Sangha—preceded by faith in the particularly Mahayanist teaching about the Absolute, or Suchness, which is all-inclusive, unconditional, transcendent, and immanent. This work, attributed to Ashvaghosha, is among the most highly regarded of Buddhist scriptures in China and is used by most of the major schools.
3. **Tannisho**: Shinran was the founder of the Jodo Shinshu school of Pure Land Buddhism in Japan. The teaching that sinners have an easier time being reborn in the Pure Land than do the righteous is linked to the Buddha's teaching of No-self (*anatta*). By throwing oneself entirely on the grace of the Buddha and accounting one's own accomplishments as nothing, there is no question of any attachment to self. A wicked person who repents completely accounts his self as nothing, but good people are more likely to have residual pride in their own virtues or attainments and hence are blocked from the goal.
4. **Makkot 23b-24a**: Judaism teaches that faith is the core and concrescence of the law—it does not accept Paul's characterization that the Law is opposed to faith. Like Paul in Galatians 3.2-11, above, this passage also quotes Habakkuk 2.4, but here it is interpreted to mean that 'the righteous shall *live* by his faith' and not merely profess it.
5. **Martin Luther King, Jr.**: *Where Do We Go from Here: Chaos or Community?* (New York: Harper and Row, 1967).
6. **July 29, 1973**: This applies to the level of an individual human being. There are, of course, greater hopes for one's family, nation and world to connect with God.
7. **Song of the Spring Breeze**: Father Moon used to sing this song while a prisoner in a North Korean labor camp, to express his hope for a bright future for his long-suffering nation.
8. **Chuang Tzu 23**: It is a well-known phenomenon that people who have faced death, imprisonment, or absolute disgrace sometimes rise above ordinary notions of good and evil and become people of profound wisdom.
9. **Chuang Tzu 19**: Based on this tradition, the drunken man who is so pliant that he can stagger about and always escape harm is a stock character in Chinese drama.
10. **One Hundred Poems on the Jeweled Spear**: Amaterasu the Sun Goddess is the chief Shinto deity; Toyouke-no-kami is the Food Goddess worshipped at the outer shrine of the temple at Ise; together with the clan ancestors (*ujigami*) they represent the productive forces of nature and humanity which provide our food.
11. **May 29, 1977**: This parable is found in Chapter 13: *Forgiveness*.
12. **Qur'an 3.102**: In Arabic the word for 'submission' is *islam*. See note 1, above.

13. **Isaiah 8.12-13**: The prophet Isaiah was accused of conspiracy for his harsh messages attacking the corrupt government and priesthood. Yet God tells him not to fear man's designs, but rather fear God.

14. **Qur'an 2.8-12**: "We are only peacemakers": these were the lukewarm Muslims of Medina who wanted to maintain their peaceful lives and a comfortable coexistence with the unbelievers, when Muhammad was calling the people to total commitment to the cause of Islam. They were hypocrites in professing Islam only for personal benefit.

15. **Qur'an 30.31-32**: The schismatic, by exalting in human opinions, is in effect joining other gods with God.

16. **Hadith of Bukhari**: This is from a description of the *Mi'raj*, Muhammad's Night Journey.

17. **Baba Metzia 59ab**: Rabbi Joshua's rebuke of the divine voice means that God has left the divine law in human hands and open to human interpretation regardless of what God might reveal about the matter—for who but human beings can judge whether a word purportedly from God truly is of God? The report of Elijah is based upon the tradition that, having been taken up to heaven in a whirlwind (2 Kings 2.11), he lives with God and enjoys his confidence.

18. **Job 1.6**: "Sons of God" refers to the angels, of which Satan is one.

19. **Ashvaghosha, Buddhacarita 13**: This account of the Buddha's temptation by Mara, the Buddhist Satan, is noteworthy because the Devil appears first as a Tempter who uses sweet infatuations before revealing his hostile form as a demon.

20. **October 13, 1957**: For the full passage, see Chapter 9: *Jesus*.

21. **Ramayana, Yuddha Kanda 118-20**: Rama's wife Sita had been kidnapped by Ravana and languished in his palace through ten long years of war as Rama battled to defeat Ravana and take her back. Although Sita had remained chaste while in captivity, Rama still was unwilling to take her back. Rama is God incarnate; why would he not know of her chastity and fidelity and accept her? The text says that he was swayed by the suspicions and scruples of the crowd, and that he momentarily doubted his true identity as Vishnu. Thus it was up to Sita herself to prove her innocence through an ordeal by fire.

22. **Qur'an 18.65-82**: This parable about Moses has no parallel in the Bible. The biblical Moses had a weakness of anger, but he was a patient man. Here Moses seeks out a teacher: tradition assigns him the name *al-Khidr*. He has such spiritual insight that he can see the reality behind appearances. For Moses, and all of us who lack such unusual powers of insight, the truth is hidden, and we make mistakes if we rely on our own judgment. Only through faith can we have insight into the true reality.

23. **Berakot 5a**: This passage explicates the proper attitude with which to face suffering based upon Isaiah 53.10, a verse from Isaiah's portrayal of the Suffering Servant.

Chapter 16

1. **Qur'an 2.186**: God is the one who is 'Close' to man. Close is one of the Ninety-nine Beautiful Names of God; see note 24.

2. **Lotus Sutra 25**: On the merits of worshipping the bodhisattva Kwan Yin (Skt. Avalokitesvara), see Chapter 7: *Help and Deliverance*.

3. **Qur'an 11.114**: These are the *salat*, the five obligatory prayers for every Muslim.

4. **Qur'an 114**: This is the concluding sura of the Qur'an.

5. **January 1, 1968**: The 'invisible enemy' is Satan, who is hidden behind our thoughts and actions unless we discern his presence.

6. **Mohandas K. Gandhi**: *Young India*, January 23, 1930.

7. **Mumonkan 1**: Zen stresses the immediacy of the experience of enlightenment, which is not dependent upon logical progression or reflection. It can only be realized through intense meditation. This passage describes what must be done to understand the koan, "Has a dog the Buddha Nature?"

8. **Samayika Patha** This is one of many recitations inwardly repeated during the layperson's meditation. Usually performed at dusk, when the day's activities have come to an end, the layperson sits in a yoga posture, asks forgiveness of all beings, puts his mind in a state of calm, and begins his meditation. This Jain practice allows laypeople a taste of the ascetic life.

9. **Chuang Tzu 15**: Ch'i (Qi) is the spiritual energy pervading all things. Taoist meditation called Chi Gong and martial arts such as T'ai-chi, employ physical exercises in order to cultivate the ch'i, unite with its flow, and harness its power, resulting in inner tranquility and spiritual vigor. In meditation controlling the ch'i begins with controlling the breath.

10. **Katha Upanishad 3.13**: Yoga is a process of absorption into Brahman. Sense activities and outward expression (words) should be stopped and attention drawn into the mind. Then the mind should be concentrated on the *buddhi*, or the highest spiritual faculty of the soul, the individualized Atman. This too should be submerged into the Great Self or Cosmic Mind, thereby losing all notions of separate individuality. Finally, this Great Self, which still knows itself, is to dissolve into the Absolute, the Peaceful Self which is devoid of any distinction or difference whatsoever.

11. **Katha Upanishad 4.1-2**: The 'Self within' is not the ego or personal self, but the divinity that transcends the individual self. Meditation fixes one's attention on this inner divine self by turning us away from the deceptive and transient phenomena of the world. This is the most fundamental statement of Upanishadic philosophy.

12. **Great Learning**: Confucian meditation, called Quiet Sitting, has as its aim neither to find the Self nor to empty the mind, but rather to make the mind level and receptive to knowledge. According to the school of Wang-yang Ming, investigation of outward reality should begin with the investigation of one's own mind.

13. **Majjhima Nikaya 1.55-63**: This teaches the distinctively Buddhist technique of meditation called the Four Arousings of Mindfulness.

14. **Meditation on Buddha Amitayus 9-11**: Meditating upon the Pure Land of Amitabha in the western direction through contemplating the setting sun was a popular practice in ancient Japan. The western gate of Shi-tenno-ji in Osaka was believed to be the gate to the Pure Land, and it is said that many followers gathered there at the spring and autumn equinoxes when the sun set directly through the gate. The meditation itself continues through sixteen stages, dwelling in turn upon the exquisite beauty of the Pure Land, the glory of the Buddha and the great Bodhisattvas, and the destinies of beings of various grades of character.

15. **February 2, 1975:** "Mind" in this context is the higher mind, the divine mind that lies at the core of the human spirit. This idea is similar to the Hindu distinction between the *atman*, the divine mind within, and the *jiva*, the individual soul. See passages from the Upanishads in Chapter 3, *Temple of God* and *Conscience and Inborn Goodness*.

16. **February 2, 1975:** This describes the force that draws people together for a common purpose or destiny, and not merely the chemistry that attracts people of the opposite sex.

17. **February 2, 1975:** This is Father Moon's unique contribution, bringing together the insights of monastic discipline and family life: the spiritual practice of meditation should connect with life in the world of people.

18. **Yasna 51.22:** This translation portrays an historical conception of the religion of Zarathustra which may differ from the monotheism of modern Parsees; here the Wise Lord Ahura Mazda is served by subordinate deities.

19. **Hadith of Muslim:** These words are spoken in the five obligatory daily prayers, called *salat* and in phrases which the Muslim continually repeats throughout the day. Each repetition (*rakat*) of the *salat* begins with the words, "God is most great," and ends with the words "Glory be to my Lord, the Most High." It includes a recitation of the opening sura of the Qur'an, which includes the words, "Praise be to God, Lord of the Worlds." The *Shahadah*, or declaration of faith, reads "There is no god but God, and Muhammad is His prophet."

20. **Katha Upanishad 1.2.15-16:** The Upanishads praise the mystic syllable OM, which is chanted at the beginning of all sacred discourse. See *Invocation*, Rig Veda 3.62.10 and note 4.

21. **Mandukya Upanishad:** Although OM is not pronounced 'AUM,' in Sanskrit the vowel O is a dipthong contracted from A-U. Hence the Upanishad can analyze OM as three letters A-U-M, investing them with mystical significance. The last non-element is the end of the sound, unutterable, fading away, merging with silence. Hence, uttering the mystic syllable OM corresponds with the movement of the soul from the external senses through successively deeper levels of being towards ultimate merging with the pure Self, which is Brahman.

22. **Nichiren:** Buddhist reformer in Japan (b. 1222) who set up these five words as the *Daimoku* chant; the words mean "Homage to the Lotus Sutra."

23. **Mahabharata**: Reciting a list of God's Thousand Names, each one an attribute of the divine, is a major form of Hindu devotion.

24. **Qur'an 59:22-24**: These are some of Allah's Ninety-nine Most Beautiful Names, each one drawn from the Qur'an.

25. **Grace of the Holy Garden:** Father Moon composed the hymns reprinted here in the early days of his ministry.

26. **May 1, 1975:** *Jeongseong* includes devotional acts such as prayers, prostrations, fasting and penances, as well as charity and service to others, all done with a sincere mind to love and serve God.

27. **Basavanna:** The chakora is a mythical bird who subsists on moonbeams. These birds are a common feature of Indic idyllic scenes and love poetry.

28. **Chandidasa:** The love between Radha and Krishna is emblematic of devotion to God in Vaishnava Hinduism. This devotional poem by the 15th-century Bengali poet Chandidasa is one of many songs of Radha's love for Krishna that are sung, often accompanied by dance, in devotion to the deity. In this song Radha expresses her undying love for Lord Krishna, but Krishna is an elusive lover who leaves her for another at the blink of an eye. As is customary, the poet adds his own signature line called a *bhanita*; in this poem Chandidasa identifies himself, a humble worshipper, entirely with Radha.

    Unificationists could thus interpret the long-suffering devotion of Radha to the inconstant deity as fulfilling an indemnity condition to restore God's long-suffering efforts to love treacherous humanity who betrayed Him in the Garden of Eden.

29. **Srimad Bhagavatam 10.3**: The last line from this account of an episode from the life of Krishna expresses an important truth: love is the one power which can control even the Almighty God.

30. **Song of Solomon 3.1-4:** This book, also called by its Hebrew name Song of Songs, is a collection of some 25 love songs such as might have been sung at weddings. Despite its secular origins, Song of Solomon has been prized by mystics as lyrically portraying the intimate experience of the soul's love for God. In Judaism it is often regarded as an expression of Israel's love for God, and Christians have similarly interpreted it this way based on the doctrine that the Church is the Bride of Christ.

31. **Vidyapati:** Radha expresses her undying love for Krishna in this Vaishnavite poem. Here the poet Vidyapati in his signature line echoes the opening line "As the mirror to my hand" that describes the couple's inseparable oneness. Yet Radha's questioning at the end shows that she is still far from comprehending the depth of their unity. She accents it by calling him Madhava, an epithet of Krishna normally used to evoke his power as a warrior god rather than a gentle lover. *Tambul* is a kind of red lipstick and *kohl* an eyeshadow.

32. **Mark 14.3-9**: The woman is elsewhere identified as Mary Magdalene; see Chapter 9: *Women of the Bible*.

33. **Ramayana:** Sita expresses her undying love for Rama. Since Rama is God incarnate, Sita's devotion is representative of every true devotee of the Lord.

34. **February 14, 1960**: Attendance in Korean culture begins with the way children care for their aged parents. It means to comfort their parents by caring for their needs, to carry on their life's work, and to achieve the dreams and goals they were unable to fulfill. Thus, attendance to God means far more than merely serving God; it means to share God's deepest heart and seek to comfort God by fulfilling the ideal of creation that was left unfulfilled due to the Fall.

35. **Psalm 24.3-6:** This psalm was sung in ancient Israel by pilgrims as they reached the Temple gates, where they would proclaim their qualifications to enter its holy precincts. The conditions

enumerated here correspond to the Ten Commandments.

36. **Oracle of Temmangu:** Here *makoto* is translated 'truth,' but it in fact connotes sincerity and inner coherence.

37. **Oracle of the Kami Hachiman:** This is one of the Oracles of the Three Shrines, printed on hanging scrolls and found hung in homes throughout Japan.

38. **Israel Baal Shem Tov:** The founder of Hassidic Judaism, his name is an epithet meaning 'Master of the Good Name.' This passage is from his last testament.

39. **Revelation 3.16**: This letter, sent to the wealthy church of Laodicea, complains that their lukewarm Christianity is nauseating. It is the antithesis of sincerity and purity of intention.

40. **Forty Hadith 1:** The 'migration' was the *hegira* of Muhammad and his faithful Companions from Mecca to Medina. Yet the point of this tradition is universally applicable.

41. **As-Sharani:** Shaikh 'Abdul Wahhab ibn Ahmad as-Sharani was a Sufi author, jurist and historian in 16th century Egypt.

42. **Rabi'a:** Rabi'a al-'Adawiyyah was the greatest woman saint of Islam; she lived in Iraq in the 8th century.

43. **January 5, 1999:** On 'Sincere devotion' (*jeongseong*), see note 26 above.

44. **Qur'an 22:36-37:** Animal sacrifice is a rite of the *hajj*, the pilgrimage to Mecca. Note that the inner purpose of the ritual sacrifice is not to satisfy God's hunger for flesh, as the pagans believed, but rather as a way for the worshipper to magnify and glorify God.

45. **Haggai 1.3-8:** This was the attitude of the Pilgrims, who when they arrived in America first built their church and school before providing for their own homes.

46. **Leviticus 27.30:** The tithe, giving ten percent of one's income, is established by this verse.

47. **Exodus 31.12-17:** Jews observe the Sabbath day on Saturday as a solemn day of rest, study, and worship. Most Christians observe the Lord's Day, Sunday, as the day of Sabbath rest and worship, commemorating that it was on a Sunday that Jesus rose from the dead, and that on Sundays the early Christians met and broke bread together to commemorate his resurrection.

48. **Zohar 1.48b:** In Jewish homes, the woman of the house lights the Sabbath candles on Friday nights to begin the Sabbath. She takes the primary role in the family-centered rituals of the holy day.

49. **Rig Veda 10.9.8:** Bathing in the Ganges is efficacious in washing away sins and receiving divine grace.

50. **March 1, 1991:** Holy water is sprinkled on couples at the holy wedding ceremony, baptizing them as they enter a Blessed marriage.

51. **Deuteronomy 16.16-17:** These were the three great pilgrimage festivals in ancient Israel, when throngs of people went up to Jerusalem to worship at the Temple. They are also known as the feasts of Passover, Pentecost and Tabernacles.

52. **Jeremiah 50.4-5:** This is a prophecy that Jews would one day offer prayers at the Western Wall, or the "Wailing Wall," in Jerusalem.

53. **Qur'an 22.26-29:** These verses sanction the hajj, the pilgrimage to Mecca, and describe some of its rites. The origin of the pilgrimage to Mecca, and the Kaaba that houses the sacred black stone, goes back to Abraham. The rites had been corrupted by the pagan Arabs, who installed their idols at the Kaaba, and only with Muhammad was the pilgrimage restored to its original purpose: to magnify the One God. To journey to Mecca in one's lifetime is a religious aspiration for all Muslims.

54. **Kojiki 39.2-3:** These three sacred symbols of Shinto are in the possession of the emperor of Japan. But the mirror, a copy of which is placed at the center of Shinto altars, is especially significant. Besides being a symbol of the sun, it represents the goddess within. The reflection of the self is the reflection of goddess.

55. **Shiva Purana:** *Puja* is the rite of image worship with its many ceremonies. It is the chief style of worship in popular Hinduism. This passage is an extract from a lengthy discussion of the worship of Shiva as represented by the *lingam*. The lingam is a stylized phallus, and its base, a vulva. Nevertheless, these symbols are devoid of any connotation of sexual license; they symbolize the cosmic unity of male and female principles. They have taken on an abstract and aniconic character,

in contrast to the images of gods and goddesses that adorn much Hindu worship.

56. **Deuteronomy 14.3-21:** These commandments are the basis for the Jewish dietary laws, determining what foods are kosher. The injunction not to 'boil a kid in its mother's milk' became the basis for the law that milk and meat shall not be eaten at the same meal, or from the same dishes, or prepared in the same sink.

57. **Tanhuma Leviticus, Shemini 15b:** The rabbis knew that the ritual commandments of scripture are often arbitrary; not only were they ridiculed by educated Gentiles, but many Jews themselves found them uncomfortable. This text gives a functional meaning to rituals such as the dietary laws. The commandments have no intrinsic value in themselves, but only as a means for people to prove their sincerity towards God, to discipline and purify themselves, and to make a condition by which God can justify them.

58. **Qur'an 2.173:** The Muslim dietary laws, or laws of *halal*, resemble the Jewish kosher laws in prohibiting eating pig's flesh. However, the Qur'an is not absolute about it, allowing for exceptional situations when no halal food is available.

59. **Hitachi Fudoki:** The Fudoki are gazetteers first prepared at the order of Empress Genmei (c. 715 A.D.) to record local traditions and legends.

60. **Sutra of Hui Neng 6:** Offerings made from a desire to earn a place in heaven are tainted by selfishness; hence they still produce karma and cannot bring about lasting liberation. Their efficacy is at best temporary. Liberation comes only through internal spiritual practice to purify the mind.

61. **Bhagavad-Gita 2.42-44:** These Hindu verses have much the same sentiment as the preceding Buddhist passage.

62. **Anguttara Nikaya 4.41-45:** Zoroastrianism and Jainism similarly opposed the ritual slaughter of animals as practiced by the Vedic Aryans in ancient times. See Chapter 4, note 12.

63. **Jeremiah 7.21-24:** The essence of Israel's covenant with God was not in the sacrificial system, but in obedience to God's commandments. This radical pronouncement denies that Temple sacrifices were even part of the original Mosaic Covenant.

64. **Menahot 110a:** Judaism regards the fruit of Torah study as a holiness equivalent to the fruit of Temple sacrifice, which had become impossible after the Temple's destruction in 70 C.E.

65. **Satapatha Brahmana 11.5.6.1-3:** This text shows the progressive spiritualization of sacrifice in Hinduism. Since Brahman is higher than the gods, the sacrifice to Brahman, namely study and realization of truth, is more essential to religion than offerings of fire and animals to the gods. Similarly, feeding animals and acts of charity which are done daily in ordinary life are regarded as holy sacrifices. Animal sacrifice long ago disappeared from Hindu worship, as it did from Jewish worship.

66. *Exposition of the Divine Principle,* **Moses and Jesus 2.1.1.2:** Moses established conditions of faith through prayer and fasting 40 days, and through honoring God's Word received on Mount Sinai, not through animal sacrifices. The sacrificial system in the Old Testament was instituted for the sake of the Israelites who were not at Moses' level. (See Jeremiah 7.21-24, above) The secondary nature of the sacrificial system even in the days of the Temple allowed it to be readily supplanted in Judaism when the Temple was no more.

Chapter 17

1. **Qur'an 4.64-69:** This refers to the citizens of Medina, many of whom were reluctant to submit to Muhammad's authority, first in accepting his legal judgments, and ultimately in obeying his call to fight for the defense of Medina. Obedience to God's Will is the mark of a sincere believer.

2. **Matthew 16.24-25:** Central to Jesus' message, this saying describes the essence of Christian discipleship. Each person should 'take up his cross,' enduring suffering and all difficulties for the sake of others, just as Jesus offered himself on the cross for the salvation of all humankind.

3. See also Chapter 22: *The Futility of War.*
4. **Lotus Sutra 13**: This stanza, called the *Kanji-hon*, gave inspiration and fortitude to Nichiren, Japan's leading champion of the Lotus Sutra, when he was exiled and persecuted by the leaders of rival Buddhist schools for his dedication to spreading its message.
5. **Hadith of Muslim**: This hadith recommends *jihad*, struggle on the way to God. The meaning of such struggles for God lies not in the killing of others, but in offering one's own life to defend true religion.
6. **Berakot 20a**: The sanctification of God's Name is to suffer martyrdom with the Jewish confession of faith, the Shema, on the lips. See Chapter 1: *The One God.*
7. **Martin Luther King, Jr.,** On learning of threats on his life, St. Augustine, Florida, June 5, 1964.

Chapter 18

1. **Dov Baer of Mezirech:** This Hassidic rabbi expresses the concept of God's exile, born out of the Jewish experience of exile. Thus did the Jews cling to God in the midst of their wandering and sometimes grinding poverty.
2. **Matthew 18.1-3**: Christians do not take this text to mean that the original nature of man is innocent. Rather, the child exemplifies an attitude of simplicity and innocence by which one can easily accept the gospel.
3. **Tao Te Ching 28**: The 'Uncarved Block' is the state of primitive simplicity without any pretense or artificiality. It can also mean the purity of one's original nature.
4. **Matthew 5.38**: In Jesus' day, when Judea was under Roman occupation, Roman soldiers used to commandeer civilians whom they met on the road and require them to carry their cloaks and supplies for one mile.
5. **Romans 12.19-20**: In Qur'an 5.27-32, Abel refused to strike back when Cain sought to kill him for fear of God and divine punishment; and he recognized that Cain would ultimately be the loser for killing him.
6. **October 4, 1976**: Father Moon teaches the Cain/Abel paradigm not as a basis of judgment, but as a path to restore fractured brotherhood. The religious people whom God has blessed take the role of Abel, while the secular people who do not know God and may have grudges against religion are in the role of Cain. Yet these Cain people have many worldly capabilities that religious people may lack. The responsibility of religious people is to embrace their secular brothers and raise them up so that united, they can build a godly and prosperous society. Otherwise, they are likely to be victims of Cain's anti-religious attitudes.
7. **Matthew 3.2**: The Kingdom of Heaven is 'at hand' not only in the eschatological sense that the time of the Messiah has drawn near—as was the case in Jesus' day. The Kingdom of Heaven is also at hand for each person as he prepares himself for it.
8. **I Ching, Great Commentary 1.3.4**: The 'borderline' refers to one's scruples about what is good and what is evil. An educated conscience is a prerequisite to repentance.
9. **Isaiah 64.6**: This passage was originally a complaint by certain Israelites that they were being shunned by society despite their faithfulness to God. But in time it came to be understood as an exclamation of the worthlessness of worldly fame or knowledge as mere pretense in the presence of the divine majesty.
10. **Shinran**: Shinran (1173-1262) honestly looked into his own mind and recognized the power of evil within. He realized, contrary to the teachings of Zen Buddhism, that even the most determined saint cannot attain salvation through dependence on his or her own mind. Rather, salvation is possible only through the Power of Another—the Original Vow of Buddha Amitabha to save all sentient beings. He became the foremost proponent of Pure Land Buddhism, which teaches a form of salvation by faith.
11. **Jonah 3.3-10**: As a lesson on repentance, the story of Jonah is recited by Jews on the Day of Atonement, the day for repenting for sins. Yet the story contains an irony, for Jonah himself was unhappy that Nineveh, the capital city of Israel's most hated enemies, had heeded his message

and repented. He would rather that they had ignored him, that God might have destroyed it. Thus God sets up for Jonah a lesson about self-righteousness.

12. **Avot 2.5**: A saying of Hillel.

13. **John 8.2-11**: According to tradition, Jesus wrote on the ground the sins of each accuser.

14. **Mumonkan 46**: The issue is grasping and dependence upon the body and sense experience, and fear of going beyond its limits.

15. **Precious Garland 149-57**: Gautama Buddha himself came to such a realization about the body's loathsomeness one evening when his father tempted him with courtesans in an effort to keep him from leaving home and beginning his spiritual quest. This is an excerpt from a meditation about bodies in general, and is not intended to denigrate women.

16. **Akkamahadevi, Vacana 33**: Akkamahadevi was a twelfth-century Virashaiva saint. Once, when a certain king tried to molest her, she suddenly threw away all her clothes and stepped out into the streets nude. This act of purity so stunned the king that he repented of his foolish lust. Akkamahadevi wandered about as a naked ascetic, clad only in her long hair, enduring the taunts of the men and teaching an example of purity and devotion to God Shiva.

17. **Avot 4.1**: Quoted by Benjamin Franklin in *Poor Richard's Almanack*.

18. **Socrates**: from Diogenes Laertius, *Lives of Eminent Philosophers* II.32.

19. **January 12, 2001**: These words were spoken at the time when all Unification Church members were asked to do a burning ceremony, offering some precious item symbolizing all their possessions. Father Moon set the example by giving away thousands of his personal items to his followers.

20. **Qur'an 66.11**: Pharaoh's wife, whose name was 'Asiya, is one of the great women of the Islamic tradition, alongside Mary the mother of Jesus and Khadija, Muhammad's first wife. She is said to have spared the life of the infant Moses and arranged to have him raised in the Palace by his mother. Her victory was to remain devout in the midst of the corruptions and pressures of life in the wicked Pharaoh's palace. In the Bible's account, Moses' rescuer was Pharaoh's daughter.

21. **Tao Te Ching 52**: The nature of the world should be understood from the vantage point of knowledge of Ultimate Reality, the Tao. Then it will be seen that things of the world change naturally, in accordance with the Tao. This leads to the concept of *wu-wei*, non-action, which is to let the Tao operate and not to meddle with things according to human ambitions.

22. **October 4, 1969**: Adam and Eve fell through an illicit relationship with the archangel Lucifer, and hence their offspring are of the archangel's lineage. Adam and Eve began their family after they had been expelled from the Garden of Eden, which signifies that their marriage was not blessed by God. See Chapter 6: *The Human Fall*.

23. **November 7, 1971**: Religions are "in the archangelic realm" because they are dealing with fallen human beings who are of the lineage of the fallen archangel. Through religious practices of charity, humility, service and asceticism, religious people are elevated to the standard of the good archangels who dwell in heaven with God. Yet even the good archangels, such as Gabriel and Michael, do not have spouses.

24. **Bhagavad-Gita 17.5-6**: People given to extreme asceticism are sometimes harsh and even cruel, demanding of others the same unbending strictness that they require of themselves. This can be understood in the Principle from the fact that ascetics are living on the path to restore the archangel; see November 7, 1971, above.

25. **Mahabharata 1.220**: The juxtaposition of asceticism and procreation as incompatible yet necessary goods is typical of Hindu thought. On the kinds of indebtedness, see Satapatha Brahmana 1.7.2.1-5, in Chapter 15: *Gratitude and Indebtedness*.

26. **Qur'an 57.27**: Muslim commentators note that the Qur'an approves of the asceticism and humility enjoined by the gospels: see Qur'an 5.82. But cloistered forms of monasticism are rejected, as they take believers out of the world while they should be mingling with others and upholding the Truth through service and example. Furthermore, in Muhammad's day many Christian monks and priests were caught up in bitter doctrinal disputes and mutual strife, scandals that reflected badly on their faith.

CHAPTER 19

1. **Doctrine of the Mean 20.8**: These are the Confucian Five Relations, or Five Bonds, which define human life. Maintaining proper ethics in these five types of relationships is the measure of one's humanity. Three of the five concern relationships in the family. They are further explicated in the next passage.

2. **Atharva Veda 3.30**: This hymn sets forth the ideal of the Hindu family.

3. **November 10, 1969**: The way of filial piety that begins in the family naturally extends to patriotism on the national level, love for humanity on the world level, to finally reach the universal level of a son or daughter of God. See *Invocation*, The Family Pledge, clause 2.

4. **2 Samuel 1.26**: David spoke these words in an elegy to Saul and Jonathan after they were killed in battle. Their friendship was so strong that Jonathan had more than once saved David's life.

5. **Nupe Proverb**: Good friends should share each other's feelings.

6. **Akan Proverb**: Doing good to each other is the basis of friendship.

7. **Song of Solomon 1.2-4**: Christians and Jews understand these verses as extolling the pure love of the soul for God as well as the genuine and faithful love of a believer for his or her spouse.

8. **Rig Veda 10.85.35-47**: This is the traditional Hindu marriage vow and blessings. The bride is Surya, daughter of the solar deity Savitri; she is the prototype of all brides. 'Her husband the eleventh' means the wife will mother her husband in his old age; 'queen' describes the wife's status as head of the household.

9. **Book of Songs, Ode 1**: This ode begins by describing a lover's anxiety as he awaits his bride, and ends with the joy of friends and family at their wedding. Many interpret the ode as describing the bride's virtue, as shown by her modest disposition and retiring manner. The sound of male and female ospreys answering each other at a distance alludes to the distance between the lovers; the soft duckweed gathered and presented as an offering alludes to their union. Confucius cites this ode in the Analects (3.20) as a model of restrained pleasure, of joy not carried to extremes.

10. **February 18, 1971**: Some of Father Moon's teachings on marriage are particularly applicable to couples whose marriages were arranged, who do not start with romantic attraction. Nevertheless, even marriages that start romantically will cool, exposing undesirable traits in a spouse.

11. **Genesis 2.18-24**: These verses give divine sanction to marriage. Jesus used them to declare that divorce was not acceptable to God—see Mark 10.2-12.

12. **Zohar 1.50a**: The "Mother" is the *Shekinah*, the indwelling presence of God as the Holy Spirit.

13. **Zohar 3.104b**: The image (*tselem*) is the astral body. It contains the divine spirit given by God at conception, and impresses its shape on the features of the physical body of the child. According to many Kabbalists, the holiness or baseness of the *tselem* differs according to whether the couple is of the Jewish people; in other words, it depends upon the couple's ancestry.

14. **Raga Suhi:** These verses are part of the Sikh wedding ceremony.

15. **Ketubot 8a**: These six benedictions are recited at Jewish weddings. The 'building' refers to the creation of Eve from Adam's rib as well as the household of the family. The reference to God as the Creator of humankind denotes that marriage is God's design for the perpetuation of the human race, which began with the blessing to Adam and Eve in Eden. The last benediction connects the joy of the newlyweds with the eschatological joy at the fulfillment of God's kingdom in Jerusalem. Bridal 'canopies' are used at all Jewish weddings.

16. **Doctrine and Covenants 131.1-3, 132.19**: Latter-day Saints of pure faith who are members of the priesthood may enter into Temple Marriage, which establishes an eternal, indissoluble bond.

17. **February 1, 1994**: In other words, our minds would be entirely upright and connect with God's love; our bodies would relate freely with all people without partiality or discrimination, likes or dislikes.

18. **Blessing and Ideal Family 7.3.3**: Father Moon is speaking to single members where men and women alike have been active in public missions, either in the church or in business.

19. **Hadith of Abu Dawud**: The Islamic law on divorce is found in Qur'an 2.226-32. There a waiting period of four months is prescribed, to allow the decision to be reconsidered.

20. **Qur'an 58.1-2**: This verse was uttered after Khaulah bint Tha'laba, wife of Aus ibn Samit, brought her complaint to the Prophet that her husband had divorced her by the traditional Arab custom of *zihar*, saying, "You are to me as my mother's back." This custom degraded women, for it freed the husband from his conjugal duties and child support yet forbade the woman from leaving him to seek a second marriage. The Prophet at first demurred, but then received this revelation upholding her rights. This is not a passage opposing divorce per se, but rather one that upholds the rights of women to seek redress in situations of injustice.

21. **Laws of Manu 9.95, 101**: Divorce is permitted, but it is not done by virtuous people. According to other verses in the Laws (9.76-81), a man may divorce his wife on the grounds of adultery, profligacy, procuring an abortion, drunkenness, malicious speech, or failure to produce a male heir. A woman may divorce her husband if he becomes a religious ascetic, is impotent, is expelled from his caste, or is long absent. A waiting period of one to eight years is normally required.

22. **Book of Songs, Ode 45**: The Chinese have always considered the refusal of a widow to marry again to show her great virtue. This poem was composed by Kung Chiang, the widow of the prince Kung-po of Wei, protesting when her mother tried to force her into a second marriage.

23. **October 23, 1977**: 미래의 주인공, "Owners of the Future," p. 11.

24. **Qur'an 4.129**: The Qur'an permits a man to support as many as four wives, but this was expressly a concession in time of war, when many widows and orphans needed to be supported (Qur'an 4.3). This verse declares that monogamy is the only equitable arrangement.

25. **Yoruba Proverb**: Children are a man's protection and a measure of his prosperity; moreover, a man can be assessed by the character of his children.

26. **May 7, 1971**: True Mother is the title of Father Moon's wife, Dr. Hak Ja Han Moon.

27. **Nupe Proverb**: In other words, you must train a child from infancy when his character is pliable; as an adult his character is already set.

28. **January 1, 1989**: In Asian families, good daughters-in-law are expected to serve their husband's parents and bear with their constant criticism without complaint. Many find the burden of keeping them hard to bear.

Chapter 20

1. **May 11, 1969**: These words were spoken in a year when student unrest was sweeping the world, including Korea.

2. **Eleanor Roosevelt**: Former First Lady of the United States and wife of Franklin Delano Roosevelt.

3. **February 15, 1959**: These words were spoken in Korea only a few years after that land had been ravaged by a bitter civil war.

4. **January 22, 2000**: To 'attend God' means to understand God's suffering and to comfort God by alleviating human sin and misery wherever it may be. It means to understand and participate in God's latter-day Providence for the salvation of the entire world.

5. **John Fitzgerald Kennedy**: Inaugural address as President of the United States, January 20, 1961.

6. **Nathan Hale**: Hale, an American patriot, spoke these his last words as he was about to be hanged as a spy, September 22, 1776.

7. **Tan Shim Ga**: This fourteenth-century Korean poem about pledging loyalty to one's lord has been adopted as a Unification Church holy song pledging loyalty to God.

8. **Marcus Tullius Cicero**: Second Philippic Oration.

9. **Patrick Henry**: American patriot, from a speech in 1775 advocating independence from England.

10. **Winston Churchill**: Former Prime Minister of Great Britain, in a speech to the House of Commons at the start of the Battle of Britain, June 18, 1940.

11. **April 17, 1988**: Father Moon himself was exiled from his homeland in North Korea and spent

more than forty years working for the opportunity to return, which he did in 1991.

12. **Abot 3.2**: This is not a mild platitude but a deliberate choice in the midst of a controversy over how to regard the Roman empire, which was severely oppressing the Jews under its control. Jews who chafed under Roman rule were calling for rebellion, which when it came was disastrous; the Jewish War (68-70 C.E.) ended with the destruction of the Temple, and later the Bar Kochba rebellion (132-134 C.E.) would be brutally crushed. But the rabbis whose words were compiled in the Mishnah called for resignation to Roman rule.

13. **January 1, 1991**: The 'Three Subjects Thought' refers to the three-fold responsibilities of leadership: to be a true parent, a true teacher and a true owner. By fulfilling public responsibilities with this three-fold ethic, we take after the nature of God. See Chapter 21: *Exemplary Leadership*.

14. **Hadith of al-Soyouti**: al-Durr al-Manthoor 523.25.

15. **August 14, 2000**: Lit.: absolute partner.

16. **Leviticus 25.10**: This well-known passage, which is carved on America's Liberty Bell, was originally a proclamation of the Jubilee Year, once every fifty years, in ancient Israel. At the jubilee, all debts were forgiven, all Hebrew slaves freed, all leases expired, and all property returned to its original owners. For the larger passage, see below, *Economic Justice*.

17. **Isaiah 61.1-2**: Jesus quoted these words as he began his ministry in Galilee, signifying his mission to establish God's Kingdom, a state of universal freedom.

18. **Chief Oren Lyons**: Address to the United Nations opening The Year of the Indigenous Peoples, December 10, 1992.

19. **Clarence Darrow**: American lawyer and champion of civil liberties. From his brief in *People v. Lloyd*, 1920.

20. **Ofudesaki 13.43-45**: All mankind—the wealthy (on high mountains) and the poor (in the valleys)—emanated from one point, 'this origin': their common ancestor that was formed by God the Parent at the shrine at Tenri, navel of the world.

21. **Dhammapada 396**: The Buddha gave new, spiritual definitions to Hindu racial and caste terms like Aryan and Brahmin. An Aryan is not a member of a light-skinned race, but one who follows the Aryan Eightfold Path. A Brahmin is not a member of a privileged caste, but one who attains the stage of arahant.

22. **Amos 9.7**: The prophet Amos warns Israel not to be overly proud of its position as God's chosen people. God has been working to save even Israel's worst enemies, the Philistines and the Syrians.

23. **Rig Veda 8.51.9**: Aryans who form the highest caste have light skins, while outcastes are a dark-skinned people.

24. **W.E.B. Du Bois**: *The Souls of Black Folk* (Chicago, 1903).

25. **Publius Syrus**: A Roman slave who wrote moral aphorisms.

26. **Muhammad Ahmad al-Maula**: Umar bin al-Khattab was an early convert to Islam, having formerly persecuted the new sect. He became a close follower of Muhammad and after his death became the second Caliph. This is an old tradition retold by Muhammad Ahmad Jaad Al-Maoulah, an Egyptian author and scholar (1883-1994).

27. **Abraham Lincoln**: Speech in Peoria, Illinois, 1854.

28. **May 1, 1977**: This passage from the English edition of *God's Will and the World* is missing from the Korean text. A search discovered its presence on the original tape, and it was retranslated.

29. **Sioux Tradition of the Sacred Pipe**: Wakan Tanka is the Lakota name for the high God or Great Spirit.

30. **Holy Teaching of Vimalakirti 7**: The point of this story is not that in this world there should be equality among the sexes. Rather, Buddhism teaches that sexual differentiation belongs only to the phenomenal sphere, which is transient and illusory. In Reality, beyond all appearances, sexuality is transcended. A similar story is found in chapter 12 of the Lotus Sutra, where the daughter of a dragon king transforms herself into the form of a man to attain Buddhahood, thereby showing Shariputra that he should not regard a woman to be a 'filthy vessel' incapable of receiving the Law.

31. **Genesis 3.12-16**: As a result of the Human Fall, Eve came under the dominion of two male beings: first the archangel (the serpent), and then her husband.

32. **Ambrose of Milan**: Ambrose takes the opposite lesson from the story of the Fall, that from the time Eve tempted Adam women have been dangerous temptresses. Therefore, men should never allow themselves to be dominated by women.

33. **1 Corinthians 11.3-11**: "Because of the angels": Most likely Paul was conceiving of angels as present at worship and guarding its holy order. However, one can also infer by this a connection to the Fall, where the woman came under the dominion of an angel.

34. **Pope John Paul II**: to Synod of Bishops; Rome, October 25, 1980.

35. **1 Corinthians 11.11-12**: For more reflections on the meaning of woman created from Adam's rib, see Chapter 19: *Ethics of Married Life*.

36. **January 1, 1982**: Father and Mother Moon practice this dictum. Following his many worldwide speaking tours, beginning in the 1990s Father Moon encouraged his wife to embark on her own speaking tours, while he shared her experience over a satellite link-up.

37. **Qur'an 4.135**: Islam does not value expediency or the competing goods of loyalty to family and kindred as highly as it values honesty.

38. **Edmund Burke**: Burke, a British statesman, supported the American colonies' struggle for independence and helped the British accept their independence. However, this champion of liberty wrote against the French Revolution, because he could foresee its excesses and totalitarian tendencies. Considered the father of 18th-century liberalism, what is now called conservatism, he left many notable aphorisms.

39. **Alexander Solzhenitsyn**: Russian author, who during the Soviet era who served as Russia's conscience, exposing through his books the horrors of communist slave-labor camps, known as the Gulag.

40. **Analects 14.36**: This and the following passage dispute the notion that to love your enemy always means to do kindness, if that would not uphold justice. Confucius is here disputing the proverb from Tao Te Ching 63 (see Chapter 13: *Love Your Enemy*). Yet Confucius also praises the ideal of universal benevolence in Analects 4.3-4 (see Chapter 13: *Universal Love*). Apparently, even though a man may like an evildoer and want to help him, sometimes doing him a kindness will not be helpful; particularly if that 'kindness' only encourages him to do more evil. Tougher measures may be appropriate, but these too should be motivated by genuine love—out of concern for the wrongdoer's welfare.

41. **Frederick Douglass**: The foremost African-American abolitionist, whose lectures against slavery both in the United States and Europe in the 1830s through the 1850s helped turn public opinion against that evil institution.

42. **William Booth**: Inscribed at the entrance of the Salvation Army's office in New York City. Booth was the founder of the Salvation Army.

43. **Qur'an 5.38**: Most schools of Islamic jurisprudence no longer employ this punishment, and those that do restrict it to the most serious cases of grand larceny.

44. **Derek Eretz Zuta 2.5**: Even one's own possessions are 'not yours' because they belong to God; we have been given them as a trust.

45. **Deuteronomy 15.1-5**: The biblical institution of the Sabbatical year granted a reprieve to the poor through a periodic forgiveness of debts.

46. **Leviticus 25.10-43**: In ancient Israel every fiftieth year was a Jubilee Year. In that year all debts were forgiven, all Hebrew slaves freed, all leases expired, and all property returned to its original owners. This practice was based upon the premise that the land belongs to God, to be granted to the clans and families of Israel in perpetuity; it is not private property to be bought and sold. It prevented the impoverishment of poor farmers by wealthy creditors.

47. **Mencius III.A.3**: When a piece of land is divided into 9 parts, it looks like *jing* (井) which is the Chinese character for the word "well." Hence the system is known as "well-fields." Note that this method of taxation based upon a fixed share of the year's crops is more humane than taxation set as a fixed amount, which farmers might have trouble raising in years of crop failure—a problem faced by modern farmers indebted to banks for whom a few bad harvests can result in bankruptcy.

48. **Francis Bacon:** *Essays, Civil and Moral 41.* This statement is made within a discussion of usury, which tends to enrich the banks at the expense of working people.

49. **Qur'an 9.60:** This verse enumerates those who should receive obligatory charity (*zakat*), a regular percentage of a Muslim's income. It includes supporting those who administer the charity, as well as debtors, prisoners and "those whose hearts have been reconciled"—new converts to the faith who suffer economic loss from having lost their livelihood because their former associates were opposed to their conversion. See Qur'an 2.267-73 in Chapter 13: *Charity*.

50. **January 13, 2001:** Literally "shareholders should form a shareholders' union." The passage's description of shareholders as active participants in the company is fitting to South Korean society, where most companies are private or closely held by family members who are the major shareholders and actively manage the company. Since this would not apply to investors in a publicly-traded company, e.g. people who have no role in the day-to-day operation of the company and simply own some common stock, we have used the term "owners."

51. **Abraham Lincoln:** Speech at New Haven, Connecticut, March 6, 1860

52. **Pope Pius IX:** Declaration of September 11, 1846.

53. **Pope Pius XI, Quadragesimo Anno:** 'Socialism' here means Democratic Socialism, a moderate left-wing political movement that has always opposed Communism for its violent and totalitarian characteristics. Communists, for their part, opposed the socialists for the gains they provided the working class through the democratic process, which lessened their revolutionary fervor.

54. Even the janitor: See Chapter 20: *Labor*.

55. **Qur'an 3.103-05:** God is one unity, and humankind should similarly be united; this reconciliation comes through submission to God. The unity of God, the unity of spirit and body within the individual, the unity of society, and the ideal unity of all reality, are encompassed in the Islamic concept of *tawhid*.

56. **Benjamin Franklin:** At the signing of the Declaration of Independence, July 4, 1776

57. **Abraham Lincoln:** "A House Divided" speech, Springfield, Illinois, June 16, 1858.

58. **Martin Niemöller:** There are many versions of this well-known poem; including several that begin, "When Hitler attacked the Jews...the Catholics..." This version is probably more authentic to Pastor Niemöller's writing during the Nazi era; it is taken from the Wikipedia.

59. **Tekanawita:** Tekanawita (c. 1450), better known as Hiawatha, was the legendary chief who unified the Five Nations of the Iroquois. The Iroquois League became the most prosperous and powerful of the Native American nations in what is now the eastern United States.

60. **Njak Proverb:** Dependent, unsuccessful relatives and friends are still part of the community to be protected.

61. **Socrates:** According to Plutarch, *On Banishment*.

62. **May 8, 1994:** This is from Father Moon's explanation of the fourth clause of the Family Pledge (see *Invocation*).

63. **July 18, 1997:** In Korean, this speech is dated May 3, 1997.

Chapter 21

1. **2 Samuel 23.3-4:** These words were spoken by King David; they were a fitting motto for his leadership of Israel.

2. **Book of Songs, Ode 254:** The rulers of China owed their leadership to the Mandate of Heaven. If Heaven showed displeasure at a ruler by sending down calamities, it meant that he and sometimes even his dynasty had forfeited the Mandate and could justly be replaced.

3. **Thomas Jefferson:** from a letter to Dr. Benjamin Rush, September 23, 1800.

4. **Nahjul Balagha, Sermon 38:** Ali speaks of his mission as Caliph as carrying forward the work of the Prophet Muhammad.

5. **Analects 12.11**: This passage gives the Confucian doctrine of Rectification of Names. In other words, an office-holder is obligated to live up to the moral standards of his office.
6. **Book of History 4.8.1-3**: In the Confucian relation between prince and minister, the able minister serves his lord with good, honest advice and covers for his shortcomings. The prince, in turn, should be attentive and accepting of his minister's wise counsel. King Wu Ting is thought to have reigned around 1323 B.C.
7. **Way of God's Will 1.3**: 'Abel's position': that loyal subordinate will someday become the leader himself.
8. **March 12, 1978**: These correspond to the three laws in the Constitution of the Kingdom of Heaven; see Chapter 2: *The Ten Commandments*. 'Violating the Principle' is a euphemism for adultery or any sexual transgression.
9. **Analects 2.3**: Confucius believed in the educational value of ceremony, particularly as when the ruler observed the rites, he was demonstrating his own standard of obedience and reverence to Heaven.
10. **Great Learning 9.1**: For more on the family as the foundation and training-ground for leadership, see Chapter 19, *The Basic Form of Life*.
11. For more critiques of democracy, see Chapter 20: *Freedom*.
12. **Winston Churchill**: Speech to the House of Commons, May 13, 1940.
13. **Emma Lazarus**: This poem, "The New Colossus," (1883) is inscribed on the base of the Statue of Liberty, which has stood in New York harbor and welcomed millions of immigrants to America.
14. **June 24, 2000**: This passage implies that the government will facilitate ways for the wealthy to provide assistance for the people on the bottom. The mechanism will operate smoothly when people live by the ethic of "living for the sake of others" in a society that honors philanthropy and service. Father Moon does not specify the administrative mechanism, which could be through job assistance, wage equalization, public assistance, non-profit charities, provisions in the tax code, or other means.
15. **The Code of Hammurabi**: Hammurabi, who ruled Babylon in the 17th century B.C., promulgated one of the oldest law-codes in existence. Although the body of the code is a compilation of customary law, the prologue, from whence this verse was taken, attributes justice to will of the gods. Marduk was patron deity of Babylon.
16. **Golden Light Sutra 12**: To "show the results of karma" means, first, that the people know they will reap the consequences of the crimes, and second, that because criminals are punished for their deeds in this life it leaves them less demerit to burden their next life.
17. **May 1, 1982**: Father Moon spoke these words while he was on trial for trumped-up tax charges, for which he would later go to prison.
18. **Qur'an 1.178**: This is the governing Qur'anic legal principle regarding the punishment for murder. The Qur'an mitigated the pre-Islamic custom of the blood feud, where retaliation for a single murder could lead to indiscriminate slaughter. Punishment must be proportionate to the crime: a life for a life. But the wishes of the victim's family could mitigate the punishment. The categories of freeman, slave and woman fit the tribal society of Muhammad's day where if the murderer could not be found justice would be carried out by an act of retaliation.
19. **May 17, 2003**: Since the mid 1990s, wilderness therapy programs and wilderness boot camps have become popular alternatives for reforming juvenile delinquents. Wilderness therapy programs in particular let adolescents experience the force of nature as their teacher under the mentoring of wilderness guides, rather than using regimentation and restraint to effect rehabilitation.
20. **Ezekiel 3.16-19**: God holds His prophet responsible to give the people timely warning, just as a watchman on the city wall was responsible to warn the defenders of an approaching army.
21. **Martin Luther**: Speech at the Diet of Worms, Germany, April 18, 1521.
22. **August 27, 1991**: This is another statement of the mind-body principle that is the basis of Father Moon's prescription for good governance in the modern world, as requiring cooperation of religious and political leaders. See Chapter 22: *World Peace*.

23. **2 Samuel 12.1-10:** David first tried to conceal his adultery with Bathsheba by urging her husband Uriah to go home and sleep with his wife to allay any suspicions about who was the child's father. When that failed—Uriah was too much the proud and loyal soldier to enjoy civilian pursuits during wartime—David sent Uriah into the thick of battle and had the troops draw back so he would be exposed and killed. Thereupon follows the prophet Nathan's famous parable.

24. **Amos 7:10-17:** In this autobiographical passage, the high priest accuses the prophet Amos of treason; then he goes to Amos and warns him to flee. He says, 'Eat bread there,' accusing Amos of being a prophet for hire. Amos replies, 'I am no prophet' to state that he is not a professional prophet in the employ of any king, but an ordinary man whom God had touched and commissioned.

25. **Qur'an 14.9-15:** The Islamic conception of a prophet is one who always preaches faith in the One God as the primary message. But this does not neglect the issues of justice and righteousness, for they are implicit in God's message. Hence those who reject God are inevitably oppressive evildoers. Furthermore, since the prophet places his life in God's hands, he is vindicated in the end.

26. **Telang, M.1:** Guru Nanak prophesied that the Mughal invaders by Babur, who descended on India in Vikrami year 1578, would leave in 1597. In that year the Mughal armies were, in fact, routed by Sher Shah. (The Vikrami chronology is one of the classical calendrical systems of India; its reference point is 58 B.C.).

Chapter 22

1. **Luke 2.14:** The proclamation of the angelic host at the birth of Jesus Christ, the Prince of Peace.

2. **Zohar 3.10b:** In Hebrew, *shalom* includes the dimensions of peace, wellness and wholeness.

3. **January 4, 1976:** "Center" can denote either God or an earthly central figure (leader or employer) or a nation that is wealthier or more powerful than one's own. Each way of construing this statement gives another facet of its meaning.

4. **Chuang Tzu 5:** Only a person at peace with himself can calm others.

5. **Isha Upanishad:** 'That' is interpreted by both Shankara and Ramanuja as Brahman; 'this' as the individual soul. Hence, peace arises from the unity of 'this' and 'That,' the soul and God.

6. **Matthew 5.23-24:** Not only will God not accept our offering if we have sinned against others, he also will not accept our offering if another person has a grievance against us, though we might think our actions were justified. Therefore we should take responsibility for others' grievances against us, and avoid all temptations to self-righteousness.

7. **Atharva Veda 7.52.1-2:** The Asvins, or divine Twins, symbolize perfect unity of two.

8. **Qur'an 42.36-43:** The Qur'an exalts forgiveness as the way in which the best of people respond to being wronged, yet as a concession to human weakness it allows that to take revenge is not a sin. Muhammad in the traditions consistently praises those who would forgive rather than take revenge. The Hadith testify to Muhammad's own forgiving nature. Imam Ali, the founding saint of Shiite Islam, likewise prohibited his followers from taking revenge for his murder. See Nahjul Balagha, Letter 47, in Chapter 21: *Law and Punishments*.

9. **August 11, 1997:** The traditional Korean custom is to celebrate every holy occasion with one's ancestors present, by making an offering table piled high with fruit and other food.

10. **Mahabharata:** Krishna takes the part of an honest advisor and mediator in an effort to prevent war; yet his diplomacy fails.

11. **Winston Churchill:** Speech, February 14, 1948.

12. **Exodus 22:23-25:** These are guidelines for judgments at trial, not a sanction for taking revenge. In modern Judaism the penalties have been replaced by monetary equivalents.

13. **February 15, 1983:** While it is not in the nature of God to demand such strict repayment, it is in the nature of victimized human beings to demand it. God set up the Law for the peace of the community, not only to be reconciled with Him.

14. **Yogacara Bhumi Sutra 4:** In this parable, Nirvana is likened to the diminution of jealousy and passion with the cool of the evening. It can be a metaphor for the way peace can arise with the calm of meditation. Those great "causes" that caused people to go to war seem unimportant from a transcendent perspective.
15. **September 21, 2005:** Father Moon is referring to his proposal to build a tunnel across the Bering Strait and an international highway to link all nations; see below, *World Peace*, September 21, 2005.
16. **Qur'an 40.21-22:** The ruins of formerly prosperous cities should be an object lesson about the consequences of sin.
17. **Book of Songs, Ode 235:** The founders of the Shang dynasty were righteous kings who earned the Mandate of Heaven. But when their descendant King Yin brought corruption and troubles to the land, the Mandate of Heaven was lost and a new dynasty, the House of Chou, came to rule. In this poem the rulers of Chou and their subjects, the former retainers of Yin, are admonished to take a lesson from the fate of the previous dynasty.
18. **Amos 2.6-16:** This refers to visiting temple prostitutes, in the service of idolatrous Baal worship.
19. **Amos 2.6-16:** 'Nazirites' were people who out of devotion to the LORD vowed never to touch alcohol or cut their hair. Samson was a Nazirite.
20. **Chief Seattle:** Treaty Oration, 1854.
21. **Isaiah 11.6-9**: 'Wolf' and 'lamb' are metaphors for imperialistic nations and the small nations they conquer. All that will cease when the earth is filled with divine knowledge.
22. **September 21, 2005:** Speech given at the inauguration of the Universal Peace Federation, which has the mission of the "Abel UN"
23. **Tao Te Ching 80**: This is the ideal of simple village life rooted in tradition and interwoven with loving ties of family and friends. It is quite the opposite of life of the modern jet-setter who travels everywhere but has no roots.
24. **September 12, 2005:** The Bering Strait Tunnel Project was also proclaimed at the inauguration of the Universal Peace Federation. Yet Father Moon first articulated his vision of an international highway in 1980, with the proposal for a tunnel linking Japan and Korea that would be the first step in a highway that would eventually link Tokyo with Beijing.

List of Sources

Sources are listed by tradition in alphabetical order as follows:

African Traditional Religions
Ancient History
Baha'i Faith
Buddhism
Christianity
Christian Science
Church of Jesus Christ of Latter-day Saints
Confucianism
Hellenism
Hinduism
Humanism, Arts and Sciences
Islam
Jainism
Judaism

Korean Shamanism and Prophecy
Native American Religions
Perfect Liberty Kyodan
Scientology
Seicho-no-Ie
Shinto
Sikhism
Society of Johrei
Taoism
Teachings of Sun Myung Moon
Tenrikyo
Theosophy
Zoroastrianism

African Traditional Religions

Abimbola, Wande. "Rituals and Symbols in Yoruba Religious Thought." Paper presented at CWR Conference, Harrison Hot Springs, August 1987.

Abimbola, Wande, ed. *Yoruba Oral Tradition*. Ibadan, Nigeria: University Press Ltd., 1975.

Adegbola, E. A. "Theological Basis of Ethics," in *Biblical Revelation and African Beliefs*, by K. Dickson and P. Ellingworth. London: Lutterworth Press. 1969.

Awolalu, J. O. *Yoruba Beliefs and Sacrificial Rites*. London: Longmans, 1979.

Booth, Newell S., Jr., ed. *African Religions: A Symposium*. New York: NOK Publishers, 1937.

Ejizu, Christopher I. *Ofo: Igbo Ritual Symbol*. Enugu, Nigeria: Fourth Dimension Publishing, 1986.

Evans-Pritchard, E. E. *Nuer Religion*. Oxford: Oxford University Press, 1977.

Ikenga-Metuh, Emefie. *Comparative Studies of African Religions*. Onitsha, Nigeria: IMICO Publishers, 1987.

Jahn, Janheinz. *Muntu: An Outline of the New African Culture*. Translated by Marjorie Grene. New York: Grove Press, 1961.

Lienhardt, Godfrey. *Divinity and Experience: The Religion of the Dinka*. London: Oxford University Press, 1961.

Mbiti, John S. *African Religions and Philosophy*. London: Heinemann, 1969.

Mbiti, John S. *The Prayers of African Religion*. London: SPCK, 1975.

Meek, C. K. *Law and Authority in a Nigerian Tribe*. London: Oxford University Press, 1937.

Middleton, John. *Lugbara Religion, Ritual and Authority among an East African People*. Washington, DC: Smithsonian Institution Press, 1988.

Nadel, S. F. *Nupe Religion*. London: Routledge & Kegan Paul, 1954.

Nola, Alfonso M. di, comp. *The Prayers of Man: From Primitive Peoples to Present Times*. Edited by Patrick O'Connor. Translated by Rex Benedict. New York: Ivan Obolensky, 1961.

Opoku, Kofi Asare. *West African Traditional Religion*. Singapore: Far Eastern Publishers, 1978.

Quénum, Maximilien. *Au Pays des Fons*. Paris: Larose, 1938.

Pachocinski, Ryszard. West African proverbs collected and translated for *World Scripture: A Comparative Anthology of Sacred Texts*. New York: Paragon House, 1991.

Radin, Paul. *Primitive Religion: Its Nature and Origin*. New York: Viking Press, 1937.

Rattray, R. S. *The Ashanti*. London: Oxford University Press, 1923.

Shorter, Aylward. *Prayer in the Religious Traditions of Africa*. London: Oxford University Press, 1975.

Smith, E. W., ed. *African Ideas of God*. Cambridge: Edinburgh House Press, 1961.

Ancient History

Pritchard, James B., ed. *Ancient Near Eastern Texts Relating to the Old Testament*. 3rd ed. Princeton: Princeton University Press, 1950.

Baha'i Faith

'Abdu'l-Bahá. *The Promulgation of Universal Peace: Talks Delivered by 'Abdu'l-Bahá during his Visit to the United States and Canada in 1912*. Wilmette, IL: National Spiritual Assembly of Bahá'ís of the United States, 1982.

Bahá'u'lláh. *Epistle to the Son of the Wolf*. Wilmette, IL: National Spiritual Assembly of the Bahá'ís of the United States, 1941, 1953, 1988.

Bahá'u'lláh. *Gleanings from the Writings of Bahá'u'lláh*. Wilmette, IL: National Spiritual Assembly of the Bahá'ís of the United States, 1952, 1976.

Bahá'u'lláh. *Kitáb-i-Íqán: The Book of Certitude*. Wilmette, IL: National Spiritual Assembly of Bahá'ís of the United States, 1931, 1950.

Bahá'u'lláh. *Tablets of Bahá'u'lláh Revealed after the Kitáb-i-Aqdas*. Wilmette, IL: Universal House of Justice, 1978, 1988.

Bahá'u'lláh. *The Seven Valleys and the Four Valleys*. Wilmette, IL: National Spiritual Assembly of Bahá'ís of the United States, 1945, 1973, 1975, 1978.

BUDDHISM

Babbitt, Irving, trans. *The Dhammapada*. New York: New Directions, 1965.

Bary, William Theodore de, ed. *Sources of Indian Tradition*. Vol. 1. New York: Columbia University Press, 1958. Used by permission of Columbia University Press.

Bary, William Theodore de, ed. *The Buddhist Tradition in India, China and Japan*. New York: Random House, 1969. Copyright © 1969 by William Theodore de Bary. Used by permission of Random House, Inc.

Batchelor, Stephen, trans. *A Guide to the Bodhisattva's Way of Life: The Bodhisattvacharyavatara by Acharya Shantideva*. Dharamsala, India: Library of Tibetan Works and Archives, 1979.

Blofeld, John. *Bodhisattva of Compassion: The Mystical Tradition of Kuan Yin*. Boston: Shambhala, 1978.

Ch'an, Chu, trans. *The Sutra of Forty Two Sections*. London: Buddhist Society, 1947.

Chang, Garma C. C., trans. *The Hundred Thousand Songs of Milarepa*. Secaucus, NJ: University Books, 1962.

Chihmann, Upasika, trans. *The Two Buddhist Books in Mahayana*. Hong Kong: Rumford, 1936.

Cleary, Thomas F., trans. *The Flower Ornament Scripture: A Translation of the Avatamsaka Sutra*. 3 vols. Boston: Shambhala, 1984-1987.

Conze, Edward, ed. *Buddhist Texts Through the Ages*. New York: Philosophical Library, 1954.

Conze, Edward, ed. *Buddhist Wisdom Books: Containing the Diamond Sutra and the Heart Sutra*. London: George Allen & Unwin, 1958.

Conze, Edward, trans. *The Large Sutra on Perfect Wisdom, with the Divisions of the Abhisamayalankara*. Berkeley: University of California Press, 1975.

Conze, Edward, ed. and trans. *The Perfection of Wisdom in Eight Thousand Lines and Its Verse Summary*. San Francisco: Four Seasons Foundation, 1983.

Cowell, E. B., F. Max Müller, and J. Takakusu, trans. *Buddhist Mahayana Texts*. Sacred Books of the East, vol. 49. Oxford: Clarendon Press, 1894.

Evans-Wentz, W. Y., ed. *The Tibetan Book of the Dead*. Oxford: Oxford University Press, 1927.

Evans-Wentz, W. Y. *Tibetan Yoga and Secret Doctrines*. Oxford: Oxford University Press, 1958.

Evans-Wentz, W.Y., ed. *Tibet's Great Yogi, Milarepa*. Translated by Lama Kaji dawa-Samdup. Oxford: Oxford University Press, 1928.

Francis, H. T., trans. *The Jataka; or, Stories of the Buddha's Former Births*. 6 vols. Reprint. London: Pali Text Society, 1981.

Goddard, Dwight, ed. *A Buddhist Bible*. Boston: Beacon Press, 1970.

Gyatso, Tenzin. *Opening the Mind and Generating Good Heart*. India: Paljor Publications, 2002.

Gyatso, Tenzin. *Universal Responsibility and the Good Heart*. Dharamsala, India: Library of Tibetan Works and Archives, 1984.

Hakeda, Yoshito S., trans. *The Awakening of Faith, Attributed to Ashvaghosha*. New York: Columbia University Press, 1967.

Horne, Charles F., ed. *The Sacred Books and Early Literature of the East*. Vol. 10. New York: Parke, Austin, and Lipscomb, 1917.

Horner, I. B., trans. *Middle Length Sayings (Majjhima Nikaya)*. 3 vols. London: Pali Text Society, 1954-1959.

Horner, I. B., trans. *The Book of the Discipline*. 6 vols. London: Pali Text Society, 1938-1967.

Hsuan-hua. *A General Explanation of the Buddha Speaks: The Sutra in Forty-Two Sections*. Translated by Bhikshuni Heng Chih. San Francisco: Buddhist Text Translation Society, 1977.

Hurvitz, Leon, trans. *Scripture of the Lotus Blossom of the Fine Dharma*. New York: Columbia University Press, 1976.

Johnston, E. H., trans. *The Buddhacarita; or, Acts of the Buddha*. New enl. ed. Delhi, India: Motilal Banarsidass, 1984.

Kalupahana, David J., trans. *A Path of Righteousness: Dhammapada*. Lanham: University Press of America, 1986.

Lectures on the Sutras. Rev. ed. Tokyo: Nichiren Shoshu International Center.

Maurice, David, ed. *The Lion's Roar: An Anthology of the Buddha's Teachings Selected from the Pali Canon*. London: Rider, 1962.

Mou-lam, Wong, trans. *The Sutra of Hui Neng*. Boston: Shambhala, 1969.

Nagarjuna. *The Precious Garland and the Song of the Four Mindfulnesses*. Translated by J. Hopkins and L. Rimpoche. London: George Allen & Unwin, 1975.

Nanamoli, Bhikkhu, trans. *Khuddaka Patha*. Pali Text Translation Series no. 32. London: Pali Text Society, 1960.

Norman, K. R., trans. *The Elders' Verses II: Therigatha*. Pali Text Society Translation Series no. 40. London: Pali Text Society, 1971.

Norman, K. R., trans. *The Group of Discourses*. London: Pali Text Society, 1984.

Oldenberg, Hermann, ed. *Vinayapitaka*. Vol. 1, Sacred Books of the East, vol. 13. Oxford: Clarendon Press, 1879.

Paul, Diane Y. *The Buddhist Feminine Ideal*. Missoula, MT: Scholars Press, 1980.

Price, A. F., trans. *The Diamond Sutra*. Boston: Shambhala, 1969.

Rahula, Walpola, ed. *What the Buddha Taught*. 2nd ed. New York: Grove Press, 1974.

Rhys Davids, C. A. F., trans. *Psalms of the Sisters*. London: Pali Text Society, 1909.

Rhys Davids, T. W., and C. A. F. Rhys Davids, trans. *Dialogues of the Buddha (Digha Nikaya)*. Parts 1-3, Sacred Books of the Buddhists, vols. 2-4. London: Pali Text Society, 1956-1959.

Rhys Davids, T. W., and F. L. Woodward, trans. *Kindred Sayings (Samyutta Nikaya)*. Vols. 1-5. London: Pali Text Society, 1950-1956.

Rogers, T. E., trans. *Buddhagosa: Buddhist Parables*. London: Trübner, 1870.

Saddhatissa, H., trans. *The Sutta-Nipata*. London: Curzon Press, 1985.

Sekida, Katsuki, trans. *Two Zen Classics: Mumonkan and Hekiganroku*. Tokyo: Weatherhill, 1977.

Shastri, Lobsang Norbu. *Bibliotheca Indo-Tibetica 7*. Sarnath: Central Institute of Higher Tibetan Studies, 1984.

Shinran. *Buddhist Psalms*. Translated by S. Yamabe and L. Adams Beck. London: John Murray; New York: Dutton, 1921.

Shinshu Seiten: Jodo Shin Buddhist Teaching. San Francisco: Buddhist Churches of America, 1978.

Snellgrove, D. L. *The Hevajra Tantra: A Critical Study*. Vol. 1. Oxford: Oxford University Press, 1959.

Soothill, W. E., trans. *The Lotus of the Wonderful Law*. Oxford: Oxford University Press, 1930.

Suzuki, D. T., trans. *The Lankavatara Sutra: A Mahayana Text*. London: Routledge & Kegan Paul, 1932.

The Teaching of Buddha. 84th rev. ed. Tokyo: Bukkyo Dendo Kyokai, 1984.

Thera, Narada Maha, trans. *The Dhammapada*. Colombo, Sri Lanka: Vajirarama, 1972.

Thera, Nyanaponika. *The Heart of Buddhist Meditation: A Handbook of Mental Training Based on the Buddha's Way of Mindfulness (Satipatthana)*. York Beach, ME: Samuel Weiser, 1965.

Thurman, Robert A. F., trans. *The Holy Teaching of Vimalakirti*. University Park: Pennsylvania State University Press, 1976.

Tsunoda, Ryusaku, W. T. de Bary, and D. Keene, comps. *Sources of Japanese Tradition*. Vol. 1. New York: Columbia University Press, 1958.

Warren, Henry Clarke, ed. *Buddhism in Translations*. Cambridge, MA: Harvard University Press, 1896; New York: Atheneum, 1982.

Woodward, F. L., trans. *Minor Anthologies of the Pali Canon: Part 2, Udana: Verses of Uplift and Itivuttaka: As It Was Said*. London: Pali Text Society, 1948.

Woodward, F. L., trans. *Some Sayings of the Buddha*. London: Oxford University Press, 1973. Used by permission of Oxford University Press.

Woodward, F. L., and E. M. Hare, trans. *Gradual Sayings*. 5 vols. London: Pali Text Society, 1951-1965.

Yamamoto, Kosho, trans. *The Mahayana Mahaparinirvana Sutra*. 3 vols. Ube City: Karinbunko, 1973-1975.

Christianity

Alexandrian Christianity: Selected Translations of Clement and Origine. The Library of Christian Classics. Vol. 2. Introduction and Notes by John Ernest Leonard Oulton. Philadelphia: Westminster Press, 1954.

Ambrose. *Seven Exegetical Works*. Fathers of the Church, vol. 65. Translated by Michael P. McHugh. Washington, DC: Catholic University of America Press, 1992.

Boethius. *The Consolation of Philosophy*. Translated by V.E. Watts. Baltimore, MD: Penguin Books, 1969.

Burr, David, trans. *Medieval Sourcebook: The Rule of the Franciscan Order*. 1996. Accessed at http://www.fordham.edu/halsall/source/stfran-rule.html

Catherine of Siena. In *Heritage of Western Civilization, Volume 1: Ancient Civilizations and the Emergence of West*. 6th ed. By John L. Beatty and Oliver A. Johnson. Englewood Cliffs, NJ: Prentice Hall, 1987.

Gilby, Thomas, trans. *St. Thomas Aquinas: Philosophical Texts*. Oxford: Oxford University Press 1951.

Godwin, Joscelyn. *Harmony of the Spheres*. Rochester, VT: Inner Traditional International, 1993.

Graham, Billy. *The Courage of Conviction*. Edited with an introduction by Phillip L. Berman. Ballantine, 1986.

Hall, George Stuart. *Gregory of Nyssa: Homilies on Ecclesiastes; An English Version With Supporting Studies*. Walter DeGruyter, 1993.

Hildegard of Bingen. *Scivias*. In *Creation and Christ: The Wisdom of Hildegard of Bingen*. Translated by Columba Hart and Jane Bishop. Edited by Kathleen A. Walsh. New York: Paulist Press, 1996.

Kempis, Thomas á. *Imitation of Christ*. Milwaukee: Bruce Publishing Company, 1949.

Kempis, Thomas á. *Imitation of Christ*. Translated by Aloysius Croft Harold Bolton. Digitized by Harry Plantinga. 1994. Accessed at http://www.leaderu.com/cyber/books/imitation/imitation.html#toc

King, Martin Luther, Jr. *Strength to Love*. Philadelphia: Fortress Press, 1963.

King, Martin Luther, Jr. *Where Do We Go from Here: Chaos or Community?* New York: Harper and Row, 1967.

Luther, Martin. *The Large Catechism*. In *Trigot Concordia: The Symbolical Books of the Evangelical Lutheran Church*. Translated by F. Bente and W. H. T. Dau. St. Louis, MO: Concordia Publishing House, 1921.

Mirandola, Pico della. *Dignity of Man*. In *Heritage of Western Civilization, Volume 1: Ancient Civilizations and the Emergence of West*. 6th ed. By John L. Beatty and Oliver A. Johnson. Englewood Cliffs, NJ: Prentice Hall, 1987.

Music in the Western World: A History in Documents. Selected and annotated by Piero Weiss and Richard Taruskin. Schirmer, 1984.

Nicene and Post-Nicene Fathers. Series 2, Vol. 1. 1890. Accessed at http://www.fordham.edu/halsall/source/conv-const.html

Perry, Marvin, Joseph R. Peden, and Theodore H. Von Laue. *Sources of the Western Tradition, Volume One: From Ancient Times to the Enlightenment*. 4th ed. Boston: Houghton Mifflin Company, 1999.

Pope John Paul II. *The Gospel of Life*. Random House, 1995. Official English translation provided by the Vatican. Accessed at http://www.vatican.va/holy_father/john_paul_ii/encyclicals/documents/hf_jp-ii_enc_25031995_evangelium-vitae_en.html

Pope Paul VI. *Nostra Aetate*. Declaration on the Relation of the Church to Non-Christian Religions. October 28, 1965. Accessed at http://www.vatican.va/archive/hist_councils/ii_vatican_council/documents/vat-ii_decl_19651028_nostra-aetate_en.html

Saint Ambrose. *Ambrose: Selected Works and Letters*. Edited by Philip Schaff. Nicene and Post-Nicene Fathers Series II, vol. 10. Edinburgh: T. and T. Clarke. Accessed at http://www.ccel.org/fathers2/NPNF2-10/Npnf2-10-08.htm#P473_59585

Saint Ambrose. *Letters*. Translated by Mary Melchior Beyenka. The Fathers of the Church, vol. 26. Washington, DC: Catholic University of America Press, 1954.

Saint Augustine. *Confessions*. Translated by J. G. Pilkington. Excerpted from *Nicene and Post-Nicene Fathers*. Series 1, Vol. 1. Edited by Philip Schaff. American Edition, 1887.

Saint Augustine. *Lectures or Tractates 21–30 on the Gospel According to St. John*. Translated by John Gibb. Taken from *The Early Church Fathers and Other Works*. Edinburgh, Scotland: Wm. B. Eerdmans, 1867. Accessed at http://www.ewtn.com/library/PATRISTC/PNI7-3.TXT

Saint Augustine. *Lectures or Tractates 31–44 on the Gospel According to St. John*. Translated by John Gibb. Taken from *The Early Church Fathers and Other Works*. Edinburgh, Scotland: Wm. B. Eerdmans, 1867. Accessed at http://www.ewtn.com/library/PATRISTC/PNI7-4.TXT

Saint Augustine. *The City of God, Books VIII–XVI*. Fathers of the Church, vol. 14. Translated by Gerald G. Walsh and Daniel J. Honan. Washington, DC: Catholic University of America Press, 1952.

Saint Augustine. *The City of God, Books XVII–XXII*. Fathers of the Church, vol. 24. Translated by Gerald G. Walsh and Daniel J. Honan. Washington, DC: Catholic University of America Press, 1954.

Saint Francis of Assisi. "The Canticle of the Sun." Translated by Roger D. Sorrell. Accessed at http://www.stolaf.edu/people/edwards/francis3.htm

Saint Francis of Assisi. "Third Admonition of the Order." In *The Sources for the Life of St. Francis of Assisi*. Translated by J. R. H. Moorman. Quoted in *The Columbia World of Quotations*. Edited by Robert Andrews, Mary Biggs, and Michael Seidel, et al. New York: Columbia University Press, 1996. Accessed at http://www.bartleby.com/66/

Saint Thomas Aquinas. *The Summa Theologica.* Benziger Bros. edition, 1947. Accessed at http://www.ccel.org/a/aquinas/summa/FP/FP001.html#FPQ1OUTP1

Simpson's Contemporary Quotations. Compiled by James B. Simpson. Boston: Houghton Mifflin Company, 1988.

Tertullian. *Apologeticum.* Accessed at http://www.tertullian.org/

Tertullian. *Apologeticus.* Translated by Alexander Souter. Cambridge: 1917.

Tertullian. "On Prescription against the Heretics." In *The Ante-Nicene Fathers.* Vol. 3. Edited by Alexander Roberts and James Donaldson. Scribners, 1906.

The Apocryphya, Revised Standard Version. New York: National Council of the Churches of Christ in the USA, 1957.

The Holy Bible, Authorized King James Version. New York: Oxford University Press, 1945.

The Holy Bible, Revised Standard Version. New York: National Council of the Churches of Christ in the USA, 1946; 1971. Used by permission. All rights reserved.

The Holy Rule of St. Benedict. The 1949 Edition. Translated by Rev. Boniface Verheyen, OSB. Atchison, KS.

The Words of Martin Luther King, Jr. Selected by Coretta Scott King. New York: Newmarket Press, 1983.

Tierney, Brian. *The Middle Ages—Volume I: Sources of Medieval History.* 2nd ed. New York: Alfred A. Knopf, 1973.

Tillich, Paul. *Dynamics of Faith.* New York: Harper & Row, 1957.

Winthrop, John. *A Model of Christian Charity.* In *New World Metaphysics: Readings on the Religious Meaning of the American Experience.* Edited by Giles Gunn. New York: Oxford University Press, 1981.

CHRISTIAN SCIENCE

Eddy, Mary Baker. *Science and Health with Key to the Scriptures.* Boston: First Church of Christ, Scientist, 1875; 1934.

CHURCH OF JESUS CHRIST OF LATTER-DAY SAINTS

Smith, Joseph, trans. *The Book of Mormon.* Salt Lake City: The Church of Jesus Christ of Latter-day Saints, 1963.

The Doctrine and Covenants. Salt Lake City: The Church of Jesus Christ of Latter-day Saints, 1974.

The Pearl of Great Price: A Selection from the Revelations, Translations, and Narrations of Joseph Smith. Salt Lake City: The Church of Jesus Christ of Latter-day Saints, 1974.

CONFUCIANISM

Bahm, Archie. *The Heart of Confucius.* Carbondale: Southern Illinois University, 1977.

Bary, W. T. de, Wing-tsit Chan, and Burton Watson, comps. *Sources of Chinese Tradition.* Vol. 1. New York: Columbia University Press, 1960.

Blofeld, John, trans. *I Ching: The Book of Change.* London: George Allen & Unwin, 1965.

Chan, Wing-tsit, comp. and trans. *A Source Book in Chinese Philosophy.* Princeton: Princeton University Press, 1963.

Dafei, Gong, and Yu Feng, eds. *Chinese Maxims: Golden Sayings of Chinese Thinkers Over Five Thousand Years.* Beijing: Sinolingua, 1994.

Lau, D. C., trans. *Mencius.* London: Penguin Books, 1979. Copyright © 1970 by D. C. Lau. Used by permission of Penguin Group.

Lau, D. C., trans. *The Analects.* London: Penguin Books, 1979; New York: Dorset, 1986.

Legge, James, trans. *Confucian Analects, the Great Learning and the Doctrine of the Mean.* The Chinese Classics, vol. 1, 2nd. ed. Oxford: Clarendon Press, 1893.

Legge, James, trans. *The Sacred Books of China, Part 1: The Shu King, Religious Portions of the Shih King, the Hsiao King*. Sacred Books of the East, vol. 3. Oxford: Clarendon, 1879.

Legge, James, trans. *The Sacred Books of China, Part 4: The Li Ki, a Collection of Treatises on the Rules of Propriety or Ceremonial Usages*. Sacred Books of the East, vol. 27. Oxford: Clarendon, 1885.

Legge, James, trans. *The She King*. The Chinese Classics, vol. 4. Oxford: Clarendon, 1895; reprint, Taipei: Southern Materials Center, 1985.

Legge, James, trans. *The Works of Mencius*. The Chinese Classics, vol. 2, 2nd ed. Oxford: Clarendon, 1895; reprint, New York: Dover, 1970.

McNaughton, William. *The Confucian Vision*. Ann Arbor: University of Michigan Press, 1974.

Nivison, David S. *The Ways of Confucianism*. Chicago: Open Court, 1996.

Tame, David. *The Secret Power of Music*. Northamptonshire, England: Turnstone Press, 1984.

Waley, Arthur, trans. *The Analects of Confucius*. London: George Allen & Unwin; New York: Random House, 1938.

Waltham, Clae, trans. *Shu Ching: Book of History. A Modernized Edition of the Translations of James Legge*. Chicago: Henry Regnery, 1971.

Wilhelm, Richard, trans. *The I Ching; or, Book of Changes*. Translated into English by C. F. Baynes. Princeton: Princeton University Press, 1977.

Wittenborn, Allen, trans. *Further Reflections on Things at Hand*. Lanham, MD: University Press of America, 1991.

Wu, John C. H., trans. *Chinese Humanism and Christian Spirituality*. Jamaica, NY: St. John's University Press, 1965.

Yang-Ming, Wang. *The Philosophy of Wang Yang-Ming*. Translated by Frederick Goodrich Henke. Open Court Publishing, 1916.

Yutang, Lin, ed. and trans. *The Wisdom of Confucius*. New York: Random House, 1938.

Hellenism

Aristotle. *Nicomachean Ethics*. Translated by W. D. Ross. Oxford: Clarendon, 1908.

Aristotle. *Nicomachean Ethics*. Aristotle in 23 volumes, vol. 19. Edited and translated by H. Rackham. Cambridge, MA: Harvard University Press; London: William Heinemann, 1934.

Aristotle. *Politics*. Book 4, chap. 11. Translated by Benjamin Jowett. Accessed at http://classics.mit.edu/Aristotle/politics.4.four.html

Cicero. *On Old Age*. Translated by E. S. Shuckburgh. Vol. 9, Part 2. The Harvard Classics. New York: P. F. Collier and Son, 1909–14.

Cicero. *Second Philippic Oration*. Edited with translation and notes by W. K. Lacey. Warminster, England: Aris and Phillips Publishers, 1986.

Diogenes Laertius. *Lives of Eminent Philosophers*. Translated by C. D. Yonge. London: Henry G. Bohn, 1853.

Jowett, Benjamin, trans. *Thucydides*. 2nd ed. Oxford: Clarendon Press, 1900. Accessed at http://classicpersuasion.org/pw/thucydides/jthucbk1rv2.htm

Plato. *Apology*. Translated by Benjamin Jowett. New York: C. Scribner's Sons, 1871.

Plato. *Dialogues*. Translated by Benjamin Jowett. New York: C. Scribner's Sons, 1871.

Plato. *Five Dialogues*. Translated by G. M. A. Grube. Indianapolis: Hackett Publishing, 1981.

Plato. *Laws*. Translated by Benjamin Jowett. New York: C. Scribner's Sons, 1871. Accessed at http://classics.mit.edu/Plato/laws.9.ix.html

Plato. *Phaedo*. Translated by Benjamin Jowett. New York: C. Scribner's Sons, 1871.

Plato. *Protagoras*. In *Collected Dialogues of Plato*. Bollingen series 71. By Edith Hamilton and Huntington Cairns. Princeton: Princeton University Press, 1961.

Plato. *Protagoras*. Translated by Benjamin Jowett. New York: C. Scribner's Sons, 1871.

Plato. *Symposium*. Translated by Benjamin Jowett. New York: C. Scribner's Sons, 1871.

Plato. *The Apology, Phaedo and Crito*. Translated by Benjamin Jowett. Vol. II, Part 1. The Harvard Classics. New York: P. F. Collier and Son, 1909–14.

Plato. *The Republic*. Translated by Benjamin Jowett. New York: C. Scribner's Sons, 1871.

Plato. *Timaeus*. Translated by Benjamin Jowett. New York: C. Scribner's Sons, 1871.

Plotinus. *The Eneads.* Translated by Stephen Mackenna and B. S. Page. Accessed at http://oaks.nvg.org/enn1.html

Thatcher, Oliver J., ed. *The Library of Original Sources.* Vol. III: *The Roman World.* Milwaukee: University Research Extension, 1907.

Hinduism

Basu, B. D. *The Matsya Puranam.* Parts 1 & 2. Sacred Books of the Hindus, vol. 17. Translated by A. Taluqdar of Oudh. Allahabad, 1917; Reprint, New York: AMS Press, 1974.

Bhaktivedanta, A. C., ed. *Krsna: The Supreme Personality of Godhead.* Vol. 1. Los Angeles: Bhaktivedanta Book Trust, 1970.

Bolle, Kees W., ed. *The Bhagavadgita: A New Translation.* Berkeley: University of California Press, 1979.

Bose, Abinash Chandra, ed. *Hymns from the Vedas.* Bombay: Asia Publishing House, 1966.

Bose, Abinash Chandra, ed. *The Call of the Vedas.* Bombay: Bharatiya Vidya Bhavan, 1954.

Bühler, Georg, trans. *The Sacred Laws of the Aryas.* Sacred Books of the East, vol. 2. Oxford: Clarendon, 1882.

Bühler, Georg, trans. *The Laws of Manu.* Sacred Books of the East, vol. 25. Oxford: Clarendon, 1886.

Buitenen, J. A. B. van, trans. *The Mahabharata.* Vol. 1, The Book of the Beginning. Chicago: University of Chicago Press, 1973.

Burnell, Arthur Coke, ed. *The Ordinance of Manu.* London: Trübner, 1884.

Chinmoy, Sri. *My Life's Soul-Journey: Daily Meditations for Ever-Increasing Spiritual Fulfillment.* Aum Publications, 1995.

Dimock, Edward C., Jr., and Denise Levertov. *In Praise of Krishna, Songs from the Bengali.* Chicago: University of Chicago Press, 1967.

Dutt, Manmatha Natha, ed. *The Garuda Purana.* Calcutta: Society for the Resuscitation of Indian Literature, 1908.

Easwaran, Eknath, ed. *The Bhagavad Gita.* Petaluma, CA: Nilgiri Press, 1985.

Easwaran, Eknath, trans. *The Upanishads.* Petaluma, CA: Nilgiri Press, 1985.

Gandhi, Mohandas. *Gandhi, An Autobiography: The Story of My Experiments with Truth.* Reprint, Beacon Press, 1993.

Ganguli, Kisarai Mohan, trans. *The Mahabharata of Krishna-Dwaipayana Vyasa.* New Delhi: Munshiram Manoharlal, 1982.

Hume, R. E., trans. *The Thirteen Principal Upanishads.* Oxford: Oxford University Press, 1931.

Jolly, Julius. *The Institutes of Vishnu.* Sacred Books of the East, vol. 7. Oxford: Clarendon, 1900.

Macnicol, Nicol, trans. *Hindu Scriptures.* Everyman's Library. London: J. M. Dent, 1938.

Mahaswamiji, Shivamurthy Shivacharya. *Religion and Society at Cross-roads.* Sirigere, India: Sri Taralabalu Jagadguru Brihanmath, 1990.

Morgan, Kenneth W., ed. *The Religion of the Hindus.* New York: Ronald Press, 1953.

Müller, F. Max, trans. *The Upanishads.* 2 vols., Sacred Books of the East, vols. 1, 15. Oxford: Clarendon, 1879, 1884.

Narayan, R. K. *The Ramayana.* London: Penguin Books, 1972.

Nikhilananda, Swami, trans. *The Upanishads.* 4 vols. New York: Ramakrishna-Vivekananda Center of New York, 1949, 1952, 1956, 1959.

Pandit, M. P. *Kularnava Tantra.* Delhi: Motilal Banarsidass, 1965.

Panikkar, Raimundo, ed. *Mantramanjari: The Vedic Experience.* Berkeley: University of California Press, 1977.

Pargiter, F. E. *The Markandaya-Purana.* Calcutta: Asiatic Society, 1904.

Prabhavananda, Swami, ed. *Srimad Bhagavatam: The Wisdom of God.* Hollywood, CA: Vedanta Press, 1943.

Prabhavananda, Swami, ed. *The Spiritual Heritage of India.* Hollywood, CA: Vedanta Press, 1963.

Prabhavananda, Swami, and Christopher Isherwood, trans. *The Song of God: Bhagavad-Gita.* Hollywood, CA: Vedanta Press, 1944, 1972.

Radhakrishnan, S., ed. *The Dhammapada.* Madras: Oxford University Press, 1950.

Radhakrishnan, S., and C. A. Moore, eds. *A Sourcebook in Indian Philosophy.* Princeton: Princeton University Press, 1957.

Raghavan, V., trans. *The Indian Heritage.* Bangalore: Indian Institute of World Culture, 1963.

Shastri, Hari Prasad, trans. *The Ramayana of Valmiki.* 3 vols. London: Shanti Sadan, 1962.

The Siva Purana. Delhi: Motilal Banarsidass, 1970.

Thibaut, George, trans. *The Vedanta Sutras of Badarayana.* Commentary by Shankara. Sacred Books of the East, vols. 34, 38. Oxford: Clarendon, 1890, 1896.

"What is Vedanta?" Vedanta Press and Catalog. http://www.vedanta.com/vedanta.html

Wilson, Horace H., trans. *The Vishnu Purana.* London: John Murray, 1840; London: Trübner, 1864.

Wood, Ernest, and S. V. Subrahmanyam, eds. *The Garuda Purana: Saroddhara.* Sacred Books of the Hindus, vol. 9. Edited by B. D. Basu. Allahabad: The Panini Office, Bhuvaneswari Asrama, Bhadurganj, 1911; Reprint, New York: AMS Press, 1974.

Yogananada, Paramahansa. "A World in Transition." In *The Divine Romance (Collected Talks and Essays on Realizing God in Daily Life, Vol. II).* By Paramahansa Yogananda. Los Angeles: Self-Realization Fellowship. Accessed at http://www.yogananda-srf.org/writings/world.html

Zaehner, R. C., ed. and trans. *Hindu Scriptures.* Everyman's Library 944. London: J. M. Dent, 1966.

Humanism, Arts and Sciences

Abell, Arthur. *Talks with Great Composers.* New York: Philosophical Library, 1955.

Alighieri, Dante. *The Divine Comedy.* Translated in the original ternary rhyme by C. B. Cayley. London: Longman, Brown, Green and Longmans, 1851–1855.

Andrade, Edward N. *Sir Isaac Newton, His Life and Work.* New York: Doubleday Anchor, 1950.

Boyd, Malcolm. *Bach.* The Master Musicians. London: J. M. Dent and Sons, 1983.

Brown, Clint, comp. *Artist to Artist: Inspiration and Advice from Artists Past and Present.* Corvallis, OR: Jackson Creek Press, 1998.

Diderot, Denis. "Letter to My Brother." December 29, 1760. In *Ouevrès Completes.* Paris: Garnier Frères, 1875. Translated for marxists.org by Mitch Abidor. Accessed at http://www.marxists.org/reference/archive/diderot/1760/letter-brother.htm

Einstein, Albert. *Out of My Later Years.* In *The Harper Book of American Quotations.* By Gorton Carruth and Eugene Ehrlich. New York: Harper and Row, 1988.

Einstein, Albert. *The World as I See It.* In *The Harper Book of American Quotations.* By Gorton Carruth and Eugene Ehrlich. New York: Harper and Row, 1988.

Einstein, Albert. "What I Believe." In *Exploring the Invisible: Art, Science, and the Spiritual.* By Lynn Gamwell. Princeton: Princeton University Press, 2002.

Fromm, Erich. *Man for Himself.* In *Oxford Dictionary of Modern Quotations.* By Tony Augarde. New York: Oxford University Press, 1991.

Galen. *Hygiene.* Translated by R. M. Green. Springfield, IL: Charles C. Thomas, 1951.

Galen. *On the Humour.* In *Great Treasury of Western Thought.* Edited by M. J. Adler and C. Van Doren. New York: R. R. Bowker, 1977.

Hippocrates. *Regimen in Acute Diseases.* Edited and translated by M. C. Lyons. Cambridge: W. Heffer, 1966.

Jefferson, Thomas. "Letter to Peter Carr." Paris, August 19, 1785. In *The Life and Selected Writings of Thomas Jefferson.* Edited and with an introduction by Adrienne Koch and William Peden. New York: Random House, 1944.

Kant, Immanuel. *Groundwork for the Metaphysics of Morals.* Translated by Jonathan Bennett. Available at http://www.earlymoderntexts.com/f_kant.html

Marx, Karl. *Critique of Hegel's 'Philosophy of Right.'* Translated from German by Annette Jolin and Joseph O'Malley. Cambridge: Cambridge University Press, 1972.

Marx, Karl, and Friedrich Engels. *The German Ideology.* Edited with an introduction by R. Pascal. New York: International Publishers, 1939.

Hugo, Victor. *Preface de Cromwell and Hernani.* Edited with introduction and notes by John R. Effinger, Jr. Chicago: Scott, Foresman and Company, 1900.

Lennon, J. Michael, ed. *Conversations with Norman Mailer.* University Press of Mississippi, 1988.

Lloyd, G. E. R. *Hippocratic Writings.* Harmondsworth, England: Penguin Books, 1978.

More, Thomas. *Utopia*. Edited by Henry Morley. Cassell and Company, 1901. Transcribed by David Price. Accessed at http://www.gutenberg.org/files/2130/2130-h/2130-h.htm

Nager, Frank. *Der Heilkundige Dichter: Goethe und die Medizin*. Translated by K. Aterman. Zurich/Munich: Artemis, 1990.

Paracelsus. *Seven Defensiones: The Reply to Certain Calumniations of His Enemies*. In *Four Treatises of Theophratus von Hohenheim called Paracelsus*. By C. L. Temkin, et al. Baltimore, MD: Johns Hopkins University Press, 1941.

Riley, Dick, Pam McAllister, and Bruce Cassidy, eds. *The Armchair Companion to Agatha Christie*. New York: Ungar Publishing, 1986.

Tripp, Rhoda Thomas. *The International Thesaurus of Quotations*. New York: Thomas Y. Crowell, 1970.

Veith, I., trans. *The Yellow Emperor's Classic of Internal Medicine*. Berkeley, CA: University of California Press, 1970; Reprint, Birmingham, AL: Classics of Medicine Library, 1988.

Weber, Robert L. *More Random Walks in Science: An Anthology*. Bristol, UK: The Institute of Physics, 1982.

Islam

Ahmad, Ghazi, trans. *Sayings of Muhammad*. Lahore, Pakistan: Sh. Muhammad Ashraf, 1968.

al-Din Rumi, Jalal. *Tales from Masnavi*. Translated by A. J. Arberry. Curzon Press, 1993.

Al-Ghazzali. *The Alchemy of Happiness*. Translated by Claud Field. London: John Murray, 1909.

Ali, A. Yusuf, trans. *The Meaning of the Glorious Qur'an*. Cairo: Dar Al-Kitab Al-Masri, 1938.

Ali, Maulana Muhammad, ed. *A Manual of Hadith*. 2nd ed. London: Curzon Press, 1978.

Ali, Maulana Muhammad. *The Holy Qur'an*. 7th ed. Columbus, OH: Ahmadiyyah Njuman Isha'at Islam Lahore, 1991.

Arberry, Arthur J. *Avicenna on Theology*. London: John Murray, 1951; Reprint, Westport, CT: Hyperion Press, 1979.

Arberry, Arthur J., trans. *The Koran Interpreted*. New York: Macmillan, 1955.

Bishop, Eric F. F. "The Forty Traditions of An-Nawawi." *The Moslem World* 29, no. 2. April 1939: 163–77.

Dermenghem, Emile. *Muhammad and the Islamic Tradition*. Translated from French by J. M. Watt. Westport, CT: Greenwood Press, 1974.

Guillaume, A. *The Life of Muhammad: A Translation of Ishaq's Sirat Rasul Allah*. Oxford: Oxford University Press, 1955.

Ibrahim, Ezzeddin, and Denys Johnson-Davies, trans. *An-Nawawi's Forty Hadith*. Damascus: Holy Koran Publishing House, 1977.

Irving, Thomas Ballantine, trans. *The Qur'an: First American Version*. Brattleboro, VT: Amana Books, 1985.

Jafery, Syed Mohammed Askari, trans. *Nahjul Balagha of Hazrat Ali*. Pathergatti, India: Seerat-Uz-Zahra Committee, 1965.

Jeffery, Arthur, ed. *Islam: Muhammad and His Religion*. New York: Bobbs-Merrill, 1958.

Khan, Maulana Wahiduddin. Passages from the Qur'an translated for *World Scripture: A Comparative Anthology of Sacred Texts*. New York: Paragon House, 1991.

Khan, Muhammad Muhsin, trans. *The Translation of the Meanings of Sahih Al-Bukhari*. 9 vols. Chicago: Kazi Publications, 1976–1979.

Nurbakhsh, Javad, comp. *Traditions of the Prophet*. New York: Khaniqahi-Nimatullahi Publications, 1981.

"Oneness, Uniqueness of Allah (Tawheed)." Translation of *Sahih Bukhari*, Book 93. USC-MSA Compendium of Muslim Texts. Accessed at http://www.usc.edu/dept/MSA/fundamentals/hadithsunnah/bukhari/093.sbt.html

Ozturk, Yasar Nuri. Selected hadith translated for *World Scripture: A Comparative Anthology of Sacred Texts*. New York: Paragon House, 1991.

Pickthall, Muhammad Marmaduke, trans. *The Meaning of the Glorious Qur'an*. Mecca and New York: Muslim World League, 1977.

"Rabi'a al 'Adawiyya." Sidi Muhammad Press, 2004. Accessed at http://www.sufimaster.org/teachings/adawiyya.htm

Robson, James, trans. *Mishkat Al-Masabih*. Lahore, Pakistan: Sh. Muhammad Ashraf, 1981.

Shirazi, Muhammad. *War, Peace and Non-violence: An Islamic Perspective*. London: Fountain Books, 2001.

Siddiqi, Abdul Hamid, trans. *Sahih Muslim*. 4 vols. New Delhi: Kitab Bhavan, 1977.

Suhrawardy, Abdullah, trans. *Sayings of Muhammad*. London: John Murray, 1941, 1945, 1949.

Jainism

Bary, William Theodore de, ed. *Sources of Indian Tradition*. Vol. 1. New York: Columbia University Press, 1958.

Bhaskar, Bhagchandra Jain. Selections from Jain scriptures prepared and translated for *World Scripture: A Comparative Anthology of Sacred Texts*. New York: Paragon House, 1991.

Chakravarti, A., trans. *Pancastikaya of Kundakunda*. New Delhi: Bharatiya Jnanapeeth, 1944.

Champion, Selwyn Gurney, and Dorothy Short, comps. *Readings from World Religions*. London: C. W. Watts, 1951.

Ghosal, S. C., trans. *Dravyasangraha of Nemichandra*. Arrah: Central Jain Pubishing House, 1917.

Jacobi, Hermann, trans. *Jaina Sutras*. 2 vols., Sacred Books of the East, vols. 22, 45. Oxford: Clarendon, 1884, 1895; Reprint, New York: Dover, 1968.

Jain, S. A., trans. *Reality*. Calcutta: Vira Shasan Sangha, 1960.

Jaini, Padmanabh S. *The Jaina Path of Purification*. Berkeley: University of California Press, 1979.

Kumar, Muni Mahendra, trans. *Acarangasutra*. Delhi: Motilal Banarsidass, 1981.

Lalwani, K. C., trans. *Dasavaikalikasutra*. Delhi: Motilal Banarsidass, 1973.

Nathamal, Muni. *Shramana Mahavira*. Translated by Sri Dineshchandra Sharma. Calcutta: Mitra Parishad, 1976.

Sogani, K. C. *Ethical Doctrines in Jainism*. Solapur: Jain Sam. Samraksaka Sangh, 1967.

Judaism

Abrahams, Israel. *Hebrew Ethical Wills*. Philadelphia: Jewish Publication Society, 1948.

Baron, Joseph L., ed. *A Treasury of Jewish Quotations*. Northvale, NJ: Jason Aronson, 1985.

Birnbaum, Philip, ed. *Daily Prayer Book*. Rockaway Beach, NY: Hebrew Publishing, 1949.

Bokser, Ben Zion, trans. *The Prayer Book: Weekday, Sabbath and Festival*. Rockaway Beach, NY: Hebrew Publishing, 1957.

Bokser, Ben Zion, trans. *The Talmud: Selected Writings*. Classics of Western Spirituality. New York: Paulist Press, 1989.

Braude, William G., trans. *The Midrash on Psalms*. 2 vols. New Haven, CT: Yale University Press, 1959.

Buber, Martin, trans. *Hasidism and Modern Man*. New York: Harper & Row, 1958.

Buber, Martin. *Tales of the Hasidim: The Early Masters*. New York: Schocken, 1947.

Cohen, A., ed. *Everyman's Talmud*. New York: E. P. Dutton, 1949.

Cohen, A., ed. *The Minor Tractates of the Talmud*. 2 vols., 2nd ed. New York: Soncino Press, 1971.

Cohn-Sherbok, Dan. *Jewish Mysticism: An Anthology*. Oxford: Oneworld, 1995.

Corson, S.A., and C. E. O'Leary. "Purkyne and System-Oriented Physiology." In *Jan Evangelista Purkyne in Science and Culture*. Edited by J. Purs. Praha: CSAV, 1988.

Danby, Herbert, trans. *The Mishnah*. London: Oxford University Press, 1933.

Epstein, I., trans. *The Babylonian Talmud*. New York: Soncino Press, 1948.

Freedman, H., and Maurice Simon, trans. *Midrash Rabbah*. New York: Soncino Press, 1983.

Friedlander, M., trans. *Guide of the Perplexed of Maimonides*. New York: Hebrew Publishing Company, 1881.

Gaer, Joseph. *The Lore of the Old Testament*. Boston: Little, Brown and Co., 1951.

Glatzer, Nahum N., ed. *Hammer on the Rock: A Short Midrash Reader*. New York: Schocken Books, 1948.

Goldin, Judah, trans. *The Living Talmud: The Wisdom of the Fathers*. New York: New American Library, 1957.

Hebrew-English Edition of the Babylonian Talmud. New York: Traditional Press, 1982.

Heinemann, Joseph. *Prayer in the Talmud: Forms and Patterns*. New York: DeGruyter, 1977.

Herford, R. Travers, ed. *The Ethics of the Talmud: Sayings of the Fathers*. New York: Schocken Books, 1925, 1962.

Hertz, Joseph J., ed. *Sayings of the Fathers*. New York: Behrman House, 1945.

Kaplan, Aryeh. *Bahir*. York Beach, ME: Samuel Weiser, 1979.

Kook, Abraham Isaac. *The Zionist Idea.* Edited by A. Hertzberg. New York: Athenaeum, 1959.

Manhar, Nurho de, trans. *The Sepher Ha-Zohar or the Book of Light.* Originally published in *The Word.* Edited by H. W. Percival. New York: Theosophical Publishing Company, 1900-14.

Mishnah. New York: Judaica Press, 1964.

Montefiore, C. G., and H. Loewe, eds. *A Rabbinic Anthology.* New York: Schocken Books, 1974.

Moore, George Foote. *Judaism in the First Centuries of the Chrisitan Era.* Vol. 1. Cambridge, MA: Harvard University Press, 1927.

Newman, Louis I., and Samuel Spitz, eds. *The Talmudic Anthology.* New York: Behrman House, 1945.

Petuchowski, Jacob J. *Our Masters Taught: Rabbinic Stories and Sayings.* New York: Crossroad, 1982.

Rodkinson, Michael L., trans. *The Babylonian Talmud.* 2nd ed. Boston: Boston New Talmud Publishing, 1918.

Scholem, Gershom. *On the Mystical Shape of the Godhead: Basic Concepts in the Kabbalah.* New York: Schocken, 1991.

Scholem, Gershom, ed. *Zohar: The Book of Splendor.* New York: Schocken Books, 1949.

Sperling, Harry, and Maurice Simon, trans. and ed. *The Zohar.* New York: Soncino Press, 1934.

Tamari, Meir, trans. *The Challenge of Wealth: A Jewish Perspective on Earning and Spending Money.* Jason Aronson, 1995.

The Holy Bible, Revised Standard Version. New York: National Council of the Churches of Christ in the USA, 1946; 1971. Used by permission. All rights reserved.

Korean Shamanism and Prophecy

Koo, Sung Mo. *Who Is He?* In *The Completed Testament Age and the Ideal Kingdom.* New York: Family Federation for World Peace and Unification, 1999.

Lee, Jung Young. *Korean Shamanistic Rituals.* The Hague: Mouton, 1981.

Native American Religions

Black Elk, Nicholas. *Black Elk Speaks: Being the Life Story of a Holy Man of the Ogala Sioux.* In collaboration with John G. Neihardt. Lincoln: University of Nebraska Press, 1961.

Brown, Joseph Epes, ed. *The Sacred Pipe: Black Elk's Account of the Seven Rites of the Ogala Sioux.* Norman: University of Oklahoma Press, 1953.

Bunzel, Ruth. "Zuni Ritual Poetry." *47th Annual Report of the Bureau of American Ethnology, 1929-30.* Washington, DC, 1932.

Chief Oren Lyons. "The Year of the Indigenous People." Opening statement to delegates of the United Nations. United Nations General Assembly Auditorium, New York City. December 10, 1992. Accessed at http://www.ratical.org/many_worlds/6Nations/OLatUNin92.html

Clark, Ella E. *Indian Legends of the Pacific Northwest.* Berkeley: University of California Press, 1953.

Densmore, Frances. "Teton Sioux Music." *Bureau of American Ethnology Bulletin no. 61.* Washington, DC, 1918.

Erdoes, Richard, and Alfonso Ortiz, eds. *American Indian Myths and Legends.* New York: Pantheon, 1984.

Farrer, Claire R. "Singing for Life: The Mescalero Apache Girls' Puberty Ceremony." In *Southwestern Indian Ritual Drama.* Edited by Charlotte J. Frisbie. Albuquerque: University of New Mexico Press, 1980.

Gusinde, M. *The Yamana.* New Haven, CT: Human Relations Area Files Press, 1932.

Halifax, Joan. *Shamanic Voices.* New York: E. P. Dutton, 1979.

Howard, Helen Addison. *War Chief Joseph.* Caldwell, ID: Caxton Printers, 1941.

Lizot, Jacques. *Tales of the Yanomami.* Translated by Ernest Simon. Cambridge: Cambridge University Press, 1985.

Marriott, Alice, and Carol Rachlin, comps. *American Indian Mythology.* New York: Crowell, 1968.

McClintock, Walter. *The Old North Trail; or, Life, Legends, and Religion of the Blackfeet Indians.* Reprint, Lincoln: University of Nebraska Press, 1968.

Michelson, Truman. "Notes from the Bull Thigh, Sept. 7, 1910." MS 2684-a. Washington, DC: Smithsonian Institution.

Olson, Sigurd F. *Runes of the North*. H. H. Knopf, 1963.

Parker, Arthur C. *The Code of Handsome Lake, the Seneca Prophet*. 1913. Accessed at http://www.sacred-texts.com

Radin, Paul. *The Autobiography of a Winnebago Indian*. New York: Dover, 1920.

Radin, Paul. "The Winnebago Tribe." *37th Annual Report of the Bureau of American Ethnology, 1923*. Washington, DC; Reprint, Lincoln: University of Nebraska Press, 1970.

Rasmussen, Knud. *Intellectual Culture of the Iglulik Eskimos*. Copenhagen: Gyldendalske Boghandel, 1930.

"Respect for Life." Report of a Conference at Harper's Ferry, West Virginia, on the Traditional Upbringing of American Indian Children. Edited by Sylvester M. Morey and Olivia L. Gilliam. Garden City, NY: Waldorf Press 1975.

Schuon, Frithjof. *L'Oeil du Coeur*. Paris: Gallimard, 1950.

Tooker, Elizabeth. *Native North American Spirituality of the Eastern Woodlands*. New York: Paulist Press, 1979.

Underhill, Ruth Murray. *Red Man's Religion*. Chicago: University of Chicago Press, 1965.

Walker, James R. *Lakota Belief and Ritual*. Lincoln: University of Nebraska Press, 1980.

Watt, Roberta Frye. *Four Wagons West*. Portland, OR: Binsford and Mort, 1934.

PERFECT LIBERTY KYODAN

Hammer, R. J. "The Scriptures of 'Perfect Liberty Kyodan': A Translation with a Brief Commentary." *Japanese Religions* 3 (Spring 1963): 18–26.

SCIENTOLOGY

Hubbard, L. Ron. *Handbook for Preclears*. Los Angeles: Bridge Publications, 1989.

Hubbard, L. Ron. *Science of Survival*. Los Angeles: Bridge Publications, 1989.

Hubbard, L. Ron. *Scientology 0-8: The Book of Basics*. Los Angeles: Bridge Publications, 1988.

SEICHO-NO-IE

Taniguchi, Masaharu. *Holy Sutra Nectarean Shower of Holy Doctrines*. Rev. ed. Gardena, CA: Seicho-No-Ie Truth of Life Movement, North American Missionary Hq., 1981.

SHINTO

Aston, W. G. *Shinto: The Way of the Gods*. London: Longmans, Green and Co., 1905.

Champion, Selwyn Gurney, and Dorothy Short, comps. *Readings from World Religions*. London: C. W. Watts, 1951.

Havens, Norman, trans. *The World of Shinto*. Tokyo: Bukkyo Dendo Kyokai, 1985.

Hirai, Naofusa. Shinto oracle prepared and translated for *World Scripture: A Comparative Anthology of Sacred Texts*. New York: Paragon House, 1991.

Kato, Genchi. *Shinto in Essence*. Tokyo: Nogi Shrine, 1954.

Philippi, Donald L., trans. *Kojiki*. Tokyo: University of Tokyo Press, 1959.

SIKHISM

Encyclopedia of Sikhism. Vol. 1. Patiala: Punjab University, 1995.

Kohli, Surindar Singh. *A Critical Study of Adi Granth.* Delhi: Motilal Banarsidass, 1961.

Mansukhani, Gobindsingh. Selections from the Adi Granth prepared and translated for *World Scripture: A Comparative Anthology of Sacred Texts.* New York: Paragon House, 1991.

Singh, Harbans. *The Message of Sikhism.* Delhi: Delhi Sikhi Gurdwara Management Committee, 1978.

Singh, Kirpal, ed. and trans. *The Jap Ji: The Message of Guru Nanak.* 5th ed. Franklin, NH: Sant Bani Ashram, 1976.

Singh, Trilochan, et. al., trans. *Selections from the Sacred Writings of the Sikhs.* London: George Allen and Unwin, 1960.

Talib, Gurbachan Singh, trans. *Sri Guru Granth Sahib.* 4 vols. Patiala: Publication Bureau of Punjabi University, Patiala, 1984.

SOCIETY OF JOHREI

Okada, Mokichi. *Johrei: Divine Light of Salvation.* Kyoto: Society of Johrei, 1984.

TAOISM

Bary, W. T. de, Wing-tsit Chan, and Burton Watson, comps. *Sources of Chinese Tradition.* Vol. 1. New York: Columbia University Press, 1960. Used by permission of Columbia University Press.

Chan, Wing-tsit, trans. *The Way of Lao Tzu: Tao Te Ching.* New York, Bobbs-Merrill, 1963.

Chen, Ellen M. *The Tao Te Ching: A New Translation with Commentary.* St. Paul, MN: Paragon House, 1989.

Dafei, Gong, and Yu Feng, eds. *Chinese Maxims: Golden Sayings of Chinese Thinkers Over Five Thousand Years.* Beijing: Sinolingua, 1994.

Giles, Herbert A., trans. *Chuang Tzu: Mystic, Moralist, and Social Reformer.* 2nd ed. Shanghai: Kelly and Walsh, 1926; Reprint, New York: AMS Press, 1974.

Lau, D. C., ed. and trans. *Lao Tzu: Tao Te Ching.* London: Penguin Books, 1963.

Legge, James, trans. *The Texts of Taoism: The T'ai Shang Tractate of Actions and Their Retributions.* Sacred Books of the East, vol. 40. Oxford: Clarendon, 1891.

Suzuki, D. T., and Paul Carus, trans. *Yin Chih Wen: The Tract of the Quiet Way with Extracts form the Chinese Commentary.* Peru, IL: Open Court Publishing, 1906, 1950.

Tze, Lao. *Treatise on Response and Retribution.* Translated by D. T. Suzuki and Paul Carus. Peru, IL: Open Court Publishing, 1906; paperback, 1973.

Waley, Arthur. *The Way and Its Power: A Study of the Tao Te Ching and Its Place in Chinese Thought.* New York: Grove Press, 1958.

Watson, Burton, trans. *Chuang Tzu: Basic Writings.* New York: Columbia University Press, 1964.

Watson, Burton, trans. *Complete Works of Chuang Tzu.* New York: Columbia University Press, 1968.

TEACHINGS OF SUN MYUNG MOON

Exposition of the Divine Principle. New York: Holy Spirit Association for the Unification of World Christianity, 1996.

Lee, Sang Hun. *Lucifer, A Criminal against Humanity.* Reported by Young Soon Kim. In *The Completed Testament Age and the Ideal Kingdom.* New York: Family Federation for World Peace and Unification, 1999.

Moon, Heung Jin, "Message from the Spirit World." Cheong Pyeong Heaven and Earth Training Center, January 1, 2002.

Moon, Sun Myung. *Aboji-e Kido [Father's Prayers].* 12 volumes. Prepared by the Family Federation for World Peace and Unification. Seoul: Seong Hwa Press, 1998.

Moon, Sun Myung. *Cheon Seong Gyeong.* Prepared by the Family Federation for World Peace and Unification. Seoul: Seong Hwa Press, 2005.

Moon, Sun Myung. *Ch'eongnyeon-e Kalgil [The Way of Young People].* Seoul: Holy Spirit Association for the Unification of World Christianity, 1991.

Moon, Sun Myung. *Ch'ukbok-gwa Isang Kajan [Blessing and Ideal Family].* Prepared by the Family Federation for World Peace and Unification. Seoul: Seong Hwa Press, 1998.

Moon, Sun Myung. *Ddeut Gil [The Way of God's Will].* Prepared by the Family Federation for World Peace and Unification. Seoul: Seong Hwa Press, 1997.

Moon, Sun Myung. *God's Will and the World.* New York: Holy Spirit Association for the Unification of World Christianity, 1980. A translation of *Hananim-ui Ddeut-gwa Segye.*

Moon, Sun Myung. *Hananim-ui Ddeut-gwa Segye [God's Will and the World].* Prepared by the Family Federation for World Peace and Unification. Seoul: Seong Hwa Press, 1990.

Moon, Sun Myung. *Jisang Saenghwal-gwa Yoenggye [Earthly Life and the Spirit World].* 2 vols. Seoul: Holy Spirit Association for the Unification of World Christianity, 2000.

Moon, Sun Myung. *Moon Sun Myung Seonsaeng Malseum Seonjip [Sermons of the Reverend Sun Myung Moon].* 400+ volumes. Seoul: Seong Hwa Press, 1984-.

Moon, Sun Myung. *Nam Bok Tongil [The Way of Unification of North and South Korea].* Seoul: Holy Spirit Association for the Unification of World Christianity, 1988.

Moon, Sun Myung. *Prayers: A Lifetime of Conversation with Our Heavenly Father.* New York: HSA-UWC, 2000. A translation of *Aboji-e Kido.*

TENRIKYO

Nakayama, Miki. *Mikagura-uta: The Songs of the Tsutome.* Tenri City, Japan: Headquarters of Tenrikyo Church, 1976.

Nakayama, Miki. *Ofudesaki: The Tip of the Divine Writing Brush.* Tenri City, Japan: Headquarters of Tenrikyo Church, 1971.

Nakayama, Miki. *Osahizu.* Tenri City, Japan: Headquarters of Tenrikyo Church.

THEOSOPHY

Blavatsky, H. P. *The Key to Theosophy: An Abridgment.* Edited by Joy Mills. Wheaton, IL: Theosophical Publishing House, 1967.

ZOROASTRIANISM

Darmesteter, James, trans. *The Zend-Avesta, Part 1: The Vendidad.* Sacred Books of the East, vol. 4. Oxford: Clarendon, 1887.

Duchesne-Guillemin, Jacques. *The Hymns of Zarathustra.* Translated from French by M. Henning. London: John Murray, 1963.

Insler, S. *The Gathas of Zarathustra.* Acta Iranica 8, vol. 1. Leiden: E. J. Brill, 1975.

Mirza, H. K. Selections from the Avesta prepared and translated for *World Scripture: A Comparative Anthology of Sacred Texts.* New York: Paragon House, 1991.